THE VICTORIA HISTORY
OF THE
COUNTIES OF ENGLAND

—

A HISTORY OF
SOMERSET

VOLUME VI

Oxford University Press, Walton Street, Oxford OX2 6DP
Oxford New York Toronto
Delhi Bombay Calcutta Madras Karachi
Kuala Lumpur Singapore Hong Kong Tokyo
Nairobi Dar es Salaam Cape Town
Melbourne Auckland Madrid

and associated companies in
Berlin Ibadan

Oxford is a trade mark of Oxford University Press

Published in the United States
by Oxford University Press Inc., New York

British Library Cataloguing in Publication Data
A catalogue record for this book is available
from the British Library

ISBN 0 19 722780 5

Distributed by Oxford University Press until 1 January 1995
thereafter by Dawsons of Pall Mall

Typeset at the University of London Computer Centre
Printed in Great Britain
on acid-free paper by
H Charlesworth & Co Ltd,
Huddersfield, England

THE VICTORIA HISTORY
OF THE
COUNTIES OF ENGLAND

EDITED BY C. R. ELRINGTON

THE UNIVERSITY OF LONDON
INSTITUTE OF
HISTORICAL RESEARCH

INSCRIBED TO THE

MEMORY OF HER LATE MAJESTY

QUEEN VICTORIA

WHO GRACIOUSLY GAVE THE TITLE TO

AND ACCEPTED THE DEDICATION

OF THIS HISTORY

A HISTORY OF THE
COUNTY OF
SOMERSET

EDITED BY R. W. DUNNING

VOLUME VI

ANDERSFIELD, CANNINGTON, AND
NORTH PETHERTON HUNDREDS
(BRIDGWATER AND NEIGHBOURING PARISHES)

PUBLISHED FOR

THE INSTITUTE OF HISTORICAL RESEARCH

BY

OXFORD UNIVERSITY PRESS

1992

CONTENTS OF VOLUME SIX

NOTE. Each parish history is divided into sections. The standard sections are Introduction, Manors and Other Estates, Economic History, Local Government, Church, Nonconformity, Education, and Charities.

LIST OF ILLUSTRATIONS

Thanks are rendered to the following for permission to reproduce material in their possession or their copyright: the Blake Museum, Bridgwater; British Rail; Mr. R. Fitzhugh; Mrs. Irene Hardwick; Mr. A. F. Kersting; the National Monuments Record of the Royal Commission on Historical Monuments (England), for illustrations marked N.M.R.; Mr. G. Roberts; Mr. J. C. D. Smith; the Somerset Archaeological Society (S.A.S.); Somerset County Council (S.C.C.); Somerset County Library.

LIST OF ILLUSTRATIONS

LIST OF MAPS AND PLANS

The maps of parishes and hundreds and the maps on pages xii, 19, 133, 192, 194, 196, and 272 were drawn by K. J. Wass from drafts by M. C. Siraut using, except where otherwise stated, information taken from tithe award maps. The plans of houses were drawn by A. P. Baggs. The map on page 198 is from a photograph by permission of the British Library.

EDITORIAL NOTE

THIS IS the fourth volume to be produced as a result of the partnership between the Somerset County Council and the University of London Institute of Historical Research. That partnership is described in the Editorial Note to Volume III, which was published in 1974. The County Council's responsibility for the *Victoria History of Somerset* has, during the compilation of the present volume, been borne by the Libraries, Museums and Records Committee (until 1978 the Libraries and Museums Sub-Committee of the Education and Cultural Services Committee) under the successive chairmanship of Mrs. D. S. Prettejohn (until 1985), Dr. A. W. G. Court (1985–7), Mr. M. W. Drower (1987–9), Lady Gass (1989), and Mr. A. W. Cotton (from 1989). The University here records its most sincere thanks for the generosity with which the County Council has met and continues to meet the expense of compiling the *History*.

Many people have given valuable help in the preparation of this volume. Those who were concerned with particular parishes are named in the footnotes to those parishes; they are thanked most warmly. For more extensive help particular thanks are rendered to Mr. J. S. Cox, Mr. and Mrs. M. F. Hill, Mr. J. F. Lawrence, Mr. P. Nokes, and Miss Eileen Palmer. Thanks are also offered to the owners and staffs of the private archives at Highclere House, Ugbrooke Park, and Wimborne St. Giles, and especially to Dr. C. Shrimpton at Alnwick and to Mr. and Mrs. P. Strong at Eton College. Among the public libraries and record offices to whose librarians or archivists and their staff the thanks of the *History* are offered for their sympathetic and patient co-operation, special mention must be made of the Somerset Record Office, the Somerset Local History Library, the Blake Museum, Bridgwater, and the Architectural & Heritage and Graphics Sections in Somerset County Council's Dept. for the Environment.

The *General Introduction* to the *Victoria County History,* published in 1970, and its *Supplement* published in 1990 give an outline of the structure and aims of the series as a whole, with an account of its origins and progress.

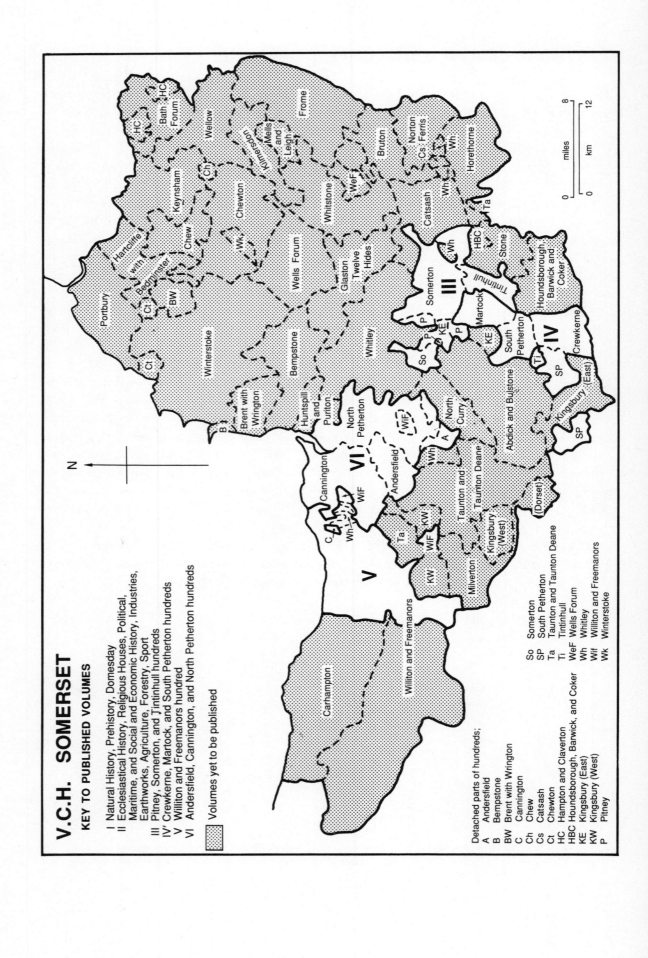

V.C.H. SOMERSET

KEY TO PUBLISHED VOLUMES

I Natural History, Prehistory, Domesday
II Ecclesiastical History, Religious Houses, Political,
   Maritime, and Social and Economic History, Industries,
   Earthworks, Agriculture, Forestry, Sport
III Pitney, Somerton, and Tintinhull hundreds
IV Crewkerne, Martock, and South Petherton hundreds
V Williton and Freemanors hundred
VI Andersfield, Cannington, and North Petherton hundreds

▓ Volumes yet to be published

Detached parts of hundreds;
A Andersfield
B Bempstone
BW Brent with Wrington
C Cannington
Ch Chew
Cs Catsash
Ct Chewton
HC Hampton and Claverton
HBC Houndsborough, Barwick, and Coker
KE Kingsbury (East)
KW Kingsbury (West)
P Pitney

So Somerton
SP South Petherton
Ta Taunton and Taunton Deane
Ti Tintinhull
WeF Wells Forum
Wh Whitley
Wif Williton and Freemanors
Wk Winterstoke

LIST OF CLASSES OF DOCUMENTS
IN THE PUBLIC RECORD OFFICE
USED IN THIS VOLUME
WITH THEIR CLASS NUMBERS

Chancery
C 1	Proceedings, Early	
C 2		Series I
C 3		Series II
C 52	Carte Antique Rolls	
C 60	Fine Rolls	
C 66	Patent Rolls	
C 85	Significations for Excommunication	
C 107	Masters' Exhibits, Senior	
C 111		Brougham
	Inquisitions post mortem	
C 132	Series I, Hen. III	
C 133	Edw. I	
C 134	Edw. II	
C 135	Edw. III	
C 136	Ric. II	
C 137	Hen. IV	
C 138	Hen. V	
C 139	Hen. VI	
C 140	Edw. IV and V	
C 141	Ric. III	
C 142	Series II	
C 143	Inquisitions ad quod damnum	
C 260	Chancery Files (Tower and Rolls Chapel), Recorda	

Court of Common Pleas
CP 25(1)	Feet of Fines, Series I
CP 25(2)	Series II
CP 40	De Banco Rolls
CP 43	Recovery Rolls

Crown Estate Commissioners and their predecessors
CRES 35	Registered Files, Estates
CRES 38	Title Deeds, etc.
CRES 39	Surveys

Duchy of Lancaster
DL 25	Deeds, Series L
DL 42	Miscellaneous Books

Exchequer, King's Remembrancer
E 117	Church Goods
E 122	Customs Accounts
E 134	Depositions taken by Commission
E 142	Ancient Extents
	Inquisitions post mortem
E 149	Series I
E 150	Series II
E 152	Enrolments of Inquisitions
E 178	Special Commissions of Inquiry
E 179	Subsidy Rolls
E 210	Ancient Deeds, Series D
E 211	Series DD

Exchequer, Augmentation Office
E 315	Miscellaneous Books
E 317	Parliamentary Surveys, Commonwealth
E 326	Ancient Deeds, Series B
E 328	Series BB
E 329	Series BS

Exchequer, First Fruits and Tenths Office
E 331	Bishops' Certificates of Institution

Exchequer, Lord Treasurer's Remembrancer and Pipe Offices
E 368	Memoranda Rolls

Registry of Friendly Societies
FS 2	Indexes to Rules and Amendments, Series I

Home Office
HO 107	Census Papers, 1841 and 1851 Census
HO 129	Census Papers, 1851 Census: Ecclesiastical Returns

Exchequer, Office of the Auditors of Land Revenue
LR 2	Miscellaneous Books
LR 3	Court Rolls
LR 14	Ancient Deeds, Series E

General Register Office
RG 9	Census Returns, 1861
RG 10	Census Returns, 1871
RG 11	Census Returns, 1881

Court of Requests
REQ 2	Proceedings

Special Collections
SC 2	Court Rolls
SC 6	Ministers' Accounts
	Rentals and Surveys
SC 11	Rolls
SC 12	Portfolios

State Paper Office
SP 12	State Papers Domestic, Eliz. I

Court of Star Chamber
STAC 2	Proceedings, Hen. VIII
STAC 3	Edw. VI
STAC 4	Mary I

Court of Wards and Liveries
WARD 2	Deeds and Evidences
WARD 7	Inquisitions post mortem

War Office
WO 30	Miscellaneous

LIST OF ACCUMULATIONS
IN THE SOMERSET RECORD OFFICE

Deposited Collections

DD/AH	Acland-Hood family of Fairfield
ALN	Alletson and Partners of Burnham-on-Sea (solicitors)
ARN	Mrs. Arundell (Everard MSS.)
AS	Lord Ashburton
AY	Alms and Young of Taunton (solicitors)
BD	Baker and Duke of Ilminster (solicitors)
BK	Mrs. E. Baker
BLM	Blake Museum, Bridgwater
BTL	Dr. R. Bartelot of Trowbridge
BV	Lt. Col. H. L. Baskerville
CC	Church Commissioners
CCH	Couch of Stogumber (solicitors)
CH	Channer, Channer, and Ligertwood of Taunton (solicitors)
CLE	P. Cole (Bowen MSS.)
CM	Combe family of Earnshill
CN	Clarke, Lukin, and Newton of Chard (solicitors)
CR	F. H. Cornish
CTV	Maj. R. E. F. Cely-Trevilian
DHR	Dodson Harding Reed of Bridgwater (solicitors)
DK	T. B. Dilks
DN	Dickinson family of Kingweston
DP	Dodson and Pulman of Taunton (solicitors)
DR	Miss J. E. Deering of Aldburgh
ED	Estate Duty copy wills
EDN	Edens of Sherborne
EDS	Department of Education and Science
ES	Esdaile family of Cothelstone
FA	G. Farr of Portishead
FD	Revd. H. E. Field of Wembdon
FS	Foster of Wells (solicitors)
GB	Gibbs family of Barrow Gurney
GC	Capt. Graham-Clarke (Hestercombe MSS.)
GJ	Goldingham and Jotcham of Wotton-under-Edge (solicitors)
GL	Gore Langton family of Newton Park
HB	Hodges of Weston super Mare (solicitors)
HC	Hancock family of Wiveliscombe
HI	Hippisley family of Ston Easton
HK	Hoskyns family of North Perrott
HLM	Helyar family of Poundisford
HM	G. Ham
HR	Miss B. M. Harris of Taunton
HS	Howard Southwood of Taunton
HWD	Howard family of Creech St. Michael
HYD	Mrs. Hayward (Dawe of Ditcheat MSS.)
JL	Mme Jullien of Gotton (Musgrave MSS.)
KW	King, Wilkinson, & Co. of Taunton (surveyors)
L	Luttrell family of Dunster
LC	Louch, Wilmott, and Clarke of Langport (solicitors)
MA	Mr. H. Maynard of Taunton
MDW	J. Meadow (St. Albyn of Alfoxton MSS.)
MI	Mildmay family of Hazlegrove
MK	Meade-King family of Walford (Tone Conservators MSS.)
MKG	Meade-King and Co. of Bristol (solicitors)
MLY	de Mauley family of Lechlade
MT	E. A. Mattock of Pitminster
MVB	Merchant Venturers of Bristol
NA	National Trust
NN	Sir Matthew Nathan
NW	Nantes and Wylde of Bridport (solicitors)
OB	Osborne, Ward, Vassall, Abbot, & Co. of Bristol (solicitors)
OS	Mrs. E. K. M. Osler
PAM	Miss E. M. Palmer of Wembdon
PC	J. D. Perceval
PH	Phelips family of Montacute
PLE	Poole and Co. of South Petherton (solicitors)
PM	Portman family of Orchard Portman
PO	Popham family of Hunstrete
POt	Popham family of Hunstrete (Thring deposit)
PT	Earl Poulett of Hinton St. George
QK	Mr. J. R. Quick of Banwell
RN	Mrs. M. O. F. Robertson
RSS	Registrar General of British Shipping (shipping records)
SAS	Somerset Archaeological and Natural History Society
SCL	Somerset County Library
SF	Sanford family of Nynehead
SFR(w)	Society of Friends (West Somerset Division)
SG	Miss Vialls-Strangeways
SH	Lord Strachie of Sutton Court
SIAS	Somerset Industrial Archaeology Society
SL	Slade family of Maunsel
SLM	Slade family of Montys Court
SOG	Society of Genealogists
SP	Sheppard family of Taunton
SPK	Speke family of Jordans
SS	Sotheby & Co.
SX	Sussex Archaeological Society
TB	Trollope-Bellew family of Crowcombe
TBL	Taunton Borough Library
TBR	W. Temple Burridge of Wellington (solicitors)
TC	Conservators of the River Tone
UK	unknown depositors
V	Vernacular Architecture Group
VN	Mr. A. W. Vivian-Neal
WBF	Bath and Wells Diocesan Board of Finance
WM	Wells Museum
WO	Trevelyan family of Nettlecombe
WRO	Wroth Charity
WY	Wyndham family of Orchard Wyndham
DD/S/BR	P. Barrett
BT	Grenville family of Butleigh
BW	H. Bristow Ltd.
CMB	Cambridgeshire Record Office
CR	Crow Ltd. of London
DA	d'Arcy Books of Marlborough
FA	E. J. Farr and Co. of Yeovil
HY	Halliday of Leicester
SH	Col. H. R. H. Southam
ST	Stradling family of Chilton Polden
VY	H. H. G. Vorley of London
WH	Lord Wharton (Halswell MSS.)

SOMERSET RECORD OFFICE ACCUMULATIONS

DD/X/ALF	P. Alford of Bristol		hnd	Capt. A. Hamond
BB	Bamber family of Castle Hill		ho	C. Hoare and Co. of London
BID	Bidwells of Cambridge		lch	Leman, Chapman, and Harrison of London
BH	T. Broomhead of Taunton		lp	Langton and Passmore of London
BKE	Mrs. R. Baker		nf	Norfolk Record Society
BOA	Miss E. R. Broadmead (W. Gresswell's papers)		pc	Mr. H. Pocock
BOK	J. Brooke		py	Perry of Brighton (solicitors)
BRC	Mrs. E. Bicknell		sh	Col. R. Southam
BRS	Mr. V. C. Burston of Bournemouth		su	Surtees and Co. of London
BTT	Mr. E. Batten		to	Torr and Co.
BUSH	Mr. R. Bush (J. Toogood's diary)		tw	A. F. and R. W. Tweedie of London
BWN	Miss L. Bowen		wa	Warrens of London (solicitors)
CAT	Mr. H. R. St. Clair Cater		wn	S. A. Warner
CHK	Chiswick District Library		wp	Winckworth and Pembertons
COR	Cornwall Record Office		wr	J. T. Warren-Potter
CRE	Mr. I. Crane			
CX	Mr. J. S. Cox of Guernsey		D/B/bw	Bridgwater Borough Records
DD	Dr. D. Davidson		D/P/	Parish Collections
DS	Major F. S. Dodson		D/PC/	Parish Council Collections
DT	T. G. C. Dougherty of Goathurst		D/PM/	Parish Meeting Collections
EDS	Miss. M. Edwards		D/R/bw	Bridgwater Rural District Council
ELT	C. B. Elliott		ta	Taunton Rural District Council
FRC	R. C. France (Bluett MSS.)			
GG	Lt. Col. J. H. N. George		**Diocesan Records**	
GST	Goathurst Charities			
GT	P. W. D. Gait		D/D/B misc	miscellaneous benefice papers
HAG	Mr. P. Haggett		B reg	bishops' registers
HAM	J. Hamilton		Bbm	benefice mortgages
HEA	G. V. M. Heap (Lord Taunton's papers)		Bg	exchanges of glebe
HMY	J. Humphrey		Bo	ordination papers
HR	Mrs. M. Hurman		Bp	presentation deeds
HU	C. R. Hudleston		Bs	clergy subscription books
HUD	C. Hudson (Greenhill papers)		Ca	act books
HUNT	Revd. C. B. Hunt of Stockland Bristol		Cd	deposition books
HUX	Mrs. M. Huxtable		Cf	faculty papers
HWK	Mrs. J. Howick of Taunton		Pd	deans' peculiar papers
JES	Mr. C. N. Jones (solicitor)		R	registration
KLT	E. L. Kelting		Rb	benefice returns
LA	Lancashire Record Office		Rg	glebe terriers
LAW	Mrs. S. Lawson		Rm	meeting house licences
LTT	Miss D. M. Lott		Rr	bishops' transcripts of parish registers
LY	Lyte family of Lytes Cary		Va	visitation returns
MCO	Surrey Record Office		Vc	visitation acts
MDX	Middlesex Record Office			
ME	Mullings, Ellett, & Co. of Cirencester (solicitors)		**Quarter Sessions Records**	
NL	Newport Library		Q/AB	bridges
OA	E. C. Oaten		AD	diseases of animals
OS	Ordnance Survey		AP	police
OSPC	Over Stowey Church School		RDd	enrolled deeds
PORT	Porter family of Broomfield		RDe	inclosure awards
PRD	Mrs. E. W. Paradine of Taunton		REl	land tax assessments
RHO	Mr. and Mrs. Rhodes		RL	victuallers' recognizances
ROBN	G. Robinson		RLa	alehousekeepers' recognizances
RY	G. Rye		RLh	hemp and flax recognizances
SMIT	J. C. D. Smith of Spaxton		RR	recusants' lands, meeting house licences
SQ	W. L. Squire (Wembdon parish records)		RRp	recusants' lands
SR	Somerset Record Society		RSc	charities
STR	Mrs. H. G. Straton		RSf	friendly society returns
SU	Miss V. Sully		RUa	company accounts
TCR	A. R. Tucker		RUi	warrants and inquisitions
VEA	Mr. Vearncombe of North Petherton		RUo	orders and acts
VIN	Vinters of Cambridge		RUp	deposited plans
VN	Mrs. A. W. Vivian-Neal		SO	order books
WG	Waldegrave family of Chewton Mendip		S Pet	petitions
WI	Wiltshire Record Office		SR	sessions rolls
DD/BR/bi	Bird and Bird of London (solicitors)		**County Council Records**	
bn	Blathwayt MSS.			
da	Druce and Attlee		C/C	property deeds
ds	Mrs. R. Bickerdyke and Miss Dawson		C/E	education department
ely	Peirs Ellis and Jackson Young (Bouverie, Pym, and Hale MSS.)		C/T	treasurer's department
en	Mr. M. Engleman		GP	general purposes
gh	Godden, Holme, and Co. of London		M	minutes

Other Deposits

D/H	hospital records
D/N/bmc	Bridgwater Methodist circuit records
brc	Broomfield Congregational records
bw. chch	Christchurch Bridgwater records
np. c	North Petherton Congregational records
tmc	Taunton Methodist circuit records
D/RA	rivers authority
D/T	turnpike trusts

buc	Buckinghamshire Record Office
dev	Devon Record Office
dst	Dorset Record Office
dut	G. Duthie of Bromley
ea	Mr. W. Earp
es	Esdaile of Cothelstone
hdn	Mrs. J. Hudson of Cannington
lawe	Mr. J. Lawrence of Bridgwater
no	Northamptonshire Record Office
sog	Society of Genealogists
vch	Victoria County History

Photostats and Microfilms

T/PH/ay	J. Ayres
bb	E. K. Barber of Maynard and Barber, Taunton

Typescripts

TS/EVD	Everard Papers

xvi

NOTE ON ABBREVIATIONS

Among the abbreviations and short titles used, the following may require elucidation:

A.O.N.B.	Area of Outstanding Natural Beauty
A.-S.	Anglo-Saxon
A.-S. Chron.	*Anglo-Saxon Chronicle*, ed. D. Whitelock and others (1931)
Abbrev. Plac. (Rec. Com.)	*Placitorum Abbreviatio*, ed. W. J. Illingworth (Record Commission, 1811)
Abbrev. Rot. Orig. (Rec. Com.)	*Rotulorum Originalium in Curia Scaccarii Abbreviatio, Henry III–Edward III* (Record Commission, 1805–10)
Abs.	Abstract
Acct.	Account
Acts of P.C.	*Acts of the Privy Council of England* (H.M.S.O. 1890–1964)
Agric.	Agriculture; Agricultural
Alum. Cantab.	*Alumni Cantabrigienses*, ed. J. and J. A. Venn
Alum. Oxon.	*Alumni Oxonienses*, ed. J. Foster
Ann. Rep.	*Annual Report*
Ann. Rep. B. & W. Dioc. Assoc. S.P.C.K.	*Annual Report of the Bath and Wells Diocesan Association of the Society for the Promotion of Christian Knowledge*
Arch.	Archaeology
Archit. Hist.	*Architectural History*
B.L.	British Library
Bapt.	Baptist
Bd.	Board
Bd. of Educ., List 21	*Board of Education, List 21* (H.M.S.O.)
Bk. of Fees	*The Book of Fees* (H.M.S.O. 1920–31)
Bodl.	Bodleian Library, Oxford
Bull. Inst. Hist. Res.	*Bulletin of the Institute of Historical Research*
Burke, *Commoners*	J. Burke and others, *A History of the Commoners* (London, 1833–8)
Burke, *Extinct Peerages*	J. Burke and others, *Extinct, Dormant, and Abeyant Peerages*
Burke, *Land. Gent.*	J. Burke and others, *Landed Gentry*
Burke, *Peerage*	J. Burke and others, *A Dictionary of the Peerage*
Cal. Chanc. Wts.	*Calendar of Chancery Warrants preserved in the Public Record Office, 1244–1326* (H.M.S.O. 1927)
Cal. Chart. R.	*Calendar of the Charter Rolls preserved in the Public Record Office* (H.M.S.O. 1903–27)
Cal. Close	*Calendar of the Close Rolls preserved in the Public Record Office (1892–1963)*
Cal. Cttee. for Compounding	*Calendar of the Proceedings of the Committee for Compounding etc.* (H.M.S.O. 1911–62)
Cal. Cttee. for Money	*Calendar of the Proceedings of the Committee for the Advance of Money, 1642–6* (H.M.S.O. 1888)
Cal. Fine R.	*Calendar of the Fine Rolls preserved in the Public Record Office* (H.M.S.O. 1911–62)
Cal. Inq. Misc.	*Calendar of Inquisitions Miscellaneous (Chancery) preserved in the Public Record Office* (H.M.S.O. 1916–68)
Cal. Inq. p.m.	*Calendar of Inquisitions post mortem preserved in the Public Record Office* (H.M.S.O. 1904–88)
Cal. Inq. p.m. Hen. VII	*Calendar of Inquisitions post mortem, Henry VII* (H.M.S.O. 1898–1955)
Cal. Lib.	*Calendar of the Liberate Rolls preserved in the Public Record Office 1226–67* (H.M.S.O. 1917–64)
Cal. Mem. R.	*Calendar of the Memoranda Rolls (Exchequer) preserved in the Public Record Office, 1326–7* (H.M.S.O. 1968)
Cal. Papal Pets.	*Calendar of Papal Registers: Petitions to the Pope* (H.M.S.O. 1896)
Cal. Papal Reg.	*Calendar of Papal Registers: Papal Letters* (H.M.S.O. and Irish Manuscripts Commission, 1893–1986)

Cal. Pat.	*Calendar of the Patent Rolls preserved in the Public Record Office* (H.M.S.O. 1891–1986)
Cal. S.P. Dom.	*Calendar of State Papers, Domestic Series* (H.M.S.O. 1856–1972)
Cal. Treas. Bks.	*Calendar of Treasury Books, preserved in the Public Record Office* (H.M.S.O. 1897–1955)
Calamy Revised, ed. Matthews	*Calamy Revised: being a Revision of Edmund Calamy's Account of the Ministers and others Ejected and Silenced, 1660–2*, by A. G. Matthews (1934)
Camd. Soc.	Camden Society
Cart.	Cartulary
Cat.	Catalogue
Cat. Anct. D.	*Descriptive Catalogue of Ancient Deeds in the Public Record Office* (H.M.S.O. 1890–1915)
Cath.	Cathedral, Catholic
Cath. Rec. Soc.	Catholic Record Society
Cath. Rel. in Som.	*Catholic Religion in Somerset* (1826)
Ch.	Church
Ch. Comm.	Church Commissioners
Chadwyck Healey, *Hist. W. Som.*	C. E. H. Chadwyck Healey, *The History of the part of West Somerset comprising the parishes of Luccombe, Selworthy, Stoke Pero, Porlock, Culbone and Oare* (1901)
Char. Com.	Charity Commission
Char. Dig.	*Digest of Endowed Charities* (1869–71)
Char. Don.	*Abstract of Returns of Charitable Donations made in 1787–8*, H.C. 511 (1816), xvi
Char(s).	Charities
Chyd.	Churchyard
Clifford MSS.	Clifford MSS. at Ugbrooke House, Devon, in 1983
Close R.	*Close Rolls of the Reign of Henry III preserved in the Public Record Office* (H.M.S.O. 1902–15)
Cncl.	Council
Co.	Company, County
Co. Lic. Cttee.	County Licensing Committee
Collinson, *Hist. Som.*	J. Collinson, *History and Antiquities of the County of Somerset* (1791)
Colln.	Collection
Com.	Commission
Complete Peerage	G. E. C[ockayne] and others, *Complete Peerage* (1910–59)
Corp.	Corporation
Crockford	*Crockford's Clerical Directory*
Cur. Reg. R.	*Curia Regis Rolls preserved in the Public Record Office* (H.M.S.O. 1922–79)
D.C.	District Council
D.N.B.	*Dictionary of National Biography*
Dept.	Department
Dict.	Dictionary
Dioc.	Diocesan
Dioc. Dir.	*Bath and Wells Diocesan Directory (and Almanack)* (1928– ; Almanack discontinued 1948)
Dir.	Directory
Dist.	District
Docs.	Documents
Dom. Bk. ed. Thorn	*Domesday Book, Somerset*, ed. C. and F. Thorn (1980)
Dom. Geog. SW. Eng.	*Domesday Geography of South-West England*, ed. H. C. Darby and R. Welldon Finn (1967)
Dugdale, *Mon.*	W. Dugdale, *Monasticon Anglicanum*, ed. J. Caley and others (London, 1817–30)
Dwelly, *Hearth Tax*	*Dwelly's National Records (i) Hearth Tax for Somerset, 1664–5*, ed. R. Holworthy (1916); *(ii) Directory for Somerset* (1929–32)
Dwelly, *Par. Rec.*	E. Dwelly, *Parish Records* (priv. print 1913–)

E.H.D.	*English Historical Documents*, ed. D. C. Douglas and others (1953–)
Econ.	Economic
Educ.	Education
Educ. Enq. Abstract	*Abstract of Educational Returns*, H.C. 62 (1835), xlii
Educ. of Poor Digest	*Digest of Returns to the Select Committee on the Education of the Poor*, H.C. 224 (1819), ix (2)
Ekwall, *Eng. Place-Names*	E. Ekwall, *The Concise Oxford Dictionary of English Place-Names* (1960)
Elect. Reg.	*The Register of Persons Entitled to Vote* (the Electoral Register)
Emden, *Biog. Reg. Univ. Cantab.*	A. B. Emden, *A Biographical Register of the University of Cambridge* (1963)
Emden, *Biog. Reg. Univ. Oxf.*	A. B. Emden, *A Biographical Register of the University of Oxford* (1957–74)
Employment of Women and Children in Agric.	*Report of the Assistant Poor Law Commissioners on Employment of Women and Children in Agriculture* [510], H. C. (1843), xii
Eng.	England, English
Eton Coll. Recs.	Records of Eton College, Bucks.
Ex. e Rot. Fin. (Rec. Com.)	*Excerpta e Rotulis Finium in Turri Londinensi asservati, Henry III, 1216–72* (Record Commission, 1835–6)
Feud. Aids	*Inquisitions and Assessments relating to Feudal Aids preserved in the Public Record Office* (H.M.S.O. 1899–1920)
Fines Imposed in 1497, ed. A. J. Howard	*Fines Imposed on Persons who assisted the Rebels during the Cornish Rebellion and the Insurrection of Perkin Warbeck in 1497*, ed. A. J. Howard (1986)
G.E.C. *Baronetage*	G. E. C[ockayne], *Complete Baronetage* (1900–9)
G.R.O.	General Register Office
Gent. Mag.	*Gentleman's Magazine* (1731–1867)
Geol. Surv.	Geological Survey
Govt.	Government
H.C.	House of Commons
H.L.	House of Lords
H.M.C. Wells	Royal Commission on Historical Manuscripts, Series 12, Calendar of the Manuscripts of the Dean and Chapter of Wells (1907–14)
H.M.S.O.	Her (His) Majesty's Stationery Office
Hamilton and Lawrence, *Men and Mining in the Quantocks*	J. Hamilton and J. Lawrence, *Men and Mining in the Quantocks* (1970)
Handbk. Brit. Chron.	*Handbook of British Chronology* (Royal Historical Society, 1986)
Harl. Soc.	Harleian Society
Hist.	History
Hist. MSS. Com.	Royal Commission on Historical Manuscripts
Hist. Parl.	*The History of Parliament* (History of Parliament Trust, 1964–)
Ho.	House
Hutchins, *Hist. Dors.*	J. Hutchins, *The History and Antiquities of the County of Dorset* (1861–70)
Ind.	Independent
Inf.	Information
Inscr.	Inscription
Intro.	Introduction
Jnl.	Journal
Jnl. Som. Ind. Arch. Soc.	*Journal of the Somerset Industrial Archaeological Society*
Kelly's Dir. Som.	*Kelly's Post Office Directory of Somerset*
Knowles and Hadcock, *Med. Religious Hos.*	D. Knowles and R. N. Hadcock, *Medieval Religious Houses of England and Wales* (1971)
L. & P. Hen. VIII	*Letters and Papers, Foreign and Domestic, of the Reign of Henry VIII* (H.M.S.O. 1864–1932)
L.J.	*Journals of the House of Lords*
Lamb. Pal. Libr.	Lambeth Palace Library
Leland, *Itin.* ed. Toulmin Smith	*Itinerary of John Leland*, ed. L. Toulmin Smith (1907–10)

Libr	Library
Lics.	Licences
List of Sch. Boards	*List of School Boards and School Attendance Committees*, H.C. (1880–1902)
Local Hist. Libr.	Local History Library, Taunton
Lond. Gaz.	*London Gazette*
Lond. Chron.	*London Chronicle*
M.I. in ch.	Monumental Inscription in church
M.V.R.G.	Medieval Village Research Group
Macdermot, *Hist. G.W.R.*	E. T. Macdermot, *History of the Great Western Railway*, revised by C. R. Clinker (1964)
Mag.	Magazine
Med.	Medieval
Min.	Ministry; Minutes
Mun.	Municipal
N.R.A.	National Register of Archives
N.S.	New Series
Nat.	National
Nat. Soc. *Inquiry 1846–7*	*Results of the Returns made to the General Inquiry made by the National Society, 1846–7* (1849)
Nat. Trust	National Trust
Nonconf.	Nonconformity
O.S.	Ordnance Survey (arch. rec. cards: archaeological record cards)
Orig. Rec. of Early Nonconf. ed. G. L. Turner	*Original Records of Early Nonconformity*, ed. G. L. Turner (1911–14)
P.C.C.	Prerogative Court of Canterbury
P.O. Dir. Som.	*Post Office Directory of Somerset*
P.R.O.	Public Record Office
P.R.S.	Pipe Roll Society
Par. rec.	Parish records
Pet.	Petition
Pevsner, *S. & W. Som.*	N. Pevsner, *Buildings of England: South and West Somerset* (1958)
Pigot, *Nat. Com. Dir.*	Pigot's *National Commercial Directory*
Plac. Coram Rege, 1297	*Placita Coram Rege apud Westmonasterium, 1297* (Index Libr. 1898)
Plac. de Quo Warr.	*Placita de Quo Warranto* (Record Commission, 1818)
Pole MS.	Photocopy and Transcript of the Collections of Sir William Pole, V.C.H. Office, Taunton
Proc. Arch. Inst.	*Proceedings of the Archaeological Institute of Great Britain and Ireland*
Proc. before J.P.s, ed. B. Putnam	*Proceedings before the Justices of the Peace in the reigns of Edward III and Richard II*, ed. B. Putnam (1938)
Proc. Dors. Arch. Soc.	*Proceedings of the Dorset Natural History and Archaeological Society*
Proc. Som. Arch. Soc.	*Proceedings of the Somerset Archaeological and Natural History Society* (from 1968 *Somerset Archaeology and Natural History*)
Public Elem. Schs.	*Return of Public Elementary Schools*, H.C. 133 (1875), lix
R.	Roll
R.D.C.	Rural District Council
R.O.	Record Office
R.S., Rec. Soc.	Record Society
Red Bk. Exch. (Rolls Ser.)	*Red Book of the Exchequer*, ed. H. Hall (Rolls Series, 1896)
Ref.	Reformed
Reg.	Register
Reg. Regum Anglo-Norm.	*Regesta Regum Anglo-Normannorum, 1066–1154*, ed. H. W. C. Davis and others (1913–69)
15th Rep. Com. Char.	*15th Report of the Charity Commissioners for England and Wales*, H.C. 383 (1826), xiii
Rep. Com. Dep. Cond. of Agric. Interests	*Report of the Royal Commission on Depressed Condition of the Agricultural Interests* [C. 3309], H. C. (1882), xiv

Rep. Com. Eccl. Revenues	Report of the Royal Commission on Ecclesiastical Revenues [67], H.C. (1835), xxii
Rep. Com. Employment in Agric.	Report of the Royal Commission on Children, Young Persons, and Women in Agriculture [4202 and 4202-I], H.C. (1868–9), xiii
Rep. Com. Mun. Corp.	Report of the Royal Commission on Municipal Corporations, H.C. 116 (1835), xxiii
Rep. Com. Poor Law	Report of the Royal Commission on the Poor Law, H.C. 44 (1834), xxvii–xxxviii
Rep. Com. Roads	Report of the Royal Commission on Roads [256, 280], H.C. (1840), xxvii
Rep. Sel. Cttee. on Poor Law	Report of the Select Committee on the Poor Law, H.L. (1837–8), xix (i–ii)
Rep. Som. Cong. Union (1896)	Annual Report of the Somerset Congregational Union and of the Evangelist Society presented at the One-Hundredth Anniversary (1896).
Return of M.P.s	Return of Every Member of the House of Commons, 1213–1874, H.C. 69-I and II (1878), lxii
Rev.	Review, Revised
Rly.	Railway
Rot. Chart. (Rec. Com.)	Rotuli Chartarum, 1199–1216 (Record Commission, 1837)
Rot. Cur. Reg. (Rec. Com.)	Rotuli Curiae Regis, 6 Richard I to 1 John (Record Commission, 1835)
Rot. de Ob. et Fin. (Rec. Com.)	Rotuli de Oblatis et Finibus in Turri Londinensi asservati, temp. Regis Johannis (Record Commission, 1835)
Rot. Hund. (Rec. Com.)	Rotuli Hundredorum temp. Hen. III & Edw. I (Record Commission, 1812–18)
Rot. Lib. (Rec. Com.)	Rotuli de Liberate ac de Misis et Praestitis, regnante Johanne (Record Commission, 1844)
Rot. Litt. Claus. (Rec. Com.)	Rotuli Litterarum Clausarum, 1204–27 (Record Commission, 1833–44)
Rot. Litt. Pat. (Rec. Com.)	Rotuli Litterarum Patentium, 1201–16 (Record Commission, 1835)
S.D.N.Q.	Somerset and Dorset Notes and Queries
Sanders, Eng. Baronies	I. J. Sanders, English Baronies, 1086–1327 (1960)
Sch.	School
Sel.	Select
Sel. Cases Eccl. Ct. Cant.	Select Cases from the Ecclesiastical Courts of the Province of Canterbury, c. 1200–1301 (Selden Society, 1981)
Ser.	Series
Soc.	Social, Society
Som. C.C.	Somerset County Council (Sites and Mons. Rec.: Sites and Monuments Record)
Som. Co. Gaz.	Somerset County Gazette
Som. Co. Herald, N. & Q.	Somerset County Herald, Notes and Queries
Som. Incumbents, ed. Weaver	Somerset Incumbents, ed. F. W. Weaver (1889)
Som. Protestation Returns, ed. Howard and Stoate	Somerset Protestation Returns and Subsidy Rolls, ed. A. J. Howard and T. L. Stoate (1975)
Som. Wills, ed. Brown	Abstracts of Somersetshire Wills etc., copied from the Manuscript Collections of the late Revd. F. Brown (priv. print. 1887–90)
Squibbs, Bridgwater	P. J. Squibbs, Squibbs' History of Bridgwater, rev. J. F. Lawrence (1982)
S.R.O.	Somerset Record Office (cf. above, page xiv)
S.R.S.	Somerset Record Society (cf. below, page xxiii)
Tax. Eccl. (Rec. Com.)	Taxatio Ecclesiastica Anglie et Wallie auctoritate P. Nicholai IV circa 1291 (Record Commission, 1801)
Trans.	Transactions, Transcripts
Trans. Anct. Mon. Soc.	Transactions of the Ancient Monuments Society
Trans. R. Hist. S.	Transactions of the Royal Historical Society
Uncat.	Uncatalogued
Univ. Brit. Dir.	Universal British Directory of Trade, Commerce, and Manufacture (1791–8)
V.C.H.	Victoria County History

Valor Eccl. (Rec. Com.)	*Valor Ecclesiasticus, temp. Hen. VIII* (Record Commission, 1810–34)
Visit.	Visitation
W. Som. Free Press	*West Somerset Free Press*
Walker Revised, ed. Matthews	*Walker Revised; being a Revision of John Walker's Sufferings of the Clergy during the Grand Rebellion, 1642–60,* ed. A. G. Matthews
Wells Wills, ed. Weaver	*Wells Wills,* ed. F. W. Weaver (1890)
Youngs, *Local Admin. Units*	F. A. Youngs, *Guide to the Local Administrative Units of England, i: Southern England* (1979)

PUBLICATIONS OF THE
SOMERSET RECORD SOCIETY
USED IN THIS VOLUME

i	*Bishop Drokensford's Register, 1309–27* (1887)
ii	*Somerset Chantries, 1548* (1888)
iii	*Kirby's Quest* (1889)
v	*Rentalia et Custumaria Glastoniae* (1891)
vi	*Pedes Finium, 1196–1307* (1892)
vii	*Cartularies of Bath Priory* (1893)
viii	*Cartularies of Bruton and Montacute Priories* (1894)
ix & x	*Register of Ralph de Salopia, 1327–63* (1896)
xi	*Somersetshire Pleas, c. 1200–56* (1897)
xii	*Pedes Finium, 1307–46* (1898)
xiii	*Registers of Bishop Giffard, 1265–6, and Bishop Bowett, 1401–7* (1899)
xiv	*Cartularies of Muchelney and Athelney Abbeys* (1899)
xv	*Gerard's Survey of Somerset, 1633* (1900)
xvi	*Somerset Wills, 1383–1500* (1901)
xvii	*Pedes Finium, 1347–90* (1902)
xviii	*Bellum Civile* (1902)
xix	*Somerset Wills, 1501–30* (1903)
xx	*Certificates of Musters, 1569* (1904)
xxi	*Somerset Wills, 1531–58* (1905)
xxii	*Pedes Finium, 1399–1485* (1906)
xxiii	*Quarter Sessions Records, 1607–25* (1907)
xxiv	*Quarter Sessions Records, 1625–39* (1908)
xxv	*Cartulary of Buckland Priory* (1909)
xxvi	*Feodary of Glastonbury Abbey* (1910)
xxvii	*Star Chamber Proceedings, Henry VII and Henry VIII* (1911)
xxviii	*Quarter Sessions Records, 1646–60* (1912)
xxix & xxx	*Register of Bishop Bubwith, 1407–24* (1913–14)
xxxi & xxxii	*Register of Bishop Stafford, 1425–43* (1915–16)
xxxiii	*The Honor of Dunster* (1918)
xxxiv	*Quarter Sessions Records, 1666–76* (1919)
xxxv	*Two Beauchamp Registers (1920)*
xxxvi	*Somersetshire Pleas, 1255–72* (1921)
xl	*Medieval Wills from Wells* (1925)
xli	*Somersetshire Pleas, 1272–9* (1926)
xliii	*Collectanea II* (1928)
xliv	*Somersetshire Pleas, 1280* (1929)
xlviii	*Bridgwater Borough Archives, 1200–1377* (1933)
xlix & l	*Register of Bishop Bekynton, 1443–65* (1934–5)
li	*Somerset Enrolled Deeds* (1936)
lii	*Registers of Bishop Stillington and Bishop Fox 1466–94* (1937)
liii	*Bridgwater Borough Archives, 1377–1400* (1938)
liv	*Register of Bishop King and Bishop de Castello 1496–1518* (1938)
lv	*Bishops' Registers, 1518–59* (1940)
lvi	*A Wells Cathedral Miscellany* (1941)
lvii	*Collectanea III* (1942)
lviii	*Bridgwater Borough Archives, 1400–45* (1943)
lix, lxiii, lxiv	*Great Chartulary of Glastonbury* (1947, 1952, 1956)
lx	*Bridgwater Borough Archives, 1445–68* (1945)
lxi	*Stogursey Charters* (1946)
lxii	*Somerset Wills from Exeter* (1952)
lxv	*Somerset Assize Orders, 1629–40* (1959)
lxvii	*Sales of Wards, 1603–41* (1965)
lxviii	*Hylle Cartulary* (1968)
lxx	*Bridgwater Borough Archives, 1468–85* (1971)
lxxi	*Somerset Assize Orders, 1640–59* (1971)
lxxv	*Somersetshire Quarterly Meeting 1668–99* (1978)
lxxvi	*Somerset Maps* (1981)
lxxvii	*Calendar of Somerset Chantry Grants, 1548–1603* (1982)
lxxix	*The Monmouth Rebels, 1685* (1985)
extra ser.	*Some Somerset Manors* (1931)

INTRODUCTION

ANDERSFIELD, Cannington, and North Petherton hundreds together occupy the Lower Parrett valley stretching from the Quantock ridge in the west to King's Sedgemoor in the east, and from the Bristol Channel in the north to the river Tone in the south. Roman river ports at Combwich and Crandon bridge and farming settlements at Bawdrip, Spaxton, and Wembdon indicate early exploitation both of alluvial grasslands and corn-growing uplands. Changes in water levels after the 4th century left the lower ground more liable to flooding, and field boundaries in Bridgwater, Chilton, Pawlett, and Wembdon parishes suggest that the course of the Parrett may have been subject to frequent and significant change over a long period.

By the late 11th century the settlement pattern was dense, especially between the Quantocks and the Parrett, an area crossed by the Saxon 'herpath' in the north and including the 10th-century strongholds of Athelney and Lyng in the south and the Domesday royal manors of Cannington, North Petherton, and Creech St. Michael. The origin of the medieval royal park at North Petherton can be traced to a pre-Conquest royal forest on the Quantocks, and North Petherton was an extensive minster parish which included the later parishes of Chedzoy, Pawlett, Thurloxton, and probably St. Michaelchurch.

Bridgwater, a chartered borough from 1200, is the only significant town, although Stogursey acquired borough status by 1225 and a burgage at North Petherton was mentioned in 1251–2. By the later Middle Ages Bridgwater's port served central, south, and west Somerset, and until the 19th century heavy goods continued to be transported along the Parrett, the Tone, and the Bridgwater and Taunton canal into Dorset and Devon.

The pattern of settlement is varied: a few nucleated villages like Bawdrip, Cannington, North Petherton, North Newton, and Stogursey; roadside villages like Chedzoy, East Lyng, Durston, and Creech St. Michael; and parishes with dispersed hamlets like Broomfield, Charlinch, and Otterhampton. Interlocking parish boundaries, notably between Bridgwater, Chilton, Durleigh, and Wembdon, and between Cannington, Otterhampton, and Stockland Bristol, indicate complex economic units and late parochial formation.

Agriculture was also varied: arable farming predominated until the 16th century, partly in open arable fields, two of which survive in Chedzoy. In the 17th century there was an emphasis on stock rearing and an increase in dairying and orchards, largely the result of improved drainage. Cheese was an important product of the area in the 18th century, and in the 19th baskets from locally grown willow. Medieval Bridgwater provided an outlet for surplus food products, notably for military operations; in the 19th century it imported fertilizer and animal feeding stuffs for the farming community.

Local woollen cloth was the most significant product of the area in the later Middle Ages and production continued into the 17th century. Attempts at copper mining and silk production in the early 19th century were largely unsuccessful, but from the late 17th century the alluvial clays of the Parrett valley provided material for the bricks and tiles for which Bridgwater became well known in the 19th century.

There was no dominant medieval landowner, but among the substantial estates built up in the later Middle Ages were those whose houses wholly or partially survive, including Fairfield, Gothelney, Gurney Street, West Bower, and Sydenham. Halswell House was from the later 17th century the grandest mansion in the area. Enmore Castle was the creation of the earls of Egmont in the later 18th century and the Quantock Lodge estate of Lord Taunton derived in part from the Egmonts' estate.

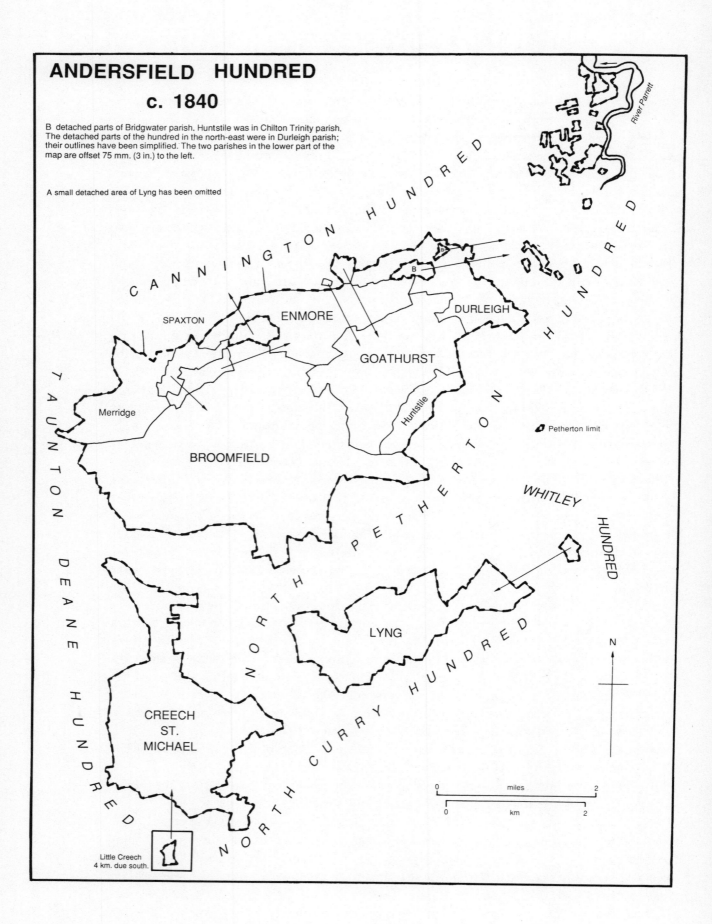

ANDERSFIELD HUNDRED
c. 1840

B detached parts of Bridgwater parish. Huntstile was in Chilton Trinity parish. The detached parts of the hundred in the north-east were in Durleigh parish; their outlines have been simplified. The two parishes in the lower part of the map are offset 75 mm. (3 in.) to the left.

A small detached area of Lyng has been omitted

River Parrett

CANNINGTON HUNDRED

HUNDRED

SPAXTON

ENMORE

DURLEIGH

GOATHURST

Merridge

Huntstile

Petherton limit

BROOMFIELD

TAUNTON DEANE HUNDRED

WHITLEY

HUNDRED

NORTH PETHERTON

LYNG

CREECH
ST.
MICHAEL

NORTH CURRY HUNDRED

N

Little Creech
4 km. due south.

miles

0   2

km

0   2

ANDERSFIELD HUNDRED

THE hundred lies east of the Quantock Hills and takes its name from the hamlet of Andersfield in Goathurst parish. It occupies part of the eastern slopes in a band stretching from the centre of the Quantock ridge to the outskirts of Bridgwater, and also includes Creech St. Michael and Lyng on the northern bank of the river Tone east of Taunton. Settlements include both scattered hill farms on the Quantocks and nucleated villages in the flood plain of the Tone. Although the area is predominantly agricultural, cloth production was an important activity until the mid 18th century and quarries and mines have been worked on the higher ground. Some settlements have grown rapidly in the 20th century because of their proximity to Taunton and Bridgwater. The Quantock Hills were designated an Area of Outstanding Natural Beauty in 1957.[1]

The Domesday hundred of Andersfield included just over 9 hides, probably in the northern area.[2] Creech St. Michael was included in the hundred from 1569[3] and Lyng from 1640;[4] both were formerly free manors. In the mid 13th century Broomfield and Durleigh manors secured temporary independence from the hundred[5] and Broomfield answered separately at the eyre as a free manor in 1242–3.[6] In 1284–5 Andersfield hundred comprised Broomfield with Heathcombe and Oggshole, Durleigh, Enmore with Blaxhold, Goathurst with Lexworthy and Halswell manors, Huntstile in Chilton Trinity, and Merridge in Spaxton.[7] Castle in Broomfield was recorded as part of the hundred in 1316 and 1327.[8] By 1569 Creech had been included in the hundred which was divided into three groups of tithings: Broomfield; Creech with Merridge; and Goathurst with Heathcombe, Lexworthy, Huntstile, Durleigh, Dukesse or Duke Fee, and Sydenham in Wembdon. A similar division was recorded in the 17th century.[9] Sydenham was part of the hundred until 1652.[10] In 1664–5 Andersfield comprised Broomfield with Heathcombe and Oggshole, Durleigh with Duke Fee, Enmore with Blaxhold, Goathurst with Lexworthy, Huntstile in Chilton Trinity, Merridge in Spaxton, Chilton (probably what was later called Chilton limit in Wembdon, which may have been the same as Sydenham), Creech St. Michael, and Lyng.[11] Duke Fee was probably absorbed into Durleigh after 1696.[12] Petherton limit, part of North Petherton village but in Andersfield hundred, was a separate tithing for land tax purposes from 1767,[13] and was recorded in 1670.[14] Petherton limit was last mentioned in 1847.[15]

Andersfield was said in John's reign to be a member of Somerton as royal demesne.[16] It was granted in 1448 to John, Lord Stourton (d. 1462), and descended to successive lords Stourton with Williton hundred[17] until 1835 when Andersfield hundred was sold to Charles Kemeys-Tynte. No reference to its ownership has been found after the 1840s.[18]

[1] Som. C.C. *County Development Plan, First Review* (1964), 2–3.
[2] *V.C.H. Som.* i. 534.
[3] *S.R.S.* xx. 241–4.
[4] S.R.O., DD/SG 58–9.
[5] *Rot. Hund.* (Rec. Com.), ii. 121, 126, 137.
[6] S.R.O., DD/S/WH 28; *S.R.S.* xi, p. 314.
[7] *Feud. Aids*, iv. 292–3.
[8] Ibid. 301, 331–2; *S.R.S.* iii. 162–4.
[9] *S.R.S.* xx. 241–4; S.R.O., D/P/broo 13/1/1; DD/DP 24/5.
[10] P.R.O., E 317/Som. 3.

[11] Dwelly, *Hearth Tax*, i. 41–55; S.R.O., Q/REl 2/4, 10. Part of Durleigh parish was known later as Chilton limit: below, Durleigh, local govt.
[12] S.R.O., DD/DP 24/5. Estates in the west of N. Petherton parish were described as in Duke Fee *c.* 1770: ibid. DD/SLM (C/1795).
[13] Ibid. Q/REl 2/4, 8.
[14] Dwelly, *Hearth Tax*, ii. 44.
[15] S.R.O., D/P/pet. n 9/1/3.
[16] *Bk. of Fees*, i. 261–2.
[17] *Cal. Pat.* 1446–52, 160; *V.C.H. Som.* v. 11.
[18] S.R.O., DD/S/WH 285.

The sheriff's tourn for Andersfield with Cannington and North Petherton hundreds was held at Lypestone or Limestone Hill in Cannington parish twice a year before 1652 when it was 'much discontinued'.[19] The court still met at Lypestone in 1696 but at Lady Day or Easter only five tenants owed suit, four with a 'post' or juror, and at Michaelmas eight had to attend. Twice yearly courts both at Enmore and at Andersfield were each attended by a further three tenants, presumably instead of going to Lypestone.[20] The sheriff's tourn had been discontinued by 1726[21] and in 1758 it was said that courts for the three hundreds had been separated and those for Andersfield met at Andersfield Green or at Enmore.[22] In 1760 one of the earl of Egmont's tenants at Andersfield owed suit to the hundred or manor court of Andersfield.[23] The earl held courts leet with view of frankpledge and court baron annually in October. From 1762 until 1827 they were held at Enmore, between 1784 and 1786 at the Castle inn there. Charles Kemeys-Tynte held his hundred court at Andersfield in the 1840s, in the bailiff's house. Court rolls survive for 1762–1827 and 1842–3.

Each tithing was represented by its tithingman and its posts or jurors who were to take cognizance of nuisances,[24] but by 1728 only the tithings of the northern area attended the court and Durleigh and Broomfield were also absent.[25] Blaxhold, Enmore, Goathurst, Heathcombe, Huntstile, Lexworthy, Merridge, and Oggshole tithings were required to attend court in 1762 but in 1764 it was said that the omission of Durleigh was an error and the tithing was always summoned thereafter. Business was limited to the formal appointment of constables, bailiff, and tithing-men and the very occasional presentment of nuisances.[26]

In the 17th century all tithings paid rents of between 1d. and 2s. called tithing silver or certain money at Easter and again at Michaelmas. Sydenham manor paid 1s. at each court and that vill paid an additional 6d. at Easter. The hundred also paid 2s. 6d. a year for the sheriff's aid.[27] Certain money was still paid in 1720[28] and continued to be claimed until 1779 but was thereafter omitted from the court record. Tithingmen were last recorded in 1843.[29]

Henry III granted the bedelry of the hundred, also known as of West Parrett, to John de la Linde (d. 1272), lord of Broomfield, who was followed by his son Walter.[30] Hugh of Bicknoller was hundred bailiff in 1345.[31] The bailiff was appointed in the hundred court from 1762 until 1843. In 1836 and 1842 he also served as hayward and was responsible for the pound, but in 1843 a separate hayward was appointed.[32] The high constable was recorded in 1626 when he contributed towards ammunition for the Bridgwater magazine.[33] In the late 18th century two high constables were chosen, one for each part of the hundred.[34] From 1765 the parts were known as the higher, apparently the southern, and the lower divisions.[35]

The hundred pound lay in Enmore parish and was rebuilt c. 1828, probably near the Castle inn. It remained in use until 1843.[36] The fire beacon for the hundred stood on Wind Down in Broomfield parish and its site was recorded until 1791.[37]

[19] P.R.O., E 317/Som. 3.
[20] S.R.O., DD/DP 24/5.
[21] Ibid. DD/S/SH 11.
[22] Ibid. DD/RN 67.
[23] Ibid. DD/S/WH 37.
[24] Ibid. DD/RN 67.
[25] Ibid. DD/X/HU 1.
[26] Ibid. DD/RN 67.
[27] P.R.O., E 317/Som. 3.
[28] S.R.O., DD/S/WH 220.

[29] Ibid. DD/RN 67.
[30] *Rot. Hund.* (Rec. Com.), ii. 121, 126; below, Broomfield, manors.
[31] S.R.O., DD/L P35/1, P36/3.
[32] Ibid. DD/RN 67; DD/S/WH 285.
[33] Ibid. D/B/bw 1960.
[34] Collinson, *Hist. Som.* i. 71.
[35] S.R.O., DD/RN 67.
[36] Ibid. DD/S/WH 285.
[37] Ibid. DD/X/CAT 5; DD/S/WH 285.

BROOMFIELD

BROOMFIELD parish occupies part of the south-eastern end of the Quantocks, where steep-sided, wooded valleys cut deep into the surrounding high ground. Broomfield hamlet, in the south-western part of the parish, is 7 km. north of Taunton and 6 km. west of North Petherton. The parish is irregularly shaped, the only natural boundary being the King's Cliff stream in the south-east. It measures c. 7.5 km. from east to west at its widest and 5 km. from north to south. In 1838 it was reckoned to be 4,274 a.[1] In 1881 the almost detached area to the north-west around Holwell and Blaxhold (3 houses and 10 persons) was transferred to Enmore, leaving 4,080 a. (1,651 ha.).[2] In 1981 minor changes to the boundary with Spaxton, also in the north-west, brought part of Merridge into Broomfield.

Broomfield parish straddles the Quantock ridge where the Devonian Ilfracombe slates lie at 290 m. at Broomfield Hill near its western boundary. South-east of the hill springs feed a stream flowing east, known as the King's Cliff stream at its lower end, forming a long cleft between two spurs which fall gently east and south-east. A similar valley, Nailscombe, runs south from the western end of the parish, and a smaller one, known as Heathcombe, runs from Broomfield Hill. There are narrow strips of valley gravels in Heathcombe and along the King's Cliff stream[3] and pockets of limestone, notably at Holwell, in the north-west, where a cavern is the only one in Britain to contain anthodites, clusters of aragonite formed where slate and limestone meet.[4] Limestone and tile-stones were quarried at Rooks Castle in the 14th century[5] and at Nailscombe in the later 16th. In the 17th century there was some illegal quarrying and lime was also sold without leave of the manor court.[6] There was a limekiln in 1705, possibly near Heathcombe, and others at Holwell by 1838.[7] Iron and copper ore were mined in the 19th century at Wort wood and near Raswell Farm.[8]

The parish is rich in prehistoric remains from the Mesolithic period onwards. There are Iron Age hillforts at Ruborough, Rooks Castle, and Castles;[9] land known as Stanborough, in the south-east of the parish, may indicate a fourth site.[10] Broomfield parish seems to have been partly or wholly in the pre-Conquest Quantock

forest.[11] The names Kingslands and Kingshill indicate a royal connexion[12] and still in the 13th century there was a royal piggery (porcheria) at Rooks Castle,[13] which by the early 16th century had been transformed into the common pound for the county.[14] The estate at Denesmodeswelle had formed part of the royal manor of Somerton before 1086.[15] Kingshill paid rent to Somerton until 1204,[16] Oggshole was a member of Somerton manor in 1212,[17] Rooks Castle remained a Crown holding until the 17th century,[18] and Melcombe was in the 16th century part of Creech manor, itself royal demesne in 1086.[19] Most of these estates lay to the south and east of the parish and adjoining North Petherton, where a royal park continued until the 16th century.[20]

The medieval settlement pattern was of scattered valley farmsteads, their names often incorporating the elements 'combe' or 'hole', as in Heathcombe, Nailscombe, Holwell, and Oggshole. The parish church, Fyne Court, the former school, and a few cottages constitute the hamlet of Broomfield. Many of the valley farmsteads were built or rebuilt in the 16th and 17th centuries,[21] and cottages were built on commons and roadside wastes, often illegally.[22] A house at Patcombe was built in the Palladian style for the bailiff of Halswell in 1771 but in 1861 was used as workers' cottages.[23] Broomfield Hall, which replaced a substantial house standing in 1664, was built in 1803 and is of five bays and three storeys in brick.[24] Since the mid 19th century many of the cottages have been abandoned, and the hamlets of Ivyton and Westleigh have shrunk to single farmsteads.[25]

The roads in the parish mainly follow spurs and ridges, only a few descending into the wider combes. The principal routes, linking Bishop's Lydeard with Bridgwater[26] and North Petherton, and Taunton with Nether Stowey, the latter only a halter path in 1547,[27] crossed below Broomfield Hill.

There is no evidence of open-field farming. Several large downland areas were divided into small fields probably at the end of the Middle Ages[28] and at least two farmstead sites at Binfords and Duckspool have remnants of infields nearby.[29] Before the 19th century there was common pasture at Broomfield Hill and

[1] S.R.O., tithe award. This article was completed in 1988.
[2] Census, 1891.
[3] O.S. Map 1/50,000, sheet 182 (1974 edn.); Geol. Surv. Map 1", drift, sheet 295 (1956 edn.).
[4] Proc. Som. Arch. Soc. ii. 14–32; W. A. Macfadyen, Geol. Highlights of the W. Country, 246.
[5] S.R.O., DD/SAS NP 1, m. 12; S.R.S. iii. 162–3; liii, p. 229.
[6] S.R.O., DD/S/WH 326.
[7] Ibid. 193; ibid. tithe award.
[8] Below, econ. hist.
[9] Som. C.C., Sites and Mons. Rec.; L. V. Grinsell, Arch. of Exmoor (1970), 91.
[10] S.R.O., tithe award.
[11] Rot. Hund. (Rec. Com.), ii. 122, 129, 134.
[12] Below, manors.
[13] Rot. Hund. (Rec. Com.), ii. 122, 134.
[14] S.R.S. xxvii, p. 268.

[15] V.C.H. Som. i. 435.
[16] P.R.O., C 52/24, no. 16.
[17] Bk. of Fees, i. 84.
[18] S.R.O., DD/S/WH 20, 95.
[19] Ibid. 21; below, Creech St. Michael, manors.
[20] Below, N. Petherton, intro.
[21] e.g. S.R.O., DD/V/BWr 4.2–3.
[22] Ibid. DD/S/WH 130–1, 209, 219; ibid. Q/S Pet 1; S.R.S. xxxiv. 23, 34, 50.
[23] S.R.O., T/PH/vch 73; P.R.O., RG 9/1622.
[24] Dwelly, Hearth Tax, i. 53; S.R.O., DD/SAS JK 21; DD/SAS (C/2645) 24.
[25] S.R.O., tithe award; P.R.O., HO 107/1924; Highclere Castle, Carnarvon MSS., U/C 2, 8.
[26] S.D.N.Q. xxxi. 463.
[27] Hants R.O., ECCLES I 85/5.
[28] S.R.O., DD/L P35/3; ibid. tithe award.
[29] R. R. J. McDonnell, The Quantock Hills A.O.N.B.: Arch. Survey (Som. C.C. 1989), 10.

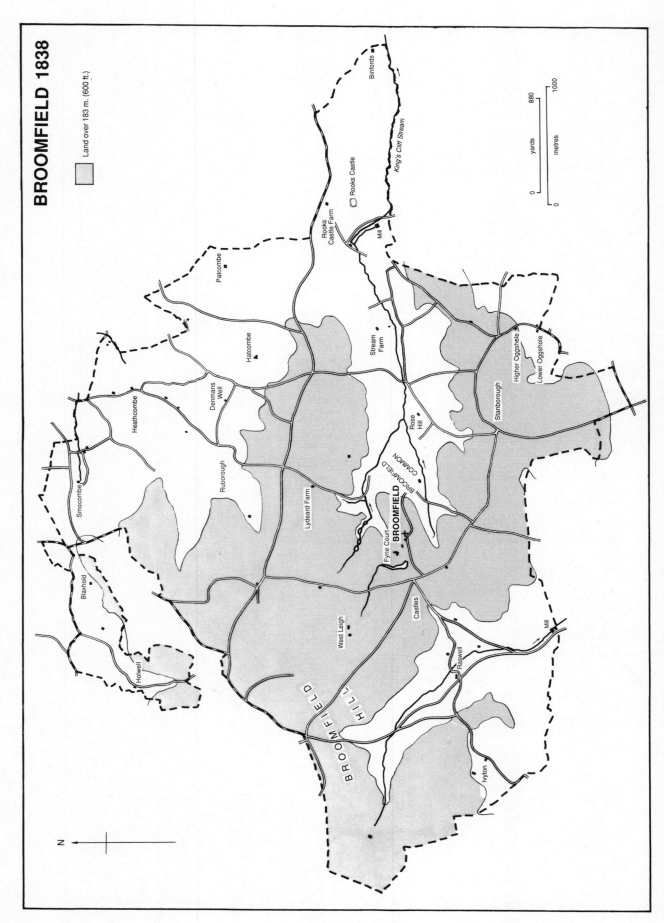

BROOMFIELD 1838

Land over 183 m. (600 ft.)

N

King's Cliff Stream

Rooks Castle

Binfords

Rooks Castle Farm

Mill

Patcombe

Stream Farm

Hatcombe

Higher Oggshole

Lower Oggshole

Dennans Well

Stanborough

Rose Hill

Heathcombe

BROOMFIELD COMMON

Ruborough

Smocombe

Lydeard Farm

Fyne Court

BROOMFIELD

Blaxhold

Castles

West Leigh

Holwell

Raswell

Mill

BROOMFIELD HILL

Ivyton

yards   880   1000

metres

0   0

6

Buncombe in the west and at Broomfield Common east of the church, and common woodland at Wood Common, and probably also at Broomfield Hill.[30] Common land had shrunk by 1838 but still covered 303 a. at Broomfield Hill and Broomfield Common.[31] Some common land remained in 1988, but few inhabitants had common rights.

In 1086 Broomfield and Blaxhold between them had woodland reckoned at a square league and 60 a.,[32] and farm and field names throughout the parish indicate the extent of former woodland. In 1580 there were trees or underwood on Buncombe Hill, Broomfield Common, and Lyeforde, and 'great woods' called East and West Broomfield and West Churchmans woods. Some woodland had been cleared by 1653[33] and some more at Patcombe and Rooks Castle in the mid 18th century,[34] but in the earlier 19th century trees were planted at Kingshill, Priors Down, and elsewhere. In 1838 there were c. 500 a. of woodland, mainly coppice, at Wort wood, near Broomfield church, Ivyton, Binfords, and Rooks Castle.[35] In 1905 there were 589 a. of woodland in the parish; by that date Priors Down and Kingshill had been cleared but Buncombe Hill and Broomfield Common were well covered.[36] The parish was extensively wooded in 1988, some woodland being managed by the Forestry Commission. John de la Linde, lord of Broomfield manor, received a grant of free warren in 1259 and there may have been a warren on Ivyton manor.[37]

There was an inn (hospicium) in 1407 with brewing equipment.[38] No licensed premises are recorded but a house called the Travellers Rest, later Home Farm, was said to have sold cider and there may have been a public house at Raswell called the Carnarvon Arms.[39]

The estimated population was 330 in 1791[40] and 369 in 1801. Numbers rose by over a third between 1811 and 1821 to 489 and then for forty years remained stable, reaching a peak of 525 in 1861. After 1871 the total fell steadily to 342 in 1901 and then more sharply in the mid 20th century to 199 in 1981.[41]

Twenty-three men were fined for complicity in the 1497 rebellion,[42] and five were punished for their involvement in the Monmouth rebellion, three with transportation to the West Indies.[43] Andrew Crosse (d. 1855) carried out experiments on electro-crystallization in and around Fyne Court.[44]

MANORS AND OTHER ESTATES. The identifiable Domesday estates in the parish are Broomfield, Blaxhold, and possibly Denesmodeswelle, while Heathcombe manor first occurs in the later 12th century and Ivyton manor by the later 13th.

BROOMFIELD was held by Alnod in 1066 and by William de Mohun in 1086.[45] It was claimed as part of Dunster honor until 1777 or later although in 1460 it was said to be held in chief.[46] It was probably one of the fees held in 1166 of William de Mohun (d. 1176) by Gerbert de Percy (d. 1179) in right of his wife Maud Arundel,[47] and they were succeeded at Broomfield by one of their daughters Alice, wife of Robert de Glastonia.[48] Alice's daughter Maud married Roger de Newburgh (d. 1194) and held the manor as a widow in John's reign,[49] and was followed by her son Robert de Newburgh (d. 1246). In 1227 Robert gave the manor in fee to his sister Margery, wife of William Belet,[50] creating a mesne lordship in which he was succeeded by his son Henry (d. 1271). William de Montagu (d. 1270) appears to have acquired it and was succeeded by his son Simon.[51] The Montagu family, which held Kingslands and Oggshole elsewhere in the parish, held the mesne lordship until 1415 or later.[52]

The terre tenancy of Margery Belet passed on her death (after 1241) to her son Robert (d. c. 1256).[53] Robert's son William granted it to John de la Linde (d. 1272) who was succeeded by his son Walter.[54] Walter held the manor in 1285 and 1316 but in 1303 it was said to be held by William de Welle, Walter de la Linde's bailiff in 1279.[55] In 1330 Broomfield was said to be held by Robert de Burgh and Walter de la Linde, although the latter was dead. Robert was bailiff of the manor in 1313 and the highest taxpayer in 1327.[56]

Walter died c. 1317 leaving five daughters, Joan, Cecily, Margery, Isabel, and Amice.[57] Amice died in 1332 and in the same year Isabel, then wife of Philip Parsafey, sold her quarter share to John of Stoford and his wife Alice.[58] In 1344 the manor was held by Robert of Lydgate, Herbert of Flinton, husband of Cecily de la Linde, John of Stoford, and Robert Dallingrigge, probably an error for Roger, son of Joan de la Linde by her husband John.[59] By 1346 Roger Dallingrigge held the whole manor.[60] By 1350 John Biccombe held the manor, and Broomfield descended with Crowcombe Biccombe manor,

30 S.R.O., DD/S/WH 19, 219, 246; ibid. Q/SR 122/23–4.
31 Ibid. tithe award.
32 V.C.H. Som. i. 491, 506.
33 S.R.O., DD/S/WH 246.
34 Ibid. 41.
35 Ibid. tithe award.
36 Statistics supplied by the then Bd. of Agric., 1905; O.S. Map 6", Som. LX. NE. (1890 edn.).
37 Cal. Pat. 1258–66, 110–11; S.R.O., tithe award; but Warren House may be named after 16th-century tenants: S.R.O., DD/L P35/8.
38 S.R.S. xvi. 29.
39 A. Mead, The Story of Fyne Court and Broomfield (1979), 15.
40 Collinson, Hist. Som. i. 72.
41 Census.
42 Fines Imposed in 1497, ed. A. J. Howard, 7.
43 S.R.S. lxxix. 9, 65, 94.
44 D.N.B.
45 V.C.H. Som. i. 506.
46 S.R.S. xxxiii, p. 351; P.R.O., C 139/177, no. 44.
47 Red Bk. Exch. (Rolls Ser.), ii. 226.
48 Sanders, Eng. Baronies, 72.
49 Plac. de Quo Warr. (Rec. Com.), 692, where Maud is called Margery.
50 Sanders, Eng. Baronies, 72; S.R.S. vi. 61, 362; ibid. extra ser. 281.
51 Pole MS. 245; S.R.S. xxxvi. 38; S.R.O., DD/L P35/1.
52 Below; Cal. Inq. p.m. ii, p. 1; Cal. Fine R. 1413–22, 94–5.
53 Close R. 1237–42, 364; Cal. Close, 1272–9, 185.
54 S.R.S. vi. 167; Cal. Inq. p.m. ii, p. 1; Rot. Hund. (Rec. Com.), ii. 121; S.R.O., DD/X/CH 4.
55 Feud. Aids, iv. 292, 301, 331; S.R.S. xli. 212.
56 S.R.S. iii. 162; xxxiii, p. 73; Cal. Inq. p.m. viii, p. 389.
57 Cal. Close, 1318–23, 100.
58 S.R.S. extra ser. 287; xii. 161.
59 Cal. Inq. p.m. vii, p. 449; viii, p. 389.
60 Feud. Aids, iv. 345.

which John had acquired by his marriage with Iseult of Crowcombe,[61] until the death of Hugh Biccombe in 1568 when, under a settlement of 1556, Broomfield passed to Hugh's daughter Maud, wife of Hugh Smythe (d. 1581).[62] Maud probably predeceased her husband, and the heir on his death was their daughter Elizabeth, wife of Edward Morgan.[63] Elizabeth was probably dead by 1596 when Edward (d. 1633) settled the estate on their son William for his marriage. William settled it on his eldest son Edward in 1611 and in 1633 on his second son Henry. William died in 1634[64] and a month later his eldest son Edward, with Henry and William Morgan, sold Broomfield manor to Walter Granger probably on behalf of Andrew Crosse and William Towill. William Towill the elder died in 1649, and in 1653 his son William and Andrew Crosse and his wife Mary made a partition of the manor.[65]

One half of the manor, later the *FYNE COURT* estate, descended in the Crosse family in the direct male line from Andrew (d. 1689) to Andrew (d. 1705), Richard (d. 1716), Richard (d. 1766), Richard (d. 1800), Andrew (d. 1855), the scientist,[66] and John. John took his mother's name of Hamilton and died in 1880 leaving a widow Susan (d. 1916), on whom the estate had been settled. Her grandson John Hamilton sold the estate in 1952 to F. J. C. Adams but there is no record of a sale of lordship. In 1972 the estate was acquired by the National Trust under an earlier agreement with Adams.[67]

Fyne Court was built by the Crosse family probably in the late 17th century. It had a main eastern elevation of seven bays, with the central bays recessed, and a secondary elevation of seven bays to the south. The south front was extended westwards by five bays when a music room was added. The room was rebuilt in 1849. Outbuildings and stables to the north and west of the house enclosed a court by the 19th century. The outbuildings, music room, and library, remnants of a stone building, survived a fire which destroyed most of the house in 1894.[68] The gardens, north and west of the house, are probably of the 18th century.[69] They are mostly wooded but include a walled kitchen garden and, along part of the western border, a small serpentine lake with a boathouse and adjacent castle-like summerhouse.

After the partition of 1653 William Towill sold parts of the estate, including the capital messuage, to members of his own family.[70] Among them was the former leasehold farm known as Hollams and Lakes which by 1799 had been acquired by Thomas Mullins (d. 1811) and had become part of the Halswell estate in 1813. Mullins probably built the house known as Rose Hill by 1810.[71] It comprises two storeys with attics and its main front is of three bays with a central, pedimented porch. What remained of the Towill share of the manor was sold in 1659 to Hugh Halswell of Goathurst and descended like Halswell manor.[72]

In 1508 Lydeard Farm, the name recorded in 1327, was described as a capital messuage.[73] At the partition in 1653 it passed to William Towill, and remained with a younger branch of the family until the 1720s.[74] In 1734 it was owned by Ann Crosse, and by 1750 by her son Andrew, and descended with the Crosse estate.[75] The cob house may have a medieval core but was rebuilt in the 17th century when a carved staircase was installed. The house was greatly altered in the 19th and 20th centuries.[76]

IVYTON manor was held of Broomfield manor in 1283 and continued to be so held until 1790 or later, although suit and rent had probably been unpaid for many years and it was not recorded as a manor after 1662.[77] Ivyton was held by Hugh de la Tour (d. 1283), possibly in succession to his brother Henry (d. by 1280).[78] Hugh's son Thomas was succeeded by his son Hugh who died c. 1321 leaving a son William.[79] William died in 1349 leaving a daughter Alice, wife of John Roche. Alice was dead by 1375 but had had a child.[80] That child may have been Isabel, wife of John Haddecombe, who released her claim to Ivyton to John Roche in 1375 and again in 1390.[81] Later in 1390 Roche gave Ivyton to John Luttrell who in 1392 assigned the rents to John Haddecombe and his wife Isabel for her life, and granted the estate in 1394 to Joan, Roche's second wife, by then married to Thomas Trowe of Plainsfield. In 1404 Richard Roche, son of John, quitclaimed Ivyton to Joan's feoffees.[82] In 1429 John Luttrell gave the reversion after Joan's death to his kinsman Richard Luttrell; Joan was dead by 1439 when Richard took possession.[83] Ivyton then descended with Over Vexford in Stogumber until 1570 when the manor was sold to William Lovel.[84]

William Lovel (d. 1590) was succeeded by his son John who conveyed Ivyton to James Clarke, his sister Emmot's husband, c. 1596.[85] Emmot's sons John, James, and Thomas Clarke sold it in 1611[86] to Sir Bartholomew Michell (d. 1616) who was followed by his daughters Jane, wife of William Hockmore, and Frances, wife of Alexander

61 *Cal. Inq. p.m.* ix, p. 371; *S.R.S.* extra ser. 288.
62 *V.C.H. Som.* v. 57; S.R.O., DD/S/WH 19.
63 P.R.O., C 142/193, no. 87.
64 S.R.O., DD/S/WH 19; P.R.O., C 142/476, no. 139; G. T. Clark, *Genealogies of Glam.* (1886), 322.
65 S.R.O., DD/S/WH 19; *Som. Wills,* ed. Brown, iii. 95.
66 S.R.O., D/P/broo 2/1/1; D/P/can 2/1/3.
67 Inf. from Nat. Trust.
68 Fyne Court, photo. of ho.; *Western Gaz.* 7 Sept. 1894.
69 Fyne Court, map 1812.   70 S.R.O., DD/S/WH 19.
71 Ibid. 209, 242.   72 Ibid. 19.
73 *S.R.S.* iii. 162; S.R.O., DD/AH 11/9.
74 S.R.O., DD/S/WH 19; D/P/broo 2/1/1; Highclere Castle, Carnarvon MSS., U/C 9; *Som. Wills,* ed. Brown, iii. 96.
75 S.R.O., D/P/broo 4/1/1; DD/S/WH 221A.

76 Ibid. DD/V/BWr 4.3.
77 *Cal. Inq. p.m.* ii, p. 278; S.R.O., DD/S/WH 219, 226; Highclere Castle, Carnarvon MSS., U/C 2.
78 *S.R.S.* xliv. 285; *Cal. Inq. p.m.* ii, p. 278; S.R.O., DD/S/WH 68.
79 *Cal. Inq. p.m.* iii, p. 59, where Thomas's son is erroneously called Thomas; ibid. vii, p. 481; *Cal. Fine R.* 1319–27, 58.
80 *Cal. Inq. p.m.* ix, p. 371; S.R.O., DD/L P35/1.
81 S.R.O., DD/L P35/1; *S.R.S.* xvii. 140–1.
82 S.R.O., DD/L P35/1–3.   83 Ibid. 4.
84 *V.C.H. Som.* v. 182; P.R.O., CP 25(2)/204/12 Eliz. I Hil.
85 S.R.O., DD/S/WH 209.
86 P.R.O., C 142/440, no. 159; ibid. CP 25(2)/346/10 Jas. I East.; Highclere Castle, Carnarvon MSS., U/C 2.

STOGURSEY CHURCH: THE CHOIR IN 1836

BROOMFIELD CHURCH, *c.* 1910

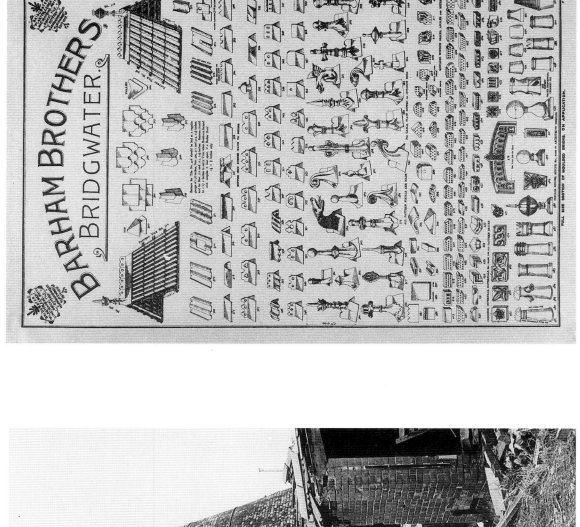

Barham Bros. brick and tile products, c. 1900

Barham Bros. brick and tile kilns, c. 1980

BRIDGWATER

Popham.[87] In 1635 Frances released Ivyton to Gregory Hockmore.[88] Between 1647 and 1662 Hockmore divided and sold the estate. Nicholas Brown bought the capital messuage but forfeited it under a mortgage to Dr. Thomas Dyke who had purchased the lordship and remaining lands from Hockmore in 1662. Dyke also bought some of the other Ivyton lands and his widow Joan purchased more in 1698.[89] Most of Ivyton passed on Dyke's death in 1689 to his kinsman Thomas Deane or Dyke of Tetton in Kingston St. Mary.[90] The rest went to another kinsman Edward Dyke (d. 1728). In 1721 Thomas married Edward's daughter Mary and their only child Elizabeth inherited the shares of both her father and an uncle, Edward Dyke (d. 1746).[91] Elizabeth, who married Sir Thomas Acland, died in 1753 and was succeeded by her son John Dyke Acland (d. 1778). John's widow Harriet (or Harriot) held the estate until her death in 1815 when it passed to her son-in-law Henry Herbert, 2nd earl of Carnarvon, formerly husband of Harriet's daughter Elizabeth Kitty (d. 1813). Henry was succeeded by his son also Henry, the 3rd earl (d. 1849).[92] Alan Herbert (d. 1907), a younger son of the 3rd earl, left Ivyton to his nephew Mervyn (d. 1929), a younger son of the 4th earl, and Mervyn's son, Mervyn, was the owner in 1988.[93]

A capital messuage was recorded probably early in the 16th century and in 1677.[94] Ivyton Farm, with a garden front of three bays and a rear service wing, dates from the early 18th century.

RASWELL, formerly Rawleshill or Rawshill,[95] was a freehold of Broomfield manor. It belonged to John Towill or at Well in 1507–8.[96] John (d. 1535) was followed by his son William (d. 1591) and grandson Edward Towill (d. 1647).[97] Edward was succeeded by his son William (d. 1649) who left it to his wife Mary for life. Mary died in 1677[98] and was followed by William Towill (d. 1685), probably her grandson. William's son, also William, and his wife Margaret sold Raswell to Thomas Dyke in 1697 but took a lease of the premises which the Towill family occupied until *c.* 1740.[99] Raswell descended in the Dyke family with Ivyton.[1]

Raswell farmhouse, which is rendered apparently over rubble, probably dates from the 16th century and has a roof of jointed-cruck construction with a framed ceiling in the hall. The three-room cross-passage plan house was extended in the 17th century by the addition of a rear north wing and an eastern room, probably a kitchen, with a jettied first floor.[2]

In 1066 *BLAXHOLD* was held by Leofric and in 1086 by Geoffrey of Roger de Courcelles.[3] A separate manor until 1451 or later, it descended with Enmore manor and by the late 17th century had become a leasehold of Enmore manor.[4] The tenant, Jasper Porter, seems to have acquired the farm by 1744 and left it to his daughter Susanna (d. 1805), wife of Richard Crosse.[5] Susanna left it to her second son Richard, who died childless, and it passed on his death to his elder brother Andrew Crosse. Andrew sold Blaxhold in 1853 to Meshach Brittan of Bristol, from whom it passed to his sons William and Charles. They conveyed the estate in 1870 to Thomas Palfrey Broadmead and it descended with the Enmore Castle estate.[6]

There was a house on the farm in 1637 with wainscotted hall and parlour.[7] The capital messuage in 1810 was Lower Blaxhold House, in Enmore parish.[8] Hill House, built at Blaxhold before 1819 by Richard Crosse in the form of a double cube, appears to have been demolished by 1890.[9]

In 1086 *DENESMODESWELLE* was held of Alfred d'Epaignes; formerly it had been part of the royal manor of Somerton.[10] It is thought to have been the estate called Denman's or Deadman's Well, possibly from the personal name Denman recorded in the parish in the early 15th century,[11] but that estate can be traced only from 1649, when it was left by Thomas Collard to his wife Frances.[12] It was held with an adjoining farm called Heathcombe by the Thorne family until after 1761[13] and passed from Margaret Jeanes (d. 1769) to her nephew Lancelot St. Albyn.[14] It descended with Alfoxton in Stringston until *c.* 1910 when it became part of the Halswell estate.[15] The site of the farm was later abandoned.

HEATHCOMBE, described in 1284–5 as ¼ fee and from 1359 as a manor,[16] was shared in 1211 between Hilary wife of Nicholas Avenel, Joan wife of Henry Furneaux, and Lettice wife of John son of Gerard of Earnshill,[17] the three daughters of Robert son of William (d. *c.* 1185–6). With Robert's manor of Kilve the estate was held of Compton Dundon manor until 1510 or later,[18] and descended in the Furneaux family

87 P.R.O., C 142/440, no. 89.
88 Ibid. CP 25(2)/480/11 Chas. I Mich.; Highclere Castle, Carnarvon MSS., U/C 2, 8.
89 Highclere Castle, Carnarvon MSS., U/C 1–2, 8, 12.
90 Ibid. FF/A 5; U/C 7–8; *Som. Wills*, ed. Brown, ii. 115.
91 Highclere Castle, Carnarvon MSS., FF/A 8, 10; U/C 2, 5.
92 S.R.O., Q/REl 2/1; ibid. tithe award; Burke, *Peerage* (1949), 359.
93 S.R.O., D/P/broo 13/1/2; *Elect. Reg.* (1905); Burke, *Peerage* (1949), 359; M.I. in Kingston St. Mary ch.
94 S.R.O., DD/L P35/3; Highclere Castle, Carnarvon MSS., U/C 2.
95 S.R.O., DD/AH 11/9; DD/S/WH 338.
96 Ibid. DD/AH 11/9–10.
97 Ibid. D/P/broo 2/1/1; *Wells Wills*, ed. Weaver, 82; M.I. in Broomfield ch.
98 S.R.O., D/P/broo 2/1/1; *Som. Wills*, ed. Brown, iii. 95.
99 S.R.O., DD/S/WH 338; D/P/broo 2/1/1; Highclere

Castle, Carnarvon MSS., U/C 2, 10.
1 Above.
2 S.R.O., DD/V/BWr 4.4.
3 *V.C.H. Som.* i. 491.
4 S.R.O., DD/NN H/20; below, Enmore, manors.
5 S.R.O., DD/PLE 63; DD/BR/ely 11/6.
6 Ibid. DD/PLE 63; below, Enmore, manors.
7 S.R.O., DD/SP inventory, 1637.
8 Ibid. DD/PLE 63.
9 C. A. Crosse, *Memorials of Andrew Crosse* (1857), 47.
10 *V.C.H. Som.* i. 435; *Dom. Bk.* ed. Thorn, 350.
11 S.R.O., DD/SAS FA 75.
12 Ibid. T/PH/dut 1.
13 Ibid. DD/S/WH 41, 338.
14 Ibid. Q/REl 2/1; M.I. in Enmore ch.
15 S.R.O., D/R/bw 15/3/4; DD/S/WH 205; below, Stringston, manors.
16 *Feud. Aids*, iv. 293; *Cal. Inq. p.m.* x, p. 395.
17 *Cur. Reg. R.* vi. 142.
18 *V.C.H. Som.* v. 98; *Cat. Anct. D.* v, A 12575.

and their descendants with Perry Furneaux in Wembdon until *c.* 1485.[19] It then passed to the Stawell family with Merridge in Spaxton[20] and was one of the estates confiscated from Sir John Stawell during the Interregnum and sold to Edward Jenkins in 1652.[21] It was recovered at the Restoration, but was sold in 1698 to Francis Bennet who dismembered the holding. The lordship was not recorded thereafter.[22]

William de Say was a tenant on the estate in the later 12th century[23] and was succeeded before 1211 by his sister Emme, wife of Roger Reimes. She died without issue before 1227.[24] That holding may have been the capital messuage and lands on the estate known as the farm of Heathcombe, which Matthew Furneaux granted to William of Sutton, heir of Hugh of Heathcombe, *c.* 1251, and William conveyed to William Malet of Enmore. From William Malet the estate passed to his son, also William, and the latter's widow Mary gave it to Raymond Malet and his wife Millicent.[25] Raymond's great-nephew Baldwin Malet settled it on Raymond and his then wife Joan *c.* 1306[26] but the holding, which came to be known as *HEATHCOMBE* manor, reverted to the main line of the Malets and descended as a holding in fee of the main manor until 1603 or later.[27] In 1602 John Malet sold to John Colford (d. 1622) most of the Heathcombe land, which was included in the later Willoughby's and Wood farms.[28]

Buckland priory appropriated the church before 1334,[29] and in 1539 the rectory estate, comprising the tithes of the parish and some glebe, passed to the Crown. It was granted in 1549 to Silvester Taverner,[30] from whom it had passed by 1557 to Humphrey Colles. Colles conveyed it to William Towill.[31] The *RECTORY* descended with Raswell until 1675, when it was settled on Jeffrey Towill, a younger son.[32] He died without issue in 1683 and by 1691 it was owned by Matthew Baron, later mayor of Wells.[33] He or another Matthew Baron held it until 1750,[34] and was succeeded by John Moss, who was in possession until 1784.[35] Richard Crosse of Fyne Court probably owned it by 1786, and it remained in the Crosse and Hamilton families.[36] Between the 1820s and 1840s it was held by John Hamilton, possibly in trust for Andrew Crosse's first wife Mary Hamilton and her children. The tithes were commuted for a rent charge of £379 in 1838.[37] In 1619 the glebe consisted of two gardens and 6 a. of land. By 1838 there were nearly 30 a. of glebe,[38] which were later absorbed into the Fyne Court estate.

A house on the rectory was mentioned in 1557 and 1619.[39] It was known in the 19th century as Parsonage Farm, or Old Parsonage, and was occupied by the lay rector in 1754.[40] Known by the end of the 19th century as the Cottage[41] and later as Fyne Court Cottage, it stands behind a small green north-west of the church. The house, which dates from the 17th century, was in 1988 occupied as two dwellings.

Buckland priory had at least three tenements in the parish attached to their manor of North Petherton.[42] The tenements were known as *BUNCOMBE*, and perhaps also included Holwell.[43] In 1544 the Crown granted the reversion to Sir John Fulford and Humphrey Colles and licensed alienation to Thomas Hill.[44] Hill was succeeded by his son George.[45] Some or all of the land passed to the Slape family and has not been traced after 1604.[46]

An estate described in the 16th century as *HOLWELL* manor and perhaps before 1539 owned by Buckland priory came into the possession of Thomas Hill (d. 1565), and he sold part of it to Edward Jenkins (d. *c.* 1572).[47] Andrew Jenkins (d. 1593) held other land of George Hill, Thomas's son.[48] By the 17th century three separate holdings at Holwell may have derived from Hill's estate. One, later known as Nether, Lower, or Middle Holwell, was assigned in 1602 by John Malet and his wife Mary to John Colford, in succession to John Jenkins.[49] The Colfords, who are said to have held the land in chief by knight service, remained in possession until the later 17th century, but by 1710 had sold to George Buller.[50] George's great-nephew, also George Buller, sold it in 1789 to John Barrell, and John's son, also John, in 1857 conveyed it to the Revd. Henry Codrington. Henry conveyed it to trustees.[51]

A second holding, known as Great or Higher Holwell, descended with Enmore manor in the late 17th century[52] but in 1743 was purchased by William Duddlestone Skinner. Twelve years later Skinner sold to John Perceval, earl of Egmont (d. 1770), and until 1835 Holwell remained part of the Enmore Castle estate. John Jeffereys bought it in that year.[53]

19 Below, Wembdon, manors.
20 Below, Spaxton, manors.
21 *Cal. Cttee. for Compounding*, ii. 1429.
22 S.R.O., DD/PC 14; DD/DHR 19; below, econ. hist.
23 Pole MS. 1002.
24 *S.R.S.* vi. 163; ix, p. 9; *Cur. Reg. R.* vi. 42, 316.
25 *S.D.N.Q.* iii. 256; Pole MS. 445, 944, 994, 1000, 1003, 4451.   26 *S.R.S.* vi. 360.
27 Below, Enmore, manors; Pole MS. 4229; P.R.O., WARD 2/18/70/11.
28 S.R.O., DD/S/WH 40; DD/SAS JK 13; P.R.O., C 142/423, no. 72; below, econ. hist.
29 *S.R.S.* ix, p. 224.   30 *Cal. Pat.* 1549-51, 36.
31 P.R.O., CP 25(2)/77/660/4 & 5 Phil. & Mary Mich.
32 Ibid. CP 25(2)/717/27 Chas. II East.
33 S.R.O., D/D/Pd 30; *S.D.N.Q.* v. 60.
34 S.R.O., DD/S/WH 222.
35 Ibid. D/D/Bo; ibid. Q/REl 2/1.
36 Ibid. DD/SAS (C/238) 69; D/R/bw 15/3/4; ibid. Q/REl 2/1; above.
37 Ibid. Q/REl 2/1; ibid. tithe award.

38 Ibid. D/D/Rg 261; ibid. tithe award.
39 P.R.O., CP 25(2)/77/660/4 & 5 Phil. & Mary Mich.; S.R.O., D/D/Rg 261.
40 P.R.O., HO 107/1924; ibid. RG 9/1622; RG 10/2383; S.R.O., D/P/broo 13/6/1.
41 O.S. Map 6", Som. LX. NE. (1890 edn.).
42 P.R.O., SC 6/Edw. VI/402.
43 Ibid. C 3/273, no. 29; below.
44 *L. & P. Hen. VIII*, xix (1), pp. 496, 506.
45 P.R.O., C 142/143, no. 24.
46 *Cal. Pat.* 1575-8, p. 27; P.R.O., C 142/279, no. 455; ibid. WARD 7/38/16.
47 P.R.O., C 3/104, no. 7; C 3/273, no. 29; C 142/143, no. 24; *Som. Wills*, ed. Brown, v. 59.
48 P.R.O., C 142/409, no. 83.
49 S.R.O., DD/SAS JK 19; P.R.O., C 3/327, no. 28.
50 *S.R.S.* lxvii, pp. 14-15; *Som. Wills*, ed. Brown, ii. 37-8; S.R.O., DD/S/WH 338.
51 S.R.O., DD/PLE 62; DD/DP 127.
52 Ibid. DD/X/HU 2.
53 Ibid. DD/PLE 62, 64.

A third holding, later known as North or Little Holwell or Diddicks Down, passed from the Malets to Charles White on his marriage to Jane Malet in 1655, but later in the century it was held by the Thorne family.[54] Roger Thorne sold it to John Perceval, earl of Egmont (d. 1770), c. 1761, but by 1838 it had been acquired by John Jeffereys.[55]

Jeffereys, a nabob from Hertfordshire, died c. 1852 and his whole estate passed to his illegitimate children John and Mary.[56] They acquired Great and Little Holwell direct and Lower Holwell through trustees. John was dead by 1861 and his widow Anne in 1879, leaving Holwell in trust for Mary for life. She died in 1900 and her surviving trustee sold Great and Little Holwell to William Broadmead of Enmore Castle.[57]

A house at Lower Holwell had seven hearths in 1664 but the site was abandoned probably in the 1870s.[58] A house attached to Little Holwell was in Spaxton parish. Great Holwell house was built between 1841 and 1851 but had probably been demolished by 1881.[59] Great Holwell farm dates probably from the early 17th century and has a main range of three rooms, of which the easternmost, the kitchen, is beneath a lower roof; the parlour wing is at the west end. The principal rooms retain intersecting ceiling beams with heavy chamfers.

CASTLE, later ROOKS CASTLE, was a Crown estate associated with Somerton manor.[60] Its tenants, nominally copyholders, claimed in the 17th century to hold in fee simple, and Crown ownership ceased to be recorded after 1662.[61] Tenants in the 13th and 14th centuries may have been members of the Rok family, but by 1403 the estate was held by Richard, son and heir of John atte Castell.[62] Richard atte Castell (d. c. 1467) was succeeded by his son Richard (d. 1476). Richard's widow Edith and her son Robert were followed by John atte Castell (d. c. 1529), and by his son John. Robert atte Castell (d. c. 1617) was succeeded by his son Thomas, perhaps the Thomas Acastle who sold Rooks Castle probably in trust for Philip Yard. Philip and mortgagees sold it to John Tynte in 1662 in trust for Hugh Halswell.[63] Rooks Castle descended as part of the Halswell estate, to which was added by 1764 a neighbouring holding known as Rooks Castle or Steven's Place which had belonged to the Bragge family in the 17th and early 18th century.[64] Rooks Castle farmhouse was built on the site of Steven's Place in 1893.[65]

Part of the Rooks Castle estate was sold, probably in the later 17th century, and was known as BINFORDS by 1662.[66] It was owned by the Catford family until 1700, and later by the Paynes and the Jeanes. Charles Tynte bought the estate from the Revd. Thomas Coney and his wife Elizabeth Jeane in 1811, and it descended like Rooks Castle.[67]

Binfords house was built before 1662.[68] There were fishponds near it in 1700, and by 1791 it was an 'elegant seat' surrounded by pleasure grounds, and later a 'desirable place for retirement'.[69] Occupied by labourers in 1881, it was later abandoned and was in ruins by 1959.[70] The house had a main front of seven bays with a central, two-storeyed porch.[71]

KINGSLANDS formed part of Thurlbear manor in 1320[72] and descended with the earldom of Salisbury until the death of Edward Plantagenet in 1484. He was succeeded by Cecily Bonville, Baroness Harrington and Bonville (d. 1529), granddaughter of Richard Neville, earl of Salisbury (d. 1460), and wife in turn of Thomas Grey, marquess of Dorset (d. 1501), and Henry Stafford, earl of Wiltshire (d. 1523). Her son Thomas Grey, marquess of Dorset (d. 1530), was succeeded by his son Henry (cr. duke of Suffolk 1551, d. 1554). Following Suffolk's attainder Thurlbear was granted to William Howard, Baron Howard of Effingham (d. 1573), who in 1556 conveyed it to Sir William and Henry Portman.[73] In 1557 Henry Portman sold the Broomfield lands to Nicholas Halswell and his son Robert.[74] The land was held by the Halswells until c. 1638 and from then until after 1751 with Clavelshay in North Petherton.[75] It later reverted to the Halswell estate by being absorbed into Hatcombe farm, a holding which Nicholas Halswell had acquired from John Stawell in 1560.[76]

MILCOMBE or MELCOMBE STREAM formed part of the manor of Creech in 1558 when it was sold to John Pyleman the tenant, and was held of Creech until 1592 or later, but in 1691 it was said to be held of the queen in chief. Richard Pyleman, John's son, conveyed half the estate, called Helliers Place, to his brother Thomas and in 1574 sold the rest, including the Cross House, to Richard Kebby. Kebby died in 1586 leaving his share to his son Giles (d. c. 1595).[77] Thomas Pyleman died in 1575 leaving an infant son Eleazer. In 1612 Eleazer sold his share to Robert Kebby, son of Giles, and Giles sold to his brother Hugh in 1614 and 1616.[78] Hugh Kebby (d. 1645) was

54 Ibid. DD/X/CAT 2; DD/DP 24; DD/S/WH 41, 338.
55 Ibid. DD/ES 3; DD/PLE 64; DD/S/WH 285; ibid. tithe award.   56 Ibid. DD/PLE 62.
57 Ibid. DD/DP 127; DD/PLE 62; P.R.O., RG 9/1622.
58 Dwelly, Hearth Tax, i. 43; P.R.O., RG 10/2383; RG 11/2372.
59 P.R.O., HO 107/929, 1924; ibid. RG 11/2372.
60 Rot. Hund. (Rec. Com.), ii. 122.
61 S.R.O., DD/S/WH 20, 95.
62 S.R.S. iii. 162; xi, p. 313; S.R.O., DD/S/WH 18.
63 S.R.O., DD/S/WH 20.
64 Below, Goathurst, manors; Dors. R.O., D 104/M 2; S.R.O., DD/S/WH 147, 269.
65 O.S. Map 1", sheet XX (1809 edn.); S.R.O., DD/X/BID 1.
66 S.R.O., DD/X/BKE 16; D/P/pet. n 13/3/5.

67 Ibid. DD/RN 8; DD/S/FA 20, 48; DD/S/WH 193.
68 Ibid. DD/X/BKE 16.
69 Ibid. DD/S/FA 48; DD/S/WH 326; Collinson, Hist. Som. i. 72.
70 P.R.O., RG 11/2372; O.S. map 1/25,000, ST 23 (1959 edn.).
71 Som. Co. Libr., copy (1937) of 1756 sketch.
72 Cal. Inq. p.m. vi, p. 142.
73 R. Sixsmith, Hist. of Thurlbear (1959), 3–5, 13–14; Cal. Pat. 1555–7, 5.
74 S.R.O., DD/S/WH 5.
75 Ibid. 170; DD/S/BW 5; below, North Petherton, manors.
76 S.R.O., DD/S/WH 6, 21/3, 189, 225; ibid. tithe award.
77 Ibid. DD/S/WH 21, 209; P.R.O., C 142/278, no. 21.
78 S.R.O., DD/S/WH 21; P.R.O., C 142/263, no. 84.

succeeded by his son Hugh (d. 1658) and his grandson Hugh Kebby (d. *c.* 1675). In 1676 the last Hugh's daughter Mary and sister Jane conveyed Helliers Place and the Cross House and their lands to Sir Halswell Tynte.[79] The Melcombe Stream land formed Stream farm on the Halswell estate by 1797.[80]

OGGSHOLE was held by William de Montagu in 1212 of the Crown as a member of Somerton,[81] and was so held by successive earls of Salisbury until 1409 or later.[82] The land was in part subinfeudated to Richard Fromond, as heir to his father Robert and grandmother Margery.[83] Richard was alive *c.* 1285 but his estate had passed to John Gyan by 1316 and to Robert Gyan by 1344.[84] In 1397 Robert Tilley was holding Oggshole and he remained in possession in 1409.[85] In 1540 it belonged to William Hody as son and heir of Richard (d. 1536). William sold Oggshole to Nicholas Halswell in 1556 and 1558 and it descended with the Halswell estate.[86] Oggshole farmhouse was rebuilt in 1868.[87]

Athelney abbey owned land at Oggshole by grant of King Henry II and John of Erleigh in the 12th century.[88] The land descended after the Dissolution with Clavelshay in North Petherton.[89]

William son of Walter and Engelois, William Fichet, and King John made grants of land at *KINGSHILL*, once part of the Fichets' manor of Merridge, to Taunton priory in the early 13th century.[90] By 1275 the priory also had a small tenement in Melcombe with common pasture at Oggshole.[91] In 1544 the Crown granted the Kingshill land and perhaps the rest to William Portman and Alexander Popham.[92] Kingshill formed part of an exchange between Nicholas Halswell and John Stawell in 1560, and on the break-up of the Stawell estate in the late 17th century passed to the Thorne family.[93] Priors, East, or Great Down, possibly also once part of the priory estate,[94] were acquired with Kingshill *c.* 1798 by John Ryall (d. *c.* 1813), and John Hamilton bought them before 1882 from John Ryall Mayo, adding them to the Fyne Court estate.[95]

ECONOMIC HISTORY. Thirteen ploughlands were recorded on the two Domesday estates of Broomfield and Blaxhold in 1086, but there were only 7 ploughteams to support the 20 tenant farmers. The livestock on Broomfield manor were 135 sheep, 16 goats, 17 pigs, 13 cattle, and a riding horse. More than half of the land taxed was in demesne, but there was only one demesne ploughteam. The estates had increased in value by half since 1066.[96]

By the end of the Middle Ages, the large downs or 'balls', mostly under furze and heath, were used like the woodland for pasturage. At Ivyton there were pasture grounds up to 70 a. in extent, with very small closes for meadow.[97] Small areas of common land on the high ground, such as a plot of 14 a. on Buncombe Hill in 1515, were probably brought under cultivation and in 1593 tenants of Broomfield manor had to hedge their hill plots within three weeks of sowing.[98] Encroachments on the commons for tillage and settlement continued in the 17th century, and oats were grown there in 1637.[99]

From the mid 16th century land was acquired by the Halswell family of Goathurst, and farmsteads were established in the remoter parts of the parish. Hatcombe, Melcombe Stream, Oggshole, and Patcombe were bought by Nicholas Halswell between 1556 and 1560, and the Halswells and their successors the Tyntes continued their purchases on the division of Broomfield manor and the dismemberment of other estates until *c.* 1910.[1] Other farms seem to have been formed in the 17th century with the break-up of the Heathcombe estates. They included a farm successively called Smocombe, Heathcombe, and Broaddown, another called Gillards, now Smocombe farm, Smocombe House, Willoughbys and Wood farms, and the land which came to be attached to Broomfield Hall.[2]

Tenants on the Halswell estate at Patcombe in the 1660s were required to apply lime and soap ashes and to plant clover to improve the soil, and Broomfield Down may by then have been ploughed.[3] Common rights for as many as 700 sheep on Wood Common had been shared between 11 tenants *c.* 1600[4] and sheep were numerous on one farm at Ivyton in 1686, where pigs and bees were also recorded in an inventory of a prosperous tenant, who grew wheat and barley on his arable land.[5] The owner of Binfords also kept pigs and bees, the latter producing 60 lb. of honey a year, and among his crops were apples and hops.[6] Peas were grown on 20 a. at Patcombe in 1711, hops at Heathcombe and elsewhere later in the century, and flax at Ivyton.[7]

Improvements in the 18th century included the inclosure of Priors Down by 1755[8] and the creation of catch meadows on the hillsides above

79 S.R.O., DD/S/WH 21; D/P/broo 2/1/1.
80 Ibid. DD/S/WH 193.
81 *Bk. of Fees*, i. 84; *Cal. Inq. p.m.* vi, p. 143.
82 *Cal. Close*, 1405–9, 456.
83 *S.R.S.* xli. 6; xliv. 206.
84 *Feud. Aids*, iv. 293, 332; *Cal. Inq. p.m.* viii, p. 389.
85 P.R.O., C 136/94, no. 35; *Cal. Close*, 1405–9, 456.
86 P.R.O., LR 3/123; S.R.O., DD/S/WH 3; below, Goathurst, manors.
87 S.R.O., DD/S/WH 204.
88 *S.R.S.* xiv, p. 172; *Tax. Eccl.* (Rec. Com.), 204.
89 Below, N. Petherton, manors; S.R.O., Q/REl 2/1.
90 *S.R.S.* vi. 18; *Cal. Chart. R.* 1327–41, 315; *Bk. of Fees*, i. 84; *Proc. Som. Arch. Soc.* ix. 8–9; P.R.O., C 52/24.
91 *S.R.S.* xli. 6.
92 *L. & P. Hen. VIII*, xix (2), p. 313.
93 S.R.O., DD/SAS (C/112) 5; DD/S/WH 41; D/P/broo 2/1/1; D/P/spax 2/1/2.

94 Ibid. DD/S/WH 246, 338; DD/WO 11/3; Highclere Castle, Carnarvon MSS., U/C 2.
95 S.R.O., Q/REl 2/9; ibid. DD/PLE 63; D/P/broo 13/1/2; ibid. tithe award; above.
96 *V.C.H. Som.* i. 491, 506.
97 S.R.O., DD/L P35/3, 6, 8.
98 Ibid. DD/AH 11/10; DD/S/WH 209.
99 Ibid. DD/S/WH 19, 209.
1 Ibid. 6; above, manors.
2 S.R.O., DD/S/WH 285; DD/PLE 64; DD/SAS JK 2, 18, 22, 32.
3 Ibid. DD/S/BW 5; ibid. Q/SR 133/10.
4 Ibid. DD/S/WH 246.
5 Highclere Castle, Carnarvon MSS., U/C 12.
6 S.R.O., D/D/Pd 13.
7 Ibid. DD/S/WH 45, 253; ibid. Q/RLh 7, 20, 55, 77; Bristol R.O., 21789 (18).
8 S.R.O., DD/WO 11/3.

Rose Hill and west and north-east of Stream Farm.[9] Farm amalgamation took place, notably on the Halswell estate, where the larger units were let at rack rents. By 1835 several of the farms had been amalgamated at Ivyton, and Stream had absorbed five other holdings.[10] In 1838 there were still 20 holdings of under 50 a. and a further 16 of under 100 a.; nine more measured between 100 a. and 200 a., and three were over 200 a. including Ivyton (361 a.) and Stream (338 a.). Broomfield Common covered 303 a. despite encroachments.[11]

Significant changes took place in the later 19th century. In 1838 there were 2,478 a. of arable and 764 a. of meadow, pasture, and orchard.[12] By 1881 the number of farms over 300 a. had increased to four and the number of recorded farm labourers had dropped from 92 in 1871 to 79.[13] Between 1838 and 1905 the arable land in the parish had been reduced by more than half and converted either to grass or to woodland, grass amounting in 1905 to 1,536 a.[14] During the 20th century the number of farms shrank still further, the population fell sharply, and many isolated farm sites, including Hatcombe, Willoughbys, and Denman's Well were abandoned. Returns for 1982 covering about half the parish showed a predominance of grassland and livestock husbandry, but a variety of crops was also grown. The main crop returned was winter barley but some wheat and oats were grown together with potatoes, beans, turnips, swedes, and fodder crops. Of the 13 holdings recorded, 7 were over 50 ha. (c. 124 a.) and 3 were worked only part-time. There were 8 specialist dairy farms and 2 holdings rearing cattle and sheep. Livestock comprised 1,189 sheep, 992 cattle, 106 poultry, and 12 pigs.[15]

Woodland management can be traced from the later 16th century. Copyholders had the right to shroud trees in certain areas and in 1580 some rights to shrouds on Buncombe Hill and other places were let in return for manuring and tillage and later some small-scale felling. Broom was also sold.[16] Woodland near Binfords was coppiced in the early 18th century,[17] and felling at Buncombe c. 1815 produced 516 oaks.[18] Timber from the parish may have been used to build two vessels at Bridgwater c. 1879 and continued to be exploited c. 1910.[19] The parish provided employment for several carpenters in the later 19th century.[20]

In 1814 iron and copper ores were found in the parish;[21] c. 1825 Andrew Crosse attempted to mine copper by means of a 100-yard adit, and two shafts were sunk into the hill at Wort wood. In 1845 the mine was revived using a steam engine and Cornish miners, but it was abandoned because the engine could not cope with the water in the mine.[22] In 1853 local landowners agreed to work three mines including an old one near Raswell Farm. The Broomfield Consols Copper and Silver-Lead Mining Co. was formed and later in 1853 it was claimed that good quality ore had been raised. Not only copper and lead but malachite and silver were said to be present, the last at 30 oz. per ton of ore. Mining was abandoned in 1854.[23]

The only evidence for clothmaking was a fulling mill recorded in the 15th century and the survival into the 19th century of the field names Rack House at Holwell and Rack Close adjoining Priors Down.[24]

MILLS. Nailscombe mill, said to have been given to Henry de la Tour (d. by 1280) by Margery de Newburgh,[25] descended with Ivyton manor until the 16th century.[26] The miller, John Needs, built a second mill before 1591, and was succeeded by William Needs (d. 1597) and Emmanuel Needs.[27] In 1612 lower and higher mills were recorded, and in 1653 a middle mill. A mill, probably the higher mill, was burnt down c. 1649, and an adjoining house was later known as Burnt Mill. Only one mill was recorded at Nailscombe in 1681.[28] It was named Bradford mill after 18th-century tenants and later Broomfield mill.[29] It continued working until the 1930s.[30] The mill, beside the Taunton road adjoining the boundary with Kingston St. Mary parish, was converted to a dwelling and the head pond was filled in.

There was a fulling mill called Nailscombe in Ivyton in 1447.[31] It was probably the mill held by the Warren family in the 1500s and forfeited c. 1523.[32] It was not recorded thereafter.

There was a mill at Heathcombe in 1293.[33] Both Broomfield and Enmore manors claimed ownership of part of a mill in the 15th and 16th centuries.[34] Heathcombe or Ford mill was held by the Towill family for three generations in the 17th century.[35] They recovered ownership in the 18th, although it was known as Cox's mill after a former owner.[36] Before 1838 it became part of the Tynte estate, but by 1851 it had gone out of use and had become labourers' cottages.[37] They had been demolished by 1953.[38]

Rooks Castle mill was recorded in 1619.[39] It

9 McDonnell, *Quantock Hills A.O.N.B.: Arch. Survey*, 9–10, 39.
10 S.R.O., DD/S/WH 235.
11 Ibid. tithe award.   12 Ibid.
13 P.R.O., RG 10/2383; RG 11/2372.
14 Statistics supplied by the then Bd. of Agric., 1905.
15 Min. of Agric., Fisheries, and Food, agric. returns, 1982.
16 S.R.O., DD/S/WH 132; D/D/Cd 51.
17 Ibid. D/D/Pd 13.
18 Ibid. DD/S/WH 256.
19 Ibid. DD/FA 11/1; DD/PLE 63.
20 P.R.O., RG 9/1622; RG 10/2383; RG 11/2372.
21 S.R.O., DD/S/WH 326.
22 Ibid. DD/X/HAM 1; Hamilton and Lawrence, *Men and Mining in the Quantocks*, 72–5.
23 S.R.O., DD/S/WH 326; DD/X/HAM 1; DD/WY 158; Hamilton and Lawrence, *Men and Mining in the Quantocks*, 72–5.
24 Below; S.R.O., tithe award.
25 *S.R.S.* xliv. 28.
26 *Cal. Inq. p.m.* ii, p. 278; S.R.O., DD/L P35/1, 3.
27 S.R.O., DD/S/WH 209; P.R.O., C 142/279, no. 449.
28 S.R.O., DD/S/WH 19, 131, 209; Highclere Castle, Carnarvon MSS., U/C 2, 4, 8; box 2.
29 S.R.O., Q/REl 2/1; ibid. D/P/broo 13/1/2; *Kelly's Dir. Som.* (1883, 1894).
30 Local inf.   31 S.R.O., DD/L P35/5.
32 Ibid. DD/L P23/16, 19; P35/8.   33 *S.R.S.* vi. 288.
34 Ibid. xxii. 118; S.R.O., DD/S/WH 209.
35 Highclere Castle, Carnarvon MSS., U/C 9; S.R.O., DD/S/WH 19, 246.
36 S.R.O., DD/DP 23/6; DD/SAS JK 18; ibid. Q/REl 2/1.
37 Ibid. tithe award; P.R.O., HO 107/1924.
38 S.R.O., DD/X/BID 21.
39 Ibid. DD/S/WH 20.

was also known as Gard's mill, after an early 19th-century lessee, and was occupied by a millwright in 1881.[40] It was driven by the King's Cliff stream, and remains of a shaft and an overshot wheel could be seen in the 1970s.[41] Binfords mill, further down the same stream, was recorded in 1662.[42] There was no record of it after 1775.[43] There may have been a mill north-west of Fyne Court on the stream that fills an ornamental canal where fields called Mellis were recorded in 1838.[44]

FAIRS. In 1259 John de la Linde, lord of Broomfield manor, received a grant of a three-day fair at All Saints.[45] There is no further record of the fair until 1606 when men from Glastonbury attended.[46] A tolsey was recorded in 1665[47] and in 1717 the site was let with the profits of the standings set up at fair time.[48] Sheep, cows, and horses were sold there in the mid 18th century and in 1748 tolls, shared between Broomfield manor and the Halswell estate, amounted to 27s. 8d.[49] In the late 18th century the main commodities of the fair, then held on 13 November, were coarse cloth and cattle, but horses were also sold.[50] During the 19th century it declined as a stock fair and by 1883, when it was last recorded, it was known for toasted biscuits and cider.[51] A small fair may have been held in the 1890s.[52]

The fair appears to have been held on the Fair Close or Fair Field, part of Broomfield green west of the church.[53]

LOCAL GOVERNMENT. Broomfield was described as a free manor in the 13th century and sent its own jury to the eyre in 1242–3.[54] In the early 14th century the parish was divided into five tithings: Broomfield, Blaxhold, Castle, Heathcombe, and Oggshole.[55] By the 16th century it was often regarded as a single tithing[56] but Heathcombe, and sometimes Oggshole, continued to be used as tithings for some purposes and in the mid 17th century Heathcombe had its own tithingman elected by rota.[57] Blaxhold was regarded as a sub-tithing of Enmore tithing in the 17th century and continued to form part of Enmore tithing for tax purposes in the 18th and 19th centuries.[58] The constable of the higher division of Broomfield was recorded c. 1647.[59]

Court rolls survive for Broomfield manor for 1409,[60] 1507, 1515,[61] 1591–1602, and 1612–28.[62]

The court usually met twice a year, three times in 1591, and a court dinner was mentioned in 1619. The tithingman and constable were sworn in the court, and a hayward was appointed in 1627. The butts and the pound were regularly presented as being in need of repair during the early 17th century and use of the commons was regulated.[63] Courts continued to be held until 1656 or later and a court dinner was kept on the Tynte share of the manor in 1710.[64] There are court records for Ivyton for 1447, 1483–4, 1500–1, 1503, 1505, 1509, 1516–17, 1523, and 1572. Courts met up to three times a year and dealt almost entirely with tenures.[65] There are copies of court rolls for Rooks Castle for various dates between 1461 and 1662.[66] One court roll for 1603 survives for the Stawells' manor of Heathcombe, and suit of court was owed twice a year until 1672 or later.[67] Court records for Oggshole survive for 1540–1.[68]

Churchwardens were sworn at the annual visitation of the dean of Wells in the later 18th century.[69] The overseers paid for clothing and medical bills and in 1638 towards building one man's house.[70] The former church house was probably used as a poorhouse by 1664–5 when it was said to be occupied by almspeople.[71] Variously called almshouse, poor cottage, or poorhouse, it was last mentioned in 1861.[72] It stood on the western boundary of the churchyard and had been demolished by 1887.[73]

The parish formed part of Bridgwater poorlaw union in 1836, Bridgwater rural district in 1894, and Sedgemoor district in 1974.[74]

CHURCH. There was probably a church at Broomfield in the late 11th century.[75] Maud Arundel, wife of Gerbert de Percy, gave Broomfield church to Wells cathedral c. 1175 at the request of Bishop Reginald to endow a prebend.[76] In the event Broomfield was excluded from the foundation and the Wells chapter seems to have retained only a pension of 2s. a century later,[77] although the parish was within the spiritual jurisdiction of the Dean of Wells until the 19th century.[78] The living was a rectory in 1296 but by 1334 the church belonged to Buckland priory which had earlier been given mortuaries of the tenants of Sir Matthew Furneaux.[79] From the 14th century the parish was served by chaplains or curates appointed and

40 S.R.O., Q/REl 2/1; P.R.O., RG 11/2372.
41 Som. C.C., Sites and Mons. Rec.
42 S.R.O., DD/X/BKE 16.   43 Ibid. DD/RN 8.
44 Ibid. tithe award; Som. C.C., Sites and Mons. Rec.
45 Cal. Pat. 1258–66, 110–11.
46 S.R.O., Q/SR 2/104.   47 Ibid. 108/37.
48 Ibid. DD/S/WH 131.   49 Ibid. 253, 255.
50 Collinson, Hist. Som. i. 72; S.R.O., DD/X/VEA 1.
51 Taunton Courier, 18 Nov. 1857; Kelly's Dir. Som. (1883); Proc. Som. Arch. Soc. lxxxii. 145.
52 Local inf.
53 S.R.O., DD/S/WH 246; ibid. tithe award.
54 Ibid. DD/S/WH 28; S.R.S. xi, p. 314.
55 S.R.S. iii. 162–3.   56 Ibid. xx. 241.
57 S.R.O., DD/S/WH 388; ibid. Q/S Pet. 1.
58 S.R.S. xxviii. 69–70; S.R.O., Q/REl 2/5.
59 S.R.O., D/P/broo 13/1/1.
60 Ibid. DD/SAS FA 75.
61 Ibid. DD/AH 11/9–10.
62 Ibid. DD/S/WH 209.

63 Ibid.
64 Ibid. 132, 209, 252.
65 Ibid. DD/L P23/15–16, 19; P35/5–6.
66 Ibid. DD/S/WH 20.
67 P.R.O., WARD 2/18/70/11; Highclere Castle, Carnarvon MSS., U/C 11.
68 P.R.O., LR 3/123.
69 S.R.O., D/D/Pd 25.
70 Ibid. D/P/broo 13/2/1–3.
71 Dwelly, Hearth Tax, i. 53.
72 S.R.O., D/D/Rr, Broomfield; P.R.O., HO 107/1924; ibid. RG 9/1622.
73 S.R.O., tithe award; O.S. Map 6", Som. LX. NE. (1890 edn.).
74 Youngs, Local Admin. Units, i. 671, 673, 676.
75 S.R.S. vii, p. 38.
76 H.M.C. Wells, i. 25, 27; Sanders, Eng. Baronies, 72.
77 H.M.C. Wells, i. 149, 307.
78 Ibid. 203, 533; S.R.O., D/D/Pd 24–5; D/D/Vc 15.
79 Pole MS. 3766, 3777; S.R.S. ix, p. 224.

paid by the priory or the farmers[80] and after the Dissolution by the lay rectors, who from the later 18th century were the lords of Broomfield manor.[81] An endowment in 1764[82] created a perpetual curacy, known as a vicarage from c. 1892, the patronage of which the Hamilton family transferred to the bishop c. 1964.[83] The redemption of a rent charge of £30 by John Hamilton in 1919 was probably to extinguish the lay rector's obligation to pay a curate.[84] From 1953 the benefice has been held with Kingston St. Mary,[85] and from 1981 also with Cheddon Fitzpaine.[86]

The church was valued at 10 marks in 1334[87] and was farmed for £8 5s. in 1534.[88] To augment the stipend paid by the lay rector, Queen Anne's Bounty made grants of £200 in 1764, 1789, 1849, and 1858 to match sums and land given by Mrs. Horner's trustees (£100 in 1764), Mrs. Pincombe's trustees (£50 in 1764, £100 in 1789, £100 in 1858), the lay rector John Moss (£50 in 1764), the curate John Blundell (£100 in 1789), John Hamilton (land worth £360 in 1849, £270 in 1858), Miss Hamilton (£130 in 1858), and John Crosse (later Hamilton) (land worth £45 in 1858).[89] The income was £78 c. 1830,[90] and further gifts by the Hamiltons in the early 20th century increased it to £206 in 1931.[91]

William de Mohun (d. after 1190) gave half the tithes to endow Dunster priory,[92] but the grant was probably not fulfilled. The tithes of the whole parish belonged to Buckland priory at the Dissolution and thereafter formed part of the lay rectory.[93] By 1841 a small piece of land at Wembdon belonged to the Broomfield curacy.[94] In 1849 John Hamilton and in 1858 John Crosse (later Hamilton) augmented the curacy with gifts of land in the parish and by 1933 there was also glebe land in Creech St. Michael, the whole totalling nearly 15 a.;[95] the land remained glebe in 1976.[96]

A house was built for the curate before 1861 some distance east of the church on the edge of Broomfield common.[97] It was occupied by the incumbent until c. 1953[98] and in 1988 was a private dwelling.

Broomfield had two priests c. 1175[99] but from the earlier 14th century the parish was served by a succession of parochial chaplains.[1] In 1450 there was also an anniversary chaplain[2] and an endowed light in 1547.[3] In the later 16th century there were difficulties in finding priests to serve the church: a French priest lasted six weeks and 'upon the soden departed'.[4] In 1576 the church lacked a communion cup and there were no quarterly sermons.[5] Among the curates of the 17th century, some resident, were Hannibal Potter, ousted as president of Trinity College, Oxford, for reading the Book of Common Prayer,[6] and John Prince, removed at the Restoration.[7] George Hellier, curate c. 1678–c. 1710, was accused, probably unfairly, of being a nonjuror.[8] Thomas Milward, curate 1778–85, held four other local livings.[9] In 1815 only one service was held each Sunday, but by 1827 both morning and afternoon services were held.[10] There were resident priests from 1861 to 1953.[11]

A church house is mentioned in 1597; it belonged to Broomfield manor[12] and by 1664–5 appears to have been a poorhouse.[13]

The church of ST. MARY AND ALL SAINTS, apparently so called in 1443 as in the 20th century,[14] but known simply as All Saints in 1313,[15] is built of rubble with ashlar dressings. It comprises a chancel with north chapel, a nave with north aisle and south porch, and a west tower. The nave may retain a 12th-century plan, but a blocked 14th-century doorway in the chancel and the tower of the earlier 15th century are the earliest surviving parts, the nave, chancel, and porch having been rebuilt in the early 16th century and the north aisle c. 1535.[16] Richard Dulverton (d. 1443), chaplain of Broomfield who repaired and decorated the church, is commemorated by a brass in the church.[17] Nave and aisles retain their late-medieval roofs, and there are fragments of glass of the same period, including an inscription to Alice Reskymer, prioress of Buckland in 1436 and 1457,[18] and some early 16th-century heraldic glass. The bench ends, one with the name of the carver, Simon Warman (d. 1585),[19] are of the mid 16th century. The chancel was partially rebuilt and furnished in the 18th century[20] and the east window, inserted in 1913 in place of an altarpiece, was glazed by Morris and Co.[21] A gallery was removed in 1854.[22]

A cup and cover are dated 1635 and there are two patens of 1709 and a flagon of 1721.[23] There were five bells, the oldest by George Purdue

80   S.R.O., D/D/Vc 20; P.R.O., SC 6/Hen. VIII/3137.
81   S.D.N.Q. xv. 161; S.R.O., D/D/Pd 30; above, manors.
82   Below, this section.
83   Rep. Com. Eccl. Revenues, pp. 128–9; Kelly's Dir. Som. (1906); Dioc. Dir.
84   S.R.O., D/P/broo 3/3/1.
85   Crockford (1959–60).   86   Dioc. Dir.
87   S.R.S. ix, pp. 224–5.
88   P.R.O., SC 6/Hen. VIII/3137.
89   C. Hodgson, Queen Anne's Bounty (1864), pp. xix, xli, clxv, clxxvi; S.R.O., D/D/Bo; D/P/broo 10/3/1; ibid. tithe award.
90   Rep. Com. Eccl. Revenues, pp. 128–9.
91   Kelly's Dir. Som. (1931).
92   S.R.S. vii, p. 38.   93   Above, manors.
94   S.R.O., tithe award, Wembdon.
95   C. Hodgson, Queen Anne's Bounty (1864), suppl. p. xli; S.R.O., D/P/broo 3/1/2; board in ch.
96   Inf. from Dioc. Office.
97   P.R.O., RG 9/1622.
98   Crockford (1959–60).
99   H.M.C. Wells, i. 27.   1   Cal. Inq. p.m. vii, p. 481.
2   S.R.S. xlix, p. 40.   3   Ibid. ii. 53.

4   S.D.N.Q. xv. 161.   5   S.R.O., D/D/Ca 57.
6   Ibid. D/D/Rr, Broomfield; Walker Revised, ed. A. G. Matthews; Alum. Oxon. 1500–1714.
7   Calamy Revised, ed. A. G. Matthews.
8   Collinson, Hist. Som. i. 73; M.I. in ch.; S.R.O., D/D/Pd 30; S.D.N.Q. xvii. 182–3.
9   S.R.O., D/D/Bs 44; D/D/Vc 88.
10   Ibid. D/D/Rb 1815, 1827.
11   P.R.O., RG 9/1622; Crockford (1959–60).
12   S.R.O., DD/S/WH 209.   13   Above, local govt.
14   Proc. Som. Arch. Soc. lxxxvii. 73; Dioc. Dir.
15   Cal. Inq. p.m. vii, p. 481.
16   Wells Wills, ed. Weaver, 82; for a photo., above, plate facing p. 8.
17   Proc. Som. Arch. Soc. lxxxvii. 72–3, rendering Dulverton as Silverton; cf. S.R.S. xxx, p. 499.
18   S.R.S. xxv, p. xxvi; C. Woodforde, Stained Glass in Som. (1946), 41, 97.
19   S.R.O., D/P/bic 2/1/2; Som. Co. Gaz. 27 Feb. 1987.
20   S.R.O., D/P/broo 4/1/1.
21   Ibid. 6/1/1; Pevsner, S. & W. Som. 102.
22   Crosse, Memorials of Andrew Crosse, 332.
23   Proc. Som. Arch. Soc. xlvii. 154.

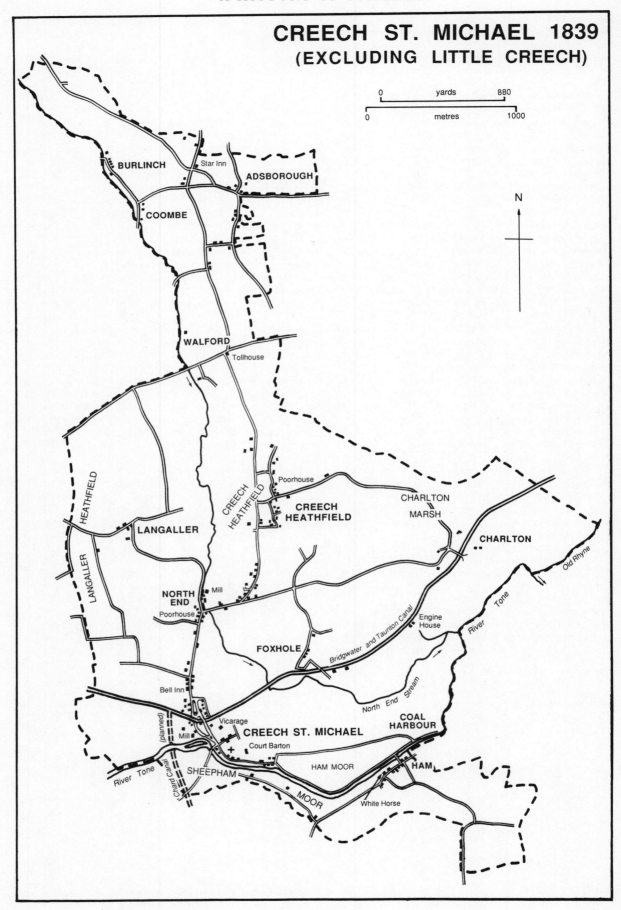

CREECH ST. MICHAEL 1839
(EXCLUDING LITTLE CREECH)

dating from 1606, and there are two early 18th-century bells.[24] The registers begin in 1630 and are complete.[25]

The churchyard cross is of the late 13th or early 14th century.[26]

NONCONFORMITY. Two houses were licensed for use by Presbyterians in 1672, although the teacher was also said to be a Baptist, four houses were licensed for unspecified denominations in 1689, and one in 1707. There were 40 Presbyterian members in a single congregation in 1718, but the group had ceased to exist by 1729.[27] Further licences for unspecified congregations were issued in 1743 and 1799.[28] Congregationalists held cottage services c. 1866 and a chapel was built at Shellthorn, 1.5 km. north of Broomfield church, in 1870.[29] Services ceased c. 1949 and the small brick building was sold in 1963.[30] Bible Christians had evening preachings in the parish in 1868.[31]

EDUCATION. There was no school in 1819 but by 1825 there was a day school for 26 children.[32] In 1835 it had 20 pupils, with a teacher paid by the Hamilton family. A Sunday school was attended by 18 children.[33] In 1846 a National day school had 20 pupils and a further 10 attended on Sundays.[34] A new schoolroom was built in 1849 and in 1903 there were 55 children on the books.[35] Numbers declined to 22 in 1932 when the school was closed and the children transferred to Kingston.[36] The building, near the church, was sold in 1957 for use as a village hall.[37]

CHARITIES FOR THE POOR. Jeffrey Towill, by will dated 1682, left an annual charge of £5 4s. on the rectory for loaves for 12 poor people each week. The charge remained until c. 1919 when a sum was invested to provide the same income. Towill also gave £20 to the parish to yield an annual income for the poor but that gift was lost.[38] Gifts by Mary Jeane, by will dated or proved 1785 for bread, and by Elizabeth Jeane in 1811 were probably lost before 1826. In 1982 cash was distributed at Easter and Christmas and a harvest supper was held from the income of the Towill charity and four other charities, £100 given by Sir Charles Kemeys-Tynte by will dated 1776, £190 by Mary Escott by will dated 1809 for the poor and for lying-in women, an unknown sum by Frances Coombe by will dated or proved 1853 for dinners for six poor men and six poor women at Easter and Christmas, and £50 by Charles Sweeting by will dated 1869, and from the former education endowment given by Frances and Charles Coombe.[39] John Jeane by will dated 1790 gave money to help buy tools for the poor, and grants towards the cost of tools were made in the 1980s.[40]

CREECH ST. MICHAEL

CREECH St. Michael lies mostly on the north bank of the Tone 5 km. east of Taunton. The simple name Creech was normally used during the Middle Ages, but Muchel (i.e. Great) Creech was used in the early 16th century,[41] presumably in distinction from Little Creech, a detached part of the parish, and the adjective appeared in the later 16th century as Michel and in the later 17th as Michael.[42] The form Creech St. Michael was in normal use from the 19th century.[43] Irregular in shape, the parish measures 3.5 km. from east to west at its widest point and c. 3 km. from north to south, with a narrow peninsula c. 3 km. long running north into the Quantocks. Most of the parish lies on ground sloping gently from the 30-m. contour to the Tone, drained by several streams, the largest known in 1753 as the Reen and later as the North End stream.[44] The peninsula occupies the east side of a combe north of Walford as far as the 122-m. contour and includes the hamlets of Burlinch and Coombe.[45] Little Creech, an area of 25 a., lies between West Hatch and Bickenhall parishes 5.5 km. south of Creech church.[46] Little Creech was transferred to West Hatch in 1884, and the present civil parish measures 931 ha. (2,300 a.).[47]

Most of the parish lies on Upper Keuper marl and valley gravels with alluvium along the Tone and the North End stream.[48] Small pools and field names suggest digging for marl and gravel. The Upper Sandstone and Ilfracombe slates were quarried at Coombe and Burlinch.[49] 'Flint' was said to have been dug at Heathfield in the early 19th century, and clay for brick and tile

24   S.R.O., DD/SAS CH 16/1. A sixth bell was added in 1990.
25   S.R.O., D/P/broo 2/1/1–4.
26   Som. C.C., Sites and Mons. Rec.
27   Orig. Rec. of Early Nonconf. ed. G. L. Turner, i. 512; A. Gordon, Freedom after Ejection, 93; S.R.O., Q/RR meeting ho. lics.
28   S.R.O., Q/RR meeting ho. lics.; ibid. D/D/Rm 2.
29   Rep. Som. Cong. Union. (1896).
30   Char. Com. files; S.R.O., D/N/brc 4/3/1–2.
31   S.R.O., D/N/tmc 3/2/5.
32   Educ. of Poor Digest (1819), p. 775; Ann. Rep. B. & W. Dioc. Assoc. S.P.C.K. (1825–6), 41.
33   Educ. Enq. Abstract (1835), p. 796.
34   Nat. Soc. Inquiry, 1846–7, Som. 4–5.
35   S.R.O., C/E 4/380/50.
36   Ibid. 4/64, 102.
37   Char. Com. files.

38   Ibid.
39   Ibid.; Char. Don. pp. 1048–9; 15th Rep. Com. Char. 343; inf. from the vicar, the Revd. G. C. H. Watson.
40   Char. Com. files; V. Waite, Portrait of the Quantocks (1964), 37, plate facing p. 32; inf. from the vicar.
41   S.R.O., DD/DP 114/16/5. This article was completed in 1984.
42   P.R.O., C 142/170, no. 23; S.R.O., DD/BR/wr 8.
43   S.R.O., DD/HWD 1.
44   The supposed name Preen results from misreading an 18th-cent. map: Our Village: A Study of Creech St. Michael, ed. D. B. Smith (c. 1970), 40.
45   O.S. Map 1/50,000, sheets 182, 193 (1976–9 edn.).
46   O.S. Nat. Grid ST 277197.
47   Census, 1891, 1981.
48   Geol. Surv. Map 1", drift, sheet 295 (1956 edn.).
49   Ibid.; O.S. Map 6", Som. LXXI. NW. (1887 edn.); S.R.O., DD/GC 90; ibid. tithe award.

was extracted near the Tone east of Creech village.[50] The Tone and a stream which may be the earlier course of that river mark much of the southern boundary of the parish and the North End stream is the western boundary of the peninsula north of Walford. The remainder of the western boundary is possibly the eastern boundary of the West Monkton estate which in the 7th century followed the course of a stream part of which may survive near Langaller. Other boundaries rarely follow natural features.[51]

Settlement in the parish was scattered: six settlements were evidently early, of which Creech village, Charlton, and Langaller were to some extent nucleated. Creech village, where the parish church stood by 1102, comprised in the later 18th century a group of houses west and south of the church along Bull Street, following the line of the river, and others north of the church along a lane which led to the fields. Further cottages lay along the road running west to Husk or Hurst Green.[52] In the 20th century new houses have been built along the village streets.

From the north-west end of the village and from Hurst Green two roads ran north to converge: the eastern one had by 1814 been replaced by a lane further east,[53] but was apparently reinstated, probably when the canal was built in 1827, and became part of the main street. The western road, formerly Pigs Barrow or Pigs Barrel Road, was renamed Curvalion Road in 1962.[54] The easternmost road was severed by the canal and the railway. Until the 1960s a few farmhouses and detached houses lay along the road north to North End:[55] a 17th-century farmhouse, altered in the 19th and 20th centuries, survived as a dwelling and a shop in 1984. In the later 20th century many new houses were built on the west side of the village between the canal and North End.

Creech Heathfield, probably a squatter settlement on the edge of the Heathfield, includes a 17th-century house, now the Crown inn, and had a poorhouse from 1652.[56] During the 20th century many houses were built east of the road.

East of Creech village, Ham, recorded in 1303, lies along the eastern end of White Street[57] on the south bank of the Tone; it is partly in North Curry parish. Charlton, north-east of Creech village, and Langaller, north-west, were both mentioned in 1327,[58] but the name Charlton suggests a pre-Conquest community of either free peasants or villeins.

There are four settlements on the higher ground in the north. Walford was recorded as Wealaford in 682,[59] and Adsborough as Tetes-

berge in the 11th century.[60] Coombe and Burlinch are small settlements in the valley north of Walford. Foxhole, a small scattered hamlet between Creech village and Charlton, now divided by the Bridgwater and Taunton canal, may have been a squatter settlement on the edge of ancient woodland.

Langaller contains several early houses. Langaller Farm, now called Langaller Manor, is a late-medieval house altered in the 17th century and again in the 20th. It probably originated as an open-hall house, later ceiled to provide a three-roomed, cross-passage house.[61] Langaller Manor Farm and Langaller House date from the 17th century. Langaller House is an **L**-shaped house, much altered in the late 18th or early 19th century. In 1868 it was said to have been recently improved.[62] Adsborough contains several houses dating from the 17th century or earlier including at least one medieval house.[63]

A common field called Ferringdons, north of Creech Heathfield, was recorded in 1604[64] and strips survived in Creech field, west of Creech village, in 1839.[65] Field boundaries suggest open arable cultivation between Creech field and Langaller and between Langaller and Walford.[66] Common meadows, pastures, and moors lay beside the Tone in the south. Creech and Langaller Heathfields, common pastures at Ham, Sheepham, shared with Ruishton, and Charlton Marsh, and several greens, probably former manorial waste, were inclosed in 1814.[67] New Mead and Mermead remained in multiple ownership in 1839.[68]

Woodland may have governed the settlement pattern of the parish. There was woodland in 1086 measuring a furlong square.[69] Creech wood, which may formerly have occupied a large area on the east side of the present village street between the church and North End, still measured 50 a. in 1559. Oak, ash, and other timber was sold in 1619, the purchaser having to make good the ground after the removal of roots.[70] Ancient boundary banks, a hedge surviving from ancient woodland, and lichen species indicate the considerable former extent of the timber cover.[71] The names Creech Heathfield and Langaller Heathfield may suggest earlier, and less effective, woodland clearance. There were nearly 7 a. of woodland in 1839,[72] 4 a. in 1905,[73] 12 a. in the 1940s,[74] and only 1 ha. (c. 2.5 a.) in 1982.[75] A field east of Court Barton was called Coneygar.[76]

Two routes crossed at Creech village. An east–west route from the North Curry ridge crossed the Tone at Ham and led to Creech

50 S.R.O., D/P/crch 14/5/2; D/R/ta 9/1/1; below, econ. hist.
51 O.S. Map 1/50,000, sheets 182, 193 (1976–9 edn.); *Proc. Som. Arch. Soc.* lxxxiv. 104–6.
52 S.R.O., DD/GC 90.
53 Ibid. D/R/ta 9/1/1.
54 Ibid. D/PC/crch 1/2/3; *Our Village*, 40.
55 O.S. Map 1/25,000, ST 22 (1959 edn.).
56 Below, local govt.
57 O.S. Map 6", Som. LXXI. SW. (1887 edn.); *H.M.C. Wells*, i. 316.
58 S.R.S. iii. 186.
59 *Proc. Som. Arch. Soc.* lxxiv, suppl. 51.
60 *V.C.H. Som.* i. 501. Tetesberge probably included Thurloxton: below, Thurloxton.

61 S.R.O., DD/V/TAr 10.5. 62 Ibid. DD/HWD 18.
63 Ibid. DD/V/TAr 10.2, 4, 6.
64 *S.R.S.* lxvii. 106. 65 S.R.O., tithe award.
66 Ibid.; O.S. Map 6", Som. LXXI. NW. (1887 edn.).
67 S.R.O., D/R/ta 9/1/1.
68 Ibid. tithe award.
69 *V.C.H. Som.* i. 436.
70 S.R.O., DD/GC 6.
71 Inf. from Mrs. P. A. Wolseley, Nettlecombe.
72 S.R.O., tithe award.
73 Statistics supplied by the then Bd. of Agric., 1905.
74 P.R.O., CRES 35/1150, 1155.
75 Min. of Agric., Fisheries, and Food, agric. returns (1982).
76 S.R.O., tithe award.

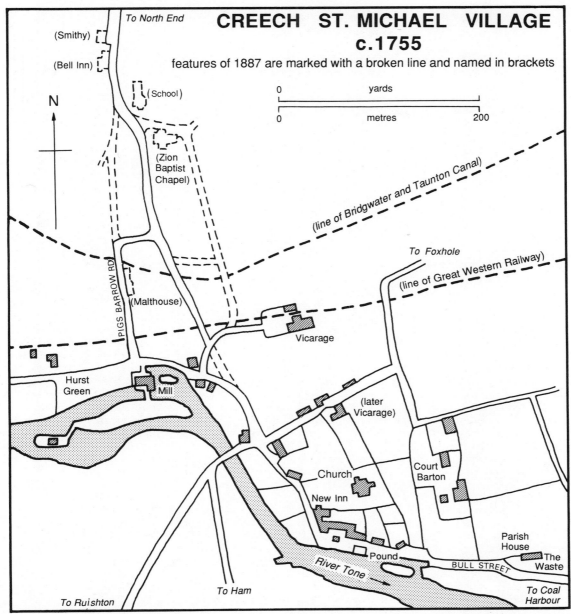

CREECH ST. MICHAEL VILLAGE
c.1755

features of 1887 are marked with a broken line and named in brackets

To North End

(Smithy)

(Bell Inn)

N

(School)

(Zion Baptist Chapel)

0   yards

0   metres   200

(line of Bridgwater and Taunton Canal)

To Foxhole

(line of Great Western Railway)

PIGS BARROW RD

(Malthouse)

Vicarage

Hurst Green

Mill

(later Vicarage)

Church

Court Barton

New Inn

Parish House

Pound

River Tone

BULL STREET

The Waste

To Ruishton

To Ham

To Coal Harbour

village through Ham moor. An alternative led through Ham and along the southern side of the Tone to Creech bridge. From the bridge the route led west along Husk Green Drove towards Hyde Lane in Bathpool and Taunton. A north–south route runs from the Quantocks through Creech Heathfield and North End to cross the east–west route before going over the Tone into Ruishton. The importance of the riverside route presumably depended on river traffic at Ham.[77] At North End the road divided to serve Langaller to the north-west and Charlton and Creech Heathfield to the east and north-east respectively, the latter continuing north to Adsborough. The roads from Taunton to Bridgwater and Glastonbury, which pass through the northern tip of the parish, were turnpiked by the Taunton trust in 1751–2[78] and posts and a tollgate erected at Walford where the two roads divided.[79] The Taunton turnpike trust ceased in 1875. The

tollhouse, rebuilt c. 1850, was moved to Durston c. 1874.[80] The old pattern of lanes in the parish has been disrupted by the canals, railway, and motorway. Creech or Tone Bridge was repaired by the hundred of Andersfield in the 1620s.[81] It was improved in 1830 and enlarged in 1848.[82] There was a bridge at Ham before 1709 and two more were ordered to be removed that year.[83] A new bridge at Ham was built in 1758 but by 1839 it had been replaced by a bridge further east on the site of the present footbridge.[84] A private suspension bridge linking Coal Harbour with Ham was built in 1968[85] to replace an earlier bridge.[86]

The parish enjoyed relative prosperity in the 17th and 18th centuries, based apparently on a mixed economy involving river traffic. Land called Colehouse, on the north bank of the Tone opposite Ham, was evidently by 1559 a landing place for coal and probably other heavy goods

77   Ibid. D/R/ta 9/1/1.   78   25 Geo. II, c. 54.
79   S.R.O., tithe award.
80   Maytree Cottage in 1984: J. B. Bentley and B. Murless, *Som. Roads*, i. 53, 96; inf. from Mrs. M. Miles, Durston.
81   *S.R.S.* xxiv. 44–5, 75–6; lxv. 1.
82   S.R.O., Q/AB 6, 10.   83   Ibid. DD/TC 7.
84   Ibid. DD/DP 23/6; D/P/crch 13/2/1.
85   Plaque on bridge.
86   S.R.O., DD/X/HAR 9/12; DD/HWD 12.

from Bridgwater.[87] Coal Harbour House appears to date from the early 17th century, and its ornamental plasterwork includes the arms of the Merchant Adventurers Company and a fireplace with the initials 'R.M.B.' and the date 1679.[88] In 1684 Richard Bobbett took a lease of the 'back river' and a moor, with the right to land coal.[89] By 1714 there were warehouses, a salt house, pans, and cellars, a smithy, and landing areas.[90] A warehouse was built c. 1783[91] but business declined in the 19th century and by 1839 there were only three coal yards along the river.[92] Coal Harbour House alone remained in 1984.

The river Tone was improved for navigation by the Tone Conservators under proposals drawn up in 1698 with Ham as the point of toll between Bridgwater and Taunton. Tolls for traffic from Bridgwater were paid at Ham Mills in North Curry and for traffic going up to Taunton at Coal Harbour.[93] At Coal Harbour the river was widened leaving an island between the old and new branches linked by bridges.[94] The western branch had been filled in by the late 19th century.[95] Locks were constructed to improve navigation near Ham and at Creech mills.[96] After serious flooding in 1960 the river was deepened and widened, and New Cut was made south of Creech Bridge to carry excess water.[97] The Bridgwater and Taunton canal running east–west through the parish was cut in 1827, with a pumping station between Foxhole and Charlton to lift water from the river.[98] The engine house survives. The Chard canal opened in 1842[99] and closed in 1866.[1] To its junction with the Bridgwater and Taunton canal it was carried by buttressed walls which survive, together with nearby buildings converted for defence during the Second World War.

Alongside the Bridgwater and Taunton canal runs the railway, opened in 1842.[2] A halt in Creech village was opened in 1928 and closed c. 1969.[3] The branch line to Chard alongside the Chard canal was opened in 1866 and closed in 1963.[4]

In 1619–20 there were two inns in the parish, the Fiery Dragon and the Prince's Arms.[5] The first, probably that in Creech village later known as the Green Dragon or Creech Inn, and formerly the church house,[6] still belonged to the lord of the manor in 1794.[7] It was rebuilt before 1768 and thereafter was also called the New Inn.[8] The names Creech Inn and New Inn were both used until the early 20th century.[9] It was renamed the Riverside Tavern in 1986. During the late 17th century there were up to five inns or alehouses in the parish and up to three in the early 18th century.[10] There were four in 1750, including two disreputable alehouses at Ham,[11] one called the White Horse established by 1726.[12] The Ship, next to the New Inn, was opened by 1768,[13] but had become a malthouse by 1774.[14] The Ball or Blue Ball was recorded between 1779 and 1786.[15] The Bell inn, in Creech village, was first licensed in 1823 and remains in business.[16] There was an alehouse on a coal wharf beside the Bridgwater and Taunton canal in 1831[17] and another, called the White Lion, at its junction with the Chard canal.[18] By 1851 there were six public houses in the parish,[19] and in the 1860s and 1870s as many as eight.[20] They included the Lane End beerhouse at Ham, open until c. 1963, another beerhouse there,[21] and one at Coombe.[22] The Star at Adsborough, open by 1839, was renamed the Maypole in 1981[23] and the Crown at Creech Heathfield was open by 1871;[24] both were in business in 1984. There was a beerhouse at Walford by 1910 which was still open in 1914.[25]

A friendly society for Creech, West Monkton, Thornfalcon, and Ruishton was founded in 1787. It met at the New Inn in 1820 and held a Whit Monday feast.[26] It was refounded in 1827 as the Creech Union Club, claiming in the 1830s to have members from a large number of surrounding parishes.[27] The Creech Young Club was founded in 1822 and was still active in 1837, and the Commendable Society was in existence in 1836.[28] During the 19th century a village revel was held in September.[29] Adsborough men's institute and reading room was set up in 1904 and was wound up in 1916.[30] The Creech Institute was recorded in 1914.[31]

There were 63 taxpayers in the parish in 1327,[32] 161 in 1377,[33] and 89 in 1526.[34] In 1664–5 110 householders were liable for hearth tax and

87 S.R.O., DD/GC 6; D/B/bw 1438, 1489, 1491, 1493–4, 1497, 1506.
88 Ibid. DD/V/TAr 10.3.
89 V.C.H. Som. ii. 456.
90 S.R.O., DD/TC 10.
91 Ibid. DD/HWD (S/2399), survey 1783.
92 Ibid. tithe award.
93 Ibid. DD/MK 12, 'Short Account of Conservators'.
94 Ibid. DD/TC 10; ibid. Q/RUi.
95 O.S. Map 6", Som. LXXI. SW. (1887 edn.).
96 S.R.O., DD/TC 14.
97 Our Village, 18.
98 C. A. Buchanan, Bridgwater and Taunton Canal, 16; below, plate facing p. 25.
99 C. Hadfield, Canals of S. Eng. 232.
1 Our Village, 19–20.
2 S.R.O., DD/MK 14.
3 Our Village, 24.
4 S.R.O., DD/X/GG 4; Our Village, 24.
5 S.R.O., Q/RLa 33; ibid. T/PH/buc 1.
6 Ibid. D/P/crch 23/2.
7 Ibid. Q/REl 2/3; ibid. DD/HWD 2.
8 Ibid. D/P/crch 13/2/1; DD/HWD 2.
9 Ibid. Q/RL; P.O. Dir. Som. (1861–75); Kelly's Dir. Som. (1883–1939).

10 S.R.O., Q/RL.
11 Ibid. D/P/crch 23/2.
12 Ibid. Q/RL.
13 Ibid. D/P/crch 13/2/1.
14 Ibid. DD/HWD 12.
15 Ibid. Q/RL; ibid. DD/DP 114/16/1.
16 Ibid. Q/RL; Kelly's Dir. Som. (1883–1931).
17 S.R.O., DD/TC 15.
18 Our Village, 21.
19 P.R.O., HO 107/1922.
20 P.O. Dir. Som. (1861–75).
21 P.R.O., RG 10/2369; S.R.O., D/P/crch 23/2; P.O. Dir. Som. (1861–75); local inf.
22 P.O. Dir. Som. (1861–75).
23 S.R.O., tithe award; Kelly's Dir. Som. (1883–1939); local inf.
24 P.R.O., RG 10/2368.
25 Kelly's Dir. Som. (1910, 1914).
26 S.R.O., Q/RSf 6.
27 M. Fuller, W. Country Friendly Socs. 40, 161; below, N. Petherton.
28 Som. Co. Gaz. 17 June 1837; P.R.O., FS 2/9.
29 E. Jeboult, Hist. W. Som. 38.
30 S.R.O., DD/CH 78/3.
31 O.S. Map 1/2,500, Som. LXXI. 6 (1914 edn.).
32 S.R.S. iii. 186.
33 P.R.O., E 179/238/150.
34 Ibid. E 179/169/150.

41 were exempted.[35] In 1760 154 male residents were recorded.[36] There were 133 houses in the parish in 1781[37] and 166 in 1821. The population rose from 608 in 1801 to 812 in 1821 and to 1,116 in 1831. Railway labourers accounted for the increase to 1,296 in 1841, and thereafter the total declined to 1,073 by 1871. The opening of the paper mills led to an increase to 1,166 in 1881, and subsequent decline was slower than in many neighbouring parishes. New building in the later 20th century caused the population to rise again, reaching 2,279 in 1981.[38]

MANORS AND OTHER ESTATES. A grant of land in 882 by King Alfred to Athelstan has been identified, probably incorrectly, as Creech.[39] In 1066 *CREECH* was held by Gunild, daughter of Earl Godwin, and at the Conquest passed to the Crown.[40] William, count of Mortain, had acquired the manor by *c.* 1102, when it formed part of his endowment of Montacute priory.[41] Montacute retained the manor until 1539, receiving a grant of free warren in 1252.[42] In 1542 the manor was granted for a term of years to Sir Thomas Wyatt (d. 1542), who left it to his widow Elizabeth.[43] Elizabeth (d. 1560) and her second husband, Sir Edward Warner, sold her interest in 1557 to William Knapman the younger, who had already acquired the reversion of the manor, which the Crown had granted in reversion to Sir Edward Hastings.[44] It was then subject to a fee farm rent payable to the Clothworkers Company and a charge of £53 11s. 10d. a year in favour of Hastings's hospital at Stoke Poges (Bucks.).[45] The manor was divided, probably by Knapman, half passing in 1558 to John Radford (d. 1565) and later to John's son Lawrence,[46] and half to John Harris, whose share in 1585 was sold by Nicholas Harris and Henry Shattock to Lawrence Radford.[47] Lawrence died in 1590 and his son Arthur sold the manor in 1598 to Robert Cuffe,[48] owner of the capital messuage and other lands, which his father, also Robert (d. 1593), had purchased.[49]

Robert Cuffe the younger (d. 1639) was succeeded by his son, also Robert, who died *c.* 1664.[50] His trustees sold the lordship in 1666 to Sir John Coventry, who held large mortgages on

the Cuffe estates. The manor house and demesne were excluded from the sale.[51] Sir John (d. 1682)[52] was succeeded by his cousin Francis Coventry (d. 1686).[53] Francis's heir was his sister Elizabeth, wife of Sir William Keyt, Bt. (d. 1702). Elizabeth's son William died in 1702, one month before his father, leaving his inheritance in Creech to his three younger sons John, Francis, and Hastings, who held the manor jointly.[54] John died in 1733 leaving a son William under age.[55] Francis and Hastings died without issue.[56] William died in 1740[57] and the manor passed successively to his uncle Sir William Keyt, Bt. (d. 1741), and to Sir William's sons Sir Thomas and Sir Robert, who held the manor jointly with John's widow Mary under a settlement of 1718. Sir Thomas died in 1755 leaving his share to his brother Sir Robert.[58] Mary died *c.* 1758[59] and in 1768 Sir Robert and his wife Margaret sold the manor to William Hussey of Salisbury. Between 1771 and his death in 1813 Hussey sold lands to tenants but reserved quit rents. He devised the manor to his nephew Henry Hinxman and to his great-nephews Edward Hinxman and James Hussey in trust for sale. Land was sold *c.* 1818, and in 1834 Edward Hinxman sold the manor, consisting almost entirely of quit rents, to William Howard of West Monkton.[60] Howard died in 1869 and the manor passed in turn to his grandson Edwin Thomas Howard[61] (d. 1920), E. T. Howard (d. 1956), and Mrs. N. T. Howard (d. 1975). The lords of the manor in 1984 were Mr. G. T. Howard, Mrs. I. M. Richards, and Mrs. K. P. Griffiths.[62]

The capital messuage, recorded in 1303,[63] was let to farm in 1535 to John Cuffe (d. 1557).[64] His son Robert died in 1593 in possession of the house and demesnes of 160 a., half of which he had bought from William Knapman in 1559.[65] Robert's son Robert (d. 1639), lord of the manor from 1598,[66] rebuilt the house, which was described in 1633 as new and the greatest ornament of the parish.[67] The capital messuage and demesnes were excluded from the sale of the manor in 1666.[68] Robert Cuffe's son Robert died unmarried in 1676.[69] His heir was his sister Anne (d. 1690), first wife of Sir Francis Warre of Hestercombe (d. 1718).[70] Their son John died *c.* 1710 leaving his interest in the estate to his

35 Dwelly, *Hearth Tax*, i. 46–50; ii. 44.
36 S.R.O., DD/HWD 12.
37 Ibid. D/P/crch 23/10.   38 *Census.*
39 Birch, *Cart. Sax.* ii, p. 170; H. P. R. Finberg, *Early Charters of Wessex*, p. 127. *Proc. Som. Arch. Soc.* lvii, suppl. 142–9, suggests that the charter relates to land W. of Taunton.   40 *V.C.H. Som.* i. 438.
41 *S.R.S.* viii, p. 119; *V.C.H. Som.* iii. 213; cf. *Reg. Regum Anglo-Norm.* i, no. 397.
42 *Cal. Chart. R.* 1226–57, 408; S.R.O., DD/DP 114/16/5.
43 *S.R.S.* viii, pp. xxiii–iv; *L. & P. Hen. VIII*, xvii, p. 107.
44 *Cal. Pat.* 1555–7, 57–8, 113; P.R.O., C 142/228, no. 63; ibid. CP 25(2)/77/660/4 & 5 Phil. & Mary Mich.
45 S.R.O., DD/HWD 26; Bodl. MS. Ash. 1126, f. 122b; P.R.O., C 142/228, no. 63; inf. from Bucks. R.O.; *V.C.H. Bucks.* iii. 313. Some sources give £53 9s. 10½d.
46 *Cal. Pat.* 1558–60, 261; P.R.O., CP 25(2)/204/18 & 19 Eliz. I Mich.; ibid. C 142/170, no. 23.
47 *Cal. Pat.* 1558–60, 137; P.R.O., C 3/37, no. 40; C 3/211, no. 10; ibid. CP 25(2)/206/27 Eliz. I East.; S.R.O., DD/GC 6; DD/CH 89/1.
48 P.R.O., C 142/228, no. 63; ibid. CP 25(2)/207/40 & 41 Eliz. I Mich.
49 Ibid. C 142/238, no. 54.

50 Ibid. C 142/531, no. 4; S.R.O., DD/GC 6.
51 S.R.O., DD/SAS H/202 2; DD/GC 6.
52 *D.N.B.*
53 Burke, *Extinct Peerages* (1840), 140–1.
54 S.R.O., DD/HS 3/4; DD/SF 913; DD/MK 1; G.E.C. *Baronetage*, iii. 140.
55 S.R.O., DD/MK 1; M.I. in ch.
56 S.R.O., DD/HS 3/4.
57 M.I. in ch.
58 G.E.C. *Baronetage*, iii. 140; S.R.O., DD/HWD 1; DD/BR/sh 1.
59 S.R.O., DD/SAS H/202 2; DD/HWD 12.
60 Ibid. DD/HWD 1; DD/HS 3/4; DD/MK 17.
61 Letter from E. T. Howard, in V.C.H. office, Taunton; S.R.O., DD/HWD 22, 25.
62 Inf. from Mr. G. T. Howard, London.
63 P.R.O., SC 11/798.
64 Ibid. SC 6/Hen. VIII/3137; ibid. C 142/114, no. 43.
65 Ibid. C 142/238, no. 54; S.R.O., DD/GC 6.
66 Above.   67 *S.R.S.* xv. 62.
68 S.R.O., DD/SAS H/202 2.
69 Ibid. D/P/crch 2/1/1.
70 Ibid. DD/GC 7; DD/SAS H/202 2; *Proc. Som. Arch. Soc.* lxxxvii. 93.

father.[71] It then descended to Francis's daughter Margaret, wife of John Bampfylde.[72] Margaret died in 1758[73] and was succeeded by her son Copplestone Warre Bampfylde. He died in 1791 leaving his land to his nephew John Tyndale, son of his sister Margaretta, who was to take the name Warre.[74] John Tyndale Warre held the estate, known as Court Barton, until 1816 when he sold it to Thomas Dyer who conveyed it to John Snook in 1825. Snook released the estate in trust for sale in 1832. It was bought by George Bickham who sold it to John Dunning in 1837.[75] Court Barton farm was held by the Dunning family until 1901 when it was broken up and sold.[76]

The house, which lies east of the church, was known as Creech farm in 1798[77] but later as Court House[78] and Court Barton. The north-west corner of the house is early or mid 16th-century and may have been the kitchen and service wing of a substantial house. It retains two large mullioned and transomed windows on the north gable end and a kitchen fireplace on the east side. In the later 18th century, but not simultaneously, additional ranges were added to the south and east by which time the western part of the original house had been demolished.

BURLINCH manor may have formed part of the estate of John Paulet, marquess of Winchester, in 1573.[79] It was conveyed by Thomas Wood to George Palmer in 1688[80] possibly in trust for the Sanford family who owned it in 1713.[81] By 1755 it had been divided.[82] In 1780 the manor, then called Ballcombe probably by confusion with a neighbouring estate in North Petherton, was held by John Muttlebury who left it to his eldest son John.[83] Comprising a smallholding and chief rents, it was owned by James Loveless in 1839 and sold in 1845.[84] There is no record of a capital messuage but a dovecot was recorded in 1755.[85]

Richard Wrotham held ½ virgate under Montacute priory in 1247[86] and his great niece Evelyn Durant held a free tenement in 1312.[87] That may have been the origin of the *CREECH* manor held by Thomas Wroth in 1664,[88] which comprised lands formerly part of the main manor and an estate at Adsborough.[89] The manor descended with Newton Wroth in North Petherton.[90] Lordship is not recorded after 1723 when it was

apportioned to Cecily Wroth and her husband Sir Hugh Acland,[91] and some of the land and a farm were sold.[92] The largest farm, bought from the Taylor family, probably in the 1740s,[93] was at Charlton and was retained until 1799 when Lady Harriet Acland sold it to George Coombe.[94] Known as Aclands in 1839,[95] and later as Charlton House, it remained in the Coombe family until 1929 when it was sold.[96] Charlton House is a large 19th-century villa.

LITTLE CREECH manor was conveyed by George Farwell to Thomas Warre in 1609.[97] By 1612 it had passed to Sir John Portman, Bt. (d. 1612), who was succeeded by his son Henry. It was said to be held of the king in chief[98] and descended in the Portman family with Clavelshay in North Petherton until 1665 or later.[99] By the early 18th century it was part of Creech manor.[1] The land was owned by 1780 and in 1800 by John Bowering,[2] by John Philips in 1804,[3] and in 1839 by Mary Nixon.[4] In 1963 the farm was purchased by the R.S.P.C.A. and in 1984 it housed an animal centre and wildlife unit.

Montacute priory appropriated Creech church in 1362 and until the Dissolution held the rectory, comprising two thirds of the corn tithe and 7 a. of arable in 1362,[5] but only tithes in 1539.[6] In 1539 it was leased to John Cuffe, whose son Robert obtained a lease from the Crown in 1577.[7] Robert's son, also Robert, purchased the reversion before 1636 and the rectory descended with the Creech manor demesnes until 1816 or later.[8] The estate in the 1780s consisted of the great tithes of overland and two thirds of the tithe on 'place lands'.[9] Early in the 19th century, probably in 1816, the rectory was acquired by Thomas Dyer, who in 1818 sold the tithe of 'place lands' to the Revd. Richard Formby but retained the tithe of overlands.[10] By 1839 several landowners, notably George Coombe in 1817, had purchased the tithes of their own lands, accounting for one quarter of the rectorial estate.[11] In 1839 the Revd. Miles Formby and Mary, widow of Thomas Dyer, holders of the remaining rectorial tithes, were awarded rent charges of £120 and £40 respectively.[12]

During the 16th century several estates were created out of the medieval manor of Creech including Charlton, Ham, Langaller, and possibly

71 S.R.O., DD/GC 7.
72 Ibid. DD/SAS FA 127; DD/GC 7.
73 *Proc. Som. Arch. Soc.* lxxxvii. 99.
74 S.R.O., DD/AS 4.
75 Ibid. DD/DP 50/4, 51/1, 55/4.
76 Ibid. tithe award; ibid. DD/SAS (C/1401) 55; Devon R.O. 547 B/P 2929.
77 S.R.O., DD/AS 4.
78 Devon R.O. 547 B/P 2929.
79 P.R.O., CP 25(2)/204/15 Eliz. I Hil.
80 Ibid. CP 25(2)/795/3 & 4 Jas. II Hil.
81 Ibid. CP 25(2)/962/12 Anne Trin.
82 Ibid. CP 43/687, rot. 381.
83 S.R.O., DD/X/NL (C/364).
84 Ibid. tithe award; ibid. DD/HWD 17.
85 P.R.O., CP 43/687, rot. 381.
86 *Cal. Inq. p.m.* i, p. 54.
87 Ibid. v, p. 192.
88 Devon R.O. 1148 M/add 2/59.
89 Ibid. 6/17.
90 Below, N. Petherton, manors.
91 S.R.O., DD/AH 1/3.
92 Ibid. DD/CH 89/1; Devon R.O. 1148 M/add 2/59.

93 Devon R.O. 1148 M/add 2/59; S.R.O., DD/DP 114/16/1.
94 S.R.O., DD/CH 67/1.
95 Ibid. tithe award.
96 Ibid. DD/CH 73/6; Devon R.O. 547 B/P 2929.
97 S.R.O., DD/CR 17; P.R.O., CP 25(2)/345/7 Jas. I Hil.
98 *S.R.S.* lxvii. 140.
99 P.R.O., C 142/406, no. 67; below, N. Petherton, manors.
1 S.R.O., DD/DP 114/16/1; D/P/hat. w 4/1/1.
2 Ibid. D/P/crch 23/10; ibid. Q/REl 2/3.
3 Ibid. D/P/crch 3/2/1.
4 Ibid. tithe award.
5 *S.R.S.* viii, p. 203.
6 *Valor Eccl.* (Rec. Com.), i. 196.
7 *Cal. Pat.* 1575–8, p. 223; P.R.O., C 142/278, no. 21; ibid. SC 6/Edw. VI/402.
8 P.R.O., C 142/531, no. 4; S.R.O., D/P/crch 4/1/1; DD/SAS H/202 2; DD/SAS FA 127; DD/AS 4; DD/DP 44/8, 114/16/2.
9 S.R.O., DD/DP 114/16/4–5.
10 Ibid. 44/8, 114/16/2.
11 Ibid.; ibid. tithe award.
12 Ibid. tithe award.

Walford. In 1558 William Knapman was licensed to grant a house, dovecot, and 138 a. in *CHARLTON* to Alexander Sydenham.[13] John Sydenham (d. 1547), probably Alexander's father, had been a tenant of the manor in 1539, and was the largest taxpayer in the parish in 1526.[14] Alexander Sydenham (d. 1584)[15] was succeeded by his daughter Elizabeth, wife of Sir John Poyntz.[16] Charlton descended with Moorland in North Petherton until 1627 or later,[17] when it was probably sold to John Pocock, tenant in 1603. Pocock (d. 1631) left Charlton to his wife Joan for life and then to his younger daughter Rachel.[18] Rachel married Edward Cely (d. 1679)[19] and was succeeded by her grandson William Cely, a minor. William died *c.* 1723 and his son John in 1723.[20] John's twin brother Edward had succeeded by 1733 but died in 1746[21] leaving it to his brother Maurice. It was sold to a younger brother, Trevilian Cely, before 1752. Trevilian died unmarried before 1767 when his heir was his eldest surviving brother William.[22] William, who took the name Trevilian as heir to his uncle John Trevilian (d. 1749) of Midelney in Drayton, held Charlton until his death in 1774[23] and left it to his nephew William Southey, son of his sister Elizabeth. William took the surname Cely and died in 1781[24] leaving Charlton to his mother Elizabeth, who by her will dated 1782 devised it to her niece Mary Ann Dewbury. In 1783 Mary Ann sold Charlton to John Bullen of Greenwich (Kent). By the 1820s it had been forfeited to mortgagees and in 1831 was left to John Matthew Quantock by his father John, nephew of the original mortgagee.[25] John Matthew Quantock conveyed part of the estate to George Coombe in 1846 and Charlton farm in 1858 to James Bond (d. *c.* 1876).[26] It was probably bought by George Coombe's son George, who held Charlton until his death in 1929 when the estate was divided and sold, although his widow kept the house until she died in 1934.[27]

The capital messuage was known as Charlton Farm in 1603.[28] Now called Charlton Manor, it is an **L**-shaped brick house with a seven-bayed front of two storeys and an attic. The earliest part of the house appears to be the later 17th-century west range, with the projecting stair turret close to the centre of the east side. It probably had a service wing running eastwards from its north end, and had 10 hearths in 1664, although 3 were no longer in use.[29] The wing

was rebuilt and possibly lengthened early in the 18th century, and the house was refitted later in the century. In the earlier 19th century the west front was remodelled, its northern half being largely rebuilt.

In 1557 William Knapman sold lands at *HAM* to Thomas Marshall[30] who probably sold them to Robert Cuffe. They descended in the Cuffe family as Ham manor but were probably re-absorbed into Creech manor after 1598.[31] A house called the Court House at Ham was let in 1760 and sold in 1790 by the lord of Creech manor.[32] The cottage called Courthouse may be on the site.

In 1559 William Knapman sold half the estate at *LANGALLER* to Robert Cuffe.[33] It descended with the Creech manor demesne until 1666 and then once again with Creech manor.[34] In 1598 Arthur Radford conveyed lands, probably the other half of the same estate, to William White[35] (d. *c.* 1629), from whom the lands passed probably in the direct male line to Francis[36] (d. by 1664), William[37] (d. *c.* 1676), William, and Francis White.[38] By 1767 the White estates were held by Samuel Richards, who had married Susanna, sister of Francis White.[39] Samuel was succeeded *c.* 1775[40] by his sons John and Francis White Richards jointly. Francis was dead by 1836, and John (d. 1844) held the whole estate in 1839.[41] John was succeeded by his son Francis White (d. 1850), and Francis by his son John Simon, on whose death in 1915 the estate was broken up and sold.[42]

The house now known as Langaller Manor Farm was partially rebuilt of stone in the 17th century but the lower east end is of cob and is probably part of an earlier house. The house was greatly altered in the 19th century.[43]

WALFORD PLACE was owned by Nicholas Raymond (d. 1612). His son Samuel (d. 1633)[44] added further land there and at Adsborough and Langaller by purchase in 1621 from Hugh Elliott, son of John (d. 1604) who had held it in 1598.[45] Samuel was succeeded by his son George (d. by 1651) whose widow Dorothy survived until 1677.[46] George's son Dr. Samuel Raymond (d. 1690)[47] was followed by his son Samuel who sold Elliott's lands to James Trivet in 1701 and Walford Place to William Cornish in 1706.[48] By 1733 Walford Place was known as Walford farm and was owned by George Bubb Dodington (cr. Lord Melcombe 1761, d. 1762).[49] It descended

[13] *Cal. Pat.* 1557–8, 233.
[14] P.R.O., SC 6/Hen. VIII/3137; ibid. E 179/169/150.
[15] Ibid. C 142/207, no. 99.
[16] S.R.O., DD/BR/pc 1.
[17] Below, N. Petherton, manors.
[18] P.R.O., C 142/490, no. 171; C 60/523, no. 28; M.I. in ch.
[19] S.R.O., D/P/crch 4/1/1; D/P/cur. n 2/1/1; *Som. Wills,* ed. Brown, iv. 75.
[20] Collinson, *Hist. Som.* i. 77; *Som. Wills,* ed. Brown, iv. 75; S.R.O., D/P/dton 2/1/1.
[21] S.R.O., DD/DP 114/16/1; D/P/crch 2/1/1.
[22] Ibid. DD/CH 89/1; DD/HWD 4.
[23] Ibid. D/P/dton 2/1/2.
[24] Ibid. DD/DP 114/16/1; DD/CH 89/1; D/P/crch 2/1/1.
[25] Ibid. DD/CH 89/1; DD/DP 39/11.
[26] Ibid.; DD/SAS (C/2273) 1/C 17/1.
[27] Devon R.O. 547 B/P 2929; local inf.
[28] S.R.O., DD/BR/pc 1.
[29] Dwelly, *Hearth Tax,* i. 48.

[30] P.R.O., CP 40/1172, Carte rot. 6.
[31] S.R.O., DD/GC 6.   [32] Ibid. DD/HWD 1–2.
[33] Ibid. DD/GC 6–7.   [34] Above.
[35] S.R.O., DD/MKG 4.
[36] Ibid. DD/SAS FA 22/1.
[37] Ibid. D/P/crch 4/1/1.
[38] Ibid. DD/MK 1; DD/SP inventory, 1676.
[39] Ibid. DD/HWD 4; DD/MK 1; D/P/crch 2/1/2.
[40] *Taunton Wills* (Index Libr. xlv), 342.
[41] S.R.O., DD/MKG 4; ibid. tithe award.
[42] Ibid. DD/CCH 68; DD/HS 3/4; D/P/crch 2/1/7–8.
[43] Ibid. DD/V/TAr 10.1.
[44] P.R.O., C 142/411, no. 160; C 142/469, no. 142.
[45] S.R.O., DD/X/NL (C/364); DD/DP 28; *S.R.S.* lxvii. 106.
[46] *Som. Wills,* ed. Brown, ii. 63; S.R.O., D/P/crch 4/1/1; DD/SAS H/202 2; M.I. in ch.
[47] S.R.O., D/P/crch 2/1/1.
[48] Ibid. DD/X/NL (C/364); DD/BR/wn 3.
[49] Ibid. DD/DP 114/16/1.

with Dodington manor[50] until 1797 when it was sold to Thomas Warren (d. c. 1825). Thomas's sons Joseph and William (d. c. 1844) succeeded jointly, and in 1858 Joseph sold it to Charles Chapman of North Petherton.[51] It probably then descended with Shovel in North Petherton until the late 19th century.[52]

Walford Farm, known as Walford Place until 1754 or later,[53] has been divided into two dwellings. The house has at its centre a low range with jointed upper cruck roof which was rebuilt, probably by Nicholas Raymond, c. 1600. There are extensions of the 18th and early 19th centuries at each end, and at the back extensive cider houses, probably of the 19th century, form part of the boundary of a walled garden.

ECONOMIC HISTORY. In 1086 there were 8 ploughlands and as many teams, a square league of pasture, and 8 a. of meadow. There were 6 hides in demesne with 2 ploughteams and six *servi*. There were 10 cattle, 10 swine, 48 sheep, and a riding horse. Twenty *villani* and 10 bordars worked the rest of the land with 6 ploughteams.[54] In 1303 Montacute priory's demesne in Creech comprised 304 a. of arable and 51 a. of meadow with some pasture. There were also 26 free holdings on about 11 virgates of land, 31 customary and ferling tenants with another 11 virgates, 9 villeins each having a house and 6 a., and 10 cottars.[55] Creech was prosperous: in 1327 it paid almost as much tax as Taunton,[56] and in 1334 it was one of the most highly taxed places in the county.[57] By 1526 it was still wealthy and the manor bailiff had the second highest tax assessment.[58] In 1535 the capital messuage and woodland were let to farm and the rental distinguished between tenements, later called 'place lands',[59] and overland.[60] In 1535–8 the rental of Creech was over £70, higher than any other of Montacute priory's estates and accounting for about 15 per cent of the priory's income.[61] During the later 16th century Creech manor was divided and sold. Many holdings remained divided and some were part free and part lease or copyhold until the late 18th or early 19th century when successive lords of the manor sold their estates.[62]

The moorlands on both sides of the Tone were regularly flooded in winter and provided rich grass in summer.[63] The tenants of Ham in the 14th century had common rights for draught animals on Westhay moor in North Curry.[64] Creech moor was said to measure c. 45 a. in 1638 and Ham moor c. 49 a.[65] Dairying and cheese-making were important: in 1679 one man had 30 cheeses and another had 72, in 1687 a third had 46, and in 1688 a herd of 8 cows produced 2 cwt.

of raw milk cheese and 2 cwt. of household cheese. Oxen were rarely listed before the 18th century but horses were plentiful and were presumably the preferred plough beast. Pigs were kept on the byproducts of cheesemaking. Edward Cely the younger had 90 sheep at Charlton in 1677. One man had 46 geese in 1687 and in 1690 a flock worth 8s. was recorded. Most farmers combined stock rearing with arable husbandry. Bearded barley was recorded in 1645, dredge in 1648, and clover from the 1670s. Apple orchards were common and both apples and cider feature in most inventories. One husbandman in 1681 worked for his landlord ploughing and sowing at 17s. an acre. Many farmers in the 17th century enjoyed considerable prosperity, reflected in their books, furnishings, linen, and plate. One of the wealthier farmers died in 1647 possessed of a quantity of silverware, jewelry, and fine clothing. John Crosse of Langaller, probably the wealthiest man in the parish when he died in 1679 with goods worth over £1,400, possessed silver plate, a clock, and books.[66]

In 1733 the arable in the parish was estimated at 1,361 a.[67] In 1781 grass covered 1,045 a., arable 1,016 a., turnips and clover 115 a., and gardens and orchards 205 a. A crop survey of 1784 gave the following acreages: meadow 585½, wheat 365½, barley 174½, fallow 140½, orchard 104, peas 80½, beans 40½, vetches 33½, oats 14, clover 3½, and flax 2.[68] In 1787 one man grew 47 stone of flax in the parish.[69] At the end of the 18th century the vicar collected tithe from potatoes and flax and in 1787 he received 87 bags of apples in tithe. In 1800 he recorded over 47 a. of potatoes.[70] At Little Creech, a farm of c. 25 a., pasture and meadow predominated but crops of potatoes, wheat, barley, and vetch were grown, livestock comprised horses, plough oxen, heifers, steers, ewes, pigs, poultry, and 4 cows which produced an average of 336 gallons of milk a year between 1801 and 1806.[71] In 1813 artificial, Dutch, and rye grasses were grown in the parish, 30 a. of flax in 1816, and 25½ a. of flax on Sheepham moor in 1817 when 67½ a. of potatoes were tithed in the parish.[72] There were 74 a. of water meadow on the Court Barton estate in 1825, over a third of the acreage.[73]

The moors by the Tone, Creech and Langaller Heathfields, and other small areas of common and waste totalling 200 a. were inclosed under an award of 1814.[74] By the 1820s the newly inclosed moors were growing crops of wheat and beans, and wheat was grown on Creech Heathfield.[75] The tithe award of 1839 recorded 1,137 a. of arable out of 2,152 a.[76]

Landholding was fragmented by the division of the manor in the 16th century[77] and there were few compact farms apart from the old freeholds

50 *V.C.H. Som.* v. 66; S.R.O., Q/REl 2/3.
51 S.R.O., DD/DHR 17; DD/HWD 17.
52 Below, N. Petherton, manors.
53 S.R.O., DD/AH 24/8.   54 *V.C.H. Som.* i. 438.
55 P.R.O., SC 11/798.   56 *S.R.S.* iii. 186, 274.
57 *Subsidy of 1334*, ed. R. E. Glasscock, 265.
58 P.R.O., E 179/169/150.   59 S.R.O., DD/DP 114/16/2.
60 P.R.O., SC 6/Hen. VIII/3137.
61 Devon R.O. 123 M/O 2; *Valor Eccl.* (Rec. Com.), i. 195.
62 S.R.O., DD/HWD 1–2.   63 *S.R.S.* xv. 63, 220.
64 *H.M.C. Wells*, i. 269, 316.

65 P.R.O., LR 2/202.   66 S.R.O., DD/SP inventories.
67 Ibid. DD/DP 114/16/1.
68 Ibid. D/P/crch 23/10.   69 Ibid. Q/RLh 21.
70 Ibid. D/P/crch 3/2/1.
71 Ibid. DD/DP 114/16/2.
72 Ibid. D/P/crch 3/2/2.
73 Ibid. DD/DP 55/4.
74 Ibid. D/R/ta 9/1/1; DD/BD 102.
75 Ibid. D/P/crch 3/2/6.
76 Ibid. tithe award.
77 Above, manors.

STOCKLAND BRISTOL CHURCH IN 1845

CREECH ST. MICHAEL CHURCH IN 1837

The Bridgwater–Taunton canal, *c.* 1950

Floods on the railway, 1894
CREECH ST. MICHAEL

at Walford and Charlton and the Court Barton estate. In 1839 only 26 holdings were over 25 a. and only 8 over 50 a. The largest farms were Charlton House farm (124 a.), Court Barton (146 a.), and Charlton farm (149 a.).[78] There was, however, some consolidation during the 19th century. The Coombe family of Charlton were farmers and graziers and bought several estates.[79] In 1813 they had over 168 a. in Creech[80] and George Coombe's estates in the parish and elsewhere were worth about £15,000 of which £1,200 was in livestock.[81] By 1839 the Coombe holdings covered nearly 200 a. and in 1851 George Coombe (d. c. 1857) farmed 250 a. in Charlton, having bought part of Charlton farm in 1846.[82] In 1881 his son George was farming 401 a. and employing 16 labourers.[83] George Coombe (d. 1929) held the largest farms in the parish at Charlton and Court Barton.[84] During the late 19th century the size of the other farms increased: 6 were over 100 a. by 1851,[85] and 8 by 1871 of which 2 were over 200 a., but the number of labourers declined.[86] Court Barton employed fewer hands in 1881 than 10 years earlier although the acreage had increased and on at least one other farm employment had halved.[87]

Drainage was poor and divided ownership inhibited improvement. On Charlton farm before 1834 several large fields were flooded every winter and one year in seven summer floods destroyed half the produce.[88] Improvements in the late 19th century alleviated sheep rot, though reducing the number of snipe.[89] An agricultural society for Creech and neighbouring parishes was set up in the 1880s to encourage skilled labour; ploughing and shearing matches were held at Court Barton and Walford, and an annual dinner was given.[90] By 1905 more land was under grass and only 769 a. were arable,[91] a figure which had declined still further to 182 ha. (c. 450 a.) in 1982.[92] Nurseries and market gardens were established, mainly at Creech Heathfield, in the later 19th century.[93] During the 20th century orchards were established at Charlton, growing apples, pears, plums, damsons, and soft fruit.[94] In 1982 two specialist fruit farms covered c. 25 ha. (62 a.). The main crops were wheat and winter and spring barley. There was no further consolidation of farms, most of which specialized in dairying and stock rearing. There were 758 cattle, 445 sheep, 345 poultry, and 34 pigs.[95]

MILLS AND FISHERY. A mill at Creech in 1086[96] presumably descended with the manor. By the mid 16th century there were two distinct mills, Creech mills and North End mill. Creech mills, also called Philberds or Filberts mills, on the Tone near Creech Bridge,[97] were probably a pair of mills under one roof. William Knapman sold a half share in two mills to Lawrence Radford in 1578;[98] in 1585 Henry Shattock and Nicholas Harris sold to Lawrence what was described as three water mills but was probably the other half share.[99] Lawrence's son Arthur sold the mill with the manor to Robert Cuffe in 1598.[1] Creech mill descended with the Court Barton estate until 1816.[2] By 1831 the mill building had doubled in size and a long extension, probably the cottages surviving in 1984, had been built along the river bank.[3] In 1861 and 1866 the miller was also a seed and manure merchant[4] and by 1872 milling had ceased.[5] The river was divided by an island; the northern branch serving as a mill pond was called the Creech river. The other branch, with a lock and towpath, was a navigable waterway called the Ham river.[6] By 1984 flood prevention schemes had closed the northern branch, leaving the mill without water. The early 19th-century mill house and the mill have been converted to residential use.

North End mill, probably the Creech customary mill, seems to be the mill of which William Knapman sold half to the elder Robert Cuffe in 1558[7] and Henry Shattock sold half to Robert Seager, possibly in trust for Robert Cuffe, in 1584; at his death in 1593 Cuffe owned the customary mill.[8] North End mill descended with the Court Barton estate until 1710 or later but by 1731 was again part of Creech manor.[9] The miller bought one third of the mill from the lord in 1788[10] and the remainder before 1800.[11] The mill was still in use, converted to steam, in 1906 but probably closed soon afterwards.[12] In the 1920s it was used as a carpenter's shop and for making cider.[13] The mill, on the stream at North End, has been partly demolished and the pond filled in. The main building has been converted into flats.

Oil mills were recorded on the North End stream in the late 18th century, presumably producing linseed oil from flax.[14]

The Tone fishery was recorded in 1086[15] and probably descended with the manor. Sir Thomas Wyatt let it to John Cuffe (d. 1557),[16] and William Knapman sold it to Robert Cuffe in

---

78 S.R.O., tithe award.
79 Ibid. DD/CH 67/1, 69/6.
80 Ibid. 67/1.
81 Ibid. 73/7.
82 Ibid. 73/6; ibid. tithe award; P.R.O., HO 107/1922.
83 P.R.O., RG 10/2368–9.
84 Devon R.O. 547 B/P 2929.
85 P.R.O., HO 107/1922.
86 Ibid. RG 10/2368–9.
87 Ibid. HO 107/1922; ibid. RG 10/2368–9; RG 11/2365.
88 S.R.O., DD/CTV 59.
89 Jnl. Bath & West of Eng. Soc. x (ii), 77; M. Williams, Draining of the Som. Levels, 172.
90 S.R.O., D/P/che. f 23/4.
91 Statistics supplied by the then Bd. of Agric., 1905.
92 Min. of Agric., Fisheries, and Food, agric. returns, 1982. Some land had been lost to housing.
93 P.R.O., RG 10/2368–9.
94 Local inf.

95 Min. of Agric., Fisheries, and Food, agric. returns, 1982.
96 V.C.H. Som. i. 438.
97 S.R.O., DD/SAS H/202 2.
98 P.R.O., CP 25(2)/204/18 & 19 Eliz. I Mich.
99 Ibid. CP 25(2)/206/27 Eliz. I East.
1 Ibid. CP 25(2)/207/40 & 41 Eliz. I Mich.
2 S.R.O., DD/SAS H/202 2; DD/SAS FA 22.
3 Ibid. DD/GC 90; DD/TC 15.
4 P.O. Dir. Som. (1861, 1866).
5 Morris & Co. Dir. Som. (1872).
6 S.R.O., DD/GC 90; DD/TC 15.
7 Ibid. DD/GC 7.   8 Ibid. 6.
9 Ibid. DD/SAS FA 82; DD/GC 87.
10 Ibid. DD/HWD 1–2.   11 Ibid. Q/REl 2/3.
12 Kelly's Dir. Som. (1906, 1910).   13 Local inf.
14 Collinson, Hist. Som. i. 74.
15 V.C.H. Som. i. 438.
16 P.R.O., E 134/33–4 Eliz. I Mich./23, no. 5.

1559.[17] Freeholders may have had fishing rights, and Edward Cely the younger had a boat at Charlton worth 30s. in 1677.[18] Fishing rights were sold with the manor in 1767[19] and were retained until 1908 or later.[20]

TRADE AND INDUSTRY. Goods brought up the river Tone between the 17th and 19th centuries were usually landed at Coal Harbour or at Ham Mills in North Curry, formerly the upper tidal limit. The Bobbett family imported coal through Coal Harbour from the early 17th century.[21] Tolls proposed by the Tone Conservators after 1698 brought objections from importers of coal, culm, and salt to Devon, Dorset, and South Somerset, who feared that prices would rise. Coal Harbour then regularly served towns and villages in a 20-mile radius; two Devon villages imported 1,800 lb. of culm each year for lime-burning, and dyers and maltsters at Bridport (Dors.) used coal landed there.[22] Among the traders there from 1714 was a salt merchant of Bewdley (Worcs.).[23]

Over 40 boatmen petitioned unsuccessfully against the imposition of tolls,[24] and in 1717 tolls were paid at Coal Harbour on about 800 boat-loads of coal and 200 tons of general cargo. The amount of toll collected suggests a decline in volume of trade during the 18th century, and from the 1780s merchants were beginning to use other sites along the river for landing coal and timber.[25] Most business by the early 1830s had been transferred to Ham Mills,[26] but still in 1878 the tenant at Coal Harbour was one of the two principal toll payers on the river.[27]

The Bridgwater and Taunton canal, opened in 1827, took business from the river, and the canal company obtained control of river trade in 1832.[28] By 1839 a coal wharf and timber yard were established near the canal bridge in Creech village.[29] The canal company was in turn bought out by the railway company in 1866, but no goods yard was built in the parish.[30]

In the later 17th century spinning, weaving, and dyeing were all done in the parish: one man in 1677 had a comb shop, over 166 lb. of yarn, 100 lb. of wool out in 'spinning houses', yarn out with weavers, pieces of finished cloth, and dyestuffs.[31] There is not much evidence of cloth-making in the 18th century. Silkweavers were recorded between 1843 and 1871,[32] and a few glovemakers in the later 19th century.[33] In the late 17th century there were two families of tanners,[34] and in 1695 a shop sold fruit, spice, and silk tape.[35] In 1821 only 26 families out of 166 were not employed in agriculture.[36] By 1851 there were several shopkeepers and dealers.[37] Small manufacturers in the late 19th century included basketmakers, one of whom employed two others, a matmaker, cabinet makers, and pipemakers, and there was a gas fitter.[38] There was a small brewery by the canal in 1831[39] and in 1851 there were several maltsters in the parish.[40] A lemonade manufacturer was recorded in 1866.[41] A brickyard at the eastern end of Bull Street was open in 1851 making bricks and drainage pipes,[42] and in the 1870s bricks and tiles.[43] The yard had closed by 1904.[44]

A paper mill, opened west of Creech village in 1875, produced writing, cartridge, and fine printing paper.[45] In 1881 it employed 140 men and women as rag cutters, grass sorters, washers, labourers, firemen and engine drivers, machine boys, a blacksmith, and beaters.[46] New machinery was installed in 1948 to produce a wider variety of papers[47] including by the later 20th century 'bulky' papers for books and lighter paper for stationery and advertising literature. The mill, owned by the British Printing and Communications Corporation and employing 62 people, closed in 1982.[48] The building was later acquired by Taunton Deane borough council to house small industries.

In 1269 Montacute priory was granted a Tuesday market at Creech and a three-day fair around the feast of St. Matthew (21 Sept.).[49] The priory's 14th-century copy of the charter gives the date of the fair as St. Augustine's day (26 May).[50] There is no evidence that markets or fairs were ever held.

LOCAL GOVERNMENT. Until 1526 or later Creech was a free manor, independent of any other hundred[51] and it was recorded as a hundred of itself in the 12th century.[52] By 1538 it was in Andersfield hundred, and by 1569 formed a tithing with Merridge.[53] By 1641 Creech was a tithing by itself and remained so into the 19th century.[54] Montacute priory in 1537–8 made a payment to Whitley hundred for lands in Creech,[55] perhaps those which

17 S.R.O., DD/GC 7.
18 Ibid. DD/SP inventory, 1677.
19 Ibid. DD/HWD 4.
20 Letter in V.C.H. office, Taunton.
21 S.R.O., D/B/bw 1489, 1493–4, 1497, 1506.
22 Ibid. DD/TC 7, 9/2.
23 Ibid. 10.
24 Ibid. 9/2.
25 Ibid. DD/MK 13, 17; DD/HWD 12; DD/TC 2.
26 Ibid. DD/TC 42–3.
27 Ibid. Q/RUa 11.
28 C. A. Buchanan, *Bridgwater and Taunton Canal*, 16; C. Hadfield, *Canals of S. Eng.* 210.
29 S.R.O., tithe award.
30 *Our Village*, 19–23.
31 S.R.O., D/D/Cd 71; D/P/crch 23/5; DD/SP inventories, 1634, 1647, 1677, 1684.
32 Ibid. DD/HWD 15; P.R.O., HO 107/1922; ibid. RG 10/2368.
33 P.R.O., RG 11/2365.
34 S.R.O., DD/CH 89/1; DD/X/NL (C/190); ibid. Q/SR 153/39.
35 Ibid. DD/SP inventory, 1695.
36 *Census*, 1821.
37 P.R.O., HO 107/1922.
38 Ibid. RG 11/2368–9.
39 S.R.O., DD/TC 15.
40 P.R.O., HO 107/1922.
41 *P.O. Dir. Som.* (1866).
42 P.R.O., HO 107/1922.
43 Ibid. RG 10/2369; Morris & Co. *Dir. Som.* (1872).
44 O.S. Map 1/2,500, Som. LXXI. 10 (1904 edn.).
45 *S.D.N.Q.* xxv. 249.
46 P.R.O., RG 11/2365.
47 *S.D.N.Q.* xxv. 249.
48 *Som. Co. Gaz.* 9 July 1982.
49 *Cal. Chart. R.* 1257–1300, 116.
50 *S.R.S.* viii, p. 132.
51 *V.C.H. Som.* v. 11; P.R.O., E 179/169/150.
52 *S.R.S.* viii, pp. 119–20, 123–4.
53 Devon R.O. 123 M/O 2; *S.R.S.* xx. 242.
54 *Som. Protestation Returns*, ed. A. J. Howard and T. L. Stoate, 186; S.R.O., Q/REl 2/3.
55 Devon R.O. 123 M/O 2.

Glastonbury abbey had claimed as part of West Monkton manor in Whitley hundred.[56]

A court for Creech manor was held in the church house twice a year in the 1580s,[57] and in the later 19th century it met in October at the Bell inn.[58] Presentments or agenda survive for the period 1755–1874 and include the appointment of a hayward, tithingman, and constable.[59] A court was held for Ham in 1594.[60]

Parishioners with common rights were responsible for repairing the churchyard wall. The obligation was probably obsolete before 1814, when rights in the common then being inclosed were claimed in proportion to the length of wall that each commoner had maintained.[61] Initialled stones, which survive, marked the sections.

The parish was served by two churchwardens, two overseers, and two waywardens in the 18th and 19th centuries.[62] In the later 17th century there were two constables,[63] and a hayward kept the common pound in 1714.[64] In 1816 the vestry appointed a keeper of the pound,[65] which lay between Bull Street and the river and was a garden in 1984. In 1652 a wounded soldier was allowed to build a house on waste at Creech Heathfield; the house had reverted to the parish as a poorhouse by 1659.[66] A scheme to buy the Ship and the New Inn for a workhouse in 1768 does not appear to have been adopted.[67] The parish paid for medical attention for the poor and in 1818 agreed to vaccinate children whose parents could not afford to pay. In 1822 a select vestry was established and an assistant overseer was employed.[68] In 1830 the vestry decided to build a poorhouse on the Heathfield. In 1839 the parish still owned two poorhouses, at Creech Heathfield and North End,[69] but they were probably sold soon afterwards.

The vestry appointed parish officers in the 19th century including a church rate collector in 1854 and three constables in 1862,[70] and formed a nuisance removal committee in 1856.[71] The parish formed part of the Taunton poor-law union in 1836, Taunton rural district in 1894, and Taunton Deane district (later borough) in 1974.[72]

CHURCH. The church of Creech formed part of the endowment of Montacute priory c. 1102.[73] The priory as patron of the rectory was licensed to appropriate the church by the king in 1336 and by the pope in 1344, but only when the church became vacant. A new rector was admitted in or shortly before 1354 on the presentation of the earl of Salisbury, evidently acting as the priory's patron in time of war with France, the priory being regarded as alien. The king also presented a rector in 1354, ten days before confirming the priory's appropriation of the church, but in 1359 he ratified the title of the earl's presentee. A vicarage was ordained in 1362.[74] The living remained a sole vicarage in 1984.[75]

The advowson of the vicarage belonged to Montacute priory until the Dissolution. The king presented a vicar in 1370, in time of war with France.[76] In 1546 Roger Bluet presented by grant of the former priory,[77] but from 1557 the advowson was held with the manor,[78] although it was let in 1632.[79] In 1666 the right of presentation was held by trustees, but afterwards descended with the rectory.[80] The bishop collated in 1738[81] and thereafter the advowson was held by the incumbents or their appointees, possibly under a deed of Sir Francis Warre in 1710.[82] In 1928 the patronage was sold to Canford School Ltd., Wimborne (Dors.), which is closely linked with the Martyrs Memorial Trust. The trust held the advowson in 1984.[83]

In 1291 the church was valued at £19 13s. 4d.[84] and in 1362 it was claimed that the value was under £20.[85] The vicarage was worth £18 a year gross in 1535,[86] c. £100 c. 1668,[87] and £600 a year net at the end of the 18th century.[88] Average income fell to £500 in 1829–31.[89]

In 1362 the vicar was given tithes of hay, wool, milk, mills, and fisheries, other small tithes except those on the priory demesne, and one third of the corn tithe of the whole parish, but he had to bear all the burdens which previously fell on the rector including repair of the chancel.[90] In 1535 vicarial tithes amounted to £13, half of which came from personal tithes and oblations.[91] In 1596 the tithes were let.[92] In 1639 the vicar was entitled to tithe on pasture in North moor, which was commuted for 6s. in 1841.[93] From the 1780s to the 1830s vicars insisted on tithe in kind instead of moduses; the parishioners' legal actions to assert their rights to pay by modus were unsuccessful, but in the 1830s the vicar, Henry Cresswell, failed to insist on payment in kind,[94] and that may be why the living fell in value. In 1794 the vicar's tithes,

56   *Proc. Som. Arch. Soc.* lxxiv, suppl. 51–4; lxxxiv. 104–6.
57   S.R.O., DD/GC 6, 15.
58   Ibid. DD/HWD 12; E. Jeboult, *Hist. W. Som.* 38.
59   S.R.O., DD/HWD 5, 12.
60   Ibid. DD/GC 6.
61   Ibid. D/P/crch 23/6.
62   Ibid. 6/3/1, 14/2/1.
63   Ibid. 4/1/1.
64   Ibid. Q/SR 270/1.
65   Ibid. D/P/crch 9/1/1.
66   *S.R.S.* xxviii. 178; S.R.O., D/P/crch 4/1/1.
67   S.R.O., D/P/crch 13/2/1.
68   Ibid. 9/1/1.
69   Ibid. tithe award.
70   Ibid. D/P/crch 9/1/1–2, 13/2/3; D/PC/crch 6/2/1.
71   Ibid. D/PC/crch 6/2/1.
72   Youngs, *Local Admin. Units*, i. 673, 675–6.
73   *S.R.S.* viii, p. 119; *Reg. Regum Anglo-Norm.* ii, p. 50.
74   *S.R.S.* viii, pp. 201–4; *Cal. Papal Pets.* i. 42; *Cal. Pat.* 1358–61, 193.

75   *Dioc. Dir.*   76   *Cal. Pat.* 1367–70, 399.
77   *S.R.S.* lv, p. 115.
78   Ibid. pp. 143–4; *Som. Incumbents*, ed. Weaver, 340; above, manors.
79   S.R.O., DD/GC 6.
80   *Som. Incumbents*, ed. Weaver, 340; above, manors.
81   S.R.O., D/D/Vc 88.
82   Ibid. D/P/crch 3/1/1, 3/2/1; DD/GC 15; *Rep. Com. Eccl. Revenues*, pp. 134–5.
83   Inf. from Martyrs Memorial Trust.
84   *Tax. Eccl.* (Rec. Com.), 198.
85   *S.R.S.* viii, pp. 202–3.
86   *Valor Eccl.* (Rec. Com.), i. 171.
87   S.R.O., D/D/Vc 24.   88   Ibid. D/P/crch 3/2/1.
89   *Rep. Com. Eccl. Revenues*, pp. 134–5.
90   *S.R.S.* viii, p. 203.
91   *Valor Eccl.* (Rec. Com.), i. 171.
92   B.L. Eg. MS. 223, f. 16.
93   S.R.O., D/D/Rg 377; ibid. tithe award, N. Petherton.
94   Ibid. DD/DP 114/16/2–5; DD/GC 15.

including the value of apples paid in kind, were worth over £420.[95] In 1839 they were commuted for £380 a year,[96] after a lengthy dispute in which the vicar tried unsuccessfully to claim tithe from Court Barton and the overlands.[97]

In 1362 the glebe lands, except 7 a. of arable, were assigned to the vicarage, with grazing for 8 oxen on the manorial and common pastures.[98] The glebe was valued at £5 in 1535.[99] In 1571 there were 78 a., and 82½ a. in 1639.[1] In 1794 the vicar received £135 in rent from 72½ a. of glebe,[2] and 68½ a. were recorded in 1839.[3] The rectory house was assigned to the vicar in 1362.[4] In 1412 it had a hall and kitchen, with a new chamber by the hall door, which was given to a retired incumbent.[5] The vicarage house was described as fit in 1835[6] but was demolished to make way for the railway c. 1841.[7] It was replaced by a cob and brick house closer to the church. That house was largely demolished and rebuilt, and extended in 1877. It was replaced by a new house in 1966.[8]

Gilbert of Shepton, rector 1327–53, was in the bishop's household in the 1330s.[9] Walter Gregory was vicar for 42 years and on his resignation in 1412 was given a pension and accommodation from the living.[10] George Sydenham, vicar from 1490 until his death in 1524, had several livings including the wardenship of de Vaux college, Salisbury, and was archdeacon of Salisbury.[11] David Marler, vicar 1565–1627, was regularly presented for preaching without a licence and for not catechizing.[12] Henry Masters was deprived in 1646 but was restored after the Restoration.[13] Edmund Archer, vicar 1702–4, was later archdeacon of Wells and was an antiquary.[14] Thomas Exon, vicar 1781–1806, was an absentee and was for some years a prisoner at Verdun.[15] Henry Cresswell, vicar 1813–51, was an eccentric who engaged in cudgel playing, wrote a play which was performed at Taunton, and was suspended for bankruptcy and violent behaviour in 1844.[16] During his incumbency services were held twice on Sundays and communion was celebrated three times a year.[17] In 1851 attendance on Census Sunday was 175 in the morning and 201 in the afternoon with 76 Sunday school children attending each service.[18] In the 1900s additional services were held at Adsborough reading room.[19]

In the 1530s there was a gilded high cross,[20] and before 1548 a lamp was maintained in the church.[21] In 1582 half the church house was let by Henry Shattock to Robert Cuffe with a proviso that the churchwardens might sell bread, beer, and victuals in the house and use it for the church ale.[22] It had become an inn, probably by 1620, and was later rebuilt.[23]

The church of *ST. MICHAEL*, so dedicated by 1742, but All Saints in 1532,[24] is built of rubble with ashlar dressings and has a chancel with north chapel and a nave with north tower and aisle and south porch. The nave and chancel were probably undivided in the early 13th century. The south doorway and the piscina survive from that period. The tower and a one-bay chapel on its east side were added later in the century. That chapel was extended eastward by one bay and a two-bay aisle was built to the west of the tower in the 15th century. It was probably at the same time that new windows were put into the older parts of the church and that the south chapel was added and the tower raised by one stage. The chancel arch is a 15th-century insertion and it is possible that the earlier division, which is not marked structurally, was one bay further west. The roofs of the nave and chancel are late medieval. Fifteenth-century fittings include the base of the rood screen, the font, and richly carved bench ends now in the chancel. A reading desk was formed from older fragments in 1634 and the south chapel has a 17th-century moulded plaster ceiling. There are traces of 17th-century wall paintings.

The tomb of Robert Cuffe (d. 1593) is in the north chapel, known as the Cuffe or Court Barton aisle and in private ownership until 1901 or later.[25] The south transept was known as the Cely or Charlton aisle and was originally separated from the church by a stone screen.[26] The east window was inserted in 1825[27] and the gallery was probably refronted in 1868.[28] The arms of Charles I of 1636 and Queen Anne c. 1710 hang in the church.[29] There are six bells, the earliest dated 1590, 1609, and 1614.[30] The plate includes a chalice of 1573 inscribed 'I.P.' and two salvers dated 1762 and 1791.[31] The registers begin in 1668 but were very badly kept before the 19th century and there are several gaps.[32]

NONCONFORMITY. In 1669 there was a conventicle, probably at Charlton, with 4 teachers and 200 hearers.[33] Two meeting houses were

95 S.R.O., D/P/crch 3/2/1.
96 Ibid. tithe award.
97 Ibid. DD/DP 114/16/4.
98 *S.R.S.* viii, p. 203.
99 *Valor Eccl.* (Rec. Com.), i. 171.
1 S.R.O., D/D/Rg 377.
2 Ibid. D/P/crch 3/2/1.
3 Ibid. tithe award.
4 *S.R.S.* viii, p. 203.
5 Ibid. xxix, p. 117.
6 *Rep. Com. Eccl. Revenues*, pp. 134–5.
7 S.R.O., Q/RDd 40.
8 Ibid. D/P/crch 3/4/1; D/D/Bbm 236; local inf.
9 *S.R.S.* ix, pp. 81, 233.
10 Ibid. xxix, p. 117.
11 Ibid. lii, p. 162; Emden, *Biog. Reg. Univ. Oxf.*
12 *S.D.N.Q.* xv. 162; *Som. Incumbents*, ed. Weaver, 340; S.R.O., D/D/Ca 160, 175, 180.
13 *Walker Revised*, ed. A. G. Matthews, 316.
14 *S.D.N.Q.* ii. 241–2; xvii. 280–1; *H.M.C. Wells*, i, p. xii.
15 S.R.O., DD/DP 114/16/2.
16 Ibid. DD/AH 60/11; *Som. Co. Herald*, 6 Apr. 1929.
17 S.R.O., D/D/Rb 1827; D/D/Va 1840, 1843.
18 P.R.O., HO 129/315/2/9/14.
19 S.R.O., DD/CH 78/3.
20 *Wells Wills*, ed. Weaver, 63–4.
21 *S.R.S.* ii. 36.
22 S.R.O., DD/GC 6.
23 Above, intro.
24 *S.D.N.Q.* iii. 10; above, plate facing p. 24.
25 S.R.O., D/P/crch 3/2/2, 4/1/2; DD/SAS (C/2401) 55.
26 Collinson, *Hist. Som.* i. 76; F. B. Bond and B. Camm, *Roodscreens and Roodlofts*, i. 160.
27 S.R.O., D/P/crch 3/2/2.
28 Ibid. D/D/Cf 1868/8.
29 *Proc. Som. Arch. Soc.* lxxxiv, suppl. 26–7.
30 S.R.O., DD/SAS CH 16/1.
31 *Proc. Som. Arch. Soc.* xlvi. 164–5.
32 S.R.O., D/P/crch 2/1/1–8.
33 *Orig. Rec. of Early Nonconf.* ed. G. L. Turner, i. 6.

licensed in 1689, one probably for Presbyterians[34] and one for Quakers who had been meeting in the parish by 1674.[35] Meeting houses were licensed at Ham in 1699 and elsewhere in the parish in 1700.[36] The Quaker meeting house, at North End, continued in use throughout the 18th century but was sold in 1804.[37]

A group of nonconformists met at Adsborough in 1701.[38] Adsborough Congregational chapel, built in 1868, was under the care of the Taunton village evangelist in 1896[39] but was affiliated c. 1947 to North Petherton.[40] In 1982 it was a United Reformed church with two members.[41]

John Wesley was an occasional visitor to Charlton where he preached four times between 1754 and 1770.[42] A Wesleyan chapel was built at North End in 1842. Attendances in 1851 were 22 in the morning and 19 in the evening.[43] The chapel closed in 1855, but was still standing in 1876.[44] A house at Ham was licensed for worship, possibly for Methodists, in 1832. Methodist services were held in a cottage there by 1851 and there were 25 at morning service and 27 in the evening.[45] Services continued except for a short break in the 1870s and a chapel had been built by 1899. Congregations declined and in 1915 the chapel was closed. By 1982 the building formed part of a dwelling. In 1876–8 Methodists worshipped in a cottage at Creech Heathfield.[46]

A house was registered by Baptists in 1816 and a chapel was built in 1824.[47] In 1851 attendances were 59 in the morning, 25 in the afternoon, and 125 in the evening; there were 13 Sunday school children.[48] A manse was purchased in 1978.[49] Zion Baptist chapel, a plain building, was demolished in 1983, and was replaced by a new building on a slightly different site.

EDUCATION. There was a school in the parish in 1609.[50] Henry Masters, the deprived vicar, was said to have kept a school during the Interregnum.[51] Henry Stodgell, by will of 1701, gave a rent charge to teach 4 poor children but the endowment had been lost by 1776. Ann Seager's bequest in 1714 of a £2 rent charge to teach poor children maintained a small school with 8 pupils in 1776,[52] and one with 5 pupils in 1819.[53] The endowment presumably supported a day school with 47 pupils in 1825,[54] and it supported 5 out of the 41 boys at a day school in 1835.[55] It was transferred to the National school, but was lost between 1903 and 1962.[56] In 1819 there were two other day schools teaching 30 children; four schools were started in 1829 and 1830, and in 1835 there were 5 day schools besides the endowed school.[57] There was also a Baptist Sunday school, opened in 1824 and closed soon after. A Sunday school was held at the Baptist chapel between 1827 and 1856 jointly by the Baptist and parish churches; it had 60 pupils in 1835.[58] The Baptists took it over in 1856 and built a new schoolroom in the chapel in 1858. It was removed in 1875 and another new room was built in 1884.[59]

By 1846 a National school had been established with 30 children but the premises, a cottage on the glebe, were inadequate.[60] A new school was built north of Zion Baptist chapel between 1871 and 1873.[61] In 1903 there were 99 children on the books with two classrooms and four teachers. Subjects taught included basket making and poultry keeping and the school received the Seager endowment.[62] Numbers fluctuated but rose to 127 in 1945 and fell to 72 in 1955 after the removal of senior pupils. By 1975 numbers had risen to 307 and there were 260 children on the register in 1981.[63] A new building was opened in Hyde Lane c. 1972 but the old one remained in use until 1983.[64]

There was a girls' boarding school at Creech Heathfield between 1861 and 1881 and a private elementary school in 1882.[65]

CHARITIES FOR THE POOR. An unknown donor, said in 1869 to have been named Hurley, gave a £1 rent charge to the poor. The money was used to buy bread at Christmas.[66] Jane Dowlin, by will of 1850, gave £275 to the poor and John Wheadon, by will proved 1866, gave £250 to the poor. Those charities, two of which were usually used to buy coal, formed the United Charities in 1909.[67] Mr. C. C. H. Cresswell, by will proved in 1907, gave over £465 stock for various purposes including the provision of coals and other necessaries for the poor.[68] The income from the United and Cresswell charities was distributed among the elderly in 1984.[69]

34 S.R.O., Q/RR meeting ho. lics.; A. Gordon, *Freedom after Ejection*, 93.
35 *S.R.S.* lxxv. 69, 71, 73; S.R.O., Q/RR meeting ho. lics.; DD/SFR (w) 10/4.
36 S.R.O., Q/RR meeting ho. lics.
37 Ibid. DD/SFR (w) 4.
38 Ibid. DD/SAS RF 3(1/1), 96.
39 *Rep. Som. Cong. Union* (1896).
40 S.R.O., D/N/np. c (S/2356), mins.
41 *United Ref. Ch. Yearbk.* (1982).
42 Zion Baptist Ch., newsletter, Oct. 1974, 2–3; *Christianity in Som.* ed. R. Dunning (Som. C.C. 1976), 68.
43 P.R.O., HO 129/315/2/9/15; local inf.
44 S.R.O., D/N/tmc 3/2/1.
45 Ibid. D/D/Rm, box 2; P.R.O., HO 129/315/2/9/16.
46 S.R.O., D/N/tmc 3/2/1, 4/2/1–2.
47 Zion Bapt. Ch., newsletter, Oct. 1974, 2–6.
48 P.R.O., HO 129/315/2/9/17.
49 Char. Com. files.
50 S.R.O., D/D/Ca 160.
51 *A Compleat Hist. of Som.* (1742), 10.
52 S.R.O., D/D/Vc 88; *Char. Don.* pp. 1044–5.

53 *Educ. of Poor Digest*, p. 781.
54 *Ann. Rep. B. & W. Dioc. Assoc. S.P.C.K.* (1825–6), 80.
55 *Educ. Enq. Abstract*, p. 802.
56 Char. Com. files.
57 *Educ. of Poor Digest*, p. 781; *Educ. Enq. Abstract*, p. 802.
58 W. M. Wigfield, *Bapt. Ch. at Hatch Beauchamp*, 18; *Educ. Enq. Abstract*, p. 802.
59 Zion Bapt. Ch., newsletter, Oct. 1974, 7.
60 Nat. Soc. *Inquiry, 1846–7*, Som. 6–7; S.R.O., D/D (S/2340), sale partic. 1870.
61 S.R.O., DD/EDS 5753; *P.O. Dir. Som.* (1875).
62 S.R.O., C/E 4/380/123.
63 Ibid. 4/64.
64 Local inf.
65 *P.O. Dir. Som.* (1861, 1875); P.R.O., RG 10/2368; RG 11/2365; *Our Village*, 40.
66 *Char. Don.* pp. 1044–5; *15th Rep. Com. Char.* 344; Char. Com. files; S.R.O., D/P/crch 17/2/1.
67 Char. Com. files; S.R.O., D/P/crch 17/2/1, 3; 17/3/1.
68 Char. Com. files.
69 Inf. from the Revd. K. Jones, vicar.

DURLEIGH

THE parish of Durleigh lies principally west and south-west of Bridgwater astride the Durleigh brook which since 1938 has been dammed to form Durleigh reservoir (77.5 a.).[70] The parish church and Durleigh Farm stand overlooking the dam on the south side of the brook c. 2.5 km. ESE. from the centre of Bridgwater. The sites of three houses, standing together on the north side of the stream in 1839, are now submerged below the reservoir.[71] The ancient boundary of the principal area of the parish is irregular, in part following the Durleigh brook and other watercourses. Part of the boundary with Goathurst, in the south-west, was marked in the earlier 18th century with stones.[72] Smaller parts of the ancient parish, linked by common ownership in the 11th century,[73] lay in and around Chilton Trinity village, north of Bridgwater, and included a substantial part of Chilton common and land further north beside the Parrett. There were also isolated fields in Wembdon and Bridgwater parishes, including arable strips in Haygrove and in St. Matthew's fields.[74] The total area of the parish in 1881 was said to be 886 a., evidently less than the true area because of an error over the boundaries of Chilton parish. In 1886 most of the detached parts of the parish were transferred: that part within Bridgwater borough (including 7 houses and 36 persons) became part of Bridgwater, unspecified lands were absorbed by Wembdon, and the remainder (including 8 houses and 36 persons) passed to Chilton Trinity. Durleigh gained West Bower, a detached part of Bridgwater largely surrounded by Durleigh, and in 1891 the total area was 755 a.[75] Modifications to the civil parish in 1933, by which land (162 a. and 20 people) was added from Bridgwater Without, and in 1952, when part of Durleigh was absorbed in the extension of Bridgwater borough, left the parish with 355 ha. (877 a.) in 1981, a figure which did not take account of further unspecified changes made in the same year.[76]

The principal part of Durleigh parish occupies undulating ground drained by the Durleigh brook and Cobb's Cross stream, their alluvial valleys below the 15-m. contour cutting through Keuper marl. Both north and south of the brook the land rises above 30 m. on harder Upper Sandstone, reaching over 46 m. on the northern boundary with Wembdon at a possibly

prehistoric earthwork known in the 20th century as Danesborough and in the 16th as Castle Acre or Sturton's Castle.[77] Most of the outlying areas of the parish lay on alluvium and on the 'island' of marl around Chilton Trinity village.[78]

Two routes westwards from Bridgwater crossed the parish, the northern passing beside a site known as Durleigh Elms towards Spaxton, the southern crossing the Durleigh brook near Haygrove Farm in Bridgwater and running south of Durleigh church towards Enmore. In 1730 a turnpike trust was proposed for both roads,[79] the northern regarded c. 1758 as part of the London–Barnstaple route. A toll gate was then proposed at Three Crosses, east of Durleigh Elms.[80] Both roads were included in a second turnpike proposal in 1759, but in 1782 only the southern seems to have been adopted.[81] The northern route was described as a turnpike road in 1796[82] although it was not maintained by the trust in 1839.[83] By 1782 a new route towards Enmore began at Three Crosses and ran south down Goose Pit hill and between Durleigh mill and the parish church.[84] Minor routes led from Durleigh Elms west to West Bower and south to the brook. Goose Pit hill also formed part of a north–south route from Chilton common through Greenway in Wembdon to Rhode in North Petherton parish.[85]

The names of three medieval settlements in the principal part of the parish, Durleigh, Rexworthy, and Everley, seem to indicate woodland clearings:[86] Durleigh and Rexworthy existed in the mid 11th century,[87] Everley as a settlement only in 1256.[88] The settlement at Durleigh comprised on the south side of Durleigh brook the church, Durleigh Farm, and the mill, and by the late 18th century a contracting group of dwellings in Durleigh street on the north side. By 1930 the street contained a single farmstead.[89] The house called Durleigh Elms was built and extended by the Gooding family on a site acquired by them in 1796.[90] From the later 19th century, and increasingly from the 1930s, houses were built in the north-eastern corner of the parish on the north side of Enmore Road as part of the suburban expansion of Bridgwater.[91]

The name of a furlong survived on Durleigh farm in the 18th century,[92] but in the 16th century the land around Durleigh village and stretching towards Goathurst had been divided into closes.[93] There was open arable belonging

70 West Som. Water Bd. *Ann. Rep.* 1963–4, 30. This article was completed in 1987.
71 S.R.O., tithe award.
72 Ibid. D/P/gst 4/1/1 (1721).
73 Below, manors.
74 S.R.O., tithe award; cf. below, map on p. 192.
75 *Census*, 1881, 1891.
76 S.R.O., GP/D, box 19; Youngs, *Local Admin. Units*, i. 425; *Census*, 1981.
77 O.S. Nat. Grid 269371; *Cal. Pat.* 1553, 54–8; S.R.O., DD/S/BW 5; DD/S/WH 2, 219; Longleat House, Seymour Papers, XII, rental (1540), f. 14v.
78 Geol. Surv. Map 1", drift, sheet 295 (1956 edn.).
79 3 Geo. II, c. 34.
80 S.R.O., DD/TB 17/8, 18/7.

81 32 Geo. II, c. 40; *S.R.S.* lxxvi, Day and Masters map.
82 S.R.O., DD/BR/ely 5/20.
83 *Rep. Com. Roads*, H.C. (1840), xxvii.
84 *S.R.S.* lxxvi, Day and Masters map.
85 O.S. Map 6", Som. LXI. NW. (1886 edn.).
86 A. H. Smith, *Eng. Place-Name Elements*, i. 94, 130–1; ii. 21, 275–6.
87 *V.C.H. Som.* i. 485, 521.
88 *S.R.S.* vi. 176–7.
89 O.S. Map 1/2,500, Som. L. 13–14 (1930 edn.).
90 S.R.O., DD/BR/ely 5/20.
91 *Kelly's Dir. Som.* (1894); S.R.O., DD/SAS (C/2273), 1/13.12.1.
92 S.R.O., DD/S/WH 246.
93 Ibid. 3, 5; DD/SF 942; Pole MS. 2753.

to Durleigh in 1540 in the east, west, and south fields at Chilton Trinity, evidently lying between Chilton moor and Chilton common and located in the parishes of Durleigh and Bridgwater.[94] Parts of Chilton common, which was divided and allotted in 1801,[95] lay in Durleigh parish because Durleigh tenants had grazing rights there. There were 26 a. of woodland in Durleigh and Rexworthy in 1086[96] when none was recorded on the two estates called Chilton. In 1839 there were just over 11½ a. of wood.[97]

A tippling house was reported in the parish in 1623.[98] In 1664–5 there were 11 houses in the tithing of Durleigh and Duke Fee.[99] The population of the parish rose gradually from 104 in 1801 to 208 in 1881, with a slight fall in the 1830s, the rise from the 1840s the result of the expansion of Bridgwater suburbs into the parish. Boundary changes in 1886 seem to account for a reduction to 158 in 1891, and there was a significant fall from 396 in 1911 to 328 in 1921.[1] Meanwhile there had been changes in the number of houses in Durleigh village: in 1839 there were 2 cottages in Durleigh Street, 1 in West Bower Lane, 2 houses at Durleigh Elms, 1 cottage on Goose Pit hill, and 2 near the mill, together with farmhouses at Rexworthy, Durleigh Farm, and Moggs.[2] In 1909 there were 6 cottages near Durleigh Farm in Rhode Lane.[3] In 1931 the total population was 348. Between 1961 and 1981 the population of what remained outside Bridgwater rose from 300 to 517, the result of building along Enmore Road.[4]

Eight people from the parish were accused of complicity in the Monmouth Rebellion of 1685.[5]

MANORS AND OTHER ESTATES. Alsi had in 1066 an estate called *DURLEIGH* which by 1086 was held as a serjeanty by Ansger the cook.[6] Ansger's estate was perhaps the land which Geoffrey of Durleigh seems to have held in 1201,[7] probably in succession to Durand of Durleigh, possibly his father.[8] Odo of Durleigh may have succeeded Geoffrey; he was later said to have held the vill of the honor of Trowbridge;[9] and William Longespée (d. 1226), earl of Salisbury, was said to have held it, apparently in succession to Durand, for 20 years.[10] It is therefore probable that Durleigh formed part of the grant made in 1214 by King John to William Longespée comprising the lands of the knights

of Trowbridge honor who had rebelled with Henry de Bohun, earl of Hereford.[11]

The estate descended like Trowbridge to Margaret, daughter of William Longespée (III) and wife of Henry de Lacy, earl of Lincoln (d. 1311). Henry was said to hold the manor in 1274 and the capital messuage in 1284–5.[12] Henry's successor Alice married first Thomas Plantagenet, earl of Lancaster (d. 1322). In 1319 Thomas granted the land, but not the fee, to John de Warenne, earl of Surrey (d. 1347), for his life.[13] The fee was granted in 1325 by Alice and her second husband Ebles Lestraunge to Hugh le Despenser the younger, who already had the reversion of the land.[14] At the same time Warenne made over to Despenser his 'foreign court' of Trowbridge and the court of Durleigh.[15] In 1337, after the Despensers' forfeiture, the Crown granted the reversion of Trowbridge, and presumably its members, after Warenne's death to William de Montagu on his creation as earl of Salisbury.[16]

Joan de Bar, wife of John de Warenne, acquired a life interest in her husband's estate in 1327[17] which in 1348 she leased to Edward, prince of Wales. On Joan's death in 1361 Edward surrendered his lease to William de Montagu, who thus acquired both the land and the fee or foreign court. Durleigh presumably followed the descent of Trowbridge, which was recovered by Blanche, daughter of Henry Plantagenet, duke of Lancaster, and her husband, John of Gaunt, in 1365, and which passed with the Duchy of Lancaster to the Crown.[18] It is not certain how much land was involved: the Duchy received rents from Durleigh in 1536–7 and a small estate described as in North Bower and Durleigh, probably in the north part of Bridgwater parish, was in 1553 held of the honor of Trowbridge, parcel of the Duchy of Lancaster.[19] The estate may by then have been absorbed into West Bower manor, which was known as Bower with Durleigh.[20]

Two estates called *CHILTON* in 1086 may have lain partly or wholly in Durleigh. One was held in 1066 by Godric and in 1086 by Ansketil of Roger de Courcelles. The other was held in 1066 by Alwine and in 1086 as a serjeanty by Ansger the cook of the king.[21] No further trace of either estate has been found until 1208–9 when a rather larger holding comprising land in Chilton and Bower was held by Robert of Chilton,[22] possibly a successor to Jordan of Chilton.[23] In 1284–5 another Robert of Chilton was

94 Longleat House, Seymour Papers, XII, rental (1540), ff. 12–13v.; S.R.O., Bridgwater and Durleigh tithe awards.
95 S.R.O., Q/RDe 29.
96 *V.C.H. Som.* i. 485, 521.
97 S.R.O., tithe award.
98 *S.R.S.* xliii. 97.
99 Dwelly, *Hearth Tax*, i. 44–5; for Duke Fee, above, Andersfield hundred.
1 *V.C.H. Som.* i. 341; *Census,* 1891, 1911, 1921.
2 S.R.O., tithe award.
3 Ibid. D/R/bw 15/3/9.
4 *Census,* 1931–81.
5 *S.R.S.* lxxix. 204.
6 *V.C.H. Som.* i. 521.
7 P.R.O., DL 42/11, ff. 5, 7; *Cur. Reg. R.* ii. 34; *S.R.S.* vi. 11; xxv. 81–2.
8 *Rot. Hund.* (Rec. Com.), ii. 121, 137.
9 B.L. Add. Ch. 20418.

10 *Feud. Aids,* iv. 293; *Rot. Hund.* (Rec. Com.), ii. 121, 137.
11 *V.C.H. Wilts.* vii. 128.
12 *Rot. Hund.* (Rec. Com.), ii. 121, 137; *Feud. Aids,* iv. 293.
13 *Cal. Pat.* 1317–21, 319; R. Somerville, *Duchy of Lancaster,* i. 337.
14 *S.R.S.* xii. 122; *Cal. Pat.* 1324–7, 102; *Cal. Chart. R.* 1300–26, 450.
15 *Cal. Pat.* 1327–30, 21.
16 Ibid. 1334–8, 550.
17 Ibid. 1327–30, 21; Somerville, *Lancaster,* i. 35.
18 *Cal. Pat.* 1361–4, 131; Somerville, *Lancaster,* i. 36.
19 P.R.O., SC 6/Hen. VIII/3073; *Cal. Pat.* 1553, 154–8.
20 Below, Bridgwater, manors.
21 *V.C.H. Som.* i. 485, 521.
22 *S.R.S.* vi. 25–6.
23 Below, Bridgwater, West Bower manor.

holding ½ fee in Chilton of Hugh Lovel, whose barony of Castle Cary the Lovels held in succession to Walter of Douai.[24]

Hugh Lovel (d. 1291) was followed by his son Richard,[25] and Richard in 1351 by his granddaughter Muriel, wife of Sir Nicholas Seymour (d. 1361). Muriel was followed by her son Richard, but no further trace of the overlordship has been found after 1371.[26]

Robert of Chilton held ½ fee in Chilton in 1284–5 and 1295.[27] He was said in 1303 to hold ¼ fee.[28] Another Robert held ¼ fee in 1346.[29] In 1412 Sir William Besyles held ¼ fee there which in 1431 was shared between John Besyles, Alice Northlode, and John Michell.[30] The holding, however, had evidently been divided: at least three small estates held of the Seymours had emerged in the 1370s: Joan, widow of John Modesley (d. 1362), Robert de la Mare (d. 1371), who held in right of his wife Joan, and Edward (d. 1372), son of Eleanor Cary, all held land in Chilton and Bower.[31]

In 1455 William Dodesham bought a substantial amount of land from Thomas Hall, William Besyles, and William's wife Agnes which included property described as in East Chilton,[32] presumably Chilton village and so called in distinction from West Chilton or Chilton Trivet. It probably included some or all of the former Chilton manor, but by 1487 was known as *EAST CHILTON* manor and was said to be held as of North Petherton manor. Dodesham died in 1480 when his heir was his niece Agnes, wife of Walter Michell (d. 1487).[33] Walter Michell was followed in succession by three sons, William, John (d. 1492),[34] and Thomas (d. 1503).[35] Thomas Michell, son of the last, in 1539 murdered both his wife and her sister and then committed suicide.[36] Richard Michell, his son and heir, died in 1563 leaving the manor, then called simply Chilton, to his son Tristram.[37] Tristram died in 1574 and was succeeded by his brother Bartholomew, later knighted. On the latter's death in 1616 his heirs were his two daughters, Jane, wife of William Hockmore (d. 1626), of Buckland Baron (Devon), and Frances, wife of Alexander Popham.[38]

William Hockmore died in 1626 in possession of Chilton manor and the manors of North Bower, Chilton Trivet in Cannington, Wembdon, and West Stretcholt in Pawlett.[39] His heir was his son Gregory, then under age.[40] Gregory was still alive in 1676[41] and had been succeeded

by 1680 by William Hockmore.[42] William was dead by 1714 when his estate was shared between his three daughters, Mary, wife of Brent Reynell Spiller (d. 1736), Honor, wife of David or Davidge Gould, and Jane Palmer, widow, later wife of William Pitt.[43] Samuel Pitt, only son of Jane, died without issue c. 1737, and by 1753 the estate was shared between Mary and Elizabeth Reynell, daughters of Mary, who had taken the name Reynell, and the six children of Honor and Davidge Gould. By 1791 Mary Reynell had devised her share to her nephew Henry Reynell,[44] who by 1801 seems to have become the sole owner.[45] He died in 1842 leaving a daughter Caroline, whose husband, the Revd. David Williams, took the name and arms of Reynell. David Reynell was the owner of North Bower, East Chilton, and Wembdon manors in 1839.[46]

By 1857 the estate had passed through a distant cousin of Caroline Reynell, Sir Thomas Reynell, Bt. (d. 1848), to Sir Thomas's widow Elizabeth (d. 1856) and to Elizabeth's son by her first marriage, Arthur John Pack, who took the name Reynell in 1857.[47] Arthur Denis Henry Heber Reynell-Pack succeeded his father in 1860 and sold the estate, then amounting to over 520 a. of land in Durleigh, Bridgwater, Chilton, Cossington, and Weston Zoyland, in 1911, when the property was divided. The part in Durleigh parish included Manor Farm immediately north-west of Chilton Trinity church.[48]

In 1066 Godric held *REXWORTHY*. In 1086 Robert was tenant there of Roger de Courcelles.[49] In 1499 Rexworthy was held of the Crown, presumably in right of the Duchy of Lancaster, as of Durleigh manor. In 1423 Thomas Plush held land there of East Postridge manor in Aisholt in succession to Richard Rexworthy, and Margaret Plush, widow of William Harding, died holding the manor in 1499. Margaret's heirs were her daughters Joan, Agnes, and Joan.[50] In the 16th century the estate passed to the Malet family. Sir Hugh Trevanion (d. 1561–2) held it for life in right of his second wife Anne, widow of Baldwin Malet (d. 1533), the reversionary interest belonging to Baldwin's son John Malet (d. c. 1570) of Wolleigh in Beaford (Devon). John Malet transferred his interest to his brother Thomas.[51]

In 1738 Rexworthy farm was occupied and probably owned by Thomas Trego, who was succeeded in 1753 by John Trego. Members of

24 *Feud. Aids*, iv. 278; Sanders, *Eng. Baronies*, 27.
25 *Cal. Inq. p.m.* ii, p. 490; *Feud. Aids*, iv. 300.
26 *V.C.H. Som.* iv. 134; *Cal. Inq. p.m.* xiii, pp. 74, 161; P.R.O. SC 6/970/4.
27 *Feud. Aids*, iv. 278; *Cal. Inq. p.m.* ii, p. 490.
28 *Feud. Aids*, iv. 300.
29 Ibid. iv. 345.
30 Ibid. iv. 434; vi. 514.
31 *Cal. Inq. p.m.* xiii, pp. 19–20, 74, 161; P.R.O., SC 6/970/4.
32 *S.R.S.* xxii. 119–20.
33 P.R.O., C 140/77, no. 78; *Cal. Inq. p.m. Hen. VII*, i, pp. 114–15.
34 *Cal. Inq. p.m. Hen. VII*, i, pp. 318–20.
35 *S.R.S.* xix. 51.
36 Ibid. xxvii. 216–25.
37 P.R.O., C 142/67, no. 114; C 142/143, no. 25; *Som. Wills*, ed. Brown, vi. 3.
38 P.R.O., C 142/167, no. 97; C 142/440, no. 89; S.R.O.,

D/P/can 2/1/1 (1610); *Som. Wills*, ed. Brown, v. 39; *S.R.S.* lxvii, p. 178.
39 P.R.O., C 142/440, no. 89.
40 *S.R.S.* lxvii, pp. 178–9.
41 Hants R.O. 7M54/198.
42 S.R.O., DD/X/OS 4.
43 P.R.O., CP 25(2)/988/13 Anne East.; CP 25(2)/1087/1 Geo. I Trin.; CP 25(2)/1087/4 Geo. I Mich.; Burke, *Commoners*, iv. 455.
44 Devon R.O. 1148 M/add 1/49, 7/38; S.R.O., DD/SAS (C/59) 24; Burke, *Commoners*, iv. 455.
45 S.R.O., Q/RDe 29.
46 Burke, *Commoners*, iv. 455; S.R.O., tithe award.
47 Burke, *Land. Gent.* (1937), 1734–5.
48 S.R.O., DD/TBL 53.   49 *V.C.H. Som.* i. 485.
50 P.R.O., SC 2/200/27; *Cal. Inq. p.m. Hen. VII*, iii, pp. 114–15.
51 P.R.O., C 3/127/23; *S.R.S.* xxi. 17–18; J. L. Vivian, *Visit. Cornw.* 212, 501.

the Holcombe family held it between 1757 and 1795, and they were followed by John Gooding.[52] Richard Gooding was owner and occupier in 1839, and W. B. Broadmead of Enmore owned it in 1909.[53]

Land in Everley belonged to Athelney abbey in the earlier 12th century.[54] Richard Wasun of Bridgwater acquired a messuage and land there in 1256[55] which passed to a family called Everley.[56] At his death in 1461 Sir Alexander Hody held *EVERLEY* manor of Athelney abbey in right of his wife Margaret, the heir of John Coker.[57] Margaret still held it at her death in 1489, and tenants in the parish owed suit to the Hody family at Gothelney in 1540–1.[58] Fields east of Durleigh Farm were called Great Everley and Everley Orchard in 1839.[59]

St. John's hospital, Bridgwater, held what was called *DURLEIGH* manor c. 1480.[60] Following the dissolution of the hospital in 1539 the Crown sold the estate in 1543 to John Smythe of Bristol.[61] John was succeeded in 1556 by his son Hugh, then of Long Ashton, and Hugh in 1580 by his daughter Elizabeth, wife of Edward Morgan.[62] Edward settled the manor in 1596 on his son William, who survived until 1634 leaving a son, another Edward Morgan.[63] In 1635 Edward sold the manor to Warwick Fownes, and in 1638 Thomas Fownes died in possession.[64] Thomas's heir was his grandson and namesake.[65]

Charles Brune of Plumber in Lidlinch (Dors.) succeeded Thomas Fownes in 1746.[66] He was succeeded in 1770 by his nephew Charles Pleydell Brune. The latter was followed by his nephew the Revd. Charles Prideaux (1760–1833), who took the additional name of Brune in 1799.[67] The Revd. Charles Prideaux-Brune was followed in the direct male line by Charles (1790–1875), Charles Glynn (1821–1907), and Charles Robert (1848–1936), the last of whom sold Durleigh in 1913 to Sidney Denning, owner until c. 1970.[68]

Durleigh Farm, standing south-east of Durleigh churchyard, is a square, symmetrical stone building of the later 18th century, adjoining the stock yards and buildings of the later 19th century.

St. John's hospital, Bridgwater, by 1535 also owned the *RECTORY* estate, comprising the tithes of the parish.[69] The Crown in 1542 leased the rectory to John Bourchier, earl of Bath. It was sublet to William Blanchflower and later to Humphrey Colles.[70] In 1556 Alexander Popham of Huntworth in North Petherton owned the rectory which he devised to his son (Sir) John

Popham (d. 1607), but a Crown grant was made, probably in error, to Thomas Wood and Thomas Fare in 1560.[71] Sir John held the rectory c. 1594 and his son Sir Francis seems to have occupied it by 1603, the outcome of a settlement made in 1590.[72]

The rectory descended in the direct male line from Sir Francis (d. 1644) to Alexander (d. 1669), Sir Francis (d. 1674), and Alexander (d. 1705). Alexander was succeeded by his father's brother, also Alexander, and that Alexander by his son Francis (d. 1735).[73] Francis's son Edward Popham, who let the estate to Philip Baker of Bridgwater in 1746, sold it in 1775 to Dr. John Dunning of Bridgwater, who married Baker's daughter Susanna. John died in 1821 and Susanna in 1824, when the rectory passed under her will to Wyndham Goodden (d. 1839). Wyndham's widow Mary held it until her death in 1844 and was succeeded by her son John, who in 1845 sold the tithe rent charge to Robert Gooding.[74] Robert Gooding was succeeded in 1854 by his great-nephew William Gooding (d. 1902) and William by his son William Forbes Gooding of Durleigh Elms,[75] who held the rent charge in 1909.[76]

Land in the parish was held of manors in other parishes, namely Puriton in 1561,[77] West Bower or Bower de la Mare in Bridgwater in the 17th century,[78] and Chipley in Langford Budville in 1839.[79]

ECONOMIC HISTORY. In 1066 the largest estate, called Durleigh, was assessed at 2¾ virgates but in 1086 had land for 3 ploughteams: the demesne had 1¾ virgate with 1 team and the tenants, enumerated as 4 *villani*, 2 bordars, and 3 *servi*, had the rest of the land and 2 teams. The three other Domesday estates which may be assigned to Durleigh, Rexworthy and two called Chilton, however, had land for 1 team, 1¾ virgate of demesne, and a bordar as a tenant, while Ansger's estate called Chilton had land for 1 team, ¾ virgate of demesne with 1 team and a *servus*, and a *villanus* with ¾ virgate and ½ team; on that estate 3 cows, 14 a. of meadow, and 5 a. of pasture were recorded. Rexworthy had land for ½ team and 2 bordars as tenants. Two of the estates had woodland, 20 a. at Durleigh and 6 a. at Rexworthy.[80]

In the later Middle Ages some substantial estates were created in and around Durleigh. In 1444 Richard Walshawe, for example, held over 200 a. in Durleigh, Wembdon, Bridgwater, and

52 S.R.O., D/P/durl 4/1/1.
53 Ibid. tithe award; ibid. D/R/bw 15/3/9.
54 *S.R.S.* xiv, pp. 147–8.   55 Ibid. vi. 176–7.
56 Ibid. xi, pp. 171, 222, 294, 412; xiv, p. 148.
57 P.R.O., C 140/4, no. 34.
58 *Cal. Inq. p.m. Hen. VII*, i, pp. 266–7; S.R.O., DD/S/WH 65; P.R.O., LR 3/123, f. 13.
59 S.R.O., tithe award.   60 *S.R.S.* lxx, pp. 58–9.
61 *L. & P. Hen. VIII*, xviii (1), p. 535.
62 P.R.O., C 142/108, no. 109; C 142/193, no. 87.
63 Ibid. C 142/476, no. 139.
64 Ibid. CP 25(2)/480/11 Chas. I Trin.; *S.R.S.* lxvii, pp. 113–14.
65 *S.R.S.* lxvii, pp. 113–14; P.R.O., C 142/486, no. 116.
66 S.R.O., D/P/durl 4/1/1.
67 Hutchins, *Hist. Dors.* iv. 190; Burke, *Land. Gent.*

(1914), 257.
68 Burke, *Land. Gent.* (1965), 92–3; inf. from Mr. C. Sellick, Durleigh.
69 *Valor Eccl.* (Rec. Com.) i. 208.
70 *L. & P. Hen. VIII*, xvii, p. 704; S.R.O., DD/POt 39.
71 *S.R.S.* xxi. 181; P.R.O., C 142/303, no. 128; *Cal. Pat.* 1558–60, 455–6.
72 S.R.O., D/D/Ca 98, 134; P.R.O., C 142/303, no. 128.
73 Burke, *Land. Gent.* (1914), 1527.
74 S.R.O., DD/DP 38/10.
75 Ibid. D/P/durl 2/1/6; *Kelly's Dir. Som.* (1906).
76 S.R.O., D/R/bw 15/3/9.
77 Ibid. DD/SF 1026.
78 Ibid. DD/S/WH 121, 211.
79 Ibid. DD/RN 19.
80 *V.C.H. Som.* i. 485, 521.

elsewhere,[81] and in 1461 Sir Alexander Hody's holding, partly his own inheritance and purchase, partly the inheritance of his wife, included Everley manor and the tenancy of Durleigh mill, the manors of West Bower in Bridgwater and Wembdon, mills in Spaxton, and scattered lands in Chilton, Enmore, Goathurst, Bridgwater, North Petherton, and beyond.[82] St. John's hospital, Bridgwater, had a demesne farm at Durleigh, the nucleus of Durleigh farm, and rents in Chilton marsh and Wembdon.[83] A copyhold farm at Chilton, part of the manor of Bower with Durleigh, in 1540 centred on an empty toft, with 12½ a. of arable in three fields, 2½ a. of meadow in separate yardlands said to be 'between the doles', and common pasture on Chilton moor.[84]

Small-scale farming is implied by 17th-century inventories, the largest, that of John Woodland (d. 1693), including 15 sheep and lambs, 3 cows, 1 heifer and 2 calves, 1 pig, and 8 a. of corn.[85] In 1666 tithes were payable for cows, heifers, calves, lambs, piglets, and colts, fleece, stored fruit, cider, hops, corn, honey, and wax.[86] In the 18th century there was some consolidation of farms, and by 1794 the Tyntes had five formerly separate tenements west of Durleigh village,[87] although holdings around Chilton remained fragmented.[88]

By 1839 Durleigh farm measured nearly 223 a., followed in size by the Tyntes' 191 a. north, east, and south of West Bower. Rexworthy farm was 79 a. and the Gooding family's lands at Durleigh Elms 63 a. Groomhouse (46 a.) and Chilton (42 a.) were the only two consolidated holdings at Chilton. In the whole parish there were 536 a. of meadow and pasture, 313 a. of arable, and 36 a. of orchards.[89] In 1905, after boundary changes, there were 647 a. of grass and 354 a. of arable.[90] The loss of land near Chilton and along Enmore Road for house building and the creation of Durleigh reservoir c. 1938 left Durleigh and Rexworthy farms as the principal farms in the ancient parish. In 1982 there were within the altered parish parts of six farms, one specializing in dairying, another in cattle rearing.[91]

Durleigh mill was recorded in 1461[92] when it formed part of Sir Alexander Hody's holding in Wembdon. By 1540 it had passed to the Seymours and was held with West Bower.[93] In 1553 the Crown sold it to Nicholas Halswell of Goathurst[94] and it descended in the Halswell and Tynte families.[95] The mill, standing north-west of Durleigh church and driven by the Durleigh brook, seems to have continued in operation until c. 1936 when the construction of the reservoir began.[96] Some of the buildings survive below the dam at no. 8 Durleigh.

Two isolated fields beside the Parrett at Crowpill, between Bridgwater and Chilton, were occupied in 1839, one as a brickyard by John Browne & Co., the other as a timber yard.[97] By 1886 the Crowpill Brick and Tile works there included a kiln and a jetty,[98] but the yard was no longer in operation by 1930.[99]

LOCAL GOVERNMENT. Durleigh, a single tithing in Andersfield hundred until the 16th century, had been united by 1640 with Duke Fee or Dukesse tithing,[1] which lay partly in the parish and was recorded in 1569;[2] it probably represented the jurisdiction of the former Duchy of Lancaster estate.[3] The name Duke Fee was in use in 1674.[4] In 1670 part of the parish was in Haygrove tithing in Bridgwater.[5]

The Duchy of Lancaster held a manor court at Durleigh in 1536–7.[6] Suit was claimed of a tenant by East Chilton manor court in 1721.[7]

In 1732 the parish vestry agreed to appoint two churchwardens and two overseers of the poor.[8] The part of the parish located within Bridgwater borough appointed two separate overseers in the 1830s.[9] The parish was divided for rating purposes between the main part, referred to as Durleigh, and the parts around Chilton Trinity village, known as Chilton Limit. In the mid 18th century the parish received rent from a parish garden.[10] A cottage on part of the site was used as a poorhouse until 1837 when it was sold.[11] The parish became part of Bridgwater poor-law union in 1836, of Bridgwater rural district in 1894, and of Sedgemoor district in 1974.[12]

CHURCH. The plan of the church and the record of a chaplain show that it existed in the 12th century.[13] In the 16th century the living was described as a chapelry,[14] but its occupant was variously called a stipendiary and a vicar.[15] In the 18th and 19th century it was sometimes called a vicarage or a donative, but from 1792 it was legally a perpetual curacy, and from 1968 a vicarage.[16] In 1976 the living became part of the united benefice of Bridgwater St. Mary and Chilton Trinity and Durleigh.[17]

The patronage presumably descended with the rectory[18] until 1845 when Dr. John Dunning's trustee conveyed it to John J. Harrison.[19] In 1857 it was exercised by Capt. H. H. Bingham, R.N.,[20] and by 1866 by the Revd. G. R. Harding (d.

81 S.R.S. xxii. 107, 148.   82 P.R.O., C 140/4, no. 34.
83 Valor Eccl. (Rec. Com.), i. 207–8.
84 Longleat House, Seymour Papers, XII, rental (1540), f. 13v.
85 S.R.O., DD/SP inventory, 1693/9.
86 Ibid. D/P/durl 3/2/1.   87 Ibid. 4/1/1.
88 Ibid. DD/X/ROBN 1; DD/BR/py 60.
89 Ibid. tithe award.
90 Statistics supplied by the then Bd. of Agric., 1905.
91 Min. of Agric., Fisheries, and Food, agric. returns, 1982.   92 P.R.O., C 140/4, no. 34.
93 Hist. MSS. Com. 58, Bath, iv, p. 339; below, Bridgwater, manors.   94 Cal. Pat. 1553, 54–8.
95 Below, Goathurst, manors.   96 Kelly's Dir. Som. (1935).
97 S.R.O., tithe award, nos. 254–5.
98 O.S. Map 6", Som. L. SE. (1886 edn.).
99 O.S. Map 1/2,500, Som. L. 13 (1930 edn.).

1 S.R.O., DD/SG 58–9.   2 S.R.S. xx. 243.
3 Above, Andersfield hundred.
4 Dwelly, Hearth Tax, ii. 219–20.
5 Ibid. i. 42–3.   6 P.R.O., SC 6/Hen. VIII/3073.
7 S.R.O., DD/SAS (C/59) 24.   8 Ibid. D/P/durl 4/1/1.
9 Ibid. 13/2/1.   10 Ibid. 4/1/1.
11 Ibid. 13/2/1.
12 Youngs, Local Admin. Units, i. 424–5, 671, 676.
13 Below (building); S.R.S. lxviii, p. 25; Cat. Anct. D. ii, B 2966.   14 S.R.O., D/D/Vc 20.
15 P.R.O., SC 6/Hen. VIII/3137; Valor Eccl. (Rec. Com.), i. 208.
16 S.R.O., DD/PO 2D/1, 2E; Rep. Com. Eccl. Revenues, pp. 136–7; Dioc. Kal.; below.   17 Dioc. Dir.
18 Above, manors.   19 S.R.O., DD/DP 38/10.
20 Clergy List, 1859.

1884).[21] William Gooding (d. 1902) had acquired the patronage by 1891 and was succeeded by his son William Forbes Gooding. Gooding transferred his interest in 1913 to the Bath and Wells Diocesan Trust, which in turn passed the patronage to the Diocesan Board of Patronage in 1939.[22] The interest of the Board in the united benefice was extinguished in 1985.[23]

About 1535 the vicar was paid a pension of 26s. 8d. from the rectory.[24] By 1539 he had a stipend of £5, which continued to be paid later in the century.[25] By 1772 the lay rector was paying £10,[26] and by 1815 £20.[27] About 1831 the average income, augmented by lot from the Bounty in 1792, was £22,[28] and in 1931 it was £20.[29] There was no glebe attached to the living and no house.

The chancel was said to be in great ruin in 1554 and its roof and windows were in decay in 1576.[30] Quarterly sermons were neglected in the later 16th and the earlier 17th century,[31] but in 1613 prayers were said both on Sundays and weekdays.[32] In the 1730s communion was celebrated four times a year, but by the 1770s only three times, for six or seven communicants.[33] From the mid 18th century neighbouring incumbents either served the cure themselves or employed curates. John Coles (by 1757, until 1788 or later) was vicar of Bridgwater and Henry Parsons (by 1813, until 1826) held Wembdon and Goathurst; J. D. Oland Crosse (1845–56) was vicar of Pawlett. James H. Gregg (1826–42), H. J. G. Young, M.D., M.R.C.S. (1857–9), and Henry Trend, D.D., LL.D. (1860–8), the last formerly the Baptist minister of Bridgwater, served Durleigh as a sole cure.[34] From the 1870s the living was again held by neighbouring incumbents except for 1911–15 when W. G. Deighton was vicar and lived in Durleigh Road, Bridgwater. From 1940 the living was held by the vicars of St. Mary's, Bridgwater.[35]

The church, of unknown dedication, comprises a chancel, a nave with south porch, and a small west tower with saddle roof. The proportions of the chancel, nave, and tower suggest a 12th-century date, but the chancel was rebuilt in the 13th century and the nave, refenestrated in the 14th century, was altered again in the later 15th, when both chancel and tower arches were inserted, together with the south door and doorway, the font, and the upper storey of the tower. A rood loft was also added, approached by a stair on the north side lit by a quatrefoil window. The furnishings date from 1870; the pulpit in use up to that date was probably that made in 1754 from carved pew ends.[36]

There are four bells: (i) medieval, from the Bristol foundry; (ii) 1739, Thomas Wroth of Bridgwater; (iii) 1530–70, Roger Semson of Ash Priors; (iv) 1631, George Purdue.[37] A bell was delivered in 1526.[38] The plate includes a cup and cover made by 'I. P.' in 1573.[39] The registers date from 1683. In the 1730s the curate was reported as 'far from keeping the register regularly'.[40]

The churchyard, its walls maintained by local farmers in the 17th century,[41] includes a yew tree planted in 1724.[42]

NONCONFORMITY. None known.

EDUCATION. There was a Sunday school with 20 children in 1819.[43] In 1846 there was a day school with 22 and a Sunday school with 5 children.[44] Between 1861 and 1883 a Sunday school was held in a house near the church.[45] An infant school was recorded in 1889 but in 1894 children were said to attend schools in Bridgwater.[46]

CHARITIES FOR THE POOR. None known.

ENMORE

THE main part of Enmore parish occupies a diamond-shaped area on the lower, eastern slopes of the Quantock ridge, 3.5 km. WSW. from Bridgwater at the nearest point. A detached area to the south-west occupied the slope of Broomfield Hill above Holwell Combe. The parish, which includes Enmore village at its centre and the roadside hamlet of Lexworthy at its eastern end, is just over 5 km. from east to west and 1.5 km. from north to south. The ancient parish was reckoned to be 1,112 a.[47] but the addition of Quantock Durborough from Spaxton in 1878 and of Blaxhold and Holwell from Broomfield in 1887[48] increased its size to 1,426 a. (577 ha.) and joined the detached area to the main part.[49]

Almost the entire north-western and northern boundaries follow the course of the Durleigh

21 Crockford, *Clerical Dir.* (1869); *Alum. Cantab. 1752–1900*.
22 *Dioc. Dir.*; corresp. in office of the Editor, V.C.H. Som.
23 Inf. from Mr. P. Nokes, Dioc. Office.
24 *Valor Eccl.* (Rec. Com.), i. 208.
25 P.R.O., SC 6/Hen. VIII/3137; S.R.O., DD/POt 39; S.D.N.Q. xiii. 271.
26 S.R.O., DD/DP 38/10.
27 Ibid. D/D/Rb 1815.
28 C. Hodgson, *Queen Anne's Bounty* (1826), 229; *Rep. Com. Eccl. Revenues*, pp. 136–7.
29 Crockford, *Clerical Dir.* (1931).
30 S.R.O., D/D/Ca 22, 57.
31 Ibid. 57, 98, 134, 151.   32 Ibid. 180.
33 Ibid. D/P/durl 4/1/1; D/D/Vc 88.
34 Ibid. D/P/durl 2/1/5, 6; *Alum. Oxon. 1715–1886*;

Alum. Cantab. 1752–1900.
35 *Dioc. Dir.*; *Kelly's Dir. Som.* (1914).
36 S.R.O., D/P/durl 4/1/1; photo. in vestry.
37 S.R.O., DD/SAS CH 16/1; D/B/bw 1511.
38 Ibid. D/B/bw 1433.
39 *Proc. Som. Arch. Soc.* xlvii. 157.
40 S.R.O., D/P/durl 2/1/1–6.
41 Ibid. D/D/Ca 274.
42 Ibid. D/P/durl 2/1/1.
43 *Educ. of Poor Digest*, p. 782.
44 Nat. Soc. *Inquiry, 1846–7*, Som. 8–9.
45 P.O. *Dir. Som.* (1861); *Kelly's Dir. Som.* (1883).
46 *Kelly's Dir. Som.* (1889, 1894).
47 S.R.O., tithe award. This article was completed in 1987.
48 *Kelly's Dir. Som.* (1889).
49 *Census, 1981*.

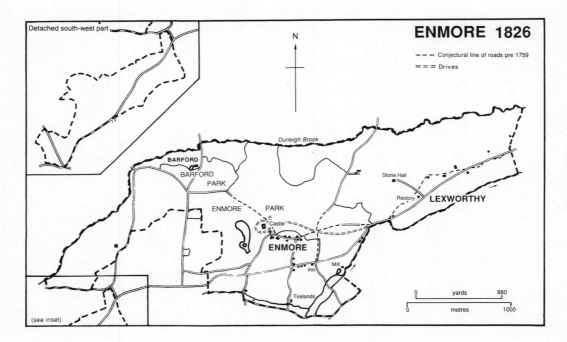

ENMORE 1826

--- — Conjectural line of roads pre 1759
=== Drives

brook from very near its source in Holwell Combe to the Durleigh reservoir, and parts of the south-eastern and southern boundaries also follow a stream. The land falls from 244 m. in the far south-west below the Quantock ridge at Broomfield Hill, steeply at first over Ilfracombe slates, to the centre of the parish, at c. 75 m., west of the village; and then more gently over Upper Keuper marls to c. 25 m. There is a narrow band of sandstone along the line of the present Bridgwater road and strips of valley gravel indicating former stream courses. Limestone from a small pocket in the west was quarried and burnt there in 1837,[50] and there were quarries south of Barford and east of the village.[51]

The name Enmore may derive from a mere, from which the lake in Enmore park may have been created. The name Lexworthy may indicate woodland clearance.[52] Enmore village lay beside the church on a small spur from which roads and paths radiated in all directions. Isolated farmsteads lay north-west at Barford, south at Tirelands, and east at Stone Hall; the medieval hamlet of Grobham, east of Enmore village, is indicated only by the field names Grabhambury.[53]

Enmore village lay on a route from Bridgwater to the Quantocks which was turnpiked to the west end of the village in 1730.[54] The expansion of Enmore park and the creation of drives across it caused the closure of a route from the village north towards Barford and culminated in the unpopular diversion of the turnpike road in 1759. The new route by-passed Lexworthy village and Enmore village street and turnpike jurisdiction was extended to Bishop's Lydeard.[55] Probably the road to Barford also dates from the same time. The old route was retained for some of its length as a footpath until 1980,[56] and other parts remain as an earthwork.

There were 112 a. of woodland in 1086[57] and at least 40 a. in 1276.[58] Timber on one estate in 1828 comprised at least nine species including witch elm, Spanish chestnut, and hornbeam.[59] There were several plantations in 1833 in addition to Roughmoor wood, north of the park, but much valuable timber was said to have been felled in 1834.[60] In 1837 there were 116 a. of woodland,[61] but later in the century more felling reduced the timber to 63 a. by 1905 and most of Roughmoor wood had been cleared.[62] Only 5 ha. (13 a.) of woodland were recorded in 1982.[63]

A warren was mentioned in 1656.[64] Parks were laid out around the houses at both Barford and Enmore. Barford park, probably created when the house was rebuilt in the early 18th century, measured c. 40 a. in 1837, and survived in 1987.[65] Enmore park had been created by 1711[66] and it was extended significantly, probably by John Perceval, earl of Egmont (d. 1770), to include most of the land between the Barford road on the west, the Durleigh brook to the north, Lexworthy to the east, and the original village

50 Geol. Surv. Map 1", drift, sheet 295 (1956 edn.); S.R.O., tithe award.
51 S.R.O., D/P/enm 14/5/1; O.S. Map 1/2,500, Som. LX. 4 (1904 edn.).
52 Ekwall, *Eng. Place-Names* (1960), 160, 283.
53 *Cal. Inq. p.m.* vii, p. 482; P.R.O., C 1/447, no. 49; C 1/566, no. 89; S.R.O., DD/HWD 19.
54 3 Geo. II, c. 34.
55 32 Geo. II, c. 40; S.R.O., DD/TB 18/7.
56 S.R.O., M 464.

57 *V.C.H. Som.* i. 472, 491.
58 *S.R.S.* xli. 66.   59 S.R.O., D/D/Bg 40.
60 Ibid. DD/HWD 19; ibid. T/PH/es.
61 Ibid. tithe award.
62 Statistics supplied by the then Bd. of Agric., 1905; O.S. Map 6", Som. XLIX. SE. (1887 edn.).
63 Min. of Agric., Fisheries, and Food, agric. returns, 1982.   64 *S.R.S.* xxviii. 309.
65 S.R.O., tithe award; *Country Life*, 7 Nov. 1974.
66 S.R.O., DD/PC 11.

street to the south, taking in some of the churchyard in 1767.[67] Further expansion south of the church was evidently contemplated: some houses were demolished c. 1791, the rectory house and glebe were acquired, and provision was made for rehousing their occupants.[68] In the event the land south of the village street was never taken into the park, which by 1833 measured 286 a. and seems to have been enclosed with a high fence.[69] By 1837 the land south of the street with the parkland west of the house called Enmore Castle had been used to create a farm, and parkland east of the house was later incorporated into Castle farm.[70] In 1932 the remaining parkland to the east became a golf course,[71] leaving a small area of parkland between Enmore Castle and the lake.

There is no record of open-field farming in the parish. Rights to common pasture were disputed between the lord of Enmore manor and another landowner before 1261, and in 1276 pasture rights in woodland in the parish were the subject of litigation.[72]

The Enmore club was recorded in 1807 and a friendly society, meeting at the Castle inn in 1804, was dissolved in 1893.[73] Enmore golf club opened in 1932 and in 1987 the course occupied the former Lower and Middle Parks and Roughmoor wood.[74]

An inn was recorded in 1619[75] and 1630,[76] and by the end of the 17th century there were three, the Bell, the Enmore, and the George inns. The Bell, whose licensee in 1683 also owned a mercery warehouse, had two butteries.[77] The Bell may well have originated as the parish brewhouse, standing at the west end of the church house. It remained open until after 1779 but had probably been demolished by 1833.[78] The Enmore inn, recorded in 1684, was owned or occupied by the Moone family. It closed c. 1765.[79] The George inn, recorded in 1696, continued until 1779 or later. It stood at the upper end of the village street and marked the end of the turnpike from Bridgwater.[80] The New Inn was recorded between 1769 and 1782.[81] Shortly before 1782 the Castle inn was built on the south side of the turnpike road, south-east of the village, and was let with a few acres of land. It was the sole licensed house in the parish between 1786 and the early 19th century.[82] It was still open in 1833 but as Castle Inn House it seems to have been a private dwelling in 1837.[83] Castle House, extended in the later 19th century, is a five-bayed house of two storeys with a three-storeyed porch, battlemented wings, and arcaded outbuildings. The Tynte Arms, probably the former Pound Cottage, had opened by 1848,[84] and the Enmore inn at Lexworthy by 1851.[85] Both were in business in 1987.

There were 29 taxpayers in 1327;[86] there were probably 63 houses in the 1660s,[87] but only 45, with c. 220 inhabitants, in 1791.[88] The population was 254 in 1801, and rose gradually to 302 in 1841 and more sharply to 343 in 1851. There followed a gradual decline to 261 in 1901. After several decades of stability the total fell to 191 in 1971; the normally resident population was 203 in 1981.[89]

Fifteen people from the parish were fined for their involvement in the 1497 rebellion.[90]

MANORS AND OTHER ESTATES. Algar held *ENMORE* in 1066 and Geoffrey was the tenant under Roger de Courcelles in 1086.[91] Like Kilve it was held of Compton Dundon manor until 1541 or later.[92] The terre tenant was Baldwin Malet in 1166,[93] and William Malet by 1200.[94] William (d. c. 1223)[95] was succeeded by a second William Malet (d. c. 1252–3)[96] and by William's son, also William, who may have died c. 1260–1.[97] Baldwin Malet was succeeded as lord in 1279 by John Malet (d. c. 1288),[98] who left an infant son Baldwin (d. 1343).[99] Baldwin was followed by his son John (d. c. 1349) and John by Baldwin Malet, a minor.[1] In 1405 the manor was settled on the same or another Baldwin Malet (d. 1416) and his third wife, Avice or Amice, Baldwin's son John having predeceased him.[2] Avice held the manor until 1431 or later but by 1452 she had been succeeded by Baldwin's granddaughter Eleanor, daughter of John Malet and wife of Sir John Hull.[3] In 1455 following the death of her son, Sir Edward Hull, Enmore was settled on Eleanor for life with remainder to Hugh Malet, son of Baldwin and Avice.[4] Eleanor died c. 1461 and Hugh in 1465.[5] Hugh's widow Joan held the manor until her death in 1496 when she was succeeded by her son Thomas Malet.[6] Thomas (d. 1501)[7] was

67 Ibid. D/D/Cf 1767.
68 Ibid. DD/PC 5, 9; D/D/Bg 11, 40; D/P/enm 14/5/1.
69 Ibid. DD/HWD 19; O.S. Map 1", sheet XX (1809 edn.).
70 S.R.O., tithe award; ibid. DD/EDN 53.
71 Below.
72 Pole MS. 905; *S.R.S.* xi, p. 66.
73 S.R.O., DD/S/WH 326; P.R.O., FS 2/9; M. Fuller, *W. Country Friendly Socs.* 143.
74 P. J. Squibbs, *Hist. Bridgwater*, ed. J. F. Lawrence, 126; S.R.O., DD/HWD 19.
75 S.R.O., Q/RLa 33.
76 Ibid. Q/RL.
77 Ibid. DD/SP inventory, 1683.
78 Ibid. Q/RL; ibid. DD/DP 24/5; DD/HWD 19.
79 Ibid. Q/SR 157/37; Q/RL; ibid. DD/NN 3; D/P/enm 2/1/1; DD/S/WH 285.
80 Ibid. DD/DP 24/5; ibid. Q/RL; Q/REl 2/5.
81 Ibid. Q/REl 2/5.
82 Ibid. Q/RL; ibid. DD/PC 10.
83 Ibid. DD/HWD 19; ibid. tithe award.
84 Ibid. D/P/enm 13/2/3; DD/HWD 19; ibid. Q/SR

Mich. 1848.
85 Ibid. D/P/enm 13/2/3.
86 *S.R.S.* iii. 163–4.
87 Dwelly, *Hearth Tax*, i. 41–4; ii. 43.
88 Collinson, *Hist. Som.* i. 95.
89 *Census*.
90 *Fines Imposed in 1497*, ed. A. J. Howard, 8.
91 *V.C.H. Som.* i. 491.
92 Ibid. v. 97–8; P.R.O., C 142/63, no. 19.
93 *Red Bk. Exch.* (Rolls Ser.), i. 227.
94 *Cur. Reg. R.* i. 259.
95 *S.R.S.* xi, p. 412.
96 Pole MS. 944.
97 Ibid. 4452; *Abbrev. Plac.* (Rec. Com.), 150; *S.D.N.Q.* iii. 256.
98 *Feud. Aids*, iv. 292–3; *Cal. Fine R. 1272–1307*, 244; Pole MS. 906; Burke, *Peerage* (1949), 1317.
99 *Feud. Aids*, iv. 301; *Cal. Inq. p.m.* viii, p. 322.
1 *S.D.N.Q.* iii. 257.
2 *S.R.S.* xxii. 19; ibid. extra ser. 128.
3 *Feud. Aids*, iv. 370, 433; Pole MS. 957.
4 *S.R.S.* xxii. 118.
5 Ibid. extra ser. 274–5; P.R.O., C 140/16, no. 8.
6 *Cal. Inq. p.m. Hen. VII*, ii, p. 50.
7 Ibid. pp. 249–50; *S.R.S.* xix. 10–11.

followed by William Malet (d. 1510), who settled Enmore on his wife Alice (d. 1524).[8] Their son Hugh (d. 1540) was succeeded in turn by his sons Thomas (d. 1540)[9] and Richard (d. 1551), and by Richard's wife Elizabeth.[10] Elizabeth was dead by 1586 when her grandson (Sir) John Malet, son of Thomas (d. 1580), was under age.[11] Sir John died in 1615[12] and was succeeded by his son John (d. 1644). John, son of the last, died in 1656 leaving a daughter Elizabeth who in 1665 married John Wilmot, earl of Rochester (d. 1680). Elizabeth died in 1682 leaving three daughters Anne, Elizabeth, and Mallett.[13]

Baynton the right to add lives to certain leaseholds and to take reversionary leases on some of his former lands.[20] The earl, an Irish peer created Lord Lovel of Holland and Enmore in the peerage of Great Britain in 1762, was succeeded by his son John James (d. 1822), the 3rd earl who, like his father, bought back many of the former manor lands.[21] John James was succeeded by his son John Perceval, the 4th earl. In 1833 and 1834 the estate, including the castle and its contents, were put up for sale to pay debts.[22] Castle and demesne were purchased by Nicholas Broadmead of Milverton.[23] He appears

VIEW OF ENMORE CASTLE, 1783

The manor, vested in trustees until 1691 or later,[14] passed to Lady Anne Wilmot, wife successively of Henry Baynton and Francis Greville.[15] She was dead by 1708 when her son John Baynton was under age.[16] John died in 1717 without issue and his heir was his sister Anne, wife successively of Edward Rolt (d. 1722) and of James Somerville, Baron Somerville (d. 1765).[17] Anne (d. 1734) was succeeded by her son Edward Bayntun Rolt (otherwise Edward Baynton, cr. Bt. 1762, d. 1800),[18] who broke up the estate.[19] In 1751 the manor was owned by John Perceval, earl of Egmont (d. 1770), although for the next three years he allowed Edward

to have been succeeded in 1850 by his brothers Philip (d. 1866) and James (d. 1892).[24] Philip's son Thomas Palfrey Broadmead occupied the estate after his father's death in part as tenant to his uncle.[25] James had no children and on his death Thomas (d. 1898) became the sole owner. He was succeeded in turn by his sons William Bucknell Broadmead (d. 1919) and the Revd. Philip Palfrey Broadmead (d. 1922), whose son Harold died in 1954,[26] when the estate was broken up and sold. The lordship had been purchased, probably in 1834, by Sir Charles Kemeys-Tynte and descended with Halswell, but was not recorded after 1899.[27]

8   P.R.O., C 142/25, no. 28; C 142/41, no. 12.
9   Ibid. C 142/63, no. 19.
10 Ibid. C 142/97, no. 101.
11 Ibid. C 142/210, no. 114.
12 S.R.O., D/D/Rr, Enmore.
13 *Complete Peerage*, xi. 47. Her son Charles died before her in 1681.
14 S.R.O., DD/NN 3; DD/PC 6.
15 Ibid. DD/BR/wp 1.   16 Ibid. DD/NN 3.
17 *Complete Peerage*, xii (i), 104–5.

18 G.E.C. *Baronetage*, v. 123.
19 S.R.O., DD/PC 1, 4.
20 Ibid. DD/NN 3; DD/PC 19.
21 Ibid. DD/NN 3; DD/PC 1; Burke, *Peerage* (1949), 690.
22 S.R.O., DD/S/WH 285; DD/PLE 64.
23 Ibid. tithe award; ibid. D/P/enm 18/1/1.
24 Ibid. D/P/milv 2/1/18; M.I. in ch.
25 S.R.O., D/P/enm 2/1/4; DD/PLE 64.
26 Burke, *Land. Gent.* (1937), 243; M.I. in ch. & chyd.
27 S.R.O., DD/S/WH 285; *Kelly's Dir. Som.* (1899).

Baldwin Malet's hall was recorded in 1396,[28] an oratory or chapel in 1404, 1415, and 1500.[29] In 1664 the house had 20 hearths,[30] and was called the Great House in 1727.[31]

Enmore Castle was built in the 1750s by John Perceval, earl of Egmont, to his own design and may have incorporated an earlier gatehouse.[32] Its plan was a hollow square with embattled square towers at the corners and semicircular turrets flanking the entrance and in the centres of the other sides. The building was surrounded by a dry moat 40 ft. wide whose flat floor was level with the castle basement. The moat gave access

tiers of Doric columns and a main entrance under a portico to the north. The interior included a large first-floor library.[38] The house was further reduced in size and remodelled inside and out before 1936 by Harold Broadmead,[39] who retained part of the western side of the building with the principal rooms. The insertion of extra walls and floors removed most of the original interiors but a few mid 18th-century fittings, of conventional character, survive. The 18th-century basement service area with part of the dry moat on the west of the house also survives. The

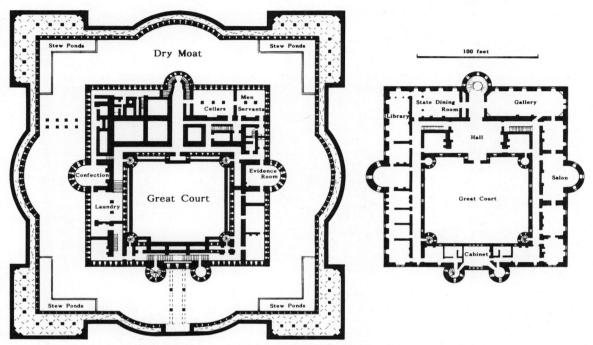

PLANS OF ENMORE CASTLE, BASEMENT AND FIRST FLOOR

to the stables and store rooms in its outer walls and was entered by a tunnel from the park.[33] The inner court was 86 ft. by 78 ft. and had circular stair turrets at each corner. The principal rooms were on the first floor and were approached by staircases leading from either side of the two-storeyed hall. There were nearly 70 rooms on three floors including an armoury, music and picture galleries, a library, and a state dining room.[34] Furnishings included tapestries later hung at Combe Sydenham and after 1950 in Bridgwater council chamber.[35] A garden and bowling green were recorded in 1770.[36] In 1834 the new owner, Nicholas Broadmead, demolished the Castle, described by a neighbour as 'very ugly ill built',[37] except for one side. He converted what remained into a three-storeyed house with an eight-bayed east front with two

house was divided into two in the 1950s.

There were three estates at Lexworthy in the 11th century. Two, held by Ordgar and Athelstan in 1066 and by Geoffrey of Roger de Courcelles in 1086,[40] descended in the Malet family with Enmore in which after 1451 they were absorbed. In the late 13th century part was held by a younger son, Richard Malet.[41] The third estate, known as LEXWORTHY or SOUTH LEX-WORTHY,[42] was held in 1066 by Alweard, who was tenant in 1086 under Eustace, count of Boulogne.[43] Until the early 13th century the manor, described as a knight's fee, continued to be part of the honor of Boulogne.[44] In 1565 the manor was said to be held of Enmore.[45]

A mesne tenancy was created in the late 12th century and was held by Gervase of Sparkford. He was succeeded by Robert of Ewyas or

28 *S.R.S.* lxviii, p. 24.
29 Ibid. xiii, p. 52; xix. 10–11; xxix, p. 203.
30 Dwelly, *Hearth Tax,* i. 43.
31 S.R.O., D/P/enm 4/1/1.
32 Ibid. DD/TB 18/7; DD/PLE 64; DD/S/WH 285; *Archit. Hist.* xxxiii. 109–10.
33 Collinson, *Hist. Som.* i. 94; S.R.O., D/P/car 23/4.
34 Taunton Castle, Braikenridge colln., plans of castle, n.d.; S.R.O., DD/PLE 64.

35 *S.D.N.Q.* xxvi. 16.   36 S.R.O., D/P/enm 14/5/1.
37 Ibid. T/PH/es.   38 Ibid. DD/CM 93.
39 *Som. Co. Herald,* 14 Mar. 1936.
40 *V.C.H. Som.* i. 491.   41 Pole MS. 937, 957, 990.
42 *S.R.S.* vi. 350; S.R.O., DD/S/WH 219.
43 *V.C.H. Som.* i. 472.
44 *Bk. of Fees,* i. 241; ii. 1435; *Red Bk. Exch.* (Rolls Ser.), ii. 577.
45 P.R.O., C 142/141, no. 18.

Rivaus, who died in 1198 leaving a daughter Sibyl (d. 1231), wife of Robert de Tregoz. Robert (d. 1213–14) was succeeded by his son Robert II Tregoz (d. 1265) and by his grandson John Tregoz (d. 1300). Lexworthy was held of John's manor of Burnham in 1306.[46] A further mesne tenancy had been created by 1284–5 when John Tregoz held of John de Cogan.[47] No further trace of Cogan's interest has been found.

The terre tenancy has not been traced between 1086 and 1285 when William of Lexworthy held the manor, probably in succession to John of Lexworthy (alive 1256) and possibly also following members of the Furnell or Fulwell family.[48] A William of Lexworthy held the manor in 1306; his son John, tenant in 1332,[49] was still alive in 1355 and had a son, also John. By 1412, however, the manor had passed to William Godwin the younger, who was succeeded after 1428[50] by his daughter Alice, wife of Robert Mompesson. Her son John Mompesson (d. 1500) was succeeded by his grandson, also John Mompesson, who died in 1511. Edmund, son of the last, died c. 1553 when his heirs were his sisters Anne, Mary, Elizabeth, and Susan.[51] In 1554 three of the sisters and probably the son of the fourth conveyed the manor to Edmund's uncle Richard Mompesson.[52] Richard sold it in 1555 to Sir Thomas Dyer and John Ewens who sold it a few days later to Nicholas Halswell.[53] The manor then descended with Halswell in Goathurst.[54] Lordship was last recorded in 1800.[55] There is no record of a capital messuage and much of the land was in Goathurst parish.

Two estates known in the 17th century as *GREAT* and *LITTLE BARFORD*[56] may derive from a virgate of land there given to Philip Sydenham in 1247.[57] Richard Barford also owned land to which his son Richard had succeeded by 1253.[58] Maud Barford, possibly Richard's widow, granted land there to Guy of Taunton before 1280 when her son Richard and Guy's son William disputed ownership.[59] William Barford held the estate in 1284, and he or a namesake in 1317. In 1331 a William Barford, retaining a life interest, settled the remainder on his brother John and on Walter of Taunton.[60]

Possibly some of the same land was held in the later 14th century by William Power, whose daughter Joan was married first to Nicholas Paris and by 1403 to John Ellis.[61] Richard Grobham quitclaimed an estate in Barford to Baldwin Malet in 1395 but it was held by William Hastings in 1405. In 1455 Barford was held of Enmore manor by Thomas Hill, and by 1475 had passed to Thomas Plush.[62] Margaret Plush, possibly daughter of the last, died in 1499 and her husband William Harding in 1500. Their three daughters, Joan, Agnes, and another Joan, were then all under age.[63]

The descent of Barford is uncertain thereafter until 1696 when Great and Little Barford were held by Edward Jenkins, who lived in the parish in 1698.[64] They were later sold, probably before 1748, by Edward Bayntun Rolt, owner of Enmore manor, to James Jeanes (d. 1759).[65] Jeanes was followed in turn by his widow Margaret St. Albyn (d. 1769) and his nephew Andrew Guy (d. 1810).[66] Andrew's daughter and heir Anne (d. 1820) married John Evered. Their son Robert Guy Evered (d. 1887) devised Barford to his second son John (d. 1931), whose younger children Robert and Gertrude Everard[67] died in possession and unmarried in the 1950s. In 1958 Barford was bought by Mr. and Mrs. M. Stancomb, the owners in 1987.[68]

There was a house at Barford in 1253.[69] A stone house was substantially rebuilt in brick with stone dressings early in the 18th century, providing a central block of five bays and originally of two storeys with attics. A little later in the century the main front was raised by one storey and single-storey wings forming quadrants were added with swept-up parapets over pediments. A walled kitchen garden to the north is probably 18th-century and Victorian pleasure grounds include an archery glade.[70]

In 1422 William Payne, whose ancestors had held a freehold in 1276, settled a holding called *WATERLAND* on his son John for life.[71] In 1467 William Payne, later described as son of John, was in possession of Paynesplace and Waterplace.[72] John Payne, possibly his son, was alive in 1497,[73] but the descent is thereafter uncertain. Part of the holding seems to have passed by 1596 to Arthur Towill or Towills.[74] He owned Waterlands in 1623 and 1640, and may have been succeeded by his younger son William c. 1664.[75] William's nephew Arthur held it in 1682, and added the leasehold farm of Tirelands, held of Enmore manor.[76] Arthur (d. by 1753) was succeeded by his son, also Arthur.[77]

46 *Cal. Close*, 1302–7, 362; *Bk. of Fees*, i. 237, 241; ii. 1435; *Red Bk. Exch.* (Rolls Ser.), ii. 577; *Cal. Inq. p.m.* iii, p. 456; *S.R.S.* iii. 32; Sanders, *Eng. Baronies*, 43.
47 *Feud. Aids*, iv. 293.
48 *S.R.S.* vi. 176; xi, p. 454; xli. 49; xliv. 50; *Rot. Hund.* (Rec. Com.), ii. 121; *Feud. Aids*, iv. 293.
49 *Cal. Close*, 1302–7, 362; *S.R.S.* vi. 350; xii. 165.
50 *S.R.S.* xvii. 30; *Feud. Aids*, iv. 435.
51 *Wilts. Pedigrees* (Harl. Soc. cv–cvi), 132.
52 P.R.O., CP 25(2)/77/656/1 Mary I Trin.
53 S.R.O., DD/S/WH 4.
54 Below, Goathurst, manors.
55 S.R.O., DD/S/WH 230.
56 Ibid. DD/DP 24/5.
57 *S.D.N.Q.* iii. 256; Pole MS. 996.
58 *S.R.S.* xi, p. 407.
59 Ibid. xliv. 40.
60 *Feud. Aids*, iv. 292, 301; *S.R.S.* viii, p. 216; xii. 158.
61 P.R.O., E 210/4258.
62 Pole MS. 4144; *S.R.S.* xxii. 19, 118; P.R.O., SC 6/977/16.
63 *Cal. Inq. p.m. Hen. VII*, iii, p. 555.
64 S.R.O., DD/DP 24/5; DD/S/WH 22.
65 B.L. Add. MS. 47051; M.I. in ch.; S. W. Rawlins, *Sheriffs of Som.* (1968), 51.
66 M.I. in ch.; S.R.O., D/P/enm 2/1/2; D/P/hun 2/1/2.
67 John had changed his name to Everard: Burke, *Land. Gent.* (1914), 627.
68 Burke, *Land. Gent.* (1914), 627; ibid. (1937), 243; *Country Life*, 7 Nov. 1974.
69 *S.R.S.* xi, p. 407.
70 *Country Life*, 7 Nov. 1974. A weather vane on the house is dated 1666.
71 *S.R.S.* xli. 66–7; S.R.O., DD/DP 64/2.
72 S.R.O., DD/DP 23/5; Pole MS. 979.
73 S.R.O., DD/DP 52/14; *Fines Imposed in 1497*, ed. A. J. Howard, 8.
74 S.R.O., DD/DP 52/14.
75 Ibid. DD/DP 76/7; Dwelly, *Hearth Tax*, i. 44.
76 S.R.O., DD/DP 77/4; DD/NN 3; D/P/enm 2/1/1.
77 Ibid. DD/BR/py 64.

The combined holding, known as Tirelands by 1767, had been acquired before 1782 by Andrew Guy, and thereafter descended with Barford.[78]

Tirelands Farm has a 16th-century main east–west range of cross-passage plan and retains part of its original jointed upper-cruck roof. Some of the internal walls are timber framed with large square panels. Behind the east end there is a short wing with a jointed base-cruck roof. The ground-floor room has an elaborately moulded coffered ceiling and a fireplace with a five-centred moulded arch. In the angle between the ranges a small turret housed a newel stair and a garderobe.

The estate later known as *CHARERS* at Lexworthy was probably held by Nicholas le Charer in 1327.[79] Walter Charer was in possession in 1364 and in 1399 he or a namesake released his estate in South Lexworthy to Baldwin Malet.[80] Charers place was recorded in 1405 when it was exempted from a settlement of Enmore manor.[81] In 1461 it belonged to the Hody family of Gothelney in Charlinch[82] and in 1540–1 was administered with Gothelney, with which it descended until 1571 when it was sold to Nicholas Chute.[83] His son Robert sold Charers to Nicholas Halswell in 1594 and it descended in the Halswell family with their manor of West Bower in Bridgwater.[84]

A separate holding called *STONE HALL* was held by the Malets in 1455.[85] It may have been sold by John Malet to Robert Farthing in 1601 and was held by the Farthing family until 1664 or later.[86] By 1696 it had been let to the Burland family and by 1752 had been sold to Anne Sweeting, probably by Edward Bayntun Rolt.[87] Between 1782 and 1841 it belonged to the North family.[88]

The name Stone Hall, occurring in 1455,[89] suggests a significant house. The present farmhouse is of the late 16th or earlier 17th century and has a central room with a moulded and coffered ceiling. It was extended in the 19th century and remodelled and refenestrated in the early 20th century.

ECONOMIC HISTORY. Three of the four Domesday estates, all called Lexworthy, seem to have occupied the valley at the eastern end of the parish; they accounted for more than two thirds of the cultivated area and for most of the recorded population. Together the four holdings comprised 10 ploughlands but there were only 9 teams. Demesne and tenant estates on the Lexworthy holdings were of equal size. Only 8 a. of meadow were recorded, all at Lexworthy, and 6 cattle and 5 pigs there were the only stock

mentioned. There were 8 *servi*.[90] A serf on Enmore manor was manumitted *c.* 1381.[91]

The quality of the 16th-century buildings at Tirelands and Stone Hall suggests agricultural prosperity in the later 16th century. The wealthiest farmers in the 17th century appear to have concentrated on livestock: one had a substantial house, grain worth over £100, and cattle, horses, sheep, pigs, and poultry valued at more than £160.[92] A hop garden was recorded in 1656.[93] Holdings remained small throughout the later 17th and the 18th century although a few farmers had leases of more than one. During the 1740s some of the larger farms on Enmore manor became freehold but most were bought back by John, earl of Egmont, before 1765.[94] In the early 19th century Tirelands farm, one of the larger holdings, was a mixed farm which produced for sale wheat, barley, oats, peas, clover seed, onions, broad beans, kidney potatoes, cider, bacon, butter, cheese, and wool. The tenant bred his own cattle and pigs and bought bulls, rams, and horses. He let his own grass and put livestock in one of the parks, possibly Barford as the owner was his landlord. The farmer also bought soap ashes and lime from several kilns. In 1814 and 1815 over 2,000 lb. of cheese were sold and between 1810 and 1820 sales of wool totalled 1,111 fleeces weighing *c.* 5,000 lb. and over 1,140 lb. of lamb's wool. His flock in 1818 comprised 102 sheep and 62 lambs. It had increased to 218 in 1823 and 389 fleeces weighing over 2,000 lb. and 500 lb. of lamb's wool were sold in 1828 to Fox and Sons of Wellington.[95] On Lexworthy manor rack renting began in the 1730s and by the 1780s almost the entire estate was let for years.[96] Small tenants were being evicted on Enmore manor and houses allowed to decay *c.* 1809.[97] Rack renting on Enmore manor had been introduced by 1833 but there was only one large farm, Enmore Park farm (133 a.), and the smaller holdings continued to be held on leases for lives. The park had been divided up and was let for grazing.[98]

After the sale of the Egmont estate the Broadmeads reorganized the farms. At first the park was divided and let, and by 1837 a farm was established which included the former glebe and the land called Quantock Durborough, the whole managed from Quantock, later Castle, farm.[99] Tirelands had more than doubled in size between 1837 and 1851 and by 1871 there were four holdings in the parish with over 100 a., two with over 200 a. In 1851 Tirelands gave employment to 8 labourers, Quantock farm to 7.[1] In 1868 housing conditions for labourers in the parish were considered good, women worked at harvest and dug potatoes and turnips, and boys

78 Ibid. Q/REl 2/5; above.
79 *S.R.S.* iii. 164.
80 Pole MS. 837, 1077.   81 *S.R.S.* xxii. 19.
82 P.R.O., C 140/4, no. 34.
83 Ibid. LR 3/123; S.R.O., DD/S/WH 3.
84 S.R.O., DD/S/WH 3; below, Bridgwater, manors.
85 *S.R.S.* xxii. 118.
86 S.R.O., DD/DP 23/7; DD/S/WH 292; Dwelly, *Hearth Tax*, i. 41.
87 S.R.O., DD/DP 25/5; DD/SAS (C/112) 9/4; B.L. Add. MS. 47051.
88 S.R.O., DD/PC 9; ibid. Q/REl 2/5; P.R.O., HO 107/929.

89 *S.R.S.* xxii. 118.
90 *V.C.H. Som.* i. 472, 491.
91 Pole MS. 903.
92 S.R.O., DD/SP inventories, 1635, 1640.
93 *S.R.S.* xxviii. 309.
94 S.R.O., DD/S/BW 5; DD/S/WH 285; DD/NN 3; DD/PC 3.
95 Ibid. D/P/enm 23/1.
96 Ibid. DD/S/WH 221A, 230; DD/X/TCR 4.
97 *Paupers and Pigkillers*, ed. J. Ayres, 185.
98 S.R.O., DD/VN (H/134); DD/PLE 64.
99 Ibid. tithe award.
1 P.R.O., HO 107/1924; ibid. RG 10/2383.

over 12 worked full-time on farms.[2] In 1871 and 1881 there were 34 farm labourers.[3]

The titheable land in the parish amounted in 1837 to 341 a. of arable, 567 a. of meadow and pasture, and 65 a. of orchard and garden.[4] In 1905, after the inclusion of Quantock Durborough and Blaxhold, there were 862 a. of permanent grass, the amount of arable remaining unchanged.[5] In 1982 grassland still accounted for over 60 per cent of recorded land.[6]

In 1960 Castle farm, the largest in the parish, specialized in pedigree beef cattle and among the farm buildings was a 70-ton granary with a diesel driven mill.[7] There were three dairy farms in 1982, and at least 1,051 sheep. Wheat, barley, and fodder crops accounted for most of the arable.[8]

Woodland provided grazing for pigs in the later 13th century and timber was sold.[9] In 1813 nursery trees for sale included larch, Scotch spruce, silver fir, and Balm of Gilead.[10]

There were four mills at Lexworthy in 1086, and the rent was paid in iron.[11] During the 13th century both William Malet and William of Lexworthy appear to have had mills at Lexworthy and Malet gave Richard Furnell of Lexworthy priority at his mill in return for being allowed a watercourse through Richard's land.[12] In 1696 two mills were recorded at Lexworthy, one probably on Trokes farm and the other, called Cutters, probably on the northern boundary stream.[13] Neither mill was recorded again. Methuens or Prowses mill existed by 1767. It belonged to Sir Charles Kemeys-Tynte but was not included in his manor of Lexworthy. Prowses mill was kept by the Collard family from 1782 or earlier until its closure, probably just before 1914.[14] The mill house survived in 1987 as Mill Farm, south-west of Enmore village, but the machinery, including an iron overshot wheel probably driving two pairs of stones, has been removed.[15]

In 1401 Baldwin Malet obtained a grant of a Monday market and a two-day fair at Midsummer,[16] but there is no evidence that either was ever held.

Rents for mills paid in iron in 1086 suggest iron making,[17] and from the mid 15th century iron was imported through Bridgwater, including in 1607 an iron furnace.[18] There were smithies beside the road at Enmore and Lexworthy in the 19th century.[19] A clothier was mentioned in the 16th century and a weaver in the mid 17th.[20] Rack Close near Prowses mill possibly indicates a former fulling mill on the site.[21] Tanning was practised in the late 17th and the early 18th century; one tanner had a horse mill and leather and bark worth £35 and another had stock valued at £300; his father and brother were also tanners.[22] Harnessmaking was recorded in 1841 and a saddlery in 1861.[23] Malting was recorded from the later 17th century.[24] There was a soapboiler in 1725 and a chairmaker in 1753.[25] In 1821 only 27 out of 55 families were employed in agriculture.[26]

In the earlier 20th century a sawmill at Enmore employed 20 men including a smith, a wheelwright, and a carpenter, and produced gates, fences, carts, window frames, and coffins. The firm also sank wells and installed hydraulic rams, built houses and the village hall, acted as undertakers, and later kept a petrol pump. The sawmill closed in the 1950s.[27]

LOCAL GOVERNMENT. Enmore parish was divided between the tithings of Enmore and Lexworthy by the 14th century.[28] Blaxhold tithing in Broomfield parish was declared a sub-tithing of Enmore in 1648, but by 1767 all three were united in a single tithing of Enmore, Blaxhold, and Lexworthy for the land tax.[29] Baldwin Malet had assize of bread and ale in Enmore manor in 1275[30] and suit of court was required of tenants until the early 18th century.[31] Court records survive for 1735–9, mainly presentments and appointments of tithingmen for Enmore, Lexworthy, and Blaxhold. A hayward was appointed in 1736. A pound was recorded in 1696 and stocks in 1739.[32] The pound lay near the turnpike road where Pound Cottage had been built by 1833.[33] Records of Lexworthy manor court survive for 1564 and 1611.[34]

In the 17th and 18th centuries tithingmen and churchwardens were appointed in an established rotation, and tithingmen in the 18th century were presented and sworn at Enmore manor court.[35] In 1782 the vestry administered the income from parish land for the benefit of the poor and other objects. In 1794 it was agreed to pay to house the poor and in 1801 the vestry bought grain for sale to the poor at reduced prices.[36]

2 *Rep. Com. Employment in Agric.* 481–2.
3 P.R.O., RG 10/2383; RG 11/2372.
4 S.R.O., tithe award.
5 Statistics supplied by the then Bd. of Agric., 1905.
6 Min. of Agric., Fisheries, and Food, agric. returns, 1982.   7 S.R.O., DD/EDN 53.
8 Min. of Agric., Fisheries, and Food, agric. returns, 1982.
9 *S.R.S.* xli. 66; lviii, p. 52; lx, p. 45; S.R.O., DD/S/WH 211.
10 *Taunton Courier*, 14 Jan. 1813.
11 *V.C.H. Som.* i. 472, 491.
12 Pole MS. 939, 4450.
13 S.R.O., DD/DP 24/5.
14 Ibid. Q/REl 2/5; ibid. tithe award; *Kelly's Dir. Som.* (1897–1914).
15 Som. C.C., Sites and Mons. Rec.
16 *Cal. Chart. R.* 1341–1417, 416.
17 *V.C.H. Som.* i. 472, 491.
18 S.R.O., D/B/bw 1437, 1439, 1442, 1474, 1491, 1502.
19 Ibid. DD/HWD 19; ibid. tithe award; P.R.O., HO

107/1924.
20 P.R.O., C 1/546, no. 93; S.R.O., DD/X/SR 5.
21 S.R.O., tithe award.
22 Ibid. DD/SP inventories, 1683, 1685; DD/DP 52/14.
23 P.R.O., HO 107/929; RG 9/1622.
24 S.R.O., DD/SP inventory, 1687; DD/PC 6; DD/SAS (C/2645) 24; ibid. tithe award; *P.O. Dir. Som.* (1861); *Kelly's Dir. Som.* (1897).
25 S.R.O., DD/NN 3; DD/BR/py 64.
26 *Census*, 1821.
27 S.R.O., D/P/chlch 3/4/2; *Bridgwater Mercury*, 20 Mar. 1984.   28 *S.R.S.* iii. 163–4.
29 Ibid. xxviii. 69–70; S.R.O., D/P/broo 13/1/1; ibid. Q/REl 2/5.
30 *Rot. Hund.* (Rec. Com.), ii. 126.
31 S.R.O., DD/PC 1.
32 Wilts. R.O. 473/53; S.R.O., DD/DP 24/5.
33 S.R.O., DD/HWD 19.
34 Ibid. DD/S/WH 210–11.
35 Ibid. DD/DP 24/5; Wilts. R.O. 473/53.
36 S.R.O., D/P/enm 13/2/1.

The church house may have been used as a poorhouse but in 1657 the parish was given the lease of half another house.[37] A poorhouse, also called the parish house and the almshouse, was recorded in 1755 and was maintained by the church-wardens until 1826 or later. The overseers seem to have been running it by 1836.[38] The house, at the east end of the village street, was owned by them in 1837 and was sold c. 1844.[39] In 1987 it was a private dwelling known as Park Gate.

The parish was part of the Bridgwater poor-law union from 1836, Bridgwater rural district from 1894, and Sedgemoor district from 1974.[40]

CHURCH. The earliest evidence for a church at Enmore is the late Norman south doorway. The benefice, a rectory, was united with Goathurst in 1956; the united benefice was further united with Spaxton and Charlinch in 1981.[41]

The advowson was held by Baldwin Malet, lord of Enmore manor, in 1329[42] and descended with that manor until 1833,[43] although the Crown appointed by lapse in 1570[44] and kinsmen of the previous rector presented a relative in 1678.[45] The patronage was not sold with the Castle estate in 1834 and may have been retained by the earl of Egmont.[46] Between 1861 and 1902 it was held by John Levien, rector 1860–75, and after his death by his trustees.[47] It was bought, probably c. 1904, by William Broadmead and descended with Enmore Castle until c. 1954.[48] In 1957 the arch-bishop of Canterbury presented by lapse[49] and between then and 1981 the bishop of Bath and Wells presented on alternate vacancies. The bishop in respect of Enmore presented jointly to the united benefice from 1981.[50]

The church was valued at £4 in 1329,[51] £8 in 1414,[52] and £8 14s. 8d. gross in 1535.[53] About 1668 the benefice was said to be worth c. £70[54] and was augmented in 1819 with £100 given by Mrs. Pincombe's trustees and £100 given by the rector.[55] Average income 1829–31 was £242.[56] Tithes were commuted for £224 in 1837.[57]

The glebe was valued at £1 1s. 6d. in 1535.[58] In 1620 it consisted of a house, buildings, and 19 a.[59] The land, mainly south of the church but also east of the village in the later park, was exchanged in

1806 and 1828 for 24 a. at Lexworthy.[60] It had been sold by 1978.[61] A priest's house was mentioned in 1319.[62] In 1620 the house lay south-west of the church near the southern end of the lake.[63] It was described as ruinous and unfit in 1806 when it was exchanged for a house at Lexworthy built by the earl of Egmont for the rector c. 1803; the old house was demolished.[64] The house was sold c. 1956 and divided into two dwellings.

The deanery chapter met at Enmore in 1195 when Gocelin, chaplain of Enmore, was present.[65] John of Drayton, rector in 1327, was described as worn out and a coadjutor was appointed.[66] There was an anniversary chaplain in 1450. John Roche or Ryche, rector 1463–7, was a canon of Wells.[67] There were both a rector and a stipendiary priest c. 1535, and the parish supported a fraternity, known as Our Lady's service or the brother-hood.[68] Thomas Rawlins, rector in 1554, was incapable because 'distracted of his wits'.[69] His successor, Justinian Lancaster, rector 1558–70, was later archdeacon of Taunton.[70] The church was served by curates in the 1570s, including two men who were not even deacons and another who had no licence.[71] Henry Atwood, rector 1601–13, failed to preach and the church bible was said to be faulty.[72] His successor, Bartholomew Safford, was accused of preaching afternoon sermons which did not finish until 5 p.m. and of failing to wear a surplice. He also altered the form of services.[73] Late 17th-century rectors were resident but the parish was served by curates in the early 18th century.[74] There were only 20 or 30 com-municants in the time of the pluralist Thomas Milward, rector 1778–9.[75] In 1789 the church band needed reeds and strings and in 1800 the principal inhabitants paid for a bassoon; an organ had been installed by 1826.[76] John Poole, rector 1796–1857, who lived at Over Stowey until the new rectory was available c. 1803, augmented the living, and established a school. Poole held two Sunday services in 1815 and was then resident although by 1835 he also held Swainswick rec-tory.[77] In 1840 communion was celebrated four times a year but John Levien had increased celebrations to six a year by 1870.[78]

A church house, recorded in 1546[79] and in 1696, probably stood south of the church.[80] It may have

37 Ibid. DD/S/WH 189.
38 Ibid. D/P/enm 4/1/1, 13/2/1, 13/2/3.
39 Ibid. tithe award; ibid. D/P/enm 13/2/3.
40 Youngs, *Local Admin Units*, i. 671, 673, 676.
41 S.R.O., D/P/car 23/8; *Dioc. Dir.*
42 *S.R.S.* ix, p. 142.
43 Above, manors.
44 *Cal. Pat.* 1569–72, p. 61.
45 *Som. Wills*, ed. Brown, ii. 11, 30; *Som. Incumbents*, ed. Weaver, 366.
46 *Co. Gaz. Dir. Som.* (1840).
47 *P.O. Dir. Som.* (1861, 1866); *Kelly's Dir. Som.* (1883, 1910).
48 *Kelly's Dir. Som.* (1906); *Crockford.*
49 S.R.O., D/P/car 23/8.
50 *Dioc. Dir.*
51 *S.R.S.* ix, p. 42.
52 S.R.O., D/D/B misc. 1.
53 *Valor Eccl.* (Rec. Com.), i. 214.
54 S.R.O., D/D/Vc 24.
55 C. Hodgson, *Queen Anne's Bounty* (1864), p. cxcvi.
56 *Rep. Com. Eccl. Revenues*, pp. 136–7.
57 S.R.O., tithe award.
58 *Valor Eccl.* (Rec. Com.) i. 214.
59 S.R.O., D/D/Rg 269.

60 Ibid. D/D/Bg 11, 40; ibid. tithe award.
61 Inf. Dioc. Office.
62 *S.D.N.Q.* xxxi. 464.
63 S.R.O., D/D/Rg 269; DD/HWD 19.
64 Ibid. D/D/Bg 11; DD/HWD 19; *Paupers and Pig-killers*, ed. J. Ayres, 78.
65 *S.R.S.* xxv, p. 90. 66 Ibid. i. 282; ix, p. 42.
67 Ibid. xlix, pp. 139, 405.
68 Ibid. liv, p. 27; *Wells Wills*, ed. Weaver, 82; S.R.O., DD/X/SR 5; D/D/Vc 20. 69 S.R.O., D/D/Ca 22.
70 *S.R.S.* lv, p. 151; Le Neve, *Fasti, 1541–1847, Bath and Wells*, 16.
71 *S.D.N.Q.* xiii. 270; S.R.O., D/D/Ca 57.
72 S.R.O., D/D/Ca 134, 151, 160.
73 T. H. Peake, 'Som. Clergy and Church Cts. in Dioc. of Bath and Wells 1625–42' (Bristol Univ. M. Litt. thesis, 1978), 284–5; *V.C.H. Som.* v. 17–18; *Alum. Oxon. 1500–1714.*
74 S.R.O., D/P/enm 2/1/1. 75 Ibid. D/D/Vc 88.
76 Ibid. D/P/enm 4/1/1, 13/2/1.
77 Ibid. D/D/Rb 1815; *Rep. Com. Eccl. Revenues*, pp. 136–7; below, educ.
78 S.R.O., D/D/Va 1840, 1870.
79 *S.R.S.* xxvii. 259.
80 S.R.O., DD/DP 24/5.

been used as a poorhouse but it continued to be maintained by the churchwardens until 1811.[81] It may have been demolished shortly after.[82]

The church of *ST. MICHAEL*, so dedicated by 1348,[83] comprises a chancel, a nave with north aisle, including vestry and organ chamber, and south porch, and a west tower. Before 1872, when all but the tower was rebuilt, the church comprised a 14th-century chancel, a nave whose south wall included a 12th-century doorway,[84] and a tower, possibly built in 1455 when a crane was hired from Bridgwater,[85] apparently designed for a narrower nave. The north nave wall may have been rebuilt in the 15th or early 16th century at the same time as a new, panelled chancel arch, a narrow, transomed south window for the rood screen, and a rood stair on the north were inserted. After 1783 the rood stair was destroyed to make an entrance to a north vestry, and a south porch was added.[86] A singing loft was recorded in 1756,[87] lit in the 1780s by a high-level domestic-style window.[88] The rebuilding in 1872–3 was to the designs of Benjamin Ferrey.[89] The south doorway, the Jacobean pulpit, and the panelled chancel arch were retained but the screen was sent to Huish Episcopi[90] and the rood screen window blocked up. Battlements were added to the tower.

In the church are a medieval chest and two early 17th-century helms and a chair from Enmore Castle. The font, possibly of the 13th century, replaced a Victorian font in 1937.[91] The statue of St. Michael was placed in the tower niche in 1979.[92]

There are six bells: one by William Purdue dated 1647 was recast in 1739 by Thomas Bayley who recast two others in 1752. Two were recast in 1796 by George and Thomas Davis, and the tenor was installed in 1897.[93] The plate includes a cup and cover of 1618, a saucer of 1727, and a tankard given by James Jeanes of Barford in 1751 and engraved with the arms of himself and his wife.[94] The registers date from 1653 and are complete.[95]

The churchyard cross dates probably from the 15th century and consists of a headless shaft in a square socket carved with blank shields standing on three octagonal steps.

NONCONFORMITY. Two houses, one the George inn, were licensed for worship in 1722, but the denomination of neither congregation is known.[96] The Wesleyans had a preaching station in 1863–4 and by 1867 the Bible Christians had a chapel, probably the cottage they gave up in 1889.[97] The undenominational Gospel hall, built beside the Bridgwater road in 1901, has been used by the Plymouth Brethren since the 1930s,[98] and in 1987 two services were held there each Sunday.

EDUCATION. In 1676 a man was licensed to teach a grammar school.[99] Before 1810 there were a day and a Sunday school, where 35 to 40 children were taught to read and write and to do needlework, established by the rector John Poole, with Lord Egmont's support. Children of 3 or 4 years were taught to read and write and cast accounts using a sand table. Older children learnt grammar, mental arithmetic, and chronology and were taught to teach the younger pupils. Children attended school for seven hours a day and had a holiday every alternate Saturday and for a week at each of the three major feasts.[1] By 1819 the day school had 100 pupils and the Sunday school up to 60.[2] By 1835 these two schools had 49 and 44 children respectively, a second day school 18, and there were 16 attending a mixed boarding school begun in 1826.[3]

In 1846 there were 36 children at the Sunday school and 31 children at a dame school, and a National school was under construction.[4] It was finished in 1848, enlarged in 1888, and had 52 children on the books in 1903.[5] Numbers fell to 40 in 1935 but rose to 71 in 1975. In 1981 there were 51 children on the register.[6]

A boarding school for young children at Lexworthy between 1841 and 1861 may have been that begun in 1826.[7]

CHARITIES FOR THE POOR. An unknown donor gave 1 a. in Bridgwater before 1455.[8] The rent was distributed to the poor until 1789 when the vestry decided to use the money to provide clothing.[9] The land was later sold and the capital had been lost by 1869.[10] Catherine Clark (d. before 1724) gave £70 for labouring men and distributions were made during the 18th century. Jasper Porter by will dated 1746 gave money for bread but the charity had ceased by 1786, probably on the death of his son in 1781. Elizabeth Moon by will dated 1780 gave £200 for the poor. The Clark and Moon charities were lost between 1826 and 1869.[11] William Skynner by will dated 1829 gave £100 for the poor; and Sarah Wood by will proved 1891 provided for a bread distribution. The last two charities were still active in 1987.[12]

81 S.R.O., D/P/enm 4/1/1.
82 Ibid. DD/HWD 19.
83 P.R.O., E 210/6893.
84 One of the columns was replaced in 1726: S.R.O., D/P/enm 4/1/1.
85 *S.R.S.* lx, p. 88.
86 S.R.O., D/D/Cf 1872/3; Taunton Castle, Pigott colln., J. Buckler, drawing 1838; above, p. 38.
87 S.R.O., D/P/enm 4/1/1.
88 Above, p. 38.
89 S.R.O., D/D/Cf 1872/3; D/P/enm 4/1/2, 6/1/1.
90 *V.C.H. Som.* iii. 11.
91 Plaque on font.   92 Plaque in ch. porch.
93 S.R.O., D/P/enm 4/1/1; DD/SAS CH 16/1.
94 *Proc. Som. Arch. Soc.* xlvii. 158.
95 S.R.O., D/P/enm 2/1/1–6.
96 Ibid. Q/RR meeting ho. lics.
97 Ibid. D/N/bmc 3/2/3, 3/2/5; Whitby, *Dir. Bridgwater* (1883).

98 Hamlin & Whitby, *Baptists in Bridgwater*, 81; *Kelly's Dir. Som.* (1919); G.R.O., worship reg. no. 41955.
99 S.R.O., D/D/Bs 42.
1 *Paupers and Pigkillers*, ed. J. Ayres, 219; J. Poole, *The Village School Improved* (Oxford, 1815), *passim*.
2 *Educ. of Poor Digest*, p. 782.
3 *Educ. Enq. Abstract*, p. 805.
4 Nat. Soc. *Inquiry, 1846–7*, Som. 8–9; S.R.O., DD/X/HEA, box 33; D/P/enm 18/1/1.
5 S.R.O., C/E 4/380/161; *Kelly's Dir. Som.* (1889).
6 S.R.O., C/E 4/64.
7 P.R.O., HO 107/929; ibid. RG 9/1622; above, this section.   8 *S.R.S.* lx, no. 780.
9 S.R.O., DD/S/SH 2; D/P/enm 4/1/1, 13/2/1.
10 *15th Rep. Com. Char.* 344; *Char. Digest* (1869–71), Som. 28.
11 *Char. Don.* pp. 1044–5; *15th Rep. Com. Char.* 344–5; *Char. Digest* (1869–71), Som. 28–9; S.R.O., DD/X/PORT 1.   12 Char. Com. Reg.

GOATHURST

GOATHURST parish lies on the northern side of the eastern end of the Quantocks, the main part stretching 3 km. north from Goathurst Down[13] beside Rooks Castle Farm into the broad, undulating valley west of Bridgwater.[14] It contained Goathurst village at its centre, Halswell House and park south of the village, and Andersfield hamlet north-west of the village. Two small detached areas each containing a farmstead, Roughmoor Farm and Crossfield Farm, 2 km. north-west of the village, belonging to Goathurst perhaps as a result of intercommoning, were absorbed respectively in 1882 by Aisholt parish and in 1885 by Spaxton. Huntstile, an area of c. 220 a. east of Halswell park and containing 3 houses and 27 inhabitants in 1881, was transferred from Chilton Trinity to Goathurst in 1886.[15] The civil parish measured 677 ha. (1,673 a.) in 1981.[16]

The parish boundary is marked on the south by the ridge road between Broomfield and North Petherton, on the east and north partly by streams. Eastwards across the parish flows Cobb's Cross stream, into which two other streams flow from the south. A narrow band of sandstone near the village divides the Morte slate of the Quantock ridge and the Mercia mudstones of the valley.[17] Both slate and sandstone were quarried, the sandstone in the late 16th century,[18] and bricks were made north of the village in 1744 and until the earlier 19th century.[19]

Goathurst, Halswell, and Andersfield were recorded in the 11th century.[20] None shows traces of open arable fields. Goathurst village, since the earlier 18th century a nucleated settlement along a single street, may earlier have comprised only the church, manor house, rectory house, and a few cottages. The cottages on the north side of the western end of the street were built on land which had earlier been the barton and orchard of Goathurst manor house, and cottages on the south side were also built in the 18th century.[21] Old Cobb, at the east end of the street, is the only house of medieval origin. The present village street, including a 19th-century terrace, consists mainly of rendered cottages with a few brick houses.

The mansion house at Halswell and its associated buildings were in multiple occupation in the later 20th century. Andersfield, in 1990 a straggling settlement of brick bungalows divided by a single field from Goathurst village, was in the 1840s a scatter of cottages and a farm along a lane called Andersfield Green.[22] Andersfield Farm probably dates from the 15th century but was altered in the 16th and 17th.[23] Two smaller settlements were Frodger, recorded in 1304[24] and later represented by Flatgate Cottages, and Oakenford, mentioned in 1327[25] and a small hamlet in 1756,[26] but now a single farm.

Andersfield, Goathurst village, and Oakenford were perhaps linked together by a route running from Enmore and the west to Bridgwater. The road north from the village to Durleigh was made in 1763 in place of a route further south-west.[27] A route between Rooks Castle and Oakenford through Halswell park was closed in 1809.[28] A footpath between the same places past Halswell House may mark another route.[29]

There were 76 a. of woodland recorded in 1086[30] and field names suggest that the north part of the parish once contained much woodland.[31] Also north of Goathurst manor house in the 17th and early 18th centuries were a warren and park.[32] Halswell manor also had a warren in 1597 and in 1708–9,[33] which lay immediately south of the village street[34] and may have formed the nucleus of the park. The park, probably created in the later 17th century, was greatly extended and planted by Sir Charles Kemeys-Tynte from 1740. It measured 30 a. in 1744,[35] more than doubled in the 1750s, and later in the century was 132 a.[36] A plantation called the Thicket was created in two sections in 1754 and 1764, part of a wood to the west was established in 1762, and in 1761 the park was extended east into Huntstile. Chestnuts and firs were planted in Huntstile Bottom, in the Thicket, and along Park Lane, between Goathurst village and Huntstile, in 1766, and more were planted on the eastern boundary in 1778.[37] Within the picturesque setting of wood and undulating parkland Sir Charles introduced temples and other features and dammed streams to create lakes and waterfalls. The buildings in the park included a rotunda and a bridge (1755), the Druid's Temple (1756), the Temple of Harmony (1764), and Robin Hood's House (1765).[38] By 1756 an avenue of trees led west from the house and a drive was created to Patcombe, in Broomfield.[39] A second avenue led north to Goathurst village,

[13] S.R.O., D/D/Rg 271. This article was completed in 1990.
[14] O.S. Map 1/50,000, sheet 182 (1974 edn.).
[15] S.R.O., tithe award; *Census*, 1891; below, Chilton Trinity.
[16] *Census*, 1981.
[17] O.S. Map 1/50,000, sheet 182 (1974 edn.); Geol. Surv. Map 1/50,000, solid and drift, sheet 295 (1984 edn.).
[18] S.R.O., DD/S/WH 242; ibid. tithe award; O.S. Map 6", Som. LXI. NW. (1887 edn.).
[19] S.R.O., DD/S/WH 255–6, 258, 262, 269; ibid. tithe award.
[20] *V.C.H. Som.* i. 513, 534.
[21] S.R.O., DD/RN 26, 28; DD/S/WH 38, 147.
[22] Ibid. D/D/Rg 271; DD/S/WH 37; DD/RN 22.
[23] Ibid. DD/V/BWr 18.3.

[24] *Cal. Inq. p.m.* iv, p. 159.
[25] *S.R.S.* iii. 164, which has Woltuford for Wolcnford.
[26] S.R.O., DD/S/WH 248.
[27] Ibid. T/PH/vch 73.
[28] Ibid. DD/X/DT 1; ibid. Q/SO; Q/SR Jan. 1809.
[29] O.S. Map 6", Som. LXI. NW. (1887 edn.).
[30] *V.C.H. Som.* i. 495, 513.   [31] S.R.O., tithe award.
[32] Ibid. DD/RN 64; DD/S/WH 25, 147, 266; ibid. tithe award.
[33] Ibid. DD/S/WH 218, 242.
[34] Ibid. DD/X/DT 1.   [35] Ibid. DD/S/WH 258.
[36] MS. tithe receipts in possession of Miss B. Harris, Taunton; S.R.O., DD/S/WH 269.
[37] S.R.O., T/PH/vch 73.
[38] *Country Life*, 9 Feb. 1989, 82–7.
[39] S.R.O., DD/X/DT 1; above, Broomfield.

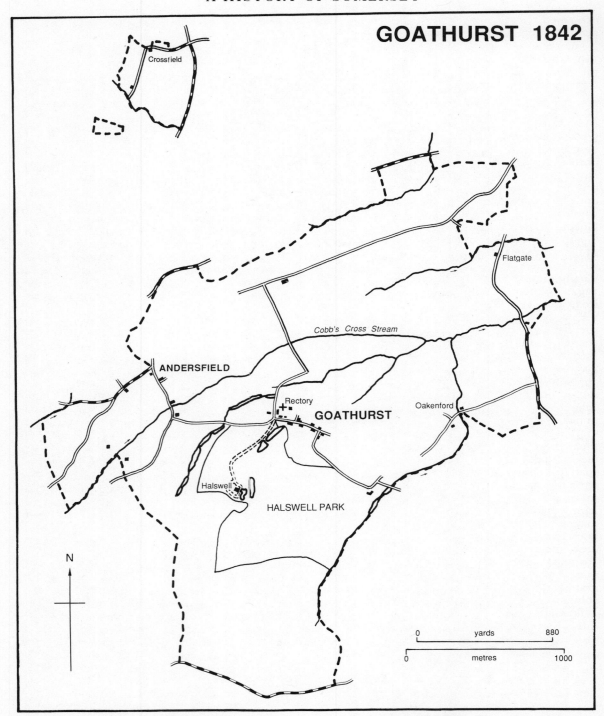

GOATHURST 1842

where a rustic lodge replaced an earlier building *c.* 1825.[40] In 1892 the park measured 194 a. and by the early 20th century had increased to 220 a.[41] Deer were kept in the late 18th century[42] and both red and fallow deer were there *c.* 1911.[43] Since 1945 much of the woodland has been felled and the parkland has been returned to arable cultivation. Several of the temples and other buildings have been damaged or destroyed.

There may have been an alehouse in the parish

in 1502[44] and a house was licensed during the 17th century,[45] but there is no later record of a public house in the parish. There was a friendly society called the Goathurst club in the 19th century and a reading room was in use in 1905.[46]

The population rose from 296 in 1801 to a peak of 349 in 1831, fell sharply between 1841 and 1851 to 303, then declined gradually to 202 in 1931. New building in the later 20th century and the division of Halswell House into flats

40 MS. tithe receipts in possession of Miss B. Harris.
41 Greswell, *Forests and Deerparks of Som.* (1905), 259; *V.C.H. Som.* ii. 569.
42 S.R.O., DD/S/WH 230, 270.
43 *V.C.H. Som.* ii. 569.
44 S.R.O., DD/X/ELT 2.   45 Ibid. Q/RL.
46 M. Fuller, *W. Country Friendly Socs.* 93, 144; S.R.O., DD/RN 70.

explained the rise to 280 in 1971; in 1981 238 people were normally resident.[47]

The rector and ten others were fined after the 1497 uprising[48] and three men were involved in the Monmouth rebellion, two of them being transported.[49]

MANORS. Alfred d'Epaignes held *GOATHURST* in 1086[50] and the overlordship descended with his lordship of Nether Stowey until 1571 or later.[51] Walter d'Epaignes held the larger part of the manor in 1086 under his brother Alfred and Ansger held the remainder, both in succession to Alwine, the tenant of the whole in 1066.[52] In 1166 Hugh son of Malger of Goathurst held a knight's fee.[53] Roger of Goathurst had succeeded by 1198 and died probably *c.* 1208.[54] Another Roger of Goathurst, alive in 1276,[55] was succeeded by William of Goathurst, probably his son, between 1286 and 1292.[56] William held the fee in 1303 and his son Roger in 1316.[57] Roger died *c.* 1325[58] and was followed by Walter of Goathurst who had been succeeded by his son Richard by 1360.[59] Richard's daughter and heir Joan married John Fittelton who in 1378–9 acquired an estate in Goathurst from John Popham.[60] Richard was apparently dead by 1382 when the manor was settled on John and Joan and their children.[61] John had died by 1412 when his son John, a minor, was permitted to marry Isabel, daughter of William Paulet of Beere. John later granted the manor to William.[62] William Paulet held the fee in 1428, having secured a quitclaim from Joan Fittelton's heirs.[63] He devised Goathurst in trust for his wife Margaret and after her death to his grandson John Fittelton.[64] In 1431 William was dead and his trustees were holding the manor.[65] John Fittelton died in 1435 leaving, as heirs to Goathurst, Joan and Agnes Sydenham, descendants of William of Goathurst.[66] Both Joan and Agnes released their rights in the manor to William Paulet of Melcombe who granted it to his son Sir John (d. 1437).[67] In 1456 John's son, also John, settled it on his brother William (d. 1483),[68] from whom it passed in the direct male line to John (d. 1542),[69] William (d.

1571),[70] and Edward Paulet (d. 1580).[71] Edward's widow Alice married Thomas Jenkins and they held Goathurst until it was settled on Edward's daughter Elizabeth for her marriage to her kinsman Sir George Paulet *c.* 1584.[72] In 1612 the manor was given to their son Edward but Sir George (d. 1644) and Elizabeth retained part of the capital messuage, which was settled on Sir George's second wife Mary Trowbridge (d. 1647).[73] Edward died in 1635 leaving five daughters: Alice, Jane, Anne, Mary, and Katharine.[74]

Alice died unmarried in 1643[75] and the manor descended as four shares which were all eventually sold to the Tyntes, owners of the Halswell estate.[76] Jane Paulet married John Payne,[77] who outlived her and was succeeded in 1674 by their son Paulet Payne (d. 1707). The Paynes' quarter share descended with Rhode in North Petherton until 1787 when the lordship was probably settled on Thomas Jeane (d. 1791) and his son John (d. 1798). John's heir in 1798 was his sister Elizabeth who married Robert, son of John Buncombe.[78] Her son Thomas Jeane Buncombe sold his Goathurst estate to Sir Charles Kemeys-Tynte between 1827 and 1831.[79] Anne Paulet married first William Bragg (d. 1641)[80] and secondly Henry Trenchard. By 1662 they had been succeeded by her elder son William Bragg.[81] William (d. 1713) was succeeded by his grandson William Bragg (d. 1726), whose brother John sold his share of Goathurst to Sir Halswell Tynte in 1730.[82] Mary Paulet married first John Buncombe and second John Glassbrook, and in 1691 succeeded to the share of her sister Katharine.[83] Mary died in 1706 having outlived her eldest son John Buncombe and was followed, under the terms of a settlement, by her daughter Millicent Buncombe (d. 1708), wife of Richard Stevens, and then by her younger son Edward Buncombe.[84] In 1712 Edward settled his share on his son John who sold off what remained of the land with his half share of the lordship to Sir Charles Kemeys-Tynte in 1753.[85]

The capital messuage was recorded in 1612.[86] It lay east of the church and was occupied by John and Mary Buncombe in the mid 17th century.[87] After the sale of their estate to Sir

47 *Census.*
48 *Fines Imposed in 1497*, ed. A. J. Howard, 8.
49 *S.R.S.* lxxix. 51, 88, 112.
50 *V.C.H. Som.* i. 513.
51 Ibid. v. 193; P.R.O., C 142/159, no. 60.
52 *V.C.H. Som.* i. 513.
53 *Red Bk. Exch.* (Rolls Ser.), i. 231.
54 *Pipe R.* 1198 (P.R.S. N.S. ix), 222; *Pipe R.* 1208 (P.R.S. N.S. xxiii), 104.
55 *S.R.S.* xli. 49.
56 *Feud. Aids*, iv. 293; *S.R.S.* vi. 284; S.R.O., DD/S/CR 1.
57 *Feud. Aids*, iv. 301, 331; S.R.O., DD/S/CR 1.
58 *S.R.S.* i. 233; lxviii, p. 29.
59 *Feud. Aids*, iv. 345; S.R.O., DD/S/CR 1.
60 *S.R.S.* xvii. 102; S.R.O., DD/S/CR 1.
61 *S.R.S.* xvii. 119.
62 S.R.O., DD/S/CR 1.
63 *Feud. Aids*, iv. 370; S.R.O., DD/S/CR 1.
64 S.R.O., DD/S/CR 1.
65 *Feud. Aids*, iv. 439.
66 P.R.O., C 139/74, no. 22.
67 S.R.O., DD/S/CR 1; P.R.O., C 139/88, no. 49.
68 S.R.O., DD/S/CR 1; *S.R.S.* xxii. 90; P.R.O., C 141/3, no. 29.

69 P.R.O., C 142/67, no. 116.
70 Ibid. C 142/159, no. 60.
71 S.R.O., D/P/gst 2/1/1.
72 P.R.O., C 3/362/15.
73 S.R.O., DD/S/WH 114; D/P/gst 2/1/1; *S.R.S.* li, p. 247.
74 S.R.O., DD/X/SR 5; *Som. Wills*, ed. Brown, vi. 97.
75 S.R.O., D/P/gst 2/1/2.
76 Below, this section.
77 P.R.O., CP 25(2)/592/1653 Trin.
78 Below, N. Petherton, manors; S.R.O., DD/S/WH 266; ibid. tithe award.
79 S.R.O., DD/BR/pa 1; ibid. Q/REl 2/6.
80 Ibid. D/P/gst 2/1/2; P.R.O., CP 25(2)/480/16 Chas. I East.
81 S.R.O., DD/S/WH 266.
82 Ibid. DD/RN 30; *Proc. Dors. Arch. Soc.* lxiv. 56–68; below.
83 *Som. Wills*, ed. Brown, iii. 121; S.R.O., DD/S/WH 25.
84 S.R.O., DD/RN 24.
85 Ibid. DD/S/WH 25, 34–5, 39; DD/RN 25.
86 Ibid. DD/S/WH 114.
87 Ibid. DD/RN 24; DD/S/WH 25; Dwelly, *Hearth Tax*, i. 42.

Charles Kemeys-Tynte in 1753 it was leased to John Buncombe for three years.[88] John died *c.* 1756 and the house, described as the mansion house or the court house, was occupied by the estate steward and his widow until *c.* 1810.[89] In 1811 it became the rectory house.[90] In the later 20th century it was divided into two dwellings known as Dower House and Church Close.

In the 17th century the house appears to have had a central range of one storey with two-storeyed projecting cross wings. The central range has a coved plaster ceiling with a projecting cornice moulding and the elaborate arms of the Paulet family. A two-storeyed block was built between

1086 Wido held it of Roger.[96] Peter of Halswell, who successfully claimed in 1280 to be heir to Ralph son of Robert (d. by 1242–3), in 1285 held Halswell for ¼ knight's fee.[97] In 1303 William of Halswell held ⅛ knight's fee[98] and had land in Halswell in 1314 and 1327.[99] He or a namesake died between 1329[1] and 1346, and another William Halswell was recorded in 1394 and may have held the fee in 1428.[2] Thereafter the descent is obscure but both John and Robert Halswell were recorded in the early 15th century and another Robert later in the century was said to be father of John whose son Nicholas held the manor on his death in 1564.[3] Nicholas's widow

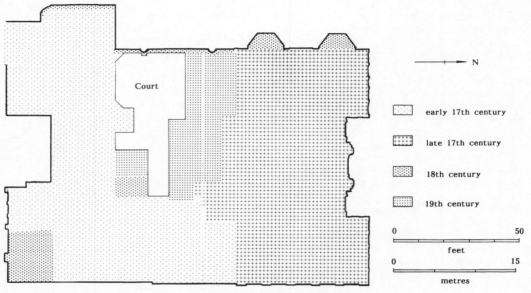

Court

→ N

early 17th century

late 17th century

18th century

19th century

0	50
feet	
0	15
metres	

PLAN OF HALSWELL

the projections of the cross wings in the 18th century. The northern cross wing was demolished in 1871 when the house was remodelled to designs by C. Knowles of Bridgwater. He left part of the south cross wing and adjacent, possibly 18th-century, service rooms but rebuilt and extended the wing westward to make a new staircase and other rooms.[91]

Roger Arundel held *HALSWELL* in 1086[92] and the overlordship descended with that of Huish Champflower to Henry de Newburgh.[93] Henry gave a mesne tenancy to Taunton priory, which was recorded only in 1285.[94] In 1565 and 1633 the manor was said to be held as of Goathurst.[95]

Alweard occupied Halswell in 1066, and in

Margery held Halswell until her death in 1573 when she was succeeded by Sir Nicholas, son of her son Robert (d. 1570).[4] Sir Nicholas (d. 1633) conveyed Halswell to his eldest surviving son Henry in 1628.[5] Henry died unmarried in 1636 and was followed by his only surviving brother the Revd. Hugh Halswell.[6] Hugh (d. 1672) appears to have settled Halswell on his daughter Jane (d. 1650), who married John Tynte, and in 1667 the manor was put in trust for her son Halswell Tynte.[7] Halswell (cr. Bt. 1673) died in 1702 and was succeeded by his eldest surviving son Sir John (d. 1710)[8] who was followed in turn by his sons Sir Halswell (d. 1730), the Revd. Sir John (d. 1740), and Sir Charles (d. 1785), and by his daughter's child Jane Hassell, wife of John

88 S.R.O., DD/S/WH 25, 198.
89 Ibid. 144, 248, 266.
90 Ibid. 266; DD/RN 64.
91 Ibid. D/D/Bbm 189; plans in possession of Mrs. D. Woods, Church Close.
92 *V.C.H. Som.* i. 495.
93 Ibid. v. 83; *Feud. Aids,* iv. 293.
94 *Cal. Chart. R.* 1327–41, 316; *Feud. Aids,* iv. 293.
95 P.R.O., C 142/141, no. 18; Halswell extent in possession of Miss B. Harris.
96 *V.C.H. Som.* i. 495.
97 *S.R.S.* xi, p. 155; xliv. 115; *Cal. Chart. R.* 1327–41, 316; *Feud. Aids,* iv. 293.
98 *Feud. Aids,* iv. 301.

99 *S.R.S.* iii. 164; xii. 43.   1 *Cal. Inq. p.m.* v, p. 126.
2 *Feud. Aids,* iv. 345, 370; S.R.O., DD/S/WH 5.
3 *S.R.S.* lviii, pp. 22, 92; S.R.O., DD/S/WH cat.; P.R.O., C 142/141, no. 18.
4 P.R.O., C 142/154, no. 86; S.R.O., DD/X/SR 5; D/P/gst 2/1/1.
5 S.R.O., D/P/gst 2/1/2; P.R.O., C 142/475, no. 96; *S.R.S.* li, p. 248.
6 *Som. Wills,* ed. Brown, vi. 94; P.R.O., C 3/399/182; C 142/492, no. 121.
7 *Som. Wills,* ed. Brown, vi. 95; S.R.O., DD/S/WH 268; DD/SAS (C/63) 8; D/P/gst 2/1/2.
8 *S.R.S.* extra ser. 45–6, 293–4; *Som. Wills,* ed. Brown, vi. 93.

Johnson. Johnson took the name Kemeys-Tynte on his wife's succession. From Jane (d. 1825) the estate passed in the direct male line to Charles Kemeys (d. 1860), Charles John (d. 1882), Charles Kemeys (d. 1891), Halswell Milborne (d. 1899), and Charles T. H. Kemeys-Tynte, in whose favour the barony of Wharton was revived in 1916. Lord Wharton was succeeded in 1934 by his son Charles J. H. Kemeys-Tynte, but he had vested the estate in Hoare's Bank which sold it in 1950 and it was broken up.[9] Lord Wharton was described as lord of the manor in 1939 but there is no further record of the lordship.[10]

Halswell Court was mentioned in 1318 when an oratory was licensed there.[11] Comprising north, east, and south ranges around three sides of a courtyard, it is of rubble, in places rendered, with the north front of ashlar. Probably the central part of the east range was by the mid 17th century the main range of a house which had wings running westwards from both ends and possibly a west range, which is suggested by the cellars beneath the later service court. Building is known to have been undertaken c. 1536[12] and lias, freestone, and tile were brought by sea through Bridgwater between 1595 and 1610.[13] The east, south, and part of the north ranges of the early 17th-century house survive, but the remainder of the north range was replaced in 1689[14] by a block containing the principal rooms, possibly designed by William Taylor of London.[15] The block has a north front of three storeys and seven bays. The three central bays are recessed and the window surrounds and doorcase are in baroque style. The principal staircase has a moulded string and twisted balusters, the secondary stair has heavy turned balusters and ball finials on the newels. Many of the ceilings have coved cornices and ornate plasterwork.[16]

In the mid 18th century, probably in 1754 to designs by Francis Cartwright of Blandford,[17] alterations were made to the west front. Canted bays were added to the ground floor of the block of 1689 and a tall screen of rendered brick with ornamental niches was built across the service court. Both court and house were given heavily rusticated doorways. The presumed western range of the earlier house may have been demolished then. During the 18th century a brick-cased staircase was added in the south-east corner of the court and rooms on the first floor of the east wing were panelled and re-fenestrated.[18] A servants' hall was built in the court in 1771[19] and other minor intrusions were made in the court in the 19th century.

In 1923 the house was severely damaged by fire. The block of 1689 was completely gutted and one outer wall collapsed.[20] It was rebuilt in 1924–6 under the direction of George and T. S.

Vickery of London,[21] the principal rooms in much the same form as before the fire except that Chinese wallpaper was used in the former chintz room. At about the same time mullioned windows replaced sashes in the older parts of the house. The house was converted into flats in the 1950s; some rooms were divided, but most of them were later reunited.

Extensive 18th-century outbuildings include a symmetrical stable block with gabled cross wings in brick and a castellated central gateway in stone. Facing it is a brick riding school, possibly designed by John Johnson c. 1770,[22] behind which is a 17th-century circular pigeon house of rubble with a bell-shaped roof. To the north a stepped pyramid was built in the 1740s to cover the main water supply for the house.

The stream ran east of the house, and probably in the later 17th century it was used to create a straight-sided canal beside the house. A formal parterre with terraces, known as the Lawn, was laid out in front of the new north range. Other features of the formal design included a triple gateway leading to a straight wide avenue to the west and other walled enclosures, and two pavilions, one perhaps facing down a walk beside the canal.[23] The layout, probably put in hand by Sir Halswell (d. 1702) or his son Sir John (d. 1710), was converted to a 'natural' landscape by Sir Charles Kemeys-Tynte who inherited in 1740. By 1756[24] the canal had become a gently curving lake bridged towards its southern end and dammed at its northern, the water flowing into a circular pool below the dam. The dam was faced with an arched rustic screen presumably to match the rockwork grotto built at the head of the lake in 1753. The formal terrace was reduced in size in 1769.[25] The circular pond was filled in before 1842 but the gardens beside the house remained a mixture of formal and informal planting until the mid 20th century.

St. John's hospital, Bridgwater had a holding called Playfield by 1362 and another elsewhere in the parish.[26]

ECONOMIC HISTORY. Goathurst manor in 1086 had 6 ploughlands and some woodland; neither meadow nor pasture were recorded although the demesne estate, which had a third of the arable and was worked by 4 *servi*, had 9 cattle, 10 sheep, 60 pigs, and 16 goats. Halswell was smaller with only 2 ploughlands, half in demesne with 2 *servi*, and some woodland; again no pasture nor meadow was recorded although 2 cattle and 10 sheep were on the demesne. All but 5 of the 23 tenants (15 *villani*, 8 bordars) were on Goathurst manor.[27]

Goathurst was taxed at only 9s. 6d. in 1327, less than half the total of Huntstile, and seven

9 Burke, *Peerage* (1949), 2119; S.R.O., DD/HR 10.
10 *Kelly's Dir. Som.* (1939).
11 *S.R.S.* i. 17.
12 S.R.O., DD/S/WH 91.
13 Ibid. D/B/bw 1480, 1487–9, 1491, 1494.
14 Date cut in stone above central window.
15 H. M. Colvin, *Biog. Dict. of Brit. Architects, 1600–1840* (1978), 819.
16 *Country Life*, 21 Nov. 1908.
17 Ibid. 9 Feb. 1989, 85.

18 S.R.O., DD/S/WH 253–5, 259–61.
19 Ibid. T/PH/vch 73.
20 *Som. Co. Gaz.* 3, 10 Nov. 1923.
21 Plaque on house; agreement in possession of Mrs. J. Silby, Goathurst; for a photo., below, plate facing p. 137.
22 *Country Life*, 9 Feb. 1989, 87.   23 Ibid. 82.
24 S.R.O., DD/X/DT 1.   25 Ibid. T/PH/vch 73.
26 P.R.O., SC 6/Hen. VIII/3137; *L. & P. Hen. VIII*, xix (2), p. 313; xx, p. 125; S.R.O., DD/S/WH 5, 16.
27 *V.C.H. Som.* i. 495, 513.

people out of nine paid the minimum tax. William of Halswell was assessed at ⌐s.[28] The Halswell demesne in 1597 consisted of a large number of small fields including oat and rye closes, meadow, orchard, a hopyard, and woodland.[29] Holdings were small in the 17th century,[30] and inventories show a high level of stock keeping but only small acreages under corn.[31] William Hite, rector (d. 1689), had cattle worth over £85 as well as horses, pigs, hay, and corn. He produced cider, cheese, and bacon.[32] Livestock continued to dominate inventories in the 18th century, and clover was recorded.[33]

The acquisition of parts of Goathurst manor by the Halswells from 1730 onwards and the expansion of the park from the 1740s led to changes in the balance of agriculture in the parish and to the reorganization of tenant holdings. The demesne farm in the early 18th century had surplus pigs, sheep, horses, and oxen for sale, and a dairy was maintained.[34] Cider was produced and a nursery garden established.[35] By the end of the century a wide variety of exotic fruit was grown in the hothouses.[36] In the 1760s, however, the home farm was not large enough to support the house, and barley for malting, oats, peas, and straw were bought in. At the same time timber on the estate was valued at £600 and rents from tenants produced £1,400.[37]

In the 1750s some farms on Goathurst manor were let at rack rents after enlargement, and a similar plan was proposed for Halswell.[38] By 1756 there were seven farms with over 50 a. in the parish, excluding the demesne holding, some tenants having more than one farm, while many small holdings survived.[39] In 1846 the largest tenant holding was 155 a., four others were over 100 a., and a further four over 50 a.[40] Wheat, oats, clover, potatoes, and 5 a. of flax were subject to tithe in 1789.[41] In 1846 arable (579 a.) and grass (571 a.) were nearly equal in area. By 1905 the area under grass had much increased.[42] In 1982 there were at least four dairy farms, but arable had increased in importance through the conversion of much of the park. Grassland accounted for 266 ha. (657 a.) of the enlarged parish and arable for 221 ha. (546 a.). At least two farms were over 100 ha. (247 a.).[43]

A cooper combined a workshop with farming in the mid 17th century.[44] There was a smithy

in the village and the blacksmith in 1684 had 1,262 lb. of new and old iron besides 98 lb. of spikes and nails.[45] In 1831 trade and manufacture supported 15 out of 58 families[46] and in 1851 there were a draper and grocer and a poulterer in the parish.[47] Other 19th-century occupations included a music teacher and fishmonger in 1861 and a basketmaker and threshing machine proprietor in 1881.[48] Large numbers of people worked on the Halswell estate: Lady Tynte employed 20 servants in 1787,[49] and there were 20 indoor servants in 1841.[50] During the 19th century estate workers included gamekeepers, gardeners, a lodgekeeper, bailiffs, a clerk of works, and a steward.[51]

MILLS. There was a mill on the Halswell estate in 1314[52] which was last recorded in 1597.[53] It may have stood on the stream west of Halswell House where a series of ponds was later made in Mill Wood.[54] Ely Mill on Goathurst manor was recorded in 1556.[55] There was a water mill on the manor in the 18th century but in 1780 it was decided not to let it and it was later taken down.[56] It may have stood north of the church.[57]

LOCAL GOVERNMENT. Goathurst parish normally formed a single tithing which was linked in 1569 with Durleigh, Huntstile, and four other places and in 1641 with Huntstile.[58] In the 1270s Roger of Goathurst claimed gallows, assize of ale (but not of bread), and waifs and strays.[59] Rolls and books for Goathurst manor court, held once or twice a year, for 1493–4, 1502–4, and 1556–60 record breaches of the assize of ale, strays, repairs, and tenants' pleas.[60] In 1676 the manor claimed money for harvest work as well as suit of court from a tenant.[61] Books for Halswell manor courts survive for 1556–64 and 1611. The court was held once or twice a year and was concerned with repairs and strays.[62] There was a pound at Andersfield in 1887.[63]

In the early 17th century the overseers gave relief mainly in cash and clothing.[64] The highway surveyors collected money in lieu of statute labour by 1756 but repairs seem to have been organized by Sir Charles Kemeys-Tynte's steward, who was paid by the surveyors. From 1762

28 *S.R.S.* iii. 164.
29 S.R.O., DD/S/WH 242.
30 Ibid. DD/S/BW 5.
31 Ibid. DD/SP inventories, 1648, 1677, 1683–4, 1692.
32 Ibid. 1688.
33 Ibid. 1734; MS. tithe receipts in possession of Miss B. Harris.
34 S.R.O., DD/S/WH 252, 254, 258; DD/X/TCR 4.
35 Ibid. DD/S/WH 34, 258; DD/SP inventory, 1721; MS. tithe receipts in possession of Miss B. Harris.
36 S.R.O., DD/S/WH 267.
37 Ibid. 262, 269.
38 Ibid. 25, 269.
39 Ibid. 248.
40 Ibid. tithe award.   41 Ibid. D/P/gst 3/2/2.
42 Ibid. tithe award; statistics supplied by the then Bd. of Agric., 1905.
43 Min. of Agric., Fisheries, and Food, agric. returns, 1982.
44 S.R.O., DD/S/WH 146; DD/SP inventory, 1683.
45 Ibid. DD/SP inventory, 1684.

46 Ibid. D/P/gst 23/5.   47 P.R.O., HO 107/1924.
48 Ibid. RG 9/1622; RG 11/2373.
49 S.R.O., DD/X/TCR 4.
50 P.R.O., HO 107/929.
51 Ibid. HO 107/1924; ibid. RG 9/1622; RG 10/2383; RG 11/2372; *Kelly's Dir. Som.* (1894).
52 *S.R.S.* xii. 43.
53 S.R.O., DD/S/WH 210, 242.
54 Ibid. tithe award.
55 Ibid. DD/S/WH 210.
56 Ibid. 25, 147, 225, 248.
57 Ibid. tithe award.
58 *S.R.S.* iii. 164; xx. 243; *Som. Protestation Returns*, ed. Howard and Stoate, 186.
59 *Rot. Hund.* (Rec. Com.), ii. 126; *Plac. de Quo Warr.* (Rec. Com.), 693.
60 S.R.O., DD/X/ELT 1–2; DD/S/WH 210.
61 Ibid. DD/S/WH 147.
62 Ibid. 210–11.
63 O.S. Map 6", Som. LXI. NW. (1887 edn.).
64 S.R.O., D/P/gst 4/4/1.

the surveyors were arranging the repairs and in 1786 financial difficulties led to a decision to levy a rate.[65]

A poorhouse, recorded c. 1705 and belonging to Goathurst manor, may have been the former church house.[66] It lay on the south side of the churchyard at the west end of the village street. It was let as a private dwelling in 1729, and after 1756 a second house was built in its garden. The poorhouse was probably demolished in 1780. It was replaced by a new poorhouse on the site of the second house, which Sir Charles Kemeys-Tynte let to the parish at a nominal rent.[67] During the 19th and early 20th centuries it housed old people and poor families and was sometimes known as the almshouse.[68] It appears to have been sold c. 1953[69] and was divided into two private dwellings known as Dorford House and the Almonry. The two-storeyed, seven-bayed house was built in the Gothick style with Y-traceried windows. Over the original ogee-headed entrance is a dated panel recording that Sir Charles provided the house.

The parish became part of the Bridgwater poor-law union in 1836, Bridgwater rural district from 1894, and Sedgemoor district from 1974.[70]

CHURCH. A church was recorded in 1266.[71] The benefice was a sole rectory until 1956 when it was united with Enmore. Since 1981 it has also been united with Spaxton and Charlinch.[72]

The advowson was held with Goathurst manor from 1321 or earlier.[73] Following the division of the manor in the early 17th century the advowson was held jointly, the husbands and sons of the co-heirs presenting together in 1660 and 1662.[74] From c. 1664 the holders of each quarter of the manor were entitled to present in turn.[75] The Tyntes acquired all four shares, that of Paulet Payne in 1678 by lease, that of the Braggs in 1730, and those of the Buncombes in 1753, both by purchase. In 1845 Charles Kemeys Kemeys-Tynte bought the reversionary interest of the Paynes to acquire the sole right of presentation.[76] The advowson descended with Halswell and remained vested in trustees for Hoare's Bank until 1981, when they apparently ceded their right on the creation of the united benefice, whose joint patrons in 1991 were the bishop, the Martyrs Memorial Trust, and the Church Trust Fund.[77]

The church was valued at £10 3s. 7d. gross in 1535[78] and was said to be worth about £80 c.

1668.[79] In 1810 the rectory was valued at over £316 gross and average annual income 1829–31 was £412.[80] In the 18th century some tithes were paid in cash and in 1789 it was said that the previous rector had agreed on a composition in cash. After a dispute cash payments were resumed in the 1790s.[81] In 1846 moduses were payable for some small tithes until all the tithes were commuted for £235.[82]

The glebe lands were valued at £3 4s. in 1535.[83] In 1606 the glebe consisted of a house with a new barn, orchards, gardens, a hopyard, and 81 a., half together near the house and the rest scattered across the parish.[84] In 1755 and 1811 substantial exchanges were made with the Halswell estate and in 1846 there were 62½ a. of glebe mainly at Andersfield and north of the church.[85] It remained church land in 1978.[86]

In 1603 the rector was said to be building a new parsonage house but probably completed only a barn and outbuildings. The house in 1606 comprised a hall with open roof, parlour, buttery, and milkhouse, with study and chambers over them and a separate kitchen.[87] By 1612 the hall had been ceiled to provide another chamber.[88] Major work was carried out in the 1740s including new doors, windows, floors, and ceilings.[89] By 1809, however, the house was said to be both in ruins and dismantled. In 1811 it was exchanged for Goathurst manor house.[90] The former parsonage house was later divided into three cottages now known as nos. 1–3 Old Rectory. About 1957 a new house, east of the former manor house, was provided. It was sold after the benefice was united with Spaxton in 1981.

A chantry in the patronage of John Popham of Huntworth was recorded in 1352[91] but no further reference to it has been found. There was also an anniversary, possibly founded by William Paulet of Beere, of which the endowment was sold to Nicholas Halswell in 1550[92] but was later claimed to have been concealed.[93] A fraternity had been formed by 1530.[94] The churchwardens had an income from church ales, lands, and gifts.[95]

Richard Martin, rector 1603–13, a pluralist, was frequently accused of neglecting his duties.[96] John Bragg was resident rector from 1613 until his death in 1651; his successor Thomas Blanchflower was confirmed in the living in 1660.[97] In the time of James Minifie, who succeeded his father as rector in 1768, there were generally more than 40 communicants.[98] He was followed

65 Ibid. D/PM/gst 6/1/2.
66 Ibid. DD/S/WH 25.
67 Ibid. 56, 147, 225, 248.
68 P.R.O., HO 107/929; ibid. RG 9/1622; RG 11/2372; S.R.O., D/R/bw 13/1/3.
69 S.R.O., DD/X/GST (S/1372).
70 Youngs, *Local Admin. Units*, i. 671, 673, 676.
71 *S.R.S.* xiii. 10–11.
72 S.R.O., D/P/car 23/8; *Dioc. Dir.*
73 *S.R.S.* i. 190; above, manors.
74 S.R.O., DD/S/WH 266.
75 Dors. R.O., D 104/M 2; S.R.O., DD/S/WH 266.
76 S.R.O., DD/S/WH 25, 266.
77 Above, manors; *Dioc. Dir.*
78 *Valor Eccl.* (Rec. Com.), i. 215–16.
79 S.R.O., D/D/Vc 24.
80 Ibid. DD/S/WH 266; *Rep. Com. Eccl. Revenues*, pp. 138–9.

81 S.R.O., DD/S/WH 266; D/P/gst 3/2/2.
82 Ibid. tithe award.
83 *Valor Eccl.* (Rec. Com.), i. 215–16.
84 S.R.O., D/D/Rg 271.
85 Ibid. DD/S/WH 266; ibid. tithe award.
86 Inf. from Dioc. Office.
87 S.R.O., D/D/Ca 134; D/D/Rg 271.
88 Ibid. D/P/gst 3/1/1.
89 Ibid. DD/S/WH 258/1–2.
90 Ibid. 266; above, manors.   91 *S.R.S.* x, p. 701.
92 *Cal. Pat.* 1549–51, 274; S.R.O., DD/S/CR 1; DD/S/WH 15.
93 *Cal. Pat.* 1572–5, p. 409; *S.R.S.* lxxvii, p. 110.
94 *Wells Wills*, ed. Weaver, 89.
95 S.R.O., D/P/gst 4/4/1.
96 Ibid. D/D/Ca 134, 160, 175.
97 Ibid. D/P/gst 2/1/2; DD/S/WH 266.
98 Ibid. D/D/B reg. 28, f. 63v.; D/D/Vc 88.

by Henry Parsons, 1789–1845, resident in the parish, curate of Durleigh, and later also rector of Wembdon, who held two Sunday services at Goathurst.[99] He was succeeded by his son Francis Crane Parsons, rector 1845–71.[1]

A church house was rented by the wardens from Goathurst manor before 1550. It may later have been used as a poorhouse.[2]

The church of ST. EDWARD, so dedicated by 1559,[3] is built of rubble with ashlar dressings and comprises a chancel with north aisle, a nave with south transept and porch, and a west tower. The proportions of the nave suggest a date earlier than the oldest feature, a 14th-century piscina in the chancel; the doorways and windows are all of the 15th and 16th centuries. The transept was probably added in the late 15th or early 16th century and the north aisle in 1559 when, following a dispute between the lords of Halswell and Goathurst manors, it was agreed that the south transept belonged to Goathurst and that Nicholas Halswell should build an aisle north of the chancel.[4] The aisle contains Halswell and Tynte family monuments from the 17th to the 19th century. In 1424 William Paulet of Beere bequeathed money for the tower, which dates from this period, and three bells.[5] The western doorway was put into the tower in the 16th century. The church was damaged in the great storm of 1703. There was a gallery by 1707.[6] In 1758 a pew was built for Sir Charles Kemeys-Tynte in the south transept following his purchase of half the manor and advowson of Goathurst.[7] The ceiling of the transept was decorated c. 1830 in Gothick style. In 1884 the church was restored by J. Houghton Spencer. The gallery and a wall between the Halswell aisle and the chancel were removed, and the chancel arch was renewed with Decorated mouldings. Carved bosses were fitted to the roof and the tower was given a parapet.[8]

The 15th-century font and rood stair survive. There is an early 17th-century pulpit with an early 18th-century tester. Painted panels under the tower may have come from the former gallery and there are also several hatchments for the Tyntes. There are monuments to members of the Halswell and Tynte families by J. M. Rysbrack, Joseph Nollekens, and Raffaele Monti.

Five of the bells were cast at Gloucester in 1705 or 1706, possibly after storm damage to the belfry. The sixth was recast in 1783.[9] The 18th-century church plate given by the Tyntes includes two communion cups of 1729 by James Wilkes.[10] The registers date from 1539 and are complete.[11]

A socket stone for a medieval cross survives in the churchyard. The site of a chapel was mentioned in 1494 and 1502 but has not been located.[12]

NONCONFORMITY. None known.

EDUCATION. In 1819 a school for 25 or 30 children was supported out of the sacrament money and voluntary contributions.[13] By 1825 the school taught 38 children and parents paid 1d. a week.[14] By 1835 numbers had increased to 59[15] but fell to 30 in 1846; a further 12 attended on Sundays. From 1844 the school was supported by an endowment of land at Chilton Polden.[16] A National school, in existence in 1872, was rebuilt in 1876 and in 1903 had 45 children on the books.[17] Numbers fell to 30 in 1925, 15 in 1935, and 9 in 1952 when the school was closed.[18] In 1982 it was a private house named Old School House.

CHARITIES FOR THE POOR. Sir Charles Kemeys-Tynte, Dame Anne Tynte, and Jane Busby by their wills dated 1776, 1794, and 1798 respectively left a total of £600 to the poor. In 1837 the money was invested in land in North Petherton parish, some of which was sold in 1981. The income was distributed in cloth and came to be known as the dowlais charity. Mary Escott, by a codicil dated 1809, gave £100 for lying-in women, to provide a nurse for two weeks after confinement, and to keep up the stock of linen she had previously provided. By the 20th century the income was distributed to elderly women and a baptismal grant was paid to mothers.[19] John Jeanes c. 1831 and James Culverwell by will proved 1867 each gave £100 to the poor and Louisa Campbell gave £300, by will proved 1872. The income from those gifts was distributed in bread and coal until the 1940s or later.[20] All the above charities and the proceeds from the sale of the poor house were combined in a scheme of 1974 to form the Goathurst Relief in Need charity. The income, from land at Hedging in North Petherton and the interest on £1,468 in consolidated stock, is distributed when required.[21]

Richard Escott and Mary Jeane by their wills dated 1784 and 1785 respectively gave a total of £125 to provide the poor with bread. The money was in the hands of a churchwarden and was lost when he went bankrupt before 1866.[22] In 1866 the vestry decided that half the income from parish property in Bridgwater should be given to the poor.[23] The estate, known as Timberlakes garden, was later sold and the money invested for the benefit of the parish.[24]

99 S.R.O., D/D/Rb 1815; D/D/Vc 88; ibid. T/PH/ay 1; *Rep. Com. Eccl. Revenues*, pp. 138–9.
1 P.R.O., HO 107/929; HO 107/1622; S.R.O., DD/S/WH 266; D/P/gst 4/1/2.
2 S.R.O., D/P/gst 4/4/1; above, local govt.
3 S.R.O., DD/RN 91.   4 Ibid.
5 Ibid. DD/S/CR 1.   6 Ibid. D/P/gst 4/1/1.
7 Ibid. 2/1/4; above, manors.
8 S.R.O., D/P/gst 8/3/1, 8/4/1.
9 Ibid. DD/SAS CH 16/1 (has 1705); R. D. Ansdell, *St. Edward's Ch., Goathurst* (1982).
10 *Proc. Som. Arch. Soc.* xlvii. 159.
11 S.R.O., D/P/gst 2/1/1–8.   12 Ibid. DD/X/ELT 1–2.
13 *Educ. of Poor Digest*, p. 784.

14 *Ann. Rep. B. & W. Dioc. Assoc. S.P.C.K.* (1825–6), 42.   15 *Educ. Enq. Abstract*, p. 806.
16 Nat. Soc. *Inquiry, 1846–7*, Som. 10–11; S.R.O., DD/X/GST (S/1372).
17 S.R.O., C/E 4/380/182; Morris & Co. *Dir. Som.* (1872).
18 S.R.O., C/E 4/64, 186.
19 *15th Rep. Com. Char.* 345–6; S.R.O., DD/X/GST (S/1372).   20 S.R.O., DD/X/GST (S/1372).
21 Ibid.; above, local govt.
22 *15th Rep. Com. Char.* 345–6; S.R.O., D/P/gst 23/3; inf. from Mr. R. Thomae, Goathurst, clerk to chars.
23 S.R.O., D/P/gst 4/1/2, 5/1/1.
24 Ibid. DD/RN 64; Char. Com. reg.; inf. from Mr. Thomae.

LYNG

THE ancient parish of Lyng included a Saxon *burh* now occupied by East Lyng village, the 'island' of Athelney with its Alfredian monastic foundation and stronghold, and the detached settlement of Burrow, a possible defensive outpost of Athelney abbey.[25] The name Lyng derives from the Old English *hlenc*, meaning a hill; Athelney means 'the island of the princes'.[26]

The parish occupies a ridge *c.* 3 km. long which protrudes north-eastwards as an extension of the Quantocks into the moors of the Parrett basin between North Petherton to the north and North Curry and Stoke St. Gregory to the south. East from the end of the Lyng ridge and attached to it by a causeway lies Athelney hill, where Athelney abbey stood east of the Alfredian fortress.[27] The monument to Alfred on the eastern end of the hill was erected by John Slade in 1801.[28] Just over 1 km. further north-east on the east bank of the Parrett and formerly a detached part of Lyng parish is Burrow, named after Burrow Mump or Mount,[29] a rocky outcrop forming a flat-topped hill with a ruined chapel on its summit.[30] The hamlet below the hill, formerly known as Burrow, was called Burrowbridge by the early 19th century after the bridge there.[31] A smaller detached part of the parish, lying 0.5 km. north-west of Burrow on the west bank of the Parrett in Salt moor[32] and including 2 houses and 8 persons, was in 1885 transferred to Stoke St. Gregory. In 1886 Burrowbridge (14 a., 8 houses, and 44 persons) was transferred to Othery. In 1882 uninhabited parts of North moor, including a large triangular area north of East Lyng village, had been transferred to Lyng parish from North Petherton, and a detached part of Lyng parish had been added to North Petherton; in 1888 Priestwood, formerly in Durston parish, was also added to Lyng.[33] In 1981 the parish measured 592 ha. (1,463 a.).[34]

The ridge which forms the thin spine of the parish is made up of Keuper marl with two pockets of valley gravel.[35] At its western end, where clay was dug in the 19th century for brickmaking,[36] the ridge reaches just over 30 m. in height and is nearly 1 km. wide; further east it falls and narrows, and beyond East Lyng village it ends abruptly at the 7-m. contour.

Burrow Mump, also of Keuper marl, reaches 31 m.

The boundary described in the perambulation of Lyng attached to a charter of 937 has not been identified on the ground, but does not seem to coincide with the later parish boundary.[37] The southern boundary is now in part the Old Rhyne, the eastern end of which is probably the former course of the West Yeo,[38] that branch of the Tone which flowed between East Lyng and Athelney. The boundary further east follows the Baltmoor wall built *c.* 1154 presumably to prevent flooding in Higher Salt moor to the north.[39] The wall was faced in stone in 1675.[40] The boundary with North Petherton in the north, agreed *c.* 1204,[41] follows man-made watercourses in North moor. Burrow was bounded on the west by the Parrett and on the north and east by the former course of the river Cary.[42]

Settlement has been confined since earliest times to those areas above the flood plain. Two bronze palstaves and a Roman bronze mask were found on Athelney island, and several sherds of Romano-British pottery were discovered at the foot of Burrow Mump.[43] Permanent settlement was established in the later 9th century. In 878 King Alfred built a stronghold on Athelney island when it was still 'surrounded on all sides by very great swampy and impassable marshes',[44] the fortress probably sited at its western end. To complement that fortress, another was later built, probably before 893, at the eastern end of the Lyng ridge, the two joined across the river then flowing between them by a bridge 'made with laborious skill'. The second fortress, 'very strong' and 'of most beautiful workmanship', has been convincingly identified as the compact settlement of East Lyng, where traces of a defensive bank and ditch west of the village coincide with reasonable accuracy with the dimensions of a *burh* listed in the Burghal Hidage.[45] At the eastern end of Athelney island King Alfred established a monastery *c.* 888, possibly in succession to a hermitage.[46] The monastery, possibly refounded *c.* 960 after destruction in Danish raids, was dissolved in 1539.[47]

The charter of 937 described the estate west of the 'town', an estate later known as West Lyng manor.[48] By the 17th century four settlements were named in the main part of the parish: East

[25] Ekwall, *Eng. Place-Names* (1960), 310. This article was completed in 1985.
[26] Ekwall, *Eng. Place-Names*, 18.
[27] Below.
[28] S.R.O., DD/SLM 14; *Proc. Som. Arch. Soc.* cxxix. 19–20.
[29] *V.C.H. Som.* ii. 499. The name King Alfred's Fort is not substantiated.
[30] M. Williams, *Draining of the Som. Levels* (1970), 53–4, 146–8; National Trust, *Guide*.
[31] *S.R.S.* lxxvi (Greenwood's map, 1822).
[32] S.R.O., Stoke St. Gregory tithe map.
[33] *Census*, 1891; 48–9 Vic. c. 6 (Local); 50–1 Vic. c. 59 (Local). [34] *Census*, 1981.
[35] Geol. Surv. Map 1", drift, sheet 295 (1956 edn.); S.R.O., DD/SAS SE 113, p. 23 for marine and other faunal remains found in 1826.
[36] O.S. Map 6", Som. LXXI. NE. (1888 edn.).
[37] H. P. R. Finberg, *Early Charters of Wessex*, pp. 130–1.

[38] P.R.O., E 134/33 & 34 Eliz. I Mich./23.
[39] *Reg. Regum Anglo-Norm.* iii, no. 28; *S.R.S.* xiv, p. 168; M. Williams, *Draining of the Som. Levels*, 59–60.
[40] *S.R.S.* xxxiv. 183–4.
[41] *Pipe R.* 1204 (P.R.S. N.S. xviii), 135.
[42] *Draining of Som. Levels*, 53–4, 146–8.
[43] *Proc. Som. Arch. Soc.* lxvii, p. lxxv; Som. C.C., Sites and Mons. Rec.; S.R.O., D/D/Bbm 236.
[44] *E.H.D.* i (1979), pp. 196, 299.
[45] Ibid. p. 299; *Proc. Som. Arch. Soc.* cxi. 64–6; cxx. 29–38; A. J. Robertson, *A.-S. Charters*, 246–8.
[46] *V.C.H. Som.* ii. 99; D. Knowles and R. N. Hadcock, *Medieval Religious Hos.* (1971), 59.
[47] *Medieval Religious Hos.* 59; R. W. Dunning, 'The abbey of the Princes: Athelney abbey, Som.', *Kings and Nobles in the later Middle Ages*, ed. R. A. Griffiths and J. Sherborne (1986), 295–303.
[48] Finberg, *Early Charters of Wessex*, pp. 130–1; *S.R.S.* xiv, pp. 155–6, 188; below, manors.

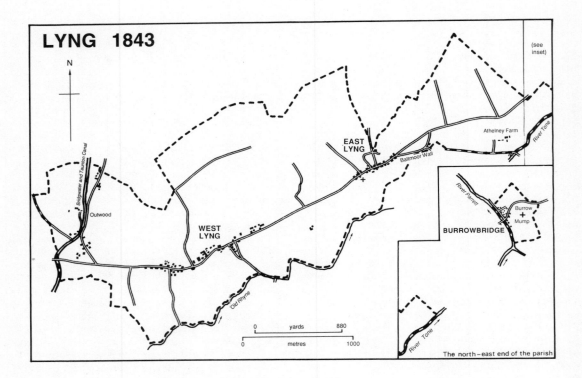

LYNG 1843

The north-east end of the parish

Lyng (so called by 1334),[49] Middleton, and West Lyng all lay along the crest of the ridge, and Outwood in the north-western end of the parish, a scatter of cottages around a green.[50] Outwood may be the 'Prostrat' Lenge' mentioned in 1497,[51] the name either suggesting desertion or referring to its site on ground falling towards North moor and the Durston stream. East and West Lyng in the 20th century were the main settlements, on the Taunton–Wells road, the latter (probably including Middleton) a group of regularly spaced farmhouses, the former school, and local-authority and private houses nearly all on the north side of the road. Outwood expanded with the building of the Bridgwater and Taunton canal and later of the railway and with the exploitation of the brick field.[52] Tenements below Burrow Mump were referred to in the early 16th century,[53] and later included at least two inns in Lyng parish.[54]

The Taunton–Wells road keeps to the crest of the ridge and forms the main route through the parish. Its course until the early 19th century, turnpiked by the Taunton trust from 1752 to 1875, passed through West and East Lyng and then ran along the Baltmoor wall south of Athelney Farm to cross the Tone at Athelney Bridge.[55] A new road was built between 1803 and 1806 across Salt moor from the eastern end of East Lyng village direct to Burrowbridge.[56] Improved alignment there involved a new toll-gate in 1804–5 and a tollhouse c. 1805.[57]

From the central spine, roads or lanes lead north and south into the droves of the moors. At Outwood a lane to Hedging in North Petherton was cut by the Bridgwater and Taunton canal, and was replaced by a footpath beside the later brickfields.[58] Further east Hitchings Drove leads north into the moors of West Lyng. A field lane south from Lyng Court Farm to Curry moor was established by 1427[59] and was later known as Streaked or Streaky Lane.[60] A second southward route from West Lyng to North Curry was planned in 1829 but was not made until c. 1869.[61] The north side of East Lyng village is an irregular rectangle formed by lanes, but only one lane, formerly called the Lane or Lyng Drove Lane, survived in use in 1985 and has recently been called Hector's Lane.[62] It leads to the former demesne lands of Athelney abbey beside Lyng Drove in an area known as Culer or Cular.[63]

The bridge over the Parrett at Burrow consisted until the earlier 19th century of three high arches with cutwaters.[64] It was replaced in 1826 by a wider bridge slightly to the north, designed

49 Cal. Chart. R. 1327–41, 314.
50 S.R.O., D/D/Cd 75; DD/DK 9; P.R.O., SC 12/34, no. 21.
51 Cal. Inq. p.m. Hen. VII, ii, p. 93.
52 Below, econ. hist.
53 P.R.O., SC 6/Hen. VIII/3144.
54 Below, this section.
55 J. B. Bentley and B. J. Murless, Som. Roads, i (1985), 56.
56 S.R.O., D/T/ta 7–8; DD/SAS TN 2/1.
57 Ibid. D/T/ta 7.
58 Ibid. tithe award; ibid. DD/MK, box 14 (map

1838); O.S. Map 6", Som. LXXI. NE. (1888 edn.).
59 H.M.C Wells, i. 329; S.R.S. xiv, pp. 197–9.
60 S.R.O., D/P/lyn 13/1/2; O.S. Map 6", Som. LXXI. NE. (1888 edn.); cf. Stackinge Lane, 1611: S.R.S. xxiii. 57.
61 S.R.O., Q/RUp 98, 106; ibid. D/RA 4/3/23; H. P. Olivey, North Curry (1901), 207–8.
62 Inf. from Mrs. J. I. Palmer, East Lyng.
63 P.R.O., SC 6/Hen. VIII/3144.
64 Collinson, Hist. Som. i. 86; S.R.O., D/RA 9/19, map, 1826.

by P. B. Ilett of Taunton.[65] Tolls, let annually by sand-glass auction, were charged until 1945.[66] New Bridge, rebuilt c. 1876, takes the road over the old course of the river Cary NNE. of Burrow Mump.[67] Athelney bridge, where the former turnpike crossed the Tone south-east of Athelney island, was a two-arched wooden structure in 1791.[68] The present bridge is of concrete. There was a wharf at Athelney bridge in the 18th century[69] and another at Burrowbridge until the mid 19th.[70]

The Bridgwater and Taunton canal, cut through the western edge of the parish at Outwood, was opened in 1827. It ceased to be used commercially after 1892.[71] The Bridgwater–Taunton section of the Bristol and Exeter railway, on a roughly parallel course, was opened in 1842. A branch line from Yeovil entered the parish south of East Lyng village, and at its junction with the main line Durston Junction station was opened in 1853. A loop line avoiding the junction was built further south in 1906 joining the main line at Cogload junction in Durston.[72] Durston Junction station and the original branch line were closed in 1964.[73]

There is no evidence of open-field arable in the parish. The grasslands to the north and north-west of the Lyng ridge were recovered during the Middle Ages from North moor and Higher Salt moor.[74] There were 50 a. of woodland on the estate in 1086,[75] some of which may have been on the northern moor land where timber trunks are still discovered under the pastures.[76] The name Outwood, used by 1543, may represent part of the former woodland including the adjoining Priestwood in Durston. By 1543 there were two areas of wood, Walbarough wood (7 a.) and Conygath copse (6 a.),[77] the latter perhaps recalling the grant of free warren made to the abbot of Athelney c. 1136–9.[78] The inclosed parts of the parish were said c. 1791 to be 'very woody', but by 1905 woodland had been reduced to less than 2 a.[79]

Later 17th-century inventories refer to several houses of two and three-roomed plan, one having a two-storeyed hall with a chamber and buttery 'within' it.[80] Two cottages at Outwood, Half Thatch and Outwood Cottage, remain relatively unaltered from that period. Modernization in 1912 obliterated the three-roomed plan of Council Farm, West Lyng.[81] Church Farm, East

Lyng, remains of traditional plan. A number of substantial houses, including Winchester House, were built in brick in East Lyng village early in the 19th century,[82] and further building took place there in the 1980s.

There were two tipplers in the parish in 1619.[83] A victualler was licensed in 1630 and another in 1660, two in 1657 and 1674, and three in 1675–6. One of the victuallers in 1657 was at Burrow, where in 1686 the inn had 8 beds and stabling for 16 horses.[84] By 1708 an inn called the Anchor or Burrow inn was established at Burrow. By 1797 it was known as the Bell and by 1806 as the King Alfred. The building was modified to accommodate the new turnpike road in that year, and was still in business in 1985.[85] The Lyng inn at East Lyng was so named by 1709 and was renamed the Rose and Crown by 1786. It was in business in 1985 and occupies a building dating from c. 1600.[86] In the mid 18th century there was a third victualler in the parish and in the 1830s two other inns, the White Hart at East Lyng and the King John (possibly later the Bell) at Burrow.[87] There were beer houses at Outwood and West Lyng in 1851 and a beer retailer at Burrowbridge by 1875.[88] The Railway Hotel was established at Durston Junction by 1861[89] and was in business as an inn in 1985.

In 1563 there were 53 households attached to the parish church and 12 to the chapel at Burrow.[90] About 1791 there were 22 houses at West Lyng, 16 at East Lyng, 8 at Outwood, and 18 at Burrow, with a total of c. 340 inhabitants.[91] In 1801 the total was 253. From that date there was a continuous increase until 1851 (the 1841 figure including 40 men working on the railway), and only a small decrease by 1861. Thereafter a slow decline brought the total in 1901 to 327.[92] By 1911 the number had fallen to 285 but from that date it remained roughly stable; between 1971 and 1981 the total rose to 315.[93]

The bridge at Burrow was recognized as of strategic importance during the Civil War, and a fort was built, presumably on the hill above. It was taken from the royalists after the battle of Langport in 1645.[94] In 1685 Lord Feversham secured the Parrett crossing shortly before the battle of Sedgemoor.[95]

St. Ethelwin, brother of King Cenwealh, may have been a hermit on Athelney island.[96] The 'fen fastnesses' there were the refuge of King

[65] S.R.O., Q/AB 31–2; ibid. D/RA 9/19, map; ibid. DD/SAS SE 113, p. 23.
[66] *S.D.N.Q.* xxiv. 193.
[67] S.R.O., Q/AB 15/5, 17.
[68] Collinson, *Hist. Som.* i. 84.
[69] S.R.O., D/P/lyn 4/1/1 (1714, 1738).
[70] Ibid. DD/X/ME 2.
[71] C. Hadfield, *Canals of SW. Eng.* (1967), 49, 65.
[72] E. T. Macdermot, *Hist. G.W.R.* rev. C. R. Clinker (1964), ii. 73, 84, 226.
[73] C. R. Clinker & J. M. Firth, *Reg. Closed Stations*, ii.
[74] Below, econ. hist.
[75] *V.C.H. Som.* i. 469.
[76] Inf. from Mrs. A. Jones, Lyng Court Farm.
[77] *L. & P. Hen. VIII*, xix (1), p. 39.
[78] *Reg. Regum Anglo-Norm.* iii, no. 27; *S.R.S.* xiv, p. 169; *Cal. Pat.* 1405–8, 95.
[79] Collinson, *Hist. Som.* i. 84; statistics supplied by the then Bd. of Agric. 1905.
[80] S.R.O., DD/SP inventories, 1667/93; 1681/29, 86; 1685/12.

[81] Ibid. D/R/bw, box 22/1/8.
[82] Ibid. DD/AH 22/13.
[83] Ibid. Q/RL 2, 33.
[84] Ibid. Q/RL; P.R.O., WO 30/48.
[85] S.R.O., DD/S/WH 218; DD/X/ME 2; DD/X/VEA; DD/CH 96/1, 4; ibid. Q/RL.
[86] Ibid. D/P/lyn 4/1/1; ibid. Q/RL.
[87] Ibid. Q/RL; ibid. D/P/lyn 23/6; Taunton Castle, Som. Co. Libr., engraving by A. Picken of 'intended new chapel', c. 1836.
[88] P.R.O., HO 107/1924; *P.O. Dir. Som.* (1875).
[89] *P.O. Dir. Som.* (1861).   [90] *S.D.N.Q.* xxx. 91.
[91] Collinson, *Hist. Som.* i. 84.
[92] *V.C.H. Som.* ii. 341.   [93] *Census*.
[94] *S.R.S.* xviii. 7; *V.C.H. Som.* ii. 215; *Cal. Cttee. for Compounding*, ii. 1008; D. Underdown, *Som. during Civil War and Interregnum*, 104, 107–8; *S.D.N.Q.* iii. 23; xx. 5; *Proc. Som. Arch. Soc.* lxxxv. 100–1.
[95] Hist. MSS. Com. 49, *Stopford-Sackville*, i, p. 391.
[96] Collinson, *Hist. Som.* i. 86 quoting an Athelney register now lost.

Alfred in the winter of 877–8 before the battle of Edington.[97] George Marston (1882–1940), artist and explorer, member of Sir Ernest Shackleton's two expeditions to the Antarctic 1907–9, 1914–16, and co-author and co-illustrator of *Antarctic Days* (1913), was buried in the parish.[98]

MANOR AND OTHER ESTATES. Athelney abbey seems to have acquired its estate in Lyng through two grants. King Alfred presumably gave the 'island' site when he founded the abbey *c.* 888.[99] A *mansio* called Relengen, identified with the later manor of *LYNG* or *WEST LYNG*,[1] was granted in 937 by King Athelstan in free alms in return for the prayers of the community for Alfred's soul.[2] In the 12th century the abbot was said to hold his lands in return for prayers for the then king,[3] and in 1485–6 to hold in free alms.[4]

The estate passed to the Crown on the surrender of the abbey in 1539 and it was later divided, the site of the monastery and its demesnes forming one holding.[5] The remainder, described as the manor and capital messuage, together with some woodland, were in 1544 granted to (Sir) John Leigh, the king's servant.[6] Leigh (d. *c.* 1563)[7] settled the manor on his nephew also John who died in 1576.[8] A claim by Sir John's daughter Agnes, wife of Edward FitzGarrett,[9] was evidently defeated, since John Leigh's widow Margery, who was still alive in 1612, held Lyng as jointure.[10] The manor was presumably let by Margery Leigh, since by 1598 the manor court was held in the names of John Pyne, (Sir) Jasper, Robert, and Geoffrey Moore, sons of Thomas Moore of Taunton, and Lancelot St. Albyn.[11] In 1602 only Pyne and St. Albyn were described as lords, from 1604 to 1608 only the three Moores.[12] Robert and Geoffrey Moore were lords in 1609, and between 1611 and 1615[13] Thomas Moore of Heytesbury (Wilts.). Thomas died *c.* 1627[14] and was succeeded at Lyng by two sons, Thomas and Francis Moore.[15] Thomas was lord in 1651.[16]

Meanwhile John Leigh (d. 1576) was followed by his son Sir John (d. 1612) and by his grandson Thomas (d. 1640).[17] Thomas's son Philip succeeded as a minor, and he was followed by his son Edward, on whom the manor was settled in 1659.[18] In 1697 Edward, of Testwood in Eling (Hants), sold the heavily mortgaged[19] manor,

amounting to nearly 1,000 a. of land including tenements attached to the former abbey holdings in Burrow, Langport, and North Petherton, to William Harrison of North Petherton.[20] Harrison died in 1740 leaving the manor in trust for his sister and then for three nieces, but it seems likely that much of the land had already been sold.[21] No further reference to the manor has been found until 1861 when Richard Gatcombe of North Petherton held the lordship. He held it until 1875 or later, but by 1883 and until 1923 Clifford Symes of Bridgwater was described as lord.[22]

In 1697 Edward Leigh sold to Sir Thomas Wroth of Petherton Park a holding described as the court leet and view of frankpledge and royalty of the manor, together with chief rents, fee farm rents, and the former farm of Lyng Court.[23] Sir Thomas died in 1721 leaving the whole estate to be shared by his two daughters Cecily and Elizabeth. In 1723 Lyng was awarded on partition to Elizabeth, and to her husband Thomas Palmer of Fairfield in Stogursey.[24] Elizabeth died in 1738,[25] leaving her father's estate in trust to her brother-in-law Peregrine Palmer, first to carry out the terms of her will and then successively for the benefit of her kinswoman Anne and of Anne's daughter Elizabeth. Anne, who married first William Oxenham of Newhouse (Devon) and then Wadham Wyndham of Fyfield (Wilts.), died in 1748. In 1752 her daughter Elizabeth Oxenham married Arthur Acland (d. 1771).[26] Their son (Sir) John Palmer Acland succeeded on Elizabeth's death in 1806.[27]

Acland died in 1831 and his trustees sold the court leet and Lyng Court farm to Anna Gatcombe (d. 1847).[28] Anna left the property in trust for Mary, wife of Thomas Mullins of Goathurst.[29] Their son, also Thomas, of Weston super Mare, was dead by 1903, and Lyng Court and other farms in Lyng and Durston passed to his widow Lucie Margaret, of Minehead. She sold Lyng Court in 1911 to her tenant Richard Gatcombe Turner (d. 1930). The farm then descended successively to Turner's son James Gadd Turner (d. 1954) and his grandson Richard John Dunning Turner (d. 1972). In 1985 it was owned by Anne, daughter of the last and wife of Mr. R. Lloyd Jones.[30]

The capital messuage, known as the Court by 1529,[31] was rebuilt in 1808.[32] It is of brick, with two storeys and attics over cellars. To the rear

[97] *A.-S. Chron.* ed. Whitelock, Douglas, and Tucker.
[98] Tombstone in chyd.; J. Murray and G. Marston, *Antarctic Days* (1913); J. Johnson and A. Greutzner, *Dict. British Artists, 1880–1940.*
[99] D. Knowles and R. N. Hadcock, *Medieval Religious Hos.* 59; *S.R.S.* xiv, p. 115.   [1] *S.R.S.* xiv, p. 188.
[2] H. P. R. Finberg, *Early Charters of Wessex,* pp. 130–1; *S.R.S.* xiv, pp. 155–6.   [3] *Bk. of Fees,* i. 86.
[4] P.R.O., E 149/889, no. 7.
[5] Below, this section (Athelney).
[6] *L. & P. Hen. VIII,* xix (1), p. 39.
[7] *Cal. Pat.* 1563–6, p. 167.
[8] S.R.O., DD/AH 8/4.
[9] *Cal. Pat.* 1563–6, p. 301; 1566–9, p. 45.
[10] *S.R.S.* lxvii, p. 124.
[11] P.R.O., SC 12/34, no. 21, ff. 15–19.
[12] Ibid. ff. 39v.–40v., 52–55v.; SC 2/227/115; *Visit. Wilts. 1623* (Harl. Soc. cv & cvi), 137.
[13] P.R.O., SC 2/227/115; *S.R.S.* xxiii. 57.

[14] *Visit. Wilts. 1623* (Harl. Soc. cv & cvi), 137.
[15] P.R.O., C 3/23, no. 71; ibid. REQ 2/38, no. 22.
[16] S.R.O., DD/DP 71/2.
[17] *S.R.S.* lxvii, p. 124; S.R.O., DD/AH 8/4; Hants R.O., IM 31/32 (copy will of Thomas Leigh).
[18] S.R.O., DD/AH 8/4.   [19] Ibid. 1/3.
[20] Ibid. DD/SL 11, 12.
[21] Ibid. DD/SAS RF 3 (1/1), pp. 93–5.
[22] *P.O. Dir. Som.* (1861, 1866, 1875); *Kelly's Dir. Som.* (1883, 1923).   [23] S.R.O., DD/AH 1/3, 16/7.
[24] Ibid. 7/1.   [25] M.I. in Stogursey ch.
[26] S.R.O., DD/AH 4/3, 54/6.   [27] Ibid. 1/3, 55/5.
[28] Ibid. 23/1; M.I. in Lyng ch.
[29] S.R.O., DD/DHR, box 26: will of Anna Gatcombe; M.I. in Lyng ch.
[30] S.R.O., DD/X/CRE 1–2; MSS. in possession of Mrs. A. Jones, Lyng Court Fm.; M.I. in Lyng chyd.
[31] P.R.O., SC 6/Hen. VIII/3144.
[32] S.R.O., DD/AH 23/3.

is a contemporary smoking house. North-east of the house is a large barn, its west porch entry and wide-splayed stone-framed openings indicating a late-medieval origin. The idea that there was a chapel on the farm[33] was probably inspired by the surviving medieval fragments.

John Tuchet, Lord Audley (d. 1557), who seems to have contemplated living at Athelney abbey while at least part of the community remained, was given temporary charge of the abbey by the king's visitors on its surrender in 1539.[34] He still held the site and demesne at farm in August 1544, but from March in that year what was later called *ATHELNEY* farm was held in fee by John Clayton or Clutton,[35] who shortly afterwards had licence to alienate them to John Tynbery or Tymbury.[36] Clutton died later in that year and was succeeded by his brother David, of Westminster.[37] David sold the estate to Tynbery in 1545, the price including a sum to discharge all leases granted by Lord Audley.[38] Tynbery died in possession of the site and a fishery in 1553.[39] His son and heir Henry died in 1567 still under age. Henry was followed by his brother William, who took possession in 1573.[40] Before 1610 William and his wife conveyed the holding to Simon Court, and in that year Simon and Edward Court were in possession.[41] Edward died in 1619 leaving a son, Simon, a minor.[42] Simon took possession in 1635 and was followed by his son Thomas, of Shepton Mallet, by 1664. The estate, then called Athelney farm, was sold in the following year to John Hucker, a Taunton merchant.[43] Hucker was executed in 1685 for his support for the duke of Monmouth, and his land was forfeit to the Crown.[44] A Treasury warrant for a grant to be made to John Churchill, Baron Churchill, later Duke of Marlborough (d. 1722),[45] was evidently frustrated by the previous creation of a trust in favour of Hucker's son Robert,[46] himself a Monmouth supporter.[47] Robert Hucker was in possession in 1692 and sold the farm in 1698 to Thomas Burge of Long Sutton. Burge mortgaged it in 1706 to Richard Brodrepp of South Mapperton (Dors.) and failed to repay the loan, but he remained in occupation until his death in 1713. He was succeeded as tenant by his son John (d. 1715) and by John's only child Mary, wife of Lawrence Brome. John Evered of Bridgwater bought the farm from Brodrepp's heirs in 1739.[48] Evered died in 1785[49] and his eventual

heir was his daughter Jane, wife of the Revd. Francis Crane Parsons of Yeovil. In 1791 Parsons sold the farm to John Slade of North Petherton. The farm descended in the Slade family until 1863 when it was sold, apparently to the Barrett family of Moredon in North Curry;[50] it was sold again in 1918 to the tenant.[51] The descent has not been traced further.

No remains of the abbey buildings survive above ground. Parts remained standing in 1674 and the ruins of a chapel still existed until *c.* 1770. The present farmhouse was built in the later 18th century.[52]

In the 16th century the *RECTORY* comprised tithes and casual cash payments, and until the Dissolution belonged to Athelney abbey.[53] It was leased by the Crown to Thomas Ansell in 1546[54] and was sold to Sir Christopher Hatton in 1579.[55] Before 1596 it had passed to Sir Nicholas Halswell, who leased it to William Goble (d. 1626), of Bridgwater.[56] The descent of the rectory thereafter is uncertain until 1676, although in 1662 the patronage was exercised by Henry and John Stallington and in 1669 by John Ellis and John Stallington, possibly heirs of Goble. Richard Jeane and Alexander Atkins presented in 1675,[57] and in the following year the rectory and advowson were sold by Benjamin Hart of Bridgwater to Alexander Atkins. Alexander, son and heir of the last, conveyed it in 1688 to his mother Margaret[58] although his younger brother Samuel was patron in 1692 and 1719.[59] Margaret died in 1718 leaving the rectory to be divided between her grandchildren. Half was shared between John Leigh and James Potter in 1737,[60] and both were among the eight patrons who presented in 1746.[61] Another patron then was William Moore, who in that same year acquired the whole rectory[62] which he added to a farm of some 100 a. inherited from his father Andrew Moore (d. 1743) of North Newton in North Petherton, formerly part of Lyng manor.[63]

William Moore died in 1768[64] and the rectory and advowson passed to his widow Elizabeth, of Bourton-on-the-Water (Glos.). She made over the estate in 1792 to Hill Dawe of Ditcheat, Moore's nephew.[65] Hill died in 1820 and was succeeded by his son and heir, also Hill Dawe.[66] The latter died in 1851 and was followed in succession by his nephew the Revd. Hill Richard Dawe (d. 1857) and by his brother Charles Dawe

33 Collinson, *Hist. Som.* i. 85.
34 W. A. J. Archbold, *Som. Religious Houses* (1892), 80–2; *L. & P. Hen. VIII*, xiv (1), p. 117.
35 *L. & P. Hen. VIII*, xix (2), p. 72.
36 Ibid. xix (1), p. 287.
37 P.R.O., C 142/71, no. 103; *L. & P. Hen. VIII*, xx (1), p. 304.
38 P.R.O., REQ 2/4, no. 50.
39 Ibid. C 142/101, no. 109; *Cal. Pat. 1553–4*, 11.
40 P.R.O., C 142/148, no. 36; C 60/389, no. 83.
41 Ibid. CP 25(2)/345/8 Jas. I Trin.; *S.R.S.* lxvii, p. 18.
42 *S.R.S.* lxvii, pp. 17–18.
43 P.R.O., C 60/530, no. 47; S.R.O., DD/SL 11, 12.
44 *S.R.S.* lxxix. 90; Hist. MSS. Com. 49, *Stopford-Sackville*, i, p. 28.
45 *Cal. Treas. Bks.* viii (2), pp. 1090–1.
46 S.R.O., DD/SL 11, 12.
47 *S.R.S.* lxxix. 90.
48 S.R.O., DD/SL 11, 12.
49 Ibid. D/P/lyn 13/2/1; ibid. Q/REl 2/7.
50 Ibid. DD/SL 11, 12; DD/X/BTT; *Bath & Wells Ruri-Decanal & Parochial Mag.* Sept. 1883, 75.
51 Sale cat. in possession of Mrs. A. Jones, Lyng Court Fm.
52 Collinson, *Hist. Som.* i. 88.
53 *Valor Eccl.* (Rec. Com.), i. 207.
54 *L. & P. Hen. VIII*, xxi (1), p. 781.
55 P.R.O., C 66/1185, m. 3.
56 *Som. Wills*, ed. Brown, ii. 65.
57 *Som. Incumbents*, ed. Weaver, 396.
58 S.R.O., DD/HYD 29.
59 *Som. Incumbents*, ed. Weaver, 396.
60 S.R.O., DD/HYD 29.
61 Ibid. DD/SAS (C/77) 16.
62 Ibid. DD/HYD 29.
63 Ibid. 28–9, 40.
64 Ibid. DD/GC 24.
65 Ibid. D/D/B reg. 28, f. 72; DD/HYD 28. Cf. *V.C.H. Glos.* vi. 79, where Hill is described as Moore's illegitimate son.
66 S.R.O., DD/HYD 28; D/P/dit 2/1/10.

(d. 1869).[67] By 1861[68] the estate had been acquired by Richard King Meade-King (d. 1887), of Walford in West Monkton, and passed successively to his son Lt.-Col. W. O. Meade-King (d. 1913) and grandson (Sir) William O. E. Meade-King (d. 1940).[69] Richard E. B. Meade-King died c. 1972 and his executors sold the land.[70]

A manor of *BURROW* was mentioned in 1786.[71] It may have comprised Burrow Hill, which belonged to the Harris family by 1767 and until 1780, when it came to John Chard.[72] A descendant married Capt. William Barrett of Moredon in North Curry, and the land passed to their son, Major A. G. Barrett, of Trull, who gave it and the chapel on its summit to the National Trust in 1946 as the county War Memorial.[73]

In 1528 the bishop of Winchester, the abbot of Glastonbury, the prior of Taunton, the warden of Eton College, and William Moleyns were freeholders of Lyng manor.[74] The Winchester holding, acquired by 1208,[75] comprised a messuage in Lyng and a fishery called Tappingweir, which was said to be on the Parrett,[76] and probably lay near the present Tappingwall Drove in Othery. The messuage remained part of the Winchester estate, administered with Ruishton tithing, until 1868 or later.[77] The Glastonbury estate has not been identified. The prior of Taunton acquired land in North moor early in the 13th century.[78] It presumably passed with the priory holding to John Ogan in 1540 and its reversion was granted to Humphrey Colles in 1543.[79] John Colles was a freeholder of the manor in 1604.[80] Eton College held a small piece of land near North moor by 1431 which was administered with Stogursey Priory manor, later Monkton Home manor, in Stogursey.[81] It was sold in 1922.[82] William Moleyns's holding was part of a family estate owned by 1429[83] which continued in their possession until after 1541.[84] John Phelips held land of the manor in 1601 which the family still retained in 1797 and which was the nucleus of Church farm,[85] its fields approached from East Lyng village along Phillips's Drove.[86] The chantry of Our Lady at North Curry owned land in the parish by 1314[87] which passed from the Lyte family to Hugh Isaacs in 1560.[88]

In the 14th and 15th centuries the chapter of Wells owned a small piece of meadow in the parish.[89] The Hospitallers had tenants of unspecified land in the early 16th century.[90]

ECONOMIC HISTORY. Hedges, ditches, old watercourses, and at least one bridge mentioned in the perambulation attached to the charter of West Lyng of 937 indicate the progress of agriculture on the Lyng ridge and the beginnings of encroachment on the moors.[91] Encroachment and improvement of moor land continued throughout the Middle Ages against a background of disputes, notably in the Tone valley, between Athelney abbey and neighbouring landowners.[92] The Domesday estate at Lyng measured only 1 hide, half in demesne worked by 6 *servi* with 2 ploughteams. Three *villani* and 4 bordars with 2 teams worked the remainder. Apart from the arable, only 12 a. of meadow were recorded.[93] By 1349 the demesne arable measured 80 a. and there were 20 a. of enclosed meadow and 8 a. of pasture.[94] A *nativus* was manumitted in 1481.[95] Modest expansion seems to have occurred on the tenant holdings: in the early 13th century the prior of Taunton acquired from Henry of Erleigh 15 a. north of East Lyng village which Henry had enclosed with a 7-ft. ditch.[96] The Erleighs continued to hold small pieces of land on the ridge in the 13th century[97] but in 1213 Athelney acquired from them 100 a. of moor in a narrow strip under the ridge and a share in common pasture, brushwood, and firewood in North moor.[98] Some Lyng graziers paid rent for land on the moor to the demesne hundred of North Petherton in the earlier 14th century.[99] Further grants from Henry of Erleigh gave the abbot an extensive holding in North moor, mostly outside the parish in the wedge-shaped area of North Petherton around Lyng Drove, immediately north of East Lyng village.[1]

South and east of the ridge the diversion of the western branch of the Tone by building the Baltmoor wall between East Lyng and Athelney island[2] was followed by several stages of diversion and straightening of the Tone and by agreements with the chapter of Wells and the Aller family over rights in Salt moor and Stan moor.[3] Further alterations to the Tone's course in Curry moor were made in the 14th and 15th centuries.[4] Most of the grassland there lay outside the parish but some was part of Lyng

67 Burke, *Land. Gent.* (1882), 436; S.R.O., D/P/dit 2/1/10.
68 *P.O. Dir. Som.* (1861).
69 Burke, *Land. Gent.* (1952), 1440. 70 Local inf.
71 S.R.O., DD/X/ME 2; DD/CH 96/4.
72 Ibid. Q/REl 2/7; ibid. D/P/lyn 13/2/1.
73 *Proc. Som. Arch. Soc.* lxxxv. 105 n.; *Som. Co. Herald, N. & Q.* 27 July 1946; 17 Apr., 15 May 1948.
74 S.R.O., DD/WY 45/1/15/15.
75 *Winchester Pipe Roll 1208–9*, ed. H. Hall, 64.
76 W. Dugdale and C. N. Cole, *Hist. of Imbanking and Draining* (1772), 106; *S.R.S.* lxiii, p. 522.
77 S.R.O., DD/SP 184; inf. from Mr. T. Mayberry.
78 *S.R.S.* xiv, p. 157.
79 *L. & P. Hen. VIII*, xviii, p. 196.
80 P.R.O., SC 12/34, no. 21.
81 Eton Coll. Rec. 6/196.
82 S.R.O., DD/MVB 68.
83 *S.R.S.* xvi. 133–4.
84 S.R.O., DD/WY 45/1/15/16.
85 P.R.O., SC 12/34, no. 21; S.R.O., DD/PH 169; ibid. tithe award.

86 O.S. Map 6", Som. LXI. SE. (1888 edn.).
87 *H.M.C. Wells*, i. 333. 88 *S.R.S.* li, p. 56.
89 *H.M.C. Wells*, i. 318–19, 325, 329.
90 S.R.O., DD/AH 11/9.
91 H. P. R. Finberg, *Early Charters of Wessex*, pp. 130–1.
92 Below, this section.
93 *V.C.H. Som.* i. 469.
94 P.R.O., E 152/78/3.
95 *S.D.N.Q.* viii. 111.
96 *Cal. Chart. R.* 1327–41, 314; *S.R.S.* xiv, p. 157.
97 S.R.O., DD/SL 1.
98 *S.R.S.* xiv, pp. 156–7.
99 S.R.O., DD/SAS NP 1, mm. 11–13, 16–18; 2, mm. 2–6.
1 *S.R.S.* xiv, pp. 153, 158–9.
2 Above, intro.
3 *Cur. Reg. R.* xvi, nos. 1270, 1702; *Reg. Regum Anglo-Norm.* iii, no. 28; *S.R.S.* vi. 108–9; xiv, pp. 167–8; *H.M.C. Wells*, i. 317–18.
4 *H.M.C. Wells*, i. 318–19, 325, 329; *S.R.S.* xiv, pp. 197–9; *Cal. Pat.* 1307–13, 265.

manor, which benefited by an increased area for taking fuel and for grazing stock.[5] A piggery was established on Salt moor in 1241–2,[6] but pigs were specifically excluded from Curry moor in 1427.[7]

The Athelney abbey estate at Lyng in 1529 comprised the site and demesne lands on the island and around Lyng Drove, the rectory, the capital messuage later called Lyng Court Farm, and tenants' rents. There were 96 separate tenant holdings in Outwood, West and East Lyng, and Hitchings, on the edge of North moor, of which 46 were in Hitchings. In addition there were 11 tenements at Burrow.[8] An incomplete survey of 1598[9] recorded 604 a. Most holdings in West and East Lyng were described as old auster tenements, probably charged with drainage works in North moor,[10] but only 35 a. of 138 a. in Hitchings were so described. There were 11 holdings each at East and West Lyng, at the former of 10 a. or less, at the latter up to 27 a. and probably more. Hitchings was divided between 24 holdings.

A survey of 1697 covered 949 a. but included land outside the parish in Salt moor and West Salt moor. There were then 9 farms, all copyholds, measuring between 20 a. and 30 a., including one held by John Leggatt, the origin of the present Leggatt's farm, and one of 48 a. at Outwood. Thomas Pocock held a total of 53 a., probably the largest farm in the parish after Lyng Court and Athelney farms. Among other tenants were members of the Batten and Meade families.[11]

The importance of meadow and pasture is evident from 17th-century inventories. John Gill (d. 1684), probably tenant of Athelney farm, the holding with most arable, left corn worth £115, cows and horses worth £120, sheep worth £100, a few pigs, and hay and wool valued at £27.[12] More typical was John Meade (d. 1681), who left 3 plough steers, 6 milking cows, 6 heifers, 3 calves, and 15 sheep, but an insignificant amount of grain in store and only 7 a. of wheat in the ground.[13] Edmund Wiltsheere's stock in 1668 included 5 milking cows, 2 yearlings, and 2 calves, and Gregory Ryall's in 1685 comprised 6 cows, 1 yearling, and 3 calves, as well as 3 horses and some sheep, pigs, geese, and poultry.[14] Many farmers left cheese (one inventory included 10 cheese boards), most kept pigs, and several had orchards.[15]

An outbreak of cattle distemper involving five farmers who grazed stock on North moor in 1757[16] and the perennial problems of flooding[17] may have been why, in the late 18th century, agriculture was said to be 'badly attended to'.[18] Lyng Court farm was the largest holding, measuring 278 a. in the 18th century and 258 a. in the 19th.[19] Six other farms paid land tax of over £2 in 1767.[20] By 1833 after Lyng Court farm there were three others measuring just over 100 a. including Athelney farm, one holding of 98 a., and three of c. 70 a.[21] The total acreage of Athelney farm was 172 a. in 1818 and included rights outside the parish on Stan moor, King's Sedgemoor, West Sedgemoor, Curry moor, and Week moor.[22] The farm, in 1827 measuring 119 a., was let for seven years subject to covenants against changing grass to tillage and against growing hemp, flax, teazels, and potatoes.[23]

The tenant at Athelney farm in 1827 specialized in dairying. He produced 163 cheeses in 1836 and sold butter in Taunton and Bridgwater.[24] A corn and cheese factor was in business in Burrowbridge in 1851[25] and a 'considerable' amount of cheese was made in Lyng in the 1870s.[26] Farmers with common rights in North moor early in the 19th century pastured cattle, sheep, sows, ducks, geese, and hens there.[27] Meadow, pasture, and orchards constituted three quarters of the titheable area of the parish in 1838.[28] The pattern of holdings continued stable throughout the 19th century, with 12 farms in 1851 and 11 in 1881, although Lyng Court farm had absorbed land to become a unit of 317 a.[29] At the sale of the Mullins estate in 1911–12 involving farms at the west end of the parish and in Durston, West Lyng farm was divided into 12 lots and Lyng Court farm measured 254 a.[30] There were still 12 principal farms in 1923 with 3 small holdings.[31] In 1982 there were 16 farms.[32] In 1905 arable covered 176 a. and grassland 1,053 a.;[33] in 1982 arable had increased to about a fifth of the total area, more than half producing wheat.[34]

The inclosure of the moors north and south of the parish in the 1790s[35] resulted in the establishment of small withy beds and the production of rods sold to basket makers, at first locally and by the 1860s further afield.[36] Production of baskets in Lyng had begun by 1889 and in the following three decades the manufacture, locally confined to the parishes of Lyng, Burrowbridge, and Stoke St. Gregory, involved growers, merchants, hauliers, and the makers of baskets and chairs.[37] The Hector family, based first at Durston station and later at Willow House, Hector's

5 S.R.S. xiv, pp. 190–1.
6 Ibid. vi. 108–9; xiv, pp. 190–1.
7 H.M.C. Wells, i. 329; S.R.S. xiv, pp. 197–9.
8 P.R.O., SC 6/Hen. VIII/3144.
9 Ibid. SC 12/34, no. 21.
10 See S.D.N.Q. xxix. 157–62; M. Williams, Draining of the Som. Levels, 120–1.
11 S.R.O., DD/SL 11/12.
12 Ibid. DD/SP inventory, 1684/70.
13 Ibid. 1681/86, 1685/12.
14 Ibid. 1668, 1685/71.
15 Ibid. 1645, 1668, 1674, 1684/70, 1685/12, 49, 51, 71, 75.
16 Ibid. Q/AD 2.
17 e.g. ibid. DD/SLM box 2.
18 Collinson, Hist. Som. i. 84.
19 S.R.O., DD/AH 16/7, 23/3, 41/10, 65/13, 16.
20 Ibid. Q/REl 2/7.   21 Ibid. D/P/lyn 23/6.

22 Ibid. DD/SLM box 2, bk. of maps, 1795.
23 Ibid. DD/SL 23.   24 Ibid. DD/S/DA 2.
25 P.R.O., HO 107/1924.
26 E. Jeboult, Valley of the Tone (1873), 61.
27 S.R.O., DD/HYD 47.
28 Ibid. tithe award.
29 P.R.O., HO 107/1924; ibid. RG 11/2373.
30 S.R.O., DD/X/CRE 1–5.
31 Kelly's Dir. Som. (1923).
32 Min. of Agric., Fisheries, and Food, agric. returns, 1982.
33 Statistics supplied by the then Bd. of Agric., 1905.
34 Min. of Agric., Fisheries, and Food, agric. returns, 1982.   35 Below, N. Petherton.
36 Proc. Som. Arch. Soc. cxxix. 169; Rep. Com. Employment in Agric. (1868–9), 484.
37 Kelly's Dir. Som. (1889 and later edns.); S.R.O., D/P/lyn 2/1/5.

Lane, produced baskets and wicker chairs, and at least four other families of craftsmen found employment in the trade, which was probably at its peak during the First World War.[38] Production in Lyng continued in 1985.[39]

The Taunton–Wells road and the rivers Parrett and Tone brought commercial traffic to the parish. A Lyng chapman was involved in business with a man from Berkshire in 1435.[40] About 1540 a local smith was importing iron up the Parrett through Bridgwater, and the same route was used by a Lyng butcher importing herring in 1620–1.[41] There were four shops at Burrow by 1539,[42] and a coal shop there by 1697.[43] Coal barges of up to 50 tons came to Burrow at the end of the 18th century, when a resident excise officer was rated highly for land tax.[44] Coal continued to be taken up the Tone to Ham in Creech St. Michael until the 1860s or later.[45] Tile, iron, brick, stone, lime, and made-up carpentry came along the same route to the wharf at Athelney bridge until the 1820s or later,[46] and to another at Burrowbridge which was still in use in 1855.[47] Philip Woodrow (d. 1645) was both a bargeman and a farmer.[48] Nine boatmen subscribed to the rebuilding of Burrow chapel in 1793, and 15 had their children baptized in the parish between 1813 and 1827, although only two were actually resident in the parish.[49] One Lyng man was still active as a boatman in 1851, and boatmen continued to work on the Tone until 1895.[50]

In the earlier 19th century Burrowbridge was home to a chaise driver and a mason, and Lyng to a shoemaker, a blacksmith, and a saddler.[51] By 1851 there were a 'horse and a cow doctor', three pig dealers, three tanners, two smiths, and an auctioneer, all relating to agriculture, and three bakers, a milliner, a tailor, a mantua maker, a dressmaker, and a staymaker.[52] Bricks were made at Outwood in the 1870s.[53] By 1881 there was a shirtmaker[54] and three shops were trading in Burrowbridge in 1889.[55] The railway company by 1881 had opened refreshment rooms at Durston station and employed an inspector, an engine driver, a ticket collector, 5 porters, a switchman, and 3 labourers all living at Outwood.[56] In the 1930s the increasing road traffic brought a motor engineering business and a commercial temperance hotel at East Lyng[57] and by 1985 a restaurant and guest house at the former King John inn at Burrowbridge.

Two mills were recorded in 1349[58] and they were still in use, although less valuable, in 1399.[59] Alterations to the course of the Tone may have led to the disappearance of the mills thereafter.

A weekly market on Mondays was established at Lyng in 1267.[60] By 1349 there was no market, but an annual fair at the Exaltation of the Holy Cross (14 Sept.).[61] That fair was apparently no longer held by 1399,[62] and no income from it was recorded later. A fair at Lyng on the first Monday in August was established by 1861.[63] It declined for some years before 1907 when neither cattle nor farmers appeared.[64] It was not revived, although a ginger bread stall was erected on fair day by the Rose and Crown inn until the Second World War.[65] By 1861 there were two fairs at Burrowbridge, on the last Tuesdays in March and August.[66] The August fair was 'good' in 1875 and survived in 1899.[67] A ginger bread stall was set up at the King Alfred inn on fair day until the Second World War.[68]

LOCAL GOVERNMENT. The status of *burh*[69] given to East Lyng in the 10th century persisted into the late Middle Ages in the description of the 'tithing and burgus' of Lyng in 1498–9,[70] and possibly in the existence of a halimote court in 1541–2.[71] Lyng manor was represented at the eyre by a separate jury in 1225,[72] and Athelney abbey's bailiffs would not permit the coroners to make inquests there.[73] In the later 13th century Lyng was described as a free manor,[74] and in 1327 was in Freemanors hundred.[75] It had become part of Andersfield hundred by 1640.[76]

By 1327 the abbey courts dealt with breaches of the assize of bread and ale and with cases of bloodshed, but from that year the tenants of Wells chapter were ordered to attend at North Curry and had only to appear at Lyng on the two lawdays.[77] Rolls for the Michaelmas and Easter lawdays, courts leet, and views of frankpledge survive for 1528–9, 1541–2,[78] 1598–1604,[79] 1605–9, and 1611–15,[80] with copies of admissions for 1651,[81] 1654, 1673, 1680, and

38 *Kelly's Dir. Som.* (1889 and later edns.); S.R.O., D/P/lyn 2/1/5, 13/1/2; DD/X/BWN 1; DD/X/BTT 5; D/R/bw, box 22/1/8; inf. from Mrs. E. Champion, Lyng.
39 Inf. from Mrs. Champion.
40 *Cal. Pat.* 1429–36, 436.
41 S.R.O., D/B/bw 1436, 1440, 1503.
42 P.R.O., SC 6/Hen. VIII/3144.
43 S.R.O., DD/SL 11/12.
44 Collinson, *Hist. Som.* i. 85; S.R.O., Q/REl 2/7 (1767).
45 Above, Creech St. Michael, econ. hist.
46 S.R.O., D/P/lyn 4/1/1 (1714, -1738); DD/PH 169; DD/S/DA 2 (1824).
47 Ibid. DD/X/ME 2; *Proc. Som. Arch. Soc.* lv. 175.
48 S.R.O., DD/SP inventory, 1645.
49 Ibid. D/P/lyn 2/1/4.
50 P.R.O., HO 107/1924; E. Hembrow, *Winter Harvest* (1990), 19.
51 S.R.O., D/P/lyn 2/1/4.   52 P.R.O., HO 107/1924.
53 S.R.O., D/D/Bbm 236; O.S. Map 6", Som. LXXI. NE. (1888 edn.); *Bridgwater Mercury*, 4 May 1870.
54 P.R.O., RG 11/2373.
55 *Kelly's Dir. Som.* (1889).
56 P.R.O., RG 11/2373; S.R.O., DD/X/BTT.
57 *Kelly's Dir. Som.* (1931).   58 P.R.O., E 152/78/3.

59 *Proc. Som. Arch. Soc.* xliii. 141.
60 *Cal. Chart. R.* 1257–1300, 85.
61 *Cal. Inq. Misc.* iii, p. 15.
62 *Proc. Som. Arch. Soc.* xliii. 141.
63 *P.O. Dir. Som.* (1861).
64 V.C.H. office, letter from the Revd. E. A. M. Godson, Vicar of Lyng (1908).
65 Inf. from Miss P. I. Champion, Stoke St. Gregory.
66 *P.O. Dir. Som.* (1861).
67 *P.O. Dir. Som.* (1875); Burrowbridge sch., log bk. 1868–99.
68 Inf. from Miss Champion.   69 Above, intro.
70 *Fines Imposed in 1497*, ed. A. J. Howard, 20.
71 S.R.O., DD/WY 45/1/1.
72 *S.R.S.* xi, pp. 41, 301.
73 *H.M.C. Wells*, i. 318–19.
74 *S.R.S.* xiv, p. 163.
75 Ibid. iii. 179–80.
76 S.R.O., DD/SG 58–9.
77 *H.M.C. Wells*, i. 318–19.
78 S.R.O., DD/WY 45/1/15/15, 16.
79 P.R.O., SC 12/34, no. 21.
80 Ibid. SC 2/227/115.
81 S.R.O., DD/DP 71/2.

1690.[82] A court dinner was held at Lyng Court Farm for the manors of Lyng and Bankland in North Petherton between 1741 and 1746.[83] Courts were said to be held in the barn there c. 1761.[84]

Part of Lyng in North moor was subject in the later 14th and the early 15th century to the swanimote jurisdiction of North Petherton park, administered as a royal forest and known as Parkhouse.[85] The Hospitallers' tenants at Lyng and the tithingman of Lyng were present at a court leet at Buckland in Durston in 1508.[86]

A tithingman was chosen for Lyng at the Michaelmas court leet in 1528, and the manor was administered by a bailiff and two constables.[87] By 1601 only one constable was appointed, in that year and in 1614–15 two surveyors of buildings, and in 1605 and 1607–8 surveyors of river banks.[88] By the early 18th century the parish was administered by a body described either as the parish meeting or the vestry meeting.[89] In 1835 it became a select vestry of seven members.[90] Two churchwardens, one nominated by the curate or vicar from 1841, two overseers, and waywardens[91] served in the parish, and from 1835 a salaried overseer was employed. In the earlier 18th century the churchwardens accounted for all parish expenditure including repairs to the stocks and the whipping post, the repair of the poorhouse, and medical treatment for a pauper.[92] Accounts for poor relief were kept separately from 1771.[93] The vestry was rarely chaired by the incumbent until the late 1860s.[94]

A poorhouse was mentioned in 1725 and 1772.[95] There were two houses in 1833, one on the north side of East Lyng village street opposite the church, the other isolated at the north end of Hector's Lane at the beginning of Lyng Drove.[96] A house divided into two tenements was sold to Bridgwater poor-law union in 1838.[97] The parish became part of that union in 1836, of Bridgwater rural district in 1894, and of Sedgemoor district in 1974.[98]

CHURCH. Lyng church, standing on the defences of the Saxon *burh* of East Lyng,[99] was described as a chapel in 1291,[1] presumably dependent upon the monastic church of Athelney. A vicarage was ordained by 1348.[2] The living was held with Burrowbridge between 1852 and 1872[3] and with Durston between 1970 and 1977. In 1978 it became part of the united benefice of Stoke St. Gregory with Burrowbridge and Lyng.[4]

Until the Dissolution the patronage belonged to Athelney abbey.[5] The Crown presented thereafter until 1579 when Sir Christopher Hatton had a grant of the rectory and advowson.[6] The patronage descended with the rectory,[7] and the executors of Richard Meade-King have the right to present on the first turn in every three to the united benefice.[8]

In 1291 the chapel was valued at £5,[9] and the vicarage in 1445 at £5 6s. 8d.[10] The net value was £10 8s. 4d. in 1535 and comprised a pension of £6 from Athelney abbey and the remainder from tithes and offerings.[11] The reputed value was £40 c. 1668,[12] but the living was described by the incumbent in 1705 as 'a very poor vicarage worth c. £15'.[13] A gift of £200 from Sir Thomas Wroth and Mr. G. Gill in 1719 was matched by Queen Anne's Bounty,[14] giving an additional £16 a year by 1725.[15] Further augmentations from the patron and Mrs. Horner's trustees in 1808 totalling £150, and from the patron, the vicar, and Mrs. Pincombe's trustees in 1810 of £200, all matched by Queen Anne's Bounty,[16] gave an average income of £81 c. 1831.[17] In 1838 the vicar was awarded a rent charge of £41 in lieu of moduses on unmown pastures and of tithes of allotments in North moor in North Petherton parish belonging to tenements in Lyng.[18] In 1923 the value was increased by £9 a year from the Ecclesiastical Commissioners and the Broadmead Trust.[19]

A garden and yard formed the glebe in the early 17th century.[20] By 1838 there were nearly 27 a. of glebe, presumably bought with augmentations, and by 1889 over 31 a., small areas of which were in the parishes of North Petherton and St. Mary's, Taunton.[21] A small plot opposite the church, possibly the site of the former vicarage house, was sold for a burial ground in 1953.[22] In 1978 there were 30 a. of glebe.[23]

In 1638 the vicarage house comprised a hall and a buttery with two rooms above and an

82 Ibid. DD/MK 1.
83 Ibid. DD/AH 22/13, 24/11.
84 Collinson, *Hist. Som.* i. 85.
85 P.R.O., SC 2/200/13.
86 S.R.O., DD/AH 11/9.
87 Ibid. DD/WY 45/1/15/15.
88 P.R.O., SC 12/34, no. 21.
89 S.R.O., D/P/lyn 4/1/1, 13/2/1.
90 Ibid. 9/1/2.
91 Ibid. 9/1/3, 13/2/1, 14/5/1.
92 Ibid. 4/1/1.
93 Ibid. 13/2/1.
94 Ibid. 9/1/3.
95 Ibid. 4/1/1, 13/2/1.
96 Ibid. 23/6; ibid. DD/MK 14, map of Lyng.
97 Ibid. D/P/lyn 9/1/2.
98 Youngs, *Local Admin. Units*, i. 671, 673.
99 *Proc. Som. Arch. Soc.* cxi. 66 n.
1 *Tax. Eccl.* (Rec. Com.), 198.
2 *S.R.S.* x, p. 559. No source has been found for the statement that it ceased to be a chapel in 1337: *Proc. Som. Arch. Soc.* xliii (1), p. 52.
3 S.R.O., D/P/lyn 2/1/4; Burrowbridge par. rec. The incumbent of Burrowbridge was curate of Lyng from 1846:

S.R.O., D/P/lyn 1/2/2.
4 *Dioc. Dir.*
5 *Som. Incumbents*, ed. Weaver, 396.
6 *S.R.S.* lv, p. 142; *Som. Incumbents*, 396; P.R.O., C 66/1185, m. 3.
7 *Som. Incumbents*, 396; *Som. Wills*, ed. Brown, ii. 65.
8 *Som. Incumbents*, 396; S.R.O., DD/HYD 29; *Dioc. Dir.*
9 *Tax. Eccl.* (Rec. Com.), 198.
10 *S.R.S.* xlix, p. 34.
11 *Valor Eccl.* (Rec. Com.), i. 216.
12 S.R.O., D/D/Vc 24.
13 *Proc. Som. Arch. Soc.* cxii. 83–4.
14 C. Hodgson, *Queen Anne's Bounty* (1864), p. clxxxii.
15 S.R.O., D/P/lyn 2/1/1, memo. at end.
16 Hodgson, *Queen Anne's Bounty* (1864), pp. clxxxii, clxxxiv.
17 *Rep. Com. Eccl. Revenues*, pp. 144–5.
18 S.R.O., tithe award.
19 Ibid. D/P/lyn 3/3/1.
20 Ibid. D/D/Rg 275.
21 Ibid. tithe award; inf. from Dioc. Office, Wells.
22 S.R.O., D/P/lyn 3/5/1.
23 Inf. from Dioc. Office.

THE CHURCH IN 1888

adjoining barn and stall.[24] By 1705 the house had been demolished,[25] and there was no residence for the incumbent until 1872 when a house was built east of the churchyard. It was exchanged in 1969 for a bungalow called 'Three Ways', in 1985 known as 'Fairburn', at the eastern end of the village. The bungalow was sold in 1978.[26]

A figure of St. Catherine, a light of St. Bartholomew, and a rood were objects of devotion in the church in the 1530s.[27] The vicar was

24 S.R.O., D/D/Rg 275.
25 *Proc. Som. Arch. Soc.* cxii. 83–4.
26 Inf. from Dioc. Office.
27 *Wells Wills*, ed. Weaver, 100; S.R.O., DD/X/SR 5.

deprived in 1554 for being married.[28] The parish was commonly served by curates in the later 16th century,[29] and vicars in the early 17th also served either St. Michaelchurch or Durston.[30] Hatton Balch, vicar from 1621 to 1636 or later, was several times complained of for failure to preach and teach.[31] Curates were responsible for the parish by the later 17th century, one serving it with St. Michaelchurch from 1689, another with Broomfield from 1763.[32] During the 18th century communion was celebrated three or four times a year,[33] and by 1776 there were 12 communicants.[34] Aaron Foster, vicar 1812–15,[35] lived at Kingston St. Mary, where he was vicar. His curate held a service at Lyng each Sunday, alternately morning and evening. Several of the curates lived at Creech St. Michael and also served Durston, including George Baring, 1813–15,[36] who personally bought food for the poor in 1815,[37] and William Henry Havergal, 1816–20, who later composed sacred music.[38] Other curates lived in Thurloxton or West Monkton;[39] only one resided in Lyng.[40] The parish was in 1846–7 said to have been in 'a wild and neglected state' because of non-resident clergy.[41] From 1846 the curate was the resident incumbent of Burrowbridge.[42] Services were held once each Sunday in 1870, with communion four times a year.[43] From 1977 the church was in the pastoral care of a non-stipendiary minister living in North Curry.[44]

By 1684 a church house was being maintained by the parish, retaining that name until 1740 but probably serving by 1725 as a poorhouse.[45] It stood opposite the church beside the site of the former vicarage house, and was later replaced by the Sunday-school room.[46]

The church of *ST. BARTHOLOMEW*, so dedicated by 1531,[47] comprises a chancel, a nave with north porch and south vestry, and a west tower. The nave windows, the piscina and sedilia in the sanctuary, and the window above them date from the earlier 14th century, together with the chancel arch, its western side left plain perhaps to accommodate a tympanum board. The remaining windows in the chancel were replaced in the 15th century. The ornate tower, added c. 1500, is of lias with Ham stone dressings. A screen and rood loft were introduced in the 15th century, involving the addition of a

large stair and the creation of a chapel on the south side of the nave. The plain lower sections of the screen survive. The ornate pulpit also dates from c. 1500. Probably from the early 17th century it formed part of a three-decker arrangement, complete with tester.[48] The clerk's desk and choir stalls incorporate medieval work. The carved bench ends include a wide variety of medieval and Renaissance motifs; one is dated 1614, but most belong to the early 16th century.[49] The plain font is of the 12th century, and there is a dug-out chest. There are fragments of medieval glass in the chancel, preserved when glass by Michael O'Connor was inserted in 1870.[50] A small area of decorated medieval plaster also survives in the chancel. The former south porch seems to have been rebuilt as a vestry c. 1884.[51]

There are six bells, including one by George Purdue (1612) and two by Thomas Wroth (1721, 1725). Another by George Purdue (1609), was replaced in 1969.[52] Two bells from Burrow chapel, dated 1607 and 1625, were at Lyng in the later 18th century.[53] The plate includes a cup and cover of 1691.[54] The registers date from 1691, the earliest entries transcribed in 1716 from an earlier register, parts of which were 'through negligence obliterated and torn out'.[55]

St. Michael's chapel on Burrow Mump was described in 1548 as a free chapel but was treated as a chantry.[56] It was let by the Crown until 1631–2 when it was granted to Christopher Favell and others.[57] It continued in use for worship,[58] and was in 1645 regarded as an independent church. Continued use of the church is suggested by rebuilding c. 1663[59] and c. 1793[60] but it was described as in ruins by 1733[61] and was probably never finished.[62] It was replaced in 1836–7 by a new church at the foot of the hill which became the parish church of Burrowbridge in 1840.[63]

The living of Burrowbridge, endowed by local subscription, was valued at £60 in 1857,[64] and was increased in 1859, 1874, and 1875 by grants from the Ecclesiastical Commissioners. Two pieces of land, amounting to just over 4 a., were given in 1874.[65] A vicarage house, built c. 1840 to designs by Richard Carver, was sold c. 1976.[66] Between 1960 and 1975 the benefice was held with Northmoor Green and from 1978 formed

28 S.R.O., D/D/Ca 18.
29 *S.D.N.Q.* xiii. 270; xxx. 90.
30 S.R.O., D/D/Ca 134, 310.
31 Ibid. 266, 274, 310; *Som. Incumbents*, ed. Weaver, 396.
32 S.R.O., D/D/Bs 42, 43; D/P/lyn 2/1/3, 4; *Som. Incumbents*, 396.
33 S.R.O., D/P/lyn 4/1/1.
34 Ibid. D/D/Vc 88.
35 *Alum. Oxon. 1715–1886.*
36 S.R.O., D/D/Rb 1815, 1827; D/P/lyn 2/1/4.
37 *Som. Co. Herald*, 28 Apr. 1962, quoting from *Lond. Chron.* 4 Jan. 1815.
38 *D.N.B.*
39 S.R.O., D/P/lyn 1/1/1; E. Green, *Bibliotheca Som.* ii. 188.
40 S.R.O., D/D/Va 1870.
41 Nat. Soc. *Inquiry*, 1846–7, Som. 12–13.
42 S.R.O., D/P/lyn 1/1/2.
43 Ibid. D/D/Va 1870.
44 *Dioc. Dir.*
45 S.R.O., D/P/lyn 4/1/1.
46 Ibid. DD/MK 14, map of Lyng.
47 *Wells Wills*, ed. Weaver, 100.

48 Drawing opposite.
49 Below, plate facing p. 153.
50 *Proc. Som. Arch. Soc.* xxiii. 49; S.R.O., D/P/lyn 8/2/3.
51 S.R.O., D/P/lyn 9/1/3.
52 Ibid. DD/SAS CH 16/1; local inf.
53 Collinson, *Hist. Som.* i. 89.
54 *Proc. Som. Arch. Soc.* xlvii. 159–60.
55 S.R.O., D/P/lyn 2/1/1.
56 *S.R.S.* ii. 53, 226; P.R.O., E 117/12, no. 21.
57 P.R.O., C 66/1451, m. 4; C 66/2572, m. 24.
58 *S.D.N.Q.* xxx. 91; S.R.O., DD/SAS CH 16/1; D/D/Ca 134, 180; *S.R.S.* lxxvii, p. 123.
59 *Proc. Som. Arch. Soc.* lxxxv. 100; above, intro.
60 S.R.O., DD/SAS PR 22.
61 *Proc. Som. Arch. Soc.* lxxxv. 100.
62 *Som. Co. Herald N. & Q.* 8 Sept. 1923; Taunton Castle, Som. Arch. Soc., print (1801) after E. Garvey.
63 Inscr. and subscription brochure in vestry.
64 Subscription brochure in vestry; *Clergy List* (1857).
65 *Dioc. Kal.* (1888).
66 B.L. Add. MS. 36379, f. 154; inf. from Mr. R. Lillford, Som. C.C.

part of the united benefice of Stoke St. Gregory with Burrowbridge and Lyng.[67] In 1870 two sermons were preached each Sunday and communion was celebrated every six weeks.[68]

The chapel of *ST. MICHAEL* on Burrow Mump, probably so dedicated by the later Middle Ages,[69] and certainly by 1548,[70] appears by the 18th century to have comprised a chancel, a central tower with a south transeptal chapel and octagonal stair turret, and a nave.[71] Excavation of the site suggested the previous existence of a chapel on the north side of the chancel and of a crypt outside the north wall of the nave.[72] The building seems to have been of the late 15th or the earlier 16th century. It was replaced *c.* 1793 by a single-cell structure with a porch in the centre of its south wall and a west tower, the remains of which still stand, owned since 1946 by the National Trust.[73]

The church of *ST. MICHAEL* in Burrowbridge village, originally comprising a small chancel, a wide nave with a west gallery, and a western porch with vestries and bellcot, was designed in 13th-century style by Richard Carver and built of coursed blue lias with Ham stone dressings. In 1888 a stone chancel arch and two side arches were erected at the east end of the nave to give the effect of a Tractarian chancel with north and south chapels.[74]

There is one bell. The plate was given in 1838, and the registers begin in the same year.

NONCONFORMITY. A Quaker lived in the parish between 1682 and 1690,[75] and houses were licensed for worship by unspecified denominations in 1689 and 1691.[76]

EDUCATION. In 1819 there was a day school at Lyng with 34 children and a Sunday school attended by between 16 and 20 children.[77] Both schools appear to have closed by 1825.[78] In 1831 a National day school and a Sunday school were started, held in a room opposite the church;[79] in 1835 both had 18 children on the books,[80] and in 1846 there were 14.[81] The school continued in the 1860s,[82] but evidently did not survive. In 1874 a school board was formed and a new school was built at West Lyng in the following year, comprising two schoolrooms and a teacher's house. By 1903 there were 50 children on the books.[83] Numbers fell to 38 in 1925, to 29 in 1945, and to 17 in 1965, when the school closed.[84] The children were transferred to Burrowbridge or to North Curry.[85] In 1985 the former school was a private house.

There were unlicensed schoolmasters at Burrow in 1609 and 1613.[86] By 1846 there were two day schools there: a Sunday school and day school with 49 children and a Sunday school with 31 children. They were known together as St. Michael's Church schools and they were taught by 12 teachers, all but two unpaid. Financial support came from subscriptions and school pence.[87] The site of the school, to be maintained in union with the National Society, was assigned to the vicar and churchwardens in 1848.[88] The school continued until after 1851[89] but then seems to have lapsed, resuming for a few months in 1858, and again continuously from 1864.[90] The buildings were extended in 1893, and in 1903 there were 86 children on the books, with an average attendance of 68.[91] From 1958 the school accepted voluntary controlled status.[92] In 1983 the estimated number on the register was 34.[93]

There were two private schools at Burrowbridge in the earlier 19th century,[94] and a private school for girls was opened in 1882.[95]

CHARITIES FOR THE POOR. William Moore, by will dated 1766, left £10 to the poor. The charity was lost after 1786.[96]

67 *Dioc. Dir.*
68 S.R.O., D/D/Va 1870.
69 W. Worcestre, *Itineraries*, ed. J. H. Harvey, 123.
70 *S.R.S.* ii. 53, 226.
71 Taunton Castle, Som. Arch. Soc., Tite colln., engravings by C. W. Bampfylde (1763) and S. Hopper (1785).
72 *Proc. Som. Arch. Soc.* lxxxv. 95–132.
73 Above, manors (Burrow).
74 Inf. from Mr. A. Rome, Nailsea, former church architect.
75 *S.R.S.* lxxv. 144, 206.
76 S.R.O., Q/RR meeting ho. lics.
77 *Educ. of Poor Digest*, p. 789.
78 *Ann. Rep. B. & W. Assoc. S.P.C.K.* (1825–6).
79 S.R.O., D/P/lyn 23/6.
80 *Educ. Enq. Abstract*, p. 813.
81 Nat. Soc. *Inquiry, 1846–7*, Som. 12–13.
82 *P.O. Dir. Som.* (1861, 1866).

83 *Lond. Gaz.* 8 May 1874, p. 2446; S.R.O. C/E 4/380/244; *Kelly's Dir. Som.* (1889).
84 Ibid. C/E 4/64.
85 Ibid. 331.
86 Ibid. D/D/Ca 160, 180.
87 Nat. Soc. *Inquiry, 1846–7*, Som. 12–13.
88 S.R.O., C/E 4/380/309; R. Birch, 'A Study of the Life and Development of a Village School' (TS. in possession of Burrowbridge sch.), 8–9.
89 Birch, op. cit. 11.
90 S.R.O., DD/X/BWN 1 (admissions reg. 1858–78). Log bks. dating from 1868 are at the sch.
91 S.R.O., C/E 4/380/309.
92 Birch, op. cit. 95.
93 S.R.O., C/E 4/64.
94 Birch, op. cit. 12–13.
95 Burrowbridge sch., log bk.
96 *Char. Don.* pp. 1046–7.

CANNINGTON HUNDRED

CANNINGTON hundred occupies an area bordering the Bristol channel between the Quantock ridge on the west and the river Parrett on the east. It ranges between the flood plain of the lower Parrett, where flood prevention schemes have checked the changes in boundaries that formerly resulted from coastal erosion and river movement, and the higher ground of the Quantock scarp. The close settlement pattern in the 11th century was of villages, hamlets, and isolated farms,[1] some of the farms sited on outcrops of gravel in the Parrett basin. At least three sites have not been identified.[2] The hundred interlocks with Williton hundred on the west, a demonstration of the links between Cannington and Williton through ownership of both by the West Saxon royal house from the time of King Alfred if not earlier.[3] A detached part of Whitley hundred marked the presence at Durborough in Stogursey of a Glastonbury abbey estate.[4] In the Middle Ages agriculture and cloth production dominated the area and there was some commerce through Bridgwater's out-port at Combwich. Cloth was produced until the later 17th century; agriculture continued to be of prime importance in the mid 20th century, but forestry had been introduced extensively on the Quantocks.

Richard I granted the hundred to Hugh de Neville 'the elder',[5] possibly Hugh de Neville of Essex (d. 1234) who was referred to as lord of the hundred in the early 13th century.[6] The hundred descended with Stogursey manor[7] until 1541 when Edward Rogers of Cannington obtained a 21-year lease from the Crown. In 1545 the lease was converted into a grant in tail male.[8] A grant of the hundred in fee tail was made to Edward Courtenay, earl of Devon, in 1553 on the assumption that Rogers still held under lease.[9] Courtenay died in 1556 and a grant in reversion was made to Thomas Percy, earl of Northumberland, in 1557.[10] Rogers died in 1567 leaving the hundred to his heir George.[11] The hundred then descended, apart from a gap following its sale in 1652 to William Cox, with the manor of Cannington through the Rogers and Clifford families.[12] Charles, Lord Clifford, still claimed ownership in 1871.[13]

In 1086 Cannington hundred comprised just over 45 hides of which 10½ hides were free of geld. It included an estate belonging to Cannington church, William de Mohun's estate at or near Shurton in Stogursey, William de Falaise's at Stogursey, and possibly also Stockland and Spaxton.[14] In 1212 the hundred included Stogursey, Stockland Bristol, and the lands of the Hostiaria or Usher family,[15] presumably those later identified as at Huntstile in Chilton Trinity.[16] In 1242–3 Aisholt and Fiddington were part of the hundred; Stogursey borough attended the eyre by its own jury.[17]

By 1284–5 the hundred comprised Aisholt, Cannington (together with Chilton Trivet, Combwich, and Rodway tithings), Currypool tithing in Charlinch, Idstock tithing in Chilton Trinity, Otterhampton, Spaxton, Stockland Bristol, Shurton and Wick tithings in Stogursey, Adscombe and Plainsfield in Over Stowey, and Stringston.[18] In the earlier 14th century West Postridge in Aisholt, Charlinch, Fiddington with Bonson,

---

[1] *Dom. Geog. SW. Eng.* ed. H. C. Darby and R. Welldon Finn, 146–7.
[2] Colgrim's land, Alwine's land, and Theodric's land, all held of Roger de Courcelles: *V.C.H. Som.* i. 485–7.
[3] *E.H.D.* i. 535; H. P. R. Finberg, *Early Charters of Wessex*, pp. 126–7; *V.C.H. Som.* i. 435–6.
[4] *V.C.H. Som.* i. 462.
[5] *Rot. Hund.* (Rec. Com.), ii. 137.
[6] *S.R.S.* lxi, p. 44; Sanders, *Eng. Baronies*, 143.
[7] Below, Stogursey, manors.

[8] *L. & P. Hen. VIII*, xvi, p. 328; *Cal. Pat.* 1557–8, 186.
[9] *Cal. Pat.* 1553–4, 252.　　[10] Ibid. 1557–8, 186.
[11] P.R.O., C 142/148, no. 28.
[12] Ibid. E 317/Som. 3; below, Cannington, manors.
[13] S.R.O., D/RA 1/5/6.
[14] *V.C.H. Som.* i. 532–3; below, Stogursey, manors.
[15] *Bk. of Fees*, i. 83.
[16] Ibid. ii. 1266; below, Chilton Trinity, manors.
[17] *S.R.S.* xi, pp. 320–1.
[18] *Feud. Aids*, iv. 281–2.

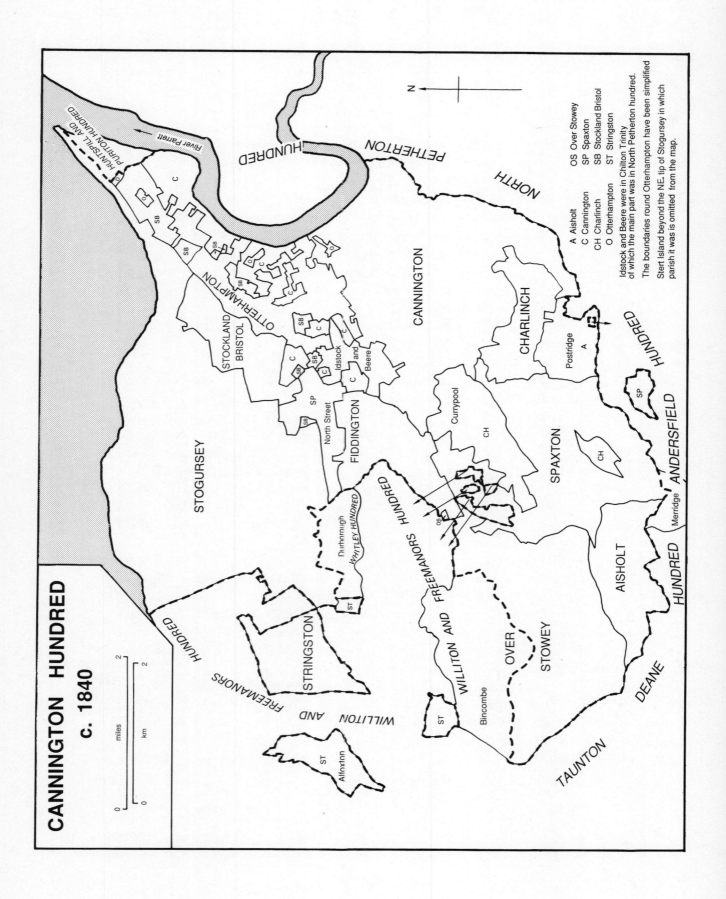

CANNINGTON HUNDRED
c. 1840

A Aisholt   OS Over Stowey
C Cannington   SP Spaxton
CH Charlinch   SB Stockland Bristol
O Otterhampton   ST Stringston

Idstock and Beere were in Chilton Trinity
of which the main part was in North Petherton hundred.

The boundaries round Otterhampton have been simplified
in which the tip of Stogursey in which

Stert Island beyond the NE. tip of Stogursey in which
parish it was omitted from the map.

Farringdon in Stogursey, and Aley in Over Stowey were also mentioned as in the hundred.[19] There were a few minor changes in the constituent parts of the hundred in the 16th and 17th centuries.[20] In 1742 the parishes within the hundred were listed as Aisholt, Cannington, Charlinch, Enmore, Fiddington, Otterhampton, Spaxton, Stockland, Stogursey, Over Stowey, and Stringston, together with the tithings of Alfoxton, Bincombe, Goathurst, Honibere and Fairfield, and Idstock and Beere. Alfoxton, Bincombe, and Honibere and Fairfield were otherwise recorded as in Williton and Freemanors hundred,[21] and Goathurst (rendered as Goathouse) was perhaps included in error for Lexworthy in Enmore parish and in Andersfield hundred.[22] In the later 18th century and until 1832 Cannington hundred comprised for fiscal purposes Aisholt, Cannington (including Chilton Trivet, Combwich, Orchard, Rodway Home, and Rodway Quarter tithings), Currypool tithing in Charlinch, Idstock and Beere tithing in Chilton Trinity (the rest of the parish being in Andersfield and North Petherton hundreds), Fiddington (including Bonson tithing), Otterhampton, Spaxton parish (including North Street, Pightley, and Tuxwell tithings but excluding Merridge in Andersfield hundred), Stockland Bristol, Stogursey (including Cock and Idson, Monkton, Shurton, and Wick tithings but excluding Durborough in Whitley hundred), Over Stowey (including Adscombe, and Higher and Lower Plainsfield tithings), and Stringston (excluding Alfoxton in Williton and Freemanors hundred).[23]

The sheriff's tourn for the hundred was held at Lypestone Hill, probably north of Clayhill in Cannington, by the 1370s.[24] Robert, Lord Poynings (d. 1446), held two 'legal' courts a year and a 'baronial' court every three weeks for the hundred.[25] Before 1652 the sheriff's tourn for the three hundreds of Andersfield, Cannington, and North Petherton had been held together at Lypestone Hill, but by that date was 'much discontinued'.[26] Charles, Lord Clifford (d. 1831), held a court at Stolford in Stogursey concerning rights on the foreshore in 1796–7.[27] At Christmas 1829 Charles, Lord Clifford, gave the usual hundred court dinner and lord's feast.[28] The court met at the Anchor inn in Cannington in 1834.[29]

In 1301 the income from the hundred included payments at the Purification called 'horderzeld', at Hockday called 'borghryst' or 'burghryzt', and at Michaelmas called 'austage'.[30] The lords claimed rights on the shore over seaweed (oare) and fishing in the 15th and earlier 18th centuries.[31] In the later 15th and early 16th century payments, known as 'borowryght' at Easter and as 'harderle' or 'harderhyll' at Michaelmas, were due from some tithings in the hundred and some manors. Additional income came from payments for watercourses and oare-burning licences.[32] Tithing silver was payable from the hundred in 1652.[33] In 1828–9 the hundred court jury ordered the levy of money from 'tithing acres' in the hundred.[34] The lords licensed a quarry in 1770–1 and fined a tenant in the same year for taking a cable found on the shore.[35]

A serjeant or bailiff of the hundred was recorded in 1225,[36] a bailiff in 1531,[37] a beadle c. 1608,[38] constables in the 17th century,[39] and a salaried bailiff in 1829.[40] There was a hundred pound in 1771–2.[41]

[19] *Feud. Aids*, iv. 308, 334–5; *S.R.S.* iii. 140–4; *Subsidy of 1334*, ed. R. E. Glasscock, 267–8.
[20] S.R.O., DD/BR/bn 10; *S.R.S.* xx. 244–54; *Som. Protestation Returns*, ed. Howard and Stoate, 193–4; P.R.O., E 317/Som. 3.
[21] *S.R.S.* iii. 298–9; *V.C.H. Som.* v. 7.
[22] *S.R.S.* iii. 296; above, Andersfield hundred.
[23] S.R.O., Q/REl 7.
[24] *Cal. Inq. p.m.* xiv, p. 142.
[25] P.R.O., C 139/126, no. 24.
[26] Ibid. E 317/Som. 3.
[27] Clifford MSS., Som. estate.
[28] Ibid. IV/6/7/X 1A.
[29] S.R.O., DD/DHR 36.
[30] *Cal. Inq. p.m.* iv, p. 342; *S.R.S.* lxviii, p. 33; S.R.O.,

DD/BR/bn 10.
[31] W. Suss. R.O., PHA 5730; S.R.O., Q/RR, papists' estates.
[32] W. Suff. R.O. 449/E3/15.53/2.2–3, 5–20; W. Suss. R.O., PHA 5730.
[33] P.R.O., E 317/Som. 3.
[34] Clifford MSS., IV/6/7/X 1A.
[35] Ibid. Som. estate, 1770–1.
[36] *S.R.S.* xi, p. 67.
[37] P.R.O., E 315/427.
[38] *S.R.S.* xxiii. 10.
[39] S.R.O., D/B/bw 1960; ibid. Q/SR 105/20; *S.R.S.* xxxiv, pp. 42, 151.
[40] Clifford MSS., IV/6/7/X 1A.
[41] Ibid. rental & accts. 1771–2.

AISHOLT

THE ancient parish of Aisholt or Asholt lay in two parts: the larger included Aisholt village on the eastern side of the Quantock ridge 4 km. south of Nether Stowey; the smaller was 4.5 km. north-east of Aisholt village, east of Spaxton village. The larger area, irregular in shape, measured 3.5 km. from east to west and 1 km. from north to south, the smaller was roughly oval, 1.7 km. east to west.[1] In 1885 the smaller area (11 houses, 53 persons) was transferred to Spaxton, leaving the civil parish of Aisholt with 875 a.[2] In 1933 the civil parish was absorbed into Spaxton.[3]

The larger part of the parish is divided into three by two streams which flow in steep-sided valleys, the land between rising at Black Knap on the Quantock ridge to 335 m. In the centre it reaches 198 m. at Aisholt wood, and in the east 220 m. on Hawkridge Hill. The valley bottoms, converging in the north-east where Hawkridge reservoir was completed in 1964,[4] lie at 30 m. above sea level. The land is largely on Cutcombe slates with bands of limestone, but Aisholt common is on Hangman grits.[5] The parish boundary on the east and south followed a footpath, lanes, and a stream, on the west an earth bank,[6] and on the north Parsons' Lane, probably an ancient route to the Quantock ridgeway.[7]

The smaller area, on the more fertile lower slope of the Quantocks, included a shallow valley watered by a tributary of the Durleigh brook, between the 61-m. and 30-m. contours bounded on the south by the Durleigh brook, on the west by the road between Enmore and Four Forks, and on the east by a lane.[8] It lies on marl with pockets of gravel.[9]

Aisholt village, named from its position in or near an ash wood, lies sheltered on the side of a valley called Holcombe running north-east. It comprises the church, the former rectory house, and a few cottages. Holcombe was the name of an estate with at least eight households in 1086,[10] and West Holcombe, possibly a settlement around Durborough Farm at the head of the valley, was named in the 15th century.[11] Holcombe Street was recorded in the 18th century[12] and several cottages stood at the upper end of the valley in 1833.[13] By the 20th century only Durborough Farm and two cottages, one probably medieval, the other with 16th-century

origins, survived.[14] Durborough Farm is a T-shaped house in which the short central arm appears to survive from a house of the late 16th or the early 17th century and the long range was rebuilt in the late 17th or the early 18th century. Lower Aisholt comprises a farm and a cottage on the Nether Stowey road.

In the smaller part of the parish a Roman villa west of Roughmoor Farm was occupied in the 3rd and 4th centuries.[15] There were two farms at Postridge in the Middle Ages, and a smallholding called Longthorns, on the road towards Bridgwater, recorded c. 1461.[16] Roughmoor and Crossfield farms had emerged by the 18th and 19th centuries respectively.[17] Several houses were built along the Four Forks to Enmore road; they included two rows built in the later 19th century behind a house called Barford Villa[18] and demolished in the later 20th.

At Holcombe in 1086 15 a. of woodland were recorded.[19] Field names current in the 19th century suggest former coppices and woodland cleared and converted to arable.[20] In 1791 the parish was described as well wooded[21] but by 1842 Aisholt wood and small plantations covered only 50 a. in all.[22] By 1905 there were over 100 a.[23] William de Reigny was granted free warren in his demesne of Aisholt in 1268.[24] In the 17th century there were commons at Hawkridge Hill and at Holcombe, later called Aisholt common, small areas of which were ploughed, including c. 23 a. in 1602.[25] By 1696 a quarter of Hawkridge common was let.[26] In 1721 a lessee was required to plant an oak, ash, or elm sapling every year.[27] In 1842 inclosed areas of former common were called Breaches, but there were still 240 a. of common at Aisholt common and Hawkridge Hill.[28] Aisholt common measured c. 171 a. in 1920 and 1986.[29]

In 1652 a woman was licensed to continue her limekiln for three years.[30] In 1842 there was a quarry near Durborough and quarries and kilns on Hawkridge Hill, beside Parsons' Lane, and by the road to Lower Aisholt.[31] Quarrying and limeburning continued on the side of Hawkridge Hill until 1930 or later.[32] Marl was dug at Postridge.[33] There was some mining in the early 18th century.[34]

There was a licensed victualler in the parish in 1657.[35]

Thirty-one households were recorded in the

[1] O.S. Map 1/50,000, sheet 181 (1976 edn.); sheet 182 (1976 edn.); S.R.O., tithe award. This article was completed in 1986.   [2] *Census* (1891).
[3] Youngs, *Local Admin Units*, i. 414.
[4] Inf. from Wessex Water.
[5] Geol. Surv. Map, 1/50,000, solid and drift sheet 295 (1984 edn.).   [6] *S.D.N.Q.* xxix. 239.
[7] O.S. Map 1/50,000, sheet 181 (1976 edn.) 1/25,000, ST 13 (1962 edn.).
[8] Ibid. 1/50,000, sheet 181 (1976 edn.).
[9] Geol. Surv. Map 1/50,000, solid and drift, sheet 295 (1984 edn.).   [10] *V.C.H. Som.* i. 486.
[11] Pole MS. 1036. Durborough Farm probably takes its name from the 17th-century tenants: S.R.O., DD/WG, box 8, survey c. 1682.   [12] S.R.O., Q/RRp 3/2.
[13] Ibid. DD/PLE 64.   [14] Ibid. DD/V/BWr 31.1.
[15] *Archaeology of Som.* ed. M. Aston and I. Burrow (1982), 65.
[16] P.R.O., E 326/6012, 6091; ibid. SC 2/200/29.

[17] S.R.O., Q/REl 7/1; O.S. Map 6", Som. XLIX. SE. (1887 edn.).
[18] S.R.O., tithe award; ibid. DD/KW 2; O.S. Map 6", Som. XLIX. SE. (1887 edn.).
[19] *V.C.H. Som.* i. 486.   [20] S.R.O., tithe award.
[21] Collinson, *Hist. Som.* iii. 237.
[22] S.R.O., tithe award.
[23] Statistics supplied by the then Bd. of Agric. 1905.
[24] *Cal. Chart. R.* 1257–1300, 92.
[25] S.R.O., DD/WG, box 8, survey c. 1682; box 9, survey; 15/3; 16/16–17.
[26] Ibid. 9, survey 1696.
[27] Ibid. 7/1.   [28] Ibid. tithe award.
[29] Ibid. DD/X/DD 2; Som. C.C., register of common land.
[30] S.R.O., DD/WG, box 13.
[31] Ibid. tithe award.   [32] Ibid. D/R/bw 13/1/1.
[33] Ibid. tithe award.   [34] Below, econ. hist.
[35] S.R.O., Q/RL.

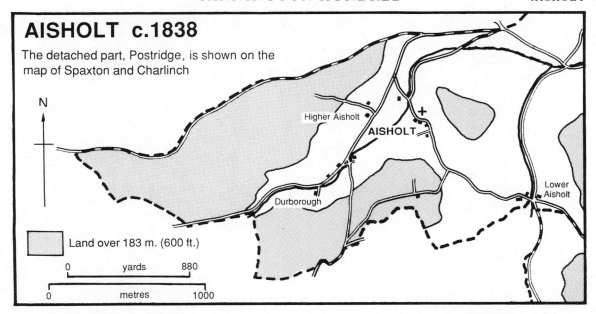

AISHOLT c.1838

The detached part, Postridge, is shown on the map of Spaxton and Charlinch

N

Higher Aisholt

AISHOLT

Lower Aisholt

Durborough

Land over 183 m. (600 ft.)

0   yards   880

0   metres   1000

later 17th century.[36] In 1801 the population was 136; it rose to a peak of 228 in 1831 and then fell steadily to 180 in 1871 and more rapidly to 121 in 1881. By 1921 the population of the reduced parish was 60.[37]

The poet and author Sir Henry Newbolt (1862–1938) lived in the Old School House in Aisholt from c. 1927 until his death.[38]

MANORS AND OTHER ESTATES. In 1086 the land of Roger de Courcelles included *HOLT* (*Olta*, probably the later Aisholt) and *HOL-COMBE*. Alweard had held both in 1066 and held Holcombe of Roger in 1086, when Roger's tenant at Holt was one Robert.[39] The two estates seem to have been combined in the manor of *AISHOLT*, probably a fee of William de Curci's barony of Stogursey in 1166,[40] and later held as of Stogursey manor, as in 1472.[41] In 1275, however, it was said to be held by the serjeanty of following the king in the army.[42]

William de Reigny held of William de Curci in 1166 a fee which was identified as Aisholt in 1186[43] and descended with Doniford in St. Decumans[44] to Sir William de Reigny (d. 1275), on whose death Aisholt was divided. Land at Aisholt, Lower Aisholt, and Holcombe, with the advowson, passed to his illegitimate daughter Joan, wife of Robert de Acton. Joan was followed by her son Robert (d. c. 1303), her grandson Robert de Acton (d. c. 1316), and her great-grandson Richard de Acton.[45] Richard settled the estate in 1384 on himself and his wife Margaret, with remainder to Sir Thomas Fichet,

lord of Spaxton. The Fichets had possession by 1395,[46] and the manor descended with Spaxton.[47]

Land called in 1202 Postridge and later *WEST POSTRIDGE* seems to have descended from Roger de Reigny to his grandson John de Reigny.[48] It may have been the ½ knight's fee which the heirs of Sir William de Reigny (d. 1275) held of Robert Walerand's heirs, lords of Rodway in Cannington and mesne tenants of the barony of Dunster, in 1284–5.[49] It was said in 1294 to be held of Rodway[50] but in 1472 to be held of John FitzJames and his wife Joan, widow of Hugh Malet.[51] In 1431 it was held by John Hill.[52]

Roger de Reigny gave land later called *EAST POSTRIDGE* manor to Plympton priory (Devon) before 1166.[53] The priory acquired more land but in the 13th century granted the whole estate to Walter of Kentisbere in return for an annuity which they probably sold before 1372.[54] East Postridge descended to Gillian of Kentisbere, who in 1280 assigned it to her daughter Joan, wife of Hugh Popham.[55] In 1326[56] Joan's son John Popham (d. c. 1345) held it. John's son Hugh (d. c. 1361) left a widow Hawise (d. c. 1389) with a life estate in East Postridge. Their sons sold their reversionary interests to Sir Thomas Fichet in 1384.[57] In 1372 Fichet redeemed the annuity charged on the estate from Katharine FrIf raunceys but in 1381 he granted it back to her for her life.[58] In 1398 the estate was settled on Robert Hill and his wife Isabel, daughter of Sir Thomas.[59] Robert's son John held East and West Postridge as two estates in 1431,[60] but they were later a single manor and

36 Dwelly, *Hearth Tax*, i. 73.
37 *Census.*
38 *D.N.B.*; V. Waite, *Portrait of the Quantocks* (1969), 90; *Kelly's Dir. Som.* (1927–39).
39 *V.C.H. Som.* i. 486–7; *Dom. Bk.* ed. Thorn, 361.
40 *Red Bk. Exch.* (Rolls Ser.), i. 225.
41 *S.R.S.* iii. 16; P.R.O., C 140/42, no. 51.
42 *Cal. Inq. p.m.* ii, pp. 94–5.
43 *Pipe R.* 1186 (P.R.S. xxxvi), 140; *Red Bk. Exch.* (Rolls Ser.), i. 225.
44 *V.C.H. Som.* v. 152; *S.R.S.* xxxiii, p. 10.
45 *S.R.S.* vi. 395; lxviii, p. 30; extra ser. 309–10.
46 Ibid. xvii. 126; below, Over Stowey, manors.

47 P.R.O., E 212/14; below, Spaxton, manors.
48 *S.R.S.* vi. 20; *Cur. Reg. R.* ii. 90.
49 *Feud. Aids*, iv. 28.   50 *Cal. Inq. p.m.* iii, p. 142.
51 P.R.O., C 140/42, no. 51.
52 *Feud. Aids*, iv. 393.   53 B.L. Harl. Ch. 49 B 23.
54 P.R.O., E 210/3754; *S.R.S.* lxviii, p. 46.
55 B.L. Add. Ch. 20230; *S.D.N.Q.* xxi. 464; below, N. Petherton, manors.   56 *S.R.S.* xii. 110.
57 *S.R.S.* xvii. 134; lxviii, p. 46; below, N. Petherton, manors.
58 *S.R.S.* lxviii, p. 45; Pole MS. 4142.
59 *S.R.S.* xvii. 174.
60 *Feud. Aids*, iv. 435.

descended with Spaxton, merging with it by the 18th century.[61] In 1920 Postridge farm was sold by E. A. V. Stanley to Somerset county council, the owner in 1986.[62]

Postridge Farm has a double-pile plan incorporating a south range of late 16th or 17th-century origin, remodelled when the parallel north range was added in the later 18th century. There was further refitting in the early 19th century.

Part of William de Reigny's estate at Postridge and Aisholt was divided after his death in 1275 among some of the heirs who received shares of Doniford:[63] an estate at Aisholt descended in the Huish family until 1627 or later,[64] and one called Horsey's Postridge[65] in the Horsey family until 1507 or later.[66]

Lands at West Holcombe were conveyed by John, son and heir of John of Holcombe of Dunster, to Sir Edward Hull in 1443–4, and probably descended in the Malet family with Enmore. It may be the estate known as Holcombe Colford or Holcombe and Colford in the later 15th and early 16th century.[67]

LITTLE POSTRIDGE was owned by the Malet family in the 16th century like Hulkshay in North Petherton.[68] With the addition of Longthorns and other land in Postridge held by the Cridland family in the 17th century,[69] Little Postridge descended as part of Enmore manor.[70] A house stood at Little Postridge in 1833 but the land had been added to Postridge farm.[71] The house had gone by 1887.[72] The house at Longthorns is a 19th-century Italianate villa, probably built between 1861 and 1866.[73]

Joan, William de Reigny's illegitimate daughter, gave an estate at Lower Aisholt to a villein tenant, Robert Tropenel, in 1292.[74] By the 15th century it was held with Plainsfield in Over Stowey[75] and in 1492 was said to be held of the bishop of Bath and Wells.[76] After the death of Nicholas Williams without male issue it reverted to the Crown.[77] By 1601 the estate had been acquired by Humphrey Blake and appears to have descended with the advowson until 1842 or later.[78] The rest of Lower Aisholt remained part of Aisholt manor until that manor was divided and sold in 1833[79] when it was probably bought by Mary Stephens, the owner in 1834.[80] Both farms at Lower Aisholt became part of the Quantock estate; in 1933 they were sold as a single farm. One house, since demolished, was then being used for storage and the owner was

said to have used an adjacent building with panelled ceilings as a cider cellar.[81] The other house probably dates from the 16th century and has 19th- and 20th-century additions.

ECONOMIC HISTORY. In 1086 Holcombe and Holt, apparently Aisholt, were each recorded as having been assessed at 1 virgate. Postridge was not recorded. Holt, with land for 1 ploughteam, was all in demesne except for 10 a. occupied by 2 bordars, and had 1½ a. of meadow. Holcombe, where there was land for 2 teams, was divided equally between the demesne, with 1 team on ½ virgate and 2 *servi*, and 1 team on ½ virgate shared between 1 *villanus* and 5 bordars. There were 12 beasts, 12 she-goats, 4 sheep, and 3 swine, and 75 a. of pasture.[82]

By the early 15th century East Postridge manor[83] appears to have been entirely enclosed and over 400 a. were shared between 14 tenants producing rents of £10 12s. 6d. in 1448.[84] Farming inventories of parishioners in the 17th century included oats as well as wheat; few holdings were over 30 a.[85] By 1842 half the parish was arable and there were 138 a. of meadow, mainly at Postridge, and 160 a. of pasture, some at Aisholt possibly former meadow. There were 21 a. of orchards.[86] Almost half the reduced parish in 1905 was arable,[87] producing wheat, barley, and roots.[88]

By the earlier 19th century holdings were being amalgamated. By 1833 Little Postridge was reduced to a landless cottage while Postridge farm included land in Charlinch and amounted to over 200 a. Lower Aisholt farm was then 180 a. and Higher Aisholt 110 a.[89] A further 9 farms were over 30 a.[90] By 1851 the three largest farms totalled over 720 a., including land outside the parish, and employed 22 labourers.[91] Numbers employed on farms had fallen to about 10 by 1881, coinciding with a fall of over 30 per cent in the population since 1871.[92] By 1919 farms had been further amalgamated; one old farm house was used for storage and a cottage as a fowl house.[93]

A licence for mining copper and other ores in Aisholt was granted in 1714[94] and a short-lived mining venture in Aisholt and Over Stowey operated by two partnerships produced £45 for the lord of the manor between 1716 and 1719.[95] A tanner, probably at Postridge, was recorded

61 Below, Spaxton, manors; S.R.O., DD/WG 8.
62 Som. C.C., deed 1920.
63 *V.C.H. Som.* v. 152–3.
64 *Cal. Close,* 1429–35, 285; P.R.O., CP 25(2)/207/40 Eliz. I Trin.; S.R.O., DD/BR/bn 10; *S.R.S.* lxvii, p. 27.
65 P.R.O., SC 2/200/28; ibid. SC 6/977/1.
66 *Cal. Inq. p.m.* xix, p. 142; *Cal. Close,* 1374–7, 159; 1435–41, 159; 1500–9, 303; *S.R.S.* xxii. 88.
67 Pole MS. 1036; W. Suss. R.O., PHA 5730; S.R.O., DD/BR/bn 10; W. Suff. R.O. 449/E3/15.53/2.16.
68 *S.R.S.* xxi. 129–30; Devon R.O. 1148 M/add 2/65; P.R.O., C 3/127, no. 23; below, N. Petherton, manors.
69 *S.R.S.* li. 281–2.
70 S.R.O., DD/PC 13, 16; above, Enmore, manors.
71 S.R.O., DD/PLE 64.
72 O.S. Map 6", Som. XLIX. SE. (1887 edn.).
73 S.R.O., DD/KW 2; *P.O. Dir. Som.* (1861, 1866).
74 P.R.O., E 210/6978.
75 Ibid. C 142/23, no. 5; below, Over Stowey, manors.

76 *Cal. Inq. p.m. Hen. VII* i, p. 348.
77 e.g. *Cal. Pat.* 1569–72, p. 130; 1572–5, pp. 451–2.
78 e.g. *Som. Wills,* ed. Brown, ii. 13; S.R.O., tithe award; below, church.
79 S.R.O., DD/PLE 64.
80 Ibid. DD/SAS (C/238) 52.
81 Ibid. DD/KW 2.   82 *V.C.H. Som.* i. 486–7.
83 By then probably including West Postridge.
84 P.R.O., E 326/6012; ibid. SC 6/977/8.
85 S.R.O., DD/SP inventories, 1637, 1646, 1684–5; DD/WG, box 8, survey c. 1682.
86 Ibid. tithe award.
87 Statistics supplied by the then Bd. of Agric., 1905.
88 *Kelly's Dir. Som.* (1906).   89 S.R.O., DD/PLE 64.
90 Ibid. tithe award.   91 P.R.O., HO 107/1924.
92 Ibid. RG 11/2369; *Census,* 1871–81.
93 S.R.O., DD/KW 2.
94 Ibid. DD/WG, box 7.
95 Ibid. 15/5–6.

in 1705.[96] A tanyard established at Postridge by 1832 belonged to South Holmes farm in Spaxton.[97] The name Rack close recorded near Aisholt village in 1842 suggests clothmaking.[98] In 1851 there were carpenters, a cattle dealer, and a grocer in the parish,[99] the last surviving until 1866 or later.[1] A millwright lived at Postridge in the later 19th century.[2]

A mill at Holcombe in 1086[3] was not recorded again. A miller was mentioned in 1674.[4]

LOCAL GOVERNMENT. The two manors of Aisholt and Holcombe Colford answered separately at Cannington hundred court in 1473–4 but in 1521 the tithingman answered for both together.[5] In the 18th century Aisholt tithing lay in three separate parishes.[6] Courts were held at Postridge in 1362[7] and court rolls survive for East Postridge manor for 1423–4, 1426–7, and probably for 1461,[8] but Postridge was administered with Spaxton by the 1680s.[9] Aisholt manor was administered with Aley by the end of the 16th century and court rolls for Aley and Aisholt survive for 1579, 1588, 1592, and 1599–1604.[10]

The tithingman, two wardens, and two overseers were appointed in rotation by the later 16th century.[11] The overseers provided relief in cash and kind in the early 18th century and supervised the apprenticeship of pauper children,[12] but there was no record of a poorhouse before the 1830s,[13] and there was no vestry in 1840.[14] The poorhouse, unoccupied in 1842,[15] was later divided into cottages, but by 1986 was a single dwelling known as Shepherds Cottage.

The parish formed part of the Bridgwater poor-law union in 1836 and the Bridgwater rural district in 1894.[16]

CHURCH. There was a chaplain at Aisholt in 1267.[17] The living was a rectory by 1291.[18] It was held with Over Stowey from 1919 and united with it in 1921.[19] From 1969 it was served by the vicar of Cannington, who on retirement from Cannington served Aisholt from 1980 until 1989 as acting curate-in-charge of an independent benefice.[20]

On the death of Sir William de Reigny in 1275

his cousin and coheir Alice, wife of William le Pruz, conveyed the advowson to Thomas Fraunceys and his son Thomas.[21] In 1313 the advowson was exercised by John of Membury, son of Sir William de Reigny's mistress Joan le Botiller.[22] In 1405 the advowson was held by Thomas Trowe.[23] John Trowe presented in 1453[24] and his trustees in 1474.[25] The advowson passed to Hugh Trowe (d. by 1493) and his wife Elizabeth (d. 1493). Their heir was Hugh's brother Thomas[26] but John Courtenay presented in 1493.[27] Thomas Trowe was attainted in 1504[28] and in 1506 the advowson was granted to Sir John Williams.[29] Sir John died in 1508 leaving a son Reginald under age.[30] Reginald (d. 1559)[31] was succeeded in turn by his sons John (d. 1560),[32] Nicholas (d. 1568), and Richard (d. 1568). On Richard's death the advowson reverted to the Crown,[33] which granted its rights to Thomas Freke and Henry Starr in 1600.[34] Humphrey Blake, who was dealing with the advowson in 1601[35] and 1613,[36] by will proved 1620 left it to his son Edmund.[37] In 1620, however, John Toogood presented.[38] In 1638 Edmund Blake with others conveyed the advowson, probably for the next presentation, to the rector, William Hite.[39] Later that year Hite died and the Crown claimed the right of patronage, probably for simony, but presented jointly with John Hite.[40] In 1640 the Crown presented again[41] but by 1660 the Blakes had recovered the advowson.[42] Humphrey Blake in his will proved 1665 left it to his son Nathaniel (d. 1705), who presented in 1668 and was himself presented in 1670. In 1706 and 1707 Nathaniel's trustees presented. His daughter Katharine married John Brice (d. 1761), rector 1707–56,[43] and the advowson descended in the Brice family to John's son Nathaniel (d. 1790), rector 1756–84, and to the latter's daughter Betty.[44] Her heir was her cousin John Brice, rector 1800–32.[45] The patronage appears to have passed to Brice's successor as rector,[46] but by 1888 it had been acquired by E. J. Stanley, whose son E. A. V. Stanley held it in 1919.[47] In 1920 the patronage was vested in the Martyrs Memorial Patronage Trust.[48]

The church was valued at £5 in 1291,[49] £7 12s. 3d. net in 1535,[50] £60 c. 1668,[51] and £280 in 1829–31.[52] The tithes, worth £6 2s. in 1535,[53]

96 Ibid. 7/1.
97 Below, Spaxton, econ. hist.
98 S.R.O., tithe award.
99 P.R.O., HO 107/1924.
1 *P.O. Dir. Som.* (1866).
2 Ibid. (1866, 1875).
3 *V.C.H. Som.* i. 486.
4 S.R.O., Q/SR 121/13.
5 Ibid. DD/BR/bn 10; W. Suss. R.O., PHA 5370.
6 S.R.O., Q/REl 7/1.
7 P.R.O., E 326/6062.
8 Ibid. SC 2/200/27–9.
9 S.R.O., DD/WG, box 8, survey c. 1682.
10 Ibid. 16/8–9, 11–12, 16–17.
11 Ibid. D/P/aish 2/1/2, 13/2/1.
12 Ibid. 13/2/1.
13 Ibid. D/D/Rr Aisholt.
14 Ibid. D/D/Va 1840.
15 Ibid. tithe award.
16 Youngs, *Local Admin. Units*, i. 671, 673.
17 *Cal. Pat.* 1266–72, 103.
18 *Tax. Eccl.* (Rec. Com.), 198.
19 S.R.O., D/P/o. sty 22/1; *Dioc. Dir.* (1921–2).
20 *Dioc. Dir.*; local inf.
21 S.R.O., DD/CN 5/10.
22 *S.R.S.* i. 49, 154–5; extra ser. 295–8.
23 Ibid. xiii, p. 59.
24 Ibid. xlix, pp. 206–7.
25 Ibid. lii, p. 56.
26 P.R.O., C 142/23, no. 5.
27 *S.R.S.* lii, p. 181.
28 *Cal. Inq. p.m. Hen. VII*, iii, p. 418.
29 *Cal. Pat.* 1494–1509, 447.
30 P.R.O., C 142/22, no. 64.
31 Ibid. C 142/128, no. 67.
32 Ibid. C 142/128, no. 69.
33 Ibid. C 142/152, no. 124.
34 Ibid. C 66/1540.
35 Ibid. CP 25(2)/207/43 Eliz. I Hil.
36 Ibid. CP 25(2)/346/11 Jas. I Mich.
37 *Som. Wills*, ed. Brown, ii. 13.
38 *Som. Incumbents*, ed. Weaver, 306.
39 P.R.O., CP 25(2)/480/13 Chas. I Hil.
40 S.R.O., D/D/B reg. 20, p. 40.
41 Ibid. pp. 65–6.
42 *Som. Incumbents*, ed. Weaver, 307.
43 Ibid.; *Som. Wills*, ed. Brown, ii. 13; S.R.O., DD/X/SR 5.
44 S.R.O., D/P/aish 2/1/2; ibid. T/PH/ay 1.
45 Ibid. T/PH/ay 1; ibid. D/D/Rr Aisholt.
46 *Rep. Com. Eccl. Revenues*, pp. 124–5.
47 S.R.O., DD/SAS PR 26.
48 Inf. from trust.
49 *Tax. Eccl.* (Rec. Com.), 198.
50 *Valor Eccl.* (Rec. Com.), i. 215.
51 S.R.O., D/D/Vc 24.
52 *Rep. Com. Eccl. Revenues*, pp. 124–5.
53 *Valor Eccl.* (Rec. Com.), i. 215.

were commuted for £210 in 1842.[54] The glebe, valued at 40s. in 1535,[55] included land at Doniford in St. Decumans,[56] given to the rector for serving a chapel at Doniford.[57] In 1842 there were 38 a. of glebe at Aisholt[58] and over 20 a. at Doniford.[59] The rector still held the land when the benefices of Aisholt and Over Stowey were united.[60] The parsonage house was recorded in 1626 and 1639 when it had a hopyard and orchard.[61] The house was said to be in perfect repair in 1815[62] and fit in 1835.[63] After the union with Over Stowey in 1921 it was sold.[64] Now called Aisholt House, it dates from the 18th century and has a main south front of three bays and three storeys. Its recessed end blocks of two storeys with swept gables may have been added when the house was remodelled in the 19th century and the grounds were planted with specimen trees.

Nicholas Savage succeeded his brother Simon as rector in 1315 while still a deacon and was licensed to study for a year.[65] In 1389 the rector employed a chaplain, possibly to serve the chapel at Doniford.[66] In 1554 the church lacked a portuas and a processional.[67] From 1566[68] the parish was served by curates, one of whom was presented in 1576 for disturbing his neighbours, for failing to catechize, keep the register, or conduct weekday services, and for marrying non-parishioners without licence.[69] He became rector in the same year.[70] William Hite, rector 1620–38, was resident and had a library worth nearly £20.[71] Henry Bennet, rector 1638–40, was ousted by Edmund Estcourt,[72] who married into a prominent local family and appears to have lived at Plainsfield at Over Stowey.[73] From 1707 to 1832 the Brice family was normally resident.[74] There were 12 communicants c. 1776.[75] John Reeks was inducted in 1784 on the day of his marriage to the patron's daughter.[76] He was frequently unable to perform his duties and the parish was served until 1805 by William Holland, vicar of Over Stowey. Congregations were often augmented by Holland's parishioners.[77] By 1815 John Brice held one service each Sunday, alternately morning and afternoon,[78] but by 1840 his successor held two services and celebrated communion four times a year.[79] By 1870 celebrations had doubled and two Sunday services continued to be held[80] but in 1921 when the rector also served Over Stowey[81] only one service was held. In 1980 there were about 30 communicants at morning service.[82]

The church house, ruinous in 1636,[83] was bought, probably in the mid 17th century, by Amery's charity.[84] It was last recorded in 1696.[85]

The church of *ALL SAINTS*, dedicated to St. Michael in 1530,[86] is built of rubble with freestone dressings and consists of a chancel, a nave with north vestry, south aisle, and south porch, and a west tower. With the possible exception of the chamfered chancel arch the whole church appears to be of the 15th century. New windows were put into the nave and south aisle in the 17th century. A singing gallery had been built by 1812[87] but was later demolished. Some restoration was carried out in 1895. Fragments of medieval glass survive in the aisle windows and there are a 15th-century door and font. The chamber organ dates from c. 1820 and was made by Samuel Parsons of Bloomsbury, London. The plate dates from 1844 and there were four bells until c. 1965 when one was sold.[88] The registers date from 1652.[89]

NONCONFORMITY. None known.

EDUCATION. The rector was licensed to keep a school in the parish in 1662.[90] There was no school in 1819 but in 1825 a day school had 10 children and a Sunday school 17. Other children went to the school at Nether Stowey at the rector's expense.[91] There was no day school in 1835 but 29 children attended Sunday school.[92] In 1846 a small cottage school, possibly in the Old School House, taught 29 children and a further 4 boys attended only the Sunday school.[93] In 1859 there was a small day school for girls.[94] From 1874 children from Aisholt attended the Aisholt and Merridge district school at Lower Merridge in Spaxton.[95]

CHARITIES FOR THE POOR. Anthony Amery, rector 1577–1620, gave £15 to the poor. The bequest was used to buy the church house, the rent from which was distributed to the poor on the Sunday before Christmas.[96] By 1786 the

54 S.R.O., tithe award.
55 *Valor Eccl.* (Rec. Com.), i. 215.
56 S.R.O., DD/WY 12/F4.
57 *V.C.H. Som.* v. 153.
58 S.R.O., tithe award.
59 Ibid. tithe award, St. Decuman's.
60 *Kelly's Dir. Som.* (1923).
61 S.R.O., D/D/Rg 259.
62 Ibid. D/D/Rb 1815.
63 *Rep. Com. Eccl. Revenues*, pp. 124–5.
64 S.R.O., D/P/o. sty 22/1.
65 *S.R.S.* i. 83, 101.
66 P.R.O., C 85/83/40; above, this section.
67 S.R.O., D/D/Ca 22.
68 *Som. Incumbents*, ed. Weaver, 306; S.R.O., DD/X/SR 5.
69 S.R.O., D/D/Ca 57.
70 *Som. Incumbents*, ed. Weaver, 306.
71 S.R.O., DD/SP inventory, 1658 (should be 1638).
72 Ibid. D/D/B reg. 20, pp. 40, 65.
73 *Som. Wills*, ed. Brown, vi. 7.
74 S.R.O., DD/SAS PR 26; D/D/B reg. 27, p. 49.
75 Ibid. D/D/Vc 88.

76 Ibid. D/P/aish 2/1/2.
77 Ibid. T/PH/ay 1.
78 Ibid. D/D/Rb 1815, 1827.
79 Ibid. D/D/Va 1840, 1843.
80 Ibid. 1870.
81 Ibid. DD/SAS PR 26.
82 Ibid. D/P/aish 2/5/2.
83 Ibid. D/D/Ca 310.
84 Ibid. D/P/aish 17/2/1.
85 Ibid. DD/WG box 9, survey 1696; below, charities.
86 *S.D.N.Q.* iii. 91.
87 S.R.O., T/PH/ay 1.
88 Ibid. DD/SAS CH 16/1; D/P/aish 9/1/2.
89 Ibid. D/P/aish 2/1/1–5.
90 Ibid. D/D/Bs 39.
91 *Educ. of Poor Digest*, p. 771; *Ann. Rep. B. & W. Dioc. Assoc. S.P.C.K.* (1825–6), 41.
92 *Educ. Enq. Abstract*, p. 790.
93 J. J. B. Clarke, *Acct. of Church Educ. among Poor* (1846), 29; Nat. Soc. *Inquiry, 1846–7*, Som. 2–3.
94 Harrison, Harrod, & Co. *Dir. Som.* (1859).
95 S.R.O., C/E 4/380/4; below, Spaxton, educ.
96 S.R.O., D/P/aish 17/2/1.

CANNINGTON: GURNEY STREET MANOR

CHARLINCH: GOTHELNEY MANOR

CANNINGTON: BLACKMOOR FARM

DURLEIGH: WEST BOWER MANOR, *c.* 1958

charity seems to have been confused with the £20 given by Thomas Good in 1689.[97] Amery's charity had probably been lost but the name continued as an alternative name for Good's charity.[98] William Brice (d. 1774) left £100 for a weekly bread distribution. The rector held the capital in the early 19th century[99] but it was later invested in consols. Charity distributions ceased c. 1930 and the income has been allowed to accumulate.[1]

CANNINGTON

THE large ancient parish of Cannington lies on the west bank of the river Parrett, the village itself 5 km. north-west from Bridgwater. The name, which is also borne by the hundred, seems to be derived from the Quantocks,[2] and Cannington was linked with two other royal estates, Williton and Carhampton, in King Alfred's will.[3] From the 12th century it was the site of a Benedictine nunnery.[4] Leland in the earlier 16th century described it as a pretty uplandish town,[5] and in the 1840s it was known as a genteel village admired for its unrivalled salubrity of air.[6] The parish formerly included part of the village of Combwich, with its port and ferry terminal.[7] In 1881 the parish contained 4,980 a. (2,015 ha.), much of which lay in detached pieces, particularly in the marshes north of Combwich. Detached and peninsular pieces were transferred to other parishes, the part of Combwich and lands to the north, with 45 houses and 226 people, to Otterhampton in 1882 and 1886, Coultings, with 1 house and 4 people, to Fiddington in 1884, and part of Knaplock, with 1 house and 7 people, to Stockland Bristol in 1886. Also in 1886 Idstock and Beere, forming a detached part of Chilton Trinity with 3 houses and 21 people, were transferred to Cannington.[8] The modern civil parish measures 1,650 ha. (4,077 a.).[9]

The parish drains ENE. into the river Parrett, which with Fenlyns rhyne (otherwise Perrymoor brook) forms much of the eastern boundary. Across the centre runs Cannington brook and across the north Combwich pill into which two smaller streams flow north across Wild moor (otherwise South moor). The land rises from the floodplain of the Parrett only a few metres above sea level to the summit of Cannington Hill at 80 m. between Cannington brook and Combwich pill, to 65 m. at Woodcock Downs on the south boundary, and to nearly 50 m. west of Cannington Hill. The low-lying land is alluvium, with river deposits along Cannington brook. The higher land lies mostly on sandstone (Mercia Mudstone in the south and south-west, Otter Sandstone on the north side of Cannington Hill and in the south-east) and limestone (Rodway Siltstone on the south side of Cannington Hill

and further west, an outcrop of carboniferous limestone at the top of the hill).[10] In the north blue lias was quarried, and there were limekilns in the north-west. Quarrying for building and road stone on Cannington Hill began in the late 18th century,[11] and continues for road stone, gravel, and aggregate in the later 20th.[12]

Mesolithic material has been found at Brymore and in a cave at Cannington Hill. The hill is crowned with an Iron Age hillfort, called Cynwir or Cynwit Castle or Cannington Camp, which has field systems nearby and seems to have been in use during the Roman period. Also nearby was a cemetery of up to 2,000 graves, in use from the mid 4th to the 8th century with some earlier material. There may have been a Roman temple near the cemetery. Both hillfort and cemetery have been damaged by quarrying. At Combwich there was a settlement from the 1st to the 4th century.[13]

The Saxon 'herpath' entered the parish via the Parrett crossing at Combwich and seems to have passed south of Cannington Hill through Knoll to Ashford.[14] Settlement at Cannington may have originated where a road south from Combwich and the 'herpath' crossed an east-west route. The church and the later nunnery were built on a gentle south-facing slope above a stream. The village street north of the church and nunnery was called King Street in the 15th century, Cannington and Frog streets in the early 19th, and High, Fore, and East streets in the later 19th. Church Street may have been part of the original north-south route; Brook Street, to the east of the church and so named by 1861, was part of the turnpike road by the 18th century. Northwards there were routes to Rodway and Combwich along Rodway Lane; and further west along Conduits Lane, later Chads Hill, through Knap to Cannington Hill.[15] The route from Bridgwater through the village to Watchet was turnpiked by the Bridgwater trust in 1759[16] and improved in 1822, notably by cutting the New Road from Sandford bridge towards Chilton Trivet.[17] A turnpike gate was recorded in 1841 and 1861, probably between East and Fore Streets at the end of Rodway Lane.[18] The road through Rodway north to

[97] *Char. Don.* pp. 1048–9; *15th Rep. Com Char.* 351; S.R.O., D/P/aish 17/1/1.
[98] Char. Com. files.   [99] *15th Rep. Com. Char.* 351.
[1] S.R.O., D/P/can 23/11; Char. Com. files.
[2] Ekwall, *Eng. Place-Names* (1960), 81; *S.D.N.Q.* xviii. 177–8. This article was completed in 1989.
[3] *E.H.D.* i. 535.   [4] *V.C.H. Som.* ii. 109.
[5] Leland, *Itin.* ed. Toulmin Smith, i. 163.
[6] *Taunton Courier*, 20 July 1842.   [7] Below, econ. hist.
[8] S.R.O., tithe award; *Census*, 1881, 1891. Combwich is treated as a single unit in this article.
[9] *Census*, 1981.
[10] O.S. Map 1/50,000, sheet 182 (1974 edn.); Geol. Surv.

Map 1/50,000, sheet 295 (1984 edn.).
[11] Clifford MSS., Som. estate papers; ibid. IV/6/7/X 1A; S.R.O., tithe award; O.S. Map 6", Som. XXXVII. SE. (1886 edn.); XLIX. NE. (1887 edn.); L. NW. (1889 edn.).
[12] *Bridgwater Mercury*, 7 Mar. 1989.
[13] Som. C.C., Sites and Mons. Rec.
[14] S.R.O., DD/X/BOA.
[15] *S.R.S.* lvii, p. 50; S.R.O., DD/BW 461; Clifford MSS., III/10/1–3; ibid. acct. 1802/3; P.R.O., RG 9/1621.
[16] 32 Geo. II, c. 40.
[17] S.R.O., Q/AB 35; ibid. tithe award.
[18] P.R.O., HO 107/935; ibid. RG 9/1621; S.R.O., D/R/bw 22/1/47.

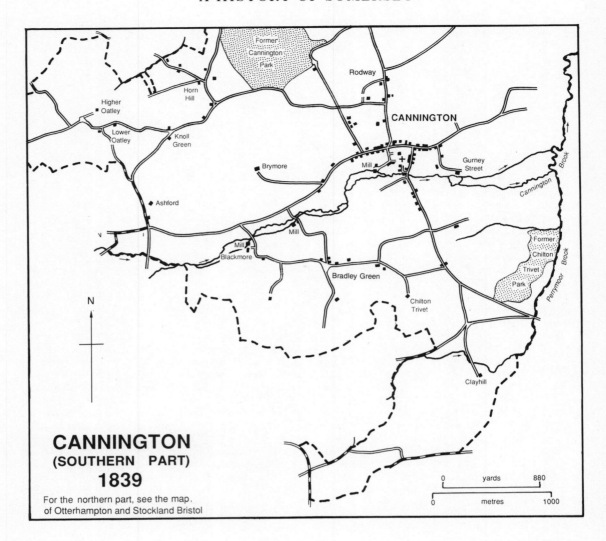

CANNINGTON
(SOUTHERN PART)
1839

For the northern part, see the map
of Otterhampton and Stockland Bristol

Combwich increased in importance when the power station at Hinkley Point was begun in the late 1950s. To the south, Malt Shovel Lane bypasses the village and serves Blackmoor Farm, crossing Blackmoor bridge. It was suggested as a bypass for Cannington in 1822.[19] The bridge was mentioned in 1632[20] and was replaced in 1792.[21] Brook bridge, recorded in 1708,[22] was probably Cannington bridge on the Bridgwater road, which was rebuilt further east in 1929.[23]

Apart from the church, Cannington Court, and the almshouses, most of the buildings in the centre of Cannington date from the late 18th or 19th century and are of brick or local stone. Frog Cottage in East Street and two cottages in Church Street probably date from the 17th century and 1 Fore Street is of the mid 18th.

Further north, Combwich seems to have been confined to the north side of the pill until the later 20th century and appears to be on a regular grid, its eastern boundary defined by an earlier

line of the river bank. Brookside probably represents a quay; Ship Lane, extended into School Lane, is the northern street, and the two were joined by 1851 by May Pole Street, renamed Church Street after 1868.[24]

Of three 11th-century farmsteads or hamlets Blackmoor was still a small hamlet in the later 18th century,[25] when Chilton and Clayhill were single farms. Other 11th-century sites, Dodesham, Pedredham, and Pillock, did not survive the Middle Ages, perhaps partly because of flooding in the 15th century, notably c. 1427 and in the 1480s.[26] Pedredham was recorded in the later 14th century[27] and the name was still in occasional use in the early 17th century,[28] but thereafter only Petherhams Marsh is recorded. Brymore, Withiel, Forde (later Ashford), Knaplock, Orchard, and Putnell occur in the earlier 13th century,[29] Knoll by 1333, and Oatley in the 15th century.[30] Knoll and Oatley both seem to have developed as scatters of houses around a

19 S.R.O., Q/AB 35.
20 *S.R.S.* xxiv. 181.
21 S.R.O., D/P/can 14/5/1.
22 Ibid. 4/1/1.
23 Ibid. DD/SIAS 60.
24 P.R.O., HO 107/1924; ibid. RG 9/1621.

25 S.R.O., DD/S/WH 218, 249.
26 *Cal. Papal Reg.* vii. 512; W. Suff. R.O. 449/E3/15.53/2.8.
27 *S.R.S.* xlviii, pp. 199, 230–1.
28 S.R.O., DD/DK 1.
29 Below, manors.
30 *Cal. Close,* 1441–7, 272; *S.R.S.* lvii, pp. 34–5.

green, and a similar settlement had emerged at Bradlake, later Bradley Green, by 1494.[31] The first two disappeared, Knoll Green in the early 19th century.[32] Rodway was a small hamlet perhaps arranged around a green and in existence by the early 13th century.[33] Rodway Farmhouse, formerly Lower Rodway, and Park Farm, formerly Higher Rodway, are three-bayed houses of two storeys with attics probably dating from the 17th century but with later alterations.

Open arable fields, implied at Rodway in 1301,[34] have not been found on other estates in the parish and were not mentioned again at Rodway, although furlong names survived in the later 14th century.[35] Common pasture on Alden Hill, that part of Cannington Hill outside the park, belonged to Rodway manor between the 13th and the 17th century.[36] Bradley Green, also known as Customary Green, provided common for Chilton Trivet manor in the 16th century.[37] It had been encroached on by the early 19th century and only a small area, called the common, remained in 1839.[38] Various people could feed sheep on Combwich common, and it was used for village sports and festivities. An attempt to claim ownership by the purchaser of the sheep leazes failed in 1903 and the common remains public open space. Knoll Green may have been common but had been enclosed by 1839.[39] There appear to have been several areas of common meadow in the marshes mainly at Wild moor, north of Cannington Hill, which was the subject of a private inclosure award in 1818.[40] Common meadows east of Gurney Street were apportioned by agreement c. 1856.[41]

There were at least 36 a. of wood or underwood recorded in 1086[42] and there were 40 a. of wood on Rodway manor in 1301.[43] The whole parish had only 67 a. of woodland in 1839[44] and 68 a. of woods and plantations in 1905.[45]

The park at Cannington Hill may have been in existence in the 14th century[46] and the park pale was recorded in 1664.[47] Described as Old Park in the early 18th century, it was divided into the Higher and Lower Parks and let out.[48] Chilton Trivet park lay detached from the farm east of the Bridgwater road. In the 1480s there was a rabbit warren on a low hill south-east of Gurney Street, where the name Conygars survived into the 19th century.[49] A warren east of Cannington Hill, recorded in the 17th and 18th centuries, was destroyed by quarrying.[50] There was a decoy pond on the edge of the marsh north of Cannington Hill; it was partly planted with willows in the early 19th century.[51]

The river crossing at Combwich, alternatively called White House passage after the inn on the Pawlett side, was made by either boat or causeway. A ferry was probably in operation by the mid 13th century.[52] By the 16th century its ownership was shared, half belonging to Pawlett Gaunts manor[53] and half divided between the owners of Combwich in proportions which appear to go back to a division of property between Walter Romsey and William Trivet in 1285.[54] Thus in 1569 a quarter share in the ferry boat had formed part of the copyhold lease granted by Sir Robert Whitney (d. by 1568) as part of his manor of Combwich.[55] The same share descended on the dismemberment of the manor to successive owners of the Anchor inn until 1786 or later.[56] One sixth share had passed by 1730 to Sir George Chudleigh as owner of the former Trivet lands absorbed into Otterhampton manor.[57] The remaining share formed part of Otterhampton Romsey manor.[58] Ralph Dyaper left ferry profits to his wife and daughter in 1630, together with possession of the wharf.[59]

Both cattle and passengers were conveyed across the river in the 16th and 17th centuries.[60] In the later 18th century the churchwardens of Otterhampton paid for repairs to the slip, possibly at the end of the causeway where the ferries docked. The crossing was evidently still in use in the late 19th century.[61]

In 1608 there were three licensed tipplers in Cannington and three in Combwich[62] but of seven licensed in 1609 five were at Combwich.[63] There were six or seven licensees until the 1630s but in 1649 the inhabitants petitioned to have only two at Cannington. An unlicensed aleseller was punished in 1651.[64] Numbers fluctuated but in 1687 there were seven licensed victuallers in Cannington parish and one or two in Combwich in Otterhampton parish.[65]

The Red Lion in Cannington was recorded in 1706 and may have been open in 1674;[66] it ceased to be an inn in the later 18th century[67] although the name was still in use in 1883, probably for a private house.[68] The Anchor, also called the Blue Anchor or Old Blue Anchor, was recorded

31 S.R.O., DD/S/WH 58.
32 Ibid. tithe award; O.S. Map 1", sheet 20 (1809 edn.).
33 S.R.O., tithe award; below, manors.
34 P.R.O., E 142/8; ibid. SC 6/1090/4.
35 *S.R.S.* lxviii, p. 47.
36 P.R.O., SC 6/1090/4; S.R.O., DD/DP 50/9.
37 P.R.O., CP 25(2)/207/41 Eliz. I East.
38 S.R.O., D/P/bw. jo 8/4/1; ibid. tithe award.
39 Ibid. DD/SAS PR 45; DD/MVB 47; ibid. tithe award.
40 Ibid. D/P/can 20/1/1.
41 Ibid. tithe award, altered apportionment.
42 *V.C.H. Som.* i. 471–2, 485–6, 510.
43 P.R.O., E 142/8.   44 S.R.O., tithe award.
45 Statistics supplied by the then Bd. of Agric., 1905.
46 *Proc. before J.P.s*, ed. B. Putnam, 191.
47 S.R.O., DD/DP 50/9.
48 Ibid. D/P/can 4/1/1; ibid. Q/RR papists' estates, 1731; ibid. tithe award.   49 *S.R.S.* lxx. 65; S.R.O., tithe award.
50 S.R.O., DD/BR/bn 10; D/P/can 4/1/1; ibid. tithe award.

51 Ibid. tithe award. Recorded in the name Coy Farm.
52 P.R.O., E 210/3677.
53 S.R.O., DD/S/HY 6/163; below, Pawlett, intro.
54 Below, manors.   55 P.R.O., C 3/109/7.
56 S.R.O., DD/ARN 4.
57 Bailey-Everard MSS. in possession of Messrs. Crosse & Wyatt, S. Molton, Devon.
58 S.R.O., DD/SL 10; P.R.O., CP 25(2)/1057/10 Geo. I Mich.
59 *P.C.C. Wills (Scroope)*, ed. J. L. Morrison (1934), 136.
60 *Smythe Corresp.* (Bristol R.S. xxxv), p. 132; Bristol R.O. 2067(5)C; S.R.O., Q/AD 2.
61 S.R.O., D/P/otn 4/1/1; DD/AH 4/3; O.S. Map 6", Som. XXXVIII. SW. (1886 edn.).
62 S.R.O., Q/SR 3/107.   63 Ibid. Q/RL.
64 Ibid. Q/RL; Q/RLa; *S.R.S.* xxviii. 100, 131; lxxi, p. 16.
65 S.R.O., Q/RL.
66 Ibid. D/P/can 13/2/1; ibid. Q/RL.
67 Ibid. D/P/can 4/1/1; ibid. Q/REl 7/2.
68 Clifford MSS. 3/10/1–3.

in 1767 and was kept by the May family until the 1840s.[69] It was renamed the Friendly Spirit in 1986 and remained open in 1989. The White Horse was recorded in 1724 but had probably been open since c. 1700. It was last recorded in 1743.[70] A house called the Black Horse near Clayhill was recorded in 1773 and 1861.[71] The New Inn in Frog Street and the Globe inn in Church Street were recorded in 1861. The former may have been open in 1851[72] and was last recorded in 1939.[73] The latter was open in 1989. The Malt Shovel between Bradley Green and Blackmoor was recorded as a public house in 1861;[74] the King's Head and the Rose and Crown in High Street were recorded in 1841 and 1881 respectively.[75] All three remained open in 1989.

The Mermaid at Combwich was recorded in 1668 but had ceased to trade by 1708.[76] The Three Mariners inn was open in 1673 but was not recorded again.[77] The Anchor, formerly the Blue Anchor, stood on the riverside at Combwich probably by 1690.[78] It was still open in 1989 and its 18th-century brick fives wall survives beside the forecourt. The Fleur de Luce at Combwich, recorded between 1727 and 1831,[79] was substantially repaired between 1775 and 1782 when it was probably a private house.[80] The Passage Boat was recorded in 1702,[81] possibly the Ship or Old Ship named in 1730[82] and still open in 1989. The Bakers Arms was open in 1871[83] and was last recorded in 1939.[84]

The Cannington friendly society or Loyal Union was founded by 1808 and met at the Anchor inn. It may have ceased in 1834. The British Society, probably also known as the 13 May Club and dating from 1810, originally met in the Anchor but later in the National school. It had 83 members in 1872, but was dissolved in 1874. The Combwich Club was disbanded in 1901.[85] A free library with c. 500 books was established at Cannington by the incumbent in 1888 but was disused by 1905.[86] The Cannington village club or institute, east of the church, was rebuilt in 1905–6 to create a hall with a skittle alley beneath, a reading room, a games room, a shop, and a dwelling.[87] There was a billiard room in Brookside, Combwich in 1939.[88]

A powder house by the river north of Combwich recorded in 1886 was later used by the Bridgwater port sanitary authority as a cholera hospital.[89]

In 1563 there were said to be 120 households

in Cannington and 20 at Combwich.[90] In 1801 the population was 868 rising to 1,215 in 1821 when over three quarters were under 40 and a quarter of the houses had been built since 1811.[91] After reaching a peak of 1,548 in 1851 the population declined to 871 in 1921 but rose to 2,038 normally resident in 1981.[92]

Three men from Combwich and two from Cannington were involved in the Monmouth rebellion in 1685.[93]

MANORS AND OTHER ESTATES. King Alfred (d. 899) devised *CANNINGTON* to his heir Edward the Elder.[94] In 1066 it was a royal manor and by 1086 it had been increased in size by land formerly belonging to Otterhampton.[95] By the 12th century Cannington was held, like Stogursey, by the Curci family,[96] and c. 1138 Robert de Curci[97] gave part of his estate to found a house of Benedictine nuns at Cannington. By the early 16th century the nuns' estate included lands round the priory, the manor,[98] and the rectory and vicarage.[99] When the priory was dissolved in 1536 some land had been let to (Sir) Edward Rogers for 21 years.[1] In 1539 the Crown granted the site of the nunnery, the manor, rectory, and advowson and the former priory lands in the parish and elsewhere to Rogers in tail male at fee farm.[2]

Rogers (d. 1567) was succeeded in the direct male line by Sir George (d. 1582),[3] Edward (d. 1627),[4] Sir Francis (d. 1638), and Hugh Rogers (d. 1653).[5] From Hugh the estate passed under the entail to his uncle Henry Rogers (d. 1672).[6] Henry left no children and Cannington reverted to the Crown, which had already let the reversion in 1661 and the future rent in 1666,[7] but a few months before Rogers died the king gave the reversion to Thomas Clifford, Baron Clifford (d. 1673).[8] Thomas may have been followed by his widow Elizabeth (d. 1709). Their son Hugh died in 1730 and the manor descended to successive Barons Clifford, namely Hugh (d. 1732), Hugh (d. 1783), Hugh (d. 1793), Charles (d. 1831), Hugh (d. 1858), Charles (d. 1880), and Lewis Clifford (d. 1916). William, the 10th baron, leased Cannington Court in 1919 and Court farm in 1920 to Somerset county council for a college of agriculture. Court farm was sold to the council in 1926. Lord Clifford was succeeded in 1943 by his son Charles.[9] Lordship was

69   S.R.O., Q/RL; Q/REl 7/2; ibid. tithe award; P.R.O., HO 107/935.
70   S.R.O., Q/RL; ibid. D/P/can 4/1/1, 13/2/1.
71   Ibid. DD/PAM 1; P.R.O., RG 9/1621.
72   P.R.O., HO 107/1924; ibid. RG 9/1621.
73   *Kelly's Dir. Som.* (1939).
74   S.R.O., D/P/can 13/1/1; P.R.O., RG 9/1621.
75   P.R.O., HO 107/935; ibid. RG 11/2371.
76   S.R.O., DD/S/WH 121, 218.   77 Ibid. Q/SR 118/79.
78   Ibid. Q/RL; Q/REl 7/2B; ibid. D/P/can 4/1/1.
79   Ibid. DD/SL 10; ibid. Q/RL; Q/REl 7/5.
80   Ibid. DD/SAS PR 45.   81 Ibid. DD/HYD 34.
82   Ibid. D/P/can 4/1/1; ibid. Q/RL.
83   P.R.O., RG 10/2380.   84 *Kelly's Dir. Som.* (1939).
85   *Rep. Com. on Poor Law*, 1834, p. 446A; P.R.O., FS 2/9; M. Fuller, *W. Country Friendly Socs.* 139, 143, 150.
86   Whitby, *Dir. Bridgwater* (1897); *Kelly's Dir. Som.* (1906).
87   S.R.O., D/R/bw 22/1/1; Som. C.C., deeds 103A.
88   *Kelly's Dir. Som.* (1939).
89   O.S. Map 6″, Som. XXXVIII. SW. (1886 edn.);

S.R.O., C/C 42/3; Whitby, *Dir. Bridgwater* (1897).
90   B.L. Harl. MS. 594, f. 55.   91 S.R.O., D/P/can 9/1/1.
92   *Census.*
93   *S.R.S.* lxxix. 197, 201.
94   *E.H.D.* i. 535; H. P. R. Finberg, *Early Charters of Wessex*, pp. 126–7.
95   *Early Charters of Wessex*, 126; *V.C.H. Som.* i. 435–6, 525.
96   *V.C.H. Som.* ii. 109; *Pipe R.* 1187 (P.R.S. xxxvii), 164.
97   Dugdale, *Mon.* iv. 416; *Proc. Som. Arch. Soc.* xi. 3.
98   *Valor Eccl.* (Rec. Com.), i. 209; *Proc. Som. Arch. Soc.* xi. 73.
99   P.R.O., SC 6/Hen. VIII/3127.
1   Dugdale, *Mon.* iv. 417–18; P.R.O., SC 6/Hen. VIII/3127.
2   *L. & P. Hen. VIII*, xiii (1), p. 409.
3   P.R.O., C 142/148, no. 28; C 142/197, no. 52.
4   Ibid. C 142/440, no. 91.   5 *S.R.S.* lxvii, p. 145.
6   S.R.O., DD/BR/bn 2; *S.D.N.Q.* xxvi. 230–1; xxvii. 9–10.
7   *Cal. S. P. Dom.* 1660–1, 531; 1661–2, 59; 1666–7, 69, 340.
8   Ibid. 1672, 263; *D.N.B.*; Burke, *Peerage* (1949), 429.
9   Burke, *Peerage* (1949), 429–30; Som. C.C., deeds ED 103A.

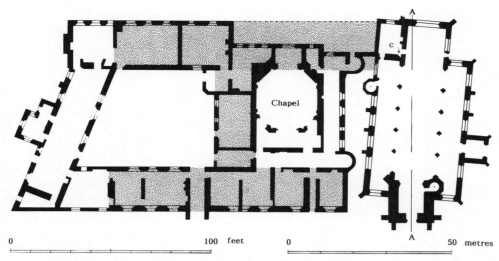

PLAN OF CANNINGTON COURT

A–A Axis of medieval church; C Respond of 12th-century chancel arch

retained by the Cliffords with Park farm and probably remains with Thomas Hugh, 14th Baron Clifford.

Cannington Court, formerly Court House, originated in the remains of the priory and has a twelve-bayed, three-storeyed west front of sandstone rubble except for the top storey which is of brick with keyed oval openings.[10] The buildings of the nunnery lay immediately to the north of the parish church to which they were linked before their post-Dissolution conversion. Whether the 12th-century church abutted the south side of the cloister or was divided from it by an open passage is not now clear but that appears to have been the arrangement after the rebuilding of the church on a new alignment in the later 15th century. The eastern claustral range has been demolished, although the outline of its gable can be seen on the church, but the western and northern ranges survive in a much-altered form. The north range, presumably the refectory, has an arch-braced roof which was formerly open. On the first floor of the west range there is a much restored and reset early 16th-century fireplace with a frieze of quatrefoiled panels enclosing shields and the initials of the Cliffords. The west range continues northwards and with the east and north ranges, which both appear to be of medieval origin, it now encloses a second courtyard. The north range is not aligned with the other buildings and it was not originally joined to the west range.

The conversion into a house for the Rogers family was centred on a first-floor hall in the northern half of the east range. There were service rooms to the north and other principal rooms on the first floor of the central and western ranges.[11] The northern court was entered by a gateway with a two-storeyed porch in limestone ashlar. Soon after the house passed to them the lords Clifford made further alterations,[12] extending the west range northwards and adding a second floor to the

west range and porch. At its southern end the added floor is only a façade.

The description of the house as 'a ruin' in the 1790s[13] may relate to the demolition of the southern end of the east range. A chapel in existence by 1776 was rebuilt by John Peniston in 1830. It is now a lecture room known as the Clifford Hall. The room is octagonal, with a domed and coffered ceiling rising to an octagonal lantern, and two large Corinthian columns flank the opening to the former chancel. The octagonal nave was probably constructed within the walls of the earlier chapel. The most prominent addition arising from the conversion of the buildings to school use is a block of single-storeyed cloakrooms in the north courtyard.[14]

The monastic precinct was bounded by a buttressed wall which survives as the garden wall adjacent to the road on the east and north. To the south-west later stables incorporate a buttressed wall which is on the presumed boundary of the precinct. The water supply was reputedly by a conduit controlled by a sluice at the mill.[15]

CANNINGTON RECTORY, which formed part of the endowment of the priory, comprised in the 18th century a tithe barn, 13½ a. of land, and the great tithes.[16] In 1839 the tithes were commuted for a rent charge of £965.[17]

Candetone, held by Saemer in 1066 and by Robert of John the usher in 1086, may have been at Cannington.[18]

Ralph le Power apparently had land in the 12th century at *KNAPLOCK*, perhaps part of the Curcis' estate. Ralph's sons Robert and William confirmed rent from Knaplock to Stogursey priory *c.* 1180; Robert was followed by his sons John and Robert.[19] By 1170 the Powers may have had as tenant William of Knaplock, who was followed by perhaps three namesakes.[20] About 1280 the wardship of William of Knaplock's son Henry was given to Richard Wason. The land passed to the

10 Below, plate facing p. 88.
11 Dwelly, *Hearth Tax*, i. 68.
12 Rainwater head dated 1714.
13 Collinson, *Hist. Som.* i. 232; W. G. Maton, *Observations in W. Co. of Eng.* (1797), ii. 111.
14 Below, R. Cath.; educ.

15 Inf. from staff at College.
16 S.R.O., Q/RR papists' estates 1731, 1748.
17 Ibid. tithe award.
18 *V.C.H. Som.* i. 521.
19 *S.R.S.* lxi, pp. 13–16, 52–3.
20 Ibid. pp. 16, 26, 52; *Cat. Anct. D.* iv, A 9285.

Wason family. Richard was dead by 1305 leaving a son Philip.[21].William Wason and his wife Joan probably held the estate in 1329[22] and may have been succeeded by another William (d. by 1431).[23] In 1449 John Assheford did fealty for Knaplock in right of his wife Margaret, William's daughter, who was still alive in 1472.[24] In 1543 John Appleton appears to have held Knaplock, possibly in succession to a Mr. Mone.[25] In 1593 the estate was shared between one Perceval, possibly George, and one Bowyer, possibly John, but in 1599 was held by John Pyne.[26] Lewis Pyne, son and heir of Philip (d. 1600), died in possession in 1608 when his heir was his brother Edward, a minor.[27] Edward (fl. c. 1640) had been succeeded by 1700 by another Edward, whose son John sold Knaplock to Robert Evered of Farm, Spaxton, in 1736.[28] Knaplock descended with Farm until c. 1808 when it was acquired by John Evered and was held with his Otterhampton estates.[29] Knaplock Farm is a rendered L-shaped house with a two-storeyed, three-bayed main range and a lower kitchen wing behind. The rent given to Stogursey priory in the 12th century was still paid to Eton College in 1773.[30]

The part of Cannington retained by the Curci family after their foundation of the priory was known by the early 13th century as *RODWAY* or Radway, and later as *RODWAY FITZPAYN*.[31] It was held in chief of the Crown in 1284–5 and 1638.[32] Ownership descended with Stogursey until 1541 when the king granted it for life to Edward Rogers.[33] The grant was renewed in 1545 in tail male.[34] Possession was temporarily lost in 1553 because of Rogers's involvement in Sir Thomas Wyatt's rebellion, when the grant in fee tail was ignored,[35] but had been secured by 1567.[36] The manor was thereafter held with Cannington manor, and lordship was last recorded in 1858.[37] Rodway farm formed part of the estate of the Somerset College of Agriculture from 1946.[38]

The capital messuage was let in 1301[39] and in the 15th[40] and 18th centuries.[41] Park Farm, formerly Higher Rodway, was described as Rodway Manor House c. 1805.[42]

BRYMORE manor was held of Rodway for ¹⁄₁₀ fee in the 15th century[43] and quit rent was paid to Rodway until 1604 or later.[44] Geoffrey of Brymore was recorded c. 1200[45] and ownership is said to have passed to the Pym family either by purchase or through the marriage of Ellis Pym to Maud, Geoffrey of Brymore's daughter.[46] In 1299 Ellis's eldest son Roger granted Brymore to his father Ellis for life with remainder to himself and his heirs.[47] Ellis was probably dead by 1318[48] and his son Roger (d. c. 1349) was succeeded by his son Henry (fl. 1359).[49] Brymore then descended in the direct male line to Philip (d. c. 1413), Roger (d. 1431), Philip (d. 1471),[50] Roger (d. 1486),[51] Alexander (d. 1504), Reginald (d. 1527),[52] Erasmus (d. 1579), Alexander (d. 1585),[53] John, the parliamentarian (d. 1643), and Alexander who died without issue c. 1660.[54] Alexander's brother, Sir Charles (cr. Bt. 1663, d. 1671), was followed by his children Charles, murdered in 1688, and Mary, wife of Sir Thomas Hales, Bt.[55] Mary (d. 1729) was followed by her son Sir Thomas (d. 1762). His son Sir Thomas Pym Hales died without male issue in 1773 and his brother Sir Philip succeeded to Brymore.[56] Sir Philip died in 1824 leaving a daughter Elizabeth who died in 1836. Brymore then passed to Philip Pleydell Bouverie, great-grandson of Sir Thomas Hales (d. 1762). Philip (d. 1872) was followed by his son Philip (d. 1890) and his grandson Henry (d. 1925). Henry left the estate to his nephew Philip Hales Pleydell Bouverie who sold it in 1928.[57] Lordship was last recorded in 1814.[58]

A house was recorded in 1299[59] and 1413.[60] It was described as a capital messuage in 1579[61] but during the 17th and 18th centuries was usually let as a farmhouse,[62] the owners reserving the use of certain rooms and stables.[63] The great storm of 1703 destroyed the dovecot and damaged the house.[64] In the later 18th century Sir Philip Hales took up residence at Brymore and probably rebuilt the house, except for the porch. In 1836 the house contained about thirty rooms with cellars and outhouses.[65] The Bouveries added to the house considerably and in 1892 the

21 *S.R.S.* lxi, pp. 32–3.
22 Ibid. xii. 132.
23 Ibid. xvii. 113, 167; Eton Coll. Rec. 6/196.
24 Eton Coll. Rec. 6/153; *S.R.S.* xxii. 141.
25 Eton Coll. Rec. 6/177.
26 Ibid. 6/201, 203.
27 *S.R.S.* lxvii, p. 193.
28 P.R.O., C 3/423, no. 17; S.R.O., DD/ARN 4.
29 Below, Otterhampton, manors; Spaxton, manors; Bailey- Everard MSS., in possession of Messrs. Crosse & Wyatt, S. Molton, Devon.
30 *S.R.S.* lxi, pp. 32–3; Eton Coll. Rec. 6/269.
31 *S.R.S.* lxi, pp. xix, 29–30; *L. & P. Hen. VIII*, xvi, p. 280.
32 *Feud. Aids*, iv. 281; *S.R.S.* lxvii, p. 145.
33 Below, Stogursey, manors; *L. & P. Hen. VIII*, xvi, p. 280.
34 *L. & P. Hen. VIII*, xx (2), p. 117; *Cal. Pat.* 1557–8, 186.
35 *Cal. Pat.* 1553–4, 252; 1554–5, 293; 1557–8, 186.
36 P.R.O., C 142/148, no. 28.
37 Above; S.R.O., DD/DHR 20.
38 Som. C.C., deeds 103A.
39 P.R.O., E 142/8.
40 W. Suff. R.O. 449/E3/15.53/2.6.
41 S.R.O., D/P/can 4/1/1.
42 Clifford MSS., survey book c. 1805; above, intro.
43 *Feud. Aids*, iv. 436; *Cal. Inq. p.m. Hen. VII*, i, p. 89; W. Suff. R.O. 449/E3/15.53/2.6.

44 S.R.O., DD/BR/bn 10.
45 *S.R.S.* lxi, p. 20.
46 S.R.O., DD/BR/ely 21/1; Collinson, *Hist. Som.* i. 233.
47 B.L. Add. Ch. 20401, 22551.
48 Ibid. 20223.
49 *Cal. Inq. Misc.*, iii, p. 353; P.R.O., E 210/7787. S.R.O., DD/BR/ely 21/1 gives a slightly different descent and Collinson, *Hist. Som.* i. 233 has several uncorroborated differences.
50 S.R.O., DD/SAS NP 10, m. 6; DD/BR/ely 21/1; *Feud. Aids*, iv. 436; *Cal. Fine R. 1422–30*, 330.
51 B.L. Add. Ch. 20226; *Cal. Inq. p.m. Hen. VII*, i, p. 89.
52 *Cal. Inq. p.m. Hen. VII*, ii, p. 590; P.R.O., C 142/46, no. 115.
53 P.R.O., C 142/187, no. 61; C 142/206, no. 20.
54 *D.N.B.*
55 G.E.C. *Baronetage*, iii. 281; S.R.O., DD/BR/ely 4/2.
56 G.E.C. *Baronetage*, iii. 79–80; S.R.O., DD/BR/ely 5/33.
57 Burke, *Peerage* (1949), 1650–1; Som. C.C., deeds 247; S.R.O., DD/DHR 43.
58 S.R.O., DD/BR/ely 20/6.
59 B.L. Add. Ch. 20222.
60 *S.R.S.* lxvii, p. 37.
61 P.R.O., C 142/187, no. 61.
62 S.R.O., DD/BR/ely 4/1–2; 5/1, 3–4, 8; 14/1.
63 Ibid. DD/BW 766.
64 Ibid. DD/BR/ely 5/8.
65 Ibid. 5/33, 20/6.

two-storeyed, 19th-century end was enlarged, with the addition of a third floor, and was redesigned by Basil Cottam to provide twelve bedrooms, servants' hall, and service rooms. In 1928 the house contained 28 bedrooms, and the grounds included tennis and croquet lawns, two lodges, and 250 feet of heated glasshouses.[66] Gordon Cecil Hart bought the house but sold it to Richard Penoyzen in 1936. In 1951 Penoyzen sold Brymore House to Somerset county council which opened it as a technical school of agriculture.[67]

The south front of Brymore House has a porch of c. 1500, much altered; a new entrance arch was inserted in the 19th century and the porch may have been restored in 1896.[68] To the west are five roughcast bays of the later 18th century, probably built in two stages; to the east are three bays of rubble with brick dressings of the later 19th century. There are extensive walled kitchen gardens, one section dated 1753, a late 18th-century orangery, and a canal which was built with an island between 1775 and 1814.[69] There is a large late 19th-century stable block.

PUTNELL, was held between the late 15th and the early 17th century of Rodway manor.[70] Probably half the estate was said to have been divided between the two daughters of John of Eston and his wife Denise, possibly in the 13th century. One apparently died childless and Putnell was divided between the other's daughters, Denise wife of William Furtherede and Isabel wife of Walter Galhampton. The children of Denise's son John died without issue and her share of Putnell passed to her daughter Nichole, who married Walter's brother Robert Galhampton; Robert was followed by John, John's son John, and the latter's son John. Isabel was succeeded by her son John and his son Thomas. Thomas's son John was followed by his son, also John.[71] One John Galhampton was dead by 1473 leaving a daughter Rose whose share was held in 1486 by Richard Symon.[72] Possibly held by Robert Brent (d. 1508),[73] it was owned by Robert Broughton in 1604, perhaps by purchase from James Peppin, and may have descended with Sandford Bickfold in Wembdon.[74] Another John Galhampton in 1486 held land at Putnell which had passed to David Galhampton by 1604.[75] By the later 18th century both estates had probably

been acquired by Lord Clifford and absorbed into his Rodway estate.[76]

The other half share of Putnell was probably held by John Ivythorne in 1333, possibly in succession to William son of Walter of Ivythorne.[77] It had passed to another John Ivythorne by 1382 and to that John's son Richard by 1422.[78] Richard was succeeded by Elizabeth, probably his daughter, wife of John Marshall (d. 1471) and mother of John Marshall who was holding land at Putnell in 1486.[79] The estate may have been held by William Edwards (d. 1547) and his son John, by a Mr. Edwards in 1604,[80] and by Katharine Edwards in 1641.[81] Putnell farm was held by the Coles family in the later 18th and the 19th century.[82]

WITHIEL manor was held of Rodway manor in 1486 and 1538.[83] In the mid 13th century William of Knaplock released his claim to land in Withiel given by his son Hugh to Hugh le Lyf, clerk.[84] He or a namesake settled estates in Rodway on Walter le Lyf in 1288.[85] Walter was dead by 1327 when Lucy le Lyf, probably his widow, held estates in Cannington.[86] They were followed by Godfrey le Lyf and his son Richard (d. by 1401).[87] Richard's widow Margery retained a life interest in Withiel and Walter Tilley, husband of Richard's daughter Joan, held land there in 1412.[88] When Joan died in 1426 Withiel passed to her younger son Leonard Tilley (d. by 1486) who was succeeded by his son Thomas (d. 1536).[89] Thomas's son William (d. 1534)[90] left a son James (d. 1557),[91] whose son George (d. 1590) had two daughters Anne wife of William Walton and Elizabeth who married Edward Parham.[92] In 1602 Elizabeth sold her half to Edmund Bowyer.[93] Anne sold her share in 1604 to Edward Rogers who later bought the other half from Bowyer.[94]

The manor descended in the Rogers family to Henry (d. 1672),[95] who was succeeded by Alexander Popham, son of Helena (d. 1668), daughter of Henry's nephew Hugh Rogers. The manor probably descended with Chadmead in North Petherton until 1720 when it was sold to John Eyre whose son, also John, sold the lordship to Jeremiah Dewdney in 1752.[96] Lordship was last recorded in 1753[97] but the lands had been sold c. 1730 to John Ruscombe.[98] Ruscombe was dead by 1766 and c. 1775 Lord

66   Ibid. DD/DHR 43.
67   Som. C.C., deeds 247; below, educ.
68   S.R.O., DD/BR/ely 20/13–14.
69   Ibid. 14/4, 20/4.
70   W. Suff. R.O. 449/E3/15.53/2.5; S.R.O., DD/BR/bn 10.
71   S.R.O., DD/S/WH 247.
72   W. Suss. R.O., PHA 5370; W. Suff. R.O. 449/E3/15.53/2.5.
73   Cal. Inq. p.m. Hen. VII, iii, p. 310.
74   S.R.O., DD/BR/bn 10; DD/DP 33/3; below, Wembdon, manors.
75   W. Suff. R.O. 449/E3/15.53/2.5; S.R.O., DD/BR/bn 10.
76   Above; S.R.O., Q/REl 7/2E; ibid. tithe award.
77   S.R.S. vi. 225; Pole MS. 4030.
78   S.R.S. xvii. 112–13; B.L. Add. Ch. 15845.
79   P.R.O., C 140/37, no. 28; W. Suff. R.O. 449/E3/15.53/2.5.
80   P.R.O., C 142/99, no. 34; S.R.O., DD/BR/bn 10.
81   Som. Protestation Returns, ed. A. J. Howard and T. L. Stoate, 193.
82   S.R.O., Q/REl 7/2E; ibid. tithe award; ibid. D/P/can

13/1/2.
83   W. Suff. R.O. 449/E3/15.53/2.6; P.R.O., SC 6/Hen. VIII/6164.
84   Cat. Anct. D. iv, A 9285.
85   S.R.S. vi. 271–2.   86   Ibid. iii. 142.
87   Cal. Pat. 1358–61, 507; Pole MS. 1007; S.R.S. xxii. 158, 161.
88   Feud. Aids, vi. 503, 514.
89   Cal. Close, 1461–8, 253–4; W. Suff. R.O. 449/E3/15.53/2.6; P.R.O., C 142/59, no. 79.
90   P.R.O., C 142/57, no. 69.
91   Ibid. C 142/114, no. 53.
92   Ibid. C 142/228, no. 78.
93   Ibid. CP 25(2)/207/44 Eliz. I East.
94   Ibid. CP 25(2)/345/2 Jas. I East; S.R.O., DD/MVB 20.
95   Above.
96   Below, N. Petherton, manors; S.R.O., DD/AH 1/3, 30/3.
97   S.R.O., DD/AH 30/3.
98   Ibid. 12/5; DD/BW 766; DD/BR/ely 5/14, 14/1.

Clifford held Withiel.[99] By 1784 it had been acquired by Sir Philip Hales, possibly by exchange, and was absorbed into the Brymore estate.[1]

The capital messuage of Withiel was let to Hugh Biccombe, son-in-law of Thomas Tilley, in the 1530s.[2] A cottage, called the Bakehouse, was the only house recorded in 1766.[3] The capital messuage had probably stood near the barton east of Brymore House,[4] where a new house, Withiel Farm, was built in the late 19th century as the farmhouse for the Brymore estate.[5]

FORDE, later ASHFORD, was granted to Adam of Bernakes in 1227 by Henry de la Roche and his wife Basilia and Adam of Tappelegh to be held of Hamelin of Tappelegh and his wife Beatrice and her heirs.[6] Adam appears to have given it to Walter of Forde, whose niece Aubrey, wife of Dorion of Stogursey, conveyed Forde to Hugh Fichet of Spaxton.[7] Another of Walter's heirs, Gunilla, with her husband Stephen de la Gulie, sold land there to Hugh Fichet.[8] Hugh also obtained from Philip de Columbers and Mariot de Bonville, widow of Adam of Bernakes, a release of rent from Forde.[9] Forde appears to have descended in the Fichet family with Spaxton manor until 1431 or later.[10]

In 1567 Giles Milburne of Somerton sold Ashford to Robert Halswell, in whose family it descended until 1631 when it was sold to the Revd. Benjamin Vaughan.[11] By 1709 it belonged to a Mr. Sindercombe, the owner in 1751, but by 1766 to Jonas Coles whose son, also Jonas, owned it in 1784.[12] James Merryman owned the estate in the 1830s and his widow Catherine in 1861 but it was later absorbed into Brymore.[13]

Ashford House, which stood on a lane to Oatley, was rebuilt further east c. 1830 with a lodge near the main road.[14] The house is stuccoed under a slate roof and has a two-bayed, three-storeyed front with central pedimented wooden porch on pilasters.

BLACKMOOR was held by Aelfric in 1066 and by Ansketil of Roger de Courcelles in 1086.[15] In the late 12th century Geoffrey of Durleigh confirmed a grant by his father Durand of land at Blackmoor to Geoffrey of Brymore as 1/10 fee.[16] In 1201 Geoffrey recovered it from the Crown after confiscation for indebtedness.[17] By 1214, however, it seems to have come into the hands of Philip de Burcy.[18] Thurstan de Burcy was recorded in

1242[19] and Robert de Burcy (fl. 1295) was described as of Blackmoor.[20] By the mid 14th century it belonged to Lucy (d. c. 1370), widow of Richard Malet. She was succeeded by her daughter Margaret, a minor, who married in turn Richard Cressebien, Thomas Hatfield, Nicholas atte More, and John Kenne (d. 1438).[21] Margaret was dead by 1440 when Blackmoor was held by her son Hugh More.[22] By his will Hugh gave Blackmoor to his wife Gillian for life, then to the churchwardens of Cannington for a year, with reversion to his half-brother Robert Kenne (d. 1453) and his issue.[23] Robert's son John sold the manor in 1476 to (Sir) Thomas Tremayle.[24]

Tremayle (d. 1508) settled Blackmoor on his younger son John and on John's wife Elizabeth.[25] In 1517 John settled the manor on himself and his second wife Mary, widow of John Halswell,[26] and died in 1534 leaving a daughter Margery, wife of Nicholas Halswell.[27] In 1535 Margery gave the manor to Mary who leased it to her son Nicholas Halswell for 20 years.[28] The manor was settled, probably in 1565, on Robert son of Nicholas and Margery, and it thereafter descended with Halswell.[29] Lordship was last recorded c. 1832.[30]

There was a house at Blackmoor in the 14th century[31] and in 1417 it had an oratory.[32] In 1534 the chapel had two bells, a holy water bucket, a chalice, two pairs of vestments, books, and other furnishings.[33] Blackmoor Farm is a late 15th-century, two-storeyed house, of red sandstone rubble, with a main range of three rooms and entry facing east, a chapel wing to the north-east, and a slightly later kitchen wing to the south-west. Both angles contain stair turrets, that on the west having a garderobe. The hall has a moulded, framed ceiling and the roofs are of jointed crucks, that of the main range being arch-braced and with windbracing. The chapel has been partitioned but retains a framed ceiling, niches, and a piscina. It was probably built by Thomas Tremayle (d. 1508), whose son John may have added the kitchen wing. Apart from the porch and the insertion of a gallery in the chapel c. 1600, the house has hardly been altered structurally since John died in 1534.[34]

CHILTON, later CHILTON TRIVET, was probably one of Ansketil's two holdings called Chilton held of Roger de Courcelles in the 11th century.[35] It was held of Stogursey from 1208 to 1301 or later,[36] and from 1434 until 1564 was

99 S.R.O., DD/BR/ely 5/14, 20/4.
1 Ibid. 20/4, 6; ibid. Q/REl 7/2E; ibid. tithe award.
2 Ibid. DD/L P36/4.
3 Ibid. DD/BR/ely 5/14.
4 Ibid. 20/6; ibid. tithe award.
5 O.S. Map 6", Som. L. NW. (1887 edn.); Som. C.C., deeds 247; S.R.O., DD/DHR 43.
6 S.R.S. vi. 67.
7 P.R.O., E 210/1999, 2158, 2896.
8 Ibid. E 210/7625.   9 Ibid. E 210/2158, 6043.
10 Ibid. E 210/2880, 4246, 10803, 70179.
11 S.R.O., DD/S/WH 14.
12 Ibid. D/P/can 4/1/1; ibid. Q/REl 7/2E.
13 Ibid. D/P/can 13/1/1; DD/DHR 43; ibid. tithe award; P.R.O., RG 9/1621.
14 S.R.O., D/P/can 3/2/9; ibid. tithe award.
15 V.C.H. Som. i. 487.
16 B.L. Add. Ch. 20418.
17 Cur. Reg. R. ii. 15, 41; S.R.S. vi. 11.
18 Cur. Reg. R. vii. 225.

19 S.R.S. xi, p. 321.
20 B.L. Add. Ch. 19980, 40615; S.R.S. lxiii, p. 394.
21 Cal. Fine R. 1369–77, 102; Cal. Inq. Misc. v. 155; S.R.O., DD/S/WH 1; P.R.O., C 139/86, no. 37.
22 S.R.O., DD/S/WH 1.
23 Ibid.; Cal. Inq. p.m. (Rec. Com.), iv. 253, 360.
24 S.R.O., DD/S/WH 1, 366.
25 P.R.O., C 142/22, no. 45.
26 S.R.O., DD/S/WH 1.
27 P.R.O., C 142/57, no. 82.
28 S.R.O., DD/S/WH 1.
29 Above, Goathurst, manors.
30 S.R.O., DD/RN 43.
31 Cal. Fine R. 1369–77, 102.
32 S.R.S. xxix, p. 290.
33 S.R.O., DD/S/WH 115.
34 Ibid. DD/V/BWr 5.2; DD/S/WH 115; for a photo., above, plate facing p. 73.
35 V.C.H. Som. i. 486; Proc. Som. Arch. Soc. xcix–c. 40.
36 S.R.S. vi. 25; Cal. Inq. p.m. iv, p. 342.

said to be held of Rodway.[37] In 1208 it was one of the fees of William of Eston,[38] possibly a descendant of Ansketil,[39] and it had passed by 1285 to his niece Sarah of Eston, wife of William Trivet.[40] The manor descended with Cock in Stogursey to John Compton (d. 1548).[41] John's son Richard died in 1564 leaving a son James, who let the manor in 1587 for the benefit of his son Henry and Henry's wife Mary.[42] In 1599 James, Henry, and Mary sold the manor to Bartholomew Michell and most of the land to Henry Andrews or Fry.[43] The manor passed on Michell's death in 1616 to his daughters Jane and Frances, but Jane's husband William Hockmore held the whole manor at his death in 1626 and was succeeded by his son Gregory, a minor.[44] The manor descended with Chilton in Durleigh until the mid 18th century,[45] after which it descended with Gurney Street.[46] Lordship was last recorded in 1887.[47]

The capital messuage, recorded in 1316,[48] descended with lands of the manor from Henry Fry to Jane, daughter of Edward Fry. In 1655 she married Francis Cridland and settled her estate on her husband and his heirs.[49] Francis died in 1667 and Jane in 1675 leaving a daughter Mary.[50] Mary had died without issue by 1703 when Jane's heirs conveyed land in Chilton Trivet to Francis's niece and heir Margaret, wife of John Burland.[51] Margaret died in 1703 and by 1707 the estate was held by Robert Codrington, who settled it in 1709 on the marriage of his son John to Elizabeth Gorges.[52] By 1724 it had been acquired by George Dodington and descended with Dodington manor until 1801 when it was sold to Solomon Pain in trust for George Pain.[53] George died c. 1817 leaving Chilton Trivet in trust for his son Robert for life. In 1830 Charles Knight bought the life interest, but on Robert's death in 1842 the estate reverted to his children Robert, George Tucker, Betty, Christian, and Alfred Pain.[54] In 1848 the estate was sold to Henry Prince[55] of the Agapemone, Spaxton. A burial ground was established for the sect at Chilton, and the deceased were said to have been interred in an upright position. In 1948 the Princites sold the estate except for the burial ground.[56]

The south range of the former manor house, now Chilton Trivet Farm, may be of the 16th century. The western room on the ground floor has a moulded plaster ceiling over intersecting beams, in the room above it the ceiling is richly decorated and has a central pendant and a plaster overmantel with the date 1662 and the initials of Francis and Jane Cridland. The house was remodelled in the later 19th century when it was given a new staircase hall and service rooms.

CLAYHILL was held by Ordgar in 1066 and by Ansketil of Roger de Courcelles in 1086.[57] Clayhill was held of Stogursey in 1208[58] and 1488.[59] In 1542 Clayhill was said to be held of Chilton Trivet manor.[60] William Testard was terre tenant in 1285; Robert Testard (d. by 1346) and Richard le Hare were lords in 1303.[61] Matthew Michell is said to have married Joan, Robert's daughter and heir, and Thomas Michell was possibly married to Richard's daughter Joan.[62] In 1412 Thomas Michell held the manor but in 1428 it was shared between Michell, William Stapleton, and Isabel Hare.[63] In 1470 Walter Michell bought one third of the manor from Joan wife of Adam Hamlyn.[64] In 1474 he settled the whole manor on his wife Agnes[65] and it descended like East Chilton in Durleigh until 1616 when lordship was last recorded.[66]

By the 18th century the estate was divided between Clayhill and Little Clayhill.[67] In 1709 Clayhill was held by William Ruscombe, who by 1733 had been succeeded by Joseph (d. 1763).[68] Joseph's daughter Elizabeth married John Poole (d. 1792), and by 1826 their son the Revd. John Poole (d. 1857) was in possession.[69] John's nephew Gabriel Poole sold Clayhill to William Gooding (d. 1902) of Durleigh.[70] In 1916 Gooding's son William and other members of the family sold it to Harry Nation, who put it up for sale in 1943.[71] It was bought by the Irish family, owners in 1989.

LITTLE CLAYHILL continued to descend with East Chilton[72] until 1791 when it was sold in trust for Thomas Symes of Nether Stowey.[73] In 1792 it was held by James Holloway, in 1794 by Sir Philip Hales, and from 1795 until 1867 or later by successive Lords Clifford with Cannington manor.[74]

In 1086 Ansketil held of Roger de Courcelles DODESHAM or Dudesham, which had been held by three thegns in 1066.[75] William of Eston may have been the lord[76] and was probably

37 P.R.O., C 139/64, no. 35; C 142/140, no. 160.
38 S.R.S. vi. 25.
39 Below, Stogursey, manors.
40 Feud. Aids, iv. 281.
41 Below, Stogursey, manors; P.R.O., C 142/99, no. 25.
42 P.R.O., C 142/140, no. 160; ibid. CP 25(2)/206/29 Eliz. I Trin.
43 Ibid. CP 25(2)/207/41 Eliz. I East.
44 Ibid. C 142/440, no. 89; S.R.S. lxvii, pp. 178–9.
45 Above, Durleigh, manors.   46 Below.
47 S.R.O., DD/BR/tw 6.
48 P.R.O., C 134/56, no. 4.
49 S.R.S. li, pp. 282–3.
50 Som. Wills, ed. Brown, iv. 91–2; S.R.O., D/P/can 2/1/3.
51 S.R.O., DD/SAS (H/104) 14.
52 Ibid. D/P/can 4/1/1; DD/DP 33/6, 34/2.
53 Ibid. D/P/can 4/1/1; DD/DHR 33; V.C.H. Som. v. 66.
54 S.R.O., DD/DHR 9, 33; ibid. tithe award.
55 Ibid. DD/SAS SE 25; D/P/can 13/1/2.
56 Below, Spaxton; Som. Co. Herald, 20 Nov. 1948; 26 May 1952.

57 V.C.H. Som. i. 485.
58 S.R.S. vi. 25; Feud. Aids, iv. 279.
59 P.R.O., E 149/891, no. 10.
60 Ibid. C 142/67, no. 114.
61 Feud. Aids, iv. 279, 301.
62 Proc. Som. Arch. Soc. lxxiii. 81.
63 Feud. Aids, iv. 364; vi. 514.
64 S.R.S. xxii. 139–40.
65 S.R.O., DD/S/WH 65.
66 Cal. Inq. p.m. Hen. VII, i, p. 114; above, Durleigh, manors.
67 P.R.O., C 142/440, no. 89; S.R.O., DD/BW 778; DD/BR/ely 5/19.
68 S.R.O., D/P/can 4/1/1.
69 Collinson, Hist. Som. i. 236; S.R.O., D/P/can 2/1/2, 4; ibid. Q/REl 29/9C; ibid. tithe award.
70 S.R.O., D/P/can 23/6.
71 Above, Durleigh, manors; S.R.O., DD/DHR, box 22.
72 Above, Durleigh, manors.
73 S.R.O., DD/BR/ely 5/19.
74 Ibid. Q/REl 29/9C; ibid. tithe award; ibid. DD/PAM 2.   75 V.C.H. Som. i. 486.
76 Cur. Reg. R. vii. 225.

followed by his son Robert (fl. 1242) and grandson, also Robert.[77] No further trace of the estate has been found until 1474 when Walter Michell held it in succession to his father William.[78] The estate descended like East Chilton manor in Durleigh and was last recorded in 1563.[79]

John de Gurney held a fee in Cannington,

when his heirs were John Peryman, grandson of his sister Joan, and Alexander Pym, grandson of his sister Eleanor, but he left a large estate in trust for his niece Agnes Peryman, daughter of his sister Joan and wife of Walter Michell.[92] John Peryman (d. 1512) lived in Cannington, possibly in the house at Southbrook, and in 1507 part of

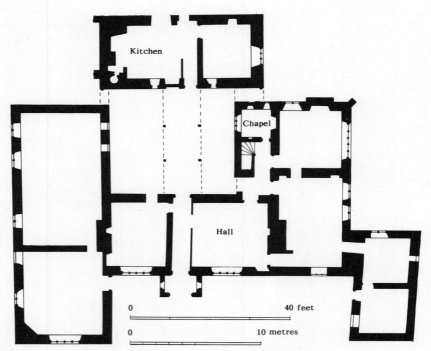

PLAN OF GURNEY STREET

possibly the later *GURNEY STREET* estate, in the late 13th century,[80] perhaps in succession to Richard de Gurney and his son Robert.[81] John was alive in 1327[82] and seems to have been followed by Hugh de Gurney by 1358.[83] Hugh or a namesake with his wife Beatrice held land in Cannington in 1401[84] and Robert de Gurney in 1443,[85] but no later record of the family has been found in Cannington. Hugh le Lyf (fl. 1292), who appears to have been granted a tenancy in the Gurney fee, had been succeeded by his son Walter by 1311.[86] Walter was dead by 1327 when his widow Lucy held a considerable estate in Cannington.[87] She may have been followed by John le Lyf and his son Richard (fl. 1358–68).[88] The Lyf holding descended with Currypool in Charlinch to Joan, wife of Walter Tilley, and Amice, wife of Baldwin Malet,[89] and may have passed to the Dodesham family,[90] which had amassed an estate from the later 14th century.[91]

William Dodesham the younger died in 1480

the Dodeshams' estate was settled on him and his wife Edith who survived him. John was eventually succeeded by his daughters Joan (d. 1561), wife of Bartholomew Coombe, and Dorothy, wife of Philip Courtenay, who partitioned their estate c. 1543, possibly after Edith's death.[93] Joan had the Cannington land and, being childless, she gave it in reversion to Nicholas Halswell who held it with Blackmoor, except Southbrook which was given to her kinsman Richard Michell.[94] Southbrook descended with Gurney Street and was last recorded as a separate estate in the 1740s. The name was preserved in 1831, although the land had probably been absorbed into Gurney Street farm much earlier.[95]

The land at Gurney Street settled on Agnes Peryman, wife of Walter Michell, descended like East Chilton until c. 1714.[96] Gurney Street and Southbrook were then held by Davidge Gould in right of his wife Honor, daughter of William

77 *S.R.S.* xi, p. 196.   78 S.R.O., DD/S/WH 65.
79 *Som. Wills*, ed. Brown, vi. 3; above, Durleigh, manors.
80 *Cat. Anct. D.* iv, A 8939.
81 *S.R.S.* xi, pp. 195, 209.   82 Ibid. iii. 140.
83 P.R.O., C 260/79, no. 14.   84 *S.R.S.* xxii. 159.
85 *Cal. Close*, 1441–7, 124.
86 P.R.O., E 326/6004; *Cat. Anct. D.* iv, A 8939; Pole MS. 5163, 5165.
87 *S.R.S.* iii. 142.   88 P.R.O., C 260/79, no. 14.
89 Below, Charlinch, manors.
90 *Cal. Close*, 1441–7, 124.

91 P.R.O., E 315/38/50; S.R.O., DD/S/WH 59; *S.R.S.* xxii. 119–20, 145.
92 S.R.O., DD/S/WH 115; P.R.O., C 140/77, no. 78; *S.R.S.* lxx, p. 51.
93 *S.R.S.* liii, pp. 60–1; P.R.O., C 142/27, no. 107; C 3/47, no. 26.
94 P.R.O., C 3/32, no 14; C 3/47, no. 26; *Som. Wills*, ed. Brown, iv. 12.
95 S.R.O., DD/DHR, box 3; ibid. Q/REl 7/2A; ibid. tithe award.
96 Above, Durleigh, manors.

Hockmore.[97] By 1751 he had been succeeded by (Sir) Henry Gould whose daughter and coheir Honora Margaretta (d. 1813) married Richard Lambart, earl of Cavan (d. 1837). She was succeeded by her son George, Viscount Kilcoursie (d. 1828), and by his son Frederick, Viscount Kilcoursie, later earl of Cavan (d. 1887). Frederick's son Frederick, the 9th earl, was followed in 1900 by his son, also Frederick,[98] who sold Gurney Street in 1925. The estate has since had several owners and been divided.[99]

In 1482 a group of buildings and surrounding orchards and lands at Gurney Street, formerly belonging to William Dodesham, included the capital messuage where he had lived, two other houses, one called the Crossed house, a tenement called Gourneys place, a chapel of St. Margaret, and a water mill.[1] About 1561 and in 1740 a capital messuage or mansion of Southbrook was recorded, apparently on or near the same site.[2] The present Gurney Street Farm or Gurney Manor, probably but not certainly the home of William Dodesham, was in 1989 under restoration by the Landmark Trust, having been divided since the late 1940s, not for the first time, into separate dwellings.

The house is irregularly disposed around four sides of a courtyard and has to the north an entrance court flanked by short wings.[3] The plan and some of the walling of the medieval open hall survive in the north range. Its parlour end was to the west and there were presumably service rooms beyond the screens passage to the east. Early in the 16th century a new solar block was added beyond the parlour containing a small chapel, another ground-floor room, and a spiral stair leading to a larger room with an open timber roof on the first floor. Late in the 16th century the block was remodelled, probably by Sir Bartholomew Michell (d. 1616). An attic floor was put in and new windows were inserted in the west wall at all three floors. The east end of the first-floor room was partitioned off to form a lobby at the head of the stairs and the lobby and chapel were given new plaster decoration. The lobby provided access to a bridge leading to the first floor of a new south range which had a kitchen and a storage room on the ground floor and a single chamber, perhaps a gallery, with an open timber roof on the first floor. Two early 16th-century windows to the first floor may have been re-used from the solar block. Early in the 17th century the upper floor and new screens wall were put into the hall which was completely refenestrated and provided with a two-storeyed porch on the north side. The chimney stack, on the wall against the parlour, may have been modified to serve the hall at this time. The parlour, which retained its low medieval ceiling height, seems to have been

of little importance by the 17th century but a new block forming the western wing of the entrance court was added then. It provided an additional chamber with a garderobe on the first floor. At the other end of the north range the matching wing formed part of an early 17th-century range on the east side of the main courtyard. Its function is not certain but it may have been in part for storage of produce. A later 16th or early 17th-century timber pentice runs across the courtyard from the south doorway of the screens passage to the kitchen.

The house appears to have been divided into several dwellings in the 1660s.[4] In the 18th and 19th centuries it was a farmhouse. Additional doorways and windows were put in, rooms were subdivided, and additions were made on the south side of the courtyard to provide more service rooms so that the house could be used as several dwellings. A staircase was built against the north-east corner of the old kitchen block so that the partitioned and ceiled upper floor could be used for farm storage.

Godwin held *PERREDEHAM*, later Pedredham or Petherhams Marsh, in 1066 and Ansketil held it of Roger de Courcelles in 1086.[5] Throughout the Middle Ages estates were recorded at Pedredham and at Petherhams Marsh in Cannington, Otterhampton, and Stockland Bristol parishes.[6] In 1227 land in Pedredham was held by Adam of Bernakes partly of Hamelin of Tappelegh and his wife Beatrice and partly of Robert of Eston for 1/20 fee.[7] The estate has not been traced later and ownership of Pedredham was very fragmented.

PILLOCK was held by Godric in 1066 and by Ansketil of Roger de Courcelles in 1086.[8] It may have been held by a family called Pillock from the late 12th to the early 15th centuries.[9] In 1280 land there was in dispute between William Pillock and Simon Michell and in 1428 Simon Byrt and William Michell and his son Walter went to arbitration over Pillocks place and lands.[10] In 1446 Walter was in possession[11] and in the later 15th century Robert Michell, possibly Walter's eldest son, released his claim to the estate to Walter (d. 1487).[12] Pillock, also called Pillock Nynes and sometimes a manor,[13] descended with East Chilton manor in Durleigh, but is not recorded after the death of Bartholomew Michell (d. 1616). Most of the land was absorbed into Gurney Street farm.[14]

Pillocks place, recorded in 1428 and *c.* 1483,[15] may have survived in the 16th century.[16] It may have been on or near the site of the house known in the late 18th and early 19th centuries as Shepherds,[17] which was replaced in the 1860s by the Grange, probably built for the solicitor James Ruscombe Poole.[18]

In 1066 Leofwin held one part of *COMBWICH*,

97 S.R.O., D/P/can 4/1/1; DD/DHR, box 3.
98 Ibid. D/P/can 4/1/1; DD/BR/tw 6; ibid. Q/REl 7/2A; Burke, *Peerage* (1949), 369–70.
99 Devon R.O. 547 B/P 2340, 3484.
1 *S.R.S.* lxx, p. 51.
2 P.R.O., C 3/47, no. 26; S.R.O., DD/DHR, box 3.
3 Above, plate facing p. 72.
4 Dwelly, *Hearth Tax*, i. 66–7.
5 *V.C.H. Som.* i. 486.   6 Below, Stockland Bristol.
7 *S.R.S.* vi. 63–4, 67.   8 *V.C.H. Som.* i. 486.

9 *S.R.S.* xi, pp. 79, 171, 301; xxii. 160; lxi, p. 28; P.R.O., E 326/5762.
10 *S.R.S.* xliv. 300–1; P.R.O., C 1/11, no. 384.
11 S.R.O., DD/L P36.   12 *S.R.S.* lxx, pp. 65, 75.
13 P.R.O., C 142/143, no. 25; C 142/440, no. 89.
14 Ibid. C 142/440, no. 89; *S.R.S.* lxx, p. 65; S.R.O., tithe award.   15 P.R.O., C 1/11, no. 384; *S.R.S.* lxx, p. 65.
16 S.R.O., DD/SH 108/1.
17 Ibid. Q/REl 7/2A; ibid. tithe award.
18 P.R.O., RG 9/1621, RG 10/2380.

which in 1086 Alfred of Marlborough held of Eustace, count of Boulogne.[19] It belonged to the honor of Boulogne until the 13th century when Alfred's successors became overlords and it was held under the honor of Ewyas until 1370 or later.[20] In 1303 it was held of Burnham manor, owned by the lords of Ewyas.[21]

In 1285 the terre tenant was Eustace of Whitney, and he or a namesake in 1346.[22] Sir Robert Whitney held the manor in 1370[23] and another of the same name held it in 1431.[24] Robert died in 1441 and was followed in the direct male line by Eustace (d. c. 1481),[25] Robert (d. c. 1494), James (d. 1500), and Robert.[26] Sir Robert Whitney was dead by 1568[27] and Sir James Whitney died in 1588 leaving his brother Eustace as his heir.[28] Eustace (d. 1608) left a son Sir Robert[29] who in 1617 sold the manor to Constance Lucy.[30] Her son Sir Richard Lucy, Bt., died in 1667 and was succeeded by his son Sir Kingsmill (d. 1678) and by the latter's son Sir Berkeley, who sold Combwich to William Harrison in 1702.[31] William was succeeded by Ames Harrison (d. 1731) and Ames's son Alexander (d. 1740), who left the lordship to his brother-in-law Richard Cridland in trust for his nieces. Both William and Alexander dismembered the manor.[32] The lordship was last recorded in 1778 when Richard Cridland and his daughters Sarah and Elizabeth sold lands at Combwich, probably all that remained of the former manor, to John Evered.[33]

In 1066 Leofwara held the other part of COMBWICH, which in 1086 Walter Arblaster held of Ralph de Limesi.[34] Overlordship descended with the Cavendish honor to the d'Odingselles family, which held it in 1285.[35] John Droxford, bishop of Bath and Wells (d. 1329), acquired the lordship of the d'Odingselles family in Combwich, but held it of Stogursey as a mesne tenant. His heir was his brother Philip,[36] but that lordship was not recorded again and the terre tenants held lands directly of Stogursey until 1491 or later.[37] The terre tenancy was divided between Walter Romsey and William Trivet and his wife Sarah in 1285.[38] The Romsey share had been absorbed into their manor of Otterhampton by 1333. The Trivet share descended with Crook in Bawdrip until 1462 when the lordship was last recorded and most of the

land was probably absorbed into Otterhampton manor.[39]

SALTY or Salthay manor, variously said to be held of Lord FitzWaryn in 1412,[40] of the Crown in chief in 1426,[41] and possibly of Wick manor in 1486 and 1537, may have originated as land reclaimed from the Parrett estuary, possibly by the Lyf family.[42] Recorded in 1412 as ½ knight's fee held by Richard Boyton in right of his wife Margery, widow of Richard Lyf, it may have been Boyton's land at Pedredham.[43] Salty formed part of the share of Richard Lyf's daughter Joan (d. 1426)[44] from whom it passed to her younger son Leonard Tilley and his son Thomas (d. 1536).[45] Thomas settled Salty manor on his son William (d. 1534) for his marriage to Joan who survived her husband.[46] Joan was succeeded by her son James Tilley (d. 1557) and the manor descended with Withiel. The lordship was last recorded in 1753.[47]

An estate at Pedredham or Petherhams Marsh was held of Salty manor for a fraction of a knight's fee.[48] It was held by John Steyning who died before 1464 leaving his son Richard under age.[49] Richard had been succeeded by 1534 by John Steyning who in 1544 sold his estate to his tenants John Lawrence and his wife Maud. In 1550 Lawrence settled the remainder on his younger son Robert.[50] Both Robert and his parents were dead by 1593 when his son John and his brother John sold STEYNINGS to Simon Venn and Hugh Saffin, probably Robert's sons-in-law. Saffin sold his half share in 1594 to his wife's sons John and George Chilcott[51] and they sold it to John Burland in 1615.[52] Simon Venn died before 1614 when his son, also Simon, did homage for his land.[53] In 1615 Burland purchased it from Simon and his mother Maud.[54] Burland already held Kitners in Petherhams Marsh which he had inherited with Steyning in Stogursey and which had probably belonged to the Kitnor family between 1339 and 1449.[55] Burland's estates in Petherhams Marsh descended with Steyning in Stogursey until the later 18th century when they were mostly sold.[56]

By 1715 land in Cannington Marsh and around Oatley, owned by the Napier family by the mid 17th century, had come to be known as CANNINGTON manor.[57] Sir Gerard Napier and his

[19] V.C.H. Som. i. 472.
[20] Bk. of Fees, i. 237, 241; Sanders, Eng. Baronies, 43; Cal. Inq. p.m. xiii, p. 43.
[21] Feud. Aids, iv. 308.
[22] S.R.S. iii. 15; Feud. Aids, iv. 352.
[23] Cal. Inq. p.m. xiii, p. 43.
[24] Feud. Aids, iv. 435.
[25] J. C. Wedgwood, Hist. Parl. Biogs. 1439–1509, 943.
[26] Cal. Fine R. 1485–1509, 199; Cal. Inq. p.m. Hen. VII, ii, pp. 174–5.
[27] P.R.O., C 3/109, no. 7.
[28] Ibid. C 142/219, no. 76.
[29] Ibid. C 142/305, no. 109.
[30] Ibid. CP 25(2)/346/15 Jas. I Trin.
[31] G.E.C. Baronetage, i. 113–14; S.R.O., DD/ARN 4.
[32] S.R.O., DD/ARN 4, 7; DD/SAS RF 3/1/1; D/P/n. pet 2/1/3; V.C.H. Som. v. 133.
[33] S.R.O., DD/ARN 7.
[34] V.C.H. Som. i. 510.
[35] Sanders, Eng. Baronies, 29–30; Feud. Aids, iv. 281.
[36] Cal. Inq. p.m. vii, p. 161.
[37] Cal. Inq. p.m. Hen. VII, i, pp. 327–8.
[38] Feud. Aids, iv. 281.

[39] S.R.O., TS/EVD 4, 8; below, Bawdrip, manors; Otterhampton, manors.
[40] Cal. Close, 1409–13, 368.
[41] Cal. Fine R. 1422–30, 147.
[42] W. Suff. R.O. 449/E3/15.53/2.6; P.R.O., C 142/59, no. 79; S.R.O., DD/L P36/4.
[43] Cal. Close, 1409–13, 368; Feud. Aids, vi. 503.
[44] Cal. Fine R. 1422–30, 147.
[45] Cal. Close, 1461–8, 253–4; P.R.O., C 142/59, no. 79.
[46] P.R.O., C 142/57, no. 69.
[47] Above; S.R.O., DD/AH 30/3.
[48] S.R.O., DD/SAS (H/104) 14.
[49] Cal. Close, 1461–8, 204.
[50] S.R.O., D/B/bw, Steyning MSS. 12.
[51] Ibid. DD/SAS (H/104) 14.
[52] Ibid. DD/DK 1.
[53] Ibid. DD/SAS (H/104) 14.
[54] Ibid. DD/DK 1.
[55] S.R.S. lvii, pp. 31–2, 39, 45; S.R.O., D/B/bw, Steyning MSS. 12.
[56] Below, Stogursey, manors; S.R.O., Q/REl 7/2F; ibid. tithe award.
[57] S.R.O., DD/PH 43.

wife Margaret held it in 1656. It descended with Woolstone in Stogursey and was held as a manor by Sir Nathaniel Napier in 1715.[58] It continued in the family until 1765 when it passed to Edward Phelips of Montacute and descended with Montacute until 1874 or later.[59] The lordship was last recorded in 1795.[60]

Buckland priory received a pension of 7s. from the tithes of Clayhill by 1334. The charge was not recorded after the Dissolution.[61]

ECONOMIC HISTORY. Arable seems to have predominated in the later 11th century, with substantial areas of meadow on the holding of Erchenger the priest, the estate called Candetone, and one of the two holdings at Combwich. No moor and only small areas of pasture land were recorded but several flocks of sheep together with goats, pigs, and cattle. There were unbroken mares on one of the estates called Chilton. Bordars were recorded in greater numbers than *villani* on all estates save one at Combwich, and there were *servi* at Chilton and Combwich. Cannington, Williton, and Carhampton shared 11 *servi* between them.[62]

In 1276–7 Rodway manor produced over 60 qr. of peas;[63] twenty years later the main crops there were wheat and oats but rye, barley, peas, and beans were also grown. Cattle, geese and poultry, meadow, pasture, and works were sold. The manor was owed 1,431 days of spring work and 441½ days at autumn; a considerable demesne employed a hayward, reeve, reaper, carter, and two drovers. There were 7½ ploughteams in use. Money was spent on making and repairing ploughs, mending carts, buying seed barley for sowing and salt for the household pottage, roofing the grange, cattle shed, and granary, threshing, winnowing, hoeing, mowing, reaping, ditching, and maintaining sea defences in the marsh. The following season wheat was to be sown at 1½ bu. to the acre on 79½ a., rye on 10 a., barley on 9 a., peas and beans on 30 a., and oats on 47 a.[64] The meadows were common pasture after the hay was carried and there was also pasture on Alden or Cannington Hill. In 1296–7 there were 58 a. of fallow, and in 1301 the manor had 324 a. of arable, 39½ a. of meadow, and 20½ a. of pasture. Six customary tenants paid churchset.[65] The Chilton Trivet demesne was largely arable in 1316. Rents accounted for more than two thirds of manorial income.[66] By 1473 Rodway manor demesne was farmed and spring and autumn works were sold.

The manor continued to maintain the drainage and in 1485 repaired the pound.[67] By the early 16th century even the pound was farmed.[68] In 1485 all rents were in cash and more than half came from overland[69] and demesne.[70] A neif at Rodway obtained permission to live out of the manor in 1532,[71] and in 1541 eleven men and their families there were manumitted.[72]

In 1539 Thomas Michell's livestock at Gurney Street included 14 oxen, a bull, and 36 other cattle, sheep, 8 horses, and 19 pigs.[73] The Cannington priory estate was let to farm in the 1530s, when the demesne measured 93 a.,[74] and continued to be let by its lay owners.[75] Early 17th-century farming inventories record wheat, peas, beans, butter and cheese, pigs, cows, and sheep. One man had a flock of 21 sheep but the wealthiest yeoman, from a family manumitted in 1514, had two thirds of his wealth in cash.[76] A tenant farmer in 1664 had to work on the rhynes and was allowed to till only half his holding.[77] Inventories of the later 17th century show an increase in wealth; crops such as clover and meadow grass were recorded, and there were greater numbers of livestock, especially sheep.[78] One farmer in 1684 had 165 sheep, some fattening in the marsh, 8 plough oxen, cattle, horses, pigs, crops of wheat, barley, oats, peas, and hay, and cheese. There were two new rooms in his house and he held several leases.[79]

On the Brymore estate in the early 18th century tenant holdings were very small but the demesne farm measured 224 a.[80] Cannington manor was also divided into a large number of small holdings and the demesne lands were also let, including the park.[81] Early 18th-century inventories include clover, trefoil or vetch, and flax. Most farmers made cheese. One farmer kept ducks and geese in the marsh with young cattle and sheep.[82]

At the end of the 18th century improvements were made to farmhouses on the Clifford estate and the holdings were reorganized to form larger farms. One tenant held a piece of land for keeping the gates and another had a decoy.[83] In 1823 farmers were said to be 'opulent' and the parish to contain 1,100 a. of arable, 860 a. of ancient meadow, and 120 a. of orchard.[84] Between 1825 and 1830 c. 26 new houses were built and others were improved.[85] There were 1,670 a. under arable in 1839, 2,502 a. under grass, 86 a. of orchard, and 69 a. of gardens. Of the grassland, 670 a. were ancient meadow. Twenty-four holdings were 20–50 a., 9 were 50–100 a., 8 were 100–200 a., and three over 200 a., Gurney

58 Ibid.; below, Stogursey, manors.
59 S.R.O., DD/PH 224/114; 293; *V.C.H. Som.* iii. 214; G.E.C. *Baronetage*, ii. 91–2.
60 S.R.O., DD/PH 169.
61 *S.R.S.* ix, p. 225; *Valor Eccl.* (Rec. Com.), i. 211.
62 *V.C.H. Som.* i. 435–6, 471–2, 485–7, 510, 521, 525.
63 P.R.O., SC 6/974/8.
64 Ibid. SC 6/1090/4.
65 Ibid. SC 6/1090/4; E 142/8.
66 Ibid. C 134/56, no. 4.
67 W. Suss. R.O., PHA 5370; W. Suff. R.O. 449/E3/15.53/2.2.
68 W. Suff. R.O. 449/E3/15.53/2.17.
69 Land not part of a tenement.
70 W. Suff. R.O. 449/E3/15.53/2.6.
71 W. Suss. R.O., PHA, ct. roll.

72 *L. & P. Hen. VIII*, xvi, p. 383.
73 *S.R.S.* xxvii. 223–4.
74 P.R.O., SC 6/Hen. VIII/3127.
75 S.R.O., DD/BR/bn 10.
76 Ibid. DD/SP inventories, 1634–7, 1645; *L. & P. Hen. VIII*, xvi, p. 383.
77 S.R.O., DD/DP 50/9.
78 Ibid. DD/SP inventories, 1671, 1674–6.
79 Ibid. 1684.
80 Ibid. DD/BW 461, 806.
81 Ibid. Q/RR papists' estates, 1717, 1731, 1748.
82 Ibid. DD/SP inventories, 1713, 1720–1, 1725, 1738.
83 Clifford MSS., estate acct. and survey bk. c. 1805; S.R.O., Q/REl 7/2E; above, intro.
84 S.R.O., DD/BR/da 8.
85 Ibid. D/P/can 13/1/1.

Street (233 a.), Brymore and Withiel (323 a.), and Higher Rodway (363 a.).[86] By 1851 there were 7 farms of over 200 a. and 7 more over 100 a.[87] Arable had shrunk to 1,286 a. in 1905 and there were said to be only 2,183 a. under grass.[88] In the mid 20th century Chilton Trivet farm produced crops of wheat, mixed oats, barley, peas and beans called balanced dredge, linseed, kale, mangolds, sugar beet, swedes, and turnips. Some meadow had been reseeded and one field of oats and barley was cut green.[89] Of 26 holdings covering 1,769 ha. (4,371 a.) in 1982 8 were over 100 ha. (247 a.) and 5 were under 10 ha. (25 a.), 10 were worked part time, 7 were dairy farms, 4 raised sheep and cattle, two specialized in cereals, and one in horticultural crops. The main crop was wheat (368 ha.), followed by barley (184 ha.), oats, potatoes, fodder roots and brassicas, and oilseed rape. There were nearly 12 ha. of horticultural crops including vegetables, glasshouse crops, apples, pears, and soft fruit. Livestock comprised 4,492 sheep, 2,272 cattle, 979 pigs, and 266 poultry.[90] At Rodway are the large grain stores of Cannington Grain Ltd., a co-operative storing and marketing grain from south-west England.

Combwich pill had attracted trade by the mid 14th century when both local and foreign vessels were shipping corn from there to Ireland and elsewhere.[91] It was part of the port of Bridgwater. In 1543 Combwich had 13 mariners,[92] and by 1601 its seamen were impressed for the navy.[93] Ships called there regularly in the 16th and early 17th centuries with coal, wine, iron, millstones, beans, woad, and oil,[94] and salt was a prominent commodity which was stored and weighed there before being transshipped to Bridgwater.[95] Irish boats were at Combwich in 1543[96] and a trader from Cannington was taking goods to London in 1609.[97] Combwich traded by river with Langport and with Ham Mills on the Tone, despite plague, in 1625.[98] In 1678 a ropemaker worked at Combwich.[99] A ship was built there in the 1690s.[1]

In the later 18th century tile, coal, and culm were unloaded at the wharf in the pill,[2] and among the leading merchants of the period was William Emmet (d. c. 1758).[3] Henry Leigh, the largest shipowner in the 19th century, built up trade and added harbour facilities,[4] but vessels

were owned or part-owned by a wide range of landowners, farmers, merchants, and even a labourer.[5] The vessels themselves ranged from small cutters to ships of over 400 tons which were unloaded at moorings in Combwich Reach and the cargoes lightered upstream, often as far as Langport.[6] By 1832 bricks were being exported from the yard of Henry Leigh the younger on the south side of the pill, and brick and tile became Combwich's main export.[7] In the 1860s Leigh's fleet sailed to Cardiff, Newport, Saundersfoot (Pemb.), Bristol, and Lydney (Glos.). Coastal trade extended as far as Sharpness (Glos.) and Bideford in the 1890s.[8] Coal was brought from Wales until the early 20th century and other goods were imported by the Combwich and District Farmers Association.[9] In the later 1950s the wharf was acquired by the Central Electricity Generating Board to bring in materials for Hinkley Point power station. By that date the brickyards of Colthurst, Symons, & Co., formerly Leigh's, had been closed for 20 years and clay extraction ceased in 1963.[10]

A Cannington shoemaker and farmer had leather worth £10 in 1640 and over £65 due on his shop book.[11] A fuller was recorded in 1649[12] and a fellmonger in 1662.[13] There were several clothworkers in the parish in the later 17th and the early 18th century,[14] a blacksmith in 1725, and a sievemaker in 1777.[15] Occupations included bookbinding and watchmaking in 1871.[16] A brush factory in Combwich, operated by Morgan Brushes Ltd. in the later 20th century, closed in the 1980s.[17]

MILLS. In 1086 there was a mill on John the usher's estate and a half mill at Chilton, perhaps Chilton Trivet.[18] In 1370 John Horsey sold a watermill in Cannington.[19] The mill of Bosecroft, recorded in 1225, may have been the later Gurney's mill, recorded in 1482.[20] Gurney Street mills and Southbrook water mill were recorded in 1740,[21] probably south of Gurney Street Farm on the two branches of Cannington brook. Gurney Street mill was rebuilt in 1872.[22]

A watermill at Blackmoor was recorded in 1370.[23] There was also a tucking mill at Blackmoor, probably adjoining the grist mill, between 1579 and 1647.[24] In 1775 the miller sold meal in Bridgwater and was said to have 'grown from a

86 S.R.O., tithe award.
87 P.R.O., HO 107/1924.
88 Statistics supplied by the then Bd. of Agric., 1905.
89 S.R.O., DD/DHR, box 12.
90 Min. of Agric., Fisheries, and Food, agric. returns, 1982.
91 *Proc. before J.P.s*, ed. B. Putnam, 191; *Cal. Fine R.* 1356–69, 291; *Cal. Pat.* 1364–7, 72, 78.
92 *Cal. Pat.* 1399–1401, 8; 1401–5, 462; *L. & P. Hen. VIII*, xviii (1), p. 319.
93 *Acts of P.C.* 1601–4, 137.
94 S.R.O., D/B/bw 1438, 1440, 1442, 1456–7, 1464, 1471–2, 1477, 1498.
95 Ibid. 1438, 1450, 1481, 1484.
96 Ibid. 1442.
97 Ibid. 1493.
98 *S.R.S.* xxiv. 9.
99 S.R.O., DD/SP inventory, 1678.
1 Wimborne St. Giles, Shaftesbury MS. L79 (1702).
2 S.R.O., DD/ARN 8; Clifford MSS., Som. estate papers.
3 S.R.O., DD/AH 12/5; DD/FA 11/1.

4 Ibid. DD/FA 11/2; P.R.O., HO 107/935; ibid. RG 11/2371.
5 S.R.O., DD/FA 11/1–2.   6 Ibid. 11/2.
7 Ibid. DD/X/HMY 17.
8 Ibid. DD/RSS 2, 20, 46, 67.
9 *Kelly's Dir. Som.* (1906, 1939).
10 Som. C.C., Sites and Mons. Rec.
11 S.R.O., DD/SP inventory, 1640.
12 Ibid. DD/WG 13/1.   13 Ibid. Q/SR 102/55.
14 Ibid. DD/SP inventories, 1672, 1675, 1716; DD/DN 463.
15 Ibid. DD/SP inventory, 1725; DD/SAS (H/104) 14.
16 P.R.O, RG 10/2380.
17 *Bridgwater Mercury*, 17 Jan. 1989.
18 *V.C.H. Som.* i. 486, 521.
19 *Cal. Pat.* 1367–70, 457.
20 *S.R.S.* xi, pp. 209–10; lxx, p. 51.
21 S.R.O., DD/DHR, box 3.
22 Devon R.O. 547 B/P 2340, 3484.
23 *Cal. Fine R.* 1369–77, 102.
24 S.R.O., DD/S/WH 243; DD/S/BW 5.

beggar to a gentleman'.[25] The mill went out of use in the later 19th century,[26] was demolished, and the site levelled.

The Cannington priory mill, recorded in 1536,[27] was later known as Coles's or Town mill.[28] Milling ceased in 1913 but the following year the mill was used to pulverize spar from Cannington quarry for use in munitions. It was operated by gas and then from a water-powered dynamo and both oil and steam engines. The mill employed c. 10 people and the ground spar was hauled to Bridgwater station by a steam traction engine. After 1918 the mill became derelict and in 1930 it was rebuilt as a dwelling and the pond filled in.[29]

Chilton mill, later Cook's mill, was recorded in 1494 and was attached to Chilton Trivet manor.[30] It may have been a fulling mill in 1599.[31] Like Town mill it was taken over for spar-crushing during the First World War but was later converted to a cheese factory powered by electricity from a turbine. The mill formerly had an overshot wheel.[32]

There was a mill at Combwich in the early 16th century,[33] probably on the north bank of the pill where Mill orchard was recorded in the 19th century.[34] The mill was last recorded in 1682.[35]

LOCAL GOVERNMENT. Between the 14th and 16th centuries Cannington was divided between the four tithings of Cannington, Chilton, Combwich, and Rodway.[36] Blackmoor, however, was said to be in Adscombe tithing in 1389.[37] Orchard tithing, recorded in 1455,[38] may have been an alternative name for Chilton tithing, which was known as Orchard and Chilton in 1641 and separated into two tithings by 1665.[39] By the mid 18th century Rodway was divided between Home and Quarter, the latter consisting of the marshes.[40] The Rodway tithingman was elected in Rodway manor court in the 16th century.[41] In 1675 neither the tithingman nor the constable of Cannington lived in the parish and their duties were done by the churchwardens.[42]

Courts leet for Rodway manor were held twice a year in 1485 and court rolls survive for Rodway for 1532–3.[43] The court was then concerned with maintaining buildings, ditches, hedges, and gates, controlling livestock, and appointing the reeve. Lord Clifford held courts in the early 19th century for Cannington and Rodway. His tenants were given a treat at the Anchor and he paid a bailiff and a woodward.[44] Blackmoor manor court records survive for 1556–7 and 1611: the court was concerned with repairs, livestock, and illegal felling.[45] Tenants of Chilton owed suit of court in 1338[46] and a court roll survives for 1817 when a bailiff was appointed.[47]

Poor relief was provided in cash and kind at the beginning of the 18th century but by the end it was almost entirely in cash.[48] In 1731 the parish proposed setting up a workhouse;[49] the vestry again considered building a poorhouse in 1816, when a surgeon was employed to inoculate poor children.[50] A select vestry was appointed from 1821 to 1835.[51] In the early 20th century Cannington House was let to the Bridgwater guardians to house children.[52] By 1866 Cannington had a burial board and was later part of the Cannington and Wembdon drainage district.[53] Cannington formed part of Bridgwater poor-law union in 1836, Bridgwater rural district in 1894, and Sedgemoor district in 1974.[54]

CHURCH. In 1086 Erchenger the priest held of the king in the church of Cannington 2½ virgates which Aelfric the priest had held in 1066.[55] Robert de Curci evidently gave the church c. 1138 as part of the endowment of Cannington priory, which appropriated the rectorial estate.[56] Parochial incumbents were known as vicars from the 13th century although no vicarage was ordained.[57] The living remained a sole benefice until 1984 when it was united with Otterhampton and Combwich, Stockland and Steart, the incumbent thereafter becoming a rector.[58]

The advowson belonged to the priory until the Dissolution and then passed to successive owners of Cannington manor. Elizabeth, Baroness Clifford, presented in 1685[59] but her successors were Roman Catholics and by 1707 let the right of presentation.[60] At vacancies in 1735 and 1766 vicars were appointed by Oxford University.[61] Lessees presented in 1798, and in 1804 the lessee, Charles Henry Burt, presented himself.[62] In 1872 Philip Pleydell Bouverie (d. 1890) acquired the advowson which he gave to the bishop of Bath and Wells.[63] The bishop was patron of the united benefice from 1984.[64]

In 1535 the vicarage was worth £7 10s. 8d.,

25   Ibid. DD/FD 16.
26   P.R.O., RG 9/1621; RG 10/2380; RG 11/2371.
27   Ibid. SC 6/Hen. VIII/3127.
28   S.R.O., D/P/can 4/1/1; ibid. tithe award.
29   Ibid. D/P/can 23/6; D/R/bw 22/1/21; ibid. T/PH/hdn 1.
30   Ibid. DD/S/WH 58; D/P/can 4/1/1; DD/DHR, box 3.
31   P.R.O., CP 25(2)/207/41 Eliz. I East.
32   S.R.O., T/PH/hdn 1; Som. C.C., Sites and Mons. Rec.
33   P.R.O., LR 3/123.
34   S.R.O., tithe award.   35   Ibid. DD/ARN 5.
36   S.R.S. iii. 140, 142, 144; xx. 246–7, 249.
37   Ibid. xiv, pp. 200–1.
38   J. C. Wedgwood, Hist. Parl., Biogs. 276, n. 6.
39   Som. Protestation Returns, ed. A. J. Howard and T. L. Stoate, 193; Dwelly, Hearth Tax, i. 65–70.
40   S.R.O., Q/REl 7/2, 2A–F.
41   W. Suss. R.O., PHA, ct. roll.

42   S.R.O., Q/SR 127/16.
43   W. Suff. R.O. 449/E3/15.53/2.5; W. Suss. R.O., PHA, ct. roll.
44   Clifford MSS., estate accts.; ibid. IV/6/7/X 1A.
45   S.R.O., DD/S/WH 210–11.
46   S.R.S. lvii, p. 30.   47   S.R.O., D/P/bw. jo 8/4/1.
48   Ibid. D/P/can 13/2/1–2, 4.   49   Ibid. 4/1/1.
50   Ibid. 9/1/1.   51   Ibid. 9/4/1.
52   Som. C. C., deeds 103A; Kelly's Dir. Som. (1931).
53   S.R.O., D/P/can 23/2; D/RA D3A.
54   Youngs, Local Admin. Units, i. 671, 673, 676.
55   V.C.H. Som. i. 471.
56   Above, manors (Cannington).
57   Cat. Anct. D. iv, A 9825.   58   Dioc. Dir.
59   Som. Incumbents, ed. Weaver, 324.
60   Clifford MSS., IV/2/38.
61   Som. Incumbents, ed. Weaver, 324; S.R.O., D/D/B reg 28, f. 40v.; D/D/Vc 88.
62   S.R.O., DD/BR/da 8; P.R.O., E 331/Bath and Wells/33.
63   S.R.O., D/P/can 3/1/2.   64   Dioc. Dir.

mostly in the form of a stipend from the prioress,[65] by composition said to have been made in the 1520s to replace an earlier one which gave the vicar small tithes and oblations, and corn in lieu of Candlemas offerings.[66] The composition, challenged in 1582–3[67] and varying between £7 and £8, continued to be paid until 1922.[68] Successive vicars of Cannington also held the lease of some or all of the tithes until 1865.[69] About 1668 the vicar had c. £40 a year,[70] and his average net income was £371 between 1827 and 1830.[71] Philip Pleydell Bouverie (d. 1872) paid the vicar the sum of £122 a year from 1865, presumably in lieu of the leased tithes, and his son established from 1872 a permanent endowment, himself giving capital sums to secure grants from the Ecclesiastical Commissioners.[72]

A garden and orchard belonging to the vicar were mentioned in the 15th century.[73] Vicarial glebe was worth 4s. in 1535.[74] There were 7 a. in 1571 but by 1626 only a garden and another small piece of ground, the gift of the lay rector.[75] They remained glebe until 1906 when the kitchen garden east of the churchyard was sold.[76]

In 1536 the vicar appears to have found his own lodging,[77] and there was no house in 1571. In 1638 there was a 'decent' house on the south side of the churchyard, possibly that which the lay rector had provided in 1626.[78] In 1735 it comprised a hall, parlour, oriel, service rooms, a study, and six chambers.[79] In the early 19th century the house was unfit[80] but after repairs[81] was described as fit but small and a pretty cottage.[82] It was totally rebuilt in 1879 with the help of Philip Pleydell Bouverie.[83] The house was sold c. 1980 and was replaced by a smaller house, no. 27 Brook Street.[84]

In 1333 Robert FitzPayn, Lord FitzPayn, gave land to the priory for a chaplain to pray for his family in the parish church.[85] In 1450 there were two anniversary chaplains,[86] one of whom became vicar in 1452.[87] Thomas Tremayne, a former fellow and rector of Exeter College, Oxford, was appointed vicar in 1504 and became vicar of Witheridge (Devon), also in the patronage of the priory and probably in plurality, in 1517.[88] The three stipendiary priests recorded c. 1535 included probably two who served the

priory.[89] In 1479 the Holy Trinity fraternity with its own altar in the church and in 1533 the store of Our Lady of Pity were mentioned.[90] There was also a light endowed with land in Spaxton.[91]

Robert Reason, vicar from 1619, was resident rector of Otterhampton, and Cannington was served by curates; in 1629 the parishioners could not name their vicar. Reason was probably deprived in 1648.[92] Under John Rugge, vicar 1698–1706, communion was celebrated five times a year.[93] The number of communicants was said in 1729 to have increased but there were only 25 in the later 18th century.[94] In 1735 Gregory Larkworthy, vicar 1711–35, agreed, after a dispute with the parishioners, to begin morning service at 10 a.m. and evening service at 3 or 3.30 p.m.[95] He died the same year leaving a comfortably furnished house and 180 books.[96] During the late 18th century the parish was usually served by curates; one vicar, Henry Poole, was described as being of 'not much religion, yet good tempered'.[97] In the 1820s there were two Sunday services.[98] In 1843 communion was celebrated six times a year but by 1870 it was celebrated monthly and on feast days.[99] In 1886 after the restoration of the church many parishioners threatened to leave as they disliked the new arrangements.[1] In the early 20th century three and sometimes five Sunday services were held, including a children's service. By the 1950s there were four services and between 10 and 30 communicants. During the 1960s and 1970s Lent lectures were given by distinguished speakers. In 1983 there were usually c. 80 communicants each Sunday.[2]

A tenement held by the churchwardens in 1536[3] may have been the church house which from 1688 was used for charitable purposes. The name church house survived until 1746.[4]

The church of ST. MARY, so dedicated by 1336,[5] comprises a structurally undivided chancel and nave, with north vestry, north and south aisles, and south porch, and a western tower. The north respond of the 12th-century chancel arch, visible in the vestry, and the weathering of the earlier nave roof on the tower, are evidence of the size and form of the church before the

65 *Valor Eccl.* (Rec. Com.), i. 209, 214.
66 *L. & P. Hen. VIII*, xi, pp. 576–7.
67 P.R.O., C 2/Eliz. I/Bb3/28.
68 S.R.O., D/D/Rg 262; D/P/can 2/9/1.
69 Ibid. D/D/Rg 262; D/P/can 3/2/1–2; DD/BR/da 8; Clifford MSS., Cannington vicarage corresp.
70 S.R.O., D/D/Vc 24.
71 *Rep. Com. Eccl. Revenues*, pp. 130–1.
72 Clifford MSS., Cannington vicarage corresp.; S.R.O., DD/BR/ely 16/4; D/P/can 3/1/2.
73 *Cal. Close*, 1441–7, 124; *S.R.S.* lxx, p. 51.
74 *Valor Eccl.* (Rec. Com.), i. 214.
75 S.R.O., D/D/Rg 262.
76 *S.R.S.* lxx, p. 51; S.R.O., tithe award; ibid. D/P/can 3/1/3, 3/3/1, 3/4/1.
77 *L. & P. Hen. VIII*, xi, pp. 576–7.
78 S.R.O., D/D/Rg 262.
79 Ibid. DD/SP inventory, 1735.
80 Ibid. D/P/can 1/6/1–2.
81 Ibid. D/D/Bbm 36.
82 Ibid. D/D/Rb 1815; DD/BR/da 8.
83 Ibid. D/P/can 23/6; DD/BR/ely 16/9.
84 *Dioc. Dir.*
85 *Cal. Pat.* 1330–4, 394.

86 *S.R.S.* xlix, p. 139.
87 Ibid. p. 177.
88 Ibid. liv, p. 91; Emden, *Biog. Reg. Univ. Oxf.* iii. 1895.
89 S.R.O., D/D/Vc 20; P.R.O., SC 6/Hen. VIII/7298.
90 S.R.O., DD/S/WH 115; *S.R.S.* xvi. 363; *Wells Wills*, ed. Weaver, 39–40.
91 *S.R.S.* ii. 55.
92 *Walker Revised*, ed. A. G. Matthews, 318; S.R.O., D/D/Rg 262; D/D/Ca 266, 274; *S.R.S.* lxv, p. 22; below, Otterhampton, church.
93 S.R.O., D/P/can 4/1/1, 13/10/1.
94 Ibid. 4/1/1; D/D/Vc 88.
95 Ibid. D/P/can 3/2/1.
96 Ibid. DD/SP inventory, 1735.
97 Ibid. D/P/can 2/1/3, 5; *Paupers and Pigkillers*, ed. J. Ayres, 35.
98 S.R.O., DD/BR/da 8; D/D/Rb 1827.
99 Ibid. D/D/Va 1843, 1870.
1 Ibid. DD/BR/ely 16/9.
2 Ibid. D/P/can 2/5/1–4; 2/8/1; 2/9/1.
3 P.R.O., SC 6/Hen. VIII/3127.
4 *Proc. Som. Arch. Soc.* cxvii. 107; below, charities.
5 *S.R.S.* xlviii, p. 87; for a photo. of c. 1860, plate opposite.

Cannington Court and Church, c. 1860

Over Stowey: Quantock Lodge, c. 1870

BRIDGWATER: CHRIST CHURCH UNITARIAN CHURCH, 1973

SPAXTON: THE AGAPEMONE CHAPEL INTERIOR, *c.* 1890

15th century when it was apparently unaisled. Everything except the 14th-century tower was demolished when the church was rebuilt in the later 15th century on a new alignment. The new work bearing the Poynings badges may indicate the involvement of Eleanor Poynings (d. 1484), wife of Henry Percy, earl of Northumberland (d. 1461).[6] The chancel is of one bay only and the church was divided liturgically by a screen and loft which added a second bay to the chancel and created chapels at the end of each aisle. The south aisle may have been the Trinity aisle.[7] By 1840 the pulpit stood on the north side of the nave and there were galleries in front of the tower arch,[8] over the south door, and over the former north chapel. Box pews occupied the aisles and the east end of the nave, and the chancel formed a large sanctuary with the communion rail on three sides of the altar. There was also a large screened enclosure for the Clifford vault.[9] The architect Richard Carver refurnished the church in 1840, turning what remained of the central section of the screen into parcloses for private pews occupying the former aisle chapels. He greatly reduced the size of the sanctuary and reseated the whole church, placing the pulpit and reading desk at the centre of the entrance to the chancel, directly in front of the altar. A vestry on the north side of the former north chapel was altered to incorporate the former rood stair turret and, after prolonged disputes,[10] the 18th-century wrought iron screen of the Clifford vault was replaced in a less prominent position.[11] In 1885, under the architect Edwin Down, the screen, including fragments of original work, was restored to its original position,[12] the whole church reseated with a central aisle, the 19th-century pulpit removed to the north side of the screen, and a new vestry built on the north side of the chancel. The iron screen became a parclose between new choir stalls and the organ in the former north chapel. The rood stair was again altered and the former vestry became a fuel store.[13]

The font is of the early 15th century, and there is a fragment of a memorial brass to Joan (d. 1472), wife of William Dodesham, and another to William's parents William (d. 1440) and Ellen.[14] The stone altar front under the tower probably came from the 18th-century chapel in Cannington Court, and the reredos of 1893 incorporates the faces of the donors, Joanna and Philip Pleydell Bouverie. The rood, designed by Tom Preater, was installed in 1983.

The plate includes a cup and cover of 1632 by 'I.M.', a salver and dish, both probably of 1725 by 'T.M.', and a flagon of 1729, the latter by Robert Lucas and bought because the number of communicants had greatly increased.[15] There are six bells, the oldest dated 1619 by George Purdue.[16] The registers date from 1559 but there are gaps in the 17th century.[17]

The chapel of *ST. LEONARD*, Combwich, so dedicated by 1524,[18] was recorded in 1336.[19] It was served by a chaplain paid by Cannington priory in 1536.[20] Bequests were made to the chapel until 1546[21] but in 1549 the chapel and chapel house were granted to two Londoners[22] who probably sold it to Robert Cuffe. Robert died in 1593 holding the chapel house and a dovecot but the chapel was not mentioned.[23] His son, also Robert, died in 1639 in possession of the house,[24] which has not been traced further; the chapel site is unknown.

In 1868 part of Combwich was transferred to Otterhampton for ecclesiastical purposes and St. Peter's, Combwich, was built.[25]

ROMAN CATHOLICISM. There was a recusant teacher in the parish in 1612.[26] The Cliffords were recusants and in 1715 there were two Roman Catholic landowners. Three members of the Knight family were ordained priests in the 18th century.[27] Nine Catholics were recorded in 1767 and six in 1776 when the chapel at Court House had a monthly service.[28] In 1795 a chaplain was paid £15 a year and 2 gn. for wine for the chapel, which was probably refitted in 1805.[29] In 1807 a group of Benedictine nuns came to Court House at the invitation of Lord Clifford and remained until *c.* 1835.[30] Apartments were used by the bishop of the Western district in 1847.[31] The house was again occupied by nuns from 1863 to 1867.[32]

The chapel in the Court House was rebuilt in 1830 and opened for public worship in 1831, dedicated to the Holy Name.[33] The chapel register survives from 1779 to 1838.[34] There were 127 Catholics in 1858 and 73 excluding schoolchildren in 1896.[35] The chapel closed *c.* 1919.[36] In 1982 services were held in the village hall by a priest from Bridgwater.

PROTESTANT NONCONFORMITY. An Independent meeting house was registered in 1799.[37] It may have closed before a chapel was

6 *Proc. Som. Arch. Soc.* civ. 76.
7 *Som. Wills*, ed. Brown, iv. 54.
8 S.R.O., D/P/can 4/1/8, 9/1/1.   9 Ibid. DD/FS, plan 1.
10 Ibid. D/D/Va 1840; DD/FS, box 55; DD/BR/ely 16; DD/X/BUSH.
11 Ibid. D/P/can 4/1/1; 6/1/1, 3; 23/12; DD/FS, plan 1; Taunton Castle, Pigott colln., drawing by J. Buckler, 1832; Braikenridge colln., drawing by W. W. Wheatley, 1845.
12 F. B. Bond and B. Camm, *Roodscreens and Roodlofts*, 153.
13 S.R.O., D/P/can 6/1/3, 23/14; D/D/Cf 1885/5.
14 Ibid. D/P/can 9/1/3; *Proc. Som. Arch. Soc.* lxxxvii. 73; xc. 78–9.
15 *Proc. Som. Arch. Soc.* xlvii. 155; S.R.O., D/P/can 4/1/1 (1727, 1729).   16 S.R.O., DD/SAS CH 16/1.
17 Ibid. D/P/can 2/1/1–15.   18 *S.R.S.* xix. 230–1.
19 Ibid. xlviii, p. 87.
20 Ibid. lii, p. 28; *Valor Eccl.* (Rec. Com.), i. 209; P.R.O., SC 6/Hen. VIII/3127.

21 S.R.O., DD/X/SR 5; *S.R.S.* xl. 203.
22 *Cal. Pat.* 1549–51, 145–6.   23 S.R.O., DD/GC 6.
24 P.R.O., C 142/531, no. 4.
25 Below, Otterhampton, church.   26 S.R.O., D/D/Ca 175.
27 *Cath. Rel. in Som.* (1826); G. Oliver, *Hist. Cath. Religion* (1857), 341.
28 H.L.R.O., list of papists, 1767; S.R.O., D/D/Vc 88.
29 Clifford MSS., acct. 1795–1809.
30 *Cath. Rel. in Som.* 40–1; *Taunton Courier*, 19 Aug. 1835.
31 Clifford MSS., IV/6/3.
32 *Proc. Som. Arch. Soc.* civ. 86; Clifford MSS., Som. estate corresp.
33 Oliver, *Hist. Cath. Religion*, 60; H. M. Colvin, *Biog. Dict. Brit. Architects* (1978), 630; S.R.O., Q/RR meeting ho. lics.; above, manors (Cannington).
34 S.R.O., T/PH/sog 1231.
35 *SW. Cath. Hist.* ii. 48–9.
36 *Kelly's Dir. Som.* (1919).   37 S.R.O., D/D/Rm 2.

opened in 1826.[38] That building, later used as a Sunday school, was sold in 1952.[39] A new chapel was built in 1869 for 300 people but by 1896 the cause was 'very weak'.[40] The chapel, at the west end of the village, belonged to the United Reformed church and remained open in 1989.

A meeting house for no stated denomination was licensed in 1825 and Wesleyans opened a chapel in 1847.[41] The Bible Christians planned a preaching place in 1867.[42]

EDUCATION. There were unlicensed schoolmasters in 1606 and 1635, a recusant woman was teaching in 1612,[43] and in 1662 a man was licensed to teach reading, writing, accounts, and ciphering.[44] In 1732 the vestry agreed to pay a master to teach six children and the overseers paid for furnishing a schoolroom at the almshouse.[45] The school appears to have continued throughout the 18th century[46] and the parish paid £1 6s. a quarter out of the church rates for the education of eight boys in 1776. There was also a school for Roman Catholic boys and girls.[47] Sarah Warren by will of 1794 gave £50 for poor girls to learn reading, knitting, and plain needlework. Mary Warren in 1801 gave £100, since lost, partly to provide a salary for a schoolmaster, and £50 to support the Sunday school. In 1968 Sarah's gift benefited Cannington primary school and Mary's gift for the Sunday school was being paid in 1964.[48]

By 1819 the Sunday school had up to 80 pupils and 8 boys continued to be taught at parish expense by the parish clerk and his wife.[49] In 1825 there were 80 children at the Sunday school supported partly out of Lady (Jane) Rogers's charity,[50] but the number had doubled by 1835. There were four day schools in 1835; one, with 38 children, was a Roman Catholic school supported by the convent.[51] This school survived until 1841 or later.[52] The other three day schools had a total of 124 children and one had an endowment, possibly Mary Warren's gift and other charity income.[53]

The almshouse schoolroom remained in use until c. 1836,[54] when a National school was built. An infant class was added in 1871. In 1903 there were 163 children on the books and an evening school was held. The school had a small endowment, possibly the gift of Sarah Warren.[55] Numbers rose to 173 in 1935 and 271 in 1975. In 1981 there were 178 children on the register. After 1947 the school accepted voluntary controlled status.[56] A Roman Catholic school established by 1875 had an average attendance of 86 in 1889. It was open in 1897 but had closed probably by 1900 when provision was made for the children at the National school.[57] John Tucker had a boarding school at Cannington which he moved to Crowcombe in 1789. In 1815 a Mr. Strong prepared boys for Oxford.[58] A boarding school for girls may have been in existence from 1839 to 1841.[59] A Roman Catholic boarding school for boys was formed in 1868. Known as the West of England and South Wales Industrial School for Catholic boys it occupied Court House until 1919 when it removed to Bath.[60] In 1881 there were 81 boarders aged between 7 and 14.[61]

The Somerset College of Agriculture and Horticulture, originally known as the Somerset Farm Institute, was founded in 1919 and occupied Court House, Court farm, and Rodway farm in 1982 and substantial new buildings, built in 1970, north of High Street. In 1928 a crop testing station was opened.[62] Brymore school was opened in Brymore House in 1953 as a technical school for boys aged 13 to 16 specializing in agriculture. Numbers rose from 38 in 1953 to 198 in 1981.[63]

CHARITIES FOR THE POOR. In 1713 and 1715 marsh lands in Cannington, Combwich, and Stockland Bristol were bought with the capital of four parish charities: Lady (Jane) Rogers, who by deed of 1601 gave £26 for the poor every Sunday; Sir Bartholomew Michell (d. 1616), who gave £20 for the poor on Christmas Eve; Margery Duddlestone (d. 1711), who gave £10 for bread on New Year's day; and Richard Tilley or Tapp (d. 1598), who gave £40 for the poor on Good Friday.[64] By 1826 the income was given to the poor and supported the almshouse, and any surplus was used to pay a schoolmaster to teach the poor and was later given to the National school.[65] In 1982 the lands were sold.[66] In 1989 the Cannington combined charities, comprising all the surviving charities except those of Henry Rogers and Benjamin Vaughan, administered the almshouse and gave small grants to the school and the elderly.[67]

Benjamin Vaughan, rector of Charlinch (d. 1639), gave £50 for apprenticing two children in husbandry. By 1826 the charity was used to bind one apprentice from Cannington in alternate

38 Rep. Som. Cong. Union (1896).
39 Char. Com. files.
40 Rep. Som. Cong. Union (1896).
41 S.R.O., D/D/Rm, box 2; D/N/bmc 3/2/1. The Independent chapel was recorded in error as Wesleyan in 1861 and 1875: P.O. Dir. Som. (1861, 1875).
42 S.R.O., D/N/bmc 3/2/5.
43 Ibid. D/D/Ca 151, 175, 301.
44 Ibid. D/D/Bs 39.
45 Ibid. D/P/can 4/1/1, 13/2/2.
46 Ibid. 2/1/3.
47 Ibid. D/D/Vc 88.
48 Char. Com. files.
49 Educ. of Poor Digest, p. 777.
50 Ann. Rep. B. & W. Dioc. Assoc. S.P.C.K. (1825–6); below, char.
51 Educ. Enq. Abstract, p. 798.
52 Robson's Dir. Som. (1839); P.R.O., HO 107/935.

53 Educ. Enq. Abstract, p. 798; 15th Rep. Com. Char. 358–9.
54 Proc. Som. Arch. Soc. cxvii. 107; S.R.O., tithe award.
55 S.R.O., C/E 4/380/64; ibid. D/P/can 18/1/1.
56 Ibid. C/E 4/64.
57 P.O. Dir. Som. (1875); Kelly's Dir. Som. (1889); Whitby, Dir. Bridgwater (1897); S.R.O., D/P/can 18/7/1.
58 S.R.O., D/P/crow 23/2; ibid. T/PH/ay 1.
59 Robson's Dir. Som. (1839); P.R.O., HO 107/935.
60 Lond. Gaz. 27 Nov. 1868, 6112; Kelly's Dir. Som. (1919).   61 P.R.O., RG 11/2371.
62 Kelly's Dir. Som. (1931); S.R.O., C/E 2/2/18–19.
63 S.R.O., C/E 4/64; 74.
64 Char. Don. pp. 1048–9; Som. Wills, ed. Brown, v. 68; 15th Rep. Com. Char. 358–9.
65 15th Rep. Com. Char. 358–9; S.R.O., D/P/can 17/3/2.
66 Char. Com. files.
67 Inf. from rector, the Revd. P. Martin.

years, half the income going to Bridgwater corporation to apprentice a Bridgwater boy, and many boys were apprenticed to shoemakers.[68] The capital was invested in the Bridgwater market house from 1787 until 1851.[69] In 1898 the charity formed part of the United Charity of Bridgwater and Cannington and by 1976 was used to benefit a youth under 18 resident in Cannington, employed in agriculture, and having the longest service with one employer.[70] The charity was for providing tools in 1989 but had not been claimed for some time.[71]

By will dated 1672 Henry Rogers left £7,500 for charity of which £2,350 was to maintain 20 poor aged persons. Half of them were to be residents of the manors of Withiel, Steart, and Salty in Cannington. In 1685 the capital was invested in land and by 1776 each recipient had c. £8 a year.[72] In 1816 the number of recipients was doubled and by 1880 all elderly parishioners were eligible.[73] In 1946 payments of £5–£10 a year were made to 32 old people and in 1971 recipients were made pensioners of the charity for 3–6 years.[74] Under a scheme of 1984 £30 a year is paid in instalments to 40 elderly people in the parish; the remaining income supports a playgroup, adapts housing for the disabled, or meets other needs. In 1989 c. £1,500 a year was being distributed.[75]

Henry Rogers also gave £600 to maintain a workhouse for the Cannington poor and in 1691 an estate was purchased. The church house was repaired for use as a workhouse c. 1688 but by the later 18th century it housed almspeople. Nine aged women were in the house in 1826 receiving 2s. or 3s. a week with clothing and fuel.[76] In 1920 the charity lands were sold.[77] In 1937 the house had room for seven inmates who received free coal and £12 a year.[78] In 1955 the almshouse was divided into five dwellings.[79] The building was modernized in 1971–2 to provide five double units. The almshouse stands on the north side of the main street and comprises a range parallel with the street, originally an open hall of eight bays built c. 1500. Part of the hall was floored in the 16th century, the remainder possibly c. 1688, when probably the two-storeyed north wing was built at the east end. A stone recording Henry Rogers's gift and a weather vane dated 1699 were added. Few early features survived reconstruction in 1971.[80] In 1989 the almshouses were administered by the Cannington combined charities.[81]

Mary Ruscombe by will dated 1725 gave £10 to the poor. By 1826 the income was used to distribute bread on Easter Sunday.[82] An unknown donor gave £182 before 1786 but the charity had been lost by 1826.[83] In 1794 Sarah Warren gave £10 to provide bread at Candlemas and in 1801 her sister Mary Warren gave £10 for the same purpose and £120 for fuel and bedding.[84] Mary's gift, put into Consols in 1865, was in existence in 1896 but has since been lost.[85] A distribution of 40s. on 25 October was recorded in 1623 but was not mentioned again.[86]

CHARLINCH

THE ancient parish, which may have taken its name from the hill on which the church stands, lay in three parts in undulating countryside 4 km. west of Bridgwater. The two largest parts, both irregular in shape, included most of the settlements, and were divided from each other by a narrow strip of Spaxton parish. One included Charlinch hamlet and Gothelney and measured 3 km. from east to west and 1 km. from north to south. The second, to the north-west, included Rowden, Currypool, Padnoller, and Swang, in an area measuring 3 km. from east to west and 1.5 km. from north to south at its widest point. The third, known as Bush, lay south-west beyond Spaxton village, 3 km. from Charlinch church.[87] The parish contained c. 1,450 a. (587 ha.), all of which was by stages added to Spaxton: in 1882 Bush (95 a., with 2 houses and 6 inhabitants),[88] in 1933 Currypool (731 a.),[89] and in 1981 the remainder (624 a.).[90]

The boundaries of the parish seldom followed natural features. Roads north-west of Bush and south-east of Currypool marked divisions with Spaxton. Currypool lies on gravel in the valley of the Cannington brook, the land rising gently from there south-west towards Rowden, reaching 76 m. and north-west to a spur 76 m. high on marls and Leighland slates dividing it from a second shallow valley. The land rises again to the north above Swang reaching 75 m. Charlinch church is on the western end of a knoll, at a height of 72 m., from which the land falls gently east to Gothelney, in an area of marls, slates, limestone, and gravels. Bush occupies an area of slates, grits, and marls on the steeper, higher, Quantock slopes between 76 m. and 183 m.[91]

68   15th Rep. Com. Char. 359; S.R.S. xxxiv. 197; S.R.O., D/P/can 17/3/2.   69   S.R.O., D/P/can 17/1/3.
70   Char. Com. files.   71   Inf. from the rector.
72   15th Rep. Com. Char. 352–3; S.R.O., D/D/Vc 88.
73   S.R.O., DD/AH 24/4; Char. Com. files.
74   S.R.O., D/P/can 17/6/1, 17/7/1.
75   Inf. from the rector.
76   15th Rep. Com. Char. 355–7.
77   Char. Com. files.
78   Som. Co. Herald, 13 Mar. 1937.
79   Char. Com. files.
80   Proc. Som. Arch. Soc. cxvii. 107.
81   Inf. from the rector.
82   15th Rep. Com. Char. 357.
83   Char. Don. pp. 1048–9.

84   15th Rep. Com. Char. 359–60.
85   S.R.O., D/P/can 17/6/2.
86   Ibid. DD/S/WH, box 33.
87   O.S. Map 1/50,000, sheet 182 (1974 edn.); S.R.O., tithe award; cf. below, map on p. 111. This article was completed in 1987.
88   Census, 1891; the acreage is of the area shown on S.R.O., tithe award, measured on O.S. Map 6", Som. XLIX. SE. (1887 edn.).
89   S.R.O., D/R/bw 16/20/1, giving 740 a.; the correct acreage of the two parts of the parish is given in O.S. Map 6", Som. index (1892 edn.), matching the acreage in Census, 1891.   90   Census, 1981.
91   O.S. Map 1/50,000, sheet 182 (1974 edn.); Geol. Surv. Map 1/50,000, solid and drift, sheet 295 (1985 edn.).

Marl digging may account for ponds in the north part of the parish[92] and there was a quarry at Bush in 1822.[93]

The settlement pattern of scattered farmsteads had probably been established by 1086 when Charlinch, Currypool, Gothelney, and Swang were in existence.[94] Padnoller was recorded in 1199.[95] There is no nucleated village in the parish and the largest settlement was probably Gothelney where in 1837 a group of houses, now reduced to one, lay around the green south of the manor house. Only the rectory house and a cottage adjoin the church. There may also have been a concentration of houses around the junction of Charlinch lane and the road to the church,[96] and there is a scatter of houses along Charlinch lane, mostly of the 20th century, especially at the western end by Four Forks. The remainder of the parish consists of compact farms with a few roadside cottages. The name Bush may indicate medieval clearance on the hillside.[97] It has been a single farm since the 17th century, probably in succession to two tenements, Holminbush and Northbarn.[98] New farm buildings were erected possibly c. 1871.[99] The name Rowden has not been found before the late 18th century.[1]

In 1648 and 1649 large numbers of people from Ireland who were relieved by the parish[2] were probably using the Nether Stowey to Bridgwater road. The road known as Oldway[3] formed the parish boundary for two short stretches east and south of Currypool, and parts of the two Bridgwater turnpike roads, from Nether Stowey and Four Forks in Spaxton also ran through the parish. All the settlements, however, lie on minor roads.[4]

No evidence of open-field arable has been found and the pattern of farmsteads surrounded by their fields is probably ancient. There was a park at Currypool, probably by 1327 when Robert the parker was recorded.[5] In 1569 it was said to be a mile in circumference,[6] but it appears to have been divided into fields c. 1618 although fallow deer remained in the area after that date.[7] The field names Lawn, Park ground, and Rail close still in use in 1837 suggest that the park lay west of Currypool Farm. The field names Warren and Park hill at Gothelney suggest a warren and possibly a park there. A small part of Radlet Common lay in the parish but it had been inclosed and was the property of Henry Labouchere in 1837.[8]

Fifteen acres of wood were recorded in 1086.[9] Timber at Currypool, including timber in the park, was being felled in the early 17th century,[10] and the tenant of Currypool in 1689 was required to plant two oak, ash, or elm every year.[11] Higher Wood, recorded in 1837, may be the site of ancient woodland, and by the same date over 45 a. of plantation and willow had been established at Currypool.[12] In 1905 41 a. of woodland remained[13] and some woodland survives near Currypool.

Twenty taxpayers were recorded in 1327[14] and 36 houses were charged for or exempted from hearth tax in 1665 and 1670.[15] In 1791 130 people were said to live in 25 houses, but that probably did not include detached areas.[16] The population rose between 1801 and 1821 from 183 to 251, fluctuated 1831–91 between 200 and 240, and fell to 158 in 1901.[17] In 1921 the total was 182 of whom 63 lived in the area transferred to Spaxton in 1933.[18] The population in the remaining portion of the parish had fallen to 49 in 1981 when the civil parish was abolished.[19]

MANORS AND OTHER ESTATES. In 1066 both *CHARLINCH* and *CURRYPOOL* were held by Alwig Banneson, and in 1086 by Roger de Courcelles.[20] Both were probably fees of Hugh Vautort in 1166[21] and both descended in the Vautort family, usually as Currypool manor although the name Charlinch manor continued in occasional use until 1803.[22] Currypool was held like Kilve[23] of the barony of Compton Dundon and overlordship was recorded in 1363.[24]

Joel Vautort was probably lord of Currypool between 1225 and 1245[25] and was followed by Philip.[26] John Vautort had succeeded Philip by 1285, and Hugh was lord possibly in 1299 and certainly by 1303.[27] Hugh Vautort granted the estate to Adam Brett, possibly his brother-in-law, in 1310–11 and died shortly afterwards. In 1311 Adam settled it on Hugh's widow Lucy for life, with successive remainders to Hugh's children John, Beatrice, and Gillian, who were probably then under age.[28] A fourth child, Egelina, may by 1316 have been married to Richard Champernowne, who then held a fee at Charlinch.[29] The manor was in the hands of the Crown in 1320[30] possibly after the death of Lucy. John Vautort, the heir, seems to have died without issue before 1332, and his sister

92 O.S. Map 6″, Som. XLIX. NE. (1887 edn.).
93 S.R.O., DD/X/OA 1; ibid. tithe award.
94 *V.C.H. Som.* i. 485, 487.
95 *Rot. Cur. Reg.* (Rec. Com.), ii. 45.
96 S.R.O., tithe award; Som. C.C., Sites and Mons. Rec.
97 Ekwall, *Eng. Place-Names* (1960), 75.
98 S.R.O., DD/S/WH 292.
99 P.R.O., RG 10/2379; O.S. Map 6″, Som. XLIX. SE. (1887 edn.). 1 S.R.O., Q/REl 7/3A.
2 Ibid. D/P/chlch 4/1/1. 3 Ibid. DD/PLE 64.
4 J. B. Bentley and B. J. Murless, *Som. Roads*, i. 25.
5 *S.R.S.* iii. 40.
6 Ibid. xx. 248.
7 P.R.O., E 134/2 Chas. I/Mich. 2.
8 S.R.O., tithe award.
9 *V.C.H. Som.* i. 485, 487.
10 P.R.O., E 134/2 Chas. I/Mich. 2; S.R.O., D/P/chlch 4/1/1.
11 S.R.O., DD/SAS HV 23.
12 Ibid. tithe award.
13 Statistics supplied by the then Bd. of Agric., 1905.
14 *S.R.S.* iii. 140.
15 Dwelly, *Hearth Tax*, i. 66, 70; ii. 53.
16 Collinson, *Hist. Som.* i. 241.
17 *Census.*
18 S.R.O., D/R/bw 16/20/1.
19 *Census.*
20 *V.C.H. Som.* i. 485.
21 *Red Bk. Exch.* (Rolls Ser.), i. 233.
22 *Cal. Close,* 1429–35, 232; S.R.O., DD/NN (H/20).
23 *V.C.H. Som.* v. 98.
24 *Cal. Close,* 1360–4, 449.
25 *S.R.S.* xi, p. 193; lxviii, p. 2.
26 Pole MS. 1041.
27 *Feud. Aids,* iv. 281, 308; B.L. Add. Ch. 22551.
28 *S.R.S.* xii. 21.
29 *Visit. Devon,* ed. J. L. Vivian, 160; *Feud. Aids,* iv. 335.
30 *Cal. Pat.* 1317–21, 445.

Beatrice, wife of Simon of Bradney, then held the estate.[31] She and Egelina Champernowne were still holding land in Charlinch in 1344[32] and Beatrice survived until 1360 or shortly afterwards.[33] She seems to have died without issue and by 1367 the inheritance had passed to her nephew Richard Lyf, son of her sister Gillian, who had married Godfrey Lyf.[34] In 1396–7 Richard granted the manor to trustees[35] and died soon afterwards, leaving two daughters, Amice or Avice, wife of Baldwin Malet, and Joan, wife of Walter Tilley.[36] In 1401 the estate was divided between them but Richard's widow Margery, later wife of Richard Boyton, retained a life interest[37] and Boyton held the manor until 1412.[38] In 1406 the whole manor was settled in reversion on Baldwin Malet and Avice,[39] although Walter Tilley and Joan secured a settlement of their share of the advowson c. 1416.[40] Avice held the manor from 1428 until c. 1436 when she granted it to Alexander Hody and others, probably in trust for her sons.[41] In 1433 her son Hugh Malet (d. 1465)[42] had released his inheritance to his brother Thomas for the latter's life [43] but Thomas presumably died and Hugh was lord of Currypool c. 1440.[44] Hugh was succeeded by his son Thomas (d. 1501),[45] and Thomas by his son William (d. 1510).[46] Currypool descended thereafter with Enmore until 1833 when it became part of Henry Labouchere's Quantock estate. Lordship was last recorded in 1833.[47] At the sale of the Quantock estate in 1920 Currypool farm was bought by Somerset county council but was sold in the same year to the tenant, William Jeanes,[48] whose family owned it in 1987.

The capital messuage of Currypool was recorded in 1521[49] and appears to have been the Malet family's home in the 16th century,[50] but by the early 18th century it was let as a farmhouse.[51] In 1664 half its 14 hearths were said to have fallen down.[52] Currypool Farm lies within a large enclosure which is moated on the north and east. Close to the north-east corner of the house the remains of a stone wing demolished c. 1960 incorporate a late medieval piscina and a 16th-century doorway, suggesting that it was the solar wing of the medieval house with a chapel. The present kitchen wing, which is probably of the 17th century, may be on the site of the main range, to which a new southern block containing the principal rooms was added early in the 19th century.

GOTHELNEY was held by Alweard in 1066 and by Geoffrey Vautort of Roger de Courcelles in 1086.[53] Overlordship was not recorded again until the 16th century when it was claimed by the lords of Enmore manor.[54] Gothelney may have been held by Hugh Vautort in 1166[55] but by the late 13th century it belonged to the Malet family and Richard Malet was fined c. 1275 for not keeping hospitality there.[56] In 1307 an estate at Gothelney was settled on Raymond Malet and his wife Joan and their issue with remainder to Baldwin Malet of whom they were to hold it.[57] Gothelney probably descended in the Malet family like Enmore until c. 1400 when Baldwin Malet gave the manor to Ralph Durburgh (d. 1432) and his wife Joan.[58] After the death of his son Robert c. 1410, Ralph granted Gothelney to Hugh Mortimer and others, presumably in trust for his daughter Joan, who with her husband John Courtenay secured a grant of the manor c. 1421.[59] Joan Durburgh was still alive in 1451[60] but may have granted Gothelney to her daughter Isabel (d. before 1436) who married Edward Greville (d. 1436–7) but had no children.[61] The manor had been acquired by Alexander Hody by 1439[62] possibly under a settlement of 1432.[63] Alexander died in 1461 in possession of the manor[64] which descended in the Hody family with Newnham in Stogursey[65] until 1622 when John Hody sold Gothelney to Roger Bourne.[66]

Roger Bourne (d. 1624) was followed in turn by his nephew John Bourne (d. 1656) and by John's son Roger (d. 1672–3).[67] Roger's daughter Florence, wife of Edward Baber, died without issue in 1713 leaving the manor to her kinsman Thomas Bourne (d. c. 1728).[68] His wife Anne (d. 1730)[69] devised Gothelney to her brother William Gore[70] (d. 1768) who left the manor to his kinsman Edward Gore.[71] Edward (d. 1801) was succeeded by his second son Charles (d. 1841) and by Charles's son Montagu (d. 1864).[72] By 1894 the estate was owned by the Cann family and John Henry Cann was the owner in 1923.[73] It passed through several hands and lordship was last recorded in 1943 when it belonged to Mr. S. Nation.[74] In 1987 the house was owned by the Hallet family.

A house was recorded c. 1275[75] and there was a chapel at Gothelney, associated with but not

31 *S.R.S.* xii. 160.
32 Ibid. 220–1.
33 *Cal. Close*, 1360–4, 449.
34 *S.R.S.* iii. 271–2; lii, p. 45; Pole MS. 1007, 1025.
35 Pole MS. 1007.
36 Ibid. 1008.
37 *S.R.S.* xxii. 158, 161.
38 *Feud. Aids*, vi. 503.
39 *S.R.S.* xxii. 23.
40 Ibid. 178.
41 *Feud. Aids*, iv. 393; Pole MS. 966.
42 P.R.O., C 140/16, no. 8.
43 *Cal. Close*, 1429–35, 232.
44 Pole MS. 995.
45 *Cal. Inq. p.m. Hen. VII*, ii, p. 250.
46 P.R.O., C 142/25, no. 28.
47 Above, Enmore, manors; below, Over Stowey, manors; S.R.O., DD/PLE 64.
48 S.R.O., C/C 45/2.
49 P.R.O., C 142/63, no. 19.
50 Ibid. C 142/97, no. 102; *S.R.S.* xix. 10, 250; xxi. 129–30.
51 Norfolk R.O., NRS 8082, 24 B 4.
52 Dwelly, *Hearth Tax*, i. 70.
53 *V.C.H. Som.* i. 485.
54 P.R.O., C 142/97, no. 42; C 142/183, no. 70.

55 *Red Bk. Exch.* (Rolls Ser.), i. 233.
56 *Rot. Hund.* (Rec. Com.), ii. 128.
57 *S.R.S.* vi. 360.
58 Pole MS. 972.
59 Ibid. 1051–3; *S.R.S.* extra ser. 262.
60 *S.R.S.* extra ser. 263.
61 Ibid. 262–3; ibid. xvi. 140–7.
62 *Cal. Close*, 1435–41, 33.
63 *S.R.S.* xxii. 83.
64 P.R.O., C 140/4, no. 34.
65 Below, Stogursey, manors.
66 P.R.O., CP 25(2)/347/20 Jas. I Mich.
67 *Som. Wills*, ed. Brown, v. 78–9.
68 *S.D.N.Q.* v. 179–80.
69 S.R.O., DD/GB 149.
70 *Som. Wills*, ed. Brown, v. 81.
71 Ibid. 87–8.
72 S.R.O., tithe award; ibid. DD/BR/lch 22; ibid. Fitz-James pedigrees; *D.N.B.*
73 S.R.O., DD/DHR 22; *Kelly's Dir. Som.* (1923).
74 S.R.O., DD/DHR 22.
75 *Rot. Hund.* (Rec. Com.), ii. 128.

necessarily within the house, in 1436.[76] During the Second World War the house was requisitioned by the War Department[77] and was later used as a kindergarten.[78] Gothelney Hall, restored by the Hallet family in the 1950s,[79] has a complex structural history. At the centre of the main, north–south, range there is a tall house of the later 15th century which has a central, ceiled hall with a cross passage, entered from the east through a porch. There was a room at each end of the hall and above each another at mezzanine level. On the first floor a great chamber, open to the roof, extended over the hall and the northern mezzanine room, and there were first and attic floors over the southern room. The roof of the great chamber is richly decorated with arch-braced main and intermediate trusses and three rows of cusped windbraces. The great chamber was lit by two-light windows on each side and on the west there was a fireplace whose flue was bracketed out from the wall. Access to the upper rooms was by a large stair turret against the eastern entry to the cross passage and there were garderobe turrets at the south-west corner and the north end of the building. That house was probably built by Alexander Hody, his widow, or his nephew, and most of the later additions were probably made during the period of the Hody family's ownership. One of the first was a room with a traceried window on top of the stair turret. It may have been used as a chapel or oratory. A 16th-century extension at the south end was probably intended for storage rather than domestic use and additions to the north and east are of similar date and appear to have contained kitchen and service rooms. The most notable 17th-century insertion is a ribbed plaster ceiling in the northern ground floor room. In the 18th century there was much internal refitting and sash windows were put into the east side of the great chamber. The porch and two-storeyed passage next to it, which may be of 16th-century origin, appear to have been rebuilt in the early 19th century.

PADNOLLER manor was settled on Hugh Cary and his wife Edith for their lives in 1427 with reversion to Thomas Horsey and his wife Alice.[80] Hugh held Padnoller in 1431[81] but by 1461 it was held with Gothelney by Alexander Hody[82] and there was no later reference to a manor. Padnoller continued to descend with Gothelney until the 16th century or later[83] but by 1649 it was part of Currypool manor.[84] When the Quantock estate was sold in 1920 Padnoller was bought by Somerset county council but was later sold to the White family, the owners in 1987.[85]

The eastern range of Padnoller House appears to be of the 18th century but it may be an older building which has been reconstructed and refitted. It became the service wing in the early 19th century when the north range, which is of the 18th century or earlier, was remodelled to provide the principal rooms.

SWINDON, later *SWANG*, was held by Alweard in 1066 and by Ranulf of Roger de Courcelles in 1086.[86] It was held of Compton Dundon barony like Kilve, and the Furneaux family had a mesne lordship.[87] In 1375 the overlordship had been lost and the mesne lords were said to hold in chief.[88] The terre tenancy was held by the Horsey family. In the mid 13th century William Avenel granted to William Horsey the lands of Swindon which had been held by Horsey's father, also William Horsey.[89] John, probably the younger William's son, lord in 1287,[90] was succeeded, though possibly not directly, by William Horsey (d. 1327),[91] John (d. by 1338),[92] Ralph (d. 1354), and John Horsey (d. 1375).[93] Henry Horsey in 1435 sold Swindon and other estates to William Bochell and his wife Alice.[94] In 1507 William Aylward of Totnes (Devon) released his rights in Swindon to John Horsey.[95] The subsequent descent is uncertain, but by 1551 it was held with Currypool.[96] Known as Swangdon in 1714[97] and Swang by 1766,[98] it was purchased by Henry Pleydell Bouverie of Brymore in Cannington and in 1928 it was bought by Somerset county council.[99]

The capital messuage was recorded in 1327[1] but there was no record of a house in 1714.[2] Swang Farm, which has a main front of brick, was extensively rebuilt, perhaps after a fire, in the early 19th century.

ECONOMIC HISTORY. The four estates recorded in 1086 comprised 10 ploughlands, 137 a. of pasture, 11 a. of meadow, and 15 a. of woodland. There were 10½ ploughteams of which 4½ were in demesne with 7 *servi*. Recorded animals comprised a riding horse, one cow, 10 beasts, 22 pigs, 54 she-goats, and 130 sheep. The value of the estates in hand had been maintained, but of the others Gothelney had fallen and Swang had risen in value since 1066.[3]

Surviving sources for the 17th century suggest that most of the parish was divided between Currypool manor and Gothelney and that tenant farmers were not generally prosperous. Arthur Blake, who probably lived at Padnoller, had a clock, books, leather chairs, and round tables, but his six-roomed house had no parlour. Other farmhouses were small and poorly furnished, and only one had a parlour.[4] Tithes were payable on cattle, sheep, pigs, geese, wool, milk, grain,

76 *S.R.S.* xvi. 140–2; below, church.
77 S.R.O., DD/DHR 22.   78 Local inf.
79 *Proc. Som. Arch. Soc.* cv. 10; for a photo., above, plate facing p. 72.   80 *S.R.S.* xxii. 70.
81 *Feud. Aids*, iv. 436.   82 P.R.O., C 140/4, no. 34.
83 Ibid. LR 3/123; ibid. STAC 3/7/38.
84 S.R.O., DD/S/WH 292.
85 Above, Enmore, manors; Som. C.C., deeds; local inf.
86 *V.C.H. Som.* i. 487.
87 Ibid. v. 98 and sources there cited.
88 *Cal. Inq. p.m.* xiv, p. 146.
89 B.L. Harl. MS. 4120, p. 69.
90 *S.R.S.* xxxv. 29.
91 *Cal. Inq. p.m.* vii, p. 29.
92 *S.R.S.* iii. 140; B.L. Add. Ch. 15927.
93 *Cal. Inq. p.m.* xi, p. 142.
94 *S.R.S.* xxii. 88; *Cal. Close*, 1435–41, 159.
95 *Cal. Close*, 1500–9, 303.   96 *S.R.S.* xxi. 129–30.
97 Norf. R.O., NRS 8082, 24 B 4.
98 S.R.O., Q/REl 7/3A.
99 Som. C.C., deeds, ED 103A.
1 *Cal. Inq. p.m.* vii, p. 29.
2 Norf. R.O., NRS 8082, 24 B 4.
3 *V.C.H. Som.* i. 485, 487.
4 S.R.O., DD/S/WH 292; DD/SP 364; DD/SP inventories, 1669, 1670, 1674, 1678, 1680, 1686.

fruit, hops, cider, eggs, honey, and wax,[5] but inventories suggest there were few cattle and only small flocks of sheep; pigs were kept by many. Wheat and barley were the commonest grain crops, and clover was grown, probably at Padnoller.[6] In 1786 one man produced 137 stone of flax and in 1794 another produced 58 stone at Bush.[7]

Most of the farms were small and held on leases for lives, but Currypool demesne, Swang, and other lands were rack rented in 1714.[8] By 1837 some small farms had been amalgamated: of 10 farms over 20 a. two were under 50 a., two between 50 and 100 a., five between 100 and 200 a., and one, Currypool, 367 a. Arable amounted to 844 a., meadow 492 a., and common 18 a.[9] During the 19th century the number of holdings declined as the larger farms expanded: in 1861 Currypool was said to cover 1,000 a. and employ 45 labourers.[10] In 1881 the largest farms were Gothelney (430 a.) and Currypool (520 a.), employing between them 34 labourers. The total number of labourers then employed had not declined since 1851.[11]

By 1905 there were 688 a. of arable and 694 a. of grass.[12] The main farms in the 20th century were Currypool, Padnoller, Swang, and the Gothelney estate.[13] In 1982 there were at least two dairy farms and livestock included sheep, cattle, pigs, and poultry. The main crops, apart from grass, were wheat, barley, and potatoes; oilseed rape, fodder crops, turnips and swedes for human consumption, and maize were also grown.[14] Potatoes continued to be a major crop in 1987 and one farm specialized in growing and processing them.

Cloth was made in the later 17th century, a man in 1691 possessing a wool chamber and a workshop containing yarn, wool, worsted, combs, and weights.[15] The field names Rack close survived at Currypool in 1714[16] and near Gothelney in 1837.[17] Malt was made in 1693.[18] In the 19th century a blacksmith, a sawyer, a cordwainer, a maltster, a carter, and a grocer were recorded.[19]

MILLS. Mills were recorded in 1086 at Swang, at Gothelney, and on the Charlinch estate.[20] No further trace of the first two has been found but the last may be the mill recorded in the 13th century and in 1379,[21] which was later part of Currypool manor.[22] The mill was kept by William Crosse (d. c. 1559), grandfather of Admiral Sir Robert Crosse.[23] It was recorded in 1714[24] and in 1832 when it may have been disused.[25] It had been demolished by 1837. The mill stood beside the brook north of Charlinch church.[26] A second mill, Solomon's mill, was recorded on the Currypool demesne in 1714.[27] There was a grist mill with an undershot wheel on Currypool farm until 1920 or later. A pond-fed wheel at Swang may have been used for milling or driving machinery, possibly at the same period.[28]

LOCAL GOVERNMENT. Most of Charlinch lay in Currypool tithing but Gothelney was included in Orchard tithing in Cannington parish from the 17th to the 19th century.[29] In the 16th century courts for Gothelney and Padnoller were held jointly with other Hody estates and court records survive for 1540–1 and 1546.[30] Courts were held for Currypool manor in the 17th century[31] and at Gothelney in the 18th century[32] but no court records have been found.

The parish had two churchwardens, two overseers, and two waywardens by the 18th century.[33] A poorhouse was recorded in 1769 but was not mentioned after 1771.[34] The vestry employed someone to keep order on Sundays at 1s. a day in 1833.[35]

The parish became part of the Bridgwater poor-law union in 1836, Bridgwater rural district in 1894, and Sedgemoor district in 1974.[36]

CHURCH. The fabric shows that the church existed in the 12th century. By 1245 the benefice was a rectory and it remained a sole rectory until 1957, when it was united with Spaxton.[37] The church closed in 1981, when the united benefice was further united with that of Enmore and Goathurst.[38]

The advowson evidently belonged to the lords of Currypool manor in the 13th and 14th centuries, being held or exercised by Joel Vautort in 1245,[39] Hugh Vautort in 1310,[40] Richard Champernowne in 1318,[41] the Crown in 1320[42] and Simon of Bradney in 1324.[43] A dispute over the advowson was resolved by 1322 in favour of Robert Brent, and Robert Brent the younger presented in 1324.[44] Thereafter for

5　Ibid. D/D/Rg 263.
6　Ibid. DD/SP inventories, 1637, 1667, 1669, 1674, 1678, 1680, 1686; DD/SAS HV 58.
7　Ibid. Q/RLh 21, 24, 51, 55.
8　Norf. R.O., NRS 8082, 24 B 4.
9　S.R.O., tithe award.
10　P.R.O., RG 9/1621.
11　Ibid. HO 107/1924; ibid. RG 11/2371.
12　Statistics supplied by the then Bd. of Agric., 1905.
13　Kelly's Dir. Som. (1906, 1931).
14　Min. of Agric., Fisheries, and Food, agric. returns, 1982.
15　S.R.O., DD/SP inventory, 1691.
16　Norf. R.O., NRS 8082, 24 B 4.
17　S.R.O., tithe award.
18　Ibid. DD/SP inventory, 1693; ibid. Q/SR 289/1.
19　P.R.O., HO 107/1924; ibid. RG 9/1621; RG 10/2379.
20　V.C.H. Som. i. 485, 487.
21　P.R.O., E 210/2880; Cat. Anct. D. iii, D 986.
22　S.R.S. xxi. 129–30.
23　S.R.O., DD/X/SR 5; Visit. Som. 1531 & 1575, 165.

24　Norf. R.O., NRS 8082, 24 B 4.
25　S.R.O., DD/X/OA 1.
26　Ibid. tithe award; O.S. Map 1", sheet XX (1809 edn.).
27　Norf. R.O., NRS 8082, 24 B 4.
28　S.R.O., C/C 45/2; Som. C.C., Sites and Mons. Rec.
29　S.R.S. iii. 140; Dwelly, Hearth Tax, i. 66, 70; S.R.O., Q/REl 7/2D.
30　P.R.O., LR 3/123.
31　S.R.O., DD/SAS HV 23.
32　Ibid. DD/DHR, box 9, lease 1756.
33　Ibid. DD/X/OA 1; DD/SAS HV 35/1; 37.
34　Ibid. DD/SAS HV 35/2.
35　Ibid. D/P/chlch 9/1/1.
36　Youngs, Local Admin. Units, i. 671, 673, 676.
37　S.R.O., D/P/chlch 2/9/3.
38　Below, this section.
39　Above, manors; S.R.S. lxviii, p. 2.
40　S.R.S. i. 30.　　　41　Ibid. 14.
42　Cal. Pat. 1317–21, 445.
43　S.R.S. x, p. 448.
44　Ibid. i. 181, 197, 231.

more than a century the advowson descended with Currypool manor. On the partition of the estate between Richard Lyf's daughters Avice Malet and Joan Tilley, the advowson was to be shared, each presenting alternately.[45] Avice Malet presented in 1427[46] and Thomas Blanchard, Joan's son by her first husband, at the next vacancy. Thomas Malet, Avice's grandson, presented in 1472,[47] on the death of Blanchard's presentee. About 1490 there was a dispute between John Blanchard, Thomas's son, and Thomas Tilley, probably son of Thomas's half brother Leonard Tilley, Thomas Tilley having appointed to the living. Tilley seems to have conceded to Blanchard in 1494[48] although his presentee remained rector until 1526, when Hugh Malet appointed his successor.[49] The Tilleys, perhaps through failure of Blanchard's heirs, retained the right to alternate patronage. In 1562 George Speke presented after two rival presentations the previous year by George Tilley's guardian Humphrey Walrond and by Erasmus Pym,[50] and in 1581 John Malet presented by grant of a turn by George Tilley.[51] In 1604 Sir John Malet acquired the share of Tilley's two daughters, and the whole was acquired by 1634.[52] The advowson thereafter descended with Currypool manor until 1681 when Edward Clare and John Haviland presented. In 1689 the patrons were Henry Baynton and his wife Anne,[53] granddaughter and coheir of John Malet (d. 1656).[54] Henry had died by 1709 leaving a son John under age.[55] John (d. 1717) was succeeded by his nephew Edward Rolt who added the name Baynton. Edward, later Sir Edward Baynton Rolt, Bt., was succeeded in 1800 by his nephew Sir Andrew Baynton Rolt and on Andrew's death in 1816 by the latter's daughter Mary Barbara, wife of the rector John Starkey.[56] Starkey held the advowson in 1835[57] but it was later acquired by Henry Labouchere and descended with the Quantock estate.[58] Since 1920 it has been vested in the Martyrs Memorial Trust, which exercises alternate patronage of the united benefice.[59]

The church was valued at £10 in 1291,[60] at £11 6s. 8d. gross in 1535,[61] and at £120 c. 1668.[62] In 1827 the benefice was said to be worth no more than £300 a year[63] but the average income in 1829–31 was £400.[64] The tithes were valued at £45 a year in 1626,[65] and were commuted in 1837 for a rent charge of £283 3s. 8d.[66] In 1626 the house and 86 a. of glebe were said to be worth £56 a year.[67] In 1837 the glebe measured 82 a. which remained church land in 1976.[68] The former Rectory, sold and divided since 1951[69] and known as Charlinch House and Tudor House, dates probably from the later 14th or the earlier 15th century. Tudor House, the eastern part of the building, had a three-bayed open hall with an arch-braced cruck roof. Its east end was altered and a smoke bay was built in the earlier 16th century. The south front, with stone mullioned windows, was an addition of the later 17th century, when the house comprised a hall, parlour, and entry, all with chambers over, and study, closet, and larder.[70] The house was enlarged on the west in the later 18th or earlier 19th century, possibly c. 1807 when the rector was living at Padnoller.[71]

Two members of the Vautort family held the living between 1292 and 1318: Joel was a pluralist and William took at least four years' study leave before seeking ordination as a deacon.[72] Two other early 14th-century rectors had only minor orders.[73] There were two stipendiary priests before 1534 besides the rector and a curate,[74] and one of the stipendiaries became rector in 1534.[75] There was an All Souls light in the church in 1536.[76] John Moore held two other benefices in 1562[77] and was non-resident in the 1570s, when he employed a curate.[78] His successor, John Parsons, was said to be the brother of Robert Parsons the Jesuit martyr[79] and was resident though a pluralist.[80] Francis Crosse was ejected in 1662.[81] John Baynton, rector 1769–1806, was the son of the patron: he lived in the parish for a time but towards the end of his incumbency Charlinch was served by a resident curate.[82] There were 20 communicants in 1776.[83] Baynton's successor John Starkey, rector 1806–34, was also patron but was often absent because of his poor health. The parish was served by a resident curate who held two Sunday services.[84] John's son Samuel, rector 1834–46, was at first non-resident, and his curate Henry Prince became notorious for his unorthodox teaching and behaviour and had his licence revoked in 1842.[85] In 1843 there were two Sunday services and communion was celebrated four times a year.[86]

45 Above, manors; *Som. Incumbents*, ed. Weaver, 329; *S.R.S.* lii, p. 45.
46 *S.R.S.* xxxi, p. 42.
47 Ibid. lii, p. 45.
48 P.R.O., CP 40/919, rot. 328.
49 *S.R.S.* lv, p. 47.
50 *Som. Incumbents*, ed. Weaver, 329–30.
51 Ibid. 329.
52 P.R.O., CP 25(2)/345/2 Jas. I Trin.; *Som. Incumbents*, ed. Weaver, 329.
53 Above, manors; *Som. Incumbents*, ed. Weaver, 329–30.
54 G.E.C. *Baronetage*, v. 123.
55 S.R.O., DD/PC 16.
56 G.E.C. *Baronetage*, v. 123.
57 *Rep. Com. Eccl. Revenues*, pp. 130–1.
58 S.R.O., D/P/chlch 6/1/1; *Kelly's Dir. Som.* (1906).
59 *Crockford*; *Dioc. Dir.*
60 *Tax. Eccl.* (Rec. Com.), 198.
61 *Valor Eccl.* (Rec. Com.), i. 215.
62 S.R.O., D/D/Vc 24.
63 Ibid. D/D/Rb 1827.
64 *Rep. Com. Eccl. Revenues*, pp. 130–1.
65 S.R.O., D/D/Rg 263.
66 Ibid. tithe award.
67 Ibid. D/D/Rg 263.
68 Ibid. tithe award; inf. from Dioc. Office.
69 S.R.O., D/P/chlch 3/4/4.
70 Ibid. DD/SP inventory, 1681.
71 Ibid. Q/REl 7/6B; *Paupers and Pigkillers*, ed. J. Ayres, 142.
72 *Cal. Papal Reg.* ii. 551; *S.R.S.* i. 14, 30, 37, 41, 48, 65, 79.
73 *S.R.S.* i. 231; x, p. 448.
74 S.R.O., D/D/Vc 20.
75 *Valor Eccl.* (Rec. Com.), i. 215.
76 S.R.O., D/P/chlch 6/1/1.
77 Cambridge, Corpus Christi Coll., MS. 97.
78 *S.D.N.Q.* xiii. 271; S.R.O., D/D/Ca 57.
79 *Cath. Religion in Som.* (1826), 71.
80 S.R.O., D/D/Rg 263; D/D/Ca 175.
81 T. G. Crippen, *Nonconf. in Som.* 21.
82 S.R.O., D/P/chlch 2/1/1.
83 Ibid. D/D/Vc 88.
84 Ibid. D/D/Rb 1827.
85 H. J. Prince, *The Charlinch Revival* (1842).
86 S.R.O., D/D/Va 1843.

Samuel Starkey joined Prince's community at Spaxton in 1846.[87] During the early 20th century two services continued to be held but the number of Easter communicants declined from 51 in 1927 to 11 in 1941.[88] The last public service was held in the church in 1981[89] and the building was then declared redundant. It was sold for conversion to a house.[90]

The former church of *ST. MARY*, so dedicated by 1533,[91] is of local rubble and at its closure comprised a chancel with north vestry and organ chamber, a nave with south aisle or transept and south porch, and a west tower. The unbuttressed tower, taken down and rebuilt in 1863,[92] may, like the nave and chancel, be of 12th-century origin. There were transepts to north and south, the former demolished, possibly in the 17th century, the latter perhaps rebuilt as an aisle in the 15th or early 16th century. The chancel was rebuilt in the 14th century. A gallery recorded in 1833[93] may have been removed when the tower was rebuilt.[94] Restoration in 1886 included rebuilding the chancel arch and walls, adding an organ chamber and boiler room to the north, replacing flooring and seats, and rearranging fittings. The rood stair was uncovered and the porch was restored as a memorial to the 1887 jubilee.[95] Further restoration took place in 1955.[96]

Church fittings formerly included a 12th-century font and a cover made in 1622.[97] The altar railings were provided in 1634 following Archbishop Laud's visitation;[98] the communion table had been replaced in 1629.[99] The reredos was erected in 1893 in memory of Lady Taunton and contained a copy of a 15th-century Italian painting presented in 1887.[1] There are traces of 15th-century glass in the south aisle.

The church plate included a chalice of 1630 and a flagon of 1766, now at Spaxton church.[2] There were five bells; one dating from the late 14th century is now in a new church in Reykjavik, Iceland, and another was an early 16th-century Bristol bell.[3] In 1538 five bells were brought from Bridgwater to Charlinch.[4] One was recast at Charlinch by Robert Austen in 1627,[5] there was another bell by Thomas Bayley of 1743, and a fifth bell was added in 1919.[6] The bells were removed after 1981. The registers date from 1744 but there are large gaps in the marriages.[7]

Fragments of a churchyard cross were recorded

in 1791[8] and three steps were shown in a drawing of 1845[9] but nothing now survives.

A chapel at Gothelney dedicated to St. John the Baptist was mentioned in 1436[10] and 1541.[11]

NONCONFORMITY. A meeting house was licensed in Charlinch lane in 1845,[12] probably for the Princites before they moved to Spaxton.[13]

EDUCATION. Thomas Stoodleigh was licensed to teach grammar in Charlinch in 1678.[14] There was no school in 1819 but by 1824 there were 14 children attending day and Sunday school at their parents' expense.[15] In 1835 only the Sunday school survived, with 25 children, but by 1846 a school supported by the rector taught 21 children on weekdays and a further 5 attended on Sundays.[16] That school was enlarged in 1884.[17] In 1903 there was only one teacher although an average of 31 children worked in two classrooms. Closure was suggested in 1915, but in 1919 the parish bought the building at the sale of the Quantock estate.[18] Attendances fell to 19 in 1925 and 14 in 1945. There were 20 children on the register in 1948 but the school closed in the following year. The children were transferred to Cannington and Spaxton.[19] The building, south of the church, was in domestic use in 1987.

CHARITIES FOR THE POOR. In 1629 several people were presented for withholding legacies to the parish including Ursula Boldey's gift of £5 to the poor.[20] Further gifts totalling £40 were made to the poor by Sir John Malet (d. c. 1685) and the Revd. John Taylor (d. 1737).[21] Malet's charity was used to provide tools. The Boldey, Malet, and Taylor charities were amalgamated in 1959.[22] Florence Baber, by will of 1713, gave £100 for apprenticing poor children. In 1867 the income was distributed to labourers but in the later 20th century it was used to help young people to earn their own living.[23] Anne Bourne (d. c. 1730) gave a rent charge of £2 10s. to poor widows, paid out of land at Gothelney, but the rent charge was redeemed c. 1966.[24] All the charities were active in 1989.[25]

87 Below, Spaxton, nonconf.; C. Mander, *The Revd. Prince and his Abode of Love*, pp. 1, 4, 88, 100–1.
88 S.R.O., D/P/chlch 2/5/1–2.
89 Ibid. DD/X/SMIT 2.
90 *Bridgwater Mercury*, 21 May 1986.
91 *Wells Wills*, ed. Weaver, 46.
92 S.R.O., D/P/chlch 8/4/1; Taunton Castle, Pigott colln., drawing by J. Buckler (1840).
93 S.R.O., D/P/chlch 6/1/2.
94 Ibid. 8/4/1.   95 Ibid.[3] 6/2/1; D/D/Cf 1886/12.
96 Ibid. D/P/chlch 6/1/2.   97 Ibid. 4/1/1.
98 Ibid.; *S.D.N.Q.* i. 9.
99 S.R.O., D/P/chlch 4/1/1.
1 Ibid. 6/2/2–3; 8/4/2.
2 Pevsner, *S. & W. Som.* 120.
3 S.R.O., DD/SAS CH 16/1; inf. from Dioc. Office.
4 S.R.O., D/B/bw 1440.   5 Ibid. D/P/chlch 4/1/1.
6 Ibid. DD/SAS CH 16/1.
7 Ibid. D/P/chlch 2/1/1–5.
8 Collinson, *Hist. Som.* i. 241.

9 Taunton Castle, Braikenridge colln., wash drawing (1845).   10 *S.R.S.* xvi. 140–2.
11 P.R.O., LR 3/123.
12 S.R.O., D/D/Rm, box 2.
13 Below, Spaxton.
14 S.R.O., D/D/Bs 42.
15 *Educ. of Poor Digest*, p. 777; *Ann. Rep. B. & W. Dioc. Assoc. S.P.C.K.* (1825–6), 41.
16 *Educ. Enq. Abstract*, p. 798; Nat. Soc. *Inquiry, 1846–7*, Som. 4–5.
17 *Kelly's Dir. Som.* (1889, 1894); S.R.O., D/P/chlch 9/1/2.
18 S.R.O., C/E 4/380/73; ibid. D/P/chlch 18/7/1.
19 Ibid. C/E 4/64, 187.   20 Ibid. D/D/Ca 266.
21 *Char. Don.* pp. 1048–9.
22 S.R.O., D/P/chlch 9/1/2; Char. Com. reg.
23 *Char. Don.* pp. 1048–9; S.R.O., D/P/chlch 9/1/1; Char. Com. reg.
24 S.R.O., DD/GB 151; D/P/chlch 9/1/1; Char. Com. files.
25 Inf. from the rector, the Revd. J. S. Barks.

FIDDINGTON

THE ancient parish of Fiddington, including the hamlets of Whitnell and Bonson, formerly Bonstone,[26] lay between Cannington on the east and Nether Stowey on the west, 9 km. north-west of Bridgwater. Parts of Spaxton lay to the north and south.[27] The parish, irregular in shape, occupied a shallow valley falling northwards from 76 m. to 15 m., drained by a stream which formed part of its western boundary before curving east through Fiddington village and

was transferred from Spaxton. The acreage of Fiddington civil parish thus increased to 1,314 a.[30]

Most of the parish lies either on valley gravels or Keuper marl, with an outcrop of sandstone around Whitnell. There may have been a quarry in the east, and pits in several places suggest marl digging.[31] Two principal roads lead northwards through the parish from the same point on the southern boundary, one passing through Fiddington village towards Stogursey, the other

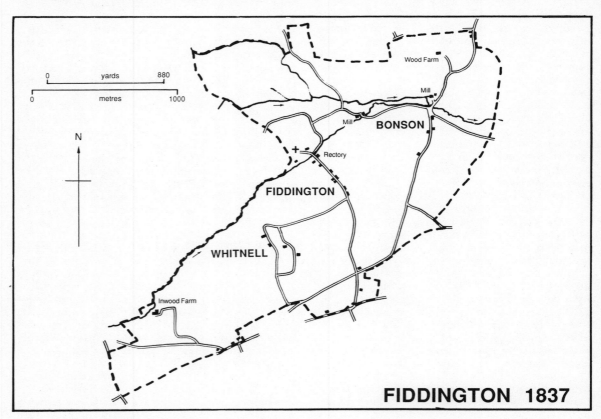

FIDDINGTON 1837

north of Bonson. The southern boundary seems to have been influenced by two ancient routes from the east, the Anglo-Saxon 'herpath' from Cannington Hill to the Quantocks and another roadway from Combwich and the Parrett crossing, which not only converged within the parish but were joined for part of their common route by the road between Bridgwater and Nether Stowey. The last route had become important by the 18th century and was turnpiked in 1759.[28]

The ancient parish was said to measure 874 a.[29] In 1878 some land at Coultings, in the northeast, was added from Cannington, and a larger area in the north, known as North Street and including the Farm estate and Bonson Wood,

through Bonson to Coultings and thence to Combwich. Fiddington was in existence by the later 11th century, Bonson by the later 12th.[32] Whitnell, south-west of Fiddington village, was recorded in 1327.[33] Inwood Farm, first mentioned in 1558,[34] lies further south-west; Wood Farm, referred to by 1652,[35] is in the extreme north-east. Keenthorne House, Heathfield Villa, and the Cottage inn are outlying houses on the Nether Stowey to Bridgwater road. All three main hamlets, Fiddington, Whitnell, and Bonson, have modern infill development; at Fiddington, arranged along a single street, bungalows and houses replaced almost all the older cottages in the 20th century although one house

26 O.S. Map 6", Som. XLIX. NE. (1887 edn.). This article was completed in 1988.
27 S.R.O., tithe award.
28 O.S. Map 1/50,000, sheet 182 (1974 edn.); V.C.H. Som. v. 191.
29 S.R.O., tithe award.
30 Ibid. D/P/fid 23/1; Census, 1891.

31 Geol. Surv. Map 1", sheet 295, drift (1956 edn.); O.S. Map 1/25,000, ST 24 (1959 edn.); S.R.O., tithe award.
32 Below, manors.
33 S.R.S. iii. 142.
34 S.R.O., DD/MVB 25.
35 Ibid. DD/BR/rd 2.

survives from the 17th century and another, probably used by the clergy when the rectory house was unfit, may be earlier. There is a large caravan and camping site at Mill Farm. One house at Whitnell may date from the late 16th century.[36]

No references have been found either to open-field arable or to common pasture. There were 42 a. of woodland in 1086,[37] and the farm names Wood and Inwood and the field names Copse and Wood close in the north-east indicate its former significance. There was no woodland in 1837.[38]

There was a licensed tippler in Fiddington in 1607 and a single licence was granted during the 17th and 18th centuries except between 1740 and 1753 when there were two. The last licence was issued in 1753 and there was no public house in the parish thereafter until the mid 19th century.[39] The Cottage inn, also known as the Keenthorne inn, was first recorded in 1861 when there was also a retailer of small beer, possibly at Bonson.[40] The Cottage inn remained open in 1988.

Ten Fiddington men were fined following the 1497 rebellion.[41] The Fiddington revel was recorded in 1675.[42] A number of people were presented for playing fives against the church walls on Sunday in 1623.[43]

The population rose from 147 in 1801 to a peak of 260 in 1851. Thereafter there was a general decline to 156 in 1901 despite the increase in the size of the parish. During the later 20th century, however, the population increased considerably to 243 normally resident in 1981.[44]

MANORS AND OTHER ESTATES. *FIDDINGTON* was held by Alfward in 1066 and in 1086 by Roger Arundel.[45] From 1303 to 1358 or later it was held of the manor of Whitelackington but in 1559 it was said to be held of Cannington manor, probably only because it was in Cannington hundred.[46]

Hugh held Fiddington of Roger Arundel in 1086. It may have been held later by the eponymous Fiddington family. William and Hugh were recorded in the late 12th century.[47] Henry (fl. 1272–85) was described as lord of Fiddington and son of Ralph of Fiddington.[48] Matthew Furneaux was lord by 1303 and was succeeded by his son Simon (d. 1358).[49] The manor

probably descended like the Furneaux share of Shurton in Stogursey to Eleanor wife of Ralph Bush.[50] In 1433 it was settled on Ralph and Eleanor for life and then on their son William, who probably died soon afterwards, and on his wife Joan, daughter of Sir Thomas Brooke.[51] In 1439 the reversion after Ralph's death was settled on John Hody, possibly in trust for John Carent (d. 1483), Joan Brooke's second husband. The manor appears to have been held by the Carent family in 1518[52] and in 1538 was settled on Sir William Carent who, with his younger son Leonard, sold it to James Downham in 1558.[53] James (d. 1558) left two thirds to his nephew Thomas Downham while his son William was a minor.[54] William, possibly son of William, sold the manor to John Shere in 1637.[55] It was bought c. 1647 by Roger Mallack who in his will of 1651 left it to his grandson Rawlyn, son of Roger Mallack the younger.[56] In his will of 1689 Rawlyn left the manor in trust for his son, also Rawlyn, who died unmarried in 1699, with remainder to the family of his kinsman Roger Mallack of Exeter. Roger's son Rawlyn (d. 1749) was followed by his son, also Rawlyn, who mortgaged the estate heavily between 1751 and 1757.[57] Further mortgages were made in the 1760s and in 1772 Fiddington was sold to Joseph Champion, who dismembered the estate.[58] The lordship appears to have been bought by John Williams who, by will dated 1788, left it in trust for his wife Sarah for her life, his daughter Jane, wife of John Tatchell, and her children.[59] Lordship was last recorded in 1822 when it was vested in John Tatchell and his four daughters.[60]

There is no record of a capital messuage. Brook Farm, now known as Manor Farm, is a 17th-century house with a main range and two short rear wings. The front was remodelled in the earlier 19th century.

BONSON manor, formerly Bothemeston or Bodmeston,[61] was held like Fiddington of Whitelackington until 1508 or later, but in 1604 it was said to be held of Rodway Fitzpayn.[62] It may have been held in the later 12th century by Ranulph of Bonstone whose successor was his nephew William of Beere.[63] Joan, daughter of Ralph FitzBernard and widow of William Braunche, held land in Bonson in the 13th century, and Richard FitzBernard was probably lord of Bonson in 1272.[64] John FitzBernard was lord of it in 1276, 1303, and probably in

36 Ibid. DD/V/BWr 16.1, 5; C. W. H. Rawlins, *Family Quartette*, 94.
37 *V.C.H. Som.* i. 494.
38 S.R.O., tithe award.
39 Ibid. Q/SR 3/107; Q/RLa 33; Q/RL; ibid. D/D/Va 1840, 1843.
40 Ibid. DD/AH 51/7; ibid. tithe award; P.R.O., RG 9/1621.
41 *Fines Imposed in 1497*, ed. A. J. Howard, 13.
42 S.R.O., Q/SR 126/8.
43 *S.R.S.* xliii. 98, 130.
44 *Census.*
45 *V.C.H. Som.* i. 494.
46 *Feud. Aids*, iv. 308; *Cal. Inq. p.m.* x, p. 395; P.R.O., C 142/119, no. 159.
47 *V.C.H. Som.* i. 494; *S.R.S.* lxi, pp. 17, 28.
48 *Cal. Pat.* 1266–72, 700; *S.R.S.* xli. 34; *Feud. Aids*, iv. 281; Pole MS. 2544.
49 *Feud. Aids*, iv. 308, 335; *S.R.S.* xii. 6; Pole MS. 2546;

Cal. Inq. p.m. x, p. 395.
50 Below, Stogursey, manors; *S.D.N.Q.* xvi. 284.
51 *S.R.S.* xxii. 191.
52 Ibid. 195; W. Suff. R.O. 449/E3/15.53/2.17; J. Hutchins, *Hist. Dors.* iv. 112.
53 P.R.O., CP 25(2)/52/372/29 Hen. VIII Hil.; Devon R.O. 48/13/1/5/1.
54 P.R.O., C 142/119, no. 159; ibid. REQ 2/38/96.
55 Ibid. CP 25(2)/480/13 Chas. I East.
56 Devon R.O. 48/13/1/6/1, 48/13/3/5/31, 48/13/4/4/1.
57 Ibid. 48/13/1/11/3, 11A; 48/13/1/14/7A, 7B, 24–5.
58 Ibid. 48/13/1/14/26–32, 34, 36; S.R.O., DD/DHR 10.
59 S.R.O., DD/ES 2.
60 P.R.O., CP 43/957, rot. 228.
61 *S.R.S.* xliv. 170; *Cal. Inq. p.m.* xi, p. 390.
62 *Cal. Inq. p.m. Hen. VII*, iii, p. 312; S.R.O., DD/BR/bn 10.
63 *S.R.S.* lxi, p. 3.
64 *Cal. Pat.* 1266–72, 700; S.R.O., DD/AH 65/1.

1316. By 1346 Peter Trivet held the manor[65] but, possibly by descent from Joan Braunche, Bonson was held by the coparceners who had Durborough in Stogursey in 1361 and until 1404 when John, son of Peter Trivet, successfully claimed the estate.[66] In 1420 his daughters held the manor. By deeds of 1423 and 1429 it was settled on Margaret, wife of Roger Tremayle, although her sister Joan, wife of Roger Pym, may have received a rent as her descendants did in the 16th century.[67] Margaret died c. 1430 and was succeeded by her son John Tremayle[68] (fl. 1472), and by her grandson Thomas Tremayle (d. 1508).[69] Thomas's son Philip died in 1520 leaving a daughter Florence, wife of William Ashleigh, whose title was disputed by her uncle John Tremayle.[70] Richard Buckland held the manor court in 1552[71] but in 1560 the estate was settled on Nicholas Halswell and his wife Margery, daughter of John Tremayle. Nicholas died in 1564 and was succeeded by his eldest son Robert.[72] In 1579 the manor was shared between Robert's son Nicholas and Edward Popham.[73]

The Halswells' half descended like Halswell in Goathurst until 1620 when it was sold to John Mullens.[74] There is no record of that half after the sale to Mullens but most of the land was at Oatley in Cannington.[75] Half shares of land in Bonson were sold to the Score family in the 17th and 18th centuries and two small farms there remained in separate ownership.[76] That known as Bonson farm was acquired by Somerset county council, which sold it in 1922.[77]

Edward Popham died in 1586[78] and his half manor descended like the Popham share of Woolmersdon in North Petherton until 1636 when Popham's mortgagees sold it to Robert Williams or Score.[79] On his death in 1640, Robert left his share to his younger sons John and Thomas who were minors. The eldest son, also Robert, and his uncle John Parsons held the estate from 1643 during John's minority following the deaths of his mother and brother Thomas. John died in 1662 and his son William before 1724 when William's son William mortgaged his half of the manor.[80] In 1730 William purchased further lands in Fiddington formerly the property of the Grove family, but those lands were also mortgaged and in 1746 he was said to have absconded and his estate was put up for sale. The mortgages were assigned, however, and William Williams retained his equity of

redemption until 1773 or later but it was eventually forfeited.[81] By 1779 Bonson was probably in the absolute possession of the Revd. Henry Rawlings who had acquired the mortgages, but lordship was not recorded after 1773. By his will of 1807 he left Bonson to his son the Revd. Henry William Rawlings, under whose marriage settlement of 1819 and will of 1855 the estates, then amalgamated as Wood farm, were settled on his widow Eliza and then on his son Thomas. Eliza died in 1878 and in 1901, after Thomas's death, the estate was put up for sale. It remained unsold until 1909 or later.[82]

The chief tenement of Bonson was let in 1472 but there is no further record of a manor house.[83] Wood Farm was rebuilt at the end of the 19th century.[84] Bonson Farm is an early 17th-century, L-shaped house.

INWOOD was held by the Columbers family with their manor of Nether Stowey.[85] In 1620 Mervyn Tuchet, earl of Castlehaven, sold part to Margaret Dodington, in whose family it descended with Dodington.[86]

In the 17th century John Coles (d. 1627) had property at WHITNELL which descended with Woolstone in Stogursey.[87] John Tuxwell also had land there which descended with Coultings in Spaxton until 1666 when it was sold to John Ruscombe.[88] In 1781 the estate was held by William Poole who had been succeeded by George Poole by 1787. In 1829 George was succeeded by Thomas Poole.[89] Following Thomas's death in 1837 Whitnell was sold, part of it passing to Henry Godfree, who also possessed land which had belonged to Richard Wickham before 1647.[90]

Cannington priory held land in Fiddington which was granted to Edward Rogers in 1538.[91] Later known as Kilcott Oak, it descended with Rogers's Cannington estate.[92]

ECONOMIC HISTORY. In 1086 Fiddington was taxed at 4 hides, of which the demesne answered for 3 hides. The whole estate was assessed at 6 ploughlands, and the demesne supported 2 teams. There were 21 a. of meadow, 80 a. of pasture, and 43 a. of moor. The recorded livestock comprised 12 cattle, 11 pigs, 60 sheep, and 40 goats and the value was unchanged from 1066. In 1086 there were 6 villani and 5 bordars sharing 3 ploughteams.[93] By the later 12th century there were two separate estates, Fiddington

65 Cal. Pat. 1266–72, 700; S.R.S. xli. 54, 194–5, 207; Feud. Aids, iv. 308, 335, 352.
66 Below, Stogursey, manors; Cal. Close, 1402–5, 249, 362.
67 S.R.S. xxii. 183; lvii, pp. 39–40, 43; P.R.O., C 142/187, no. 61; C 142/206, no. 20.
68 Feud. Aids, iv. 394, 436; S.R.S. lvii, p. 43.
69 Devon R.O. 2530 M/L 6/6/1A; P.R.O., C 142/22, no. 45.
70 P.R.O., C 1/459, nos. 24–5; L. & P. Hen. VIII, xiii (1), pp. 405–6.
71 P.R.O., LR 3/123.
72 S.R.O., DD/S/WH 7.
73 P.R.O., CP 25(2)/205/21 & 22 Eliz. I Mich.
74 Above, Goathurst, manors; S.R.O., DD/S/WH 7.
75 S.R.O., DD/S/WH 7.
76 Above; S.R.O., Q/REl 7/4A; ibid. tithe award.
77 S.R.O., C/C 46/1.
78 P.R.O., C 142/211, no. 156.
79 Below, North Petherton, manors; S.R.O., DD/BR/rd 2.

80 S.R.O., DD/BR/rd 2; D/D/Rr Fid.
81 Ibid. DD/BR/rd 2–3; Devon R.O. 48/13/4/6/19–20.
82 S.R.O., DD/BR/rd 2–3; D/R/Bw 15/3/12; ibid. Q/REl 7/4A.
83 Devon R.O. 2530 M/L 6/6/1A.
84 S.R.O., DD/BR/rd 3.
85 V.C.H. Som. v. 193–4.
86 Ibid. 66; S.R.O., DD/AH 37/6.
87 S.R.S. lxvii, pp. 96–7; Devon R.O. 48/13/4/4/1; below, Stogursey, manors.
88 Som. Wills, ed. Brown, v. 68; S.R.O., DD/VN (C/10); below, Spaxton, manors.
89 S.R.O., Q/REl 7/4.
90 Ibid. DD/SAS (C/909) 135/1; ibid. tithe award; ibid. Q/REl 7/4; Devon R.O. 48/13/4/4/1.
91 Valor Eccl. (Rec. Com.), i. 209–10; L. & P. Hen. VIII, xiii (1), p. 408.
92 S.R.O., Q/RRp 1/30; above, Cannington, manors.
93 V.C.H. Som. i. 494.

and Bonson.[94] In 1579 Bonson manor comprised a main farm of 210 a. and 10 other holdings, only two over 50 a. and the rest under 30 a., although additional overland was available.[95] Holdings remained small during the 18th century and in 1745 there were difficulties in renewing leases on Fiddington manor, possibly because the harvest was bad. In 1746 several tenants were in debt, some had abandoned their holdings, one man was in gaol, one in danger of imprisonment, and another was impoverished. The tenants were said to be mostly poor and estates fetched low prices although the manor was valued at over £331 a year.[96]

Inventories of the 17th century suggest mixed farming; in 1639 a farmer had 6 cattle, 22 sheep, 3 pigs, and 2 horses and had sold some young animals. A wealthy clothworker who also farmed had a flock of 60 sheep, 19 cattle and a dairy, 10 pigs, and 3 horses, with hay and corn worth £30. Rye and oats were grown besides wheat and barley,[97] and in 1685 a tenant of Fiddington manor was required to plant an orchard.[98] In the 1780s large quantities of flax were grown; in 1784 two men produced 385 stone on 9½ a., in 1786 output was 442 stone, and in 1787 one man produced 317 stone.[99]

In 1837 there were 408 a. of arable, 387 a. of meadow and pasture, and 39 a. of orchard and garden. Of the 17 holdings over 10 a., 9 were under 25 a., 4 between 25 a. and 50 a., 1 between 50 a. and 100 a., and 3 were over 100 a. but under 150 a.[1] Most of the tenants, however, occupied more than one holding. In 1851 four farmers worked most of the land in the parish and employed 23 labourers. Later in the 19th century only two farmers had less than 100 a.[2] By 1905 the parish had almost doubled in size and most of the land was laid to grass, which covered 1,055 a. There were 593 a. of arable.[3] In 1982 there were 12 holdings, half of which were worked part-time and 3 of which specialized in poultry. Eight holdings were under 50 ha. (123.5 a.) but one was over 300 ha. (741 a.). Arable land had increased to cover half the parish, with wheat on 215 ha. (531 a.), barley on 84 ha. (207.5 a.), and oilseed rape on 28 ha. (69 a.). Poultry numbered 241,736 birds of which 49,700 were laying hens. There were also 756 cattle and 692 sheep.[4] Poultry farming with egg packing remained an important industry in 1988.

Cloth was made in the parish in the 17th and early 18th centuries, giving rise to field names such as Weavers acre and Dyers close.[5] One woman in 1636 died in possession of a pair of looms and wool and she also kept a few sheep. A clothier was recorded in 1667.[6] Another died in 1670 with wool out for spinning and large quantities of wool, yarn, dyestuffs, soap, and fuel. He had a furnace, combs, scales, a warping bar, and other tools, together with 116 serges worth £260. A sergemaker's inventory of 1714 included two furnaces, scales in a warping shop, a shop fitted out with a counter, yarn, and white and coloured wool; 1,521 lb. of wool had been sold.[7] Tanners were recorded in the parish in 1638 and 1656, possibly at Inwood, where there were field names such as Tanhouse mead and Tanners plot.[8]

MILLS. Two mills were recorded in 1086 paying 2s.[9] In 1242 the Fiddington miller died after falling under the wheel.[10] Fiddington manor mill, recorded in 1309,[11] was known in 1473–4 and 1518 as Galpin mill and by 1705 as Dunstone mill.[12] Manorial tenants still owed suit of mill in 1681.[13] In 1772 the mill was sold by Joseph Champion to the brothers Richard and Gregory Score. Richard (d. 1807) left his share to his brother who in 1819 gave the mill to his sons John (d. 1834) and William; William probably sold it to the miller before 1837.[14] It was in use in 1899 but milling seems to have ceased by 1906.[15] The mill was later demolished and the pond and leats were filled in. Bonson mill, recorded in 1403 and in 1458 when tenants of Bonson manor owed mill suit,[16] remained part of the manor until 1773 when Henry Rawlings sold it to William Kebby. The new owner had to repair the sluices and turn the water on the vendor's lands between Saturday evening and Monday morning.[17] During the 19th century the mill was kept by the Bowering family but it appears to have gone out of use by 1923.[18] It was driven by an internal overshot wheel. The mill building bears the date 1734 but it was totally rebuilt in the early 19th century.

FAIRS. In 1242 it was said that fairs were held at Fiddington and customs taken without warrant.[19] The fairs were not recorded again.

LOCAL GOVERNMENT. The parish formed a single tithing by the 16th century but Bonson, with land in Cannington, formed a separate division for land tax purposes.[20] Tithingmen were chosen in the 17th century according to a rota of ten holdings.[21] Court records for Bonson manor survive for 1540–1, 1552, and 1611,[22] and

94 Above, manors.
95 S.R.O., DD/S/WH 243. Overland was land not part of a tenement.
96 Devon R.O. 48/13/4/4/4, 7; 48/13/4/6/13, 19–20.
97 S.R.O., DD/SP inventories, 1636, 1639, 1670.
98 Devon R.O. 48/13/3/5/8.
99 S.R.O., Q/RLh 6, 22, 55.   1 Ibid. tithe award.
2 P.R.O., HO 107/1924; ibid. RG 11/2371.
3 Statistics supplied by the then Bd. of Agric., 1905.
4 Min. of Agric., Fisheries, and Food, agric. returns, 1982.   5 S.R.O., tithe award.
6 Ibid. DD/SP inventory, 1636; DD/DP 52/4.
7 Ibid. DD/SP inventories, 1670, 1714.
8 Taunton Archdeaconry Wills, ed. H. R. Phipps, 19; S.R.S. xxviii. 296; S.R.O., tithe award.
9 V.C.H. Som. i. 494.

10 S.R.S. xi, p. 320.
11 Ibid. xii. 6.
12 W. Suss. R.O., PHA 5370; W. Suff. R.O. 449/E3/15.53/2.17; Devon R.O. 48/13/4/6/1.
13 Devon R.O. 48/13/3/5/18.
14 S.R.O., D/P/fid 2/1/1; D/D/Rr Fid.; DD/DHR 10; ibid. tithe award.
15 Kelly's Dir. Som. (1899, 1906).
16 S.R.S. xxii. 8–9; Devon R.O. 2530 M/L 6/6/1.
17 Above, manors; S.R.O., DD/BR/rd 3.
18 S.R.O., tithe award; P.R.O., HO 107/1924; ibid. RG 11/2371; Kelly's Dir. Som. (1923).
19 S.R.S. xi, p. 321.
20 Ibid. xx. 244–5; S.R.O., Q/REl 7/4, 7/4A.
21 Devon R.O. 48/13/3/5/27.
22 P.R.O., LR 3/123; S.R.O., DD/S/WH 211.

rolls survive for Fiddington manor for 1647–8. Courts continued to be held at Fiddington twice a year until the mid 18th century or later.[23]

During the earlier 19th century watchmen were appointed and constables were elected.[24] The overseers gave relief in cash and in kind in the later 17th century. In 1684 they repaired what had probably been the church house for which they paid rent to Fiddington manor in 1702 and in the 1740s.[25] In 1839 it was sold to the rector Henry Rawlings and became the site of the school.[26]

Fiddington became part of Bridgwater poor-law union in 1836, Bridgwater rural district in 1894, and Sedgemoor district in 1974.[27]

CHURCH. Fiddington church was first recorded in 1272.[28] The living was a sole rectory until 1964 and from that year it was held with Stogursey. Since 1976 the benefices have been united.[29]

The advowson probably belonged to the lords of Fiddington manor but in 1272 Henry of Fiddington's title was challenged by Richard FitzBernard of Bonson.[30] Henry gave the advowson to William of Edington, clerk, who granted it to John de Columbers and his wife Alice. She presented in 1316 but in 1319 the advowson was settled on her son Philip de Columbers and his heirs.[31] By 1340, however, it had been recovered against Philip de Columbers and Simon Furneaux by Geoffrey of Stawell who claimed that Alice de Columbers had given it to him and that he had secured a release from Philip.[32] It was later bought by Simon Farway who sold it to Robert Crosse, and Robert enfeoffed Sir Thomas Fichet c. 1383.[33] The advowson descended with Spaxton manor until 1756 or later.[34] By 1776 it was owned by William Yorke who later became rector.[35] Thereafter the advowson was held by successive incumbents or their relatives.[36] Since 1939 it has been held by the Diocesan Board of Patronage.[37]

The church was valued at £8 in 1414[38] but at only £6 10s. 2½d. net in 1535.[39] By 1668 it was valued at c. £60[40] and in 1765 at £90,[41] but by 1831 had risen to £215.[42] In 1837 tithes were commuted for a rent charge of £200.[43]

In the later 13th century Henry of Fiddington gave 4 a. of arable with the advowson to William of Edington. The land, later described as 14 a., was said to be the glebe but was let by the patron in the later 14th century.[44] It had probably been given to the rector before 1535 when the glebe was worth 43s.[45] In 1613 the glebe measured 35 a.[46] and in 1837 nearly 39 a.[47] The land remained church property in 1978.[48] The glebe house was recorded in 1613 and in 1815 it was said that it had not been occupied by the incumbent for a century.[49] It was described as unfit in 1835 and was let in 1837 but it had been repaired by 1840 when it was occupied by a curate.[50] The house, east of the village street, was sold in 1968[51] and later demolished.

The first recorded incumbent, Richard Anselm, had licence to study in 1317 and to serve Philip de Columbers in 1319.[52] Matthew Cote, appointed in 1342, had only received the first tonsure.[53] Thomas Abendon, rector 1452–64, was an Augustinian canon and theologian and by 1463 had left the parish in the care of a chaplain.[54] Thomas Puffe, instituted in 1516, was charged with superstition for having used earth from the graveyard on his fields.[55] In 1557 the churchyard was insufficiently enclosed and the chalice had been taken out of the church. The church was still without a communion cup in 1576.[56] Richard Reeks was ejected from the rectory in 1642 but was restored in 1660.[57] Most rectors were non-resident in the 18th century and the parish was served by curates. Matthew Hole, rector 1709–11, was vicar of Stogursey and a fellow of Exeter College, Oxford.[58] John Woolcott was rector for 53 years; his successor in 1765, Richard Lewis, lived at Honiton and failed to provide a curate. The one Sunday service was held at 1 p.m. which the parishioners described as 'unseasonable, improper and an inconvenient hour'.[59] There were between 10 and 15 communicants in 1776.[60] In 1815 the curate was living at Charlinch. In 1827 the rector lived at Staplegrove and the curate was vicar of Over Stowey; there was only one Sunday service, held alternately morning and afternoon.[61] By 1840 a resident curate provided two Sunday services and celebrated communion at least three times a year. Celebrations had increased to six by 1870 when there was a resident incumbent.[62] In 1891 there was a bible class and a Sunday school besides two Sunday services. In 1951 there were three Sunday services and the average number of communicants was 5.[63]

The church house, probably called the parish house, had been let to the overseers by 1684.[64]

The church of *ST. MARTIN*, so dedicated by

23 Devon. R.O. 48/13/4/4/1; 48/13/4/6/4.
24 *S.R.S.* xxviii. 360; S.R.O., D/P/fid 9/1/1.
25 S.R.O., D/P/fid 4/1/1; Devon R.O. 48/13/4/4/3, 6, 8.
26 S.R.O., D/P/fid 9/1/1; DD/BR/rd 3; below, educ.
27 Youngs, *Local Admin. Units*, i. 671, 673, 676.
28 Cal. Pat. 1266–72, 700.   29 *Dioc. Dir.*
30 Cal. Pat. 1266–72, 700.
31 *S.R.S.* i. 111, 133; lxviii, p. 39.
32 Ibid. x, pp. 441, 448–9; lxviii, p. 39.
33 Ibid. lxviii, pp. 41–2.
34 Ibid. extra ser. 315–16; below, Spaxton, manors.
35 S.R.O., D/D/Vc 88.
36 *Rep. Com. Eccl. Revenues*, pp. 138–9; *P.O. Dir. Som.* (1866, 1875).
37 *Kelly's Dir. Som.* (1939); *Dioc. Dir.*
38 S.R.O., D/D/B misc. 1.
39 *Valor Eccl.* (Rec. Com.), i. 215.
40 S.R.O., D/D/Vc 24.   41 Ibid. D/D/C pet.
42 *Rep. Com. Eccl. Revenues*, pp. 138–9.
43 S.R.O., tithe award.
44 *S.R.S.* lxviii, pp. 16, 39, 41.
45 *Valor Eccl.* (Rec. Com.), i. 215.
46 S.R.O., D/D/Rg 270.   47 Ibid. tithe award.
48 Inf. from Dioc. Office.
49 S.R.O., D/D/Rg 270; D/D/Rb 1815.
50 *Rep. Com. Eccl. Revenues*, pp. 138–9; S.R.O., tithe award; ibid. D/D/Va 1840.
51 S.R.O., D/P/fid 3/4/6.   52 *S.R.S.* i. 111, 133, 305.
53 *H.M.C. Wells*, i. 250; *S.R.S.* x, p. 441.
54 Emden, *Biog. Reg. Univ. Oxf. to 1500*; *S.R.S.* xlix, pp. 399, 420.
55 *S.R.S.* lvi. 158.   56 S.R.O., D/D/Ca 27, 57.
57 *Walker Revised*, ed. A. G. Matthews, 318.
58 *D.N.B.*   59 S.R.O., D/D/C pet.
60 Ibid. D/D/Vc 88.   61 Ibid. D/D/Rb 1815, 1827.
62 Ibid. D/D/Va 1840, 1870.
63 Ibid. D/P/fid 2/9/2, 6.
64 Above, local. govt.

the early 14th century,[65] comprises a chancel with north vestry, nave with north aisle and south porch, and a west tower. Despite a planned rebuilding of all except the tower in 1860 the church retains older fabric. The south walls of the nave and chancel appear to be medieval and include an area of possible herringbone masonry, the chancel arch is 14th century, and the roofs are probably 16th century. Much work was done between 1727 and 1732, partly as a result of storm damage in 1729. Coloured screens were placed under the chancel and tower arches. A door beside the pulpit was walled up and a new window was put in the south wall.[66] At the restoration in 1860, for which John Norton was the architect, a north aisle was added, the south porch was rebuilt, and most of the windows were renewed. A west gallery was removed and the south doorway into the chancel was reopened.[67] The tower was rendered and the church restored in 1977.

There is a sheela-na-gig in the external south wall.[68] Internal fittings include early 16th-century bench ends and a Jacobean pulpit. The shaft and base of an early 14th-century cross remain in the churchyard. Part of a figure survives in a canopied niche on the east side of the shaft.

The plate includes a cup of 1765 by 'J.F.'[69] There is a late medieval bell from the Bristol foundry.[70] The peal was increased from four to six in 1979. The registers date from 1706 but there are many gaps in the first volume.[71]

NONCONFORMITY. There were recusants in the parish in the 1630s and in 1641.[72] A meeting house was licensed in 1819 for an unspecified denomination.[73] Providence General Baptist chapel was opened at Whitnell in 1837. It was served from Burton in Stogursey but closed between 1923 and 1931.[74] The building, in agricultural use in 1982, had been converted into a dwelling by 1987. The Wesleyans began services at Coultings in 1868 and a chapel and schoolroom were built c. 1874.[75] In 1898 there were 11 members and one weekday and two Sunday services. By 1900 there was only one service a week and by 1920 services had ceased. The chapel was in bad condition in 1924 and was put up for sale in 1928.[76] In 1932 it was converted to a private house[77] and so remained in 1988. There was an Independent chapel in the parish by 1861;[78] it was probably at Coultings and was last recorded in 1896 when it was in the care of an evangelist from Stogursey.[79]

EDUCATION. In 1676 a man was licensed to teach in the parish.[80] There was a day school in 1819 where 19 pupils were taught at parish expense.[81] In 1825 there was a Sunday school but no day school was recorded.[82] Ten years later there was a day school with 12 children taught at their parents' expense.[83] In 1847 the village school, on the site of the former church house purchased by the rector in 1839, was supported by subscriptions and had 40 pupils on weekdays and a further 10 boys who attended on Sundays only. In 1850 the Sunday school taught 60 children and had a clothing club to which women might also belong.[84] The school, affiliated to the National Society, was supported by donations and a voluntary school rate from 1873.[85] In 1873 the parish agreed to pay the rector a rent.[86] The school was rebuilt on an adjoining site to the north-west in 1891 when there were 48 children at the day school and 41 at the Sunday school. In 1903 there were 40 children on the books with one teacher.[87] Numbers fell to 19 in 1925, 11 in 1945, and 6 in 1954 when the school was closed. The children were transferred to Cannington.[88] The school, south-west of the church, became the village hall and remained in use in 1988.

CHARITIES FOR THE POOR. John Grove, probably in 1680, gave money for apprenticing a poor boy in the woollen trade, and agreed that any residue should be used to provide woollen cloth and clothing for the poor. By a deed of 1705 the sum of £50 was secured for this purpose.[89] In the 18th and 19th centuries the income was used to distribute cloth and blankets.[90] Distributions of flannel were made until 1904 when cash was given. The last recorded distribution of cash was in 1974.[91]

Eliza Rawlings by will dated 1878 gave £50 to the poor, the interest to be distributed at Christmas. After 1942 the income was distributed with Grove's charity.[92]

65 S.R.S. lxviii, p. 39.
66 S.R.O., D/P/fid 4/1/2.
67 Ibid. D/P/fid 6/1/1; 8/3/1; D/D/Cf 1860/7.
68 Proc. Som. Arch. Soc. cxxiii. 111–13.
69 Ibid. xlvii. 165.
70 S.R.O., DD/SAS CH 16/1; D/P/fid 4/1/2.
71 Ibid. D/P/fid 2/1/1–4.
72 Ibid. D/D/Ca 266, 274, 310; Som. Protestation Returns, ed. A. J. Howard and T. L. Stoate, 194.
73 S.R.O., D/D/Rm, box 2.
74 Baptist Handbk. (1900); H. J. Hamblin and A. J. Whitby, Baptists in Bridgwater, 84; Kelly's Dir. Som. (1923, 1931).
75 S.R.O., D/N/bmc 3/2/3, 4/2/1; P.O. Dir. Som. (1875).
76 S.R.O., D/N/bmc 2/3/11, 3/2/2, 4/2/3.
77 Ibid. D/R/bw 22/1/23.
78 P.O. Dir. Som. (1861).

79 Rep. Som. Cong. Union (1896).
80 S.R.O., D/D/Bs 42.
81 Educ. of Poor Digest, p. 784.
82 Ann. Rep. B. & W. Dioc. Assoc. S. P. C. K. (1825–6), 42.
83 Educ. Enq. Abstract, p. 806.
84 Nat. Soc. Inquiry, 1846–7, Som. 8–9; S.R.O., D/P/fid 18/3/6; DD/BR/rd 3.
85 S.R.O., D/P/fid 2/9/2, 17/3/2, 18/3/2.
86 Ibid. 9/1/2.
87 Ibid. C/E 4/380/169.
88 Ibid. 4/64, 188.
89 Ibid. D/P/fid 4/1/1, 17/3/1; 15th Rep. Com. Char. 361–2.
90 S.R.O., D/P/fid 4/1/1, 18/3/6.
91 Ibid. 17/3/1.
92 Char. Com. reg.; S.R.O., D/P/fid 17/3/1.

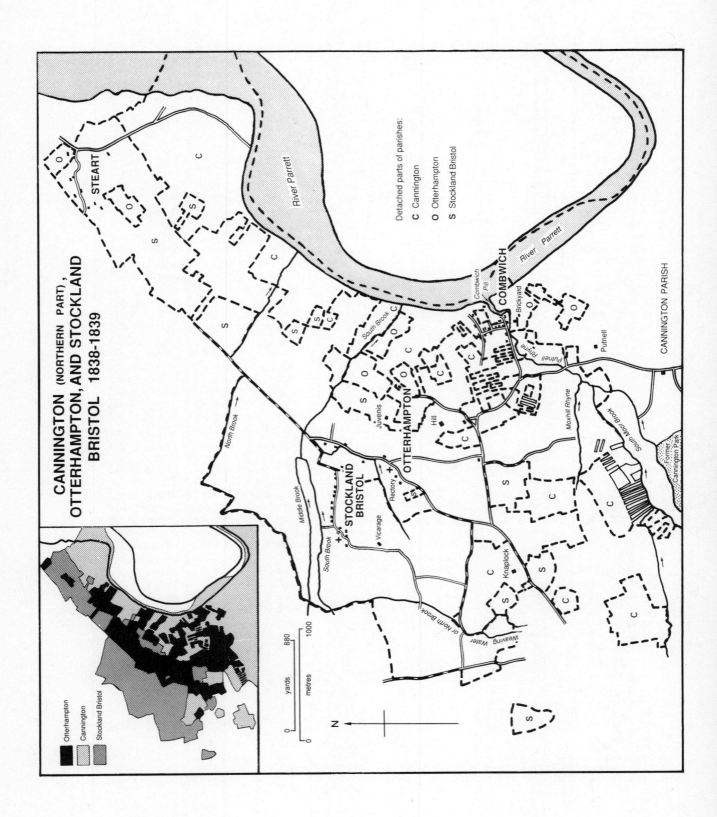

CANNINGTON (NORTHERN PART), OTTERHAMPTON, AND STOCKLAND BRISTOL 1838-1839

Detached parts of parishes:

C Cannington
O Otterhampton
S Stockland Bristol

OTTERHAMPTON

THE ancient parish of Otterhampton lay between Stockland Bristol and the river Parrett 2.5 km. north of Cannington village and 8 km. north-west of Bridgwater.[93] It included Otterhampton village, a small settlement at Hill, now centred on Hill House, and parts of Combwich. The eastern half of the parish beside the river interlocked with Cannington parish, the result of at least one division of holdings between the estates of Cannington and Otterhampton between 1066 and 1086 and of the common ownership of one of the Combwich estates and Otterhampton Rumsey manor.[94] The parish also interlocked with Stockland Bristol, upon the church of which it was formerly dependent.[95] Between Otterhampton and Stockland villages the boundary follows a footpath, a stream, and a road, and part of the south-western boundary followed South Moor Brook.[96] The ancient parish measured 983 a.[97] In 1886 Otterhampton acquired Steart and other detached areas from Stockland and exchanged lands with Cannington, bringing the whole of Combwich into Otterhampton civil parish which in 1891 was said to measure 2,026 a.[98] In 1933 the area of Huntspill parish west of the Parrett at Steart estimated at 218 a. was transferred to Otterhampton.[99] The present civil parish covers 934 ha. (2,308 a.).[1]

From Combwich village (7 m.) the land rises on marl and Blue Lias over sandstone to 38 m. at Hill House. The remainder of the parish is flat marshland, in the south-west on marl, alluvium, and valley gravels, and in the north and north-east on alluvium, all below the 7.5-m. contour. The higher ground was quarried for lime and building stone, and brick and tile were made from the alluvium. The southern part of the parish is drained by the Moxhill and Putnell rhynes and the marshlands to the north by the South and North brooks. The flat lands along the Parrett are protected by sea walls which have been moved as land has been lost or gained.[2]

The name Otterhampton may indicate the settlement of the people of the Otterham, the marshes.[3] Otterhampton village comprising the church, former rectory house, and one farm which was probably the capital messuage of the main Domesday estate, seems to have been larger, since there is evidence of former buildings around the church.[4] There was a small estate at Moxhill in the 11th century.[5] A settlement, known as Twye in 1348 and Twyhouse in 1620, came to be known as Hill.[6] Combwich, the largest settlement and a small port, was shared with Cannington until 1886. Its ancient chapel was in Cannington parish and the history of the village is included under Cannington. The school and village hall bore the name Otterhampton in 1989.

The main route through the parish took traffic to and from the port and ferry at Combwich westwards to Nether Stowey and Stogursey. A road from Cannington crossed this route west of Combwich and may have led directly to Hill before the later 18th century. This road continued through a scattered roadside settlement north of Otterhampton village to the Steart marshes. The road from Cannington has from 1957 led to Hinkley Point power station, and has therefore become the principal route through the parish. Otterhampton village lay on a road from Coultings in Spaxton to Steart, a route which was closed south of the rectory after 1887.[7]

Combwich Down, west of the village, was an arable field shared between Cannington and Otterhampton into the 19th century. The meadows of North and South moors were similarly shared. They were not inclosed until 1867, and parts of South moor remained divided in strips into the 20th century.[8] A park was laid out around Hill House in the late 18th century, possibly for deer, and was sheltered on the north by plantations.[9]

There was a licensed tippler in the parish in 1607 and possibly in 1630. Later public houses were in Combwich.[10] There was said to have been an Otterhampton club whose poles were converted into churchwardens staves.[11]

The population rose from 176 in 1801 to 221 in 1831 when there was a shortage of houses, only 32 for 46 households.[12] Thereafter it fluctuated between about 210 and 240; most people lived at Combwich.[13] The growth of Combwich during the 20th century and the inclusion of the whole village in the civil parish account for the increase in population to 422 in 1931, to 551 in 1971, and to 697 in 1981.[14]

Six men were fined for involvement in the 1497 rebellion,[15] and Thomas Charnock, the alchemist, was buried at Otterhampton.[16]

MANORS AND OTHER ESTATES. There were three holdings called Otterhampton in 1066. The first, held by Edwin, had passed to

---

93 This article was completed in 1989.
94 Below, manors.
95 Below, church.
96 O.S. Map 1/25,000, ST 24 (1959 edn.).
97 S.R.O., tithe award.
98 Census, 1891.
99 S.R.O., GP/D, box 19.
1 Census, 1981.
2 O.S. Map 1/25,000, ST 24 (1959 edn); Geol. Surv. Map 1/50,000, solid and drift, sheet 279 and parts of 263 and 295 (1980 edn.); Proc. Som. Arch. Soc. xxiii. 65–7; S.R.O., D/RA 1/6/1.
3 Ekwall, Eng. Place-Names (1960), 336.
4 Som. C.C., Sites and Mons. Rec.

5 V.C.H. Som. i. 512.
6 S.R.O., TS/EVD; DD/SAS (C/77) 29.
7 S.R.S. lxxvi, maps 1782, 1822; S.R.O., tithe award; O.S. Map 6", Som. XXXVII. SE. (1887 edn.); O.S. Map 1/25,000, ST 24 (1959 edn.).
8 S.R.O., Q/RDe 156; ibid. tithe award; O.S. Map 1/25,000, ST 24 (1959 edn.).
9 Som. C.C., Sites and Mons. Rec.; S.R.O., tithe award.
10 S.R.O., Q/SR 3/107; Q/RL; above, Cannington.
11 Ch. guide.
12 S.R.O., D/P/otn 2/1/2.
13 Census; P.R.O., HO 107/1924.   14 Census.
15 Fines Imposed in 1497, ed. A. J. Howard, 14.
16 D.N.B.; Som. Wills, ed. Brown, v. 56.

Roger de Courcelles by 1086 when it was held of him by Robert. The second, whose owner was unnamed in 1066, had been divided by 1086, two thirds passing to the royal estate of Cannington and the remainder to the previous owner's son Osmer. The third, and the only one that can be traced further, had been held by Estan in 1066 and was held by Herbert of Alfred d'Epaignes in 1086.[17]

The estate held by Herbert of Alfred d'Epaignes came to be known as *OTTERHAMPTON* manor, and was held of the honor of Nether Stowey until 1577 or later.[18] William, son of Terry of Mudford, held a fee of Nether Stowey in 1166, and was succeeded by his son Terry and by Terry's son Henry.[19] In 1216 Henry's lands were given to William of Eston, but in 1225 Henry laid claim to land in Otterhampton.[20] Beatrice of Otterhampton, probably widow of Robert of Eston, held a fee of Nether Stowey in 1262,[21] and her daughter Sarah held Otterhampton with her husband William Trivet *c.* 1285.[22] The estate descended with Cock in Stogursey until 1433 and may have been sold by William Trivet to Alexander Hody (d. 1461). Thereafter it descended with Newnham in Stogursey until 1650.[23] In 1651 the manor was held by Hugh Hody, who had purchased it from Gilbert Hody. In 1664 Hugh settled it on his son Gilbert. Hugh died *c.* 1670 and Gilbert by 1697 leaving as his heirs Anne, wife of Hugh Pomeroy, and Joan, both probably his daughters.[24] It was settled by Joan in 1713 and 1714 on her marriage to George Chudleigh.[25] Sir George Chudleigh, Bt., died in 1738 and the estate was held by his second wife Frances Davie (d. *c.* 1748).[26] Margaret Chudleigh, one of their four daughters, sold the manor to Robert Evered in 1755.[27] Robert was dead by 1766 and his son John died in 1782 leaving the estate in trust for his son John, a minor.[28] John died in 1848 and was succeeded by his son Robert who settled the manor on his son Andrew upon his marriage in 1865.[29] Andrew died in 1925 and was succeeded by his son Robert who was described as lord of the manor in 1931. Lordship was not recorded again and the estate was broken up and sold, mainly to tenants, in 1946.[30]

A capital messuage was recorded in 1316.[31] It was let during the 18th century, in 1729 to Robert Evered. It continued to be recorded until 1782.[32] It was probably the house known in the 19th century as Otterhampton Farm,[33] which lies immediately south-west of the church and is now known as Manor Farm. It is a late 17th-century, three-bayed house with extensive 19th-century alterations.[34]

Part of Otterhampton manor,[35] known later as *OTTERHAMPTON RUMSEY* manor, was held in 1286 by Walter of Romsey, son and heir of Sir Walter of Romsey. Walter or another of the same name died *c.* 1333 and his son Sir John died in 1334 leaving a son Walter under age.[36] Sir Walter died in 1403 having settled Otterhampton on his wife Alice (d. 1404) and on his grandson Walter, son of Thomas Romsey, who had predeceased his parents.[37] Walter died probably without issue as the estate was held by his elder brother Thomas (d. 1420) and Thomas's wife Joan (d. 1441). Their daughter and heir Joan married Thomas Paine but died childless *c.* 1447 having granted her Somerset estates in 1443 to Henry Champeneys and his wife Elizabeth, probably widow of Walter Romsey, for life.[38] Joan's heir to her Somerset estates was Joan wife of Roger Wyke, granddaughter of Sir Walter Romsey (d. 1403). Joan and Roger settled certain lands on Joan, wife of John Cayleway and possibly their daughter, but remained in possession of most of the former Romsey lands in 1462.[39]

William Cayleway and his wife Anne sold an estate described as one third of Otterhampton Rumsey manor in 1542 to John St. Clere who in 1547 sold it to James Bowerman.[40] James died in possession in 1548 leaving a son Andrew who sold it later that year to his brother Henry.[41] Henry died in 1589 leaving it to his brother William who died in 1591 leaving a son Andrew.[42] In 1620 Andrew Bowerman sold the manor, sometimes described as one third of Otterhampton manor, to William Bacon and thereafter it descended with Maunsel in North Petherton until *c.* 1733 when Alexander Seymour left it to his brother William, a minor.[43] By 1752 it was held by William's nephew Alexander Seymour Gapper who sold it to John Evered the elder in 1759. The estate, also known by then as Hill, was settled in 1774 by John on his son Robert, who held it in 1809.[44] Robert appears to have sold part to his cousin John Evered *c.* 1812, possibly for the construction of Hill House, and by 1838 he had sold Hill Farm and most of the land. There is no record of a sale of lordship, which was not recorded after 1809.[45]

The capital messuage called Twyhouse, recorded

17 *V.C.H. Som.* i. 485, 512, 525.
18 Ibid. i. 512; v. 193–4; P.R.O., C 142/183, no. 70.
19 *Red Bk. Exch.* (Rolls Ser.), i. 231; *S.R.S.* lxi, p. 17.
20 *Rot. Litt. Claus.* (Rec. Com.), 245; *S.R.S.* xi, p. 86.
21 Below, Stogursey, manors; *Close R.* 1261–4, 90.
22 *Feud. Aids*, iv. 281.
23 *S.R.S.* liv, pp. 6–7; below, Stogursey, manors.
24 S.R.O., DD/ARN 2, 5, 6.
25 Bailey-Everard MSS., in possession of Messrs. Crosse & Wyatt, S. Molton, Devon.
26 G.E.C. *Baronetage*, i. 207.
27 S.R.O., D/D/B reg 27, f. 14v.; DD/ARN 2.
28 Ibid. DD/X/MCO; DD/ARN 2.
29 Ibid. DD/BR/gh 3. Andrew later changed his name to Everard.
30 M.I. in ch.; *Kelly's Dir. Som.* (1931); S.R.O., DD/KW 1946/38.
31 *Cal. Inq. p.m.* vi, p. 43.
32 S.R.O., DD/ARN 2, 6; DD/X/MCO.

33 Ibid. tithe award.   34 Ibid. DD/V/BWr 24.1.
35 *Feud. Aids*, iv. 308, 353; S.R.O., DD/NW 64.
36 S.R.O., TS/EVD; *S.R.S.* ix, pp. 188–9; xii. 62, 163, 189; *Cal. Fine R.* 1327–37, 386–7.
37 *Cal. Inq. p.m.* xviii, pp. 328–9, 378–9; *Cal. Close*, 1402–5, 434.
38 *V.C.H. Hants*, iv. 459; P.R.O., C 138/61, no. 76; C 139/131, no. 26; *S.R.S.* xxii. 105.
39 *V.C.H. Hants*, iv. 459; *S.R.S.* xxii. 110–11, 206.
40 P.R.O., CP 25(2)/36/241/34 Hen. VIII Trin.; CP 25(2)/36/242/38 Hen. VIII Hil.
41 Ibid. C 142/85, no. 35; S.R.O., DD/SAS (C/238) 45.
42 *Som. Wills*, ed. Brown, i. 68; P.R.O., C 142/228, no. 94.
43 S.R.O., DD/SX 52/1; below, N. Petherton, manors; *Som. Wills*, ed. Brown, iv. 11.
44 Bailey-Everard MSS., in possession of Messrs. Crosse & Wyatt, S. Molton, Devon; S.R.O., DD/ARN 2.
45 S.R.O., Q/REl 7/5; ibid. tithe award; P.R.O., CP 25(2)/1402/49 Geo. III Trin.

in 1620, and possibly in 1608, was the residence of the Bacon family and was probably William Bacon's mansion house at Hill recorded in 1609.[46] By the 18th century the house was known as Hill Farm.[47] Hill Farm is of the early or mid 17th century and has a long central range, which may incorporate part of an earlier building, with cross wings which project southwards and a near-central rear wing. The principal ground-floor room in the western, parlour wing has a compartmented, beamed ceiling which was subsequently plastered, probably in 1666 when an ornamental plaster overmantel was put in. The house has been divided into three dwellings. The central section was partly refitted in the later 19th century and the west wing was renovated c. 1988.

There was a mansion on the site of Hill House in 1782,[48] but the present house dates from the early 19th century, possibly c. 1812. It is sited at the eastern end of a spur of high ground and the principal rooms have extensive views to the south and east. The house is built around an open courtyard which is entered through a central carriageway in the two-storeyed north-west range. The main house forms the south-east range and has a tall stuccoed front of five bays with lateral segmented bays. It has a spacious central hall and staircase flanked by the principal rooms, one of which has a ceiling in Adam style. A small park had been established around the house by 1822[49] and there is an early 19th-century stable block. The house was sold c. 1946 and became a school but in 1976 it was bought by the Bristol Christian Youth Trust and is used as a teaching and conference centre.[50]

MULSELLE, later Moxhill, was held by Alwine in 1066 and by Hugh of Alfred d'Epaignes in 1086.[51] In 1201 William le Poer sold it to Terry of Mudford[52] and it continued thereafter as part of Otterhampton manor.[53]

Stogursey priory received two grants of land in the parish in the later 12th century, one by Helewise, sister of Robert FitzBernard and wife of Hugh Pincerna, and her daughter Cecily, and the other by Alexander son of Viel.[54] The land was later administered as part of its manor of Monckton in Stogursey.[55]

ECONOMIC HISTORY. The four 11th-century estates at Otterhampton together had land for 5½ ploughteams but 6 teams were recorded, of which 3 were on the demesnes where there were also 3 *servi*. There were 22½ a. of meadow, 15 a. of pasture, 10 a. of wood and underwood. Livestock included 5 cattle, 11 pigs, and 45 sheep. There were 9 *villani* out of a

recorded population of 20.[56] In 1316 the Trivet manorial demesne at Otterhampton comprised 90 a. of arable, 30 a. of meadow, and 20 a. of pasture. There were then eight neifs who owed three days' work in autumn; and of the £4 8s. rent, £1 14s. was paid by free tenants.[57] In the 1330s a widow's dower in the manor included 10 a. of wheat and 4 cattle and had produced crops of wheat, oats, hay, and fodder.[58] In the 1540s the manor court attempted to regulate livestock: outsiders were presented for putting animals on the marshes and the rector was accused of allowing his pigs to go unringed; he also kept geese. A neif was recorded as late as 1546.[59] In the early 17th century tithes were levied on corn, cattle, calves, wool, lambs, pigs, geese, honey, wax, and apples. In 1634 the corn tithes were worth £30 and the small tithes £26.[60] In 1636 one woman had corn worth over £19, a large quantity of cheese and bacon, 11 cattle, horses, sheep worth £30, and 2 pigs.[61] Cheese and dairy cattle appear in other inventories but also wheat, sheep, wool, and poultry.[62] During the 18th century holdings were small apart from Hill farm on the Otterhampton Rumsey estate, which covered about 130 a. There were a few rack-rented estates on Otterhampton manor by 1755 but rents of capons, pepper, and cumin were still being charged.[63]

During the agricultural protests of 1801 labourers marched to Hill House where John Evered addressed them. With other magistrates he tried to make farmers bring their corn to market to reduce prices and shortages.[64] In 1824 one farmer had over £175 of livestock in the parish, possibly on the marsh, mainly sheep but also cows and a colt.[65] In 1839 there were 681 a. of meadow and pasture, 242½ a. of arable, 18 a. of orchard, 17 a. of woodland, and 4 a. of garden. Most holdings were under 25 a., but some of them were only tracts of marsh; only two were over 100 a., of which the larger was Otterhampton farm with 191½ a.[66] During the next 40 years the larger holdings absorbed some of the smaller: Moxhill farm reached 190 a. by 1861, Higher Hill farm 100 a. by 1871, Otterhampton farm 229 a. and Moxhill farm 231 a. by 1881.[67] By 1905, after the inclusion of Steart marsh, the parish comprised a total of 1,353 a. of grass, 212 a. of arable, and 28 a. of wood.[68] Six holdings covering two thirds of the parish in 1982 had 294 ha. (726 a.) of grass and 105 ha. (250 a.) of arable. Most of the arable land was under wheat, but there were small amounts of winter and spring barley, oats, fodder, orchard, soft fruit, and glasshouse crops. There were 708 cattle and 691 sheep; three of the holdings were dairy farms, another specialized in rearing cattle and

46 S.R.O., DD/BR/hnd 1; DD/SAS SX 60; DD/SAS (C/77) 29.
47 Ibid. DD/ARN 2.
48 *S.R.S.* lxxvi, map 1782.
49 Ibid. map 1822.
50 S.R.O., Q/REl 7/5; *Bridgwater Mercury*, 24 Jan. 1989.
51 *V.C.H. Som.* i. 512, where the identification of Mulselle as Marsh Mills is incorrect: below, Over Stowey, econ. hist.
52 *S.R.S.* vi. 8.
53 S.R.O., DD/ARN 2, 5; D/R/bw 15/3/20.
54 *S.R.S.* lxi, pp. 18, 21.
55 Below, Stogursey, manors.

56 *V.C.H. Som.* i. 485, 512, 525.
57 P.R.O., C 134/56, no. 4.
58 Ibid. E 142/71/10.   59 Ibid. LR 3/123.
60 S.R.O., D/D/Rg 280.
61 Ibid. DD/SP inventory, 1636.
62 Ibid. 1680, 1684, 1690.
63 Ibid. DD/SL 10; DD/SLM 2; DD/ARN 2.
64 J. Hamilton and J. Lawrence, *Men and Mining in the Quantocks* (1970), 23.
65 S.R.O., DD/DP 65/4.
66 Ibid. tithe award.
67 P.R.O., RG 9/1621; RG 10/2380; RG 11/2371.
68 Statistics supplied by the then Bd. of Agric., 1905.

sheep. Two were worked part-time. All the holdings were under 200 ha. (494 a.), two were over 100 ha. (247 a.), two between 50 ha. and 100 ha. (124–247 a.), one between 20 and 30 ha. (49–74 a.), and one under 2 ha. (5 a.).[69]

Although primarily an agricultural parish the river and the growth of the wharf at Combwich provided alternative employment.[70] A man from Otterhampton was accused of selling bad fish in 1379.[71] There was a sergeweaver in the parish in 1676,[72] and bricks and tiles were manufactured in Combwich in the 19th century.[73]

A mill, probably at Combwich, was recorded on Otterhampton manor in the 1540s.[74]

LOCAL GOVERNMENT. Otterhampton tithing was recorded in 1180 and the parish remained a single tithing into the 19th century.[75] Court rolls survive for the main manor for 1540, 1541, and 1546. The court appointed a hayward in 1541 and was concerned with repairs and cases of debt and trespass.[76] Tenants owed suit of court in 1651.[77] Tenants of Otterhampton Rumsey owed suit to its manor court in 1671.[78] There was a pound in front of the church until the 19th century.[79]

The overseers gave relief in cash and kind in the early 19th century, paid for fostering and schooling pauper children, and also for cleaning the schoolroom. A poorhouse, repaired by the overseers between 1814 and 1836,[80] stood north of the church and was last recorded under that name in 1861 when it was occupied by three labourers.[81] In 1989 it was a private house called Wainbridge.

Otterhampton became part of Bridgwater poor-law union in 1836, Bridgwater rural district in 1894, and Sedgemoor district in 1974.[82]

CHURCHES. By the later 12th century Otterhampton had its own rector,[83] but the parish did not have full parochial status: the vicar of Stockland in 1377 successfully claimed to bury the dead of Otterhampton unless they had chosen to be buried elsewhere.[84] Otterhampton probably established its independence soon afterwards. Following the building of St. Peter's at Combwich c. 1868, those detached parts of Cannington parish in and around Combwich village were transferred to Otterhampton for ecclesiastical purposes only, and the new church became a chapel of ease to Otterhampton.[85] The rectory of Otterhampton with Combwich was united with Stockland in 1971 and from 1984 formed part of the united benefice of Cannington, Otterhampton, Combwich, and Stockland.[86] Otterhampton church was closed for regular services in 1985 and was declared redundant.[87]

The lords of Otterhampton and Otterhampton Rumsey manors presented to the rectory alternately.[88] By the late 15th century the lords of Otterhampton Rumsey manor had lost their right although they continued to claim the advowson until 1548 or later.[89] The advowson descended with the main manor until John Evered (d. 1848) left it to his son the Revd. Charles Evered (d. 1867) whose widow Emma sold it to her brother-in-law Robert Guy Evered (d. 1887). Robert's second son John in 1892 sold it to his elder brother Andrew (d. 1925) who left it in trust for his wife Louisa (d. 1928) and his daughter Edith (d. 1945), wife of the Revd. Frederick Rostron. The personal representatives of the trustees retained the right of patronage until the church was declared redundant.[90]

The church was valued at £5 in 1291[91] and in 1535 at £13 18s. 6d. gross.[92] The rectory was said to be worth £70 6s. a year in 1634[93] but only c. £60 in 1668.[94] In 1802 the living was valued at £175 a year,[95] rising to an average of £260 gross in 1829–31,[96] and to £300 in 1868.[97] In the later 12th century some tithes in the parish were found to belong to Nether Stowey, whose rector granted them to the chaplain of Otterhampton for life at rents of 2s. 6d. and a wax candle.[98] In 1839 the tithes were commuted for an annual rent charge of £239 14s.[99]

The glebe lands, valued at £1 2s. in 1535,[1] comprised in the early 17th century 22 a. of land, mainly arable.[2] The glebe measured 19½ a. in 1839.[3] By 1924 some glebe had been sold but 7½ a. remained in 1978.[4] In the early 17th century the parsonage house appears to have had a detached kitchen, barn, pigeon house, and stables.[5] It was burnt down c. 1623 and rebuilding remained unfinished in 1630;[6] it had probably been completed by 1634.[7] The rectory house, having been in decay for many years, was replaced in 1802 by a large L-shaped house with a symmetrical three-bayed front, paid for by the

69 Min. of Agric., Fisheries, and Food, agric. returns, 1982.
70 Above, Cannington, econ. hist.
71 S.R.S. liii, p. 52.
72 S.R.O., Q/SR 130/35.
73 Above, Cannington, econ. hist.
74 P.R.O., LR 3/123; above, Cannington, mills.
75 Pipe R. 1180 (P.R.S. xxix), 111; S.R.O., Q/REl 7/5.
76 P.R.O., LR 3/123.
77 S.R.O., DD/ARN 5.
78 Ibid. DD/SX 52/4.
79 Ibid. D/P/otn 4/1/1.
80 Ibid. 13/2/1.
81 Ibid. tithe award; P.R.O., RG 9/1621.
82 Youngs, Local Admin. Units, i. 671, 673, 676.
83 S.R.S. lxi, pp. 18–19.
84 Cart. St. Mark's Hosp., Bristol (Bristol Rec. Soc. xxi), pp. 141–2.
85 S.R.O., D/P/otn 3/6/1.
86 Dioc. Dir.; Bath and Wells Bd. of Finance, Rep. (1984), 28.

87 Bridgwater Mercury, 2 Apr. 1986; Bath and Wells Bd. of Finance, Rep. (1988), 31.
88 S.R.S. ix, pp. 93, 188–9; xxx, p. 390.
89 S.R.S. liv, pp. 6–7; P.R.O., C 142/85/35; S.R.O., DD/SAS (C/238) 45.
90 Bailey-Everard MSS., in possession of Messrs. Crosse & Wyatt, S. Molton, Devon.
91 Tax. Eccl. (Rec. Com.), 198.
92 Valor Eccl. (Rec. Com.), i. 216.
93 S.R.O., D/D/Rg 280.   94 Ibid. D/D/Vc 24.
95 Ibid. D/D/Bbm 22.
96 Rep. Com. Eccl. Revenues, pp. 148–9.
97 S.R.O., D/P/otn 3/6/1.
98 H.M.C. Wells, i. 40.   99 S.R.O., tithe award.
1 Valor Eccl. (Rec. Com.), i. 216.
2 S.R.O., D/D/Rg 280.
3 Ibid. tithe award.
4 Ibid. D/P/otn 5/2/1; inf. from Dioc. Office.
5 S.R.O., D/D/Rg 280.
6 Ibid. D/D/Ca 235, 274.
7 Ibid. D/D/Rg 280.

rector, John Jeffrey D.D.[8] By 1839 the house had been considerably extended.[9] The Old Rectory preserves its 1802 frontage with a central door under a triangular pediment. Following the union with Stockland the rector moved to Combwich and the rectory house was sold.[10]

Hugh Willings, rector, was in dispute with the vicar of Stockland in 1377[11] and was accused of involvement in the concealment of customs in 1386.[12] William Warre was instituted to the living in 1519 as an acolyte, and in the same year was licensed to hold another benefice.[13] In the 1530s there was a fraternity of St. Peter and St. Paul in Otterhampton.[14] In 1554 the rector was reported for keeping his horses in the churchyard and for not preaching sermons.[15] Robert Reason, rector from 1618 and also vicar of Cannington, was chaplain to the earl of Rutland in 1629. His curate was accused of neglecting his duties and another man sometimes took services.[16] At least one 18th-century rector was a pluralist, the registers were not kept for 20 years before 1771,[17] and John Trevor, rector 1771–94, was thought to be abroad in 1785.[18] His successor Dr. John Jeffrey, rector 1794–1861, was said to be very rich.[19] He was resident, but also served Stockland and in 1815 only a morning service was held at Otterhampton.[20] In 1827 there were two Sunday services, but by 1840 only one. Communion was then celebrated at least three times a year;[21] by 1870 there were two Sunday services and communion 14 times a year.[22] Charles Anderson, rector 1872–98, was the first chairman of Bridgwater rural district council.[23] After the opening of Combwich church attendances at Otterhampton were reduced and in 1898 there were c. 10 communicants.[24] Only morning services were held there in the 1930s and communion was celebrated monthly.[25] Two Sunday services were occasionally held later but there were usually fewer than 10 communicants.[26]

A church house was recorded in 1755 and 1766 when it was held with the capital messuage, later Otterhampton Farm.[27] It was probably the house which the vestry agreed to demolish in 1841 but which still stood in front of the church in 1845.[28]

The church of St. Peter or St. Peter and St. Paul, so dedicated in the 1530s,[29] but later renamed ALL SAINTS, is built of rubble and comprises a chancel with north vestry, a nave with south porch, and a west tower. The nave is probably of 12th-century origin although no original features survive except perhaps the rear

arch of the south doorway. The south doorway is 14th-century and the tower is early 15th-century. The chancel roof was in need of repair in 1629 and in 1630 was reported to be in such a bad state that it endangered those receiving communion.[30] In 1804 the roofs and north wall of the church were taken down and rebuilt and the tower was repaired. There was a singing gallery in 1816 and new seating was provided in 1827.[31] In 1840 the church was undergoing repair and the chancel was rebuilt using some of the older materials including the 15th-century east window.[32] By 1881 the church was said to be in a very bad state largely through damage from damp, the floor being below the level of the churchyard.[33] In 1894 a major restoration included the insertion of new windows in the north wall to match those in the south, new glass, pulpit, and seats, the raising of the chancel floor, and repairs to the screen.[34] The church contains a 12th-century font with an early 17th-century cover, 14th-century niches either side of the chancel arch, a much repaired late-medieval west door with fragments of tracery, a 16th-century screen,[35] 17th-century communion rails, and the arms of George VI.

There are four bells including one from the medieval Bristol foundry and two, dated 1617 and 1647, by members of the Purdue family. They were rehung in the 1920s.[36] The cup and cover date probably from the late 17th century.[37] The registers begin in 1656 but there are gaps, notably 1751–71.[38]

The chapel of ST. PETER at Combwich, from 1988 the parish church,[39] was built between 1868 and 1870 to a design by C. Knowles for Susan Jeffrey, widow of Dr. John Jeffrey, rector of Otterhampton. She also provided an endowment to pay a curate's stipend.[40] Services were held weekly and communion was celebrated monthly in 1898–9. During the 20th century there were weekly communions but usually fewer than 10 communicants.[41] The church comprises a chancel with polygonal apse and south vestry, a nave with north and south transepts, and a two-storeyed south porch surmounted by an octagonal belfry with spire. The interior includes later 19th-century stained glass and furnishings. There is a peal of five bells. The marriage registers date from 1944.[42]

NONCONFORMITY. There were two recusants in the parish in the 1590s.[43] A meeting

8 Ibid. D/D/Bbm 22.
9 Ibid. tithe award; ibid. D/P/otn 3/4/1; D/R/bw 22/1/23.   10 Dioc. Dir.
11 Cart. St. Mark's Hosp., Bristol (Bristol Rec. Soc. xxi), pp. 141–2.   12 P.R.O., SC 6/968/26.
13 S.R.S. lv, p. 4; B.L. Stowe Ch. 587.
14 Wells Wills, ed. Weaver, 115.
15 S.R.O., D/D/Ca 22.   16 Ibid. 266, 274.
17 Ibid. D/D/B reg. 27, f. 14v.; D/P/otn 2/1/2.
18 Ibid. D/D/Bo.
19 Ibid. D/D/Vc 88; ibid. T/PH/ay 1; M.I. in ch.
20 S.R.O., D/D/Rb 1815.
21 Ibid. D/D/Rb 1827; D/D/Va 1840.
22 Ibid. D/D/Va 1870.   23 Squibbs, Bridgwater, 102.
24 S.R.O., D/P/otn 2/5/1.
25 Ibid. 2/9/2.   26 Ibid. 2/5/1.
27 Ibid. DD/X/MCO; DD/ARN 2.

28 Ibid. D/P/otn 4/1/1; ibid. tithe award; Taunton Castle, Braikenridge colln., drawing by W. W. Wheatley, 1845.
29 S.D.N.Q. iii. 11; xv. 143; Wells Wills, ed. Weaver, 115; S.R.O., DD/X/SR 5.   30 S.R.O., D/D/Ca 266, 274.
31 Ibid. D/P/otn 4/1/1.
32 Ibid. D/D/Va 1840.   33 Ibid. D/P/otn 8/3/1.
34 Ibid. 8/3/2, 13/2/1; Kelly's Dir. Som. (1897).
35 F. B. Bond & B. Camm, Roodscreens and Roodlofts, 182.
36 S.R.O., DD/SAS CH 16; D/P/otn 6/1/1, 8/3/3.
37 Proc. Som. Arch. Soc. xlvii. 168.
38 S.R.O., D/P/otn 2/1/1–5.
39 Bath and Wells Bd. of Finance, Rep. (1988), 30.
40 S.R.O., D/P/comw 3/3/1; D/P/otn 3/6/1; Bridgwater Mercury, 26 Oct. 1870.
41 S.R.O., D/P/comw 2/5/1, 5; D/P/otn 2/9/2.
42 Ibid. D/P/comw 2/1/1.
43 Recusant Roll, ii (Cath. Rec. Soc. lvii), 141; S.D.N.Q. v. 114.

house with Sunday school, possibly at Combwich, was licensed in 1822 for an unspecified congregation. The Bethel Congregational chapel was built in 1838, probably as a Mariners Christian chapel, and licensed in 1848.[44] Services ceased, probably before 1870 when the Wesleyans took Combwich within their circuit.[45] In 1879 the chapel was loaned to the Wesleyans.[46] It was still used by the Methodists in 1989.

EDUCATION. A day school supported by subscriptions taught 20 children in 1819 and the same number, including some from Stockland Bristol, were attending in 1825.[47] There was a nonconformist Sunday school in 1822, probably at Combwich.[48] In 1835 there was no day school but 18 children attended a Sunday school, possibly in the schoolroom recorded in 1832, the number increasing to 27 in 1846.[49] A day school was built

at Combwich in 1857, and in 1880 it was taken over by a school board. In 1903 there were 52 children on the books with two teachers in two rooms.[50] Numbers fluctuated, rose to 58 in 1915 and fell to 44 in 1945. By 1975 there were 68 children on the books and as many were registered in 1981. The school was known as Otterhampton school in 1989.[51]

St. Hilda's school, a private mixed school but intended primarily for girls, moved from Westcliffe-on-Sea (Essex) to Hill House c. 1946 and closed in the early 1970s.[52]

CHARITIES FOR THE POOR. The rector, Dr. John Jeffrey, by will dated 1861 left £200 for the poor and Jane Evered, by deed of 1887, gave £100 for a distribution in cash or kind to six of the deserving poor.[53] The charities have since been combined but were not being distributed in 1989.[54]

SPAXTON

THE ancient parish of Spaxton comprises scattered hamlets and farmsteads on the eastern side of the Quantocks. The main part of the parish included settlements at Spaxton, Four Forks, Merridge, with Lower Merridge and Courtway, Pightley, Radlet, and Tuxwell, and entirely surrounded a detached part of Charlinch called Bush. A detached area to the north, the former manor of Stockland Lovel and later known as North Street, included Coultings and Farm. There was also a smaller area to the south-east, surrounded by Enmore parish, which was the 11th-century holding of Quantock, later Quantock Durborough.[55] The highly irregular boundaries and their relationship with other parishes in the immediate vicinity suggest that Spaxton parish may be the residue of a larger unit, possibly with a minster at its centre,[56] which included Charlinch and perhaps Postridge and part of Nether Stowey.

The main part of the parish measured up to 4 km. from west to east and nearly 6 km. from north to south. North Street was 3 km. from west to east and 1.5 km. from north to south, and Quantock Durborough 1 km. by 0.5 km. In 1839 the total area was reckoned as 3,387 a.[57] In 1878 North Street (11 houses, 51 persons) was transferred to Fiddington, and Quantock Durborough (no population) to Enmore. Two years later detached parts of Nether Stowey at Radlet (4 houses, 18 persons) were added to Spaxton and in 1882 the detached part of Charlinch at

Bush (2 houses, 6 persons) was also added. In 1885 Spaxton acquired Postridge (11 houses, 53 persons) from Aisholt and small areas from Goathurst (1 house, 4 persons) and Nether Stowey. In 1891 the parish measured 3,646 a.[58] In 1933 the civil parish of Aisholt (875 a.) and Currypool and Rowden from Charlinch (740 a.) were added to Spaxton, making a total of 5,261 a.[59] The civil parish of Charlinch was taken into Spaxton in 1981, but the extreme south-west part of Spaxton ancient parish was transferred to Broomfield, making a total of 5,876 a. (2,378 ha.).[60]

West and south-west of Spaxton village and Pightley the land rises up a spur formed between two streams flowing from the Quantocks, one through Holwell Combe where it marks the boundary with Enmore, the other called Peartwater. Hawkridge Hill[61] rises in 2.5 km. over slates and grits to more than 213 m. and then falls abruptly into a valley at Lower Merridge, where a stream divides the parish from Bishop's Lydeard and Aisholt. In the south, where the parish reaches the Quantock ridge, the land rises to over 244 m. near the Travellers Rest inn, further south-west to above 228 m. on Gib Hill, and then up the scarp to the boundary ridge which gave Merridge its name on the 305-m. contour just below the summit of Cothelstone Hill. North of Peartwater is a smaller spur shared with Over Stowey parish, a shallow valley of gravels and marls occupied by Radlet common

44   S.R.O., D/D/Rm, box 2; *Rep. Som. Cong. Union* (1896); below, Bridgwater, nonconf.
45   S.R.O., D/N/bmc 3/2/3.
46   Ibid. 3/2/2, 4/3/37, 4/3/50; *Rep. Som. Cong. Union* (1896).
47   *Educ. of Poor Digest*, p. 792; *Ann. Rep. B. & W. Dioc. Assoc. S.P.C.K.* (1825–6), 42–3.
48   S.R.O., D/D/Rm, box 2.
49   *Educ. Enq. Abstract*, pp. 822–3; Nat. Soc. *Inquiry, 1846–7*, Som. 14–15; S.R.O., D/P/otn 13/2/1.
50   S.R.O., C/E 4/380/312; *Lond. Gaz.* 22 June 1880, 3538.
51   S.R.O., C/E 4/64.

52   *Bridgwater R.D.C. Guide* (1969); Char. Com. reg.; above, manors.
53   Char. Com. reg.; S.R.O., D/P/otn 17/1/1.
54   Inf. from rector.
55   S.R.O., tithe award. This article was completed in 1987.
56   Below, church.
57   S.R.O., tithe award.   58   *Census*, 1891.
59   Youngs, *Local Admin. Units*, i. 414; S.R.O., D/R/bw 16/20/1.
60   *Census*, 1981.
61   The name Merridge Hill is used of the road over it to Merridge.

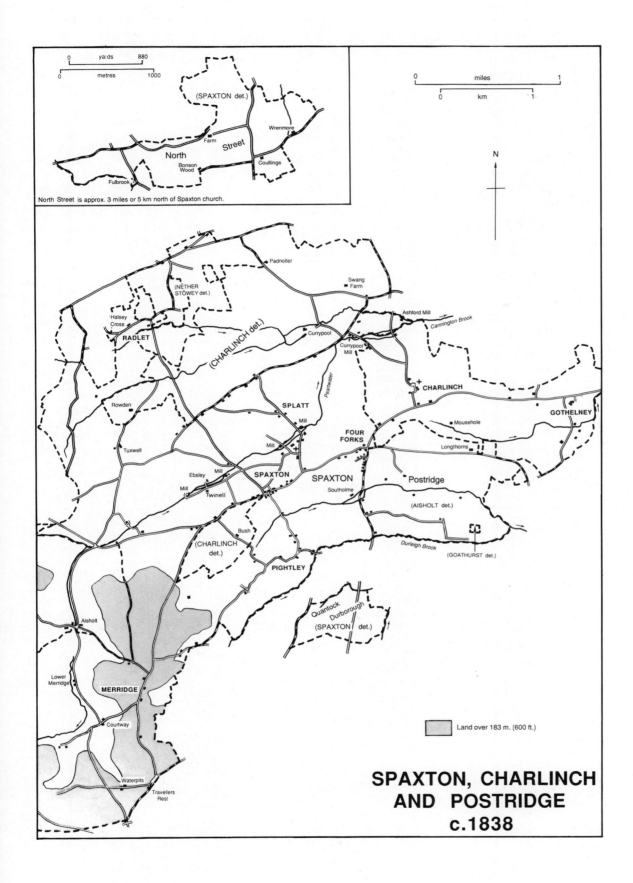

0 yards 880
0 metres 1000

(SPAXTON det.)

Wrenmore

Farm   Street

North

Bonson
Wood   Coultings

Fulbrook

North Street is approx. 3 miles or 5 km north of Spaxton church.

0 miles 1
0 km 1

N

Padnoller

Swang
Farm

(NETHER
STOWEY det.)

Ashford Mill

Halsey
Cross   Currypool   Cannington Brook

RADLET
(CHARLINCH det.)   Currypool
                                       Mill
                                                              CHARLINCH
Rowden   SPLATT
                                                         Mousehole   GOTHELNEY
                          Mill
                                    FOUR
             Tuxwell   Mill   FORKS   Longthorns
                    Mill
        Ebsley   Mill   SPAXTON   SPAXTON
        Mill   Postridge
              Twinell   Southolme
                                                   (AISHOLT det.)
                    Bush
              (CHARLINCH
                det.)   Durleigh Brook
                    PIGHTLEY   (GOATHURST det.)

                              Quantock
                              Durborough
                              (SPAXTON det.)

Aisholt

Lower
Merridge

MERRIDGE

Courtway   Land over 183 m. (600 ft.)

Waterpits

Travellers
Rest

**SPAXTON, CHARLINCH
AND POSTRIDGE
c.1838**

and wood,[62] and then a small ridge of slates and grits. The north-western and eastern part of the parish, below the 91-m. contour, lies largely on marl and valley gravels with a band of sandstone running along the Peartwater through Spaxton village. The North Street area is on marl, Quantock Durborough on slates and grits.[63] Pockets of limestone were worked at Merridge in the 18th and 19th centuries,[64] and licences to mine near Spaxton were granted in 1714.[65] Black Pit, north of Four Forks, may be the result of marl digging.[66] A mine at Merridge is said to have produced iron, copper, malachite, and possibly silver in the 19th century,[67] and sulphur ore was extracted at Merridge.[68]

Flints have been found on the Quantock ridge and bronze torcs and palstaves are said to have been discovered within the parish.[69] Evidence of Iron Age occupation was found at Peartwater near Court Farm. By the later 11th century there were at least seven settlements, of which the most populous was Spaxton, followed by Pightley and Tuxwell.[70] By the 13th century farmsteads or hamlets had been established, possibly by woodland clearance at Ebsley,[71] and at Durland or Durnland[72] and Pleabury,[73] called Claybury Castle in 1838,[74] the last on marginal land near the 122-m. contour. By the later Middle Ages at least four farmsteads were named: Coultings, Wrenmore, Southam,[75] now Holmes Farm, and Clarkes Farm.[76] Halsey and Twinell farms and the hamlet of Splatt were recorded in the 17th century.[77]

Until the 19th century there was no significant nucleated settlement. Spaxton village comprised the church, manor house, rectory, church house, two mills, and some cottages beside the Peartwater, all on a loop running from the Old Way,[78] a road from Cannington which led directly to the Quantock ridgeway. The road from Bridgwater and Durleigh to the Quantocks ran slightly south of the village. There a roadside settlement grew up, known from the 15th century to the 18th as Fursegate,[79] and later as High Street. In the 20th century it formed an almost continuous built-up street for a mile from the 19th-century crossroads settlement of Four Forks.[80] This last hamlet expanded rapidly in the 1840s when the community known as the Agapemone was estab-

lished there.[81] Lower Merridge and Courtway hamlets were roadside settlements on the Taunton to Nether Stowey road, and there was similar development in the 17th century at Keenthorne, Halsey Cross,[82] and Cuckolds Row.[83]

The scattered settlements produced the complex network of roads in the parish. Three parallel routes from Bridgwater and Cannington crossed the parish to the Quantock ridge. The most northerly was the only one to be turnpiked, in 1759.[84]

There was woodland on all the 11th-century estates in the parish[85] with the exception of Pightley. That name suggests pre-Conquest clearance, and field names indicate that clearance continued.[86] In 1380 a tenant on Spaxton manor had to dig up tree roots.[87] Felling was carried out in the later 15th century to the east of Spaxton park and at Stockland Lovel, where timber was sold with faggots and underwood.[88] Coppices at Merridge were cut for charcoal burning in the 1650s[89] and there were over 40 a. of wood there in 1709.[90] Shortly before 1833 acorns were sown on 145 a. for coppice, and 40 a. of oak coppice were sold with the earl of Egmont's Spaxton estate, together with small plantations on many of the tenant farms.[91] In 1838 there were 90 a. of woodland, mainly plantations and coppices, the largest plantations being on Hawkridge Hill and encroaching on Merridge common.[92] Between then and 1887 there was more planting on the lower ground but some woodland at Merridge was cleared.[93] By 1905 only 80 a. of woodland were recorded[94] and some was later cut down both at Hawkridge and Merridge.[95]

A park including woodland belonging to Spaxton manor, probably north of Spaxton village between Peartwater and the Old Way boundary, had been established by the mid 13th century.[96] It had been let by 1440 and was partly ploughed by 1475.[97] By the 17th century the 74-a. park had been entirely converted to agricultural use.[98] John de Columbers was granted free warren at Stockland Lovel in 1304[99] and a park there produced an income of 54s. 4d. in 1484–5.[1] No further trace of it has survived. There was a park at Tuxwell in 1540[2] and a field at Merridge was known as the Park in 1838.[3]

62 The name Radeflode (1308) perhaps signifying a stream: Ekwall, *Eng. Place-Names* (1960), 174.
63 Geol. Surv. Map 1", drift, sheet 295 (1956 edn.).
64 S.R.O., DD/PC 15; ibid. tithe award; O.S. Map 6", Som. LX. NE. (1890 edn.).
65 S.R.O., DD/WG 13/10.
66 O.S. Map 6", Som. XLIX. SE. (1887 edn.).
67 J. Hamilton and J. F. Lawrence, *Men and Mining in the Quantocks* (1970), 72–7.
68 S.R.O., DD/X/BOK (S/2326).
69 Som. C.C., Sites and Mons. Rec.
70 *V.C.H. Som.* i. 485, 494, 512, 523.
71 *S.R.S.* vi. 20; *Cur. Reg. R.* 1201–3, 90, 185.
72 *Cat. Anct. D.* iii, D 1287.
73 *S.R.S.* lxviii. 2.
74 S.R.O., tithe award.
75 Ibid. DD/AH 11/9; P.R.O., SC 6/977/16.
76 Below.
77 S.R.O., D/P/spax 2/1/1, 23/1; ibid. T/PH/dut 1; *Som. Wills*, ed. Brown, v. 68.
78 S.R.O., DD/WG 8/2A, 9/4; DD/PLE 64.
79 Ibid. D/P/spax 23/1; P.R.O., C 140/42, no. 51; E 326/5978.
80 *S.R.S.* lxxvi, map 1782; S.R.O., tithe award; P.R.O.,

HO 107/935.
81 Below, nonconf.
82 S.R.O., DD/WG 8/2A, 9/4, 13/1.
83 O.S. Map 6", Som. XLIX. SE. (1887 edn.).
84 J. B. Bentley and B. J. Murless, *Som. Roads*, i. 25.
85 *V.C.H. Som.* i. 485–7, 494, 512–14, 523.
86 Bonson wood and White wood, Shortalregrove, Ebsley: S.R.O., tithe award; *S.R.S.* lxviii, p. 15.
87 P.R.O., E 210/2493.
88 Ibid. SC 6/1116/2.
89 G. D. Stawell, *A Quantock Family* (1910), 400.
90 S.R.O., D/P/spax 23/1; DD/ES 2.
91 Ibid. DD/PLE 64.   92 Ibid. tithe award.
93 O.S. Map 6", Som. XLIX. SE. (1887 edn.).
94 Statistics supplied by the then Bd. of Agric., 1905.
95 Cf. O.S. Map 1/25,000, ST 23 (1959 edn.).
96 *S.R.S.* lxviii, pp. 3–4.
97 P.R.O., SC 6/977/5, 16.
98 S.R.O., DD/SAS (C/112) 5.
99 *Cal. Chart. R.* 1300–26, 45.
1 P.R.O., SC 6/1116/2.
2 Longleat House, Seymour Papers, XII, rental (1540), f. 9.
3 S.R.O., tithe award.

A gore on the area known as Spaxton Down and small crofts elsewhere may have been remnants of open-field arable.[4] There was common pasture at Radlet and on Merridge Hill. Radlet common remained open until the late 19th century, but by 1919 belonged solely to Radlet farm.[5] Merridge common measured 161 a. in 1720.[6] By 1838 half remained while a further 50 a. were shared between a few proprietors, who let pasture rights.[7] Land at Merridge remained common in 1987.

A water works and pumping station were established near Ashford mill, on the northern boundary of the parish, in 1879 to provide water for Bridgwater. The small Ashford reservoir was opened in 1934.[8]

A friendly society, probably started in 1807, had been dissolved by 1834 for fear of government intervention, but another had been formed by 1845 and existed in 1857.[9] A tradesmen's friendly society was recorded in 1897, together with a working men's club and parish reading room.[10]

There were two licensed tipplers in the parish in 1607.[11] A cottage on the waste mentioned in 1651 may have become the Bell at Keenthorne by 1680,[12] and licences were granted to a man at Radlet in 1674 and to one in Merridge in 1690.[13] The Bell had probably been licensed by 1726[14] and remained in business until 1798. There were two, and occasionally three, licensees in the 18th century. One ran the Crown, also known as the Three Crowns or the Fursegate inn, in High Street, established by 1750 and the sole inn in the early 19th century.[15] It was still open in 1919 but had closed by 1926,[16] and was a private house in 1987. The King William IV inn had opened by 1851[17] but by 1866 was called the Victoria Arms.[18] In 1987 it was known as the Victoria or the Victoria at Spaxton. The Lamb at Four Forks had been opened by 1856[19] and was in business in 1987. There was also a beerhouse at Four Forks in the earlier 1860s and another at Courtway in 1861.[20] The Travellers Rest on the ridge route above Merridge had been opened by 1837, having been recently converted from cottages.[21] It remained open in 1987. The Bell at Courtway, opened by 1841, was closed c. 1962.[22]

Among the houses not attached to substantial estates in the parish are some dating from the 16th century or earlier including Peacock Cottage at Pightley, Jack O'Knights at Lawyer's Hill, Hawkridge, and Tuckers in Splatt Lane, north of the church. Clarkes Farm, east of Pightley, has a late-medieval open hall of two bays with a jettied upper room at the dais end, and a wing added in the 16th century. Several 'Arts and Crafts' style houses were built at Four Forks in the early 20th century by Joseph Morris (d. 1913) and his daughter Violet (d. 1958), both members of the Agapemone.[23]

There were 392 communicants in the parish in 1623.[24] The population increased steadily from 662 in 1801 to a peak of 1,080 in 1851, partly through the growth of Four Forks and the Agapemone. There was a gradual decline in the later 19th century to 797 in 1901 and a further fall to 666 in 1931. The incorporation of Aisholt civil parish with 60 people and of Currypool from Charlinch with 63 in 1933, and later 20th-century housing led to an increase in population to 920 in 1971, but only 831 people were normally resident in 1981.[25]

Ten Spaxton people were implicated in the revolt of 1497[26] and one man in the Monmouth rebellion in 1685.[27]

MANORS AND OTHER ESTATES. In 1086 there were nine separate estates held under four lordships.

Alfred d'Epaignes held all of *SPAXTON* in demesne in 1086 except for 1½ hide occupied by an unnamed knight.[28] In 1166 Robert Fichet held the fee and in 1227 Hugh Fichet.[29] The latter or another Hugh died c. 1261–2 and was succeeded by his son Robert[30] (d. c. 1272) and by his grandson Hugh Fichet,[31] who held the fee c. 1285 and in 1303.[32] By 1314 Hugh had been succeeded by his son (Sir) John,[33] who was followed by his son (Sir) Thomas before 1344.[34] Sir Thomas was dead by 1367[35] and was followed by his son Sir Thomas (d. 1386)[36] and by his grandson also Thomas Fichet.[37] Thomas died under age in 1395 when his heir was his sister Isabel, wife of Robert Hill.[38] Isabel predeceased her husband, who died in 1423 leaving a son John.[39] John Hill (d. 1434)[40] was succeeded by his son John who died in 1455 leaving as his heir his daughter Genevieve, wife of Sir William Say.[41] Genevieve died in 1480,[42] but her husband occupied the estates until his death in 1529.[43]

4 *S.R.S.* lxviii, pp. 13–15.
5 S.R.O., DD/SCL 9.
6 Ibid. D/P/spax 23/1.
7 Ibid. tithe award.
8 Squibbs, *Bridgwater*, 91, 127.
9 *Rep. Com. Poor Law*, H.C. 44, p. 446 (1834), xxviii (2); P.R.O., FS 2/9.
10 *Kelly's Dir. Som.* (1897, 1899).
11 S.R.O., Q/SR 3/107.
12 Ibid. DD/WG 8/2A, 13/1.
13 Ibid. Q/RL; Q/SR 126/4.
14 Ibid. DD/WG 13/9; Q/RL.
15 Ibid. Q/RL.
16 Ibid. DD/SCL 9; D/R/bw 16/16/1.
17 P.R.O., HO 107/1924; *P.O. Dir. Som.* (1861).
18 *P.O. Dir. Som.* (1866).
19 S.R.O., D/P/spax 9/1/1.
20 *P.O. Dir. Som.* (1861, 1866).
21 S.R.O., DD/ES 3.
22 P.R.O., HO 107/935; *Bridgwater Mercury*, 4 Sept. 1984.

23 S.R.O., D/R/bw 22/1/1, 4; *Trans. Anct. Mon. Soc.* xxxiii. 72–9, 92–3.
24 S.R.O., D/P/spax 2/1/1.
25 *Census*.
26 *Fines Imposed in 1497*, ed. A. J. Howard, 8, 13.
27 *S.R.S.* lxxix. 74.
28 *V.C.H. Som.* i. 512.
29 *Red Bk. Exch.* (Rolls Ser.), i. 231; *S.R.S.* vi. 53.
30 *Ex. e Rot. Fin.* (Rec. Com.) ii. 360, 384.
31 *S.R.S.* lxviii, p. xvi.
32 *Feud. Aids*, iv. 281, 308.
33 *S.R.S.* lxviii, p. 20; P.R.O., E 210/2419, 70179.
34 *S.R.S.* xii. 222; lxviii, pp. xvi, 29.
35 Ibid. lxviii, p. 8.   36 P.R.O., C 136/71, no. 5.
37 *Cal. Inq. p.m.* xvi, pp. 401–2.
38 P.R.O., C 136/87, no. 24.
39 *S.R.S.* lxviii, p. xix; P.R.O., C 139/4, no. 31.
40 P.R.O., C 139/71, no. 36.
41 *Cal. Fine R.* 1452–61, 135; *S.R.S.* lxviii, p. xxvii.
42 P.R.O., C 142/19, nos. 68–70.
43 Ibid. E 326/6558; C 142/51, no. 35.

The heirs were then the descendants in the female line of John Hill (d. 1434),[44] half the manor going to John Waldegrave and half being divided between Thomas Hussey, William Clopton, and Ellen, wife of George Babington.[45] John Waldegrave (d. 1543) acquired Ellen's share and his son Sir Edward (d. 1561) obtained the remaining shares.[46]

Sir Edward's son Charles succeeded as a minor and died in 1632.[47] The manor passed in the direct male line to Sir Edward (cr. Bt. 1643, d. 1647), Henry (d. 1658), Charles (d. 1684), Henry (cr. Baron Waldegrave 1686, d. 1689), James (cr. Earl Waldegrave 1729, d. 1741)[48] and James, who sold Spaxton manor to James Smith. After Smith's death the estate was sold in 1756 to John Perceval, earl of Egmont.[49] The earl (d. 1770) was followed by his son John (d. 1822) and John's son John, whose estates with the lordship were sold in 1833.[50] The Spaxton lands were bought by Henry Labouchere and became part of the Quantock estate;[51] no reference to lordship has been found after 1852.[52]

Court Place was recorded in the late 14th century, having gardens inside and outside its gates.[53] Robert Hill appears to have lived at Spaxton and had an oratory there in 1408.[54] In 1423 the house contained a hall, parlour, principal chamber, and second chamber,[55] and a kitchen and pigeon house were recorded in 1476. The house was repaired in 1477 and was let by 1493.[56] By the mid 17th century the capital messuage called Manor House was leased to the Cridland family.[57] A lease of 1662 included a gatehouse and park and the tenant was obliged to entertain the lord and his officers twice a year.[58] The house, with dried-up fishponds, the Court Garden, and demesne lands continued to be leased to the Cridlands and their heirs the Burlands until 1737 when it was known as Spaxton Farm, but as early as 1717 the farm was sub-let.[59] The farm was bought by Somerset county council in 1920.[60]

Court Farm or Court House is formed by two ranges at right angles. Both have pairs of opposed medieval doorways suggesting cross passages but neither retains any other evidence for an open hall. The north–south range has a large room, which may have been a ground-floor hall, and there is a projection, now housing a staircase, from its western side which has a medieval window at first-floor level. The room

to the north also has opposed doorways, both now blocked, and to the north again the room which is at the intersection of the two ranges has a medieval window in its west wall. The east–west range was probably once joined to a building, now a barn, a short distance to the east. Both contain a number of late medieval windows and were originally two-storeyed. The buildings were once more extensive, and it is possible that what remains are ranges of chambers for the estate officials in the later 15th century.[61]

In 1314 John Fichet gave to John Tremenet in fee a farm called *SOUTHAM* or *SOUTH HOLMS*, in Spaxton and Aisholt, which was held of Spaxton manor in the 15th century.[62] John Tremenet's son John had been followed by 1385 by Henry Tremenet or Tremelet.[63] Henry died c. 1424 and his son John was alive in 1476.[64] The land may have passed to William Halswell (d. 1606),[65] but by 1656 had been transferred from another William Halswell to John Cridland and his family, and by 1698 to John Codrington.[66] Codrington sold it to Richard Musgrave and it descended with Stamfordlands in North Petherton.[67] Sir James Langham, Bt., sold it in 1795 to William Ford, owner in 1838.[68] The house, now Holmes Farm, was rebuilt soon after 1711.[69]

MERRIDGE, held in 1066 by Alwig Banneson, was in 1086 held of Alfred d'Epaignes by Ranulph, probably Ranulph of Stringston.[70] The overlordship descended with Nether Stowey, and Merridge was held of that honor until the early 17th century.[71] From Ranulph Merridge probably descended with Stringston to a branch of the Fichet family in the 12th century and later to the Furneaux family. It continued to be held with Stringston and in 1421 was assigned with Perry in Wembdon and Shurton in Stogursey to Robert Greyndour (d. 1443) and his wife Joan.[72] Joan, who married secondly Sir John Barre, died in 1485,[73] but by that date Merridge seems to have passed to the Stawells, coheirs of the Furneaux family.[74] In 1508 Robert Stawell, son of Edward and grandson of Robert (d. 1506), died leaving the manor to his son John, then a minor.[75] John was succeeded in 1541[76] by his grandson (Sir) John. The manor descended with Durston[77] until 1653 when it was sold to Richard Bovet after forfeiture.[78] The Stawell family recovered the manor after the Restoration and it continued to descend with Durston until

44 *S.R.S.* lxviii, p. xxvii; P.R.O., C 142/51, no. 33.
45 P.R.O., C 142/51, no. 35.
46 Ibid. C 142/68, no. 54; C 142/133, no. 130; *V.C.H. Som.* v. 138.
47 P.R.O., C 142/467, no. 173.
48 *V.C.H. Som.* v. 138.
49 *S.R.S.* extra ser. 315–16; S.R.O., DD/PC 19.
50 S.R.O., DD/PLE 64.
51 Ibid. tithe award; below, Over Stowey, manors.
52 Deeds in possession of Mr. Ebsary, Ebsley Fm., Spaxton.
53 *S.R.S.* lxviii, pp. 15–16.
54 Ibid. xiii, p. 79; lxviii, p. xix.
55 Ibid. xvi. 403.
56 P.R.O., SC 6/977/16, 18; SC 6/Hen. VII/551–2.
57 S.R.O., DD/WG 13/5; DD/SAS (C/112) 5.
58 Ibid. DD/WG 13/2; DD/SAS (C/112) 5.
59 Ibid. DD/WG 7/1, 8/2A, 13/9; ibid. Q/RRp 1/30.
60 Ibid. DD/SCL 9; D/R/bw 16/6/1.
61 Cf. P.R.O., SC 6/977/11, 13, 16, 18, 20–3.

62 *S.R.S.* lxviii, p. 14; P.R.O., E 210/2052; ibid. SC 6/977/16.
63 P.R.O., E 210/2419; E 326/5768.
64 *S.R.S.* lxviii, p. 14; P.R.O., SC 2/200/27; SC 6/977/16.
65 S.R.O., DD/WG 16/17; D/P/spax 2/1/1.
66 Ibid. D/P/spax 23/1; DD/DP 34/2; DD/SAS (C/112) 5; *S.R.S.* li, p. 21.
67 S.R.O., DD/DP 33/6; below, N. Petherton, manors.
68 S.R.O., Q/REl 7/6; ibid. T/PH/no 3; ibid. tithe award.
69 Ibid. DD/SAS (C/112) 5.
70 *V.C.H. Som.* i. 513.
71 *S.R.S.* lxvii, p. 60.
72 *S.D.N.Q.* xvi. 284.
73 P.R.O., C 141/5, no. 10.
74 *S.D.N.Q.* xvi. 284.
75 G. D. Stawell, *A Quantock Family*, 336; *Cal. Inq. p.m. Hen. VII*, iii, pp. 161, 324.
76 P.R.O., C 142/66, no. 71.
77 Below, Durston, manors.
78 *Cal. Cttee. for Compounding*, ii. 1430.

the death of John, Lord Stawell, in 1692.[79] In 1702 the trustees for the sale of Stawell's estates conveyed the manor to Francis Bennet, who dismembered it.[80] Bennet left the remnant of the manor, after the death of his wife, to William, Lord Stawell, and his male heirs. William was in possession by 1733[81] and was succeeded in 1742 by his brother Edward, Lord Stawell (d. 1755). Edward left Merridge in trust for his daughter Mary, wife of Henry Bilson Legge and later Baroness Stawell. Mary (d. 1780) was succeeded by her son Henry, Lord Stawell, who in 1789 sold the lordship to William Hawker of Poundisford in Pitminster.[82] In 1790 Hawker agreed to sell it to Sir James Esdaile and others,[83] probably in trust for Edward Jeffries (d. c. 1812), and Edward's grandson, Edward Jeffries Esdaile.[84] E. J. Esdaile died in 1867 leaving a son, also Edward Jeffries Esdaile (d. 1881),[85] whose successor Charles E. J. Esdaile was succeeded c. 1923[86] by his son William. The lands were divided and sold in 1924. Lordship and sporting rights were retained by the Esdaile family but the lordship was not recorded later.[87]

A moated platform at Courtway may be the site of the Fichets' house at Merridge.[88] A house at Waterpits in Merridge was described as a capital messuage in 1783. It had been sold away from the manor in 1702 but was purchased by Edward Jeffries in 1793.[89]

QUANTOCK, later QUANTOCK DURBOROUGH, was held in 1066 by Alwig Banneson and in 1086 by Robert of Alfred d'Epaignes.[90] John Durburgh held it of Spaxton manor in 1328, probably in succession to his father Walter (d. by 1313),[91] and the land descended in the Durburgh family with Stogursey Hadley manor[92] until 1384 or later.[93] By 1412 and probably by 1399 it was held by Sir Thomas Brooke.[94] Sir Thomas died in 1418 and his widow Joan in 1437. Their son Sir Thomas (d. 1439)[95] was succeeded by his son Edward, Lord Cobham (d. 1464). Edward probably settled the manor on his daughter Elizabeth for her marriage to Robert Tanfield. Elizabeth (d. 1502)[96] was followed in turn by her grandson William Tanfield (d. 1529)[97] and by her great-grandson Francis Tanfield (d. 1558). Francis left two young sons, John and Clement, both of whom probably died childless. Clement's widow Anne was in possession in 1588,[98] and there is no

further reference to lordship. The land had become part of the Enmore estate by 1720[99] and some was absorbed into Enmore park.

In 1384 Sir Hugh Durburgh gave rents and reversions to William Taillour of Dunster.[1] The estate came to be called Little Quantock, and by 1476 it had been acquired by William Dodesham.[2] In 1560 it was held by one of his heirs, Joan Coombe, and from her passed to the Halswell family. They held it until 1754[3] when it was sold to John Perceval, earl of Egmont, and was absorbed into the Enmore estate.[4] A small holding at Quantock Durborough formed part of Williton Hadley manor by 1542[5] and descended like that manor in the Wyndham family. Before 1763 Charles Wyndham, earl of Egremont (d. 1763), sold it to the earl of Egmont.[6] There is no record of a manor house at Quantock Durborough.

Estan held an estate called RADLET in 1066, and in 1086 Herbert held it of Alfred d'Epaignes.[7] A small holding described as at Tuxwell could be the same estate. It was held with Alfoxton manor in Stringston in 1310 and was still so held in 1499.[8] It has not been traced further.

PIGHTLEY, later known as PIGHTLEY MALET, was held in 1066 by Aelmer and in 1086 of Roger de Courcelles by Geoffrey de Vautort.[9] It probably descended with Enmore manor until the death of John Malet in 1656,[10] and may then have been divided. One part continued with Enmore manor until 1833[11] but some land had passed to Robert Kidner by 1720[12] and to Andrew Guy before 1766,[13] after which it was probably absorbed into the Barford holding in Enmore.[14]

Godric held an estate called RADLET in 1066 which Robert held of Roger de Courcelles in 1086.[15] It may have been that estate which Margaret de la Tour held in 1308 and in which Hugh of Kilve and William Colne or Kilve had interests later in the 14th century.[16] The de la Tour family in 1346 made over their rights to Henry Halswell and John of Somerton,[17] both of whom already had a life interest in other Halswell family lands there.[18] In 1390 Joan Luttrell acquired an estate at Radlet from John Roche which had formerly been held by Isabel, wife of John Haddecombe.[19] After a series of grants for life Richard Luttrell secured the

79 P.R.O., CP 25(2)/760/13 Chas. II Trin.
80 S.R.O., DD/ES 1, 2; DD/SAS (C/112) 5.
81 Ibid. DD/ES 2.
82 Stawell, Quantock Fam. 125, 128; S.R.O., DD/ES 1–2.
83 S.R.O., DD/ES 2.
84 Ibid. 3.
85 Ibid. 13.
86 Proc. Som. Arch. Soc. lxix, p. xii.
87 S.R.O., DD/ES 3; Devon R.O. 547B/2307.
88 O.S. Nat. Grid ST 203338; Som. C.C., Sites and Mons. Rec.
89 S.R.O., DD/ES 2, 11.
90 V.C.H. Som. i. 513–14.
91 S.R.S. lxviii, p. 12; S.R.O., DD/L P36/4.
92 Below, Stogursey, manors.
93 B.L. Harl. Ch. 49. G. 6.
94 Ibid. Cott. Ch. xxiii. 31; S.R.S. lxviii, p. 13.
95 S.R.S. xxii. 194; extra ser. 301; Cal. Close, 1435–41, 87, 189.
96 S.R.S. xxxiii. 260; extra ser. 302; Cal. Inq. p.m. Hen. VII, ii, p. 495.

97 P.R.O., C 142/50, no. 126.
98 Ibid. C 142/121, no. 131; S.R.O., DD/BR/py 7.
99 S.R.O., D/P/spax 23/1.
1 B.L. Harl. Ch. 49. G. 6.
2 S.R.O., DD/S/WH 65.
3 Ibid. 115.   4 Ibid. 218.
5 L. & P. Hen. VIII, xvii, p. 563.
6 V.C.H. Som. v. 151; S.R.O., DD/S/WH 285.
7 V.C.H. Som. i. 512.
8 S.R.S. xii. 21; xvi. 365–6; xvii. 5; S.D.N.Q. vii. 149–50; below, Stringston, manors.
9 V.C.H. Som. i. 485; S.R.O., DD/BR/bn 10.
10 Above, Enmore, manors.
11 S.R.O., DD/PC 14; DD/PLE 64.
12 Ibid. D/P/spax 23/1.   13 Ibid. Q/REl 7/6B.
14 Ibid. tithe award; above, Enmore, manors.
15 V.C.H. Som. i. 486–7.
16 S.R.O., DD/L P35/1; S.R.S. xvii. 120.
17 S.R.O., DD/L P36/3.
18 S.R.S. xii. 22; S.R.O., DD/L P35/1, P36/3.
19 S.R.S. xvii. 141; S.R.O., DD/L P35/1.

reversion in 1430,[20] and the property descended in the Luttrell family with Over Vexford in Stogumber, together with land held of Stogursey Hadley manor there,[21] until 1551, when it was probably sold to George Sydenham and descended as part of Tuxwell and Radlet.[22]

Two thegns held in 1066 an estate called *STOCKLAND*, probably in Stogursey and Spaxton, which Ansketil held of Roger de Courcelles in 1086 and which probably included the later *STOCKLAND LOVEL* manor.[23] From the 17th century the estate was known as *FARM*. Stockland, part of Nether Stowey honor in 1166,[24] was held of the king in chief between 1285 and 1303[25] and by 1342 was shared between the Trivets' manor of Otterhampton, Stockland Bristol manor, and Stogursey priory.[26] The Crown assumed overlordship after the forfeiture of James Tuchet, Lord Audley, lord of Nether Stowey, in 1497.[27] Thereafter overlordship of the whole estate was no longer mentioned, but some land there was claimed as part of Dunster honor in 1625.[28]

In 1166 William Lovel held the fee.[29] By the mid 13th century it had probably passed to William de Columbers of Stockland (fl. 1254),[30] almost certainly a younger son of Maud de Chandos and Philip de Columbers of Nether Stowey. William (d. by 1262)[31] was succeeded by his son Philip.[32] Philip died probably c. 1279 and William, possibly his son, was dead by 1280.[33] Although Philip had a grandson Hugh de Vautort,[34] Stockland Lovel passed c. 1280 to Philip's cousin John de Columbers, lord of Nether Stowey.[35]

The manor descended with Nether Stowey until the attainder of Edward Seymour, duke of Somerset, in 1552[36] when it was granted to Thomas Dannet.[37] Thomas died in 1569 leaving a son, also Thomas,[38] who in 1584 conveyed the manor to John Walker and his wife Elizabeth.[39] They sold in 1586 to William Syms[40] and Syms in turn to Robert Burgoyne in 1591.[41] Burgoyne is said to have sold the estate, possibly in 1596, to Henry Hensley who died in 1623 leaving a son John.[42] Despite claims by the Bowyer and Walker families,[43] John Hensley leased Stockland Lovel to Robert Everard (d. 1663),[44] whose widow Joan (d. c. 1687) held the estate for life and whose brother Henry (d. c. 1679) appears to have purchased the freehold. The estate, called

Farm, passed to Henry's cousin John Everard (d. 1696).[45] John was succeeded by his son Robert (d. 1726) whose wife, Susanna, was lady of Nether Stowey manor. Farm and the lordship again descended with Nether Stowey until 1832.[46] In that year the manor was sold to Daniel Fripp of Bristol, who in 1861 sold it to the Merchant Venturers of Bristol.[47] There is no further reference to the lordship. In 1919 the Merchant Venturers sold Farm to Isaac Hill who was succeeded in 1930 by his sons Froude and Clifford. Michael, son of Froude, and his wife Lavinia took over the business in 1967 and were owners in 1987.[48]

The capital messuage was named Bockham or Byckhams in the 16th century after tenants,[49] in the 17th and 18th centuries simply as Farm,[50] in the 19th as Stockland Lovel farm,[51] and in the 20th as Farm Estate. It is a late-medieval house of five bays with an open hall and service room occupying four bays and an inner room with a chamber over the eastern bay beyond the hall. In the later 16th century a cross passage was formed, and probably the porch was added on the north side. In the 17th century a rear wing was built north of the east end to provide a parlour and stair. A contemporary extension at the west end comprised a room in line with the original house and a second rear wing, including a large room with three ovens, probably a brew-house, and a dairy with cheese and flour chambers above. By 1696 the chamber over the hall had been decorated with a painted representation of the firmament. The parlour ceiling has 'particularly rich' decorative plasterwork of the 17th century.[52] North of the house are the remains of a formal walled garden.

Two farms, Coultings and Wrenmore, were part of Stockland Lovel manor in the 16th century. Robert Tuxwell held *COULTINGS* in 1507 and John Tuxwell by 1513.[53] John Tuxwell, possibly son of the last, died in 1565 and his son, also John, in 1566. Alice, widow of the first, retained possession until her death in 1608 and was followed by her granddaughter Mary (d. 1641), who was succeeded in turn by her sons Francis (d. by 1666) and Joseph Cox.[54] Joseph sold the farm to William Prowse in 1666, and Mrs. Prowse was in possession in 1720.[55] Thomas Prowse (d. 1767) was followed by his son George and in 1770 by his daughter Mary.[56] The

20 S.R.O., DD/L P35/1, 2, 4.
21 *V.C.H. Som.* v. 182; S.R.O., DD/L P36/4.
22 P.R.O., C 142/106, no. 55; below.
23 *V.C.H. Som.* i. 486; below, Stogursey, manors.
24 *Red Bk. Exch.* (Rolls Ser.), i. 231.
25 *S.R.S.* iii. 48; *Feud. Aids,* iv. 311.
26 *Cal. Inq. p.m.* viii, p. 268; P.R.O., C 137/26, no. 56; C 137/73, no. 47; C 137/84, no. 36.
27 P.R.O., C 142/152, no. 131; S.R.O., DD/SAS (C/96) 18.
28 S.R.O., DD/MVB 2.
29 *Red Bk. Exch.* (Rolls Ser.), i. 231.
30 *S.R.S.* vi. 158.   31 Ibid. lxviii, p. 18.
32 Ibid. xxxvi. 133; lxviii, p. 19.
33 Ibid. xli. 198, 207; xliv. 72, 144.   34 Ibid. xlix, p. 144.
35 Ibid. iii. 48; vi. 249; xliv. 158–9.
36 *V.C.H. Som.* v. 193; *L. & P. Hen. VIII,* v, p. 150.
37 *Cal. Pat.* 1551–3, 298.
38 P.R.O., C 142/152, no. 131.
39 Ibid. CP 25(2)/206/26 & 27 Eliz. I Mich.; S.R.O., DD/SAS (C/96) 18.
40 Ibid. CP 25(2)/206/28 Eliz. I Hil.

41 Ibid. CP 25(2)/206/33 & 34 Eliz. I Mich.
42 Ibid. WARD 7/69, no. 222, where the date is given in error as 1586.
43 e.g. P.R.O., C 3/107, no. 24; C 142/257, no. 57; ibid. CP 25(2)/592/1653 Hil.
44 S.R.O., DD/X/SR 5.
45 Farm Estate, Fiddington, deeds of Mr. and Mrs. M. Hill, marked as box 14, bundle A, nos. 1–2.
46 *V.C.H. Som.* v. 194.
47 Farm Estate, deeds, box 17, bundle B, no. 21; bundle C, nos. 2–15.
48 Inf. from Mr. Hill, Farm Estate, Fiddington.
49 S.R.O., DD/SAS (C/96) 18; DD/AH 11/9–10.
50 Farm Estate, deeds, box 17, bundle A, nos. 1–2, 4.
51 Ibid. bundle B, nos. 14–15.
52 *Proc. Som. Arch. Soc.* cxxix. 132–6.
53 S.R.O., DD/AH 11/9.
54 Ibid. D/P/spax 2/1/1; DD/VN; *Som. Wills,* ed. Brown, v. 68; *S.R.S.* lxvii, pp. 101–2.
55 S.R.O., D/P/spax 23/1.
56 Ibid. Q/REl 7/6A; DD/S/WH 111.

farm thereafter passed through several hands until part was acquired in 1865 by the Merchant Venturers of Bristol.[57]

Coultings Farm, where a small farmhouse survives, was described as a capital messuage in 1666 and 1794.[58] One of the barns may be of the 16th century.

WRENMORE belonged to Thomas Courtenay, earl of Devon, at the time of his death in 1461, and it seems to have passed to his brother Henry. Henry was attainted and executed in 1467 and the land, which passed to the Crown, was granted in 1470 to John Lambard.[59] Edward Courtenay, a distant relative of the last earl, was restored to the family estates and title in 1485 and was holding Wrenmore at the time of his death in 1509.[60] His grandson Henry, earl of Devon (cr. marquess of Exeter 1525), was attainted in 1538 and executed in 1539. His estates reverted to the Crown, and Wrenmore seems to have passed to Sir Thomas Moyle of Eastwell (Kent), a prominent government official.[61] He was succeeded at Wrenmore by his daughter Katharine, wife of Sir Thomas Finch, also of Eastwell.[62] In 1561 Finch sold it to John Kaynes of Compton Pauncefoot,[63] who in turn sold it to John Kene of Spaxton in 1566. Kene died in 1580 and his son, another John, sold it in the following year to John Bowyer, who already held other interests in the manor, including Bonson Wood farm.[64]

John Bowyer was succeeded in 1599 by his son Edmund.[65] The holding descended with the manor of Moorland in North Petherton[66] in the Bowyer family until 1707, when it was transferred to Edward Colston, who leased it back to Edmund Bowyer in 1709.[67] In 1723 Colston's executors recovered the estate following legal proceedings,[68] and it was thereafter considered part of the holding of the Merchant Venturers of Bristol.[69]

Beorhtric's holding at TUXWELL in 1086 had been held in 1066 by Godwin.[70] Its descent has not been traced between the 11th century and the 14th, but in 1372 some land there and at Moorland was held by Sir Thomas Fichet of the duchy of Lancaster, presumably as part of Trowbridge honor.[71] Robert Hill held it at his death in ·1423 as of the duchy manor of Durleigh.[72]

A second estate at TUXWELL, later known as EAST TUXWELL,[73] was held in 1066 by Estan, who also held land at Radlet, and in 1086 by Hugh of Roger Arundel.[74] The overlordship descended with that of Huish Champflower to Henry de Newburgh, and in 1276 passed to Queen Eleanor,[75] although Robert de Newburgh disputed the Crown's claim in 1326.[76] The overlordship has not been traced thereafter. The estate may have been held with Huish Champflower by the Champflower family as mesne lords, and from them passed to the FitzJames family: in 1361 it was held of John FitzJames as of his manor of Wyke Champflower.[77] The FitzJameses retained an interest in the estate until 1552 or later.[78]

Before 1291 John FitzGeoffrey was succeeded as terre tenant by his son William.[79] William's successor was probably Gilbert or Gibon of Edington.[80] Gilbert's son, also Gilbert, died in 1361 when his heir was his brother Thomas.[81] Family disputes followed,[82] and ownership of Tuxwell has not been traced until 1461 when Tuxwell manor was held by Alexander Hody,[83] possibly in right of his wife Margaret, daughter and heir of John Coker, whose ancestor Richard Coker had held land in the parish in 1328.[84] The estate passed, with Moorland manor in North Petherton, to Sir John Seymour, and from him to his son Edward, duke of Somerset.[85] On the duke's attainder and execution in 1552 his son John claimed the manor as the inheritance of his mother, the duke's first wife.[86] The subsequent dispute may have caused the estate to be divided, parts being added later to Tuxwell cum Radlet.

PLEABURY was held of East Tuxwell in 1540.[87] It was sold in 1558 by William Hody to Nicholas Halswell, the owner in 1587.[88] Pleabury was held by Thomas Trott in 1618 and the adjoining estate of Twinell by Thomas Collard (d. 1654).[89] By 1658 both estates were held by Thomas Collard's son John,[90] who was succeeded in 1679 by his son the Revd. Thomas Collard (d. 1691).[91] In 1720 Pleabury was held jointly by Thomas Graunt, husband of Thomas Collard's eldest daughter Alice, and Francis Wilkins who married her sister Elizabeth, but Twinell was held by a Mr. Collard, probably their cousin John.[92] Alice (d. 1752) had inherited both estates by 1750 and left Twinell and other lands to her grandson Thomas Graunt and Pleabury to her son Thomas (d. 1753).[93] Thomas the younger was holding both estates in 1766 and died in 1780,[94] probably childless, and was

57   Ibid. Q/REl 7/6A; ibid. tithe award; P. V. McGrath, *The Merchant Venturers of Bristol* (1975), 355.
58   S.R.O., DD/VN; DD/MLY 13.
59   *Cal. Pat.* 1467–77, 187; J. L. Vivian, *Visit. Devon*, 245.
60   S.R.O., DD/AH 11/9.
61   e.g. *L. & P. Hen. VIII*, xx, *passim*.
62   *Visit. Kent 1619–21* (Harl. Soc. xlii), 68; *Visit. Kent 1574, 1592* (Harl. Soc. lxxv), 13.
63   S.R.O., DD/SF 1026.
64   Ibid. DD/MVB 3.
65   P.R.O., C 142/257, no. 57.
66   Below, N. Petherton, manors.
67   S.R.O., DD/MVB 1.
68   Ibid. 14.
69   Ibid. 29.
70   *V.C.H. Som.* i. 523.
71   *S.R.S.* lxviii, pp. 11, 16.
72   *Cal. Close*, 1422–9, 100; P.R.O., C 139/4, no. 31.
73   *Cal. Inq. p.m.* xi, p. 202.
74   *V.C.H. Som.* i. 494.

75   Ibid. v. 83.
76   *Cal. Mem. R.* 1326–7, p. 108.
77   *Cal. Inq. p.m.* xi, p. 202.   78   *S.R.S.* li, p. 46.
79   *Cal. Close*, 1288–96, 204.
80   *S.R.S.* iii. 119; lxviii, p. 49.
81   *Cal. Close*, 1360–4, 365; *Cal. Inq. p.m.* xi, p. 417.
82   *S.R.S.* lxviii, p. 49.
83   P.R.O., C 140/4, no. 34.
84   *S.R.S.* xii. 134.
85   Below, N. Petherton, manors.
86   *Cal. Pat.* 1551–3, 278–9.
87   Longleat House, Seymour Papers, XII, rental (1540), f. 10.   88   S.R.O., DD/S/WH 3, 91.
89   Ibid. D/P/spax 23/1; ibid. T/PH/dut 1.
90   Ibid. D/P/spax 23/1.
91   Ibid. 2/1/2; 23/1; D/P/wyco 2/1/1; ibid. T/PH/dut 1.
92   Ibid. D/P/spax 23/1; D/P/wyco 2/1/1; D/P/mis 2/1/1; D/P/du 2/1/3.
93   Ibid. DD/DP 34/3; D/P/spax 2/1/3.
94   Ibid. D/P/spax 2/1/3.

succeeded by Thomas Poole,[95] son of Alice Graunt's daughter Mary.[96] Thomas (d. 1795) was succeeded by his son Thomas (d. 1837),[97] whose trustees held Pleabury and Twinell in 1838.[98] It was later absorbed into the Quantock estate.[99]

A third estate at Tuxwell, later known as *WEST TUXWELL* manor, was held by Thomas Trowe in 1431[1] and until 1506 descended with Plainsfield manor in Over Stowey.[2] In 1506 it was absorbed into Plainsfield manor, and formed part of the land sold to John Perceval, earl of Egmont, in 1761. The sale included part of *TUXWELL CUM RADLET* manor,[3] which included much of East Tuxwell, and passed to George Sydenham from the Seymour family. George conveyed it to Humphrey Blake in 1556 as a holding of the Crown.[4] Humphrey died in 1558, leaving the estate to his son Robert, but it appears to have passed to another son, John (d. 1571), and to John's brother Thomas.[5] In 1572 the manor was settled on Thomas, who sold it to his brother Robert in 1577.[6] Robert Blake died in 1592 and his son William sold the manor in 1602 to John Malet of Enmore.[7] The manor descended like Enmore until 1833 when Tuxwell and Radlet farms were bought by Henry Labouchere to form part of his Quantock estate.[8] There is no further reference to the lordship; and after the break-up of the Quantock estate in 1919 Tuxwell was bought by Somerset county council and Radlet by Alfred Gooding.[9]

In 1412 an estate called *EBSLEY* was held by Matthew Coker, and it probably passed to Margaret Coker, wife of Alexander Hody.[10] It descended like East Tuxwell manor, and following the division of the duke of Somerset's estate it had come into the hands of Barnabas Leave by 1602. He also held part of Pleabury, which had also formed part of the Seymour manor of East Tuxwell.[11] Barnabas was succeeded in 1615 by his son John (d. 1635). John's son John was holding Ebsley in 1658, and a Mrs. Leave was the owner in 1687. By 1720 it was held by John Thomas,[12] in 1766 by William Rich, and in 1781 by James Rich.[13] James died in 1815 leaving the farm in trust for Mary and Elizabeth, daughters of his cousin John Rich.[14] Elizabeth, who survived her sister, died in 1846 leaving her land in trust for William Rich of Ebsley.[15] It was later part of the Quantock estate and in 1920 Somerset county council sold the farm to the tenant.[16]

Ebsley Farm, made smaller and remodelled in the 20th century, is a 17th-century house

formerly extending further south. There is an 18th-century staircase in the square projection at the rear.

An estate called *KEENTHORNE* was given before 1498 to maintain a lamp in Cannington church.[17] It was granted by the Crown in 1550 to Edward Isaake and William Moryce who in the same year sold it to Nicholas Halswell.[18] It appears to have been held of the duke of Somerset's manor of Tuxwell.[19] The land descended with Halswell in Goathurst until 1622 when it was sold to Margaret Dodington and descended with her estates in Stogursey until 1638 or later.[20]

ECONOMIC HISTORY. AGRICULTURE. In 1086 the nine estates in the parish, of which Stockland may have extended into Stogursey and two at Radlet may have been partly in Over or Nether Stowey, comprised a total of 23 ploughlands, 128 a. of pasture, and 70 a. of meadow. Among the stock recorded were 124 sheep, 46 goats, and 16 pigs. Most of the estates were evenly divided between demesne and tenanted land. Two holdings, parts of Radlet and Tuxwell, had declined in value since 1066, but Stockland had more than doubled. The largest holdings were Spaxton and Pightley; Tuxwell had the greatest area of pasture and woodland.[21]

The Halswell family, tenants at Radlet by 1311, held 87 a. of arable, 5 a. of meadow, 10 a. of pasture, and 8 a. of moor,[22] but smaller holdings were more typical, 40 a. on Spaxton manor[23] and 40 a. and 30 a. at Tuxwell in 1464.[24] By 1412 Spaxton manor comprised 29 separate tenant holdings at rents varying between 1d. and 26s. 8d., including two of 40 a., the whole rental amounting to £13 15s. About 1390, when the lord was a minor, the demesnes of Spaxton manor had been divided between 12 tenants and were let for a total of £7 11s. 5d. Serfdom and labour services had disappeared from Spaxton manor by the early 15th century.[25] By 1440 the whole estate was let to farm, and surviving accounts from the 1440s and the 1470s indicate a consistent income of just under £40, although the total included rent from land outside the parish. The estate during that period was evidently administered in differing ways: in 1439–40 income was listed from arable, meadow, pasture, cottages, and mills; in 1447–8 it was arranged by place, the largest amounts coming from the established tenant holdings in Spaxton and East Postridge

95 S.R.O., Q/REl 7/1, 6c.
96 Ibid. DD/DP 34/3.
97 *V.C.H. Som.* v. 195.
98 S.R.O., tithe award.
99 Ibid. DD/SCL 9.
1 *Feud. Aids*, iv. 436; P.R.O., C 142/23, no. 5.
2 Below, Over Stowey, manors; S.R.O., DD/SE 27.
3 S.R.O., DD/NN (H/20); below, Over Stowey, manors.
4 P.R.O., CP 25(2)/77/659/3 & 4 Phil. & Mary Mich.; C 142/119, no. 163.
5 *Som. Wills*, ed. Brown, i. 59; S.R.O., D/P/o. sty 2/1/1.
6 *Cal. Pat.* 1575–8, pp. 266, 270.
7 P.R.O., C 142/236, no. 56; ibid. CP 25(2)/207/44 Eliz. I Hil.
8 Above, Enmore, manors; S.R.O., DD/PLE 64.
9 S.R.O., DD/SCL 9; D/R/bw 16/16/1.
10 *Feud. Aids*, vi. 513; P.R.O., C 140/4, no. 34; *S.R.S.*

xxii. 127–9, 145–6.
11 P.R.O., C 142/413, no. 44; Longleat House, Seymour Papers, XII, rental (1540), f. 10.
12 P.R.O., C 142/258, no. 13; S.R.O., D/P/spax 23/1.
13 S.R.O., Q/REl 7/1.   14 Ibid. DD/CH 52.
15 Ibid. DD/ED 219/856.
16 Ibid. DD/SCL 9; D/R/bw 16/16/1; inf. from Mr. Ebsary, Ebsley Farm.
17 S.R.O., DD/S/WH 15.
18 *Cal. Pat.* 1549–51, 274; S.R.O., DD/S/WH 15.
19 *S.R.S.* lxxvii, p. 70.
20 S.R.O., DD/S/WH 8; DD/AH 11/3; below, Stogursey, manors.
21 *V.C.H. Som.* i. 485–7, 494, 512–14, 523.
22 *S.R.S.* xii. 22; S.R.O., DD/L P35/1, P36/3.
23 *S.R.S.* lxviii, p. 14; P.R.O., E 210/4513, 5778, 9363.
24 *S.R.S.* xxii. 127–9.
25 Ibid. lxviii, pp. 13–16.

while the demesne rents were recorded in detail.[26]

The income from Stockland Lovel manor in 1484–5 was largely from fixed rents, the only variables being the agistment of the park, sales of wood, and perquisites of courts.[27] Lands called waterleats, recorded from the 13th century,[28] had in places been converted to arable by 1540.[29] In the meadows of Spaxton manor in the early 15th century some tenants were allowed 18d. rent for securing the haycocks after gleaning.[30]

The six principal farms on Tuxwell manor in 1540 ranged in size between 18 a. and 80 a., the two largest including tracts of downland pasture. The other farms were predominantly arable, with parcels scattered in crofts in former open fields.[31] Pressure on traditional arable land presumably resulted in the tillage of parcels on Merridge Hill in the early 17th century to grow rye.[32]

Spaxton farmers seem to have prospered during the 17th century and the early 18th, and inventories suggest well furnished houses. Silver spoons appear in several,[33] a dulcimer in one.[34] Dairies were common,[35] and one farmer left cheese worth £4 10s.[36] In 1639 a wealthy man, John Fisher the younger, had livestock worth over £200 including nearly 100 sheep, and was owed money for milk.[37] Wheat, barley, and oats were regularly sown, with smaller quantities of peas, clover, and onions.[38] Thomas Reason (d. 1716) possessed 10 plough oxen, 115 sheep and lambs, and grain worth £111, and he seems to have made malt, cheese, and cider.[39] Robert Curry (d. 1738) had recently altered his house and had created a new first-floor parlour furnished with a dozen chairs.[40]

In 1720 there were said to be 3,279 a. of arable, 605 a. of meadow and pasture, 49 a. of orchard, and 40 a. of wood,[41] but the total acreage exceeded that of the parish. By 1838 arable measured 1,800 a., meadow and pasture 1,336 a., and orchards 70 a.,[42] a change perhaps in part due to restrictions on ploughing in leases from the 1730s.[43] By the early 19th century over two thirds of the parish belonged to the earl of Egmont. Wages were said to be low, averaging £15–£18 a year, and many labourers were on piece work. Women and children found occasional work but most families barely subsisted, although several owned their own cottages. Wages for living-in labourers were also said to be inadequate.[44]

In 1838 there were 38 holdings of over 25 a., of which only six were over 100 a. The largest were Tuxwell farm with 330 a., Farm with 258 a., and Spaxton farm with 242 a. By then Henry Labouchere owned c. 1,200 a.[45] The number of large farms remained fairly constant during the 19th century, but the number of labourers dropped from 66 in 1861 to 38 in 1871.[46] The tenant at Wrenmore was said in 1847 to have introduced 'implemental husbandry', and in 1871 new machinery for chaff cutting, threshing, pulping roots, and grinding for animal feed was introduced at Farm.[47] By 1905 the amount of arable land had contracted to 1,470 a. and permanent grassland covered 1,735 a.[48] There was little change in the size of farms after the mid 19th century. In 1982 dairy farming was predominant, followed by cattle and sheep rearing; wheat and barley were the main arable crops, and a wide range of vegetables was grown.[49]

INDUSTRY. By the 16th century Spaxton was a centre of cloth working, especially dyeing and finishing, as illustrated by a contemporary bench end in the church. The plentiful supply of water powered fulling mills[50] and served the dyeing process. Imports of madder and woad were made through Bridgwater in the later 16th and the earlier 17th century,[51] and there was a dyehouse on Spaxton manor in 1721.[52] Among the clothiers were the 17th-century Collard family, from Taunton, and a man who was presented for stretching cloth in 1631.[53] Cards, spinning wheels, and looms occur in inventories, and one man had five pairs of fullers' shears. Cloth working seems to have declined after the 17th century.[54]

The Trutch family were blacksmiths, probably at Fursegate,[55] from the 16th until the 18th century. John Trutch imported large quantities of iron through Bridgwater in the late 16th and the early 17th century, including 2 tons in 1603.[56] David Trutch had a smithy with two anvils in 1645 and Richard Trutch (d. 1741) had 1,371 lb. of iron, shoeing tools, and horse shoes besides anvils, bellows, vices, tongs, and hammers.[57] An edgetool forge was set up near Ebsley by the Lillycrap family, possibly on the site of a former fulling mill, using a water wheel to power the bellows and grindstone. The area may earlier have been used for smelting iron.[58] The forge was in business between 1841 and 1861,[59] but the family

26 P.R.O., SC 6/977/5, 8, 11, 13, 16, 18, 20, 22–3; SC 6/1119/17; SC 6/Hen. VII/549–50.
27 Ibid. SC 6/1116/2.
28 Cat. Anct. D. iii, D 1287; P.R.O., E 210/8116.
29 Longleat House, Seymour Papers, XII, rental (1540), ff. 8–10.
30 S.R.S. lxviii, p. 16.
31 Longleat House, Seymour Papers, XII, rental (1540), ff. 8–10.
32 P.R.O., WARD 2/18/70/11.
33 S.R.O., DD/SP inventories, 1635, 1641, 1690.
34 Ibid. 1690.
35 Ibid. 1690, 1695.
36 Ibid. 1639.
37 Ibid. 1640, inventory made in 1639.
38 Ibid. 1670, 1678, 1691, 1695.
39 Ibid. 1716.
40 Ibid. 1738.
41 Ibid. D/P/spax 23/1.

42 Ibid. tithe award.   43 Ibid. DD/WG 13/9.
44 Rep. Com. on Poor Law, H.C. 44, p. 405 (1834) xxx–xxxiii.
45 S.R.O., tithe award.
46 P.R.O., HO 107/1924; ibid. RG 9/1621; RG 10/2379.
47 McGrath, Merchant Venturers, 354.
48 Statistics supplied by the then Bd. of Agric., 1905.
49 Min. of Agric., Fisheries, and Food, agric. returns, 1982.
50 Below, this section (mills).
51 e.g. S.R.O., D/B/bw 1480, 1493, 1506–7.
52 Ibid. DD/WG 2.
53 S.R.S. xxiv. 164; Cal. Cttee. for Money, ii, pp. 826–7; Som. Wills, ed. Brown, v. 4; S.R.O., D/D/Cd 81.
54 S.R.O., DD/SP inventories, 1667–8, 1681.
55 Ibid. D/P/spax 23/1.   56 Ibid. D/B/bw 1480.
57 Ibid. DD/SP inventories, 1645, 1741.
58 Som. C.C., Sites and Mons. Rec.
59 P.R.O., HO 107/935; ibid. RG 9/1621.

appears to have turned to baking[60] and the forge and mill had gone by 1919.[61]

Leather was produced at a large tannery at South Holmes. In 1832 it was described as new and well managed. Bark was plentiful in the area and the yard could tan 30 hides a week.[62] The tanyard appears to have occupied land opposite the farmstead, in Aisholt parish.[63] In 1851 the tanner employed 22 men but some of them may have worked on the farm.[64] In 1861 he was also dealing in timber and had 25 employees.[65] The tannery was probably in use in 1872 but had closed by 1881 although the timber business continued[66] and the yard survived.[67] Other tradesmen recorded in the parish included a fellmonger in 1841[68] and two millwrights in 1861.[69] There was a sawmill near Four Forks in 1887[70] and another at Keenthorne near Radlet in 1927.[71] In 1987 a small firm called Thursday Cottage made preserves.

MILLS. Mills were recorded in 1086 at Radlet and Merridge. The former may have been either in Spaxton or in Nether Stowey.[72] There was a mill at Radlet in 1311[73] and two fulling mills there in the 17th and 18th centuries, one in Nether Stowey and one in Spaxton.[74] The mill at Merridge was mentioned in 1201[75] and 1225[76] and may be Cornwell's mill, held by Charles Barrell in 1720.[77] John Williams held two mill houses at Merridge in 1787[78] but the mill may have gone out of use by 1816[79] and none survived by 1838. There was a Mill close at Lower Merridge.[80]

Ashford mill, also called Ford, Doe's, and Street's,[81] on the boundary with Cannington, was recorded in the 13th century, was rebuilt c. 1359,[82] and descended with Spaxton manor.[83] It was a fulling mill from 1650 or earlier[84] until 1696 but by 1702 had become a grist mill[85] and continued in use until c. 1875.[86] It had an overshot wheel, but only the wheel pit and the mill building remained in 1976.[87]

Pightley mill, referred to in 1328,[88] stood probably on Durleigh brook. Its later history is unknown.

Splatt mill, also called Legge's, east of Court Farm, may have been the Spaxton manor mill recorded in 1329.[89] It was let in the 15th century, when it was known as Spaxton mill, and was repaired in 1477.[90] Ownership descended with Spaxton manor and the mill used an overshot wheel and had a bakery in the 19th century.[91] In the early 20th century the mill ground 300 sacks of wheat and barley each week including Russian, Persian, and American grain. Six horses were kept for transport to and from Bridgwater railway station twice a day. During the First World War stone from Cannington quarry was ground at the mill. In the 1950s the mill was grinding barley, oats, and beans for cattle feed.[92] In 1985 the building was converted for residential use. The mill dates from the 18th century with 19th-century additions and machinery. The mill house dates from the 16th or 17th century but was altered in the 18th.

Crockers mill, later known as Spaxton[93] or Twinell mill,[94] lay west of Spaxton village near Ebsley. It was held with Tuxwell manor in the 15th century[95] and was known as Hoby's mill in the early 16th.[96] It remained in use until 1899[97] or later and retained equipment, including an iron overshot wheel and a set of stones, in 1919.[98] It was last recorded as a mill in 1937,[99] and was later gutted and used as a barn. Another mill called Spaxton mill was mentioned in 1851 and 1861[1] but its site is unknown.

A manor mill at Stockland Lovel in 1521, when its roof was defective,[2] has not been found recorded later.

Jebb's mill, also called Erle's,[3] lay north-west of the church and was mentioned in 1687.[4] It belonged to Spaxton manor. It had a malthouse by 1833,[5] and probably remained in use until 1851[6] but was demolished before 1887.[7] The house and former malthouse remained in 1987.

Currypool mill, also known as Poke's,[8] may have existed by 1579.[9] It also belonged to Spaxton manor and remained in use until 1939[10] or later. A turbine was installed in 1934 and was used to power a saw bench in 1976.[11] In 1987 the mill house survived but the site had been landscaped for a caravan park.

Cowd's mill, also called Clyve mill, was part

60 P.O. Dir. Som. (1866).
61 S.R.O., DD/SCL 9.
62 Taunton Courier, 28 Mar. 1832.
63 S.R.O., tithe award, Aisholt.
64 P.R.O., HO 107/1924.
65 Ibid. RG 9/1621.
66 Morris & Co. Dir. Som. (1872); P.R.O., RG 11/2367, 2369.
67 O.S. Map 6", Som. XLIX. SE. (1887 edn.).
68 P.R.O., HO 107/935.
69 Ibid. RG 9/1621.
70 O.S. Map 6", Som. XLIX. SE. (1887 edn.).
71 Kelly's Dir. Som. (1927).
72 V.C.H. Som. i. 486, 513.
73 S.R.S. xii. 22.
74 Below, this section.
75 S.R.S. vi. 18.
76 Cur. Reg. R. xii. 71.
77 S.R.O., D/P/spax 23/1.
78 Ibid. Q/REl 2/9A.
79 Ibid. D/P/spax 14/2/1.
80 Ibid. tithe award.
81 Ibid. DD/WG 13/7, 16/3; DD/PLE 64.
82 P.R.O., E 210/2880, 7019, 7787.
83 S.R.O., DD/WG 16/3.
84 Ibid. 13/1.

85 Ibid. 8/2A, 9/4.   86 P.O. Dir. Som. (1875).
87 Som. C.C., Sites and Mons. Rec.
88 S.R.O., DD/L P36/3.
89 S.R.S. lxviii, p. 12.
90 P.R.O., SC 6/977/13, 16, 18.
91 Ibid. HO 107/1924; P.O. Dir. Som. (1866, 1875).
92 B. Lawrence, Quantock Country (1952), 147–8.
93 Kelly's Dir. Som. (1894, 1899).
94 S.R.O., DD/SCL 9.
95 P.R.O., C 140/4, no. 34; S.R.S. xxii. 127–9, 145–6.
96 Longleat House, Seymour Papers, XII, rental (1540), f. 9.
97 Kelly's Dir. Som. (1899).
98 S.R.O., DD/SCL 9.
99 Bridgwater & Dist. Dir. (1937–40).
1 P.R.O., HO 107/1924; ibid. RG 9/1621.
2 S.R.O., DD/AH 11/10.
3 Ibid. D/P/spax 23/1.
4 Ibid. DD/WG 13/5.
5 Ibid. DD/PLE 64.
6 Ibid. tithe award; P.R.O., HO 107/1924.
7 O.S. Map 6", Som. XLIX. SE. (1887 edn.).
8 S.R.O., DD/PLE 64.
9 Ibid. DD/WG 16/8.
10 Kelly's Dir. Som. (1939).
11 Som. C.C., Sites and Mons. Rec.

of the manor of Tuxwell cum Radlet in 1633.[12] It was held by the Jones family[13] and in 1818 was put up for sale with house and bakehouse.[14] The mill probably went out of use then, and in 1833 the house and land formed part of the earl of Egmont's estate in the parish.[15] The mill was probably standing in 1838[16] but had been demolished by 1887.[17] The site is beneath Hawkridge reservoir, largely in Aisholt.

There was a fulling mill with racks on Spaxton manor in the 13th century.[18] In 1355 the site of a fulling mill with watercourse and racks was let to two men who were to rebuild the mill.[19] This may be the mill recorded in 1412 and repaired in 1481.[20] At Pleabury in Tuxwell manor there were three fulling mills in 1461 and 1540.[21] One, in need of repair in 1540–1, was sold in 1558 by William Hody to Nicholas Halswell[22] and another was acquired by Robert Blake in 1577.[23] Robert's son William sold two fulling mills to Barnabas Leave in 1597.[24] Barnabas, whose family had been tenants of one mill in 1540,[25] died in 1615 leaving a son John.[26] John (d. 1635) was succeeded by his son John[27] who held an estate in the area in 1658.[28] The Pleabury fulling mills were not recorded thereafter but one was probably the site of the edgetool manufactory.[29] A fulling mill at Radlet formed part of the estate purchased by Thomas Collard from Charles Steyning and was sold by Thomas's grandson John Collard to the trustees of Cannington almshouse.[30] In 1694 it was described as a decayed clothing mill[31] and was probably demolished. It stood probably on the stream south of Halsey Cross Farm where Mill meadow lay in 1838.[32]

Buttles mill mentioned in 1725[33] and Blunts mill recorded in 1766 [34] cannot be identified but may be alternative names for other Spaxton mills.

LOCAL GOVERNMENT. Until the 16th century or later part of the parish was in Merridge tithing in Andersfield hundred and part in Spaxton tithing in Cannington hundred.[35] During the 17th and 18th centuries it was divided into 10 divisions or tithings for administrative purposes: Ebsley, Fursegate, Merridge, North Street, Padnoller, Pightley, Radlet, Spaxton,

Splatt, and Tuxwell.[36] For the land tax there were 7 tithings: Merridge, North Street, Pightley, Lower Plainsfield, comprising Radlet and Padnoller, Spaxton, including Splatt and possibly Fursegate, Tuxwell, and the Spaxton division of Aisholt tithing which included Ebsley.[37] The tithingman of Spaxton paid 'burghright' and other taxes for Pightley Malet at Cannington hundred court in 1521.[38] In 1650 the Spaxton tithingman complained that his expenses in repairing stocks and conveying prisoners had not been paid.[39]

Extracts from court rolls for Spaxton manor survive from between 1328 and 1403,[40] and rolls for 1423–5, 1427, 1459,[41] 1531,[42] 1579, 1587–8, 1592, 1594, and 1599–1605.[43] Courts were still held in the later 17th century when the tenant of the capital messuage had to entertain the lord and his officers twice a year.[44] The 1425 court roll contained a separate entry for Fursegate. There was a hayward in 1425 and in 1427 a neif was reported living away from the manor.[45]

Court rolls for Stockland Lovel survive for the years 1507–23 and courts were held once, and sometimes twice, a year.[46] Court rolls for Merridge survive for 1603[47] and 1632[48] and there are presentments of courts held at Waterpits, Merridge, 1812–33 mainly concerning abuse of the commons and waste.[49] Courts were held twice a year at Radlet in the 14th and 15th centuries[50] and suit was owed to Tuxwell cum Radlet manor in 1580 and 1633.[51] Pleabury was administered with the Hody family estates in the area and court records survive for 1540–1 and 1546.[52]

There was a parish beadle in 1607.[53] Churchwardens were being appointed on a property rota by 1636, absentee owners having to pay a fine for not serving or to provide a deputy.[54] Shortly before then collectors for the poor were recorded[55] and by 1697 the overseers were four in number. Four highway surveyors divided the parish between them in 1699. In 1700 the number of overseers was changed to two to reduce the cost, and in 1706 a new rota of 15 principal inhabitants was established to serve as wardens and overseers. In 1735 the number of eligible people was brought down to 12, and each year the two overseers were to receive £4 in expenses to work within the parish, and on retiring at the end of the year were to serve as churchwardens.[56]

12 S.R.O., DD/SX 57.
13 Ibid. Q/REl 7/1.
14 Deed formerly in S.R.O. and now destroyed.
15 S.R.O., DD/PLE 64.
16 Ibid. tithe award.
17 O.S. Map 6", Som. XLIX. SE. (1887 edn.).
18 P.R.O., E 210/10249.
19 Ibid. E 210/10248.
20 S.R.S. lxviii, p. 115; P.R.O., SC 6/977/23.
21 Ibid. C 140/4, no. 34; Longleat House, Seymour Papers, XII, rental (1540), f. 9.
22 P.R.O., LR 3/123; S.R.O., DD/S/WH 3.
23 P.R.O., CP 25(2)/205/19 Eliz. I Trin.
24 Ibid. CP 25(2)/207/39 & 40 Eliz. I Mich.
25 Longleat House, Seymour Papers, XII, rental (1540), f. 9.
26 P.R.O., C 142/413, no. 44.
27 Ibid. C 142/528, no. 13.
28 S.R.O., D/P/spax 23/1.
29 Above, this section (industry).
30 S.R.O., D/P/can 17/1/1; DD/S/WH 296; DD/BR/ely 5/5.
31 Ibid. DD/BR/ely 5/5.
32 Ibid. tithe award.
33 Ibid. DD/WG 13/9.
34 Ibid. Q/REl 7/6.
35 S.R.S. iii. 140–1, 163; xx. 245.
36 S.R.O., D/P/spax 23/1.
37 Ibid. Q/REl 2/9A; 7/1, 6, 6A–C, 9C.
38 DD/BR/bn 10.
39 S.R.S. xxviii. 124.
40 Ibid. lxviii, pp. 12–13.
41 P.R.O., SC 2/200/27–9.
42 S.R.O., DD/AH 11/9.
43 Ibid. DD/WG 16/8, 11–13, 16–17.
44 Ibid. 13/2, 5.
45 P.R.O., SC 2/200/28.
46 S.R.O., DD/AH 11/9–10.
47 P.R.O., WARD 2/18/70/11.
48 B.L. Add. Ch. 28283.
49 S.R.O., DD/ES 3.
50 Ibid. DD/L P35/1, 4.
51 Ibid. DD/MVB 3; DD/SX 57.
52 P.R.O., LR 3/123.
53 S.R.S. xxiii. 10.
54 S.R.O., DD/SAS PR 343.
55 S.R.S. xxiv. 181–2.
56 S.R.O., D/P/spax 14/2/1, 23/1.

The 15 principal inhabitants of 1706 were also to act as a vestry concerned with poor relief and church repairs, and each in turn had to provide a meal for his fellows. Poor relief from 1706 was to be administered on the first Friday of every month at a certain tombstone in the churchyard. From 1735 relief was given monthly on Sundays.[57]

Spaxton formed part of the Bridgwater poor-law union in 1836, Bridgwater rural district in 1894, and Sedgemoor district in 1974.[58]

CHURCH. The existence of a rural deanery of Spaxton in the later 12th century[59] suggests that the church may have begun as a minster, and the building appears to be of the 11th century. The benefice remained a rectory and in 1957 was united with Charlinch[60] and in 1981 with Enmore and Goathurst.[61]

By 1329 the advowson was owned by the lords of Spaxton manor.[62] The Crown granted out the patronage during a minority in 1531[63] and presented in 1576 by lapse.[64] Throughout the 17th and the early 18th century the advowson was let by the Waldegraves[65] but had passed from James Smith[66] before 1773 to James Yorke and Edward Leave Yeo.[67] Yorke's representatives held it until 1817 when it was put up for sale[68] and was acquired by the next rector, William Gordon.[69] Successive rectors held the patronage until c. 1900. From then it was vested in the Church Trust Fund,[70] which from 1957 appointed on alternate vacancies. Since 1981 the patronage of the united benefice has been exercised jointly by the bishop, the fund, and the Martyrs Memorial Trust.[71]

The church was valued at £13 6s. 8d. in 1291,[72] at £25 gross in 1535,[73] and at £120 c. 1668.[74] In 1803 the living was thought to be worth at least £800 a year.[75] The average net income 1829–31 was £594.[76] Tithes were valued at £21 13s. 4d. in 1535.[77] In 1838 the tithes were commuted for a rent charge of £663.[78]

The church had 2 a. of land in 1250[79] and by 1535 the glebe was valued at 66s. 8d.[80] By 1636 it comprised the parsonage house, 39 a. of land, a second house, and Blindwell, 22 a. with a house.[81] In 1670 there were 3 houses and 62 a.[82] and in 1838 the glebe was nearly 65 a.[83] Exchanges of land between the rector and the owners of Spaxton farm in 1883 reduced the size

of the glebe considerably,[84] and land at North Street had been sold by 1928.[85] In 1956 the glebe comprised the rectory house, the parish room, 2 cottages, and 37 a.,[86] of which 29½ a. remaining in 1976 were sold c. 1982.[87]

The rectory house may have been repaired c. 1470 when the rector purchased 5,000 lath nails.[88] In 1638 it was described as a mansion and its outbuildings and grounds included a malthouse, pigeon house, stables, two courts, two gardens, a woodyard, and a barn.[89] In 1954 it was divided into four dwellings, one of which was for the rector.[90] In 1967 the house, later Peart Hall, was sold. The central range, which has a south front of five bays with central doorway, was built in the 18th century, perhaps incorporating some walls from an earlier house. Early in the 19th century, probably in 1803 and in the 1830s,[91] it was refitted and enlarged to the west, north, and east. The eastern extension, in the form of a cross wing, provided a new entrance front of five bays whose central doorway was protected by a trellis-work porch, since removed. Later in the 19th century a conservatory was added to the south end of the east wing, additional bedrooms were provided on the west and detached stables and a coach house were built beyond them. A new house was built for the rector in 1967.

Thomas de l'Aleton, rector in 1317 and a pluralist, was given leave of absence provided that he visited Spaxton and maintained a chaplain.[92] Henry of Littleton, rector while still a subdeacon in 1329, had leave to study for three years and was not priested until 1332; in 1340 he was licensed to serve the prior of Merton (Surr.).[93] In 1423 five service books were bequeathed to the church.[94] Leonard Say, a relative of the patron, was probably under age when instituted in 1478, but in the following year, having attained his majority, was allowed to hold a second benefice.[95] His immediate successor appears to have been only a subdeacon when instituted in 1493.[96] There was an anniversary chaplain employed in 1450 and in the 1530s,[97] and until 1549 a light was maintained out of wax rents granted by 1359 and from land called Church Lands which may have been given for repairs.[98] Land given to maintain a light was sold to Crown grantees in 1575.[99]

The living was served by curates from the 1560s,[1] and among the non-resident rectors John

57 S.R.O., D/P/spax 23/1.
58 Youngs, *Local Admin. Units*, i. 671, 673, 676.
59 *H.M.C. Wells*, i. 38, 41, 432.
60 S.R.O., D/P/chlch 2/9/3.   61 *Dioc. Dir.*
62 *S.R.S.* i. 297.   63 *L. & P. Hen. VIII* v, p. 148.
64 *Cal. Pat.* 1575–8, p. 68.
65 S.R.O., DD/WG 13/2, 10.
66 Above, manors.   67 S.R.O., D/D/Vc 88.
68 Devon R.O. 1148 M/add 36/260.
69 *Rep. Com. Eccl. Revenues*, pp. 152–3.
70 *Kelly's Dir. Som.* (1899, 1902); *Dioc. Dir.*
71 *Dioc. Dir.*
72 *Tax. Eccl.* (Rec. Com.), 198.
73 *Valor Eccl.* (Rec. Com.), i. 214.
74 S.R.O., D/D/Vc 24.   75 Ibid. T/PH/ay 1.
76 *Rep. Com. Eccl. Revenues*, pp. 152–3.
77 *Valor Eccl.* (Rec. Com.), i. 214.
78 S.R.O., tithe award.   79 *Bk. of Fees*, ii. 1210.
80 *Valor Eccl.* (Rec. Com.), i. 214.
81 S.R.O., D/D/Rg 282.

82 Ibid. D/P/spax 3/1/3.
83 Ibid. tithe award.
84 Deeds in possession of Mr. Ebsary, Ebsley Fm., Spaxton.
85 S.R.O., D/P/spax 9/1/1.
86 Ibid. DD/WBF 4.
87 Inf. from Dioc. Office; local inf.
88 *S.R.S.* lxx, p. 30.
89 S.R.O., D/D/Rg 282.
90 Ibid. DD/WBF 3, 4.
91 Ibid. T/PH/ay 1; *Rep. Com. Eccl. Revenues*, pp. 152–3.
92 *S.R.S.* i. 175.
93 Ibid. ix, pp. 9, 58, 76, 106, 373.
94 Ibid. xvi. 403.
95 Ibid. lii, p. 78; *Cal. Papal Reg.* xiii (2), p. 632.
96 *S.R.S.* lii, p. 182.
97 Ibid. pp. 28, 49; S.R.O., D/D/Vc 20.
98 *S.R.S.* ii. 54–5, 227; lxxvii, p. 25; S.R.O., DD/S/WH 15.
99 *Cal. Pat.* 1572–5, p. 409; *S.R.S.* lxxvii, pp. 110, 123.
1   *S.D.N.Q.* xiii. 271; S.R.O., D/D/Ca 57.

Woolton, rector 1576–9, was bishop of Exeter 1579–94,[2] and Thomas Bartlett, rector until 1603, visited the parish occasionally and was a royal chaplain and archdeacon of Exeter.[3] Richard Powell, 1604–22, was the first of a long succession of resident rectors. His son Richard, rector from 1624, was deprived and died in prison, possibly by poison. Richard's son, also Richard, presented in 1645, was refused admission in favour of his brother-in-law John Carlisle. Carlisle died in 1668 and was succeeded by Joseph Cooke, who married Carlisle's widow.[4] Carlisle's son Henry succeeded Cooke as rector in 1709. He was followed by William Yorke, presented in 1713 by Mary Carlisle, probably Henry's daughter and later William's wife.[5] William Yorke died in 1772.[6] About 1788 there were 20 communicants.[7] A second William Yorke, rector 1803–17 and probably related to his namesake, also held Fiddington but lived at Spaxton.[8] Two Sunday services were held in 1815,[9] and between 1840 and 1843 celebration of communion was increased from at least three to twelve times a year.[10]

There was a church house in the 16th century which belonged to Spaxton manor.[11] It was badly damaged in the great storm of 1703 and was only partly rebuilt.[12] In 1731 an extension was added to the north, later rebuilt in two storeys.[13] The house was sold in 1833,[14] probably to the rector, who owned it in 1838.[15] It was later divided into two dwellings, known in 1987 as Glebe and St. Margaret's cottages.[16]

The church of *ST. MARGARET*, so named by 1742,[17] was dedicated in the Middle Ages and until 1536 or later to St. Mary.[18] It comprises a chancel with north vestry and south chapel, a nave with south aisle and south porch, and a west tower. The narrow nave and the herringbone masonry at the east end of the north wall suggest a date in the 11th century. The nave was later extended westwards and both nave and chancel were altered in the early 14th century. The tower was built or heightened probably in the 1430s.[19] North and south chancel chapels were formed in the later 15th century, the former evidently associated with the panelled and elaborately carved canopy over an earlier tomb.[20] The chapel was extended, probably twice: it was used as a vestry

by 1606[21] and was enlarged to take the organ in 1894.[22]

The south chancel chapel may have been extended from its original plan when the south aisle and two-storeyed porch were added, possibly c. 1536, the date of the pews. Bench ends in the nave are dated 1561.[23] Among them is one depicting a fuller or shearman with his cloth-finishing tools. The date 1720 and the names of pew owners are to be found on several book rests. The pulpit includes panels of the late 16th or the 17th century.

There are a cup and almsdish of 1662 and a flagon dated 1708 and given in 1755.[24] There are six bells, the two oldest of the later 17th century.[25] Parts of the clock mechanism are said to date from c. 1600[26] and the clock was recorded in 1655.[27] The registers date from 1558 but there is a gap between 1652 and 1668 and the first two registers are severely damaged.[28]

A building at Courtway, Merridge, probably earlier the Baptist chapel, was opened in 1876 as St. Andrew's chapel.[29] One service was held on Sundays during the earlier 20th century but by the 1960s numbers of communicants had fallen to c. 10[30] and the chapel closed. The building, clad in corrugated iron, had quarters for a caretaker at the rear.[31] It was demolished in 1985.[32]

NONCONFORMITY. There was a Roman Catholic in Spaxton in 1740, probably the recusant recorded in 1767.[33]

A house was licensed for protestant worship in 1701.[34] Wesleyan Methodist services were held as part of the Taunton circuit by 1838.[35] Premises were acquired in 1847[36] and in 1858 a chapel was built. A Sunday schoolroom was added in 1922 as a war memorial.[37] In 1960 there were two Sunday services, attended by an average of 23 and 19 people respectively.[38] The chapel was still in use in 1987.

A shared Baptist and Congregational chapel was built at Merridge in 1839. It was closed c. 1860 but restored and reopened as a Congregational church in 1883.[39] It closed c. 1938.[40] The chapel was being converted into a house in 1987.

There was a Baptist chapel in Merridge between 1861 and 1875, probably established after

2   S.R.O., D/D/Ca 134; *Cal. Pat.* 1578–80, p. 55.
3   S.R.O., D/D/Ca 134; *Som. Incumbents*, ed. Weaver, 436.
4   S.R.O., D/P/spax 2/1/1; DD/WG 13/5; *Walker Revised*, A. G. Matthews, 317.
5   S.R.O., D/P/spax 2/1/2–3; *Som. Incumbents*, ed. Weaver, 436.
6   S.R.O., D/P/spax 2/1/3 (21 Aug. 1772).
7   Ibid. D/D/Vc 88.
8   Ibid. D/D/Rb 1815; *Paupers and Pigkillers*, ed. J. Ayres, 284.
9   S.R.O., D/D/Rb 1815.
10 Ibid. D/D/Va 1840, 1843.
11 Ibid. DD/WG 8/2A, 9/4; *Proc. Som. Arch. Soc.* cxix. 62.
12 S.R.O., DD/WG 13/8.
13 Ibid. 13/9.
14 Ibid. DD/PLE 64.
15 Ibid. tithe award.
16 *Proc. Som. Arch. Soc.* cxix. 62.
17 Ibid. xvii. 118.
18 *S.R.S.* xxxvi. 183; *Proc. Som. Arch. Soc.* li. 131.
19 *S.R.S.* xix. 334.

20 *Proc. Som. Arch. Soc.* lxviii. 60–1 and pl. xiii; lxx. 81–2 and pl. viii.
21 S.R.O., D/D/Ca 151.
22 Ibid. D/P/spax 6/1/1.
23 Ibid. 23/1; cf. below, plate facing p. 153.
24 S.R.O., D/P/spax 9/1/1.
25 Ibid. 4/1/1, 6/1/1, 23/1; DD/SAS CH 16/2.
26 M. Odlum, *Hist. of Ch. and Village of Spaxton* (1974), 76.
27 S.R.O., D/P/spax 23/1.
28 Ibid. 2/1/1–11.
29 Odlum, *Hist. Spaxton*, 421.
30 S.R.O., D/P/spax 2/5/1, 5, 6.
31 Ibid. 1/3/1.
32 Local inf.
33 S.R.O., D/P/spax 23/1; H.L.R.O., recusant list, 1767.
34 S.R.O., Q/RR meeting ho. lics.
35 Ibid. D/N/bmc 7/2.
36 Ibid. 4/3/47.
37 Ibid. 4/3/50.
38 Ibid. 3/2/2, 4/3/50.
39 *Rep. Som. Cong. Union* (1896).
40 S.R.O., C/E 4/380/4; local inf.

the closure of the joint chapel.[41] It was described as an iron chapel in 1872[42] and was probably the later Church of England chapel opened there in 1876.[43]

The Trinity Free Church at New Charlinch, Four Forks, was licensed in 1845,[44] but was probably built a few years earlier, and was used by the Revd. George Thomas, a follower of the Revd. Henry Prince. In 1846 the group of houses and chapel known as the Agapemone was built by William Cobbe, and Prince and his followers occupied the site from the end of that year.[45] In 1851 there were 65 people living on the site,[46] a number which had fallen to 36 by 1881.[47] Prince died in 1899; John Smyth-Pigott took over leadership of the community and further houses were built,[48] but he spent part of his time in London where he had claimed to be the Messiah in 1902, and the Agapemone declined. A hospital was opened there during the Second World War but in 1957 the Agapemone was sold.[49] It was divided and the chapel was converted to a dwelling. The main house is a two-storeyed, Tudor style building with crenellated bay windows.

EDUCATION. Teachers at an English school were licensed in 1675 and 1676.[50] Joseph Cooke, the rector, by will of 1708 left a sum to provide 2s. 6d. a week to teach 15 poor children.[51] A charity school supported by the endowment had 25 children in 1825 and 15 in 1835.[52] Its income, augmented in 1879, was later enjoyed by the National school.[53] A Sunday school with between 40 and 50 children had been established by 1819[54] and had 65 children in 1825.[55] By 1835 there were only 20 children.[56]

In 1835 there were also a day school with 10 children and another with 25 boys. Between that date and 1846 a single school was established which in that year had a total of 111 children, 36 of whom attended only on Sundays.[57] A new school was built in 1860 in association with the National Society. In 1903 there were 100 children with three teachers.[58] Numbers fell to 66 in 1925 and to 47 in 1945 but rose to 77 in 1965. In 1981 there were 44 children on the register but it was estimated that there would be 57 in 1988. In 1947 the school accepted voluntary controlled status.[59]

A school, described as at Courtway in 1871,

was held in Merridge Baptist chapel in 1872.[60] Aisholt and Spaxton district school at Merridge opened in 1874. There were 48 children on the books in 1903 but numbers fell and it closed in 1938 when the remaining children were transferred to Spaxton.[61] In 1987 the building was used as the Aisholt and Merridge village hall.

A private school was kept in Spaxton village in 1851 and 1861 and in the same years a small boarding school was held at Four Forks, attended by children from the Agapemone.[62] There was a private school at the Mount, Courtway, primarily for foreign girls, by 1928 and until c. 1939.[63]

CHARITIES FOR THE POOR. Before 1392 land called Kytcotts at Holwell was said to have been bought for the poor.[64] In 1719 accumulated rents from the Parish or Poor's Land, evidently the same land, were used to buy a house and land at Waterpits, and the estate produced an income of £32 in 1786 and £48 in 1826, when sums of between 5s. and £2 were distributed.[65] The land was sold in 1919 and the money was invested in stock. In 1977 the income was distributed in vouchers.[66]

Elizabeth Rich (d. 1846) of Ebsley left £100 to the poor and distributions were made at Christmas in the 1890s. A further £300 was given to the poor in 1911 by Miss M. O. Galloway, a relative of the then rector.[67] Distributions of the Galloway charity were made in cash and in kind until 1958 or later.[68] In 1987 the charities were about to be amalgamated.[69]

In 1683 Joseph Cooke, the rector, leased some waste land north of the church house to build an almshouse.[70] The house was not then built, but under his will dated 1708 he left rents on lands in Stogursey for a house to be built south-east of the church for six poor people. Each of the six was to receive 2s. a week, fuel, and candles, and clothing or an allowance. A room was set aside for a reader paid to read prayers twice a day. Every year a banquet was provided for the six inmates and the trustees of the charity.[71] By 1928 the almshouse lands had been sold and the money invested in stock.[72] In the late 1950s improvements were made to the two-roomed dwellings, in 1981 the number of dwellings was reduced to four in order to enlarge them, and c. 1988 they were modernized.[73]

41 P.O. Dir. Som. (1861, 1875).
42 Morris & Co. Dir. Som. (1872).
43 Above, church.
44 S.R.O., D/D/Rm, box 2.
45 W. H. Dixon, Spiritual Wives (1868), i. 295; C. Mander, The Revd. Prince and his Abode of Love (1976), 70, 72, 87; for a view of the chapel, above, plate facing p. 89.
46 P.R.O., HO 107/1924.
47 Ibid. RG 11/2369.
48 S.R.O., D/R/bw 22/1/4.
49 Mander, Abode of Love, passim; Som. Co. Herald, 29 Sept. 1948.
50 S.R.O., D/D/Bs 42.
51 Char. Com. files.
52 Ann. Rep. B. & W. Dioc. Assoc. S.P.C.K. (1825–6), 42; Educ. Enq. Abstract (1835), p. 822.
53 Char. Com. reg.; S.R.O., D/P/spax 18/5/1.
54 Educ. of Poor Digest, p. 798.
55 Ann. Rep. B. & W. Dioc. Assoc. S.P.C.K. (1825–6), 42.
56 Educ. Enq. Abstract, p. 822.
57 Ibid.; Nat. Soc. Inquiry, 1846–7, Som. 16–17.
58 S.R.O., C/E 4/380/370.
59 Ibid. 4/64.
60 Morris & Co. Dir. Som. (1872); P.R.O., RG 10/2379.
61 S.R.O., C/E 4/64, 159, 380/4.
62 P.R.O., HO 107/1924; ibid. RG 9/1621.
63 S.R.O., D/R/bw 22/1/18; local inf.
64 S.R.O., D/P/spax 23/1.
65 Char. Don. pp. 1048–9; 15th Rep. Com. Char. 364–5.
66 Char. Com. files.
67 S.R.O., DD/ED 219/856; Char. Com. files.
68 S.R.O., D/P/spax 17/3/12.
69 Inf. from the rector, the Revd. J. S. Barks.
70 S.R.O., DD/WG 13/5.
71 15th Rep. Com. Char. 362–4.
72 S.R.O., D/P/spax 17/1/4, 18/5/2.
73 Ibid. 17/6/5; Char. Com. files; Bridgwater Mercury, 14 Feb. 1989.

STOCKLAND BRISTOL

THE ancient parish of Stockland Bristol, former-ly Stockland Gaunts, derived its secondary names from its former owners, first the Gaunts hospital, Bristol, and later Bristol corporation.[74] The main part of the parish lay between Otter-hampton and Stogursey, 9 km. north-west of Bridgwater; the remainder comprised several detached parts mostly to the east and north-east, including the hamlet of Steart, on the coast 4 km. north-east of Stockland village. The ancient parish covered c. 1,150 a.[75] In 1886 the detached land around Steart (including 8 houses and 46 persons) was transferred to Otterhampton parish and parcels in the south-west passed to Fidding-ton. Knaplock was added from Cannington parish.[76] The area of the resultant civil parish is 335 ha. (828 a.).[77]

The principal part of the parish lies in the south-west across a low ridge reaching 30 m., from which the land falls to the flat marshes at c. 7 m. in the north-east. Weaving water or North brook flows down the hill and then forms part of the western and northern boundary. The eastern boundary is marked in part by a stream and in part by the road from Stockland to Steart. Much of the southern boundary followed the road between Combwich and Stogursey. The boundaries of the detached area at Steart were the coast and the sea wall which protected Wall common in Stogursey and gave its name to fields called Wallsend in Stockland parish.[78]

The sloping ground is clay overlying Blue Lias with pockets of limestone.[79] Much of it was formerly woodland,[80] full of springs, and was described as cold clay, not very productive, and benefiting neither from lime nor, if wet, even from animal manure.[81] Quarrying was obstruct-ing roads in 1575 and 1646, and in 1577 the lessee of the rectory sold 60 cartloads of stone from the estate, possibly from the land north of the church. In 1637 tenants were forbidden to sell paving stones outside the manor without licence. In 1579 three men were accused of building two unlicensed lime kilns and of mak-ing 700 bu. of lime in each. In 1774 a tenant of the manor was given permission to build a limekiln.[82] The alluvium of the marsh land was good both for arable and for sheep provided that it was well drained.[83] Maintenance of the clyces or sluices and watercourses was of considerable importance and an earth wall to protect an outwarth[84] was constructed in 1445.[85] The marsh

north of Stockland village, known formerly as Pederham or Petherhams Marsh,[86] is drained by North, Middle, and South brooks, which flow eastwards into the Parrett through North and Combwich clyces. In the 1630s and 1640s Stock-land manor court ordered hollow trees to be laid to improve field drainage.[87] The manor was responsible not only for the drainage within the parish but also for Stockland clyce, probably either the present North clyce or Combwich clyce.[88] By 1741, however, responsibility for the clyce was shared with other landowners and Stockland manor paid only half the cost of rebuilding it that year.[89]

Stockland village, a single street running along the edge of the marsh eastwards from the church, may originally have extended further west, where earthworks north of the church suggest the original nucleus. The surviving street, with nearly all the houses, farmyards, and paddocks on the north side running down to South brook, faced an open arable field whose nearest furlong was called Burgage.[90] A survey of 1547 described 17 dwellings in Stockland manor, probably the whole village except the vicarage house. At least four were single store-yed, a further seven appear to have had halls open to the roof, and one seems to have had two halls to accommodate two related households. Two dwellings appear to have been longhouses, many had ground floor chambers, and only one parlour and one buttery were recorded. Four houses had kitchens, one of which might have been separate from the dwelling.[91] Surviving houses include Rosemary Cottage, a medieval building enlarged in the 16th century, and two of the 17th century, the Poplars and Rogers Farm, the second having plasterwork dated 1675.[92] Most houses remained small in the 18th century and in 1833 several were described as old and thatched although one had had a new roof and another had new farm buildings.[93]

Steart hamlet appears to have been called Marsh in 1377[94] and in 1762 and 1822 the Marsh houses were recorded.[95] By the mid 19th century the hamlet was known as Steart Marsh and in 1881 also as Steart Bay; from the late 19th century it has usually been called Steart.[96] It is a remote settlement of widely spaced farms and cottages.

The road from Combwich to Stogursey ran through or along the southern edge of the parish

74 Below, manors. This article was completed in 1988.
75 S.R.O., tithe award; above, map on p. 104.
76 Census, 1891; Kelly's Dir. Som. (1906).
77 Census, 1981.
78 O.S. Map 1/25,000, ST 24 (1959 edn.); 1/50,000, sheet 182 (1974 edn.); S.R.O., tithe award; ibid. DD/DHR 36.
79 Geol. Surv. Map 1/50,000, solid and drift, sheet 279 and parts of 265 and 295 (1980 edn.).
80 Below, this section.
81 Bristol R.O. 04203, 04246.
82 Ibid. 04403–4; S.R.O., DD/DHR 37.
83 Bristol R.O. 04237.
84 Reclaimed salt marsh, probably outside the sea wall.
85 S.R.S. lvii, p. 44; below, local govt.

86 S.R.O., DD/AH 35/32, 65/9.
87 Bristol R.O. 04404.
88 S.R.O., DD/DHR 36.
89 Ibid.; Bristol R.O. 2067 (24).
90 S.R.O., tithe award.   91 Bristol R.O. 4490.
92 S.R.O., DD/V/BWr 32.1–3.
93 Ibid. DD/SP inventories, 1731, 1732, 1737; Bristol R.O. 04246.
94 Cart. St. Mark's Hosp., Bristol (Bristol Rec. Soc. xxi), pp. 141–2.
95 S.R.O., DD/DHR 36; S.R.S. lxxvi, map 1822.
96 P.R.O., HO 107/1924; ibid. RG 11/2371; Kelly's Dir. Som. (1906); O.S. Map 6", Som. XXXVIII. NW. (1886 edn.); O.S. Map 1/25,000, ST 24 (1959 edn.).

and was joined there by the road from Steart through Stockland village. Both were evidently well used in the 17th century as gifts to travellers by the parish officers in 1655 amounted to most of the annual parish expenditure.[97] The parish was indicted in 1809 for failure to repair the first route.[98] The second, straightened in the 1860s south-west of the village to improve the grounds of the new Vicarage, later Stockland Manor,[99] led along Marsh or Steart drove to Wall common and then along the beach to Steart, a route which was vulnerable to erosion and storms such as that of 1869.[1] During the later 19th century attempts were made to prevent Lord Clifford allowing pebbles to be removed from Steart beach for road repair as this was said to be weakening the sea defences.[2] There was no made-up road across Wall common and the fields until the 20th century and it was not metalled until c. 1961.[3]

The field names Beaverland and Midfurlong indicate an open arable field on the rising ground south of the village street, where small strips were still cultivated in 1547.[4] A common meadow north of the village was still in strips in the 1820s.[5] There may originally have been common grazing on the marshes but there was apparently none in the 17th century,[6] although some manor holdings were awarded allotments in Steart common in 1803.[7]

No woodland was recorded in 1086[8] but field names show that the southern part of the parish was once well wooded, largely with oak. Timber was still plentiful in the 17th century,[9] and 602 timber trees were sold in 1813, mostly oak and elm but also ash, aspen, and walnut.[10] Stockland moor, described as peaty and unimprovable in 1801, had been planted by 1837 when there were 60 a. of woodland, most owned by Bristol corporation.[11] In 1947 over 25 a. of woodland was felled, but at least 25 a. survived in 1982.[12]

The Stockland friendly society had been disbanded by 1921 when it was decided that its poles and flags should be kept in the church.[13]

The population rose in the first three decades of the 19th century from 144 in 1801 to 202 in 1831 but fell thereafter to 181 in 1851, 142 in 1861, and 138 in 1871. By 1881 there had been a sharp increase to 188 but following the transfer of Steart to Otterhampton in 1886 the total was 140 in 1901 and it declined during the 20th century to 97 in 1971. Ten years later the population totalled 130,[14] because of new building in the village and the subdivision of Stockland Manor.

Ten men were fined for alleged involvement in the 1497 rebellion.[15] The alchemist Thomas Charnock is said to have lived in Stockland after his marriage in 1562.[16]

MANOR AND OTHER ESTATES. The manor of *STOCKLAND* was held by Ralph de Reuilly from Ralph Pagnell in 1086. Its Saxon owner is unknown.[17] The manor subsequently descended with East Quantoxhead to Maurice de Gaunt (d. 1230), who left Stockland in his will to the hospital of St. Mark at Bristol.[18] Maurice's heir, Andrew Luttrell, successfully claimed the manor in 1232 but agreed to sell it to the hospital.[19] Geoffrey, Andrew's son, released his rights in Stockland c. 1265 to his brother Alexander, who was said to have been given the manor by his father,[20] notwithstanding charters of 1259 and 1267–8 confirming the hospital's ownership. In 1271 Alexander Luttrell disseised St. Mark's but they recovered possession and bought Luttrell off with an annuity.[21] The hospital remained in possession of the manor, known from the late 13th century as *STOCKLAND GAUNTS*.[22] A further claim to the manor was made by the Luttrell family between 1337 and 1340, which the hospital bought off with a second annuity.[23] In 1541, following the dissolution of the hospital, the king granted Stockland manor to the mayor and commonalty of Bristol.[24] The manor remained in the ownership of Bristol corporation, from which it derived its alternative name of *STOCKLAND BRISTOL*, until 1839 when it was sold to Thomas Daniel.[25] Thomas (d. 1872) was succeeded by his son the Revd. Henry Arthur Daniel (d. 1912).[26] Henry's son Henry Thomas (d. 1952) gave his land in Stockland to his son Henry Cave Daniel, who dismembered the manor, selling mainly to the tenants, in 1947 and 1952.[27]

The court house was recorded in 1317.[28] There is no later record of a capital messuage or court house. During the 18th century the corporation officers appear to have stayed in Stogursey or elsewhere when keeping courts.[29] The vicarage house, renamed Stockland Manor after 1884 when a new house was built for the incumbent,

97 S.R.O., D/P/stoc. b 4/1/1.
98 Ibid. DD/AH 23/4.
99 *P.O. Dir. Som.* (1866); S.R.O., tithe award; O.S. Map 6", Som. XXXVI. SE. (1886 edn.).
 1 S.R.O., DD/DHR 36, map 1744; P.R.O., RG 9/1621; *Proc. Som. Arch. Soc.* xxiii. 67.
 2 S.R.O., D/RA 1/5/6.
 3 Ibid. 29/9/34; DD/EDN 90; O.S. Map 1/25,000, ST 24 (1959 edn.).
 4 S.R.O., tithe award; Bristol R.O. 4490.
 5 S.R.O., DD/DHR 36, map 1822.
 6 Bristol R.O. 04237.
 7 S.R.O., DD/DR 61; ibid. Q/RDe 68.
 8 *V.C.H. Som.* i. 510.
 9 Bristol R.O. 04203, 04237.
10 Ibid. 32079 (224).
11 S.R.O., tithe award.
12 Ibid. DD/DHR 43; Min. of Agric., Fisheries, and Food, agric. returns, 1982.
13 S.R.O., D/P/stoc. b 4/1/3.

14 *Census*; above.
15 *Fines imposed in 1497*, ed. A. J. Howard, 14.
16 *D.N.B.*
17 *V.C.H. Som.* i. 510.
18 Ibid. v. 122; *Cart. St. Mark's*, pp. xxviii, 29.
19 *Close R. 1227–31*, 437; 1231–4, 59; *Cal. Inq. Misc.* i, p. 8; *Cart. St. Mark's*, pp. 125–6.
20 *Cart. St. Mark's*, pp. 136–7.
21 Ibid. pp. xxviii–xxix, 127–8; *S.R.S.* xxxvi. 148–9.
22 *Feud. Aids*, iv. 282.
23 *Cart. St. Mark's*, pp. 129–33.
24 *L. & P. Hen. VIII*, xvi, p. 418.
25 S.R.O., DD/DHR 37.
26 Burke, *Land. Gent.* (1914), 493; S.R.O., D/P/stoc. b 4/1/3; DD/DHR 43.
27 S.R.O., DD/DHR 43; DD/KW 1947/37; DD/X/PRD 2.
28 *S.R.S.* i. 129.
29 Bristol R.O. 2067 (5)c.

was the residence of Henry Daniel. A small park was established on former glebe land south of the house.[30] In 1912 the rooms included four reception rooms, study, schoolroom, nursery, fifteen bedrooms, and servants hall. The Tudor-style house of stone and slate has a six-bayed entrance front and is of four storeys including attic and basement. It retains many decorative features both inside and out including coffered ceilings and oriel windows.[31] The house was sold by Henry Cave Daniel in 1952[32] and was divided into three dwellings.

An estate called *JUVENIS*, Jouverney, or Juffnies,[33] may have belonged to the Iuvernay or Gyverney family in the 13th century. Richard and William Gyverney were recorded in the area in 1286 and 1297, and in 1338 an estate in Otterhampton and Stockland was settled on Richard Gyverney and his third wife Margaret.[34] Richard was succeeded by Maud, said to be his sister, and her husband Henry Power (d. 1361). Their daughter Joan married William Shareshull, who is said to have sold his Somerset estates to William Bonville.[35] In 1408 Juvenis belonged to William Bonville and descended with the manor of Idstock in Chilton Trinity.[36] Edmund Bowyer sold Juvenis with Idstock to Edward Colston in 1707 and it formed part of the estate of Colston's hospital, Bristol, until 1919.[37] In 1920 Juvenis was divided among several owners.[38]

A house, described as an old mansion house and probably the capital messuage, had gone out of use by 1616 but a new house on a slightly different site may have been built by 1621.[39] The house called Juvenis probably dates from the 19th century.

The *RECTORY* was appropriated to St. Mark's hospital, the lords of the manor, in 1316.[40] It comprised in 1547 the great tithes, three fields, a barn, and a dovecote.[41] Barn and dovecot were in decay in 1573, and by the 17th century there was only one field but the tithes were retained.[42] The dovecot, standing west of the church, belonged to Stockland manor in 1657.[43] The field had been absorbed into one of the farms of the manor by the early 19th century.[44] The tithes, demanded in kind in 1820[45] and commuted for a rent charge of £60 in 1837, were sold with the manor by Bristol corporation to Thomas Daniel in 1839.[46]

ECONOMIC HISTORY. In 1086 there was land at Stockland for five ploughteams. Two

teams with four *servi* worked the demesne estate of 2½ hides; seven *villani* and four bordars had three teams and ½ hide. There were 50 a. of meadow and 80 a. of pasture. Six cattle, 20 pigs, and 40 sheep were recorded.[47] There were at least 13 oxen in 1241 and in 1547 arable land accounted for two thirds of the recorded land of the manor.[48]

In 1317 and 1454 small tithes were payable on hay, reed beds, hemp, flax, wool, milk, apples, calves, foals, swine, geese, and doves.[49] In 1547 there were c. 25 holdings, of which 7 were over 50 a. and 15 were under 20 a. Six farms had oxhouses, two had sheep houses, and one had a cowhouse. One farm had a whitehouse where cheese and butter were made.[50]

In the 17th century the rector was supposed to keep a bull and a boar on the rectory field by the church for the use of the tenants and certain tenants were responsible for returning those animals to the field at night.[51] Sheep were kept on Steart common and in 1613 eight men held a total of 590 sheep leases of which half paid tithe to the vicar.[52] In 1655 it was said that the manor was divided into woodland and marshland. The marsh was deep earth and healthy for sheep as well as producing wheat, barley, beans, and peas. Stockland moor in the south-west end of the parish was poor marshland and worth as little as 3s. 4d. a year. It was said that less land should be kept under tillage. Rents were very high.[53] In the 17th century one woman had a cheese press and another kept a variety of livestock.[54] Sheep were the predominant stock in the early 18th century but there was also cider making and dairying. Houses remained small and poorly furnished.[55]

In 1744 the number and size of holdings had changed little since the 16th century.[56] In 1745 it was agreed that tenants should not be granted shares in Stockland moor and the common meadows but that these should be kept in hand until they could be enclosed and rack rented. Nevertheless, in 1801 the common meadows were still being fed in common after mowing.[57] By the end of the 18th century the largest farms were rack rented[58] and by 1801 at least three holdings had been amalgamated to create Stockland farm. Much of the land was cold or in need of drainage and a large number of fields which had been oak woodland were said to be unsuitable for agriculture. It was said that anyone with the capital needed to stock Stockland farm, about £2,000, would prefer to buy than to pay the high rent. In 1826 most of the corn grown

30 Below, church; O.S. Map 1/25,000, ST 24 (1959 edn.).
31 S.R.O., DD/DHR 37, 43; D/P/stoc. b 4/1/3.
32 Ibid. DD/DHR 43.
33 P.R.O., C 142/53, no. 4; S.R.O., D/P/stoc. b 3/2/1.
34 S.R.O., TS/EVD; *Plac. Coram Rege, 1297* (Index Libr. xix), pp. 119–20; *S.R.S.* xii. 25, 33, 80.
35 *Proc. Som. Arch. Soc.* xxxiii. 142–3; *Cal. Inq. p.m.* xi, p. 159.
36 P.R.O., C 142/53, no. 4; below, Chilton Trinity, manors.
37 Below, Chilton Trinity, manors; S.R.O., DD/MVB 1; D/P/stoc. b 3/2/1.
38 S.R.O., D/P/stoc. b 3/2/1.
39 Ibid. DD/MVB 34.
40 *S.R.S.* i. 129.
41 Bristol R.O. 4490.
42 Ibid. 04403; S.R.O., DD/DHR 36.
43 Bristol R.O. 4490; S.R.O., DD/DHR 36.
44 S.R.O., DD/DHR 36; ibid. tithe award.
45 Bristol R.O. 04203.
46 S.R.O., tithe award; ibid. DD/DHR 37.
47 *V.C.H. Som.* i. 510.
48 *S.R.S.* xi, p. 191; Bristol. R.O., 4490.
49 *H.M.C. Wells*, i. 385; *S.R.S.* xlix, p. 226.
50 Bristol R.O. 4490.
51 S.R.O., DD/DHR 36.
52 Ibid. D/D/Rg 284.　　　53 Bristol R.O. 04237.
54 S.R.O., DD/SP inventory, 1691.
55 Ibid. 1731–2, 1737.
56 Above, intro.
57 S.R.O., DD/DHR 36; Bristol R.O. 04203; 2067 (i)L.
58 S.R.O., DD/DHR 36.

was wheat but there were small acreages of barley, beans, and oats.[59] In 1833 the meadow and pasture in the marsh were said to be good and although liable to flood were little damaged as the water subsided quickly, indicating that drainage had improved. The lands of the manor continued to be divided between one large farm and several small holdings.[60]

In 1837 306 a. of titheable land were arable, 754 a. were meadow and pasture. Stockland manor comprised over 700 a. but most of the remainder of the parish around Steart and in the marsh was still divided between many different owners. Stockland farm measured over 300 a., and there was one other farm of over 100 a., but in contrast there were 14 farms of between 10 a. and 25 a.[61] Grazing, dairying, and corn growing were the main activities.[62] In the later 19th century the marshes around Steart were used for grazing cattle and sheep and a herdsman was employed to look after them. There was also a dairywoman at Steart and by 1881 two shepherds.[63] The size of holdings remained little changed until the 1870s. In 1871 the six largest farms employed 22 labourers but in 1881 the three largest farms together had increased in size to over 560 a. and employed 18 labourers.[64] In 1905, in the smaller civil parish, arable had shrunk to 131½ a. and there were 584 a. of permanent grass.[65] A return of 9 holdings totalling 244.7 ha. (605 a.) in 1982 indicated a further shrinkage of arable to only 26 ha. (64 a.), most of which was under wheat. The largest holding was over 100 ha. (247 a.), one had between 30 and 40 ha. (74–99 a.), and the rest were under 20 ha. (50 a.). Seven holdings were worked part-time and of the remainder one specialized in dairying and the other in cattle rearing. There were 2,122 cattle, 220 sheep, 3 pigs, and 42 poultry.[66]

There were two windmills in the parish in 1317[67] and the sites of two medieval mill mounds are known, one at the east end of the village street, the other further north.[68] Both mills still stood in the 16th century, but one, the customary mill of the manor, which was probably the nearest to the village, had been blown down by the 17th century.[69] The other, rebuilt c. 1568, was standing c. 1614, but in 1655 the site was said to have been flooded by the sea.[70] Land called Milland in the 14th century and in the 19th century incorporated into the grounds of Stockland Manor, may also have been the site of a windmill.[71] Field names suggest the existence of a water mill on the boundary with Stogursey parish near Lower Cock Farm.[72]

During the 16th century some shipping put into Steart bay[73] and in the 19th century a mariner from Steart owned a small ship and a half share in a French prize. A Stockland butcher and grazier was a Cannington merchant's partner in a ship which foundered in 1864.[74] Stockland had fishing weirs with 17 butts and a fishery with 5 nets which were last recorded in 1700.[75] Fishing provided employment for many families at Steart, who probably used the same methods as at neighbouring Stolford: a mud horse was recorded in 1922.[76] There were four fishermen at Steart in 1851 and in 1871 and 1881 there were nine.[77] A clothier was recorded in 1641[78] and a tanner in 1702.[79] A grocer and a cooper each had a shop in the parish in 1881.[80]

LOCAL GOVERNMENT. In the 1220s Maurice de Gaunt was granted freedom from suit to Cannington hundred. In 1247 Maurice's widow, Margaret de Sumery, agreed that the men in her dower estate of Stockland should pay suit to the foreign hundred of the hospital of St. Mark, Bristol, although she was to receive all the amercements.[81] It was later said that the king had confirmed Stockland's freedom from suit to the sheriff's tourn.[82]

Court books for Stockland manor survive for 1547–91, 1595–8, 1603–4, 1606, 1609, 1617–33, 1637–52, and 1757–1853. Courts met once or twice a year and combined tenurial business with courts leet and view of frankpledge. In 1581 the court ordered that a pillory and a cucking stool be set up. The tenants complained that the lords held courts less frequently than twice a year, as was customary, and in 1603 that the lords failed to give a court dinner; they also said they should maintain the pound which lay south of the village street east of the church. Court business consisted mainly of seeing that watercourses and bridges were maintained and preventing nuisances.[83] The tithingman, chosen by a rota of tenants of Stockland manor between the 16th and 18th centuries, served as hayward in the following year.[84]

The overseers paid relief in cash and kind including house rent and doctor's bills. In the 1860s an assistant overseer was employed.[85]

The church house appears to have been used as a poorhouse from the later 17th century. It comprised west, north, and south chambers, and was extensively repaired in 1697–8.[86] In 1702 bricks were provided for an oven. The overseers paid rent for the building and in 1713 a doctor

59 Bristol R.O. 04203.
60 Ibid. 04246.
61 S.R.O., tithe award.
62 Ibid. DD/DHR 36.
63 P.R.O., HO 107/1924; ibid. RG 9/1621; RG 11/2371.
64 Ibid. RG 10/2380; RG 11/2371.
65 Statistics supplied by the then Bd. of Agric., 1905.
66 Min. of Agric., Fisheries, and Food, agric. returns, 1982.
67 S.R.S. i. 129.
68 O.S. Nat. Grid ST 249439, 259448; Som. C.C., Sites and Mons. Rec.
69 S.R.O., DD/DHR 36.
70 Ibid. DD/X/WI 34; Bristol R.O. 04237, 04403.
71 H.M.C. Wells, i. 518; S.R.O., tithe award.

72 S.R.O., D/D/Rg 284; DD/DHR 36; DD/AH 51/7; ibid. tithe award.   73 Ibid. D/B/bw 1456, 1469.
74 Ibid. DD/FA 11/1.
75 S.R.S. lxvii, p. 14; S.R.O., DD/WY 84.
76 Below, Stogursey, econ.; S.R.O., DD/BR/ds 1.
77 P.R.O., HO 107/1924; ibid. RG 10/2380; RG 11/2371.
78 Som. Wills, ed. Brown, iii. 29–30.
79 S.R.O., Q/SR 222/1.   80 P.R.O., RG 11/2371.
81 Cart. St. Mark's, pp. 123, 142.
82 Rot. Hund. (Rec. Com.), ii. 118.
83 Bristol R.O. 04403–4; S.R.O., DD/DHR 36; DD/BR/ely 20/17.
84 S.R.O., DD/DHR 36; Bristol R.O. 04203, 04403.
85 S.R.O., D/P/stoc. b 4/1/2, 13/2/1.
86 Ibid. 4/1/1–2.

was paid to treat seven of the almshouse people.[87] The building was described as an almshouse in 1744 but was maintained by the parish in the early 19th century.[88] The house and an adjoining cottage were demolished *c.* 1845.[89]

Stockland formed part of the Bridgwater poor-law union from 1836, Bridgwater rural district from 1894, and Sedgemoor district from 1974.[90]

CHURCHES. The parish church was probably a mother church, as suggested by the claim in 1377 that people from Otterhampton and the Marsh should normally be buried in Stockland churchyard and that the vicar was entitled to all offerings for requiems.[91] St. Mark's hospital, Bristol, had acquired the advowson by 1259, and in 1316 appropriated the rectory,[92] valued at £6 13s. 4d. in 1291.[93] In 1317 the bishop ordained a vicarage,[94] the advowson of which was held with Stockland manor until 1971 when the bishop became patron on the union of Stockland with Otterhampton and Combwich. Since 1984 the living has been held with Cannington also.[95]

In 1317 the vicarage was endowed with tithes which in 1535 were valued at £4 5s. 3d.[96] It was augmented in 1454 with 28s. a year from the hospital.[97] Its gross value in 1535 was £6 9s. 3d.,[98] in 1668 c. £30,[99] and the average 1829–31 was £161.[1] The income included the augmentation, paid by Bristol corporation in succession to St. Mark's hospital, although in 1819 payment was in arrears.[2] In 1864 the lay rector gave the vicar his annual tithe rent charge of £60 but the benefice continued to be known as a vicarage.[3]

The vicarial tithes were paid by composition in the 1640s.[4] In 1817 tenants complained to Bristol corporation that the vicar demanded 2s. in the pound from rack rents and had abandoned the composition for small tithes[5] which were commuted in 1837 for £153 18s.[6]

In 1633, as in 1317, the vicar had 20 a. of glebe;[7] some was exchanged with the lord of the manor in 1864 and 1883,[8] more land was bought, and in 1884 there was over 35 a., all of which had been sold by 1978.[9]

A house was assigned to the vicar in 1317.[10] In 1815 the vicarage house was said to be small and ruinous, a mere cottage, very old and thatched, with unceiled rooms, and in bad repair.[11] It had

been demolished by 1822. An adjoining thatched timber barn was almost a ruin. About 1816 Bristol corporation contributed towards the cost of a new house, built near the road. It was of two storeys, three bays long, and two rooms deep.[12] This house was replaced on the same site in 1860–1 by a much larger one, later known as Stockland Manor.[13] In 1884, when Henry Daniel resigned the living, he built a new vicarage house nearer the church so that he might remain in occupation of his home.[14] The new vicarage remained part of the living until 1971. In 1989 it was a residential home known as the Old Vicarage.

In addition to the vicar there was a stipendiary priest *c.* 1535.[15] Robert Banks, vicar 1572–95, and his wife were very unpopular in the village[16] and in the early 17th century there were complaints against the vicar for insufficient preaching.[17] Richard Marlowe, vicar 1627–47, left a library worth £20.[18] In 1776 there were 15–20 communicants.[19] In 1815 the vicar was non-resident and there was only one Sunday service.[20] There were two Sunday services by 1840, with communion three times a year.[21] By 1870 celebrations had increased to eight a year.[22] Charles Whistler, vicar 1895–1909, was an antiquary and writer.[23]

The church house was let to the parishioners for 1d. in 1549 but was in decay in 1613.[24] It was still used by the parish in the 1650s and the overseers rented it in 1692, suggesting that by this date it was used as a poorhouse.[25]

The former church, dedicated to *ALL SAINTS* in 1316,[26] in the 19th century comprised a chancel, a nave with south transept, south porch, and north aisle, and a west tower. Most of the windows appear to have been of the 14th century.[27] In 1865–6 Thomas Daniel, lay rector and patron, rebuilt the church at his own expense.[28] The new church, on the site of the old and dedicated to *ST. MARY MAGDALENE*, was said to be by Mr. Arthur of Plymouth. It was built of lias in the early 14th-century style and comprises a chancel with south transept or organ chamber and north vestry, a nave with north aisle and south porch, and a west tower. Original fittings from the earlier church include the 15th-century font and fragments of the screen. The screen was restored

87 Ibid. 4/1/2.
88 Ibid. 13/2/1; DD/DHR 36, survey 1744; Bristol R.O. 04246.
89 Taunton Castle, Braikenridge colln., drawing by W. W. Wheatley, 1845.
90 Youngs, *Local Admin. Units*, i. 671, 673, 676.
91 *Cart. St. Mark's*, pp. 141–2.
92 Ibid. p. 136; *S.R.S.* xv. 33; Lincoln's Inn, Hale MS. 185 (Bath cartulary), p. 237. The calendared version in *S.R.S.* vii (2), p. 122 is inaccurate.
93 *Tax. Eccl.* (Rec. Com.), 198.
94 *H.M.C. Wells*, i. 385; *S.R.S.* i. 129.
95 S.R.O., D/P/otn 3/6/5; above, manors; *Dioc. Dir.*
96 *S.R.S.* i. 129; *Valor Eccl.* (Rec. Com.), i. 215.
97 *S.R.S.* xlix. 226.
98 *Valor Eccl.* (Rec. Com.), i. 215.
99 S.R.O., D/D/Vc 24.
1 *Rep. Com. Eccl. Revenues*, pp. 152–3.
2 Bristol R.O. 04203.   3 S.R.O., DD/DHR 36.
4 Ibid. DD/SP inventory, 1647.
5 Bristol R.O. 04203.
6 S.R.O., tithe award.

7 *S.R.S.* i. 129; xlix, p. 226; S.R.O., D/D/Rg 284.
8 S.R.O., DD/DHR 36, 37.
9 Ibid. D/P/stoc. b 4/1/3; inf. from Dioc. Office.
10 *H.M.C. Wells*, i. 385.
11 S.R.O., D/D/Rb 1815; D/D/Bbm 44; Bristol R.O. 04203.
12 S.R.O., D/D/Bbm 44; DD/DHR 36, map 1822.
13 P.R.O., RG 9/1621; above, manors.
14 S.R.O., DD/DHR 37, 43; D/P/stoc. b 4/1/3.
15 Ibid. D/D/Vc 20.   16 Bristol R.O. 04403.
17 S.R.O., D/D/Ca 160, 175.
18 Ibid. DD/SP inventory, 1647.
19 Ibid. D/D/Vc 88.   20 Ibid. D/D/Rb 1815.
21 Ibid. D/D/Va 1840.   22 Ibid. 1870.
23 *Som. Co. Herald*, 10 Oct. 1921.
24 Bristol R.O. 04403; S.R.O., D/D/Ca 180.
25 S.R.O., D/P/stoc. b 4/1/1–2; above, local govt.
26 *Cart. St. Mark's*, pp. 138–9.
27 Taunton Castle, Pigott colln., drawing by J. Buckler, 1843; S.R.O., DD/DHR 36, map 1822; cf. above, plate facing p. 24.
28 S.R.O., D/P/stoc. b 4/1/3, 13/2/1; *P.O. Dir. Som.* (1866).

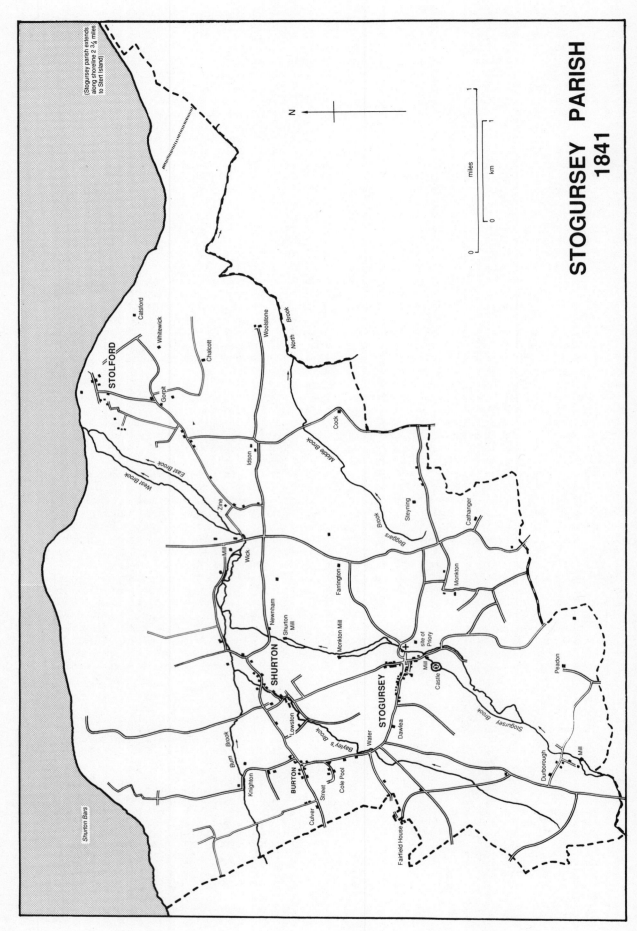

STOGURSEY PARISH
1841

Shurton Bars

(Stogursey parish extends along shoreline 2 3/4 miles to Stert Island)

Catsford
Whitewick
STOLFORD
Chalcott
Gorpit
Woolstone
North Brook
Idson
Cock
Middle Brook
West Brook
East Brook
Zine
Steyning
Brook
Beggars
Cathanger
Mill
Wick
Farrington
Monkton
Newnham
Shurton Mill
Monkton Mill
SHURTON
Monkton Mill
site of Priory
STOGURSEY
Peadon
Castle
Mill
Lowston
Bayley's Brook
Water
Dawlea
Stogursey Brook
Burn Brook
Knighton
BURTON
Street
Cole Pool
Durborough
Mill
Culver
Fairfield House

miles
km

and considerably enlarged in 1920 by F. Bligh Bond.[29] The east window of 1867 is by Clayton and Bell.[30]

There are five bells only one of which, dated 1827, pre-dates the rebuilding of the church.[31] There is an Elizabethan cup and a salver and a flagon of 1750 and 1754 respectively, apparently given in 1755.[32] The registers date from 1538 and are complete.[33]

A chapel at Steart which had gone out of use by 1611[34] was presumably the chapel in the parish described in 1613 as having no services because 'dissolved' and used to house pigs;[35] in 1756 it was used as a barn.[36]

The church of *ST. ANDREW* at Steart was built by the Revd. Henry Daniel in 1882 and endowed by him with over £1,000 on condition that at least one Church of England service was held there each Sunday. The brick building comprised an undivided chancel and nave with south porch and bell turret. In 1986 the turret was struck by lightning and the church was badly damaged by the ensuing fire. It was later restored, but without the bell turret. Henry Thomas Daniel gave a set of plate to the church in 1917.[37]

NONCONFORMITY. Two houses were licensed for Presbyterian worship in 1672.[38] The Bethel Congregational chapel at Steart was built in 1847 and licensed in 1848, probably for use by the Mariners Christian sect. In 1896 it was said to be submerged during high tides.[39] It closed c. 1938.[40] The small rubble and pantiled chapel survived in 1982 as a domestic outbuilding.

EDUCATION. A schoolhouse was recorded in 1787 and 1788.[41] In 1819 a school for 10 children was supported by the vicar and parents. The children were educated until the age of 10 when parents were in need of their labour.[42] In 1825 the children were said to be educated in Otterhampton at the expense of the vicar.[43] He was paying for the education of 9 out of 18 children at a day school in Stockland in 1835; the rest were paid for by their parents. A Sunday school, begun in 1829, had 27 pupils in 1835, and was supported by the vicar, the lords of the manor, and a parishioner.[44] A church school existed between 1861 and 1872 but in 1873 a request was made for children from the parish to have a room at Combwich school.[45] A new school was built at Stockland in 1880 and had 54 children on the books in 1903.[46] Numbers fell to 25 in 1925, to 17 in 1935, and to 4 in 1941 when the school closed.[47] The building was later used by the Stockland sports club, which bought it in 1950 and was in possession in 1988.[48]

CHARITIES FOR THE POOR. None known.

STOGURSEY

STOGURSEY is a large parish on the Bristol Channel coast west of the river Parrett. It includes the substantial village and former borough of Stogursey, with its castle and priory, and a number of hamlets of which the largest are Shurton, north of Stogursey village, and Stolford, on the coast, and Hinkley Point nuclear power station.[49] The name, in the 11th century Stoche or Estocha,[50] acquired the suffix Curci from its owners in the later 12th century.[51] The ancient parish was shaped like an inverted triangle whose base lay along the coast, its apex 5.5 km. inland. East of Stolford it tapered to a narrow coastal strip largely confined to the foreshore but including at its eastern end part of Steart common on the promontory at the mouth of the Parrett. That promontory continued north-east to Steart warren until the peninsula was breached c. 1798, to form Stert Island.[52] The island was transferred from Stogursey to Huntspill parish in 1885.[53] The coastal strip remaining in the parish was either lost to the sea by coastal erosion or absorbed into Otterhampton parish. The present civil parish measures 2,414 ha. (5,965 a.).[54]

The inland boundaries are irregular. Much of the parish lies on low, undulating land near the 15-m. contour, watered by Bum, Bailey's, Stogursey, and Middle brooks, and comprising Blue Lias and alluvium, with areas of brown loamy and silty sands with some gravel around Fairfield, Burton, Shurton, and Stolford. Higher ground to the south, comprising marls known as Mercia Mudstone, reaches above the 61-m. contour at Tet Hill, Monk wood, and Farringdon Hill, and

29 S.R.O., D/D/Cf 1920/135.
30 Pevsner, *S. & W. Som.* 297.
31 Ibid. DD/SAS CH 16/2.
32 *Proc. Som. Arch. Soc.* xlvii. 168–9.
33 S.R.O., D/P/stoc. b 2/1/1–6.
34 Ibid. DD/S/WH 210.
35 Ibid. D/D/Ca 180.
36 Ibid. DD/AH 11/1.
37 Ibid. D/P/stoc. b 4/1/3; *Som. Co. Gaz.* 2 Dec. 1882; *Bridgwater Mercury*, 25 June 1986.
38 *Orig. Rec. of Early Nonconf.* ed. G. L. Turner, i. 547, 613; *Cal. S.P. Dom.* 1672, 475.
39 *Rep. Som. Cong. Union.* (1896); S.R.O., D/D/Rm, box 2; below, Bridgwater, nonconf.
40 S.R.O., D/N/scu 7/6/17.
41 Bristol R.O. 2067 (16)F.
42 *Educ. of Poor Digest*, p. 798.

43 *Ann. Rep. B. & W. Dioc. Assoc. S. P. C. K.* (1825–6), 43.
44 *Educ. Enq. Abstract*, pp. 822–3.
45 *P.O. Dir. Som.* (1861); Morris & Co. *Dir. Som.* (1872); S.R.O., D/P/stoc. b 18/7/1.
46 S.R.O., C/E 4/380/377.
47 Ibid. 4/64.
48 Ibid. DD/DHR 43.
49 O.S. Map 1/25,000, ST 14 (1962 edn.); ST 24 (1959 edn.). This article was largely written in 1985.
50 *Proc. Som. Arch. Soc.* xcv. 121.
51 *S.R.S.* lxi, pp. 15–16, 19–20, 22.
52 S.R.O., DD/SAS SE 113/2; *S.R.S.* lxxvi, intro. 24–5. The name of the village and moors is pronounced locally with two syllables, that of the point and island with one.
53 *Census*, 1891.
54 *Census*, 1981. Earlier measurements have varied: S.R.O., tithe award; *Census*, 1841, 1891, 1901, 1931.

above the 76-m. contour near Durborough. There are bands of marls north of Knighton, and Catsford and Wall commons are on deposits of Storm Gravels.[55] Marl was used for dressing land at the end of the 13th century.[56] There was a location named Claypits at Durborough in the later 14th century[57] and the clay was used by potters there in the 15th.[58] Limestone, found at the junction of marls and lias, was quarried for building in and near Stogursey village from the 15th to the 18th century[59] and elsewhere it was dug for burning in the 17th century.[60] There was a kiln on the coast near Shurton Bars in the 18th century[61] and the limestone there was described as valuable.[62] In the later 19th century there were five kilns near Shurton Bars and two inland near Steyning.[63] The name Sandpits, found south of Stogursey village in the early 18th century, presumably indicated extraction there,[64] and in the mid 19th century there was a field called Brick Yard at Knighton.[65] In 1792 coals, probably sea coal, were said to have been discovered, also near Knighton.[66] In 1909 the Bridgwater Collieries Co. Ltd. leased mining and mineral rights on Sir Alexander Acland-Hood's lands in Stogursey but the lease was surrendered in 1911.[67] Gravel was quarried in several places in the parish, and beach pebbles were used for road repairs.[68]

On the beach near Stolford are the remains of a submerged forest dated to 2500 B.C., part of the evidence for a coastline constantly changing since prehistoric times.[69] In 1614 the bounds of Wick manor could not be perambulated because of coastal erosion, although there were sea walls which lord and tenants were supposed to repair.[70] Those defences frequently failed to protect coastal cottages[71] and in the 1660s Steart common was said to be liable to flood almost as far as Steart House.[72] A proposal to cut a channel through the promontory west of Steart village in 1723[73] was not accepted, but changes continued, notably the breach of c. 1798,[74] until modern sea defences were built in the late 1950s. They involved the construction of a sea wall and the consolidation of soil with Spartina grass. Stert Island and the Stogursey foreshore became part of the Bridgwater Bay National Nature Reserve in 1954.[75]

There is evidence of Bronze Age and Roman occupation in the parish, much of the prehistoric material found near the present shore line.[76] The higher ground to the south and south-east had attracted a number of settlements by the later 11th century, several sharing the element 'stoche' in their names.[77] Stochelande (later Shurton, from 'sheriff-tun'),[78] Estochelande (probably the later Steyning), Estocha, and Suntinstoch (representing the later Stogursey village) may have been formerly parts of a single unit, and Durborough, Idson, 'Sedtammetone', Woolstone, and Wyndeats had also been settled by the later 11th century.[79] Fairfield and Wick, both hamlets established by the 13th century, were later known like Shurton and Stogursey to have had their own arable fields.[80] There were also houses at Burton,[81] Cock,[82] Culver Street,[83] Lowston,[84] Knighton,[85] and Monkton by the mid 14th century, the last named from the priory founded after 1100.[86] Other settlements include West Wall, later Wallsend, recorded in 1423,[87] and Stolford in 1431–2.[88] By 1614 Wick and Stolford each comprised several houses,[89] and Durborough was still a hamlet in the mid 18th century[90] although by the 19th it had been reduced to a single farm.[91] After 1614 cottages were lost along the coast at Stolford and Wallsend,[92] and others were abandoned at Shutternford, also known as Fairfield village,[93] and at Wick.[94] In the 1840s there was some new building at Shurton,[95] and roadside settlement increased along the Combwich road beyond Steyning.[96]

Stogursey village lies at the junction of two ancient routes, one between the Quantocks and the coast, the other from the river crossing at Combwich. East of the junction and beside a brook a church is known to have existed by the early 12th century.[97] Upstream, south of the junction, Stogursey castle was built by 1204, and probably by 1166 in succession to a building of the early 12th century.[98] At the convergence of the two routes a market place was formed, perhaps in the 12th century, and a borough had been created by 1225[99] bounded by a watercourse fed from St. Andrew's well and known as the Town Ditch or Law Ditch, part of which still runs on the south.[1] There were said to be 60 burgages in 1301.[2] The borough seems to have extended beyond the ditch by the later Middle Ages, northwards along Lime Street and westwards along High Street, where building plots were fitted into the strips of the adjoining common arable fields.[3] In 1614 there were over 80 burgages.[4] By the end of the 18th century the borough included three open-field furlongs, called burgages, and other adjoining fields.[5]

A large, rectangular market place was formed at the centre of the borough, entered from the east via

55   Geol. Surv. Map 1/50,000, solid & drift, sheet 279 and pts. of 263 and 295 (1980 edn.); sheet 295 (1984 edn.).
56   P.R.O., SC 6/1090/4.   57   *S.R.S.* lxi, p. 60.
58   Below, econ. hist. (other trade and industry).
59   W. Suss. R.O., PHA uncat.; Alnwick Castle, Northumberland MS. X.II.12.9C; Eton Coll. Rec. 6/196, 230, 269.
60   S.R.O., DD/X/WI 34.
61   Eton Coll. Rec. 51/363.   62   S.R.O., DD/MY 35.
63   O.S. Map 6", Som. XXXVII. NW. (1886 edn.); SE. (1886 edn.); S.R.O., tithe award.
64   S.R.O., tithe award; ibid. D/P/stogs 4/1/2.
65   Ibid. tithe award.   66   Ibid. DD/MY 35.
67   Ibid. DD/AH 36/23.   68   Ibid. D/P/stogs 9/1/2, 14/5/2.
69   *Proc. Som. Arch. Soc.* cxii. 13.
70   S.R.O., DD/X/WI 34.   71   e.g. ibid. D/P/stogs 9/1/3.
72   Ibid. D/RA 9/24; D/RA (C/2259).
73   Ibid. D/RA 9/24.
74   *S.R.S.* lxxvi, intro. 24–5; S.R.O., DD/SAS SE 113/2.
75   *Proc. Som. Arch. Soc.* cxii. 18; inf. from warden.
76   Som. C.C., Sites and Mons. Rec.; *Proc. Som. Arch. Soc.* cxvii. 47–64.   77   Besides Stockland Bristol, above.

78   S. W. Rawlins, *Sheriffs of Som.* 4–5; *Dom. Bk.* ed. Thorn, 364.   79   *V.C.H. Som.* i. 462, 486–7, 501, 505, 508.
80   Below, econ. hist. (agriculture).
81   *S.R.S.* vi. 313.   82   P.R.O., E 142/71/10.
83   S.R.O., DD/AH 65/7.   84   *Cal. Inq. p.m.* iv, p. 341.
85   *H.M.C. Wells*, i. 513.   86   *S.R.S.* lxi, pp. xiii, 58.
87   S.R.O., trans. file 2, no. 62.
88   Eton Coll. Rec. 49/272.   89   S.R.O., DD/X/WI 34.
90   Ibid. DD/AH 14/7, 32/5.   91   Ibid. tithe award.
92   Ibid. DD/X/WI 34; D/P/stogs 9/1/3; Bristol R.O. 04404.
93   S.R.O., DD/AH 13/1, 32/22, 34/20, 66/5; *Bridgwater Times*, 13 May 1847.   94   S.R.O., DD/X/WI 34.
95   Ibid. DD/AH 60/11.
96   Ibid. 3/4.   97   Below, church.
98   Below, castle.   99   *S.R.S.* xi, p. 40.
1   S.R.O., DD/AH 31/10; 32/9–10; 33/5, 7; 34/3; 35/15, 21.   2   Ibid. 17/11.
3   Eton Coll. Rec. 6/196; Alnwick Castle, Northumberland MS. X.II.12.9A(i).   4   S.R.O., DD/X/WI 34.
5   Ibid. DD/AH 65/12, from which the map opposite is taken.

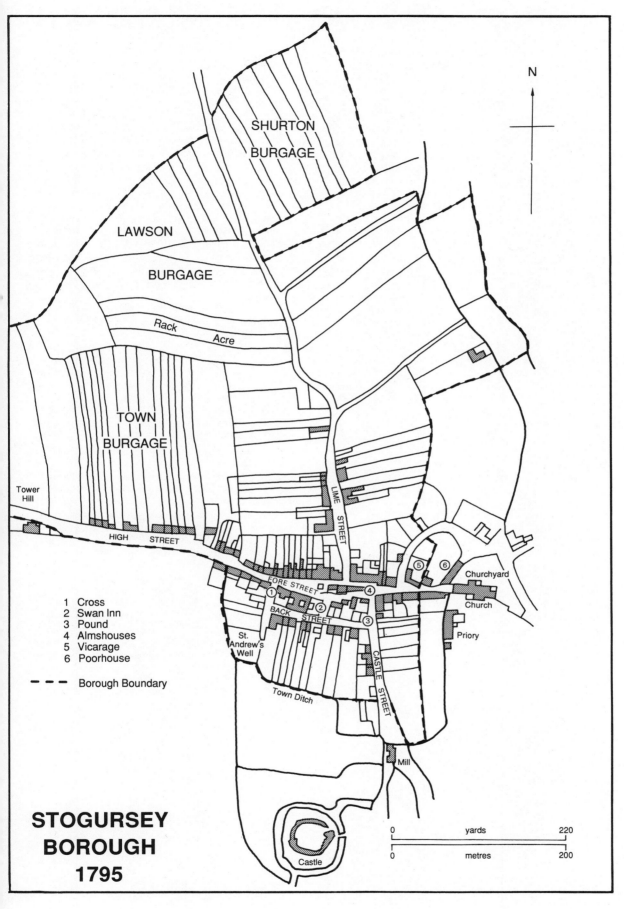

N

SHURTON
BURGAGE

LAWSON

BURGAGE

Rack   *Acre*

TOWN

BURGAGE

Tower
Hill

HIGH   STREET

LIME STREET

FORE STREET

BACK   STREET

St.
Andrew's
Well

Town Ditch

CASTLE STREET

Mill

Castle

Churchyard

Church

Priory

1 Cross
2 Swan Inn
3 Pound
4 Almshouses
5 Vicarage
6 Poorhouse

– – –   Borough Boundary

| 0 | yards | 220 |
| 0 | metres | 200 |

**STOGURSEY
BOROUGH
1795**

Harpe Lane, so named in 1440, and St. Mary Street[6] (renamed Church Street *c*. 1861).[7] Routes from the north converged on Lime Street, so named in 1431,[8] and from the west on High Street, recorded in the early 16th century.[9] From the south, a road passing the castle and the castle mill was called Castle Street in 1431[10] and Mill Street in the 19th century.[11] Encroachments on the market place had probably begun by the 15th century when the almshouse occupied part of an island site in the north-eastern corner.[12] By 1614 there was a larger group of buildings on the south side. A grid of streets was thus formed. The widest street, to the north, was known as Fore Street at its wider, western end, and probably as East Street at its east end in the early 16th century.[13] In the centre, south of the almshouse, was Alms Street or Middle Street[14] and in the south Back Street.[15] Well Street, recorded in the early 16th century,[16] led to St. Andrew's well. Part of it was called St. Andrew's Street by 1871,[17] a name extended to Back and Well streets by the later 20th century.

In 1865 the Combwich road was diverted from its course west of the old vicarage through the site of the church house around the churchyard.[18] At about the same time Sir Peregrine Acland bought the almshouse and the adjoining buildings[19] and demolished them leaving the site open. Courts were built off Well and Lime streets in the later 19th century;[20] in the later 20th new housing was sited in the former open fields north of the village.

The cross at the western end of the market place survives only as the worn stump of an octagonal shaft on a square plinth. It dates from the 13th or the 14th century.[21] St. Andrew's well was so named by 1473.[22] A garden was associated with it in 1532[23] and the well lake was mentioned in 1614[24] and 1742.[25] During the later 18th century the well heads were enclosed and the water was piped. In 1870 the area was enclosed and an arched entrance built bearing the arms of Acland and Egmont, the latter transferred from the 18th-century well house. The wells were restored in 1979 and consist of two well houses and three outlets with stone troughs.[26]

Most of the 100 a. of woodland on the Stogursey estate in 1086 was probably on the Quantocks in Over Stowey; only small areas were recorded at Durborough, Idson, Shortmansford, and Shurton.[27] Kete

wood, later Cat wood, between Stogursey and Steyning, was mentioned in 1258–9,[28] and Monk wood, west of Cat wood, in 1378.[29] There were *c*. 130 a. of woodland at Fairfield in the 18th century,[30] but Little Fairfield wood (12 a.) was felled, possibly in the 1780s,[31] and Great Fairfield wood perhaps at the same time. Both were converted to tillage although chestnut, beech, fir, and oak standards were retained.[32] Great Fairfield wood had been replanted by 1840 and small plantations had been established around Fairfield House and lodges. The total of *c*. 138 a. of woodland in the parish in 1840 included Monk wood and copses at Wick park.[33] In 1905 there were 147 a. of woodland in the parish.[34]

There was a park near the castle in 1295.[35] The land, known as Old Park and later part of the Wyndeats estate, continued to be called the park or the king's park into the 16th century.[36] Field names indicate its position west of the castle site.[37] Wick park, north-east of Stogursey village, measured 120 a. in 1301.[38] Part of the area was wooded and income was received from timber and pannage.[39] The maintenance of its fence was the responsibility of tenants of adjoining land. The park was divided and let for agricultural use by the late 16th century,[40] and in 1681 it was sold to the owners of the Steyning estate.[41] By 1840 it was partly shared between several farms and partly woodland.[42] The names Wick Park covert and Wick Park cottages indicate the position of the park south-east of Wick hamlet. William Verney is said to have been licensed to enclose 200 a. for a park at Fairfield in 1473[43] and a deerpark there was referred to in 1516.[44] Much of the parkland around the house by 1822 was outside Stogursey parish, but within the parish was an area south of the house which had been emparked by Sir John Acland when the road to Stringston was diverted away from the house between 1806 and 1822.[45]

The route from the Parrett crossing at Combwich may originally have passed south of Stogursey village and near the castle site; it presumably ran near Steyning, and beyond Peadon westwards it is traceable as a green way north of Durborough.[46] That route from Combwich may in the 12th century have been diverted northwards to Stogursey village when the market was established there,[47] and may have continued to Shurton and along the remarkably

6 S.R.O., DD/AH 65/2.   7 P.R.O., RG 9/1604.
8 Eton Coll. Rec. 6/196.
9 Alnwick Castle, Northumberland MS. X.II.12.9A(i).
10 Eton Coll. Rec. 6/196.
11 P.R.O., RG 10/2354; S.R.O., DD/AH 35/21.
12 Below, char.
13 W. Suss. R.O., PHA uncat.; W. Suff. R.O. 449/E3/15.53/2.17.
14 S.R.O., DD/SAS (C/112) 9/1; P.R.O., HO 107/935.
15 S.R.O., DD/AH 65/12.
16 Alnwick Castle, Northumberland MS. X.II.12.9A(i).
17 P.R.O., RG 10/2354.   18 S.R.O., D/P/stogs 9/1/3.
19 Ibid. DD/AH 34/17; below, char.
20 P.R.O., RG 10/2354; O.S. Map 6", Som. XXXVII. SE. (1886 edn.).
21 Som. C.C., Sites and Mons. Rec.
22 Eton Coll. Rec. 6/162.   23 S.R.O., DD/L P36/4.
24 Ibid. DD/X/WI 34.   25 Ibid. DD/AH 32/19.
26 Taunton Castle, Braikenridge colln., drawing, 1845; notice at well.
27 *V.C.H. Som.* i. 462, 486, 501, 505, 508; *Dom. Bk.* ed.

Thorn, 364.
28 *S.R.S.* lxi, p. 31.
29 Eton Coll. Rec. 6/195; S.R.O., tithe award.
30 S.R.O., DD/AH 4/9, 13/4.   31 Ibid. 40/6.
32 Ibid. 65/12; DD/HC 138.
33 Ibid. tithe award.
34 Statistics supplied by the then Bd. of Agric., 1905.
35 *Cal. Close*, 1288–96, 467; P.R.O., SC 6/1090/4; S.R.O., DD/AH 17/11.
36 *Cal. Inq. p.m.* iv, p. 341; W. Suss. R.O., PHA 5730; S.R.O., DD/AH 17/11.
37 S.R.O., DD/X/WI 34; ibid. tithe award.
38 *Cal. Inq. p.m.* iv, p. 341.
39 W. Suff. R.O. 449/E3/15.53/2.5, 9–10, 17.
40 S.R.O., DD/X/WI 34.
41 Ibid. DD/S/WH (N/152).
42 Ibid. tithe award.
43 Ibid. DD/AH 23/19.   44 Ibid. 11/10.
45 Ibid. 65/12; *S.R.S.* lxxvi, map 1822.
46 S.R.O., tithe award.
47 Below, econ. hist. (market and fairs).

straight road via Burton and Culver Street to Lilstock, Stringston, and the coast road to Watchet. A second route from Stogursey market place passed via Fairfield to Holford, along a road still known in the 20th century as Portway Lane.[48] Portway Lane led both to Watchet and to the Quantocks. A more direct route to Over Stowey from Burton through Durborough was known in the later 18th century as the great road from Stogursey to Stowey.[49] A new route, made necessary by the construction of Hinkley Point nuclear power station, comes from Cannington and runs across the site of Wick park.

In 1824 a ship canal was proposed, and a route surveyed by Thomas Telford linking Stolford with Beer (Devon).[50] A rail link between Stolford and Bridgwater was suggested in 1845.[51] In 1888 a ship canal between Lilstock and Seaton (Devon) via Stolford was supported by the Board of Admiralty.[52] A railway between Bridgwater and Stogursey, with an extension further west, was under consideration for several years after 1899.[53]

In 1957 building began on a nuclear power station for the Central Electricity Generating Board at Hinkley Point, a site on the coast almost due north of Stogursey village and formerly known as Botestall.[54] Generating began in 1965. A second station on the site, opened in 1976, had the first advanced gas-cooled reactor to supply the national grid. The two stations have a combined output capacity of 3,400 megawatts and 1,300 people are employed on the site.[55] A third station was proposed in 1985 and was the subject of a public inquiry in 1989–90.

There were two licensed victuallers in 1608[56] and an unlicensed house was suppressed in 1614.[57] By 1630 the number of licensed premises in the parish had increased to four[58] and in 1647 the number in the borough alone was reduced to three.[59] Included was the Swan, named in 1622 and probably in existence by 1619,[60] which stood in Stogursey market place. Its name was changed to the Acland Arms c. 1865[61] and to its present name, the Acland Hood Arms, by 1889.[62] It remained open in 1985. By 1675 and for most of the 18th century there were six licensed houses, including the Corner Inn at the junction of Church and Castle streets, first recorded in 1654, which was called the Three

Choughs by 1713[63] and the Queen's Head by 1744.[64] The White Horse, east of the last, had opened by 1673.[65] The Lamb, probably in business between 1746 and 1786, and the Rose and Crown, possibly in Castle Street and named in 1754,[66] did not survive into the 1790s. There was then only one licensed house in the parish, and during the unrest of 1800–1 the men of Stogursey complained that there were no more.[67] In the mid 19th century several beerhouses came into being[68] and by the later years of the century there were c. 10 public houses, including the Greyhound[69] and the White Lion[70] in Lime Street, the Fox and Hounds[71] in High Street, and the Castle in Castle Street.[72] The Greyhound was still in business in 1985.

The earliest recorded public house outside the village was Steart House, on Steart warren, which was licensed between 1779 and 1792.[73] The Burton inn was licensed in 1850[74] and remained open in 1939.[75] It probably closed soon afterwards and was a private house in 1985. There was a beerhouse at Stolford, possibly at the junction of Gorepit and Whitewick lanes, between 1850 and 1861.[76] The beerhouse at Cockwood was open between 1851 and 1872.[77] The Shurton inn was probably open from 1861[78] and remained open in 1985. Another beerhouse at Shurton, at the east end of the hamlet, was open by 1871[79] and possibly by 1851.[80] By 1890 it was known as the King Tree, and is said also to have been called the First and Last.[81] It probably closed soon after 1906[82] and in 1985 was called Lower House Farm.

The Stogursey Women's friendly society was established in 1806 and met at the Swan. It provided pensions for members over 70 and there were initially 51 members.[83] It was dissolved in 1868.[84] The Stogursey friendly society had been founded by 1811 and also met at the Swan.[85] It was disbanded, probably in 1845, when the Stogursey New friendly society was formed with over 100 members. The society ceased to take new members c. 1920 and was wound up in 1952 when 17 surviving members each received c. £34.[86] Painted 'battle boards', possibly belonging to the Stogursey friendly society, are preserved in the parish church.[87]

There was a reading room and library in Church Street in 1872,[88] and in 1928 both old

48 V.C.H. Som. v. 89; below, Stringston.
49 S.R.O., DD/AH 35/32.
50 Ibid. DD/X/KLT 3.
51 C. Hadfield, Canals of S. Eng. 310, 313.
52 S.R.O., DD/AH 3/7.
53 Ibid. Q/RUo 7; ibid. DD/AH 5/2, 17/13.
54 Ibid. D/RA 9/24, maps 1723, 1784.
55 Inf. from C.E.G.B., Hinkley Point.
56 S.R.O., Q/RL.
57 S.R.S. xxiii. 116.
58 S.R.O., Q/RL.
59 S.R.S. lxxi, p. 15.
60 Devon R.O. 1050A, ct. roll.
61 S.R.O., DD/AH 40/6; P.O. Dir. Som. (1861, 1866).
62 Kelly's Dir. Som. (1889).
63 S.R.O., DD/AH 32/8.
64 Ibid. DD/SP inventory, 1737; DD/OB, map 1744; ibid. Q/RL.
65 Eton Coll. Rec. 6/191, 211, 213; S.R.O., Q/SR 118/5; Q/RL; ibid. DD/MVB 62.
66 S.R.O., DD/AH 23/17; D/P/stogs 4/1/2; ibid. Q/RL.
67 Ibid. Q/RL; ibid. DD/AH 59/12.
68 Ibid. DD/SAS PR 482/2.

69 Ibid. DD/SF 4548.
70 Ibid. DD/SAS PR 482/2; P.R.O., RG 9/1604; P.O. Dir. Som. (1875).
71 S.R.O., DD/SAS PR 482/2; D/P/stogs 3/1/1; P.R.O., RG 10/2354.
72 P.O. Dir. Som. (1859, 1875).
73 Below, manors (Steart).
74 S.R.O., DD/SAS PR 482/2.
75 Kelly's Dir. Som. (1939).
76 S.R.O., DD/SAS PR 482/2; P.O. Dir. Som. (1861).
77 P.R.O., HO 107/1920; Morris & Co. Dir. Som. (1872).
78 P.R.O., RG 10/2354; P.O. Dir. Som. (1861).
79 P.R.O., RG 10/2354.
80 S.R.O., DD/SAS PR 482/2.
81 Ibid. DD/CCH 1/8; DD/V/WLr 24.8.
82 Kelly's Dir. Som. (1906).
83 S.R.O., DD/AH 66/18.
84 Ibid. DD/SAS PR 492; P.R.O., FS 2/9.
85 S.R.O., DD/AH 11/6; P.R.O., FS 2/9.
86 S.R.O., D/P/stogs 23/1, 6; P.R.O., FS 2/9.
87 S.R.O., D/P/stogs 9/3/2; M. Fuller, W. Country Friendly Socs. pl. facing p. 85.
88 Morris & Co. Dir. Som. (1872).

and new reading rooms were mentioned.[89] They were not recorded again. A maypole was erected in the village in 1764,[90] and mummers performed in the early 19th century.[91]

In 1340 the borough was taxed at 30s., more than twice Nether Stowey. In 1377 130 people paid poll tax.[92] There were 646 communicants in 1548, the total probably including the communicants of Lilstock,[93] and in 1563 there were 174 households in Stogursey alone.[94] In 1801 the population was 1,168. The figure rose to 1,496 in 1831 and remained fairly constant until 1881, when it fell to 1,262. The decline continued, reaching 1,034 in 1901, but in the later 20th century new housing brought about an increase. By 1961 the population was 1,391. It rose to 1,454 in 1971 but by 1981 had fallen to 1,196.[95]

King John stayed at Stogursey in September 1210 with Warin FitzGerold, possibly at the castle.[96] Sixty-three men were fined for involvement in the Cornish rebellion in 1497.[97] Two supporters of the duke of Monmouth were executed at Tower Hill, probably on the site now occupied by the school.[98] The cross was the site of a Jacobite disturbance in 1719.[99] In 1801 men from Stogursey marched to Bridgwater to ask for lower prices.[1] Sir John Burland of Steyning (d. 1776) was Chief Baron of the Exchequer.[2] Sir Wroth Palmer Acland (d. 1816) was a younger son of Arthur Acland of Fairfield and served under the duke of Wellington, becoming K.C.B. and Lieutenant-General in 1814.[3] Samuel Taylor Coleridge wrote his 'Ode to Sara' at Shurton Bars in 1795.[4] The emperor of Abyssinia, Haile Selassie, visited Stogursey in 1938.[5]

CASTLE. Although there is no known record of the building until 1204,[6] Stogursey castle was presumably in 1166 the *caput* of the honor, including more than 27 knights' fees, of William (III) de Curci, lord of Stogursey.[7] On William's death in 1171 the honor passed to his infant son William (IV) who took possession in 1189 and died without issue in 1194.[8] His sister and heir Alice had married Warin FitzGerold, who forfeited the honor before his death in 1216.[9] In that year the Crown ordered the destruction of the castle,[10] which therefore may have been excluded from the grant of Stogursey manor[11] in the same year to Fawkes de Breauté, husband of Margaret, Alice's daughter by Warin. Fawkes's rebellion led to the siege of the castle, which in 1224 the constable was ordered to deliver to the sheriff.[12] Half the honor, including Stogursey, was claimed for Joan, Alice's daughter by Henry of Cornhill; by 1228 Joan's husband Hugh de Neville of Essex (d. 1234) was in possession of Stogursey lands[13] and in 1233 the Crown ordered him to fortify the castle.[14] His son and heir John died in 1246 leaving a son Hugh who came of age in 1256, forfeited his lands for rebellion, and died childless in 1269. He had been pardoned but in 1266 surrendered Stogursey, which the Crown granted to Robert Walerand (d. c. 1273). Robert's nephew and namesake was both a minor and an idiot,[15] and the Crown made temporary grants of Stogursey to Ames of Savoy, Thomas Button, archdeacon of Wells, and Queen Eleanor until 1297 or later.[16]

When Robert Walerand died c. 1301 the Crown was in possession of Stogursey castle and borough, and the Crown retained control since Robert's brother and heir John was also an idiot.[17] In 1308 the king granted custody to Robert (III) FitzPayn of Poorstock (Dors.), and in the following year, on John's death, Robert retained the estate which, by the time of his death in 1315, he held in chief.[18] Robert (IV) FitzPayn, Lord FitzPayn, son of the last, died in 1354 leaving a widow Ela (d. 1356) and a daughter Isabel. The estate passed on Ela's death to Robert's nephew Robert Grey of Codnor (Essex), who assumed the name FitzPayn.[19] His daughter and heir Isabel (d. 1394) married Richard Poynings, Lord Poynings (d. 1387), and Isabel's son Robert, Lord Poynings (d. 1446), was succeeded by his granddaughter Eleanor, daughter of Richard Poynings and wife of Henry Percy, later earl of Northumberland (d. 1461). Eleanor died in 1484 and was followed by her son Henry (d. 1489), Henry's son Henry Algernon (d. 1527), and Henry Algernon's son Henry (d. 1537), successive earls of Northumberland.[20] By 1514 the estate was described as the manors of Stogursey, Wyndeats, and Wick.[21]

On the death of the earl of Northumberland in 1537 his lands passed by his gift to the Crown,[22] and those in Stogursey were granted first to Sir

89 S.R.O., D/PC/stogs 1/2/2.
90 Ibid. D/P/stogs 2/1/4.
91 Ibid. 23/19.
92 *S.D.N.Q.* xxix. 11–12; P.R.O., E 179/169/31.
93 *S.R.S.* ii. 53.
94 B.L. Harl. MS. 594, f. 55.
95 *Census.*
96 *Rot. Lib.* (Rec. Com.), 231.
97 *Fines Imposed in 1497*, ed. A. J. Howard, 14.
98 S.R.O., D/P/stogs 2/1/2.
99 Ibid. Q/SR 288/4.
1 Ibid. DD/AH 59/12.
2 *S.D.N.Q.* iii. 268–9.
3 *D.N.B.*
4 S. T. Coleridge, *Poems on Various Subjects* (1797), pp. 88–93.
5 S.R.O., D/P/stogs 23/10.
6 *S.R.S.* lxi, p. 75; cf. D. F. Renn, *Norman Castles in Britain*, 316, where the building mentioned in 1090 refers to the castle of Curci-sur-Dives (Calvados).
7 *Red Bk. Exch.* (Rolls Ser.), i. 224–5.
8 Sanders, *Eng. Baronies*, 143; *S.R.S.* xli. 4; *Pipe R.* 1189–90 (Rec. Com.), 7.

9 Sanders, *Eng. Baronies*, 143.
10 *Rot. Litt. Claus.* (Rec. Com.), i. 239; *Rot. Litt. Pat.* (Rec. Com.), 186, 190.
11 *Rot. Litt. Claus.* (Rec. Com.), i. 293.
12 *Pat. R.* 1216–25, 456, 462–4, 490; *Rot. Litt. Claus.* (Rec. Com.), i. 617, 619; ii. 6, 16; *Roll of Divers Accts.* (P.R.S. N.S. xliv), 1; Sanders, *Eng. Baronies*, 143.
13 *Proc. Som. Arch. Soc.* lxvi. 118–19; *Close R.* 1227–31, 43; Sanders, *Eng. Baronies*, 143.
14 *Close R.* 1231–4, 546.
15 Sanders, *Eng. Baronies*, 143; *Cal. Pat.* 1258–66, 609; *Cal. Inq. p.m.* ii, pp. 6, 8.
16 *Cal. Pat.* 1272–81, 272, 463; *Cal. Close*, 1288–96, 22; *Feud. Aids*, iv. 282; P.R.O., SC 6/1090/4.
17 B.L. Add. Ch. 19302; *Cal. Inq. p.m.* iv, p. 341; v, p. 73; *Feud. Aids*, iv. 308.
18 *Cal. Close*, 1307–13, 33–4, 169; *Cal. Inq. p.m.* v, pp. 73, 388.
19 *Cal. Inq. p.m.* v, p. 388; *S.R.S.* xii. 120–1; *Complete Peerage*, v. 463–4.
20 *Complete Peerage*, ix. 721 and n.
21 P.R.O., CP 25(2)/51/360/6 Hen. VIII East.
22 *Complete Peerage*, ix. 721 and n.

STOGURSEY CASTLE IN 1845

BRIDGWATER CASTLE, *c.* 1800

STOGURSEY: FAIRFIELD HOUSE

GOATHURST: HALSWELL HOUSE

Richard Gresham and almost immediately afterwards to Henry Courtenay, marquess of Exeter, who had had an interest in them from 1532.[23] Courtenay was attainted in 1538[24] and the estate was granted in 1541 to Queen Catherine Howard (d. 1542).[25] It was later granted to Queen Catherine Parr on whose death in 1548 the castle (then called Wyndeats), together with the borough and Stogursey, Wick FitzPayn, and Wyndeats manors passed to Edward Seymour, duke of Somerset (d. 1552).[26] They reverted again to the Crown in 1552, and in the following year Stogursey castle and manor were presumably subsumed in a grant of Wick and Wyndeats manors and Stogursey borough to Edward Courtenay, earl of Devon, who died without issue in 1556.[27]

The earldom of Northumberland was revived in 1557 in favour of Thomas Percy, nephew of the previous earl, with remainder to Henry Percy, Thomas's brother, and Thomas was granted an estate described as the manors of Wick FitzPayn and Wyndeats and the borough, manor, and castle of Stogursey.[28] Thomas died in 1572 and Henry in 1585. Henry was followed by his son, also Henry (d. 1632), that Henry's son Algernon (d. 1668), and Algernon's son Joceline (d. 1670), successive earls of Northumberland.[29]

Following Joceline's death without male heir the estate was divided and sold by trustees largely from 1681.[30] Ownership of the castle is unknown until 1724, when it belonged to John Willis of Goathurst (d. 1761). He bequeathed it to George Davis (d. c. 1786), whose son William sold it in 1820 to (Sir) Peregrine Acland.[31] It was sold by Lord St. Audries in 1952[32] and in 1981 was bought by the Landmark Trust.[33]

The castle, which stands on low ground to the south of Stogursey village, comprises a roughly circular motte with two baileys, the inner protecting the motte on the south and east, the outer at a higher level further east, both surrounded by earth banks and watercourses. A third embanked enclosure lies north and west. The character of the earthworks and the evidence of structures beneath the motte suggest that the site was occupied and defended before the present castle was built,[34] and that it was, perhaps, the dwelling of William de Falaise mentioned c. 1100.[35]

The standing buildings of the castle, confined to the motte, comprise a curtain wall strengthened by a circular tower on the west side and a gatehouse to the east, to which a house was later added. The curtain wall contains work of the 12th century[36] but may have been rebuilt in the 14th. The towers appear to be of the 13th century, the gatehouse evidently succeeding a single, circular tower.[37] Those works may be related to the order of 1233 to fortify the castle.[38] In 1304 the constable was ordered to have its bridges repaired.[39] In the 1490s a new tower was built, two others re-roofed, and other rooms were fitted up when the castle was in use as a centre of estate administration. Among the rooms were an audit room, a wardrobe, and a prison besides domestic quarters which included a nursery.[40] Repairs were made in 1519[41] and a constable was paid until 1530[42] but by 1538 the building was said to be in decay.[43] By the later 16th century destruction was evidently advanced and rabbits were kept within the castle walls.[44] Before 1614 the gatehouse was extended to form a house,[45] which was inhabited in 1684.[46] The house was rebuilt c. 1878[47] and has been restored by the Landmark Trust for use as holiday accommodation.[48]

BOROUGH. The borough of Stogursey was recorded from 1225 when it answered at the eyre.[49] In 1301 it paid a small sum called 'burghright' to Cannington hundred.[50] It belonged to the lords of Stogursey until 1833 when it was last recorded,[51] except for the period 1550–2 when it was held by William Barlow, bishop of Bath and Wells, by grant of Edward Seymour, duke of Somerset.[52] In 1559 it was said that the earls of Northumberland had made Stogursey a 'borough town' although their charter had been burned.[53]

In the early 17th century the lord of the borough claimed deodand, treasure trove, and felons' goods.[54] Borough rents and profits totalled £9 1s. 6d. in 1276–7,[55] £8 18s. 5d. in 1500,[56] and £7 6s. 2d. c. 1542.[57] Rents were worth £6 4s. 9d. in 1559[58] and £5 0s. 1d. in 1614, when the lord also claimed deodand, treasure trove, and felons' goods.[59]

MANORS. In 1066 Beorhtsige (Brixi) held *STOKE*, which William de Falaise held in

---

23 P.R.O., E 150/928, no. 18; E 328/283.
24 Ibid. E 150/928, no. 18; S.R.S. lxi, pp. 76, 91.
25 L. & P. Hen. VIII, xvi, p. 241.
26 Cal. Pat. 1547–8, 126, 173.
27 Ibid. 1553–4, 181, 251, 256.   28 Ibid. 1557–8, 189.
29 Complete Peerage, ix. 728–40.
30 S.R.O., DD/AH 16/1, 28/1, 32/21; DD/BV 10; DD/HLM 8; DD/NN (H/20); DD/PC 17; DD/SAS (C/112) 9/2; DD/S/SH (N/152–3); DD/X/BH 2; P.R.O., CP 25(2)/761/21 Chas. II East.; MSS. in possession of Mr. J. S. Cox, Guernsey.
31 S.R.O., DD/AH 33/16, 55/2; D/P/gst 2/1/4; inf. from the Landmark Trust.   32 S.R.O., DD/X/HUX 1.
33 Inf. from the Landmark Trust.
34 The suggestion of Mr. Richard McDonnell, archaeologist.
35 S.R.S. lxi, p. 1.
36 D. F. Renn, Norman Castles in Britain, 316.
37 V.C.H. Som. ii. 150; there is no evidence, either documentary or archaeological, to support the claim for its destruction in 1457, despite Collinson, Hist. Som. i. 251;

Proc. Som. Arch. Soc. xxiii (1), 67.
38 Above, this section.   39 Cal. Close, 1302–7, 121.
40 W. Suff. R.O. 449/E3/15.53/2.2, 6, 9–10, 12.
41 Ibid. 2.17; W. Suss. R.O., PHA uncat.
42 P.R.O., E 315/427, f. 58.
43 L. & P. Hen. VIII, xiii (2), p. 293.
44 S.R.O., D/D/Cd 129.   45 Ibid. DD/X/WI 34.
46 Ibid. DD/SP inventory, 1684.
47 Proc. Som. Arch. Soc. xxiii (1), 67; for a view before the rebuilding, above, plate facing p. 136.
48 Inf. from the Landmark Trust.
49 S.R.S. xi, p. 40.   50 Cal. Inq. p.m. iv, p. 341.
51 e.g. S.R.S. lxvii, p. 193; S.R.O., DD/PLE 64.
52 Cal. Pat. 1549–51, 205; 1552, 456.
53 B.L. Harl. MS. 71, ff. 63–4.
54 S.R.O., DD/X/WI 34.   55 P.R.O., SC 6/974/8.
56 W. Suss. R.O., PHA uncat.
57 P.R.O., SC 6/Hen. VIII/6397.
58 B.L. Harl. MS. 71, f. 64.
59 S.R.O., DD/X/WI 34.

1086.[60] Emme, daughter and heir of William de Falaise, married William (I) de Curci. William (I) died c. 1114, and their son William (II) was dead by 1120. That William's son was William (III) de Curci who held the honor in 1166, and *STOGURSEY* manor descended with the honor and castle until c. 1680.[61] In 1686 Robert Siderfin bought the manor together with that of Wick FitzPayn.[62] Siderfin sold the lordship to Edward Habberfield in 1704.[63] By 1744 the manors were owned by Thomas Darch (d. 1752), whose widow Mary sold them to John Perceval, earl of Egmont, in 1758.[64] The lordship descended to successive earls, but it was not recorded after 1833.[65]

A manor called *WICK*, later *WICK FITZPAYN* after its lords in the earlier 14th century, was held in 1228 by Hugh de Neville with Stogursey,[66] with which it descended and was sold to Robert Siderfin in 1686; like Stogursey, its lordship is not recorded after 1833.[67] Estates which had been held of Stogursey honor in the Middle Ages were by the early 17th century said to be held of the manor of Wick FitzPayn.[68]

In 1066 Edric had an estate called Widiete. William held it of Roger de Courcelles in 1086,[69] but by 1301 it had become part of the demesne holding of Stogursey castle[70] and came to be known as *WYNDEATS* manor from 1514.[71]

Wyndeats manor passed in 1681 to John Day of Knighton, Stogursey,[72] who in 1714 settled it on the children of his daughter Elizabeth Holbech.[73] One of them, Day Holbech, left the estate by will of 1761 to John Coffin of Somerton, but the lordship was not recorded after 1741.[74] John's daughters Mary and Catherine held the estate in 1771. Catherine's heir was her son Brian Coombe (d. 1818) and Mary's her niece Jane Purlewent. In 1820 Jane and four heirs of Brian Coombe sold the property in trust for Frances Spurway, one of their number.[75] In 1846 Frances sold to the trustees of the late Sir John Palmer-Acland, and thereafter Wyndeats descended with Fairfield manor.[76]

Dawlea Farm was the capital messuage of the estate in the later 18th century[77] and probably dates from that period; a house stood on the site in 1614.[78]

An estate descended from the Trivet family to Robert Pokeswell (d. 1429), whose son John held courts for *CHALCOTT* manor in the 1440s.[79] The Chalcott manor held by Walter Steyning at his death in 1537[80] may have been the same estate. Edmund Wyndham bought lands at Chalcott in the later 17th century.[81]

The Pokeswells had a capital messuage in 1448,[82] as did Edmund Wyndham in 1689.[83] Chalcott Farm is a 17th-century house substantially rebuilt and enlarged in 1802.[84]

William Trivet held a fee at *COCK* as part of Stogursey honor in 1301,[85] in right of his wife Sarah, possibly daughter of Robert of Eston.[86] William was still in possession in 1312[87] but died shortly afterwards. His grandson and heir, Thomas Trivet, died in 1316 and was succeeded by his own posthumous son (Sir) John,[88] who was still alive in 1371.[89] Sir Thomas, son of Sir John, died in 1388[90] having settled his estate on himself and his second wife Elizabeth and their children. Their two daughters died without issue, probably before 1422, when Elizabeth gave Cock to her husband's kinsman John Trivet.[91] He was Elizabeth's heir when she died in 1433.[92] The estate is said to have passed with the marriage of a Trivet heir to John Compton in 1446–7.[93] John Compton, possibly John's son, with his wife Elizabeth sold what was called Cock manor in 1505 to William Nethway,[94] a Taunton merchant who in 1510 conveyed it to trustees to maintain a chantry and chapel at Taunton priory.[95] In 1548 the Crown sold the manor to Edward Bury, probably in trust for Robert Whetstone, a London haberdasher.[96] The Nethway family tried to regain possession against Whetstone,[97] who died in 1557 leaving Cock to his younger son Francis, a minor.[98] Margaret Matthews and Jane Haskins, granddaughters of William Nethway, revived their claim in 1563.[99] In 1579 Stephen Kay and his wife Margaret, possibly Margaret Matthews, conveyed half the manor to Edmund Wyndham, who bought the other half in 1586 from Francis Whetstone.[1]

Whetstone seems to have retained land called Cock Grounds, probably the former demesne holding, which was conveyed to Sir John Popham and Thomas Palmer in 1595.[2] Palmer's share in 1605 was described as half the manor,[3] and was known after more land had been added

60 *V.C.H. Som.* i. 508.
61 Sanders, *Eng. Baronies*, 143; *Red Bk. Exch.* (Rolls Ser.), i. 224–5; above, castle.
62 S.R.O., DD/PC 17.
63 P.R.O., CP 25(2)/961/3 Anne Mich.
64 S.R.O., DD/JL 121; DD/MY 42; DD/PC 17; Eton Coll. Rec. 6/267.
65 Above, Enmore, manors; S.R.O., DD/AH 19/9, 31/10; DD/PLE 64.
66 *S.R.S.* xli, p. 44; P.R.O., E 150/928, no. 18.
67 Above, this section.
68 S.R.O., DD/X/WI 34.
69 *V.C.H. Som.* i. 487.
70 *Cal. Inq. p.m.* iv, p. 341; above, castle.
71 P.R.O., CP 25(2)/51/360/6 Hen. VIII East.
72 S.R.O., DD/AH 28/1.
73 Ibid. 27/1.
74 Ibid. 28/1; DD/S/FA 20.
75 Ibid. DD/AH 27/1.
76 Ibid. 28/1; below, this section (Fairfield).
77 S.R.O., DD/AH 28/1.
78 Ibid. DD/X/WI 34.
79 P.R.O., C 139/45, no. 30; Dors. R.O., D/WLC/M 244–5.

80 P.R.O., C 142/59, no. 92.
81 S.R.O., DD/WO 5/3.
82 Dors. R.O., D 10/M 245.
83 S.R.O., DD/WO 5/3.
84 Ibid. DD/AH 23/3.
85 *Cal. Inq. p.m.* iv, p. 341.
86 P.R.O., C 137/83, no. 35.
87 *Cal. Inq. p.m.* v, p. 196.
88 Ibid. vi, p. 43.
89 B.L. Harl. Ch. 49. F. 31.
90 *S.R.S.* lxviii, pp. 36–7; *Proc. Som. Arch. Soc.* xxviii. 214.
91 *Cal. Close, 1419–22,* 234.
92 P.R.O., C 139/64, no. 35.
93 Collinson, *Hist. Som.* iii. 89.
94 P.R.O., CP 25(1)/202/42/20 Hen. VII East.
95 S.R.O., DD/AH 30/4; *S.R.S.* xix. 177–8.
96 *S.R.S.* ii. 22–3; *Cal. Pat.* 1549–51, 121; S.R.O., DD/AH 30/4; P.R.O., C 3/26, no. 44.
97 S.R.O., DD/AH 30/4.
98 Ibid.; P.R.O., E 150/944, no. 19.
99 S.R.O., DD/AH 30/4.
1 P.R.O., CP 25(2)/205/21 Eliz. I Hil.; S.R.O., DD/AH 30/4.
2 S.R.O., DD/AH 30/4.
3 *S.R.S.* lxvii, p. 45.

as *COCK AND GOREPIT* manor. It thereafter descended with Fairfield.[4] The Wyndham holding descended with Kentsford in St. Decumans until 1703, when it was sold to Richard Musgrave (d. 1727).[5] It probably then descended like Stamfordlands in North Petherton until 1795 when it was sold to John Acland.[6] There is no further reference to lordship.

A grange at Cock was recorded in 1316,[7] and a capital messuage in 1557 which came to be called Cock Farm and later Upper Cock Farm.[8] It is a double-pile house of the 18th century.

In the later 10th century King Edgar granted two hides at *DURBOROUGH* to Ealdred or Aelfhelm which passed to Glastonbury abbey.[9] The abbey claimed lordship until the 14th century,[10] and one of the two later divisions of the manor, Durborough Dodington, was said in 1554 to be held in chief but later to be held of the hundred of Whitley, formerly Glastonbury abbey's.[11] The other division, Durborough Verney, became linked with Fairfield, and was said in 1508 to be held of the earl of Northumberland, lord of Stogursey.[12] A mesne lordship held by the Forz family was treated in 1303 and 1428 as the chief lordship;[13] Simon Furneaux, one of the Forz heirs, held it in 1320–1[14] and Sir Baldwin Malet in 1363.[15]

Oswald held Durborough of the abbey in 1066 and Roger de Courcelles in 1086.[16] Baldwin de Vere may have been the tenant in 1234,[17] but by 1256 Thomas Trivet was lord probably in right of his wife Eleanor, daughter of Joan Braunche, the granddaughter and heir of Wandril de Courcelles.[18] Thomas was still alive in 1280.[19] Another Thomas Trivet held the estate in 1328 and 1338,[20] and was said to have left as coheirs his daughter Maud wife of Ralph Verney,[21] Eleanor Pokeswell, probably his granddaughter by another daughter,[22] and the three daughters of Cecily (d. 1361), probably a third daughter.[23]

Maud Verney's third share, known as *DURBOROUGH VERNEY*[24] and later as *DURBOROUGH* manor,[25] descended with Fairfield in the Verney and Palmer families.[26] Eleanor Pokeswell's share descended with her share of Woolmersdon in North Petherton until the death of Thomas Pokeswell in 1537,[27] when

it was divided between his two daughters, Elizabeth, wife of Richard Howe, and Eleanor, wife of John Roynon.[28] George Smythe of Woolmersdon bought the Roynon share in 1584 and had by 1590 acquired the other, possibly from Elizabeth Howe's daughter Dorothy, wife of John Killigrew.[29] The shares then descended with Smythe's share of Woolmersdon, but before 1639 Nicholas Smythe sold the land to Jane, wife of Sir Francis Hele. Hele in that year sold to Sir Francis Dodington and it became part of Durborough Dodington manor.[30]

Cecily's three daughters, Cecily or Christine Crewkerne, Alice Orchard, and Maud Dodington, each had one ninth share of Durborough, which also descended with Woolmersdon.[31] Cecily or Christine Crewkerne held a share in 1366[32] which seems to have been sold to another of the coparceners by 1431.[33] Alice Orchard's share was sold to Nicholas Halswell in 1564, and passed from his grandson Nicholas Halswell to Margaret Dodington in 1622.[34] Margaret sold it to her son (Sir) Francis in 1625.[35] Maud Dodington's share probably descended with Dodington manor[36] and was known as *DURBOROUGH DODINGTON* by 1514[37] and later as Durborough or Durborough alias Woolmersdon manor.[38] The Dodington lands, only partly in Stogursey parish,[39] descended from the Dodington family to Richard Grenville, duke of Buckingham and Chandos (d. 1839), and were sold by him to the trustees of the late Sir John Acland in 1837.[40]

A capital messuage was recorded on the Pokeswell manor in 1446 when it was let.[41] Durborough Farm, which belonged to Durborough Verney manor,[42] is probably medieval in origin but was extensively altered in the early 17th century to form a three-roomed cross-passage house whose hall has a framed and panelled ceiling.[43]

In 1166 Goslan held a fifth of a fee of William de Curci,[44] and his son Martin of Fairfield held *FAIRFIELD* of Maud de Chandos, lady of Nether Stowey.[45] By the later 13th century the estate comprised land in Stogursey, Lilstock, and Stringston.[46] In 1301 part was held of Stogursey manor[47] and in 1507 it was said to be

4   S.R.O., DD/AH 4/9, 16/5, 30/5; below, this section.
5   *V.C.H. Som.* v. 155; S.R.O., DD/AH 3/3; DD/WO 5/2.
6   Below, N. Petherton, manors; S.R.O., DD/AH 2/2.
7   P.R.O., C 134/56, no. 4.
8   S.R.O., DD/AH 30/4, 32/23.
9   H. P. R. Finberg, *Early Charters of Wessex*, p. 143.
10   *V.C.H. Som.* i. 462; *Rot. Hund.* (Rec. Com.), ii. 135; *S.R.S.* xxvi. 62.
11   *Cal. Pat.* 1553–4, 7; P.R.O., WARD 7/24, no. 129; *S.R.S.* lxvii, p. 45.
12   *Cal. Inq. p.m. Hen. VII*, iii, pp. 258–9.
13   *Feud. Aids*, iv. 306, 349, 365.
14   S.R.O., DD/L P36/4, 32.
15   *Cal. Inq. p.m.* xi, p. 390; Pole MS. 933, 4458.
16   *V.C.H. Som.* i. 462.
17   *Close R.* 1231–4, 540.
18   *S.R.S.* vi. 178, 374; *Proc. Som. Arch. Soc.* lxxviii, pp. 15–16.
19   B.L. Add. Ch. 20230; *S.R.S.* xliv. 139–40; S.R.O., DD/AH 65/1.
20   Pole MS. 4458; *S.R.S.* xii. 198.
21   S.R.O., DD/AH 65/6, 66/9.
22   Below, N. Petherton, manors.
23   *Cal. Inq. p.m.* xi, p. 390.

24   S.R.O., DD/AH 11/9.
25   P.R.O., C 142/21, no. 66.
26   Below, this section (Fairfield).
27   Below, N. Petherton, manors.
28   P.R.O., CP 25(2)/93/710/1 & 2 Phil. & Mary Mich.; CP 25(2)/205/20 Eliz. I East.
29   Ibid. CP 25(2)/260/20 Eliz. I Trin.; CP 25(2)/206/32 Eliz. I East.; Hutchins, *Hist. Dors.* i. 112.
30   S.R.O., DD/AH 33/19.
31   Below, N. Petherton, manors.
32   *Cal. Close*, 1364–8, 220.
33   Below, N. Petherton, manors.
34   Ibid.; P.R.O., C 142/154, no. 86; S.R.O., DD/S/WH 8.
35   S.R.O., DD/AH 35/32.
36   *V.C.H. Som.* v. 66.
37   S.R.O., DD/AH 11/9.   38   Ibid. 55/2.
39   Ibid. 40/4; *V.C.H. Som.* v. 66.
40   S.R.O., DD/AH 55/2.
41   Dors. R.O., D 10/M 244.
42   S.R.O., DD/AH 35/32.
43   Ibid. DD/V/WLr 24.2.
44   *Red Bk. Exch.* (Rolls Ser.), i. 225.
45   *V.C.H. Som.* v. 104, 193; S.R.O., DD/AH 60/19.
46   S.R.O., DD/AH 66/5.
47   *Cal. Inq. p.m.* iv, p. 342.

held of the earl of Northumberland.[48] Later in the century and in 1605 it was said to be held of Nether Stowey manor.[49]

Martin of Fairfield was followed, probably between 1212 and 1216, by William Russell, and William by his son Ralph (d. 1287).[50] Ralph's daughter and heir Margaret married first William Verney (d. by 1280) and secondly William de la Pyle.[51] Her son William Verney died in 1333 leaving a son Ralph (d. 1350), who was succeeded by his sons William (d. 1351) and John (d. 1392). John's son, also John, was probably a minor, for his mother Avice held the manor court.[52] John (d. 1448) was succeeded by his son John (d. 1462) and his grandson William Verney (d. 1489).[53] William was followed in direct line by John (d. 1507),[54] Robert (d. 1547),[55] John (d. 1551),[56] and Hugh Verney (d. 1556). Hugh's heir was his infant daughter Elizabeth, later wife of William Palmer.[57]

Elizabeth's son Thomas Palmer succeeded as a minor on his mother's death in 1592[58] and when he died in 1605 his son William was also under age.[59] William died in 1652[60] and was followed by his brother Peregrine (d. 1684)[61] and by Peregrine's son Nathaniel (d. 1718). Nathaniel's son Thomas, an antiquary who wrote a history of parts of the county,[62] died without issue in 1734 and his wife Elizabeth, who had held the estate jointly with him, in 1738.[63] Thomas's brother Peregrine succeeded but died without issue in 1762, leaving the estate to his kinsman Arthur Acland in tail male.[64] Arthur died in 1771 and his son John (cr. Bt. 1818 and from then known as Palmer-Acland) in 1831.[65] Sir John's son Sir Peregrine Fuller-Palmer-Acland was succeeded in 1871 by his only daughter Isabel (d. 1903), wife of Sir Alexander Fuller-Acland-Hood, Bt. Her son Alexander (cr. Baron St. Audries, 1911) died in 1917 and was succeeded by his elder son Alexander Peregrine, Baron St. Audries,[66] who died unmarried in 1971. His heir was his niece Elizabeth Acland-Hood, later the wife of Sir Michael Gass, K.C.M.G. (d. 1983). Lady Gass owned Fairfield and a considerable estate in the parish in 1985.

William Verney (d. 1489) is said to have had licence c. 1473 to encircle his house at Fairfield with a wall and seven round towers.[67] The plan of that house is probably incorporated within the present building. Part of the richly decorated, late 15th-century beams of two first-floor rooms survive in the south-west wing, and there is a blocked arch of similar date in the wall between the former screens passage and the dining room. Three of the towers remained in the earlier 18th century on the boundary of a walled court east of the house.[68]

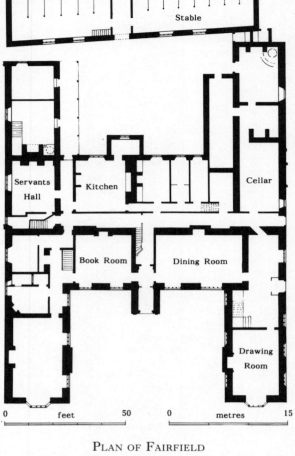

PLAN OF FAIRFIELD

Elizabeth Verney (d. 1592) may have begun remodelling the house to give it, though not completely symmetrical, the conventional form of an **E**. The porch is dated 1589, and above it was a tower of three further storeys. A hall block lay to the north-east. The medieval house may have continued beyond the south-west wing and probably contained service rooms.[69] The lower back court had service rooms on the south-west and north-east, and the stables on the north-west side may have been contemporary with the remodelling, but are more likely to have been a 17th-century addition. The work on the house was said to have been unfinished in 1633.[70] Nathaniel Palmer (d. 1718) or his son Thomas (d. 1734) altered the interior, adding new staircases in each main wing. The quality of that to the south-west, at the service end of the house, suggests that the rooms were being converted for family use.

About 1780[71] and again c. 1815[72] Sir John Acland made extensive alterations, in the second phase

48 P.R.O., C 142/21, no. 66.
49 Ibid. WARD 7/24, no. 129; *S.R.S.* lxvii, p. 45.
50 S.R.O., DD/AH 60/19; *V.C.H. Som.* v. 193; *S.R.S.* xli. 24.
51 *S.R.S.* xliv. 270.   52 S.R.O., DD/AH 60/10, 66/5.
53 Ibid. 60/10, 65/2.
54 *S.R.S.* xix. 102–5; *Cal. Inq. p.m. Hen. VII*, iii, pp. 258–9.
55 P.R.O., C 142/85, no. 52.   56 Ibid. C 142/97, no. 92.
57 Ibid. C 142/112, no. 86; S.R.O., DD/AH 13/5.
58 P.R.O., C 142/237, no. 129.
59 *S.R.S.* lxvii, p. 45.
60 Ibid. xv. 35.

61 M.I. Stogursey ch.; S.R.O., DD/AH 54/1.
62 S.R.O., DD/AH 60/10.
63 M.I. Stogursey ch.
64 S.R.O., DD/AH 54/3; D/P/stogs 2/1/4.
65 Ibid. DD/AH 23/1, 60/10.
66 Burke, *Peerage* (1949), 1760–1.
67 S.R.O., D/P/stogs 23/19.
68 Ibid. DD/AH 23/4 map; 60/10.
69 Fairfield House, early 18th-century painting.
70 *S.R.S.* xv. 35.   71 S.R.O., DD/AH 40/6.
72 Ibid. 66/12; for a photo., above, plate facing p. 137.

to the designs of Richard Carver. The rooms to the south-west were demolished and a new kitchen range was built behind the hall. Roofs were reconstructed, dormers were removed, and the porch tower was reduced in height by one storey. Many rooms were redecorated and coloured marble fireplace surrounds were introduced. A new entrance front was probably created on the north-east side of the house during the same period.

A 17th-century barn and a granary of the earlier 18th century survive behind the house. In the early 18th century a short canal was dug, parallel to the entrance front but separated from the house by the Stringston road. Sir John Acland extended his park southwards to the new line of the Stringston road between 1806 and 1822, some 350 metres from the house. Lodges, remodelled or rebuilt in the later 1830s, were placed at the eastern and southern entrances, and sheltering belts of trees were planted.[73]

A chapel at Fairfield was served by a priest paid by William Verney in 1333.[74] The last chaplain was mentioned in 1562. The building was described as 'fair' in the later 16th century but even its site was not known by the 1730s.[75]

FARRINGDON was held of Stogursey honor in 1301,[76] and it was later said to be held of Wick FitzPayn manor or Stogursey castle until 1615.[77] It may have been held by William of Eston in 1226.[78] William of Greenham and Raymond Trivet, possibly coheirs, shared the fee in 1301.[79] Raymond Trivet was named as lord with Walter Bluet in 1346[80] but Thomas Trivet had succeeded by 1354[81] and in 1379 Sir Thomas Trivet, perhaps the same man, conveyed his property to John Fittleton, possibly in trust for sale, since the Bluets had sole interest there by 1428.[82]

The share of William of Greenham passed on his death before 1341[83] to Walter Bluet, then a minor and son of Sir Walter Bluet and Christian of Greenham.[84] Walter may still have been under age when Simon Furneaux was described as lord in 1344,[85] but he was evidently of age in 1346[86] and was later knighted. He was dead by 1397 when his heir was his son John Bluet.[87] John was still alive in 1428 but dead by 1431 when the manor was held by his widow Agnes, then wife of John Bevyle.[88] Agnes's son John Bluet succeeded on her death in 1442 and the manor then descended with North Petherton manor until the death of John Bluet in 1634.[89]

By that date Farringdon had been settled on John Bluet's daughters Anne, Mary, and Elizabeth, but at the time of his death two more daughters, Dorothy and Susan, had been born, and Elizabeth had died.[90] The estate was therefore shared so that Anne and Mary each had one third share as under the settlement and one quarter share of Elizabeth's third, while Dorothy and Susan each had one quarter share of Elizabeth's third. Mary's share, described as half the manor, by 1674 had passed to John Selleck, archdeacon of Bath (d. 1690),[91] and from him it descended to his son Nathaniel (d. c. 1691) and to Nathaniel's son John (d. 1732).[92] In 1779 the heirs of John's two daughters, Susan and Elizabeth, sold to William Poole of Shurton, and in 1792 William's devisees sold to (Sir) John Acland, already owner of the other share. Farringdon thereafter descended with Fairfield.[93]

Anne Bluet and her sister Dorothy conveyed their estate to George Pollard in 1677. George died in 1685 when his heir was his grandson Henry Sweeting of Kilve.[94] Henry (d. c. 1732) was followed in turn by his sons Henry (d. 1739) and Thomas (d. 1758), and by Thomas's son Henry (d. 1785). Henry's son Henry sold his half share to John Acland in 1788.[95]

The manor house, known as Farringdon Hill and recorded in 1653, was probably on the site of the present house, which dates from the 19th century. A chapel was let with the manor house in 1653[96] and the field name Chappelhayes was recorded in 1840.[97]

In 1066 *IDSON* was held by Alwine, and in 1086 by Ansketil of Roger de Courcelles.[98] The Trivets' estate was held as a fee of Stogursey honor in 1301,[99] but later divisions gave rise to claims to overlordship by the owners of Spaxton and Otterhampton manors.[1]

In the mid 13th century Beatrice of Eston, possibly a descendant of Ansketil[2] and widow of Robert of Eston, gave the capital messuage and land to her daughter Sarah.[3] Sarah married Robert Fichet of Spaxton (d. 1271–2),[4] and she or a daughter of the same name had by 1301 married William Trivet (d. 1314–15).[5] In 1307 William Trivet's son William released his rights in the estate to the tenant, Gilbert of Beere,[6] and Gilbert was succeeded in the direct male line by Robert (fl. 1334–5), Thomas, and John (fl. 1401–12).[7] The subsequent descent of the holding has not been traced.

William of Beere gave land at Idson to Stogursey priory in 1170 and his son Peter granted a

73 *S.R.S.* lxxvi, map 1822.
74 S.R.O., DD/AH 65/10, 66/10.
75 Ibid. 60/10.
76 *Cal. Inq. p.m.* iv, pp. 341–2.
77 P.R.O., C 139/105, no. 10; C 140/81, no. 56; C 142/39, no. 87; S.R.O., DD/X/WI 34.
78 *Cur. Reg. R.* xii. 331.
79 *Cal. Inq. p.m.* iv, pp. 341–2.
80 *Feud. Aids*, iv. 353.
81 *Cal. Chart. R.* 1341–1417, 133.
82 *S.R.S.* xvii. 100; *Feud. Aids*, iv. 394.
83 *S.R.S.* xi, pp. 399–400.
84 Ibid. x, p. 443; Collinson, *Hist. Som.* iii. 29.
85 Pole MS. 2464.
86 *Feud. Aids*, iv. 353.
87 S.R.O., DD/SF 1453–5.
88 *Feud. Aids*, iv. 435; P.R.O., C 139/105, no. 10.
89 Below, N. Petherton, manors; P.R.O., C 142/475, no. 105.

90 P.R.O., C 142/475, no. 105; ibid. CP 25(2)/617/1655 Hil., 1656 Mich.; *S.R.S.* lxvii, p. 10.
91 *S.R.S.* lxxii, pp. xiii–xiv; S.R.O., DD/BR/lp 4; P.R.O., CP 25(2)/717/24 Chas. II Mich.
92 S.R.O., DD/BR/lp 4; DD/AH 32/1.
93 Ibid. DD/AH 16/1, 32/21, 34/19; DD/L 2/18/100.
94 Ibid. DD/AH 13/1, 32/21; DD/L 2/18/100; *Som. Wills*, ed. Brown, iii. 14.
95 S.R.O., DD/AH 12/6, 13/1, 32/21; D/P/kve 2/1/2–3; DD/L 2/18/100; *V.C.H. Som.* v. 99.
96 S.R.O., DD/BR/lp 4.   97 Ibid. tithe award.
98 *V.C.H. Som.* i. 486.   99 *Cal. Inq. p.m.* iv, p. 341.
1 *S.R.S.* lxviii, pp. 6, 10; P.R.O., C 137/74, no. 50.
2 Below, other estates (Steyning).
3 *Cat. Anct. D.* iii, A 5865.   4 *S.R.S.* lxviii, p. 19.
5 P.R.O., C 139/64, no. 35.
6 *S.R.S.* lxviii, p. 11 (where the date is given as 1361); P.R.O., E 326/5976.
7 *S.R.S.* lxviii, pp. 11, 13.

holding to William, son of Hugh of Idson, a former tenant, in the early 13th century.[8] Peter was still alive in 1242–3[9] and had been succeeded by his son William by 1281.[10] The Idson family retained their interest[11] until William Idson conveyed his lands there to John Verney in 1387[12] and the estate was thereafter considered a manor.[13] It descended with Fairfield until 1417 when Ralph Verney vested it in trustees[14] who in 1428 gave it to the executors of Nicholas Bubwith, bishop of Bath and Wells. They in turn gave the estate to the chapter of Wells in 1430.[15] Idson remained in the possession of the dean and chapter until 1866 when it was vested in the Ecclesiastical Commissioners.[16] In 1870 the commissioners sold Idson to George Burges, the lessee, who in the same year conveyed it to Sir Alexander Acland-Hood,[17] and it again formed part of the Fairfield estate.

Beatrice of Eston had a capital messuage at Idson in the mid 13th century.[18]

In 1295–6 the heirs of Walter de Burges as mesne lords held *KNIGHTON* as ½ knight's fee of Stogursey honor.[19] The overlordship was recorded until 1638.[20]

The heirs of John de Tornie held part of Knighton in 1295–6[21] and John Brun by 1301;[22] it was that part which Robert Oldmixon (d. 1555) held, possibly in succession to his father William (d. 1544) and grandfather John Oldmixon (d. 1511). Robert's son John succeeded his father as a minor[23] and sold to Sir George Rogers in 1576.[24] Sir George (d. 1582)[25] was followed by his son Edward (d. 1627), and Edward by his son Sir Francis (d. 1638). During the ownership of Sir Francis the estate came to be known as Knighton manor.[26]

Francis Rogers's son Hugh died without male issue in 1653 and the manor passed to his uncle Henry, descending like Chadmead in North Petherton[27] until 1720 when the trustees for the sale of Sir Copplestone Warwick Bampfylde's estate sold Knighton to John Eyre. In 1752 John's son John sold Knighton to Jeremiah Dewdney. John and William Hawkins bought Dewdney's Knighton farm in 1753 and two other farms in Knighton in 1764 and 1768. In 1787 the enlarged estate was sold to James Knight of Cannington who in 1823 settled it on his son Charles.[28] In 1840 Charles sold it to William Hawkins who put it up for sale in 1876.[29] Knighton farm was bought by Sir Alexander Acland-Hood.[30] Knighton Farm house is

of medieval origin and has smoke-blackened trusses; it was extensively altered in the 17th century.[31]

Another estate at Knighton belonged to William Cordwent in the later 13th century[32] and in 1307, and to Robert Cordwent in 1372.[33] John Cordwent held an estate in Knighton in 1410 and 1430[34] and was probably succeeded by his son John (d. c. 1468)[35] and the latter's son John (d. c. 1507).[36] John's son John (d. 1544) was succeeded by his grandson John, son of his deceased son John,[37] who sold Knighton and other estates in Stogursey to John Dodington in 1571.[38] The estate was absorbed into Stogursey Dodington manor and was later known as Poole's.[39]

The land and tithes given between 1100 and 1107 by William de Falaise and Geva his wife with Stogursey church to Lonlay abbey (Orne)[40] formed the main endowment of the priory at Stogursey which had been established as a cell of Lonlay by c. 1120.[41] During the 12th century were added gifts of land at Monkton, Steyning, and Tet Hill[42] and by the late 14th century the priory held c. 155 a. mainly at Monkton and Sowden.[43] The estates were evidently in Crown hands in 1438 and were handed over to Eton College in or before 1440.[44] Thereafter the estate was known variously as *STOGURSEY* or *STOGURSEY PRIORY*, from 1562 *STOGURSEY RECTORY alias MONKTON HOME* manor, and from the later 17th century more usually as Monkton Home manor.[45] From 1713 the Merchant Venturers of Bristol as trustees of Colston's hospital held the manor at farm. In 1921 Eton College and the Merchant Venturers acted together and sold the manor, the college buying back some of the land including Priory farm.[46] No later reference to lordship has been found.

The priory's endowment also included tithes described as the tithe of rents of Stogursey lordship and of Rodway in Cannington,[47] and were worth 35s. 4d. in 1301.[48] Tithe rents were still claimed c. 1540 with a payment in lieu of pasture on Wick moor.[49] By 1599, however, the rectors were receiving corn tithe and a modus from all meadows.[50] In 1840 the Merchant Venturers, as lessees of the rectory, received a rent charge of £800.[51]

The priory buildings evidently lay on the south side of the church. In 1314 the prior had a hall, chamber, storeroom, kitchen, brewhouse, bake-

---

8 *H.M.C. Wells*, i. 512.   9 *S.R.S.* xi, pp. 214, 225.
10 *H.M.C. Wells*, i. 512–14.
11 Ibid. 512, 514–15, 517–19.
12 Ibid. 507–8, 513, 515–16.   13 Below, local govt.
14 *H.M.C. Wells*, i. 506.   15 Ibid. 424, 508–9.
16 S.R.O., DD/AH 16/6.   17 Ibid. 12/8.
18 *Cat. Anct. D.* iii, A 5865.   19 S.R.O., DD/X/WI 34.
20 Ibid. DD/AH 11/9; P.R.O., C 142/171, no. 189;
S.R.S. lxvii, pp. 144–5.   21 S.R.O., DD/X/WI 34.
22 *Cal. Inq. p.m.* iv, p. 341.
23 P.R.O., C 142/25, no. 37; C 142/104, no. 80; *S.R.S.* xl. 1;
Som. Wills, ed. Brown, iv. 106.   24 S.R.O., DD/POt 39.
25 P.R.O., C 142/197, no. 52.
26 Ibid. CP 25(2)/479/8 Chas. I East.
27 Below, N. Petherton, manors.
28 S.R.O., DD/AH 30/3.   29 Ibid. 14/11, 16/8, 40/6.
30 Ibid. 30/3.
31 Ibid. DD/V/WLr 24.4.
32 N.R.A. Spencer Bernard MSS. 112.
33 S.R.O., DD/AH 66/5, 6.
34 N.R.A. Spencer Bernard MSS. 118, 121.
35 S.R.O., DD/AH 65/2, 66/5.
36 Ibid. D/P/stogs 4/1/1.
37 Ibid. DD/AH 11/9; P.R.O., C 142/71, no. 189.
38 *S.R.S.* li, p. 91.
39 Below; S.R.O., tithe award.
40 *S.R.S.* lxi, p. 1.
41 Ibid. p. 46; *V.C.H. Som.* ii. 169–71.
42 *S.R.S.* lxi, pp. 24, 27, 38, 42.
43 Eton Coll. Rec. 6/195.
44 *Cal. Pat.* 1436–41, 556; *Cal. Close*, 1441–7, 163.
45 *S.R.S.* lxi, pp. 77–85.
46 S.R.O., DD/BR/ely 20/17; DD/MVB 55, 68; inf. from
Mr. P. Strong, archivist of Eton College.
47 *S.R.S.* lxi, p. 1; *Cal. Close*, 1272–9, 88.
48 *Cal. Inq. p.m.* iv. p. 341.
49 Eton Coll. Rec. 6/151.   50 Ibid. 6/203.
51 S.R.O., tithe award.

house, and a barn.[52] In 1383 a chamber with a latrine and fireplace and a solar adjoining the west side of the hall were recorded,[53] and there was a gatehouse in 1431.[54] In 1455 the prior's house comprised a great hall, kitchen, chambers, and stable under a single roof.[55] By 1599 it was called Priory House.[56] In 1607 the tenants agreed to insert an upper floor in the hall and glaze the windows.[57] In 1775 the house, said to be too large for the occupier of Priory farm,[58] consisted of a hall with two parlours to the south and a large room west of the hall converted into a dairy and passage, with a kitchen to the south. A bakery, brewhouse, and granary were ruinous and it was suggested that they be removed.[59] The house was demolished c. 1810 and a new farmhouse was built on a different site.[60]

In 1432–3 John, son of John FitzJames, though under age held a freehold at Moorhouse, of Wick FitzPayn manor and in 1466–7 another John FitzJames paid fine in lieu of homage on entry.[61] A John FitzJames who held Moorhouse in 1485–6[62] was perhaps the John (d. 1510) whose son Sir John FitzJames (d. c. 1542) had what was described in 1540 as *MOORHOUSE* manor.[63] Nicholas FitzJames, cousin and heir of Sir John, died in 1550 holding land in Stogursey, Cannington, Wembdon, Spaxton, and Stockland Bristol which passed to his son James.[64] James sold the estate, no longer described as a manor, to John Wylly in 1552[65] and by 1614 it was held by Humphrey Willis, one of the two free tenants at Moorhouse holding between them only 66 a. of land by knight service of Wick FitzPayn manor.[66] The Moorhouse estate appears to have been dismembered.[67]

Thomas Trivet (d. 1316) held 1 knight's fee at *NEWNHAM* of the honor of Stogursey,[68] of whose lords it was held until 1614 or later.[69] Thomas's father William may have held the fee; Thomas's posthumous son John[70] was followed by his son Sir Thomas Trivet who sold Newnham with other estates in 1379 to John Fittleton.[71] By 1399 John had left a son William a minor.[72] In 1431 Agnes Bevyle, who held the Bluet family's Farringdon manor, was returned as lady of Newnham,[73] but in 1452 Sir Alexander Hody (d. 1461) settled Newnham on himself and

his wife Margaret.[74] Margaret, later wife of Sir Reynold Stourton, died in 1489[75] and Newnham passed to her first husband's nephew Sir William Hody, Chief Baron of the Exchequer (d. 1524),[76] and in turn to Sir William's younger son William (d. 1535) and that William's son Richard (d. 1536). Richard's son William, under age in 1536,[77] was succeeded in 1577 by his son Henry[78] who was succeeded in 1615 by his brother Richard. Richard was dead by 1621 when John Hody mortgaged the manor. Newnham had passed to Gilbert Hody by 1638.[79] Gilbert, probably Gilbert's son, was in possession in 1650[80] but appears to have dismembered the manor[81] and there is no later reference to lordship. The capital messuage was let in 1540[82] but was not recorded thereafter.

SHORTMANSFORD was held of William de Mohun in 1086[83] and continued to be held of the honor of Dunster until 1520.[84] A mesne lordship was granted to Cleeve abbey before 1285[85] but is not otherwise recorded. Beorhtric was tenant in both 1066 and 1086.[86] In 1256 it was held by Thomas Trivet[87] and descended with Durborough. After the death of Thomas Trivet (fl. c. 1330)[88] it seems to have been totally absorbed into that manor and the name was no longer used for the estate. It survived as a field name in Holford parish in the early 16th century.[89]

William de Mohun held in 1086 an estate called Stochelande which Algar had held T.R.E.[90] By 1219 it was known as Schirreveton,[91] later contracted to *SHURTON*, the name deriving from the office of sheriff which William de Mohun had held.[92] The estate was held of Dunster honor until 1777 or later.[93]

Robert of Glaston, son of William of Glaston, gave dower in Shurton to his wife Azilia. Her grandson and heir, Robert de Newburgh, son of Roger de Newburgh, secured his right to the lordship after a prolonged dispute.[94] He was dead by 1247 and his son Henry subinfeudated the land and later surrendered the mesne lordship in 1271.[95]

From 1271 Shurton was held of Dunster honor by Agnes Bausan, widow of Sir Stephen Bausan and wife of Sir Anketil de Martival.[96] It passed to Joan Bausan, daughter of Sir Stephen's

52 *S.R.S.* lxi, p. xxx.
53 *Cal. Pat.* 1381–5, 221.
54 Eton Coll. Rec. 6/196.
55 Ibid. 6/155.
56 S.R.O., DD/MVB 55; Eton Coll. Rec. 6/203.
57 Eton Coll. Rec. 49/273.
58 Ibid. 6/230.
59 Ibid. 6/220.
60 Ibid. 6/19; S.R.O., T/PH/ay 1.
61 S.R.O., DD/X/WI 34.
62 W. Suff. R.O. 449/E3/15.53/2.6.
63 Longleat Ho., Seymour Papers, XII, rental (1540), f. 8.
64 *S.D.N.Q.* xvi. 97, 128.
65 *S.R.S.* li, p. 46.
66 S.R.O., DD/X/WI 34.
67 e.g. ibid. DD/AH 28/11; DD/HM 28.
68 *Cal. Inq. p.m.* vi, p. 43.
69 S.R.O., DD/X/WI 34.
70 *Cal. Inq. p.m.* vi, p. 43.
71 *S.R.S.* xvii. 100.
72 *Cal. Pat.* 1396–9, 568.
73 *Feud. Aids*, iv. 435.
74 P.R.O., C 140/4, no. 44.
75 *Cal. Inq. p.m. Hen. VII*, i, p. 267.

76 P.R.O., C 142/41, no. 42.
77 Ibid. C 142/58, no. 34.
78 Ibid. C 142/183, no. 70.
79 *Som. Wills*, ed. Brown, i. 60; Hutchins, *Hist. Dors.* ii. 233; S.R.O., DD/GB 45.
80 S.R.O., DD/AH 3/8; DD/X/GT; DD/SAS (C/112) 9/1.
81 e.g. ibid. DD/AH 26/7, 66/14.
82 P.R.O., LR 3/123.
83 *V.C.H. Som.* i. 505.
84 *S.R.S.* xxxiii, pp. 49, 53, 271.
85 Ibid. p. 60.
86 *V.C.H. Som.* i. 505.
87 *S.R.S.* vi. 178.
88 Ibid. xxxiii, p. 71.
89 *Cal. Inq. p.m. Hen. VII*, i, pp. 293–4; S.R.O., DD/AH 11/9. The field was later Shiphamford: ibid. tithe award, Holford.
90 *V.C.H. Som.* i. 501. For the identification, *Dom. Bk.* ed. Thorn, 364.
91 *Pipe R.* 1219 (P.R.S. N.S. xlii), 179.
92 S. W. Rawlins, *Sheriffs of Som.* 4–5.
93 *S.R.S.* xxxiii, p. 35.
94 Ibid. pp. 19–21; ibid. extra ser. 336–7.
95 Ibid. xxxiii, pp. 42–4; S.R.O., DD/L P35/1, 36/4.
96 *S.R.S.* extra ser. 338; S.R.O., DD/L P35/1.

brother and heir Sir Richard, and in 1279 she and her son Richard Huish held the fee.[97] Joan, who in 1283 or earlier had subinfeudated half the fee to Hawise Ralegh, was dead by 1285, and Richard held half the fee in demesne and half as mesne lord.[98] Richard (d. 1297) was followed in turn by his son Richard (d. c. 1331), Richard's son also Richard (d. 1361), and that Richard's son William, each being a minor at his father's death.[99] William died without issue, and in 1379 his share was granted to his widow Ricarda and her second husband Sir Thomas Fichet.[1] Sir Thomas died in 1386 and Ricarda in 1390, leaving an infant son Thomas (d. 1395). Half of Shurton then passed to their daughter Isabel, wife of Robert Hill. The estate descended with Hill's manor of Spaxton through Isabel's son John (d. 1434) to her grandson John Hill (d. 1455).[2] That John's daughter Genevieve (d. 1480) evidently inherited one third of his estate, for her husband Sir William Say held the third by curtesy of England until his death in 1529.[3] John's widow Margaret held two thirds of the estate at her death in 1497 when her heirs were her husband's nieces, Joan wife of Sir Richard Pudsey and Isabel wife of Edward Waldegrave.[4] Isabel's share was held by her husband Edward Waldegrave for life but their son John Waldegrave (d. 1543), who predeceased his father in 1543, had acquired a third of Joan's share.[5] John's son Edward probably bought the rest of Joan's share from her heirs. The estate descended in the Waldegrave family like Spaxton until 1726 when James Waldegrave, then Baron Waldegrave, sold it to Joseph Ruscombe.[6] It was thereafter dismembered and there is no later trace of lordship.

The half subinfeudated to Hawise Ralegh, herself possibly related to the Huish family, appears to have passed by 1296 to her daughter Maud, wife of Matthew Furneaux (d. 1316).[7] Maud died probably in 1340 when her daughter Maud, wife of Roger le Warde, held half Shurton manor with remainder to her brother (Sir) Simon Furneaux (d. 1358).[8] Roger was still alive in 1358[9] and was succeeded in or before 1371 by Elizabeth, daughter and heir of Simon and wife of John Blount.[10] From Elizabeth the half share descended with Stringston manor[11] until the death of John Strode in 1581 when it was probably retained by his widow Margaret (d. 1607), formerly wife of Thomas Luttrell.[12] John

Strode's son Robert had succeeded by 1608[13] and died in 1616 leaving it to Sir Richard Strode of Newnham (Devon), who had married Robert's daughter Catherine, by then deceased. Sir Richard sold it in 1626 to William Strode of Barrington.[14] William still held it in 1656[15] but there is no later reference to ownership.

There was a court house at Shurton in the early 13th century.[16] The capital messuage, recorded in 1435, then belonged entirely to John Hill's share of the estate.[17] In 1717 it was called Shurton Farm[18] and by 1789 had been renamed Shurton Court.[19] The northern part of the house contains a roof of arch-braced collars of the 16th century. A west wing was added to the house in the 17th century and in the late 18th a new south front of five bays and three storeys replaced the original south end to form a large, double-pile house. The south front has a central pedimented door beneath a Venetian window and Ionic pilasters at each end. The house had been divided into two dwellings by 1985.

The estate called *STEART* manor in 1584 seems to have evolved from a virgate which Walter le Lyf held of Stogursey honor in 1301.[20] The estate, held of the lords of Stogursey in 1614,[21] descended in the Tilley family with their estate in Moorland in North Petherton until the death of George Tilley in 1590.[22] George's daughter Elizabeth, wife of Edward Parham, sold half the manor to Edmund Bowyer in 1602,[23] and her sister Anne, wife of William Walton, sold her share to Edward Rogers in 1604. In 1623 the whole manor was held by Edward Rogers who had purchased Steart warren from Edmund Bowyer in 1604,[24] and it descended with Cannington manor until 1653. The land continued to descend with Cannington but the lordship passed from Hugh Rogers (d. 1653) to his daughter Helena and from her to her son Alexander Popham (d. 1705). It was sold in 1720 to John Eyre, whose son John sold it to Jeremiah Dewdney in 1752. The lordship was not recorded again.[25]

A manor house was referred to in 1584.[26] Known as Warren House in the 18th century,[27] it was used as a watch house by customs officers possibly between 1686 and 1796[28] and as Steart House was licensed as an inn in the later 18th century.[29] It was demolished between 1829 and 1840.[30]

A second manor of *STEART* was held of the lords of Stogursey by Walter Michell (d. 1487)[31]

---

97 *Cal. Inq. p.m.* ii, p. 177; *S.R.S.* extra ser. 338.
98 *Cal. Inq. p.m.* ii, p. 352; *S.R.S.* vi. 363.
99 *S.R.S.* extra ser. 340.
1 Ibid. lxviii, pp. 42–3.
2 P.R.O., C 139/71, no. 36; above, Spaxton, manors.
3 P.R.O., C 1/594, no. 64; C 142/51, no. 35.
4 *Cal. Inq. p.m. Hen. VII*, ii, pp. 51–2.
5 Ibid. C 142/68, no. 54; *S.R.S.* xxi. 77; ibid. extra ser. 315.
6 S.R.O., DD/DP 33/7, 34/5; DD/AH 12/5, 16/1; above, Spaxton, manors.
7 *Cal. Chart. R.* 1257–1300, 465; *S.R.S.* extra ser. 347; *Feud. Aids*, iv. 308, 334.
8 *Cal. Inq. p.m.* vii, p. 167; *S.R.S.* iii. 14; xii. 204; ibid. extra ser. 347; Pole MS. 2569.
9 *Feud. Aids*, iv. 353; *S.R.S.* xxxv. 97.
10 *S.R.S.* extra ser. 348; *Cal. Inq. p.m.* x, p. 395.
11 Below, Stringston, manors.
12 *S.R.S.* extra ser. 351.
13 Ibid. xxxiii. 315.
14 P.R.O., CP 25(2)/479/1 Chas. I Hil.
15 Hutchins, *Hist. Dors.* ii. 131 n., 132 n.
16 Eton Coll. Rec. 49/270.
17 P.R.O., C 139/71, no. 36.
18 S.R.O., Q/RRp 3/2.
19 Ibid. DD/AH 60/1.
20 Ibid. D/D/Cd 129; *Cal. Inq. p.m.* iv, p. 342.
21 S.R.O., DD/X/WI 34.
22 Below, N. Petherton, manors.
23 P.R.O., CP 25(2)/207/44 Eliz. I East.
24 Ibid. CP 25(2)/345/2 Jas. I East.; S.R.O., DD/MVB 20.
25 P.R.O., C 142/340, no. 91; S.R.O., DD/AH 30/3; DD/BR/su 14; above, Cannington, manors.
26 Ibid. D/D/Cd 129.
27 Ibid. DD/X/KLT 1; Eton Coll. Rec. 51/363.
28 *Cal. Treas. Bks.* 1685–89 (1), 429; Clifford MSS. Som. estate, rentals; S.R.O., DD/X/KLT 1; ibid. Q/RRp.
29 S.R.O., Q/RL; above, intro (inns).
30 S.R.O., DD/DHR 8; ibid. tithe award.
31 *Cal. Inq. p.m. Hen. VII*, i, p. 115.

in succession to William Michell, owner in 1474.[32] It descended with Chilton manor in Durleigh to Bartholomew Michell (d. 1616)[33] but has not been traced later.

The manor of *STOGURSEY DODINGTON*, recorded in 1523,[34] appears to have been formed out of the scattered holdings of the Dodington family in Stogursey including a number of burgages,[35] and from 1571 a large estate at Knighton, which was a freehold of Wick FitzPayn manor.[36] It was held with Durborough Dodington manor[37] and tenants owed suit to either court in the early 17th century.[38] Lordship was last recorded in 1801.[39]

Walter Durburgh (d. probably by 1313), his son John (d. 1352), John's son Sir Hugh (d. *c.* 1388), and Sir Hugh's son James held land in Stogursey and elsewhere[40] which thereafter passed with Williton Hadley in St. Decumans to the Hadley family.[41] The land, called *STOGURSEY HADLEY*, was not said to be a manor but had its own court;[42] the part in Stogursey was held of the lords of Stogursey by knight service in 1524[43] and 1614.[44] The estate was much reduced in size after the early 16th century,[45] and by the 19th had been absorbed into Williton manor.[46] In 1857 it was sold to the trustees of the will of Sir John Acland Bt.[47] There is no record of a capital messuage.

In 1066 Ulf held *WOOLSTONE*. In 1086 Robert held it of Roger de Courcelles,[48] with whose lands it formed part of the barony of Compton Dundon until 1490 or later.[49] By 1276 Woolstone was in the possession of Egelina, widow of Philip de Columbers,[50] and the manor descended with Nether Stowey manor until the attainder of the duke of Somerset in 1552.[51] In 1554 Woolstone was let to Edmund Timewell, yeoman of the guard, and was said to have been in the tenure of Thomas Dannet.[52] Thomas had apparently purchased the estate by 1570 and in 1588 he sold it to Humphrey Wyndham of Wiveliscombe.[53] Humphrey died in 1622 leaving his lands to his daughter Elizabeth, wife of John Colles.[54] Elizabeth died in 1634 leaving several daughters including Margaret, wife of (Sir) Gerard Napier.[55] Margaret died in 1660, evidently in possession of the whole estate, and her husband in 1673. Their son Sir Nathaniel Napier, Bt. (d. 1709)[56] left his estates in trust for his

grandson William,[57] who died unmarried in 1753. He was succeeded in turn by his brother Gerard (d. 1759) and his nephew, also Gerard (d. 1765).[58] The last left his estates to Edward Phelips of Montacute, his mother's half-brother.[59] Edward (d. 1797) was succeeded by his son William[60] (d. 1806). In 1808 William Helyar, Edward Phelips's trustee, sold Woolstone to John Acland of Fairfield, but there is no later reference to the lordship.[61] Woolstone farm was sold to the tenant in 1920[62] and *c.* 1971 it was bought by the Hill family and added to Farm estate, Fiddington.[63] The capital messuage mentioned in 1735[64] was described as small.[65] The present house, which has some evidence of a 17th-century structure, is largely of the late 19th and the early 20th century.

OTHER ESTATES. After 1193 Alice, sister of William de Curci, gave to Richard son of Hugh of Buveny land at *CATHANGER* which continued to be held of the lords of Stogursey and in the late 15th century owed rent of a pair of spurs, or wax, or cash. Richard's brother Geoffrey (d. by 1248) gave the land to Barlinch priory, which retained it until the house was dissolved in 1536.[66] The Crown granted the reversion in 1543 to Humphrey Colles (d. 1570) and his son John was probably in possession in 1599.[67] By 1690 Cathanger had come to Edmund Wyndham and was probably sold *c.* 1703 to Bartholomew Farthing (d. 1718).[68] Benjamin Farthing (d. 1730) was succeeded by his widow Mellior (d. 1783) and his daughter Sarah Kebbey.[69] Samuel Kebbey, Sarah's son, sold to Samuel Poole (d. 1808) in 1799,[70] and Samuel's son Henry sold to William Fripp in 1830. The Society of Merchant Venturers of Bristol acquired the farm from Fripp in 1862, and probably sold it with Farm estate to the Hill family in 1919.[71]

A capital messuage was recorded in 1690.[72] The present house, divided into two cottages, has a main range of the later 16th or early 17th century with a cross-passage plan. A short cross wing at the west end was reconstructed in the 18th century.

By the early 14th century an estate called Loveleston, later *LOWSTON*, was held by Taunton priory of the heirs of Matthew Furneaux who

32 S.R.O., DD/S/WH 65.
33 Above, Durleigh, manors.
34 S.R.O., DD/AH 11/10.
35 Ibid. 14/7, 30/1, 33/10.
36 *S.R.S.* li, p. 91; S.R.O., DD/X/WI 34.
37 Above, this section.
38 S.R.O., DD/AH 30/1, 31/4.
39 Ibid. 11/1.
40 Ibid. DD/L P36/4; *Cal. Inq. p.m.* x, p. 17.
41 *V.C.H. Som.* v. 151.
42 S.R.O., DD/L P36/4.
43 Ibid. P33/1.
44 Ibid. DD/X/WI 34.
45 Ibid. DD/L P33/1.
46 Ibid. DD/AH 17/6.
47 Ibid. 31/16.
48 *V.C.H. Som.* i. 486.
49 *S.R.S.* xxxv. 30; *Cal. Inq. p.m. Hen. VII,* i, p. 247.
50 *Rot. Hund.* (Rec. Com.), ii. 137.
51 *V.C.H. Som.* v. 193.
52 *Cal. Pat.* 1553–4, 108.
53 S.R.O., DD/PH 44.
54 *Som. Wills,* ed. Brown, ii. 41.

55 Ibid. i. 34.
56 G.E.C. *Baronetage,* ii. 91–2.
57 S.R.O., DD/AH 2/4.
58 G.E.C. *Baronetage,* ii. 91–2.
59 Ibid.; S.R.O., DD/AH 2/4.
60 S.R.O., DD/AH 2/4; DD/PH 40.
61 Ibid. DD/AH 2/4.
62 Ibid. DD/X/LAW 1.
63 Inf. from Mr. M. and Mrs. L. Hill, Farm, Fiddington.
64 S.R.O., DD/AH 2/4.
65 Dors. R.O., D 438 A/F 13.
66 *Proc. Som. Arch. Soc.* lxvi. 113; *Tax. Eccl.* (Rec. Com.), 204; *S.R.S.* xi, p. 337; Dugdale, *Mon.* vi. 386; *Valor Eccl.* (Rec. Com.), i. 219; W. Suff. R.O. 449/E3/15.53/2.5–6.
67 *L. & P. Hen. VIII,* xviii (1), p. 197. A grant of 1544 to Sir William Stourton probably did not take effect: ibid. xix (1), p. 40; P.R.O., WARD 7/13, no. 32; Eton Coll. Rec. 6/203.
68 S.R.O., DD/WO 5/3; DD/AH 3/3, 21/4.
69 Deeds in possession of Mr. & Mrs. Hill, Farm, Fiddington.
70 Ibid.; S.R.O., DD/AH 29/14.
71 Deeds in possession of Mr. & Mrs. Hill.
72 S.R.O., DD/WO 5/3.

held of the heirs of William de Forz, and they in turn of Glastonbury abbey.[73] No later record of this estate has been found.

STEYNING was probably part of the 11th-century estate of Stockland, evidently in Stogursey and Spaxton, which was held by two thegns in 1066 and by Ansketil of Roger de Courcelles in 1086.[74] Steyning was held of William Malet, from whom the lords of Stogursey held a mesne lordship, in 1208, of Matthew Furneaux in 1300,[75] and of Glastonbury abbey in 1512.[76] Between 1338 and 1578 the main holding there was held of Chilton Trivet manor.[77]

Ansketil son of Herbert held land at Steyning in the early 12th century.[78] He was followed in turn by his son William of Eston (d. by 1166), by William's son Osbert (d. by 1181), and by Osbert's son William of Eston.[79] By 1200 the Estons had disposed of their land, partly to Stogursey church and partly to William of Steyning. William was succeeded by his son Roger de Solers. About 1200 the abbot of Lonlay (Orne), the appropriator of Stogursey church, confirmed to Roger the house and land once held by Ansketil son of Herbert.[80] Lonlay's cell Stogursey priory in 1284–5 held what was called Steynings Place,[81] probably let to the family called Steyning.[82]

Roger de Solers was probably followed by William of Steyning (fl. 1260).[83] John of Steyning died c. 1338,[84] having settled Steyning in 1300, subject to his own life interest, on Maud, daughter of Warin Ralegh.[85] In 1340 Maud's son Henry Furneaux conveyed it to his brother (Sir) Simon whose daughter and heir Elizabeth, wife of John Blount, held it in 1386.[86] After the death of Elizabeth's daughter Alice, wife of Richard Stury, without children in 1414 the whole Furneaux inheritance became subject to division between the heirs of Sir Simon Furneaux. Steyning seems to have been the share of the heirs of his sister Margaret, and to have passed in 1421 to John Roynon.[87] William Roynon (d. 1512) was succeeded by his grandson Thomas Roynon, who in 1545 sold the estate to the lessee William Poole.[88]

Poole (d. 1550) settled Steyning on himself and his wife Alice (d. 1562). Their daughter Joan (d. 1570) was followed by her son John Burland (d. 1604)[89] from whom Steyning passed in the direct male line to John (d. 1648), John (d. 1649), John (a minor in 1649, d. 1713), John (d. 1746), Sir John (d. 1776), and John Berkeley Burland (d.

s.p. 1804). The next heir was John Burland Harris, infant great-grandson of John Burland (d. 1746) who in 1835 took the additional surname Burland[90] and died in 1871. His heir was his son William (d. 1890) whose son John Burland Harris-Burland offered the estate for sale in 1897.[91] Part was bought by Sir Alexander Acland-Hood in 1904.[92]

Roger de Solers had a house at Steyning c. 1200[93] and there was a chief messuage in 1338.[94] Steyning Manor is a small, earlier 17th-century building with a double-pile plan, a gabled south elevation of three bays with mullioned and transomed windows, and a central porch. Many original fittings survive including panelling and richly ornamented plasterwork in the south-eastern room on the ground floor. At the back is a detached earlier house with a three-roomed plan which has a cross passage and a projecting newel stair.

In 1301 Henry and Walter Everard held land of the lords of Stogursey,[95] whose lordship of West Wall or *WALLSEND* was recorded until 1614.[96] That land might have been at Wildmarsh where the Hatherick family had an estate in 1318 part of which was held by Henry Everard.[97] In 1423 John Everard settled land in Westwall on his son John.[98] By the later 15th century there were three estates at Wallsend. One, later known as Wallhouse and Kilwall, descended in the Everard family until the later 18th century and was subsequently divided and sold.[99] A second estate, sometimes known as Curwell's Place after its 15th-century owners, belonged to the Lyte family in the 16th century[1] but from 1622 probably descended with Durborough Dodington manor.[2] Another estate at Wallsend, possibly traceable to a holding of John Pokeswell in 1472 and of Humphrey Colles (d. 1570), was held by John Day in 1614.[3] Day died in 1654 and was followed by his son John (d. 1668) and his grandson, also John Day. The estate then descended like Wyndeats manor until 1761 when it was divided.[4]

ECONOMIC HISTORY. AGRICULTURE. The eight Domesday estates that are thought to have lain partly or wholly within the parish[5] contained 30½ ploughlands assessed at 16 hides. The various demesnes had 11 ploughteams, with 20 *servi*, on land assessed at nearly 10 hides, and 56 *villani*, 18 bordars, and 3 coliberts had 17 teams

73 *S.R.S.* xxvi. 62.
74 *V.C.H. Som.* i. 486; above, Spaxton, manors (Stockland Lovel).
75 *S.R.S.* vi. 25, 311.
76 P.R.O., C 142/27, no. 101.
77 *S.R.S.* lvii, p. 30; S.R.O., D/B/bw Steyning MSS. 12.
78 *S.R.S.* lxi, pp. 1, 8, 44–5.
79 *Red Bk. Exch.* (Rolls Ser.), i. 227; *Bradenstoke Cart.* (Wilts. Rec. Soc.), 192.
80 *S.R.S.* lvii, pp. 25–6; lxi, pp. 27–9; below, church.
81 Eton Coll. Rec. 6/152.
82 S.R.O., D/B/bw Steyning MSS. 12.
83 *S.R.S.* lxi, p. 38.
84 Ibid. lvii, p. 33.
85 Ibid. vi. 311.
86 Ibid. lvii, pp. 31, 33; *S.D.N.Q.* xvi. 281–2.
87 *S.D.N.Q.* xvi. 281, 283.
88 S.R.O., D/B/bw Steyning MSS. 12.
89 Ibid.; D/P/stogs 2/1/1.

90 *S.D.N.Q.* iii. 268–9.; S.R.O., D/B/bw Steyning MSS. 14; DD/DK 1; DD/GJ 2.
91 *S.D.N.Q.* iii. 268–9; S.R.O., DD/SAS (C/2401) 64.
92 S.R.O., DD/AH 28/7.
93 *S.R.S.* lxi, pp. 27–8.
94 Ibid. lvii, p. 30.
95 *Cal. Inq. p.m.* iv, p. 34.
96 S.R.O., DD/X/WI 34.
97 B.L. Add. Ch. 26760–1.
98 S.R.O., trans. file 2/62.
99 Burke, *Land. Gent.* (1914), 626; S.R.O., DD/X/WI 34; ibid. Q/REl 7/8D; ibid. tithe award.
1 S.R.O., DD/X/LY 3; DD/S/WH 9.
2 Ibid. DD/S/WH 8; DD/AH 35/32; above, manors (Durborough).
3 Deeds in possession of Mr. & Mrs. Hill, Farm, Fiddington.
4 S.R.O., DD/AH 28/1; *S.R.S.* lxvii, p. 102.
5 *Dom. Bk.* ed. Thorn, p. 364.

on the remaining land. The meadow recorded was 279 a., pasture 81 a., and woodland 140 a.; the livestock recorded was 5 riding horses, 47 beasts, 34 swine, 404 sheep, and 14 goats. The principal manor of Stoke accounted for roughly half of these totals, with 15 ploughlands assessed at 5 hides, of which the demesne had 2 hides with 4 teams and 5 *servi* and the tenants (38 *villani*, 4 bordars, and 3 coliberts) had 11 teams; there were 150 a. of meadow, 19 a. of pasture, and 100 a. of woodland, 3 riding horses, 29 beasts, 10 swine, and 250 sheep. Woolstone manor with only ½ ploughland included half of all the recorded pasture and 17 a. of meadow; there were also large amounts of meadow at Idson (40 a.) and at what became Shurton (61 a.). The aggregate value of all the estates had fallen from £37 11s. to £33 16s., of Stoke manor from £25 to £20; two of the estates had risen in value.[6]

In the later 13th century sales of grain accounted for the largest part of the income of Stogursey manor, and sales of cheese, fish, pigeons, fleeces, livestock, and pasture for more than rents. In 1277 there was a demesne flock of 302 ewes, herds of 59 cattle with 24 calves and 63 pigs with 24 piglets, and 4 mares. Six ploughmen, a shepherd, a herdsman, and a dairymaid were employed on the demesne farm.[7]

By 1297 the dovecot was let to farm, works were being sold, and the number of servants had increased, to include a parker at Wick and 3 carters. Sheep were not recorded. Game was kept in the park and hay was supplied as feed in winter. Income from rents was about the same as in 1277, but grain sales had fallen although they still provided the largest item of income. It may have been a bad year for crops, for although there were 370 quarters of grain in the grange, mainly wheat and oats but also barley, peas, beans, and dredge, some seed was purchased. Nearly 26 quarters of maslin and barley came from the mill together with 3½ bu. of flour which was used by the household. Poultry, geese, and capons were sold. Less seed was used than twenty years earlier, probably because of its higher price, and the major crops were wheat sown on 195 a. and oats on 180 a.; there were 34 a. of peas and beans, 18 a. of dredge, 14 a. of barley, and 6 a. of vetches. Nearly 9,000 mowing, reaping, ploughing, and carrying works were performed but extra labour was needed for threshing, hoeing, mowing, and reaping. Rents in iron for land on the Quantocks were used in repairing ploughs, mill gear, and other equipment. The granges at Wick and Wyndeats and a cattle house at Wyndeats also needed repair that year.[8] By 1301–2 more works were being

sold and more money was spent on seed. Wheat was sown on 205 a., oats on 180 a., with smaller acreages of barley, beans and peas, and vetches.[9] In 1301 on Wick manor over 5,000 day works were recorded, worth about the same as manor rents.[10]

On the smaller estates, which are much less well documented, there was a wide variety of stock and cropping. Tenants at Steart in the 13th century owed rents in geese, garlic, and cheese,[11] and geese were kept at Stolford.[12] The owner of a farm at Cock in 1331 had 40 a. of standing wheat and quantities of wheat, barley, oats, and beans in stock from a farm equipped with two carts and two ploughs.[13] Wheat and beans were the main contents of the priory barn in 1324, some of it collected as tithes. The priory farm was equipped with two ploughs and three carts, and livestock included 12 oxen, 58 pigs, a bull, and two boars.[14] In 1332 the prior of Stogursey complained that Robert FitzPayn had illegally impounded a horse, a colt, 18 oxen, 200 sheep and lambs, a boar and 30 pigs.[15]

The demesne at Wick was let at farm in the mid 15th century[16] and that at Newnham by 1540.[17] Tithes were payable to the vicar in the 1450s on a wide variety of stock and produce including squabs and rabbits, leeks and onions, fisheries, linen, flax, and hemp. By far the largest in value were milk and cheese, amounting to nearly 40 per cent of the income, followed by wool and lambs.[18]

Harvest works were demanded on the former priory estate by Eton College in the mid 15th century, and part of the rent was in kind.[19] Ploughing and carrying works at Wick were sold in 1421–2 and 1500–1,[20] and in 1578 tenants there paid work silver.[21] Tenants at Stolford and neighbouring Whitewick owed works and 'gi-vose', probably goose, silver in 1614. Wick manor, the largest estate in the parish, comprised 1,309 a. in 1614, of which 601 a. were arable, 510 a. were pasture, and 198 a. were meadow. Most farms were under 35 a., but Wick farm was over 160 a. and let to tenants in half shares.[22]

By the 16th century there were common arable fields at Fairfield,[23] Newnham,[24] Stogursey,[25] Wick,[26] and in the north-west of the parish where the people of Burton, Culver Street, Knighton, and Shurton cultivated in an in- and out-field system.[27] Wick fields were known in 1614 as Howndsborough, Seaberton or Skevington, Stolford, and Idmeston or Yedmyster fields.[28] Between Shurton and Stogursey village Lowelstone field, mentioned in the 14th century, and Shurton fields in 1541[29] later became Lawson and Shurton burgages, like Stogursey's

6 *V.C.H. Som.* i. 462, 486–7, 501, 505, 508.
7 P.R.O., SC 6/974/8.
8 Ibid. SC 6/1090/4.
9 Ibid. SC 6/1090/6.
10 Ibid. E 142/8.
11 Ibid. E 326/10463.   12 Ibid. E 142/8.
13 Ibid. E 142/71, no. 10.
14 *S.R.S.* lxi, pp. xxx–xxxi.
15 *Cal. Pat.* 1330–4, 288.
16 Eton Coll. Rec. 49/272.
17 *S.R.S.* xxi. 148–9.
18 Eton Coll. Rec. 6/260.
19 Ibid. 6/211; *S.R.S.* lxi, pp. 67, 69–70.

20 Eton Coll. Rec. 49/272; W. Suss. R.O., PHA uncat.; W. Suff. R.O. 449/E3/15.53/2.8.
21 W. Suss. R.O., PHA uncat.
22 S.R.O., DD/X/WI 34.
23 Ibid. DD/AH 11/10.
24 P.R.O., LR 3/123.
25 S.R.O., DD/AH 65/12.
26 W. Suff. R.O. 449/E3/15.53/2.6; S.R.O., DD/X/WI 34; DD/SAS (C/112) 9/1.
27 Survey Bk. 1582 in possession of Mr. J. S. Cox, Guernsey; S.R.O., DD/BV 10.
28 S.R.O., DD/X/WI 34.
29 Ibid. DD/AH 65/2; P.R.O., LR 3/123.

Town or West burgage[30] all within Stogursey borough.[31] By the later 16th century tenants of Wick manor, the largest holding, had access to over 250 a. of land on the coast at Wall, Sharpham, Salt, and Goose commons, Little Common in Redham moor, and an enclosed area called Stolford Ham. They also had the after-shear grazing of South moor and access to nearly 900 a. in Over Stowey.[32] Other commoners could graze cattle on Wick and North moors, Redham moor, and Horseham.[33]

Inventories of the 17th century suggest a growing prosperity although the farmer who owned 102 sheep and lambs, 31 cows, calves and other young cattle, 6 plough steers, 6 pigs, and a horse was exceptional.[34] Dairying was still predominant, and clover had been introduced by 1689,[35] but mixed arable farming was widely practised[36] and a hopyard had been established on the Fairfield estate by 1720.[37] Surplus dung was sold by one dairy farmer in the early 18th century[38] and a yeoman dying in 1731 left 100 cheeses in a cheese chamber, a dairy with two cheese wrings, and cows and calves valued at £60.[39] More land was laid to pasture later in the century, 'nothing at this time paying as well as a dairy farm',[40] and rectorial income was affected by the increase in livestock at the expense of corn. Some land was said to have been impoverished by constant ploughing and want of manure.[41] The Eton College estate remained largely arable, cultivated in a regular rotation of wheat, oats, beans, barley, or clover for two years, with the third year fallow.[42] Peadon farm, on higher ground in the south, was mainly grass in the later 18th century, with only one field in wheat and two ploughed for barley in any one year.[43]

Cropping was said in 1831 to have been possible in only three years out of five on the coastal lands, and the poor clay there could successfully grow only vetches.[44] In 1840 of the titheable land 2,677 a. were arable, 1,221 a. were meadow, and 1,198 a. were pasture. Most of the farms were under 50 a. and none over 250 a. Thirty were 10–25 a., 23 were 25–50 a., 17 were 50–100 a., and 10 were 100–150 a. The five largest were part of the Fairfield estates and had in most cases absorbed smaller holdings. Bullen farm was 157 a., Peadon 210 a., Water 213 a., Cock 214 a., and Chalcott 230 a.[45] By 1851 the number of farms over 150 a. had doubled, with Cock farm (240 a.) the largest. A total of 122 people were employed on c. 30 farms.[46] By 1861 the number of farms over 100 a. had increased to 23 and 130 labourers were employed on farms in the parish.[47] In 1863 farms on the Fairfield estates were said to be mixed arable and pasture

with the meadows used for rearing horses and fattening cattle and sheep.[48] The Acland family at Fairfield were the largest landowners by the 1830s and by 1867 owned c. 2,660 a., nearly half the parish. Farms had been enlarged by amalgamation and exchange, and in 1867 most were over 100 a. and produced a rental of £1,775.[49] By 1881 the two upland farms at Peadon and Durborough measured over 200 a., Bullen and Farringdon farms had increased to over 350 a., presumably by absorbing neighbouring holdings, and a number of farmers described themselves as out of business.[50] In 1880 a report on Wick farm stated that the pasture was tart and caused purging in cattle, and that it was too wet for sheep.[51]

The depressed state of agriculture in 1882 was said to be due in part to the continuing division of open fields, moors, and commons into landshires or raps subject to common rights, and also to heavy, badly drained soil. The arable fields were farmed on a three-year rotation of wheat, lentcorn or a pulse, and fallow when the fields lay open the whole year. The moors were mown and then pastured, some known as hopping meadows which were enjoyed by two owners alternately, and the permanent common pasture was stinted. Some land near the cliffs formerly arable was being left uncultivated in spite of high tithe charges. The sheep were said to be in poor condition but the multiplicity of owners prevented improvements in drainage.[52]

At Knighton in the 1890s turnips and swedes were grown for seed and to feed a flock of nearly 400 sheep, and beans, oats, vetches, and sainfoin were sown. Milk, butter, eggs, and poultry were sold locally and some butter was sent to London. The fields were dressed with lime, dissolved bone, nitrate of soda, and superphosphate.[53] By 1905 permanent grassland had increased to 3,307 a. with arable accounting for only 1,814 a.[54] By this time fewer arable strips survived, but the last baulks were not ploughed out until the 1930s.[55] Mushrooms were grown commercially at Shurton in 1939.[56] By 1982 there had probably been a slight increase in arable. Farms remained small, only 11 out of 31 recorded were more than 50 ha. (c. 123 a.) and over half were farmed part-time, 6 were mainly dairy farms, with 4 concentrating on stock-rearing, and others on pigs, poultry, or horticulture. About 60 per cent of the arable land recorded was under wheat, with barley accounting for c. 20 per cent. Other crops were rape, oats, potatoes, maize, and vegetables. There were 218,112 poultry, mainly broilers, 3,021 sheep, 2,254 cattle, and 1,604 pigs on the recorded holdings.[57]

Tenants had common rights both within and

30 S.R.O., DD/X/WI 34. 31 Ibid. DD/AH 65/12.
32 S.R.O., DD/X/WI 34.
33 Ibid. DD/AH 3/5, 14/11–12; DD/DHR 22.
34 Ibid. DD/SP inventory, 1672.
35 Ibid. Q/SR 179/1.
36 e.g. ibid. DD/SP inventory, 1693.
37 Ibid. DD/AH 34/1.
38 Ibid. DD/SP inventory, 1721. 39 Ibid. 1731.
40 Eton Coll. Rec. 6/236.
41 S.R.O., DD/AH 66/11. 42 Eton Coll. Rec. 6/269.
43 S.R.O., DD/AH 14/7. 44 Ibid. 59/12.
45 Ibid. tithe award. 46 P.R.O., HO 107/1920.

47 Ibid. RG 9/1604.
48 S.R.O., DD/AH 14/11. 49 Ibid. 64/4.
50 P.R.O., RG 10/2354; RG 11/2356.
51 S.R.O., D/P/spax 17/7/2.
52 Rep. Com. Dep. Cond. of Agric. Interests [C. 3309], pp. 43–4, H.C. (1882), xiv.
53 S.R.O., DD/DHR, box 40.
54 Statistics supplied by the then Bd. of Agric., 1905.
55 Local inf.
56 Kelly's Dir. Som. (1939).
57 Min. of Agric., Fisheries, and Food, agric. returns, 1982.

outside the parish. The former Quantock forest land in Over Stowey provided grazing and timber in the 16th and earlier 17th centuries.[58] Tenants of Durborough manor had common in Dodington parish,[59] and in a common in Durborough hamlet, later called the Green, which had been inclosed by 1840.[60] There was extensive grazing for sheep on the coast, and after the dismemberment of Wick manor common rights became detached from the holdings to which they had belonged,[61] although tenants of Fairfield manor retained common rights until the 19th century or later.[62] Some of the commons were available only after haymaking, while in others tenants had the right to all the grass.[63] The rights, named but not defined, of foreshear, vesture, and stockage remain: commoners have registered rights on Redham for 46 bullocks and 94 sheep and on Ham for 46 cattle and 94 sheep, c. 50 rights on Wick moor, each for 6 bullocks or 4 bullocks and a horse, and 44 rights on North Ham, Goose marsh, Catsford and Wall commons each for 20 sheep. On Sharpham there were 42 horse rights which have been sold. All the rights are controlled by a hayward appointed by the commoners.[64]

MILLS. There were two mills in 1086, one on Stogursey manor, one on Wyndeats manor.[65] The first was possibly Wick mill, recorded in 1301[66] and possibly in 1277,[67] which was the customary mill for all tenants in 1614.[68] By the 18th century, after the dismemberment of Wick manor, the mill was owned by Cook's charity for Spaxton parish.[69] The mill was probably in use until soon after 1881.[70] Driven by Stogursey brook with an overshot wheel, it had been partially demolished by 1985.[71]

The Wyndeats mill was later known as Castle[72] or Town mill. It paid 6d. in 1086,[73] in 1301 it was worth 53s. 4d.,[74] and in 1474 it was farmed for 60s.[75] In 1614 the manor tenants were not certain whether the mill was a customary one.[76] On the sale of the manor in 1681 the mill was conveyed to Alexander Marshall of Nether Stowey, possibly in trust for the tenant, Agnes Farthing.[77] By his will dated 1748 John Acreman left the mill to his mother Grace for life and then to John Farthing of Bristol. John Farthing was dead by 1784 when his daughters sold the mill to James Knight, miller. By 1789 the mill had

been acquired by William Elson who, by his will of 1809, left it to his nephew William Elson. William sold the mill in 1822 to Thomas and William Powell of Bristol who in 1836 sold it to the trustees of the will of Sir John Acland.[78] The mill remained in use until 1948 but by 1952 was no longer working.[79] It was bought c. 1982 by the Landmark Trust. The building probably dates from the early 18th century. The frame of the overshot wheel and much machinery survive.

Monk or Monkton mill, probably the new mill recorded in the mid 12th century,[80] was later said to have been given to Stogursey priory church by the lord of Shurton manor in return for masses.[81] The machinery was extensively repaired in 1446[82] and stones were bought in 1488 and 1538.[83] The mill remained in use until 1861[84] but by 1871 the mill house was occupied by a labourer.[85] The mill house was still let in 1888[86] but the mill had been demolished by 1886.[87] The mill lay on the Stogursey brook south of Shurton mill. Fragments of walling survived in 1985.

Shurton mill existed in the early 13th century.[88] Ownership descended with the manor and was shared between the two halves when the manor was divided.[89] Before 1434 it was apparently let with a large estate to Sir John Coleshill.[90] The mill was described as two mills in 1653.[91] It was owned by John Simonds in 1714 and 1722[92] and in 1755 by William Poole (d. 1768) of Shurton Court.[93] After the death of Poole's son William in 1789[94] the mill appears to have been sold to Charles Knight.[95] Joan Knight, probably his widow, married George Bishop, miller, in 1807 and was the owner of Shurton mill in 1819.[96] By 1840 the mill had been conveyed to Mary Westcombe[97] and she employed her three sons and another man in the mill in 1851.[98] The mill continued to be worked by the Westcombe family in 1931 but milling had ceased by 1939.[99] The two-storeyed mill, south-west of Newnham Farm, was later converted into a private house and the attached mill house, a 17th-century house enlarged in the 18th century and extensively altered in the 19th and 20th centuries, was in 1985 empty and overgrown.

Durborough mill existed by the mid 13th century when Thomas Trivet bought a share from William of Beere who had inherited it from his father Adam. Philip de Columbers bought another share from Christine, widow of Simon

58   S.R.O., DD/X/WI 34.
59   Ibid. DD/AH 32/4–5; ibid. T/PH/vch 56.
60   Ibid. DD/AH 2/6, 35/32; ibid. tithe award.
61   e.g. ibid. DD/AH 3/5; DD/PC 17.
62   Ibid. DD/AH 65/12.
63   Ibid. 14/11–12; DD/DHR 22.
64   Som. C.C., common lands register; local inf.
65   V.C.H. Som. i. 487, 508.
66   S.R.O., DD/AH 17/11.
67   P.R.O., SC 6/974/8.
68   S.R.O., DD/X/WI 34.
69   Ibid. D/P/spax 17/1/2.
70   P.R.O., RG 11/2356.
71   Som. C.C., Sites and Mons. Rec.
72   W. Suss. R.O., PHA uncat.
73   V.C.H. Som. i. 487.
74   P.R.O., E 142/8.
75   W. Suss. R.O., PHA 5370 and uncat.
76   S.R.O., DD/X/WI 34.
77   Ibid. DD/PC 17.
78   Ibid. DD/AH 21/7, 31/11.

79   Ibid. D/P/stogs 23/19; DD/X/HUX 1.
80   S.R.S. lxi, p. 5.
81   P.R.O., SC 2/20/27.
82   Eton Coll. Rec. 61/RR/A/34.
83   Ibid. 61/RR/E/4; 61/RR/G/24.
84   P.R.O., RG 9/1604.
85   Ibid. RG 10/2354.
86   S.R.O., DD/MVB 64.
87   O.S. Map 6", Som. XXXVII. SE. (1886 edn.).
88   Eton Coll. Rec. 49/270.
89   P.R.O., SC 6/977/14, 16; SC 6/Hen. VII/539, 543; S.R.O., DD/AH 11/10.
90   P.R.O., C 141/4, no. 42.
91   S.R.O., DD/SOG 984.
92   Ibid. DD/AH 28/2; P.R.O., CP 25(2)/1057/8 Geo. III Trin.   93   S.R.O., DD/AH 21/4, 60/1.
94   Ibid. 60/1.   95   Ibid. Q/REl 7/8C.
96   Ibid. DD/AH 26/9; D/PC/stogs 6/1/2.
97   Ibid. tithe award.
98   P.R.O., HO 107/1920.
99   Kelly's Dir. Som. (1931, 1939).

of Durborough, and probably sold it to Trivet.[1] Ownership descended with Durborough manor.[2] By the early 18th century one third was held with Durborough Verney and two thirds with Durborough Dodington,[3] the profits including the sediment from the mill pond.[4] Milling appears to have ceased between 1866 and 1871.[5] The mill stood on the Stogursey brook south of Durborough, but nothing remains of the buildings.

Fairfield mill was recorded in 1471 at Shutternford[6] and in 1658.[7] In 1682 it was said to have been destroyed many years before[8] but it continued to be recorded until 1777.[9] It was probably near Water Farm.

There was a fulling mill on Fairfield manor which was out of repair in 1401. A fulling mill on Durborough Verney manor was recorded in 1467[10] but it was said to be in total decay in 1508 and was last recorded in 1513.[11]

There was a windmill mound at Chalcott in 1448.[12] Theat windmill, standing further east near Wall Common and named after a nearby watercourse,[13] was bought by Nicholas Halswell from John Lyte in 1561 and was held of the lord of Stogursey estate in 1614.[14] It had passed to Margaret Dodington by 1625[15] and was sold in 1736 by John Eyre to Jonathan Bacon.[16]

A 'watermill called the horse mill' was within Stogursey borough between 1500 and 1523.[17]

MARKET AND FAIRS. A market was held on Saturdays in 1301.[18] In 1559 the market was said to have decayed, and profits from the market and fairs in 1686 totalled only 10s.[19] The market was recorded in the early 18th century[20] but probably ceased soon afterwards. In 1800 an attempt was made to provide a provision market for the poor on Mondays.[21]

A fair was held on the feast of St. Andrew (30 Nov.) in 1301[22] but by the 16th century fairs were held on 3 May and 14 September. In 1559 those fairs were said to have decayed,[23] but both fairs, still held early in May and in mid September, continued into the mid 19th century.[24] Neither was recorded again.

WOODLAND. Both Eton College and the earls of Northumberland exploited the timber on their estates. In 1565 sales of wood on Wick manor produced £53 16s.[25] The woods of Wick and Stogursey manors were let for 21 years from 1572, the tenant to take two cuttings and to sell the timber to manorial tenants for 20s. an acre, but leaving at least half of the 7-year old trees at the end of the term.[26] Wick Park then had over 100 a. of trees mainly 20 years old, though 10 a. had been felled in the previous two years.[27] Tenants took underwood there, and sales of timber produced £8 in 1577–8.[28] Timber in Monk wood was sold by Eton College in 1532, the purchaser undertaking to remove all timber in the wood and oak standards in the hedges within five years.[29] Monkton manor in 1607 had c. 780 hedgerow trees, mainly oak and elm,[30] and in 1670 Monk wood contained 20 a. of which 4 a. were for the use of tenants of the manor who were each entitled to a share of the woodland.[31] In 1764 the Merchant Venturers of Bristol as farmers of the manor received over £15 from sales of coppice wood[32] and in 1773 the under-tenant of Monk wood felled 1 a. a year. The oak timber was valued highly but the brushwood was taken by the poor.[33] By 1792 the 20-a. wood had been cleared and was let with Priory farm, whose tenant was allowed to plough after clearing the underwood.[34] The land was evidently replanted shortly afterwards, and by 1831 there was said to be a lot of oak in the wood, but the soil would not produce large timber.[35] A valuation of the manor in 1859 recorded that the woodland was in a bad state on account of cattle eating the young saplings.[36] Sales of timber from Peadon farm raised over £730 in 1808.[37]

FISHERIES. The Stert flats, fished by means of weirs with basketwork butts or putchers, and by nets stretched over frames and known as 'hangs' or 'netstalls', seem to have been divided into three 'rows' or 'renes' by the mid 16th century.[38] Stogursey priory owned fishing rights at Stolford by 1431 and c. 1455 the vicar received an average of over 10s. a year from the tithe of all fisheries.[39] A succession of fishermen at Stolford between 1551 and 1720 had a cottage, 12 'netstalls', and 9 weirs.[40] Wick, Newnham, and Stogursey Dodington manors each had a share in the fisheries in the 17th century.[41] The three fisheries, each over 1,000 a. in extent, were defined by sight lines in the later 18th century and were known as Stolford, William Rawlins's or Glover's, and John Merchant's. By the later

1 S.R.O., DD/AH 65/1.
2 Above, manors.
3 S.R.O., DD/AH 32/2, 35/25.
4 Ibid. 33/12.
5 P.O. Dir. Som. (1866); P.R.O., RG 10/2354.
6 S.R.O., DD/AH 65/2.
7 Ibid. D/P/stogs 13/2/1.
8 Ibid. DD/AH 16/5.
9 Ibid. 13/4.
10 Ibid. 65/5.
11 Ibid. 11/9.
12 Dors. R.O., D 10/M 245.
13 S.R.S. iii. 141; S.R.O., DD/DHR 36.
14 P.R.O., C 3/111, no. 73; ibid. CP 25(2)/204/4 Eliz. I Hil.; S.R.O., DD/X/WI 34.
15 S.R.O., DD/AH 35/32.
16 Ibid. 31/15, 33/9.
17 W. Suss. R.O., PHA uncat.; W. Suff. R.O. 449/E3/15.53/2.17–19.
18 Cal. Inq. p.m. iv, p. 341.
19 B.L. Harl. MS. 71, f. 63; S.R.O., DD/PC 17.
20 Eton Coll. Rec. 49/273B.
21 S.R.O., DD/AH 59/12.
22 Cal. Inq. p.m. iv, p. 341.
23 B.L. Harl. MS. 71, f. 63.
24 Bath and West and Southern Cos. Jnl. II. xii (1865), 267–8.
25 Alnwick Castle, Northumberland MS. X.II.12.1E.
26 Cal. Pat. 1572–5, p. 88.
27 Alnwick Castle, Northumberland MS. X.II.12.9C.
28 W. Suss. R.O., PHA uncat.
29 Eton Coll. Rec. 6/99.   30 Ibid. 6/206.
31 Ibid. 6/208.   32 Ibid. 6/236.
33 Ibid. 6/269.
34 S.R.O., DD/MVB 58.
35 Eton Coll. Rec. 6/191.   36 Ibid. 6/216.
37 S.R.O., DD/AH 23/3.
38 Ibid. DD/BW 71, 520: one was called Middle Row.
39 Eton Coll. Rec. 6/260.
40 S.R.O., DD/BW 71, 520.
41 P.R.O., CP 25(2)/207/43 Eliz. I Trin.; S.R.O., DD/X/GT; DD/AH 33/9.

17th century Stogursey Dodington manor was letting 12 butts and fishing rights at Stolford.[42] In 1841 there were eight fishermen at Stolford and one at Steart,[43] but the number at Stolford fell.[44] By 1985 only one fisherman was in business in the parish, using a wooden 'mud horse' to reach his nets and the principal catch was shrimp; bass, cod, eel, and mullet were also caught.[45] A fish farm specializing in eels, using warm water from Hinkley Point power station, was established in 1977; 20 tons of eels were produced in 1985.[46]

Seaweed (or ore) was collected and burnt by licence from the later 15th century.[47] It was said in the later 18th century to be gathered in great quantities,[48] and was still being exploited in 1819.[49]

OTHER TRADE AND INDUSTRY. From the beginning of the 16th century men of Stogursey were involved in overseas trade through Bridgwater in a wide variety of goods[50] and both Steart and Stolford provided landing places. A merchant of Minehead shipped beans from Steart in 1543[51] and Stolford was used to import stone in 1446[52] and pigs in the later 17th century.[53] Coal was brought to the quay at Shurton Bars in the later 18th century both to fuel limekilns and for domestic use,[54] and by the mid 19th century two coal merchants were in business at Stolford.[55] Throughout the 19th century parishioners invested in local shipping, one farmer having three sloops between 1797 and 1803.[56]

The clothing industry was established in the 15th century. A vestment maker was in business in 1456[57] and a weaver and a mercer were pardoned for a trespass in 1465.[58] A dyer was a tenant at Durborough in 1473[59] where there was a fulling mill.[60] By 1495 a dyehouse had been built near Stogursey castle and continued in use into the 1520s in association with racks built c. 1518.[61] A Stogursey clothier was recorded in 1631[62] and others worked in the parish in the 17th century.[63] Looms, yarn, and unfinished cloth were mentioned in many inventories.[64] Evidently the principal product was serge[65] but worsted wool in many colours was stolen in

1681,[66] and there is said to have been a silk mill near the castle.[67] Chapmen and mercers were working in the parish in the 17th century.[68]

Tanning and gloving had been established by the mid 15th century.[69] William Burland (d. 1549) left to his son, also William, his tanning vats,[70] and several generations of the Rawlins family bore the alias Glover.[71] Thomas Symons (d. c. 1691) of Shurton had a tanhouse with dressed leather, calfskins, leather, hides, and white hides worth nearly £84 and a bark mill, trough, and bark valued at £9.[72] A tanhouse had been built near St. Andrew's well in Stogursey village by 1689 and a tanyard had been established by the 1760s.[73] A tanyard near the Castle mill operated for much of the 19th century[74] and there was a leather house at Shurton in 1853.[75]

There was a potter in the parish in the later 14th century[76] and several potters were working at Durborough in the 1440s.[77]

Maltsters are mentioned from the mid 18th century, and later in the century there were malthouses in Back Street in Stogursey village and at Water House, now Little Water Farm.[78] In 1840 there were at least three maltings in Stogursey village and breweries attached to at least two inns.[79] A brewery in High Street had closed by 1867.[80]

There was a family of instrument makers in the parish in the 17th century[81] and a button-maker in the 18th.[82] There were tallow chandlers at Shurton in the 18th century[83] and tallow chandlers and soap boilers in Stogursey village,[84] probably occupying the soap factory later used as a Congregational chapel.[85] There were two watchmakers in the parish in the 1860s,[86] and other 19th-century craftsmen included a biscuit maker, a cutler,[87] and a carriage builder.[88] In the later 20th century, besides the nuclear power station at Hinkley Point, industries included picture framing and welding in the village.

Medieval retail trade presumably centred on Stogursey market. A shambles and a wine cellar were recorded in 1475.[89] At least three men issued trade tokens in the 17th century.[90] An inventory of 1681 recorded the varied stock of a general shop which sold foodstuffs, clothing,

42 S.R.O., DD/FD 16.
43 P.R.O., HO 107/935.
44 Ibid. RG 10/2354; RG 11/2356; *Kelly's Dir. Som.* (1894); Clifford MSS. III/10/1–3, rents 1883.
45 *Bridgwater Mercury*, 29 Jan. 1985.
46 Ibid. 5 Mar. 1986. It has since closed.
47 e.g. W. Suff. R.O. 449/E3/15.53/2.5, 8, 17.
48 Eton Coll. Rec. 6/251.
49 Clifford MSS. IV/6/7/X 1A.
50 *S.R.S.* xix. 61; S.R.O., D/B/bw 1480–1, 1493, 1500, 1505.
51 P.R.O., STAC 2/27/63.
52 Eton Coll. Rec. 61/RR/A/34.
53 S.R.O., Q/SR 135/23.
54 Ibid. T/PH/ay 1.
55 P.R.O., HO 107/1920.
56 S.R.O., DD/FA 11/1.
57 Eton Coll. Rec. 6/155.
58 *Cal. Pat.* 1461–7, 414.
59 S.R.O., DD/AH 65/5.
60 Above, this section (mills).
61 W. Suss. R.O., PHA uncat.; W. Suff. R.O. 449/E3/15.53/2.17–18.
62 *S.R.S.* xxiv. 165.
63 S.R.O., DD/AH 27/1, 28/1, 33/5; D/P/stogs 2/1/3.
64 Ibid. DD/SP inventories, 1640, 1645, 1647, 1670,

1681, 1686.
65 Ibid. 1696, 1785; ibid. Q/SR 149/2.
66 Ibid. Q/SR 149/1.
67 B. Lawrence, *Quantock Country*, 139.
68 S.R.O., DD/AH 34/2–3, 7; ibid. Q/SR 102/23.
69 Eton Coll. Rec. 6/153, 155, 162; *Cal. Pat.* 1461–7, 414.
70 S.R.O., DD/SAS RF 3/2/1.
71 Ibid. DD/SP inventory, 1674; D/P/stogs 2/1/1; DD/AH 28/11, 33/8.
72 Ibid. DD/SP inventory, 1691.
73 Ibid. D/P/stogs 13/3/3; DD/AH 33/5.
74 Ibid. DD/DHR, box 44.   75 Ibid. box 4.
76 *H.M.C. Wells*, i. 514, 518–19; S.R.O., DD/AH 65/5.
77 Dors. R.O., D 10/M 244.
78 S.R.O., DD/AH 26/1, 40/4.
79 Ibid. tithe award.   80 Ibid. D/P/stogs 4/3/1.
81 Ibid. DD/SAS (C/112) 9/1; ibid. Q/SR 112/39.
82 Ibid. DD/AH 28/11.
83 Ibid. D/P/stogs 2/1/4; DD/AH 26/9.
84 Ibid. DD/AH 3/1, 29/3; ibid. T/PH/ay 1.
85 Below, nonconf.
86 *P.O. Dir. Som.* (1861, 1866).
87 P.R.O., HO 107/1920.
88 Ibid. RG 11/2356.
89 S.R.O., DD/AH 65/2.
90 *Proc. Som. Arch. Soc.* lxxxvii. 12.

stationery, earthenware, tobacco, and dye-stuffs.[91] In 1819 seven people were rated on their shops[92] and in 1851 there were two drapers and grocers in Fore Street and shopkeepers in Fore Street and Back Street, and at Stolford.[93] By 1861 there were a grocer and spirit merchant at Shurton and a grocer and shopkeeper at Burton,[94] and in 1871 there were also two shops at Stolford.[95] In 1881 Stogursey village included the shops of a grocer, a china dealer, a saddler, a butcher, a baker, and a chandler.[96] Shops survived at Burton and Shurton until the 1930s[97] and there was a variety of small shops in High Street and Lime Street in Stogursey village in 1985.

During the 1930s the parish became popular with holidaymakers, and by 1939 many farms and guesthouses were offering accommodation.[98] Proposals for holiday camps in 1947 were rejected[99] but there were several camping sites in operation in 1985.

LOCAL GOVERNMENT. In 1327 there were five tithings within the parish, Stogursey or Borough, Wick, and Shurton, all in Cannington hundred,[1] Durborough in Whitley hundred,[2] and Fairfield in Williton hundred.[3] In 1521 a tithingman of Farringdon also answered at the Cannington hundred view of frankpledge,[4] but the tithing was not mentioned in 1560 when Wick, Stogursey, and Shurton were complete tithings within the parish and Durborough was held with Cossington.[5] Wick tithing was subdivided in the 17th century to form the quarter tithings of Newnham and Woolstone.[6] Woolstone had been part of Stockland tithing in Stockland Bristol until the mid 13th century.[7] Some Chalcott tenants paid rent called 'hardurzild' to Chilton Trivet tithing in Cannington parish in 1445–6.[8]

The lord of Stogursey claimed wreck of the sea in the 13th and the early 14th century,[9] and as lord of Wick manor in the 16th century.[10] The sale of the manor in 1681 included profits of wreck, stone, and timber from the shore, and new land 'accruing by violence of the sea'.[11] In the mid 18th century the lord of Wick manor claimed to control the coast from Lilstock to the Parrett,[12] a right which was exercised later in the century by the lords of Cannington hundred who also claimed jurisdiction over fishing and gathering seaweed.[13] The lord of Wick in the 17th century claimed deodands, felons' chattels, and strays, for which pounds were built at

Stogursey, Wick, and on the Quantocks in Over Stowey parish.[14]

Nine borough courts were held a year in the late 13th century[15] and in 1301–2 they were called portmotes.[16] Four courts were recorded in 1485–6[17] and there are court rolls for June and September 1532,[18] and for October 1576 and April 1577.[19] In 1614 it was noted that the lord might keep courts at his pleasure,[20] but no further record of courts has been found. A portreeve, said in the 16th and the early 17th century to have been chosen at each Michaelmas court in rotation according to his tenement, accounted for rents and profits.[21] There were

BOROUGH SEAL OF STOGURSEY

also two bailiffs, two constables, two clerks of the market, two breadweighers, two aletasters, and two well keepers.[22] In the 18th century one of the bailiffs had to attend the reeve 'in the nature of a serjeant', the other attended the constables. The second clerk of the market then acted as scavenger and inspector of nuisances.[23] A seal of the 13th and 14th centuries, depicting a four-tiered, embattled tower or castle, bears the legend SIGILL' COMMUNE BURGENSIUN DE STOKES CURCI.[24] A copper-gilt and engraved seal matrix was recorded in 1559 which bore a legend SIGILLUM GOMIT... DE STOKE SURSEY (sic).[25] An 18th century description mentions the castle with the legend SIGILLUM COMITIS DE ... DOMINI DE STOKE CURCY.[26]

Shurton manor had leet jurisdiction until the

91 S.R.O., DD/SP inventory, 1681.
92 Ibid. D/P/stogs 6/1/2.
93 P.R.O., HO 107/1920.   94 Ibid. RG 9/1604.
95 Ibid. RG 10/2354.   96 Ibid. RG 11/2356.
97 Kelly's Dir. Som. (1931, 1939).
98 Ibid. (1939).
99 S.R.O., D/P/stogs 1/2/2.
1 S.R.S. iii. 141, 143, 276.
2 Ibid. 45; Rot. Hund. (Rec. Com.), ii. 135.
3 S.R.O., DD/AH 60/10; S.R.S. iii. 314.
4 S.R.O., DD/BR/bn 10.
5 S.R.S. xx. 65, 250.
6 S.R.O., DD/X/WI 34; Bristol R.O. 04404.
7 Rot. Hund. (Rec. Com.), ii. 137.
8 Dors. R.O., D/WLC/M 246.
9 Rot. Hund. (Rec. Com.), ii. 119; Cal. Pat. 1307–13, 254.

10 W. Suss. R.O., PHA 6911.
11 S.R.O., DD/PC 17.   12 Ibid. DD/AH 17/11.
13 Ibid. 3/10; DD/DHR, box 33; Clifford MSS., III/10/1–3 and Som. estate, rental 1796–7.
14 S.R.O., DD/X/WI 34.
15 P.R.O., SC 6/1090/4.   16 Ibid. SC 6/1090/6.
17 W. Suff. R.O. 449/E3/15.53/2.5.
18 W. Suss. R.O., PHA uncat.   19 Ibid. 6911.
20 S.R.O., DD/X/WI 34.
21 B.L. Harl. MS. 71, f. 63; S.R.O., DD/X/WI 34.
22 W. Suss. R.O., PHA 6911.
23 Eton Coll. Rec. 49/273B.
24 B.L. Seals, clii, no. 7; for a drawing see S.R.O., D/P/stogs 23/14, reproduced above.
25 B.L. Harl. MS. 71, f. 64.
26 Eton Coll. Rec. 49/273B.

The church and Market Place

The Almshouses in 1845

STOGURSEY

Bench ends: Lyng, Stogursey, and Spaxton

North Petherton: North Newton Church, *c.* 1860

mid 13th century,[27] but there is no later evidence of it. Court rolls for Shurton manor survive for 1424–7[28] and for shares of it for 1507–8,[29] 1579, 1588, 1592, 1594, and 1599–1605.[30] Fairfield and Stogursey Priory manors had leet jurisdiction with view of frankpledge. Records of a three-weekly court of Fairfield manor survive for 1275–1349;[31] from 1386 all Fairfield manor courts were called courts leet and included twice-yearly views of frankpledge 1457–1547.[32] One free tenant paid a rent called 'hardurzild' in 1302.[33] For the priory estate extracts from what appear to have been thrice-yearly courts survive for 1384–98,[34] and from 1449 until 1841 the thrice-yearly sessions held for Eton College were called courts leet and view of frankpledge.[35] The court records continued until 1918;[36] a tithingman and two aletasters were chosen every Michaelmas in the 15th century[37] but only one aletaster by the 1590s.[38] From the 17th century business was largely confined to admissions and surrenders. A tithingman continued to be chosen in a fixed rotation, and a hayward was similarly chosen from 1829.[39]

Manor courts were held twice a year on the Pokeswell share of Chalcott manor and rolls survive for 1445, 1448,[40] and 1517.[41] Manor courts were kept at Cock in 1514[42] and twice a year on the Palmers' manor there in the 1650s.[43] Owners of the shares of the divided Durborough manor each held courts. For the later Durborough Dodington manor records of courts survive for 1365 and 1514.[44] From Durborough Verney manor there are rolls for various years between 1392 and 1518,[45] where courts were normally called manor courts but were held in the later 14th century only at Easter and Michaelmas. In April 1467 the court was called a leet, but thereafter sessions were held irregularly. For the Pokeswells' share rolls for annual manor courts survive for 1445–8,[46] and there is a record of a single manor court for part of Durborough Dodington manor for 1611.[47] Tenants owed suit to Farringdon manor in the 18th century[48] but no court rolls survive.

Two courts were held each year at Newnham in 1540–1[49] and suit was still owed in the 17th century.[50] Two courts were also held for Stogursey Hadley in the 14th and 15th centuries[51] but no records have been found. There is a draft

court roll for Stogursey Dodington for 1523[52] but by the early 17th century tenants owed suit to either of the two Dodington manors, Stogursey or Durborough.[53] In the late 18th century the earl of Egmont claimed that the marquess of Buckingham could not hold court for the former as it 'had been given up for many years past'. The marquess held his court, however, and Egmont's steward was sworn foreman of the jury.[54]

The parish was divided into ten areas for tithe collection in 1431 and into 13 c. 1490.[55] From the mid 17th century the parish officers operated through ten tithings: Borough, Burton, Cock and Idson, Durborough, Knighton, Monkton, Shurton, Stolford, Whitewick, and Wick.[56] Land tax was assessed in five units: Borough, Cock and Idson, covering the whole eastern part of the parish, Monkton, Shurton, and, the largest, Wick.[57]

There were two churchwardens by 1502 and decisions on church affairs were made by a group of 24 parishioners.[58] That group approved all purchases and distributions for the poor in the mid 17th century, and vestrymen were chosen from their number.[59] By 1693 the vestry and the 24 appear to have been synonymous[60] and all were known as vestrymen by the 1730s.[61] The vestry had appointed a salaried clerk by 1797,[62] and in 1820 a select vestry of 15 was elected.[63] In the mid 17th century there were four overseers, two chosen from the 24. Their number had been reduced to two by 1738,[64] and a paid overseer who was also parish surveyor was appointed in 1779.[65] In 1749 it was agreed to restrict parish work to those on relief or with large families.[66] The poor were badged from 1780 and an apothecary was employed for their care in 1781.[67] Spinning wheels were supplied to poor women in 1784[68] and provisions were sold to the poor at reduced prices in the 1790s.[69] In 1816 the parish paid for inoculating poor children[70] but in 1832 gave up apprenticing pauper children. In 1840 the parish considered establishing a fund for pauper emigration.[71]

There were four highway surveyors in the mid 17th century,[72] each assigned by the later 18th century to one of the four areas of Borough, Durborough, Monkton, and Wick or Shurton.[73] By 1828 there were 10 waywardens, a number

27 S.R.S. lxviii, p. 43–4.
28 P.R.O., SC 2/200/27–8.
29 S.R.O., DD/AH 11/9.
30 Ibid. DD/WG 16. A court of survey was held on the Strode manor in 1582: MS. in possession of Mr. J. S. Cox, Guernsey.
31 S.R.O., DD/AH 65/6, 66/5.
32 Ibid. 11/9–10; 65/2, 5; 66/5.
33 Ibid. 66/5.
34 Eton Coll. Rec. 6/152.
35 Ibid. 6/97, 101, 153, 156–89; S.R.O., DD/AH 11/9.
36 Eton Coll. Rec. 49/273B–C.
37 Ibid. 6/153.
38 Ibid. 6/184.
39 Ibid. 6/189–90.
40 Dors. R.O., D 10/M 244–5.
41 S.R.O., DD/AH 11/10.
42 Ibid. 30/4.
43 Ibid. DD/SAS (C/112) 9/1; DD/AH 32/23.
44 Ibid. DD/AH 11/9, 65/5.
45 Ibid. 11/9–10, 65/5, 66/5.
46 Dors. R.O., D 10/M 244–5.
47 S.R.O., DD/S/WH 211.

48 Ibid. DD/AH 12/6, 32/21.
49 P.R.O., LR 3/123.
50 S.R.O., DD/AH 3/8.
51 Ibid. DD/L P36/4.
52 Ibid. DD/AH 16/10.   53 Ibid. 33/7.
54 Ibid. 24/8.   55 Eton Coll. Rec. 6/197, 219.
56 S.R.O., D/P/stogs 4/1/2, 13/2/1.
57 Ibid. Q/REl 7/8, 8A–D.
58 Ibid. D/P/stogs 4/1/1.
59 Ibid. 13/2/1–2.
60 Ibid. DD/AH 21/4.
61 Ibid. D/P/stogs 13/2/2.
62 Ibid. 13/2/4.   63 Ibid. 9/1/1.
64 Ibid. 13/2/1–2.
65 Ibid. 14/5/1.
66 Ibid. 13/2/2.
67 Ibid. 13/2/3.
68 Ibid. DD/AH 21/4.
69 Ibid. D/P/stogs 13/2/4.
70 Ibid. 13/2/6.
71 Ibid. 9/1/2.
72 Ibid. 13/2/1–2.
73 Ibid. 14/5/1.

reduced in 1839 to 5.[74] A paid surveyor had been appointed from 1779.[75] Road work was offered to paupers at established rates in 1822.[76]

In 1843 the vestry was concerned in the appointment of two borough constables, and provided an additional two pairs of handcuffs by subscription. It was active in improving roads in the 1860s and in 1867 erected a building over the brook in the churchyard as a place to distribute what was called parish relief, to store coal, and to act as a mortuary for bodies washed ashore.[77] The parish council elected from 1894 concerned itself with the condition of parish bridges, the maintenance of the village pump, and the use of the parish pound.[78]

The church house was in use as a dwelling, probably a poorhouse, by the later 17th century.[79] It was repaired by the churchwardens in 1707 when it had 7 chambers, a workroom, and 2 'fore' rooms.[80] It continued to be called the church house for much of the 18th century,[81] but by 1830 it was known as the poorhouse when five rooms were to be partitioned. It was decided to demolish the building in 1838,[82] but it was still standing in 1844 when its sale was approved. Its site was incorporated in the new road around the churchyard agreed in 1865.[83]

The parish became part of the Williton poor-law union in 1836, Williton rural district in 1894, and West Somerset district in 1974.[84]

CHURCH. Between 1100 and 1107 William de Falaise and Geva his wife gave the church with land and tithes to Lonlay abbey (Orne).[85] The abbey had a priory at Stogursey by c. 1120[86] and the parish church was extended apparently for use by the monks.[87] A vicar was serving the cure by c. 1280[88] and the prior and monks presented vicars until 1352 when the Crown assumed the patronage because the house was alien.[89] The priory and patronage of the vicarage passed to Eton College, which presented in 1453 for the first time, and remained lay rector in 1985.[90] Until 1881 Lilstock church was treated as a chapelry under the vicar of Stogursey.[91] From 1964 Stogursey was held with Fiddington, and in 1976 the benefices were united, Eton College presenting on alternate vacancies.[92]

The vicarage was valued at £6 13s. 4d. in 1414 and was said to be poor in 1433.[93] In 1454 the gross income was £16 0s. 10¼d.,[94] in 1535 £29 9s.,[95] in 1548 £35 6s. 8d.,[96] about 1668 it was valued at c. £60,[97] and the average annual income in 1829–31 was £389.[98] In 1454 the vicar received, besides the small tithes from the parish, four cartloads of hay and tithe sheaves from the former priory estate.[99] In 1584 small tithes were no longer received from the former priory estate.[1] In 1840 the vicar received a rent charge of £370 in lieu of all his tithes and loads of hay.[2]

In 1535 the glebe was worth 2s. 8d.[3] In 1607 it comprised a barn and 1½ a. in Lime Street,[4] later described as a half and a quarter burgage in the common field of Easter Burgage.[5] In 1840 there remained just over 1 a. and the churchyard.[6] Some 11 a. around the new vicarage house were added in the 1860s[7] but part of the Lime Street property was sold in 1942.[8] The rest remained church property in 1978.[9]

In the 1450s and 1460s the vicar rented the house formerly occupied by the prior.[10] By 1487, however, Eton College had provided a house.[11] In 1729 it was let to a wheelwright.[12] Although in good repair in 1840[13] it was abandoned by the vicar for another house and was sold to Eton College in 1868.[14] The Old Vicarage, west of the church, is a 16th-century building with an 18th-century wing partly demolished in the early 20th century. A new and larger house, designed by John Norton, was built in 1869.[15] Structural problems caused it to be demolished and replaced in 1912 on an adjoining site, using some of the old materials.[16] The new house in turn was sold in 1979 after a replacement had been built in part of its garden.[17]

Chaplains were recorded in the parish c. 1175[18] and in the late 12th and early 13th century[19] before the appearance of a vicar c. 1280.[20] The prior was appointed curate and guardian for an infirm vicar in 1402.[21] By 1444 Eton College was supporting a chaplain,[22] presumably the chaplain recorded in 1463.[23] In 1465 the new vicar was required to find one for the parish[24] but in 1474 the college agreed to do so. The chaplain's salary, usually paid by the farmers of the rectory, was maintained until 1567.[25] Chaplains were necessary when the living was held by pluralists

74 S.R.O., D/P/stogs 9/1/2.   75 Ibid. 14/5/1.
76 Ibid. 9/1/1.
77 Ibid. 9/1/3.
78 Ibid. D/PC/stogs 1/2/1, 3/4/1.
79 Ibid. D/P/stogs 2/1/3.
80 Ibid. 4/1/2.
81 Ibid. 2/1/4.   82 Ibid. 9/1/2.
83 Ibid. 9/1/3.
84 Youngs, *Local Admin. Units*, i. 674–6.
85 *S.R.S.* lxi, pp. 1–2.
86 Ibid. p. 46.
87 Ibid. pp. 2, 6; below, this section.
88 *S.R.S.* lxi, p. 34.
89 *Som. Incumbents*, ed. Weaver, 446.
90 *S.R.S.* xlix, p. 210.
91 *V.C.H. Som.* v. 106.
92 *Dioc. Dir.*
93 *S.R.S.* xxxi. 152; S.R.O., D/D/B misc 1.
94 Eton Coll. Rec. 6/260.
95 *Valor Eccl.* (Rec. Com.), i. 214. Includes Lilstock as do probably all valuations until the late 19th century.
96 *S.R.S.* ii. 53.
97 S.R.O., D/D/Vc 24.
98 *Rep. Com. Eccl. Revenues*, pp. 152–3.
99 Eton Coll. Rec. 6/260.   1 S.R.O., D/D/Cd 129.
2 Ibid. tithe award.
3 *Valor Eccl.* (Rec. Com.), i. 214.
4 Eton Coll. Rec. 6/206.
5 S.R.O., DD/OS 19.
6 Ibid. tithe award.
7 Inf. from Dioc. Office; below.
8 S.R.O., D/P/stogs 3/1/1.
9 Inf. from Dioc. Office.
10 Eton Coll. Rec. 6/197, 260.
11 Ibid. 6/203, 219.   12 Ibid. 6/251.
13 S.R.O., D/D/Va 1840.
14 Ibid. DD/X/RHO.
15 Ibid. DD/CC E1349; D/D/Bbm 169.
16 Ibid. DD/CC E1349; D/P/stogs 3/4/1; 23/2, 19.
17 Ibid. DD/WBF 2 Stogursey.
18 *S.R.S.* lxi, p. 13.
19 Ibid. pp. 11, 14, 22.
20 Ibid. p. 34.
21 Ibid. xiii, p. 30.
22 Eton Coll. Rec. 61/RR/A/19.
23 *S.R.S.* xlix, p. 399.
24 Ibid. lii, p. 28; lxi, p. 65.
25 Ibid. lxi, p. 65; Eton Coll. Rec. 61/RR/D/1; 61/BR/K/7.

such as Thomas Machy, vicar 1485–6 and headmaster of Eton, and Robert Blackwall, 1486–8.[26] It was complained in the early 16th century that the parish was without 'a goode hed and a sade curate and lernyd'.[27] Henry Handley (d. 1539–40) and William Witherton, vicar 1540–44, both seem to have been in the parish when they died, but the first had been a fellow of King's College, Cambridge, and the second held another Eton living.[28] About 1535 the clergy in the parish comprised the vicar, a curate, a stipendiary chaplain, and a chantry chaplain.[29]

Church ales, bequests, offerings, and land provided income for church maintenance and decoration in the early 16th century: an organ was repaired in 1507–8, and a bible and its chain were bought in 1539–40, and five volumes of the litany in 1543–4.[30] The rood had not been replaced by 1557 when three parishioners abused the altars.[31] Richard Wickham, vicar 1582–99, was accused of not wearing a surplice, of leaving out parts of the liturgy, and of unjust dealings.[32] Richard Meredith, vicar from 1628, and Elias Batchelor, vicar 1671–87, were Etonians and former fellows of King's College, Cambridge. Meredith's incumbency was interrupted by two intruded clergy in 1649 and 1652. He was also rector of West Bagborough and from 1660 held the archdeaconry of Dorset.[33] Matthew Hole, vicar 1687–1730, appointed to the living as a friend of a fellow of Eton,[34] was a canon of Wells and a fellow of Exeter College, Oxford, for the whole of his tenure of the vicarage, and he was also rector of Fiddington 1709–11. In 1715, when he was elected rector of Exeter College, he was temporarily suspended from his living for neglect and for absence from a visitation.[35] Absentee pluralist vicars in the 18th and early 19th century left the parish to curates who claimed c. 1776 that there were between 70 and 80 communicants, and who celebrated communion c. 7 times a year.[36] In 1799 the duty consisted of a morning service each Sunday and between Lady Day and Michaelmas afternoon prayer, to which a sermon had been added between 1788 and 1799 at the joint cost of the vicar and Mr. John Acland.[37] In 1815 the resident curate also served Lilstock and Kilton.[38] John Barnwell, vicar 1826–66, was also rector of Holford and vicar of Sutton Valence (Kent).[39] By 1840 there were two services with a sermon each week, and by 1843 it was intended to increase communion services from seven a year to twelve.[40] In 1851 average attendance was

said to be 400 in the morning and 430 in the afternoon.[41] In 1854 communion was celebrated in church 17 times with an average of 41 communicants, and also in private homes.[42] By 1870 both vicar and curate were resident and there were monthly and festal celebrations of communion.[43]

A chantry priest was employed by c. 1535,[44] possibly in connexion with a brotherhood or guild of Our Lady, established by 1519–20, which had grown out of a calendar of deceased parishioners.[45] The chantry was dissolved in 1548 and its lands, including a field called Chantry in Chalcott, were sold.[46] There were altars or aisles of Our Lady and the Holy Trinity, and lights were maintained before images of St. Anne, St. George, St. Erasmus, Our Lady of Pity, the Trinity, and the rood.[47]

Eton College gave a site on the edge of the churchyard in 1516 and the parish built a church house there.[48] It was described in 1680 as a church house and shop[49] and was probably then being used as a poorhouse.[50]

The church of *ST. ANDREW*, so dedicated by c. 1100,[51] is built of random rubble with ashlar dressings and has a sanctuary with north vestry, a choir with north and south aisles, a crossing tower with north and south transepts, and a nave with a former north porch now used as a store. The tower, which is capped by a spire, and the transepts survive from the late 11th century,[52] the transepts formerly having eastern apses which flanked a short, apsidal chancel. The east end was reconstructed in the late 12th century when the chancel was lengthened to form a choir and the transepts were extended eastwards as choir aisles or chapels of two bays, later known as the Lady and Trinity aisles.[53] The enlargement was presumably to provide a choir for the monks after the church had become conventual. The present floor level in the choir is the result of excavation in the 1940s, and probably marks the level of a vault beneath the original choir. There is no evidence of further building until after the closure of the priory c. 1440.[54] About 1500 the nave was rebuilt and a north porch was added, joined to the north transept by the rood stair. On the south side a chapel was built in the angle between the nave and the south transept. Both choir aisles were reconstructed, and that on the north was extended eastwards as a two-storeyed vestry.

By the early 19th century the interior fittings included a three-decker pulpit on the north side

26 Emden, *Biog. Reg. Univ. Cantab. to 1500*; Emden, *Biog. Reg. Univ. Oxon. to 1500*.
27 *S.R.S.* lxi, p. 87, from Eton Coll. Rec. 6/223.
28 *S.R.S.* xxi. 23; lv, p. 162; S.R.O., DD/X/SR 5; *Alum. Cantab. to 1751.*
29 S.R.O., D/D/Vc 20.
30 Ibid. D/P/stogs 4/1/1.
31 Ibid. D/D/Ca 27.
32 Ibid. 98; P.R.O., C 3/242, no. 55; C 3/247, no. 74.
33 *Som. Incumbents*, ed. Weaver, 313, 446; *Som. Wills*, ed. Brown, iii. 97; *Walker Revised*, ed. A. G. Matthews.
34 *D.N.B.*
35 Phipps, *Taunton Archdeaconry Probate Rec.* 74.
36 Eton Coll. Rec. 6/269; S.R.O., D/D/Bo; D/D/Bp; D/D/Vc 88; D/P/stogs 2/1/5, 4/4/1.
37 Eton Coll. Rec. 6/251.
38 S.R.O., D/D/Rb 1815.
39 *Rep. Com. Eccl. Revenues*, pp. 152–3.

40 S.R.O., D/D/Va 1840, 1843.
41 P.R.O., HO 129/313/4/5/4.
42 S.R.O., D/P/stogs 4/4/1.
43 Ibid. D/D/Va 1870.   44 Ibid. D/D/Vc 20.
45 Ibid. D/P/stogs 4/1/1; D/D/Vc 20.
46 *S.R.S.* ii. 52; lxxvii, p. 81; S.R.O., DD/WO 17/2; DD/SAS (C/432) 17.
47 S.R.O., DD/X/SR 5; D/P/stogs 4/1/1; *S.R.S.* ii. 226; *Wells Wills*, ed. Weaver, 148.
48 S.R.O., D/P/stogs 4/1/1; Eton Coll. Rec. 6/203.
49 Eton Coll. Rec. 6/212.
50 Above, local govt.
51 *S.R.S.* lxi, p. 1.
52 M. Baylé, 'Les Chapiteaux de Stogursey (Somerset) Ancien Prieuré de Lonlay L'Abbaye', *Bulletin Monumental* (1980), cxxxviii. 405–16.
53 S.R.O., D/P/stogs 4/1/1; cf. above, plate facing p. 8.
54 W. Suss. R.O., PHA 5730.

of the crossing, a pew built in the later 17th century by Peregrine Palmer of Fairfield[55] in the nave chapel, and a west gallery built c. 1740.[56] The tower, possibly weakened by the removal of the rood beam in 1703,[57] had been unsafe for nearly a century when Richard Carver rebuilt two of its piers in 1815–16.[58] In 1824 he rebuilt most of the walls and renewed the roof.[59] In 1864 John Norton inserted windows in the east wall of the sanctuary, removed the Palmers' family pew and south chapel, and added choir stalls, a pulpit, and a low screen in an elaborate Norman style. Parapets to the tower, north transept, and north choir aisle probably date from that restoration. The church was reopened in 1865.[60] In the 1930s and 1940s the building was again restored, when all the interior Victorian work was removed, the choir floor lowered, and old memorials, probably brought from the churchyard, were introduced.[61]

The oldest furnishings in the church are a Norman tub font with four faces, standing on reset medieval tiles in the north transept, and a second Norman font from Lilstock. The bench ends in the nave are probably of the early 16th century and depict a wide range of tracery and plant motifs, birds, including a spoonbill, and Renaissance themes. A carver named Glosse was paid in 1524–5 for work on the church.[62] A blocked doorway on the north side of the nave marks the site of the rood stair. The screen was still in place in 1735[63] and the panelled recess beside it probably held a tomb. The recess was possibly matched by another on the south side, perhaps altered to make an entrance to the chapel, later the Fairfield pew, which occupied the angle between the nave and transept.[64] The recesses may have contained the two effigies of members of the Verney family now under the choir arcades: that identified as of William Verney (d. 1333) was provided with a plain tomb chest in 1864,[65] and that identified as of John Verney lies on a 15th-century tomb-chest but has been badly damaged. In the early 18th century there was another tomb, said to be of Ralph Verney.[66] The south aisle of the choir, sometimes called the Verney aisle,[67] contains monuments to owners of Fairfield including Peregrine Palmer (d. 1684) in the style of Gibbons, Nathaniel Palmer (d. 1718), and Sir Thomas Wroth of Petherton Park (d. 1721) with his daughter Elizabeth (d. 1737) and her husband Thomas Palmer (d. 1734). A painting was said to have decorated the east wall of the north aisle of the choir and fragments of painted plaster and of wooden carvings were discovered in the 1940s.[68]

The church has two flagons, two dishes, a paten, and a chalice, all given by Thomas Palmer in 1723 to commemorate his marriage to Elizabeth Wroth.[69] There were at least four bells in the early 16th century.[70] The oldest of the present six was cast by George Purdue in 1611.[71] In 1761 two bells were found to be broken because of the practice of tying them for funerals.[72] The registers date from 1598 but have a gap between c. 1630 and 1653.[73]

A chapel of St. John the Evangelist adjoined the church in the early 12th century.[74] No later evidence of it has been found. A chapel at Durborough in 1316 belonged to Stogursey priory.[75] A tenement called the Chapel was mentioned in the early 17th century,[76] and a field west of the stream at Durborough was called Chappelhayes in 1841.[77]

Probably after 1316 the lords of Wick manor built a chapel at Stolford, later dedicated to St. Michael.[78] The chapel, repaired in 1490,[79] was described as ruinous in 1577–8.[80] It belonged to Henry Percy, earl of Northumberland (d. 1585), in 1579 and descended with Stogursey manor after the dismemberment of Wick; from 1758 it was claimed by the earls of Egmont, who maintained the chapel for the benefit of local fishermen.[81] It had evidently been demolished by 1824,[82] but its location is marked by Chapel cottages built on adjoining land owned by Eton College.[83] Further inland, on the road between Stolford and Wick, the church of *ST. PETER,* Stolford, was provided in 1866 by Sir Peregrine Fuller-Palmer-Acland, whose family continued to support it directly until 1912.[84] It was closed in 1945 and reopened in 1955.[85] It is a small timber building, formerly known as St. Andrew's Mission Church, comprising a chancel, nave, and south-west tower, with a west porch added in 1983.[86] It was apparently brought from West Quantoxhead, where it had been used while the church there was being rebuilt in 1854–6.[87] The Perpendicular font was formerly in Stogursey church.[88] In 1985 services were held fortnightly with communion once a month.

NONCONFORMITY. There were two recusants in the parish in the 1590s[89] and two Roman Catholics at Shurton in 1715.[90]

Two meeting house licences were issued in 1689 and a Presbyterian meeting was held in the parish c. 1690.[91] The meeting comprised 100

55 S.R.O., D/P/stogs 23/18.   56 Ibid. 4/1/2.
57 *Notes on Hist. of Ch. of St. Andrew, Stogursey*, ed. B. Tucker (1925), 8.
58 S.R.O., D/P/stogs 4/1/2–3; DD/AH 19/8.
59 Ibid. D/P/stogs 4/1/3, 9/1/2; Eton Coll. Rec. 6/191.
60 Ibid. DD/AH 21/15.
61 Ibid. D/P/stogs 6/1/1, 6/2/2.
62 Ibid. 4/1/1; cf. above, plate facing p. 153.
63 *Stogursey Ch*. ed. Tucker, 8.
64 Taunton Castle, Pigott colln., J. Buckler, drawing 1836.
65 S.R.O., D/P/stogs 6/2/1.
66 Ibid. DD/AH 60/10.   67 Ibid. D/P/stogs 6/2/1.
68 *Stogursey Ch*. ed. Tucker, 13.
69 S.R.O., D/P/stogs 2/1/3, 9/1/3.   70 Ibid. 4/1/1.
71 Ibid. DD/SAS CH 16/2.
72 Ibid. D/P/stogs 4/1/2.   73 Ibid. 2/1/1–14.
74 *S.R.S.* lxi, p. 44.   75 Ibid. i. 8.

76 S.R.O., DD/AH 33/19, 35/32; DD/S/WH 8.
77 Ibid. tithe award.
78 *Cal. Pat.* 1330–4, 288; Eton Coll. Rec. 6/159; *S.R.S.* i. 8.
79 Eton Coll. Rec. 61/RR/E/6.
80 W. Suss. R.O., PHA uncat.
81 S.R.O., DD/AH 17/11.
82 Ibid. DD/X/KLT 3, map 1824.
83 Eton Coll. Rec. 6/157, 159, 197, 206; 51/363.
84 S.R.O., DD/AH 59/8 and box 2; D/P/stogs 3/4/1.
85 Inf. from Mr. J. Ley, Stolford, Stogursey.
86 S.R.O., D/P/stogs 9/9/3; *Dioc. Dir.*; local inf.
87 *P.O. Dir. Som.* (1866); *V.C.H. Som.* v. 135.
88 Taunton Castle, Pigott colln., J. Buckler, drawing 1836.
89 *S.D.N.Q.* v. 115; *Recusant Roll*, ii (Cath. Rec. Soc. lvii), 141.   90 *Cath. Religion in Som.* (1826), 33.
91 S.R.O., Q/RR meeting ho. lics.; A. Gordon, *Freedom after Ejection* (1917), 93.

members and a minister in 1718, when a second meeting was said to have ceased.[92] There is no further record of Presbyterians but an Independent meeting house was licensed in 1786.[93] It had closed by 1822 when Congregationalists held cottage services in the parish. In 1823 a church was formed and a soap factory was bought for use as a chapel. It was enlarged in 1835 but services had ceased by 1851. In 1863 the chapel was reopened and in the 1890s a Sunday school was built.[94] The chapel, in Castle street, was still open in 1973 and was registered as a United Reformed church in 1974.[95] It closed in 1977, following an agreement to unite with the congregation of the parish church,[96] and the building became a community meeting room. A Congregational chapel at Stolford was recorded in 1872 and 1896 and services were held in the same period at Burton and Shurton.[97]

A Particular Baptist chapel was built at Burton in 1833 following weekly prayer meetings. The church had 11 members and a minister when it joined the Western Baptist Association in 1836.[98] In 1851 attendance was 81 at morning service and 72 in the evening; 29 children attended the Sunday school.[99] The chapel was still open in 1985 but did not belong to the Baptist Union.[1] It has a small graveyard with an adjoining manse.[2]

In 1846 a small Primitive Methodist chapel was built at Stolford. In 1851 there were 29 people at morning service and 35 in the afternoon; 9 children attended the Sunday school in the morning and 11 in the afternoon.[3] The chapel was acquired by Baptists in 1884 and had a congregation of between 30 and 50. It was served by the minister of Burton chapel and was still in use in 1937[4] but may have closed soon afterwards. It was ruinous in 1985.

EDUCATION. The parish clerk taught 3 or 4 small children in 1606.[5] Francis Rawlins was licensed as a schoolmaster in 1662 and remained until his death in 1710.[6] Two other masters were licensed in 1662, and a schoolmistress died in 1706.[7] By 1759 two teachers were each receiving £2 a year from offerings at communion services and in that year taught 20 poor children. Extra

payments were made to teach sewing, but all support ceased in 1827.[8] By will of 1764 William Daniel provided for the education of 10 poor children, but the charity had been lost by 1826.[9] In 1772 the vicar also supported poor children and in 1795 the vestry agreed to establish a Sunday school.[10] By 1819 there were two National schools, supported by charitable contributions, with a total of 84 pupils,[11] one in Stogursey village, the other probably at Burton.

In 1825 the Stogursey school was held on Sundays and weekdays, supported by weekly payments and subscriptions; 94 children attended, 6 of them on Sunday only.[12] It was probably the largest of the four schools in the parish in 1835, with 102 children and a library,[13] and had 111 pupils and an endowment in 1846. On Sundays there were as many as 89 pupils in 1846 and 128 in 1851.[14] A new Stogursey school was built in 1860, designed by John Norton in a flamboyant Gothic style, of Quantock stone with Bath stone dressings.[15] In 1903 it received contributions from the Society of Merchant Venturers of Bristol and from Eton College, and there were 200 children on the books.[16] By 1945 the number had fallen to 112 but by 1955 had risen to 152. From 1957 the school took juniors and infants only and in 1965 there were 142 on the books. In 1988 there were 89.[17]

The National school at Burton, probably established by 1819,[18] had 52 pupils in 1835[19] and 57 in 1846.[20] It was still open in 1883[21] but has not been traced later. In 1829 an infant school was established in High Street, Stogursey, which closed c. 1871.[22] There were several small schools in the hamlets: a school with 10 pupils at Wick in 1835,[23] a boarding school at Shurton in 1841,[24] a day school there by 1861 and until 1872,[25] a boarding school for infants at Burton between 1851 and 1871,[26] and an infant school at Stolford in 1871–2.[27] In Stogursey village a boarding school for girls and infants with 35 pupils in 1841 survived until c. 1860.[28]

CHARITIES FOR THE POOR. William Paulet (fl. 1412–16) of Beere in Chilton Trinity endowed almshouses for six poor people.[29] One of them was to ring the bell and read prayers

92 T. G. Crippen, Nonconf. in Som. 39.
93 S.R.O., D/D/Rm 1.
94 Rep. Som. Cong. Union (1896); P.R.O., HO 129/4/5/12.
95 S.R.O., D/N/np. c (S/2356); G.R.O., worship reg. no. 10415.
96 S.R.O., D/N/scu 7/16/18.
97 Morris & Co. Dir. Som. (1872); Rep. Som. Cong. Union (1896).
98 H. J. Hamblin & A. J. Whitby, Baptists in Bridgwater (1937), 83–4; F. H. Cockett, Partnership in Service [n.d., after 1973], 30.   99 P.R.O., HO 129/4/5/5.
1 Baptist Union Dir. (1981–2).
2 Hamblin & Whitby, Baptists in Bridgwater, 84. The chapel closed in 1989.
3 P.R.O., HO 129/4/5/5.
4 H. J. Hamblin, Romance of a Wayside Sanctuary, 8, 12; Hamblin & Whitby, Baptists in Bridgwater, 84.
5 S.R.O., D/D/Ca 151.
6 Ibid. D/D/Bs 39; DD/HM (N/14); D/P/stogs 2/1/3.
7 Ibid. D/D/Bs 39; D/P/stogs 2/1/3.
8 Ibid. 4/4/1.   9 Char. Don. pp. 1048–9.
10 S.R.O., D/P/stogs 4/1/2.
11 Educ. of Poor Digest, p. 799.

12 Ann. Rep. B. & W. Dioc. Assoc. S.P.C.K. (1825–6), 43.
13 Educ. Enq. Abstract, p. 823.
14 Nat. Soc. Inquiry, 1846–7, Som. 16–17; P.R.O., HO 129/313/4/5/4.
15 S.R.O., DD/AH 51/7; Morris & Co. Dir. Som. (1872); J. Whitby, Dir. Bridgwater (1883); Pevsner, S. & W. Som. 301, where the date is given incorrectly as 1865
16 S.R.O., C/E 4/380/380.
17 Ibid. 4/64.
18 Educ. of Poor Digest, p. 799.
19 Educ. Enq. Abstract, p. 823.
20 Nat. Soc. Inquiry, 1846–7, Som. 16–17.
21 J. Whitby, Dir. Bridgwater (1883).
22 Educ. Enq. Abstract, p. 823; S.R.O., tithe award; DD/AH 5/1; P.R.O., RG 10/2354.
23 Educ. Enq. Abstract, p. 823.
24 P.R.O., HO 107/935.
25 P.O. Dir. Som. (1861); Morris & Co. Dir. Som. (1872).
26 P.R.O., HO 107/1920; ibid. RG 10/2354.
27 Ibid. RG 10/2354; Morris & Co. Dir. Som. (1872).
28 P.R.O., HO 107/935; ibid. RG 9/1604; P.O. Dir. Som. (1859); S.R.O., DD/AH 5/1.
29 S.R.O., D/P/stogs 17/7/14; DD/AH 65/2; below, Chilton Trinity.

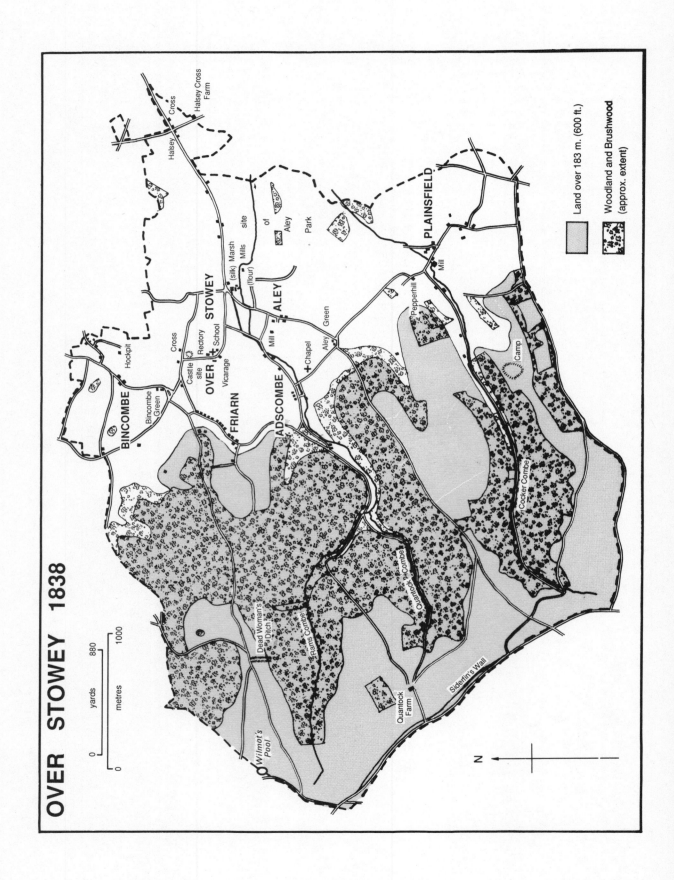

OVER STOWEY 1838

BINCOMBE

Bincombe
Green

Hockpit

Halsey
Cross

Halsey Cross
Farm

Cross

Castle
site

School

Rectory

OVER

Vicarage

FRIARN

STOWEY

Marsh
(silk) Mills
(flour)

site
of
Aley
Park

ALEY

Mill

Chapel

Aley
Green

ADSCOMBE

PLAINSFIELD

Mill

Pepperhill

Wilmot's
Pool

Dead Woman's
Ditch

Rams Combe

Quantock Combe

Quantock
Farm

Sidenfin's Wall

Cocker Combe

Camp

N

Land over 183 m. (600 ft.)

Woodland and Brushwood
(approx. extent)

0   880   1000
yards

0   metres   1000

twice a day; the surviving bell is said to be medieval. By 1823 the endowment comprised lands in Stogursey, Nether Stowey, and Over Stowey producing c. £190. The estate was sold in 1919 when the income was c. £240, and the money invested in stock. A charity founded under the will of Maud Stodden dated 1727 for poor spinsters or widows was in 1826 distributed weekly to eight women. The charity lands, worth c. £54 a year, were sold in 1919 and the proceeds invested. In 1978 the two charities were combined to form a housing association but a Christmas distribution is also made from the Stodden charity.[30]

The almshouses, rebuilt in the 16th century,[31] stood in the main street of Stogursey at the east end of an island of buildings. They were demolished in 1869 and the women's almshouse, for six women, was built in Lime Street.[32] An almshouse for three men was built in 1821 at the corner of Castle Street and St. Andrew's Road. Both houses were remodelled in 1981.[33]

Richard Tilley or Tapp of Stockland Bristol gave £40 to the poor of Stogursey by his will dated 1599[34] and Walter Walford gave £10 in 1618.[35] By 1658 these gifts together with those of John Burland and John Burland, senior, Widow Currill, Baldwin Hillman, George Hobbes, John Shurt, Thomas Symons, and Walter Tapscott totalled £105 10s. and by 1673 Joan Burland, John Day, Mary Hobbes, and Thomas Hobbes had given another £33.[36] John Meredith of Taunton, by will dated 1677,[37] left £100 to provide the poor with clothing and William Hellier gave £10 to the poor in 1689.[38] Sir John Wroth and Peregrine Palmer gave £20 each to the poor on the deaths of their wives. All those charities, many still regularly distributed in 1705,[39] had been lost by 1786.[40] William Daniel gave a £5 rent charge in 1764 for a sermon and bread for the poor on Ash Wednesday and for poor children to be taught to read;[41] it had been lost by 1826.

James Morgan by will of 1727 gave £50 to be invested in land to relieve 10 poor householders and to provide a Good Friday sermon: £5 was distributed annually between 1797 and 1894. John Mascol by will of 1731 gave a rent charge to be distributed to 30 poor families twice a year;[42] by 1950 this charity, also known as the Candlemas Bread, was restricted to 6 poor persons and was distributed in cash or in kind.[43] In 1989 the Mascol and Morgan charities were given to elderly women at Easter.[44] Frances Palmer, by will dated 1760, gave £100 to be invested in land for the poor and Robert Banks, butler at Fairfield, by will of 1815, gave £200 to be invested in land for 10 poor persons.[45] Both charities were declared void in 1820; the land passed to the Acland family and Peregrine Acland invested a sum in consols c. 1825, the income to be distributed to the poor as the Palmer and Banks charities.[46] Under a trust of 1965 the Palmer and Banks charities were to be used for charitable purposes in the parish and in 1989 were distributed to elderly women.[47]

OVER STOWEY

THE parish of Over Stowey, also called Upper Stowey,[48] lies on the heavily wooded eastern side of the Quantocks immediately south-west of Nether Stowey and c. 12 km. west of Bridgwater. It is roughly rectangular in shape, extending for 5 km. from east to west and 3.5 km. from north to south. The western boundary follows the Quantock ridgeway and the southern a road from the ridgeway to Spaxton. The northern boundary reaches the southern side of Nether Stowey castle.[49] Land at Stowey Rocks (2 houses, 11 persons) was transferred to Nether Stowey in 1886, and the total area was 3,697 a. in 1891.[50] There have been no later changes and in 1981 the parish covered 1,496 ha.[51]

Most of the parish lies on the higher slopes of the Quantock ridge, the land falling eastwards from 350m. on the summit to 91m. on the eastern boundary. The slope is pierced by a succession of steep-sided combes, Bin Combe in the north, Rams Combe and Quantock Combe joining together in the centre, and Cockercombe in the south.[52]

Most of the higher ground comprises Hangman grits, with Upper Keuper marls and valley gravels lower down the slopes. At the junction of grits and marls are areas of sandstone, Ilfracombe slates with grits and limestones, and a small pocket of Schalstein.[53] Stone was quarried for building by 1614[54] and in the 19th century there were quarries at Adscombe and 0.5 km. south of Adscombe. The second produced green igneous rock used in the construction of Quantock Lodge.[55] Road stone was extracted at Bincombe by the mid 19th century[56] and limestone was dug for burning by the later 17th

30 S.R.O., DD/AH 11/16; D/D/Vc 88; D/P/stogs 17/3/2–3; 15th Rep. Com. Char. 365–71; Char. Com. reg.
31 Taunton Castle, Braikenridge colln., drawing 1845; cf. above, plate facing p. 152.
32 S.R.O., tithe award; ibid. D/P/stogs 17/3/1, 17/3/12/2, 17/7/4.
33 Ibid. D/P/stogs 17/3/12/2; stone on building.
34 Som. Wills, ed. Brown, v. 17.
35 S.R.O., D/P/stogs 2/1/1.   36 Ibid. 13/2/1.
37 15th Rep. Com. Char. 372.
38 S.R.O., D/P/stogs 4/1/2.   39 Ibid. 17/1/4.
40 Char. Don. pp. 1048–9.
41 S.R.O., D/P/stogs 4/1/2, 17/1/4; above, educ.
42 15th Rep. Com. Char. 372; S.R.O., D/P/stogs 4/1/3–4; DD/AH 28/4, 29/1.   43 Char. Com. reg.

44 Inf. from the Revd. A. E. Applegarth, rector.
45 15th Rep. Com. Char. 372; S.R.O., D/P/stogs 4/1/4.
46 S.R.O., D/P/stogs 17/7/40.
47 Char. Com. reg.; inf. from rector.
48 Cal. S.P. Dom. 1634–5, 54. This article was completed in 1986.
49 O.S. Map 1/50,000, sheet 181 (1974 edn.); below.
50 Census, 1891.
51 Ibid. 1981.
52 O.S. Map 6", Som. XLIX. NW., SW. (1887 edn.).
53 Geol. Surv. Map 1", drift, sheet 295 (1956 edn.).
54 S.R.O., DD/X/WI 34.
55 Proc. Som. Arch. Soc. xliii. 11.
56 P.R.O., HO 107/935; O.S. Map 6", Som. XLIX. NW. (1887 edn.).

on Aley manor and elsewhere.[57] Malachite was said to have been found at Pepperhill quarry c. 1920.[58]

Copper is said to have been extracted at Bincombe between 1690 and 1724,[59] and licences to mine on Aley manor, possibly in Aisholt parish, were granted in 1716 and 1720.[60] Other licences were granted in 1755 and 1758 to mine on Friarn manor in Bincombe, and a mine there, possibly on Dodington manor lands, was operating near Walford's Gibbet by 1790.[61]

Several barrows and cairns, the linear earthwork known as Dead Woman's Ditch, a small iron-age enclosure called Cockercombe or Plainsfield camp, and traces of a group of huts at the head of Rams Combe are evidence of the prehistoric exploitation of the Quantock ridge within the parish.[62] The claim that weapons and burials were discovered near Plainsfield and that they marked the site of an early Saxon battle has not been substantiated, although a field called Deadman's field there might seem to give colour to the story.[63]

The limited area of level ground in the parish dictated the pattern of medieval settlement. With one exception, dwellings were in small clusters at the mouth of each combe. The exception is the hamlet of Over Stowey, which lies on a small spur commanding an extensive view of the coast and the Parrett. It included by the later 12th century both the parish church and the 'old castle precinct' on the Stowey 'herpath'.[64] The castle may have been the *caput* of the estate of Alfred d'Epaignes at Stowey in the later 11th century and the precursor of the castle at Nether Stowey.[65] It survives as a large, flat mound to the north of Over Stowey village. Aley and Plainsfield hamlets were recorded in 1086,[66] Adscombe in the 13th century,[67] and Bincombe in 1327.[68] Adscombe in 1547 comprised only two houses and a ruined tenement.[69] The settlement called Peppestake (later Pepperhill) was recorded in 1316[70] and Hockpit or Hogpit by 1655.[71] Building on roadside waste was widespread in the 18th and 19th centuries at Friarn, Bincombe Green, and along the road eastward from Marsh Mills to Halsey Cross, although some of the cottages did not stand for long.[72] In the 20th century permanent camping sites were established near Rams Combe.

At least four ancient routes run beside or across the parish. The most significant at an early date

was the Anglo-Saxon 'herpath' or military road, which gave the parish its name.[73] The 'herpath' followed a roughly east–west route, entering the parish at Halsey Cross on the eastern boundary, skirting the castle north of Over Stowey hamlet,[74] and running directly up a great spur to Dead Woman's Ditch and thence to Crowcombe Gate on the Quantock ridgeway.[75] A second east–west route branched south-west from the 'herpath' east of Over Stowey hamlet and passed through Aley Green, a route known in the 12th century as the great way of Solmere.[76] The second route may later have been diverted southwest from Aley Green to the Triscombe stone on the ridgeway and thence to Taunton.[77] There were also two north–south routes. The Quantock ridgeway, known as Alferode in 1314,[78] continued to be used until the beginning of the 19th century when the lower routes were impassable.[79] The second, largely abandoned in the 19th century, ran south from Nether Stowey castle, and where it crossed the 'herpath' by Over Stowey castle gave its name to a holding called Cross. It ran through Over Stowey hamlet and Aley Green to Plainsfield. A bridge was built c. 1640 at Rooksford, where the route crossed the Seven Wells stream, which runs down through Adscombe.[80] The part of the route between Nether Stowey and Cross and known as Millers Lane had been abandoned by 1782.[81] A route further east between Plainsfield and Halsey Cross had probably been abandoned by 1838[82] and before 1842 was replaced by a more direct route north between Plainsfield and Marsh Mills.[83] Those changes were probably connected with the improvement of the Quantock estate culminating in the building of Quantock Lodge, the disappearance of Aley Green, and the closure of other routes within the newly created grounds. The road from Aley to Triscombe, for example, was closed in 1864, and in 1877 that from Adscombe through Seven Wells to Quantock Farm was declared private.[84]

The high ground to the west and north-west, shared in the early Middle Ages between the honors or lordships of Stogursey and Nether Stowey,[85] seems to have been part of a pre-Conquest forest of Quantock.[86] The Stogursey share, c. 1,000 a. stretching south-east along the ridge from West Hill above Rams Combe, was partly open ground and was common to the tenants of Wick manor in Stogursey until the 17th century.[87]

57 S.R.O., DD/WG 13/1; ibid. tithe award.
58 J. Hamilton and J. Lawrence, *Men and Mining in the Quantocks* (1970), 30.
59 Ibid. 31.
60 S.R.O., DD/WG 7/9; DD/X/HAM 1; above, Aisholt.
61 S.R.O., DD/AH 37/3; DD/S/SH (N/152); DD/X/HR 37; ibid. tithe award; Hamilton and Lawrence, *Men and Mining in the Quantocks*, 30.
62 *Proc. Som. Arch. Soc.* cxiii, suppl. 38; cxxx, 142; B. L. Add. MS. 39172; S.R.O., DD/X/WI 34.
63 *Som. Co. Herald*, 24 Oct. 1936; S.R.O., tithe award.
64 *Cart. St. Mark's Hosp., Bristol* (Bristol Rec. Soc. xxi), p. 160.
65 *Proc. Som. Arch. Soc.* cxxv. 124–5.
66 *V.C.H. Som.* i. 501, 512.
67 *S.R.S.* xiv, p. 150.
68 Ibid. iii. 165.
69 Bristol R.O. 4490.
70 *Cat. Anct. D.* iii, A 5997.
71 S.R.O., DD/WO 17/3.
72 Ibid. DD/SAS (C/1207); ibid. tithe award; O.S. Map

6", Som. XLIX. NW. (1887 edn.).
73 Ekwall, *Eng. Place-Names* (1960), 427.
74 *Cart. St. Mark's Hosp., Bristol*, p. 160.
75 *S.R.S.* lxi, p. 19; *V.C.H. Som.* v. 191.
76 *S.R.S.* lxi, p. 19.
77 S.R.O., DD/SAS (C/923); *S.R.S.* lxxvi, map 1782.
78 *H.M.C. Wells*, i. 184.
79 S.R.O., T/PH/ay 1; DD/SAS (C/923); map by George Withiel, 1687, in possession of Col. G. W. F. Luttrell, Court Ho., E. Quantoxhead.
80 S.R.O., DD/SAS RF 3/1/2.
81 Ibid. DD/SAS (C/1207), 18th-cent. map; *S.R.S.* lxxvi, map 1782.   82 S.R.O., tithe award.
83 Ibid. Q/SR Mich. 1842.
84 Ibid. Spring 1864, Mids. 1882; ibid. D/H/ta 2/3/1; D/P/o. sty 4/1/1.
85 Below, manors (Quantock Farm).
86 S.R.O., DD/X/WI 34; Pole MS. 2957; above, Broomfield, intro.
87 P.R.O., E 178/5623; S.R.O., DD/X/WI 34.

In the 1630s at least 180 a., part of Plainsfield Hill and presumably the ground later known as Aisholt Hill or the Slades,[88] was divided and allotted in fee to local landowners including the lord of Plainsfield, in return for the surrender of their claims to common over the whole area.[89] By 1683, and probably by 1656, about half the remainder of the Stogursey land had been inclosed and let, and Quantock farm was created soon after 1686. The owner, Robert Siderfin, probably built the wall which marked the western boundary of both the farm and the parish.[90]

The Nether Stowey share, known as the Stowey Customs and covering Robin Upright's Hill and Great Bear,[91] remains largely uninclosed, although Warren House, recorded in 1672,[92] had become the centre of a small farm by 1838.[93] Attempts to inclose the area in the 1800s led to disputes between the lord of Nether Stowey and the vicar of Over Stowey, the latter claiming the right to cut wood there.[94] The assumed transfer of ownership of the soil of the commons from the honor to the manor of Nether Stowey in the early 17th century seems to have given rise to the claims of tenants of that manor to commons there. In the later 20th century the parish councils of Over and Nether Stowey registered rights to estovers, turbary, and bracken cutting on behalf of all householders in their parishes.[95]

In 1086 Aley and Plainsfield had 25 a. of woodland and the Stowey estate wood measuring 1½ league square.[96] Woodland belonging to the rectory on the lower slopes had largely disappeared by 1655 and what remained was scrub rather than timber.[97] Friarn wood was said to cover 220 a. in the mid 17th century, but 46 a. had been 'lately grubbed up' by 1688 and the remainder was coppice.[98] At about the same time half of the newly created Quantock farm was woodland fit for sale.[99] In 1739 only half Parsonage wood was actually timbered and the trees, six years old or less, were decayed.[1] Fifty years later most of the woodland on Quantock farm was said to be suitable only for oak coppice.[2] The sale of part of the Enmore estate to Henry Labouchere in 1833 brought together some 660 a. of woodland, of which 4 a. was fir plantation and the remainder oak coppice.[3] In addition there were similar woodlands on the Stowey Customs further north. In 1838 about 900 a. were under wood, mostly oak coppice,[4] but by the 1880s firs had been planted widely

on the Quantock estate,[5] a policy which the Forestry Commission continued in the 20th century despite local protest.[6] In 1905 there were 920 a. of woodland in the parish.[7] Clear felling took place during the First World War but replanting began in 1922.[8] The hills remained extensively wooded and in 1986 were used both for recreation and for commercial purposes.

Aley park measured 100 a. in 1275[9] and occupied land east of Aley hamlet, probably as far as the eastern boundary of the parish. In 1357 at least 36 people were accused of breaking into it, hunting deer, and killing a foal and cattle grazing there.[10] Throughout the 15th century the pale was regularly repaired and the deer were fed as necessary.[11] By the early 17th century the park had been divided.[12] West of Bincombe in Nether Stowey lordship the names Warren House and Great and Little Warren suggest the site of a warren established after the grant of free warren to Philip de Columbers in 1248. It is possible also that the Nether Stowey deer park extended into Over Stowey in the north-east corner of the parish.[13]

There was a tavern at Aley in 1201[14] and a victualler was recorded in the early 17th century.[15] In 1673 the keeper of a licensed alehouse in the parish offered no lodging, sold beer during service time, and allowed cards.[16] In 1676 four victuallers lost their licences.[17] In 1686 the parish had one inn offering two beds and stabling,[18] but three years later there were five licensed houses. By 1690 the number had been reduced to four and by 1736 to two.[19] One of them may have been the Squirrel inn at the junction of Rams Combe and Quantock Combe.[20] The Dial at Aley Green and the White Horse on the Bridgwater road served the parish in the 18th century. The latter was last licensed in 1779[21] and later became a farmhouse with the same name. The Dial, later the Aley Green public house, was briefly closed c. 1800[22] but remained until 1851 when it was probably demolished during the building of Quantock Lodge.[23] It was replaced by a beerhouse at Halsey Cross, licensed in 1849, which later became the Albion and in 1881 the Pear Tree inn.[24] It appears to have closed by 1894.[25] There is said to have been a public house at Bincombe, probably in the early 19th century.[26]

A reading room and news room with a library of 150 books was established in 1896; it appears

88 S.R.O., tithe award; O.S. Map 6", Som. XLIX. SW. (1887 edn.).
89 P.R.O., E 178/5623; S.R.O., DD/S/SH (N/153).
90 S.R.O., DD/HC (N/42); DD/SAS (C/923), map 1688.
91 O.S. Map 6", Som. XLIX. NW. (1887 edn.).
92 S.R.O., Q/SR 116/72.
93 Ibid. tithe award.
94 Ibid. T/PH/ay 1.
95 R. R. J. McDonnell, *Quantock Hills A.O.N.B.: an Archaeological Survey* (Som. C.C. 1989), 4.
96 *V.C.H. Som.* i. 512–13.
97 Bristol R.O. 04237.
98 S.R.O., DD/X/BB 6.
99 Ibid. DD/HC (N/42); DD/SAS (C/923), map 1688.
1 Bristol R.O. 04241.
2 S.R.O., DD/HC (N/42).
3 Ibid. DD/PLE 64.
4 Ibid. tithe award.
5 O.S. Map 6", Som. XLIX. NW. (1887 edn.).
6 *Proc. Som. Arch. Soc.* xciv. 34.

7 Statistics supplied by the then Bd. of Agric., 1905.
8 *Quantock Forest Trail* (c. 1960s), Forestry Com. pamphlet.
9 P.R.O., C 133/11, no. 11.
10 *Cal. Pat.* 1354–8, 616.
11 P.R.O., SC 6/977/8, 11, 13, 15, 20.
12 S.R.O., DD/WG 16/8; P.R.O., C 3/400, no. 103.
13 *V.C.H. Som.* v. 191; S.R.O., tithe award.
14 *S.R.S.* xi, p. 23.   15 S.R.O., Q/RL.
16 Ibid. Q/SR 118/92.
17 *S.R.S.* xxxiv. 208.
18 P.R.O., WO 30/48.
19 S.R.O., Q/RL.
20 Ibid.; ibid. DD/X/BOA; ibid. tithe award.
21 Ibid. Q/RL.
22 Ibid. T/PH/ay 1.
23 Ibid. DD/PLE 64; P.R.O., HO 107/1924.
24 S.R.O., DD/SAS PR 482/2; P.R.O., HO 107/1924; ibid. RG 9/1621.
25 *Kelly's Dir. Som.* (1889, 1894).
26 S.R.O., DD/X/BOA.

to have closed c. 1925.[27] There was a cricket club in the parish between 1897 and 1902.[28]

There were 115 adult males in the parish in 1641[29] and in 1801 the population was 468. It had risen to 592 by 1831 but had fallen to 561 in 1851. The increase to 613 in 1861 was due in part to the staff of Quantock Lodge and the estate, but the total declined steadily thereafter to 433 in 1891. The establishment of a hospital and later a school at Quantock Lodge led to an increase in the 20th century, and the total was 511 in 1971. The normally resident population in 1981 was 360, many of them probably living in the north where new housing in Nether Stowey village extended over the parish boundary.[30]

In 1645 the rectory and probably the church tower were fortified for the king by the Selleck family[31] and in 1668 a local man was pensioned for injury in the king's service.[32] Christopher Rich (1647–1714), attorney and theatrical manager, and the Revd. John Poole (d. 1857) were born in Over Stowey.[33] Henry Labouchere (cr. Baron Taunton 1859, d. 1869), the builder of Quantock Lodge, was M.P. for Taunton 1830–59 and a cabinet minister.[34]

MANORS AND OTHER ESTATES. Three tenants in chief had land in Over Stowey in 1086, Alfred d'Epaignes, lord of Stowey, William de Falaise, lord of Stogursey, and William de Mohun, lord of Dunster.

Alfred d'Epaignes held STOWEY in 1086 in succession to Earl Harold.[35] His lands, including Over Stowey and Plainsfield and extending both sides of the Quantocks,[36] may have centred on the castle at Over Stowey, the only one known on his estate. Later the honor centred on the new castle at Nether Stowey and took its name.[37] Alfred and his immediate successors seem to have divided and subinfeudated the estate.

PLAINSFIELD, which had been held in 1066 by Edred, was occupied in 1086 by Hugh d'Epaignes under Alfred.[38] It was held of Nether Stowey honor until that was forfeited to the Crown in 1497,[39] and was held of the Crown from then until 1627 or later, in that year as of the manor of Hampton Court.[40]

Richard son of Ralph held ½ fee at Plainsfield in 1166.[41] In 1262 Walter of Plainsfield was

probably owner[42] and by 1285 had been succeeded by Adam de Chandos, probably also known as Adam of Plainsfield.[43] In 1300 Adam de Chandos settled the manor on himself for life with remainder to William de Chandos, son of Adam the elder.[44] Adam held the estate in 1303,[45] William in 1304,[46] and Adam de Chandos, possibly a third, between 1310 and 1318.[47] Another William Chandos held the manor in 1346[48] and by 1393 had been succeeded by Joan Trowe, daughter of William Chandos.[49] Joan's son Thomas Trowe seems to have been in possession by 1402, although his mother may still have been alive.[50] Thomas continued in possession until 1431 or later[51] but by 1447 had been succeeded by John Trowe.[52]

In 1489–90 the manor was settled on Hugh Trowe and Elizabeth Malet, widow of Thomas Ashley, probably for their marriage.[53] Elizabeth survived her husband but died in 1493, when her husband's brother Thomas was heir.[54] Thomas was involved in the rebellion of 1497 against Henry VII and was attainted in 1504. Plainsfield manor was granted to Sir John Williams in 1506,[55] and on his death two years later it passed to his son Reginald, then a minor.[56] Reginald died in 1559 leaving sons John (d. 1560), Nicholas, and Richard.[57] Nicholas and Richard both died in 1568 without male issue and the manor reverted to the Crown.[58]

By 1601 Humphrey Blake (d. 1620), whose family had been tenants of the demesne probably from the mid 16th century, had acquired the manor.[59] Humphrey's son Humphrey and their kinsman Robert Blake (d. 1627) seem to have shared the estate. Robert left a son, also Robert, a minor,[60] but in 1639[61] the manor was held by the younger Humphrey's son or grandson, also Humphrey, who was succeeded in 1665[62] by his son John.[63] John Blake died in 1695 and his son, also John, in 1704.[64] A third John Blake, son of the last, by his will of 1722 left the manor in trust for his nephew John Rich. John Rich by will dated 1747 gave Plainsfield to his brother Nathaniel who with his wife Joan sold the manor in 1761 to John Perceval, earl of Egmont (d. 1770).[65] The manor thereafter descended like Enmore; the lordship was not, however, mentioned in the sale of the estate in 1833.[66]

John Trowe was licensed to have an oratory in his house at Plainsfield in 1447,[67] and in 1511

27 Kelly's Dir. Som. (1897, 1923, 1927).
28 Ibid. (1897, 1902).
29 Som. Protestation Returns, ed. A. J. Howard and T. L. Stoate, 172–3.
30 Census.
31 Cal. Cttee. for Money, iii. 1424.
32 S.R.S. xxxiv. 52.
33 D.N.B.; above, Enmore, church.
34 D.N.B.
35 V.C.H. Som. i. 512–13.
36 Proc. Som. Arch. Soc. cxxv. 124–5.
37 V.C.H. Som. v. 193–4.
38 Ibid. i. 512; Dom. Bk. ed. Thorn, 306.
39 Cal. Pat. 1494–1509, 447.
40 S.R.S. lxvii, p. 8.
41 Red Bk. Exch. (Rolls Ser.), i. 231.
42 Close R. 1261–4, 90.
43 Feud. Aids, iv. 281; B.L. Add. Ch. 22551.
44 S.R.S. vi. 311.
45 Feud. Aids, iv. 308.
46 Cal. Chanc. Wts. 229.

47 Cal. Inq. p.m. v, p. 126; S.D.N.Q. xxi. 464.
48 Feud. Aids, iv. 352.
49 S.R.O., DD/AH 65/8; S.R.S. xiv, p. 178.
50 S.R.S. xxix, pp. 276, 283; P.R.O., E 326/6080.
51 Feud. Aids, iv. 393, 436.   52 S.R.S. xlix, pp. 80–1.
53 Pole MS. 872.   54 P.R.O., C 142/23, no. 5.
55 Cal. Inq. p.m. Hen. VII, iii, p. 418; Cal. Pat. 1494–1509, 447.
56 Cal. Inq. p.m. Hen. VII, iii, pp. 323–4.
57 P.R.O., C 142/128, nos. 67, 69, where Nic. is called Wm.
58 P.R.O., C 142/152, no. 124.
59 S.D.N.Q. xxix. 141; Cal. Pat. 1566–9, p. 176; Som. Wills, ed. Brown, ii. 13; P.R.O., CP 25(2)/207/43 Eliz. I Hil.
60 S.R.S. lxvii, p. 8; P.R.O., C 142/436, no. 5.
61 P.R.O., CP 25(2)/480/15 Chas. I Mich.; ibid. E 178/5623.
62 Ibid. CP 25(2)/715/15 Chas. II Trin.; M.I. Aisholt ch.
63 P.R.O., CP 25(2)/795/4 Jas. II Trin.
64 S.R.O., D/P/o. sty 2/1/3.
65 Ibid. DD/SAS (C/82) 43.
66 Ibid. DD/PLE 64; above, Enmore, manors.
67 S.R.S. xxix. 283; xlix, pp. 80–1.

the buildings there included the chapel house, pigeon house, and gatehouse.[68] The house was leased to the tenant of the demesne in 1571.[69] Plainsfield Court, in 1986 called Plainsfield Court Farm, dates probably from the 17th century and formerly included plaster work dated 1663.[70] There appear to have been considerable alterations and additions between 1833 and 1887, including the building of a large south wing.[71]

An estate was held by Ralph, his son Hamon, and grandson Hugh de Bonville who in the mid 12th century gave lands to Over Stowey church.[72] Alice, widow of Hugh de Bonville, in 1220 granted her dower lands in Stowey to St. John's hospital, Bridgwater.[73] The hospital surrendered in 1539, and its lands in Stowey passed to the Crown. As the manor of *OVER STO-WEY or FRYRON*, later simply *FRIARN* manor, it was sold to Emmanuel Lucar, a London merchant, in 1544.[74] Lucar died in 1574 and was succeeded by his son Mark (d. 1600).[75] Mark's son Emmanuel divided the estate in 1646, selling the manor and some land to Edward Rich the elder and Edward Rich the younger.[76] Edward Rich the younger died in 1696[77] and was followed in turn by his son and grandson both named Thomas Rich.[78] The manor, together with an estate called Chapel, was held with Hartrow manor in Stogumber until 1758 or later,[79] but in 1786 the Revd. Henry Ward and his wife Susanna conveyed the manor to John Vernon.[80] In 1791 Vernon sold it to John James Perceval, earl of Egmont (d. 1822), and it descended with the Egmont estate until 1833[81] when it was sold to Henry Labouchere. The lordship was not recorded thereafter. Chapel, meanwhile, had been bought by John Perceval, earl of Egmont, before 1765[82] and it too became part of the Quantock estate in 1833.

The capital messuage of the hospital estate was mentioned in 1538–9.[83] It may have been later known as Chapel House, for it stood beside the former chapel of Adscombe[84] and was the home of the Rich family in the 17th and early 18th centuries.[85] It was said to have been dated 1529 and to have contained an oak staircase and mantelpiece,[86] but it had been demolished by 1887.[87]

Friarn farm, sold by Emmanuel Lucar to Lewis Sweeting in 1646,[88] passed from Sweeting and his wife to Edward Coward in 1674 and from Edward to the Revd. Christopher Coward c. 1695.[89] It descended to Bridget Coward, wife of George Hamilton, but between 1759 and 1765 became part of the Egmont estate.[90]

Friarn House, recorded in 1660,[91] was described as a capital messuage in 1730.[92] It stood probably east of the road from Bincombe to Adscombe, and was demolished before 1833, when Friarn farm was united with Adscombe.[93]

Soon after the mid 12th century the church and land, which had probably formed part of the d'Epaignes estate, had come into the possession of Hugh de Bonville, in succession to his grandfather Ralph and his father Hamon.[94] Between c. 1155 and 1189 Hugh gave arable, pasture, and woodland to Over Stowey church, and before 1181 gave the church and more land to Stogursey priory.[95] The land presumably passed in 1239 with the patronage of the church from the priory to the bishop of Bath and Wells,[96] and the *RECTORY* was exchanged in 1326 with St. Mark's hospital, Bristol, for lands elsewhere. The hospital held a house, the great tithes, and most of the former church land, with a share of common pasture,[97] until 1539; two years later the rectory passed to the mayor and commonalty of Bristol.[98] The city corporation sold the estate to the tenant in 1840,[99] and by 1919 it had been absorbed into the Quantock estate.[1]

Parsonage Farm is a late 16th- or early 17th-century house of cross-passage plan, with one-roomed back wings. A square stair wing projects from the rear wall, lit by a large 17th-century window, probably reset. The southern room of the main range has a 17th-century moulded plaster overmantel depicting Adam and Eve. In 1816 the front of the house was taken down,[2] and other alterations at the time included a new staircase and the remodelling of the southern ground-floor room of the main range.

Pasture and wood on Quantock, amounting to a third of the parish, was part of the medieval lordship of Stogursey, and was presumably attached to the Domesday estate of Stogursey which William de Falaise held in 1086.[3] William granted rights there with Stogursey church to the abbey of Lonlay (Orne) at the beginning of the 12th century.[4] The tract of land, regarded in

68 S.R.O., DD/AH 11/9.
69 *Cal. Pat.* 1566–9, p. 176; 1569–72, p. 242.
70 S.R.O., DD/SCL 9; *Proc. Som. Arch. Soc.* xliii. 13; plaster work said to have been taken to Yeovil c. 1921: inf from Mrs. Dalley, Plainsfield Ct. Fm.
71 S.R.O., DD/PLE 64; O.S. Map 6", Som. XLIX. SW. (1887 edn.).
72 Below, church.
73 *S.R.S.* vi. 41–2.
74 Devon R.O. 1148 M/add 1/60.
75 *Cal. Pat.* 1566–9, p. 196; P.R.O., C 142/167, no. 124.
76 P.R.O., C 3/458, nos. 63, 65; C 142/259, no. 77; ibid. CP 25(2)/480/22 Chas. I Mich.
77 S.R.O., D/P/o. sty 2/1/3.
78 Ibid. DD/X/ALF 6; P.R.O., CP 25(2)/961/2 Anne Hil.
79 *V.C.H. Som.* v. 70; S.R.O., D/P/o. sty 4/1/1; DD/X/HR; DD/X/BB 6.
80 P.R.O., CP 25(2)/1400/26 Geo. III East.
81 Ibid. CP 43/831/31 Geo. III Hil.; S.R.O., DD/PLE 64.
82 S.R.O., Q/REl 7/9; DD/S/WH 285.
83 P.R.O., SC 6/Hen. VIII/3137.
84 Below, church.

85 S.R.O., DD/WO 17/3; DD/X/ALF 6.
86 Ibid. DD/X/BOA.
87 O.S. Map 6", Som. XLIX. SW. (1887 edn.).
88 P.R.O., C 3/458, nos. 63, 65; C 3/462, no. 101; *S.R.S.* xxviii. 276.
89 S.R.O., DD/S/BR 2.
90 Ibid. DD/X/CX 4; DD/DN 91; DD/X/BB 6; DD/S/WH 285; ibid. Q/REl 7/9.
91 Ibid. Q/SR 99/46.
92 Ibid. DD/DN 91.
93 Ibid. DD/PLE 64.
94 *Cart. St. Mark's Hosp., Bristol*, pp. 160–1.
95 Ibid. 159–61, 275.
96 Ibid. 162–3; *Sel. Cases Eccl. Ct. Cant.* (Selden Soc. xcv), pp. 207–25.
97 *Cart. St. Mark's Hosp., Bristol*, pp. 163–7.
98 *L. & P. Hen. VIII*, xvi, p. 418.
99 S.R.O., DD/DHR 24; DD/DP 5/1.
1 Ibid. DD/SCL 9.
2 *Paupers and Pigkillers*, ed. J. Ayres, 270–1.
3 *V.C.H. Som.* i. 508.
4 *S.R.S.* lxi, p. 1.

the late 16th century as being a quarter share of the royal forest of Quantock, presumably of pre-Conquest date,[5] descended with the barony of Stogursey and the manor of Wick FitzPayn until 1686 when it was sold to Robert Siderfin, who created *QUANTOCK FARM* out of some of the former common land. The farm descended like Wick manor, and in 1758 was bought by John Perceval, earl of Egmont (d. 1770).[6] His grandson sold it with other Egmont estates to Henry Labouchere in 1833.[7]

Quantock Farm was built probably between 1686 and 1688, and was a three-storeyed, double-pile house of four or five bays, with a forecourt flanked by stables, and a central gateway leading to a tree-lined avenue.[8] The house was replaced in the late 18th or early 19th century by two nearly identical, double-fronted houses abutting end to end. About 1930 the southern house was encased, heightened, and extended, and in 1987 the two were in single occupation.

ALEY was held by Algar in 1066 and by Garmund of William de Mohun (I) in 1086.[9] It continued to be held of the barony of Dunster until c. 1520 or later,[10] but it was also said to be held of the honor of Stogursey, almost certainly in confusion with Aisholt.[11]

Aley may have been held by William de Curci in 1166.[12] It was held by Sir William de Reigny (d. 1275)[13] and his widow Akyna until 1280 or later,[14] and by 1285 it had passed by Sir William's gift to Robert of Acton, son of Joan, his illegitimate daughter.[15] By 1303 Robert had been succeeded by Stephen Beaumond (d. 1310), husband of Robert's widow Joan (d. 1308).[16] Alice, daughter of Stephen and Joan, married John de Bures, who had Aley in 1318[17] and 1332.[18] By 1340, probably following John's death, Aley had been recovered by Richard of Acton,[19] grandson of Robert (d. c. 1303).[20] In 1384 Richard settled Aley on himself and his wife Margaret for life, with remainder to Sir Thomas Fichet of Spaxton.[21] Sir Thomas's son, also Thomas (d. 1395), succeeded to the manor, which descended with Spaxton.[22] The lordship was not mentioned in the sale of 1833.[23]

There was no house on the manor in 1275.[24] A lodge in the park, recorded in the later 15th century,[25] was standing in 1587[26] but not in 1685;

a field was called Lodge Court in the late 17th century.[27] Aley Farm was described as a capital messuage in 1696 and 1721.[28] The present Aley Farm, on the other side of the lane, is a small 18th-century house which has been reduced in size.

Athelney abbey held land at *ADSCOMBE* by grant of several people in the mid 13th century including William Fichet and Gillian, wife of Roger de Amaray.[29] It was held of the Crown c. 1285[30] but later partly of Aley manor.[31] The rents of the estate were assigned to the conventual kitchen.[32] After the Dissolution, Adscombe was granted with Hamp in Bridgwater to Bristol corporation.[33] Successive tenants paid fee farm rents to the city probably until the sale of Hamp manor in 1698. The Rich family, tenants by 1655, then became owners, and remained so until 1761 when Nicholas Rich sold it to John Perceval, earl of Egmont (d. 1770).[34] By 1833, when the Egmont estate was sold, Adscombe had been amalgamated with Chapel and Friarn.[35]

A holding later known as *CROSS* may have originated in land given by Alice Childecote to her son Robert in 1438. In 1450 and 1454 Robert Childecote and his son John conveyed their land in the parish to John Capron, clerk. Thomas Capron, John's nephew, in 1478 released the holding to Thomas Tremayle (d. 1508) and Roger Pym.[36] Philip Tremayle, son of Thomas, sold an estate in Over Stowey, Bincombe, and Adscombe to Baldwin Malet (d. 1533). Baldwin's son John may have held Cross c. 1577,[37] and it descended to his great-great-grandson Baldwin Malet of St. Audries. In 1692 Baldwin mortgaged the house and land to Thomas Rich, a kinsman of the tenant Samuel Rich; in 1696 on failure to repay the loan he released the property to Samuel.[38]

Samuel Rich was succeeded by his son, also Samuel (d. 1765),[39] and by the latter's sons Thomas (d. 1813) and James (d. 1815).[40] James left Cross to his kinsman Edmund Rich (d. 1842) who was followed by his son Samuel (d. 1886) and the latter's son, also Samuel (d. 1912).[41] The farm was later acquired by E. J. Stanley and became part of the Quantock estate. In 1920 it passed with that estate to Somerset county council, the owners in 1986.[42]

5 S.R.O., DD/X/WI 34; above, Broomfield.
6 Above, Stogursey, manors; S.R.O., DD/PC 17.
7 S.R.O., DD/PLE 64.
8 Ibid. DD/HC (N/42); DD/PC 17; DD/SAS (C/923).
9 *V.C.H. Som.* i. 501.
10 *S.R.S.* xxxiii, p. 272.
11 Ibid. lxviii, p. 30.
12 Ibid. extra ser. 306.
13 Above, Aisholt, manors; P.R.O., C 133/11, no. 11.
14 *Cal. Inq. p.m.* iii, p. 178; *S.R.S.* xxxiii, p. 49.
15 *S.R.S.* xxxiii, p. 60; P.R.O., CP 40/433, m. 367.
16 *Feud. Aids*, iv. 308; *S.R.S.* xii. 6; ibid. extra ser. 309–10.
17 *Cal. Close*, 1300–26, 388.
18 Ibid. 1330–3, 481.
19 *Cat. Anct. D.* i, B 282; P.R.O., E 210/7125.
20 P.R.O., E 329/285; ibid. CP 40/433, m. 367; *S.R.S.* extra ser. 310–11; lxviii, pp. 30–1.
21 P.R.O., E 326/4365; *S.R.S.* lxviii, pp. 31–2.
22 Above, Spaxton, manors.
23 S.R.O., DD/PLE 64.
24 P.R.O., C 133/11, no. 11.

25 Ibid. SC 6/977/11, 22.
26 S.R.O., D/P/o. sty 2/1/1.
27 Ibid. DD/WG 8/2A.
28 Ibid. 7/2, 9/4; ibid. Q/RRp 3/2.
29 *S.R.S.* xiv, pp. 150–1.
30 *Feud. Aids*, iv. 282.
31 S.R.O., DD/AH 11/9.
32 *S.R.S.* xiv, p. 163.
33 *Cart. St. Mark's Hosp., Bristol*, p. 60.
34 S.R.O., DD/SAS (C/82) 43; Bristol R.O. 4490, 04237, 00570/24.
35 S.R.O., DD/PLE 64; ibid. tithe award.
36 Ibid. DD/S/WH 62; *Cal. Inq. p.m. Hen. VII*, iii, p. 312.
37 P.R.O., C 1/541, no. 13; S.R.O., D/P/stogs 17/7/1; *S.R.S.* xxi. 17–18.
38 *V.C.H. Som.* v. 131; S.R.O., DD/L 2/16/89.
39 *Som. Wills*, ed. Brown, iii. 11; S.R.O., DD/L 2/16/89.
40 S.R.O., Q/REl 41/33A; M.I. in ch.
41 S.R.O., DD/CH 52; DD/ED 189/7075; D/P/o. sty 2/1/5.
42 Ibid. DD/SCL 9.

Cross Farm has a 17th-century cross-passage plan and two back wings. The partly walled garden incorporates an 18th-century gazebo. The house appears to have had two southern wings in 1744 which had gone by 1822.[43]

PEPPERHILL, by the later 16th century including land in Spaxton,[44] may be traced to a grant of land by Sir Walter of Romsey to Walter le Lyf and his wife Lucy in 1312.[45] A further grant in 1316 by Robert FitzPayn was described as at Peppestake, a name which persisted until the later 16th century.[46] By 1614 it was known as Pepperhill.[47]

Walter le Lyf was dead by 1327.[48] By the mid 15th century the land was held by Leonard Tilley[49] and in 1485 by Thomas Tilley.[50] Thomas died in 1536,[51] and he was followed by his grandson James Tilley (d. 1557), and James by his son George (d. 1590).[52] George left two daughters Anne, wife of William Walton, and Elizabeth, later wife of Edward Parham. In 1604 Elizabeth released her share to William Walton.[53] By 1614 the estate was occupied by Richard Lawrence or Dyer (d. 1641),[54] and his successor Hugh Lawrence or Dyer (fl. 1683)[55] was followed by his son John. John may have sold the estate to Edward Rich.[56] By 1713 Pepperhill was owned by Edward's son Thomas Rich and it descended with Friarn manor.[57]

The house was a substantial one in 1641 with at least five chambers.[58] It was rebuilt in 1859 in Tudor style by Henry Clutton for Lord Taunton as a home dairy house for Quantock Lodge. The octagonal dairy had a Minton tile floor and double roof to ensure coolness.[59]

The earl of Egmont (d. 1770) and his son acquired many of the estates in the parish, which the 4th earl sold in 1833 to Henry Labouchere, later Baron Taunton, who also bought land formerly in Nether Stowey manor in 1838. Labouchere held what was sometimes called the manor of *OVER STOWEY* or *OVER AND NETHER STOWEY*, but was usually known as the *QUANTOCK* estate, with c. 2,800 a. in Over Stowey.[60] Labouchere was succeeded in 1869 by his daughter Mary (d. 1920), wife of Edward James Stanley.[61] In 1919 and 1920 the whole estate was sold. Several of the farms were bought by Somerset county council to provide small holdings, and Quantock Lodge, the principal residence, with 2,045 a.,[62] was also bought by the council under the Public Health Act. The building was opened as Quantock Lodge Sanatorium in 1925.[63] The hospital closed in 1962;

Quantock independent school opened there in 1963[64] and remained in 1986.

The house, designed in a 'free Tudor style' by Henry Clutton, was started in 1857 and built in stages during the 1860s, mostly of stone quarried on the estate. It has an **L**-shaped plan, two storeys with attics, and a projecting two-storeyed porch.[65] It includes a great hall, library, and other rooms in a mixture of Gothic and Tudor styles with tiled floors, coffered and plaster ceilings, and elaborate chimney pieces and overmantels. West of the house a stable block, later partly demolished, was built in 1860. There is a large Gothic gatehouse and lodge on the Nether Stowey road, and outside the parish there are further lodges on an ornamental drive to Spaxton.[66] Part of the stable block has been demolished, and modern school buildings occupy much of the space between it and the house.

ECONOMIC HISTORY. The parish was probably divided for farming in 1086 into four: Plainsfield, the holding of Alfred d'Epaignes called Stowey, Aley, and the land on the Quantock Hills. Together, the first three had land for 9 ploughs, Alfred's holding comprising more than half the total. Only 9 a. of meadow were recorded, but each estate had some woodland; and the Stowey estate also had 100 a. of pasture. There were 8 *villani*, 13 bordars, and 9 *servi*. Apart from a cob at Aley, the only livestock recorded was at Stowey: 9 cattle, 7 pigs, and 90 sheep.[67] The Quantock holding of Stogursey may not have been included in the Domesday survey.

By 1275 Aley manor had 4 villein tenants owing both rent and works, 130 a. of arable worth between 2d. and 6d. an acre, 17 a. of meadow, and woodland and a park amounting together to nearly half the total area and forming the most valuable part of the estate.[68] Income from the park declined in the 15th century, expenditure often exceeding income from pigs or from the sale of wood. In the middle of the century cash was raised through the sale of mowing works and of small quantities of wood, meadow, and pasture, but most income was from rents and the farm of the demesne.[69] Works were still sold in the 1480s on Aley manor,[70] and mowing services were owed by nine tenants on Plainsfield manor c. 1510.[71]

On the Quantock ridge tenants of Wick FitzPayn

43 Ibid. DD/DHR box 36, map; DD/SAS (C/1207).
44 P.R.O., SP 12/288/42.
45 *Cat. Anct. D.* iv, A. 8375–6.
46 Ibid. iii, A 5997.
47 S.R.O., DD/X/WI 34; P.R.O., SP 12/288/42.
48 *S.R.S.* iii. 140.
49 S.R.O., DD/X/WI 34; *Cal. Close*, 1461–8, 454.
50 *Cat. Anct. D.* i, B 274.
51 P.R.O., C 142/59, no. 79.
52 Ibid. C 142/114, no. 53.
53 Ibid. C 142/228, no. 78; ibid. CP 25(2)/345/2 Jas. I Mich.
54 S.R.O., DD/X/WI 34; D/P/o. sty 2/1/1; DD/SP inventory, 1640 (1640/1).
55 Ibid. DD/PC 17.
56 Ibid. DD/S/WH 285.
57 Ibid. DD/SAS PD 64; above.

58 Ibid. DD/SP inventory, 1640 (1640/1).
59 Ibid. DD/X/DD 2.
60 *V.C.H. Som.* v. 194; S.R.O., DD/PLE 64; ibid. tithe award.
61 S.R.O., D/P/o. sty 2/1/8; ibid. C/C box 30; Burke, *Land. Gent.* (1914), 1764.
62 S.R.O., DD/X/DD 2.
63 Ibid. D/H/ta 2/3/1.
64 Inf. from Quantock school.
65 Above, plate facing p. 88.
66 S.R.O., DD/X/DD 2.
67 *V.C.H. Som.* i. 501, 512–13.
68 P.R.O., C 133/11, no. 11.
69 *S.R.S.* lxviii, p. 33; P.R.O., SC 2/200/277; SC 6/977/8, 11, 13.
70 P.R.O., SC 6/977/24; SC 6/Hen. VII/539–43.
71 S.R.O., DD/AH 11/9.

manor in Stogursey and various landowners had grazing rights in pasture and wood within the honor of Stogursey by the late 13th century.[72] By 1484–5 there were small areas of arable and by 1518–19 rye and oats were being grown.[73] A century later tillage was still permitted and the tenants of Wick manor in Stogursey claimed exclusive rights to graze 30 sheep each there. Claims by tenants of Plainsfield manor to similar rights were resisted, but by 1614 nine were paying rent to use the common.[74] In the 1630s the lord of Plainsfield among others received allotments of former Stogursey common on Plainsfield Hill.[75]

Aley park was divided and let by 1604[76] and in 1647 it was ploughed for the first time after a lime dressing.[77] Grazing was increased at the expense of the woodland on the rectory estate and at Friarn and in 1688 it was proposed to convert former woodland at Friarn into water meadows.[78] Grain was prominent in some 17th-century inventories,[79] but the yeoman who perhaps occupied Aley farm in 1696 had only 50 a. of wheat, barley, dredge, peas, and hay.[80] A poor husbandman had rented a small piece of hill ground for corn by 1684; more prosperous farmers had small flocks of sheep.[81] Farming was evidently small-scale: only one house in the later 17th-century inventories had more than four rooms.[82]

The inclosure of Stogursey commons on the Quantocks in the later 17th century created a new farm of 560 a., later known as Quantock farm, half of which was woodland. The remainder of the commons, some 440 a., was divided and let.[83] In the early 18th century rack renting began on Aley manor, but the leasing and sub-leasing of small holdings continued.[84] There is some evidence of farming improvement, such as the growing of clover on Aley farm in 1706,[85] and a lease of land at Adscombe, for which the rent was to be paid partly in cider and reed, required dunging with 160 seams per acre after four crops.[86] Nearly half of Quantock farm was heath in 1784, but its arable land was said to be good for corn.[87] Flax was grown at Bincombe in the 1780s.[88] In 1800 the vicar commented on the lack of horses in the parish and the continuing use of oxen, and also noted the primitive method employed to sow wheat, the children dropping seed into holes made by men and women with iron-tipped sticks.[89]

Henry Labouchere in the 1830s bought c. 2,796 a. in the parish, of which 1,625 a. were to form the pleasure grounds of Quantock Lodge. Of the 640 a. outside the Quantock estate, over half was common land belonging to Nether Stowey manor. There were in 1838 only four small freeholds. Plainsfield Court Farm was the largest farm, 234 a., and Aley farm had 206 a., three had 100–200 a., seven had 50–100 a., and four 20–50 a. By that date arable accounted for 819 a., meadow and pasture for 1,099 a.[90] In 1851 ten farmers employed 54 labourers, and the Quantock estate provided employment and housing for gamekeepers, building workers, and woodmen.[91] Arable had shrunk by 1905[92] but in 1982 the size and number of holdings was almost the same as in 1838. Most land was under grass, primarily for dairying, and the principal arable crop was wheat, followed by turnips and swedes for human consumption.[93]

MILLS. There was a mill on Alfred d'Epaignes' estate of Stowey in 1086.[94] Its successor may have been that owned by Bridgwater hospital in 1539[95] and known as Chapel mill, which descended with Friarn manor until 1655.[96] No further trace of it has been found. There was probably a mill at Plainsfield in 1508[97] and 1655;[98] one belonged to Plainsfield manor in 1833.[99] In 1838 it was owned by Robert Hill but had probably ceased milling by 1841.[1] The surviving leat behind the cottage indicates an overshot mill. Mill Cottage dates from the 17th or 18th century. Aley mill, recorded in 1604 on Aley manor,[2] was later known, after successive tenants, as Tratt's or Kebby mill,[3] and by 1838 as Marsh mills.[4] It was probably demolished when the new road from Plainsfield was built before 1842, and business was transferred to the former silk mill, a short distance northwest.[5] It was sold as a working mill in 1919, but it was probably not worked later.[6] A grist mill at Adscombe had been converted from a fulling mill by 1649.[7] The Perrett family, who operated it, employed an assistant who competed for custom with rival millers.[8] After 1793 it was sold to Richard Nation,[9] and from 1805 it was occupied by Thomas Hurley who was succeeded by his son Samuel, the owner in 1838.[10] Milling appears to have ceased by 1851.[11] The mill had no pond but was said in 1767 never to want for water.[12]

72 P.R.O., SC 6/974/8, 1090/4; ibid. E 142/8.
73 Alnwick Castle, Northumberland MSS. X.II.12.9A (iii); W. Suff. R.O. 449/E3/15.53/2.17–18.
74 Alnwick Castle, Northumberland MSS. X.II.12.9A (viii), 9C; S.R.O., DD/X/WI 34.
75 P.R.O., E 178/5623; S.R.O., DD/S/SH (N/153).
76 S.R.O., DD/WG 16/17.
77 Ibid. 13/1.
78 Ibid. DD/DHR box 36, map 1744; DD/X/BB 6; Bristol R.O. 4490, 04237.
79 S.R.O., DD/SP inventories, 1645, 1677.
80 Ibid. 1696.
81 Ibid. 1675, 1677, 1684.
82 Ibid. 1675, 1677, 1684, 1689.
83 Ibid. DD/HC (N/28); DD/SAS (C/923), map 1688.
84 Ibid. DD/WG 8/2A, 9/4; ibid. Q/RRp 3/2.
85 Ibid. DD/WG 15/3.   86 Ibid. DD/DR 31.
87 Ibid. DD/HC (N/42).
88 Ibid. Q/RLh 17.
89 Paupers and Pigkillers, ed. J. Ayres, 33–4, 49.

90 S.R.O., tithe award.
91 P.R.O., RG 9/1621; RG 10/2380; RG 11/2371.
92 Statistics supplied by the then Bd. of Agric., 1905.
93 Min. of Agric., Fisheries, and Food, agric. returns, 1982.
94 V.C.H. Som. i. 512–13.
95 P.R.O., SC 6/Hen. VIII/3137.
96 Devon R. O. 1148 M/add 60; above, manors.
97 Cal. Inq. p.m. Hen. VII, iii, p. 324.
98 S.R.S. xxviii. 276.   99 S.R.O., DD/PLE 64.
1   Ibid. tithe award; P.R.O., HO 107/935.
2   S.R.O., DD/WG 16/17.
3   P.R.O., C 3/400/103; S.R.O., DD/WG 8/2A.
4   S.R.O., tithe award.
5   O.S. Map 6", Som. XLIX. SW. (1887 edn.).
6   S.R.O., DD/SCL 9.   7 Ibid. DD/AH 34/22.
8   Ibid. 34/22; ibid. Q/SR 121/13.
9   Ibid. DD/AH 34/22, 40/41; ibid. Q/REl 7/9A.
10 Ibid. Q/REl 7/9A; ibid. tithe award.
11 P.R.O., HO 107/1924.
12 S.R.O., DD/AH 66/11.

A fulling mill and land called Rackhays at Adscombe were conveyed in 1451 by the lord of Plainsfield to John Verney of Fairfield.[13] The mill, held by Hugh Lawrence in 1547,[14] had become a grist mill by 1649.[15] Another fulling mill, in operation at Plainsfield c. 1510,[16] was still in use c. 1614. A third fulling mill stood at the junction of Ramscombe and Quantock Combe c. 1614, when it was occupied by Richard Lawrence or Dyer;[17] a fourth seems to have been established at Chapel mill in the 1640s in association with a dyehouse;[18] and a fifth, called French's, stood at Cockercombe, but had been converted to a dwelling by 1696.[19] Marsh mills, established between 1648 and 1676,[20] was evidently occupied by a clothier in 1681 and included a fulling mill.[21] Fields near the mill were known as Rack close and Rackbridge meadows. The Poole family, occupiers until the early 19th century, were later tanners.[22]

Between 1812 and 1816 new buildings and a large leat called a 'new canal' were constructed at Marsh mills for a silk mill, probably established by Thomas Ward, a Nether Stowey tanner.[23] The mill was said to have provided employment for hundreds of women and girls, but in 1839 only a few workers remained.[24]

Land called the Blademill, part of Aley park, was recorded in 1685.[25]

TRADE AND INDUSTRY. Sales of wood contributed to the income of Aley manor and the Stogursey estate in the 15th century;[26] in the later 17th there was some conversion of woodland to arable on Friarn farm. Part of Friarn wood was coppiced at 12 years' growth and the product sold to charcoal burners at £4 an acre, while there were also 300 standards.[27] In 1605 wood worth over £80 was sold on the Quantock land of Wick manor, some for charcoal burning.[28] The woodland on Quantock farm by 1784 was suitable for oak coppice and for producing bark, charcoal, poles, and faggots.[29] The bark went to local tanneries, one established in Bin Combe by 1716, whose owner left on his death 111 calfskins, horse hides, and clout leather worth over £66 and equipment worth £39.[30] In 1838 a tanyard at Marsh Mills was worked by the Poole family.[31] Among the charcoal burners were at least two generations of the Walford family.[32] Broom making was of some local significance. In 1851 17 men from 9 households, mostly members of the Palmer family living at Bincombe and Friarn, earned a precarious living as broomers or broom squires.[33] Demand for their products was said in 1868 to be falling, but broomers remained in the parish until the 1880s.[34]

Cloth was fulled at Adscombe from the 15th century, and in the 16th there were a dyehouse and racks at Pepperhill.[35] The Lawrence or Dyer family was engaged in the clothing trade in the later 16th and the 17th century, and the Blakes of Plainsfield in the early 17th.[36] A clothier was accused in 1631 of stretching his cloth and of using inferior materials.[37] Several clothiers, weavers, and fullers were active in the later 17th century.[38] Matthew Poole of Marsh Mills was probably one of the wealthier men in the parish with goods worth over £300, including cloth, wool, and flock worth over £90. The presence of yarn, cards, and other equipment indicates that others probably carded wool and may have been engaged in spinning and weaving. There were 2 racks, 4 pairs of shears, and a smoothing box on the premises.[39] A weaver's inventory of 1683, with a pair of looms and husbandry tools, suggests that weaving was a part-time occupation.[40] A weaver was recorded in 1704[41] but the cloth trade had probably declined by then. In 1807 an old woman from Aley spun for a Taunton clothier.[42]

A pottery was established in the 13th century in a field adjoining Nether Stowey parish but locally in Over Stowey.[43] A potter living in the parish in 1591 and probably originating in Flanders[44] may have been responsible for introducing a particular continental style into south-west England. Bricks were made at Bincombe in 1780,[45] and it was perhaps there that what were called Stowey bricks in 1688 were made.[46]

In the early 19th century the parish was poor and overcrowded.[47] In 1821 there were only 71 houses for 132 families after the population had increased by over a quarter in ten years.[48] During the 1830s one pauper family numbering about 40 people had built seven dwellings, little more than huts, on the roadside.[49] In 1838 there were nearly 60 landless cottages of which 37 were on the waste and often divided into as many as five

13 Ibid. 65/4.
14 Bristol R.O. 4490.
15 S.R.O., DD/AH 34/22.
16 Ibid. 11/9.
17 Ibid. DD/X/WI 34.
18 P.R.O., C 3/458, no. 63; S.R.O., DD/S/WH 285.
19 S.R.O., DD/S/WH 285; DD/L 2/16/89.
20 Ibid. DD/WG 13/1; D/P/l. st. 1 2/1/1.
21 Ibid. DD/SP inventory, 1681.
22 Ibid. tithe award.
23 Paupers and Pigkillers, ed. J. Ayres, 70, 270, 274–5.
24 Robson's Dir. Som. (1839); Employment of Women and Children in Agric. [510], p. 125, H.C. (1843), xii.
25 S.R.O., DD/WG 8/2A.
26 P.R.O., SC 2/200/27; SC 6/977/8, 11, 13; Eton Coll. Rec. 6/222.
27 S.R.O., DD/X/BB 6.
28 Alnwick Castle, Northumberland MSS. X.II.12.9C.
29 S.R.O., DD/HC (N/42).
30 Ibid. DD/SP inventory, 1716.
31 Ibid. tithe award.
32 Ibid. DD/X/HWK.

33 P.R.O., HO 107/1924.
34 Ibid. RG 10/2380; RG 11/2371; Rep. Com. Employment in Agric. 482.
35 P.R.O., SP 12/288/42; above, mills.
36 Bristol R.O. 4490; S.R.O., DD/AH 37/7; DD/X/WI 34; D/P/o. sty 2/1/1; D/P/stogs 17/7/23; ibid. Q/SR 115/131; P.R.O., C3/409, no. 134; Cal. Pat. 1558–60, p. 162.
37 S.R.S. xxiv. 137.
38 S.R.O., Q/SR 115/37, 131; 126/8; ibid. DD/SP inventories, 1681, 1683.
39 Ibid. DD/SP inventory, 1681.
40 Ibid. 1683.
41 Ibid. Q/SR 232/7.
42 Paupers and Pigkillers, ed. J. Ayres, 159.
43 V.C.H. Som. v. 195.
44 S.R.O., D/B/bw 1305.
45 Ibid. DD/AH 37/3.
46 Ibid. DD/SP inventory, 1688.
47 Employment of Women and Children in Agric. [510], p. 125, H.C. (1843), xii.
48 Census, 1821.
49 S.R.O., D/P/o. sty 13/3/2.

dwellings.[50] Even the new cottages on the Quantock estate were cramped, with only one downstairs room and attic bedrooms with sloping ceilings.[51] Most of the 21 indoor servants at Quantock Lodge in 1881 were recruited outside the parish leaving locals to find subsistence employment.[52] Among traditional village craftsmen in the later 19th century was a blacksmith.[53]

LOCAL GOVERNMENT. The parish lay in four tithings; Adscombe, Aisholt, and Plainsfield in Cannington hundred and Bincombe in Williton and Freemanors hundred, the last three including land outside the parish.[54] Aley was a division of Aisholt tithing by 1766, by which date Plainsfield tithing had been divided for land tax collection into Higher Plainsfield, containing the hamlet, and Lower Plainsfield, comprising the manor lands outside the parish.[55] The tithingman of Bincombe was from 1638 to be chosen from the tenants in rotation.[56]

Court rolls survive for Aley manor for the years 1423–4, 1426, 1459,[57] 1507,[58] 1579, 1582, 1592, and 1599–1604.[59] By the later 16th century,[60] and probably by c. 1400, the manor included land at Aisholt.[61] Court records for Plainsfield survive for various years between 1508 and 1522 and courts were held there annually.[62] The Athelney abbey estate of Adscombe was administered as part of Lyng free manor in the 14th century[63] and by 1535 with Hamp.[64]

There was a poorhouse by 1799, possibly the former church house. In 1816 it was decided to whitewash it and to inspect it each month.[65] It appears to have been no longer a poorhouse by 1838.[66]

The parish became part of the Bridgwater poor-law union in 1836, of the Bridgwater rural district in 1894, and of Sedgemoor district in 1974.[67]

CHURCH. There was a church at Over Stowey in the time of Ralph, whose grandson Hugh de Bonville between c. 1155 and 1189 endowed it, and before 1181 gave it to Stogursey priory.[68] In 1239 the priory surrendered the church to Jocelin, bishop of Bath and Wells, in return for an annuity.[69] In 1326 Bishop John Droxford

exchanged the rectory with St. Mark's hospital, Bristol, but retained the advowson and the following year ordained a vicarage.[70] Successive bishops exercised the patronage of the living until 1865 when it was transferred to Henry Labouchere, Baron Taunton. On his death in 1869 the patronage passed to his daughter Mary (d. 1920), wife of E. J. Stanley, and on her death was vested in the Martyrs Memorial Patronage Trust.[71] The benefice was held with Aisholt from 1919 and united with it in 1921, having the same patron.[72] In 1973 the two livings were disunited, Over Stowey becoming part of the united benefice of Nether Stowey with Over Stowey. The Martyrs Memorial and Church of England Trust nominates on alternate vacancies.[73]

In 1291 the church was valued at £8 13s. 4d.[74] but in 1326 it was said to be worth only £6 13s. 4d.[75] The vicarage was assessed at £9 1s. 4d. in 1535[76] including a pension of 13s. 4d. paid by the rectors under the terms of the 1327 ordination.[77] The living was augmented in 1828 with £200 by the vicar, W. B. Buller, and by Mrs. Horner's trustees.[78] The average income of the benefice c. 1831 was £165.[79] The vicarage was endowed with all the small tithes in 1327[80] and tithes and oblations were valued at £8 15s. in 1535.[81] By 1625 the vicar also had the great tithes of Plainsfield and of several fields at Radlet, Halsey Cross, and Bincombe which had possibly belonged to Plainsfield manor. Moduses for meadow had been introduced by 1678 and the vicar then received 20s. in lieu of tithes in Friarn wood.[82] In the late 18th century the vicar refused to accept a modus for the 1,000-a. estate of the earls of Egmont and demanded tithe in kind.[83] William Holland, vicar 1779–1819, collected his tithes in kind, but the farmers of the rectory tried to withhold tithe, claiming that the 13s. 4d. paid by Bristol corporation was in lieu of tithe.[84] In 1838 the vicar was awarded a rent charge of £165 1s. in lieu of small tithe, the great tithe of Higher and Lower Plainsfield tithings within the parish and Hare close at Bincombe, meadow moduses, and the 13s. 4d. from the rectory.[85]

In 1327 the vicar was given a croft adjoining his house and the right to pasture his animals with those of the rector.[86] The vicarial glebe was worth 3s. in 1535[87] and in 1625 measured 2 a.[88] In 1838 the vicar also rented the rectory land.[89]

50 S.R.O., tithe award.
51 *Rep. Com. Employment in Agric.* 482.
52 P.R.O., RG 10/2380; RG 11/2371.
53 Ibid. RG 10/2380; S.R.O., D/P/o. sty 2/1/9; *P.O. Dir. Som.* (1875); Taunton Castle, Som. Co. Museum.
54 *S.R.S.* iii. 140, 142–3, 165.
55 S.R.O., Q/REl 7/1, 7/9B–C.
56 *S.R.S.* lxv, p. 40.
57 P.R.O., SC 2/200/27–9.
58 S.R.O., DD/AH 11/9.
59 Ibid. DD/WG 16/8–9, 11–12, 16–17.
60 Ibid. 16/8.
61 *Cat. Anct. D.* v, A 11505; P.R.O., E 326/6080; above, Aisholt.
62 S.R.O., DD/AH 11/9–10.
63 *S.R.S.* xiv. 163.
64 *Valor Eccl.* (Rec. Com.), i. 206; below, Bridgwater, local govt.
65 *Paupers and Pigkillers*, ed. J. Ayres, 19, 21, 278.
66 S.R.O., tithe award.
67 Youngs, *Local Admin. Units*, i. 671, 673, 676.

68 *Cart. St. Mark's Hosp., Bristol*, pp. 159–60, 275.
69 Ibid. pp. 162–3.
70 *H.M.C. Wells*, i. 205, 402.
71 *Lond. Gaz.* 10 Jan. 1865, 110; *Dioc. Dir.*
72 S.R.O., D/P/o. sty 22/1.
73 *Dioc. Dir.*
74 *Tax. Eccl.* (Rec. Com.), 198.
75 *Cal. Pat.* 1324–7, 317.
76 *Valor Eccl.* (Rec. Com.), i. 216.
77 *S.R.S.* lxviii, p. 34.
78 C. Hodgson, *Queen Anne's Bounty* (1864), p. ccviii.
79 *Rep. Com. Eccl. Revenues*, pp. 148–9.
80 *S.R.S.* lxviii, p. 34.
81 *Valor Eccl.* (Rec. Com.), i. 216.
82 S.R.O., D/D/Rg 281.
83 Ibid. DD/TB 18/10; DD/HC (N/28).
84 Ibid. T/PH/ay 1.   85 Ibid. tithe award.
86 *S.R.S.* lxviii, p. 34.
87 *Valor Eccl.* (Rec. Com.), i. 216.
88 S.R.O., D/D/Rg 281.
89 Ibid. tithe award.

The vicar was assigned a house in 1327.[90] In 1713 the vicarage house comprised a hall, kitchen, parlour, buttery, and three chambers.[91] It lies south-west of the church and was rebuilt before 1744 with a south-east main front of three bays facing a formal garden, and a short back wing, incorporating service rooms and a staircase.[92] Early in the 19th century bays were added to the ground-floor front and the rooms were refitted. Later in the 19th century a block was added on the south-west side and the gabled dormers were rebuilt. The house ceased to be used as a vicarage and was sold c. 1973.

Twelfth-century clergy included Robert, probably later archdeacon of Wells c. 1155–69.[93] By the early 14th century the rector may have been regularly absent, as a chaplain was resident with his own house.[94] In 1321 the rector was given leave of absence because of his slender income and the licence was renewed in 1323, possibly to study canon law.[95] In 1554 the church lacked service books.[96] The vicars were normally resident in the 16th century but during their absence the rector of Aisholt was paid to take to take Sunday and Friday services.[97] Richard Penny was resident vicar for nearly 40 years from 1568[98] but towards the end of his incumbency the church was served by a curate who lived in the parish.[99] Richard Floyd was deprived in 1649 and restored in 1660.[1] Caradoc Butler, vicar 1671–1713,[2] bought extensive lands and royalties but later sold or mortgaged them.[3] At his death his goods were valued at less than £20.[4] From 1722 to 1763 the parish was served by Thomas Coney and his son John who also succeeded each other as prebendaries of Buckland Dinham. Thomas was a pluralist and author of 25 published sermons.[5] There were at most 16 communicants c. 1778.[6] William Holland, vicar 1779–1819, lived in the parish between 1779 and 1792 and again from 1798 until his death in 1819. His diary survives for the years 1799 to 1818. He held one Sunday service at Over Stowey and regularly served neighbouring churches. Services were then accompanied by a fiddler and other musicians.[7] Holland was succeeded by William Beadon Buller (1819–56) who, like most of his predecessors, was a pluralist, but he lived in Over Stowey.[8] By 1840 two services were held on Sunday and communion was celebrated three times a year. Buller was then assisted, and in 1856 succeeded by, his son William Edmund Buller who served the parish until 1878. By the 1870s communion was celebrated weekly.[9]

By 1393 an acre of land at Bincombe, probably given to the parish by the Nowlibbe family, was charged with an annuity of 4d. for obits for members of the family in the church.[10] By 1440 the land was known as Peter's Acre.[11] The land passed to John Verney in 1451 and probably descended with Fairfield.[12] The annuity was lost but the name Church Acre was recorded in the late 18th century[13] and in 1838 one acre of land, probably the same, was said to belong to the parish overseers.[14] By 1872 the land had been absorbed by the Fairfield estate but was said to belong to the poor.[15]

In 1535 vats, a barrel, and other vessels were given to the church, possibly for use in the church house.[16] In 1636 the church house was said to be decayed and ruinous.[17] It may have become the poorhouse, later used for the Sunday school.

The church of *ST. PETER AND ST. PAUL*, so dedicated by 1532,[18] had been dedicated to St. Peter alone in the 12th century.[19] It is built of rubble with freestone dressings and has a chancel with north chapel and vestry, a nave with north aisle and south porch, and a west tower. The short, narrow nave may be of 12th-century origin but its earliest feature is a 14th-century window in the south wall. The chancel was probably rebuilt in the 14th century[20] and the north aisle and tower were added in the 15th or early 16th century. In 1750 a window was inserted to give light to the pulpit.[21] In 1800 there was a gallery which was taken down probably in 1840. The tower was roughcast and whitewashed in 1806.[22]

In 1840 the church was restored by Richard Carver; the north vestry and south porch may then have been added, and new windows were inserted in the south wall.[23] The chancel was restored by C. E. Giles in 1857[24] and was extended in 1902.[25] Some bench ends are in the Perpendicular style and the brass chandelier of 1775 is by Street and Pyke of Bridgwater.[26] There is glass by Hardman of Birmingham dated 1857 and 1902 in the chancel, and by Morris and Co. in the north aisle (in memory of Lord Taunton 1870 and 1874) and elsewhere. A large monument to Thomas and James Rich by H. Wood of Bristol, dated 1815, bears carvings of farm implements.

There are six bells including two from the medieval foundry at Exeter and one dated 1714 by Thomas Wroth.[27] The church plate includes a cup and cover of 1574 by J. Ions of Exeter and

90 *S.R.S.* lxviii, p. 34.
91 S.R.O., DD/SP inventory, 1713.
92 Ibid. DD/DHR, box 36, map 1744.
93 *Cart. St. Mark's Hosp., Bristol*, p. 159; J. A. Robertson, *Som. Hist. Essays* (1921), 76.   94 *S.R.S.* i. 270.
95 Ibid. 306.   96 S.R.O., D/D/Ca 22.
97 *S.D.N.Q.* xiii. 271.   98 *Som. Incumbents*, ed. Weaver, 450.
99 S.R.O., D/P/o. sty 2/1/1.
1 *Walker Revised*, ed. A. G. Matthews, 313.
2 *Som. Incumbents*, ed. Weaver, 450.
3 S.R.O., DD/BV 10; DD/PC 17.
4 Ibid. DD/SP inventory, 1713.
5 Ibid. DD/SAS PD 125; Le Neve, *Fasti, 1541–1857*, Bath and Wells, 27; *Som. Incumbents*, ed. Weaver, 450.
6 S.R.O., D/D/Vc 88.
7 Ibid. T/PH/ay 1. Extracts printed as *Paupers and Pigkillers*, ed. J. Ayres (Gloucester, 1984).
8 S.R.O., D/D/Rb 1827.

9 Ibid. D/D/Va 1840, 1870; D/P/o. sty 2/1/8.
10 Ibid. DD/AH 65/8.   11 Ibid. 65/7.
12 Ibid. 65/4.   13 Ibid. D/P/o. sty 4/1/1.
14 Ibid. tithe award.   15 Ibid. DD/AH 51/7.
16 *Wells Wills*, ed. Weaver, 116.
17 S.R.O., D/D/Ca 310.
18 *Wells Wills*, ed. Weaver, 116.
19 *S.R.S.* lxi, p. 19; S.R.O., DD/AH 65/7.
20 Taunton Castle, Pigott colln., drawing by J. Buckler, 1836.
21 S.R.O., D/P/o. sty 4/1/1.
22 Ibid. T/PH/ay 1; ibid. D/P/o. sty 4/1/1.
23 Ibid. D/D/Va 1840; Taunton Castle, Pigott colln., drawing by J. Buckler, 1836; ibid. Braikenridge colln., drawing by W. W. Wheatley, 1855; Church Com. Rec., file 21744/8.
24 *Taunton Courier*, 10 June 1857.
25 S.R.O., D/P/o. sty 4/1/2.
26 Pevsner, *S. & W. Som.* 269.
27 S.R.O., DD/SAS CH 16/2.

a small 18th-century paten.[28] The registers date from 1558 but the years 1654–86 are missing and there are no burial records 1753–78.[29]

A churchyard cross was recorded in 1535;[30] the present one was dedicated in 1902.[31]

The chapel of Our Lady at Adscombe, so dedicated by 1534,[32] was built possibly in the late 13th century. Much of the west end was standing in the late 19th century[33] but little remained in 1986 except the wall footings and the bases of two buttresses at the western corners.

NONCONFORMITY. In 1668 a conventicle was held at Over Stowey.[34] For a time during the early 19th century Cornish miners who came to work in neighbouring copper mines introduced Methodism,[35] and Particular Baptists opened a meeting house in the parish in 1817.[36]

EDUCATION. In the late 17th or early 18th century a school was kept by the vicar Caradoc Butler.[37] A Sunday school in 1795 served as a model for a proposed school at Stogursey. In 1813 James Rich gave £100 towards its support.[38] The school was also supported by the earl of Egmont and had 17 pupils in 1819.[39] In 1825 the Sunday school was attended by 80 children[40] and by 1835 by 60. There was a day school with 20 children

by 1835.[41] The Sunday school was held in the poorhouse before 1840.[42] The National school was built in 1840 east of the church on the site of the poorhouse and had 90 pupils in 1846.[43] In 1903 there were 88 children on the books and three teachers.[44] Numbers fell rapidly, reaching 51 in 1915, 24 in 1935, 16 in 1955, and 13 in 1978 when the school was closed.[45] The building became the village hall.

Quantock independent school at Quantock Lodge[46] was open in 1986.

CHARITIES FOR THE POOR. John Blake of Plainsfield by will dated 1722 gave money to the poor, which was probably what was described in 1786 as a rent charge of 10s. given by an unknown donor; it had been lost by 1826.[47] Thomas Rich, by will dated 1715, gave a £1 rent charge to the poor. James Rich, by will dated 1813, gave £500 and Thomas Landsey, by will of 1801, gave half the interest on £100 to the poor.[48] Part of James Rich's bequest to the Sunday school was later converted into the Over Stowey Coal and Clothing club. The bequests of Thomas and James Rich and Thomas Landsey to the poor were united under a scheme of 1932 as the Parochial Charities.[49]

The Mary Stanley Sick Poor Fund, begun c. 1920, was used in 1981 to provide gifts for those in hospital.[50]

STRINGSTON

THE ancient parish of Stringston, west of and detached from Cannington hundred at the northern edge of the Quantocks, was divided into four separate parts.[51] The largest, roughly square and measuring c. 650 a., included Stringston village and the hamlets of Dyche and Corewell, and had as its northern boundary in 1839 the line of a road, in 1886 only a footpath, called Harford Lane between Shurton in Stogursey and Putsham in Kilve, and as its southern boundary the course of a stream.[52] About 1.5 km. west lay the tithing of Alfoxton, an irregular area of c. 360 a., nearly 3 km. from north to south and at most 1 km. wide, between Kilve parish on the west and the stream flowing down Hodder's Combe and the Holford stream on the east. Its south-western boundary was marked in 1839 by the course of the Hunting Path. The tithing included a house, known as

Alfoxton Park, the home of the St. Albyn family. The third part of the parish, 0.5 km. south-east of Stringston village, comprised in 1839 eight fields between Dodington and Stogursey parishes near Perry Mill. The fourth part, 2 km. south of Holford village and 3.5 km. from Stringston village, is an irregular block of land on the top of the Quantock scarp, c. 124 a. in extent,[53] including the hill fort known as Dowsborough. Its boundary with Holford common was marked in the 18th century by heaps of stones.[54] The four parts together measured 1,193 a.[55] In 1883 the Dowsborough and Perry Mill areas, both without houses, were transferred to Dodington, and in 1886 Alfoxton, said to contain 1 house and 5 persons, was transferred to Holford. The detached part of Kilton at Plud was added, forming the civil parish of Stringston measuring 859 a.[56]

28 Proc. Som. Arch. Soc. xlvii. 168.
29 S.R.O., D/P/o. sty 2/1/1–10.
30 Wells Wills, ed. Weaver, 116.
31 S.R.O., D/P/o. sty 4/1/2.
32 Wells Wills, ed. Weaver, 116.
33 S.D.N.Q. ii. 239.
34 S.R.S. xxxiv. 46.
35 Paupers and Pigkillers, ed. J. Ayres, 28, 33, 270, 292; S.R.O., T/PH/ay 1.
36 S.R.O., D/D/Rm, box 2.
37 Ibid. DD/HC (N/28).
38 Ibid. D/P/stogs 4/1/2; Char. Com. reg.
39 Educ. of Poor Digest, p. 800.
40 Ann. Rep. B. & W. Dioc. Assoc. S.P.C.K. (1825–6), 42.
41 Educ. Enq. Abstract, p. 817.

42 S.R.O., DD/CLE 5, memoir of Kath. Ward.
43 Nat. Soc. Inquiry, 1846–7, Som. 16–17; S.R.O., C/E 4/380/313.   44 S.R.O., C/E 4/380/313.
45 Ibid. 4/64; ibid. DD/X/OSPC 16.
46 Above, manors.
47 Char. Don. pp. 1048–9; S.R.O., DD/SAS (C/82) 43.
48 15th Rep. Com. Char. 373–4.
49 Char. Com. reg.
50 Ibid.; inf. from the Revd. R. Parker.
51 S.R.O., tithe map. This article was written in 1986.
52 S.R.O., tithe map; O.S. Map 6", Som. XXXVII. SW. (1886 edn.). John Harford occurs 1400–1: Pole MS. 2567.
53 S.R.O., tithe map.
54 Ibid. T/PH/vch 57/3, photograph of map of 1765.
55 V.C.H. Som. ii. 342.
56 Census, 1891.

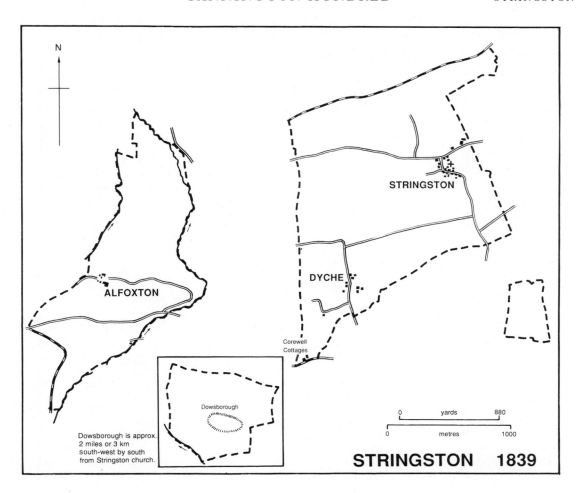

N

STRINGSTON

DYCHE

ALFOXTON

Corewell
Cottages

Dowsborough

Dowsborough is approx.
2 miles or 3 km
south-west by south
from Stringston church.

0   yards   880

0   metres   1000

STRINGSTON   1839

In 1933 Kilton-cum-Lilstock civil parish was added to form an enlarged civil parish of Stringston.[57]

The main part of the parish lies on ground rising from Stringston village northwards to a slight ridge of just over 107 m. on its northern boundary at Harford Lane. The slope comprises bands of valley gravel, Lower Lias, limestone, and marls.[58] Limestone was quarried in that part of the parish by 1662[59] and two quarries survived into the 19th century. There was a limekiln north of Prior's Farm and another in a marlpit further west.[60] Valley gravels predominate south and south-west of Stringston village, the land rising gently to 107 m.[61] Sand was dug on the edge of Stringston common, south of the village, by 1519[62] and gravel at an unknown site by 1651.[63]

The Alfoxton part of the parish rises from just below the 46-m. contour at Putsham up the Quantock scarp to 244 m. on Longstone Hill, whose steep and wooded south-eastern slope,

known as Willoughby Cleeve, forms one side of Hodder's Combe. The slope was known as Wildway Edge in 1681[64] and as Willine Cleeve in 1839.[65] Hodder's Combe is named after Anthony Hodder, tenant of a house and land there by 1809 and in 1839.[66]

The Perry Mill part of the parish included fields called claypits, and was largely on marl.[67] Dowsborough, formerly common land and coppice[68] and in 1986 oak scrub, occupies a steep hill rising to 333 m., and is composed of Hangman Grits.[69]

Within the single bank and ditch of the probable Iron-Age hill fort at Dowsborough are two earthworks, one a ditched round barrow, the other possibly a saucer-barrow.[70] In the later 16th century the site was called Dolesbery or Dolebery, and in the 17th Deuxbarrow or Dewsbarow.[71] Late forms such as Danesborough have given rise to speculation about Danish invasions.[72] A late-Roman coin hoard is said to have been discovered above Alfoxton,[73] apparently

57   *Som. Review Order*, 1933.
58   Geol. Surv. 1", drift, sheet 295 (1956 edn.).
59   S.R.O., DD/AH 11/11.
60   O.S. Map 6", Som. XXXVII. SW. (1886 edn.).
61   Geol. Surv. 1", drift, sheet 295 (1956 edn.).
62   S.R.O., DD/AH 11/4, 66/2; Sandpitts orchard nearby was recorded in 1839: ibid. tithe award.
63   Ibid. DD/AH 11/11.
64   Ibid. DD/MDW 17.
65   Ibid. tithe award.

66   Ibid. D/P/stn 4/1/1; ibid. tithe award.
67   Ibid. tithe award; Geol. Surv. 1", drift, sheet 295 (1956 edn.).
68   Below, this section.
69   Geol. Surv. 1", drift, sheet 295 (1956 edn.).
70   L. V. Grinsell, *Arch. of Exmoor* (1970), 66, 88.
71   S.R.O., T/PH/vch 65; Dors. R.O., D 1. MW/M4, f. 51v.
72   Grinsell, *Arch. of Exmoor*, 116.
73   W. Gresswell, *Land of the Quantocks* (1903), 25.

near the Great Road which, until the later 18th century, was the main route westwards from Bridgwater to Watchet.[74]

Two roughly parallel east-west roads cross the main part of the parish, both from Stogursey; the southern road, leading to Holford and the Great Road, was called Portway Lane.[75] Two parallel north–south roads may also have existed, but only parts survive. Stringston village lies at the junction of the eastern and northern routes, and comprises the church, Stringston Farm, and a cluster of small houses around a now enclosed green. No. 1 Stringston and the Cottage are medieval in origin; nos. 5 and 9–11 (originally one house) are probably of the 16th century. Dyche lies on the eastern route whose junction with Portway Lane is a staggered crossroads. That crossroads was mentioned in the mid 12th century in association with land called 'Aladich' and with meadow 'on the lower way',[76] the way perhaps now represented by the footpath between Dyche and Corewell. Dyche Farm is an 18th-century building; an adjoining barn has one jointed-cruck truss. Corewell, a group of cottages, was mentioned in 1275–6 and there was a house at Gugglemoor, adjoining to the north, in 1317 and 1592.[77]

In the Alfoxton area of the parish are the former capital messuage, now the Alfoxton Park Hotel, reached from Holford by a long woodland drive, and Granfield's Tenement, a house on the edge of Hodder's Combe, mentioned in 1629.[78]

There were small areas of open-field arable at Dyche in the early 14th and the 17th century, at Shortridge, west of Stringston village below the road to Kilton, also in the 14th century,[79] and at the Raps, immediately north of Stringston village. Traces of strips remained in all three places in the 19th century,[80] but most arable was inclosed by the later 16th.[81] The field at Alfoxton, probably in open cultivation, was mentioned in 1242.[82]

There were commons at Stringston, Alfoxton, and on the Quantocks. Stringston Heathfield, south of Stringston village, was already being encroached upon by 1519,[83] but part of it still remained in 1751. In 1807 it was said that 13 a., probably the last to survive, had been recently inclosed.[84] Four acres of Alfoxton common, on Longstone Hill, 'measured out by an ancient measure called Quantock measure', were inclosed c. 1629;[85] there were probably further inclosures later in the 17th century,[86] and by 1839 just over 34 a., then known as Stringston

common, had been absorbed in the Alfoxton estate.[87] In the mid 12th century a holding in the parish claimed housebote and haybote in the wood of Quantock.[88] Dowsborough, c. 1620 comprising some 80 a. of coppice and the remainder of 'clear down', was all subject to common rights for sheep pasture.[89] Dowsborough woods, 60 a. in extent, were let from 1717 to a Nether Stowey innholder for 99 years,[90] and by 1812 comprised stunted oak coppice on and within the ramparts, and 60 a. of hill pasturage outside.[91] By 1839 there were 167 a. of wood in the whole parish, including four copses north of Stringston village and woods near Alfoxton at Willoughby Cleeve and further north at Dog Pound, part of the Alfoxton estate.[92] Willoughby Cleeve and other land, acquired from the St. Albyns, was given to the National Trust by Mr. G. A. Falk in 1951,[93] and other woodland was bought by the League Against Cruel Sports in 1981. The Dog Pound, a small walled enclosure by the entrance to the drive to Alfoxton Park, was restored and presented to Holford village in memory of Mr. J. L. Brereton, the former owner of the Alfoxton estate, in 1982.[94]

Fields west of Stringston village, probably held with the capital messuage, seem by their names and shape to have formed a park.[95] A park at Alfoxton had been created by 1797 which, under the terms of the will of Lancelot St. Albyn (d. 1878), was to be stocked with at least 50 head of deer.[96] About 1900 there were 80 fallow deer in the park.[97]

A victualler in the parish was licensed in 1676 and there were two more in 1690. An innkeeper was in business between 1735 and 1756.[98] There was no inn by 1802.[99]

There were 14 households in the parish in 1563.[1] By 1801 the population was 121. It rose gradually to 159 in 1851 but fell rapidly to 114 in 1881. The population of the civil parish was 121 in 1891, but fluctuated to 92 in 1921. In 1931 it stood at 155.[2]

William and Dorothy Wordsworth occupied Alfoxton House between July 1797 and April 1798, and S. T. Coleridge and other members of their literary circle visited them there.[3]

MANORS AND OTHER ESTATES. In 1066 Alwig Banneson had 1 hide at Stringston and 2 hides in Alfoxton and Dyche. All that land was held in 1086 by Alfred d'Épaignes, and of Alfred by Ranulph,[4] probably Ranulph of Stringston;[5] by then a further ½ hide, held in 1066 by

74 *V.C.H. Som.* v. 2, 97, 129.
75 Ibid. 26; S.R.O., tithe award.
76 Pole MS. 2362, 2364. The surname *de fossato* was borne locally in the 12th century: ibid. 2570.
77 S.R.O., DD/AH 65/5; DD/MDW 17.
78 Ibid. DD/MDW 15.
79 Ibid. DD/AH 65/5, 65/7, 66/2.
80 Ibid. tithe award.
81 Ibid. T/PH/vch 65.
82 *S.R.S.* xi, p. 304.
83 S.R.O., DD/AH 66/2.
84 Ibid. 7/3.
85 Ibid. DD/MDW 15.
86 Ibid. 17.
87 Ibid. tithe award.
88 Pole MS. 2361.
89 Dors. R.O., D 1. MW/M5, f. 51v.

90 S.R.O., DD/AH 7/3.
91 Ibid. 11/7.
92 Ibid. tithe award.
93 *Properties of the National Trust* (1973), 129.
94 Inf. from Mrs. M. P. Brereton, Sidmouth.
95 S.R.O., tithe award.
96 *Collected Letters of S. T. Coleridge*, ed. E. L. Griggs (1966), i. 334; S.R.O., DD/NA, box 2.
97 W. Gresswell, *Forests and Deerparks of Som.* (1905), 259; *V.C.H. Som.* ii. 570.
98 S.R.O., Q/RL.
99 Ibid. Q/REl 7/10.
1 *S.D.N.Q.* xxx. 91.
2 *V.C.H. Som.* ii. 342; *Census*, 1911–31.
3 *Jnls. of Dorothy Wordsworth*, ed. M. Moorman, 4; *Letters of Coleridge*, ed. Griggs, i. 336, 339n.; B. Lawrence, *Coleridge and Wordsworth in Som.* (1970), 140–85.
4 *V.C.H. Som.* i. 512–13.
5 Ibid. 532.

Bristive, had been added to the hide in Stringston and may perhaps be identified as the detached part of the parish near Perry Mill. Another hide in Stringston, held in 1066 by Siward and in 1086 by Roger de Courcelles and of Roger by one William, has not been traced later and was presumably absorbed in the main estate.[6] Alfred d'Epaignes' overlordship descended like Nether Stowey manor to the Columbers family. Alfoxton was held by Philip de Columbers in 1166,[7] and Alfoxton and Stringston were still held of the honor or manor of Nether Stowey in the early 17th century.[8]

From Ranulph the undertenancy of *STRINGSTON* apparently descended in the earlier 12th century to Adam of Stringston, who was probably also known as Adam de Conteville and whose daughter Aubrey married successively Hugh Thurlac of Stringston and Hugh Fichet.[9] Hugh Fichet held a fee in Stringston in 1166 and was still alive in 1201.[10] Aubrey's son and heir Sir William Fichet was still alive in 1245[11] but by 1249[12] had probably been succeeded by another William, who held ½ fee there in 1284–5.[13] William, son and heir of the last and probably of Merridge in Spaxton, held ½ fee in 1303.[14] William, his son and heir, was mentioned in 1314–15.[15] In 1324–5 he granted Stringston manor and the advowson of the living to (Sir) Simon Furneaux, heir to Kilve manor.[16]

From Sir Simon (d. 1358)[17] the manor passed with Kilve to his daughter Elizabeth Blount and her daughter Alice Stafford, later Stury (d. 1414). When the estate was divided in 1421 Stringston was assigned to Joan, great-great-granddaughter of Simon's sister Hawise, and her husband Robert Greyndour (d. 1443).[18] Joan, who married Sir John Barre as her second husband, died in 1485, when her heir at Stringston was William Strode of Somerton.[19]

William Strode died in 1499 leaving his manor for life to a younger son, John, subject to the life interest of his widow Alice (d. 1517).[20] Stringston apparently descended to John's nephew John Strode, to that John's son Robert (d. 1559), to Robert's son John (d. 1581),[21] and to John's son Sir Robert, who died in 1616 leaving the manor to his brother Sir John Strode (d. 1642).[22] Sir John's son, also Sir John (d. 1679), was followed in succession by three of his children, William (d. 1706), Thomas (d. 1718), and Anne

(d. 1731).[23] Anne died unmarried and was succeeded by George Strode, Sir John's nephew. George died childless in 1753 and his brother Thomas also childless in 1764. The heir was Sir John Oglander, Bt., of Nunwell (I.W.), son of Sir John Strode's daughter Elizabeth.[24] Sir John Oglander was succeeded in 1767 by his son Sir William (d. 1806) and Sir William by his son, also Sir William (d. 1852), whose son Sir Henry after prolonged negotiations sold the manor and lordship with Stringston farm to Sir Alexander Hood in 1867.[25] The manor thereafter descended with the Fairfield estates to Elizabeth, Lady Gass, owner in 1986.[26]

The capital messuage was let for lives in 1398–9 and 1433–4.[27] It continued to be let in the 16th century, though in the 17th the tenant was a member of the Strode family.[28] Stringston Farm dates from the later 18th century.

Alfoxton may, like Stringston, have passed from the Domesday undertenant, Ranulph, to Adam de Conteville, since in 1201 Richard de Conteville had a claim to land there and was later thought to have released his rights to William son of Jordan.[29] William had ½ fee in Alfoxton in 1166 and may have been known as William of Alfoxton.[30] John of Alfoxton was recorded in 1275–6,[31] and in 1311 he or a namesake settled his estate at Alfoxton on himself and his wife Maud and his issue, with contingent remainders to Richard of Birland.[32] John died c. 1332. In 1342 Richard settled the manor on his brother Thomas and on Thomas's sons William and John,[33] and in 1347 Thomas settled it on himself and his wife Joan, with reversion to William and his wife Alice in tail. The heir of William and Alice may have been Christine, wife of William Cornu, who had established ownership by 1374. William Cornu was dead by 1383 and Christine married Edward Brightley, and she is said to have settled Alfoxton in 1385–6 on James Ayshe of Chagford (Devon). The Ayshe family remained in possession until 1419–20 when John Ayshe sold it to Richard Popham of Porlock.[34]

Richard Popham's daughter and heir Joan married first John Sydenham (d. 1464) and second John St. Albyn of Parracombe (Devon). Joan died in 1499 and in 1503 her estates were divided, Alfoxton passing to John St. Albyn, possibly her grandson.[35] That John, described as of Chilton Trivet having married Elizabeth

6 Ibid. 487.
7 *Red Bk. Exch.* (Rolls Ser.), i. 231; *V.C.H. Som.* v. 193.
8 P.R.O., C 142/652, no. 190; C 142/764, no. 3; S.R.O., DD/AH 11/9; Dors. R.O., D 1. MW/M4, f. 51v.
9 S.R.O., DD/AH 21/2; Pole MS. 2361, 2475.
10 *Red Bk. Exch.* (Rolls Ser.), i. 231; *S.R.S.* vi. 18.
11 *S.R.S.* lxviii, p. 4.
12 *S.D.N.Q.* vii. 149.
13 Pole MS. 2556; *Feud. Aids*, iv. 281.
14 Pole MS. 2552; *Feud. Aids*, iv. 308.
15 Pole MS. 2554.
16 Ibid. 2512, 2537, 2836; *Cal. Close, 1323–7*, 511; *V.C.H. Som.* v. 98.
17 *Cal. Inq. p.m.* x, p. 395; not 1359 as in *V.C.H. Som.* v. 98.
18 *Cal. Close, 1441–7*, 177; *S.D.N.Q.* xvi. 282; *V.C.H. Som.* v. 98.
19 P.R.O., C 141/5, no. 10; Dors. R.O., D 1. MW/M4, f. 47.
20 *Cal. Inq. p.m. Hen. VII*, ii, p. 203; P.R.O., C 142/32, no. 85.

21 P.R.O., C 142/193, no. 67; *S.R.S.* extra ser. 350–1.
22 J. Hutchins, *Hist. Dors.* ii. 131 n., 132 n.
23 Dors. R.O., D 279/E4; ibid. D 1. MW/M5; Hutchins, *Hist. Dors.* ii. 130.
24 Dors. R.O., 438A/T22; S.R.O., DD/AH 11/11; Hutchins, *Hist. Dors.* ii. 130.
25 S.R.O., DD/AH 1/4; Burke, *Land. Gent.* (1914), 1421–2.
26 Above, Stogursey, manors.
27 Pole MS. 2557, 2743.
28 Dors. R.O., D 1. MW/M4, f. 49; S.R.O., T/PH/vch 65.
29 *Cur. Reg. R.* ii. 2; S.R.O., DD/AH 21/2: 18th-cent. notes based on charters at Alfoxton.
30 *Red Bk. Exch.* (Rolls Ser.), i. 231; Pole MS. 2361–2, 2592.
31 *S.R.S.* xli. 61.   32 Ibid. xii. 21.
33 *S.D.N.Q.* vii. 149–50.
34 *S.R.S.* xvii. 5; *S.D.N.Q.* vii. 150; S.R.O., DD/AH 21/2.
35 S.R.O., DD/AH 21/2; DD/WY 1/30–1; *S.R.S.* xvi. 363–5.

Trivet, was still in possession in 1507.[36] His son, also John (d. c. 1540), was followed by John's son George,[37] and George by his son John (d. 1601) and his grandson Lancelot (d. 1624).[38] John (d. c. 1652), son of Lancelot,[39] was succeeded in turn by two of his sons, John (d. 1708) and Lancelot (d. c. 1709). John, son of Lancelot, died in 1723 and was followed by his sons John (d. 1744) and Lancelot (d. 1745). The last, of Nether Stowey, was followed by his sons John (d. 1768) and the Revd. Lancelot (d. 1791).[40]

Lancelot St. Albyn died without issue, and for a long time the estate was let.[41] In 1806 his heir, his great-nephew Langley Gravenor, came of age and took the name St. Albyn.[42] Langley died in 1874, and on the death of his elder son Lancelot in 1878 Alfoxton passed to Lancelot's widow Jane (d. 1891) for her life, with remainder to his elder sister Anne, wife successively of Birt Jenner (d. 1863) and William Prichard (d. 1888). Anne was succeeded in 1905 by her son Birt St. Albyn Jenner. After his death without children in 1924 Birt's widow made over the estate to his nephew John Lancelot Brereton (d. 1973). Much of the estate was sold in 1920 but the house, park, and woods were retained, the house being let to a succession of tenants and becoming a private hotel in 1930. Between 1939 and 1946 it was occupied by Wellington House preparatory school from Westgate-on-Sea (Kent), and then reverted for use first as an hotel and until 1958 as a Christian Endeavour holiday home. The house and c. 55 a. of land were sold by the Brereton trustees in 1958, and since that date the house has been an hotel. The remaining parts of the estate in the parish were sold in 1978 and 1981.[43]

Alfoxton Park hotel, standing on a prominent site with extensive views northwards across the Bristol Channel, is a large house of two storeys, cellars, and attics. It comprises a south range of seven bays, with a three-bayed pediment and central Tuscan porch of the early 18th century, and to the north a parallel range built probably before 1797–8 when the house comprised nine lodging rooms, three parlours, and a hall.[44] A 'most superb room' was said to have been lately built and furnished in 1810.[45]

In King John's reign one William, perhaps son of Jordan, granted land in Dyche and 'Lymmbery' to John of Alfoxton.[46] It had presumably been part of the 2 hides in Alfoxton recorded in Domesday.[47] In 1500 John St. Albyn held a manor called *LYMBER* or Lymbards which in 1503 comprised land in Burton in Stogursey, Dodington, Holford, and Stringston.[48] It was merged with Alfoxton manor by the earlier 18th century, and in the 19th the name was confined to two fields in Dodington parish, between Dodington village and Dyche and adjoining both Holford and Stringston parishes.[49]

Two other holdings, Gugglemoor and Corewell or Currill, were probably part of Dyche in 1086. *GUGGLEMOOR*, held by Gilbert of the marsh and his sons Henry and William in the mid 13th century,[50] descended to John Gilbert of Gugglemoor (fl. 1284) and to John's son John of Gugglemoor (fl. 1321). By 1427 the estate had passed to Thomas Gilbert of Exeter, whose daughter married Nicholas Biccombe. The Biccombes are said to have held it in Henry VII's reign.[51] John St. Albyn was owner by 1592[52] and it was still held with Alfoxton in 1839.[53] *CORE-WELL*, partly in Holford parish,[54] included a farm in Stringston which belonged to John St. Albyn by 1608[55] and was still held with Alfoxton in 1724.[56]

Hugh Fichet and his wife Aubrey gave a virgate of land and its tenants to Taunton priory in the mid 12th century.[57] The priory's estate, called Kingshill in 1535, still paid chief rent to the lord of Stringston.[58] Montacute priory had some land in the parish in 1291.[59] Neither estate has been identified nor traced further. From the 13th century the Verney family acquired rents and land, some associated with Barnsworthy in Dodington, which John Verney of Fairfield in Stogursey sold in 1416.[60] The land was partitioned in 1519 and part was thereafter known as Coles's tenement.[61] That holding, with additional lands, remained in the Coles family until 1740 and was bought by (Sir) John (Palmer) Acland in 1791.[62] Land at Dyche, also formerly held by the Coles family, was owned by Nicholas Palmer of Fairfield by 1699 and descended with the Fairfield estate.[63] Sir Francis Dodington had a freehold tenement in 1651 which in 1705 comprised a farm of 73 a. at Dyche.[64] It descended with Dodington manor and in 1786 was owned by George Grenville, marquess of Buckingham (d. 1813).[65] The farm seems to have been sold before 1827[66] and was later absorbed into the Fairfield estate.[67] George Prior, whose family had been resident at Stringston in 1497[68] and

36 Devon R.O., DD/4183; S.R.O., DD/AH 11/9; Collinson, *Hist. Som.* i. 265.
37 P.R.O., C 3/162/57; ibid. C 142/67, no. 113; Collinson, *Hist. Som.* i. 265.
38 P.R.O., C 142/271, no. 150; C 142/652, no. 190; *Som. Wills*, ed. Brown, i. 85.
39 S.R.O., DD/AH 11/11.
40 Ibid. D/P/stn 2/1/2–3; *Som. Wills*, ed. Brown, i. 85–6; M.I.s in Stringston ch.
41 S.R.O., D/P/stn 4/1/1; above, intro.
42 *Paupers and Pigkillers*, ed. J. Ayres, 93, 197–8; fuller text in S.R.O., T/PH/ay 1.
43 S.R.O., DD/AH 41/10; DD/NA, box 2, abs. of title 1920; Burke, *Land. Gent.* (1914), 1045; *Walford's County Families* (1891); inf. from Mrs. M. P. Brereton, Sidmouth; H. Riley, *Alfoxden Days* (priv. print. n.d.).
44 *Collected Letters of Coleridge*, ed. Griggs, i. 334.
45 *Paupers and Pigkillers*, ed. J. Ayres, 197.
46 S.R.O., DD/AH 21/2.
47 Above.

48 Devon R.O., DD/4183; S.R.O., DD/WY 1/30–1.
49 S.R.O., DD/AH 37/32; DD/MDW 21; ibid. Dodington tithe award; *V.C.H. Som.* v. 3.
50 S.R.O., DD/AH 21/2; Pole MS. 2364.
51 S.R.O., DD/AH 21/2.
52 Ibid. DD/MDW 17.
53 Ibid. tithe award.   54 *V.C.H. Som.* v. 3.
55 S.R.O., DD/MDW 16.   56 Ibid. 21.
57 *Cal. Chart. R.* 1327–41, 315; *Tax. Eccl.* (Rec. Com.), 204.
58 *Valor Eccl.* (Rec. Com.), i. 169.
59 *Tax. Eccl.* (Rec. Com.), 204.
60 S.R.O., DD/AH 65/5, 7; 66/15.
61 Ibid. 66/2.   62 Ibid. 11/4.
63 Ibid. 35/19.
64 Ibid. 11/11, 37/23.
65 Ibid. 7/3, 37/23; *V.C.H. Som.* v. 66.
66 S.R.O., DD/HWD 19; ibid. T/PH/vch 57/2; ibid. tithe award.
67 Ibid. DD/AH 2/6.
68 *Fines imposed in 1497*, ed. A. J. Howard, 14.

were tenants of part of Alfoxton manor in 1567[69] and part of the glebe in 1613,[70] owned the freehold of Prior's farm in 1765.[71] John Prior owned it in 1839.[72] The house is a 17th-century building with plaster work bearing the dates 1641 and 1658.

ECONOMIC HISTORY. The holdings in the parish in 1086 amounted together to 7 ploughlands, 13 a. of meadow, 86 a. of pasture, and 35 a. of wood. Stock was recorded on only the 1 hide at Stringston: 8 beasts, 15 pigs, and 193 sheep. There were three demesne farms: 3 virgates with 4 *servi* and 2 ploughteams at Stringston held by Ranulph, 1½ hide with 1 *servus* and 1 ploughteam at Alfoxton and Dyche, and ½ ploughland at Stringston held by William. Of the 11 recorded tenants 6 were at Alfoxton and Dyche.[73] By the later 12th century one of the tenant farms comprised 18 a. of arable at Dyche, 6 a. of land 'on the hills', and 2 a. of meadow.[74] That and another farm of 12 a. were held in fee.[75] Other farms were smaller and equally scattered: the Bolimer family in 1317 had 4 a. at Stringston, 3 a. at Dyche, and 1½ a. 'on the hill towards Kilton'.[76] Two larger holdings were the virgate given to Taunton priory in the 12th century[77] and the farm of 54 a. held by John Nichol until his outlawry in 1369, perhaps in succession to Robert Nich in 1327.[78] The capital messuage of Stringston manor was let with 17 a. in 1434.[79]

Two fields called Ryecroft had been inclosed from Stringston Heathfield by 1519;[80] by 1620 other parts of the common were under plough, and rye was grown on the Quantocks at Dowsborough.[81] Inclosure of Alfoxton common had begun by 1629 when Granfield's tenement was formed, the tenant then having common for 50 sheep, 1 horse, 1 colt, and 6 bullocks.[82] Another Alfoxton tenant had grazing for 6 sheep on Longstone (then Alfoxton) Hill, with the right to cut ferns and furze.[83] Tithes were payable in the 17th century on cows, calves, sheep, lambs, pigs, gardens, honey, wax, apples, pears, and hops.[84] Thomas Paddon (d. 1716) left 2 horses, 2 oxen, 2 cows, 6 ewes and lambs, 1 pig, some poultry, and corn both growing and in store, and among his goods were harrows and a putt.[85]

By 1582 Stringston manor comprised the capital messuage with a substantial farm let for £4

a year and seven holdings ranging between 1 a. and 36 a. let for rents between 3s. and 23s.[86] The manor, and also the parish, was by that time dominated by one family of tenant farmers, the Govetts, who from the late 15th century held land there.[87] Margaret Govett, widow, occupied the capital messuage of Stringston from 1546 and was followed in 1578 by her grandson William.[88] Richard Govett had a lease of scattered fields from the Alfoxton estate by 1636 which his descendants still held in 1718.[89] George Govett succeeded his parents in the tenancy of Stringston farm in 1749, and Richard Govett, and later his widow Joan, farmed other lands at Dyche and elsewhere in the 1740s.[90] Three members of the family held seven leaseholds in 1765 including Stringston farm,[91] and from 1807 John Govett combined several tenancies with an enlarged Stringston farm, then measuring 280 a.[92] In 1839 Robert Govett occupied nearly 366 a.[93] William Govett of Stringston farm employed 12 labourers on his 300 a. in 1851,[94] and by 1861 Edwin Govett occupied the same farm.[95] The Govetts continued to farm in the parish until c. 1870.[96]

Rack renting was introduced on the Strode estate in 1731 and by 1766 half was held on lease and divided between five farms.[97] By 1839 the estate totalled just over 470 a. The Alfoxton estate was then just over 416 a. including nearly 150 a. of woodland and park around Alfoxton House, and Sir Peregrine Acland owned seven separate holdings totalling just over 80 a.[98] Sir Alexander Acland-Hood bought 424 a. with Stringston manor in 1867 and thus became the largest landowner in the parish.[99]

In 1705 a 21-year lease of a farm at Dyche limited the tenant to two corn crops in succession and specified adequate lime and dung.[1] An 8-year lease of Stringston farm in 1807 required the removal of mole and ant hills and the destruction of ferns, thistles, and rushes, all necessary measures to improve the recently inclosed parts of the common.[2] In 1839 arable (466 a.) and grassland (453 a.) were almost equal in area,[3] but in 1905 grass was slightly more extensive than arable in the Stringston part of the parish.[4]

Small fields near Alfoxton were let to craftsmen from neighbouring parishes in the 17th century: a pasture in 1645 to a Kilve clothier, and Granfield's tenement to Hugh Granfield,

69 S.R.O., T/PH/vch 65.
70 Ibid. D/D/Rg 283.
71 Ibid. D/P/stn 4/1/1.
72 Ibid. tithe award.
73 *V.C.H. Som.* i. 487, 512–13.
74 Pole MS. 2364.
75 Ibid. 2561.
76 Dors. R.O., D 438A/T26; cf. Pole MS. 2551, 2564–5, 2568, 2592, 2747; S.R.O., DD/AH 65/5, 7.
77 Above, manors.
78 *Cal. Inq. Misc.* iii, p. 289; *Cal. Close, 1369–74,* 267; *S.R.S.* iii. 141.
79 Pole MS. 2743.
80 S.R.O., DD/AH 66/2.
81 Dors. R.O., D 1. MW/M4, f. 50v.
82 S.R.O., DD/MDW 15, deeds 1629–81.
83 Ibid. DD/MDW 17.
84 Ibid. D/D/Rg 283.
85 Ibid. DD/SP inventory, 1716/21.
86 Ibid. T/PH/vch 65; cf. Dors. R.O., D 1. MW/M4, ff.

49–51 (survey bk. c. 1620).
87 *Fines Imposed in 1497,* ed. A. J. Howard, 14; S.R.O., DD/AH 66/2 (Govett's Down); P.R.O., C 3/162/57.
88 Dors. R.O., D 1. MW/M4, f. 49.
89 S.R.O., DD/MDW 17, 21.
90 Ibid. DD/AH 7/3.
91 Ibid. D/P/stn 4/1/1; ibid. Q/REl 7/10.
92 Ibid. DD/AH 7/3.
93 Ibid. tithe award.
94 P.R.O., HO 107/1920.
95 Ibid. RG 9/1604.
96 *P.O. Dir. Som.* (1866); Morris & Co. *Dir. Som.* (1872).
97 Dors. R.O., D 1. MW/M7.
98 S.R.O., tithe award.
99 Ibid. DD/AH 12/7.
1 Ibid. 37/23.
2 Ibid. 7/3.
3 Ibid. tithe award.
4 Statistics supplied by the then Bd. of Agric., 1905.

a Holford dyer, in 1681. George Poole, a String-ston clothier, became a tenant at Alfoxton in 1681.[5] There is a field called Rackmead south of Stringston village.[6] Tanhouse Tenement at Dyche was recorded in 1765 and was the site of a tanyard in 1839.[7] By 1802 a butcher and a cordwainer lived in the parish,[8] and there was a shop at Dyche in 1839.[9] By 1851 there were a blacksmith, two cordwainers, and a thatcher,[10] and by 1861 a smith and a mason.[11] The shop continued into the 1870s,[12] and in 1906 and until the 1930s a road contractor operated from the parish. In 1923 there was a wheelwright at Dyche.[13] Farming was the sole occupation in the parish in 1986.

Alfoxton mill, driven by a race off the stream south-east of Putsham in Kilve, was built by 1676.[14] It was still in operation in 1839[15] but was no longer used by 1886.[16]

LOCAL GOVERNMENT. A court book for Stringston manor records intermittent courts baron from 1651 to 1797.[17] Business included changes in tenancies and orders for the mainten-ance of buildings, ditches, and fences and for the administration of the commons. From 1578 the tenant of the capital messuage acted as collector of rents, which he was required to deliver to the lord at Parnham (Dors.), and had to provide hospitality for the steward when he held courts twice a year for two days.[18] By 1672 rents were to be paid at the capital messuage, for the lessee was then a member of the Strode family.[19] The lessee from 1807 was obliged to provide the lord and his steward with sufficient hospitality for a day and a night once a year to keep courts.[20] One court c. 1730 was held at Parnham. During a dispute over a right of way in 1657 tenants were ordered to meet in the churchyard at 6 o'clock in the morning. A hayward was mentioned in the 17th century.[21]

No court rolls or records have been found for Lymber or Lymbards manor, but courts were held there c. 1535,[22] and suit was required of tenants until 1665.[23] A tenement in Stringston village, and probably another in Dyche, were held in the 17th century of the Palmer family for suit of court twice a year at Fairfield.[24]

Two wardens and two sidesmen held office each year in the 17th century,[25] but there was usually only one warden in the 18th century, and often only one in the 19th. There were two overseers by the 1760s who distributed to the poor weekly pay, house rent, clothing, and tools. There was a vestry of seven in 1765, six includ-ing the rector and Langley St. Albyn in 1829, and five in 1846–7. In 1767 and 1773 the parsonage house was used as a poorhouse.[26] The parish became part of Williton poor-law union in 1836 and of Williton rural district in 1894. In 1974 it formed part of West Somerset district.[27]

CHURCH. A rector of Stringston was recorded in the time of Richard I.[28] The living was a sole rectory until after 1334[29] but by 1358 it had become a chapelry linked with the college or chantry at Kilve.[30] It remained dependent on Kilve after the college had ceased to function,[31] the living being known as the rectory of Kilve with Stringston. That rectory was held with East Quantoxhead from 1946 and in 1947 was united with Kilton and Lilstock. In 1978 it became part of the benefice of Quantoxhead.[32]

Before 1334 the advowson belonged to the lords of Stringston manor and in that year was exercised by the minister and fellows of Kilve.[33] Curates from the 16th century were probably appointed by the rectors of Kilve. No separate valuation of Stringston rectory or chapel has been found, and by the 17th century all tithes in Stringston were paid to the rector of Kilve.[34] The tithe rent charge awarded in 1839 was £188 10s.[35] The glebe lands of the chapelry in the 17th century amounted to 40 a. in Stringston and 2 a. in Kilton.[36] In 1839 there were just over 43 a. in Stringston, and 46 a. in 1948.[37] The curate c. 1532 was paid £5, in the 1570s £8 or £10, and in 1827 £50 and fees.[38] The rectory house was reported as in need of repair c. 1594[39] and there were two houses on the glebe in the 17th cen-tury.[40] There was no house in 1839.[41]

The parish chaplain in 1468 was a regular canon or friar.[42] In 1547 there had been no sermons for three years.[43] Curates were appar-ently resident in the 16th and 17th centuries including Simon Batt, curate by 1598 and until his death in 1649.[44] The church house, let to the parishioners c. 1620, was in private occupa-tion by 1667, and was still standing in 1731.[45] Curates served the parish in the 18th century

5   S.R.O., DD/MDW 15, 17.
6   Ibid. tithe award.
7   Ibid. D/P/stn 4/1/1; ibid. Q/REl 7/10; ibid. tithe award.
8   Ibid. Q/REl 7/10 (window tax 1802).
9   Ibid. tithe award.
10   P.R.O., HO 107/1920.
11   Ibid. RG 9/1604.
12   Morris & Co. *Dir. Som.* (1872).
13   *Kelly's Dir. Som.* (1906, 1923, 1931).
14   S.R.O., DD/MDW 17, 19.
15   Ibid. tithe award.
16   O.S. Map 6", Som. XLIX. NW. (1886 edn.).
17   S.R.O., DD/AH 11/11.
18   Dors. R.O., D 1. MW/M4, f. 49.
19   S.R.O., DD/AH 7/3; Dors. R.O., D 1. MW/M4, f. 49.
20   S.R.O., DD/AH 7/3.
21   Ibid. 11/11.
22   P.R.O., C 3/162/57.
23   S.R.O., DD/MDW 16, 17.

24   Ibid. DD/AH 35/11, 19.
25   Ibid. D/D/Rg 283.   26   Ibid. D/P/stn 4/1/1.
27   Youngs, *Local Admin. Units*, i. 438, 674, 676.
28   *S.R.S.* lxi, p. 46.
29   Ibid. ix, p. 165.
30   P.R.O., C 260/70, no. 17; cf. *V.C.H. Som.* v. 101.
31   *S.R.S.* lv, p. 162; S.R.O., D/D/Vc 20.
32   *V.C.H. Som.* v. 101; S.R.O., D/P/stn 22/3/1.
33   *S.R.S.* i. 101; ix, p. 165; xii. 133; Pole MS. 2537, 2836.
34   S.R.O., D/D/Rg 283.
35   Ibid. tithe award.
36   Ibid. D/D/Rg 274 (Kilve), 283 (Stringston).
37   Ibid. tithe award; ibid. D/P/kve 3/1/6.
38   Ibid. D/D/Vc 20; D/D/Rb 1827; *S.D.N.Q.* xiii. 271.
39   S.R.O., D/D/Ca 98.
40   Ibid. D/D/Rg 283.
41   Ibid. tithe award.   42   *S.R.S.* lii, p. 27.
43   S.R.O., D/D/Ca 17.
44   Ibid. D/P/stn 2/1/1–2; D/D/Bs 39.
45   Dors. R.O., D 1. MW/M4, f. 51; D 1. MW/M5; D 279/E4.

176

but John Matthew, rector 1797–1837, served Stringston in person until 1827 and then employed his son as curate.[46] There were 13 communicants in the 1770s.[47] Services were held alternately at Stringston and Kilve in the earlier 19th century, but by 1840 they were held each Sunday at Stringston, either in the morning or the afternoon; sometimes there were no communicants.[48] In 1851 the usual attendance was 70 in the morning, including the Sunday school, and 50 in the afternoon.[49] The Sunday school continued until 1924; monthly celebrations of communion were established by 1910 when other services were held once each Sunday, usually in the afternoon.[50]

The small church, in 1851 and since c. 1980 named after *ST. MARY THE VIRGIN* but of unknown ancient dedication,[51] comprises a chancel with north vestry, a two-bayed nave with south transept and south porch, and a western tower with a broach spire. The tower, which contains an early medieval window on its south side, was rebuilt in 1765 in blue lias with Bath stone window surrounds and battlements.[52] Remains of a late medieval building survive in the chancel arch, part of the chancel wall plate, the outer arch of the porch, a carved head in the vestry, and the font. The transept, containing memorials of the St. Albyn family, was built or rebuilt in the 18th century, and the chancel was rebuilt and refenestrated between 1840[53] and 1845.[54] There was extensive rebuilding in 1879 at the cost of the rector, Sir Alexander Acland-Hood, Mrs. Langley St. Albyn, and the parish, when the spire was added.[55] Further restoration was undertaken in 1912 by Sir Prior Goldney, Bt., descendant of the Prior family.[56]

The plain pew ends, one dated 1602, are carved with the initials of occupiers and the names of tenements. A gallery was mentioned in 1768.[57] The pulpit dates from the 18th century. The 15th-century churchyard cross, bearing the figures of the Crucifixion, was the object of veneration in the 1840s.[58]

The oldest of the three bells is probably by Henry Jefferies of Bristol and dates from the 15th century.[59] There is a cup and cover of 1574 made by 'I.P.'[60] The registers begin in 1557 and are complete.[61]

NONCONFORMITY. In 1669 there was a conventicle under Thomas Safford.[62] A house was licensed for Methodists in 1754[63] and another, called Shutt's, for Independents in 1786.[64] The last was replaced by a chapel, apparently converted from a cottage, in 1801.[65] The chapel was probably still in use in 1865 but had become a dwelling by 1886.[66]

EDUCATION. In 1734 George Paddon left £15 by will, the interest for teaching poor children.[67] There was a teacher in the parish in 1802,[68] and in 1826 a dame school seems to have been receiving the charity money.[69] A day school was opened in 1833 for 5 boys and 5 girls, all taught at their parents' expense;[70] the educational charity was devoted by the 1850s to general poor relief.[71] In 1874 Sir Alexander Hood built a National school and schoolhouse at Dyche for children of the poorer classes from Dodington, Holford, and Stringston, and in 1903, when it was leased to the county council, there were 68 children on the books under three teachers.[72] Numbers fell to 45 in 1915 and to 20 in 1933, when the school was closed.[73]

CHARITIES FOR THE POOR. Elizabeth St. Albyn, by will dated 1738, gave £10, the interest to buy bread for the poor. John St. Albyn (d. 1744) left a similar sum for poor householders not receiving relief. The Revd. Lancelot St. Albyn in 1781 held both capital sums.[74] Between 1854 and 1863 the capital was invested, the churchwardens distributing the proceeds either in bread or in cash.[75] Mrs. Jane St. Albyn, by will proved 1891, gave £300 to be distributed at Christmas among the poor, a charity apparently shared with Holford.[76] The income from all three charities, together with that from George Paddon's educational charity, seems to have been distributed in Stringston, Kilve, and Holford in blankets, clothing, and coal,[77] but by 1931 Paddon's charity was identified as for the benefit of children.[78] By 1982 the charities were not being distributed.[79]

46 S.R.O., D/P/stn 2/1/4, 2/1/6.
47 Ibid. D/D/Vc 88.
48 Ibid. D/D/Rb 1815, 1827; D/D/Va 1840.
49 P.R.O., HO 129/313/4/7/9.
50 S.R.O., D/P/stn 2/5/1.
51 P.R.O., HO 129/313/4/7/9; Dioc. Dir.; embroidery in ch.
52 S.R.O., D/P/stn 2/5/1.
53 Taunton Castle, Pigott colln., wash drawing by J. Buckler (1840) showing Venetian window on S.
54 Ibid. Pigott colln., wash drawing by J. Buckler (1840); ibid. Braikenridge colln., watercolour by W. W. Wheatley (1845); Local Hist. Libr. photograph by R. Gillo.
55 *W. Som. Free Press*, 20 Sept. 1879.
56 Inscr. in ch.; *Kelly's Dir. Som.* (1919); S.R.O., D/P/stn 4/1/2.
57 S.R.O., D/P/stn 4/1/2.
58 *Som. Co. Herald*, 15 Dec. 1928.
59 S.R.O., DD/SAS CH 16/2.
60 *Proc. Som. Arch. Soc.* xlvii. 170.
61 S.R.O., D/P/stn 2/1/1–6.
62 *Orig. Rec. of Early Nonconf.* ed. G. L. Turner, i. 9.
63 S.R.O., Q/RR.   64 Ibid. D/D/Rm 1.
65 Ibid. One in a row of cottages, in 1986 nos. 2 and 3 Stringston.
66 Ibid. DD/AH 12/7; not marked as a chapel on O.S. Map 6", Som. XXXVII. SW. (1886 edn.).
67 S.R.O., D/P/stn 4/1/1, flyleaf.
68 Ibid. Q/REl 7/10 (window tax).
69 *15th Rep. Com. Char.* p. 374.
70 *Educ. Enq. Abstract* p. 824.
71 S.R.O., D/P/stn 4/1/1.
72 Ibid. C/E 4/380/390; ibid. DD/AH 36/23.
73 Ibid. C/E 4/64, 165.
74 Ibid. D/P/stn 4/1/1, flyleaf.
75 Ibid. regular accounts.
76 Char. Com. file.
77 S.R.O., D/P/kve 17/3/2; D/P/stn 17/1/1; above, educ.
78 S.R.O., D/P/stn 17/2/1.
79 Inf. from the rector, the Revd. W. H. Minshull.

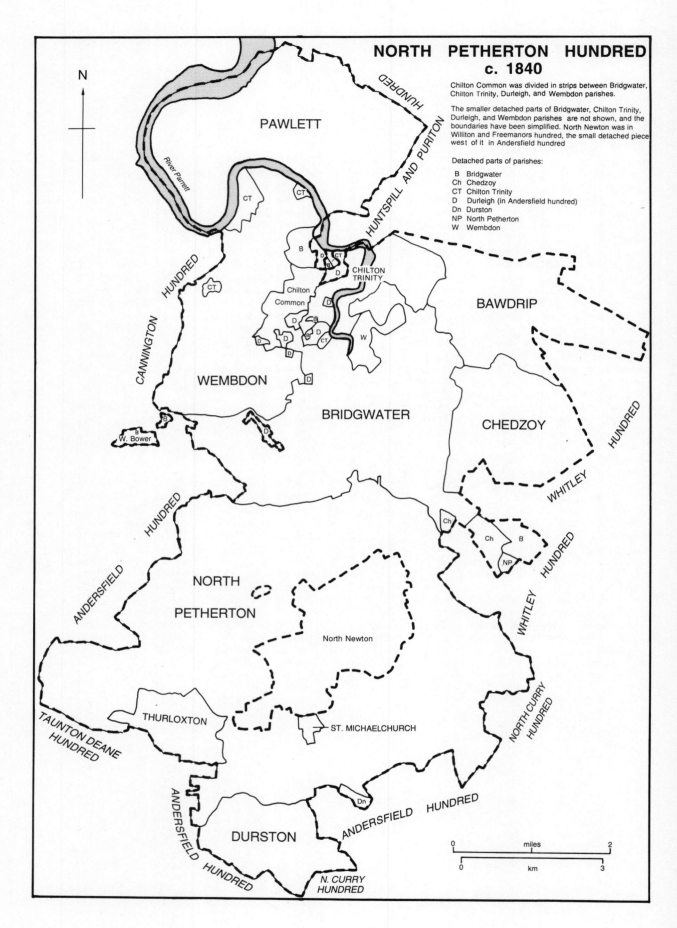

NORTH PETHERTON HUNDRED
c. 1840

Chilton Common was divided in strips between Bridgwater, Chilton Trinity, Durleigh, and Wembdon parishes.

The smaller detached parts of Bridgwater, Chilton Trinity, Durleigh, and Wembdon parishes are not shown, and the boundaries have been simplified. North Newton was in Williton and Freemanors hundred, the small detached piece west of it in Andersfield hundred

Detached parts of parishes:

B Bridgwater
Ch Chedzoy
CT Chilton Trinity
D Durleigh (in Andersfield hundred)
Dn Durston
NP North Petherton
W Wembdon

N

PAWLETT

River Parrett

HUNTSPILL AND PURITON HUNDRED

CANNINGTON HUNDRED

CHILTON TRINITY

Chilton Common

WEMBDON

W. Bower

BRIDGWATER

BAWDRIP

CHEDZOY

WHITLEY HUNDRED

WHITLEY HUNDRED

ANDERSFIELD HUNDRED

NORTH

PETHERTON

North Newton

THURLOXTON

ST. MICHAELCHURCH

NORTH CURRY HUNDRED

TAUNTON DEANE HUNDRED

ANDERSFIELD HUNDRED

ANDERSFIELD HUNDRED

DURSTON

Dn

N. CURRY HUNDRED

| 0 | miles | 2 |
| 0 | km | 3 |

NORTH PETHERTON HUNDRED

A LARGE royal estate at North Petherton constituted in 1084 a hundred assessed at 38 hides, 3 virgates, and ½ ferling.[1] Most of the estate was granted away by the Crown, including the manor of North Petherton, to which the hundred jurisdiction was later attached. Manor and hundred were granted at fee farm by Henry I to John of Erleigh (d. *c.* 1162).[2] Henry I[3] also granted Crandon in Bawdrip at farm, and Adsborough (*Tetteberg*) in Creech St. Michael, Chedzoy, the former grazing farm (*vaccaria*) of the royal estate,[4] Pawlett, and Pignes in Bridgwater in fee. An estate at North Newton, part of the barony of Odburville, came into the hands of the hereditary foresters of Petherton forest or park.[5] By the later 13th century the whole ancient estate was out of the Crown's possession with the exception of Petherton park and residual claims to forest jurisdiction on North moor[6] and until 1298 elsewhere.[7]

North Petherton hundred, which grew out of the former royal estate, was held by the family of John of Erleigh like the manor of North Petherton[8] until 1371 when another John of Erleigh was licensed to alienate the hundred and manor to John and Margery Cole.[9] The hundred continued to be held with the manor and was entailed on John Henry Slade in 1832,[10] but no claims to ownership thereafter have been found.

Adsborough, Chedzoy, Crandon, and Pignes were regarded as part of North Petherton hundred by 1212.[11] By 1284–5 the hundred comprised Bawdrip and its hamlet of Crandon, Chedzoy, Chilton and its hamlet of Pignes, Clayhill in Cannington, Durston, Pawlett and its hamlets of East and West Stretcholt, North Petherton and five hamlets (Huntworth, West Newton, Shearston, Tuckerton, and Woolmersdon), Thurloxton, Wembdon and its hamlets of Perry, Sandford, and Sydenham, and two hamlets of Bridgwater (Dunwear and Horsey).[12] West Bower in Durleigh, Bradney, Crook, Ford, and Wood in Bawdrip, Kidsbury in Wembdon, and Durston were separately named within the hundred in 1303.[13] Lyng, regarded in 1275 as a free manor,[14] and Walpole in Pawlett were included by 1316. So, in the same year, was Bridgwater borough,[15] which in 1275 had been described as a separate hundred.[16]

Durston and Wembdon and the hamlets of Clayhill, Crandon, and Sydenham were omitted from the subsidy return of 1327; Cogload in Durston was recorded as part of the free manor of Halse.[17] Durston was included again in 1334.[18] A holding described as 'Slape and Dunwear' appeared in 1346.[19] One further settlement, 'Yawesye', was added to the hundred by 1432,[20] and by 1498–9 the tithing of Haygrove in Bridgwater.[21]

Settlement changes had produced some reorganization of tithings by 1569 when

[1] *V.C.H. Som.* i. 533.
[2] *Cal. Inq. Misc.* i, p. 321. Wm. of Erleigh was the grantee according to *Rot. Hund.* (Rec. Com.), ii. 140; he, it is implied, received the estate from the *abavus* (*sic* for *atavus*) of Edw. I. See below, N. Petherton, manors.
[3] *Bk. of Fees,* i. 84.
[4] *Rot. Hund.* (Rec. Com.), ii. 140.
[5] Below, N. Petherton, manors.
[6] *Rot. Hund.* (Rec. Com.), ii. 126.
[7] Collinson, *Hist. Som.* iii. 59–60.
[8] Below, N. Petherton, manors.
[9] *Cal. Pat.* 1370–4, 136.
[10] Below, N. Petherton, manors; P.R.O., CP 43/993, rot 24.

[11] *Bk. of Fees,* i. 84–5.
[12] *Feud. Aids,* iv. 277–9.
[13] Ibid. 300–1.
[14] *Rot. Hund.* (Rec. Com.), ii. 126.
[15] *Feud. Aids,* iv. 332.
[16] *Rot. Hund.* (Rec. Com.), ii. 127.
[17] *S.R.S.* iii. 186, 240–4.
[18] *Subsidy of 1334,* ed. R. E. Glasscock, p. 260.
[19] *Feud. Aids,* iv. 361.
[20] S.R.O., DD/SAS NP 15; possibly Yearsey or Yearsley in Pawlett.
[21] B.L. Royal MS. 14 B vii.

the hundred comprised Bawdrip with Bradney, Bridgwater borough with the castle ditch, Chedzoy, Chilton Trinity with Pignes, Dunwear with (East) Bower, Durston, Hamp, Horsey, Huntworth, West Newton, Pawlett with Stretcholt, North Petherton borough with Denizen (later Free Denizen),[22] Shearston, Thurloxton, Tuckerton, Wembdon with Perry and Sandford, Woolmersdon, and an additional tithing of Buckland Fee,[23] representing the former North Petherton lands of the religious house of Buckland.[24] Further modifications were made at least for fiscal purposes in the 17th century: in 1640 Bawdrip included Crandon but not Bradney, and Durston included Cogload;[25] in 1649 Durston and Cogload were joined by St. Michaelchurch, and North Petherton included Moorland Limit while the southern part of Denizen was linked with Town Limit.[26] In both years Haygrove tithing appeared independently of Bridgwater.

Chilton Trinity, Perry, Pignes, Sandford, and Stretcholt were separately represented at the hundred in 1652 but Bower, Bridgwater borough, Buckland Fee, North Petherton borough and Denizen, and Wembdon were omitted,[27] but the tithings of North Petherton with North Newton and of St. Michaelchurch were included in 1742.[28] Parishes and tithings as constituted within the hundred from the mid 18th century for the collection of land tax reflect the expansion of Bridgwater and growing settlements in North Petherton: Bawdrip, Bridgwater (tithings of Borough, West Bower, Dunwear and East Bower, Hamp, Haygrove, and Horsey), Chedzoy, Durston, Pawlett, North Petherton (tithings of Bankland, Buckland Fee, Huntworth, Moorland, West Newton, North Petherton (or Town Denizen), Shearston, Tuckerton, and Woolmersdon), St. Michaelchurch, Thurloxton, and Wembdon (tithings of Pignes, Perry, and Sandford).[29] In 1841 it was recognized that Chilton Trinity, which had been linked with West Bower in the 1760s,[30] also extended into Andersfield and Whitley hundreds,[31] the former in respect of Huntstile.

By the later 13th century a distinction was drawn between the *intrinsecus* or within hundred, also occasionally called the manor,[32] and the *forinsecus* or foreign hundred, at least at the monthly hundred courts. The former embraced the demesne holdings of the Erleighs and their successors in North Petherton and was in practice a manorial court.[33] The latter, its courts held monthly in the later 14th century on the same days as the within courts, evidently had separate records[34] but its profits were received, like those of the within courts, by the bailiff of the manor and hundred.[35] The distinction of business in the two courts was consistently preserved in the surviving records with three exceptions: in 1382 the tithing of Stretcholt was summoned to answer for the concealment of an oak tree regarded as wreck of the sea;[36] in 1397 a man was fined for the theft of peacocks' feathers at Pawlett;[37] and in 1401 Horsey tithing was in mercy for not producing a knife involved in an assault.[38]

In the mid 15th century, and perhaps from the beginning, the law hundreds and sheriffs' tourns embraced the hundred as a single unit, but by the mid 17th century the hundred was divided for fiscal purposes: in 1650 the western division comprised the former within hundred tithings of North Petherton manor, together

[22] S.R.O., DD/SG 58–9.
[24] *Feud. Aids*, iv. 277–9.
[25] S.R.O., DD/SG 58–9.
[26] Ibid. DD/SF 1690.
[27] P.R.O., E 317/Som.3.
[28] *S.R.S.* iii. 302.
[29] S.R.O., Q/REl 29.

[23] *S.R.S.* xx. 127–39.

[30] Ibid.

[31] *S.R.S.* iii. 326–7.
[32] e.g. S.R.O., DD/SAS NP 1, m. 16 (1310–11).
[33] Below, N. Petherton, local govt.
[34] S.R.O., DD/SAS NP 12, m. 7d.
[35] e.g. ibid. 3; 4, m. 1; 5, mm. 1–3.
[36] Ibid. 10, mm. 1, 2.   [37] Ibid. 12, m. 1.
[38] Ibid. 13.

with Buckland Fee, Durston, Hamp, and Thurloxton.[39] Bankland and Moorland were named as additional tithings of the western division by 1766 when the eastern division comprised Chilton, Dunwear with Bower, Horsey, Sandford, Stretcholt, and Wembdon.[40]

Henry of Erleigh (d. 1272) remitted to the prior and convent of Taunton all fines and amercements levied on them or their men of Thurloxton in his hundred court,[41] and Philip of Erleigh (d. c. 1275) claimed strays in his hundred and manor of North Petherton.[42] Strays were taken in the foreign hundred in 1310–11.[43] Thomas Beaupyne and his heirs were in 1398 given wide jurisdiction in the hundred including the return of royal writs, the return of all Exchequer summonses and precepts not affecting royal business, and the collection of taxes.[44]

Henry de Gaunt c. 1243 withdrew suit to the hundred court in respect of Pawlett tithing, but the tithing rendered 32d. as a fine at the sheriff's tourn twice a year.[45] At the Michaelmas law hundred in 1431 the tithings of Chilton Trinity, Dunwear, Horsey, Huntworth, West Newton, Perry, Pignes, Sandford, Shearston, Stretcholt, Thurloxton, Tuckerton, and Woolmersdon each appeared by a tithingman and a varying number of other tenants or posts; Hamp was represented by its tithingman alone and Wembdon and Yearsey by free tenants. Most tithings produced either small cash payments or hens as *centum* or tithing penny; the tithingman of Bawdrip did not come.[46] The same tithings with Chedzoy, Durston, and Pawlett, but without Wembdon and Yearsey, still contributed tithing silver in 1652.[47] Bawdrip, Chedzoy, and Durston were unrepresented at the annual leet and view of frankpledge which by 1766 constituted the sole meeting of the hundred court, and no-one attended for Pignes and Wembdon. The tithingman of Durston, it was stated in 1776, needed separate notification of justices' meetings because he never attended the hundred leet.[48]

The sheriffs' tourns and the hundred leet courts for North Petherton were held with those of the hundreds of Andersfield and Cannington at Lypestone Hill, but by 1652 they were said to be 'much discontinued'.[49] Meetings were usually held on Mondays in late October in the later 18th century with occasional adjournments to early November. The court met in 1775 at the New Inn, North Petherton.[50]

The foreign hundred and the within hundred shared a steward and a bailiff in the Middle Ages,[51] and the two offices continued into the later 18th century.[52] There were two constables by 1626[53] each attached by the 1760s to the division of the hundred and occasionally then called high constables.[54] Two closes, called Ward Leazes, near Petherton park, were in the later 18th century used by the bailiff to keep strays.[55] The lord of the hundred was charged with the repair of two pounds in the former foreign hundred, one at Stretcholt and the other in the tithing of Dunwear and Bower.[56]

39 Ibid. Q/Commonwealth.
40 Ibid. DD/SL 9: court leet 1776.
41 *Cal. Chart. R.* 1327–41, 314.
42 *Rot. Hund.* (Rec. Com.), ii. 140.
43 S.R.O., DD/SAS NP 1, m. 16.
44 *Cal. Chart. R.* 1341–1417, 370–1.
45 *S.R.S.* xi, p. 215; *Rot. Hund.* (Rec. Com.), ii. 128.
46 S.R.O., DD/SAS NP 15, mm. 1 and d., 6d., 7.
47 P.R.O., E 317/Som.3.

48 S.R.O., DD/SL 9.
49 P.R.O., E 317/Som.3.
50 S.R.O., DD/SL 9.
51 e.g. ibid. DD/SAS NP 4, m. 1.
52 Devon R. O. 1936 M/M 5 (1541–2); S.R.O., DD/SL 9.
53 S.R.O., D/B/bw 1960.
54 Ibid. DD/SL 9: presentments 1767, 1769.
55 Ibid. survey c. 1760.
56 Ibid. DD/SLM 2, list of charges 1797.

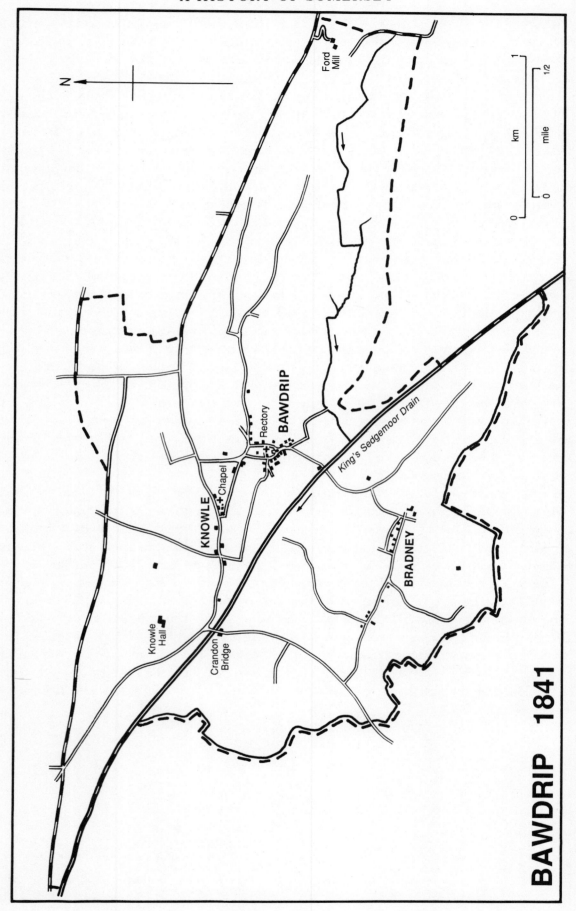

BAWDRIP 1841

BAWDRIP

BAWDRIP parish lies on the south side of the Polden ridge 5 km. north-east from Bridgwater.[1] It stretches for 5 km. along the slope from Dunball in Puriton on the west to Stawell village on the east, and for 2.5 km. from the Polden ridgeway which forms its northern boundary to Chedzoy in the south. The stream which forms its western boundary may have been a tributary of the Parrett; the southern boundary is also a natural watercourse.[2] The parish includes the village of Bawdrip and subsidiary settlements or former settlements at Knowle and Crook to the west, Horsey to the south-west, Bradney and Peasy to the south, and Ford to the east. It covered 768 ha. (1,898 a.) in 1981 before minor changes were made.[3]

Bawdrip village, Knowle, and Ford shelter below the 30-m. contour on marls between alluvium and the Blue Lias of the Polden ridge which rises to over 61 m. above Knowle.[4] There may have been quarrying on the hillside in the 15th century[5] and lias was dug in the early 19th.[6] There were limekilns at Ford in 1840[7] and at Knowle in 1841,[8] and lime was being extracted and processed in the extreme western tip of the parish under Puriton Hill by 1886 and until 1973 in association with the cement works at Dunball.[9] Salt was extracted in the early 20th century.[10] Bradney, Crook, and Peasy, their names implying slight elevations on the flat alluvial moors, are on 'islands' of marl, and Bradney is also partly on an area of Burtle Beds which extends from Chedzoy.[11]

King's Sedgemoor Drain crosses the parish from south-east to north-west, passing between Bawdrip village and Peasy Farm and under Crandon bridge. Completed by 1798 and widened during the late 19th and the 20th century,[12] it followed, at least in part, a 'great drain' which had been made in the late 16th century from the moors to Crandon bridge.[13] That drain, in the 17th century known as Peasy rhyne or Black Ditch, flowed from Great Lake near Parchey in Chedzoy.[14] It was thought to have been part of the Cary river,[15] and the lords of Bradney and Bawdrip paid rent to Castle Cary manor for the 'use' of Cary Water in the 17th and 18th centuries.[16] Below Crandon bridge the river was evidently navigable in the Roman period.[17]

Navigation was proposed in 1829 and the owner of Knowle Hall had a sailing boat for use on it.[18] Other watercourses in the parish include the stream from Stawell through Ford which flows west through Bawdrip Level and was known in the 17th century as Bawdrip Brook.[19]

A Roman road from Ilchester followed the Polden ridge and descended to the river west of Crandon bridge where a port was in use between the 1st and the 4th century A.D.[20] At the bridge, mentioned in 1614,[21] roads from Bristol and Glastonbury to Bridgwater converged and the route from the bridge was causewayed and maintained in the early 17th century jointly by Bridgwater and Bawdrip parishes.[22] The roads were turnpiked in 1730 by the Bridgwater Trust.[23] A new route from Bristol to Bridgwater avoiding Crandon bridge was built in Bridgwater parish in 1822 but the old route was retained and in 1971 was improved to provide access to the M5 motorway.[24]

Just south of the Roman ridge road on the Poldens and east of the present Bawdrip village stood a Romano-British homestead overlying an Iron-Age site; and a site at Bradney was occupied from the Iron Age until the 4th century A.D. A bronze hoard of the 1st century A.D. was discovered, probably near Crandon bridge, in 1800.[25] Bawdrip, Bradney, Crandon, and Crook were centres of estates in the 11th century.[26]

Bawdrip village may have originated as a roadside settlement on a route along the edge of the moors from Crandon to Stawell. In the 19th century most of the cottages there stood along the road, with the church and the remains of a small green to the north. Two lanes east and west of the churchyard led north to more widely spaced farmhouses and yards and to a second east–west route between Knowle and Ford which, as Eastside Lane, was built up in the 17th and in the 18th century.[27] In the 20th century houses were built along the abandoned railway track and within Bawdrip village. Arable fields called west, middle, and east fields, and Furthenfield lay on the slope north of the village, and the first three seem to have been divided by the early 17th century into north and south 'laynes'.[28] Small scattered plots, including two called North and Dock fields, two others called

1 This article was completed in 1988.
2 O.S. Map 1/50,000, sheet 182 (1974 edn.).
3 Census, 1981.
4 Geol. Surv. map 1/50,000, solid and drift, sheet 295 (1984 edn.).
5 S.R.S. lviii, p. 79.
6 S.R.O, DD/SAS (C/238) 19; ibid. tithe award.
7 Ibid. DD/CH 48.
8 Ibid. tithe award; P.R.O., HO 107/1925.
9 O.S. Map 6", Som. L. NE. (1886 edn.); Som. C.C., Sites and Mons. Rec.
10 Below, econ. hist.
11 Geol. Surv. map 1/50,000, solid and drift, sheet 295 (1984 edn.).
12 S.R.O., D/RA 1/5/1, 1/8/1; DD/SG 54–5; M. Williams, Draining of Som. Levels, 219–21, 237.
13 W. Dugdale, Hist. of Imbanking and Draining (1662), 111; S.R.O., T/PH/dst 4/2; DD/DN 163; D/RA 1/8/3.
14 P.R.O., SC 2/198/9; S.R.O., D/RA 1/8/1; map 1685,
in D. G. Chandler, Sedgemoor 1685, between pp. 108 and 109.   15 S.D.N.Q. xxxi. 233–5.
16 S.R.O., DD/CH 47.   17 Below.
18 S.R.O., D/RA 1/8/3; DD/X/LA 11.
19 Devon R.O. 96 M 4/8; S.R.O., DD/SG 54; M. Williams, Draining Som. Levels, 118.
20 Som. C.C., Sites and Mons. Rec.; M5 Research Cttee. reps.; S.D.N.Q. viii. 105–8; Proc. Som. Arch. Soc. cxv. 53–4.
21 S.R.S. xxiii. 110.
22 Ibid. 110, 134, 255–6, 320; S.R.O., Q/SR 19/101, 20/62.
23 S.R.O., DD/SAS (C/2402), 34; J. B. Bentley and B. J. Murless, Som. Roads, i. 23.
24 Bentley and Murless, Som. Roads, i. 22–3.
25 Som. C.C., Sites and Mons. Rec.; S.D.N.Q. viii. 105–8; Proc. Som. Arch. Soc. cxxiv. 121.
26 V.C.H. Som. i. 497, 499, 526.
27 S.R.O., D/P/baw 23/1.
28 Ibid. D/D/Rg 198; P.R.O., LR 3/123.

Middle and Higher furlongs, and several land-shares persisted into the 19th century.[29] Bawdrip tenants had common rights until the mid 16th century[30] in Bawdrip moor, south-east of the village and later known as Bawdrip Level, on marshland between the village and Bradney,[31] and on King's Sedgemoor, where c. 300 a. were used by Bawdrip and Bradney tenants in the 17th century.[32]

Bradney hamlet had about 12 houses in 1841 but in 1988 consisted of a farm and a few cottages built mainly of brick. North field there was mentioned in 1635[33] and Southfield Lane was so named in the later 19th century.[34] The settlement at Crandon may have been replaced by Knowle, first recorded by name in 1567.[35] A house appears to have been built at Crandon between 1430 and 1450 and may have been standing in the early 16th century.[36] Knowle Farm,[37] now called Manor Farmhouse, is an 18th-century house with a Tuscan portico. Houses have been built along the Glastonbury road at Knowle during the 20th century. Crany or Crandon and West Crandon fields were still worked in common in the early 17th century.[38] Crook seems to have been abandoned as a settlement after the 11th century.[39] There was a house at Ford c. 1300,[40] possibly on the site of the later Ford Farm.

In the 20th century a group of houses beside the Bath road on the western edge of the parish has been named Horsey after the farm and former manor to the west in Bridgwater parish.

In 1890 the Bridgwater Railway Co. opened a line between Bridgwater and Edington Burtle to link the town with the Somerset and Dorset line. The track was constructed through the middle of Bawdrip village. A passenger halt was built there in 1923. The line closed in 1954 and at least one house has been built along part of its course in the village.[41]

Two acres of underwood were recorded at Crandon in 1086,[42] and in 1324 the lord of Bradney had a willow copse.[43] Plantations on Knowle Hill to screen the new hall and park accounted for most of the 45 a. of wood in 1841.[44] In 1905 there were 34 a. of woodland.[45]

Three people were presented for breaches of the assize of ale in 1479,[46] two tapsters were recorded in 1538 although only one was licensed in 1543,[47] and an unlicensed ale seller was presented in 1612.[48] There was only one licensed house in the parish, held by one family between 1618 and 1657 and said to be used by travellers on the highway.[49] It was almost certainly the Knowle inn, so named by 1663,[50] part of Bawdrip manor until it was sold to the tenant in 1770. It was then called the Bull but had resumed its old name by 1806.[51] It remained open in 1988.

There was a friendly society at Bawdrip.[52] Horse races were held at Crook in the 19th century.[53]

There were 90 communicants in 1548.[54] The population rose from 244 in 1801 to 372 in 1821, then to a peak of 472 in 1861, falling to 340 in 1891. Numbers remained stable until the 1950s when new housing brought the total to 510 in 1961. There were 504 persons normally resident in 1981.[55]

Fifteen men from Bawdrip were fined for involvement in the rebellion of 1497.[56] The duke of Monmouth's army marched through the parish on the night of 5–6 July 1685, taking a route along Bradney and Marsh lanes and across North moor to Langmoor in Chedzoy before engaging the royal forces.[57]

MANORS AND OTHER ESTATES. *BAWDRIP* was held by Renewald from Walter of Douai in 1086; Merlesuain had held it in 1066.[58] It was held as of Castle Cary until the 16th century or later.[59] During the 17th and 18th centuries 4s. 8d., half collected from Bradney manor, was paid to the lords of Castle Cary for Cary Water. The last recorded payment was in 1776.[60]

Robert of Bawdrip held ½ knight's fee in 1166 and was succeeded by William (fl. 1194–1212)[61] whose son Robert married before 1227.[62] Gerard, probably Robert's son, succeeded between 1242[63] and 1249[64] and was followed before c. 1280[65] by his son Sir Adam of Bawdrip (d. c. 1296). William Martin, guardian of Adam's son John, was returned as holding the manor in 1303.[66] John was apparently of age by 1316.[67] He was dead by 1333 when Joan, probably his widow, held Bawdrip with her second husband John Durburgh.[68] In 1351 John, son of Hugh of Bawdrip, gave the manor to his mother Orange in dower.[69] Orange married John Cadehay before 1355 and assigned her dower to John

29 S.R.O., tithe award.
30 P.R.O., SC 2/198/6; *Cat. Anct. D.* v, A 12677.
31 S.R.O., DD/SAS (C/432) 2.
32 Ibid. D/RA 1/8/3.
33 Devon R.O. 96 M 4/8.
34 O.S. Map 6", Som. L. NE. (1886 edn.).
35 P.R.O., C 3/217, no. 49.
36 Ibid. C 139/64, no. 35; C 139/137, no. 14; ibid. STAC 2/30/132.
37 S.R.O., DD/X/MDX 4.
38 Ibid. D/D/Rg 198.
39 *Proc. Som. Arch. Soc.* cxxix. 9–10; M.V.R.G. *33rd Ann. Rep.* 12–13.
40 Pole MS. 1080.
41 J. B. Bentley and B. J. Murless, *Som. Roads*, i. 24; R. Atthill, *Som. and Dorset Rly.* 110; S.R.O., DD/CH 43.
42 *V.C.H. Som.* i. 526.
43 *Cal. Inq. p.m.* vi, p. 290.
44 S.R.O., tithe award.
45 Statistics supplied by the then Bd. of Agric. 1905.
46 P.R.O., SC 2/198/2.
47 Ibid. LR 3/123.
48 B.L. Add. MS. 15561; S.R.O., Q/RL.
49 S.R.O., Q/RL; Q/RLa 33; *S.R.S.* xxviii. 5.
50 S.R.O., Q/SR 104/42.
51 Ibid. DD/CH 47; ibid. Q/RL.
52 M. Fuller, *W. Country Friendly Socs.* 144.
53 Below, Bridgwater, intro.   54 *S.R.S.* ii. 64.
55 *Census.*
56 *Fines Imposed in 1497*, ed. A. J. Howard, 27.
57 Lamb. Pal. Libr., MS. 942/34; *S.D.N.Q.* xxviii. 17.
58 *V.C.H. Som.* i. 499.
59 Sanders, *Eng. Baronies*, 27–8; *V.C.H. Som.* iv. 134; P.R.O., C 142/249, no. 81.
60 S.R.O., DD/CH 47.
61 *Rot. Cur. Reg.* (Rec. Com.), i. 131; *Cur. Reg. R.* vi. 261.
62 Devon R.O. 96 M 83/6; *S.R.S.* vi. 64.
63 *Bk. of Fees*, ii. 752.
64 *S.R.S.* vi. 371–2.
65 B.L. Add. Ch. 74822; *S.R.S.* iii. 10; lxviii, p. 53.
66 *Cal. Pat.* 1292–1301, 187; *Cal. Inq. p.m.* iii, p. 434; *Feud. Aids*, iv. 300.
67 *S.R.S.* iii. 74.   68 Ibid. ix, p. 141.
69 Deed in possession of Mr. J. S. Cox, Guernsey.

Osborn in return for an annuity.[70] John of Bawdrip granted the reversion to Sir John of Combe in 1359, probably as security for debt, himself retaining a life tenancy. Sir John (d. 1362) left an infant son John and John of Bawdrip tried to regain the manor, but in 1371 the sheriff delivered it to Margaret, Sir John's widow, until the debt should be paid.[71] In 1372 John of Combe came of age and did fealty for two thirds of Bawdrip.[72] He probably died childless, with the debt unpaid, and in 1403 Margaret and her second husband Thomas Beaupyne settled Bawdrip on their daughter Margaret, wife of William Wroughton.[73]

William died in 1408 and his widow married John Blacket who held her estate after her death c. 1421.[74] William's son John (d. 1429) left the manor to his brothers William and Edward Wroughton during his son John's minority.[75] John (d. 1496) left a son Christopher (d. 1515) who was succeeded by his grandson[76] (Sir) William Wroughton (d. 1559). Sir William's son Sir Thomas (d. 1597) settled Bawdrip on his second son Giles for his marriage to Lady Catherine Poulett.[77] Giles and Catherine mortgaged the manor in 1602 to Henry Long and probably forfeited it. Between 1607 and 1622 possession was disputed by Long and the Horton family.[78] Henry Long (d. 1612) was succeeded by his son Henry[79] who died c. 1621 when Walter Long, probably his brother, held Bawdrip.[80] In 1634 Walter sold it to Sir Samuel Rolle, his brother Henry Rolle, and their brother-in-law Hugh Fortescue,[81] who held jointly until Samuel's death in 1647.[82] Henry (d. 1656) was followed in the direct male line by Francis (d. c. 1686),[83] Henry (d. c. 1692), and Francis (d. s.p. 1709).[84] Francis was succeeded by John Rolle (d. c. 1726), possibly his brother,[85] Samuel Rolle (d. 1729),[86] and Samuel's brother John (d. 1730) in turn. John settled Bawdrip in succession on his younger sons John, William (d. by 1742), and Denis, of whom John, who took the surname Walter, held the manor. Bawdrip passed to Denis, probably when John succeeded to the estates of his eldest brother Henry (d. 1750).[87] Between 1769 and 1771 the Bawdrip estate was broken up,[88] the lordship and remaining lands being sold to Mary Jeffreys in 1771.[89] Mary (d. 1785) was succeeded at Bawdrip by Jeffreys Allen (d. 1844), son of her sister Ann and Benjamin Allen (d. 1791),[90] and by his son

William (d. 1882). William's son Jeffreys Charles Allen-Jeffreys dismembered his estate for sale in 1903 but was called lord of the manor until 1910.[91] Francis Brake of Knowle Hall styled himself lord of the manor in the 1920s and 1930s[92] but lordship was not recorded thereafter.

Bawdrip Farm, later known as Court Farm,[93] and in 1988 Tudor Court Farm, has an L-shaped plan made up of a two-roomed eastern arm of the early 16th century[94] with a 17th-century kitchen block to the west. The 16th-century building is of high quality, both ground-floor rooms having framed ceilings of nine panels. Several areas of figurative and decorative painted plaster survive, and it may have been built as a parlour wing to an older hall on the site occupied by the later kitchen. Rooms were made in the attics in the 17th century and a single-storeyed dairy was added to the kitchen in the 18th or early 19th century. The house has been extensively restored since 1983.

Alnod the reeve held *BRADNEY* in 1066 but in 1086 it was held like Bawdrip by Renewald from Walter of Douai,[95] and was probably merged with the main estate. In 1573 it was said to be held of Bawdrip manor.[96]

In 1292 Matthew of Bradney bought land in Bradney from William Goathurst[97] and in 1303 it was held by Anthony of Bradney (d. c. 1321), canon of Wells and rector of Bawdrip,[98] who was succeeded by Joachim of Bradney (d. 1324) and his son Simon (d. 1375).[99] Simon had no children and his wife Beatrice is said to have granted what was then described as a manor to Sir John Beaumont (d. 1380), who held it jointly with his wife Joan.[1] She was dead probably by 1431 when Thomas Beaumont, Sir John's grandson, held the manor.[2] Thomas (d. 1451) also held Elworthy manor, with which Bradney descended to Thomas Muttlebury,[3] the lord in 1634. Thomas Muttlebury (d. 1652) retained Bradney, which passed from his son Thomas to another Thomas Muttlebury (fl. 1705), probably grandson of Thomas (d. 1652), and to John Muttlebury who settled the manor in trust to raise money for his four daughters before 1712.[4] In 1725 Bradney was in the possession of Harry Brydges (d. 1728); he was succeeded by his daughters Anna, who married William Ledwell before 1769, and Elizabeth, who married Thomas Hughes before 1765 and sold her share

70 *Cat. Anct. D.* ii, B 3469.
71 *V.C.H. Som.* v. 44–5; *Cal. Inq. p.m.* xiii, p. 75; *Abbrev. Rot. Orig.* (Rec. Com.), ii. 319; *Cal. Fine R.* 1369–77, 160.
72 *Cal. Close,* 1369–74, 367.
73 Ibid. 1402–5, 346; *S.R.S.* xxii. 13.
74 *Cal. Close,* 1405–9, 425–6; 1419–22, 144; *Cal. Fine R.* 1413–22, 386–7; P.R.O., C 137/74, no. 50.
75 P.R.O., C 139/42, no. 85.
76 *Cal. Inq. p.m. Hen. VII,* ii, pp. 15–16; P.R.O., C 142/30, nos. 119, 148.
77 *V.C.H. Wilts.* ix. 32; P.R.O., CP 25(2)/261/31 Eliz. I East.; ibid. C 142/249, no. 81.
78 Hants R.O. 44M69/L 17/81; B.L. Add. MS. 15561; Add. Ch. 55399.
79 P.R.O., C 142/331, no. 111.
80 Ibid. CP 25(2)/387/19 Jas. I Hil.
81 B.L. Add. Ch. 9282.
82 Devon R.O. 96 M 4/8; *Som. Wills,* ed. Brown, i. 84.
83 Hants R.O. 5M58/80; *D.N.B.*; *Som. Wills,* ed. Brown, i. 84.

84 Devon R.O. 96 M 4/6; S.R.O., DD/CH 46–7; D/P/shap 2/1/1.
85 Hants R.O. 5M58/82; S.R.O., DD/CH 45–6.
86 S.R.O., D/P/shap 2/1/1; DD/CH 46.
87 Ibid. DD/CH 47; DD/SF 70; Hants R.O. 5M58/94.
88 S.R.O., DD/CH 47–8.   89 Ibid. DD/X/EDS 2.
90 Ibid. DD/CH 47–8; ibid. tithe award.
91 Ibid. DD/CH 48, 97/6; *Kelly's Dir. Som.* (1910).
92 *Kelly's Dir. Som.* (1923, 1939).
93 S.R.O., DD/CH 46–7, 97/6.
94 The date 1532 is on an internal partition.
95 *V.C.H. Som.* i. 499.
96 P.R.O., C 142/165, no. 155.
97 *S.R.S.* vi. 287.
98 *Feud. Aids,* iv. 300; *Cal. Fine R.* 1319–27, 82; below, church.
99 *Cal. Inq. p.m.* vi, p. 290; *S.R.S.* lxi, p. 55.
1 P.R.O., C 139/28, no. 22; *Cal. Inq. p.m.* xv, p. 84.
2 *Feud. Aids,* iv. 434.
3 *V.C.H. Som.* v. 70; P.R.O., C 142/165, no. 155.
4 P.R.O., CP 25(2)/961/4 Anne Trin.; ibid. C 111/20.

probably in trust for her sister. Anna held Bradney until 1792.[5] The manor was purchased c. 1793 by Joseph Bradney but lordship was not recorded after the late 1790s.[6] Joseph was followed by his second son the Revd. Joseph (d. 1868),[7] whose son Joseph sold the estate c. 1919 when it was broken up.[8]

A capital messuage, recorded in 1324,[9] may have been Bradney Farm which included a large 'gothic' window but was burnt down in the 1890s.[10]

Aldred held *CRANDON* in 1066 and 1086.[11] Probably as a member of North Petherton it escheated to the Crown in the time of Henry I, and was given to Fulk de Alneto.[12] The Crown received 6s. 8d. for Crandon until 1317 or later.[13] By 1342 the Columbers family held a mesne tenancy[14] which descended with Stockland Lovel until 1481 or later.[15] The manor may have been granted to Robert Pokerel (fl. 1166),[16] and it descended, probably after the death of Robert's widow Constance, to their son Richard Pokerel who died before 1201. Richard's heirs were his sisters Sabina, wife of Hugh of Greinton, Rose, wife of Thomas le Border, and Amabel, wife of William of Walton, and John la Stock, husband or son of a deceased sister, Constance.[17] Eve, possibly Sabina's daughter, married Hugh Trivet (d. by 1242) before 1219.[18] Hugh left a son James,[19] but by 1242 Sabina's quarter share of Crandon had passed to Ralph Trivet, who granted it for her life to Eve, possibly daughter of Hugh Trivet and Eve, and her husband Ralph Huse.[20] Ralph had been succeeded by Thomas Trivet by 1253.[21] Peter le Border, possibly Rose's son, exchanged lands in Crandon, presumably the second share, with Adam le Ireys in 1235. Adam let his estate for a pair of white gloves[22] and the same rent was demanded by John de la Stock when he granted land in Crandon, probably Constance's quarter, to Robert of Bawdrip.[23] Robert's estate probably descended as part of Bawdrip manor.[24] Amabel Walton gave the fourth share to her son John but it later came to Amabel, widow of Jordan de Barnage, who sold her lands in 1263 to Thomas Trivet.[25] Thomas of Crandon sold an estate, possibly Peter le Border's share, to Thomas Trivet before 1253.[26]

Thomas Trivet died c. 1281 in possession of three of the four parts of the manor, though in 1272 and 1280 Hugh Trivet, perhaps his uncle, held them of him.[27] Thomas's son William in 1303 settled Crandon on his son William,[28] whose son Thomas died in 1316. Thomas's posthumous son John was granted free warren at Crandon in 1354.[29] John's son Thomas died in 1388 leaving a widow Elizabeth,[30] who granted Crandon during her life to her husband's cousin John Trivet.[31] In 1428 Catherine Trivet, probably an error for Elizabeth, was said to hold Crandon; Elizabeth died in possession in 1433 when her heir was John Trivet.[32] Alexander Hody, Robert Corffy, and Hugh Kene, possibly John's trustees, gave an estate in Crandon to William Stafford (d. 1450).[33] William's son Humphrey, earl of Devon (d. 1469), held the manor. Humphrey's heirs were his cousins Elizabeth and Anne Cheney and their half-sister, Eleanor Talboys.[34] Crandon passed before 1506 to Anne's son Robert, Baron Willoughby de Broke, who in 1530 settled the manor on his mistress Joan Pye with remainder to their son George Willoughby. Joan surrendered her interest to George (d. 1550),[35] whose son Henry conveyed the manor in 1575 to feoffees for sale to Robert Blake (d. 1592).[36] In 1593 Robert's elder son William conveyed the manor, called Crandon with Puriton, to his brother Humphrey.[37] Humphrey (d. 1625) was succeeded in turn by his sons Robert (d. 1657) and Humphrey.[38] Humphrey sold part of the land to his brother Nicholas who had been Robert's tenant.[39] The lordship was bought by their brother Benjamin Blake in 1669.[40] In 1674 Benjamin sold the manor to George Powell[41] who conveyed it to John Doble in 1682.[42] Doble was in possession in 1693[43] but by 1712 Crandon was held by George Brydges and his son George[44] possibly in trust for Harry (d. 1728), the elder George's brother. Harry's male heir was his nephew George (d. 1751)[45] and the manor descended in the family with the dukedom of Chandos probably until the death of Richard, duke of Buckingham and Chandos, in 1829. In 1843 the lordship was vested in trustees, possibly for sale,[46] but it was not recorded again.

The manor lands were acquired by Benjamin Allen (d. 1791) but in 1788 the estate was put up for sale by order of the Exchequer.[47] Knowle

5 S.R.O., DD/CH 47; P.R.O., CP 25(2)/1198/33 Geo. II East.; CP 25(2)/1397/5 Geo. III East.
6 S.R.O., D/RA 1/8/3; ibid. Q/REl 29/1.
7 Ibid. tithe award; *Alum. Cantab.* 1752–1900.
8 S.R.O., DD/DHR 43; *Som. Co. Herald*, 13 Apr. 1929.
9 *Cal. Inq. p.m.* vi, p. 290.
10 S.R.O., D/P/baw 23/1.
11 *V.C.H. Som.* i. 526.
12 *Bk. of Fees*, i. 84; ii. 1384–5.
13 Ibid. i. 84; *Cal. Close*, 1313–18, 404.
14 *Cal. Inq. p.m.* viii, p. 268.
15 Above, Spaxton, manors; *Cal. Inq. p.m.* xvi, p. 433; xviii, p. 155; *L. & P. Hen. VIII*, v, pp. 450–1.
16 *Red Bk. Exch.* (Rolls Ser.), i. 221.
17 *S.R.S.* vi. 20; xi, p. 6; *Cal. Fine R.* 1272–1307, 131.
18 *S.R.S.* vi. 112; viii, p. 154; xiv, pp. 185–6; lxiii, p. 382; *Bk. of Fees*, i. 262.
19 *S.R.S.* viii, p. 154; xxvi. 74.
20 Ibid. vi. 112; xi, p. 301.
21 Ibid. xi, p. 423.
22 Ibid. vi. 93.
23 Devon R.O. 96 M 83/6.
24 Above.

25 B.L. Add. Ch. 62218; *S.R.S.* vi. 203.
26 *S.R.S.* xi, pp. 423–4.
27 Ibid. iii. 10; xxxvi. 178; xliv. 267; *Cal. Inq. p.m.* ii, p. 238.
28 *S.R.S.* vi. 324; *Feud. Aids*, iv. 300.
29 Pole MS. 2506; *Cal. Chart. R.* 1341–1417, 133.
30 *Proc. Som. Arch. Soc.* xxviii, p. 214.
31 *Cal. Close*, 1419–22, 234.
32 *Feud. Aids*, iv. 364; P.R.O., C 139/64, no. 35.
33 P.R.O., C 139/137, no. 14.
34 Ibid. C 140/32, no. 30.
35 Ibid. CP 40/977, m. 142; ibid. C 142/97, no. 110.
36 Ibid. C 3/217, no. 49; C 142/236, no. 56.
37 Ibid. CP 25(2)/207/35 Eliz. I East.
38 Ibid. C 142/422, no. 18; *D.N.B.*; *Cal. S. P. Dom.* 1670, 686.
39 *S.D.N.Q.* vi. 226.
40 P.R.O., CP 25(2)/716/21 Chas. II Mich.
41 Ibid. CP 25(2)/717/26 Chas. II Trin.; *S.D.N.Q.* vi. 250.
42 P.R.O., CP 25(2)/718/34 Chas. II Mich.
43 S.R.O., DD/CH 81/4.
44 P.R.O., CP 25(2)/962/11 Anne Mich.
45 S.R.O., DD/CH 47; *Hist. Parl., Commons*, 1715–54, i. 499.
46 S.R.O., DD/BR/wa 3.
47 Ibid. DD/CH 47.

farm remained in the Allen family and descended with Bawdrip manor until it was sold in 1910.[48] The other farm on the estate in Bawdrip parish, Knowle Hill, with further land was bought by George Templar who sold it between 1796 and 1805[49] mainly to Benjamin Barker (d. 1805), the tenant at Knowle Hill. Barker left his estates to his daughter Ann, wife of William Smark.[50] In 1830–1 Knowle was acquired by Benjamin Greenhill,[51] already owner of Puriton and Downend manor, including land in Bawdrip.[52] Benjamin was succeeded in 1881 by his son Benjamin (d. 1884), whose brother Pelham Spencer Greenhill (d. 1916) succeeded at Knowle. Pelham's son, also Pelham, died two months later. His trustees sold part of the estate in 1921 but the Hall was retained by the family until 1959 and remaining lands descended to the younger Pelham's son Benjamin, the owner in 1988.[53]

Knowle Hall, a two-storeyed house with attics and basement, was built in Tudor style in the 1830s.[54] It was let until c. 1861 when the Greenhill family took up residence.[55] By 1886 a large park had been established around the house.[56] Knowle Tower was part of a large sham castle, since demolished, built for Benjamin Greenhill in 1870.[57] In the 20th century the house was let, first to private tenants, as a hotel by 1939,[58] and as a school from the 1950s. The St. Andrew's school education trust bought the house in 1959.[59] Since 1976 the hall has been occupied by the Institute for Brain Injured Children.[60]

In 1066 Edward held *CROOK* and in 1086 Rademer held it of Walter of Douai,[61] from whom the descent of the overlordship is obscure, John Horsey being named as overlord c. 1280[62] and William of Pawlett in 1303.[63] From the 15th century Crook was held of the lords of Puriton manor.[64]

William of Crook may have been the tenant in 1166[65] and Nicholas of Crook was recorded in the early 13th century.[66] Thomas Trivet (d. c. 1281) held it[67] and Crook descended with Cran- don until 1388.[68] By 1428 Crook had passed to Humphrey Courtenay (d. 1456)[69] possibly in right of his wife Joan. In 1461 Joan settled her estate in trust for Henry, brother of Thomas Courtenay, earl of Devon (d. 1461).[70] Henry was attainted and executed in 1467 and Crook, like Wrenmore in Spaxton, was granted in 1470 to John Lambard who held it in 1484.[71] It may have been restored to the Courtenays like Wrenmore, and by 1546 it belonged to Sir Thomas Moyle (d. 1560)[72] whose daughter Katharine, wife of Sir Thomas Finch, sold it with Puriton manor in 1561 to John Kaynes of Compton Paunce- foot.[73] In 1576 Kaynes sold Crook to William Lottisham (d. c. 1576) whose son Hugh (d. 1598) was succeeded by his cousin Oliver Lottisham.[74] Oliver (d. c. 1620)[75] was followed by his son William (d. 1635)[76] and by William's son Oliver (d. 1651).[77] Oliver's widow Mary, who married Henry Bull, released Crook to Oliver's sister and heir Elizabeth, wife of Edward Clarke, in 1660.[78] Elizabeth predeceased her husband in 1667 without issue and, under the terms of a settle- ment, Crook passed in 1675 on his marriage to Edward Clarke, Edward's son by a former mar- riage. Edward (d. 1710) was succeeded by his son Jepp (d. 1741).[79] Jepp's son Edward was in possession in 1778.[80] In 1841 Crook was owned by James Chapple.[81] By 1856 it had been ac- quired by Mrs. Greenhill of Knowle, mother or wife of Benjamin (d. 1881), and it descended with Knowle.[82] There is no record of a manor house.

FORD was in the same overlordship as Baw- drip in 1303[83] but between 1508[84] and 1650 it was held as of Bawdrip manor.[85] Adam de la Ford held Ford in 1303.[86] He or another Adam (d. c. 1325) was followed by his widow Christian (d. c. 1329) and his son Adam. Adam and Henry de la Ford, probably his brother, may have died childless before 1346.[87] Ford passed to the Brent family through the marriage of Robert Brent c. 1303 to Clarice, probably daughter of Adam de la Ford (d. c. 1325).[88] Clarice's son Robert Brent (fl. 1330–3)[89] was said to have died in 1351 and to have been followed by his son John (d. by 1373)[90] and grandson John Brent (d. c. 1413).[91] Robert (d. 1421), son of the last, left a sister Joan, wife of John Trethek.[92] In 1434–5 Joan's half brother John Brent confirmed Trethek's estate for life in Ford manor. Joan had no children and John Brent's son Robert (d. 1508) inherited.[93] Robert was followed in the direct male line by John (d. 1524), William (d. 1536),[94] and Richard

48 Ibid. 97/6.
49 Ibid. D/RA 1/8/3; ibid. Q/REl 29/1.
50 Ibid. DD/ED 1.   51 Ibid. Q/REl 29/1.
52 Ibid. DD/FS 36.
53 Ibid. DD/X/HUD 20; inf. from Mrs. Carolanne Hudson, Claverdon (Warws.).
54 S.R.O., DD/X/LA 11.
55 P.R.O., RG 9/1628; RG 11/2377.
56 O.S. Map 6", Som. L. NE. (1886 edn.).
57 S.R.O., D/P/baw 23/1; O.S. Map 6", Som. L. NE. (1886 edn.).
58 *Kelly's Dir. Som.* (1906, 1923, 1931, 1939).
59 S.R.O., DD/X/HUD 20.
60 *Bridgwater Mercury,* 9 Apr. 1986.
61 *V.C.H. Som.* i. 497.
62 *Cal. Inq. p.m.* ii, p. 238.
63 *Feud. Aids,* iv. 300.
64 P.R.O., C 140/1, no. 8; S.R.O., DD/SF 2955.
65 *Red Bk. Exch.* (Rolls Ser.), i. 234.
66 *S.R.S.* xi, p. 68.
67 *Cal. Inq. p.m.* ii, p. 238; *Cal. Fine R.* 1272–1307, 144.
68 Above (this section).
69 *Feud. Aids,* iv. 364, 434; P.R.O., C 139/167, no. 14.
70 P.R.O., C 140/1, no. 8.

71 *Cal. Pat.* 1467–77, 187; *Cal. Close,* 1476–85, 395; above, Spaxton.   72 S.R.O., DD/SF 867; *D.N.B.*
73 S.R.O., DD/SF 1026.
74 Ibid. 4032; *Cal. Pat.* 1575–8, 155; *Som. Wills,* ed. Brown, i. 16.
75 S.R.O., DD/SF 2945, 3135.   76 Ibid. 976.
77 Ibid. 4032; *Som. Wills,* ed. Brown, v. 50.
78 S.R.O., DD/SF 2946.
79 Ibid. 801, 4032; *Som. Wills,* ed. Brown, iii. 33, 35.
80 S.R.O., DD/SF 2960.
81 Ibid. tithe award.
82 Ibid. DD/SAS PR 66; D/P/baw 13/1/2.
83 *Feud. Aids,* iv. 300.
84 *Cal. Inq. p.m. Hen. VII,* iii, p. 310.
85 S.R.O., DD/CH 47.   86 *Feud. Aids,* iv. 300.
87 Ibid. iv. 344; *S.R.S.* xii. 190, 203; S.R.O., DD/AH 65/11.
88 Collinson, *Hist. Som.* iii. 91, 435.
89 Pole MS. 524, 529; *S.R.S.* lvii. 28; lx:ii, 334–5.
90 Collinson, *Hist. Som.* iii. 435; *Cal. Pat.* 1370–4, 287.
91 *Cal. Fine R.* 1405–13, 248.
92 Pole MS. 524–5, 529; P.R.O., C 138/56, no. 25; *S.R.S.* xxii. 181.
93 *Cal. Inq. p.m. Hen. VII,* iii, pp. 309–10.
94 *Som. Wills,* ed. Brown, i. 52; P.R.O., C 142/59, no. 7.

(d. 1570).[95] In 1552 Richard was declared an idiot, having settled Ford on the intended marriage of his infant daughter Anne with Robert Broughton.[96] The marriage did not take place and in 1564 Anne married Thomas Paulet (d. 1586).[97] Ford passed, after Thomas's death, to Anne's daughter Elizabeth who married Giles Hoby[98] and, after 1589,[99] to John Brent (d. 1614). John was succeeded by his son John, born in 1612,[1] who died without issue in 1692 leaving his widow Mary in possession.[2] His kinsman and heir, John Hodges (d. 1696), left the reversion to his wife Elizabeth.[3] After Mary Brent's death in 1703 Elizabeth Hodges sold the manor to Robert West[4] who was followed by Samuel West (d. c. 1756) and Mrs. West, probably Samuel's widow, who held it in 1767.[5] Benjamin Allen bought Ford before 1776 and in 1779 sold it to the Quaker philanthropist Richard Reynolds (d. 1816). Richard's daughter Hannah, widow of William Rathbone,[6] settled the manor in 1826 on her son Richard Rathbone who in 1840 sold it to Thomas Short. In 1843 Thomas conveyed part of Ford to Anna Gatcombe[7] and the remainder to John Hopkins who mortgaged the manor in 1849 and 1852.[8] The lordship was not recorded again but after 1856 Ford farm was sold to the Revd. Joseph Bradney and held with Bradney.[9]

Adam de la Ford had a dwelling at Ford c. 1300,[10] described as a manor house or court in 1326 and 1330.[11] It was probably on the site of Ford Farm which dates from the late 18th or the early 19th century and has a two-storeyed, three-bayed front of coursed lias.

In the early 13th century Robert of Bawdrip granted William Wood (de bosco) a house and land, formerly held by Emme Wood and adjoining William's own house. William granted lands in WOOD in the manors of Bawdrip and Stawell in free marriage with his daughter Joan to Geoffrey of Kitnor. Joan and Geoffrey settled Wood on their son William[12] who granted it to Adam de la Ford, his wife Isabel, and son Henry in 1301.[13] Adam held Wood with Ford in 1303.[14] Wood was not recorded again and was probably absorbed into Ford manor.

ECONOMIC HISTORY. There was land for 11 ploughteams on the four estates of Bawdrip, Bradney, Crandon, and Crook in 1086.[15] Bawdrip, the largest, had a small demesne arable farm for 1 ploughteam and the tenants, numbering 21, had 5 teams for a similar area. There were 100 a. of meadow and 40 a. of pasture. Bradney had 1 team for its 3-virgate demesne and the 7 tenants had 1½ team for their virgate. There were 25 a. of meadow.[16] Crandon was entirely a demesne holding with ½ team and small amounts of meadow and underwood.[17] Crook, assessed at 1 ploughland, had a team on its ½ virgate demesne; the 4 bordars had no team but ½ virgate. No other land was recorded.[18]

By the later 13th century the marshland pastures included 400 a. at Crandon.[19] In 1480 there were complaints against outsiders for pasturing on Bawdrip moor[20] and there was a long-running dispute between the tenants of Bawdrip and Bradney manors over the common land along the causeway between Crandon bridge and Bridgwater.[21] Inclosure of common arable began near Ford c. 1520[22] but was elsewhere evidently piecemeal, and there were still traces of open arable strips above Bawdrip village in the early 19th century.[23]

'Grypes' or baulks were ordered to be built at the ends of furlongs in the open arable fields in 1558[24] and part of a field boundary beside a brook was to be hedged, ditched, and planted in 1611.[25] Tenants let cattle into the common fields before harvest and successive rectors were reminded by the manor court in 1589 that only 20 sheep might be commoned there,[26] and in 1611 that the fold should have been removed from the corn field before Easter.[27]

Some holdings were amalgamated in the 17th century and in 1650 at least five houses were said to have been lost and their lands let with other tenements.[28] Following the sale of the Bawdrip estate c. 1770 the land was improved and although there were few holdings over 50 a. in the later 18th century there were at least nine by 1836 including two over 150 a.[29] About 130 a. of grassland remaining in common in that part of King's Sedgemoor in Bawdrip parish were allotted in 1795.[30] Agriculture employed 67 out of 79 families in 1821.[31] By 1841 there were only 449 a. of arable, 1,195 a. of meadow and pasture, and 60 a. of orchards. A modus for milk as well as for meadow suggests that dairying had been long established. The largest farm was well over 200 a. in extent and there were six over 100 a., but there were still 18 holdings under 25 a.[32] Three farms measured over 200 a. by 1861 and the five largest farms between them employed

95 P.R.O., C 142/156, no. 14.
96 Ibid. C 142/96, no. 63.
97 Ibid. C 142/156, no. 14; ibid. SC 2/198/7.
98 Ibid. C 142/215, no. 245.
99 Ibid. SC 2/198/8.
1   S.R.S. lxvii, p. 90.
2   S.R.O., DD/BR/py 13; DD/X/STR 1; D/P/coss 2/1/1.
3   Som. Wills, ed. Brown, iii. 69.
4   S.R.O., D/P/coss 2/1/1; DD/BR/py 13.
5   Ibid. DD/CH 48; ibid. Q/REl 29/1.
6   D.N.B.; S.R.O., DD/CH 48; ibid. Q/REl 29/1; ibid. transcript file 2/64.
7   S.R.O., DD/CH 48.
8   Ibid. DD/BR/en 4.
9   Ibid. DD/SAS PR 66; D/P/baw 13/1/2.
10 Pole MS. 1080.
11 S.R.S. i. 276; ix, p. 373.
12 S.R.O., DD/AH 65/11.
13 Pole MS. 1080.
14 Feud. Aids, iv. 300.
15 V.C.H. Som. i. 497, 499, 526.
16 Ibid. 499.
17 Ibid. 526.
18 Ibid. 497.
19 S.R.S. xliv. 267.
20 P.R.O., SC 2/198/2.
21 Ibid. 5, 8–9; ibid. LR 3/123.
22 Ibid. LR 3/123.
23 S.R.O., tithe award.
24 P.R.O., SC 2/198/4.
25 Ibid. 9.
26 Ibid. 8–9.
27 B.L. Add. MS. 15561, f. 115.
28 S.R.O., DD/CH 47.
29 Ibid.; DD/SAS PR 65.
30 Ibid. DD/CH 47; D/RA 1/8/1, 3.
31 Census.
32 S.R.O., tithe award.

34 labourers.[33] By 1905 the area of arable had been reduced to 347 a. and grass had correspondingly increased.[34] A return covering about two thirds of the parish in 1982 showed only 65 ha. (161 a.) of arable, mainly growing wheat but also barley, potatoes, beet, and mangolds. Half the ten holdings returned were under 20 ha. (50 a.) and only one was over 100 ha. (248 a.).[35]

There was a glover in 1610[36] and a Bawdrip man was trading in malt through Bridgwater in 1612.[37] In the early 19th century a merchant living in Bawdrip owned a Bridgwater-based schooner.[38] A lime works was established by 1886 in the extreme western tip of the parish adjoining the Downend cement works[39] and it remained in use until 1973.[40] Borings for coal, begun in 1909, produced instead a quantity of brine which was processed in a plant built by C. W. M. Greenhill in 1911 as table and industrial salt. In 1914 the business was sold to Salt Union Ltd. which continued working until the 1920s.[41]

There were mills at Bawdrip and Crandon in 1086[42] and in the early 13th century William of Bawdrip granted Robert de la Ford liberty of milling in any of his mills, water or wind.[43] There was a windmill on Bradney manor in 1324[44] and another at Bawdrip in 1552.[45] The latter was recorded in 1650 but had been dismantled by 1685.[46] It stood in East field south of the Glastonbury road, probably on land called Moat in 1841.[47]

Ford watermill was recorded in 1553[48] but may be much earlier; William atte Mill witnessed a deed of land at Ford in 1338.[49] In 1634 it was described as two water grist mills.[50] It went out of use after 1861.[51]

LOCAL GOVERNMENT. In the Middle Ages the parish formed a single tithing,[52] for fiscal purposes later sometimes called Bawdrip with Bradney or Bawdrip with Crandon.[53] In the 1670s a tithingman of Crandon attended the court of Crandon with Puriton.[54]

Court rolls for Bawdrip manor survive for 1479–82,[55] and for many years between 1530 and 1680.[56] Courts were still being held in 1768 when a man was paid for summoning suitors.[57] The court house needed repair in 1558.[58] The lord or his steward were found accommodation at the former manor house in the mid 17th century.[59] A tithingman, a hayward, and two constables were regularly appointed in the court in the 16th and 17th centuries and the business included breaches of the assize of ale, the repair of the pound, and especially the maintenance of rhynes and bridges. A cucking stool was ordered in 1555 and 1591,[60] and stocks were to be repaired in the 1630s and 1655.[61] Courts were held for Bradney manor in the 16th and 17th centuries[62] but no records have been found. A leet court book for Crandon with Puriton has entries for 1674–7 and 1681 and records the appearance of a hayward for each place.[63]

During the 19th century the number of churchwardens was reduced from two to one but two overseers continued to be appointed, supported by a salaried deputy together with a waywarden and guardian.[64] The poor were housed in the church house by 1634 and rent for it was paid by the parish until the 1760s.[65] The poorhouse recorded in 1796 may have been the same building.[66] In 1841 the overseers held a workhouse and two poorhouses on the southern edge of the churchyard.[67] One was considered in 1858 for use as a school.[68] The remaining buildings were private houses in 1988. The parish became part of the Bridgwater poor-law union in 1836, Bridgwater rural district in 1894, and Sedgemoor district in 1974.[69]

CHURCH. Bawdrip church was recorded c. 1195 when the abbot of Athelney released his claim to the advowson to William of Bawdrip in return for an annual pension.[70] The pension, amounting to £2, continued to be paid by the rectors to the abbey until the Dissolution, thereafter to the Crown until 1790, when the pension was sold to John Day Blake. It was held in trust for successive patrons until 1872 when it was bought by the Revd. John Warren and merged with the rectory.[71] The living remained a sole benefice until 1987, and since then it has been held with Cossington.[72]

The advowson was held with Bawdrip manor until c. 1770[73] when it was bought by John Stradling,[74] in whose family it remained until the death of the Revd. John Stradling, rector of Bawdrip, in 1804.[75] It was settled on the Revd. William Smith Knott, rector 1806–28, whose

33 P.R.O., RG 9/1628.
34 Statistics supplied by the then Bd. of Agric. 1905.
35 Min. of Agric., Fisheries, and Food, agric. returns, 1982.
36 S.R.O., Q/SR 9/23.
37 Ibid. D/B/bw 1497.
38 Ibid. DD/FA 11/1.
39 O.S. Map 6", Som. L. NE. (1886 edn.).
40 Som. C.C., Sites and Mons. Rec.
41 S.R.O., D/PC/baw 3/2/2; Kelly's Dir. Som. (1919, 1923); Proc. Som. Arch. Soc. cxiv. 96–9.
42 V.C.H. Som. i. 499, 526.
43 S.R.O., DD/AH 65/11.
44 Cal. Inq. p.m. vi, p. 290.
45 P.R.O., LR 3/123.
46 S.R.O., DD/CH 47.
47 Ibid.; ibid. tithe award; W. Dugdale, Hist. of Imbanking and Draining (1662), map pp. 110–11.
48 P.R.O., LR 3/123.
49 S.R.O., DD/AH 65/11.
50 B.L. Add. Ch. 71725.
51 P.R.O., RG 9/1628.
52 S.R.S. xi, p. 301; S.R.O., DD/SAS NP 13.

53 S.R.S. xx. 135; Som. Protestation Returns, ed. A. J. Howard and T. L. Stoate, 247; Dwelly, Hearth Tax, ii. 294.
54 S.D.N.Q. vi. 250–1.
55 P.R.O., SC 2/198/2.
56 Ibid. 4–9; ibid. LR 3/123; B.L. Add. MS. 15561; Devon R.O. 96 M 4/8.
57 S.R.O., DD/CH 47.　　　58 P.R.O., SC 2/198/4.
59 S.R.O., DD/CH 47.
60 P.R.O., LR 3/123; ibid. SC 2/198/8.
61 Devon R.O. 96 M 4/8.
62 P.R.O., C 3/244/4; C 111/20.
63 S.D.N.Q. vi. 250–4.
64 S.R.O., D/P/baw 9/1/1.
65 Ibid. DD/CH 47.　　　66 Ibid. D/RA 1/8/3.
67 Ibid. tithe award.
68 Ibid. D/P/baw 23/1.
69 Youngs, Local Admin. Units, i. 671, 673, 676.
70 Devon R.O. 96 M 83/7.
71 S.R.O., DD/S/ST 7; DD/DHR 44.
72 Dioc. Dir.
73 S.R.O., DD/X/EDS 2.
74 Ibid. D/D/B reg. 28, f. 85.
75 Ibid. D/D/Vc 88; M.I. in ch.

trustees presented in 1828.[76] By 1831 it had been acquired by Edward Page, rector 1835–54,[77] and succeeding incumbents were both rectors and patrons until c. 1902 when the trustees of William Brice held the advowson.[78] They remained patrons until c. 1950 when patronage passed to the bishop.[79]

The church was valued at £8 in 1291,[80] £18 12s. 8d. gross in 1535,[81] and c. £90 in 1668.[82] The tithes in 1535 were valued at £17 4s. 8d.[83] In 1703[84] and 1776 the lords of Ford paid a modus of 8s. 1½d. for tithes.[85] In 1836 Ford farm was described as 'titheless'[86] and in 1841 as exempt from tithe from time immemorial on payment of 8s. 4d. a year. Tithes of the whole parish were commuted for a rent charge of £355.[87] In 1280 the rector held an estate at Crandon.[88] The glebe was valued at £1 8s. in 1535[89] and in 1617 consisted of 44½ a. of which 12¼ a. were meadow and the rest lay in the open arable fields.[90] Following inclosure the glebe in 1841 consisted of 38 a. of scattered closes,[91] still so owned in 1978.[92]

In the mid 15th century the rector was ordered to repair his buildings[93] and in 1568 the parsonage was in decay.[94] In 1606 the buildings included bakehouse, barn, stable, and cattle stall.[95] The house was probably rebuilt in the early 19th century,[96] the barn and stables were rebuilt before 1840,[97] and the house was enlarged in 1848. By 1861 the rector had moved to Uplands House,[98] on the north side of the village. The house, recorded in 1822[99] and rebuilt, probably for the Revd. John Warren, in the late 1850s, had ten bedrooms and a large service wing. Later known as Bawdrip House, it was acquired by Somerset county council for use as a smallpox hospital[1] and in 1988 was a family residential centre. Warren's successor, the Revd. J. M. Warren, returned to the rectory house, which was occupied by successive rectors until 1987 when it was divided into two private dwellings.

The first recorded rector, William of Bawdrip, had been succeeded by 1280 by Anthony of Bradney, lord of Bradney.[2] Thomas Keke, rector 1400–20, was granted a year's study leave in 1402[3] and his successor Walter Woodward was appointed in 1420 while only an acolyte.[4] John Bulcombe, instituted in 1475, was made bishop of Waterford and Lismore in the same year but

retained the living until 1482.[5] John Pokeswell, both rector and chaplain of Ford from 1530 to 1547, employed a curate.[6] The rectory was let at farm in 1568 and curates were employed to serve the church.[7] John Atherton, rector from 1585, was the father of John Atherton, bishop of Waterford and Lismore, hanged in 1640.[8] Rectors were resident from the late 18th century and there were between 12 and 16 communicants c. 1770.[9] In the early 19th century the rector also served as curate to neighbouring churches.[10] In 1827 there was one Sunday service and a second every alternate Sunday.[11] John Bowen, instituted in 1828, was a deputy lieutenant for the county and founder president of the Royal Harmonic Society.[12] His successor employed a curate[13] and there were two Sunday services and 8 celebrations of communion by 1843,[14] rising to 14 or 15 by 1870.[15] During the early 20th century there were four Sunday services.[16]

The church house was recorded in the 16th century[17] and in 1634 it was said to have been used to house the poor.[18]

In 1330 Simon of Bradney was licensed to give land to support a chaplain celebrating for the souls of his family on five days each week in the Lady chapel, probably in the north transept.[19] No further record has been found.

The church of St. Michael the Archangel, so dedicated by 1330[20] but later known as ST. MICHAEL AND ALL ANGELS,[21] is built of lias with dressings of Ham stone and has a chancel, a central tower with north and south transepts, and a nave with south vestry and south porch. The small nave may be of 12th-century origin but has no features earlier than the 14th century. The crossing arches of the central tower are late 13th-century and have double-chamfered arches resting on foliate capitals above human corbel heads. The middle stage of the tower, the porch, the transepts, and the chancel were rebuilt or added in the 14th century, the piscinae indicating the use of the transepts as chapels. There is a blocked 14th-century doorway in the north wall of the chancel. The north transept was originally unlit but windows were inserted in both transept and nave in the 19th century. A 13th-century effigy lies in the north transept under a later cusped arch.[22] The medieval font and floor tiles were removed in 1865[23] but a small Madonna and Child, possibly from

76 S.R.O., D/P/baw 2/1/6.
77 Rep. Com. Eccl. Revenues, pp. 126–7; S.R.O., D/P/baw 2/1/6.
78 S.R.O., D/P/baw 2/1/6; Kelly's Dir. Som. (1902, 1906).
79 Kelly's Dir. Som. (1939); Crockford (1953–4).
80 Tax. Eccl. (Rec. Com.), 198.
81 Valor Eccl. (Rec. Com.), i. 212.
82 S.R.O., D/D/Vc 24.
83 Valor Eccl. (Rec. Com.), i. 212.
84 S.R.O., DD/BR/py 13.
85 Ibid. DD/CH 48.
86 Ibid. D/P/baw 13/1/1.
87 Ibid. tithe award.   88 S.R.S. xliv. 267.
89 Valor Eccl. (Rec. Com.), i. 212.
90 S.R.O., D/D/Rg 198.
91 Ibid. tithe award.
92 Inf. from Dioc. Office.
93 Proc. Som. Arch. Soc. cvi. 58.
94 S.R.O., D/D/Ca 40.   95 Ibid. D/D/Rg 198.
96 Rep. Com. Eccl. Revenues, pp. 126–7.
97 S.R.O., D/D/Va 1840.   98 P.R.O., RG 9/1628.

99 S.R.O., D/D/Rm, box 2.
1   Ibid. D/R/bw 22/1/57; D/PC/baw 3/2/2.
2   S.R.S. xliv. 267; Cal. Papal Reg. i. 587.
3   S.R.S. xiii, p. 35.   4 Ibid. xxx, p. 399.
5   Ibid. lii, pp. 58, 117; Cal. Papal Reg. xiii. 451, 838.
6   S.R.S. ii. 64.   7 P.R.O., SC 2/198/7; C 3/55, no. 85.
8   Collinson, Hist. Som. iii. 93; D.N.B.
9   S.R.O., D/D/Vc 88.
10 Ibid. D/D/Rb 1815, 1827.
11 Ibid. 1827.
12 Ibid. D/P/baw 2/1/6.
13 Rep. Com. Eccl. Revenues, pp. 126–7.
14 S.R.O., D/D/Va 1843.
15 Ibid. 1870.
16 Ibid. D/P/baw 2/5/1–5.
17 P.R.O., SC 12/22/31.
18 Above, local govt.
19 Cal. Pat. 1330–4, 17.
20 Ibid.   21 Dioc. Dir.
22 Pevsner, S. & W. Som. 86.
23 Proc. Som. Arch. Soc. lxvi, p. xxviii.

a reredos, are preserved in the chancel. A planned rebuilding in 1865 was abandoned for shortage of funds but extensive alterations were carried out by C. E. Giles. The windows were replaced, except for the west window, and the floor was dug out to increase the internal height.[24] New seating replaced box pews and a gallery in the north transept.[25] During the two-year closure of the church services were held in a barn at the rectory.[26]

The bells, housed in a late-medieval bell cage, comprise two by Roger London (d. 1448?) of Wokingham (Berks.), one of 1671 by Thomas Purdue, and one of 1745 by Thomas Bayley.[27] The church possesses a set of silver plate of 1763 by Fuller White given by Denis Rolle.[28] The registers date from 1748 and are complete.[29]

There was a chapel of *ALL SAINTS* at Bradney by 1330 when Simon of Bradney was licensed to alienate land for a chaplain to celebrate mass there on Wednesdays and Fridays for the souls of his family.[30] There is no further record of the chapel.

In 1306 Adam de la Ford was licensed to endow the newly built chapel of *ST. MARY* within the manor house or court at Ford,[31] later described as a perpetual chantry[32] and a free chapel.[33] The advowson descended with Ford manor.[34] In 1455, when the chapel was said to be desolate and ruinous, the chaplain was required to say prayers for the dead and a monthly mass for the founder.[35] The income from the endowment was worth 26s. 8d. in 1535 and 1548,[36] but in 1548 there was neither plate nor ornament.[37] The last chaplain, appointed in 1530, was already rector of Bawdrip.[38] The chapel was suppressed in 1548 and its land at Stawell was sold.[39]

NONCONFORMITY. In 1752 a house was licensed for Methodist worship and John Wesley preached in the parish in 1760.[40] A meeting house at Bradney was licensed in 1803,[41] probably for Methodists who held two services there each week in 1838. Bradney chapel was built in 1842[42] but by 1898 had only five members. Services had ceased by 1924 when it was sold.[43] It was a private house in 1988.

Meeting-house licences were granted in 1822 and 1825, the latter for Congregationalists who built Sion chapel at Knowle in 1830.[44] They had resident ministers during the 19th century and there was in addition an evangelist in the parish in 1871.[45] In 1872 the chapel had been recently restored.[46] It was in use as a United Reformed church in 1988.

EDUCATION. A parish school house, probably on Bawdrip Green, was recorded in 1763.[47] In 1819 several schools taught a total of c. 20 children and the same number attended Sunday school.[48] By 1825 43 children attended three day schools supported by parents and 45 went to the Sunday school which continued until 1846 or later.[49] A Dissenting Sunday school, begun in 1822, gave free instruction to 20 children in 1835. There was only one day school, with 11 pupils, in that year[50] but by 1846 two dame schools taught 26 children.[51]

A parochial school, built c. 1870, was enlarged in 1897 and had 53 pupils in 1903.[52] In 1913 it became a council school. Numbers fell to 29 in 1935 and were 32 in 1965. In 1966 the school was restricted to children under eight and in 1988 there were about 35 children on the register.[53]

In the 1860s there was a dame school at Bradney.[54] St. Andrew's boarding school for boys was kept at Knowle Hall during the 1950s and 1960s.[55]

CHARITIES FOR THE POOR. Elizabeth Stradling in 1805 and Grace Callow by will proved 1875 each left £100 for the poor. Dinah Ritchie gave £100 in 1856 for bread and coal and Frances Stribbling Warren provided £50 for bread, both distributed on Christmas Eve.[56] Distributions had ceased by the 1980s.[57]

24 S.R.O., D/D/Cf 1865/1; D/P/baw 6/1/1, 23/1; Pevsner, *S. & W. Som.* 86.
25 Photos. in private possession.
26 S.R.O., D/P/baw 23/1.
27 Ibid. 6/3/1; DD/SAS CH 16/1.
28 Ibid. D/P/baw 5/2/1; Pevsner, *S. & W. Som.* 86.
29 S.R.O., D/P/baw 2/1/1–6.
30 *Cal. Pat.* 1330–4, 17.
31 Ibid. 1301–7, 413 (wrongly identified in index); *S.R.S.* i. 276; ix, p. 373; P.R.O., C 143/51, no. 12.
32 *S.R.S.* xlix, p. 102.
33 Ibid. lv, p. 15.
34 *Som. Incumbents*, ed. Weaver, 22; above, manors.
35 *S.R.S.* xlix, p. 249.
36 *Valor Eccl.* (Rec. Com.), i. 213; *S.R.S.* ii. 64.
37 *S.R.S.* ii. 64.
38 *Som. Incumbents*, ed. Weaver, 22; *S.R.S.* lv, pp. 59, 61.
39 *S.R.S.* ii. 64; *Cal. Pat.* 1547–8, 407.
40 S.R.O., Q/RR meeting ho. lics.; Wesley, *Jnl.* (1901), iii. 21.
41 S.R.O., D/D/Rm, box 2.
42 Ibid. D/N/bmc 3/2/1, 4/3/45, 7/2.
43 Ibid. 2/1/4, 2/3/11, 3/2/2.
44 Ibid. D/D/Rm, box 2; *Educ. Enq. Abstract*, p. 794; *Rep. Som. Cong. Union* (1896).
45 P.R.O., HO 107/953; ibid. RG 10/2390; *P.O. Dir. Som.* (1866, 1875).
46 Morris & Co. *Dir. Som.* (1872).
47 S.R.O., DD/CH 47.
48 *Educ. of Poor Digest*, p. 773.
49 *Ann. Rep. B. & W. Dioc. Assoc. S.P.C.K.* (1825–6), 44; Nat. Soc. *Inquiry*, 1846–7, Som. 2–3.
50 *Educ. Enq. Abstract*, p. 794.
51 Nat. Soc. *Inquiry*, 1846–7, Som. 2–3.
52 S.R.O., C/E 4/380/29; ibid. DD/CH 48; D/P/baw 23/1.
53 Ibid. C/E 4/64.
54 *P.O. Dir. Som.* (1861, 1866).
55 *Bristol, Devon, Dorset, Som. Sch. Handbk.* [c. 1954]; *Ind. Schs. of Som. & Glos.* [c. 1967].
56 Char. Com. files.
57 Local. inf.

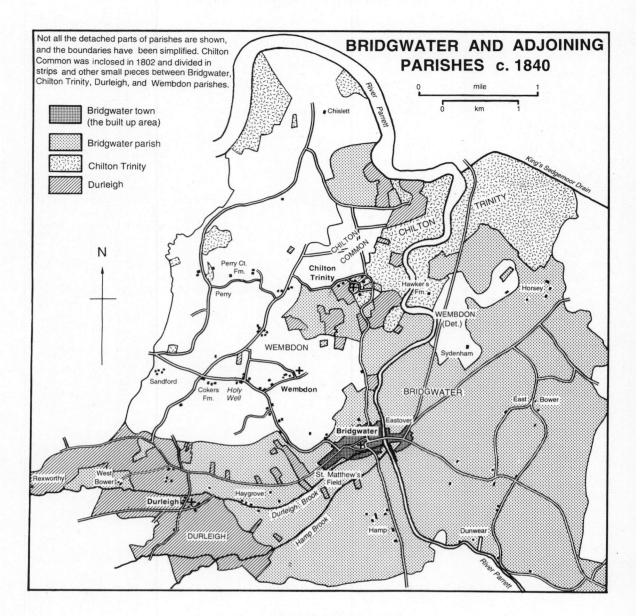

Not all the detached parts of parishes are shown, and the boundaries have been simplified. Chilton Common was inclosed in 1802 and divided in strips and other small pieces between Bridgwater, Chilton Trinity, Durleigh, and Wembdon parishes.

Bridgwater town (the built up area)

Bridgwater parish

Chilton Trinity

Durleigh

BRIDGWATER AND ADJOINING PARISHES c. 1840

BRIDGWATER

THE borough and port of Bridgwater lies in an irregularly shaped parish through which flows the tidal river Parrett.[58] It lies *c.* 18 km. by water from Bridgwater Bay. The first element of the name, commonly thought to refer to a bridge built by the Domesday lord Walter of Douai,[59] is more likely to be derived either from the Old Norse *bryggja*, meaning a quay or jetty, or from the Old English *brycg*, a gang plank between ship and shore.[60] Bridgwater, apparently agricultural at Domesday,[61] had developed into a town by 1200. A castle was built soon after that date and near its south-eastern corner a bridge crossed the Parrett. Four gates marked the principal entrances to the town. The parish included in the 11th century the secondary settlements of

Hamp in the south, Haygrove and West Bower in the west, the latter in a detached part of the parish, Horsey in the north-east, East and North Bower in the east, and Dunwear in the south-east. Horsey, its name suggesting an island,[62] Haygrove, and Hamp were probably nucleated hamlets around a single farm; the Bowers were perhaps isolated dwellings. Dunwear was a scattered riverside settlement occupying much of the east bank of the Parrett.

The boundaries of the ancient parish, which measures at its widest 6 km. from east to west and 4.5 km. from north to south, suggest that Wembdon, Chilton Trinity, Durleigh, and Bridgwater had formed a single unit, and in 1086 Bridgwater, Horsey, Bower, and Wembdon

58 This article was completed in 1991.
59 e.g. A. H. Powell, *Ancient Borough of Bridgwater* (1907), 1–2.

60 A. H. Smith, *Eng. Place-Name Elements*, i. 54.
61 Below, econ. hist. (agric.).
62 Smith, *Place-Name Elements*, i. 148–9.

were part of the estate held by Walter of Douai.[63] North of the town the boundaries either curve to suggest earlier watercourses or interlock in such a way as to imply that the Parrett may have had several channels and that intercommoning resulted on ground permanently recovered from the tidal marsh. The eastern boundary, with Bawdrip and Chedzoy, in part follows natural watercourses and in part a causeway named Park or Port Wall, created by a drainage scheme before the late 18th century. A small stretch of the southern boundary follows the Parrett, but near the hamlet of Somerset Bridge an incursion of North Petherton parish across the river, named Old River Ground, was evidently the result of natural or deliberate straightening.[64] Another part of the southern boundary, also with North Petherton, was evidently formed across Stock moor when the area was inclosed. The boundary with Durleigh partly follows streams, and that with Wembdon was marked by the northern edge of the former Queen's wood.[65] West Bower, beyond Durleigh to the west, was divided into two small, irregular areas. After transfers of land to all six adjoining areas, including West Bower to Durleigh, in 1886–7, the area of the parish was 3,967 a. in 1891.[66] The civil parish of Bridgwater Without, including Dunwear, East Bower, Chedzoy Lane, and Haygrove, was created in 1894.[67]

East of the river the parish is on low-lying alluvium c. 6 metres above sea level nearest the river and 12 metres on the north-eastern boundary at Horsey. West of the river alluvium runs across Stock moor in the south and along the Durleigh brook between Hamp and the town, both of which lie on ridges of marl, the highest point of which was occupied by Bridgwater castle. Bridgwater's marl has two small areas of terrace deposits[68] of valley gravel, which were used by the 16th century and until the 18th for building work and streets.[69] Sand was dug on the ridge in 1393–4.[70] Lime was dug in the south-east corner of the town near the 'quay above the bridge' in the 17th and 18th centuries,[71] and a kiln was in operation near Lyme Bridge by 1497.[72]

COMMUNICATIONS. The construction of Bridgwater Bridge c. 1200[73] and pontage levied on its users indicate the importance of the east–west river crossing, and routes both east and south of the town over low-lying marshes had to be

causewayed. East of the town from 1286 there was a causeway running north from St. John's hospital to the Poldens[74] and indulgences were offered in 1326 to encourage its repair.[75] It was known as the 'long causeway' in the 18th century.[76] A second causeway leading south beside the Parrett was repaired through bequests of a Taunton merchant and others from 1501,[77] and in 1622 a charge was made for use of the route.[78]

Both causeways were among the principal parish roads turnpiked in 1730, the one on the route to Taunton, the other carrying the main traffic for the east and north. The other roads turnpiked in 1730 were the Minehead route through Wembdon village, two routes to the Quantocks, and one to Langport across Sedgemoor. In 1829–30 the Taunton route was re-aligned, and a new Bristol road was built direct to Dunball in Puriton, avoiding Crandon bridge.[79] A new route to take through traffic away from the town centre was built in 1958, involving the construction of Blake Bridge. The local section of the M5 motorway, following the general routes of the railway and the Bristol road, was begun in 1971 and opened in 1973.[80]

Ships presumably discharged their cargoes on both sides of the Parrett after c. 1200. A quay, recorded in 1424, was probably then being faced and paved.[81] Another quay, on the west bank above the bridge, was made for inland traffic in 1488 and was later known as the Langport slip.[82] Old and new quays, also on the west bank, were mentioned in 1616.[83] The old quay was enlarged and repaired and work was done on Back Quay, the old Langport slip, between 1697 and 1701, and c. 1712 a new quay was built on the east bank.[84] 'Mr. Darby's' new quay had been built on the west bank, north of the old quay, by c. 1730.[85] An Act of 1794 enabled further improvements.[86] In 1845 official quays were defined, measuring 717 ft. from the town bridge on the east side and 716 ft. on the west. In addition to the quays in 1845 were a dry dock on the east bank[87] and a large wet dock on the west which comprised an outer tidal basin and an inner dock. The whole dock, with a bascule bridge and a complicated system of sluices and culverts to scour the basin of river mud, was designed by Thomas Maddicks and opened in 1841.[88]

The port had no official customs house in 1565,[89] but c. 1724 the duke of Chandos was planning to build one which seems to have been finished in 1726.[90] It probably replaced an

63 V.C.H. Som. i. 497, 499–500.
64 S.R.O., Q/REl 29/6D.
65 Ibid. tithe award.
66 Census, 1891.
67 Local Government Act, 1894, 56 & 57 Vic. c. 73.
68 Geol. Surv. Map 1/50,000, solid and drift, sheet 295 (1984 edn.).
69 S.R.O., D/B/bw 1341, 1523; ibid. 2/1/2 (4 Dec. 1758; 22 Sept. 1775).
70 S.R.S. liii, no. 475.
71 S.R.O., D/B/bw 2045 (1662); ibid. 2/1/2 (5 Dec. 1774).
72 Ibid. D/B/bw 1365, 1435; for Lyme Bridge, below, this section.
73 Below, this section.
74 Cal. Pat. 1281–92, 244.
75 S.R.S. i. 259.
76 S.R.O., D/B/bw 117, 1550, 1617, 1828, 1969, 2184; S.R.S. xxiii. 110, 133–4, 255–6, 320; Proc. Som. Arch. Soc. lxvi. 69.

77 S.R.O., DD/X/SR 5, p. 24 (1539); S.R.S. xix. 27 (1501).
78 S.R.S. xxiii. 320.
79 J. B. Bentley and B. J. Murless, Som. Roads, i (1985), 21–5.
80 M5 Motorway in the South West (Dept. of Transport, 1977).
81 S.R.S. lviii, no. 613.
82 S.R.O., D/B/bw 803, 1896.
83 Ibid. 615, 1317, 1690.
84 Ibid. Q/RUa; L.J. xvi. 248.
85 S.R.O., DD/SH 149.
86 Ibid. DD/SAS PR 221; L.J. xl. 146, 210.
87 Below, econ. hist. (industries).
88 Murless, Bridgwater Docks, 12–20; below, plate facing p. 217.   89 S.D.N.Q. xxx. 159.
90 San Marino (Calif.), Huntington Libr., Chandos MSS. ST 57, vols. 24–41, letters 21 July 1724; 4 Aug. 1726 (microfilm in Taunton Castle, Local Hist. Libr.).

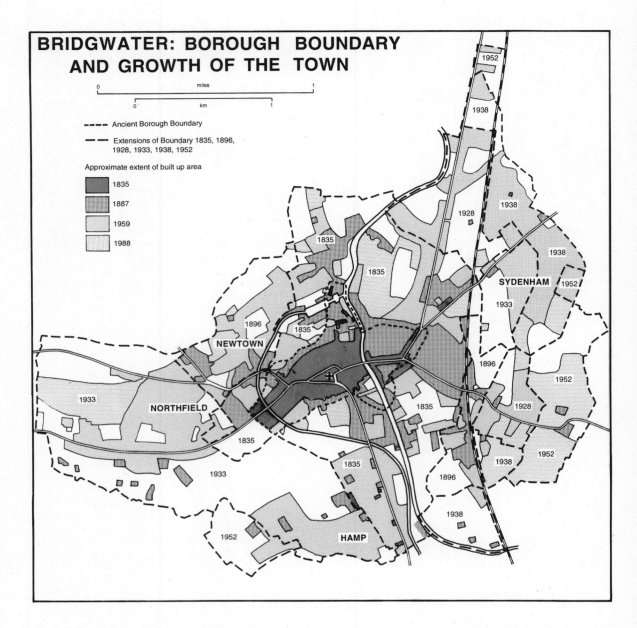

BRIDGWATER: BOROUGH BOUNDARY AND GROWTH OF THE TOWN

miles
km

- - - Ancient Borough Boundary

— - — Extensions of Boundary 1835, 1896, 1928, 1933, 1938, 1952

Approximate extent of built up area

1835
1887
1959
1988

NEWTOWN
NORTHFIELD
SYDENHAM
HAMP

earlier building on the quay belonging to the corporation.[91] From the 16th century cuts were made to straighten the river Parrett. A meander in Hamp was isolated by a new channel in 1568.[92] Thereafter improvements, effected or only suggested, concerned the lower reaches of the river, but its course from Bridgwater Bridge upstream came under private Acts passed in 1673 and 1699 to improve the navigation to Taunton.[93]

The Bridgwater and Taunton canal, which from 1827 provided an alternative to the Tone and Parrett navigation, was extended from the terminating lock and basin at Huntworth in North Petherton parish by a loop west of Bridgwater which led to a large dock north of the town

linked to the river by a tidal basin.[94] Extension and dock were opened in 1841. The canal ceased to be used commercially c. 1907, but the dock remained in use until 1971. In 1974 Somerset county council bought the dock and surrounding land. Associated buildings and machinery were subsequently restored and the dock converted to a marina.[95]

The Bristol–Exeter railway was opened as far as Bridgwater in 1841 and through the remainder of the parish to link with Taunton in 1842.[96] A branch from the railway station to wharves on the east bank of the Parrett was opened in 1845 as a horse tramway by Bridgwater corporation. From 1867 steam engines were used and from

91   S.R.O., D/B/bw 2/1/2 (4 Dec. 1758).
92   Bristol R.O. 04026 (8), pp. 256–68; R. Ricart, *Maire of Bristowe is Kalendar* (Camden Soc. [2nd ser.], v), 57–8.
93   *L.J.* xii. 539, 569–70; ibid. xvi. 373, 416; Hist. MSS. Com. 8, *9th Rep. II, House of Lords*, pp. 24–5; *Cal. S.P. Dom.* 1684–5, 126–7.

94   Below, plate facing p. 217.
95   B. J. Murless, *Bridgwater Docks and the River Parrett* (1983), *passim*; C. Hadfield, *Canals of Southern Eng.* (1955), 309–10, 357.
96   E. T. Macdermot, *Hist. G.W.R.* rev. C. R. Clinker, ii. 72, 90, 330.

ELEVATION OF BRIDGWATER BRIDGE, 1795

1871 the line crossed the Parrett by a telescopic bridge to serve the docks, with branches to a pottery, a brewery, and other businesses.[97] The railway company opened extensive carriage works on the west side of the track south of the town in 1848.[98]

In 1890 the Bridgwater Railway Co. opened a single line linking the Somerset and Dorset line at Edington with Bridgwater North station. An adjoining goods depot included sidings serving a cattle dock and a brick and tile works and linked with the dock branch of the Bristol and Exeter line. The Edington line, operated by the Somerset and Dorset Joint Railway, was closed for passengers in 1952 and for freight in 1954.[99] Only the main-line station and line have remained open; the dock sidings have been removed and built over.

The grant of pontage to William Brewer in 1200 indicates that a bridge either already existed or was planned. Brewer was later remembered as the builder of the bridge.[1] In the later 13th century there was apparently a common fund to maintain the bridge,[2] known by 1286 as the great bridge.[3] Sir John Trivet gave 300 marks to rebuild the bridge in the 1390s, and work on it was in progress in 1399–1400.[4] There were houses on both the old and the new bridge.[5] In the 1480s tides and military vehicles damaged the bridge,[6] which was repaired in 1532 and 1678.[7] It was of stone, with three arches and cutwaters. By the end of the 18th century all the houses on it had been removed.[8] The medieval bridge was replaced by an iron one cast in 1795

at Coalbrookdale by Thomas Gregory and transported by water. It stood on masonry plinths and was virtually complete in October 1798. The old bridge was difficult to demolish and its piers were then still standing. The new bridge, with an elliptical arch pierced in Coalbrookdale's characteristic style, was topped by cast iron fencing over a 75-ft. span. Increasing traffic proved too heavy for the bridge, which was replaced by the present cast iron one, designed by R. C. Else and G. B. Laffan and made by George Moss of Liverpool, which was opened in 1883.[9]

Frog Lane bridge, named in 1344, may have taken the lane across the Durleigh brook as it entered the Parrett.[10] The south bridge, over the Durleigh brook outside the south gate, was called Lyme Bridge in 1373 and 1722.[11] The east bridge, taken up in 1646–7, may have crossed the former priory ditch at Eastover.[12] Horsemill Bridge, mentioned in 1694, may have taken the Taunton road across the Hamp brook,[13] and was perhaps the Hamp bridge, of brick, transferred in 1871–2 from the turnpike trustees to the county.[14]

Four bridges cross the Parrett besides the town bridge and the M5 motorway bridge. Somerset Bridge at Huntworth was designed by I. K. Brunel for the Bristol and Exeter Railway Co. It had a flat masonry arch which was partially demolished before completion in 1843 and was replaced in 1844 by a laminated timber arch. That bridge was replaced in 1904 by one of steel girders on the original masonry foundations.[15]

97 Murless, *Bridgwater Docks*, 29–30, 32.
98 Macdermot, *Hist. G.W.R.* ii. 81–3.
99 R. Atthill, *Som. and Dors. Railway* (1985), 20, 69–70, 81, 110, 112.
1 *S.R.S.* xv. 131; xlviii, no. 1; Leland, *Itin.* ed. Toulmin Smith, i. 162.
2 *S.R.S.* xlviii, no. 10.
3 *Cal. Pat.* 1281–92, 244.
4 *S.R.S.* liii, nos. 477–9; lviii, no. 502; Leland, *Itin.* ed. Toulmin Smith, i. 162.
5 *S.R.S.* xlviii, no. 297; lviii, no. 686; lx, no. 850.

6 Ibid. lxx, no. 1071.
7 S.R.O., D/B/bw 1523, 1695.
8 Below, plate facing p. 216.
9 Murless, *Bridgwater Docks*, 5–7, 32–3.
10 *S.R.S.* xlviii, p. liii and no. 139.
11 Ibid. no. 297; S.R.O., D/B/bw 2/1/1 (Jan. 1722).
12 S.R.O., D/B/bw 1617.
13 Bristol R.O. 00904 (7); B.L. Add. Ch. 71720; S.R.O., D/B/bw 2/1/1 (18 May 1720).
14 S.R.O., Q/AB 8, 15/1, 17, 21.
15 Murless, *Bridgwater Docks*, 22–3.

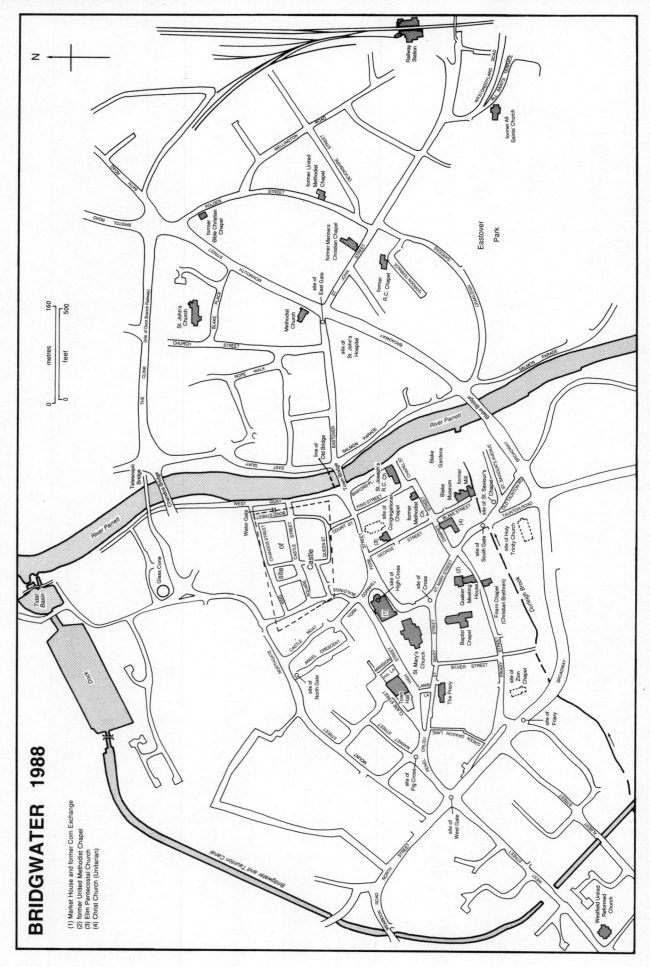

BRIDGWATER 1988

N

(1) Market House and former Corn Exchange
(2) former United Methodist Chapel
(3) Elim Pentecostal Church
(4) Christ Church (Unitarian)

metres   0   160
feet   0   500

Railway Station

WESTONZOYLAND ROAD

ALL SAINTS TERRACE

former All Saints' Church

Eastover Park

former United Methodist Chapel

WELLINGTON ROAD

STREET

DEVONSHIRE STREET

former Bible Christian Chapel

POLDEN STREET

BRISTOL ROAD

BLAKE ROAD

former Mariners Christian Chapel

MONMOUTH STREET

ST JOHN STREET

site of East Gate

former R.C. Chapel

GORDON TERRACE

GASGOD

CRANLEIGH

St. John's Church

BLAKE PLACE

CHURCH STREET

Methodist Church

ROPE WALK

site of St. John's Hospital

BROADWAY

SALMON PARADE

THE CLINK

(site of Dock Branch Railway)

Telescopic Bridge

Charles Bridge

River Parrett

Blake Bridge

SALMON PARADE

River Parrett

line of Old Bridge

EASTOVER

EAST QUAY

WEST QUAY

Town Bridge

BINFORD PL.

St. Joseph's R.C. Ch.

KING STREET

CHAPEL ST

Blake Gardens

former Mill

ST. SAVIOUR'S AVENUE

Glass Cone

Water Gate

BOND STREET

Site of Castle

CHANDOS STREET

CASTLE STREET

QUEEN ST

COURT ST

site of Congregational Chapel

GEORGE STREET

former Methodist Ch.

DAMPIET STREET

BLAKE STREET

Blake Museum

site of St. Saviour's Chapel

BROADWAY

OLD TAUNTON RD

TAUNTON ROAD

Dock

Tidal Basin

KING SQUARE

NORTHGATE

CASTLE MOAT

ANGEL CRESCENT

YORK BUILDINGS

CORNHILL

FORE STREET

site of High Cross

site of Cross

ST MARY STREET

site of South Gate

Quaker Meeting House

(2)

Friarn Chapel (Christian Brethren)

Durleigh Brook

site of Holy Trinity Church

(4)

(3)

(1)

St. Mary's Church

MANSION HO. LA.

MARY ST

Baptist Chapel

SILVER STREET

FRIARY STREET

site of North Gate

HIGH STREET

DAMPIET ST

LAMB LA.

The Priory

site of Zion Chapel

BROADWAY

MOUNT STREET

MARKET STREET

DARE STREET

GREEN DRAGON LANE

PENEL ORLIEU

site of Friary

NORTH STREET

site of Pig Cross

site of West Gate

ALBERT STREET

WEST STREET

Westfield United Reformed Church

Bridgwater and Taunton Canal

CRIBTON ROAD

North of the town bridge, the telescopic or Black Bridge was built in 1871 to take a railway across the river. It was steam-driven, retracting to allow shipping to pass upstream. The bridge, temporarily immobilized in 1942, was last opened in 1957, and from 1983 became part of a new road network. A few yards further north Chandos Bridge was opened in 1988.[16] South of the town bridge a partial town bypass crosses the river by Blake Bridge, opened in 1958.[17]

LAND USE. In 1086 there were 100 a. of underwood on Bridgwater manor and 3 a. on Hamp manor.[18] A small wood at Hamp survived in the mid 17th century.[19] The lord of Bridgwater was licensed in 1200 to enclose his wood,[20] and by 1234 part of the wood, west of the town, was a deerpark.[21] Timber, underwood, and bracken were sold from it until the early 15th century.[22] By 1635 it was known as Queen's wood.[23] There was only 10 a. of coppice and withy bed in the parish in 1847.[24]

By 1234 Bridgwater park provided livestock for North Petherton park[25] and meat for the royal household.[26] Part of the park was wooded and by 1413 was called Castle wood; the remainder was known as West park.[27] The park was mentioned in 1461[28] but was then probably let for pasture. Three fields named Parks survived in Haygrove in 1847.[29]

POPULATION. In 1327 the borough had 61 taxpayers,[30] and there were 858 payers of poll tax in 1377.[31] The population in 1444–5 has been estimated at c. 1,600,[32] but John Leland c. 1540 recorded the decay of more than 200 houses within living memory,[33] and there were 600 communicants in the parish in 1548 and a total of 352 households in 1563.[34] There were 642 males who signed the Protestation in 1641.[35] A census taken in 1695 suggested 2,200 or more inhabitants for the town and 600 for the rest of the parish.[36] In 1801 the total population was 3,634, and within ten years it had increased by over a quarter to 4,911. Increases of over one fifth followed in each of the next three decades, giving a total of 10,450 in 1841, which included 311 temporary labourers on the canal and railway and 92 in ships in the harbour. Thereafter for a time the annual increases were much smaller, the largest being over one tenth in the 1890s to a total of 14,900 in 1901.[37] Between 1901 and 1911 the total rose sharply to 17,981 but thereafter increases were smaller until 1951. In 1971 the total had risen to 22,691 and in 1981 to 23,323.[38]

THE MEDIEVAL TOWN. The town's street pattern may have been based on a large, probably planned, central market place which became less prominent as the town developed as a port. The market place seems to have formed a large, roughly square area at the eastern end of the churchyard. Roads led into it from south, east, and west. At its north-eastern corner was the main entrance to the castle, which occupied that quarter of the town. Not far from the castle entrance stood the high cross. The market place probably extended as far south as the south-eastern corner of the churchyard, marked by St. Mary's Cross.[39] The name Cornchepyng or the Cornhill was in use for the market place in the mid 14th century.[40] Encroachments made on the south and west sides of the market place, significantly limiting the commercial area, perhaps caused shops and stalls to be moved to a street on the north side of the churchyard, called the great street by the mid 13th century and later High Street.[41]

By the mid 14th century High Street, wide enough to accommodate the market overflow from the town centre, was itself encroached upon by a long 'island' of shops and stalls in the vicus cocorum and known as Cokenrewe, and by the flesh and fish shambles, buildings which survived until the earlier 19th century.[42] The 'island' may also have included shops called Chapman Row and Ratyn Rew.[43] North of High Street was Orlove Street, and from its eastern end a street was formed by the mid 13th century following the line of the castle ditch northwards and known as North Street and later as Northgate Street.[44] The increase in business in the port enhanced the status of the street between the market place and the quay, which was known either as 'between church and bridge' or, as in 1367, Fore Street. By that date merchants had established themselves along its course,[45] their stalls perhaps sited along the edge of the castle moat.

High Street ran west from the Cornhill, converged with Orlove and St. Mary streets to form a triangular area, called the Orfair in 1399, and continued as Pynel Street to the west gate.[46] Both Pynel and Orlove seem to have been personal names.[47] Orlove Street (later Back Street) was called Clare Street in the 20th century, Pynel Street (later Prickett's Lane) was called Market

16   Bridgwater Mercury, 8 Feb. 1983; 20 Sept. 1988.
17   Squibbs, Bridgwater, 136–7.
18   V.C.H. Som. i. 469, 499.
19   Bristol R.O., 4490, f. 6; 04237.
20   Rot. Chart. (Rec. Com.), i (1), 45.
21   Below, this section.
22   P.R.O., C 133/32, no. 7/6; C 133/114, no. 8; ibid. SC 6/1094/11; ibid. LR 3/58/9.
23   S.R.O., DD/S/BW 5.
24   Ibid. tithe award.
25   Close R. 1231–4, 494; 1234–7, 51, 238, 240, 279, 449.
26   Cal. Lib. 1226–40, 497; 1245–51, 155; Close R. 1247–51, 11.
27   P.R.O., SC 6/969/21; ibid. LR 3/58/9.
28   S.R.S. lx, no. 820.
29   S.R.O., tithe award.
30   S.R.S. iii. 278–9.
31   P.R.O., E 179/169/31; S.D.N.Q. xxix. 11–12.

32   T. Dilks, Pilgrims in Old Bridgwater (1927), app.
33   Leland, Itin. ed. Toulmin Smith, i. 163.
34   S.R.S. ii. 57; S.D.N.Q. xxx. 91.
35   Som. Protestation Returns, ed. Howard and Stoate, 84–7.
36   Ibid. D/P/bw. m 2/1/3.
37   V.C.H. Som. ii. 352.
38   Census.
39   For the crosses, see below.
40   S.R.S. xlviii, nos. 133, 193.
41   Ibid. e.g. nos. 16–22, 116–17, 130, 181, 235.
42   Ibid. nos. 13, 21–2, 27–8, 130, 133, 163, 207, 278; liii, no. 370; lviii, nos. 536, 547.
43   Ibid. lxx, nos. 1024, 1030.
44   Ibid. xlviii, nos. 12, 16, 48, 235.
45   Ibid. nos. 237, 260.
46   Ibid. opp. p. xlix; liii, no. 492; lviii, no. 520.
47   Ibid. xlviii, p. liv.

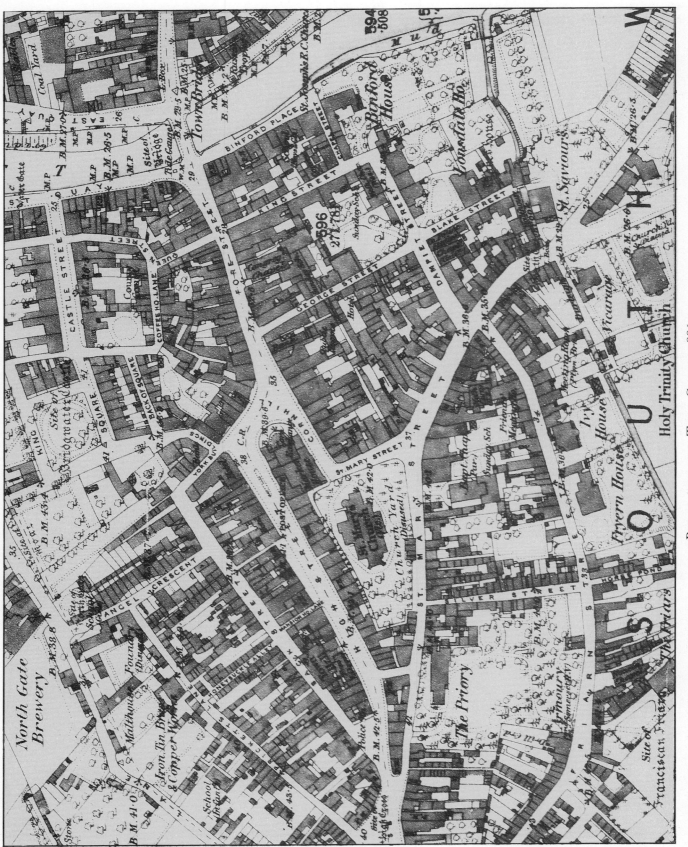

BRIDGWATER: THE TOWN CENTRE 1886

Street, and the junction with High Street and St. Mary Street was called Penel Orlieu.[48]

South of the church St. Mary Street, so named by 1299,[49] gave direct access to the cattle market from the south. Further south, Friarn Street, so named in 1298,[50] marked the line of the town ditch, beyond which was the Franciscan friary.[51] The gateway to the friary still stood in 1709.[52] Friarn Street was crossed by a road, by c. 1720 known as Silver Street,[53] from St. Mary Street to the wayer or horsepool on the Durleigh brook.[54]

The south-eastern quarter of the town was generally known as Damyet by the mid 14th century, probably in reference to the mill on its southern edge on the Durleigh brook. Damyet, later Dampiet, Street existed by 1344; it may have been the unnamed street mentioned in 1260.[55] Frog Lane, also named in 1260, probably ran along the river bank; Croniles Lane was said to be in the same area.[56]

There were three crosses in the town. The high cross, at the junction of the Cornhill and High Street, existed in 1367. It was rebuilt or altered in 1567–8.[57] By the end of the 18th century the cross comprised six columns supporting a pinnacled roof around a central column which supported a cistern holding the town's water supply.[58] St. Mary's Cross, at the south-eastern corner of the churchyard, probably marked the original entrance to the market place from the south.[59] In 1724 the corporation ordered the churchwardens to remove timber and lead from the cross, which probably formed a shelter around the cross shaft.[60] The cross was removed in 1769 to Penel Orlieu and was demolished in the 1830s.[61] A replica was built in 1989 at the east end of Fore Street. An 'old' cross stood outside West Gate c. 1480 and in 1543.[62] This may have been the cross 'on the west of the town' mentioned in 1544 and called St. Anthony's Cross. It was still so named in 1630.[63] By 1689 its name had been changed to Pig Cross, and it seems by then to have been re-sited in Penel Orlieu.[64] It was demolished in 1769 and was replaced by St. Mary's Cross.[65]

In the 1540s there were north, south, east, and west gates, but John Leland saw no other defences.[66] There had been a defensive wall, at least on the west, where before 1295 a tenant was

identified as William the smith in the walls, and in 1302 a site was bounded by the wall on the town ditch.[67] The 'common ditch of the vill' was still a clear boundary in the mid 14th century, but elm trees were growing on parts of it by the earlier 15th.[68] The 'old fortifications' were still recognizable in 1653[69] and water at high tide filled the ditch 'for a great part about the town'.[70] Water still ran from beyond the west gate via the Mount along the northern edge of the town to the river in the earlier 18th century[71] and the Mount itself seems to have been in origin a bastion in the defences,[72] possibly referred to as near the north gate in 1399.[73]

The west gate was mentioned in 1299;[74] it was repaired in 1556,[75] but has not been traced thereafter. The north gate, also mentioned in 1299,[76] was rebuilt in 1646–7 but by the 1720s it was in bad repair and was taken down to improve the road in 1798.[77] Its site was once marked by a stone near the girls' school in Northgate Street.[78] The south gate, referred to c. 1361,[79] was removed when the turnpike road was improved in 1822.[80] The east gate, mentioned in the mid 13th century and later known as St. John's Gate, still stood in 1553.[81]

The east gate marked the entrance to the town's largest suburb, Eastover, joined by the town bridge to the main part of Bridgwater on the west bank of the Parrett. Eastover was probably established after the bridge was built c.1200,[82] and the building of St. John's hospital by 1213[83] may mark its eastern extent. A ditch was licensed in 1286 from a point south of the bridge to the hospital, to provide a water-supply, and from there ran beside a causeway northwards to the river.[84] The single street in Eastover was known variously as 'beyond the bridge', 'between the bridge and the hospital', 'east of the bridge', and 'within the east gate'.[85] By the mid 14th century it was usually known as Eastover.[86] Burgages had been established there by the mid 13th century.[87]

As both the town and Eastover began to outgrow the defences, burgages were laid out beyond the east gate on the road to Horsey by the mid 13th century and beyond the north gate by 1300.[88] The extent of the town along the Horsey road was marked by 1480 by Kelyng Cross.[89] Burgages were also laid out beyond the

48 Ibid. nos. 92, 125, 164; S.R.O., D/B/bw 577, 595, 615, 619, 1317, 1615, 1748, 2251.
49 *S.R.S.* xlviii, no. 45.   50 Ibid. no. 44.
51 Below, this section (buildings).
52 S.R.O., D/B/bw 1686.   53 Ibid. DD/SH 1490.
54 *S.R.S.* xlviii, nos. 54, 114.
55 Ibid. nos. 8, 139, 383; lviii, no. 574.
56 Ibid. xlviii, nos. 8, 70, 139, 155, 245; liii, no. 346; lviii, no. 626. Croniles Lane is placed in the north-west part of the town in *S.R.S.* xlviii, p. liv.
57 Ibid. xlviii, no. 229; S.R.O., D/B/bw 1546.
58 S.R.O., DD/X/LTT 7; *Univ. Brit. Dir.* (1797), ii. 357; below, local govt. (borough).
59 S.R.O., DD/SH 1490.
60 Ibid. D/B/bw 2/1/1 (20 Nov. 1724).
61 Ibid. 2/1/2 (11 July 1769); A. H. Powell, *Bridgwater in Later Days* (1908), 194–5; S. G. Jarman, *Hist. Bridgwater*, 249.
62 *S.R.S.* lxx, no. 1030; S.R.O., D/B/bw 120.
63 *S.R.S.* li. 19; P.R.O., C 142/534, no. 167.
64 S.R.O., D/B/bw 1686.
65 Jarman, *Hist. Bridgwater*, 249.
66 Leland, *Itin.* ed. Toulmin Smith, i. 162.
67 *S.R.S.* xlviii, nos. 38, 53.

68 Ibid. no. 194; lviii, no. 642; lx, no. 746.
69 P.R.O., E 317/14.
70 J. Sprigge, *Anglia Rediviva*, 67.
71 S.R.O., D/B/bw 2/1/2 (8 Oct. 1734).
72 Ibid. DD/SH 1490, map. c. 1720.
73 *S.R.S.* liii, no. 492.
74 Ibid. xlviii, no. 47.
75 S.R.O., D/B/bw 1533.
76 *S.R.S.* xlviii, no. 48.
77 S.R.O., D/B/bw 1617; ibid. 2/1/3 (23 Jan. 1798); DD/SAS (C/1193) 4, p. 151.
78 Jarman, *Hist. Bridgwater*, 260.
79 *S.R.S.* xlviii, no. 194.
80 S.R.O., Q/AB 35.
81 *S.R.S.* ii. 232; xlviii, no. 15; lxxvii, nos. 80–1.
82 Above, this section.
83 *V.C.H. Som.* ii. 154–6.
84 *Cal. Pat.* 1281–92, 244.
85 *S.R.S.* xlviii, nos. 23, 80, 107 (p. 208), 283.
86 Ibid. nos. 184, 200–1, 203, 208.
87 Ibid. no. 23.
88 Ibid. nos. 15, 56.
89 Ibid. lxx, p. xi.

west gate,[90] along three diverging roads, North Street (named by 1299),[91] West Street (named by 1377),[92] and a way to a western horse pool.[93]

LATER GROWTH OF THE TOWN. The decay of the town *c.* 1500[94] and the reported damage in 1645[95] limited the growth of the town until the 18th century, when the gradual destruction of the castle made room for new streets. Castle, originally Chandos, Street was under construction in 1724, and the 'north back street', now Chandos Street, was projected.[96] Coffee House Lane, named after a coffee house in business in 1730, is mentioned in 1788.[97] King Square, proposed by the duke of Chandos in 1726, was eventually built between 1807 and 1830. Angel Crescent was built in 1816,[98] York Buildings by 1823, Russell Place by 1829, and Victoria and Albert streets by 1842.[99]

In the 1840s the town began to expand eastwards, encouraged by the arrival of the railway, both for residential and commercial purposes. The new parish of St. John the Baptist, Eastover, was created in 1846,[1] and by 1851 there were terraces along the Bristol and Bath roads and in Monmouth Street. St. John Street, giving access to the railway station, had become a shopping centre by 1861, and terraced streets were built north and south of it: Devonshire Street was begun in the late 1860s, Edward Street completed *c.* 1880, Rosebery Avenue completed in 1896–7, Cranleigh Gardens in 1905–6.[2] Similar building west of the town stretched into Wembdon and Durleigh parishes in the late 19th and the earlier 20th centuries.

Further expansion began in the late 1920s on the New Town estate in the north-west, where local authority housing was built for those who had lived in the slums demolished in the town centre. Other areas of public housing in the 1920s and 1930s were along the Bristol and Bath roads to the north-east and Taunton Road and Rhode Lane in the south.[3] In the 1950s the Sydenham estate east of the railway was built, and the Hamp estate south of the town centre followed from the 1960s. There was further expansion in the south and south-east in the 1980s.

BUILDINGS. A reference of 1397 to a house of three couples in Friarn Street to be built within seven years[4] and an agreement with a carver in 1515 for a new house in St. Mary Street[5] suggest that both were timber framed, perhaps with

crucks. Timber was probably the normal material for domestic buildings until the later 17th century when bricks became more common.[6] Among the few timber-framed houses to survive are nos. 2, 39, and 47 St. Mary Street, all of two storeys. No. 2 has a jettied front to the street. A more elaborate house of three storeys with jetties on two sides was demolished *c.* 1826.[7] An elaborate carved ceiling of the earlier 16th century now in the Burrell Collection in Glasgow[8] came from a house in St. Mary Street, demolished in the early 20th century.[9]

There are no houses with architectural features certainly of the later 17th century, but a number of surviving buildings may belong to that period, and more are recorded in old photographs and drawings. They are generally of two low storeys with a steep pantiled roof aligned with the street. The walls are of brick although it is possible that some have replaced or refaced timber framing, perhaps after the destruction during the Civil War.[10] The survival, in relatively large numbers, of such houses in the central streets such as Fore Street and High Street suggests that they were the common building type before the 18th century, and there is only one recorded instance of a single-storeyed cottage with attics.[11] Individual buildings no longer surviving included one with 'a cupillo or tower' of brick, described as newly erected in 1708 and still partly standing in 1802.[12] There was another building topped by a cupola in St. Mary Street by 1738.[13]

Castle Street,[14] laid out *c.* 1724 by the duke of Chandos, originally provided the site for six houses of five bays on each side of a broad roadway. All are of uniform character, of three storeys, with dressings including string courses and bolection-moulded architraves of ashlar. The main variation is in the design of the doorcases. It is probable that the south side was built some years after the north side, although presumably before 1734 when the duke sold the estate. It is likely that his architect was Benjamin Holloway, whose own house of *c.* 1730[15] was the Lions on West Quay, the most distinguished house in the town. It is of five bays and two storeys with a basement. The full-height centre piece is approached by steps which rise from a courtyard flanked by single-storeyed wings. In a similar style to the Castle Street houses is the Waterloo House public house in St. Mary Street. It is of six bays and has a large 18th-century shop front inserted into much of the ground floor. No. 5 West Quay is probably of similar

90 *S.R.S.* xlviii, nos. 39, 52.
91 Ibid. nos. 12, 49, 93, 95.
92 Ibid. nos. 118, 199; liii, no. 310; lviii, no. 525; lx, no. 751.
93 Ibid. xlviii, nos. 60, 64, 104–5; lviii, no. 522.
94 Leland, *Itin.* ed. Toulmin Smith, i. 162.
95 Below, this section (national events).
96 San Marino (Calif.), Huntington Libr., Chandos MSS. ST 57, vols. 24–41, letters 21 July 1724; 27 July 1726 (microfilm in Taunton Castle, Local Hist. Libr.).
97 S.R.O., DD/CH 47; 'Som. Insurance Policy Holders, 1714–31' (TS. in S.R.O.).
98 Inf. from Mr. J. F. Lawrence, Wembdon, based on deeds held by Sedgemoor D.C.
99 S.R.O., DD/OS 1; Pigot, *Nat. Com. Dir.* (1822–3, 1842).
1 Below, church.

2 Sidcot Sch., Winscombe, deeds and estate plans; C. Norman, 'The landscape of an area of Bridgwater' (Bristol Univ. Cert. in Arts thesis, 1978).
3 W. Locke, *Times Remembered* (priv. print. 1983), 12, 41; S.R.O., D/R/bw 22/1/42.
4 *S.R.S.* liii, no. 484.
5 S.R.O., D/B/bw 1084.
6 Below, econ. hist. (industries).
7 Squibbs, *Bridgwater*, pl. 97.
8 *Burrell Colln.* (1984), 116–17.   9 Local inf.
10 Below, this section (national events).
11 Squibbs, *Bridgwater*, pls. 35, 37, 62, 88, 103–4.
12 S.R.O., D/B/bw 1686; DD/WY 155/1.
13 Ibid. D/B/bw 1685; D/B/bw 2/1/3 (22 Feb. 1819).
14 Below, plate facing p. 232.
15 W. Halfpenny, *New Method of Perspective Made Easy* (1731).

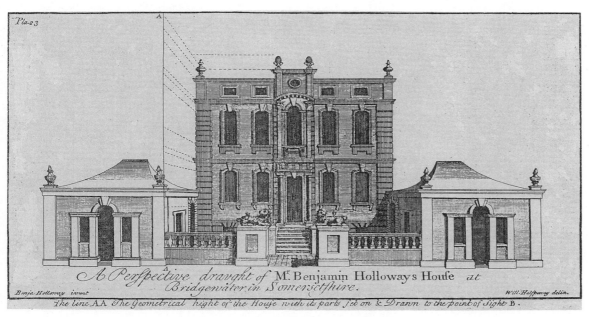

A Perspective draught of Mr Benjamin Holloways House at Bridgewater in Somersetshire.

Benja Holloway invent   Will Halfpeny delin.

The line AA The Geometrical hight of the House with its parts set on & Drawn to the point of Sight B.

THE LIONS, WEST QUAY, *c.* 1730

date and quality but much has been destroyed by an earlier 20th-century shop front.[16] The Priory in St. Mary Street has also been much altered in the 20th century but it appears to have had a pilastered, early 18th-century front of seven bays flanked by early 19th-century additions.

The most complete surviving house of smaller size is no. 15 Friarn Street, of four bays and three storeys, which does not have stone dressings but has brick plat bands and an elaborate timber shell hood above the doorway. A short terrace of plain, one-bayed, three-storeyed houses in Chandos Street is almost contemporary with the Castle Street houses whose gardens it faces, but in the earlier 18th century most small houses probably continued to be built in the two-storeyed vernacular tradition of the 17th century.

If the Chandos-influenced houses of the earlier 18th century have decorative elements which might in English terms be described as baroque, the buildings of the later 18th and early 19th century are by contrast very restrained. King Square, the one major building enterprise of the period and incomplete, is in the restrained manner, and so is the former Royal Clarence hotel in High Street. The probability is that much of the rebuilding in the town is 19th- rather than 18th-century. Many of the houses are of three storeys and in the 19th century they have stepped voussoirs to the window heads. Contemporary shop fronts were not uncommon.[17]

As in most other towns the mid 19th century marks the beginning of a period when several styles were used for commercial and domestic building. No. 9 Cornhill has a datestone for 1857 and is Italianate, four storeys high and six bays

long. The Infirmary was refronted in 1876 in a mid 18th-century style and the former Y.M.C.A. building at the corner of Eastover and Salmon Parade had ornamental brickwork and a roofline inspired by northern European gothic.[18] Most idiosyncratic is Castle House, Queen Street, late gothic in outline and decoration with early Renaissance rustication, built in 1851 to demonstrate the versatility of Portland cement.[19]

As early as the 18th century there had been a few houses standing in spacious grounds (e.g. the Priory and Hamp House) and they became more numerous as the town spread outwards in the mid 19th century.[20] Most of the growth of the built up area, however, was in the form of streets of relatively uniform terraces[21] or semi-detached pairs.[22] Ornamental bricks and tiles, manufactured in the town,[23] were used to decorate even the humbler houses. On some of the less humble houses unfaced stone is used for walling, and gables with ornamental barge-boards are common, perhaps in an attempt to be different.

The part of the town east of the river appears always to have had an architectural character inferior to that of the west. The only early buildings of quality are on the river frontage. No. 4 East Quay appears to be a design derived from the mid 18th century London pattern books, especially in its eared architraves, quasi-pilasters, and 'Gibbs' door surround, but the interior appears to be of the early 19th century. In Eastover several two-storeyed houses with steep pantiled roofs are probably late 18th-century in origin, and in Monmouth Street the demolished Rookery was probably late 18th-century and the earliest suburban terrace in Bridgwater.[24] Monmouth Terrace and adjacent

16   Photo. in R. Fitzhugh and W. Loudon, *Bygone Bridg-water and the Villages* (1987), 67.
17   Squibbs, *Bridgwater*, pls. 6, 24, 152.
18   Ibid. pl. 174.
19   *Bridgwater Mercury*, 30 Apr. 1986; 1 July 1987.

20   Squibbs, *Bridgwater*, pls. 87, 116–19, 139.
21   Fitzhugh and Loudon, *Bygone Bridgwater*, pp. 21, 27, 70.
22   Ibid. pp. 19, 21, 26.
23   Above, plate facing p. 9.
24   Squibbs, *Bridgwater*, pls. 131, 189.

houses are mostly of two or three bays with semicircular heads to the windows. Church Street and Blake Place were presumably nearly contemporary with St. John's church, erected in 1843.[25] Most of the houses are in dark brown coursed rubble with lighter stone or painted wood architraves; those nearest the church are semidetached, the remainder terraced. Nearer the railway, houses of the mid 19th century are nearly uniform two-storeyed terraces of red brick without front gardens and the only decorations are the ornamental door and window heads.

A hall of pleas in Fore Street belonged to the castle estate and was mentioned in 1347–8.[26] It may have been the building known in 1431–2 as the shire hall.[27]

A guildhall recorded in Fore Street in 1354 evidently had a first-floor room above booths.[28] Known variously in the 15th and 16th centuries as the common house, the town house, or the town hall,[29] it was called the guildhall in the 18th century, when separate rooms within the building included a burgess hall or council house, a serjeants' hall, and the 'mayor's alphabet', a small room for the corporation's library and records.[30] A room over the burgess hall was divided in 1743.[31] The building, which had an entrance with steps and columns, was in a poor state of repair by 1808, and its demolition was suggested.[32] The corporation moved to the grand jury room at the assize hall in High Street in 1822, and the guildhall was probably demolished soon afterwards. In 1823 they moved to a new building adjoining. That building, designed by Richard Carver and financed by an 'improvement committee' including Sir Thomas Lethbridge and other members of the grand jury, provided a town hall and strong room for the corporation, lodgings for the judges, and witness and jury rooms.[33] It is of limestone in a simple classical style with panelled pilasters. The corporation later extended its use of the building when the assizes ceased to be held in the town; in the 1880s part was used as a police court and part as a free library.[34] It is now used as offices by Sedgemoor district council and by the Bridgwater charter trustees. A new town hall was built behind, on the site of the former assize hall, in 1865 to the designs of Charles Knowles.[35] It is of rusticated stone and brick in a Venetian style.

Until 1720 a temporary 'boarder house' was erected for the assizes near the high cross, and in order to ensure that the judges came regularly to the town the corporation then agreed to buy out the right of the tenant of the Red Cow inn on the north side of High Street and to build there a permanent assize hall.[36] The building, 'most magnificent, large, and capacious', was said to have been erected in six weeks 'after the model of Westminster Hall'.[37] The cost was borne by local gentry and by members of the corporation, and the work was supervised, and possibly designed, by John Gosling.[38] The hall, to which a grand jury chamber was added c. 1722, was also used for quarter sessions.[39] When not in use by judges or magistrates the building was a store for wool, flax, hides, and tallow.[40] The front of the building was colonnaded, providing space for market stalls. The court room, which was galleried, was divided in 1776, and seats for a jury were added in the part used for assizes.[41] The building was demolished in 1856.[42]

There was a prison in Bridgwater c. 1210,[43] probably in the castle. A prison was claimed by both the Crown and Roger Mortimer in 1280.[44] The gaol was mentioned in 1352,[45] 1481,[46] the mid 17th century, and 1728.[47] Its condition was severely criticized by John Howard in 1789.[48] The building, on the south side of Fore Street, had an imposing rusticated classical frontage; it was closed and demolished in 1875. Cells were built at the police station in High Street, and in 1911 at the new station in Northgate.[49] A lock-up called the Cockmoyle prison was mentioned in 1575.[50] It was later said to be part of an inn of the same name, and in 1687–8 was called the borough bridewell.[51] The lock-up was evidently on an upper floor over a lane between High Street and the churchyard, since it was known as the higher prison in the 17th century and Upper Bow in the 18th.[52] In 1729 the quarter sessions established a bridewell for the borough and parish, probably an extension to the town's prison, and set up a whipping post there.[53]

An old pillory was mentioned in 1378.[54] In the early 17th century the pillory stood in High Street by the stocks and near the site of the present town hall.[55] In 1744 the corporation ordered the pillory to be removed to the Cornhill, but both pillory and stocks were in 1782 to be set up again on the old site.[56] No further record of either has been found.

St. John's hospital had been established by 1213[57] at the eastern end of Eastover. New buildings seem to have been erected c. 1350,[58] and in the mid 15th century the site included a church, chapter house, and cloister, with rooms

25 Below, churches.
26 P.R.O., SC 6/968/17, 25; SC 6/969/4, 10–11.
27 S.R.S. lviii, no. 653.
28 Ibid. xlviii, no. 172; P.R.O., SC 6/968/22; SC 6/969/17.
29 S.R.O., D/B/bw 800, 1431, 1546, 1552.
30 Ibid. D/B/bw 2238; ibid. 2/1/2 (26 Dec. 1735; 21 Feb. 1737).
31 Ibid. 2/1/2 (22 Nov. 1743).
32 Ibid. 2/1/3 (27 Apr. 1808; 18 July 1809; 2 Mar. 1810; 23 Sept. 1811; 3 May 1813; 4 Sept. 1819).
33 Ibid. 2/1/3 (23 Sept. 1822; 23 Sept., 6 Dec. 1823).
34 O.S. Map, 1/500, Som. L. 11. 21 (1887 edn.).
35 Pevsner, S. and W. Som. 98.
36 S.R.O., D/B/bw 2/1/1 (4–5 July 1720).
37 Ibid. DD/SAS (C/1193) 4, p. 151.
38 Ibid. D/B/bw 2/1/1 (12 Dec. 1721); D/B/bw 1643.
39 Ibid. 2/1/1 (22 June 1722; 1 May 1724; 26 Feb. 1725).
40 Ibid. 2/1/1 (26 Feb. 1725); 2/1/2 (4 May 1752).

41 Ibid. 2/1/1 (23 July 1723); 2/1/2 (2 July 1776).
42 Squibbs, Bridgwater, pl. 100.   43 S.R.S. lxiii. 373.
44 Plac. de Quo Warr. (Rec. Com.), 693.
45 Cal. Pat. 1350–4, 377.
46 S.R.S. lxx, no. 987.
47 S.R.O., D/B/bw 1623, 1804.
48 J. Howard, Account of Prisons in the Western Circuit (1789), 38–40.
49 Squibbs, Bridgwater, pl. 53.
50 S.R.O., D/B/bw 2231.
51 P.R.O., E 134/3 Jas. II East./26.
52 S.R.O., D/B/bw 1617, 1686.
53 Ibid. 2/1/1 (26 Aug. 1729).
54 S.R.S. liii, nos. 317–18.
55 S.R.O., D/B/bw 1278, 1283.
56 Ibid. 2/1/2 (10 July 1744; 14 Nov. 1782).
57 V.C.H. Som. ii. 154–6.
58 S.R.S. x, p. 635.

including a parlour off the cloister, the whole surrounded by gardens.[59] The church was *c.* 112 ft. long.[60] Leland described the hospital as partly outside the east gate.[61] At the Dissolution the site passed into private hands,[62] but parts of the hospital still stood in 1703.[63]

The convent of Friars Minor (Franciscans or Grey Friars) was founded in 1245–6.[64] The friars left the original site, by 1358 occupied by nine burgages,[65] for one south-west of the town, between the town ditch and the Durleigh brook.[66] Timber was given for unspecified buildings in the 1250s, for a dormitory in 1278, and for further work in 1284,[67] and land was added to the precinct in 1349.[68] The conventual church was rebuilt in the earlier 15th century, and it and its burial ground were consecrated in 1445.[69] In 1538 the buildings comprised a church and simple domestic quarters, the church measuring 210 ft. by 52 ft.[70] Some of the buildings and the lead were sold, but the domestic quarters were in the 1540s a fine dwelling house.[71] The house was owned by the Saunders family in 1571 and 1629,[72] but only the 'cemetery and churchyard' survived in 1720.[73]

INNS AND TAVERNS. A tavern on the west side of the high cross in 1367 and Robert Plympton's inn in High Street in 1376 were the earliest recorded inns in the town,[74] and the George in St. Mary Street was mentioned between 1392 and 1421.[75] In the 16th century the inns included the Bell, belonging to Holy Trinity chantry, the Saracen's Head, belonging to Athelney abbey, and the Ship, belonging to St. John's hospital; the Swan, leased late in the century to the corporation by the Crown for a rent of 4*d.*, the price of 4 iron horseshoes, and 38 iron keys; the Angel, the White Hart, and in Eastover the Three Crowns.[76]

In the 17th century the justices used to meet at the Angel in High Street, and other prominent houses were the Crown, the Lamb, the Noah's Ark, the Red Cow, and the Red Lion.[77] In 1686 the town's inns offered 143 beds and stabling for 246 horses.[78] Other inns included the Blue Anchor, the Black Boy, the Rose, the Three Cups, the Three Mariners, and the Valiant Soldier.[79]

The Red Lion and the Fighting Cocks seem to have been frequented by the rival political factions on the corporation in the early 18th century, and the Swan was the regular haunt of troops billeted in the town.[80] In the 1720s there were said to be over 120 houses selling ale and cider in the town,[81] and by 1748 the town was divided into three divisions for licensing purposes when there were just over 50 licensed houses and a single coffee house.[82] The Swan, the Castle Tavern, the King's Head, and the Fountain were regularly used for excise hearings in the 18th century.[83] There were still at least 50 licensed houses in the 1790s, and 45 in 1822–3. Seven stood on the Quay, including the Ship on Launch; 8 were in Eastover, and the remainder mostly in the town centre including 10 in and around High Street. Among those was the Valiant Soldier, which in 1790 had a fives court. The principal establishments were the George, the Swan, and the King's Head.[84] In 1825, as part of the rebuilding of the north side of High Street, the Royal (later Royal Clarence) hotel replaced the former Crown and Angel inns, and until it closed in 1984 was the principal establishment in the town.[85] Inns opened away from the town centre mark the spread of the built-up area: the Railway hotel, by the railway station, in 1839–40; the Mermaid in Bath Road in 1859, the Crowpill in Chilton Street by 1869, and eleven inns in St. John Street in the 1870s.[86] There were 71 hotels, inns, and beerhouses in the parish in 1909, 44 in 1988.[87]

SOCIAL AND CULTURAL ACTIVITIES. A play was performed in the shire hall in 1431–2,[88] and pipers from Ash Priors took part in the Corpus Christi pageant in 1449. The pageant, also called the shepherds' pageant, was last recorded in 1543.[89] The king's players visited the town in 1461–2. In 1494–5 minstrels of the king, the king's mother, the earl of Arundel, and the mayor of Bristol were rewarded for their visits.[90] Among the entertainers who visited frequently until the 1560s were the players of the duke of Somerset and of the earls of Bridgwater and Bath, whose patrons had landed interests in and around the town; the players or minstrels of the sovereign, the Lord Admiral, the marquess of Dorset, the earl of Worcester, Lord de la Warr,

59 Ibid. xlix, p. 390; l, pp. 456–7.
60 W. Worcestre, *Itineraries*, ed. J. H. Harvey, 125.
61 Leland, *Itin.* ed. Toulmin Smith, i. 163.
62 P.R.O., SC 6/Hen. VIII/3151; S.R.O., DD/POt 39; *L. & P. Hen. VIII*, xviii (1), p. 196; xix (2), pp. 86–7.
63 S.R.O., DD/X/SU; P.R.O., C 142/141, no. 17.
64 *V.C.H. Som.* ii. 151–2; *Proc. Som. Arch. Soc.* cxxix. 69, 71, 73–4; *S.R.S.* xlviii, pp. xlvi–xlix.
65 P.R.O., SC 6/968/19–22.
66 *Proc. Som. Arch. Soc.* cxxix. 69–74.
67 *Cal. Lib.* 1245–51, 299; *Close R.* 1247–51, 312; 1256–9, 221; *Cal. Close*, 1272–9, 451; 1279–81, 309.
68 *Cal. Pat.* 1348–50, 361.
69 *S.R.S.* xlix, p. 24. Money had been given for the church by John Somour (d. 1419): Worcestre, *Itineraries*, 79, 81.
70 *L. & P. Hen. VIII*, xiii (2), p. 130; Worcestre, *Itineraries*, 81, 127 and plan opp. 398; *Brit. Soc. Franciscan Studies*, 18 (1937), 211–18.
71 P.R.O., SC 6/Hen. VIII/3151; Leland, *Itin.* ed. Toulmin Smith, i. 162.
72 P.R.O., C 142/278, no. 148; S.R.O., DD/DP 75/3.
73 S.R.O., DD/SAS (C/1193) 4, pp. 149–51.
74 *S.R.S.* xlviii, nos. 229, 299.

75 Ibid. liii, no. 455; lviii, no. 603.
76 S.R.O., D/B/bw 128, 431, 492, 500, 566–8, 609, 618, 622, 632–3, 798, 800, 909, 1239, 1340, 1435, 1540, 1690; Bodl. Libr., MS. Top. Som. b. 1, ff. 8–10; P.R.O., C 142/414, no. 92; *Ledger Bk. of John Smythe, 1538–50* (Bristol Rec. Soc. xxviii), 69.
77 S.R.O., D/B/bw 1074, 1294, 1686, 1898, 1915, 2135; D/P/bw. m 2/1/3; *S.R.S.* xxxiv. 200; Dors. R.O., D104/M2.
78 P.R.O., WO 30/48.
79 S.R.O., D/B/bw 1074, 1686, 1690, 2135; D/P/bw. m 2/1/2–3; DD/DP 93/5; DD/S/WH 189.
80 *Proc. Som. Arch. Soc.* cvi. 66–74.
81 S.R.O., DD/SAS (C/1193) 4, p. 151.
82 Ibid. D/B/bw 2024, 2157; DD/CH, box 36.
83 Ibid. D/B/bw 1861.
84 *Univ. Brit. Dir.* (1797), ii. 356–61; Pigot, *Nat. Com. Dir.* (1822–3); S.R.O., DD/RN 53/1.
85 S.R.O., DD/HB 34; D/B/bw 2/1/3; Jarman, *Hist. Bridgwater*, 250.
86 D. Williams, *Bridgwater Inns Past and Present* (Oxen Books, 1987).
87 *Kelly's Dir. Som.* (1909); *Bridgwater Mercury*, 6 Apr. 1988.
88 *S.R.S.* lviii, no. 653.
89 Ibid. lx, no. 757; S.R.O., D/B/bw 1431, 1442.
90 *S.R.S.* lx, no. 830; S.R.O., D/B/bw 1431.

Lord Mountjoy, and Mr. Fortescue. A Christmas play at the mayor's house and exhibitions of lions and bears were among the other entertainments.[91] Players were not regularly recorded in the later 16th century, although one killed in the town was buried there in 1597, and Lord Berkeley's players were paid in 1603–4.[92] Some 'stage players' performed at the town hall in 1722, and a company of comedians from Bath hired the assize hall for several weeks in 1736.[93] Travelling players seem to have visited the town during the summer assizes c. 1800, and by 1813 a theatre had been established in Penel Orlieu under Henry Lee.[94] Edmund Kean performed in the town in 1816.[95] The theatre, described as in Back Street in 1834, was then lit with gas; the magistrates withdrew its licence in 1853.[96] The Bijou theatre was opened in St. Mary Street in 1912, the Palace in Penel Orlieu in 1916, both as cinemas, and by 1925 the town hall was used as a theatre. In the same year the former Bijou was reopened as the Empire, the Arcade cinema was opened in Eastover in 1929, and the Odeon in Penel Orlieu in 1936. The former Palace was reopened in 1940 as a social centre for troops. An arts centre in Castle Street, claimed to be the first of its kind in Britain, was established in 1946.[97]

Dancing at the guildhall, forbidden by the corporation after a few years in 1731, was revived in 1755 in connexion with horse races. The races, held originally in the summer and continuing in the 1780s, were later abandoned but were revived in 1813 when the Taunton races were transferred to Bridgwater. By the 1820s they took place early in September at Crook, north-east of the town, on a mile-long circular course. In 1854, after a gap, they were revived in late August and by 1867, as the Bridgwater and West Somerset races, were held at the end of September. The Bridgwater steeplechase and hurdle races were held in 1898 but were said to have been abandoned by 1905. Races were revived in July 1926 at Durleigh, but were discontinued in 1929.[98]

Tennis and fives were played in the town in the 17th century, and the corporation owned a bowling green in Eastover until the 1720s.[99] Popular entertainment is suggested in the field name Bull Baiting acre, adjoining Castle field.[1] Revels were said to have been held near Pig Cross on Oak Apple Day (29 May) until the 1830s.[2] Annual amusements, including public breakfasts, balls, and backsword play, were held on Chilton common by 1793, and a festival, probably to celebrate peace with France, was planned to entertain 10,000 people on the Cornhill in 1814.[3] Bonfires traditionally held on the Cornhill to commemorate the Gunpowder plot took on political overtones in the 1850s, and the crushing of the Indian Mutiny inspired a procession, the first to be called a carnival, in 1857 with decorative floats, a band, and firework displays known as 'squibbing'.[4] Processions in 1882 and 1883, the second to celebrate the completion of the new town bridge, were followed by a more organized carnival in 1884, beginning a tradition for which Bridgwater has become renowned.[5] The last bonfire on the Cornhill was made in 1924, but the squibbing[6] and the carnival floats, each built by competing carnival clubs from within the town and from throughout the county, have made Bridgwater carnival the most popular tourist attraction of its kind in the West of England.

Bridgwater cricket club was founded in 1832.[7] Turkish baths were opened in York Buildings in 1861, and swimming baths in Old Taunton Road in 1890.[8] The baths were replaced by the Lido in Broadway in 1960, and the Lido by the Sedgemoor Splash in Mount Street in 1991.[9] The Blake Gardens were opened in 1902, Eastover recreation ground in 1905, and Victoria Park c. 1928.[10]

There was a reading room in the market house by 1830 which by 1840 had become the Literary and Scientific Institution.[11] By 1861 there were reading rooms in St. John's Street, Taunton Road, and West Street, the first still in use in 1889.[12] By 1859 the Literary and Scientific Institution had been moved to George Street where there was a museum 1861–75 and a reading room in 1875.[13] A reading room at the town hall by 1889 remained there until 1906 when the present library was opened in Binford Place.[14] The present museum, known as the Admiral Blake Museum, was opened in Blake Street in 1926.[15]

The first newspaper in the town was the *Bridgwater and Somersetshire Herald*, founded in 1825, which continued 1831–3 as the *Alfred*. The *Bridgwater Times* was published 1846–61 and was followed by the *Bridgwater Standard* (1861–70) and the *Bridgwater Gazette* (1871–85) which, as the *Bridgwater Independent*, was continued 1885–1933. The *Bridgwater Mercury and Western Counties Herald*, begun in 1857,[16] continued in 1991.

91 S.R.O., D/B/bw 1434–6, 1440–2, 1462, 1464, 1544; DD/SAS PR 217.
92 Ibid. D/P/bw. m 2/1/1 (8 Dec.); D/B/bw 1590.
93 Ibid. D/B/bw 2/1/1–2.
94 Ibid. DD/SAS FA 185, p. 128; D/P/bw. m 4/1/49.
95 Ibid. T/PH/ay 1. 96 Squibbs, *Bridgwater*, 65, 76.
97 Ibid. 116, 121, 124–5, 128, 131, 133.
98 S.R.O., D/B/bw 2/1/2 (30 June 1755); ibid. D/B/bw 1522; DD/X/HUD 20; T. B. Dilks, *Charles James Fox and the Borough of Bridgwater* (1937), 28–9; *Taunton Courier*, 21 Aug. 1822; S.R.S. lxxvi (Greenwood's map); *Kelly's Dir. Som.* (1906); *V.C.H. Som.* ii. 595; Squibbs, *Bridgwater*, 55, 77, 104, 124–5; R. Bush, *Book of Taunton*, 105.
99 S.R.O., D/B/bw 1631; DD/S/WH 118; DD/SH 1490.
1 Ibid. D/B/bw 1686, 2055; ibid. tithe award.
2 Powell, *Bridgwater in Later Days*, 194–5; Jarman, *Hist. Bridgwater*, 249. 3 S.R.O., DD/L 2/154/13.
4 *Bridgwater Times*, 9 Nov. 1854; *Bridgwater Mercury*, 11

Nov. 1857.
5 *Bridgwater Mercury*, 11 Oct. 1983; Squibbs, *Bridgwater*, 110.
6 Sydenham Hervey, Diary (TS. in possession of R. W. Dunning, Taunton), 5 Nov. 1871; Squibbs, *Bridgwater*, pl. 71.
7 Squibbs, *Bridgwater*, 64.
8 Ibid. 100–1; *P.O. Dir. Som.* (1861).
9 Squibbs, *Bridgwater*, 137; local inf.
10 Squibbs, *Bridgwater*, 106, 111, 125; *Kelly's Dir. Som.* (1906).
11 Pigot, *Nat. Com. Dir.* (1830); *Co. Gaz. Dir. Som.* (1840).
12 *P.O. Dir. Som.* (1861); *Kelly's Dir. Som.* (1889).
13 Harrison, Harrod, & Co. *Dir. Som.* (1859); *P.O. Dir. Som.* (1861); *Kelly's Dir. Som.* (1875).
14 *Kelly's Dir. Som.* (1889, 1910).
15 Ibid. (1927); Som. C. C. *Dir. Museums in Som.* (1988).
16 L. E. J. Brooke, *Som. Newspapers 1725–1960* (1960), pp. 44–6.

Before *c.* 1820 there were seven friendly societies in Bridgwater, each based at an inn, the earliest at the Three Tuns, apparently founded in 1795. One for mariners was founded in 1805, another for carpenters and joiners in 1811, and a third based at the Baptist church in St. Mary Street in 1818. In the mid 19th century national societies for tradesmen were active.[17]

NATIONAL EVENTS. King John visited Bridgwater in 1204, 1205, 1208, and 1210, and Henry III in 1250.[18] Prests were delivered in the town to William Longespée, earl of Salisbury, in 1208–9[19] and a tax levied in Cornwall in 1234 was to be taken for safe custody to the town.[20] Letters patent were dated there in 1221.[21] Royal justices met in the town in 1204, in the 1250s, in the 1270s, and in the later 14th and earlier 15th century.[22] The assize judges sat in Bridgwater each summer from 1720 but by 1797 and until 1853 every other year.[23] The Michaelmas quarter sessions for the county met in Bridgwater by the later 16th century and until 1670, when instead the town held the Midsummer sessions.[24] The sessions continued to be held there until 1853.[25]

In 1381 Bridgwater was the scene of a serious disturbance when St. John's hospital was attacked and the master forced to surrender bonds held against townsmen.[26] In 1469 Humphrey Stafford, earl of Devon, was executed in the town.[27] In 1528 sessions of the peace in both Bridgwater and Taunton were interrupted by insurrection,[28] and in 1536 four men were executed in the town after a rising at Taunton. In 1539 part of the body of Richard Whiting, abbot of Glastonbury, was displayed at Bridgwater.[29] The town was chosen as the title for a possible suffragan bishopric in 1534, but no appointment was ever made.[30]

In June 1643 half the parliamentary garrison of Taunton, retreating before the king's army, stayed briefly in the town. Supporters of parliament were said to be 'very strong' there, but others attempted to detain the troops.[31] Some 2,000 men were said to have left at night as the marquess of Hertford advanced.[32] The royalist garrison then installed was commanded by Col. Edmund Wyndham of Kentsford, recently M.P. for the borough, and the defences of the town included four guns ordered by Prince Maurice.[33]

Some of the garrison mutinied when there were rumours of Irish troops landing at Minehead and Bristol.[34] In 1643, between June and November, 17 soldiers were buried in the town.[35]

In 1644 the governor refused to use his troops to protect excise collectors from attacks, in which some local recruits joined.[36] In August men from the garrison beat off 500 parliamentary horse who had attacked a supply column near North Petherton.[37] During the year 20 soldiers were buried in the town including two killed at North Petherton.[38]

In the year from September 1644 the town paid for 400 pairs of hose and shoes for the king's forces then at Wells.[39] Prince Rupert and the leaders of the Western Association met in Bridgwater in April 1645.[40] After his defeat at Langport on 10 July Goring brought his guns and some infantry into the town.[41] The New Model army followed up its success by a gradual investment from the south and east. Maj.-Gen. Massey established his headquarters at Hamp House, and Col. Holborne took Sydenham Manor. The defenders, behind earthworks at the east end of St. John's field and between there and Dunwear, were equipped with 40 guns, and mounted a battery between the west and north gates, at what was later called the Mount.[42] Sir Thomas Fairfax, in command of the parliamentary forces, placed troops in the fields of Horsey and Bower, and five regiments of the New Model under Cromwell were drawn up in St. John's and Castle fields.[43]

The town was stormed on 21 July 1645. Fairfax took Eastover with 600 prisoners, finding that most of the suburb had been fired. He then crossed the Parrett, forcing the royalists to yield the town. A total of 2,000 prisoners, 800 horse, and 36 guns were taken.[44] Estimates of the damage varied. Fairfax said that a third of the town had been burnt, while a royalist declared that 'most of the town' was destroyed by fire except some houses near the castle, the damage ascribed either to Col. Wyndham or to the townsmen.[45] Henry Harvey, lord of the Castle manor, claimed to have lost £4,000 including a house by the bridge, and the mayor in 1656 asked help to repair 120 houses destroyed in the town including the almshouses.[46] Many of the inhabitants had removed themselves for safety to Wembdon.[47] Between 8 January and 17 July

17 P.R.O., FS 2/9.
18 *Proc. Som. Arch. Soc.* lxiii. 39–40; *Cal. Pat.* 1247–58, 72; *Close R.* 1247–51, 311.
19 *Pipe R.* 1208 (P.R.S. N.S. xxiii), 198.
20 *Cal. Pat.* 1232–47, 42.
21 *Pat. R.* 1216–25, 300, 312.
22 *Close R.* 1256–9, 35; *Cal. Close,* 1392–6, 215; *S.R.S.* xi, p. 430; xli. 12, 147, 157, 233; lxviii. 7; *H.M.C. Wells,* ii. 35, 59.
23 S.R.O., D/B/bw 2/1/1 (4, 5 July 1720); ibid. Q/SR 599; *Univ. Brit. Dir.* (1797).
24 *S.R.S.* xxiii, pp. xxiv, 5, 85, 149; *V.C.H. Som.* ii. 43; S.R.O., D/B/bw 1551; *Cal. S.P. Dom.* 1668–9, 113–14; 1670, 213.
25 S.R.O., Q/SR 599.
26 *Proc. Som. Arch. Soc.* lxxiii. 57–69.
27 *Complete Peerage,* iv. 328.
28 *L. & P. Hen. VIII,* iv (2), p. 1830.
29 Ibid. add. i (1), p. 369; *V.C.H. Som.* ii. 96.
30 *S.D.N.Q.* xvi. 246.
31 *S.R.S.* xviii. 47–8, 85.

32 Hist. MSS. Com. 58, *Bath,* iv, p. 218; D. Underdown, *Som. in Civil War and Interregnum,* 51.
33 *S.R.S.* xviii. 47–8; Hist. MSS. Com. 41, *15th Rep. VII, Somerset,* p. 67.
34 D. Underdown, *Revel, Riot, and Rebellion,* 165.
35 S.R.O., D/P/bw. m 2/1/1.
36 Underdown, *Revel,* 149.
37 S.R.O., D/P/bw. m 2/1/1 (burials 14 Aug.); Underdown, *Civil War,* 77; below, North Petherton, intro.
38 S.R.O., D/P/bw. m 2/1/1 (burials 1 July, 14 Aug.).
39 Ibid. D/B/bw 1516.
40 Underdown, *Civil War,* 92.
41 *Richard Symonds's Diary* (Camd. Soc. [1st ser.], lxxiv), 210–11.
42 *Proc. Som. Arch. Soc.* xxiii. 12–25; Underdown, *Civil War,* 108; *Cal. S.P. Dom.* 1667–81, 199.
43 Hist. MSS. Com. 6, *7th Rep. I, Verney,* p. 451.
44 *L. J.* vii. 506, 511.
45 S.R.O., D/B/bw 141; *Symonds's Diary,* 210–11.
46 *Cal. S.P. Dom.* 1656–7, 207.
47 *S.R.S.* xxviii. 126, 135.

1645, before the siege, 68 soldiers were buried in the town; thereafter no burials were registered until 1 December.[48]

Troops remained in the town, which was used as a base for the expedition to Ireland,[49] and in 1646 blood was shed when the County Committee used them against a crowd of local people who had come to help slight the defences.[50]

In 1646–7 the corporation paid for the removal of guns from the quay and the wages of three men for three days 'towards dismantling of the garrison'. In 1647–8 it celebrated with wine when the dragoons left the town, and in 1648–9 made a gift to the 'Lord General's clerk' for 'taking of the soldiers from the town'.[51] A company was to be raised there in 1659 and Col. Richard Bovet's regiment was then in the town. Part of it was sent towards Bristol in 1660 for Gen. Monk.[52]

During Monmouth's rebellion the town was occupied twice by rebel troops and for at least a year afterwards by regular dragoons. The corporation formally proclaimed Monmouth king on 21 June 1685 and the town was more generous than any other in voluntary contributions to his cause. Monmouth himself had quarters in the castle, his army on Castle field.[53] Remarkably few townsmen were reported absent from home during the time of the rebellion or were otherwise accused of complicity.[54]

The rebels returned to the town for two days before the battle of Sedgemoor, barricading the bridge and setting up guns at the high cross, in the castle, and at the south gate.[55] After the battle the king's troops chased some of the rebels into the town and then brought their wounded for treatment. The corporation was not paid for their maintenance until 1687.[56] Nine rebels were hanged, drawn, and quartered in the town.[57] James II visited the town briefly in 1686,[58] and the corporation soon afterwards petitioned that dragoons still quartered in the town should be removed.[59]

In the early 18th century political rivalry, accusations of Jacobitism, and the presence of troops caused several riots in the town.[60] John Oldmixon (1673–1742), the Whig pamphleteer, was customs collector there 1716–30, and acted for James Brydges, duke of Chandos, who had commercial interests in the town.[61]

Robert Blake (1598–1657), admiral and general, was born in the town; John Allen (1660–1741), physician and inventor, practised and died there; and Henry Phillpotts (1778–1869), bishop of Exeter,[62] and Francis Joseph Grimshaw (1901–65), Roman Catholic archbishop of Birmingham, were born there.[63]

CASTLE. William Brewer (d. 1226) was licensed in 1200 to build a castle at Bridgwater which descended with the manor, or one third of the manor, until 1627.[64] While the Crown had custody 1233–48 it appointed constables and used parts of the castle as a prison and a store.[65] The Crown again occupied the castle 1322–6 in case Roger Mortimer should escape from the Tower and use it as a base for operations in Wales.[66] When he sold his interest in the manor in 1627 Sir George Whitmore retained the castle, which had been separately leased in 1591 to William Goble, collector and bailiff,[67] but he sold the castle in 1630 to Henry, son of William Harvey of Bridgwater, a lawyer.[68] Henry's son Henry died in 1671, and the castle passed first to his uncle Francis, owner in 1673 and 1690, and by 1699 to his nephew John Harvey[69] (fl. 1715). In 1721 John's son Francis conveyed the castle and other properties on the site and elsewhere in the town to James Brydges, duke of Chandos.[70] The duke sold the estate to Thomas Watts in 1734, and in 1738 Watts and his wife Mary conveyed it to John Anderdon, M.D. In 1777 John's son Edward was owner of two houses and extensive gardens, formerly the castle bailey, besides the remains of a substantial mansion.[71] Robert Harvey, M.D., is said to have been the owner in 1791.[72]

The castle was apparently rectangular in plan and lay in the north-east corner of the town and on the west bank of the river. Only the early 13th-century Water Gate and a stretch of curtain wall north of it survive above ground. In 1242 the constable was ordered to repair the mound upon which the castle keep stood, to mend the turrets, and to make other necessary repairs.[73] In 1246 the towers were to be roofed and the surrounding palisade renewed.[74] In 1360 the building was said to be in ruins,[75] although repairs had been made to the chapel and a barn

48 S.R.O., D/P/bw. m 2/1/1.
49 Hist. MSS. Com. 15, 10th Rep. VI, Pleydell-Bouverie, p. 95; ibid. 63, Egmont, i, pp. 297, 299.
50 Underdown, Revel, 225; S.R.S. lxxi. 17; lxxxi. 25; L.J. viii. 684, 706.
51 S.R.O., D/B/bw 1518, 1617, 1619.
52 Hist. MSS. Com. 51, Leyborne-Popham, p. 158; Cal. S.P. Dom. 1659–60, 52; 1660–85, 86.
53 S.R.O., D/B/bw 1634; J. Oldmixon, Hist. of Eng. during the reigns of the Royal House of Stuart (1730), 702; W. M. Wigfield, Monmouth Rebels (1980), 166; R. W. Dunning, Monmouth Rebellion (1985), 65–7.
54 S.R.S. lxxvii. 196; but cf. R. Clifton, Last Popular Rebellion (1984), 297.
55 Hist. MSS. Com. 49, Stopford-Sackville, i, p. 15.
56 Cal. Treas. Bks. viii (2), 532; viii (3), 1350, 1518.
57 Dunning, Monmouth Rebellion, 67; S.R.O., D/B/bw 1635.
58 Hist. MSS. Com. 4, 5th Rep. I, Sutherland, p. 187; ibid. 6, 7th Rep. I, Verney, p. 503.
59 S.R.O., D/B/bw 1636.
60 I. M. Slocombe, 'A Bridgwater Riot, 1717', Proc. Som. Arch. Soc. cvi. 66–76.
61 J. P. W. Rogers, 'John Oldmixon in Bridgwater,

1716–30', Proc. Som. Arch. Soc. cxiii. 86–98; below, econ. hist. (other trade and industry).
62 D.N.B.
63 Who Was Who, 1961–70, 463.
64 Below, manors (Bridgwater Castle).
65 S.R.S. xi, pp. 40, 42; Cal. Lib. 1226–40, 229.
66 Cal. Fine R. 1319–27, 94, 189, 358, 419; Cal. Pat. 1321–4, 230; Cal. Chanc. Wts. 537; Cal. Mem. R. 1326–7, pp. 111–12.
67 P.R.O., C 66/1379.
68 Cal. S.P. Dom. 1625–6, 369, 569; 1625–49, 501.
69 P.R.O., CP 25(2)/717/25 Chas. II Trin.; S.R.O., D/P/bw 1170; B.L. Add. Ch. 71718.
70 P.R.O., CP 25(2)/1056/1 Geo. I Trin.; S.R.O., D/D/C pet.; C. H. C. and M. I. Baker, James Brydges, First Duke of Chandos (1949), 221.
71 Baker and Baker, James Brydges, 234; P.R.O., CP 25(2)/1398/11 & 12 Geo. III Trin.; S.R.O., DD/BLM (map, 1777).
72 Collinson, Hist. Som. iii. 82.
73 Cal. Lib. 1240–45, 129.
74 Ibid. 1245–51, 21.
75 Cal. Inq. p.m. x, p. 532.

within the walls in 1347–8.[76] Part of the surrounding ditch had by then been filled and built over; other sections were used for grazing and growing timber, while the southern stretch towards the town still held water, and reeds growing there were cut to thatch some of the castle buildings.[77] In the 1380s, when the castle formed part of the network of the Mortimer estates in the West and Wales, small repairs were regularly made both to the defences and to buildings within the walls. A substantial oak palisade was rebuilt on the north side in 1394–5; the eastern wall, strengthened with at least two towers, one at a corner, was frequently repaired. The main entrance was a 'great gate' or 'outer gate towards the town', evidently detached beyond the ditch, which gave access across the outer drawbridge to the outer bailey; an 'inner bridge facing the tower within the ditch' led to a second drawbridge and the inner bailey.[78] Two other towers stood at the time.[79]

About 1400 the buildings within the inner bailey included chambers for estate officials, a kitchen, a cellar, a horse mill, and a dungeon. A barn mentioned in 1347 seems to have been replaced as a hay store in the 1390s by the castle hall, known as Mortimers Hall. Detached buildings included stables, a dovecot, and a chapel.[80] A new chamber was mentioned in 1408, and three men were ordered by the manor court to return two guns to the castle; the bailey was being used to graze cattle[81] and for archery practice.[82] Private dwellings had been established within the walls by the 1450s.[83] Successive owners from the earlier 15th century appointed their retainers to offices such as doorkeepers and constables. In the 1530s and 1540s one man was described as constable and bailiff of the ditches of the castle, and the keepership was a Crown appointment until c. 1607.[84] Before 1502 buildings had been erected on each side of the main gate of the castle, which by then gave access from the high cross to the town's north gate.[85]

Leland described the castle in the 1540s as 'all going to mere ruin',[86] and in 1548 'the old frame of the castle' was reported as having fallen down and been removed to the house of the customer of the port.[87] In 1565 royal commissioners suggested that the buildings might be demolished to provide a site and materials for a customs house and a new quay.[88] A house was being built within the castle in 1566–7 at the expense of the town,[89] but no further work has been traced until

Henry Harvey's house 'by the bridge', built c. 1637 and damaged or destroyed in the siege in 1645.[90] Harvey or his predecessor had pulled down some of the walls shortly before 1635.[91] In 1650 the castle was thought to be of possible military value.[92] Probably in the later 17th century a castellated mansion was built on the summit of the castle mound, its western front in the form of a twin-towered gatehouse. Eight rooms on the first floor were occupied in the 1720s by the estate steward and later by a schoolmistress.[93] Between the house and the eastern wall of the castle, where there had been a grove of elm trees,[94] the present Castle and Chandos steets were laid out in the early 1720s and the eastern wall was demolished in 1726 to provide access to the quay.[95] The remainder of the site was occupied by two houses and extensive gardens.[96] About 1804 the western area was an open playground surrounded by a wooden palisade. The ruins of the castellated mansion still stood surrounded by deeply pitted ground.[97] The site was subsequently laid out as King Square.[98]

In 1219 the chapel within the castle was among the churches appropriated to the newly founded St. John's hospital in Bridgwater.[99] It was dedicated to St. Mark, and in 1535 a priest celebrated there three times a week for the souls of the founder and of King John.[1] The chapel was of stone with a stone-tiled roof and a bell tower.[2]

BOROUGH. King John's charter to William Brewer in 1200 declared Bridgwater to be a free borough, in which William might levy tolls of all kinds on outsiders and whose burgesses were to be free of tolls beyond the borough except in London. The charter was confirmed in 1318, 1371, 1381, and 1400.[3] The lordship of the borough descended with the chief manor in two shares,[4] and from the 15th century was represented by a rent or fee farm.[5]

Bridgwater appeared as a borough before the justices in eyre by 1225.[6] In the later 14th century the borough paid its lords rents for burgages and stalls, tolls from port, markets, and fairs, and perquisites of courts.[7]

In 1468, allegedly because of the town's decline, the Crown granted a charter which incorporated the borough with a mayor, two bailiffs, and an unspecified number of burgesses. The charter confirmed to the mayor and

76 P.R.O., SC 6/968/17.
77 Ibid. SC 6/968/17, 21, 25, 27; SC 6/969/11.
78 Ibid. SC 6/968/27, 29; SC 6/969/2, 4; S.R.S. xlviii, nos. 226, 276.
79 P.R.O., SC 6/968/25, 27.
80 Ibid. SC 6/968/17, 25, 27, 29; SC 6/969/4, 6.
81 Ibid. LR 3/58/9.
82 Sel. Cases of Trespass from the King's Courts, 1307–99 (Selden Soc. c), 30.
83 S.R.S. lx, no. 786.
84 P.R.O., C 139/18–19, no. 32; ibid. SC 6/1113/11; L. & P. Hen. VIII, vii, pp. 146–7; xix (1), p. 374; Hist. MSS. Com. 53, Montagu, p. 77.
85 S.R.O., D/B/bw 1938.
86 Leland, Itin. ed. Toulmin Smith, i. 162.
87 P.R.O., E 117/12, no. 21.
88 S.D.N.Q. xxx. 159.
89 S.R.O., D/B/bw 1544.
90 Proc. Som. Arch. Soc. xxiii. 18.

91 Cal. S.P. Dom. 1634–5, 502.
92 Ibid. 1650, 178.
93 Baker and Baker, James Brydges, 221, 229; above, plate facing p. 136.
94 S.R.O., DD/SAS (C/1193) 4, p. 150.
95 Baker and Baker, James Brydges, 229.
96 S.R.O., DD/BLM (map, 1777).
97 Proc. Som. Arch. Soc. xxiii. 46.
98 Above, intro. (buildings).
99 S.R.S. xlix, p. 288.
1 S.R.O., D/B/bw 1424; Valor Eccl. (Rec. Com.), i. 208.
2 P.R.O., SC 6/968/17, 25, 27; SC 6/969/2, 4, 6, 11.
3 P.R.O., DL 42/1, f. 433, no. 20; DL 42/11, ff. 2v.–3; S.R.S. xlviii, no. 1; lviii, no. 504; Cal. Chart. R. 1300–26, 377; 1341–1417, 220; Cal. Pat. 1377–81, 597.
4 Below, manors.
5 Below, this section.
6 Ibid. xi, p. 41.
7 P.R.O., SC 6/968/19–26, 28; SC 6/969/1–2, 4–5, 7–20.

bailiffs the right to pay a reduced rent to the lord of one third of the borough as a fee farm. During her lifetime they were to pay £3 each year to Cecily, duchess of York, and after her death £10 to the Crown.[8] The fee farm was paid at the Exchequer until 1630, when it was part of the jointure of the queen, Henrietta Maria, and was still being claimed in 1646–7.[9]

The rent of the remaining two thirds of the borough, occasionally called a fee farm,[10] belonged to the Zouche share of Haygrove manor until 1485.[11] Giles Daubeney, Baron Daubeney (d. 1508), was succeeded by his son Henry (cr. earl of Bridgwater 1538, d. 1548). Henry retained the rent from the borough until 1544 or later, but by 1547 it was being paid to Richard Zouche (succ. as Baron Zouche in 1550, d. 1552).[12] Richard settled the rent, then amounting to £10 16s. 8d., on his two younger sons, Richard and Charles. Richard conveyed his share in 1558 to his eldest brother George, Lord Zouche (d. 1569).[13] George's share was paid to his widow Margaret 1572–7 and in 1578 to his son Edward, Lord Zouche (d. 1625).[14] Charles Zouche in 1566–7 received his share, which by 1572 had passed to John Byflete.[15] Byflete was succeeded in 1621 by his son Robert, and Robert in 1641 by his son Thomas. Thomas's heirs were paid in arrears in 1652[16] but no further payments have been traced.

The borough received a new charter in 1587, modified in 1628, and another in 1683. The corporation established under the Act of 1835 was dissolved in 1974, though the town retained a titular mayor.[17]

MANORS AND OTHER ESTATES. In 1066 Merlesuain held *BRIDGWATER*, which in 1086 Walter (or Walscin) of Douai held as one of a group of manors which lay on each side of the Parrett[18] and later formed part of the honor of Bampton (Devon).[19] Walter had no tenant recorded at Bridgwater, which may therefore have been his demesne manor; in the late 12th century and in 1234 other manors in the group were held of it.[20] From 1283 the manor, or at least the 'foreign' as distinct from what had become the borough, was known as *HAY-GROVE*.[21] Walter was succeeded c. 1107 by his

son Robert, who rebelled in 1136, and Robert's daughter Gillian carried his lands to successive husbands Fulk Pagnell and Warin de Aule.[22] Warin held the honor of Bampton in 1166[23] but Bridgwater was in the Crown's hands from 1177 to 1179. It then passed to Fulk's son Fulk Pagnell,[24] who fled the realm in 1185. The sheriff accounted for Bridgwater in 1185–6,[25] but the honor was held by the guardian of Fulk's son William in 1186–7.[26] The sheriff rendered tallage for Bridgwater and other lands in 1199–1200, and in that year Fulk recovered his lands.[27] Also in 1199 Fulk granted Bridgwater manor to William Brewer as part of an exchange, a grant which was confirmed by the Crown and by Fulk's son William.[28]

William Brewer died in 1226 and his son and heir William in 1233 without issue.[29] After a period of Crown custody between 1233 and 1248,[30] Bridgwater passed to two great-granddaughters of the elder William, namely Maud and Eve de Braose. Maud married successively Roger de Mortimer (d. 1282) and William Mortimer (d. 1297). Her share of Bridgwater was the castle and one third of the borough and manor, an estate later sometimes known as *BRIDGWATER CASTLE* manor.[31] She died in 1301 when her heir was Edmund, her son by her first husband. Edmund (cr. Baron Mortimer 1295, d. 1304)[32] held Bridgwater jointly with his wife Margaret, who survived until 1334.[33] Her heir was her great-grandson Roger Mortimer, Lord Mortimer and earl of March (d. 1360), but his mother Elizabeth (d. 1355) had a life interest in the estate.[34] Roger's widow Philippe (d. 1382) held the estate in dower.[35] From then the estate was usually held in dower by the Mortimers' widows. Philippe was followed by her grandson Roger (d. 1398), whose widow Eleanor died in 1405.[36] Her son Edmund died in 1425, and when his widow Anne died in 1432 the heir was his nephew Richard Plantagenet, duke of York.[37]

Richard's widow Cecily, duchess of York, held the castle and the third share of the borough and manor from her husband's death in 1460 until her own in 1495, when the estate merged with the Crown.[38] Queen Elizabeth, wife of Henry VII, was granted the reversion, and on her death in 1503 the lordship again passed to the Crown.[39] Catherine of Aragon as princess of

8 *Cal. Chart. R.* 1427–1516, 226–9.
9 S.R.O., D/B/bw 657, 1617, 1672, 1791, 1948, 1968–9, 2030–4, 2085.
10 Ibid. D/B/bw 125, 2058.
11 Below, manors (Haygrove).
12 S.R.O., D/B/bw 1879, 1887, 2033, 2051, 2057–63; *Complete Peerage*, xii (2), 948–9.
13 P.R.O., C 3/201/108; *Cal. Pat.* 1557–8, 343.
14 S.R.O., D/B/bw 1968, 2072–3, 2075.
15 Ibid. 1672, 1968, 2049, 2119; M. Whitfeld, *In Praise of Bratton St. Maur* (1974), 48, 52, 55.
16 S.R.O., D/B/bw 198, 1854, 1871, 1946–7, 1963, 1969.
17 Below, local govt. (borough).
18 *V.C.H. Som.* i. 497, 499–500.
19 *Pipe R.* 1179 (P.R.S. xxviii), 71; Sanders, *Eng. Baronies*, 5.
20 P.R.O., DL 42/11, f. 2 and v.; *Bk. of Fees*, i. 400.
21 *Cal. Inq. p. m.* ii, p. 265.
22 Sanders, *Eng. Baronies*, 5.
23 *Red Bk. Exch.* (Rolls Ser.), i. 256–7.
24 *Pipe R.* 1178 (P.R.S. xxvii), 44; 1179 (P.R.S. xxviii), 71; 1180 (P.R.S. xxix), 111; 1181 (P.R.S. xxx), 9; Sanders, *Eng. Baronies*, 5.

25 *Pipe R.* 1185 (P.R.S. xxxiv), 182; 1186 (P.R.S. xxxvi), 140.
26 *Red Bk. Exch.* (Rolls Ser.), i. 69.
27 *Pipe R.* 1199 (P.R.S. N.S. x), 197, 240.
28 P.R.O., DL 42/11, ff. 1, 2, 4v.; *Rot. Chart.* (Rec. Com.), 28; Dugdale, *Mon.* v. 204. 29 Sanders, *Eng. Baronies*, 123.
30 *Abbrev. Rot. Orig.* (Rec. Com.), i. 1–2, 4; *Cal. Pat.* 1232–47, 51, 99, 287; 1247–58, 8; *Bk. of Fees*, ii. 755, 1140; *Cal. Lib.* 1226–40, 380; 1240–45, 265.
31 *Cal. Pat.* 1247–58, 8; *Cal. Inq. p.m.* ii, p. 265; iii, p. 270. A third coheir, Eleanor, wife of Humphrey de Bohun, apparently had no share in Bridgwater: Sanders, *Eng. Baronies*, 8.
32 *Cal. Inq. p.m.* iv, pp. 20, 118, 158; *Complete Peerage*, ix. 276–85.
33 *Cal. Pat.* 1301–7, 33; *Cal. Inq. p.m.* iv, p. 158; *S.R.S.* vi. 393.
34 *Cal. Inq. p.m.* vii, p. 400; x, p. 532; *Cal. Pat.* 1313–17, 491.
35 *Cal. Inq. p.m.* xv, pp. 227–8.
36 *Cal. Close*, 1396–9, 452, 454; P.R.O., C 137/53, no. 23.
37 *Complete Peerage*, viii. 453; *Cal. Close*, 1422–9, 218–19.
38 *Complete Peerage*, xii (2), 909; *S.R.S.* lx, pp. viii–ix, nos. 773, 819; lxx, no. 894.
39 *Cal. Pat.* 1485–94, 369–70; *Rot. Parl.* vi. 462; *Handbk. Brit. Chron.* (1986), 38.

Wales received the share as part of her jointure in 1509,[40] but in 1511 it was given to two daughters of Edward IV, namely Katharine, recently widowed countess of Devon, and Anne, wife of Sir Thomas Howard.[41] Anne was dead by 1512 and Katharine in 1527,[42] and their estate in Bridgwater evidently reverted to the Crown and formed part of the jointure of Anne Boleyn (d. 1536), Jane Seymour (d. 1537), Anne of Cleves (marriage annulled 1540), Catherine Howard (d. 1542), and Catherine Parr (d. 1548).[43] It reverted to the Crown and was let.[44] In 1626 it was granted to Sir William and Sir George Whitmore, who had both been lessees of the estate.[45] In 1627 George conveyed the manor, but not the castle, to Sir Richard Grobham, husband of his sister Margaret.[46] Grobham died in 1629 leaving his widow in possession with remainder to his nephew George Grobham of Broomfield.[47] George died probably in 1646, and in 1652 John Howe the elder, husband of Sir Richard's sister and heir Jane, together with a Richard Grobham, were apparently in possession of the estate.[48] The manor continued in the Howe family, probably with little land, descending from John and Jane Howe to their son John (cr. Bt. 1660), to Sir John's son Sir Richard Grubham Howe (d. by 1703), and to Sir Richard's son and namesake (d. 1730), owner in 1704–5.[49] No further reference to the manor has been found.

On the partition of Bridgwater in 1248 Eve de Braose, wife of William de Cauntelo (d. 1254), received two thirds of the borough and manor.[50] In 1255 Eve was succeeded by her son George Cauntelo (d. 1273) whose sister and heir Millicent (d. 1298–9) married Eudes la Zouche (d. 1279).[51] From her son William (cr. Baron Zouche 1308, d. 1352) the estate passed to successive barons Zouche until the attainder of John, Lord Zouche, after the battle of Bosworth in 1485.[52] The Crown granted the estate in tail male to Giles Daubeney, Baron Daubeney (d. 1508).[53]

In 1538 Daubeney's son Henry (cr. earl of Bridgwater 1538, d. 1548) sold his share of Bridgwater manor to Edward Seymour, earl of Hertford[54] (attainted 1552). In 1582 his heir, Edward Seymour, earl of Hertford (d. 1621),

recovered the estate, which passed to Anne, known as Lady Beauchamp, the widow of his eldest grandson Edward Seymour.[55] Anne married secondly Edward Lewis and was still alive in 1662.[56] The manor seems to have passed by 1677 to two of the daughters of her first husband's brother, Frances, wife of Conyers Darcy, later earl of Holderness (d. 1692), and Jane, wife of Charles Boyle, Baron Clifford of Lanesborough (d. 1694). Courts were held 1683–6 in the names of Darcy and Boyle.[57] In 1687 Thomas Bruce, earl of Ailesbury (d. 1741), and his wife Elizabeth, daughter of Henry Seymour, Lord Beauchamp, sold the estate to Sir Charles Pym, Bt. (d. 1688), whose heir was his sister Mary, wife of (Sir) Thomas Hales.[58]

Sir Thomas was succeeded in 1748[59] by his son Sir Thomas (d. 1762). The estate descended with Brymore in Cannington, but by the time of Henry Hales Pleydell-Bouverie (d. 1925)[60] it was negligible in size.

By 1323 Maurice de Berkeley, Lord Berkeley (d. 1326), received a rent charge of £10 from his brother-in-law William, Lord Zouche, payable from Bridgwater park.[61] The rent charge descended in the Berkeley family[62] and in 1439 was divided between three sisters, Margaret (d. 1467), wife of John Talbot, earl of Shrewsbury, Eleanor (d. 1467), then wife of Edmund Beaufort, earl of Dorset, and Elizabeth (d. 1480), then wife of George Neville, Lord Latimer.[63]

Margaret's share descended indirectly to Sir Edward Grey (cr. Baron Lisle 1475, Vct. Lisle 1483, d. 1492), whose estate included what was later called the manors of *KIDSBURY*, Haygrove, and Bridgwater, inherited from Thomas Cheddar.[64] His son John (d. 1504) left a daughter and heir Elizabeth (d. 1519), wife of Henry Courtenay, earl of Devon. Her heirs were two aunts of whom Elizabeth, Baroness Lisle, wife of Arthur Plantagenet (cr. Vct. Lisle 1523, d. 1542) was the sole survivor by 1523.[65] Viscount Lisle, retaining a life interest after the death of his wife c. 1530, leased the estate in 1531 to his stepson Sir John Dudley, later duke of Northumberland (d. 1553),[66] a transaction which resulted in a dispute with Sir Edward Seymour.[67] Seymour acquired part of the estate after Lisle's death,[68] and exchanged it for other

40   *L. & P. Hen. VIII*, i (1), p. 49.
41   P.R.O., CP 25(2)/51/358/3 Hen. VIII Mich.; *Complete Peerage*, iv. 330.
42   *Handbk. Brit. Chron.* 38.
43   *L. & P. Hen. VIII*, vii, p. 147; xv, p. 52; xvi, p. 240; xviii (1), p. 121; xix (1), p. 374; P.R.O., LR 14/858; *Cat. Glynde Place Archives*, ed. R. F. Dell, no. 3471.
44   P.R.O. LR 14/894; ibid. E 178/4452; *Cal. Pat. 1566–9*, p. 333.
45   P.R.O., C 66/1811, 1842; Collinson, *Hist. Som.* iii. 81–2.
46   P.R.O., CP 25(2)/526/2 Chas. I Hil.; Burke, *Land. Gent.* (1914), 2014.
47   P.R.O., C 142/460, no. 53.
48   *Som. Wills*, ed. Brown, iii. 4; P.R.O., CP 25(2)/616/1652 Mich.
49   G.E.C. *Baronetage*, iii. 123.
50   *Pat. R. 1247–58*, 8; *Cal. Inq. p.m.* ii, p. 18; Sanders, *Eng. Baronies*, 40.
51   *Cal. Inq. p.m.* ii, p. 18; *Cal. Close, 1272–9*, 115; *Cal. Fine R. 1272–1307*, 18, 59; *Complete Peerage*, xii (2), 938–9.
52   *Complete Peerage*, xii (2), 938–47; *Cal. Inq. p.m. Hen. VII*, iii, p. 547.
53   *Rot. Parl.* vi. 485; P.R.O., C 142/25, no. 22.

54   P.R.O., E 328/94, 97.
55   Ibid. C 66/1218; ibid. CP 25(2)/347/19 Jas. I Mich.
56   *Complete Peerage*, vi. 507; S.R.O., DD/X/SU; D/B/bw 2045.
57   S.R.O., DD/HK 63; P.R.O., CP 25(2)/762/29 Chas. II East.; *Complete Peerage*, ii. 431; vi. 536; xii (1), 133.
58   P.R.O., CP 25(2)/795/3 Jas. II Mich.; ibid. CP 43/423, rot. 242; G.E.C. *Baronetage*, iii. 281.
59   B.L. Eg. 3129; S.R.O., D/P/can 4/1/1.
60   G.E.C. *Baronetage*, iii. 79–80; Burke, *Peerage* (1949), 1650; Som. C.C., Brymore deeds 247; above, Cannington, manors.
61   P.R.O., SC 6/1148/2, 8; *Cal. Inq. p.m.* xii, p. 193.
62   *Cal. Inq. p.m.* xii, p. 193; xvi, p. 306; *Complete Peerage*, i. 126–31; *Cal. Close, 1364–8*, 437; 1389–92, 14.
63   P.R.O., C 139/94, no. 54; C 140/26, no. 44; *Cal. Close, 1476–85*, p. 224; *Complete Peerage*, i. 131 n.
64   P.R.O., E 326/6768; ibid. SC 6/969/22; *Complete Peerage*, viii. 55–61.
65   *Cal. Inq. p.m. Hen. VII*, ii, p. 521; *Complete Peerage*, viii. 60–7.
66   P.R.O., E 328/303.
67   Ibid. E 211/371; E 326/5686, 6768, 12180; E 328/201, 272; *Cat. Anct. D.* iii, D 637; *L. & P. Hen. VIII*, vi, p. 626.
68   P.R.O., C 142/115, no. 38; ibid. SC 6/Hen. VIII/3074.

Crown land in 1547; it remained in royal possession until 1570 when it was granted in fee to Hugh Counsell and Robert Pistor.[69] No further trace of the share has been found.

Eleanor's share descended to Henry Manners, earl of Rutland (d. 1563), and has not been found recorded after 1560.[70] Elizabeth's share, with lands in Bridgwater, descended through the Nevilles[71] to Henry Percy, earl of Northumberland,[72] who still received an annuity from the manor in 1605.[73]

In 1066 Saric held an estate at *BOWER*. In 1086 Walter of Douai held it with Rademer as his tenant.[74] The overlordship seems to have descended with Bridgwater, and 2½ knights' fees in Bower, Horsey, and Pawlett were held of William Brewer's heirs in 1234.[75] William of Horsey was mesne tenant of those fees, and a namesake held ½ knight's fee at Bower in 1303. Although there is no reference to the Horsey family in 1346,[76] some land at East and West Bower, on either side of Bridgwater, was held in 1371 of John Horsey by knight service.[77]

In 1205 Christian of Bridgwater (*Bruges*), widow of Jordan of Chilton, claimed dower against Robert of Chilton in her late husband's lands in 'his Bower', Little Bower, and 'the other Bower'.[78] Robert of Chilton was holding land at Bower in 1254, and one of the same name was tenant of William of Horsey there in 1303.[79] The heirs of Robert were returned as tenants in 1346.[80]

In 1309 Hugh Godwin settled land in South Bower on his wife Margery.[81] By 1318, after Hugh's death, Margery held land there and at North Bower.[82] No further reference to the estate has been found until 1412, when William Godwin the elder was holding the manor of *GODWINSBOWER*,[83] in 1586 called Godwinsbower or *DUNWEAR*.[84] William Godwin or his namesake died in 1442 when his heir was his son William, then a minor.[85] William Godwin, possibly successor to the last, died in 1502, when his son Christopher was his heir. The manor was then described as being 'by the house of the hospital of St. John the Baptist', and was said to be held of the lord of Curry Rivel.[86] In 1507 Christopher Godwin sold the manor, including lands in East, North, and South Bower, to Robert Brent.[87] Robert (d. 1508) was followed

by his son John (d. 1524), John by Robert's grandson William Brent (d. 1536), and William by his son Richard. The manor was said in 1508 to be held of Otterhampton manor,[88] and again in 1614.[89] Richard Brent (d. 1570) had an only daughter Anne, wife of Thomas Paulet (d. 1586). Elizabeth, daughter of Thomas and Anne, married Giles Hoby and by 1586 had a daughter Anne, then a minor.[90]

In 1614 John Brent died seised of the manor, his son John being then a minor.[91] The younger John appears to have survived until 1692, when his heir was his cousin John Hodges.[92] Elizabeth Hodges, probably John's widow, had an interest in the manor in 1703, but John is said to have sold some of his land to Robert West.[93] No further owners have been traced, although the manor still existed in 1763.[94]

In 1487 Walter Michell died seised of *NORTH BOWER* manor, held of North Petherton manor.[95] The manor descended with East Chilton manor in Durleigh[96] to the Hockmore family and was held in 1723 by the last William Hockmore's three sons-in-law, Brent Reynell Spiller, William Pitt, and Davidge Gould.[97] John Peryman (d. 1512) held another manor of *NORTH BOWER*. His heirs were his daughters Joan and Dorothy.[98] Dorothy married Philip Courtenay and, as a widow, held the manor in 1555.[99] Edward Courtenay was owner in 1575, but by 1613 the estate had passed to the Chichester family, owners of Dunwear manor.[1] Sir Robert Chichester (d. 1627) held the manor as of North Petherton manor,[2] and it descended with Dunwear until 1693 or later.[3]

In 1280 Stephen le King and Maud his wife and Lettice at Cross claimed that Jordan of Chilton had disseised Eileen at Bower, greatgrandmother of Maud and Lettice, of land in Durleigh and granted it to Maslin at Bower, whom John Maslin of Bower had succeeded.[4] Hugh Maslin, son and heir of William Maslin, in 1335 granted his lands in and near *WEST BOWER* to Richard Coker.[5] Richard was succeeded by James Coker (fl. 1402–7) and James by Matthew Coker, who held the estate in 1412 and was alive in 1420.[6] John Coker, described as cousin and heir of James Coker, left a daughter Margaret, who had succeeded to West Bower manor by 1461. She married first Sir Alexander

69 *Cal. Pat.* 1569–72, p. 42.
70 *Complete Peerage*, xi. 104–8; P.R.O., E 326/12925; ibid. CP 25(2)/259/2 & 3 Eliz. I Mich.
71 *Cal. Close*, 1476–85, p. 224.
72 *Complete Peerage*, vii. 480–6; Alnwick Castle, Northumberland MSS. X. II. 12/2F, 6, 9A (xii); P.R.O., C 142/248, no. 22.
73 Alnwick Castle, Northumberland MSS. X. II. 12/9.
74 *V.C.H. Som.* i. 497.
75 *Bk. of Fees*, i. 400.
76 *Feud. Aids*, iv. 300, 344.
77 *Cal. Inq. p.m.* xiii, pp. 19–20.
78 *Cur. Reg. R.* iv. 2–3, 39; *S.R.S.* vi. 25–6.
79 *Close R.* 1253–4, 153; *Feud. Aids*, iv. 300.
80 *Feud. Aids*, iv. 344.
81 *S.R.S.* xii. 14.
82 *Cal. Pat.* 1317–21, 297, 470, 547; *Rot. Parl.* i. 372.
83 *Feud. Aids*, vi. 513.
84 P.R.O., C 142/215, no. 245.
85 Ibid. C 139/109, no. 26.
86 *Cal. Inq. p.m. Hen. VII*, iii, pp. 407–8; P.R.O., C 1/286/33.
87 *Cal. Close*, 1500–9, pp. 207, 280, 345.

88 *Cal. Inq. p.m. Hen. VII*, iii, pp. 309–11; P.R.O., C 142/41, no. 28; C 142/58, no. 6.
89 *S.R.S.* lxvii, p. 90.
90 P.R.O., C 142/156, no. 14; C 142/215, no. 245.
91 *S.R.S.* lxvii, p. 90.
92 B.L. Add. Ch. 71725; Collinson, *Hist. Som.* iii. 436–7; S.R.O., DD/MLY, box 10.
93 P.R.O., CP 40/3211, m. 20; Collinson, *Hist. Som.* iii. 436–7.   94 S.R.O., DD/AH 39/9.
95 *Cal. Inq. p.m. Hen. VII*, i, pp. 114–15.
96 Below, Durleigh, manors.
97 P.R.O., CP 25(2)/1089/9 Geo. I Hil.
98 Ibid. C 142/27, no. 107.
99 Ibid. CP 25(2)/77/658/2 & 3 Phil. & Mary Mich.; *S.R.S.* extra ser. 28.
1 P.R.O., CP 25(2)/204/17 & 18 Eliz. I Mich.; CP 25(2)/386/11 Jas. I Trin.
2 Ibid. C 142/438, no. 129; *S.R.S.* lxvii, p. 167.
3 P.R.O., CP 43/391, rot. 99; below, this section (Dunwear).
4 *S.R.S.* xliv. 182, where Durleigh is misread as Churleigh.
5 *S.D.N.Q.* xxvii. 5; *S.R.S.* lvii. 31–2.
6 *S.R.S.* lvii. 34; *Feud. Aids*, vi. 513; *S.D.N.Q.* xxvii. 5; Pole MS. 4034.

Hody (d. 1461)[7] and c. 1462 Sir Reynold Stourton,[8] and died in 1489. Her heir was her cousin John Seymour (d. 1491) whose son[9] Sir John (d. 1536) was father of Jane Seymour, Henry VIII's queen, and of Edward Seymour (cr. earl of Hertford 1537, duke of Somerset 1547). Edward held West Bower from 1536 until his attainder and death in 1552, when the manor was forfeit to the Crown.[10]

The Crown sold the manor and other lands, including some possessions of the dissolved hospital of St. John in Bridgwater, in 1553 to Thomas Sydney and Nicholas Halswell. Sydney sold his share to Halswell two weeks later[11] and the manor descended with Halswell manor in Goathurst, being let for much of the 17th century to members of the Still and Bourne families.[12] In 1938 Lord Wharton sold West Bower to Bridgwater corporation for the construction of Durleigh reservoir, and in 1963 ownership passed to the West Somerset water board. Mr. Michael Martin later bought the house and surrounding land.[13]

Richard Coker was licensed to have an oratory at West Bower for a year in 1339,[14] and the manor house included a chapel of St. John the Baptist in 1462.[15] West Bower Manor, now on the edge of Durleigh reservoir, comprises two sides of a courtyard house, the north side of which is a substantial gatehouse with added polygonal turrets flanking its southern façade. Glass in the cusped and transomed turret windows bears the initials A and M which have been interpreted as those of Alexander and Margaret Hody.[16] In 1540 the house was described as in two parts, one covered in slate, the other in lead. There was also a little court 'within the walls', a garden said to be outside the gate on the west, a small barton with another garden, an orchard, and a pond. Nearby was a former rabbit warren. The house was then let with 75 a. of land.[17] In 1635 the site included a dovecot and the house was let with 150 a. of land.[18] The dovecot, circular in plan with c. 730 nest holes, was made of cob, repaired with brick and stone; it was demolished in 1967.[19]

Robert de la Mare died in 1371 holding a small estate described as at East and West Bower of John Horsey, and leaving his son Richard as his heir.[20] Sir Alexander Hody (d. 1461) held BOWER DELAMERE or Delameres Bower as part of his estate at West Bower,[21] and the name Delamere survived on the West Bower estate until the earlier 18th century.[22]

Geoffrey the cook seems to have been lord of DUNWEAR in the 1190s.[23] The manor was held of John de Columbers as 1 knight's fee in 1284–5 and as ½ knight's fee in 1303,[24] and in 1569 and 1627 was held of the Columbers heir as of Nether Stowey manor.[25] In 1236 William de Raleigh held Dunwear in demesne,[26] Thomas de Raleigh in 1284–5 and 1303,[27] Lucy de Raleigh in 1316, and Thomas de Raleigh before 1342.[28] Thomas's unnamed heirs were lords in 1346.[29] Possibly from then and certainly from 1402[30] Dunwear manor descended with Beggearn Huish in Nettlecombe, and the Chichesters retained it when they sold Beggearn Huish in 1604. Sir Robert Chichester, K.B., died in 1627 owning both North Bower and Dunwear and leaving a son John, a minor.[31] John (cr. Bt. 1641) seems to have mortgaged or sold both manors in 1660,[32] and no further trace of either manor has been found.

In 794 Brihtric, king of Wessex, granted to his alderman Wigferth 10 cassati of land on the north bank of the Parrett. The charter recording the grant later belonged to Athelney abbey. A second Athelney charter, dated 959 and recording a grant by King Eadwig to Ceolward of a mansa at Ham, on the west bank of the Parrett, may have recorded another estate, described as 3 'perticae' at Ham, and later as the manor, which King Aethelred gave to Athelney abbey in 1009.[33] Athelney abbey held HAMME or HAMP manor until its dissolution in 1539, the holding sometimes assessed at ½ knight's fee, and the income assigned to the abbey pittancer.[34] A holding within the manor from 1225 provided a lamp for the abbey's Lady Chapel.[35]

In 1541 the Crown sold the manor, leased to Sir Richard Warre and his son Robert, to the corporation of Bristol.[36] The corporation let the estate to John Castleman, already a substantial tenant there, in 1554,[37] but from 1694 sold houses and land. In 1698 it sold the rest, including the lordship, to Roger Hoar of Bridgwater.[38] His son, also Roger, retained the manor until 1705 when he sold it to Sir John Tynte, and it descended with West Bower.[39]

In 1540 the Crown let the capital messuage of Hamp to John Soper.[40] From 1543 it was leased

7   P.R.O., C 140/4, no. 34; S.R.S. xxii. 145–6.
8   S.R.S. xlix, p. 368.
9   Cal. Inq. p.m. Hen. VII, i, pp. 266–7, 327; Burke, Peerage (1949), 1869.
10   P.R.O., C 142/115, no. 38.
11   Cal. Pat. 1553, 54–5; S.R.O., DD/S/WH 2.
12   P.R.O., C 142/475, no. 96; Som. Wills, ed. Brown, v. 77; vi. 81; S.R.S. xxviii. 297; S.R.O., D/B/bw 286; above, Goathurst, manors.
13   Inf. from Mr. Martin, West Bower.
14   S.R.S. ix, p. 360.
15   Ibid. xlix, p. 368.
16   S.D.N.Q. xxvii. 55–6.
17   Longleat House, Seymour Papers, XII, f. 14v.
18   S.R.O., DD/S/BW 5.
19   Proc. Som. Arch. Soc. cxii. 101–3.
20   Cal. Inq. p.m. xiii, pp. 19–20.
21   Pole MS. 2770, 2898.
22   S.R.O., DD/S/WH 218.
23   Pipe R. 1194 (P.R.S. N.S. v), 19; S.R.S. xxv, p. 95.
24   Feud. Aids, iv. 278, 300.

25   P.R.O., C 142/151, no. 9; S.R.S. lxvii, p. 167; V.C.H. Som. v. 193–4.
26   S.R.S. vi. 81; xiv, p. 149.
27   Feud. Aids, iv. 278, 300.
28   Ibid. 332; Year Bk. 16 Edw. III (Rolls Ser.), (2), 327–32.   29   Feud. Aids, iv. 344.
30   V.C.H. Som. v. 115; P.R.O., C 137/44, no. 36.
31   P.R.O., C 142/438, no. 129; S.R.S. lxvii, p. 167.
32   P.R.O., CP 25(2)/715/12 Chas. II Mich.
33   S.R.S. xiv, pp. 144–6, 188; H. P. R. Finberg, Early Charters of Wessex, pp. 118–20, 139–41, 149.
34   S.R.S. xiv, p. 153; Feud. Aids, iv. 300; Tax. Eccl. (Rec. Com.), 204.
35   S.R.S. xiv, p. 151.
36   L. & P. Hen. VIII, xv, p. 563; xvi, p. 418; Bristol R.O. 4490, f. 5v.
37   Bristol R.O. 04403.
38   Ibid. Common Cncl. Proc. 1687–1702, ff. 106v.–107, 161; ibid. 00570 (1–28); 00904 (2–6, 14–15).
39   S.R.O., DD/RN 1; above, this section (West Bower).
40   L. & P. Hen. VIII, xv, p. 563.

to John Castleman, and from 1569 to Robert Moleyns. Moleyns held it jointly with Robert Cuffe in 1575,[41] and another Robert Cuffe occupied Hamp Farm and demesnes in 1655.[42] In 1547 the house included a ground-floor hall with a chapel at one end.[43] No record of it after 1655 has been found.

Alweard Glebard held *HORSEY* in 1066 and Walter of Douai in 1086.[44] The overlordship descended with Bridgwater and on William Brewer's death in 1233 passed through his sister Margery to her daughter Gundrada, wife of Pain of Chaworth (d. 1237), and to Pain's son Patrick (d. 1283), whose two sons died childless. Patrick's daughter Maud (d. by 1322) married Henry,[45] earl of Lancaster from 1322, who was succeeded in 1345 by his son Henry (cr. duke of Lancaster 1351, d. 1361).[46] Horsey, granted in 1463 to George Plantagenet, duke of Clarence (d. 1478), was considered to be parcel of the duchy of Lancaster until 1641 or later.[47]

Rademer or Raimar was undertenant of Horsey in 1086.[48] In 1166 William of Horsey held 1 knight's fee there of the honor of Bampton (Devon),[49] and Philip of Horsey held ½ knight's fee of William Brewer before 1208.[50] William of Horsey had succeeded by 1236 and his son and heir William was evidently dead by 1275.[51] John of Horsey had succeeded by 1284 and died c. 1294, leaving his son William a minor.[52] William held the estate in 1303 and was followed c. 1327 by his two sons John (d. c. 1337) and Ralph (d. 1354) in turn. Ralph's son John was a minor in 1354.[53]

John, of age in 1359, held Horsey and other estates until his death in 1375, when he left Horsey settled on his widow Eleanor. His son[54] Sir John settled the manor before 1412 on his wife Eleanor, but by a further settlement of 1420 the manor passed on his death in 1422 to Joan, widow of his son William and wife of John Trethek.[55] Sir John's son and heir Henry held Horsey in 1428, and settled it on himself and his wife in 1432.[56] He died childless in 1460 and his estate passed to his brother Thomas (d. 1468),[57] and then in direct male line to John (d. 1531), Sir John (d. 1546), Sir John (d. 1564), and Sir John (d. *s.p.* 1589).[58] Under a settlement made by the last, the manor or lordship of Horsey and Pignes passed to his cousin Sir Ralph Horsey[59]

(d. 1612). Though Sir Ralph left a son George, Horsey manor passed to Sir Thomas Freke, presumably by sale, since George had assured it to Sir Thomas during his mother's life.[60] Sir Thomas's son John succeeded in 1633 and held the manor at his death in 1641, but his sons John (d. 1657) and Thomas are not known to have held the manor.[61] In 1673 Sir John Morton, Bt., owned the estate.[62] He died in 1699, leaving as his heir his daughter Anne, wife of Edmund Pleydell (d. 1726).[63] Their son John Morton Pleydell was in possession in 1703 and died in 1705. His brother and heir Edmund Morton Pleydell (d. 1754) was followed in the direct male line by two namesakes (d. 1794 and 1835). The eldest daughter of the last, Margaretta (d. *s.p.* 1871), wife of the Revd. James Michel,[64] settled Horsey and Pignes on her nephew John Clavell Mansell (later Mansel-Pleydell), on whose behalf they were sold in 1868 to Joseph Boon. Thomas Major House bought the land in 1872 and in 1877 sold it to the trustees of the late Mary Tyler Greenhill. Her grandson Pelham Spencer Greenhill succeeded in 1877. Pelham Benjamin Greenhill, son of the last, died in 1916 in the same year as his father, and the heir was Benjamin Greenhill, an infant. In 1984 Mr. Greenhill gave Horsey Manor Farm to his daughter Carol, Mrs. A. C. Hudson, owner in 1988.[65]

St. John's hospital, Bridgwater, founded before 1213 probably by William Brewer, had by then been endowed with Bridgwater church.[66] By 1215 it had also acquired 100 a. of land, a compact holding north-east of the hospital site which was still known as Hundred Acres in 1842.[67] The land may have been given in exchange for other land previously granted by Brewer to the hospital.[68] About 1349 the hospital acquired rents in the town and the reversion of small properties there.[69] By 1535 the hospital also held rents in Hamp and Horsey.[70]

John Bourchier, earl of Bath (d. 1561), farmer of the hospital site and the rectory in 1538–9,[71] received grants of both properties in 1541 or 1542,[72] but from Michaelmas 1542 the site and demesne were occupied by Humphrey Colles, who secured a reversionary lease from the Crown in 1543.[73] Colles remained in occupation of the former demesne until his death in 1570

---

41 Bristol R.O. 04403; 4490, f. 6.
42 Ibid. 04237.
43 Ibid. 4490, f. 6.   44 *V.C.H. Som.* i. 499.
45 *Bk. of Fees*, i. 400; *Feud. Aids*, iv. 278; *Cal. Inq. p.m.* iii, p. 142; Sanders, *Eng. Baronies*, 125.
46 *Cal. Inq. p.m.* x, p. 160; *Cal. Close*, 1360–4, 209; *Handbk. Brit. Chron.* (1986), 468.
47 *Cal. Pat.* 1461–7, 226; 1467–77, 457, 530; P.R.O., C 142/498, no. 22.
48 *V.C.H. Som.* i. 499.
49 *Red Bk. Exch.* (Rolls Ser.), i. 256–7.
50 P.R.O., DL 42/11, ff. 2–2v. Philip, Walter, William, and Thomas of Horsey were said to have been successive lords in Henry II's reign: Collinson, *Hist. Som.* iii. 85–6.
51 *Bk. of Fees*, i. 400; *S.R.S.* vi. 81; Pole MS. 833, 4112; *Cal. Inq. p.m.* ii, pp. 94–5.
52 *Feud. Aids*, iv. 278; *Cal. Inq. p.m.* iii, pp. 142, 383; *Cal. Close*, 1288–96, 346.
53 *Cal. Inq. p.m.* iii, p. 383; vii, p. 29; viii, p. 63; x, pp. 160, 260; *Feud. Aids*, iv. 300, 344.
54 *Cal. Inq. p.m.* x, p. 432; xiv, p. 142; *Cal. Close*, 1354–60, 573–4; 1360–4, 209; 1374–7, 159.
55 *Feud. Aids*, vi. 509; P.R.O., C 139/1, no. 20; *Cal. Close*,

1422–9, 30.
56 *Feud. Aids*, iv. 364; B.L. Add. Ch. 53143.
57 P.R.O., C 140/2, no. 25; C 140/28, no. 32.
58 J. Hutchins, *Hist. Dors.* iv. 252–3, 427–9; P.R.O., C 142/84, no. 37.
59 P.R.O., C 142/221, no. 102; *S.D.N.Q.* xix. 103.
60 P.R.O., E 178/5620.
61 Ibid. C 142/498, no. 22; *Visit. Dors. 1623* (Harl Soc. xx), 41–2.   62 S.R.O., DD/SH 108, pt. 2.
63 G.E.C. *Baronetage*, i. 121.
64 P.R.O., CP 43/482, rot. 113; Burke, *Land. Gent.* (1914), 1513–14.
65 S.R.O., DD/HUD 12; inf. from Mrs. A. C. Hudson, Claverdon (Warws.).   66 *V.C.H. Som.* ii. 154–5.
67 *Rot. Chart.* (Rec. Com.), 204; S.R.O., tithe award.
68 P.R.O., DL 42/11, f. 6v.   69 *Cal. Pat.* 1348–50, 407.
70 *Valor Eccl.* (Rec. Com.), i. 207–8.
71 P.R.O., SC 6/Hen. VIII/3151; *L. & P. Hen. VIII*, xiv (1), p. 428.
72 *L. & P. Hen. VIII*, xvii, p. 704; xviii (1), p. 196; xix (2), pp. 86–7.
73 P.R.O., SC 6/Hen. VIII/3140; *L. & P. Hen. VIII*, xviii (1), p. 196.

when Hundred Acres passed to his son John.[74] John, like his father recorder of the town,[75] died in 1627, having leased the land to his son George.[76] The Colles family held the land in 1631,[77] but under the will of Matthew de Haviland dated 1667 Hundred Acres was to pass after the death of his wife Constance first to his sister Mary Davies for two years and then was to be sold for the benefit of his four nieces.[78] Hundred Acres was acquired by the Popham family who held it and other former hospital property in and near the town until 1774 when it was divided and sold.[79]

The site of the former hospital and land in North Petherton, called *BRIDGWATER* manor and later *ST. JOHN THE BAPTIST* manor, was sold by the Crown in 1611 to Sir Richard Grobham (d. 1629). It probably descended on his death with Bridgwater Castle manor[80] and after the death of Sir Richard Grubham Howe in 1730 passed to a Mr. Howe, who held it in 1732,[81] and to Margaret Howe, probably his widow, by 1769.[82] Described as half the manor, it was sold by a Mr. Howe, perhaps Margaret's successor, to Thomas Dosson (d. 1802). Dosson's brother George sold it in 1811 to William Mogg (d. *c.* 1856).[83] No further record of the estate has been found.

In 1542 the buildings of the hospital were intended for destruction,[84] but John Newport died in 1564 in possession of the mansion, its circuit, and precincts.[85] No further references to the buildings have been found.

Although by 1546 the Crown had granted about one third of the hospital's rents in the town to William Portman and Alexander Popham, the rest, called Bridgwater manor late *PRIORY*, were still in the Crown's hands.[86]

Alexander Popham (d. 1556) was probably sublessee of the *RECTORY* from the earl of Bath.[87] After expensive negotiations in 1561 Bridgwater corporation acquired in reversion a 21-year lease of the rectory and tithes from the Crown, subject to finding two priests to serve the church.[88] In 1571 the lease was extended to 81 years, with a further obligation to appoint a schoolmaster.[89] The corporation remained lessee of the rectory until 1706 when it acquired the title in fee.[90]

From 1564 the corporation granted leases of the tithes in small units, occasionally those of a single holding but more usually those of one or more tithe collection districts. In 1564 they were defined as of wool and lambs, sheaf and corn,

oblations, offerings, and small tithes, but in the 1570s mention was made of tithing pigs, vicar's tithes, and offerings made within the borough called Easter Book or Easter duties, payable by servants, which were all usually reserved to the corporation.[91] The corporation remained impropriators in 1847 when a rent charge of £328 18s. 7d. was agreed. Until then most of the parish owed tithes at the rates of 6d. an acre from residents and 12d. an acre from others on land not growing grain or flax; tithes of Castle field were partly by modus and partly in kind, and 41 a. of the former hospital demesne were tithe free.[92]

In 1227 Dunkeswell abbey (Devon) held a messuage in Bridgwater given by William Brewer.[93] The abbey retained the messuage, receiving a rent of 12s. in 1539.[94] In the later 13th century Muchelney abbey was granted a half burgage[95] in High Street, which it still held in 1388.[96] The Monmouth family, probably in the 12th century, gave Taunton priory three burgages[97] valued at 4s. in 1535 and including a tenement in High Street.[98] Apart from its manor of Hamp, Athelney abbey held several burgages in the town including an inn called the Saracen's Head.[99] Buckland priory by 1535 had a pension paid by St. John's hospital in respect of tithes from Horsey.[1] By the 16th century the Name of Jesus chantry in St. Mary's church, Taunton, and the chantry in Woolavington church each had a burgage in the town.[2]

ECONOMIC HISTORY.

AGRICULTURE. The four Domesday manors which lay within the ancient parish, Bridgwater, Bower, Hamp, and Horsey, together measured 8½ hides. Bridgwater manor, the largest, gelded for 5 hides but comprised 10 ploughlands. Two hides were in demesne worked by 3 teams; the tenant farms, worked by 8 teams, measured 3 hides. Horsey, next in size, gelded for 2 hides but comprised 7 ploughlands. Three virgates were in demesne and the remainder was worked with 5 teams. Hamp was about half the size of Horsey and was shared equally between lord and tenants. Bower gelded for ½ hide with land for 3 teams; there was 1 on the demesne, 1 on the tenant farms. The demesnes together were worked by 7 teams with 11 *servi*; the recorded tenants totalled 25 *villani*, 24 bordars, and 9 cottars. There were 40 beasts on the combined manors, 48 pigs, and 111 sheep, the last shared only between Bridgwater

---

74 P.R.O., SC 6/Hen. VIII/3143; ibid. WARD 7/13, no. 32; *L. & P. Hen. VIII*, xix (2), pp. 86–7.
75 Jarman, *Hist. Bridgwater*, 274.
76 *S.R.S.* lxvii, p. 95; S.R.O., DD/PH 43.
77 S.R.O., D/B/bw 1868.
78 *A Chronicle of De Haviland* (*c.* 1865), 77.
79 S.R.O., DD/PO, box 21; DD/POt 134.
80 Above, this section.
81 S.R.O., D/B/bw 2/1/2 (2 May 1732).
82 Ibid. DD/SAS (C/96) 17/17.
83 Ibid. DD/PAM 5.
84 Ibid. DD/POt 39.
85 P.R.O., C 142/141, no. 17.
86 Ibid. SC 6/Hen. VIII/3143; *L. & P. Hen. VIII*, xx (1), p. 676.
87 *S.R.S.* xxi. 180–1.
88 *Cal. Pat.* 1560–3, pp. 161–2; S.R.O., D/B/bw 799, 1694, 1815.

89 *Cal. Pat.* 1569–72, p. 307.
90 S.R.O., D/B/bw 656, 938, 1280, 1745, 1820, 1872, 1968–9; *V.C.H. Som.* ii. 447.
91 S.R.O., D/B/bw 800, 1074, 1320, 1561, 1590, 1688, 1822, 2179–83, 2185.
92 Ibid. tithe award.
93 *Cal. Chart. R.* 1226–57, 18. The gift was probably made by William Brewer (d. 1233).
94 Dugdale, *Mon.* v. 680.
95 *S.R.S.* xiv, pp. 89–90.
96 Ibid. xlviii, no. 130; liii, no. 434.
97 *Cal. Chart. R.* 1327–41, 316.
98 *Valor Eccl.* (Rec. Com.), i. 169; Dugdale, *Mon.* v. 626.
99 *S.R.S.* xlviii, no. 292; Bodl. Libr., MS. Top. Som. b. 1, f. 8; *Valor Eccl.* (Rec. Com.), i. 207; *L. & P. Hen. VIII*, xviii (1), p. 535.
1 *Valor Eccl.* (Rec. Com.), i. 211.
2 *Cal. Pat.* 1549–51, 145–6; 1553–4, 153.

and Horsey. There was a riding horse at Horsey but only 2 beasts at Hamp. A total of 25 a. of pasture was found at Bridgwater and Horsey.[3]

Bridgwater manor, whose stock included 100 ewes in 1185–6,[4] was divided between two lords in the mid 13th century. Each share included an agricultural estate at Haygrove, urban rents, and market and port dues. In 1249 the demesne of the Mortimers' share, one third of the manor, measured 91 a. of arable and 24 a. of meadow. Farm rents and cash in lieu of works from customary tenants were worth 20s. in 1249, 34s. from 8 customary tenants in 1282, and 19s. from 9 tenants for rent and 5s. for works in 1304. In 1249 the estate was valued at £21 2s. 10½d.[5] In 1256–7 the other two thirds of the manor had nearly 140 a. under crops. Rents amounted to 37s. 2d. from 19 customary tenants who performed 132 works. The gross income was £85 4s. 11d., of which sales of grain, stock, and pasture accounted for over £51. The demesne was staffed by 2 ploughmen and 1 carter and the arable in that year was divided between oats (51 a.), wheat (37 a.), beans (26 a.), rye (15 a.), and barley (10 a.).[6]

By 1347–8 the demesne of the Mortimers' third was almost entirely let and total rents amounted to £23 1s. 7d., including a small sum from the rent of the demesne meadow and from the sales of wax paid for chevage.[7] Crops were lost in 1381–2 and later because of flooding north of the town around Crowpill,[8] and in the summer of 1413 income was slightly reduced because herons and sparrowhawks had not nested and bees and rabbits had disappeared.[9]

Horsey manor in the 13th and 14th centuries included a demesne farm of c. 130 a., all but 12 a. arable, and rents of free tenants amounting to 8s. There were at least 12 customary tenants in 1327; 9 tenants in 1337 had each a messuage and 8 a. and paid 2s. in lieu of services and labour.[10] Other holdings east of the town in the 13th century and later seem to have been fragmented, one in 1208–9 having 7 a. in five places and 1 a. in a new meadow apparently in Bower and Dunwear.[11] Another in the 1290s comprised 26 a. of arable and 6 a. of meadow in Dunwear and Slape.[12] A farm of similar size in the same area by 1316 survived in the 15th century;[13] holdings in North Bower, Dunwear, and nearby Slape formed part of the much larger and scattered estates of William Dodesham in 1455 and of James Hadley in 1532.[14]

Common arable cultivation was still practised in the parish in the 16th century. Blackland,

perhaps earlier known as the field by Crowpill,[15] North field, Matthew's field, and Hayle or Hey field lay north-west and west of the town.[16] Hamp field still retained some arable strips in the 1540s, but part had by then been converted to pasture.[17] Land at Bower called Pulfurlang in 1208–9[18] may have been part of a field which survived in 1847 in small and narrow inclosures collectively called Brimpsfield and Crow Lane field near Slape Cross on the boundary with Chedzoy.[19] Small parts of Horsey field remained in the 1550s[20] and Great and Little Dunwear fields, named in 1847, may have survived from the Dunwear or West field named in 1763.[21]

Common arable cultivation seems to have been abandoned in the eastern part of the parish by the early 16th century and the contrast between it and the west was then marked. In the 1530s, when corn tithes for the whole parish were worth over £25 compared with tithe hay at 17s. 4d. and tithe of wool and lambs together at 34s., Horsey, Dunwear, and North Bower accounted for nearly three quarters of corn and other arable crops tithed.[22]

By 1539 Castle field, formerly the arable demesne field of Eastover, was pasture[23] and St. John's hospital's adjoining Hundred Acres was divided into 80 customary holdings of which the largest comprised an enclosed pasture of 30 a., 13 a. of arable, and common grazing.[24]

In the 1540s Hamp manor, which lay on both sides of the river south of the town, was divided between 5 freeholds, 4 leaseholds, and 42 customary tenancies. Copyhold and leasehold land together amounted to some 620 a., of which more than three quarters were almost evenly divided between arable and pasture. The largest holding, with the capital messuage and some demesne, was 78 a., two others were c. 50 a., most were between 10 a. and 20 a. and comprised small closes. One had a sheep house and a hay house, another a barn and stall under one roof, a third a hay loft over an ox stall. One tenant was licensed to let his house fall down.[25] The lords sold 165 elms from Hamp manor in 1556–7.[26] In 1568 they organized and partly paid for making a new channel for the river.[27]

West Bower manor had been inclosed by the 1550s and its land, lying also in Cannington, Wembdon, and Durleigh, was shared between 11 tenants.[28] In 1635 the manor house was let with 115 a. Much of the rest of the estate was let in holdings of 4 a. or less.[29]

In 1655 Hamp manor contained 472 a. in 43

3 *V.C.H. Som.* i. 469, 497, 499.
4 *Pipe R.* 1186 (P.R.S. xxxvi), 140.
5 P.R.O., C 132/8, no. 4; C 133/32, no. 7/6; C 133/114, no. 8.
6 Ibid. SC 6/1094/11.
7 Ibid. SC 6/968/17.
8 Ibid. SC 6/968/21, 23; SC 6/969/3.
9 Ibid. SC 6/969/21.
10 Ibid. C 135/3, no. 6; C 135/50, no. 21; ibid. E 149/2/4, m. 2; *Cal. Close,* 1288–96, 346.
11 *S.R.S.* vi. 25–6.
12 Ibid. 292, 300.
13 *Cal. Pat.* 1313–17, 511; *Cal. Inq. p.m.* vi, p. 290; *Feud. Aids,* iv. 365.
14 *S.R.S.* xxi. 13–14; xxii. 119–20.
15 Ibid. liii, nos. 334, 352.

16 S.R.O., DD/POt 39; *S.R.S.* lx, no. 780; lxx, nos. 921, 931; P.R.O., SC 6/Hen. VIII/3137.
17 Bristol R.O. 4490.   18 *S.R.S.* vi. 25–6.
19 S.R.O., tithe award.   20 *Cal. Pat.* 1553, 54–5.
21 S.R.O., tithe award; ibid. DD/AH 39/9.
22 *Valor Eccl.* (Rec. Com.), i. 208; P.R.O., SC 6/Hen. VIII/3137.
23 P.R.O., SC 6/Hen. VIII/3073–4; SC 6/968/21; SC 6/969/3; ibid. LR 14/858; *L. & P. Hen. VIII,* xviii (1), 121; *Cal. Pat.* 1566–9, p. 333; S.R.O., DD/S/WH 1.
24 P.R.O., SC 6/Hen. VIII/3137.
25 Bristol R.O. 4490.
26 *City Chamberlains' Accts.* (Bristol Rec. Soc. xxiv), 67.
27 Bristol R.O. 04026 (8), pp. 256–68; ibid. 04403.
28 S.R.O., DD/S/WH 2; *Cal. Pat.* 1553, 54–8.
29 S.R.O., DD/S/BW 5.

holdings: the largest was just over 90 a., another 61 a., and a third 55 a. Most were under 10 a. Half the manor lay on 'deep, solid earth' which was being cropped four years in five and produced beans and good corn 'with little help'. Other land, on sand and gravel, needed less ploughing and more manuring, but produced wheat. The wet marsh supported coarse grass only. One tenant was described as 'exceeding bad', and another had 'impoverished' his tenement; a field recovered from the river was 'the choicest ground' in the manor. Meadow was cheap and rated low for tithe. There were no commons except the small Hamp green; rents and heriots were high.[30] By 1698 some holdings had been consolidated: the demesne farm was 99 a. in 1694, and by 1705 another had increased to 115 a.[31]

Sixty husbandmen and 13 yeomen in the parish contributed in 1661 to a voluntary gift to the king in comparison with 63 tradesmen.[32] By 1709 tithe payments showed a change from the 1530s: little over one third of the corn in the parish was produced east of the river and Horsey's contribution had fallen to under one fifth of the whole. Wheat in the whole parish then covered 188 a., barley 158 a., beans 72 a., pulse 61 a., peas 29 a., and there were smaller areas of vetches and oats.[33]

In 1774 Benjamin and Thomas Allen were rated between them for over 500 a. at Dunwear and Edward Pleydell for over 200 a. at Horsey. Other large holdings were at East Bower.[34] By 1788 the Allens' holdings were much reduced, Thomas's comprising a dairy farm with a new brick house, 14 a. of cider orchards, and 89 a. of land. Benjamin's was a compact farm of 76 a. including 6 common rights in King's Sedgemoor.[35] Other farms in that part of the parish were much smaller but together claimed 30 common rights until 1795 when Bridgwater parish was allotted land in the south-east beside the Weston Zoyland road in respect of claims by farmers in Horsey, East Bower, and Dunwear.[36] The only other common grazing in the parish was Chilton common, shared with Chilton Trinity, Durleigh, and Wembdon; it was partly inclosed by agreement in the 18th century and finally allotted in 1802.[37]

By 1847 meadow and pasture accounted for 3,060 a. in the parish; arable covered only 533 a., orchards 215 a. There were then six principal landowners of whom Margaretta Michel had 370 a., Sir Thomas Reynell 289 a., and John Allen 222 a. The largest farm, Dunwear, was 147 a.;

one at East Bower was 143 a. and several others were just over 100 a., including the later Foundry farm, Coxpit farm, and one at Haygrove. Horsey farm was just under 100 a. and several were just over 70 a.[38] By 1862 the Tyntes' estate centred on West Bower had been consolidated as a farm of 273 a., but small holdings persisted around Haygrove and at East Bower until the earlier 20th century.[39] By 1905 the amount of arable land had been further reduced to 383 a.,[40] and by 1982 there had been a further fall in arable. In that year there was a total of 77.5 ha. under crop, more than half winter barley. Returns were then made of 33 farms of which 2 were over 100 ha. and 12 between 30 ha. and 100 ha. Six farms specialized in dairying, 3 in stock rearing, 2 in general horticulture, and 1 in poultry.[41]

MILLS. In 1086 Walter of Douai had a mill in Bridgwater.[42] Following the division of the lordship the Mortimers held a third of two mills in 1249.[43] The two mills, probably under a single roof, were still in operation in 1395.[44] No further reference to those mills has been found.

A mill known as Little Mill, recorded c. 1361,[45] retained the name in the mid 16th century when three quarters of it belonged to Bridgwater Castle manor.[46] By the early 17th century it was known as the Town mill or Bridgwater mill.[47] The mill, at the southern end of Blake Street, was driven by a leat from the Durleigh brook.[48] In 1886 it was described as a disused sawmill.[49] It was used as a builder's store until 1988 when it was bought on behalf of the Bridgwater Museum Society for incorporation into the town's museum.[50]

A mill on Hamp manor by 1549, perhaps also known as South mill,[51] continued in use in the 17th century. Its sluice required repair in 1647 and the mill was said to be ruinous in 1655. It was evidently rebuilt, and in 1694 Bristol corporation sold it to Edward Raymond.[52] No further trace of it has been found.

A water mill at West Bower, owned by William Gascoigne in 1423,[53] passed to Sir Alexander Hody (d. 1461) and descended with West Bower manor.[54] It was still in use in 1909.[55] The mill stood west of West Bower Manor.

A water mill east of the Parrett granted by William of Horsey to William Brewer (d. 1233)[56] may be the mill at 'Arknelle', described in 1251–2 as alienated from Pignes.[57] No further reference to it has been found.

A horse mill was in use in Bridgwater castle in

30 Bristol R.O. 04237.
31 Ibid. 00570 (1–28), 00904; S.R.O., DD/RN 1.
32 S.R.O., D/B/bw 78.
33 Ibid. 1903.
34 Ibid. D/P/bw. m 13/2/15.
35 Ibid. DD/CH 47.
36 Ibid. Q/RDe 116.
37 Ibid. 29; below, Wembdon, intro.
38 S.R.O., tithe award.
39 Ibid. DD/RN 53/2; DD/TBL 53; Som. C.C., Brymore deeds.
40 Statistics supplied by the then Bd. of Agric. 1905.
41 Min. of Agric., Fisheries, and Food, agric. returns, 1982.
42 V.C.H. Som. i. 499.
43 P.R.O., C 132/8, no. 4.

44 Ibid. SC 6/968/21; SC 6/969/11.
45 S.R.S. xlviii, no. 194.
46 Bodl. Libr., MS. Top. Som. b. 1.
47 S.R.O., D/B/bw 613; S.R.S. lxvii, p. 17.
48 S.R.O., D/B/bw 1636, 1737, 1971; Bristol R.O. 00904 (7); B.L. Add. Ch. 71720.
49 O.S. Map 1/500, Som. L. 11. 21 (1887 edn.).
50 Local inf.
51 Bristol R.O. 04403 (14 Oct. 1549); Bodl. Libr., MS. Top. Som. b. 1.
52 Bristol R.O. 00904 (7, 12), 04237, 04403–4.
53 P.R.O., C 139/7, no. 56.
54 Above, manors.
55 S.R.O., D/R/bw 15/3/9.
56 P.R.O., DL 42/11, f. 4v.
57 Bk. of Fees, ii. 1266.

1304. It was said to have been ruinous in 1372 but was working in 1382 and by 1389 was leased with 12 a. of land for the support of five horses. It was still in use in 1413, but no further trace has been found.[58]

A horse mill formerly belonging to St. John's hospital was sold by the Crown in 1544 to Sir John Fulford and Humphrey Colles and by them in the same year to John Newport.[59] John Newport's son Emmanuel sold the mill to Alexander Jones in 1591.[60] No further trace has been found.

A horse mill in use on the south side of High Street in 1655 belonged to the Halswell estate.[61]

A fulling mill built c. 1409 in Bridgwater castle was still in use in 1413[62] but no further trace has been found.

In 1548 the mayor and burgesses of Bridgwater granted the site of a former mill on the bank of the Parrett for building a weir. The site, described as between a mill tail and a barn and stretching from the low water mark 14 yd. towards the middle of the river, seems to have been for a tide mill.[63]

A windmill at Horsey in 1294 belonged to the Horsey family in 1327.[64] The site, excavated in 1907 and 1971, produced 15th-century pottery.[65]

Messrs. Spiller operated steam-driven flour mills in Chilton Road, Crowpill, from 1845. The mills were disused by 1886.[66]

MARKETS AND FAIRS. William Brewer was granted a free market at Bridgwater in 1200.[67] Stalls were set up in High Street by the mid 13th century, and by 1367 some stalls were housed in a market hall (*domus stallorum*) there, while others stood in Fore Street.[68] There were separate fish stalls by 1449, and butchers' stalls were in the flesh shambles, mentioned in 1472[69] and surviving until the rebuilding of the north side of High Street in the early 1820s.[70] By 1615 a separate shambles stood in the market place, in the 1730s comprising stalls under three of the arches on the north side of the high cross.[71]

Market day was Saturday under the borough charter of 1468, but by the later 16th century it seems to have been changed to Thursday.[72] By the later 17th century cheese was sold in the Cheese Market and later bacon also.[73] Stalls in and around the high cross were from 1769 used by hide sellers.[74]

Efforts were made in the 1770s to establish extra cattle sales,[75] and by the 1790s markets were held on Tuesdays, Thursdays, and Saturdays; the principal market day remained Thursday, largely for cattle and cheese in the 1790s, and also for corn in the 1820s.[76] The town's markets were by the 1790s the 'most considerable' in the county for corn, horned cattle, sheep, pigs, and cheese.[77] Demand for food among the poor in 1800 drove prices up and forced the delivery of foreign wheat from Bristol and flour direct from Philadelphia, but only the turnip crop had actually failed. Crops of barley and wheat had improved in quality over the previous year but potatoes had doubled in price since 1798. Farmers could not leave unthreshed corn in the fields for fear of theft.[78] A special market for cattle was advertised in 1826, to be held on Thursday 30 November,[79] but contraction of business is suggested by a petition of 1839 to protect the Thursday market from competition.[80] An annual 'great market' was established in the 1880s, held on the first Wednesday in December[81] to coincide with the change in the principal market day from Thursday to Wednesday made in 1857, while at the same time the lesser market days were established as Monday and Saturday.[82] By 1902 enlarged markets on the last Wednesdays in January, March, and June and a fatstock show on the Thursday before the first Wednesday in September had replaced all but one of the ancient fairs in the town, while the 'great market' continued on the first Wednesday in December.[83] By 1914 the fatstock show and the 'great market' were combined on the first Tuesday and Wednesday in December and the special markets in January and March had ceased.[84]

A triangular area within the west gate was known by 1399 as le Orfaire, and was evidently the site of the cattle market.[85] Cattle and pigs were offered for sale in the same place, then called Penel Orlieu, in the 19th century, when the sheep market was in West Street. The cattle market was enclosed in 1875 and improved in 1889–90.[86] The market was removed to a new site in Bath Road in 1935,[87] where it operated in 1991. By 1909 meat, fish, fruit, and vegetables were sold in the market hall on Wednesdays and Saturdays, and later every weekday.[88] A general market was held at the cattle market on Saturdays in the 1980s, but an attempt to extend it to Sundays during the summer months in 1986 was

58 P.R.O., C 133/114, no. 8; ibid. SC 6/968/17, 21; SC 6/969/3, 21; *S.R.S.* xlviii, no. 269 (p. 193).
59 *L. & P. Hen. VIII*, xix (1), p. 496; xix (2), p. 86.
60 P.R.O., CP 25(2)/206/33 & 34 Eliz. I Mich.
61 S.R.O., DD/S/WH 118.
62 P.R.O., SC 6/969/21.
63 S.R.O., D/B/bw 499.
64 *Cal. Close*, 1288–96, 346; P.R.O., E 135/3, no. 6.
65 *S.D.N.Q.* xii. 314; Bristol Univ., Dept. of Extra-Mural Studies, M5 Research Cttee. Interim Rep. 1971. The site, at ST 322387, was destroyed by the construction of the M5 motorway.
66 Inf. from Mr. David Wainwright, Christon; O.S. Map, 1/500, Som. L. 11. 1 (1887 edn.).
67 P.R.O., DL 42/1, f. 433, no. 20; 42/11, ff. 2v.–3; *S.R.S.* xlviii, no. 1.
68 *S.R.S.* xlviii, nos. 13, 235, 237.
69 Ibid. lx, no. 757; lxx, no. 913.
70 S.R.O., D/B/bw 2/1/3 (24 Sept. 1821).
71 Ibid. D/B/bw 1278; 2/1/2 (14 Dec. 1733; 14 May 1734).

72 Ibid. D/B/bw 1839; *Cal. Chart. R.* 1427–1516, 229.
73 S.R.O., D/B/bw 1630; 2/1/2 (23 June 1784).
74 Ibid. D/B/bw 2/1/1 (17 Aug. 1725); 2/1/2 (21 Oct. 1769).
75 Ibid. D/B/bw 2/1/2 (23 Nov., 9 Dec. 1778).
76 Collinson, *Hist. Som.* iii. 75; *Univ. Brit. Dir.* (1797); Pigot, *Nat. Com. Dir.* (1822–3).
77 B.L. Add. MS. 28793, f. 17.
78 P.R.O., HO 42/54/53879.
79 S.R.O., D/B/bw 2/1/3 (25 Sept. 1826).
80 Ibid. D/B/bw 1839.
81 *Kelly's Dir. Som.* (1883, 1889).
82 Bridgwater Markets and Fairs Act, 20 & 21 Vic. c. 30 (Local and Personal).
83 *Kelly's Dir. Som.* (1902); for the fairs, below, this section.
84 *Kelly's Dir. Som.* (1914).
85 *S.R.S.* liii, no. 492.
86 Squibbs, *Bridgwater*, pl. 13; *Kelly's Dir. Som.* (1899, 1909).
87 *Bridgwater Mercury*, 9 May 1934; Squibbs, *Bridgwater*, pl. 38.
88 *Kelly's Dir. Som.* (1909, 1939).

The west quay and bridge, *c.* 1800

The west quay and bridge, *c.* 1950

BRIDGWATER

The launch of the ketch *Irene,* 1907

Sluicing at the tidal basin, *c.* 1902

BRIDGWATER

not successful[89] and in 1991 it was held on Saturdays only.

The old Tolsey in High Street was referred to between 1352 and 1708.[90] The Cheese Market, measuring 100 ft. by 13 ft. 6 in., stood in the centre of St. Mary Street at the east end of the churchyard by 1674.[91] It was removed between 1794[92] and 1822 and a new building erected on the corner of Friarn Street and St. Mary Street, on the site of the Three Cups inn.[93] By 1830 it had been converted into an inn.[94]

A corn market house was built in brick by 1791.[95] The north and south sides of the building were demolished for road-widening in 1825, and an Act was secured in 1826 under which a new frontage was constructed.[96] It is said to have been completed c. 1827 and to have been designed by John Bowen.[97] The present building has a portico with heavy Ionic columns leading into a corn exchange rebuilt in 1875. Behind is the earlier market house, entered from north and south through gateways flanked by Ionic columns in antis.

In 1200 William Brewer was granted an annual eight-day fair beginning on 24 June.[98] The fair seems to have lapsed c. 1359 when no merchants came.[99] It was revived by the charter of 1587, when it was to last for six days.[1] By the mid 18th century a fair was held only on Midsummer day, and it included a shoe fair, transferred in 1743 from George Lane to Dampiet Street.[2] By 1857 it was held for two days, 24 and 25 June, but from that year it was held for one day, the last Wednesday in June.[3] The fair remained in existence as a horse fair until 1936 or later.[4] In 1869 a summer fair was also held on 7 July in Eastover for horses only, but it was then said to be in decline.[5]

By 1249 the lords of Bridgwater had an eight-day fair around St. Matthew's day (21 Sept.)[6] and its site, St. Matthew's field outside the west gate, was established by 1404.[7] The fair was not mentioned in the borough charter of 1468, but was one of the three confirmed in 1587, and in 1628 was to be held for three days.[8] With the new calendar of 1752 the fair began on 2 October.[9] By 1852, perhaps only temporarily, it included a Saturday pleasure fair.[10] In 1857 the

fair was transferred to the three days beginning on the last Wednesday in September.[11] In the late 1920s it was extended to four days.[12] By 1822 the fair was claimed to be one of the largest in the West of England.[13] By c. 1900 the first day of the fair was for the sale of cattle and horses, the other two for cattle and general merchandise, but by 1914, when sheep also were sold on the first day, the other two days were solely for pleasure.[14] In the late 1920s the fair was extended to include Saturday.[15] In 1988 it was held for four days as usual.[16]

The lords of Bridgwater also had two small fairs at Ascension and Whitsun. Both existed in 1358 but thereafter declined. The Whitsun fair was held in 1403 but not in 1405; the Ascension fair was held in 1405 but very little toll was taken.[17] In 1468 the former Ascension day fair seems to have been re-established as one for five days from the Monday after Shrove Tuesday,[18] and it was continued by the borough charter of 1587.[19] In the 1740s the fair included a special sale of shoes, and in the 1780s of narrow cloths and shap.[20] In the 1790s the fair was apparently limited to the first Sunday in Lent,[21] but by 1800 it was held on the second Thursday in Lent.[22] In 1857 the fair was transferred to the last Wednesday in March; it is said to have survived until c. 1900.[23]

By the charter of 1683 a fair for all marketable goods and for large and small cattle was to be held in High Street on 28 and 29 December.[24] By the mid 18th century it was known as the Cock fair or Cock Hill fair,[25] and it continued as the Christmas fair until the later 19th century, held on 28 December until 1857 and from then transferred to the last Wednesday in January.[26]

OVERSEAS TRADE. Plausible interpretations of the town's name[27] indicate that Bridgwater already by the 11th century used the river for trade. The inclusion of lastage as part of the income of the town in 1200 has been seen as evidence that there was a port, where duty was collected on freight landed and vessels moored.[28] The lord's 'water tolls' in the later 13th century were worth rather less than the market tolls,[29] and a century later had declined both absolutely

89 *Bridgwater Mercury*, 30 Apr. 1986; inf. from Sedgemoor Dist. estates dept.
90 *S.R.S.* xlviii, no. 163; liii, no. 369; S.R.O., D/B/bw 129, 1686.
91 S.R.O., D/B/bw 1630, 1637, 2008; D/B/bw 2/1/1 (13 Sept. 1731); DD/RN 8.
92 Ibid. D/B/bw 2/1/3 (4 Nov. 1785; 30 June 1794).
93 Ibid. 2/1/3 (21 Jan. 1822).
94 Pigot, *Nat. Com. Dir.* (1830).
95 Collinson, *Hist. Som.* iii. 75.
96 S.R.O., D/B/bw 2/1/3 (16 Feb. 1825); *L.J.* lviii. 114, 138; 7 Geo. IV, c. 7 (Local and Personal).
97 *Robson's Som. Dir.* (1839); Pevsner, *S. and W. Som.*, 98, where the date 1834 is given.
98 *S.R.S.* xlviii, no. 1.
99 P.R.O., SC 6/968/19.
1 S.R.O., D/B/bw 2167.
2 Ibid. D/B/bw 2/1/2 (17 Aug. 1743).
3 20 & 21 Vic. c. 30 (Local and Personal).
4 *Proc. Som. Arch. Soc.* lxxxii. 140.
5 Squibbs, *Bridgwater*, 88.
6 P.R.O., C 132/8, no. 4.
7 *S.R.S.* lviii, no. 525.
8 S.R.O., DD/X/ME 7.
9 *Univ. Brit. Dir.* (1797); Collinson, *Hist. Som.* iii. 75.

10 Squibbs, *Bridgwater*, 64, 74.
11 20 & 21 Vic. c. 30 (Local and Personal).
12 Squibbs, *Bridgwater*, pl. 180.
13 Pigot, *Nat. Com. Dir.* (1822–3).
14 *Kelly's Dir. Som.* (1902, 1909, 1914).
15 Squibbs, *Bridgwater*, pl. 180.   16 Local inf.
17 P.R.O., SC 6/968/19–29; SC 6/969/1–19.
18 *S.R.S.* lxx, p. xii.
19 S.R.O., DD/X/ME 7.
20 Ibid. D/B/bw 2/1/2 (17 Aug. 1743; 23 June 1784).
21 *Univ. Brit. Dir.* (1797).
22 S.R.O., T/PH/ay 1, 6 Mar. 1800; Pigot, *Nat. Com. Dir.* (1822–3).
23 20 & 21 Vic. c. 30 (Local and Personal); *Proc. Som. Arch. Soc.* lxxxii. 143.
24 S.R.O., Bridgwater charters, trans. E. de G. Birch; *Proc. Som. Arch. Soc.* lxxxii. 143.
25 S.R.O., D/B/bw 2/1/2 (4 Dec. 1758); D/B/bw 1782.
26 Collinson, *Hist. Som.* iii. 75; *Bath and West and Southern Cos. Jnl.* 2nd ser. xii (1865), pp. 267–8; *Proc. Som. Arch. Soc.* lxxxii. 143; 20 & 21 Vic. c. 30 (Local and Personal).
27 Above, intro.
28 *Proc. Som. Arch. Soc.* xcix. 56–7.
29 P.R.O., C 132/8, no. 4; C 133/32, no. 7/6; C 133/79, no. 7/9.

and in relation to the market tolls.[30] Nevertheless, the town provided sailors for the Welsh campaign in 1277,[31] and on at least 13 occasions between 1301 and 1417 sent ships on military expeditions to Ireland, Scotland, France, and Spain. In 1319, when it was liable jointly with Bristol for one ship for Scotland, the only vessel available had already gone on service to Gascony; in 1342 jointly with Combwich it sent four ships and a barge to Brittany.[32]

Until the early 15th century the customs accounts for Bridgwater were subsumed in those of Bristol. The tolls payable to the lords of the town give an indication of the volume of trade: the Mortimers' estate received 16s. 2d. in 1347–8 and 12s. 8d. in 1358–9, but much less than half those sums in nearly every year 1381–1403.[33]

About 1300 Bridgwater merchants were trading in wine with Bordeaux, and in 1330 the port was a centre for victualling for the same destination.[34] The Bardi used Bridgwater as a collecting port for wool exports in the 1340s,[35] and Bridgwater merchants were involved in the export of agricultural products to southern France, northern Spain, Wales, and Ireland. David le Palmer and Hugh le Mareys were licensed in 1331 to ship 500 qr. of corn to Wales but not to foreign parts,[36] and in 1364–5 John Michel and others were licensed to export wheat, beans, and peas to Cornwall, Ireland, Bayonne, and Spain.[37] Merchants from the port evaded customs on wool, hides, and wool fells by lading them in the river and not at the quay; John Godesland of Combwich shipped quantities of corn to Ireland to the king's enemies.[38] John Cole, probably the most prosperous merchant in the town at the time, took large quantities of beans to Bordeaux and Bayonne and to the Bristol Channel ports in the 1360s and 1370s; and Richard atte Mill was licensed with a Wellington man in 1371 to load barley and beans for Waterford, Cork, Cardiff, and Carmarthen.[39]

Imports included wine brought in on a Dunwich ship in 1360 and herrings unloaded in 1382.[40] In 1396–7 the town's bailiff accounted for money charged for moorage, for the use of the bushel measure, and for the hire of planks, ropes, and skids used to take wine from ships to the town cellar. In that year a wooden gangway (*via de meremio*) was made for landing wine and stone. In the year 1399–1400 the town charged for the haulage of 101 tuns of wine.[41]

Bridgwater, a separate port from 1402, exported more than 100 cloths in each of 11 years up to 1450, and more than 200 in 1415–16 and 1422–3. For 75 years from 1472 the number of cloths leaving the port (which included creeks outside the town) never fell below 100 a year, and from 1488 to 1506 never below 300: 966 cloths were exported in 1481–2 and 974 cloths in 1500–1. The average for the period 1402–1506 was just over 200 a year,[42] and was higher 1506–47.[43] Wine imports fluctuated widely.[44] The town's income from charges for the use of moorings, quays, the crane, measures, and planks was on average between £5 and £6 in the 1420s and c. £2 10s. in the 1460s.[45] The charges made by the water bailiffs for unloading, storing, and moving imported goods show a growth of imports by the end of the century, yielding c. £20 a year,[46] but only half as much 1525–43 before rising to an average of over £25 1549–83.[47] In that period trade was said to be increasing, making the port the busiest in the county.[48] The number of ships belonging to the port, however, was only 5 in 1508–9, 'few' in 1570, and in James I's reign only 4, compared with 37 belonging to Bristol and 16 to Barnstaple.[49] The income from charges fell markedly in the mid 1580s, but a partial recovery gave an average 1600–53 of c. £15.[50]

Bridgwater's cloth exports in the later 15th and early 16th century were principally to San Sebastian, Fuenterrabia (Spain), Bayonne, Andalusia, Bilbao, Bordeaux, and the Irish ports,[51] and trade continued there in the first half of the 16th century. Serges, kerseys, and Tauntons were exported, for instance, in the last quarter of 1547,[52] Tauntons being, with Bridgwaters and Chards, cloths defined by an Act of parliament which Bridgwater corporation obtained in 1555.[53] A consignment of poldavy, canvas belonging to an Antwerp merchant, which may have been on its way to Bristol, was confiscated in 1563.[54]

Agricultural products were the other main export to both international and regional markets in the later Middle Ages. Half was to the Irish ports of Wexford, Waterford, Youghal, Galway, Limerick, and Rosse, and was mostly beans.[55] In

30 P.R.O., SC 6/968/17, 19–20, 22–4, 26, 28; SC 6/969/1, 5–7, 10, 12–13, 17–20.
31 *Cal. Pat.* 1272–81, 195.
32 Ibid. 1292–1301, 584; 1301–7, 53, 61, 75; 1307–13, 352; *V.C.H. Som.* ii. 247–9; *S.R.S.* lix, pp. lxvii, 169–71.
33 P.R.O., SC 6/968/17, 19–20, 22–4, 26, 28; SC 6/969/1, 5–7, 10, 12–13, 17–20.
34 *Cal. Close*, 1313–18, 565; 1330–3, 28–9, 86; *Overseas Trade of Bristol* (Bristol Rec. Soc. vii), p. 177.
35 *Cal. Close*, 1336–9, 323.
36 *Cal. Pat.* 1330–4, 75; *Cal. Close*, 1330–3, 284.
37 *Cal. Pat.* 1361–4, 317; 1364–7, 35, 44, 61, 72, 176; 1370–4, 94; *S.R.S.* liii, no. 362.
38 *Cal. Close*, 1346–9, 180; *Cal. Fine R.* 1366–9, 291; *Cal. Inq. Misc.* iii, p. 206; P.R.O., SC 6/976/15.
39 *Cal. Pat.* 1367–70, 109, 339, 467; 1370–4, 52.
40 *S.R.S.* xlviii, no. 190; liii, no. 375.
41 Ibid. liii, no. 483; lviii, no. 502.
42 E. M. Carus-Wilson and O. Coleman, *England's Export Trade, 1275–1547* (Oxford, 1963), 88–119.
43 Ibid.; G. Schanz, *Englische Handelspolitik gegen Ende des Mittelalters* (Leipzig, 1881), ii. 100.
44 W. Childs, 'Ireland's Trade with England in the Later Middle Ages', *Irish Econ. and Soc. Hist.* ix (1982), 22.
45 *S.R.S.* lviii, nos. 613, 641, 686, 703, 711, 718; lx, nos. 728, 757, 768, 774, 785, 793, 824, 830, 850.
46 S.R.O., D/B/bw 1429, 1431–2.
47 Ibid. DD/SAS PR 217; ibid. D/B/bw 1428, 1433–5, 1440–2, 1458, 1464, 1467–70, 1472, 1475.
48 *S.D.N.Q.* xxx. 158–9.
49 *L. & P. Hen. VIII*, i (1), p. 92; *Cal. S.P. Dom.* 1547–80, no. 74; *Trans. R. Hist. S.* N.S. xix. 336.
50 S.R.O., D/B/bw 1462, 1476–91, 1493–1510, 1513, 1515, 1517, 1519–21, 1576, 1579–80, 1585.
51 *S.R.S.* xix. 64–8; lxx, nos. 933–4; P.R.O., C 1/27/184, 28/473; W. Childs, *Anglo-Castilian Trade in the Later Middle Ages* (Manchester, 1978), 79; *Irish Econ. and Soc. Hist.* ix. 21–2.
52 P.R.O., E 122/27/25.
53 S.R.O., D/B/bw 1877, 1916; 2 & 3 Phil. & Mary, c. 12.
54 S.R.O., D/B/bw 1889, 1993.
55 *S.R.S.* lviii, nos. 517, 657, 714; lxx, nos. 938, 980; S.R.O., D/B/bw 1985.

1519 a consignment of wheat and rye destined for Cork or Kinsale was landed at Tenby.[56] Several export licences were issued in the 16th century for beans, malt, or pulse, and Leland reported that Bridgwater became a kind of staple for beans when corn was dear overseas.[57] Edward Dyer was licensed in 1568 to export 1,000 qr. of wheat and beans from Bridgwater and Minehead to any friendly country, and in 1571 Bridgwater was one of the ports for grain, butter, and cheese exports to Ireland.[58]

Hides were exported in varying quantities in Henry VIII's reign.[59] Only one of the four ships leaving the port in the last quarter of 1547 had hides, 94 doz. calfskins and 40 unspecified hides on a ship from San Sebastian. The remainder of the cargo comprised 51 serges, 34 doz. kerseys, and 32 doz. Tauntons.[60] Miscellaneous exports included a consignment of tin sent to Bordeaux in the 1480s.[61]

In the later 15th century annual wine imports averaged 102 tuns (25,704 gallons), but figures fluctuated between 366 tuns in 1475–6 and none in 1470.[62] In 1504–5 just over 285 tuns were unloaded, including small amounts of sweet white wine in Gascon and Breton ships.[63] Average annual wine imports in Henry VIII's reign amounted to just over 79 tuns[64] and still, as in the 15th century, came from La Rochelle, the Bordeaux region, Portugal, and southern Spain.[65]

In the 1470s a picard of Wexford took beans from Bridgwater and returned with red herring, salmon, conger eels, and barrels.[66] Coastal trade extended from the Bristol Channel ports around the south-west peninsula to Dartmouth, Exmouth, Melcombe Regis, and Dorchester, and there were frequent links with Bristol and London merchants.[67] Among prominent businessmen in the port in the 15th century were John Kedwelly, owner of a crayer called the *Cog John* of 24 tons and another ship of 50 tons, both evidently captured by the French in the Channel c. 1410. The first was bound for La Rochelle with wine, the other laden with 60 cloths.[68] John Hill (d. 1482) had a quarter share in two ships and an eighth share in another[69] and Denis Dwyn (d. 1504), an Irishman but a burgess and former bailiff of Bridgwater, owned a ship called the *Gabriel* and traded with Bordeaux in woad, cloth, and wine, and with a Limerick merchant in whiting and cod.[70] John Smythe

was apprenticed in the town and continued to trade through the port after moving to Bristol.[71]

Millstones and grindstones, imported from the Forest of Dean by 1503–4, were distributed from the 1550s in Devon and almost as far as the Dorset coast. During the period 1562–73 the corporation established a monopoly on their import and resale. At the end of 1572 it held a stock of 38 millstones, 45 grindstones, 19 cornstones, 4 mustard mills, and 1 horsemill stone, and in 1590–1 it sold 76 stones.[72]

About 1600 general trade improved considerably. In the 1590s imports had been erratic and depressed, hardly paying the fees of the customs collector, and only one large ship belonged to the port.[73] Export licences for trade to Ireland and resumed business with France, Spain, and Portugal, doubled the amount of customable trade from c. 1603,[74] but there was far more coastal traffic than a century earlier and direct trade with France and Spain was rare. In 1603–4 red, white, and canary wine and sack came via Bristol, salt via Barnstaple, iron via Cardiff, and iron and train oil on a Weymouth barque. Other commodities in that year included Spanish wool, raisins, sugar, and sumach.[75] In 1614–15 the range of imports was narrower, but included metheglin, probably from Wales, block wood, tombstones, copperas, and *campecha*, presumably Campeachy wood.[76] In 1639–40 roughly the same amount of goods was imported, involving 189 vessels of which 153 were local ones plying the Bristol Channel. Coal and salt were then the principal commodities, together with building materials such as cases of glass, laths and other timber, nails and iron rods, besides cloth known as Manchester ware.[77]

In the 1620s and 1630s licences to export grain and other goods to Ireland further stimulated cross-channel trade,[78] but restrictions on Irish trade were imposed during the rebellion there in 1649–50.[79] In 1656 Bridgwater tried to revive the trade in millstones, imported from South Wales.[80] Piracy sometimes caused disruption,[81] and in 1666 trade was said to be 'at a stand' except for foreign ships which could afford escorts.[82] Bridgwater was in 1661 asked to support an escort vessel for the Newfoundland fishing fleet.[83] The increase in trade which peace brought had only a limited effect on Bridgwater, the largest ships turning to foreign business such as salt and lime from La Rochelle and neglecting

56 P.R.O., REQ 2/4, no. 261; REQ 2/12, no. 1.
57 *L. & P. Hen. VIII*, i, Addenda (1), pp. 245–6; iii (2), p. 1286; xviii (1), p. 287; *Cal. Pat. 1557–8*, 309; Leland, *Itin.* ed. Toulmin Smith, i. 168.
58 *Cal. Pat. 1566–9*, p. 314; *1569–72*, p. 254.
59 Schanz, *Englische Handelspolitik*, ii. 115.
60 P.R.O., E 122/27/25.
61 *B.L. Harl. MS. 433*, ed. R. Horrox and P. W. Hammond, ii. 209.
62 *Irish Econ. and Soc. Hist.* ix. 22.
63 S.R.O., D/B/bw 1432.
64 Schanz, *Englische Handelspolitik*, ii. 144.
65 *S.R.S.* lviii, no. 519; lxx, nos. 922, 951, 982; *Rot. Parl.* iii. 643; *B.L. Harl. MS. 433*, ed. Horrox and Hammond, ii. 209; *Overseas Trade of Bristol in 16th Cent.* (Bristol Rec. Soc. xxxi), 101 and n.; Childs, *Anglo-Castilian Trade*, 52.
66 S.R.O., D/B/bw 1985.
67 *S.R.S.* lviii, nos. 653, 687–8, 699, 707–8, 719; lx, nos. 844, 849, 853–4; lxx, nos. 906, 946; P.R.O., REQ 2/12, no. 1.

68 *Rot. Parl.* iii. 643.
69 *S.R.S.* lxx, no. 1003.
70 Ibid. xix. 64–8; *Overseas Trade of Bristol in 16th Cent.* 101 and n.
71 *Ledger Bk. of John Smythe* (Bristol Rec. Soc. xxviii), 2–3, 12, 16 sqq.
72 S.R.O., D/B/bw 800, 1429–30, 1432–3, 1458, 1537–9, 1541–3, 1547, 1549–50, 1552–4.
73 *Cal. S.P. Dom. 1595–7*, 215–16, 315, 459, 525.
74 *Acts of P.C. 1599–1600*, 794; *1601–4*, 426–7; *S.D.N.Q.* xxviii. 338; S.R.O., D/B/bw 1478–83.
75 S.R.O., D/B/bw 1488.
76 Ibid. 1499.
77 Ibid. 1515.
78 *Acts of P.C. 1628–9*, 46, 230, 233, 365, 381–2; *1629–30*, 82.
79 *Cal. S.P. Dom. 1649–50*, 35.
80 S.R.O., D/B/bw 2039.
81 *Cal. S.P. Dom. 1631–3*, 146; *1634–5*, 33.
82 Ibid. *1666–7*, 197.
83 *Cal. Treas. Bks. 1660–7*, 246.

coal and cloth.[84] In 1669 a ship from Virginia was at Minehead bound for Bridgwater.[85] Bridgwater vessels were involved in French–Irish and English–Dutch trade in the 1670s and operated direct links with Spain, Ireland, and other English ports.[86] William Alloway, a general merchant of Bridgwater, between 1695 and 1704 traded in salt, tallow, Irish wool, and West Indian tobacco, and his ships visited London, Liverpool, Waterford, Cork, Dublin, Minehead, Port Isaac (Cornw.), and Barbados.[87]

Throughout the 18th century the port supported c. 1,000 tons of shipping, in 1701 made up of 33 vessels employing 171 men. Foreign trade accounted for one third or less of the tonnage until the middle of the century, but thereafter for two thirds.[88] It included 'very good' wheat exported via Bristol to Madeira, illegal rum imported from Gallipoli and Leghorn, and unspecified trade with Newfoundland.[89] About 1760 the principal foreign imports were deals, small masts, pipestaves, coal, and culm. Coasters brought in beer and cider, bottles, bricks, cheese, bacon, and wood hoops. Corn went outwards to Bristol.[90] Quantities of salt were also imported from Droitwich (Worcs.).[91] By the 1770s trade was said to be chiefly with Portugal and Newfoundland, but traders had contacts with Gibraltar, Virginia, and the West Indies, and dealt in large quantities of Irish wool.[92]

There were 32 vessels registered in the port in 1789, trading largely in coal from Wales, wool from Ireland, and timber from the Baltic and North America, and in the 1820s c. 60 vessels came regularly.[93] The growth of the brick and tile industry increased tonnage after the 1850s. Average annual trade from the 1820s was over 112,000 tons, but by the 1870s had almost doubled, in 1870–3 reaching an average of 204,809 tons a year carried in 3,793 vessels. The peak year was 1878 with 233,039 tons.[94] During the same period there were 145 ships registered in the port totalling 8,943 tons.[95]

Four companies, Stuckey and Bagehot, Haviland, Axford, and Sully dominated business in the port in the 19th century. The Havilands had a fleet of small vessels in the coal, culm, and limestone business; the Axfords, owning the London and Bridgwater Shipping Co. between 1825 and 1847, were coastal traders with fast schooners; Stuckey and Bagehot had larger vessels which used Combwich quay until the dock was built; the Sullys were coal and culm

merchants, mostly engaged in coastal trade but occasionally sailing to Scotland, Ireland, and France.[96] Joel Spiller, starting in 1840 in partnership with Samuel Browne, was described as a corn merchant. His milling business was the first to establish Bridgwater as a centre for agricultural food production.[97] In 1851 at least 199 people in the parish were directly involved in overseas trade as mariners, pilots, sailors, or seamen, and a further 28 were engaged in shipbuilding.[98]

Between the 1870s and 1904 trade fluctuated, falling in 1900 to 132,000 tons but rising to 189,000 in the last year, part of the decline following the construction of the Severn Tunnel and the active discouragement of the railway company which owned Bridgwater dock.[99] Exports of tiles to Australia and New Zealand and of tiles and Bath brick to Canada, the United States, Spain, France, and Germany involved the construction of a new quay in 1903–4, and before 1914 linseed was imported for cattle feed manufacture and foreign timber for the building trades. Total trading nevertheless declined, and on one day in 1911 only one vessel was moored in the river.[1] Tonnage was 108,000 in 1912 with 1,586 vessels visiting. Technical advances in brick and tile manufacture abroad after the First World War reduced exports, and coal came increasingly by rail. In 1937 the number of vessels nearly halved in the port as a whole and there was further decline in the following year. The last sailing vessel to berth commercially at the quay came in 1934. In 1953 tonnage had fallen to 52,766, the last year when commercial shipping passed the telescopic bridge to berth at the riverside quays. The whole port, exporting an average of 5,000 tons in the 1930s, exported none in 1968. The docks, their future already uncertain, took no more coal after 1966 and were closed in 1971.[2]

OTHER TRADE AND INDUSTRY. By 1249 the rents of burgages, shops, and stalls and the tolls from markets, fairs, and quay were a significant part of the income of Bridgwater manor.[3] By 1257 there were 313 burgages, 13 stalls, and 5 shops.[4] From the mid 13th century the town attracted settlers not only from the immediate hinterland and elsewhere in the county[5] but also from Devon and Wales.[6] In 1256–7 there were three Jews in the town: one was licensed to live there for a year, one for part of a year, and the third was fined for a trespass.[7]

84 *Cal. S.P. Dom.* 1667, 120, 534; 1667–8, 11, 254, 300.
85 Ibid. 1668–9, 345.
86 Ibid. 1671, 540; 1673–5, 479; 1676–7, 93; 1677–8, 266; 1678, 577.
87 S.R.O., DD/DN 463; see also DD/X/PG.
88 Ibid. DD/FA 11/1.
89 *Trade of Bristol in 18th Cent.* (Bristol Rec. Soc. xx), 141–2; S.R.O., D/B/bw 1861; *S.D.N.Q.* xix. 274–5.
90 S.R.O., DD/FA 11/1.
91 Ibid. D/B/bw 2040; salt discharge acct. 1817–23 in possession of J. Stevens Cox, Guernsey.
92 *Complete English Traveller* (1771).
93 S.R.O., DD/FA 11/2; B.L. Add. MS. 28793, pp. 16–17; Pigot, *Nat. Com. Dir.* (1822–3).
94 Squibbs, *Bridgwater, passim.* The figures are for the whole port, which from 1834 stretched from beyond Minehead in the west to Uphill in the east.
95 S.R.O., DD/FA 11/2.

96 Ibid. 11/1, 2; DD/RSS 1, 2, 19, 20, 46, 67; *Cal. of Bristol Apprentice Bk.* i (Bristol Rec. Soc. xiv), 51, 249; *S.D.N.Q.* xxii. 222.
97 *Co. Gaz. Dir. Som.* (1840); inf. from Mr. David Wainwright, Christon; P.R.O., HO 107/1925; S.R.O., DD/CH, box 26, lease of 1847.
98 P.R.O., HO 107/1925.
99 E. Porter, 'Bridgwater Industries Past and Present' (TS. *c.* 1970 in Taunton Castle, Local Hist. Libr.), 18, 56.
1 Ibid. 6, 20–1, 41; Squibbs, *Bridgwater*, 116.
2 Murless, *Bridgwater Docks and the River Parrett*, 42, 44–5; Porter, 'Bridgwater Ind.' 56; Squibbs, *Bridgwater*, 130.
3 P.R.O., C 132/8, no. 4.
4 Ibid. SC 6/1094/11.
5 e.g. *S.R.S.* vi. 299, 310; xli. 38; xlviii, nos. 39, 74, 134, 141.
6 Ibid. xlviii, nos. 3, 27, 65, 137, 157.
7 P.R.O., SC 6/1094/11.

The most prominent townsmen in the later 13th century seem to have been goldsmiths and dyers.[8] A tucker was recorded in 1310 and a weaver in 1318.[9] In 1327 Bridgwater was the highest taxed town in the county, but second with Bath in the number of taxpayers; in 1340 it was the fourth highest, but in 1377 was second in the number of taxpayers.[10] General indications of decline in the mid 14th century are a petition of the burgesses against an additional tax in 1347 on account of poverty,[11] the total absence of merchants from the Midsummer fair in 1359,[12] and the lower level of tolls levied in the market and at the quay after 1359.[13]

Sellers of cloth and wine were established in the town by the 1240s[14] and cloth merchants in the earlier 14th century were dealing not only in locally made 'mixed' cloth and broad cloth but also in Flemish products.[15] Six drapers, three of them from Taunton, were selling cloth illegally in the market in 1388.[16] Dyeing, spinning, and carding were practised in the later 14th century, a rack was standing outside the west gate in 1355, and a shuttle maker was in business in 1380.[17]

By the 15th century Bridgwater was part of a network of inland and overseas trade involving London merchants,[18] a Frome clothier with connexions in the Cotswolds,[19] a Salisbury embroiderer, a Wolverhampton burgess, and a Plymouth plumber.[20] A fulling mill was in use at the castle in the early 15th century,[21] and weavers, tuckers, dyers, and cardmakers continued to be active.[22] In the 1440s there were at least 12 weavers, 9 fullers, 3 dyers, and 2 cardmakers living in the town.[23] In the 1450s the town was home to a German goldsmith and a French mercer.[24] Inland trade was sufficiently important for the construction of a new slip above the bridge in 1488.[25]

By the later 15th century cloth was evidently the most important factor in the town's trade, merchants importing from Wales and North Devon and clothiers producing both undyed and violet cloth, both called Bridgwaters.[26] Among individual merchants involved in the trade were William Shore of London and Edward Goldeston of Taunton (d. 1502), the latter trading with a Lombard in Southampton.[27] Cloth finishing was carried out until the 1530s or later.[28] The general economy of the town, however, was in decline. The revenues of the borough were said

to be reduced in 1454[29] and claims that the town had fallen into 'so great poverty and decay' that people were leaving induced the owners of the fee farm to reduce their rents.[30] References to tenements in decay and defective rents were not uncommon for the next 80 years, and c. 1540 the loss of over 200 houses within living memory was reported.[31] The Crown found difficulty in selling the former chantry properties in the town because most were 'at the point of utter ruin', and the fee farm had to be further reduced because of the reduction of rent values after the confiscation of monastic estates in the town.[32]

The mayor and corporation, who purchased some of the former chantry land and who inherited from John Colverd (d. 1553) much of his estate both in the town and at East Stour (Dors.),[33] found themselves subject to heavy repair costs and owners of empty tenements. The annual gross value of their estate was over £30 in 1553, to which was added the profits of the port, but from which salaries and the cost of poor relief and entertainment had to be found.[34] In 1558 repairs and lost rents amounted to far more than the total rent income, by 1563–4 loans were needed to balance the account, and for ten years thereafter expenditure remained high.[35]

In 1505–6 65 wagons took goods from the town, mostly to Glastonbury, Wells, and Taunton but also to Old Cleeve and Warminster (Wilts.).[36] In 1526 nine went to Exeter, and goods were often sent overland to Bristol.[37] The river routes to Langport and Taunton were also used.[38] Cloth production was no longer important, but a weaver was still in business in 1581, felt was made at the same time, and a silk weaver was mentioned in 1611.[39]

In the earlier 17th century the town was again said to be decaying and in 1655 was said to have 'no eminent way of trade'.[40] The volume of inland business varied from year to year. It was usually in heavy goods such as millstones, iron, wine, oil, coal, salt, and soap, with occasional extraordinary cargoes such as freestone, an iron furnace, prunes, herring, and glass.[41] In 1648–9 charges were levied on 202 tons of iron, over 31 tuns of wine, 2 tuns of oil, and some casks which passed beneath the town bridge and up the Parrett, on 16 tuns of oil and wine which went overland to Bristol, and on 2 tuns of sack which probably went by road to Taunton.[42] In 1652–3

8 *S.R.S.* xi, p. 438; xliv. 51, 129, 299–300; xlviii, nos. 3–4, 8.
9 Ibid. xlviii, nos. 64, 85.
10 Ibid. iii. 278–9; *S.D.N.Q.* xxix. 11.
11 *Rot. Parl.* ii. 189.
12 Above, this section (markets and fairs).
13 P.R.O., SC 6/968/17, 19–20, 22–4, 26, 28.
14 *S.R.S.* xi, p. 293.
15 Ibid. xlviii, nos. 65, 80–1.
16 Ibid. liii, no. 439.
17 Ibid. xlviii, nos. 120, 129, 142, 175, 187, 305, 315; liii, nos. 348, 351.
18 Ibid. lviii, nos. 500, 599; lxx, nos. 929–30.
19 Ibid. xvi. 69–70.
20 Ibid. lx, nos. 762, 788, 805.
21 Above, this section (mills).
22 *Cal. Pat.* 1408–13, 344; 1416–22, 158; *S.R.S.* lviii, nos. 587, 592, 598, 641, 648, 657, 676, 678–9, 687.
23 *S.R.S.* lx, nos. 732–42.
24 Dors. R.O., D 10/X2, mm. 3d., 4.
25 S.R.O., D/B/bw 803.

26 *S.R.S.* lx, no. 747; lxx, nos. 930, 933–4, 1052A; *Overseas Trade of Bristol* (Bristol Rec. Soc. vii), p. 213; S.R.O., D/B/bw 191.
27 *S.R.S.* xix. 33–4; lxx, no. 930.
28 Ibid. xvi. 310; lx, nos. 771, 830; lxx, nos. 916, 921, 969, 982, 1006; S.R.O., D/B/bw 861, 1111, 1439, 1523; *Ledger Bk. of John Smythe* (Bristol Rec. Soc. xxviii), 76, 165.
29 *S.R.S.* lx, no. 773.
30 Ibid. p. xiii, nos. 819, 825.
31 S.R.O., D/B/bw 754; *S.R.S.* lxx, no. 921; P.R.O., SC 6/Hen. VIII/3074; Leland, *Itin.* ed. Toulmin Smith, i. 163.
32 S.R.O., D/B/bw 750, 795, 1684, 1831, 1878; *S.R.S.* lxxvii. 123.
33 *Cal. Pat.* 1553–4, 192; S.R.O., D/B/bw 1201.
34 S.R.O., D/B/bw 129.
35 Ibid. 1535, 1540–3, 1546, 1549–50, 1552–4.
36 Ibid. 1432.   37 Ibid. 1433, and e.g. 1439.
38 Ibid. e.g. 1434–5.   39 Ibid. 1278, 2175, 2217.
40 *Cal. S.P. Dom.* 1629–31, 40; Bristol R.O. 04237.
41 S.R.O., D/B/bw 1488, 1491, 1493, 1496; *S.R.S.* xxiv. 9.
42 S.R.O., D/B/bw 1519.

128 tons of iron and other unspecified goods passed under the bridge.[43] Quantities of coal and salt were also taken inland by river.[44] Coal and goods such as flax, hemp, grindstones, glass, long saws, and glue came through the port from the Forest of Dean to Langport in the early 18th century, and there was a similar trade with Taunton.[45]

In the 17th century merchants or mercers continued to be the leading townsmen,[46] but in the earlier 18th century professional men such as physicians and apothecaries became prominent, including John Morgan (d. 1723), founder of a grammar school, and John Allen (c. 1660–1741), inventor, both doctors of medicine.[47] Trade guilds or companies seem to have been organized by the later 17th century, perhaps in face of contracting business and rivalry from outside the town. A tailors' guild was in existence as early as 1571–2, and companies of butchers and shoemakers by 1684.[48] The cordwainers had a separate company from 1685 until 1774 for a maximum of 12 members,[49] and London shoemakers were effectively excluded when an attempt was made to introduce them in the 1720s.[50] In 1694 goldsmiths, tanners, and 12 other trades including pewterers and booksellers were incorporated into a single company, later extended for a total of 24 trades under the title of the Goldsmiths' Company, whose clear aim was to maintain a monopoly for its members.[51] The Goldsmiths' Company survived until 1736 or later, but some of its number, including grocers, mercers, drapers, and dry salters, evidently founded a merchants' company in 1732.[52]

Shipbuilding probably began long before a shipwright was recorded in 1593.[53] In 1671 Sir William Wyndham suggested the skill should be revived,[54] and c. 1697 John Trott built the *Friendship* for the merchant William Alloway.[55] In the early 18th century the corporation encouraged shipbuilding both on the east bank of the river beside the bowling green and on the east quay.[56] Dr. John Allen was involved with plans for a dock in 1728 and in 1732 John Trott negotiated successfully to build a graving and repairing dock on the east bank, which in 1743 was converted to a dry dock.[57] The Trott family were still using the dock in 1814.[58] Between 1766 and 1799 40 vessels were built in the port

ranging from 13 to 266 tons,[59] and sailmakers and manufacturers of rope and twine were in business.[60]

Brickmaking had begun in Bridgwater by 1655 when a brickmaker emigrated to the West Indies.[61] In 1686–7 bricks from Mr. Balch's yard were used for rebuilding corporation property.[62] There was a brick kiln at Hamp by 1708–9, another at Crowpill in the 1720s, and by the 1730s there were at least two on the riverside between them.[63] Other brickworks established in the 1760s and 1770s included those of Samuel Glover, who exported bricks to a coal mine near Kidwelly (Carms.) and imported anthracite dust to fire his kilns.[64] The Sealy family had a yard and kilns at Hamp before 1776, and by the early 19th century the brickyards in the neighbourhood were home to 'a whole colony of people'.[65]

James Brydges, duke of Chandos (d. 1744), opposed local monopolies by attempting from 1721 onwards to introduce glass and soap making and a distillery. The soap works failed in 1725; the distillery, east of the river, lasted little longer. Some glass makers, specializing in bottles, went bankrupt in 1728, others remained until 1733. The glasshouse survived, used by pottery and tile manufacturers, until 1943.[66]

In 1738 Thomas Bayley, tinman and brazier, was admitted a free burgess, and later founders included Thomas Pyke, George and Thomas Davis, and members of the Kingston family. Between them they produced bells, cannon, and a wide variety of castings for agriculture and the building trade.[67]

By the 1780s 7 surgeons and 5 attorneys practised in the town. There were then 6 mercers and drapers and a wide range of other businesses, often in curious combinations: John Chubb dealt in wine and timber, James Chubb was an ironmonger and hatter. Cheese and corn dealers made the town a distribution centre for agricultural produce.[68] Three banks were in business by the 1790s and by the early 19th century nine professions were represented including accountants and musicians, and other occupations were those of druggist, engraver, writing master, miniaturist, printer, bookbinder, cabinet maker, and basket maker.[69] By 1822–3 11 coaches came to the town and 9 carriers operated on 14 routes, including 2 to London.[70]

43 S.R.O., D/B/bw 1521.
44 Ibid. 1738–9, 1741, 1808–9, 2041, 2168–70.
45 Ibid. 1524, 1644.
46 Ibid. 78, 570, 619, 1748, 1785, 1793, 2024/2; *Proc. Som. Arch. Soc.* cvi. 69; cxi. 43, 45, 47.
47 S.R.O., D/B/bw 570; *D.N.B.*
48 S.R.O., D/B/bw 1552, 1634.
49 Ibid. DD/X/DN 1.
50 C. H. C. and M. I. Baker, *James Brydges, First Duke of Chandos* (1949), 231.
51 S.R.O., D/B/bw 1671, 1978, 2171–2.
52 Ibid. 1797; ibid. 2/1/2 (30 Dec. 1732; 3 July 1733); see also 2/1/1 (12 Feb. 1717/18).
53 Ibid. D/B/bw 2175.
54 *Cal. S.P. Dom.* 1671, 499.
55 S.R.O., DD/DN 463.
56 Ibid. D/B/bw 2/1/1 (8 Mar. 1725/6; 6 Dec. 1728).
57 Ibid. D/B/bw 2/1/2 (2 May 1732; 30 July 1736; 17 Dec. 1743); DD/X/KLT 1.
58 Ibid. D/B/bw 2/1/3 (26 Sept. 1814).
59 Ibid. DD/FA 11/1.
60 Ibid. D/B/bw 2/1/1 (28 May 1731); *Proc. Som. Arch. Soc.* cvi. 69.
61 Bristol R.O. 04220 (1), f. 10v.
62 S.R.O., D/B/bw 1636.
63 Ibid. D/B/bw 2116; ibid. 2/1/1–2; DD/S/WH 218; San Marino (Calif.), Huntington Libr., Chandos MSS. ST 57, vols. 24–41, letters 30 Aug., 7 Sept. 1726 (microfilm in Taunton Castle, Local Hist. Libr.); Baker and Baker, *James Brydges*, 222 n.
64 Carms. R.O., Dynevor MSS.; S.R.O., DD/S/WH 24; *D.N.B.* s.v. Hen. Phillpotts.
65 S.R.O., DD/RN 53/2; ibid. T/PH/ay 1 (June 1810).
66 Baker and Baker, *James Brydges*, 221–33; *Lond. Gaz.* 16 Mar. 1728; S.R.O., D/B/bw 1861; San Marino (Calif.), Huntington Libr., Chandos MSS. ST 57, vols. 24–41, 7, 18, 27 July, 4, 11 Aug. 1726 (microfilm in Taunton Castle, Local Hist. Libr.); F. Hawtin and B. J. Murless, 'Bridgwater Glasshouse', *Jnl. Som. Ind. Arch. Soc.* iii (1981), 2–5; above, plate facing p. 00.
67 *V.C.H. Som.* ii. 433; S.R.O., D/B/bw 2116; D/P/bw. m 2/1/7; *Taunton Courier*, 27 Mar. 1822; *Bailey's Brit. Dir.* (1784).
68 *Bailey's Brit. Dir.* (1784).
69 *Univ. Brit. Dir.* (1797); S.R.O., D/P/bw. m 2/1/7.
70 Pigot, *Nat. Com. Dir.* (1822–3).

By 1830 there were 2 fewer coaches but 15 carriers operated on 17 routes.[71] By 1842 coaches had further declined in face of the railways, but there were 18 carriers' routes from the town.[72]

By 1823 there were three brickfields at Hamp and by 1830 a fourth, worked by John Browne and William Champion, patentees of bonded ornamented bricks.[73] Bath brick, named for its resemblance to Bath stone, was made from the 1820s out of the mud deposited on the Parrett's banks.[74] Brickmaking was seasonal and wages were high in the 1830s.[75] The firms of John Sealy, Henry James Major, and Browne and Co. were the most prominent in the 19th century, producing building brick and tiles,[76] and the industry in 1840 was thought to employ some 1,300 workers, half of them habitually laid off in winter. About 1850 there were 16 brick and tile works within 2 miles of Bridgwater Bridge.[77] H. J. Major employed 120 men and 100 boys in 1881.[78] Ten local brick and tile companies made Bath bricks, used for scouring polished metal, and some 8 million were produced each year in the 1880s, increasing in the 1890s to 24 million but falling by 1900 to 17 million.[79] Poor pay resulted in a prolonged strike in the brickyards in 1896,[80] and exports of bricks, tiles, and Bath bricks were reduced after the First World War.[81] New detergents destroyed the Bath brick business, and manufacture had probably ceased by 1939. New building in the town stimulated local demand for bricks and tiles, and peak production from 13 sites within the parish was reached in 1935–7. All but two of the brickyards reopened after 1945 but in the 1960s there was a rapid decline. Colthurst Symons's yard at Castle Field was the last to close, in 1970, because the best clay was exhausted and cheaper sources were available elsewhere.[82]

Between 1800 and 1850 51 vessels were built in the port, produced by 7 shipyards, the largest vessel 459 tons. Six yards built 88 vessels 1851–1900 but only one yard, that of F. J. Carver on the east quay, remained by 1887 and only three vessels were built there between 1900 and 1944. No ships were built later.[83]

Other types of engineering continued in the 19th century and tradesmen included James Culverwell and Co., manufacturers of brickmaking machinery, Hennett, Spink, and Else, of the Bridgwater Ironworks, makers of Hampton Court Bridge, and the railway wagon works.[84]

The town was an important distribution centre for coal, timber, and cattle food until the decline of the port,[85] and from the 1930s attracted manufacturing industries to replace its traditional sources of employment including the Quantock Preserving Co. Ltd. and British Cellophane in 1937–8, both located in Wembdon parish.[86] By 1939 industrial and commercial sites on the Bristol road were occupied[87] and from the 1950s Bridgwater has been the most industrialized town in Somerset. In 1990 plans for an industrial estate south of the town were linked with large distribution depots beside the M5 motorway, located in North Petherton parish.[88]

LOCAL GOVERNMENT. BOROUGH. By the mid 13th century the lords of Bridgwater held a court with view of frankpledge and received perquisites both from the borough and from Haygrove; in 1256–7 the income was 32s. 11d. from the borough and 13s. 2d. from Haygrove.[89] In 1280 the owners of two thirds of the lordship claimed gallows, tumbrel, pillory, waifs and strays, wrecks of the sea, the assize of bread and of ale, vee de naam, return of writs within the county, and a gaol.[90] By the later 14th century the borough court met 12 or 14 times each year. Views of frankpledge were held at Hockday and Michaelmas and officers were chosen at Michaelmas. The court appointed 2 reeves, 2 bailiffs, 2 aletasters, 2 breadweighers, a janitor for each of the 4 town gates, and keepers or wardens of 12 streets or other areas into which the town was divided.[91] The court regulated the market and controlled nuisances and offences within the borough, including its meadows and fields at Crowpill and near the castle. The court was being held in 1413[92] and probably continued until subsumed in the borough court of 1468.[93]

A piepowder court was recorded in 1378[94] and continued into the 18th century. During St. Matthew's fair seven men were accused in 1735 of failing to pay toll, and receipts from hawkers of nuts, wigs, and lottery tickets were noted in 1736.[95] The town clerk was steward of the court.[96]

In 1378 the borough court roll records income from a court called Durneday. The name appears to relate to sealing the doors of burgages whose rent was in arrears. The court was mentioned 1378–88, 1416,[97] 1474–7, and 1495–6.[98] In

71 Ibid. (1830).
72 Ibid. (1842).
73 S.D.N.Q. xix. 234; Pigot, Nat. Com. Dir. (1822–3, 1830).
74 B. J. Murless, 'The Bath Brick Ind. in Bridgwater', Jnl. Som. Ind. Arch. Soc. i (1975), 18–28.
75 Rep. Com. Poor Law, H.C. 44, pp. 488a–489a (1834), xxviii (2).
76 Pigot, Nat. Com. Dir. (1842); Slater's Royal Nat. & Com. Dir. (1852–3); V.C.H. Som. ii. 353; above, plates facing p. 9.
77 E. Porter, 'Bridgwater Industries Past and Present' (TS. in Taunton Castle, Local Hist. Libr.), 10–11.
78 P.R.O., RG 11/2374.
79 Jnl. Som. Ind. Arch. Soc. i (1975), 18–28.
80 Bridgwater Mercury, 9 July 1986.
81 Above, this section (overseas trade).
82 Porter, 'Bridgwater Ind.' 20–1, 33; Som. Ind. Arch. Soc. Gazetteer (1973).
83 S.R.O., DD/FA 11/1; S.D.N.Q. xx. 127; xxii. 222;

above, plate facing p. 217.
84 Taunton Courier, 20 Apr. 1864; Kelly's Dir. Som. (1906); V.C.H. Som. ii. 360.
85 Above, this section (overseas trade).
86 Porter, 'Bridgwater Ind.' 22, 66–9, 81, 84–5.
87 Kelly's Dir. Som. (1939). 88 Local inf.
89 P.R.O., SC 6/1094/11.
90 Rot. Hund. (Rec. Com.), ii. 127; Plac. de Quo Warr. (Rec. Com.), 693.
91 P.R.O., SC 6/968/19–20, 22–4, 26; SC 6/969/5, 7, 10–13, 17–19; S.R.S. liii, nos. 317–18, 320, 322–6, 328–32, 334–7, 340, 344, 348, 350–3, 355, 357, 359, 428–31, 433–6, 438–44.
92 P.R.O., SC 6/969/21.
93 Below, this section.
94 S.R.S. liii, nos. 317–19.
95 S.R.O., D/B/bw 1718.
96 Ibid. 2/1/2 (30 Aug. 1732).
97 S.R.S. liii, pp. xviii–xix, nos. 322, 334, 351, 360, 434.
98 P.R.O., SC 6/969/22–3; SC 6/Hen. VII/1105.

the later 14th century the court met in January or February each year. The name Durneday rent given to burgage rent in the 1470s and a reference in 1495–6 to cash paid for release of suit to 'the lord of Durnaday' were apparently both archaisms.

In the third quarter of the 13th century[99] the burgesses and community agreed a series of ordinances and sealed it with their common seal. The ordinances established a guild, presided over by two stewards elected annually and assisted by a bailiff. They established fines for members convicted of certain offences, and defined trading times for the sale of meat and fresh fish. They also made members of the guild serving as steward of the altars of the Virgin and the Rood or as steward of the bridge accountable to the guild stewards. The guild stewards themselves were accountable to the community.[1] They were to dispense justice, regulate the market, and administer communal property. Offences within their jurisdiction were minor: debt, actions outside the borough against burgesses, and false accusation; and fines levied were to be paid to the community.[2] Probably the ordinances concerned only the burgesses and the guild merchant of the town. In 1373–5 the community's receiver accounted for amercements made in the community's court;[3] by the 1440s the common stewards were holding regular sessions to deal with cases of debt and the grant of freedom, and they presided over arbitrations sworn before them in the common hall of the borough and sealed with the common seal.[4]

Specific references to the guild merchant are rare. In 1373–5 the stewards of the guild authorized work on the church; in 1386 a guild meeting levied fines on absent members, and in 1392 the guild stewards leased a tenement associated with the bridge.[5] In 1394 the guild paid fines and spent money on entertainment.[6] In 1416 the Crown described the guild merchant as the Holy Trinity guild, perhaps because by then its concerns were limited to the administration of the Trinity chantry.[7] In 1441–2, however, the clerk of the common stewards of the guild of Bridgwater was mentioned.[8]

In 1256–7 there were two borough reeves and two serjeants.[9] In 1299 the burgesses used the seal of the town reeves on a charter permitting building over the west gate.[10] In 1322 there were two bedels, later called bailiffs, who replaced the serjeants.[11] By 1373, and no doubt long before, the town had its own receiver, whose income in 1373–5 derived principally from a rate levied throughout the town and from goods given to the chantry of the Rood, together with fines from the town's own court, and charges at the

bridge and for the use of the town's measures in the port.[12] In 1394 income was largely from entry fines, customs, and a collection to meet the M.P.s' expenses; a regular charge was the stipend of the permanent clerk of the community.[13] In the 1390s the receiver became known as the bailiff of the community;[14] he accounted to two stewards, known in the 1420s as the common stewards, and once in 1441–2 as the common stewards of the guild of Bridgwater. In 1460–1 John Pole was described as clerk of the stewards and of the community.[15] By 1428–9 the community's income was principally from port charges, with much smaller sums from rents, fines of the watch, and fines imposed by the stewards in the borough court.[16]

The lords of the town maintained a common oven within the borough,[17] together with a hall of pleas and a gaol. The hall was repaired in 1347–8 and again in 1389–90, but by 1394–5 it seems to have been let, and may have been replaced by the adjoining guild hall, which by 1389–90 was being used for inquests before the steward of the estate by order of either of the lords of the town.[18] The lords of the borough in 1386–7 shared the cost of rebuilding the pillory and thews, both used for offenders sentenced in the borough court in the 1370s.[19]

The borough court and the community or burgesses's court were probably both subsumed in the court established when the borough was incorporated by the charter of 1468. The new borough court, under the mayor and bailiffs, was to be held each Monday to deal with all offences, and the corporation was to have return of writs, assize of bread and of ale, and of weights and measures.[20]

The mayor and bailiffs were to be chosen each year on the Monday after 8 September and were to appoint a recorder or steward. The charter, confirmed in 1488, 1495, and 1512, assured to the corporation a guild merchant, market and fair, and the right to collect tolls on the bridge.[21] The 'brethren of the council' in 1558 comprised the mayor, two bailiffs, the customer and the searcher of the port, seventeen other men, and three women, probably the widows of recently deceased burgesses.[22] Other borough offices emerged as the corporation's business increased. By 1494–5 the mayor appointed water bailiffs[23] who levied port charges, received some rents, and, as administrators of the borough's largest source of income in the earlier 16th century, paid fees and the cost of entertainment and repairs to property.[24] By 1556, after the corporation had bought the former chantry property in 1554, a general receiver was appointed to administer the

99 *S.R.S.* xlviii, p. xiv.
1 Ibid. no. 10; for the altars or chantries, below, church.
2 *S.R.S.* xlviii, no. 10.
3 Ibid. no. 297.
4 Ibid. lx. nos. 746–7, 831.
5 *S.R.S.* xlviii, no. 297; liii, nos. 418, 458.
6 Ibid. liii, no. 476.
7 Ibid. lviii, no. 583.
8 Ibid. no. 711.
9 P.R.O., SC 6/1094/11.
10 *S.R.S.* xlviii, no. 48.
11 Ibid. nos. 95, 137, 140.
12 Ibid. no. 297.
13 Ibid. liii, no. 476.

14 Ibid. nos. 458, 483.
15 Ibid. lviii, nos. 613, 711; lx, no. 824.
16 Ibid. lviii, nos. 587, 641, 676.
17 P.R.O., SC 6/1094/11.
18 Ibid. SC 6/968/17, 25; SC 6/969/3, 4, 10–11. For the guild hall and gaol see above, intro. (buildings).
19 P.R.O., SC 6/968/27; *S.R.S.* liii, nos. 328, 330.
20 *Cal. Chart. R.* 1427–1516, 226–9.
21 Ibid.; S.R.O., D/B/bw 893; *S.R.S.* lxx, p. xi; *L. & P. Hen. VIII*, i (1), p. 396.
22 S.R.O., D/B/bw 124.
23 Ibid. 1431.
24 Water bailiffs' accts. survive for 1494–5, 1503–5, and many years between 1525 and 1652.

borough's lands, both within the borough and outside, and to account for the water bailiffs' receipts.[25] In 1556 also there was a steward.[26] Two serjeants at mace were recorded by 1535.[27]

In 1587 a new charter defined the corporation as the mayor, two aldermen, and 18 burgesses. The mayor was to be chosen each year from the capital burgesses on the Monday next before Michaelmas; the aldermen, serving for life unless removed for bad government, were to be chosen by majority vote from the capital burgesses; the capital burgesses were to be chosen for life from the 'best and wisest' of the burgesses of the town by the mayor, recorder, and aldermen, or by a majority, including the mayor and aldermen, of the existing corporation. Two bailiffs were to be appointed each year from the capital burgesses and the corporation was to choose a recorder, a common clerk, a receiver, and as many constables and other officers as it had before the charter was granted. The charter was confirmed in 1614, and again in 1628 when the jurisdiction of the corporation was extended to include the whole parish and the number of capital burgesses was increased from 18 to 24, to be chosen by the mayor and aldermen.[28]

The charter of 1587 made the borough court a court of record under the mayor, recorder, and the two aldermen; the jurisdiction was defined as the borough, the area under the castle walls known as Castle Ditch, and 'franchises' beyond the east gate formerly belonging to St. John's hospital.[29] The court, in practice often held before the mayor and a deputy recorder who was usually one of the aldermen, heard pleas of debt, trespass, theft, and other cases under 40s. Its permanent officer was the clerk or protonotary, usually the town clerk, supported by two bailiffs, two or three serjeants at mace, and a crier who was also the gaoler. After 1835 the recorder presided, and the town council appointed a registrar and other minor officials. By then only a few cases of debt were heard. There were no suits in 1838 or 1839 although the court cost the town council £52. In 1847 the court's jurisdiction passed to the county court.[30] Notes, extracts, and records of the court survive from 1693.[31]

The charter of 1468 appointed the mayor and recorder for the time being justices of the peace within the borough, and that of 1587 added the two aldermen.[32] Records of the court survive from 1749. Petty sessions were held weekly; the grand jury was appointed quarterly for all but capital cases.[33] The borough sessions were abolished under the Courts Act of 1971 and the borough commission of the peace ceased to have effect in 1974.[34]

In 1683, under pressure from Sir John Stawell and Peter Mews, bishop of Bath and Wells, who wished to secure a Tory majority, and, it was later claimed, 'by surprise and in a surreptitious and clandestine manner', the charter of 1628 was surrendered.[35] A new charter gave the king in council power to remove members of the corporation,[36] made the mayor notary public and coroner, and limited the parliamentary franchise to the common council.[37] It removed the recorder Sir John Malet, an alderman, and ten other burgesses.[38] The resulting Tory majority secured M.P.s acceptable to the Crown in 1685, but the town's failure to support the Declaration of Indulgence of 1687 is thought to have resulted in the removal of seven burgesses named in the 1683 charter. Those removed included William Masey [? Massey], mayor under the charter of 1683,[39] who was said to have 'carried himself with that insolency and tyranny to all sorts of people, that the inhabitants, whether churchmen, Presbyterian, or other joined together to ring out the bells for joy at his departure into Ireland where he was preferred and where it is thought he was poisoned'.[40] In November 1688 the corporation unsuccessfully petitioned for the restoration of their old charter.[41]

In the early 18th century the corporation appointed annually 17 constables, each in charge of an area which had not changed since the Middle Ages, 2 bread weighers, 2 surveyors of the market, 2 shambles wardens, 2 sealers and provers of leather, 3 inquisitors of hides and skins, 3 salt weighers, 1 packer of herrings, and 2 aletasters.[42] By the 1780s five men were holding all the port and market offices between them, in 1805 four men, and in 1811 three. The street constables were effectively replaced in 1829 by four elected constables and watchmen for the whole borough and parish and by four watchmen at the quays.[43]

The charter of 1683 remained the governing instrument of the town until 1835. The corporation was then in debt through the failure of the treasurer in private business; opposition was growing because its members did not 'fairly represent' the opinions of the inhabitants and because the mayor and others interfered at parliamentary elections. Members had administered public property fairly, according to government commissioners, and were repaying the debt left by the former treasurer, but expenditure at £945 exceeded income at £936. Income was principally from tithes (£316), turnpikes (£195), market and fair tolls (£145), and rents (£132); the main items of expenditure were £325 from the tithe account, including clergy stipends, and £238 on highway repairs. The

25 S.R.O., D/B/bw 928, 1533; below, church.
26 S.R.O., D/B/bw 928, 1229, 1327.   27 Ibid. 1439.
28 Ibid. Bridgwater charters, trans. Birch; ibid. DD/X/ME 7; D/B/bw 2167; Cal. S.P. Dom. 1628–9, 41.
29 S.R.O., D/B/bw 2167.
30 Proc. Som. Arch. Soc. cxi. 38–50; County, Hundred and Boro. Cts. H.C. 338–IV, pp. 12–15 (1839), xliii; Cts. of Request, H.C. 619, pp. 140–1 (1840), xli.
31 S.R.O., D/B/bw 245, 1530, 1644, 1760, 1798, 1824, 1907; ibid. 34/1/1–8.
32 Cal. Chart. R. 1427–1516, 226–9; S.R.O., D/B/bw 2167.
33 S.R.O., D/B/bw 35/1/1–17; ibid. 1530, 2312.
34 Courts Act, 1971, c. 23; Commissions of the Peace

Order, 1974.
35 S.R.O., D/B/bw 2117; Cal. S.P. Dom. July–Sept. 1683, 119, 384, 401–2, 416, 440.
36 S.R.O., D/B/bw 1632, 1634.
37 Cal. S.P. Dom. 1683–4, 93–4, 108.
38 S.R.O., Bridgwater charters, trans. Birch; ibid. D/B/bw 1978, 2117.
39 Ibid. D/B/bw 107, 119; D/P/bw. m 2/1/3; D/N/bw. chch 1/3/2; V.C.H. Som. ii. 231.
40 S.R.O., D/P/bw. m 2/1/3.
41 Cal. S.P. Dom. 1687–9, p. 363.
42 S.R.O., D/B/bw 2/1/2 (22 Sept. 1718).
43 Ibid. 2/1/2–3.

commissioners discovered small irregularities in the administration of the Court of Record, found the watch inadequate, and street lighting poor.[44]

In 1835 the borough was divided into two wards, north and south, and the corporation thereafter comprised a mayor, 6 aldermen, and 18 councillors, elected by the ratepayers. Borough officers included treasurer, recorder, town clerk, clerk of the peace, and coroner.[45] A committee of the corporation took effective control of the Parrett navigation in 1845, and the corporation took over the market and paving, watching, and lighting the streets from the market trustees under an Act of 1857.[46] Committees were responsible for health from 1867, water supply from 1876, and free libraries from 1877.[47] By the 1890s there were separate committees for allotments and town improvements,[48] from 1904 a borough education authority,[49] and later special committees for specific business such as borough extension, a proposed airport, and wartime emergencies.[50] Sedgemoor district council assumed the functions of the corporation in 1974 but councillors representing the area of the former borough constitute a body of charter trustees who elect a town mayor each year.[51]

ARMS, SEALS, INSIGNIA, AND PLATE. In 1952 the borough received a formal grant of arms, taken from the borough seal in use since the later 18th century showing a castle of three stages flanked by turrets capped by domes, above a wooden bridge of five arches. The crest is an ancient ship in full sail bearing the arms of Robert Blake, the supporters are lions holding shields with the arms of Brewer and Trivet, and the motto is 'Opes consilium parit' (Wisdom begets wealth).[52] In the 13th century and until 1393 or later the burgesses used a seal depicting a castle of three stages with a large central door, standing on a stone bridge of four round arches with water beneath. The round seal, 2 in. in diameter, bore the legend, Lombardic, SI[GILLUM] COMMUNE [DE] [BRI]GWALTER.[53] By 1464 the depiction of the castle, on a seal of the same size and shape, was slightly altered and that of the bridge had been replaced by one of a wooden structure of six arches; it bore the legend, Black Letter, SIG[I]LLUM C[OMMUNE] [V]ILLE DE BRI[GWA]LTER.[54] A further change had taken place by 1478 and probably accompanied the new charter of 1468, when, on a round seal 1½ in. in diameter, the castle was flanked by two columns and the castle door was replaced by a raised portcullis above a leopard's face. It was described as the seal of the office of the mayor of the town and bore the

legend, Black Letter, SIGILLUM MAIOR . . . [BRI]GEWAT[ER].[55] The seal in use by the mid 18th century included the three-staged castle, but its flanking columns had become turrets with domed tops placed on the lowest stage of the castle, which itself formed a stone bridge of three arches.[56] In a later version of the device, current in 1797, the turrets were placed beside the three-staged castle above a wooden bridge of five arches, with a star placed above one turret and a fleur de lis above the other.[57] The seal made in 1835, 1¼ in. in diameter, incorporating the 18th-century device, bears the legend, Roman, SIGILLUM MAJORIS BALLIVORUM ET BURGENCIUM VILLE DE BRIGEWATER.[58]

A seal in use by the burgesses on behalf of St. Mary's chantry in the 13th century and 1369 was vesica-shaped, 1½ in. by 2¼ in., and bore the figures of the Virgin and Child with the inscription, Lombardic, SIGILLUM BEATE MARIE VIRGINIS.[59] A third seal, used by the burgesses in 1299, was that of the reeves of the town. Round, 2 in. in diameter, it depicted two sailors hauling ropes on a one-masted vessel and bore the legend, Lombardic, SIGILLUM PREPOSITORUM DE BR[IGE]WATER.[60] It was used by the reeves in the early 15th century[61] and by the water bailiffs in the early 17th century.[62]

The burgesses owned a silver mace in 1444–5.[63] Of three maces in 1991, the largest is of silver gilt made by Thomas Maunday of London c. 1653 and two are of silver, bought in 1654.[64] All three bore a Commonwealth crown and the cross of St. George, but in 1660 the crown was replaced by a royal crown and the largest mace was inscribed for Charles II. The town also possesses a silver salt, the gift in 1638 of Sir Thomas Wroth, the recorder, and a pair of loving cups, the gift of Margaret Jones, widow, and hallmarked for 1640–1.[65]

MARKET HOUSE TRUSTEES. In 1778 a general meeting of inhabitants agreed to build a market house, to improve St. Mary Street and the approach to Cornhill, and to pave and light footpaths. The corporation offered a sum of £500 and a toll on some market goods; paving and lighting were to be financed either by an extra Sunday toll on turnpikes or by a rate. In 1779 an Act empowered named trustees, together with investors of £20 or more, the mayor, the recorder or his deputy, the aldermen, and the corporation's receiver and bailiff to buy buildings for demolition, to build a market house, to regulate markets, and to pave, cleanse, light, and watch the streets.[66] A market house

44   *Rep. Com. Mun. Corp.* H.C. 116, pp. 461–7 (1835), xxiii.
45   Mun. Corporations Act, 5 & 6 Wm. IV, c. 76.
46   S.R.O., D/B/bw 31/1/1; 20 & 21 Vic. c. 30 (Local and Personal).
47   S.R.O., D/B/bw 3/6/1, 3/10/1, 3/16/1.
48   Ibid. 3/9/1A, 3/13/1.
49   Ibid. C/E boxes 42–5, 184/1–17.
50   Ibid. D/B/bw 3/19/1–2, 3/20/1, 3/24/1, 8/1/2.
51   Local Govt. Act 1972, c. 70, section 246.
52   L. Jewitt and W. H. St. John Hope, *Corporation Plate and Insignia of Office* (1895), ii. 302; C. W. Scott-Giles, *Civic Heraldry of Eng. and Wales*, 323–4.
53   S.R.O., D/B/bw 92, 132, 136.
54   Ibid. 881.

55   Ibid. 872.
56   Ibid. 2214–15.
57   Powell, *Bridgwater in Later Days*, opp. 24.
58   Jewitt and Hope, *Corporation Plate and Insignia*, ii. 302.
59   S.R.O., D/B/bw 61, 259, 829–32.
60   *S.R.S.* xlviii, no. 118.
61   S.R.O., D/B/bw 90, 755, 972.
62   *S.R.S.* xlviii, p. xiii.
63   Ibid. lx, no. 728.
64   S.R.O. D/B/bw 1978.
65   Jewitt and Hope, *Corporation Plate and Insignia*, ii. 301–2.
66   S.R.O., D/B/bw 2/1/2 (23 Oct., 3, 9 Nov. 1778); 19 Geo. III, c. 36.

had been built by 1791 but no other improvements seem to have been made.[67] In 1825 the corporation ordered the trustees to demolish part of the house for road widening.[68] In 1826 the trustees obtained an Act to enlarge the building and to widen and improve the streets, with power to curb nuisances, improve drains, water streets, and contract for gas lighting.[69] In 1857 an Act placed all the markets under the corporation as a single body of trustees.[70]

MANORIAL. The lords of Bridgwater claimed the same franchises in the foreign or manor as in the borough.[71] For Bridgwater or Haygrove manor five courts were held during the year 1347–8, two between January and Michaelmas 1382, two, called halimotes, in 1389–90, three halimotes in 1394–5, and one in 1413.[72] Court rolls survive for 1371–2,[73] 1400,[74] and 1407–8.[75] By 1400 courts were held four or five times a year; an aletaster and a hayward were appointed each summer, and much of the business concerned drainage in the fields around the town and Castle Ditch.[76] The court, described as that of Bridgwater Castle manor, was meeting twice a year by 1539 and its concerns included its customary tenants in Durleigh and Dunwear as well as in Haygrove. A will was proved in the manor court in 1553.[77] Court rolls survive for 1538–9 (or 1539–40)[78] and for one session in 1541.[79]

Records of what had been the Zouches' manor of Bridgwater or Haygrove comprise a copy of court roll for 1662[80] and court books for 1683–5,[81] 1709–36,[82] and 1782–1839.[83] Courts leet and baron and view of frankpledge were normally held each autumn in the later 17th and the 18th century, and the court appointed a hayward and a tithingman. The court was concerned with agriculture, repairs to buildings, and maintenance of roads. The manor possessed a bakehouse in the town, and the manorial pound was to be repaired in 1814, 1816, and 1817.

Court papers for West Bower manor survive for 1610 and several years 1710–85. The court met principally for tenurial business, but it appointed a hayward in 1772 and made orders several times for rebuilding the pound at Hamp Green and for defending the green against encroachments. In 1727 a juryman was fined for leaving a session and abusing his fellow jurymen.[84]

About 1270 Henry of Erleigh released Athelney abbey from suit to the hundred and manor courts of North Petherton, but required the tithingman of Hamp to attend the hundred twice a year. The abbey was to continue holding its own courts at Hamp.[85] After the Dissolution, Bristol corporation held views of frankpledge

and manor courts each year until the mid 17th century. Court books record regular sessions 1549–1650, mostly in summer or autumn until the 1630s, and then less frequently. The corporation's surveyors, sometimes with the city chamberlain, presided over what was described as a view of frankpledge with manor court. In the mid 16th century the court was often called that of Hamp and Adscombe, apparently because the income from it included a payment from Adscombe in Over Stowey. A tithingman and a hayward were usually chosen in the court; tenants served as tithingman in rotation. Most of the business of the court concerned drainage, building maintenance, and the control of strays, and a committee to survey rhynes was sometimes appointed. In 1583 the court fined two men for not wearing caps on Sundays as required by the statute, and admitted a guardian to lands on condition that he maintained his ward at school and sent money each year to the city chamberlain as a trust fund for the boy. In 1584 the court seized a silver-gilt pestle belonging to a felon for delivery to the city chamberlain. In 1587 the court ordered the stocks and butts to be repaired, and in 1585 a tenant was accused of playing bowls and other games during service time. In 1609 customary tenants were reminded that they were not to sue each other for debt or trespass out of the manor court for a sum less than 40s. without leave; the lords were reminded that it had been the custom to entertain the jury to dinner. The butts were again reported as in decay in 1639, and the pound in 1646; in 1647 order was given to set up a cucking stool and stocks.[86]

No court roll of St. John's hospital has survived. An extract of a court with view of frankpledge of the former hospital's manor in 1567 records a grant in reversion by the chief steward.[87]

After the corporation acquired the rectory in fee from the Crown in 1706[88] the estate became known as the manor of Bridgwater and in 1732 the town clerk was appointed its steward, to preside over a view of frankpledge and court baron.[89]

PARISH. Although the charter of 1628 extended the jurisdiction of the borough to the whole parish, parochial and borough government remained distinct. In the earlier 18th century the parish met annually to elect 4 churchwardens, 4 overseers, and 4 highway surveyors. Two of each operated within the town, one in Dunwear and Bower and the east, and one in Hamp and the west.[90] By 1827 the parish meeting was known as the vestry, and in the early 1830s it was open, a select vestry having been tried and abandoned.[91]

67 Collinson, *Hist. Som.* iii. 75; S.R.O., T/PH/bw (map, *c.* 1806).   68 S.R.O., D/B/bw 2/1/2 (16 Feb. 1825).
69 7 Geo. IV, c. 7. (Local and Personal).
70 20 & 21 Vic. c. 30 (Local and Personal).
71 Above, this section (borough).
72 P.R.O., SC 6/968/17, 21; SC 6/969/3, 11, 21.
73 *S.R.S.* xlviii, nos. 266, 269, 272.
74 P.R.O., SC 2/198/15, mm. 2–3.
75 Ibid. LR 3/58/9.
76 Ibid. SC 2/198/15, mm. 2–3.
77 S.R.O., D/B/bw 1201.
78 P.R.O., SC 6/Hen. VIII/3074.
79 Ibid. LR 3/123.
80 S.R.O., DD/X/SU; D/B/bw 2045.
81 Ibid. DD/HK 63.   82 B.L. Eg. MS. 3129.
83 S.R.O., DD/BR/ely 14/7.
84 Ibid. DD/S/WH 211, 213.   85 *S.R.S.* xiv, pp. 148–9.
86 Bristol R.O. 00570, 04403–4, 100904 (7); *City Chamberlains' Accts.* (Bristol Rec. Soc. xxiv), 136, 147.
87 S.R.O., D/B/bw 1926.
88 Above, manors (rectory).   89 S.R.O., D/B/bw 2/1/2.
90 Ibid. D/B/bw 1826, 1997, 2003, 2024.
91 Ibid. D/P/bw. m 9/1/1 (vestry bk. 1827–1972); *Rep. Com. Poor Law*, H.C. 44, pp. 488a–489a (1834), xxviii (2).

In the late 1820s it met monthly, but by the earlier 1830s only 'when expressly assembled'. Each year it chose three of the four churchwardens, the fourth being nominated by the vicar. In 1844 it was discovered that wardens had not submitted accounts for many years. The overseers employed the governor of the workhouse as their assistant. A salaried poor-rate collector appointed in 1839 was known as assistant overseer from 1847. From 1842 the vestry appointed a salaried road surveyor.[92]

In 1693–5 the south gate almshouse was rebuilt and part may have been used thereafter as a workhouse.[93] The whole building was a parish poorhouse in 1820,[94] and in 1834 was well regulated, in 1831 holding an average of 86 people.[95] In 1836 the house was investigated by a House of Lords committee because of the high mortality rate there.[96] In 1837 it was replaced by the union workhouse in Chilton Road, which in 1948 became a hospital.[97]

PUBLIC SERVICES. In 1694 the corporation permitted Richard Lowbridge of Stourbridge (Worcs.) to take water from the Durleigh brook by means of an 'engine or waterwork' and to convey it to a cistern to be built over the high cross. George Balch, whose family had the lease of part of the brook, called Friars, from which the water was taken, acquired the system from Lowbridge in 1709.[98] The water was conveyed in hollow elm pipes.[99] From 1879 a public supply was brought from Ashford in Spaxton via the reservoir on Wembdon Hill. Reservoirs were built at Durleigh in 1938 and at Hawkridge in Aisholt in 1962.[1] Gas was produced in the town from 1834[2] and electricity from 1904.[3]

The borough police force was established in 1835; its headquarters were in Fore Street until 1875 when they moved to High Street. A new police station was opened in Northgate in 1911, near the site of the present station, opened in 1966.[4]

George Bubb Dodington gave the town a fire engine in 1725 which was at first kept in the parish church and was maintained by the parish.[5] The parish kept the engine beside the poorhouse near the south gate in the 1830s.[6] In the 1880s the engine was kept at the rear of the town hall, where a new station was opened in 1906.[7] In 1964 the new station was opened for the county fire service in Salmon Parade.[8]

In 1813 an infirmary, known in 1990 as Bridgwater General hospital, was opened in Clare Street. It was removed in 1820 to Salmon Lane, later Salmon Parade, and was extended in 1876, 1894–5, and 1934.[9] In 1840 there was an eye infirmary in Victoria Street and in 1872 an infectious diseases hospital was opened.[10] The former union workhouse was transferred in 1948 to the National Health Service and became a hospital known in 1990 as Blake hospital.[11] Between 1920 and 1988 there was a maternity unit in Castle Street.[12]

PARLIAMENTARY REPRESENTATION.

Bridgwater sent two burgesses to parliament[13] in 1295. Until 1328 the M.P.s' names indicate origins or residence outside the town, and fewer than half of them were mentioned in the borough records. In the fifty years after 1375, however, townsmen predominated. William Thomere, steward of the guild merchant and lieutenant of the Admiral of the West,[14] was returned at least 14 times 1377–1406, William Gascoigne and his son William at least 15 times 1406–29, and John Kedwelly, the town clerk, at least 7 times 1397–1414.[15] Outsiders again served for the borough later in the 15th century: lawyers from the neighbourhood like William Dodesham (1442), Sir Thomas Tremayle (1472), and William Hody (1483), landowners like John Maunsel (1449, 1453), royal servants like Thomas Driffield (1449), James FitzJames (1467), and John Hymerford (1483). The most important townsman of the later 15th century was John Kendall, chosen at least five times from 1467 and the town's first mayor.[16]

During the 16th and earlier 17th century the town's recorder usually secured the senior seat for himself or his nominee. Baldwin Malet may have influenced the choice of Henry Thornton and Hugh Trotter, customs officials and local landowners, in 1529. Sir Thomas Dyer, a royal household official, sat in five parliaments between 1545 and 1559.[17] His colleague in 1559 was Robert Moleyns, mayor and controller of the port, who managed the passage of an Act for sealing local woollen cloths.[18] Alexander, Edward, and John Popham of Huntworth, Edward's son-in-law John Court, and possibly Nicholas Halswell of Goathurst were recorders returned in Elizabeth I's reign.[19]

Nicholas Halswell in 1603 and Edward Popham in 1623, 1625, and 1626 maintained the

92 S.R.O., D/P/bw. m 9/1/1.
93 Ibid. D/B/bw 750, 1526–7, 1639, 2164.
94 Char. Don. pp. 1086–7.
95 Rep. Com. Poor Law, H.C. 44, pp. 488a–489a (1834), xxviii (2).
96 Rep. Sel. Cttee. on Poor Law, H.L. (1837–8) xix (i–ii); V.C.H. Som. ii. 332–3.
97 Co. Gaz. Dir. Som. (1840); below, this section (public services).
98 S.R.O., D/P/bw 1634, 1686, 2158–9, 2178.
99 S.D.N.Q. xvi. 14; inf. from Mr. J. F. Lawrence, Wembdon.
1 Squibbs, Bridgwater, 91, 129, 139.
2 P.O. Dir. Som. (1861).
3 Squibbs, Bridgwater, 110.
4 Mun. Corp. Act, 5 & 6 Wm. IV. c. 76; Squibbs, Bridgwater, pl. 53.
5 S.R.O., D/P/bw 2/1/2 (11 May, 26 Nov. 1725; 5 Apr. 1726).

6 Ibid. D/P/bw. m 9/1/1 (1830, 1837, 1840).
7 Kelly's Dir. Som. (1889–1939); Squibbs, Bridgwater, 111.
8 Squibbs, Bridgwater, 139.
9 S. G. Jarman, Bridgwater Infirmary (1890); Squibbs, Bridgwater, 55, 57, 127; Kelly's Dir. Som. (1914).
10 Co. Gaz. Dir. Som. (1840); Kelly's Dir. Som. (1914).
11 Local inf.   12 Inf. from Mrs. P. Searle, Bridgwater.
13 For 1295–1468, S.R.S. xlviii, pp. xxxii–iii; liii, pp. xv–xvi; lviii, pp. xi–xii; lx, p. xi.
14 S.R.S. liii, no. 210; Sel. Pleas Admiralty, i (Selden Soc. vi), 167.
15 P.R.O., E 122/25/5; E 368/195; Cal. Fine R. 1413–22, 57, 128, 161; Cal. Close, 1406–13, 434; S.R.S. xxii. 31; liii, no. 383; lviii, no. 588.
16 J. C. Wedgwood, Hist. Parl., Biog., 1439–1509, 276, 283–4, 332, 457, 461, 512–13, 571, 867–8.
17 Hist. Parl., Commons, 1509–58, i. 181–2; ii. 73; 1558–1603, i. 235.   18 S.R.O., D/B/bw 393, 601, 1916.
19 Hist. Parl., Commons, 1558–1603, i. 235.

influence of two local families; Robert Warre, the second member in 1623, presumably owed his return to the recorder Roger Warre.[20] Sir Thomas Wroth, recorder 1628–62, was returned as M.P. in 1628, probably in 1644 on the death of his brother Sir Peter, and in 1656, 1659, and 1660; he was at times 'outrageously republican' but attended only one session of Charles I's trial. His colleague in 1628 was Sir Thomas Smythe, then aged 18, who failed to be elected in 1640 for what came to be the Short Parliament. He later replaced Edmund Wyndham, elected for the second parliament of 1640 but expelled as a monopolist, and was considered by the more radical politicians of the county as 'a serviceable good member'.[21]

From 1660 to 1708 elections were often hotly contested, the result both of uncertainty as to who had the franchise and of deep political and religious divisions within the community. The mayor and capital burgesses elected the members in 1660, 1661, 1669, and 1685, but in 1679, 1681, and 1689 the electorate was widened to those paying scot and lot, amounting in 1679 to c. 380 voters. John Tynte of Halswell in Goathurst, formerly a Cavalier colonel, was returned in 1661, beginning his family's long association with the borough, and on his death in 1669 there was a contest between Francis Rolle of Shapwick, a Presbyterian member of the Convention, and Peregrine Palmer of Fairfield. Palmer lost but was returned on petition, on the grounds that several of the 24 voters were disqualified for holding conventicles in their houses.[22] At the next election, in 1679, Sir Halswell Tynte, Rolle, Ralph Stawell of Cothelstone, and William Clarke of Sandford in Wembdon contested the borough, Stawell standing for the Court party backed by the officers of his local militia, who were all sworn as freemen for the election. Tynte was returned 'on all sides', presumably elected both by the mayor and capital burgesses and by the common burgesses, and returned under the borough seal with the 'assent and consent of the commonalty'. Rolle was chosen by the common burgesses and similarly returned under the mayor's signature. Stawell was chosen by the capital burgesses and returned in the name of the mayor and capital burgesses. Tynte was declared elected without further debate and Rolle later took the second seat, the common burgesses evidently being adjudged to have the franchise.[23] In 1681 Sir John Malet, the town's recorder and a strong exclusionist with nonconformist support, was returned with Tynte,[24] but Stawell undermined Malet's interest by persuading the corporation to surrender its charter in 1683. The resulting Tory majority chose as M.P. their new recorder,

Sir Francis Warre, in 1685, but Halswell Tynte's local influence won him the other seat against Stawell's candidate. Warre and another Tory were returned for the borough in 1689.[25]

The election of the nonconformist Roger Hoar in 1695 and 1698 suggests that the Tories were not entirely successful, although Warre was returned again at a byelection after Hoar's death in 1699. In 1701 both members, George Balch and John Gilbert, were townsmen, but at the next three elections Balch shared the return with Sir Thomas Wroth and in 1708 with George Dodington.[26]

From then until 1753 two members of the Dodington family, with extensive interests in the port and customs, normally held one seat, a Tory country gentleman the other. Only three elections were contested. Dodington was returned with Nathaniel Palmer in 1710 and with Thomas Palmer in 1715. George Bubb Dodington sat with Palmer (by then recorder) in 1722, with Sir Halswell Tynte in 1727, and with Palmer again in 1734.[27] In 1726 John Poulett, Earl Poulett (d. 1743), and his associate Bernard Hutchins were elected freemen of the borough,[28] and in 1741 John's son Vere, probably with the support of Charles Seymour, earl of Egremont, successfully fought an election, the first of four Pouletts to sit for Bridgwater at intervals until 1806. Peregrine Poulett, elected in 1747, was succeeded in 1753 by Robert Balch, then of Nether Stowey but descended from Bridgwater merchants who had represented the borough in 1692–5 and 1701–10. Egremont's support continued until 1757.[29]

Elections were usually contentious in the later 18th century. There were c. 250 voters, although the members returned in 1768 claimed that the right still lay with the corporation. Most prospective candidates became freemen. John Perceval, earl of Egmont, elected freeman in 1736 'for his great merits and knowledge in antiquities and useful learning', won most votes both in 1754 and 1761, Dodington failing at the first and Balch at the second. In 1768 Benjamin Allen, a townsman, was returned top of the poll; John James Perceval, Viscount Perceval, Egmont's heir, was unseated in favour of Anne Poulett. Poulett and Allen were returned unopposed in 1774 and after a contest in 1780, but Allen was unseated in 1781 in favour of John Acland.[30] Charles James Fox, elected a freeman in 1780, stood at the same election, at the invitation of a local man, John Chubb, and representing opposition to Lord North. Fox himself took no part in the campaign, but the election of North as a freeman in 1782 was evidence of the continued strength of North's supporters in the town.[31] In 1784 Poulett and

20 Return of M.P.s, H.C. 69–I, pp. 445, 459, 465, 471; H.C. 69–II, p. xxix (1878), lxii.
21 S.R.O., DD/X/ME 7 (1628 charter); Smythe Family Correspondence (Bristol Rec. Soc. xxxv), 85, 160–1, 168, 200; Hist. Parl., Commons, 1660–90, iii. 769–70; S.R.S. lxxi. 73–4, 78–9.
22 Hist. Parl., Commons, 1660–90, i. 372–4; V.C.H. Som. ii. 232–3; Hist. MSS. Com. 29, 14th Rep. II, Portland, iii, p. 91.
23 Hist. Parl., Commons, 1660–90, i. 372.
24 Cal. S.P. Dom. 1683 (1), 387.
25 Hist. Parl., Commons, 1660–90, i. 372–4; Cal. S.P.

Dom. 1683–4, 93–4; 1685, 54, 60.
26 Return of M.P.s, i. 575, 582, 589, 596, 603; ii. 5, 13, 23.
27 Hist. Parl., Commons, 1715–54, i. 314, 429–30.
28 S.R.O., D/B/bw 2/1/2; V.C.H. Som. iv. 45–6, 51.
29 Hist. Parl., Commons, 1715–54, i. 314, 429–30; 1754–90, i. 367–8; Cat. Petworth Ho. Archives, ed. F. Steer and N. Osborne, i. 9.
30 Hist. Parl., Commons, 1754–90, i. 367–8; below, plate facing p. 233.
31 S.R.O., D/B/bw 2/1/2; T. B. Dilks, Charles James Fox and the Borough of Bridgwater (1937).

Alexander Hood succeeded against the combined opposition of Fox and Chubb, but in the following year Poulett died and was replaced by a supporter of Pitt.[32]

The Poulett family, holding the office of recorder, continued to manage the borough, but without complete success. Vere Poulett and John Langston, a London banker, were returned against the Egmont interest in 1790, and in 1796 and 1802 George Pocock, Earl Poulett's brother-in-law, and Jeffreys Allen, a local supporter of the government. Poulett and Langston won again in 1806, but later Poulett turned against his father, the earl, and in 1807 he was defeated by Pocock and William Thornton (later Astell), an East India Company director. The disaffected Poulett was supported by the duke of Buckingham and John Chubb. Pocock and Astell were returned again in 1812 and 1818 representing the Tory interest,[33] and Astell was returned at each election up to and including 1831. From 1820 he was accompanied by C. K. Kemeys-Tynte of Halswell, who was returned until 1837 and then again from 1847 until his death in 1860. His fellow Liberal member from 1857 was Alexander Kinglake, the historian, who served as member until 1869. A Conservative elected top of the poll in 1865 was later unseated; a byelection in the following year returned another Conservative, George Patton, with a very slender majority against Walter Bagehot, and a few weeks later Patton lost the byelection following his appointment as a minister. The Liberal victor, (Sir) Philip Vanderbyl, and Kinglake were returned in 1868, but in the following year they were unseated and the town was disfranchised for bribery and corruption.[34] From 1885 one of the county divisions has been named after the town.

CHURCHES. Between 1088 and c. 1107 Walter of Douai gave the church of Bridgwater with all tithes to the monastery of Bath.[35] The grant was confirmed by his son Robert of Bampton, and in 1156 by Pope Adrian IV.[36] Probably in the 1180s Walter's great-grandson Fulk Pagnell granted the church, then in his gift, to the abbey of Marmoutiers at Tours for the benefit of the priory of Tickford or Newport Pagnell (Bucks.).[37] The grant seems to have been ineffective, for in 1203 William Brewer, Fulk's successor as lord of Bridgwater, acquired the

advowson from the prior of Bath in return for an annual payment of 100s.[38] About 1214 Bath cathedral priory gave its remaining rights in the church to William Brewer's newly founded hospital of St. John in Bridgwater in return for a pension of £4 13s. 4d., which was paid until the Dissolution.[39]

From 1219 the master and brethren of the hospital undertook to serve the church both by one of their own number and by a secular chaplain.[40] There was a vicar in 1245[41] and an endowed vicarage in 1291.[42] The hospital presented secular clerks until the Dissolution except in 1498–9 when the vicarage was held by Thomas Spenser, the master of the hospital, who was presented to the living by the prior of Taunton and a canon of Wells.[43] The Crown acquired the patronage at the Dissolution and presented from 1557 onwards.[44] The Lord Chancellor exercises the patronage of the living, consolidated since 1749 with the rectory of Chilton Trinity.[45] The parishes of Holy Trinity, St. John, and St. Francis were formed from St. Mary's parish in the 19th and 20th centuries.[46]

The vicarage was assessed at £5 6s. 8d. in 1291.[47] In 1535 it was valued at £11 7s. 5½d. net;[48] it was vacant for several years from 1557 because the income had been reduced.[49] It was reputed to be worth £30 c. 1668.[50] Probably by that date and certainly by the early 18th century the vicars were regularly receiving money from other sources.[51] In 1815 the living was declared to be worth under £110 gross but in 1827 it was over £300 gross.[52] The average net income in the period 1829–31 was £342.[53]

In 1304 the bishop assigned to the vicar legacies for forgotten tithes, various offerings, the tithes of calves, geese, and garlic, and the small tithes of the chapelry of Horsey. The vicar was to bear a third of the charges of the church.[54] The offerings were worth £8 in 1535.[55] In the 1570s they comprised 2d. from every communicant, 6d. at weddings, and 3d. at churchings.[56] The vicar's tithes, valued at 78s. 8d. in 1535 including half the tithe wool and lambs from Horsey,[57] were payable on calves, geese, and garlic in the 1570s and 1613,[58] but from 1721 the tithes of Horsey and a pension of 10s. were commuted for a payment of £10 by the corporation either to the vicar or to the curate,[59] a sum considered by 1847 to be a rent charge.[60]

The vicar's glebe, valued at 8s. in 1535[61] and comprising just over 2 a. in Friern mead in the

32 *Hist. Parl., Commons,* 1754–90, i. 367–8; S.R.O., D/B/bw 2116; ibid. 2/1/2 (15 Nov. 1768); Hist. MSS. Com. 30, *13th Rep. III, Fortescue,* i, p. 252.
33 *Hist. Parl., Commons,* 1790–1820, ii. 345–6; *Paupers and Pigkillers,* ed. J. Ayres (Gloucester, 1984), 76.
34 Squibbs, *Bridgwater,* 86–8, 194; *Mins. of Evidence before Sel. Cttee. on Bridgwater Election Petition,* H.C. 247 (1866), x.
35 *S.R.S.* vii (1), p. 39; (2), p. 160.
36 Ibid. (1), pp. 39–40, 69.
37 Dugdale, *Mon.* v. 204; *V.C.H. Bucks.* i. 360–1.
38 *S.R.S.* vi. 19; vii (2), p. 20.
39 *Rot. Chart.* (Rec. Com.), 204; *Valor Eccl.* (Rec. Com.), i. 176.
40 *S.R.S.* xlix, pp. 288–9.
41 Ibid. xlviii, no. 3; cf. ibid. nos. 12, 16.
42 *Tax. Eccl.* (Rec. Com.), 198.
43 *S.R.S.* liv, pp. 13–14, 44.
44 *Cal. Pat.* 1557–8, 356.

45 S.R.O. D/P/chi. t 2/9/1; D/B/bw 2/1/2 (25 Oct., 18 Dec. 1749).
46 Below, this section.
47 *Tax. Eccl.* (Rec. Com.), 198, 202.
48 *Valor Eccl.* (Rec. Com.), i. 213.
49 S.R.O., D/B/bw 1693.
50 Ibid. D/D/Vc 24.   51 Below, this section.
52 S.R.O., D/D/Rb 1815, 1827.
53 *Rep. Com. Eccl. Revenues,* pp. 128–9.
54 *Cal. Papal Reg.* v. 201; vii. 63. A spurious ordination, evidently concocted in the later 16th century, is in S.R.O., D/B/bw 695.
55 *Valor Eccl.* (Rec. Com.), i. 213.
56 S.R.O., D/B/bw 1693.
57 *Valor Eccl.* (Rec. Com.), i. 213.
58 S.R.O., D/D/Rg 260.
59 Ibid. D/B/bw 2/1/1 (9 Jan. 1721–2) and 2087.
60 Ibid. tithe award.
61 *Valor Eccl.* (Rec. Com.), i. 213.

1570s and 1637,[62] was exchanged for two plots of the same size in 1852.[63] In 1978 there was no glebe.[64]

The vicar's house, including two courts and a garden, lay in 1613 on the south side of St. Mary Street.[65] In 1815 it was considered 'small, mean, and uncomfortable',[66] and in 1822–3 the vicar lived in Castle Street.[67] In 1851 the vicar lived at Hamp[68] and in 1881 at Haygrove.[69] In 1929 the present vicarage in Durleigh Road, formerly the Elms, was bought for the benefice.[70]

Among the vicars of Bridgwater in the Middle Ages was Richard of Exbridge, a poor acolyte, who held the living briefly during the winter of 1348–9,[71] Nicholas Frampton, outlawed for his part in the insurrection of 1381,[72] and John Colswayn, who held the benefice from 1423 until 1474.[73] Colswayn's successor Richard Croke, vicar from 1474 to c. 1498, was the first graduate to hold the living.[74] Thomas Street remained vicar 1528–57.[75] For some time after his death the living was sequestrated, John Phillips, the parish clerk or chanter, acting as sequestrator and occasionally burying the dead.[76] John Bullingham, preacher at Bridgwater 1562–3 and vicar of Creech St. Michael, was later bishop of Gloucester (1581–98) and Bristol (1581–89).[77]

From the mid 13th century subsidiary altars, fraternities, and chantries were established and endowed within the church,[78] and in 1310 there were at least three chaplains, a deacon, and two other clerks besides the vicar.[79] Four chaplains and three clerks were recorded in 1383,[80] five chaplains in 1414,[81] and in 1450 a parochial chaplain, a chantrist, and seven anniversary chaplains.[82] The parochial chaplain in 1450 and 1464 seems to have been regarded as deputy to the vicar; he lived at the vicarage house where he taught a school at the vicar's request.[83] Even after the three chantries were dissolved in 1548, three priests and three clerks were employed in 1551 in addition to the vicar.[84] The vicar and two other priests, one a former chantrist, were serving obits in 1558.[85] In 1554 the corporation acquired some former chantry land on condition that a perpetual mass was offered.[86]

There was an endowed mass before the Rood by 1296.[87] Lights before the high cross were still supported by a separate fund in 1420,[88] but they seem thereafter to have been provided by the churchwardens, who may have replaced the foundation with the Rood chapel, established by 1428.[89] The chantry of the Blessed Virgin Mary had been founded before 1260 and was endowed with rents.[90] The chantry chapel was within the chancel of the parish church, and chaplains attached to it had a dwelling house in St. Mary Street by 1349.[91] A light at the chantry altar seems to have had a separate endowment.[92] The chantry, administered by wardens in the later 14th century, seems to have been refounded in 1393, when the stewards of the guild merchant as patrons undertook to appoint a chantry priest, who was to have a permanent seat in the choir of the parish church, to find someone to maintain the church clock, and to live in a house on the west side of the vicarage house.[93] The stewards of the guild merchant appointed priests until they were succeeded by the mayor and burgesses in 1468.[94] The endowment, valued at £8 0s. 8d. in 1548,[95] passed to the Crown, and houses and land worth £5 16s. were sold to the corporation in 1554.[96]

In the 13th century there was an altar of St. James,[97] in 1310 an altar of All Saints, beside which stood a figure of the Virgin,[98] and in 1384 an altar of St. Catherine.[99] About 1414 part of the interior of the church seems to have been reorganized: the All Saints altar was probably removed and chapels of Holy Trinity and St. Anne were created;[1] by the 1480s there were others dedicated to the Holy Cross or the Rood, St. George, and St. Erasmus.[2] There were representations of the Trinity and St. Catherine in their respective chapels,[3] and fraternities and endowments supported the chapels.[4] In 1529 a representation of St. Sebastian was to be replaced by one in alabaster,[5] and in the 1540s there were more fraternities and an altar of St. Saviour.[6]

By the later 14th century the regular income of the churchwardens came principally from collections in the parish, supplemented by occasional collections in church and by gifts and legacies.[7] In 1414–15 the keepers of the Holy

62 S.R.O., D/D/Rg 260.
63 Ibid. tithe award.
64 Inf. from Dioc. Office.
65 S.R.O., D/D/Rg 260.
66 Ibid. D/D/Rb 1815.
67 Pigot, *Nat. Com. Dir.* (1822–3).
68 P.R.O., HO 107/1925.
69 Ibid. RG 11/2374.
70 S.R.O., D/P/bw. m 3/4/1.
71 *S.R.S.* x, p. 559.
72 *Cal. Close, 1377–81,* 447.
73 *S.R.S.* xxx, p. 436; xxxi, p. 109; lii, p. 55.
74 Ibid. liv, pp. 13–14.
75 Ibid. lv, pp. 52–3; *Cal. Pat. 1557–8,* 356.
76 S.R.O., D/B/bw 1541, 1693, 1767.
77 Ibid. D/B/bw 1540; D/D/B reg. 15; *S.R.S.* lv, p. 144; *S.D.N.Q.* xv. 162; *Alum. Cantab. to 1751*; *D.N.B.*
78 *S.R.S.* xlviii, nos. 8, 10, 23–4, 27–8, 40.
79 Ibid. no. 65.
80 Ibid. liii, no. 380.
81 Ibid. lviii, no. 569.
82 Ibid. xlix, p. 139.
83 S.R.O., D/B/bw 115, 1682.
84 Ibid. 1678.
85 Ibid. 1533.

86 *S.R.S.* lxxvii, p. 84.   87 Ibid xlviii, no. 40.
88 Ibid. no. 282; liii, nos. 407, 427; lviii, nos. 577, 591, 602.
89 Ibid. lviii, nos. 642, 648, 650; lxx, no. 1029B; S.R.O., D/B/bw 21, 802.
90 *S.R.S.* xlviii, nos. 8, 24, 27–8.
91 Ibid. nos. 151, 156; liii, nos. 333, 423.
92 Ibid. xlviii, no. 70.
93 Ibid. no. 244; liii, nos. 321, 333, 358, 385, 400, 462, 482; *Cal. Pat. 1391–6,* 176.
94 *S.R.S.* xiii, pp. 60–1; xxxii, p. 270; xlix, pp. 292–3, 376, 425; lii, p. 124; liv, pp. 73, 99, 103; lv, pp. 12, 108.
95 Ibid. ii. 230–2.
96 Ibid. lxxvii, pp. 83–4.
97 Ibid. xlviii, no. 24.
98 Ibid. 65.
99 Ibid. liii, no. 398.
1 Ibid. lviii, no. 576.
2 S.R.O., D/B/bw 21, 381, 1000A, 1169, 1835; *S.R.S.* xvi, 245–6.
3 *S.R.S.* lviii, nos. 574, 644.
4 Ibid. xlix, pp. 398–9; lviii, nos. 569, 644; S.R.O., D/B/bw 1000A.
5 *S.R.S.* xix. 281.
6 *Downside Rev.* xv (1896), 228–33.
7 *S.R.S.* liii, no. 406.

Trinity lights gave money for new windows in their chapel, for the rebuilding of which the stewards of the community had lent money.[8] After 1448 the churchwardens acquired houses and other property within the town, and from 1452–3 received an income from the sale of seats.[9] By 1548 most of the church's income was from rents and fines.[10]

By 1445 the income of the chapels and fraternities of St. George, St. Catherine, and the Holy Cross was being administered by the bailiff and burgesses as a single perpetual endowment.[11] In 1548 the endowment was regarded as a chantry, since a substantial part of the property had been left by John Kendall in 1489 to support a priest in St. George's chapel.[12] The chantry was dissolved in 1548 and some of the property was sold to the town in 1554.[13]

A chantry was founded in the chapel of the Trinity in the parish church in 1455 after apparently unsuccessful attempts to convert an established fraternity in 1408, 1414, and 1422.[14] The lands and tenements were administered by trustees who in 1525 conveyed them to a chaplain who was to say mass at the Trinity altar and to be present in choir with the other priests and clerks of the church.[15] The chantry was the best endowed in the church and in 1548 was valued at £9 14s. 8d. net.[16] Some of its property was sold to the town in 1554.[17]

Land in Stour Eastover (Dors.) owned by John Colswayn, vicar 1423–74,[18] passed from his trustees to the mayor and burgesses, and his obit and one established by John Colverd of West Harptree were maintained in 1558.[19]

Part of the income from the former chantry lands granted to the corporation in 1553 was to find a chaplain 'to help the vicar in the services'.[20] The lease of the rectory estate, bought by the corporation in 1561, required them to find two 'priests or ministers' to serve in the church,[21] and in 1567–8 two men were paid £18 a year.[22] Revised terms agreed in 1571 charged the corporation with stipends of £20 for a man 'to preach and teach in the town and neighbourhood', £13 6s. 8d. for a curate, and a further sum for a schoolmaster.[23] From 1593 until the 1630s the vicar enjoyed one or other of the two stipends.[24] By 1639 the payments to both preacher and curate had been doubled.[25] The corporation gave the minister which it appointed to the living in 1647 £110 a year,[26] augmented from 1657 by

£40 from the Trustees for the Better Maintenance of Ministers.[27] By 1660 the corporation was paying the minister £125, reduced to £60 when he remained in the parish after the vicar was restored. The corporation also paid the vicar £30 a year in 1661–2, and his successor £24 6s. 8d. in 1674–5 and £38 6s. 8d. from 1678,[28] including £5 under an endowment for a Sunday lecture made in 1633.[29] From 1725 the corporation paid the vicar £23 6s. 8d. including £10 for the Horsey tithes, but from 1729 paid the £10 instead to the curate, along with a present of 20 guineas each year. From 1733 the vicar received the £10, and in 1757 his successor was also nominated to the post of preacher and later received £20 as Sunday lecturer.[30] The corporation in 1772 and in 1773 paid him £43 6s. 8d., comprising £20 as preacher, £13 6s. 8d. as presbyter or reader, and £10 for the Horsey tithes. He complained that the Sunday lecturer's stipend had not been paid for several years and that no allowance had been made for a 'proper' chaplain for many years.[31] In 1783 the lecturer's stipend was restored to the vicar and he received further sums of £2 for administering the communion and 10s. for a Good Friday sermon,[32] but in the later 1780s the £20 was described as a present and in addition he received only £10 for the Horsey tithes and £1 for the sermon. Thereafter payment was usually in arrear and in varying amounts: in the early 1820s £11 a year; by 1852 the earlier lecturer's stipend of £33 6s. 8d. and the £10 from Horsey tithes.[33] The vicar received £16 13s. 4d. for the afternoon lecture in 1906.[34] In 1991 Sedgemoor district council, successor to Bridgwater corporation, paid £10 in respect of Horsey tithes and £33.34 for the afternoon lecture.[35]

The increase in clerical income encouraged ministers to stay, including George Swankin, preacher by 1595 and until 1622,[36] John Devenish, vicar 1605–c. 1644, and George Wootton, curate by 1623 and until 1645, vicar 1645–6, 1660–69.[37] Devenish was suspended for a time in 1636 after complaints of unorthodox behaviour, but both he and Wootton signed the Protestation in 1642.[38] Wootton was ejected in 1646 and was replaced by 'a pious, learned, and approved minister', John Norman, appointed by the corporation in 1647 and later by parliament.[39] In 1651 he was suspected of 'malignity and disobedience',[40] but he continued to be paid

8 S.R.S. lviii, no. 576.
9 Ibid. lx, nos. 758, 760, 769.
10 S.R.O. D/B/bw 1447.
11 Ibid. lx, no. 727; S.R.O., D/B/bw 1339. Later gifts were sometimes made to individual foundations: S.R.O., D/B/bw 381, 663, 1169.
12 S.R.O., D/B/bw 1000A, 1339; S.R.S. ii. 230–2.
13 S.R.S. lxxvii, pp. 83–4.
14 Ibid. lviii, nos. 544, 569, 574, 608; lx, nos. 779–83.
15 S.R.O., D/B/bw 1423.
16 S.R.S. ii. 234–7.
17 Ibid. lxxvii, pp. 83–4.
18 S.R.O., D/B/bw 750; S.R.S. ii. 56–7; lxx, no. 928.
19 S.R.O., D/B/bw 1533, 1535.
20 Cal. Pat. 1553–4, 192.   21 Ibid. 1560–3, 161–2.
22 S.R.O., D/B/bw 1545.
23 Cal. Pat. 1569–72, p. 307.
24 S.R.O., D/B/bw 1580–1, 1583, 1605, 1672, 1676, 1856, 1968–9, 2122.   25 Ibid. 1516, 1615.
26 Ibid. 594, 1617.   27 S.D.N.Q. xiii. 157.

28 S.R.O., D/B/bw 1626–8, 1630–3, 1636.
29 Ibid. 1527.
30 Ibid. D/B/bw 2/1/1 (6 July 1725, 21 Mar. 1729); 2/1/2 (2 Nov. 1733); D/B/bw 1783, 2087; D/D/Bs 44.
31 Ibid. D/B/bw 1522, 1737, 1971–2.
32 Ibid. 1616.
33 Ibid. 11/1/1, 3.   34 Ibid. 11/1/14.
35 Inf. from the Director of Finance, Sedgemoor D.C.
36 S.R.O., D/B/bw 1584, 1969, 2122; D/P/bw. m 2/1/1 (22 Oct. 1622).
37 Ibid. D/D/Vc 81; D/P/bw. m 2/1/2 (22 Dec. 1669); Som. Incumbents, ed. Weaver, 318.
38 V.C.H. Som. ii. 42; T. H. Peake, 'Clergy & Church Cts. in Dioc. of Bath and Wells 1625–42' (Bristol Univ. M. Litt. thesis, 1978), 286–7; Som. Protestation Returns, ed. Howard and Stoate, 87.
39 S.R.O., D/B/bw 594; Walker Revised, ed. A. G. Matthews, 321–2; L.J. ix. 228.
40 Calamy Revised, ed. A. G. Matthews, 367; Cal. S.P. Dom. 1651, 277.

Cornhill and St. Mary's Church, *c.* 1800

Castle Street, 1950

BRIDGWATER

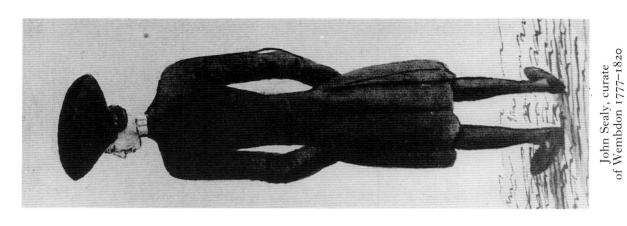

John Sealy, curate
of Wembdon 1777–1820

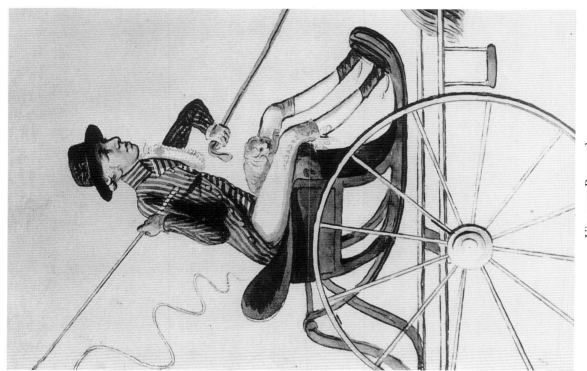

Viscount Perceval

BRIDGWATER CHARACTERS

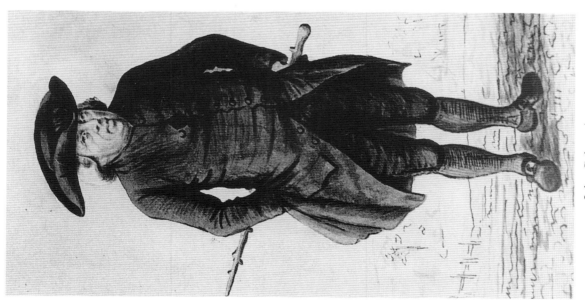

John Coles, vicar
of Bridgwater 1742–86

by the corporation after Wootton had been restored as vicar in 1660.[41] Norman left in 1662.[42] Wootton died in 1669, described as 'most vigilant pastor of this parish'.[43] In 1683 William Allen, vicar 1670–1720, was accused of holding views bordering on heresy.[44]

In 1720 the corporation unsuccessfully requested the appointment as vicar of the curate, James Knight, who remained curate until his death in 1757.[45] John Coles, vicar 1742–86,[46] and William Wollen, vicar 1786–1844, held the living in succession for more than a century.[47] About 1776 the church had 100 communicants, and in 1815 there were two sermons on Sundays and prayers on Wednesdays, Fridays, and holy days.[48] The evening sermon was given by the preacher and reader in 1827.[49] By 1840 Sunday sermons were preached in the morning and afternoon.[50] A surpliced choir was introduced in 1849.[51] From 1857 until 1864 the vicar was the Tractarian, Michael Sadler,[52] and by 1870 three services were held on Sundays, each with a sermon, and several services on weekdays. Communion was celebrated twice a month, alternately at 9 a.m. and after morning service.[53]

In 1537 a house on the north side of High Street and described as the church house was conveyed to two leading townsmen.[54] The building was maintained by the corporation, and was occasionally used for entertainments.[55] The grammar school was held by 1722 in an upper chamber of the building, for the demolition and rebuilding of which the corporation appointed a committee in 1765.[56] The school returned there probably early in 1788. At the end of 1799 it was suggested that part of the building be used as a winter soup kitchen, and early in 1801 the corporation agreed to lease the building.[57] The lease declared that the building, or probably some part of it, had been used as an inn 'for many years past'.[58] The Mansion House inn continued to occupy the building in 1989. The upper floor, approached by an outside stair at the west side until 1868,[59] seems to have included an assembly room.

The church of *ST. MARY* has a sanctuary of two and a half bays, a choir of two bays with north and south chapels, an aisled and clerestoried nave of five bays with transepts linked to porches, and a low west tower topped with a tall spire. The chancel and tower are of red sandstone; the remainder is largely of limestone, mostly with Ham stone dressings.[60]

If the jambs of the north porch doorway, with stiff-leaf capitals of the early 13th century, are *in situ* the church was already aisled. The tower arch and the slightly later north transept and the porches indicate that the nave had reached its present size by the mid 14th century and that the church was cruciform. Major rebuilding work was paid for in 1366–7 and work was in progress on the tower in 1385, when perhaps the spire was added.[61] A chapel next to the charnel house mentioned in 1385–7 had been recently completed by 1415, and work on a second chapel in 1417–18, said to be in the charnel house, was probably an adaptation of the north transept. A further chapel was planned in 1414–15.[62] The chancel roof may be dated by a carved boss between 1385 and 1416.[63] The reconstruction of the aisled nave may have followed shortly after *c.* 1420. Building continued into the 1440s, financed by tallages,[64] and the sanctuary, then called the Lady Chapel, may have been extended or altered in 1447–8.[65]

A rood screen, begun in 1414–15 and finished in 1419–20,[66] remained in its original position until restoration in the mid 19th century; some of the original parts in 1902 became the parclose screens north and south of the present choir stalls. Further chapels, probably formed by parcloses, had been created by the 1530s, at least one of them in the north aisle.[67] A second screen was erected west of the rood screen in the early 17th century, perhaps forming the new aisle mentioned in 1620.[68] Stalls for members of the corporation occupied the aisle until both stalls and screen were removed to the south side of the church in the early 1850s.[69] A pew was built above the south porch *c.* 1663 and another over the north in the 1740s.[70] There were also galleries over the north and south chapels in the choir, at the west end of the nave, and in the tower. All were removed in 1849 when the church was restored under W. H. Brakspear and the stuccoed plaster ceiling of the nave and the plain clerestory were replaced by a hammer-beamed roof and windows in Decorated style. Other roofs were heavily restored or replaced, the pulpit was removed from its prominent position on the north side of the nave, and the whole church was reseated. Windows were inserted on the north and south sides of the sanctuary, and much of the Decorated tracery in the existing windows and the north porch may have replaced 15th-century work. Brakspear also removed a square recess between the south porch and transept. The whole restoration,

41   S.R.O., D/B/bw 1626–8.
42   Ibid. DD/SFR 8/2; cf. below, prot. nonconf.
43   S.R.O., D/P/bw. m 2/1/2 (22 Dec. 1669).
44   *Cal. S.P. Dom.* 1683–4, 45–6.
45   S.R.O., D/B/bw 2/1/1 (15 Feb. 1719–20); 2/1/2 (7 Feb. 1757).
46   Plate opposite.
47   S.R.O., D/D/Vc 88; A. H. Powell, *Bridgwater in Later Days*, 256.
48   S.R.O., D/D/Vc 88; D/D/Rb 1815.
49   Ibid. D/B/bw 2/1/3 (26 Dec. 1825); D/D/Rb 1827.
50   Ibid. D/D/Va 1840.
51   *Bridgwater Times*, 26 July 1849.
52   *D.N.B.*
53   S.R.O., D/D/Va 1870.
54   Ibid. 626: description on endorsement.
55   Ibid. 1441, 1464.
56   Ibid. 2/1/1 (1 Sept. 1722); 2/1/2 (7 July 1756); cf.

D/B/bw 1736, 1971.
57   Ibid. 2/1/3 (8 Dec. 1787; 16 Dec. 1799; *c.* Jan. 1801).
58   Ibid. D/B/bw C.L. 14.
59   Inf. from Mr. J. F. Lawrence, Wembdon.
60   Below, plate facing p. 312.
61   *S.R.S.* xlviii, no. 238; liii, no. 426.
62   Ibid. liii, no. 426; lviii, nos. 576, 601.
63   Ibid. liii, p. xxii.   64   Ibid. lx, nos. 732–43.
65   Ibid. lviii, nos. 650, 660; lx, no. 754.
66   Ibid. lviii, nos. 576, 601.
67   S.R.O., D/B/bw 1000A, 1678; *Downside Rev.* xv (1896), 228–33; *S.R.S.* lx, nos. 729, 786.
68   S.R.O., DD/X/SR 5, p. 114.
69   F. B. Bond and B. Camm, *Rood Screens and Rood Lofts*, i. (1909), 150; A. H. Powell, *Bridgwater in Later Days*, opp. p. 216.
70   S.R.O., D/D/C pet., pets. of Francis Harvey and Moses Williams.

which continued until 1853, was attacked both locally and nationally.[71]

The east window of the sanctuary is blocked by a painting, given in 1780 by Anne Poulett, which he acquired from a Spanish ship taken as a prize.[72] It may be Bolognese, of the later 17th century.[73] Below it is an Elizabethan or Jacobean communion table, a 14th-century tabernacle, and seats which were formerly parts of choir stalls. There are 14th-century tomb recesses in the north aisle of the nave, matched by Victorian replicas in the south aisle. The pulpit is of the early 16th century; the pews, elaborately carved in Gothic style, were installed in 1849.

There are eight bells, all of which were recast in the 19th century from originals of the 17th century or earlier.[74] Both Thomas Jefferies of Bristol and William Purdue had been involved in making and maintaining the bells, of which there had been at least three by 1384–5.[75] The plate includes a cup and cover of 1640 by 'W.C.', a tankard of 1724 by James Wilkes, and two dishes, a cup, and a paten of 1727–8 by Robert Lucas.[76] The registers begin in 1558 and are complete.[77]

There was a chapel at Horsey in 1304 and probably c. 1280.[78] In 1415 its maintenance was a charge on the people of Horsey.[79] In 1535 the vicar of Bridgwater paid a priest to celebrate there.[80] Bread and wine for communion was found from Bridgwater rectory in the 1540s, and in 1548 the curate was serving the chapel every Sunday.[81] The chapel no longer existed in the 1570s.[82]

There was a chapel of St. Saviour outside the south gate built, it was said in the 1530s, within living memory by a merchant called William Poel or Pole.[83] It seems to have been still standing in 1703 and its site, beside a clise across the Durleigh Brook near its junction with the Parrett, was a landmark throughout the 18th century.[84] St. Saviour's Avenue was built near the site in the late 19th century.

HOLY TRINITY church, Taunton Road, was consecrated in 1840 and was assigned in 1841 a district chapelry comprising the southern part of the ancient parish.[85] It was endowed in 1842, and a glebe house was built in 1879.[86] A room for a Sunday school and other parish business was opened in St. Saviour's Avenue in 1892.[87] The church, which was designed by

Richard Carver, was of stone and comprised a chancel with north and south vestries, aisleless galleried nave with north and south porches, and a bellcot on its western gable; it was demolished in 1958.[88] Parish worship was transferred first to the mission church of the Good Shepherd, part of Greenfield House, Hamp Street, which had been in use since 1953. A new church in Greenfield, called the Holy and Undivided Trinity and designed by Caroe and Partners, was consecrated in 1961. It is of brick and concrete with a steeply pitched pantiled roof, and comprises a chancel, a nave with shallow transepts, and a bellcot.[89]

The church of ST. JOHN THE BAPTIST, Eastover, was assigned a parish and consecrated in 1846 to serve the eastern part of the ancient parish. It was built largely through the efforts of its first minister, J. Moore Capes,[90] who in the year of its consecration became a Roman Catholic.[91] In 1871–2 there were weekly services, lectures, and night schools in several parts of the parish, and a surpliced choir was introduced.[92] In 1876 there were daily services with four each Sunday, at least one a communion service.[93] A vicarage house, built at the same time as the church, was enlarged 1876–84.[94] The church, in grey stone in an Early English style, comprises a chancel with north vestry, a nave with south porch, and a west tower. The architect, John Brown of Norwich, planned a spire, which proved impossible because of poor foundations. The church was one of the first in the country to embody the principles of the Oxford movement.[95] The pulpit, font, sedilia, and reredos are in Painswick stone.[96]

St. John's church in 1882 opened the mission church of ALL SAINTS, successor to a room in Edward Street.[97] By 1966 the church had closed and was in use as a boy's club.[98] The building, in Gothic style, is tall and comprises chancel and nave, in sandstone with freestone dressings.

The church of St. FRANCIS OF ASSISI, Saxon Green, was begun in 1960 for a district formed in 1958. A parish was created in 1965. The church, of brick and tile, was designed by Peter Bradley of Taunton. It comprises a shallow chancel, added c. 1979, a nave with north Lady Chapel, and a south-west tower, to which a spire was added in 1984.[99]

[71] Taunton Castle, Braikenridge and Pigott collns., drawings by J. C. Buckler (1832) and W. W. Wheatley (1843); S.R.O., D/D/WBf 8/2; DD/X/BKP 1 (architect's drawings); D/P/bw. m 6/1/1, 9/1/1; Bridgwater Times, 3 May 1849; Proc. Arch. Inst. (1851), pp. liv–lv.
[72] Proc. Som. Arch. Soc. lxvi, p. xxiii.
[73] Pevsner, S. & W. Som. 96.
[74] S.R.O., DD/SAS CH 16/1.
[75] S.R.S. liii, no. 406; S.R.O., D/B/bw 731, 1723, 2101.
[76] Proc. Som. Arch. Soc. xlvii. 152–4.
[77] S.R.O., D/P/bw. m 2/1/1–51.
[78] Cal. Papal Reg. v. 201; Cal. Inq. p.m. iii, p. 383.
[79] S.R.S. lviii, p. 47.
[80] Valor Eccl. (Rec. Com.), i. 213.
[81] P.R.O., SC 6/Hen. VIII/3143; S.R.S. ii. 57.
[82] S.R.O., D/B/bw 1693.
[83] Leland, Itin. ed Toulmin Smith, ii. 96.
[84] B.L. Add. Ch. 71720; S.R.O., D/B/bw 1719, 1737, 1971. It was also then known as St.David's and St. Savery chapel.
[85] Taunton Courier, 17, 24 June 1840; Lond. Gaz. 2 Mar.

1841, p. 568.
[86] Lond. Gaz. 29 Apr. 1842, p. 1167; 9 May 1879, p. 3264.
[87] Squibbs, Bridgwater, p. 100.
[88] Ibid. pl. 43; B.L. Add. MS. 36379, f. 178; Som. Co. Herald, 11 May 1963.
[89] Squibbs, Bridgwater, pp. 135, 138; local inf.
[90] H. E. Field and T. B. Dilks, Parish of St. John the Baptist, Bridgwater (1946); Lond. Gaz. 4 Aug. 1846, p. 2837.
[91] Below, Rom. Cath.
[92] Diary of Sydenham Hervey, TS. in possession of editor, V.C.H. Somerset. [93] S.R.O., D/D/Va 1876.
[94] Field and Dilks, St. John Baptist Ch. 4, 12; S.R.O., D/D/Bbm 252.
[95] T. B. Dilks, Bridgwater in Brief (1927), 51; Field and Dilks, St. John Baptist Ch. 1–2; Devon R.O. 1148 M/add 36/560, 562, 585. [96] Field and Dilks, St. John Baptist Ch. 4.
[97] Ibid. 37–8; S.R.O., D/D/WBf 8/3.
[98] O.S. Map, 1/1,250 ST 3036 NE. (1966 edn.).
[99] S.R.O., D/P/bw. ht 22/3/1; D/P/bw. m 3/6/2; Dioc. Dir.; Bridgwater Mercury, 21 Feb. 1984; inf. from the Revd. D. Arnott, vicar.

ROMAN CATHOLICISM. One man was presented for recusancy in 1593–4 and another as a suspect in 1613.[1] Three male and two female papists were reported in 1767, one man a toll keeper, one woman keeping a cook's shop.[2] There was one reputed papist c. 1776.[3]

Mass was celebrated weekly in a private house from 1845 and following the conversion to Catholicism of J. Moore Capes, founder and first minister of St. John's church, a Catholic chapel, dedicated to St. Joseph, was opened in 1846 in Gordon Terrace.[4] Capes and Bishop (later Cardinal) Wiseman contributed towards the cost.[5] The church was first served from Cannington, but in 1851 it had a resident priest.[6] In 1878 there were 60 Easter communicants.[7] A new church with the same dedication was built in 1882 in Binford Place,[8] of red brick with Bath stone dressings; it was extended in 1982.[9] The church in Gordon Terrace was a workshop in 1990.

In 1850 a small group of Dominican tertiaries attempted unsuccessfully to establish a house in the town.[10] Between 1885 and 1891 Sisters of Mercy occupied a building in King Street.[11] A group of Sisters of the Holy Rosary opened a convent in Eastcroft, Durleigh Road, in 1939.[12] The convent remained open in 1990.

PROTESTANT NONCONFORMITY. The vicar held exercises in his house in 1636.[13] A Presbyterian *classis* had been established by 1647, a Baptist meeting by 1653, and a Quaker meeting by 1670.[14] In 1669 there were conventicles in 8 houses under 11 teachers attended by 260 people. Among the teachers, many of them ejected from livings in other parts of Somerset, were John Gardner, a Presbyterian, and Tobias Wells (d. 1692), a Baptist.[15] Five meetings (three Presbyterian, two Baptist) were licensed in 1672,[16] three in 1689, and five, of unspecified denomination, 1710–19.[17]

Humphrey and Robert Blake and the town's recorder, Sir Thomas Wroth, were members of the *classis* in 1647,[18] and John Norman, vicar

1647–60, was associated with a Presbyterian meeting from 1662.[19] In 1672 Presbyterians were meeting in the houses of David Bailey, Roger Hoar, and Robert Balch.[20] In 1683 Lord Stawell with his militia confined 'fanatics' to their homes and demolished a meeting house in the town, a building 'made round like a cockpit' with room for 400 people; the furniture, piled high in the Cornhill and topped by the pulpit and cushion, was burned.[21] The building is likely to have belonged to Presbyterians. In 1687 Robert Balch and Roger Hoar were acting as trustees of a house in Dampiet Street,[22] probably the building described as a meeting house from which stones were carried in 1688 for the reconstruction of the mill dam.[23] The meeting house was evidently being rebuilt at the time, and in 1689 it was licensed for worship as Christ Church.[24] An academy was established there by John Moore the elder, and by 1718 there were c. 600 members.[25] A new Presbyterian meeting house in Friarn Street, evidently the result of secession, was licensed in 1760.[26] Presbyterians were said to be numerous in the town in the 1770s.[27]

The theology of the congregation became increasingly Unitarian. From 1809 meetings of the Western Unitarian Society were held at Bridgwater,[28] and since 1815 the church and congregation have been Unitarian.[29]

Christ Church is plain and largely of brick but with older stone courses in the lower part of its south wall. The shell hood over the entrance and the main structure belong to the building of 1688, but the church has been several times remodelled, notably in 1788. A gallery pew formerly reserved for the mayor and other members of the corporation was converted for a Sunday school in 1833. Most of the internal fittings date from the 19th century. A plaque beside the entrance records the visit of S. T. Coleridge as preacher in 1797.[30]

Baptists, meeting since 1653,[31] registered two meetings in 1672,[32] were said to have built a chapel in 1687, and claimed c. 50 members.[33] They built a chapel in St. Mary Street in 1692,[34] and they claimed 200 members in 1718.[35] In the

1 *Recusant Roll*, ii (Cath. Rec. Soc. lvii), 141; S.R.O., D/D/Ca 180.
2 House of Lords R.O. 'Complete lists of papists 1767'.
3 S.R.O., D/D/Vc 88.
4 G. Oliver, *Hist. of the Catholic Religion in Som.* (London, 1857), 65; St. George's R.C. Ch., Taunton, *Parish Mag.* Summer 1982; above, churches.
5 H. E. Field and T. B. Dilks, *Parish of St. John the Baptist, Bridgwater* (1946), 5.
6 P.R.O., HO 107/1925.
7 R. I. Hancock, 'St. Joseph's R.C. Sch., Bridgwater, 1883–1983' (TS. at St. Joseph's sch., based on original sources since destroyed), 3.
8 *Lond. Gaz.* 1 Sept. 1883, 4075.
9 *Bridgwater Mercury*, May 1982.
10 Oliver, *Catholic Religion*, 65; Hancock, 'St. Joseph's Sch.' 2.
11 Hancock, 'St. Joseph's Sch.' 4–5; O.S. Map 1/5,000, Som. L. 11. 21 (1887 edn.).
12 *Bridgwater Mercury*, 15 Oct. 1985.
13 S.R.O., D/D/Ca 309, 313.
14 Below, this section.
15 *Orig. Rec. Early Nonconf.* ed. G. L. Turner, i. 9, 236; ii. 1104; *Calamy Revised*, ed. A. G. Matthews, 217, 353, 367, 521, 539; S.R.O., D/P/bw. m 2/1/2 (9 Feb. 1668/9), 2/1/3.
16 *Cal. S.P. Dom.* 1672, 42, 378, 675; *Orig. Rec. Early Nonconf.* i. 236, 239, 369, 439, 532, 561, 567, 611–12; ii. 1104, 1124; iii. 842.

17 S.R.O., Q/RR meeting ho. lics.
18 T. G. Crippen, *Nonconf. in Som.* 11; *V.C.H. Som.* ii. 49.
19 S.R.O., D/B/bw 1626–8; ibid. DD/SFR 8/2; *Cal. S.P. Dom.* 1663–4, 116; *D.N.B.*
20 *Orig. Rec. Early Nonconf.* i. 236, 239, 369, 439; *Cal. S.P. Dom.* 1672, 42. 21 *Cal. S.P. Dom.* 1683 (2), 60.
22 S.R.O., DD/OS 1.
23 Ibid. D/B/bw 1636 (1 May 1688).
24 Ibid. D/N/bw. chch 2/1/14.
25 J. Murch, *Hist. Presbyterian and General Baptist Churches of the West of Eng.* (1835), 176–8; Crippen, *Nonconf. in Som.* 39.
26 S.R.O., D/D/Rm 1.
27 Ibid. D/D/Vc 88; D/N/bw. chch 2/3/1, 4/3/6.
28 Murch, *Hist. Presbyterian and Baptist Churches*, 182–3, 568.
29 S.R.O., DD/OS 3; D/N/bw. chch 4/2/1, 4/3/1.
30 Ibid. D/N/bw. chch 2/3/1, 4/3/1–6; C. E. Pike, *Our Ancient Meeting House* (Bridgwater, n.d.); above, plate facing p. 89.
31 Crippen, *Nonconf. in Som.* 15; D. Jackman, *Baptists in the West Country*, 1; *Assoc. Rec. Particular Baptists*, ii (1973), 58, 64, 105.
32 *Cal. S.P. Dom.* 1672, 378, 675.
33 R. W. Oliver, *Strict Baptist Churches in Eng.* v (1968), 122; H. A. Hamblin and A. J. Whitby, *Baptists in Bridgwater* (c. 1937), 40, based on a church bk. destroyed in 1870.
34 Hamblin and Whitby, *Baptists in Bridgwater*, 41.
35 Crippen, *Nonconf. in Som.* 39.

1760s the minister purged the church of Arminians, and by 1780 there were only 29 members. In 1781 the remaining members signed a Calvinist declaration and in 1791 church membership had fallen still further. The chapel was demolished and replaced in 1837. Some members seceded to the Unitarians in 1853 but numbers increased from the 1870s and cottage meetings were held in Albert and Union streets. In the 1880s the church opened a house for sailors on West Quay and formed a temperance association. Membership reached 336 in 1907, and 739 children attended the Sunday school.[36] Northgate mission had opened by 1914 in some cottages, but both the mission and its Sunday school closed in 1927.[37] A chapel in Moorland Road, on the Sydenham estate, was acquired in 1965 and closed in 1972.[38] The membership of the chapel in St. Mary Street was 173 in 1982.[39] The chapel of 1837, designed by Edwin Down, is of brick, with a stone front formed by a giant pedimented entrance with plain Ionic columns, and was originally hidden from the street by cottages. Galleries were added in the 1870s, and the chapel was enlarged and the Sunday school rebuilt.[40]

In 1658 John Anderdon, a goldsmith, became a Quaker, and meetings were held at his house by 1670.[41] A meeting house was licensed in 1689.[42] William Penn held a meeting in the town hall in 1694,[43] and a meeting house for 200 was built in Friarn Street in 1722.[44] In 1737 the assize hall was licensed for use by Quakers. In 1776 Quakers used a temporary booth in the castle bailey; the licence was issued to eight individuals, all from Glastonbury or Street,[45] and about the same time there was said to be only one family of Quakers in the parish.[46] In 1801 the Friarn Street meeting house was enlarged and improved.[47] It was still open in 1991, occupying a brick building, no. 10 Friarn Street.

George Whitefield was welcomed to the town by the vicar in 1739 but suffered popular abuse there. John Wesley preached on several occasions between 1746 and 1769, and a house was licensed for worship by Methodists in 1753.[48] Bridgwater formed part of the Somerset circuit in 1777 and the Taunton circuit until 1840, when a new circuit was formed based on Bridgwater. There was a chapel in Eastover, with a Sunday school, by 1800.[49] A chapel was built in King Street in 1816 which by 1860 had been twice enlarged and seated 420. A Sunday school was added in 1924 with seating for 300, and by 1961 the premises included a gymnasium. In 1960 average attendance was 73 at morning service and 118 in the evening.[50] The chapel closed in 1980, and in 1988 was used as a furniture store. It is a plain building of brick, the main entrance through a portico added in 1860.

A Primitive Methodist chapel had been opened in Angel Crescent by 1852, and another in West Street by 1861.[51] One of them was still in use in 1875, but by 1880 that in West Street was being used by the Salvation Army, and the Primitive Methodists were meeting in St. John Street, probably in the Mariners Christian chapel. The cause had probably ceased by 1881.[52]

Wesleyan Reformers met in the market house in 1851, later in Gloucester Place, and from 1855 in St. Mary Street, where their chapel was enlarged in 1858.[53] The congregation became part of the United Methodist Free Church in 1857. The chapel closed in 1907 when the United Methodists joined the Bible Christians. The combined congregation used the Bible Christian chapel until 1911 when a new chapel was built in Monmouth Street. After Methodist union in 1932 Monmouth Street chapel became the head of a small circuit, which was united with the former Wesleyan circuit based on the King Street chapel in 1951. In 1960 average attendance at Monmouth Street was 74 at morning service and 114 in the evening. The chapel, of brick with Bath stone dressings, and designed by W. H. Dinsley,[54] was open in 1991. The chapel in St. Mary Street was after 1907 converted to a cinema, and in 1982 was part of a private club.[55] The United Methodist Free Church also had a chapel in Polden Street, recorded c. 1886. It closed probably before 1904, and the site was occupied in 1982 by a workshop.[56]

Bible Christians began their mission in the town in 1866 in an iron chapel in Bath Road. Cottage meetings held from 1873 in Chedzoy Lane increased the need for new premises and a chapel was built in Polden Street in 1876. Preaching was also undertaken at the docks in the 1880s.[57] In 1907 the Bible Christians joined the United Methodists. Until 1911 the combined congregation used the Polden Street chapel, which was then sold for use as an engineering workshop.[58]

A meeting house for Independents, in St. Mary Street near the south gate, was licensed in 1787, and another, possibly for the same congregation, in 1792. A different Independent congregation met in a disused malthouse in Friarn Street, which was also licensed in 1792.[59]

36   Hamblin and Whitby, *Baptists in Bridgwater*, 42, 48–9, 64, 72.
37   *Kelly's Dir. Som.* (1914); Hamblin and Whitby, *Baptists in Bridgwater*, 76.
38   F. H. Cockett, *Partnership in Service* (c. 1973), 30.
39   *Baptist Union Dir.* (1981–2).
40   Hamblin and Whitby, *Baptists in Bridgwater*, 56–9.
41   *S.R.S.* lxxv. 45, 57; S.R.O., DD/SFR 8/1.
42   *S.R.S.* lxxv. 69, 203; S.R.O., Q/RR meeting ho. lics.; ibid. DD/SFR(w) 41.
43   *Memoirs relating to the Sufferings of John Whiting* (1791), 504.
44   S.R.O., DD/SFR(w) 27; Crippen, *Nonconf. in Som.* 51.
45   S.R.O., Q/RR meeting ho. lics.; ibid. D/D/Rm 1.
46   Ibid. D/D/Vc 88.
47   Ibid. DD/SFR(w) 4.
48   *V.C.H. Som.* ii. 61–2; S.R.O., Q/RR meeting ho. lics.
49   S. G. Jarman, *Hist. Bridgwater*, 220; S.R.O., D/N/bmc 7/2.
50   S.R.O., D/N/bmc 2/3/1, 3/2/3, 4/3/4, 4/3/50, 7/2.
51   *Slater's Dir. Som.* (1852–3); *P.O. Dir. Som.* (1861).
52   Jarman, *Hist. Bridgwater*, 227; Whitby & Sons, *Bridgwater Almanack* (1880, 1881); *P.O. Dir. Som.* (1875).
53   Jarman, *Hist. Bridgwater*, 221.
54   S.R.O., D/N/bmc 3/2/3; 4/2/4, 11–12, 15; 4/3/50; *Bridgwater Mercury*, 12 Apr. 1911; *Monmouth Street Methodist Chapel, 1911–61* (Bridgwater, 1961).
55   O.S. Map 1/2,500, Som. L. 11 (1930 edn.).
56   Ibid. (1889 and 1904 edns.).
57   S.R.O., D/N/bmc 3/2/5, 4/2/4, 4/2/11.
58   Ibid. 4/2/4, 11–12, 15; 4/3/50; *Monmouth Street Methodist Chapel, 1911–61*.
59   S.R.O., D/D/Rm 1, 2.

Yet another group of Independents met in a malthouse in Salmon Lane, on the east bank of the Parrett, but in 1817 their leader took over the Friarn Street meeting house and the two congregations probably united. A Sunday school was added in 1818 and the chapel, known as Zion, was rebuilt in 1822.[60] It was closed in 1865 and was used as a skating rink before being taken over by the Salvation Army in 1881.[61]

A new chapel was begun in Fore Street in 1862 and was opened in 1864. Fore Street Congregational chapel was built in a Decorated style in grey limestone with Bath stone dressings, and had seating for 900. Lecture rooms were added in 1877.[62] The chapel was demolished after closure in 1964, and the congregation moved in 1966 to a new building known as Westfield Congregational chapel (later Westfield United Reformed church) in West Street, next to St. Matthew's Field.[63] It was open in 1991.

A nonconformist mission for seamen was said to have started in 1817. In 1837 the Mariners chapel was built in St. John Street by a former Primitive Methodist minister, and in the following year was vested in the Mariners Christian Society.[64] The society had apparently ceased by 1857, but the chapel continued in use.[65] In 1885 the Congregationalists tried to take over, but in the next year the minister and members asked help from the Wesleyans and invited preachers from the United Methodists in St. Mary Street. From 1889 the chapel was considered to be Congregationalist, although some of the trustees were Baptists.[66] A Sunday school was begun in the 1880s, and a schoolroom was built in 1911. The chapel continued in use until 1960 when it was sold and converted to a motor cycle shop. In 1961 work began on a new Mariners Christian chapel in Moorland Road, registered in 1963. Ownership and direction were transferred to the Baptists in 1965.[67]

Services of the Catholic Apostolic church, whose leader Henry Drummond visited the town, were held in the Grand Jury room of the town hall before 1840, when there was a chapel in Dampiet Street. Meetings were also held on West Quay. By 1889 the congregation had removed to King Street, and the chapel appears to have closed c. 1908.[68]

Plymouth Brethren came to the town in the 1840s and held their first meetings in Gloucester Place. By 1868 they had moved to Friarn Street, and meetings of Open Brethren were still held there in 1988.[69] The Brethren also had a meeting place in George Street by 1883, a Gospel Hall in West Street and rooms in Northgate by 1897, a meeting room in King's Place by 1906, and another in Court Street in the 1920s. The Gospel Hall was still in use in 1939, but the room in King's Place had recently been given up. The meeting place in George Street was licensed until 1954.[70]

The Salvation Army 'opened fire' in the town in 1880 with violently opposed meetings at the former Primitive Methodist chapel in West Street.[71] In 1881 they took over Zion chapel in Friarn Street as their citadel, and remained there until 1970.[72] The building was demolished in 1971, and in 1972 the Army acquired the former Baptist chapel in Moorland Road, which was their citadel in 1991.[73]

A National Spiritualist church was established in King's Place by 1937, possibly where the Brethren had met. A Christian Spiritualist church was meeting in the same year and by 1968 occupied a building in Queen Street,[74] which it still occupied in 1991. The Spiritualist National Union church was meeting in Green Dragon Lane in 1954.[75]

The Bridgwater Central Mission operated from St. Mary Street by 1937, but it had moved to Green Dragon Lane by 1954, when it was run by the Independent Pentecostal Fellowship.[76] By 1973 the Elim Pentecostal church had opened in George Street, and the cause continued in 1991.[77] The Bridgwater Evangelical church was founded in 1969, and in 1982 was meeting in the youth hut at Sydenham school.[78] Kingdom Hall, the meeting place of the Jehovah's Witnesses in Old Taunton Road, was licensed in 1971. It was replaced by a new building in the Drove in 1986.[79]

Between 1843 and 1851 six licences were issued for meeting houses of unspecified denominations, in Ball's Lane (later King Street), Friarn Street, King Square, Hamp, and a warehouse near the quay.[80] The Princeites held a service in Dunwear in 1872,[81] but evidently made no headway. A town missionary based in Friarn Street, possibly in connexion with the Brethren, was working in 1878 and 1882.[82] Other places of worship included a Gospel Union mission on West Quay in 1897, a Labour church at Docker's Hall in 1918, and a meeting room in Westonzoyland

60 Rep. Som. Cong. Union (1896); inf. from Mr. J. F. Lawrence, based on ch. rec.
61 Lond. Gaz. 7 Apr. 1865, p. 1942; Bridgwater Mercury, 18 Aug. 1970; below, this section (Salvation Army).
62 Rep. Som. Cong. Union (1896); Lond. Gaz. 7 Oct. 1864, p. 4786; Jarman, Hist. Bridgwater, 224–5; Squibbs, Bridgwater, pl. 198.
63 Squibbs, Bridgwater, 141.
64 Rep. Som. Cong. Union (1896); S.R.O., D/N/bmc 2/1/5.
65 Jarman, Hist. Bridgwater, 222.
66 S.R.O., D/N/bmc 3/2/16, 4/2/1; Jarman, Hist. Bridgwater, 222–3; Rep. Som. Cong. Union (1896).
67 Jarman, Hist. Bridgwater, 223; Som. Co. Herald, 2 June 1960; Bridgwater Mercury, 6 June 1961, 23 Feb. 1965; G.R.O. Worship Reg. nos. 68831, 70391.
68 Co. Gaz. Dir. Som. (1840); Jarman, Hist. Bridgwater, 226; Kelly's Dir. Som. (1906, 1910); A. H. Powell, Bridgwater in the Later Days, 249.
69 Jarman, Hist. Bridgwater, 226; P.O. Dir. Som. (1875).

70 Whitby & Sons, Dir. Bridgwater (1883, 1897); Kelly's Dir. Som. (1906, 1923, 1931, 1939); Bridgwater Dir. (1929); G.R.O. Worship Reg. no. 53205.
71 S.R.O. D/N/bmc 4/2/4; Jarman, Hist. Bridgwater, 227.
72 Bridgwater Mercury, 1 Dec. 1970.
73 F. H. Cockett, Partnership in Service (n.d.), 22; Bridgwater Mercury, 19 Oct. 1971.
74 G.R.O. Worship Reg. nos. 56189, 56907; O.S. Map 1/1,250, ST 2937 SE. (1968 edn.).
75 G.R.O. Worship Reg. no. 62406.
76 Ibid. nos. 56075, 62406.
77 Kelly's Dir. Bridgwater (1972–3).
78 Bridgwater Mercury, 1 Mar. 1983.
79 G.R.O. Worship Reg. 72245; Bridgwater Mercury, 24 Sept. 1986.
80 S.R.O., D/D/Rm 2.
81 Sydenham Hervey Diary, 1–2 Jan. 1872 (TS. in possession of the editor, V.C.H. Somerset).
82 Whitby & Sons, Bridgwater Almanack (1878, 1882).

Road for 'Christians not otherwise designated' in 1971.[83]

EDUCATION. There was a school in the town by 1298 when its rector undertook to send seven of his poor pupils to receive daily pittances at St. John's hospital, where a further 13 school-children lived on the foundation.[84] A master of schools was mentioned in the town in 1379[85] and the hospital's impropriate rectories of Morwen-stow (Cornw.) and Wembdon were charged together with the support of 13 boys in 1535.[86] The inhabitants' request for a free grammar school in 1548[87] was an attempt to secure an endowment for the existing school, probably held by 1553 in a school house belonging to the corporation.[88] The grant to the corporation, first of tithes in 1561 and later of the rectory, pro-vided an endowment for what became the free grammar school.[89] In 1819 the school had no pupils, but a school in Mount Street, established under Dr. John Morgan's will dated 1723 and originally designed as a grammar school, was by then teaching elementary subjects. In 1816 it had been increased in size by the addition of a schoolroom for 300 boys.[90] It became a second-ary school in 1871 and from 1888 received the endowment of the former grammar school, which had closed in 1869. Under a Scheme of 1910 it became an aided secondary school and in 1930, becoming a maintained school, moved to new buildings in Durleigh Road.[91] It was replaced in 1973 by Haygrove comprehensive school.[92]

In the 1460s John Wheler, the parish priest, took boys at the vicarage house and, at the vicar's behest, taught them to read and sing.[93] The curate of Chilton Trinity had a school in the town in 1609, and there was an unlicensed school in the parish in 1613.[94] Two schools for reading, writing, arithmetic, and accounting were licensed in 1662.[95]

A nonconformist academy, considered one of the principal academies in the country, was founded c. 1688 by John Moore (d. 1717), Presbyterian minister of Christ Church. Moore is said to have been arrested for keeping the academy, and its work was interrupted in 1714. Moore's son John continued it until his death in 1747, and it possibly continued later.[96]

Before 1715 Frances Safford gave £40 to the corporation to teach poor children to read. The interest of £2 provided schooling for ten child-ren by 1737, and the school continued until 1826 or later. In 1839 its endowment was attached to the grammar school.[97]

Christ Church Sunday school was founded in 1780, and there was also a Wesleyan Sunday school by 1800.[98] Private schools included Snook's writing school in 1793,[99] and Mr. Gill's writing school in 1804.[1] By 1819 there were, apart from the grammar school, three writing schools, a girls' school supported by subscrip-tions, several schools for 'little children', and Sunday schools having together 352 pupils.[2] In addition, by 1822 there were five boarding schools.[3]

ELEMENTARY SCHOOLS FOUNDED 1824–70. By 1835 the day schools of the town, including the grammar school, taught 897 pupils, and the Sunday schools 805 pupils.[4] Among the day schools was an infant school begun in 1830 with 70 children, supported partly by subscriptions and partly by school pence. It was probably the National infant school, then near Angel Cres-cent, which seems to have moved to a site between Mount Lane and Prickett's Lane c. 1841. The school had 121 pupils in 1846[5] and 149 paying school pence in 1875.[6] It merged with the girls' National school in 1891.[7]

A British school opened in 1824 was the largest day school in 1835, when it had 134 pupils in premises in Mount Street and was supported by subscriptions and fees. It was last recorded in 1852.[8] A day and Sunday school with 20 boys and 100 girls in 1835 had probably grown out of a girls' school supported by subscriptions in 1819. In 1835 80 of the girls paid fees.[9] The largest Sunday school in 1835, begun by the Independents in 1819, taught 126 boys and 150 girls; one of the two Baptist Sunday schools had 66 boys and 71 girls in 1835, and the Church boys' Sunday school, begun in 1823, had 120 pupils. The last was in Mount Street and in 1846 had 70 pupils with a paid master.[10]

In 1830 the Unitarian minister opened a day school in Friarn Street, and a schoolroom was built in 1834. In 1835 it had 60 pupils.[11] An infant school was also held there from 1838. Average attendance rose from 40 in 1840 to c. 130 in 1850; the building was enlarged c. 1842, and the infants were moved in 1850 to a building

83 Whitby & Sons, *Dir. Bridgwater* (1897); S.R.O., D/N/bmc 3/2/5; G.R.O., Worship reg. no. 71251.
84 *S.R.S.* i. 268; *V.C.H. Som.* ii. 154–5, 446.
85 P.R.O., E 179/4/4; N. Orme, *Educ. in the W. of Eng. 1066–1548*, 94.
86 *Valor Eccl.* (Rec. Com.), i. 208–9.
87 *S.R.S.* ii. 57.
88 S.R.O., D/B/bw 129.
89 *V.C.H. Som.* ii. 446–7; S.R.O., D/B/bw 1694.
90 *Educ. of Poor Digest*, 775.
91 S.R.O., E/4/6/40; E/4/6/69; *V.C.H. Som.* ii. 447–8.
92 Below, this section.
93 S.R.O., D/B/bw 115, 1682; Orme, *Educ. in the W. of Eng.* 94–5.
94 S.R.O., D/D/Ca 160, 180.
95 Ibid. D/D/Bs 39.
96 T. G. Crippen, *Nonconf. in Som.* 41; S.R.O., D/N/bw. chch 4/3/1; *D.N.B.*
97 *15th Rep. Com. Char.* 425; S.R.O., D/B/bw 1522, 1735, 1737, 1782, 1784, 1970, 2381, 2408; *Educ. of Poor Digest*, 775.
98 S.R.O., D/N/bw. chch 4/2/7, 5/2/1; D/N/bmc 7/2.
99 *Sherborne and Yeovil Mercury*, 23 Sept. 1793.
1 S.R.O., T/PH/ay 1, Dec. 1804.
2 *Educ. of Poor Digest*, 775.
3 Pigot, *Nat. Com. Dir.* (1822); *Taunton Courier*, 3, 24 Dec. 1812; 17 July 1822.
4 *Educ. Enq. Abstract*, 795–6.
5 Nat. Soc. *Inquiry, 1846–7*, Som. 4–5; S.R.O., T/PH/law (survey of 1836); ibid. DD/EDS 4773; D/B/bw C.L. 12.
6 *Public Elem. Schs.* H.C. 133 (1875), lix.
7 St. Mary's sch., girls' sch. log bk. 1863–1905; below, this section.
8 *Educ. Enq. Abstract*, 795–6; *Slater's Dir. Som.* (1852–3).
9 *Educ. of Poor Digest*, 775; *Educ. Enq. Abstract*, 795–6.
10 *Educ. Enq. Abstract*, 795–6; Nat. Soc. *Inquiry, 1846–7*, Som. 4–5.
11 *Educ. Enq. Abstract*, 795–6; S.R.O., D/N/bw. chch 4/2/1, 4/3/1.

in Provident Place, Wembdon. Adult evening classes were begun in 1850, probably in the original building in Friarn Street.[12] About 1866 the Provident Place school was demolished, and the Friarn Street school probably merged with a girls' British school in the same street; that school may have occupied the former Unitarian infant school buildings since 1852. The girls' school continued to be supported by the Unitarians; in 1875 157 pupils paid school pence. The school was transferred to Bridgwater school board in 1878. In the following year the school closed.[13]

By 1846 there were National schools for both boys and girls. The boys' school, in Mount Street by 1839, had 78 pupils both on Sundays and weekdays, and was supported by subscriptions and school pence. The school seems to have merged with Dr. Morgan's school by 1852.[14] The girls' school, founded in 1830 and in Northgate by 1839, in 1846 had 32 pupils on Sundays only and 100 on Sundays and weekdays under 4 paid and 16 unpaid teachers.[15] In 1875 it had 120 pupils paying school pence.[16] The girls' school, which also took infants, amalgamated with the infant school in Mount Street in 1891.[17] In 1907 the school had 307 pupils on the books, but in 1937 the number had fallen to 176, with average attendances of 154.[18] From 1937 the school, by then usually known as St. Mary's C. of E. school, took infants and juniors only and by 1947 had assumed voluntary controlled status. In 1959 it had 223 pupils on its books. From 1961 it took infants only, in 1973 moved to Park Road, and in 1977 amalgamated with St. Matthew's school in Oakfield Road. The school thus formed was known as St. Mary's C. of E. school and took children up to the age of 11. In 1988 the estimated number on roll was 263.[19]

In 1846 there was a school in the union workhouse where a master and mistress taught 20 girls and 38 boys.[20] In the following year schools were being built in Eastover for 240 children. The site, in St. John's Place, later Blake Place, had been bought by J. Moore Capes, first minister of St. John's, who with the Poole family and a grant from the National Society paid for the buildings.[21] The original buildings, in the early Tudor style, were extended probably in 1869.[22] In 1875 a total of 404 pupils paid school pence,[23] but average attendance was 357 in 1906–7 and 190 in 1937–8.[24] By 1947, when there were 250 children on the books, St. John's (Eastover Parochial) school

was a voluntary aided primary school. In 1975 the school transferred to new buildings in Weston-zoyland Road and from 1983 was called St. John and St. Francis C. of E. school. In 1988 the estimated number on roll was 342.[25]

Two cottages known as School Cottages in Gordon Terrace were bought c. 1846 for the newly founded Catholic mission there, and one was in use as a school by 1850. St. Joseph's school received a diocesan grant in 1859, and by the 1870s was taking pupils from both the town and Highbridge. The school occupied the former mission church in 1882, but in the following year it moved to new premises on the north side of the new Catholic church in Binford Place. There was accommodation for 70 pupils, and parents paid school pence. Between 1885 and 1891 teachers were drawn from the adjoining convent; the school gradually declined after the sisters left, and in 1894, having 41 pupils, was closed. It was reopened during the First World War for the children of Belgian refugees, but from 1918 was used only for the Sunday school and other parish purposes.[26]

In 1940 it was reopened to take the influx of evacuees, but was not considered necessary by the education authority and remained not fully recognized. The teaching staff were drawn from sisters of the Holy Rosary convent and classes were held both in the original school and in the former convent buildings in King Street. The number on roll on opening was 57 and within a year had risen to 115. By 1955 there were 205 pupils, and classes were also held in Cranleigh Gardens and Salmon Parade. In common with other schools in the town, it took only juniors and infants from 1957; in 1963 there were 131 children on the books.[27] The original buildings were finally replaced by St. Joseph's Roman Catholic aided primary school, Park Avenue, opened in 1963 for 240 pupils. An extension was built in 1973. The estimated number on roll in 1988 was 242.[28]

The West Street Ragged school was opened in 1860[29] for boys and girls, and a new classroom was added in 1870.[30] By 1875, known as the West Street National (later C. of E.) school and occasionally as Trinity National, it was for boys only and there were 169 paying school pence.[31] By 1889 girls were again taught, and in 1907 there were 173 boys and girls and 111 infants on the books.[32] Average attendances fell to 152 in 1921–2 and fluctuated in the 1930s.[33] By 1947 the school had adopted voluntary controlled

[12] S.R.O., D/N/bw. chch 4/2/1, 4/3/6.
[13] Ibid. 4/2/1–3, 4/3/1, 4/3/6, 6/3/1; D/B/bw 16/4/4; ibid. C/E 4/181/2, 334; *Public Elem. Schs.* H.C. 133 (1875), lix.
[14] *Slater's Dir. Som.* (1852–3); *V.C.H. Som.* ii. 447–8.
[15] Nat. Soc. *Inquiry, 1846–7*, Som. 4–5; *Robson's Dir. Som.* (1839); S.R.O., T/PH/law; ibid. DD/EDS 3622; St. Mary's sch., draft Scheme S.O. 8091.
[16] *Public Elem. Schs.* H.C. 133 (1875), lix.
[17] S.R.O., D/P/bw. m 18/8/1; St. Mary's sch., girls' sch. log bk. 1863–1905.
[18] S.R.O., C/E 4/184/1; *Bd. of Educ., List 21, 1908, 1938* (H.M.S.O.).
[19] S.R.O., C/E 4/64; St. Mary's sch., admission reg. girls' and inf. sch. 1937–75; managers' min. bk. 1968–75.
[20] J. B. B. Clarke, *Acct. of Church Educ. among Poor* (1846).
[21] Nat. Soc. *Inquiry, 1846–7*, Som. 4–5; H. E. Field and T. B. Dilks, *St. John the Baptist, Bridgwater, 1846–1946*, 4.

[22] S.R.O., DD/EDS 5544; Field and Dilks, *St. John the Baptist, Bridgwater*, 9.
[23] *Public Elem. Schs.* H.C. 133 (1875), lix.
[24] *Bd. of Educ., List 21, 1908, 1938*.
[25] S.R.O., C/E 4/64; inf. from Mrs. G. I. Atkins, sch. sec.
[26] R. I. Hancock, 'St. Joseph's R.C. Sch., Bridgwater, 1883–1983' (TS. at St. Joseph's sch., based on original sources since destroyed).
[27] Ibid.
[28] S.R.O., C/E 4/64; Hancock, 'St. Joseph's Sch.' 22.
[29] *Bridgwater Times*, 20 Apr. 1859; 25 July 1860; S.R.O., D/D/WBf 9/3.
[30] S.R.O., DD/EDS 3224.
[31] *Public Elem. Schs.* H.C. 133 (1875), lix; *Kelly's Dir. Som.* (1883).
[32] *Kelly's Dir. Som.* (1889); S.R.O., C/E 4/184/1.
[33] *Bd. of Educ., List 21, 1923, 1938*.

status and there were 230 children under 11 on its books. From 1958 it took juniors only, and was renamed St. Matthew's C. of E. school. In 1964 the school moved to a site in Oakfield Road and in 1977 it was joined by St. Mary's school, formerly in Park Road.[34]

BOARD SCHOOLS. A school board for the borough was established in 1870; its members visited 27 public and private schools and decided that schools were needed in the populous districts east and west of the town.[35] A united school district for the borough and the extra-municipal parts of the parish was formed compulsorily in 1875.[36]

Eastover school opened in 1873 in Cornborough Place, off Wellington Road.[37] In 1875 a total of 607 pupils there paid school pence.[38] In 1897 a new junior mixed school was established on the site, and in 1899 the school had 1,334 pupils.[39] In 1906–7 average attendance was 1,072, divided between four departments, boys, girls, junior mixed, and infants. It fell to 1,038 in 1913–14, and to 423 in 1937–8.[40] In 1947 the school was reorganized for juniors and infants; in that year there were 475 pupils on the books. In 1969 the juniors moved to new buildings in Wellington Road, and in 1975 were joined by the infant classes to form Eastover primary school. In 1988 the estimated number on roll was 347.[41]

A second board school was established, for the western side of the town, in Albert Street in 1880, for 716 pupils. It was enlarged in 1896–7, and in 1906–7 average attendance was 718, the number on the register being 846.[42] Attendance declined to 436 in 1937–8, but in 1947, when juniors and infants only were taken, there were on average 562 on the books.[43] In 1958 the school changed its name to Friarn, and in 1978 the juniors moved to the former Westover school site in Wembdon Road. The infants remained in Albert Street until 1981 when the school was reunited in Wembdon Road. In 1988 there were 307 pupils on the books.[44]

COUNCIL SCHOOLS FOUNDED SINCE 1903. A pupil teacher centre for girls opened at the Art and Technical Institute in 1904. Preparatory classes were added in 1912, and in 1913 there were 39 pupils aged 10 and over. In 1919 it became a recognized secondary school, and in 1923 had 135 pupils. In 1929 the school moved to new premises in Park Road, where pupil teaching continued. There were 226 on the register in 1933 and 266 local pupils and 21 evacuees in 1943.[45] The school closed in 1973 as part of the introduction of a comprehensive system

in the area.[46] The former school buildings became an area teachers' centre, and in 1988 the Somerset Education Centre.[47]

Westover senior council school, Wembdon Road, opened in 1937 with average attendance of 585 boys and girls.[48] As Westover secondary modern school it had 672 pupils on the roll in 1947 and 931 in 1955. The school closed in 1973. In 1978 the buildings were taken over by Friarn school.[49]

In 1944 a county secondary technical school was established in Lonsdale House, Blake Street, for boys of 13 and over. In that year there were 24 boys on roll, and 124 boys in 1959. The school, regarded as part of the technical college, closed in 1964.[50]

Three new schools were opened between 1956 and 1966 to provide secondary places for children from the north, east, and south sides of the town. Hamp secondary modern school was opened in Hamp Avenue in 1956. Its name was changed to the Blake secondary modern in 1957 and from 1973 it became a comprehensive school. In 1957 there were 324 pupils on the books, and in 1975 the number had risen to 719 aged 11–16. In 1988 the estimated number on roll was 638. Sydenham secondary modern school opened in 1961 in Parkway. In 1973 it became comprehensive, and in 1988 was a community school. There were 758 pupils on the books in 1965, 963 in 1975, and an estimated 660 in 1988. Chilton Trinity school, Chilton Street, opened as a secondary modern in 1966 and became comprehensive in 1973. In 1975 there were 925 pupils on the books and in 1988 an estimated 797.[51] Haygrove comprehensive school, Durleigh Road, was created in 1973; senior classes used the buildings of the former Dr. Morgan's boys' grammar school while junior classes were initially in the former Westover school buildings.[52] In 1975 there were 1,155 pupils on the books, and in 1988 an estimated 743.

Four new county primary schools were opened in 1952. Two shared a site in Rhode Lane, Hamp. In that year Hamp junior school had 150 pupils on the books, and Hamp infant school had 65 pupils. By 1975 the junior school had 316 pupils and the infant school 210. Numbers fell gradually thereafter, and in 1988 the numbers were 237 and 192 respectively. The other two schools opened in Bath Road, the junior school having 112 on the books and the infant 60. From 1959 the schools were renamed Sydenham, and in 1975 numbers had risen to 321 juniors and 200 infants. In 1979 the infant school was renamed Willowside, but from 1981 both were known as Sedgemoor Manor school after amalgamation with Bower infant school. In 1981

34 S.R.O., C/E 4/64; *Daily Express*, 30 Sept. 1969.
35 S.R.O., C/E 4/181/1.
36 *Lond. Gaz.* 24 Nov. 1874, 5603.
37 S.R.O., D/B/bw 2403.
38 *Public Elem. Schs.* H.C. 133 (1875), lix.
39 S.R.O., C/E 4/181/9; cf. ibid. D/B/bw 2421.
40 *Public Elem. Schs.* H.C. 133 (1875), lix; *Bd. of Educ., List 21, 1908, 1915, 1923, 1938*.
41 S.R.O., C/E 4/64; log bks. 1878–1974 are ibid. 4/185/1; 4/351/1–3.
42 Ibid. 4/181/4–5, 184/1–3; *Kelly's Dir. Som.* (1906); *Bd. of Educ., List 21, 1908*; cf. S.R.O., D/B/bw

2401, 2403.
43 *Bd. of Educ., List 21, 1938*; S.R.O., C/E 4/64.
44 S.R.O., C/E 4/64; *Bridgwater Mercury*, 20 Nov. 1984.
45 S.R.O., C/E 4/71, 184/2–3, 362.
46 Ibid. 4/71.
47 Ibid. 4/64.
48 *Bd. of Educ., List 21, 1938* .
49 S.R.O., C/E 4/64; log bk. 1966–73 is ibid. 4/362/3.
50 Ibid. 4/64; Bridgwater Coll., admission reg. 1944–64; ibid. H.M.I. rep. 1959.
51 S.R.O., C/E 4/64.
52 Ibid. 4/362.

there were 383 juniors and 204 infants. Bower infant school was opened in 1969 in Parkway, and in 1975 had 147 pupils on the books. Bower junior, on the same site, opened in 1972, with a unit for disturbed children, and in 1975 there were 259 children attending. Both were closed in 1981 and joined with Sydenham as Sedge-moor Manor school. The former infant school became the headquarters of the school library service in 1982.

There was a county nursery school in Rhode Lane in 1947 which then had 38 children. It closed in 1953. A second county nursery school, called St. John's, was established in Monmouth Street near Blake Place in 1947 with 39 children on the books. There were 50 in 1975. In 1976 it moved to Parkfield, but it had closed by 1980.

Elmwood special school, Hamp Avenue, opened in 1956, was the first purpose-built special school in the county. It took pupils from 5 to 16, and in 1981 there were 145 on the books. A second special school, taking children from 2 to 16, was opened in 1971, and is known as the Bridgwater Penrose special school, Albert Street. In 1975 there were 46 on the books.[53]

TERTIARY EDUCATION 1860–1989. In 1860 the Bridgwater School of Art was opened in George Street, possibly in association with the Literary and Scientific Institution there.[54] Another art school was established in Queen Street in 1888, and in 1891 it moved to Lonsdale House, Blake Street, where art and technical schools were formally established. In the following year continuation night schools were also held there.[55] The Bridgwater Art and Technical (later Technical and Art) Institute, from 1958 the Bridgwater Technical College, expanded to premises in Mount Street and Queen Street, and in 1959 to new buildings in Broadway. In 1975 it also occupied premises in Park Road. A new building in Bath Road was first occupied in 1978, and in 1988 most of the college departments were housed there, the Broadway site retaining the building and continuing education departments. In 1973 it became a tertiary college, and in 1989 had 667 full-time, 3,288 part-time day and evening vocational, and 3,443 part-time day and evening leisure students.[56]

PRIVATE SCHOOLS FROM 1822. Five academies were listed in 1822 and 8 in 1830, 5 of which were partly or wholly for boarders.[57] In 1861 there were 23 schools listed, many of them held in the large houses in Castle Street and King Square.[58] Several schools were conducted by clergymen, including a classical school under the Revd. Dr. Henry Trend in Northgate in 1840, or were connected with smaller churches, such as an infant school in St. John Street attached to the Mariners Christian chapel 1842–52.[59] Among the more successful private schools of the later 19th century were the Collegiate School in Blake Street, which had moved to Green Dragon Lane by 1897 and remained in the town until its move to Malmesbury (Wilts.) in 1946,[60] and a girls' school held in College House, North Street, by 1889 and until 1931 or later.[61]

There were several private schools in the parish in the 20th century, many of them short-lived. Among them were Aventicum school, Northfield, established by 1910 and open until 1924 or later, and Clarendon College or House, Dampiet Street, open between 1919 and 1937. St. Margaret's high school for girls began c. 1923 in King Street, later moving to Taunton Road, and finally to the corner of Wembdon Road and Northfield. It closed in 1987.[62] A school was held at the Holy Rosary convent, Durleigh Road, between 1939 and 1963.[63]

CHARITIES FOR THE POOR. ALMSHOUSES. An almshouse had been established outside the west gate by 1454–5. It was endowed with little or no land, but the town bailiffs undertook repairs, and from 1546 it received a small sum, later 5s., from a tenement and garden given by John Bentley.[64] In 1551 the almshouse contained four poor men and women who in that year received bedding from a testator.[65] By 1618 the inmates were four women.[66] In 1558 the building was extensively repaired, largely through gifts in cash and in kind from townsmen.[67] The building was 'utterly demolished' during the siege of the town in 1645, but the town receiver was paying the 5s. as a gift to or as rent for the last inmate in 1653–4, and the same sum for a man who was probably her son in 1655.[68] The site, let on a building lease in 1667, and occupied by a private house within a year, was on the south side of West Street, on the corner of a lane leading to Roper's Lane, opposite the Bell (later White Ball) inn.[69]

In 1483 Thomasina Hill left £40 to rebuild an almshouse for men,[70] perhaps referring to the house in West Street. A year earlier a house for 13 poor men and women was projected, but reference in 1498 to a single almshouse in the town suggests that it was not built.[71]

A second almshouse in the town had been

---

53   Ibid. 4/64.
54   P.O. Dir. Som. (1861); S.R.O., Q/RSl 1.
55   Bridgwater Coll., Min. Bks. M1–4, Letter Bks. L1–3; P. Campion, 'The Beginnings of Art and Technical Education in Bridgwater, 1887–1904' (TS. for B. Ed. in coll. libr.).
56   S.R.O., C/E 4/64, 5/45; Bridgwater Coll., Min. Bk. M6; inf. from Mrs. B. Hunt, Bridgwater Coll.
57   Pigot, Nat. Com. Dir. (1822–3, 1830).
58   P.O. Dir. Som. (1861).
59   Co. Gaz. Dir. Som. (1840); Pigot, Nat. Com. Dir. (1842); Slater's Dir. Som. (1852–3).
60   Kelly's Dir. Som. (1883); Whitby & Sons, Dir. Bridgwater (1897); Whitby, Light, & Lane, Dir. Bridgwater (1938); Som. Co. Herald, 14 Aug. 1964.
61   Kelly's Dir. Som. (1889, 1931).

62   Ibid. C/E 4/362/4–9; Kelly's Dir. Som. (1910, 1931, 1939); Dir. Bridgwater (1929); Whitby, Light, & Lane, Dir. Bridgwater (1937–40); Independent Schs. Som. & Glos. (n.d.); Bridgwater Mercury, 21 Jan. 1987.
63   Local inf.; Bridgwater Mercury, 15 Oct. 1985.
64   S.R.S. lx, nos. 785, 850; Leland, Itin. ed. Toulmin Smith, i. 163, 298; S.R.O., D/B/bw 645–6, 1533, 1540, 1591, 1607, 2291. The suggestion that it was originally a hospital of St. Giles (Knowles and Hadcock, Med. Religious Hos. 346) cannot be sustained.
65   S.R.O., D/B/bw 1678.   66   Ibid. 1607.
67   Ibid. 1768.   68   Ibid. 1516, 1617, 1619–22.
69   Ibid. 1263, 1269, 1686; D/B/bw C.L. 41, 44; ibid. T/PH/bw (map c. 1806); T/PH/law (no. 414 on plan).
70   S.R.S. xvi. 247.
71   Ibid. 364; lxx, no. 1011; S.R.O., D/B/bw 1390.

established near the south gate by *c.* 1603.[72] The corporation made weekly payments to support the almspeople and maintained the building, partly from the gift of Alexander Jones (mayor 1598, d. 1609), who *c.* 1603 paid £100 to the town, partly for the repair of the almshouse. Most of the gift was used to buy the rectory estate, but 2*s.* a week from the gift was still paid to the almspeople together in 1715.[73] In 1618 there were 12 almsfolk,[74] and from 1658 they were paid £3 a year, the interest on a sum bequeathed by Bernard Sparke to be lent to tradesmen.[75] The almshouse was said to have been 'utterly demolished', probably during the siege in 1645, but it was rebuilt in brick in 1693–5, partly paid for by the gift of £300 from Major Matthew Ingram, a native of the town. The gift was augmented in 1699 by £100 given by Mary Brent, which was laid out in the purchase of land in Hamp. The almshouse evidently remained unfinished for some years.[76] By 1800 Dorothy Holworthy's charity was being distributed to the almsfolk; by 1820 the almshouse was let to the churchwardens for use as a parish poorhouse, and both its founder and its original purpose had been forgotten.[77] The building, which stood outside the south gate, on a narrow site between the road to Taunton and the path to Hamp known as Hamp Ward,[78] was extended in 1830 by the addition of an engine house, a mortuary, and two rooms for vagrants. The building, proposed to be sold in 1851,[79] was still standing in 1865 but was then unoccupied, and it had been demolished by 1887.[80]

By trust deed dated 1952 Ernest John Waddon established the Rose Waddon Rest Home charity in memory of his wife to provide homes for female pensioners of 60 and more resident in the borough for 20 years. Three cottages were replaced by four flats, no. 21 Chilton Street.[81]

OTHER CHARITIES. By will proved 1553 John Colverd or Colvord devised to the mayor and burgesses the residue of his estate in reversion to pay 40*s.* a year to the poor. Payments from the estate had begun by 1561 and continued until 1609,[82] but thereafter seem to have been regarded as part of the general funds of the corporation. Elizabeth Prowse by will proved 1554 devised land in trust, the mayor to receive each year 20*s.* for the poor. The tenants of the land seem not to have paid the rent from *c.*

1606.[83] Robert Blake by deed dated 1592 gave £240, the interest to be partly for poor relief.[84] Gifts of cash and clothing were made from the endowment in 1605,[85] and the charity formed part of the poor stock of the corporation in the later 18th century but seems to have been lost in the 19th.[86] Richard Tapp or Tilley gave by will proved 1599 a sum which was later held by the corporation. The interest on £40 was still distributed each Good Friday and Christmas Eve in 1786, but has not been found later.[87] Margaret Blake by will dated 1599 gave £10 to the corporation, the interest to provide smocks on All Saints' day for six poor women. The endowment was transferred to the corporation in 1602, but the charity seems to have been lost by 1715.[88] Christian Shercombe (d. 1613) left £10 for the poor in the hands of the corporation.[89] From 1787 the corporation used the income to buy cloth for the poor.[90] In 1839 the charity was transferred to the Bridgwater charity trustees.[91] By will dated 1633 Richard Castleman gave £300 to the aldermen of the town to be laid out in real property, one third of the income to be for the poor.[92] The endowment, used from 1787 to buy cloth, was transferred to the Bridgwater charity trustees in 1839.[93] Richard Holworthy by will dated 1643 gave £50, the interest to be distributed weekly in bread.[94] The charity was transferred to the Bridgwater charity trustees in 1839.[95] Admiral Robert Blake (d. 1657) gave £100 to provide food and clothing twice a year. In 1826 the income was used to buy cloth.[96] Dorothy Holworthy *c.* 1662 gave £140 10*s.* to buy land, the rent to be given to the poor. From 1787 it was used by the corporation to buy cloth for the poor.[97] The charity seems to have been lost between 1826 and 1839.[98] Dr. William Blake by will dated 1667 gave the interest on £100 already held by the corporation.[99] From 1787 it was used to buy cloth and in 1839 was transferred to the Bridgwater charity trustees.[1]

Robert Balch (d. 1705) gave a rent charge of 40*s.*, initially for the new workhouse, but it later passed to the corporation. The charity survived in 1786 but was lost after 1826.[2] Sir John Bawden gave £40 to the poor before 1715.[3] The charity was distributed in cloth from 1787 and was transferred to the Bridgwater charity trustees in 1839.[4] Gilbert Bloyce by will of 1717 gave a rent charge and John Gilbert by will of 1731 gave leasehold properties for weekly bread distributions.

---

[72] S.R.O., D/B/bw 1600, 1724.

[73] Ibid. 1516, 1527, 1617, 1620–23, 1724, 1937, 2083, 2291; D/P/bw. m 2/1/1 (11 Apr. 1609).

[74] Ibid. D/B/bw 1610.

[75] Ibid. 1527.

[76] *Cal. S.P. Dom.* 1656–7, 207; S.R.O., D/B/bw 570, 1526–7, 1639; *Char. Don.* pp. 1086–7; *15th Rep. Com. Char.* p. 428; *Bridgwater Times*, 2 Oct. 1853.

[77] S.R.O., T/PH/law; *Char. Don.* pp. 1086–7.

[78] S.R.O., D/B/bw C.L. 106.

[79] Ibid. D/P/bw. m 9/1/1.

[80] Squibbs, *Bridgwater*, pl. 20; O.S. Map 1/500, Som. L. 15. 11 (1887 edn.).

[81] Char. Com. reg.; inf. from Mr. Peter Butterworth, clerk to the trust.

[82] S.R.O., D/B/bw 1201, 1540, 1549, 1591, 1594, 1597, 1605, 1766, 2291.

[83] Ibid. 1678, 1747.

[84] Ibid. 1527.

[85] Ibid. 1882.

[86] Below, this section.

[87] *Som. Wills*, ed. Brown, v. 68; S.R.O., D/B/bw 2381.

[88] S.R.O., D/B/bw 905, 1527, 2014, 2291, 2319.

[89] Ibid. 1527, 1857.

[90] *15th Rep. Com. Char.* p. 422.

[91] S.R.O., D/B/bw 2408; below, this section.

[92] S.R.O., D/B/bw 1527.

[93] Ibid. 2408; *15th Rep. Com. Char.* p. 422; below, this section.

[94] S.R.O., D/B/bw 1527.

[95] Ibid. 2408; below, this section.

[96] *15th Rep. Com. Char.* pp. 429–30.

[97] Ibid. p. 422.

[98] Ibid.; S.R.O., D/B/bw 2408.

[99] S.R.O., D/B/bw 1527; *Som. Wills*, ed. Brown, ii. 102.

[1] *15th Rep. Com. Char.* p. 422; S.R.O., D/B/bw 2408.

[2] S.R.O., D/B/bw 1527, 2164; *Char. Don.* pp. 1086–7; *15th Rep. Com. Char.* p. 425.

[3] S.R.O., D/B/bw 1527.

[4] *15th Rep. Com. Char.* p. 422; S.R.O., D/B/bw 2408.

Both survived in 1826, the first as a dole until 1939.[5] Constance Harvey (d. 1718) gave £20 for poor widows, an endowment which was spent on cloth from 1787 and which was transferred to the charity trustees in 1839.[6] Anne Holworthy (d. 1745) gave the mortgage interest on a house, payment of which had ceased by 1826.[7] Before 1757 Samuel Darby gave 10s a year for a sermon on Good Friday and £10 to pay interest for the poor;[8] the £10 had been lost by 1826.[9] A rent charge of £5 given by one Grabham before 1715 has not been traced further.[10] Jane Habberfield by will dated 1813 gave a bread dole which by 1936 was used for sermons on Ash Wednesday and Ascension Day at St. Mary's church, a bread distribution, and the general parish poor fund.[11]

In 1786–7 there were said to be 17 endowed charities for the poor in the parish including 12 with a total capital value of over £780, and three others with a total rent charge income of over £54.[12] All seem to have been administered by the corporation, which from 1787 paid out annual interest of £30 in cloth for the poor from the endowments of Robert (d. 1657) and William Blake, Richard Castleman, Dorothy Holworthy, Sir John Bawden, Constance Harvey, and Christian Shercombe, together with the interest from the apprentice charity of Benjamin Vaughan (d. 1639) which was shared with Cannington.[13] The Richard Holworthy and John Gilbert bread charities were also still continued, the latter also providing cloth from surplus income in the first week in December. By 1826 the charity of Mary Brent was no longer paid to the inmates of the south gate almshouse, but instead to 4 or 5 widows not otherwise supported, who received weekly doles of 1s. 6d.[14] Mary Brent's charity, subject to a Scheme of 1864 and Orders of 1882 and 1900, in the 1960s provided pensions to poor people over 60.[15] The charity of Robert Blake (d. 1657) was in 1826 used to buy clothing, while those of Gilbert Bloyce and Jane Habberfield, the latter invested in consols and not in the corporation, continued as bread doles.[16]

In 1839 the corporation paid to a new body called the Bridgwater charity trustees the sum of £923 13s. 6d. in the name of 12 charities, including three educational charities.[17] In 1853 after the trustees refused to disclose their accounts people complained that out of capital of c. £1,200 only £40 went to the poor and implied that the rest, for education, was not distributed.[18] In fact, in that year the trustees, in the name of eight charities, paid out £66 18s. 8d. to help Dr. Morgan's educational charity to clothe 30 poor boys.[19] Under a Scheme of 1857 the charities of Robert Blake, Richard Castleman, and Dorothy and Richard Holworthy became part of the

endowment of the grammar school, later known as the King James exhibition, to provide exhibitions and scholarships for pupils in need; and the charities of Constance Harvey, Christian Shercombe, William Blake, Sir John Bawden, and Robert Balch became part of the endowment of Dr. Morgan's school. The educational charities thus established were thereafter known as the Bridgwater Municipal Charities, and were in 1989 administered by trustees as the King James exhibition and scholarship endowment, providing assistance for Bridgwater pupils in secondary or higher education.[20]

From 1839 there is no further trace of the charity of Robert Blake (d. 1592). Under a Scheme of 1898 the sermon charities of Richard Castleman and Samuel Darby, the Benjamin Vaughan apprentice charity, and the bequest of James Hartnell, to the governors of the King James exhibition by will proved 1866, became the United Charities. Hartnell's charity was transferred to the Board of Education in 1904; and the remainder, subject to minor modifications in 1964 and 1976, were in 1989 administered by Sedgemoor district council, which paid small sums to the vicar of Bridgwater in respect of Castleman's and Darby's charities and offered half the income from Vaughan's charity to help a needy Bridgwater child to enter a trade.[21]

There also remained in 1988 the charities of Robert Blake (d. 1657), John Gilbert, Gilbert Bloyce, and Jane Habberfield. The first two, administered by trustees under a Scheme of 1908, provided food and clothing for the inhabitants of Bridgwater borough. Bloyce's charity, in the 1930s a rent charge of £5 4s., was administered by the vicar of St. Mary's in place of bread doles on Sunday mornings. Habberfield's charity, a bread dole worth £3 9s. 6d. and a poor fund worth 9s. 6d., together with a small sermon charity, were also considered part of the charity income of St. Mary's church. It was administered by the vicar and churchwardens with part of the gift of James Cook, who by will of 1912 gave capital sums to the three parishes of St. Mary, St. John the Baptist, and Holy Trinity for distributions of meat and bread on Christmas Day. At Christmas 1964 the charities of Bloyce, Habberfield, and Cook were distributed at St. Mary's in vouchers worth 3s. each.[22]

By will proved 1848 Jane Axford gave investments, the income to be given on 1 January in money, provisions, or clothing to the poor of St. Mary's parish. The income was under £5 in 1966. Before 1896 Mary Ann Smith by will endowed pensions for poor widows or spinsters born in the parish; under a Scheme of 1964 the

5   15th Rep. Com. Char. pp. 426–7, 429; S.R.O., D/P/bw. m 17/3/1; Som. Co. Herald, 19 Aug. 1939; 5 Apr. 1947.
6   15th Rep. Com. Char. p. 422; S.R.O., D/B/bw 2408.
7   S.R.O., D/B/bw 2381; 15th Rep. Com. Char. p. 431.
8   Char. Don. pp. 1086–7; S.R.O., D/B/bw 1522, 1735.
9   15th Rep. Com. Char. p. 425.
10   S.R.O., D/B/bw 1527.
11   15th Rep. Com. Char. p. 430; S.R.O., D/P/bw. m 17/3/1.
12   Char. Don. pp. 1086–7.
13   S.R.O., D/B/bw 1527, 1784; above, Cannington, charities.

14   15th Rep. Com. Char. pp. 425–8.
15   Char. Com. reg.
16   15th Rep. Com. Char. pp. 429–30.
17   S.R.O., D/B/bw 1527, 2408.
18   Bridgwater Times, 2 Oct. 1853.
19   S.R.O., Q/RSc 3/2.
20   Som. C.C., Educ. Dept., educational foundations and trusts, file S 11; Bridgwater Chars. (publ. F. G. Dowty, 1857).
21   S.R.O., D/P/bw. m 17/5/1–2; Char. Com. reg.
22   Char. Com. reg.; S.R.O., D/P/bw. m 4/4/2, 17/2/1, 17/3/1, 17/7/1–2.

endowment became known as Towell's Charity Trust.[23] By indenture of 1898 Mary Katherine Lovell-Marshall gave £30 a year for pensions for poor people of 70 and over in the parishes of St. Mary and Holy Trinity. The trustees were empowered to pay rent or give assistance in kind.[24] Mrs. L. M. Mansfield before 1932 gave an income of between £25 and £50 for pensions for people who had lived in Bridgwater for 10 years and were unable to support themselves. 'Poor

distressed persons' in Bridgwater shared the income from the Manchip Trust, established by will of 1936 and administered under a Scheme of 1970. The Emma Pearce Memorial Fund was founded by will of 1942 for distributions to the needy widows and spinsters of St. Mary's and neighbouring parishes.[25] Miss L. M. Tamlin (d. 1942) by will gave £10,000 for the use of poor residents of the borough. The income was £1,480 in 1988 and 38 pensioners each received £40 in 1989.[26]

CHEDZOY

CHEDZOY parish lies immediately east of Bridgwater parish and at the western end of King's Sedgemoor; Chedzoy village is c. 4 km. from the centre of Bridgwater.[27] The second element in the name, 'eg' or 'ieg', signifies an island[28] and the village, with its adjoining arable fields, lies on an 'island' of Burtle marine sands[29] at 7.5 m., slightly above the surrounding alluvium, which is mostly below the 4-m. contour. The parish measures 615 ha. (1,519 a.), c. 136 a. having been transferred to Weston Zoyland in 1886.[30]

Chedzoy rhyne on the north is probably the oldest boundary, following a natural watercourse. Park wall rhyne, on the west and also in part natural, may be largely the product of drainage before the late 18th century. The eastern and southern boundaries with King's Sedgemoor were roughly defined by the drove around Chedzoy east field until part of the moor was allotted to the parish. By 1798 the eastern boundary was marked by King's Sedgemoor Drain and the southern by Chedzoy New Cut.[31]

The 'island' forming the heart of the parish was settled possibly in the Mesolithic period,[32] and timber trackways in the 3rd to 1st millennium B.C. linked it with Sowy or Zoy 'island' to the south-east.[33] Roman artifacts have been found in the parish,[34] and a possible Roman building was uncovered near Slape, at the north-western tip of the 'island'.[35]

Three routes established the later settlement pattern, formed the village at the centre of the parish along the arms of a **T**, and thus defined the areas of the three open arable fields. Those fields, east, north, and west, stretched from the village to the edge of the moors. In 1988 large areas of north and east fields remained unhedged.

From the junction of the three routes Ward's

Lane runs east to the hamlet of Parchey, which may be identified with Elney, mentioned between 1332 and the 16th century.[36] The parish church and village cross stand in Ward's Lane, and beyond them the boundary bank of the north field may have been the site of the 'high row' of cottages mentioned in 1350.[37] North-west from the village Chedzoy Lane leads to Slape Cross. Slape, a scattered settlement, straddling the boundary with Bridgwater parish, was recorded c. 1329.[38] Slapeland was said to have been the site of a chapel, and the remains of a large medieval house there[39] may have been those of Cauntelos manor house.[40] South-west from the village, the route passes along Frog Street and divides, leading west to Bridgwater and south to Fowler's Plot. The Bridgwater route was known as Port Wall in the late 14th century;[41] by the mid 19th century it was a drove in Chedzoy parish; its course beyond is now a footpath.[42] The hamlet of Fowler's Plot was so named in 1373.[43] Some houses in Chedzoy village are of the 17th century or earlier and are of rendered cob or rubble;[44] 19th- and 20th-century infilling is mostly brick.

Portwall and Longwall,[45] a causeway at Slape bridge,[46] a sluice at Slape,[47] and wiers[48] were built by the later 14th century to improve drainage in the meadows and moors; another causeway and walls, stepping stones, and bridges[49] played an important part in the exploitation of this difficult terrain. Features such as the Langmoor Stone or the Devil's Upping Stock marked crossing points over watercourses.[50] Part of the moor known as Bowlake, under water in the Middle Ages, was dry by 1576[51] but flooding elsewhere in the parish was common. Significant improvements came when the low-lying land south and east of the village was inclosed

[23] Char. Com. reg.
[24] S.R.O., D/P/bw. m 17/5/2; Char. Com. reg.
[25] Char. Com. reg.
[26] Inf. from Mr. D. F. Heal, clerk to the trustees.
[27] O.S. Map 1/50,000, sheet 182 (1974 edn.). This article was completed in 1988.
[28] Ekwall, *Eng. Place-Names*, 94, 154; *S.R.S.* lxiii, p. 372; S.R.O., DD/S/WH 111.
[29] Geol. Surv. map 1/50,000, solid and drift, sheet 295 (1984 edn.).
[30] *Census*, 1891, 1981.
[31] S.R.O., DD/SG 55, map c. 1795; M. Williams, *Draining of Som. Levels*, 149–52.
[32] *Proc. Som. Arch. Soc.* cxxiii. 7.
[33] Ibid. cxii. 159, 162; Som. C.C., Sites and Mons. Rec.
[34] Collinson, *Hist. Som.* iii. 94.
[35] *V.C.H. Som.* i. 329, 359; Som. C.C., Sites and Mons. Rec.

[36] B.L. Add. Ch. 15911; *Survey of the Lands of Wm., Earl of Pembroke*, ed. C. R. Straton (Roxburghe Club), ii. 443 sqq.; S.R.O., DD/S/ST 20.
[37] B.L. Add. Ch. 15971.   [38] Ibid. 15903.
[39] W. Stradling, *Priory of Chilton super Polden* (1839), 1–4, 22; S.R.O., DD/S/ST 20.
[40] P.R.O., SC 6/974/6; SC 6/Hen. VIII/3043; below, manors.   [41] B.L. Add. Ch. 16067.
[42] O.S. Map 6", Som. L. SE. (1887 edn.); O.S. Map 1/50,000, sheet 182 (1974 edn.).
[43] B.L. Add. Ch. 16059.
[44] S.R.O., DD/V/BWr 8.1.
[45] B.L. Add. Ch. 16063, 16067.
[46] Ibid. 15971.   [47] Ibid. 16005.
[48] Ibid. 15903–4.   [49] Ibid. 15973–4.
[50] G. Roberts, *Hist. of Duke of Monmouth*, ii. 73n.; *S.D.N.Q.* xxviii. 18.
[51] *Pembroke Survey*, ed. Straton, ii. 466.

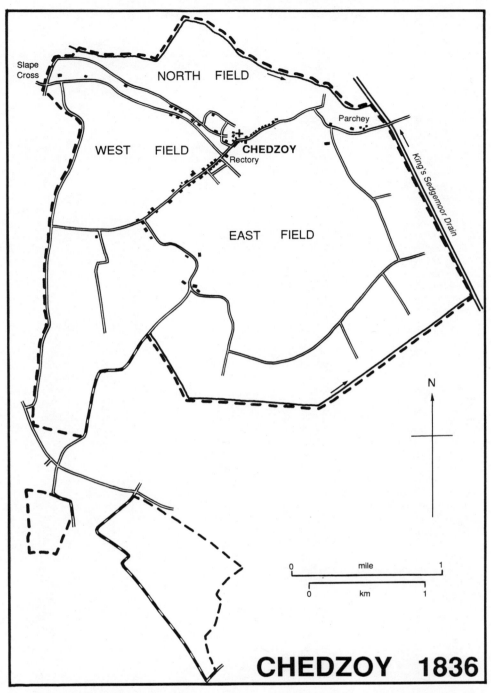

CHEDZOY 1836

under Acts of 1795 and 1797, and 344 a. of King's Sedgemoor were allotted to Chedzoy.[52] Meadows to the west of the parish were also divided and inclosed by 1836.[53] King's Sedgemoor Drain, constructed in 1797–8, proved inadequate for draining Chedzoy's moors and in 1861 the Chedzoy Internal Drainage District built a small pumping station on the Parrett, in Weston Zoyland parish, to drain the Chedzoy moors southwards.[54]

In 1331 twenty-five people were presented at the manor court for breach of the assize of ale, and a further three for selling ale by unlawful measure.[55] There was an inn or alehouse in Chedzoy in 1619 and 1629.[56] Between 1657 and 1690 the Bond family kept an inn which may have remained open until 1738 or later.[57] There is no further record of an inn until 1859 when the Crown stood beside the church.[58] It was last recorded in 1902.[59] A beerhouse was in business west of the church in 1861.[60] It had become known as the Manor House inn by 1881[61] and it

52   S.R.O., D/RA 1/8/1; D/P/chedz 20/1/2; ibid. tithe award.
53   Ibid. tithe award.
54   Williams, *Draining of Som. Levels*, 158, 211.
55   B.L. Add. Ch. 15906.

56   S.R.O., Q/RLa 33; *S.R.S.* xxiv. 91.
57   S.R.O., Q/RL.
58   *P.O. Dir. Som.* (1859); P.R.O., RG 11/2376.
59   *Kelly's Dir. Som.* (1902).   60   *P.O. Dir. Som.* (1861).
61   P.R.O., RG 11/2376.

remained open in 1988. Chedzoy friendly society, established in 1879, was still in existence in 1891.[62]

There were 240 communicants in the parish in 1548[63] and in 1683 there were 398 people of whom 62 were not native.[64] In 1801 the population numbered 457 and thereafter fluctuated reaching a peak of 549 in 1831 and declining steadily to 317 in 1891. It has remained stable since then, totalling 323 normally resident in 1981.[65]

William of Worcester stayed at Chedzoy on his travels through the area in 1478.[66] Forty-six men of the parish were fined after the 1497 rebellion.[67] After the battle of Sedgemoor on 6 July 1685 the rebels were pursued through the parish. Forty-two were killed in the east field, then under corn. Andrew Paschall, rector of Chedzoy 1662–96, wrote a description of the battle.[68] The parish was ordered to pay a share of the charges for executing the rebels and to provide labour for making a mound over a mass grave.[69] James II visited the site of the battle in 1686 and was entertained in the village.[70]

MANOR AND OTHER ESTATES. Chedzoy was a member of the royal manor of North Petherton in the 12th century, and Henry I granted it to Roger de Mandeville (d. 1130), though possibly only for life.[71]

Alfred de Pirou apparently held *CHEDZOY* manor in the 1140s.[72] Alexander de Pirou married Alice, widow of Richard de Montagu (d. by 1166) and mother of William de Montagu, who was later lord of Chedzoy. In 1195 William de Pirou paid to have possession of his inheritance in Chedzoy,[73] and was later succeeded by his son Richard who leased his land in Chedzoy to William Brewer.[74]

Chedzoy manor (from 1485 often called Chedzoy with Cauntelos)[75] was adjudged to William de Montagu in the court of John as count of Mortain; as king, John allowed William seisin in 1199.[76] William held the manor in 1212[77] but after his rebellion in 1215 he lost possession to William Brewer.[78] William de Montagu died in 1217, having apparently submitted to Henry III,

and custody of the land and of his grandson William de Montagu was given to Alan Basset.[79] Between 1219 and 1226 Brewer and Basset disputed possession of Chedzoy, Basset securing custody after Brewer's death in 1226.[80]

William de Montagu paid homage for his lands in 1234, presumably on his coming of age,[81] and died in 1270 when he was succeeded by his son Simon (d. 1317).[82] Simon's son William died in 1319[83] leaving a widow, Elizabeth (d. 1354), holding dower in Chedzoy,[84] and a son, also William (cr. earl of Salisbury 1337, d. 1344). William's two thirds passed to his widow Catherine (d. 1349).[85] On the death of William's son in 1397 the whole manor passed to his widow Elizabeth (d. 1415).[86] Thomas Montagu, earl of Salisbury, great-nephew of the last William, inherited the manor on Elizabeth's death and died in 1428 when Chedzoy became part of the dower lands of his widow Alice, later countess of Suffolk (d. 1475). An annuity from the manor was paid to Alice (d. 1462), Thomas's daughter and heir and wife of Richard Neville, earl of Salisbury.[87]

Their granddaughter and coheir Isabel, wife of George Plantagenet, duke of Clarence, inherited Chedzoy in 1475 but died in 1476 leaving an infant son Edward, earl of Warwick.[88] On his attainder in 1499 the manor was forfeit to the Crown, but his sister Margaret, widow of Sir Richard Pole, successfully petitioned for restoration in 1513–14 and became countess of Salisbury. Following her execution in 1539 the manor again reverted to the Crown.[89]

In 1553 the manor was granted to William Herbert, earl of Pembroke (d. 1570), who was succeeded in turn by his son Henry (d. 1601)[90] and Henry's sons William (d. 1630) and Philip (d. 1650).[91] Philip Herbert, earl of Pembroke and son of the last, sold the manor in 1652 to Henry Rolle and his son (Sir) Francis.[92] Sir Francis died c. 1686 leaving the manor in trust for his daughters. Priscilla, Sir Francis's widow, acquired the remaining interest in 1694 and held the manor until her death c. 1708.[93] She was followed by her brother-in-law, Denzil Onslow (d. 1721),[94] by his widow Jane (d. by 1747), by Jane's executor Henry Weston (d. by 1771),[95] and by

[62] M. Fuller, *W. Country Friendly Socs.* 139; S.R.O., DD/X/HUNT 1.
[63] *S.R.S.* ii. 55–6.
[64] S.R.O., D/P/chedz 2/1/1.
[65] *Census.*
[66] W. Worcestre, *Itineraries,* ed. J. Harvey, 37–8.
[67] *Fines Imposed in 1497,* ed. A. J. Howard, 26.
[68] Lamb. Pal. Libr. MS. 942/34; *S.D.N.Q.* xxviii. 17.
[69] MS. in possession of Mr. J. S. Cox, Guernsey. Corpses from the battle were dug up in 1872: Sydenham Hervey, diary, TS. in possession of R. Dunning.
[70] R. Dunning, *Monmouth Rebellion* (1984), 75.
[71] *Bk. of Fees,* i. 84; *Rot. Hund.* (Rec. Com.), ii. 140; for Roger de Mandeville, Sanders, *Eng. Baronies,* 42.
[72] *S.R.S.* xxv. 105.
[73] Ibid. viii, p. 105; xiv, p. 135; *Pipe R.* 1195 (P.R.S. N.S. vi), 39, 234.
[74] P.R.O., DL 25/200–1.
[75] Ibid. SC 6/974/6; Dors. R.O., D 124, box 10, acct. of ctess. of Salisbury 1529–30.
[76] *Rot. de Ob. et Fin.* (Rec. Com.), 8.
[77] *Bk. of Fees,* i. 84.
[78] *Rot. Litt. Claus.* (Rec. Com.), i. 252.
[79] Ibid. 313, 336.
[80] *Cur. Reg. R.* viii, p. 29; x, p. 125; xi, pp. 1, 233; xii,

pp. 168, 448–9; *Rot. Litt. Claus.* ii. 160.
[81] *Ex. e Rot. Fin.* (Rec. Com.), i. 257.
[82] *S.R.S.* iii. 10; *Complete Peerage,* ix. 80–2, where Simon's death is given erroneously as 1316; *Cal. Inq. p.m.* vi, p. 75; *Cal. Fine R.* 1307–19, 341.
[83] *Cal. Chart. R.* 1257–1300, 346; *Cal. Inq. p.m.* vi, p. 142.
[84] *Cal. Close,* 1318–23, 192, 194; *Cal. Inq. p.m.* x, p. 147.
[85] *Cal. Close,* 1343–6, 307; *Cal. Inq. p.m.* ix, p. 274.
[86] P.R.O., C 136/94, no. 35; *Feud. Aids,* vi. 505; *Cal. Fine R.* 1413–22, 94–5; *Cal. Inq. Misc.* 1399–1422, p. 62.
[87] *Cal. Close,* 1422–9, 422; *Cal. Pat.* 1422–9, 504; *S.R.S.* xxii. 189; *Complete Peerage,* xi. 393–5.
[88] *Cal. Pat.* 1476–85, 522, 528.
[89] P.R.O., C 142/28, no. 22; B.L. Harl. Ch. 43 F 8; *Cal. Pat.* 1553, 169; *Complete Peerage,* ix. 83; xi. 399–402; xii(2), 394–7.
[90] *Cal. Pat.* 1553, 169; 1555–7, 492; P.R.O., C 142/154, no. 79; C 142/264, no. 181.
[91] P.R.O., WARD 7/80, no. 203; *Complete Peerage,* x. 410–18.
[92] P.R.O., CP 25(2)/592/1652 East.
[93] S.R.O., DD/S/WH 111; *Som. Wills,* ed. Brown, 1. 84.
[94] Burke, *Peerage* (1949), 1529; S.R.O., DD/BR/to 2.
[95] S.R.O., DD/S/FA 5, 37; DD/S/ST 19/3.

Henry's executor, Heneage Finch, earl of Ayles-ford (d. 1777).[96] In 1775 Jane Henley, countess of Northington, with others, conveyed the manor to William Lawson[97] possibly in trust for John Dawes, the owner in 1781.[98] Dawes died c. 1788 leaving his estate to his son John who in 1791 sold the manor to Sir Robert Mackreath. Sir Robert conveyed it in 1802 to Thomas Porter,[99] on whose death in 1815 Chedzoy passed in turn to his sons William (d. c. 1821) and Henry (d. 1858). In 1860 the estate was ordered to be sold.[1] The lordship was not recorded later. Many farms were purchased by tenants c. 1861 but most were bought immediately afterwards by Oxford University, the owners in 1988.[2]

The capital messuage of the manor with garden and dovecot was recorded in 1320[3] and a hall, garderobe, and stable were repaired in 1341–2.[4] In 1344 the house was said to be ruinous.[5] In 1576 the dovecot was held with a field called Court close,[6] which may have been near Court Farm, an early 17th-century cob and stone house.[7] A house called Manor House, later probably Manor Farm, was described as newly built in 1860. It was then occupied by the estate steward and accommodated the owner when visiting the estate.[8]

By 1350 John de Cauntelo and Isabel his wife held a house and land of Chedzoy manor for their lives.[9] The capital messuage called Cauntelos probably stood at Slapeland and disappeared between 1537 and 1576.[10]

Bruton priory had an estate in Chedzoy in 1291[11] and 1362,[12] but in 1485 a messuage and 13 a. were described as formerly belonging to the prior.[13]

ECONOMIC HISTORY. In the 1270s Chedzoy was remembered as having been a dairy (*vaccaria*) of the royal estate at North Petherton in the early 12th century.[14] By 1320 the grassland there comprised 160 a. of enclosed pasture.[15] There were also parcels of overland, probably under grass, which were let to customary tenants. Grassland on the moors was shared with other lordships. In 1235 William de Montagu and the abbot of Glastonbury had agreed to divide receipts for grazing on what was called Weston Marsh or Sowy Land, an agreement

apparently still in force in the later 16th century.[16] In the early 14th century tenants of Dunwear and others were presented for grazing sheep and geese illegally on the commons.[17]

The arable land held by customary tenants in 1320 included 28 holdings of ½ virgate and 33 of a fardel. There were 16 cottagers (*cottelli*) and four other customary tenants. The tenants' cash rents amounted to over £79. There were also 2 freeholdings, one of a virgate, paying rents worth 10s. 8d. and a further tenant paying 12d. There was no demesne farm.[18]

The whole manor was worth £101 8s. 5d. net in 1320.[19] The rents remained constant between 1330 and 1378, although arrears in 1362–3 exceeded 40 per cent of the rental.[20] At least 16 tenants died in 1348 and although new tenants were admitted almost immediately further deaths led to several holdings remaining in hand. Some were later let out for short terms.[21] In 1360 there were 18 men and women who refused to do autumn work and withdrew their labour.[22] Incidental sources of income in the Middle Ages included chevage, paid in iron, wax, and cash.[23] Manumissions were granted in the later 14th century[24] but there were still at least three neifs in 1576.[25] By 1484–5 the rent income had only marginally increased.[26] In 1529–30 there was a small increase in income[27] and by 1588–9 the annual income was over £111. In 1624 arrears of nearly £127 had been accumulated and rents were static but court profits and fines reached £352.[28]

By 1576 a home farm of just over 100 a. had been established. The remainder of the estate was divided between c. 70 tenants with 76 holdings of which the largest was 42 a. and most were between 10 a. and 30 a.; the home farm and most of the tenants' lands lay in scattered strips.[29] Crops in the 17th century included peas, beans, barley, and wheat.[30] Dairy cows, pigs, and poultry were frequently recorded in probate inventories, but only two small flocks of sheep were mentioned.[31] One farmer left 40 cheeses and another 4 cwt. of cheese.[32] Movable shelters were made for summer use on the moors.[33]

Clover had been introduced by the mid 18th century[34] but cattle were still turned into the cornfields from harvest until sowing. Two men from Pawlett and Dunwear were fined in 1747

96 Ibid. DD/X/RY 4/2; Burke, *Peerage* (1949), 104.
97 P.R.O., CP 25(2)/1399/15 Geo. III Mich.
98 S.R.O., Q/REl 29/3.
99 Ibid. D/N/bmc 2/1/2; DD/MY 35.
1 Ibid. D/N/bmc 2/1/2.
2 Ibid. DD/X/HUNT 6; DD/LC 2/12; D/R/bw 15/3/6; D/P/chedz 3/1/2; ibid. C/C 43/1; *P.O. Dir. Som.* (1861); inf. from Oxford University Chest Estates Office.
3 P.R.O., C 134/65, no. 3.
4 B.L. Add. Ch. 16125.
5 P.R.O., C 135/75, no. 2.
6 *Pembroke Survey*, ed. Straton, ii. 456.
7 S.R.O., DD/V/BWr 8.2.
8 Ibid. DD/FD 18.
9 B.L. Add. Ch. 16129.
10 P.R.O., SC 6/Hen. VIII/3043; *Pembroke Survey*, ed. Straton, ii. 442 sqq.
11 *Tax. Eccl.* (Rec. Com.), 198.
12 B.L. Add. Ch. 16015.
13 P.R.O., SC 6/974/6.
14 *Rot. Hund.* (Rec. Com.), ii. 40.
15 P.R.O., C 134/65, no. 3.

16 *S.R.S.* vi. 80–1; lix. 214–15; *Pembroke Survey*, ed. Straton, ii. 466; Hants R.O. 44M69 XVII/43.
17 B.L. Add. Ch. 15906, 15942.
18 P.R.O., C 134/65, no. 3; B.L. Add. Ch. 16134.
19 P.R.O., C 134/65, no. 3.
20 B.L. Add. Ch. 16117, 16138, 16144.
21 Ibid. 15961–3, 15965, 15981.
22 Ibid. 16009.
23 Ibid. 16117, 16134.
24 Ibid. 16139.
25 *Pembroke Survey*, ed. Straton, ii. 445, 451, 464.
26 P.R.O., SC 6/974/6; SC 6/Hen. VII/1329–33, 1850, 3039–43.
27 Dors. R.O., D 124, box 10.
28 B.L. Add. Ch. 16147.
29 *Pembroke Survey*, ed. Straton, ii. 442 sqq.
30 *S.R.S.* xliii. 96; S.R.O., DD/S/ST 19/2.
31 S.R.O., DD/SP inventories, 1635, 1637, 1670, 1681, 1723, 1749.
32 Ibid. 1645, 1749.
33 Ibid. 1641, 1645.
34 Ibid. 1749.

for stocking the common beyond the limit of five sheep an acre.[35] Despite constant tillage, the arable fields were worth 30s. an acre in 1795 and produced high quality wheat and barley.[36] By the end of the 18th century some of the holdings were rack rented but the largest was only 48 a. and although some tenants combined more than one tenancy only a few had more than 50 a.[37]

Seventy-seven families in 1821 were engaged in agriculture.[38] Some strips around the edges of the three great fields had been inclosed by the earlier 19th century, and by 1840 there were 14 farms measuring more than 50 a.[39] although much poverty resulted from the disappearance of subsistence holdings.[40] By then about one third of the land was arable and moduses were paid on calves, cows, colts, and ancient meadow.[41] In 1851 eleven farmers worked more than 100 a. and two had more than 200 a.[42] By the 1880s only the central core of the north and west fields remained uninclosed, although by that date strips had disappeared. East field was a much larger undivided area, and baulks and headlands were still used for common grazing.[43] The number of farm labourers increased from 58 in 1851 to 72 in 1861 but declined to 46 in 1881.[44] There were several market gardens in the later 19th century,[45] and in 1882 coarse potatoes, wheat, barley, and beans were grown and cheese was made. Oxford University was blamed for charging rents that ruined some tenants.[46] Farms continued to be amalgamated in the 20th century.[47]

Arable still accounted for about a third of the land in 1905.[48] In 1982 a return, including land outside the parish, recorded 185 ha. (457 a.) of arable producing wheat, barley, oats, maize, potatoes, fodder, and garden crops. Grassland supported 1,855 cattle with some pigs, poultry, and sheep. There were about 10 a. of non-commercial orchard. Most holdings were over 50 ha. (124 a.) and specialized in dairying and cattle-rearing.[49]

A glover was recorded in 1394 and a weaver in 1638.[50] Men from Chedzoy, including a pump-maker, imported timber through Bridgwater in the late 16th century.[51] In the early 19th century a local man supplied malt, hops, butter, cheese, beans, fowls, cider, and seed potatoes to people

from a wide area between the Quantocks and the Poldens.[52] A Chedzoy farmer in 1847 owned a Bridgwater sloop which was broken up in 1851.[53] A smithy was still in business in 1988.

MILLS. In 1320 the manor had a windmill and, possibly at Slape, a watermill[54] which was probably replaced by a windmill before 1348.[55] By 1330 there were three windmills. One, at Slape, described as new,[56] was known as the west mill in 1363–4.[57] It was probably one of the two mills which survived in 1529[58] but had gone by 1576.[59] The second windmill in 1330 was called the south mill and was still in use in 1342–3.[60] It probably stood near Fowler's Plot.[61] The third windmill mentioned in 1330 was later called Clos mill. It was blown down in 1379 but had evidently been rebuilt by 1381 and was in use in 1384.[62] A fourth windmill, mentioned in 1349–50 and described as the east mill,[63] may have been replaced by one bought at Barrington and re-erected in 1356–7.[64] It was sited in the east field on Mill Batch.[65] It was evidently of the smock post type and was blown down and destroyed in 1827.[66]

Two horse mills, used for grinding malt,[67] were held with the south mill and Clos mill. One of them was replaced in 1356–7 by one bought at Glastonbury and rebuilt.[68] One of them may have gone out of use by 1373.[69] The horsemill at Clos mill had burnt down by 1485.[70]

MARKET AND FAIR. In 1314 Simon de Montagu obtained a grant of a Tuesday market and a three-day fair at the feast of St. Mary Magdalene (22 July).[71] No trace of either has been found.

LOCAL GOVERNMENT. Court rolls for Chedzoy manor survive for 1330–77,[72] 1379–84,[73] 1403–13,[74] 1543,[75] 1652–9, 1665–7, 1679–80,[76] 1747, and 1756.[77] In the 1330s, when up to four courts were held each year, one or two reeves, a tithingman, a hayward, and aletasters were chosen in the court, and in 1334–5 wickmen, who maintained walls and sluices.[78] In the early 15th century the court appointed three reeves and a hayward.[79] In the later 16th century, when two courts leet and two manor courts were

35 S.R.O., DD/S/ST 19/3.
36 J. Billingsley, *Agric. of Som.* 198–9.
37 S.R.O., DD/MY 35.
38 *Census* (1821).
39 S.R.O., tithe award.
40 Ibid. D/D/Rb 1827; D/P/chedz 13/1/7.
41 Ibid. tithe award.
42 P.R.O., HO 107/1925.
43 O.S. Map 6", Som. L. SE. (1887 edn.); LI. SW. (1886 edn.); *Rep. Com. on Dep. Cond. of the Agric. Interests* [C. 3309], p. 43, H.C.(1882), xv.
44 P.R.O., HO 107/1925; ibid. RG 9/1625; RG 11/2376.
45 *P.O. Dir. Som.* (1861); *Kelly's Dir. Som.* (1883).
46 *Rep. Com. on Dep. Cond. of the Agric. Interests*, 43.
47 Local inf.
48 Statistics supplied by the then Bd. of Agric. 1905.
49 Min. of Agric., Fisheries, and Food, agric. returns, 1982.
50 B.L. Add. Ch. 26868; *Taunton Archdeaconry Wills*, ed. T. Phipps, 10.
51 S.R.O., D/B/bw 1481, 1493, 1497, 1503.
52 Ibid. DD/UK 8.
53 Ibid. DD/FA 11/1.
54 P.R.O., C 134/65, no. 3.

55 B.L. Add. Ch. 15906, 15963, 15965.
56 Ibid. 15906.   57 Ibid. 16138.
58 Dors. R.O., D 124, box 10.
59 P.R.O., SC 2/198/20; *Pembroke Survey*, ed. Straton, ii. 466.
60 B.L. Add. Ch. 15906, 15942.
61 Ibid. 16059–60.
62 Ibid. 15906, 26868; P.R.O., SC 2/198/19.
63 B.L. Add. Ch. 16129.
64 Ibid. 16136.
65 S.R.O., DD/MY 35; ibid. tithe award.
66 A. J. Coulthard and M. Watts, *Windmills of Som.* 45–6; *S.D.N.Q.* xxviii. 31.
67 B.L. Add. Ch. 16000.
68 Ibid. 16136.   69 Ibid. 16059–60.
70 P.R.O., SC 6/974/6.
71 *Cal. Chart. R.* 1300–26, 241.
72 B.L. Add. Ch. 15903–16075.
73 P.R.O., SC 2/198/19; B.L. Add. Ch. 16076, 26868.
74 B.L. Add. Ch. 16077–16102.
75 P.R.O., SC 2/198/20.
76 B.L. Add. Ch. 16103–16.
77 S.R.O., DD/S/ST 19/3.
78 B.L. Add. Ch. 15906–23. Cf. *S.R.S.* v. 39n.
79 B.L. Add. Ch. 16085.

held each year, a reeve, a tithingman, two constables, and two water bailiffs were chosen at the Michaelmas tourn.[80] Two haywards were also appointed in the mid 17th century,[81] and a reeve, two constables, a tithingman, and a hayward were in office in the mid 18th century.[82]

The court in the 14th century received payments of chevage besides entry and marriage fines, dealt with breaches of the assize of ale, strays, and pleas between tenants, and gave orders for the maintenance of drains and buildings. In the later 16th century the lord claimed the chattels of felons, waifs, and suicides, deodands, strays, and the assize of bread and of ale. In the mid 17th century the court supervised the use of the open fields and commons and the maintenance of fences, drains, and paths. A pound was mentioned in 1354[83] and 1486,[84] and a court house, which the homage of the manor had to repair, was destroyed by fire before 1360.[85] Archery butts were recorded in 1576[86] and the place where the cucking stool had stood was known in 1768.[87]

From the 17th century two churchwardens, two overseers, and two highway surveyors administered the parish,[88] the last two working with the manor court on roads, bridges, and drains.[89] A vestry met regularly in the 18th century and the poor were relieved in cash and in kind.[90] A doctor was engaged to attend the poor in 1781.[91] The overseers were probably using the church house by 1740 to house the poor; a poorhouse was mentioned in 1762.[92] From 1774 until 1802 or later another house was in use for the purpose,[93] and that was succeeded before 1840 by a cottage near Fowler's Plot.[94]

Chedzoy became part of the Bridgwater poor-law union in 1836, Bridgwater rural district in 1894, and Sedgemoor district in 1974.[95]

CHURCH. The church was a dependent chapel of North Petherton and was given with the mother church to Buckland priory on its foundation c. 1166.[96] Temporary burial rights were granted to the chapel, probably during the civil war in the 1140s.[97] The church had achieved independence by the early 13th century,[98] and was a sole rectory until 1978. It was held with

St. John the Baptist's, Bridgwater, between 1978 and 1984 and thereafter with Weston Zoyland.[99]

A dispute over patronage between the bishop of Bath, Buckland priory, and the lord of Chedzoy manor was settled in 1280 in favour of the lord, Simon de Montagu,[1] and the advowson descended with the manor until 1678 or later.[2] It was acquired by John Coney (d. c. 1713),[3] and remained in his family, several members of which were rectors, until Thomas Coney, rector 1835–40, sold it to Richard Luscombe, vicar of Moorlinch.[4] By 1861 George Mullens, rector 1855–91, had acquired the patronage and his nephew and successor, George Richard Mullens, held it from 1897 until 1940.[5] He was succeeded as patron by Mrs. S. A. Rowlands, but since 1960 the bishop of Bath and Wells has held the advowson.[6]

The church was valued at £20 in 1291,[7] £38 16s. 8½d. net in 1535,[8] and c. £300 in 1668.[9] Average income had fallen to £111 in 1829–31.[10] Tithes and offerings were worth over £37 in 1535[11] paid, it was later claimed, in the form of moduses.[12] Rectorial tithes were commuted for £385 5s. in 1840; tithes on Fowler's or Vowle's Mead, inclosed under Act of 1797 and worth then £2, were due to the bishop.[13] In the mid 12th century 3 a. of land appear to have been given to the church,[14] and the rector held a cottage by 1353.[15] In 1535 the glebe was valued at £2 3s. 6d. a year;[16] in 1626 it comprised 32¼ a. in the open fields.[17] It was assessed at 29 a. in 1840[18] and remained church property in 1978.[19] A rectory house stood with two barns and other buildings in 1626.[20] The house had been recently repaired in 1815[21] but was substantially rebuilt later.[22] In 1848 Charles Knowles designed additions in the Gothic style.[23] The house was replaced c. 1957 by a new building to the north, which itself was sold in 1978.[24]

The value of the living and the prominence of the patrons attracted distinguished and absentee rectors including Godfrey Giffard, rector in the mid 13th century and later bishop of Worcester 1268–1302,[25] and Thomas de Montagu, rector by 1391 and until 1394 or later and during that time dean of Salisbury.[26] John Welles, rector from 1415, died at the council of Constance in

80 *Pembroke Survey*, ed. Straton, ii. 442sqq.
81 B.L. Add. Ch. 16103.
82 S.R.O., DD/S/ST 19/3.
83 B.L. Add. Ch. 15986, 26868.
84 P.R.O., SC 6/Hen. VII/139.
85 B.L. Add. Ch. 16000, 16004, 16010, 16125, 16133.
86 *Pembroke Survey*, ed. Straton, ii. 466.
87 S.R.O., DD/X/RY 4/4.
88 Ibid. Q/SR 138/32–3; ibid. D/P/chedz 4/1/1, 4.
89 Ibid. D/P/chedz 4/1/4, 13/2/2, 14/5/1; DD/S/ST 19/4.
90 Ibid. D/P/chedz 13/2/1–3.
91 Ibid. 13/10/3.
92 Ibid. 4/1/4.
93 Ibid. 5/1/1, 13/2/1; DD/MY 35; ibid. Q/REl 29/3.
94 Ibid. tithe award.
95 Youngs, *Local Admin. Units*, i. 671, 673, 676.
96 *S.R.S.* xxv. 7–9; below, N. Petherton, church.
97 *S.R.S.* xxv. 105.
98 Ibid. xliv. 32–3.
99 *Dioc. Dir.*
1 *S.R.S.* xxv. 106; xliv. 3, 32–3.
2 Above, manor.
3 *Som. Incumbents*, ed. Weaver, 332.
4 S.R.O., DD/X/HUNT 6; DD/CH 45; D/D/Bo;

D/D/Bp; D/D/Vc 88; DD/BR/to 2; D/P/chedz 2/1/2; *Proc. Som. Arch. Soc.* cxii. 76.
5 S.R.O., D/P/chedz 2/1/2; *P.O. Dir. Som.* (1861); *Kelly's Dir. Som.* (1906, 1939).
6 *Crockford*; *Dioc. Dir.*
7 *Tax. Eccl.* (Rec. Com.), 198.
8 *Valor Eccl.* (Rec. Com.), i. 214.
9 S.R.O., D/D/Vc 24.
10 *Rep. Com. Eccl. Revenues*, pp. 130–1.
11 *Valor Eccl.* (Rec. Com.), i. 214.
12 S.R.O., DD/S/ST 19/3.
13 Ibid. tithe award; ibid. D/P/chedz 20/1/2.
14 *S.R.S.* xxv. 105.
15 B.L. Add. Ch. 15979.
16 *Valor Eccl.* (Rec. Com.), i. 214.
17 S.R.O., D/D/Rg 264.
18 Ibid. tithe award.   19 Inf. from Dioc. Office.
20 S.R.O., D/D/Rg 264.
21 Ibid. D/D/Rb 1815.
22 Ibid. DD/X/HUNT 1.
23 Ibid. D/D/Bbm 100.
24 Ibid. D/P/chedz 3/4/1.   25 *S.D.N.Q.* xviii. 66.
26 Emden, *Biog. Reg. Univ. Oxf. to 1500*; *Cal. Papal Reg.* iv. 401, 465; *Cal. Pat. 1391–6*, 514.

1417;[27] Nicholas Upton, rector 1427–34, wrote a book on heraldry and knighthood;[28] Thomas Northwich, rector 1470–87, was also prior of Eye (Suff.). Northwich's immediate successors were Christopher Urswick, rector 1487–8, a scholar, courtier, and diplomat,[29] and Richard Nykke, rector 1489–1501, bishop of Norwich 1501–36.[30] The parish was served by a chaplain in 1450 and 1463 and by two in 1468 and c. 1535.[31] The church had endowed lights, some probably established by 1406,[32] and c. 1510 the churchwardens maintained a rood light and a fund called Our Lady's service.[33] A chantry dissolved in 1548 had land in the parish and in Bridgwater, Axbridge, and Crediton (Devon).[34] A house called Our Lady house, mentioned in the early 16th century, may have been the predecessor of the five-bayed church house which was also used for holding manor courts in the 1570s.[35] It was being maintained by the churchwardens in the later 17th century[36] but the overseers paid for repairs in 1740.[37] A piece of land at Dunwear in Bridgwater was owned by the church by 1529 and continues to be let by candle auction.[38]

Nicholas Mason, rector from 1547, was deprived in 1554 but would not leave[39] and John Cotterell, rector 1558–72, was a considerable pluralist.[40] George Montgomery spent some time in Ireland from 1609 where he was bishop of Clogher and of Meath.[41] The rectory house was plundered during the Civil War and Walter Raleigh, rector 1620–46 and dean of Wells 1642–6, was imprisoned there.[42] There were usually 12 communicants in the 1770s.[43] In 1827 there were two services each Sunday[44] and by the early 1840s celebrations of communion were held eight times a year for 30 communicants.[45] Monthly communion was celebrated by a resident rector in 1870.[46]

The church of *ST. MARY*, so dedicated by 1343,[47] is built of coursed lias and comprises a chancel with north vestry, clerestoried nave with north and south transepts and aisles, a south porch, and a west tower. The arcades and the north aisle are of the earlier 13th century but the south aisle was widened in the early 14th century, aligning it with a chapel built on the south

side of the chancel when that was restored and altered in the later 13th century. The tower[48] was added in the earlier 16th century together with the porch, the clerestory, the arch into the north transept, and windows in the north aisle. The south chapel may have been demolished at the same time. A gallery in the north transept was removed c. 1845[49] and the chancel was rebuilt in 1884.[50]

The font is of the 13th century and among the furnishings are a pulpit and bench ends of the 16th century. The former reading desk (1620) is part of the organ screen, and the altar rails (1637) are under the tower arch. The screen of the 1880s incorporates part of the late medieval screen and rood loft which were removed c. 1841.[51] There is a memorial brass, probably of Richard Sydenham (d. 1499).[52]

The church plate includes a cup and cover of 1573 and a flagon of 1758.[53] Two bells, the great bell and the Lady bell, were recorded c. 1508–9[54] but the oldest surviving bell in a peal of six is of the late 16th century by Roger Semson.[55] The registers date from 1559 and are virtually complete.[56]

NONCONFORMITY. Two meeting houses were licensed for Independents in 1821[57] and one for Methodists in 1840, but none was recorded in 1843.[58] A house opposite the school was licensed in 1861 and the Wesleyan chapel was built in 1864,[59] probably on the same site. In 1882 the Bible Christians bought it but their mission failed due to 'religious intolerance' and in 1894 the chapel was put up for sale.[60] In 1901–2 the Wesleyans returned[61] but in 1924 services ceased. In 1927 the chapel was sold and converted into a dwelling.[62]

EDUCATION. A school was recorded in 1612 and in 1662 a man was licensed to teach writing, reading, accounts, ciphering, and grammar.[63] The overseers maintained a school between 1694 and 1777.[64] In 1819 a Sunday school taught 64 children but numbers had fallen to 42 by 1825.[65] In 1835 there were 73 at the Sunday school and

---

27 *S.R.S.* xvi. 86–7.
28 Ibid. xxxi, p. 55; xxxii, p. 167; *D.N.B.*
29 *S.R.S.* lii, pp. 34, 146; *Cal. Pat.* 1485–94, 170; *D.N.B.*
30 *S.R.S.* lii, pp. 155, 189; liv, pp. 38, 66; *D.N.B.*
31 *S.R.S.* xlix, pp. 139, 399; lii, p. 27; S.R.O., D/D/Vc 20.
32 B.L. Add. Ch. 16077.
33 Ibid. 16081–3; 16092.
34 *S.R.S.* ii. 229.
35 B.L. Add. Ch. 16081–3; *Pembroke Survey*, ed. Straton, ii. 466.
36 S.R.O., DD/S/ST 19/4.
37 Ibid. D/P/chedz 4/1/4; above, local govt.
38 S.R.O., DD/S/ST 19/4; *Bridgwater Mercury*, 19 July 1988.
39 *Cal. Pat.* 1547–8, 188; S.R.O., D/D/Va 18; D/D/Ca 22.
40 Emden, *Biog. Reg. Univ. Oxf.* 1501–40.
41 *Cal. S.P. Dom.* 1603–10, 199; S.R.O., DD/WO 54/8.
42 S.R.O., D/P/chedz 2/1/1; D/D/Ca 235; D/D/Vc 81; *D.N.B.*
43 S.R.O., D/D/Vc 88.
44 Ibid. D/D/Rb 1827; D/P/chedz 2/1/2.
45 Ibid. DD/X/HUNT 1; D/D/Va 1843.
46 Ibid. D/D/Va 1870.

47 B.L. Add. Ch. 15944.
48 Emden, *Biog. Reg. Univ. Oxf. to 1500*, s.v. Hugh Pole; S.R.O., DD/X/SR 5.
49 S.R.O., DD/DN 306.
50 Ibid. DD/X/HUNT 1; for a view of the church in 1838, below, plate facing p. 313.
51 F. B. Bond and B. Camm, *Roodscreens and Roodlofts*, 155.
52 *S.R.S.* xvi. 387.
53 *Proc. Som. Arch. Soc.* xlvii. 156; S.R.O., D/P/chedz 4/1/1, 5/2/1.
54 B. L. Add. Ch. 16081–2.
55 S.R.O., DD/SAS CH 16/1; D/P/chedz 5/2/1.
56 Ibid. D/P/chedz 2/1/1–8.
57 Ibid. D/D/Rm, box 2.
58 Ibid. D/N/bmc 3/2/1; DD/X/HUNT 1.
59 Ibid. D/N/bmc 2/1/2; 3/2/1, 3.
60 *Co. Topog. Som.* (1875); S.R.O., D/N/bmc 4/2/4.
61 S.R.O., D/N/bmc 2/1/2, 3/2/2, 4/3/46–7.
62 Ibid. 2/3/11; D/R/bw 22/1/16.
63 Ibid. D/D/Ca 175; D/D/Bs 39.
64 Ibid. DD/S/ST 19/4; D/P/chedz 4/1/4, 13/2/1; D/D/Bs 44.
65 *Educ. of Poor Digest*, p. 778; *Ann. Rep. B. & W. Dioc. Assoc. S.P.C.K.* (1825–6), 41.

54 at two day schools, begun in 1818 and 1830.[66] The day schools had closed by 1843 but 90 children attended a Sunday school in a building probably erected in 1842.[67] The Sunday school had 77 pupils in 1846 but a day school was 'much wanted'.[68] A National school, in existence in 1861, was transferred to a school board in 1875[69] and rebuilt in 1876. In 1903 there were 80 children on the books[70] but numbers fell to 25 in 1945. In 1966 the school became a junior school and in 1981 there were 41 children on the register.[71]

There was a boarding school in the parish in 1859, a dame school in the 1860s,[72] and a private

school in 1883. Elizabeth Winter kept a dairy school for farmers' children between 1894 and 1910, and for several years afterwards she lectured on cheese and butter making.[73]

CHARITIES FOR THE POOR. Charity Norris (d. 1812) gave £100 the income from which was distributed to about 50 people before 1866. In 1856 Dinah Ritchie provided for a coal or bread distribution and in 1875 Charity Boon and Grace Callow left money to the poor.[74] The combined income was distributed to the elderly in 1987.[75]

CHILTON TRINITY

THE ancient parish of Chilton, known by 1329 as Chilton Trinity,[76] lay in three principal and several smaller parts. The principal parts were the three Domesday estates of Pignes, Huntstile, and Idstock (or Edstock), to the last of which Beere had been united by common ownership by the later 14th century, although Idstock church had perhaps been independent in the early 13th century.[77] Chilton village, 2 km. north of Bridgwater, lay largely outside Chilton parish, only the church and Chilton Farm standing within its ancient boundaries. The largest area of the parish lay 3 km. north and north-east of Bridgwater on both sides of the Parrett, on the rich alluvial land which included the site of the 11th-century settlement of Pignes, a name which survived as a tithing into the 19th century.[78] Six km. WNW. from Chilton church, between Cannington and Fiddington parishes, lay Idstock tithing, otherwise known as Idstock and Beere. Six km. SSW. from Chilton church was Huntstile tithing, bounded on the west by Goathurst, into which it was later absorbed, and on the east by North Petherton. Other parts of Chilton parish lay within or adjacent to Wembdon parish, including allotments in Chilton common, north and north-west of Chilton church. About 1840 the tithe survey reckoned the ancient parish at 1,012 a. excluding the 304 a. of Idstock and Beere, then described as an extra-parochial chapelry[79] but in fact part of Chilton parish;[80] Idstock and Beere were sometimes regarded in the 19th century as part of Cannington and were treated as a separate civil parish between 1866 and 1886, when, with 3 houses and 21 persons, they were added to Cannington and (a small part) Otterhampton.

Also in 1886 Chilton Trinity lost Huntstile, with 3 houses and 27 persons, to Goathurst and an uninhabited part to Wembdon, and gained parts of Bridgwater (9 houses, 44 persons), Durleigh (8 houses, 36 persons), and Wembdon (1 house, 9 persons). Those changes reduced the area of the parish from, apparently, 1,381 a. to 1,143 a. excluding foreshore and tidal water. In 1907 an uninhabited area of 32 a., called Chilton Common (it had presumably formed part of the common) and regarded as extra-parochial until 1858 when it became a civil parish, was added to Chilton Trinity, reckoned as 1,183 a. in 1911.[81] The parish was reduced in area to 799 a. in 1933, gaining 75 a. from Bridgwater Without and losing 436 a. east of the Parrett to Bridgwater Without and 23 a. to Puriton.[82] In 1971 the area of the parish was given as 324 ha. (801 a.);[83] the small increase since 1933 not accounted for by boundary changes, like that between 1886 and 1911, was presumably the result of reclamation of foreshore.

Most of the ancient parish lay on alluvium below the 15-m. contour. Chilton church and Chilton Farm, like the rest of Chilton village, occupy a small island of Keuper marl. Idstock and Beere, on gradually rising ground reaching just above the 30-m. contour, are partly on Keuper marl with a narrow ridge of sandstone. Huntstile is in a much steeper landscape, as its name may indicate,[84] on ground rising from 30 m. to 160 m., from Keuper marl at its lower end through Upper Sandstone to Ilfracombe slates.[85]

The boundaries of the ancient parish were irregular. Those of Huntstile followed two streams flowing down from the Quantocks; Idstock's were in part two brooks and, at its

66 *Educ. Enq. Abstract*, p. 799.
67 S.R.O., DD/X/HUNT 1.
68 Nat. Soc. *Inquiry, 1846–7*, Som. 6–7.
69 S.R.O., D/N/bmc 3/2/1; D/P/chedz 18/1/1; ibid. C/T 3.
70 Ibid. C/E 4/380/83.
71 Ibid. 4/64.
72 Harrison, Harrod, & Co. *Dir. Som.* (1859); *P.O. Dir. Som.* (1861, 1866).
73 Whitby, *Dir. Bridgwater* (1883); *Kelly's Dir. Som.* (1894, 1910, 1919).
74 Char. Com. files.
75 Local inf.
76 *Cal. Pat. 1327–30*, 414. This article was completed in 1987. The former parish is shown on the maps above, pp.

66, 178, 192.
77 Below, manors, church.
78 S.R.O., Q/REl 29/9A; below.
79 S.R.O., tithe awards, Chilton Trinity (1839) and Idstock (1843).
80 Below, church.
81 *Census, 1831–91*; Youngs, *Local Admin. Units*, i. 421; the acreage before 1886 is taken from *V.C.H. Som.* ii. 347, which says that too large an area was taken for the parish for Census purposes in 1881 and probably in 1871.
82 S.R.O., GP/D, box 19, Som. Review Order, 1933; *Census, 1931* pt. ii.
83 *Census, 1971*.
84 A. H. Smith, *Eng. Place-Name Elements*, ii. 152.
85 Geol. Surv. Map 1", drift, sheet 295 (1956 edn.).

western end across Wildmoor, a line of boundary stones.[86] The eastern boundary of the main part of the parish, around Horsey Level, may have followed one or more earlier courses of the Parrett. A silted-up meander south-east of Chilton village may outline the Newland reclaimed by the later 14th century.[87] On the west bank near Pignes farm 12 a. were reclaimed in the 1620s and more in the next decade, but tidal changes resulted over 30 years in the loss before 1637 of *c.* 40 a. on the west bank and a gain of only 4 a. on the east.[88] A petition from some local gentry in 1664 to remove a meander 'running a great compass' about Pignes may not have been successful,[89] and another by the owner of the farm, Sir John Morton, was opposed 'for silly reasons' by the town of Bridgwater. In 1673 Morton is said to have hired some sailors, who made a cut through the isthmus in a single night.[90] A second meander known as Viking's pill, also around part of Pignes and Horsey, was cut off by tidal action in 1679 and in consequence some 120 a. of Chilton, Bawdrip, and Puriton were reclaimed.[91]

Iron-age and Roman pottery have been found at Chilton village.[92] Chilton, Pignes, Huntstile, Beere, and Idstock were all settled by 1066.[93] The name Chilton implies a settlement for younger sons, Idstock a religious site or a secondary settlement, and Beere a woodland pasture.[94] Pignes, on the west side of the river, may suggest a meander. The settlement at Pignes may have been reduced to a single farm in the 14th century and was apparently abandoned, probably because of flooding, before 1723.[95] South of Pignes but on the east side of the Parrett stood buildings described in 1822 as Ship Pool.[96] Apparently the same site had become Hawker's (now Hawkhurst) Farm by 1829.[97] Chilton village increased in size after the establishment of the brick and tile works *c.* 1900[98] and again, from residential development, in the 1970s. Houses in the village in the 17th century included two of standard three-roomed plan, one with an additional porch entry with a room above.[99] Chilton Farm is a large 19th-century building in brick, comprising a south range with two north wings behind. Beere Manor Farm and Huntstile are more substantial.[1]

No direct evidence of open-field arable has been found in the parish. In the earlier 16th century, however, there were small closes at Idstock and Beere which might have originated as arable strips.[2] Large pasture grounds evidently lay beside the Parrett by the later 14th century.[3] In the earlier 16th century some Idstock tenants had small pieces of meadow in Combwich marsh and Wildmoor in Cannington.[4] Chilton farmers had rights in Chilton common, formerly Wildmarsh, north and northwest of Chilton village.[5] Small detached parts of the parish near Harp common and Perry green, both locally in Wembdon, suggest origins in common rights there. There were 7 a. of underwood at Idstock in 1086[6] and 6 a. of high wood and pasture at Huntstile in 1325.[7] In the early 18th century there were over 8,000 elms at Beere.[8] Huntstile was well wooded in the mid 18th century; and more trees were planted there in 1778 to form the eastern edge of Halswell park.[9]

There was a licensed tippler in the parish in 1674–5.[10] The Chilton revel was held on Trinity Monday in the later 17th century.[11] In the later 19th century a rifle range occupied part of Horsey Level in the parish.[12]

In 1563 there were 8 households at Chilton, 6 at Huntstile, and 2 at Idstock.[13] Fourteen houses were recorded in 1664–5[14] and 14 families in 1749.[15] There were said to be only three houses in the parish *c.* 1788, a figure which probably omitted Idstock and Huntstile.[16] In 1801 the population was 50. It rose from 49 in 1831 to 74 in 1841, fell to 52 in 1851 and 53 in 1861, and rose again to 88 in 1881. The boundary changes of 1886 brought a net gain of 62 persons. The population of the then civil parish remained stable until 1921, when it was 156, rising to 182 in 1931. That of the parish as constituted in 1933 was 146 in both 1931 and 1971, but rose to 282 in 1981.[17]

MANORS AND OTHER ESTATES. Three estates together seem to have formed the ancient parish of Chilton.[18] Pignes, including Chilton church, was the largest and was held with Huntstile and probably Idstock in 1086. Beere adjoined Idstock and was held with it in 1408.

Beorhtric held *PIGNES* in 1066. In 1086 John the usher held it[19] with the estates of Huntstile and probably Idstock;[20] he also held Perry in

86 O.S. Map 6", Som. XLIX. NE. (1886 edn.).
87 S.R.O., Chilton tithe award, no. 62; *Cal. Inq. p.m.* xiv, p. 142.
88 P.R.O., E 178/5619; E 178/6028, ff. 1, 2, 17.
89 *Cal. S.P. Dom.* 1664–5, 33.
90 S.R.O., DD/SH 108, pt. 2.
91 P.R.O., E 178/6028, f. 33. The date 1677 is given in M. Williams, *Draining of Som. Levels*, 93, 113 and n.
92 Inf. from Mrs. M. Langdon, Huntspill.
93 *V.C.H. Som.* i. 471, 485, 487, 520–1.
94 Smith, *Eng. P.-N. Elements*, i. 16, 94; ii. 153–4.
95 *Cal. Inq. p.m.* x, p. 397; Som. River Bd. *13th Ann. Rep.* 1962–3, 54 and map opposite. The probable site is ST. 30504010: *Proc. Som. Arch. Soc.* cxxix. 31 and plate 5 (wrongly captioned).
96 *S.R.S.* lxxvi, Greenwood's map.
97 S.R.O., Q/REl 29/9A.
98 Below, econ. hist.
99 S.R.O., DD/SP inventories, 1669/72, 94.
1 Below, manors.
2 P.R.O., E 315/385, ff. 83v.–86v.

3 *Cal. Inq. p.m.* xiv, p. 142.
4 P.R.O., E 315/385, ff. 85–85v.
5 S.R.O., Q/RDe 29. 6 *V.C.H. Som.* i. 487.
7 P.R.O., C 134/90, no. 1.
8 S.R.O., DD/MVB 46.
9 Ibid. DD/S/WH 269; ibid. T/PH/vch 73; ibid. Chilton tithe award. 10 Ibid. Q/RL.
11 Ibid. Q/SR 138/46.
12 *W. Som. Free Press*, 30 Aug. 1879; O.S. Map 6", Som. L. NE. (1886 edn.). 13 *S.D.N.Q.* xxx. 91.
14 Dwelly, *Hearth Tax*, i. 45.
15 S.R.O., D/P/chi. t 2/9/1.
16 Ibid. D/D/Vc 88.
17 *Census*, 1801–1981, including tables of boundary changes, 1891, 1931 pt. ii; cf. *V.C.H. Som.* ii. 347, stating that the figures in *Census*, 1881, and perhaps ibid. 1871, were for an area larger than the parish.
18 The estate identified as Chilton Trinity in *V.C.H. Som.* i. 521 is considered to be partly or wholly in Durleigh: above, Durleigh, manors. 19 *V.C.H. Som.* i. 520.
20 Below.

Wembdon[21] and Wigborough in South Petherton[22] together with land in Cannington, North Petherton, and elsewhere which was alienated from the holding in Henry II's reign.[23] John held Pignes of the king in chief by the sergeanty of usher or porter of the king's hall.[24] Pignes evidently passed to William the usher (fl. 1199),[25] and by 1207 to William's daughter Helen of Wigborough, who married Eustace of Dowlish.[26] Helen and Eustace still held land at Pignes in 1243 but by 1250 had been succeeded by their son Richard of Wigborough.[27] William of Wigborough followed Richard in 1270 and was in possession in 1284–5.[28] Another William, who was knighted, was lord in 1309 and died in 1324–5 leaving his brother Richard as his heir.[29] Richard was dead by 1343, and on his widow Maud's death in 1359 the manor passed to John Horsey (d. 1375) whose grandfather and namesake had bought the reversion in 1328–9.[30] The holding descended from 1359 with Horsey in Bridgwater until the death of Sir Ralph Horsey in 1612, but it then passed to Ralph's son George, who still possessed it in 1638 and who had been succeeded by Ralph Horsey by 1641.[31] By 1703 the holding had passed to the Pleydell family and descended with Horsey.[32]

Alweard held *HUNTSTILE* T.R.E. In 1086 it was held by John the usher,[33] and descended from him like Pignes until 1324–5, held as part of the sergeanty of serving as usher of the king's hall.[34] By 1431 it was said to be held for 1/20 fee.[35]

Sir William of Wigborough held Huntstile with Pignes and Wigborough at his death in 1324–5.[36] Joan, his widow, held it with land in Chilton as dower,[37] and it had passed from her to Maud, widow of Richard of Wigborough, by 1343.[38] Maud's successor was Sir Richard Cogan, who died in 1368 leaving a son William as his heir.[39] The manor then descended like Wigborough to Sir Fulk FitzWaryn (d. 1391) and then through Sir Fulk's granddaughter Elizabeth FitzWaryn to her husband Sir Richard Hankeford (d. 1431). Their daughter Thomasia, later wife of William Bourchier, succeeded to the whole of her mother's estate on the death of her sister in 1433.[40]

Fulk Bourchier, Lord FitzWaryn, son and heir of William and Thomasia, died in 1479,[41] and Huntstile descended like Wigborough to Fulk's son John, Lord FitzWaryn (cr. earl of Bath 1536, d. 1539).[42] He or one of his successors sold

Huntstile to Edward Walker of Nether Stowey, who was in possession in 1562. Walker died in 1565[43] and his son John sold it in 1571 to John Brodripp.[44] Brodripp died in 1578 leaving his son Richard a minor.[45] Another Richard Brodripp had succeeded by 1670[46] and died in 1705 leaving Huntstile to his son Robert. Robert died c. 1709 leaving unspecified lands to his brothers Thomas (d. c. 1756) and Richard (d. 1737).[47] In 1766 the manor was bought from Bennett Coombe by Sir Charles Tynte and descended with the Halswell estate in Goathurst.[48] In 1987 it belonged to the Herbert family.[49]

Huntstile Farm, a stone building, stands on a steeply sloping site which is probably the reason for the unusual arrangement of the rooms within its **L**-shaped plan. Repairs and alterations, especially the replacement of windows, and much of the roof, have made the dating of its development uncertain. In the 16th century the hall was probably the room at the north-east corner. The ground is lowest there and it is built over a cellar. The service rooms were in the south wing beyond a cross passage and the parlour was in the west wing behind the hall stack and beyond a lobby with a newel stair. The kitchen was subsequently rebuilt and the service rooms to the south of it are later still. An inventory of 1674[50] lists a number of rooms which presumably occupied the south wing although it is doubtful whether any of them were in their present form. The hall and the room above it retain an early 17th-century panelling.

IDSTOCK, formerly Ichestock, was held in 1066 by Wulfa and in 1086 by Roger de Courcelles. Roger's tenant was John,[51] probably John the usher, since by the earlier 13th century the estate was held by Helen of Wigborough, John's successor in his other Somerset holdings.[52] By 1284–5 William of Wigborough was said to hold the vill of Idstock of the king in chief, but in 1312 he was returned as holding the mesne lordship for 1/20 knight's fee of Nicholas Poyntz, successor to Robert de Courcelles in neighbouring estates.[53] That mesne lordship had apparently lapsed by 1408 when Idstock was said to be held of the countess of Kent.[54]

In 1284–5 Robert de St. Clare held Idstock of William of Wigborough.[55] By 1360 Sibyl, widow of Robert de St. Clare (d. 1359), held land there which passed on her death to her son Richard. It formed the dower of Richard's widow, Isabel,

21 Below, Wembdon, manors.
22 *V.C.H. Som.* iv. 177.
23 *Bk. of Fees*, ii. 1170–1, 1209, 1266.
24 *S.R.S.* xi, p. 301; *Bk. of Fees*, i. 261; ii. 1170; J. H. Round, *The King's Serjeants* (1911), 110–12.
25 *Pipe R.* 1199 (P.R.S. N.S. x), 240.
26 *V.C.H. Som.* iv. 177.
27 *Bk. of Fees*, ii. 1209, 1266.
28 *Cal. Inq. p.m.* i, pp. 244–5; *Feud. Aids*, iv. 277.
29 S.R.O., D/D/B reg. 1, f. 28A; *Cal. Inq. p.m.* vi, p. 373.
30 *Cal. Pat.* 1327–30, 34–5, 236; *S.R.S.* xii. 131–2.
31 Above, Bridgwater, manors; P.R.O., E 178/5620; *Som. Protestation Returns*, ed. A J. Howard and T. L. Stoate, 247.
32 P.R.O., CP 43/482, rot. 113.
33 *V.C.H. Som.* i. 521.
34 P.R.O., C 134/90, no. 1.
35 Ibid. C 139/51, no. 54.
36 Ibid. C 134/90, no. 1.
37 *Cal. Pat.* 1327–30, 14.
38 *Year Bk.* 17 Edw. III (Rolls Ser.), 109; *Cal. Inq. p.m.*

x, p. 397.
39 *Cal. Inq. p.m.* xii, p. 197.
40 *V.C.H. Som.* iv. 177; P.R.O., C 139/51, no. 54.
41 P.R.O., C 140/73, no. 76.
42 *Complete Peerage*, v. 508.
43 P.R.O., C 142/142, no. 32.
44 Ibid. CP 25(2)/204/13 & 14 Eliz. I Mich.
45 Ibid. C 142/191, no. 83.
46 Ibid. CP 25(2)/761/22 Chas. II Mich.
47 *Som. Wills*, ed. Brown, iv. 117–18.
48 S.R.O., DD/S/WH 225; ibid. T/PH/vch 73; P.R.O., CP 43/754, rot. 385; above, Goathurst, manors.
49 Local inf.
50 S.R.O., DD/SP inventory, 1674/31.
51 *V.C.H. Som.* i. 487.
52 *Cal. Inq. p.m.* i, p. 307; *V.C.H. Som.* iv. 177; above manors (Pignes, Huntstile).
53 *Feud. Aids*, iv. 282; *Cal. Inq. p.m.* v, p. 196.
54 P.R.O., C 137/68, no. 42.
55 *Feud. Aids*, iv. 282.

and in 1394 Richard's son Ralph St. Clare sold the reversion on her death to Sir William Bonville.[56] Sir William died in 1408[57] and his heir was his grandson William Bonville (cr. Lord Bonville 1449, d. 1461). Lord Bonville was succeeded by his great-granddaughter Cecily Bonville (d. 1529), wife first of Thomas Grey, marquess of Dorset (d. 1501), and secondly of Henry Stafford, earl of Wiltshire (d. 1523).[58] Cecily's heir was her son Thomas Grey, marquess of Dorset, who died in 1530 leaving as heir a minor, his son Henry (cr. duke of Suffolk 1551).[59] Henry was attainted in 1554 but Idstock did not pass to the Crown until the death of his widow Frances, then wife of Adrian Stokes, in 1559.[60]

In 1558 the Crown granted the reversion of the manor to William Honnynge, clerk of the queen's privy signet, and Nicholas Cutler. They sold it in the same year to John Bowyer, formerly a servant of the duke of Suffolk and tenant since 1553.[61] Bowyer died in 1599[62] leaving his son Edmund (d. 1625) his heir.[63] Edmund was followed by his son Edmund (d. 1665)[64] and grandson, also Edmund Bowyer (d. 1670).[65] In 1707 Edmund, son of the last, sold Idstock with Beere and other adjoining land to Edward Colston of London, remaining life tenant until his death in 1715.[66] The estate formed part of Colston's Hospital foundation at Bristol until it was sold as part of Edbrook farm in 1919.[67]

The capital messuage was let in 1557.[68]

An estate called Bera, probably *BEERE*, was held both in 1066 and 1086 by Leofa, one of the king's clerks.[69] No further trace of the holding has been found until 1369 when (Sir) William Bonville (d. 1408) owned Beere manor. It was said in 1408 to have been held as of Lady Margaret Courtenay,[70] presumably Margaret de Bohun (d. 1391), widow of Hugh Courtenay, earl of Devon (d. 1377).[71] The estate had been let to Sir John Paulet (d. 1391), and his successor there, probably his brother William, was in occupation in 1412 and probably in 1416 when he founded a chantry in Idstock chapel.[72]

The lordship of Beere descended from Sir William Bonville with Idstock, and in 1558 Frances Grey, duchess of Suffolk (d. 1559), was said to hold it in chief.[73] It passed with Idstock to the Bowyer family, and was sold by Colston's Hospital in 1920 to Charles Venner, whose family owned it in 1987.[74]

Beere Manor is probably in origin a stone house of the later 15th or earlier 16th century, with a great upper chamber above a central hall. The hall was entered from a screens passage which had a porch on the south. The porch was balanced by a projection in the south front between the hall and the parlour to the east. By the earlier 18th century both were four storeys high, perhaps as a result of remodelling in the earlier 17th century.[75] Early in the 18th century Edmund Bowyer panelled the hall and the parlour. Later additions have been made to the rear of the hall and the service wing. The main roof and the windows throughout are of the later 17th and earlier 18th centuries. The stable block adjoining the south-west corner of the house was built c. 1707.[76]

Between 1199 and 1207 William the usher gave land at Huntstile to Montacute priory. It was held by the priory in 1251–2[77] but no further reference to the land has been found.

In 1329 Simon Furneaux was licensed to grant a house and land, including some at Chilton, to form part of the endowment of a chantry at Kilve.[78] The land became part of Kilve rectory after the chantry had ceased to function before the end of the 14th century,[79] and some 28 a. in Chilton belonged to the rector in 1613.[80] There were nearly 22 a. in 1839;[81] they were sold in 1925–6.[82]

In 1326 Matthew Coker was licensed to grant land in Chilton to endow a chantry in Wembdon church.[83] No further trace of the chantry has been found. St. George's chantry in Bridgwater parish church had 1 a. at Chilton.[84]

The lands of the free chapel of Idstock were bought in 1548 by Sir John Thynne and Laurence Hyde.[85] By 1572 the chapel was owned by John Mawdley, who was succeeded in that year by his son Thomas.[86] As concealed Crown property it was sold to John Farnham, a gentleman pensioner of the queen, in 1577;[87] he in the same year sold to Christopher Peyton of London, and Peyton sold to the tenant, John Bowyer.[88] The chantry house, probably that later known as Edbrook Cottage and locally in Cannington parish, was demolished c. 1905.[89]

ECONOMIC HISTORY. The four Domesday holdings which seem to have later formed the parish of Chilton Trinity gelded together for

56 *S.R.S.* xvii. 44, 102.
57 P.R.O., C 137/68, no. 42.
58 *Complete Peerage*, ii. 218–19.
59 P.R.O., C 142/53, no. 4.
60 *Cal. Pat.* 1557–8, 163; *Complete Peerage*, iv. 421–2.
61 *Cal. Pat.* 1557–8, 163; S.R.O., DD/MVB 2; *Proc. Som. Arch. Soc.* cxxiii. 71; P.R.O., STAC 4/4/48; STAC 4/9/12.
62 J. Hutchins, *Hist. Dors.* iii. 527.
63 P.R.O., C 142/257, no. 57; C 142/419, no. 42; S.R.O., DD/MVB 2.
64 S.R.O., DD/MVB 1; *Som. Wills*, ed. Brown, iv. 82.
65 S.R.O., DD/MVB 8, 41.
66 Ibid. 1, 46.
67 Ibid. 19.
68 B.L. Harl. 607, f. 21.
69 *V.C.H. Som.* i. 471.
70 Devon R.O. 123 M/TB 478–9; P.R.O., C 137/68, no. 42.
71 *Complete Peerage*, iv. 324.

72 *Feud. Aids*, vi. 507; *Cal. Pat.* 1413–16, 405.
73 *Cal. Pat.* 1557–8, 163; *Complete Peerage*, iv. 421–2.
74 Above, manors (Idstock); S.R.O., DD/MVB 19; local inf.
75 Painting in house, reproduced below, plate facing p. 296.
76 S.R.O., DD/MVB 46.
77 *S.R.S.* viii, p. 128; *Bk. of Fees*, ii. 1266.
78 *Cal. Pat.* 1327–30, 414.
79 *V.C.H. Som.* v. 101.
80 S.R.O., D/D/Rg 224.
81 Ibid. tithe award.
82 Ibid. D/P/kve 3/1/2, 6.
83 *Cal. Pat.* 1324–7, 246.
84 *S.R.S.* lxxvii, p. 80; above, Bridgwater, church.
85 *S.R.S.* lxxvii, p. 3; below, church.
86 P.R.O., C 142/172, no. 132.
87 *Cal. Pat.* 1575–8, p. 309.
88 S.R.O., DD/MVB 4.
89 Ibid. tithe award; photo. c. 1905 in possession of Mr. A. Bye, Creech St. Michael.

2 hides. The largest, Pignes, accounted for more than half the assessment; it had 2 ploughteams, one each on the ½ hide of demesne and on the ½ hide of demesne of the priest there. There were 2 teams at Huntstile, one on the ½ virgate of demesne, the other worked by 3 *villani* and 4 bordars. A single team at Beere was shared with the tenants. There was meadow at Pignes (5 a.), Idstock (20 a.), and Beere (6 a.), and 10 a. of pasture at Huntstile. Sheep were recorded at Pignes (33), Idstock (20), and Beere (5), pigs at Pignes (16), Beere (5), and Huntstile (4), and 'beasts' at Pignes (14), Beere (4), and Idstock (3). In total the value of the estates had increased, but Pignes had fallen by a quarter and Huntstile had doubled.[90]

In 1325 the Huntstile demesne seems to have comprised the capital messuage, a dovecot, 1 a. of garden, ½ a. of meadow, and 6 a. of wood and pasture but no arable. Ten villeins and 4 cottars paid rent for the remainder of the land.[91] In 1359 the dower share of the whole estate was described as a messuage, a carucate of 40 a., 6 a. of meadow, 6 a. of wood, and 10s. rent.[92] Pignes in 1325 was a single manor with 180 a. of demesne arable and 2 a. of meadow, the remainder being let to tenants in fee, 5 other free tenants, and 11 villeins who paid quarterly rents. Labour service was valued at 11s.[93] In 1359 the same estate comprised 449 a. of arable, 6 a. of meadow, and 12d. rent, but was then worth only 66s. 8d. because of flooding,[94] and in 1373 it was said to comprise only 100 a. of pasture.[95]

About 1525 the adjoining estates of Idstock and Beere measured just over 300 a., divided almost equally between arable and pasture. Most of the demesne pasture was shared among 13 of the 16 holdings at will or for lives, the largest of which was the capital messuage of Beere with a farm of 119 a., mostly arable.[96] In 1557 the capital messuage of each estate was let and the income derived from rents of customary tenants and from a few leaseholders.[97]

By the 17th century the greater part of the parish was under grass. John Hill (d. 1669) grew wheat, barley, and beans besides hay, but his stock included 67 sheep, 7 bullocks, 7 cows, and 6 yearlings all grazing in the marsh, and there were 142 cheeses in his house. John Page of Huntstile (d. 1671), with more arable than most, had 3 yoke of oxen and quantities of wheat, barley, and peas, but he also possessed 7 cows, 6 young stock, and 84 sheep, and had in his house 80 lb. butter and c. 8 cwt. of cheese. Bartholomew Thorne (d. 1640), evidently a much less prosperous farmer, had rother cattle worth £23, 32 sheep, 2 pigs, and 2 mares, and among dead stock 'old corn', wool, and cheese.[98]

By 1715 the estate at Idstock and Beere had been divided between three farms, Beere (190 a.), Edbrook (78 a.), and Idstock (40 a.),[99] the second beginning as a small holding in the 16th century and known alternatively as East Brook.[1] Improvements recently made in 1715 included a new orchard at Edbrook and a new barn at Idstock. Beere already had a new stable for 10 to 12 horses. From the earlier 18th century the three farms were let for terms of 7, 14, or 21 years.[2] Chilton common or Wildmarsh was divided and allotted in 1802.[3]

About 1840 grassland accounted for about two thirds of the parish. The principal landowners were Margaretta Michel (587 a.), owner of Pignes manor including Chilton and Hawker's farms; the Merchant Venturers of Bristol (304 a.), administrators of Colston's Hospital and owners of Idstock and Beere; Sir Charles Tynte (224 a.), owner of Huntstile; and John Cridland (71 a.).[4] In 1905, after its boundaries had been changed, the parish comprised 990 a. of grassland and 15¼ a. of arable.[5] On Huntstile farm Thomas Danger was noted c. 1850 for having over ten years improved the production of turnips and other green crops by using a drill and a horse hoe.[6] Dairymen and cowkeepers were in business by the later 19th century, and by 1914 the county council had established a cheese school at Hawker's farm.[7] In 1910 the parish had nine farms, and the same number was returned in 1982, three of which were specialist dairy farms.[8]

There was a mill at Beere in 1086.[9] It was apparently still in use in 1707,[10] but no longer by the mid 19th century when only its site was known.[11] The mill was driven by the brook flowing from Fiddington.

There was a shop in the parish in 1875, a carpenter and a market gardener in 1894, and a haulier in 1897. By 1902 the Somerset Trading Co. had begun[12] the manufacture of bricks and by 1909 Major & Co. Ltd. were involved in clay extraction.[13] By 1923 Majors still rented a clay pit and the Somerset Trading Co. had a brickyard producing bricks, tiles, and field drainpipes which occupied over 35 a. By 1926 the area had increased to 55 a.[14] The firm built a large tile factory east of the village in 1930, and by 1939 was the only business there. The factory closed in 1968[15] and in 1987 was occupied by various small manufacturers.

90 *V.C.H. Som.* i. 471, 485, 487, 520–1.
91 P.R.O., C 134/90, no. 1.
92 *Cal. Inq. p.m.* x, p. 397.
93 P.R.O., C 134/90, no. 1.
94 *Cal. Inq. p.m.* x, p. 397.
95 Ibid. xiv, p. 142.
96 P.R.O., E 315/385, ff. 83v.–86v.
97 B.L. Harl. 607, f. 21.
98 S.R.O., DD/SP inventories, 1669/72, 1674/31, 1640/57.
99 Ibid. DD/MVB 46.
1 Ibid. 35, 46.
2 Ibid. 32–3, 35.
3 Ibid. Q/RDe 29.
4 Ibid. Chilton Trinity and Idstock tithe awards.

5 Statistics supplied by the then Bd. of Agric. 1905.
6 T. D. Acland and W. Sturge, *Farming of Som.* (1851), 33–4, 41 n.
7 *P.O. Dir. Som.* (1875); *Kelly's Dir. Som.* (1883 and later edns.); S.R.O., DD/S/FA 11 (1868).
8 *Kelly's Dir. Som.* (1910); Min. of Agric., Fisheries, and Food, agric. returns, 1982.
9 *V.C.H. Som.* i. 471.
10 S.R.O., DD/MVB 1.
11 Ibid. Idstock tithe award.
12 *P.O. Dir. Som.* (1875); *Kelly's Dir. Som.* (1894, 1897, 1902).
13 S.R.O., D/R/bw 15/3/7.
14 Ibid. 16/6/1.
15 Ibid. 22/1/20; inf. from Mr. Brian Murless, Taunton.

LOCAL GOVERNMENT. In the later 13th century Chilton parish included Chilton, Huntstile, Idstock, and Pignes tithings,[16] and in the 18th and 19th centuries the same divisions were retained for land tax collection.[17]

Idstock and Beere each had manor courts in 1557.[18] Idstock was said in 1715 never to have paid towards the church and poor rates of Chilton and to have maintained its own poor.[19] Idstock and Beere maintained a poorhouse on the northern boundary of Beere farm beside the road to Coultings.[20]

In 1852 Chilton parish vestry appointed one man as overseer of the poor and waywarden, another as churchwarden, and a third as salaried assistant overseer. There were two overseers in 1859 and the churchwarden was also waywarden. The assistant overseer administered both poor and highway rates.[21] Chilton parish formed part of Bridgwater poor-law union in 1836; all its former parts were in Bridgwater rural district from 1894 and Sedgemoor district from 1974.[22]

CHURCHES. The plan and part of the fabric of the church are of the later 11th century. A priest held land as part of Pignes manor in 1086.[23] By 1291 the benefice was called the church of Chilton and Idstock;[24] c. 1327 Chilton had dependent chapels at Idstock and Huntstile.[25] Chilton remained a sole rectory until 1749 when it was united with Bridgwater.[26] From 1976 it was also held with Durleigh,[27] and the united benefice of Bridgwater and Chilton Trinity and Durleigh was created in 1984.[28]

Sir William of Wigborough was patron in 1309.[29] About 1327 Richard of Wigborough gave the church with its dependent chapels to St. John's hospital, Bridgwater,[30] and in 1336 the hospital was licensed to appropriate.[31] No appropriation took place and the hospital continued to present rectors until the Dissolution in 1539, with the exception of two presentations in 1501 made by the prior of Witham and others under a grant of 1492.[32] The Crown has been patron since the Dissolution.[33]

Chilton and Idstock were valued at £5 6s. 8d. in 1291[34] and the gross income of Chilton was £8 0s. 2½d. in 1535.[35] It was said to be worth £60 in 1668,[36] and £42 15s. in 1748.[37] Tithes

were worth £5 8s. 6½d. in 1535[38] and in 1634 were claimed in Chilton, Huntstile, and Idstock, from the demesnes of Beere, and from the area called Horsey Limit, while a customary payment was made from land called Horsey Slime.[39] The rector was awarded £195 6s. as a rent charge in lieu of tithe in Chilton and Huntstile in 1839, and £17 7s. in Idstock and Beere in 1843.[40] Glebe in 1535 was valued at £3 11s. 8d.[41] In 1634[42] there were over 5 a. in Chilton and c. 30 a. at Idstock, the Idstock land having been disputed with the owner of Idstock chapel in 1559, c. 1594, and c. 1600 when the rector accepted an annual rent of £15.[43] The rent was still paid c. 1715.[44] In 1839 there were nearly 6 a. of glebe in Chilton and the same amount remained in 1978.[45]

A chamber on the north side of the rectory house, with use of the hall, kitchen, and garden, was assigned to the retiring rector in 1420.[46] In 1634 the kitchen was separate from the house.[47] The walls of the house, of 'mud supported by props' under a thatched roof, were allowed to fall into ruin c. 1756.[48] There was no trace of a house by 1840.[49]

Richard St. Clare, rector from 1309 until 1327 or later, was given the living before taking holy orders.[50] Simon atte Thorne of Farway (Devon), appointed rector in 1341, was a lawyer.[51] The parish was served by a curate c. 1575.[52] Richard Jones, rector from 1610 until 1636 or later,[53] was several times presented for non-residence and in 1626 took his curate to court for extortion. In 1629 he was said to be chaplain to the bishop of Winchester.[54] In 1606 seven households were accused of attendance at church only three times a year,[55] and in 1623 the residents of Idstock and Beere were reported for not attending at all.[56] In 1749 only four families went to the Sunday afternoon services, formerly held monthly but by that time fortnightly,[57] and in 1788 there were insufficient communicants for a service to be held.[58] In 1815 one service a month was held in winter and two in summer,[59] but in 1827 there was an evening service each Sunday conducted by the curate. Services were held each Sunday in 1840 but communion was given at Bridgwater. By 1870 two Sunday services were normally held.[60]

The church of HOLY TRINITY, evidently

16 Feud. Aids, iv. 277–9, 281–2, 292–3.
17 S.R.O., Q/REl 2/2A, 7/2C, 29/2B, 29/9A.
18 B.L. Harl. 607, f. 18.
19 S.R.O., DD/MVB 46.
20 Ibid. Idstock tithe award.
21 Ibid. D/P/chi. t 9/1/1.
22 Youngs, Local Admin. Units, i. 421, 671, 673, 676.
23 V.C.H. Som. i. 520.
24 Tax. Eccl. (Rec. Com.), 198, 202.
25 Cal. Pat. 1327–30, 33.
26 S.R.O., D/P/chi. t 2/9/1.
27 Ibid. 2/9/6.
28 Dioc. Dir.
29 S.R.O., D/D/B reg. 1, f. 28A.
30 Cal. Pat. 1327–30, 33; S.R.S. ix, p. 301.
31 Cal. Pat. 1334–8, 303.
32 S.R.S. liv, pp. 58, 60.
33 Som. Incumbents, ed. Weaver, 333.
34 Tax. Eccl. (Rec. Com.), 198, 202.
35 Valor Eccl. (Rec. Com.), i. 215.
36 S.R.O., D/D/Vc 24.
37 Ibid. D/P/chi. t 2/9/1.
38 Valor Eccl. (Rec. Com.), i. 215.

39 S.R.O., D/P/chi. t 3/1/1.
40 Ibid. tithe awards.
41 Valor Eccl. (Rec. Com.), i. 215.
42 S.R.O., D/P/chi. t 3/1/1.
43 Ibid. DD/MVB 4; P.R.O., C 3/10/34; ibid. E 134/36–7 Eliz. I Mich./21.
44 S.R.O., DD/MVB 46.
45 Ibid. tithe award; inf. from Dioc. Office.
46 S.R.S. xxx, p. 389.
47 S.R.O., D/P/chi. t 3/1/1.
48 Ibid. D/D/Bo 1756.   49 Ibid. D/D/Va 1840.
50 Ibid. D/D/B reg. 1, f. 28A; S.R.S. i. 27, 37; xii. 125, 129; Cal. Pat. 1327–30, 124.
51 S.R.S. ix, p. 429; Cal. Papal Reg. iii. 277, 284; Cal. Papal Pets. 136.
52 S.D.N.Q. xiii. 271.
53 Som. Incumbents, ed. Weaver, 333; S.R.O., D/D/Ca 310.
54 S.R.O., D/D/Ca 235, 266, 274, 310; P.R.O., C 3/406/76.
55 S.R.O., D/D/Ca 151.   56 S.R.S. xliii. 95.
57 S.R.O., D/P/chi. t 2/9/1.
58 Ibid. D/D/Vc 88.
59 Ibid. D/D/Rb 1815.
60 Ibid. D/D/Rb 1827; D/D/Va 1840, 1870.

so dedicated by 1329,[61] comprises chancel, nave, south porch, and west tower. The tall, round-headed rear arch to the south doorway indicates a later 11th-century origin, confirmed by proportions of chancel and nave. The chancel was extended eastwards, the chancel arch evidently enlarged, and the windows replaced in the later 15th or the earlier 16th century, the windows having square heads with carved spandrels. The tower has a pierced parapet and decorated stair turret. The font is Perpendicular in style with a Jacobean lid, and part of a late-medieval screen survived in the 1840s.[62] The pulpit dates from the earlier 17th century. In the churchyard are the remains of a font.

Registers survive for the periods 1732–46 and 1845 to date, and there are transcripts for 1599–1667.[63] Chilton entries are to be found in the registers of Bridgwater for the period 1746–1845.[64] There are five bells including one by Thomas Jefferies of the earlier 16th century and one by Roger Semson, probably of the mid 16th century.[65] The plate includes a cup and cover made by J. Ions of Exeter and dated 1574.[66]

A church at Idstock was confirmed as one of the possessions of Stogursey priory in 1204,[67] but it was held with Chilton in 1291.[68] As a chapel of Chilton it was granted by Richard of Wigborough to St. John's hospital, Bridgwater, c. 1327.[69] In 1416 William Paulet founded a chantry in a newly built Lady Chapel on the north side of the chapel of *ST. MARY*, endowing it with over 100 a. in Stogursey, Cannington, and Idstock.[70] By 1535 the chantry and chapel had been united as a free chapel under one chaplain; the income was then £6 10s. 2d. for the maintenance of the chaplain and a boy.[71] In

1548, when the chapel passed to the Crown and its demolition was ordered, the value was £6 15s. 6d.[72]

The chapel was apparently still in use in 1563,[73] but its stone-vaulted roof, the timber from its tower and bell frame, and its quoins were removed, the vaulting later used at Goathurst as a brine tank. Stone was also used to build a chamber at Beere.[74] The ruins survived in the early 20th century,[75] but in 1987 the site was overgrown with trees.

A chapel at Huntstile was given c. 1327 with Chilton church to St. John's hospital, Bridgwater.[76] It was still in existence in 1336,[77] but no further trace has been found.

NONCONFORMITY. In 1842 a house was licensed for use by an unspecified congregation.[78] Chilton was included in the Bible Christian circuit in 1873 but services were discontinued in 1875.[79]

EDUCATION. There was no school in the parish in 1835, but in 1840 a Sunday school was occasionally held in the church.[80] In 1857 a regular Sunday school was attended by 13 boys and 7 girls.[81] A room was built in 1868 for the vestry and Sunday school by J. Smith, the mayor of Bridgwater.[82] By 1883 Chilton's children attended the day school at Wembdon.[83] The school room continued to be used by the Sunday school until 1963[84] or later, and was standing in 1987.

CHARITIES FOR THE POOR. None known.

DURSTON

THE parish of Durston, on the southern edge of North Petherton hundred, lies 7.5 km. north-east of Taunton.[85] Roughly oval in shape, it measures 2.4 km. from east to west and 1.5 km. from north to south at its widest point. A detached part of the parish, lying 1 km. beyond the eastern boundary in North moor between Lyng and North Petherton and known as Priestwood (32 a.), was transferred to Lyng in 1888.[86] In 1891 and later the parish measured 1,013 a. (410 ha.).[87]

The parish lies on undulating ground where the lowest slopes of the Quantocks descend to

the valley of the Tone at Curry moor. Its northern boundary is marked by a stream and its south-eastern by a watercourse called Old Rhyne, which marks the end of Curry moor. A stream runs southwards between the highest ground to the west, rising to 47 m., and a small central ridge, from which the land falls eastwards to another stream running into the Old Rhyne. Most of the parish lies on Keuper marl, with a small area of Upper Sandstone in the extreme north-west, valley gravels in the south, and a narrow tongue of alluvium along the course of the eastern stream.[88] Limestone was

61 *Cal. Pat.* 1327–30, 414.
62 Taunton Castle, Braikenridge colln., water-colour drawing by W. W. Wheatley, 1846.
63 S.R.O., D/P/chi. t 2/1/1; D/D/Rr 104A.
64 Ibid. D/P/bw. m 2/1/5–10, 18–19.
65 Ibid. DD/SAS CH 16/1.
66 *Proc. Som. Arch. Soc.* xlvii. 156–7.
67 *S.R.S.* lxi, p. 75.
68 *Tax. Eccl.* (Rec. Com.), 198, 202.
69 *Cal. Pat.* 1327–30, 33; *S.R.S.* ix, p. 321; *Cal. Close,* 1346–9, 351.
70 *Cal. Pat.* 1413–16, 405; S.R.O., DD/SH 108, pt. 1. For estates in Stogursey, above, Stogursey, manors.
71 *Valor Eccl.* (Rec. Com.), i. 215.
72 *S.R.S.* ii. 54, 227; P.R.O., C 3/10/34.
73 *S.D.N.Q.* xxx. 91.

74 P.R.O., E 134/36–7 Eliz. I Mich./27.
75 W. H. P. Greswell, *Land of Quantock* (1903), opp. p. 201; Taunton Castle, Braikenridge colln., wash drawing and plan, W. W. Wheatley, 1845; photo. 1908.
76 *Cal. Pat.* 1327–30, 33.
77 Ibid. 1334–8, 303.
78 S.R.O., D/D/Rm, box 2.
79 Ibid. D/N/bmc 3/2/5.
80 *Educ. Enq. Abstract*, p. 800; S.R.O., D/D/Va 1840.
81 S.R.O., D/P/chi. t 2/6/1.   82 Ibid. 9/1/1.
83 *Kelly's Dir. Som.* (1883).
84 S.R.O., D/P/chi. t 2/6/1.
85 This article was written in 1985.
86 Local Govt. Bd. Order 20643.
87 *Census.*
88 Geol. Surv. Map 1", drift, sheet 295 (1956 edn.).

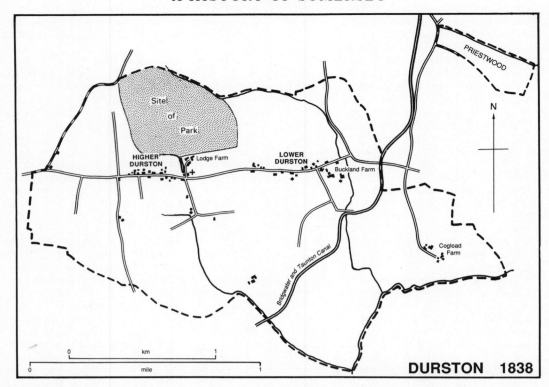

DURSTON 1838

quarried for a few years from 1650, possibly at a site later called Quarry close on the western edge of the parish,[89] and red sand was dug in the 1870s.[90]

The Taunton–Glastonbury road, turnpiked by the Taunton trust in 1752,[91] runs from east to west through the centre of the parish, entering near Durston Elms. There a road north to West Newton forms part of the western boundary; another runs south to Creech St. Michael, a modern replacement for an earlier route south from Walford Cross which was blocked in 1973 by the construction of the M5 motorway. Lanes and footpaths lead from the central spine road to the fields, including Curry Lane to Creech St. Michael and Frog Lane. At the extreme eastern edge of the parish Primmore Lane leads north towards North Petherton; Priestwood Lane leads north-east to the detached part of the parish at Priestwood.[92] Another lane leads south from the main road to Cogload. The main road was widened in the 1960s.

The Bridgwater and Taunton canal, running through the south-eastern part of the parish, was opened in 1827. It is crossed by two bridges, Headworthy and Swan's Neck, to provide access to fields. The canal was virtually unused commercially after 1892.[93] The Bridgwater and Taunton section of the Bristol and Exeter railway, entering the parish beside the canal and running roughly parallel with it, was under construction in 1841[94] and was completed the following year. Durston station, however, lay in

Lyng parish. A loop from Athelney was brought to a junction at Cogload in 1906 as part of the new London route through Castle Cary, a junction modified in 1931.[95]

The two principal settlements, Higher and Lower Durston, line the Taunton–Glastonbury road. Higher Durston, around the junction with Frog Lane and a path to West Newton, includes the church, Lodge Farm (the former manor house), the former school, and the Buckwell, the latter a source of water mentioned in 1651[96] and fed in the 19th century from a long narrow lake beside Lodge Farm. Lower Durston lies near the site of Buckland priory and preceptory and seems to have been known as Crosse by Buckland. In 1391 it comprised at least 16 messuages occupied by craftsmen such as a tanner, a smith, a skinner, and a barber, perhaps suggesting an attempt to plant an urban settlement outside the gates of the priory.[97] Cogload Farm, on the eastern edge of the parish, occupies the site of a hamlet established by the later 13th century.[98] Its name suggests that it was near a significant watercourse,[99] presumably the Old Rhyne which may thus mark the original course of the River Tone. There were several farmsteads there in the mid 18th century.[1]

Cogload Farm is a building of the 16th century or earlier with jointed crucks and two curing chambers. Froglane Farm, much altered in the 19th century, formerly had a smoke-blackened roof and Yardside, also in Frog Lane, is of three-roomed plan, with hall chimney against

89 S.R.O., DD/JL 66A; ibid. tithe award.
90 E. Jeboult, *Valley of the Tone* (1873), 47.
91 25 Geo. III, c. 54.
92 S.R.O., D/P/durn 14/5/1–2.
93 C. Hadfield, *Canals of SW. Eng.* (1967), 49, 65.
94 *V.C.H. Som.* ii. 347.
95 E. T. Macdermot, *Hist. G.W.R.* rev. C. R. Clinker

(1964), ii. 73, 84, 226 and n.
96 S.R.O., DD/PH 28. The well head was said to have been 'lately' built in 1873: Jeboult, *Valley of the Tone*, 46.
97 *S.R.S.* xvii. 144–6; lxxvi, 1822 map; below, manors (Crosse). 98 Collinson, *Hist. Som.* iii. 60–1.
99 *Eng. Place-Name Elements*, ed. A. H. Smith, ii. 9.
1 S.R.O., Q/REl 29/4.

the screens passage.[2] Hascolls Farm, Lower Durston, dates from c. 1650. Maytree Cottage, Higher Durston, was formerly a tollhouse built c. 1850 at Walford Cross, West Monkton, and removed to its present site c. 1874.[3]

The site of Buckland priory and preceptory appears to be occupied by the farmhouse and buildings of Buckland Farm.[4] A spring rising north of the site fed fishponds established in the later 12th century and then supplied the priory with water and drainage.[5] The ponds, equipped with a boat in 1540,[6] were filled in by 1725,[7] but were in use as ponds in 1985. The water supply was channelled from a conduit by the 1260s,[8] the conduit standing in a field variously known as Flaggy or Flagons Chapel.[9]

The shapes of fields in the south-west part of the parish suggest the former existence there of a common arable field.[10] In the south-east part lay medieval meadow around Cogload.[11] Buckland manor in 1544[12] included 20 a. of woodland, part known as Perifield grove, perhaps giving its name to Perry Ville farmstead,[13] later Perry-ville Barton.

A medieval park was formed north of Durston manor house c. 1223 and was stocked from Blackmore forest (Dors.).[14] Timber from the park was used to build a hall and solar at North Petherton in the early 14th century.[15] The park was said to have comprised 200 a. of wood and 60 a. of meadow in 1434.[16] The park survived as a separate farm into the later 17th century,[17] but was later incorporated into Lodge farm. Woodland called Buckland warren was referred to in 1695,[18] and a small field called Warren Kennel lay on the eastern side of the parish.[19] By 1838 it formed two small enclosures known as Warrens Plot and Kennel Plot,[20] both then tithe free because formerly part of Buckland priory estate.

There was an inn in the parish by 1613,[21] probably the inn at Buckland which in 1686 offered a single guest bed and stabling for two horses.[22] It was known as the Buckland inn by 1696,[23] and continued in use throughout the 18th century.[24] It was apparently pulled down between 1821 and 1828.[25] Another inn was opened by 1841[26] which by 1866 was called the Durston

inn.[27] It occupied the house known in 1985 as Mountlands in Lower Durston, and ceased to be an inn after 1883.[28]

In 1801 the population of Durston was 169. It rose to 258 in 1851 but thereafter declined in almost every decade. In 1981 the usually resident population was 108.[29]

MANORS. Alwig held *DURSTON*, later known as Durston Hall,[30] in 1066, and Roger Arundel held it in 1086.[31] The overlordship descended in the barony of Poorstock (Dors.) and on the death of Gerbert de Percy in 1179 Durston formed part of the barony which passed to Gerbert's daughter Sibyl and thence to the FitzPayn family.[32] Robert, Lord FitzPayn (d. 1315), was overlord in 1284–5[33] and his son, also Robert (d. 1354), in 1337.[34] The overlordship descended like the castle and manor of Stogursey[35] to Henry Algernon Percy, earl of Northumberland (d. 1527), who was overlord in 1503.[36] In 1604 Durston was said to be held of James Clarke as of his manor of Cheddon Fitzpaine,[37] a manor also formerly held by the families of FitzPayn and Percy.[38]

An undertenant, Richard, held Durston in 1086.[39] William of Erleigh possessed the manor by 1177,[40] possibly in succession to his father John of Erleigh, who had received the hundred and manor of North Petherton in Henry I's reign.[41] Ownership descended in the Erleigh family like North Petherton manor. On the death of Philip of Erleigh c. 1275[42] Philip's widow Rose, later wife of Geoffrey of Wroxhall,[43] received Durston in dower.[44] Rose was still alive in 1304–5.[45] She was succeeded by her son (Sir) John of Erleigh, who died c. 1323,[46] and by her grandson, also Sir John, who died c. 1337.[47] John of Erleigh, son of the last, born in 1322 was knighted in 1371[48] after service with the Black Prince in Spain,[49] and died c. 1410.[50] After John's death the site of the manor of Durston and woods in the park were given by John's widow Isabel to their only daughter Margaret and to her second husband Sir Walter Sandys,[51] and Sandys was holding a fee in

2 Inf. from Mrs. M. Miles, Durston.
3 J. B. Bentley and B. J. Murless, *Som. Roads*, i. 96; inf. from Mrs. Miles.
4 The farm buildings date largely from c. 1886: S.R.O., DD/MAR 3.
5 *S.R.S.* xxv, pp. 26–7.
6 P.R.O., LR 2/62, f. 182v.
7 S.R.O., DD/SS, bdle. 8.   8 *S.R.S.* xxv, p. 15.
9 S.R.O., DD/MI 5; ibid. tithe award.
10 Ibid. tithe award.   11 *S.R.S.* xxv, p. 15.
12 T. Hugo, *Hist. Mynchin Buckland Priory and Preceptory* (1861), 169–70.
13 *S.R.S.* lxxvi, 1822 map.
14 *Rot. Litt. Claus.* (Rec. Com.), i. 539.
15 S.R.O., DD/SAS NP 1, mm. 9–10.
16 *Cal. Close, 1429–35*, 327.
17 S.R.O., D/P/durn 4/1/1, 1650–78.
18 Ibid. 4/1/1, 1695.
19 Ibid. 13/2/1.   20 Ibid. tithe award.
21 Ibid. Q/SR 18/117–18.
22 P.R.O., WO 30/48.
23 S.R.O., D/P/durn 4/1/1.
24 Ibid. Q/RL; ibid. DD/SL 18; DD/SLM 2; MSS. in possession of Sir Benjamin Slade, London.
25 S.R.O., D/P/durn 13/2/1.
26 P.R.O., HO 107/953.

27 *P.O. Dir. Som.* (1866).
28 *Kelly's Dir. Som.* (1883); inf. from Mrs. Miles. The dates 1831 and 1837 appear on the building.
29 *Census*, 1801–1981.
30 *Cal. Inq. p.m. Hen. VII*, ii, pp. 92–3.
31 *V.C.H. Som.* i. 494.
32 Sanders, *Eng. Baronies*, 72.
33 *Feud. Aids*, iv. 278.
34 *Cal. Inq. p.m.*, viii, p. 58.
35 Above, Stogursey, castle.
36 *Cal. Inq. p.m. Hen. VII*, iii, pp. 413, 428.
37 *S.R.S.* lxvii, p. 60.
38 Collinson, *Hist. Som.* iii. 245–6.
39 *V.C.H. Som.* i. 494.
40 *Pipe R. 1176–7* (P.R.S. xxvi), 24.
41 Below, N. Petherton, manors.
42 *Cal. Pat. 1272–81*, 100.
43 *Cal. Fine R. 1272–1307*, 160, 457; S.R.O., DD/SAS NP 1, mm. 6, 8–10; Collinson, *Hist. Som.* iii. 60–1.
44 *Cal. Close, 1272–9*, 410; *Feud. Aids*, iv. 300.
45 S.R.O., DD/SAS NP 1, m. 10.
46 *Cal. Inq. p.m.* vi, p. 298.   47 Ibid. viii, p. 58.
48 Ibid. x, p. 181; *S.D.N.Q.* iv. 38.
49 Collinson, *Hist. Som.* ii. 199.
50 *S.D.N.Q.* iv. 38.
51 P.R.O., C 139/70, no. 32.

Durston in 1428.[52] Three years later the manor was held by Isabel, who by 1431 was the widow of Sir John of Rowdon.[53] She died in 1434, leaving Durston and the remainder of the Erleigh inheritance to Margaret.[54] Margaret married thirdly Sir William Cheyne, and both she and her husband died in 1443. The heir was Margaret's son Thomas Seymour, the issue of her first marriage.[55]

Thomas Seymour (knighted by 1456,[56] d. 1458) was succeeded by his grandson William Seymour,[57] who was then still under age and was knighted before his death in 1503.[58] Sir William's daughter Joan, his heir, married William Drury and died in 1517 leaving as her heirs her two cousins, the sons of Sir William's two sisters, John Stawell, son of Anne, and Edward Bampfield, son of Margaret.[59] Their succession to Durston was subject to a grant for lives made by Sir William to Catherine Winsor and her son Henry.[60] Edward Bampfield died in 1528[61] and was followed in turn by his sons John (d. 1532) and Richard (d. 1594).[62] Richard's son Amias sold his estate in 1598 to Sir John Stawell, who as grandson of Sir William Seymour's nephew John Stawell (d. 1541) had inherited the other half of the manor, subject to the life interest of Catherine Tyndale, possibly the Catherine Winsor of 1517.[63] Sir John Stawell died in 1604.[64] His grandson and heir, also John (later Sir John Stawell, K.B.), succeeded as a minor.[65] He suffered forfeiture after the Civil War and the manor was sold to Henry Cheeke in 1652.[66] Sir John, who recovered his land, died in 1662 and was followed by his two sons, first George (d. 1669) and then Ralph Stawell (cr. Baron Stawell 1683). Ralph's son John, Lord Stawell, died in 1692,[67] heavily in debt.[68] The family estates, including both Durston and St. Michaelchurch,[69] were evidently sold, both passing to the Seymour family, perhaps through purchase by Alexander Popham and descent to his daughter Elizabeth, wife of Francis Seymour.[70] Henry Seymour (d. 1805), son of Francis and Elizabeth, both of whom died in 1761, was lord of St. Michaelchurch by 1762[71] and of Durston by 1792.[72] Henry Seymour was succeeded by his son Henry (d. 1849) and then by his grandson Henry Danby Seymour (d. 1877), who sold the land, then amounting to 447 a. in the parish, in 1873 to Edward Portman, Viscount Portman.[73] The sale did not include the lordship of the manor, and Alfred Seymour (d. 1888), brother of Henry Danby Seymour, still owned land in the parish in 1888. Alfred Seymour was succeeded by his daughter Jane Margaret, who was still alive in 1914.[74] The Portman estate was divided and sold in 1930.[75]

The manor house at Durston was regularly occupied by the Erleigh family in the 14th century,[76] and its kitchen and oxhouse were repaired in 1328–9.[77] The present house, known as Lodge Farm by the mid 18th century,[78] stands on the north side of the church. It includes an open hall under a smoke-blackened wagon roof of thirty-one trusses, a two-storeyed porch leading to a cross entry at its lower end, and a solar over service rooms in a cross wing beyond the entry. There are traceried and transomed windows in solar and porch. Dates at both ends of the 15th century have been suggested.[79]

In or after 1170, and probably before 1176, William of Erleigh gave all his land at Buckland, Durston chapel, and land and churches elsewhere for the foundation of a house of Augustinian canons at Buckland. The canons were dispersed before c. 1180 and possession of the house and land was given to the Hospitallers to provide for a convent where all the sisters of the order were to be placed. The order also established a preceptory there, later endowed with a farm at Cogload,[80] but the sisters received endowments distinct from those of the preceptory, and some of the preceptory's land and income was assigned to them.[81] The grant to both the canons and the Hospitallers was in free alms,[82] but in 1304 Buckland was said to be part of 2 fees held by the Hospitallers of Edmund Mortimer.[83] The same two fees were claimed by successive earls of March until 1425 or later.[84] The claim may have been made in respect of land held by the preceptory. No preceptor was appointed after 1433, and after 1500 the sisters are thought to have become Augustinian.[85]

The preceptory, with manors in Devon, was leased from 1501 for 30 years to John Verney of Fairfield,[86] and the lease passed in 1506 to his younger sons John and George.[87] They were

52 *Feud. Aids*, iv. 364.
53 Ibid. 433.
54 P.R.O., C 139/70, no. 32; *Cal. Close, 1429–35*, 327.
55 P.R.O., C 139/110, no. 37; S.R.O., DD/AH 21/1 (Palmer MSS.).
56 *S.R.S.* xlix, p. 270.
57 *Cal. Inq. p.m. Hen. VII*, ii, pp. 224–5.
58 *S.R.S.* xvi. 260; *Cal. Inq. p.m. Hen. VII*, iii, pp. 413, 428.
59 P.R.O., C 142/79, no. 295.
60 G. D. Stawell, *A Quantock Family: Hist. of the Stawell Fam.* 339.
61 P.R.O., C 142/47, no. 28.
62 Ibid. C 142/75, pt. 2, no. 65; C 142/244, no. 102.
63 Ibid. CP 25(2)/207/40 Eliz. I East.; ibid. C 142/66, no. 71; *Som. Wills*, ed. Brown, vi. 73; *L. & P. Hen. VIII*, xviii (1), p. 193; Stawell, *Quantock Fam.* 62.
64 *Som. Wills*, ed. Brown, vi. 73.
65 *S.R.S.* lxvii, p. 60.
66 S.R.O., DD/PH 28; *Cal. Cttee. for Compounding*, ii. 1429.
67 *Complete Peerage*, xii (1), 26–7.
68 Hist. MSS. Com. 17, *14th Rep. VI, H.L. 1692–3*, p. 330.

69 Below, St. Michaelchurch, manor.
70 Burke, *Land. Gent.* (1914), 1696.
71 S.R.O., DD/SL 19.
72 Wilts. R.O. 1126/24.
73 Photocopy of sale cat. in possession of Mrs. M. Miles.
74 Burke, *Land. Gent.* (1914), 1696; S.R.O., Q/REr.
75 S.R.O., DD/KW 20.
76 *Cal. Inq. p.m.* x, p. 181; *S.R.S.* xxv, pp. 30–1.
77 S.R.O., DD/SAS NP 2, m. 5.
78 Ibid. Q/REl 29/4.
79 *Proc. Som. Arch. Soc.* cxxix. 129–32.
80 *S.R.S.* xxv, pp. 34–5.
81 *V.C.H. Som.* ii. 148–50; *S.D.N.Q.* xiv. 69; xvii. 41–3; *S.R.S.* xxv, pp. 1–8; 'Orig. Doc. in Lamb. Pal. Libr.' *Bull. Inst. Hist. Res.* suppl. 6 (1967), p. 11; Hugo, *Mynchin Buckland, passim*.
82 *S.R.S.* xxv, pp. 1–5.
83 *Cal. Inq. p.m.* iv, p. 164; *Cal. Close, 1302–7*, 275.
84 *Cal. Inq. p.m.* xvii, p. 457; *Cal. Close, 1360–4*, 159; P.R.O., C 136/104–5, no. 34; 139/18, no. 32.
85 Knowles and Hadcock, *Medieval Religious Houses*, 278, 284.
86 B.L. Lansd. 200, f. 84 and v.
87 *S.R.S.* xix. 102–3.

followed by Edmund Mill of Wells and his wife Anne in 1508 and by Henry Thornton of Curry Mallet in 1516.[88] Thornton's lease for 40 years was renewed in 1521.[89] He died in 1533 leaving his interest to his son-in-law Thomas Tynberry under the name of the farm and commandery of Buckland.[90] In 1539 the Hospitallers leased the same to William Hawley or Halley, Tynberry's son-in-law, for a term of 50 years[91] and on the dissolution of the order in 1540 Hawley became the Crown tenant.[92] In 1545 he and Alexander Popham bought the estate, then described as the manor and late preceptory of *BUCKLAND PRIORS*, with other former Hospitaller property.[93] The estate was conveyed solely to Hawley later in the year[94] and by 1548 he held just over 300 a. there.[95]

William Hawley died in 1567 and was followed in turn by his sons Henry (d. 1573) and Gabriel or Geoffrey (d. 1603), and by his grandson Sir Henry Hawley, son of his third son Francis.[96] Sir Henry died in 1623 having added the site of the dissolved priory and its demesnes by purchase from Edward Rogers in 1608.[97]

The priory surrendered in 1539[98] and the site and demesnes were let to farm to (Sir) Edward Rogers.[99] Rogers also leased former priory land in North Petherton.[1] In 1542 he took a Crown lease of the priory site and over 150 a. adjoining for 21 years.[2] Edward's grandson Edward Rogers sold the 'site, circuit, and curtilage' of the priory to Sir Henry Hawley in 1608.[3]

Hawley died in 1623 when his heir was his son, also Henry.[4] Henry Hawley was succeeded in 1628 by his brother Francis (cr. Bt. 1644, Baron Hawley 1645), who died in 1684 leaving his grandson, also Francis Hawley, as his heir.[5] Francis, Lord Hawley, sold his heavily mortgaged estate of Buckland to James Baker of Culmstock (Devon), clothier, in 1711 and Baker's widow Sarah and his son Christopher in 1725–6 sold it to George Parker of Boringdon (Devon).[6]

George Parker (d. 1743) was followed by his son John (d. 1768) and by his grandson, also John Parker (cr. Baron Boringdon 1784, d. 1788).[7] Thomas Gray of Earl's Court (Mdx.), a jeweller, acquired Buckland in 1809–10[8] and

died in 1820.[9] He was succeeded by his son Robert, resident rector of Sunderland (co. Dur.), who also held the living of Durston at his death in 1838.[10] Arthur Gray, then a minor and later ordained, succeeded his father in the manor[11] and sold the estate between 1860 and 1867 to Edward Portman, Baron Portman (cr. Vct. Portman 1873, d. 1888).[12] On the purchase of the Durston estate in 1873[13] the Portman family became owners of almost the entire parish.[14] Buckland farm, representing the former manor of Buckland, was sold to the tenant, Mr. G. R. Norman, by Edward Portman, Viscount Portman, in 1930.[15]

The conventual buildings at Buckland comprised two distinct parts, the nuns' church and living quarters and the church and domestic buildings of the preceptory.[16] The Augustinian canons had built a church by c. 1180 dedicated to St. Mary and St. Nicholas.[17] This came to be known as the greater church, in contrast to the chapel of the preceptory which stood with other buildings on its north side.[18] By the early 15th century, and probably since the change of ownership in the late 12th century, the nuns' church was dedicated to St. Mary and St. John or to St. John alone.[19] By 1506 there was an altar called the cross altar[20] whose two chaplains were supported by the farmer of the preceptory.[21] The site was surrounded by 'pleasure grounds', orchards, and gardens.[22] The preceptory chapel had by 1272 a light of St. Nicholas,[23] and by 1338 other buildings included a court or manor house, a bakehouse, a dovecot, and gardens.[24]

By 1675 Lord Hawley occupied a substantial house on the site.[25] It was remembered as having a wainscotted hall 'large enough to turn a coach and horses in'. The building was demolished c. 1800 together with an adjacent chapel which contained monuments 'with figures of men and arms' and a bellcot.[26] The chapel was still in use in 1798.[27] Buckland Farm, a plain house of three storeys, was built on made-up ground on or near the previous buildings presumably for Thomas Gray (d. 1820). Gravestones, probably from the nuns' burial ground, were discovered in 1836 several feet beneath the kitchen garden.[28] The present farm buildings incorporate a medieval

88 B.L. Cott. MS. Claud. E. vi, ff. 56v.–57, 168v.–169v.
89 P.R.O., LR 2/62, f. 87 and v.
90 *S.D.N.Q.* vii. 111–13.
91 P.R.O., LR 2/62, f. 181 and v.
92 Hugo, *Mynchin Buckland*, 153–6.
93 *L. & P. Hen. VIII*, xx (1), p. 125; *S.R.S.* ii. 41.
94 P.R.O., C 54/443, no. 47.
95 *Cal. Pat.* 1547–8, 267.
96 P.R.O., C 142/145, no. 18; C 142/167, no. 84; *Som. Wills*, ed. Brown, vi. 69–70.
97 P.R.O., E 368/542, rot. 112.
98 *L. & P. Hen. VIII*, xiv (1), p. 106.
99 Hugo, *Mynchin Buckland*, 128–30.
1 Below, N. Petherton manors (Buckland and Chadmead).
2 P.R.O., C 142/148, no. 28; C 142/197, no. 52.
3 Hugo, *Mynchin Buckland*, 179–80.
4 *S.R.S.* lxvii, pp. 22–4.
5 P.R.O., CP 25(2)/479/4 Chas. I Mich; *Complete Peerage*, vi. 418–19.
6 S.R.O., DD/PT 36; DD/SS, bdle. 8; West Devon R.O., Acc. 69 (Parker of Saltram), lease 1726.
7 *Complete Peerage*, ii. 220.
8 S.R.O., Q/REl 29/4.
9 M.I. in Durston ch.

10 *Gent. Mag.* (1838), i. 431–3; S.R.O., D/D/B reg. 35, f. 63.
11 *Alum. Oxon.* 1715–1886; S.R.O., D/P/durn 2/1/2, bap. 1823.
12 S.R.O., D/P/durn 3/3/1, 13/1/1; Burke, *Peerage* (1949), 1618–19.
13 Above.
14 *P.O. Dir. Som.* (1875).
15 S.R.O., DD/KW 20.
16 *Knights Hospitallers in Eng.* (Camd. Soc. [1st ser.], lxv), 17–19; *Proc. Som. Arch. Soc.* cxxix. 110–13.
17 *S.R.S.* xxv, p. 5.
18 Hugo, *Mynchin Buckland*, 13, 111; S.R.O., DD/AH 12/1.
19 Hugo, *Mynchin Buckland*, 13, 111; *S.R.S.* xvi. 403.
20 *S.R.S.* xix. 102.
21 B.L. Lansd. 200, f. 84 and v.; P.R.O., LR 2/62, ff. 87 and v., 181 and v.
22 Hugo, *Mynchin Buckland*, 128.
23 *S.R.S.* xxv, pp. 23–4.
24 *Knights Hospitallers in Eng.* 17.
25 J. Ogilby, *Britannia*.
26 Hugo, *Mynchin Buckland*, 112.
27 *Registers of Durston*, ed. R. G. Bartelot (1914), 16–17.
28 Hugo, *Mynchin Buckland*, 112.

buttressed wall, but otherwise date from the later 19th century.

In 1391 John Hayward settled 16 messuages and 21 a. of land in Crosse by Buckland and 3 messuages and 3 a. in Durston on William Frebody and his wife Clemence.[29] She may have been Clemence, widow of John de Moleyns, a South Petherton miller.[30] Nicholas Moleyns died in 1429 holding lands at Crosse and Buckland,[31] and in 1497 John Moleyns died in possession of the manor of *CROSSE* in Durston, land in North Petherton, and mills in South Petherton and Kingsbury Episcopi, held as of the manor of Durston Hall. John was succeeded by his uncle, Richard Moleyns.[32] William Moleyns owned Crosse by 1531 and died in 1553 when his heir was his son Anthony.[33] Anthony died in or before 1590 when his two daughters and coheirs sold the manor and lands in Durston and Lyng to Henry Moleyns.[34] In 1613 James Arnwood and his wife, Richard Bartholomew and Thomas Knollys, possibly acting as trustees, granted the manor to Robert Waterton.[35] Waterton settled Crosse on his grandson Robert Blatchford in 1647,[36] and Robert Blatchford, perhaps his son, still owned it in 1722.[37] It passed from the Blatchfords to Elizabeth Hascoll, whose son Robert died in 1782 dividing his estate into three parts. Hascoll's Farm in Lower Durston formed part of the estate.[38]

In 1725 part of Buckland manor, described as the manor of *COGLOAD*, was purchased by George Parker from Lord Hawley.[39] By 1752 it was owned by George Baker of Brockenhurst (Hants).[40] He was still owner in 1767 but by 1781 had been succeeded by John Baker. Both John[41] and George Baker were described as owners of the manor in 1790,[42] but thereafter the estate was known as Cogload farm. Anna Wheaton, successively wife of John Kinglake (d. 1809) and Joseph Gatcombe (d. 1820),[43] owned Cogload farm, which she expanded, from 1784[44] until her death in 1847. It passed to Mary Mullins of Goathurst[45] and later to her son Thomas. On Thomas's death by 1903 the farm and a larger estate at Lyng were sold.[46]

The Augustinian canons at Buckland were given the chapel of Durston by William of Erleigh.[47] The Hospitallers, their successors, were instituted as parsons in 1189,[48] and in 1335 they were recorded as holding the church with

the tithes of Cogload.[49] Among the chaplains supported by the preceptory in 1501 was a chaplain at Durston.[50] The impropriate rectory was leased by the Hospitallers to William Hawley in 1539[51] and descended like Buckland manor. From 1838 a tithe rent charge of £170 was payable to the lord of Buckland manor on land representing Durston manor in the west of the parish and on Cogload in the east.[52] In 1862 the rent charge was separated from Buckland manor and was transferred by the Revd. Arthur Gray to the incumbent.[53]

In 1535 the Hospitallers' estate included the rectory of Buckland with the chapel of St. Michaelchurch. The whole, comprising tithes and offerings, was worth 12s. 5d. net.[54] It was farmed by Edward Rogers by 1538[55] and was leased to him by the Crown with the priory site in 1542,[56] and sold to him and others in 1544.[57] Rogers's grandson, also Edward Rogers, retained the rectory when he sold his land in Durston parish to Sir Henry Hawley in 1608,[58] and Sir Francis Rogers was probably still in possession at his death in 1638.[59] By 1647, however, the tithes of Buckland had come into the hands of Sir Francis Hawley,[60] lord of Buckland manor, and were subsumed within the manor. By 1838 Buckland manor land was tithe free.[61]

A cottage and 45 a. of land, belonging by 1529 to St. Andrew's chantry in St. Mary's church, Taunton,[62] were sold in 1549 to George Payne of Hutton.[63] In 1620 the land was conveyed by Nicholas Halswell to Sir Henry Hawley of Buckland.[64]

ECONOMIC HISTORY. An estate at Durston was taxed at 2¾ hides in 1086 and comprised land for 4 teams. The demesne farm, assessed at 1 hide 1½ virgate, had 1 ploughteam and was staffed by 4 *servi*. Four *villani*, 5 bordars, and 4 cottars occupied the remainder. There were 15 a. of meadow, 20 a. of pasture, and 20 a. of wood.[65] In 1312 Durston manor comprised 300 a. of demesne arable, *c.* 15 a. of meadow, 30 a. of pasture in a park, 15 a. of wood, and rents totalling 40s. from 2 free and 8 customary tenants.[66] Buckland manor and Cogload, which comprise most of the low-lying land in the parish, may represent ground brought into use after the later 11th century by drainage works in

29 S.R.S. xvii, pp. 144–6.
30 V.C.H. Som. iv. 189.
31 S.R.S. xvi, pp. 133–4.
32 Cal. Inq. p.m. Hen. VII, ii, pp. 92–3.
33 P.R.O., C 142/108, no. 103.
34 Ibid. CP 25(2)/206/32 Eliz. I Trin.
35 Ibid. CP 25(2)/386/10 Jas. I Hil.
36 Inf. from Mrs. Miles, Durston, based on deeds of 'Mundays', Durston.
37 P.R.O., CP 25(2)/962/7 Anne East.; CP 25(2)/1057/8 Geo. I Trin.
38 Ibid. CP 43/677, rot. 23.
39 S.R.O., DD/SS, bdle. 8; DD/PT 36.
40 Ibid. DD/SL 18.
41 Ibid. Q/REl 29/4.
42 MS. in possession of Sir Benjamin Slade, London.
43 S.R.O., D/P/sto. st. g 2/1/2; D/P/pet. n 2/1/22.
44 Ibid. Q/REl 29/4.
45 M.I. in Lyng ch.; S.R.O., DD/CH 96/4; DD/X/CRE 1.

46 Kelly's Dir. Som. (1889); S.R.O., DD/X/CRE 1.
47 S.R.S. xxv, pp. 1–2.
48 Ibid. pp. 8–9.
49 Ibid. ix, pp. 239–40.
50 B.L. Lansd. 200, f. 84 and v.
51 P.R.O., LR 2/62, f. 181 and v.
52 S.R.O., tithe award.   53 Ibid. D/P/durn 3/1/1.
54 Valor Eccl. (Rec. Com.) i. 211.
55 P.R.O., SC 6/Hen. VIII/3137.
56 Ibid. E 315/214, ff. 33v.–34.
57 L. & P. Hen. VIII, xix (1), p. 504.
58 Above, this section.
59 S.R.S. lxvii, p. 145.
60 S.R.O., DD/MI 5.
61 Ibid. tithe award.
62 S.R.S. ii. 197; lxxvii, p. 60; P.R.O., C 1/473, nos. 22–3.
63 Cal. Pat. 1549–51, 135.
64 S.R.O., DD/S/WH 15.
65 V.C.H. Som. i. 494.
66 P.R.O., C 134/81, no. 20.

and around Curry moor, at their greatest in the later 13th century.[67] In 1338 the preceptory demesne estate at Buckland comprised 268 a. of arable land, 39 a. of meadow, and rents; the priory had 3 carucates of arable and 3 a. of meadow.[68]

An agreement of the mid 13th century gave Buckland priory the tithes of a meadow in Cogload and 'la Newmede' for horses, and limited grazing on the preceptory's fields called Oxenmoor and Cowmoor, the former for 36 oxen in return for carting manure there from their farmyard.[69] By 1338 the preceptory employed a hayward, a pig keeper, and a carter.[70] In 1539 the former preceptory demesne comprised 122 a. of wheat, 112 a. of rye, 114 a. of barley, 33 a. of oats, and 1 a. of beans. A further 39 a. lay fallow for one year and 113 a. for two, 8 a. were described as 'dunged with the corn', and 12 a. as 'dunged with the fold'. There were three meadows with hay in cocks. Among the farm buildings were rooms for male and female servants, a dairy, and a lime house, and there were pens for cocks, hens, and hawks, and cider-making equipment.[71] The site of the priory in 1542 comprised 117 a., apparently of grassland, which had been arable in 1338, and 10 a. of wood, the grassland in fields enclosed by polled elms and ashes, some said to be a hundred years old.[72]

There continued to be two main estates in the parish after the Dissolution: Buckland Priors, the former preceptory lands, measured over 300 a. in 1548.[73] By the mid 17th century Durston manor was mostly divided into small tenancies on long leases, but Henry Cheeke held the demesne farm of some 106 a.[74] The same holding, known as Lodge farm by 1766,[75] measured 112 a. in 1838.[76] Buckland farm and Cogload manor measured together 450 a. in 1725,[77] and by 1838 386 a. and 68 a. respectively when the several holdings of Cogload had been combined in the hands of Mrs. Anna Gatcombe to form Cogload farm.[78]

Inventories of the 17th century indicate small-scale mixed farming with crops of wheat, barley, peas, and small orchards of apples and pears.[79] Richard Weech (d. 1679) had at least 15 a. of arable, 2 yokes of oxen, 4 horses, 2 milking cows, 2 heifers and their calves, and 4 pigs.[80] John Slocombe (d. 1677) had a flock of sheep, a mare and colt, and some pigs, and held in store bacon, barley, cider, and clover seed.[81] Henry Bryant

(d. 1693) had 22 a. under corn and a flock of 22 old sheep and 15 lambs, while Edward Sherwood (d. c. 1713) combined mixed farming with his profession as a wood carver.[82] The inn in 1687 also housed a tobacco shop.[83]

In the 18th century the two farms whose land lay on the moors in the south concentrated on cattle raising. In the 1750s the Ruscombe family of Buckland fattened oxen for sale in Salisbury and London.[84] John Kinglake (d. 1809), who farmed at Cogload and also in Stoke St. Gregory, similarly traded in cattle over a wide area between North Devon, Dorset, and Hampshire, and occasionally as far away as London. The arable land at Cogload in his time produced wheat and, in 1809, flax.[85]

Tenements in Durston manor were sublet in the early 19th century: the largest was called Drakes and Honey Groves and amounted to 62 a. in 1815 when it was let for seven years for £105, the undertenant covenanting not to convert grassland for tillage.[86] By 1838 three farms ranging in size between 39 a. and 61 a.,[87] Hascoll or Hascoll's, Warr's, and Frog Lane, were sublet. The names, the first two based on 17th-century tenants,[88] did not indicate a single tenant for each farm, and still in 1873 three of the six named farms were held in multiple tenancies: Warr's farm was shared by 5 tenants, Lodge by 3, Frog Lane by 2. Samuel Kidner, who actually farmed most of Lodge, was then also tenant of 4 other holdings, his total acreage amounting to 210 a.[89] By 1851 the farmer at Buckland (375 a.) employed 20 labourers and Kidner had 8 labourers.[90] Kidner was involved in the experimental use of lime dressings in the 1860s,[91] and by 1881 held 300 a. on which he employed 6 men, 3 women, and 2 boys.[92]

In 1838 the balance of land use had been slightly in favour of arable in the titheable area of the parish,[93] but by 1905 there were 603 a. of permanent grass and 418 a. of arable.[94] In 1982 arable again took the largest share, most under barley and wheat but with significant areas of rape, beans, oats, and peas, and one holding devoted to horticulture. One of the farms was a specialist dairy holding.[95]

There was a single shop in the parish by 1824.[96] In 1851 there were 3 carpenters, 2 smiths, 2 basket makers, a dressmaker, and a butcher, and a father and son described as machine makers.[97] By 1861 there were 3 shops, a wheelwright, and a boot and shoe maker.[98] One shop had closed

[67] M. Williams, *Draining of the Som. Levels* (1970), 55–7.
[68] *Knights Hospitallers in Eng.* 17–19.
[69] *S.R.S.* xxv, p. 15.
[70] *Knights Hospitallers in Eng.* 18–19.
[71] P.R.O., LR 2/62, f. 182v.
[72] Ibid. E 315/214, ff. 33v.–34; SC 6/Hen. VIII/3137; Hugo, *Mynchin Buckland*, 162–3.
[73] *Cal. Pat.* 1547–8, 267.
[74] S.R.O., DD/PH 28.
[75] Ibid. Q/REl 29/4.
[76] Ibid. tithe award.
[77] Ibid. DD/SS, bdle. 8; West Devon R.O., Acc. 69 (Parker of Saltram), lease, 1726.
[78] S.R.O., tithe award.
[79] e.g. ibid. DD/SP inventories, 1646/62; 1648/51; 1684/167; 1685/28, 56A, 96; 1691/82.
[80] Ibid. 1679/54A.
[81] Ibid. 1677/11.
[82] Ibid. 1693/4; 1714–15/8.

[83] Ibid. 1679/21.
[84] Ibid. Q/AD 2.
[85] Ibid. DD/X/VEA; *Proc. Som. Arch. Soc.* cxxix. 161–70.
[86] S.R.O., DD/CH 73/3.
[87] Ibid. tithe award.
[88] Ibid. DD/SP inventory, 1668/9; ibid. Q/REl 29/4; O.S. Map 1/2,500, Som. LXXI. 2 (1888 edn.); *Proc. Som. Arch. Soc.* xlvii. 158.
[89] Photocopy of sale cat. in possession of Mrs. M. Miles.
[90] P.R.O., HO 107/1922.
[91] *Jnl. Bath & West of Eng. Soc.* 2nd ser. xii (1864), 353.
[92] P.R.O., RG 11/2365.
[93] S.R.O., tithe award.
[94] Statistics supplied by the then Bd. of Agric. 1905.
[95] Min. of Agric., Fisheries, and Food, agric. returns, 1982.
[96] S.R.O., D/P/durn 13/2/1.
[97] P.R.O., HO 107/1922.
[98] *P.O. Dir. Som.* (1861).

by 1875 and there was further contraction in the 1880s.[99] A wheelwright, a newsagent, and a chimney sweep were recorded in 1923,[1] and by 1930 there survived the village stores, the post office, a wheelwright, and a blacksmith.[2] By 1931 a petrol filling station was established at Durston Elms, and guesthouse accommodation was offered there.[3] Durston Elms garage and Durston (Somerset) Woodlands (founded in 1953)[4] were in retail business in 1985.

A windmill was built on Durston manor in 1324–5.[5] It stood on a mound south of Lower Durston village once thought to be a barrow.[6]

LOCAL GOVERNMENT. The tithing of Durston regularly constituted part of North Petherton hundred except, apparently, in 1327.[7] The parish, or more probably that detached part called Priestwood, was subject in the later 14th and early 15th century to the swanimote jurisdiction of North Petherton park, administered as a royal forest[8] and known as Parkhouse.[9] In 1327 Cogload was taxed as part of the Hospitallers' free manor of Halse,[10] and in 1508 its tithingman reported to the court leet of the manor of Buckland.[11] In 1640 Durston and Cogload formed a single tithing,[12] and in 1649 Durston, Cogload, and St. Michaelchurch were similarly linked.[13] Cogload again formed a separate tithing for land tax purposes by 1766 but only until 1781.[14]

Durston manor court met every three weeks in the 15th century.[15] Court rolls for leet, view of frankpledge, and court baron survive for March and September 1632. A tithingman, two constables, and a bailiff appeared at the courts, and business included admissions of tenants, orders for the maintenance of buildings, hedges, and ditches, and fines for playing unlawful games, for not living on tenements, and for harbouring people of ill-repute. The court also ordered the replacement of the cucking stool.[16] The whole parish was ordered to repair stocks in 1650.[17] Suit of court to Durston manor twice a year was required under a lease of 1792.[18]

Buckland manor had a twice-yearly view of frankpledge by 1269[19] and pleas and perquisites formed a small part of the preceptory's income in 1338.[20] A court leet held at Michaelmas 1508

claimed jurisdiction over Cogload and widely scattered estates of the Hospitallers.[21] In the mid 17th century Crosse manor was said to have view of frankpledge and court leet.[22] In the mid 18th century the lord of Cogload required suit of court from a tenant 'at reasonable summons' to Cogload.[23]

In the 17th century the parish was administered by a group of between six and nine men who approved the rates.[24] Five men formed the fortnightly select vestry by 1821,[25] and ten were listed as 'proper' to hold parish office in 1829.[26] In 1840 the parish officers comprised 2 wardens, 2 overseers, 2 waywardens, and two tax assessors. Two constables were chosen each year from 1842.[27] By 1797 the poor were receiving cash or clothing regularly, with occasional payments of cash for lodgings and medical services, and gifts in kind such as a spinning turn or a saucepan.[28] A cottage built on the waste in 1651 was to revert for the use of the poor.[29] The overseers were paying rent for a poorhouse by 1800; it was owned by the lord of Durston manor[30] and stood in Lower Durston on the south side of the main road.[31] In 1821 it was referred to as a workhouse.[32] Rent for the house was paid until 1836,[33] when the parish became part of the Taunton poor-law union. The parish formed part of the Taunton rural district in 1894 and Taunton Deane district (later Borough) in 1974.[34]

CHURCH. The position of Durston church beside the former manor house suggests a manorial origin. In or after 1170, and probably before 1176, William of Erleigh, lord of the manor, gave Durston chapel, possibly once dependent on North Petherton, as part of the endowment of Buckland priory.[35] The Hospitallers, replacing the canons at the priory, became perpetual parsons in 1189.[36] On the lapse of the office of preceptor after 1433 it was for a time let to the lords of the manor and described as a free chapel.[37] By 1501 it was served by a chaplain paid by the farmer of the former preceptory,[38] and after the Dissolution in 1540 was regarded as a donative by owners of Buckland manor as impropriators of Durston rectory.[39] The living was described in 1792 as a perpetual and augmented curacy,[40] in 1839 as a chapel, curacy,

99 *P.O. Dir. Som.* (1875); *Kelly's Dir. Som.* (1883, 1889, 1894); P.R.O., RG 11/2365.
1 *Kelly's Dir. Som.* (1923).
2 S.R.O., DD/KW 20.
3 *Kelly's Dir. Som.* (1931).
4 Local inf.
5 S.R.O., DD/SAS NP 2, m. 3.
6 *V.C.H. Som.* i. 182; *Proc. Som. Arch. Soc.* xcvi. 235; O.S. arch. rec. cards.
7 *S.R.S.* iii. 240–4.
8 *Cal. Pat.* 1350–4, 377.
9 P.R.O., SC 2/200/13.
10 *S.R.S.* iii. 186.
11 S.R.O., DD/AH 11/9.
12 Ibid. DD/SG 58–9.
13 Ibid. DD/SF 1690.
14 Ibid. Q/REl 29/4.
15 P.R.O., C 139/70, no. 32.
16 B.L. Add. Ch. 28283.
17 *S.R.S.* xxviii. 128.
18 Wilts. R.O. 1126/24.
19 *S.R.S.* xxv, p. 37.

20 *Knights Hospitallers in Eng.* 17.
21 S.R.O., DD/AH 11/9.
22 Inf. from Mrs. Miles based on deeds of 'Munday's', Durston.
23 S.R.O., DD/SL 18.
24 Ibid. D/P/durn 4/1/1.
25 Ibid. 9/1/1.
26 Ibid. 13/2/2.
27 Ibid. 9/1/2.
28 Ibid. 9/1/1, 13/2/1–2, 13/10/1.
29 *S.R.S.* xxviii. 152–3.
30 S.R.O., D/P/durn 13/2/1.
31 Ibid. tithe award.
32 Ibid. D/P/durn 9/1/1.
33 Ibid. 13/2/2.
34 Youngs, *Local Admin. Units*, i. 673, 675–6.
35 *S.R.S.* xxv, pp. 1–2.
36 Ibid. pp. 8–9.
37 P.R.O., C 139/70, no. 32; C 139/110, no. 37; *Cal. Close*, 1429–35, 327.
38 B.L. Lansd. 200, f. 84 and v.
39 e.g. *Rep. Com. Eccl. Revenues*, pp. 136–7; below, this section.
40 S.R.O., D/D/B reg. 32, f. 121.

or donative,[41] in 1860 as a rectory,[42] and in 1867 as a perpetual curacy.[43] The living, held with Thurloxton from 1896[44] and united with it between 1904 and 1961,[45] was held with Lyng between 1961 and 1978.[46] In 1978 it became part of the united benefice of North Newton with St. Michaelchurch, Thurloxton, and Durston.[47]

The preceptors of Buckland presumably appointed the chaplains of Durston until 1433. In 1434 and 1443 successive ladies of the manor had the right of presentation at alternate vacancies possibly in conjunction with the Hospitallers.[48] The priors of St. John of Jerusalem appear to have appointed chaplains when the preceptory was let to farm after 1501.[49] After the Dissolution the impropriators appointed and paid curates until 1930 when Edward Portman, Viscount Portman, retained the advowson on the sale of the estate.[50] Lord Portman died in 1942 and his uncle and successor, Seymour Berkeley Portman, Viscount Portman, transferred the patronage of Thurloxton with Durston to the bishop of Bath and Wells in 1944.[51] The bishop has three out of every four turns in the advowson of the united benefice.[52]

The curate was paid £2 10s. c. 1535,[53] £3 6s. 8d. and his tabling in the later 16th century,[54] and £15 in the mid 18th.[55] The average income was £20 in 1829–31.[56] By 1860 the annual stipend had been increased to £30. In that year Queen Anne's Bounty augmented the living by grant of £200 and the lay impropriator, the Revd. Arthur Gray, made over his tithe rent charge of £170, which from 1862 was payable to the incumbent.[57] In 1838 there was no glebe;[58] no house was provided for the curate.[59]

In 1420 a friar minor was licensed to be enclosed as a hermit in a cell near Buckland priory.[60] There was an anniversary chaplain at Buckland in 1450,[61] and two chaplains in the priory church and one in the preceptory chapel under the farmers after 1501.[62] In 1541 licence was given to make a churchyard round the church at Durston,[63] presumably as a result of the closure of Buckland priory where the inhabitants may have been buried. Curates were not resident in the parish and in 1630 services on Wednesdays, Fridays, and holy days were not read.[64] No church ales were held after 1634.[65] Thomas Jenkins, curate by 1688 and until 1699 or later, also served North Newton, and in 1689 declared himself a non-juror.[66] William Bampfield, curate from 1776 until 1782 or later, also served Lyng and Michaelchurch,[67] and Thomas Tregenna Biddulph, curate by 1815 and until 1838 and a leading Evangelical, was also incumbent of St. James's, Bristol.[68] In 1815 he lived in an adjoining parish for three months of the year and his assistant curate, who lived in Creech St. Michael and also served Lyng, then and later held services each Sunday at Durston.[69] By 1840 two services were held during the summer and one in winter.[70] On Census Sunday 1851 the general congregation was 100 in the morning and 146 in the afternoon, with 35 children at each from the Sunday school.[71] William Smith Tomkins, curate 1862–96, served the parish from West Monkton in 1873–4 but in 1875 lived at Castle Cary where also he was the curate. In 1881 he was boarding at Lodge Farm but by 1883 was living in Weston-super-Mare.[72] There was a resident assistant curate in 1901–2.[73]

The church house was a two-storeyed, thatched building; part was used as a school until 1644, when fruit was stored there.[74]

The church of *ST. JOHN THE BAPTIST*, dedicated in the 1540s to St. Nicholas,[75] is a small building of stone comprising chancel, nave with south porch, and western tower, all but the tower rebuilt in 1852–3 to the designs of C. H. Knowles in the Decorated style.[76] The furnishings include a communion table of 1635.[77] There was a gallery in the tower in 1873.[78]

There are five bells, the oldest dated 1633.[79] The registers date from 1712 and are complete.[80] The plate includes a cup and cover of 1695, a paten of c. 1655, and a saucer dated 1728.[81]

NONCONFORMITY. Seventeen people were fined for not taking communion in 1671.[82] There was a Quaker in the parish in 1679.[83] A

41 Ibid. D/D/B reg. 35, f. 63.
42 Ibid. reg. 38, f. 36.
43 Ibid. D/P/durn 8/4/1.
44 Ibid. 2/1/2, flyleaf.
45 Ibid. D/P/lyn 22/3/1.
46 *Dioc. Dir.*
47 S.R.O., D/P/new. n 2/9/2.
48 P.R.O., C 139/70, no. 32; C 139/110, no. 37; *Cal. Close*, 1429–35, 327.
49 B.L. Lansd. 200, f. 84 and v.; ibid. Cott. MS. Claud. E vi, ff. 168v.–169v.
50 Above, manors.
51 S.R.O., D/P/thu 2/9/2; Burke, *Peerage* (1949), 1619.
52 *Dioc. Dir.*
53 S.R.O., D/D/Vc 20.
54 *S.D.N.Q.* xiii. 271.
55 S.R.O., D/D/Vc 87.
56 *Rep. Com. Eccl. Revenues*, pp. 136–7.
57 S.R.O., D/P/durn 3/3/1–2; C. Hodgson, *Queen Anne's Bounty* (1864), suppl. p. xlviii; *Livings Augmented by Q.A.B.* H.C. 122, p. 25 (1867), liv.
58 S.R.O., tithe award.
59 e.g. ibid. D/D/Ca 22, 274; *Rep. Com. Eccl. Revenues*, pp. 136–7.
60 *Cal. Papal Reg.* vii. 180.
61 *S.R.S.* xlix, p. 140.
62 B.L. Lansd. 200, f. 84 and v.
63 *L. & P. Hen. VIII*, xvi, p. 502.

64 S.R.O., D/D/Ca 22, 274.
65 Ibid. D/P/durn 4/1/1.
66 Ibid.; Hist. MSS. Com. 32, *13th Rep. VI, Fitzherbert*, p. 26.
67 *Registers of Durston*, ed. R. G. Bartelot (1914), 32–3; S.R.O., D/D/Bo.
68 S.R.O., D/D/Rb 1815; *Alum. Oxon.* 1715–1886; E. Green, *Bibliotheca Somersetensis*, ii. 172; *Proc. Som. Arch. Soc.* cxxx. 137.
69 S.R.O., D/D/Rb 1815, 1827.
70 Ibid. D/D/Va 1840.
71 P.R.O., HO 129/315/2/7/13.
72 S.R.O., D/P/durn 2/1/2; Jeboult, *Valley of the Tone* (1873), 46; *Clergy List* (1874); *P.O. Dir. Som.* (1875); P.R.O., RG 11/2365; *Kelly's Dir. Som.* (1883, 1889).
73 *Kelly's Dir. Som.* (1902); *Dioc. Kal.*
74 S.R.O., D/P/durn 4/1/1.
75 *L. & P. Hen. VIII*, xvi, p. 502; *S.R.S.* xxi. 62–3.
76 S.R.O., D/P/durn 6/1/1; *Bridgwater Times*, 1 Apr. 1852, advert. for builders' tenders.
77 S.R.O., D/P/durn 4/1/1.
78 F. B. Bond & B. Camm, *Rood Screens and Roodlofts*, i. 166; Jeboult, *Valley of the Tone*, 46.
79 S.R.O., DD/SAS CH 16/1.
80 Ibid. D/P/durn 2/1/1–2; *Registers of Durston*, ed. R. G. Bartelot.
81 *Proc. Som. Arch. Soc.* xlvii. 157–8.
82 S.R.O., D/P/durn 4/1/1.
83 *S.R.S.* lxxv. 109.

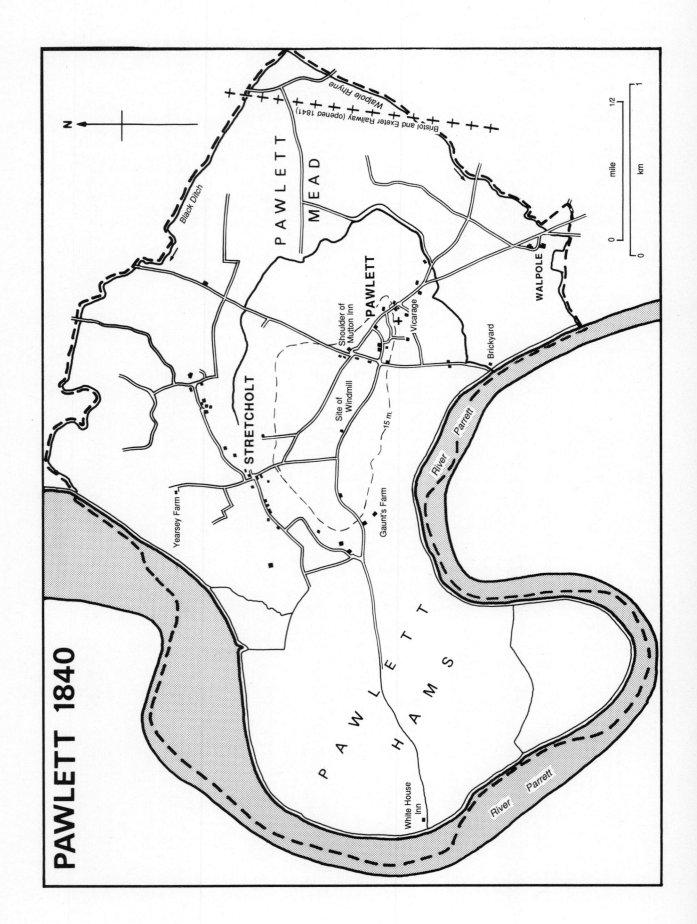

PAWLETT 1840

N

Black Ditch

PAWLETT MEAD

Walpole Rhyne

Bristol and Exeter Railway (opened 1841)

STRETCHOLT

Shoulder of Mutton Inn

PAWLETT

Vicarage

WALPOLE

Site of Windmill

Brickyard

15 m.

Yearsey Farm

Gaunt's Farm

River Parrett

P A W L E T T   H A M S

White House Inn

River Parrett

1/2   1
mile
km
0   0

house was licensed for use by Presbyterians in 1760,[84] and regular services were held by Wesleyan Methodists in 1848;[85] no later evidence has been found of either congregation.

EDUCATION. A schoolmaster left Buckland in 1554, and a teacher at Durston in 1612 was reported as unlicensed.[86] Part of the church house was used as a day school before 1644.[87] There was a dame school for 6 to 10 children in 1819.[88] By 1835 there were two day schools with a total of 12 children and a Sunday school, begun in 1823, for 30 children.[89] In 1846 there was a dame school with 14 pupils and the Sunday school, then teaching 60 children, provided clothing for poor pupils.[90] A church school was built in 1853 in Higher Durston[91] and it had 45 on the books in 1905. Numbers fell to 23 in 1925 and to 13 in 1945. The school closed in 1946,[92] and in 1985 the building was a private house.

CHARITIES FOR THE POOR. None known.

PAWLETT

PAWLETT parish lies north of Bridgwater in a bend of the river Parrett near its mouth. The river confines the parish on the west, and on the north-east and south-east the boundary follows the Black Ditch and Walpole Rhyne respectively. From north to south the parish measures 3 km.; from east to west 5.5 km. Its area is 1,258 ha. (3,108 a.).[93] At its centre is Pawlett Hill, on which Pawlett village stands. On lower ground are Stretcholt hamlet to the north and Walpole hamlet to the south.

Pawlett Hill rises to 32 m. above sea level, an outcrop of Lower Lias clay and limestone forming a detached part of the Polden ridge; it is surrounded by low-lying alluvium, marine sands, and Burtle beds. Walpole Rhyne and the Black Ditch may represent an earlier course of the Parrett, which on its present course has moved its banks, sometimes naturally, sometimes in association with man-made banks and drains.[94] The name Walpole refers to a pool or pill (creek) associated with a sea wall.[95] All the land within the meander enclosing the west side of the parish may have been reclaimed from saltmarsh, probably beginning in the 13th century. Gaunts Farm, south of Pawlett Hill and below the 15-m. contour, and Yearsey Farm, on the marshes west of Stretcholt, seem to mark the progress of land reclamation in the 18th century.[96]

A bronze palstave is said to have been found near Stretcholt. Pawlett Hill has yielded evidence of occupation from the Roman period, and there may have been a Saxon site in Pawlett Hams.[97]

Pawlett village, the name of which was that of an 11th-century estate[98] and may refer to a stream either with stakes or below a steep-sided hill,[99] stands at the south-east end of Pawlett Hill and consisted until the 19th century of a few stone farmhouses and irregular closes in a triangle of roads with the church in the south-east angle. Along the north-eastern side of the village Puriton Way ran from the pound at the top of the hill to Bourdon or Bourne Green at its foot. West from the green ran Burham Lane, and south from the pound ran Canham Lane, formerly the way to Pawlett pill.[1] Pawlett village later expanded west and north-west along the hill top, and much of the historic centre was infilled, partly with local authority housing and largely in brick. Stretcholt and Walpole were also the names of 11th-century estates.[2] Stretcholt is a road-side settlement along the probable course of the Saxon 'herpath'.[3] Walpole hamlet was partly destroyed by the building of the new road to Bridgwater in 1821–2.[4] In the mid 20th century it became the site of a fuel distribution depot.[5]

The name Stretcholt suggests that the area was anciently wooded, and coppicing was practised at Stretcholt in the later 18th century.[6] There were 12 a. of coppice in 1838.[7] There was a warren on Pawlett Gaunt's manor in 1477.[8]

Before the 18th century the main route through the parish was that which came from the north through Stretcholt and across the Hams to the river crossing opposite Combwich. The route was regarded as the king's highway by the 15th century.[9] A second route from the north to Pawlett village was causewayed and crossed the watercourse, later known as Brickyard Rhyne, by Queen Bridge, recorded in 1497.[10] A route from the east along the Polden

84 S.R.O., Q/RR meeting ho. lics.
85 Ibid. D/N/tmc 3/2/1.
86 Ibid. D/D/Ca 22, 175.
87 Ibid. D/P/durn 4/1/1.
88 *Educ. of Poor Digest*, p. 782.
89 *Educ. Enq. Abstract*, p. 805.
90 Nat. Soc. *Inquiry, 1846–7*, Som. 12–13.
91 *Kelly's Dir. Som.* (1889).
92 S.R.O. C/E 4/64; ibid. D/P/durn 18/11/1.
93 *Census*. This article was completed in 1986.
94 O.S. Map 1/50,000, sheet 182 (1976 edn.); Geol. Surv. Map 1/50,000, solid and drift, sheet 279 and parts of 265 and 295 (1980 edn.).
95 Ekwall, *Eng. Place-Names*, 470–1; A. H. Smith, *Eng. Place-Name Elements*, ii. 244.
96 O.S. Map 1/50,000, sheet 182 (1976 edn.); below, econ. hist.

97 Som. C.C., Sites and Mons. Rec.
98 *V.C.H. Som.* i. 499.
99 Ekwall, *Eng. Place-Names*, 342; Smith, *Eng. Place-Name Elements*, ii. 59.
1 Wimborne St. Giles, Shaftesbury MSS., map 1658; S.R.O., T/PH/ea map 1780.   2 Below, manors.
3 Fields nearby were called Stowey: S.R.O., tithe award; cf. *V.C.H. Som.* v. 191.
4 Below, this section.
5 O.S. Map 1/25,000, ST 34 (1959 edn.).
6 S.R.O., DD/MLY 1, 4.
7 Ibid. tithe award.
8 Wimborne St. Giles, Shaftesbury MSS., M 205.
9 *Cart. St. Mark's, Bristol* (Bristol Rec. Soc. xxi), pp. 133–4.
10 *Manorial accts. of St. Augustine's Abbey, Bristol* (Bristol Rec. Soc. xxii), p. 35.

ridge divided at Pawlett village; both branches joined the road to the river crossing in the mid 17th century.[11] The roads north and east of the village were turnpiked in 1759 to form part of the Bristol–Bridgwater road which was rerouted through Walpole in 1822.[12] The ferry, known as Combwich Passage or White House Passage, was shared between the owners of Pawlett Gaunt's manor and the Combwich manors in 1589,[13] and in 1810 a half share was let with the inn at the passage.[14]

A landing place called Pawlett pill, directly south of Pawlett village, was regarded as a creek within the port of Bridgwater by the 15th century.[15] Tenants of Pawlett Gaunt's manor were obliged to scour the pill in 1475.[16] It continued in use in the 18th century[17] but by 1780[18] it was blocked by Canham sluice and a landing stage on the river had evidently been constructed.[19] That wharf was rebuilt and probably extended when bricks were manufactured nearby in the 19th century.[20]

The Bristol and Exeter railway, opened in 1841, passed through the eastern corner of the parish.[21]

There was a victualler in the parish in 1609[22] and from 1655 the house at Combwich Passage later known as the White House was licensed.[23] In 1675 there were four victuallers, but later normally two.[24] The White House remained in business until 1897 and survived as a farmhouse until 1920 or later.[25] The Shoulder of Mutton, in Pawlett village and so called by 1779,[26] was built probably c. 1658.[27] It remained open until 1883[28] and in 1986 was known as Nevys House. A third inn was licensed c. 1740,[29] and a public house called the Jolly Sailor is said to have been at Stretcholt in the 19th century.[30] The house called the Manor House became a hotel c. 1950[31] and was in business in 1986.

The Pawlett friendly society, established in 1794 and reorganized in 1838, met at the Shoulder of Mutton in 1844.[32] In the early 20th century there were refreshment rooms and a social club in the village, and in 1935 a tennis club.[33]

In 1801 the population was 429, rising to 433 in 1811 and to 529 in 1821 when there were only 69 houses for 98 families. Numbers peaked at 597 in 1871 but fell from 483 in 1891 to 346 in 1901. The population thereafter increased to 374 in 1911, 462 in 1931, 672 in 1961, and 786 in 1981.[34]

Twenty-six men were fined for involvement in the Cornish rebellion in 1497.[35] Two men from Pawlett were implicated in the Monmouth rebellion, one of whom was transported to the West Indies.[36] About 1940 trials for cutting the cables of balloons were held over the Hams; the balloon was housed in a hangar which still stands north-west of Gaunt's Farm.[37]

MANORS AND OTHER ESTATES. Pawlett, Stretcholt, and Walpole, separately held in 1066, were all held by Walter of Douai in 1086.

PAWLETT, later PAWLETT GAUNTS,[38] was held by Saemer in 1066 and by Rademer of Walter of Douai in 1086.[39] Walter died c. 1107 and his heir, Robert, who rebelled in 1136,[40] seems to have lost the main part of his estate which passed to Robert, son of Robert FitzRoy, earl of Gloucester. Before 1147 Robert gave it to Robert FitzHarding (d. 1171).[41] Robert's younger son, also Robert (d. 1194),[42] was succeeded by his son Maurice (d. 1230), who held Pawlett of the Crown in 1212.[43] Maurice's heir was Robert de Gournay, son of his half-sister Eve. Robert died in 1269 and was followed by his son Anselm (d. 1286) and by Anselm's son John (d. 1291) in turn. John's heir was his daughter Elizabeth, wife of John ap Adam (d. 1311).[44] Their son Thomas was acknowledged as lord of Pawlett in 1335[45] but no further trace of this lordship has been found.

Maurice, son of Robert FitzHarding, known as Maurice de Gaunt, appears to have promised to give his estate to St. Mark's hospital, Bristol, a promise fulfilled by Robert de Gournay.[46] The manor was confirmed to the hospital in 1232.[47]

The hospital was dissolved in 1539 and the manor was let in 1540 and sold before 1544 to Richard Cooper or Cupper of London.[48] Richard died in 1566 and was followed by his son John (cr. Bt. 1622, d. 1631).[49] Sir Anthony Ashley Cooper, son of the last, redeemed the

11 Wimborne St. Giles, Shaftesbury MSS., map 1658.
12 S.R.O., DD/SAS (C/238); (C/2402) 34; ibid. Q/RUp 65; J. B. Bentley and B. J. Murless, Som. Roads, i. 23.
13 S.R.O., DD/S/HY 6/163; above, Cannington, econ. hist.
14 S.R.O., DD/MLY 6.
15 Cal. Chart. R. 1427–1516, 227.
16 Wimborne St. Giles, Shaftesbury MSS., M 205.
17 S.R.O., D/P/pawl 4/1/1 (1738).
18 Ibid. T/PH/ea map 1780.
19 Ibid. D/P/pawl 13/2/1 (landing coal 1783).
20 Below, econ. hist.
21 S.R.O., D/P/pawl 9/1/1.
22 Ibid. Q/RL.
23 S.R.S. xxviii. 261–2; Wimborne St. Giles, Shaftesbury MSS., L 79.
24 S.R.O., Q/RL.
25 Ibid.; ibid. DD/KW 4; Kelly's Dir. Som. (1897).
26 S.R.O., Q/RL.
27 Ibid. DD/V/BWr 27.3; Wimborne St. Giles, Shaftesbury MSS., map 1658.
28 S.R.O., DD/MLY 7, 9, 11–12, 14; Kelly's Dir. Som. (1883).
29 S.R.O., Q/RL.
30 Bridgwater Mercury, 21 Jan. 1989.

31 Local inf.
32 M. Fuller, W. Country Friendly Socs. 46, 141; Taunton Courier, 26 June 1844; P.R.O., FS 1/618/454; FS 2/9.
33 Kelly's Dir. Som. (1910, 1914); S.R.O., D/R/bw 13/2/1.
34 Census.
35 Fines Imposed in 1497, ed. A. J. Howard, 25.
36 S.R.S. lxxix. 69, 82.
37 M. Hawkins, Som. at War, 1939–45, 60–1.
38 S.R.O., DD/BR/bi 1.
39 V.C.H. Som. i. 499.
40 Sanders, Eng. Baronies, 5.
41 Cal. Pat. 1405–8, 15; Sanders, Eng. Baronies, 13; Complete Peerage, v. 683, 686 n.
42 Pipe R. 1194 (P.R.S. N.S. v), 19; Sanders, Eng. Baronies, 55.
43 Ex. e Rot. Fin. (Rec. Com.), i. 205–7.
44 Sanders, Eng. Baronies, 14–15; S.R.S. xliv. 295; Feud. Aids, iv. 276.
45 Cal. Inq. Misc. ii, p. 359.
46 S.R.O., DD/S/HY 6/163; Sanders, Eng. Baronies, 55; Cart. St. Mark's, p. xiii.
47 Cal. Chart. R. 1226–57, 170.
48 S.R.O., DD/BR/bi 1; L. & P. Hen. VIII, xix (1), p. 639.
49 P.R.O., C 142/143, no. 23; S.R.O., DD/S/HY 6/163; S.R.S. lxvii, p. 16.

manor from the Court of Wards in 1648.[50] He was created Baron Ashley in 1661 and earl of Shaftesbury in 1672 and died in 1683.[51] The manor descended with the earldom of Shaftesbury until the death of Anthony, the 5th earl, in 1811. It then passed to his only daughter Barbara, coheir through her mother of the barony of de Mauley. Lady Barbara and her successors bought most of the other estates in the parish. She married William Ponsonby (cr. Baron de Mauley 1838, d. 1855) and died in 1844 leaving as heir her son Charles. Charles was followed at his death in 1896 by his sons William (d. 1918) and the Revd. Maurice Ponsonby in turn. Maurice made over the manor in 1919 to his son Hubert William Ponsonby,[52] who sold part in 1920 and the remainder in 1922.[53] The lordship passed with the Manor House to H. Carver in 1922, W. W. Buncombe c. 1930, R. M. Smith c. 1948, and to Bass Brewery c. 1954. Bass sold the house and lordship in 1981 to Mr. A. Hunt, owner in 1986.[54]

A house recorded in 1299[55] had an oratory licensed in 1338.[56] It was known as Gaunt's Court from 1474 until 1593 and may have been divided in the 1520s. The chapel chamber was still so named in 1593.[57] The house was still standing in 1658 but had been replaced by 1780 by Gaunt's Farm on a site slightly further north.[58] That in turn was rebuilt as cottages in the 19th century which were abandoned c. 1970. Manor House, later Manor Hotel, is a villa built for the agent of the estate shortly before 1861 when it was known as the Steward's House.[59] It was sold in 1922.[60]

ALKESEYE was held by Robert FitzHarding in 1163, by his son Maurice (d. 1191), and by the latter's son Robert who died in 1220 without issue.[61] The later descent is not certain, but Maurice de Gaunt (d. 1230) granted land there, lately held by Geoffrey of Erleigh, to Hugh Trivet. Hugh or a namesake was alive in 1277 and was succeeded by James Trivet who gave the land with the services of free tenants to St. Mark's hospital, Bristol, in 1315. The land was then probably absorbed into Pawlett Gaunts manor.[62]

Cannington priory held *YEARSEY* or Yawesye, probably acquired in 1382,[63] until the

Dissolution.[64] It was granted to Edward Rogers in 1538 and descended with Cannington.[65]

Thomas Grindenham held land in 1394 in East Stretcholt, later called *GOUNDENHAM*, which had passed by 1412[66] to John Goundenham (d. by 1438) and by 1451 to Sibyl, daughter and heir of N. Goundenham and wife of John Kyghley.[67] Kyghley was still alive in 1474.[68] Goundenham may have been part of the estate which Joan, daughter of John Speke and wife of Sir Thomas Brooke, held of St. Mark's hospital, Bristol, at her death in 1527 and which in 1528 her son Hugh agreed should be assigned to Nicholas Halswell and his wife Margery, Joan Brooke's niece.[69] The property descended with Halswell in Goathurst until 1602 when another Nicholas Halswell exchanged it with John Cornish.[70] By 1660 it had passed to William Bacon,[71] and as Stretcholt farm[72] the estate descended with Maunsel in North Petherton[73] until the death c. 1731 of Alexander Seymour, who left Stretcholt farm to his sister Eleanor.[74] Eleanor had probably died without issue before 1756 when the estate was held by her nephew Alexander Seymour Gapper of Maunsel,[75] who sold off some land.[76] Stretcholt farm, however, appears to have been conveyed to Gapper's uncle Francis Seymour (d. 1761) and passed to Henry (d. 1805) and Henry Seymour (d. 1849).[77] It was later purchased by Henry Smith Sparke (d. c. 1904).[78] Ownership has not been traced further.

A capital messuage was recorded in 1602;[79] it was probably replaced by the early 18th-century farm house known as Seymours.

In 1508 Robert Brent held an estate of Pawlett Gaunts manor which came to be known as *PAWLETT* manor.[80] It may have originated in the holding of Hugh Godwin in 1286[81] and it descended like Godwinsbower manor in Bridgwater.[82] John Hodges, kinsman and heir of John Brent, sold his estate in Pawlett in 1694 to Edward Perrot and Gilbert Whitehall, and they sold to John Gooding. The land, no longer referred to as a manor, passed to the Good family,[83] and part was acquired by William Ponsonby, lord of Pawlett Gaunts, in 1832.[84]

The part of his lordship which Robert, son of Walter of Douai, retained after c. 1136 passed c. 1200 like Bridgwater manor to William

50   W. D. Christie, *Life of 1st Earl of Shaftesbury* (1871), app. II, xlvii; *Complete Peerage*, xi. 642n.
51   *Complete Peerage*, xi. 644–6.
52   Burke, *Peerage* (1949), 567, 1816–17; S.R.O., DD/X/VIN 1.
53   S.R.O., DD/KW 4, 11.
54   Local inf.; *Bridgwater Mercury*, 28 Aug. 1984.
55   *Cal. Pat.* 1292–1301, 469.
56   *S.R.S.* ix, p. 324.
57   Wimborne St. Giles, Shaftesbury MSS., LE 995, M 205; P.R.O., C 2/Eliz. I/S 19/32.
58   Wimborne St. Giles, Shaftesbury MSS., map 1658; S.R.O., T/PH/ea, map 1780.
59   P.R.O., RG 9/1626, RG 11/2377; local inf.
60   S.R.O., DD/KW 11.
61   *Pipe R.* 1163 (P.R.S. vi), 26; ibid. 1171 (P.R.S. xvi), 11; Sanders, *Eng. Baronies*, 13; *Red Bk. Exch.* (Rolls Ser.), ii. 549. The exact site of this estate is unknown but may have included Yearsey.
62   Pole MS. 3156, 3158; S.R.O., DD/S/HY 6/163.
63   *Cal. Pat.* 1381–8, 119; S.R.O., DD/SAS NP 14, 15.
64   *Valor Eccl.* (Rec. Com.), i. 209.
65   *L. & P. Hen. VIII*, xiii (1), p. 409; above, Cannington, manors.

66   S.R.O., DD/S/WH 10; *Feud. Aids*, vi. 513; *S.R.S.* lxx, p. 66.
67   *S.R.S.* xxii. 115; lxx, p. 66.
68   Wimborne St. Giles, Shaftesbury MSS., M 205.
69   S.R.O., DD/S/WH 10.
70   Ibid. 12.
71   Ibid. DD/SF 4002.
72   Ibid. DD/NW 63.
73   Below, N. Petherton, manors.
74   *Som. Wills*, ed. Brown, iv. 11.
75   S.R.O., DD/MLY 4; below, N. Petherton, manors.
76   S.R.O., DD/MLY 4, 11.
77   Burke, *Peerage* (1949), 1871; S.R.O., Q/REl 29/5; ibid. tithe award; ibid. DD/SAS (C/212), map 1800.
78   *Kelly's Dir. Som.* (1902, 1906); S.R.O., D/R/bw 15/3/21.
79   S.R.O., DD/S/WH 12.
80   *Cal. Inq. p.m. Hen. VII*, iii, p. 311; P.R.O., C 142/156, no. 14.
81   *Cal. Close*, 1279–88, 409.
82   Above, Bridgwater, manors.
83   S.R.O., DD/MLY 10, 12; ibid. Q/REl 29/5; ibid. T/PH/ea, map 1800.
84   Ibid. DD/MLY 2.

Brewer,[85] was held by his heirs as 2½ fees in Pawlett, Horsey, and Bower in 1234,[86] and descended like Bower to the duchy of Lancaster.[87] William of Horsey held a mesne tenancy in Pawlett as at Bower in 1234 and his successors held the fee of the duchy in 1401–2.[88]

The terre tenancy was held by the Pawlett family. Walter of Pawlett was succeeded by his son William in his estate at Pawlett in 1242–3.[89] William of Pawlett was one of the lords there in 1316[90] and by 1324 had perhaps been succeeded by John, son of Martin of Pawlett.[91] John, whose family became known as Paulet, was still alive in 1344.[92] Another John Paulet (d. c. 1382)[93] was followed by Sir John Paulet (d. 1391),[94] whose widow Elizabeth held *PAWLETT* in 1412.[95] Their son John and his sons John and Thomas were all dead by 1413,[96] and the manor passed to Sir John's younger son Thomas[97] and descended with Rhode in North Petherton to Sir Amias Paulet, later Poulett (d. 1538).[98] His son Sir Hugh sold the manor to John Newport in 1548.[99]

John Newport died in 1564 and his son John[1] under age and without issue c. 1566, when the estate escheated to the Crown.[2] Lucy Newport, widow of John's brother Emmanuel, and her sons had recovered the manor by 1604 when they sold it to George Dodington.[3] Pawlett descended with Dodington manor, except for the years 1652 to c. 1660 when it belonged to the Freake family by purchase after confiscation.[4] In 1802 the lordship was put up for sale[5] following the sale of most of the land,[6] and was not recorded again.

John Paulet was granted license in 1344 to have mass in his oratory.[7] The house was possibly on the site of the later Pawlett Farm which was sold to Richard Doidge in 1802. Doidge sold it to Lady Barbara Ashley-Cooper in 1814[8] and it was renamed South Farm.[9] The present house dates from the late 18th century.

STRETCHOLT was held in 1066 by Eadweald and Leofgar and in 1086 by Rainwald of Walter or Walscin of Douai.[10] Stretcholt was later divided between Bampton and Castle Cary honors.[11] One half evidently descended with Bridgwater in Bampton honor but continued in the possession of Fulk Pagnell (d. 1208) and passed to his son William (d. 1228) and to William's son William (d. 1248). Auda, sister and heir of the last and wife of John de Ballon, died in 1261, and in 1267 the barony passed to John de Cogan, heir of Christian, daughter of Fulk Pagnell (d. 1208).[12] John held ½ fee at *EAST STRETCHOLT* in 1284–5[13] and died in 1302.[14] No further reference to the overlordship has been found.

John de Marisco or Marsh held a mesne tenancy of John de Cogan in 1284–5[15] possibly in succession to William de Marisco.[16] Stephen Marsh held it in 1343[17] but no further reference has been found.

In 1284–5 John Cote was the terre tenant of East Stretcholt, where he or a namesake held land in 1242–3.[18] William Trivet's holding in 1303 may be the messuage and carucate of land held by knight service of Stephen Marsh in 1343 by Thomas Gournay through his wife Joan, widow of Thomas Trivet (d. 1316).[19] The subsequent history of the estate has not been traced.

Land at East Stretcholt, said in 1623 to be held of Hendley,[20] probably Robert Hensleigh (d. 1623), owner of Syndercombe in Clatworthy,[21] descended with Syndercombe through the Periam and Lethbridge families to Sir Thomas Buckler Lethbridge, Bt. (d. 1849), who bought the adjoining West Stretcholt estate.[22] The combined holding known as Stretcholt farm or Lethbridge's[23] passed to Sir John Hesketh Lethbridge and to his son John Periam Lethbridge. The farm was sold to Lord de Mauley in 1862.[24]

Further land, also said to be held of Hendley, was held by knight service by Sir Nicholas Smith (d. 1622). It passed to his son Nicholas (d. 1629), Nicholas's son George (d. 1631), and Sir Nicholas's second son George.[25] Possibly held by Mr. Selleck in 1658,[26] the estate appears to have been divided. Part was in possession of George Balch of Bridgwater in 1723 when it was settled on the marriage of his son John;[27] John was probably dead by 1731[28] leaving a son Robert.[29] The estate descended with Nether Stowey manor[30] until 1802 when George Balch sold most of the estate known as Stretcholt farm in small lots.[31] The remaining lands continued

85 P.R.O., DL 42/11, f. 2.
86 *Bk. of Fees*, i. 400.
87 Above, Bridgwater, manors.
88 *Feud. Aids*, vi. 630.
89 *S.R.S.* xi, pp. 151, 153–4.
90 *Feud. Aids*, iv. 332.
91 S.R.O., DD/S/HY 6/163.
92 *S.R.S.* x, p. 491.
93 Pole MS. 2560.
94 P.R.O., C 139/73, no. 54; the Som. inquisition is missing.
95 *Feud. Aids*, vi. 514; P.R.O., SC 6/1293/11.
96 *V.C.H. Som.* iv. 124, 142–3.
97 *Feud. Aids*, iv. 365; C. Winn, *Pouletts of Hinton St. George* (1976), 14–15.
98 Below, N. Petherton, manors.
99 S.R.O., DD/CH, box 46.
1 P.R.O., C 142/141, no. 17.
2 Ibid. C 142/145, no. 20.
3 Ibid. CP 25(2)/345/2 Jas. I East.
4 *V.C.H. Som.* v. 66; *Cal. Cttee. for Compounding*, iv. 2557.
5 S.R.O., DD/AH 14/3.
6 e.g. ibid. DD/MLY 1–2, 4, 7.
7 *S.R.S.* x. 491.

8 S.R.O., DD/MLY 7–8.   9 Ibid. DD/KW 4.
10 *V.C.H. Som.* i. 497.
11 Sanders, *Eng. Baronies*, 5, 27.
12 Ibid. 5 and n.   13 *Feud. Aids*, iv. 276.
14 Sanders, *Eng. Baronies*, 5.
15 *Feud. Aids*, iv. 276.
16 *S.R.S.* xliv. 48–9.
17 *Cal. Inq. p.m.* viii, p. 287.
18 *Feud. Aids*, iv. 276; *S.R.S.* xi, p. 215.
19 *S.R.S.* vi. 324; *Cal. Inq. p.m.* vi, p. 43; viii, p. 287.
20 *S.R.S.* lxvii, pp. 202, 205.
21 *V.C.H. Som.* v. 35.
22 S.R.O., Q/REl 29/5; ibid. DD/AH 60/11; DD/ES 3; ibid. tithe award; Burke, *Peerage* (1949), 1211.
23 S.R.O., DD/MLY 10; O.S. Map 6", Som. XXXVIII. SW. (1886 edn.).
24 Burke, *Peerage* (1949), 1211–12; S.R.O., DD/MLY 1, 3, 10, 14.
25 *S.R.S.* lxvii, pp. 201–3; P.R.O., C 142/486, no. 128.
26 Wimborne St. Giles, Shaftesbury MSS., map 1658.
27 S.R.O., DD/SAS (C/96) 17/19.
28 Ibid. D/N/bw. chch 1/3/2.
29 Ibid. DD/SAS (C/96) 17/19; ibid. Q/REl 29/5.
30 Ibid. DD/AH 39/9; *V.C.H. Som.* v. 198.
31 S.R.O., DD/WY 155/1; DD/MLY 4.

to descend with Nether Stowey manor until 1847 when they were sold to the de Mauleys and held with Pawlett Gaunts.[32]

The division of Walter of Douai's estates, possibly between the sons of his two marriages, brought part of Stretcholt, later *WEST STRETCHOLT* manor, into the hands of Ralph Lovel (fl. 1121) and into Castle Cary honor.[33] It was held of Hugh Lovel (d. 1291) in 1285–7[34] but no further trace of the overlordship has been found. Sir Adam of Bawdrip held a mesne tenancy in 1285 when the terre tenant was Raymond Malet.[35] Also in the late 13th century Sabina, widow of Jordan of Bradney, granted an estate at Stretcholt to her son Humphrey.[36] The descent has not been traced further.

In 1412 Thomas Michell held land at West Stretcholt[37] which seems to have descended with East Chilton in Durleigh until 1663[38] when Gregory Hockmore sold it to Humphrey Steare. Steare died in 1692 when the land passed to Robert Steare, already owner of property there.[39] Robert was succeeded by his son Samuel (d. 1745). A dispute between the heirs of Richard Limbery (d. 1774), to whom Steare had devised his land, and Steare's legatees concluded with its sale and division in 1797.[40] During the 19th century part was acquired by Sir Thomas Leth-bridge, Bt., and part, known as Black Rock, by the Revd. George Trevelyan.[41] Later in the century the Trevelyan holding was bought by the de Mauleys.[42]

In the later 13th century a family named de la Grove was settled in the parish.[43] In 1325–6 Robert de la Grove held land there[44] and William Grove was succeeded by Simon Ellis (d. by 1474).[45] John Strangeways owned an estate at *GROVE* in West Stretcholt in 1590,[46] which by 1620 was held by George Dodington.[47] The property descended with Dodington manor, and was augmented by other lands in West Stret-cholt,[48] but in 1800–1 it was divided and sold, mostly to Thomas Parker.[49] William Dod pur-chased Parker's estate and other land in 1808 and 1810,[50] and his son, also William, sold Dod's farm to Lord de Mauley, lord of Pawlett Gaunts manor, in 1853.[51]

Edward Brit held *WALPOLE* in 1066 and Rademer of Walter of Douai in 1086.[52] An estate there, held of Castle Cary honor in 1371[53] and in 1408[54] may be traced to a holding shared in 1242–3 between three daughters of Gerard of Bratton[55] which appears to have been acquired by the Bawdrip family and which by 1355 was known as *BAWDRIP AND WALPOLE* manor.[56] Dower there had been assigned to Joan, wife of Sir John Durburgh (d. 1352) and pre-viously widow of John of Bawdrip, heir to Adam of Bawdrip (d. 1296).[57] In 1355 the same land was assigned by John, son and heir of Hugh of Bawdrip, to his mother Orange.[58] The property descended with Bawdrip manor and in 1542 it may have passed, with Washford in St. Decu-mans,[59] to Sir John Wyndham, who owned Walpole manor in 1552.[60] The manor then de-scended with other Wyndham estates[61] until 1703 when it was conveyed to Sir Thomas Wroth, Bt., probably in trust for Edward Ray-mond.[62] Edward died before 1746 leaving Walpole to George Raymond (d. by 1748) whose son Edward sold it to Sir Charles Kemeys-Tynte. Sir Charles in 1753 sold it to Mary Jeane, widow.[63]

James Coker had land in Pawlett in 1350[64] which may have descended by 1461 to Margaret, daughter of John Coker and widow of Sir Alex-ander Hody. Margaret's property was said to be held of William le Eyre.[65] The holding descend-ed, with West Bower in Bridgwater, to Edward Seymour, duke of Somerset, on whose attainder in 1552 it reverted to the Crown.[66] It was granted in 1553 to Thomas Sydney and Nicholas Hal-swell and descended with Halswell in Goathurst[67] until 1746 when most of the land was sold to Edmund Jeane (d. 1754).[68] Ed-mund's son John also inherited the Walpole estates which his mother Mary bought in 1753 and died in 1790 leaving Walpole to his younger daughter Mary who in 1794 married Wyndham Gooden.[69]

In 1798 Gooden purchased more land in Walpole and in 1802 the remainder of the Tynte estate there, creating an estate called *WAL-POLE* manor in 1807.[70] By his death in 1839 Gooden had reorganized Walpole into two large farms known as the Western and Eastern; the house on the latter, now Walpole Farm, was said to be newly erected in 1844. Gooden left Walpole to be sold to benefit his younger child-ren.[71] John Ryall Mayo bought it in 1845 and sold it to Lord de Mauley, lord of Pawlett Gaunts manor, in 1856.[72]

Robert FitzHarding gave Pawlett church to St. Augustine's abbey, Bristol, probably *c.* 1140,

32 Ibid. DD/MLY 1.
33 Sanders, *Eng. Baronies*, 27 and n.
34 *Feud. Aids*, iv. 276.
35 *S.R.S.* iii. 10.
36 Pole MS. 3159.
37 *Feud. Aids*, vi. 514.
38 Above, Durleigh, manors.
39 S.R.O., DD/MLY 2, 5; DD/X/BRC 9; DD/SAS (H/202) 4; D/P/pawl 4/1/1.
40 Ibid. DD/MLY 2, 4; DD/X/BRC 9.
41 Ibid. DD/MLY 1, 4, 14; D/P/pawl 13/1/1; ibid. Q/REl 29/5; ibid. tithe award.
42 Ibid. DD/KW 4.
43 *S.R.S.* xli. 136–7.
44 S.R.O., DD/S/HY 6/163.
45 Wimborne St. Giles, Shaftesbury MSS., M 205.
46 P.R.O., C 142/229, no. 102.
47 *S.R.S.* lxvii, p. 105; S.R.O., DD/CH, box 46.
48 *S.R.S.* lxvii, p. 105; S.R.O., DD/MLY 2; DD/S/WH 172; ibid. Q/REl 29/5.

49 S.R.O., DD/BK 3/18; DD/CH 80/5; DD/MLY 4; DD/X/BRC 10.   50 Ibid. DD/MLY 1–2.
51 Ibid. 1, 14.   52 *V.C.H. Som.* i. 497.
53 *Cal. Inq. p.m.* xiii, p. 75.
54 *Cal. Close, 1369–74*, 367; P.R.O., C 137/74, no. 50.
55 *S.R.S.* vi. 114, 205.   56 *Cat. Anct. D.* ii, B 3469.
57 *V.C.H. Som.* v. 21; above, Bawdrip, manors.
58 *Cat. Anct. D.* ii, B 3469.   59 *V.C.H. Som.* v. 45.
60 P.R.O., C 142/99, no. 76.
61 *V.C.H. Som.* v. 155.
62 P.R.O., CP 25(2)/961/2 Anne Mich.
63 S.R.O., DD/MLY 1; below.
64 *Cal. Inq. p.m.* xiii, p. 209.
65 P.R.O., C 140/4, no. 34.
66 Above, Bridgwater, manors.
67 *Cal. Pat. 1553*, 55; above, Goathurst, manors.
68 S.R.O., DD/MLY 3; D/P/west m. 2/1/2.
69 Ibid. DD/MLY 12; DD/RN 8.
70 Ibid. DD/MLY 3, 12.   71 Ibid. 12.
72 Ibid. 3; *Taunton Courier*, 18 Sept. 1844.

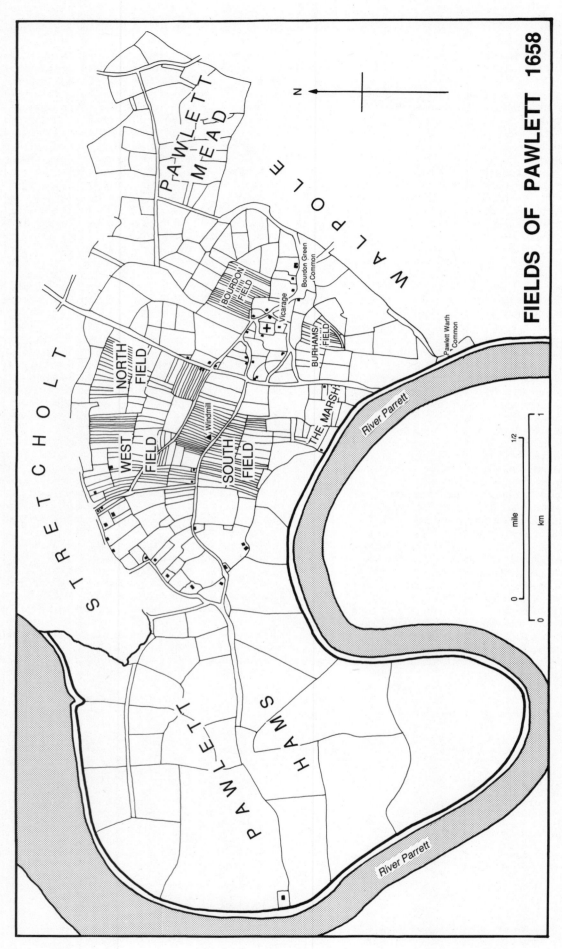

FIELDS OF PAWLETT 1658

and his son Robert gave ½ virgate in 1146.[73] Maurice de Gaunt (d. 1230) gave more land, called *PAWLETT* manor, a grant confirmed by Robert de Gournay.[74] In 1251, however, the abbey renounced its estate in favour of St. Mark's hospital, Bristol, in return for other lands which were known in 1540 as *PAWLETT* manor together with land and tithes which constituted the *RECTORY*. Manor and rectory were let together by 1529 to William and Robert Williams and Robert's wife Christine.[75] The manor was held as of East Greenwich by John Williams at his death in 1608 when it was divided between his two daughters, Joan, wife of William Avery, and Sarah, wife of Humphrey Blake.[76]

The Averys' share passed to Joan's son John (d. 1669) and included the later Shoulder of Mutton inn.[77] It passed from John's widow Grace and her son John to John Clarke (d. by 1711), who was followed by his son Robert (d. by 1721) and his grandson also Robert Clarke (d. before 1752).[78] Robert Brown, nephew of the last, sold the estate to Jasper Porter in 1758.[79] Porter's daughter Susannah sold it to the Revd. Francis Parsons for the benefit of Anne Poole who married the Revd. Charles Burt *c.* 1794.[80] In 1835 Anne and her son Augustus conveyed it to William Ponsonby, lord of Pawlett Gaunts manor.[81]

The Blakes' share, which included responsibility for the chancel,[82] passed to Arnold Brown and his wife Hannah who sold it in 1682 to John Taylor. By will of 1725 it was divided between Taylor's son Joseph and the Revd. Samuel Taylor;[83] most of the land, known as Taylor's, passed to William Doidge in 1766,[84] whose children sold most of it *c.* 1812, part going to Lady Barbara Ashley-Cooper.[85] Other parts were bought by Lord de Mauley, lord of Pawlett Gaunts, in 1843.[86]

The tithes were held by the Williams family and apparently passed on the death of John Williams in 1608 to Sir John Cooper who let them to Humphrey Blake before 1631.[87] They descended with Pawlett Gaunts manor.[88] Rectorial tithes were commuted in 1838 for a rent charge of £200.[89]

ECONOMIC HISTORY. In 1086 four estates were together assessed at 5 ploughlands, and there were 5 teams on the demesnes compared with half that number on the tenants' holdings. Only 25 a. of meadow were recorded and no woodland nor pasture. Stock comprised 24 cattle, 67 pigs, and 83 sheep.[90] Parts of the low-lying Hams were grazed in common after haymaking by the mid 12th century[91] and by the 1330s Stretcholt tithing, which included much of the grassland in the north part of the parish, was one of the most highly taxed places in the hundred.[92] In the 1390s the master of St. Mark's hospital, Bristol, kept peacocks on his estate.[93] In the 1490s the rectory estate produced wheat, oats, and beans, and tenants rendered each year 300 hens eggs, 200 stone of cheese, cattle, young pigs, poultry, and geese.[94] A quarter of the vicarage income arose from wool and lambs.[95]

In 1259 St. Mark's hospital claimed it was unable to support the poor until its lands had recovered from flooding,[96] and *c.* 358 a. of the South Hams, south-west of Gaunt's Farm, were possibly brought into use in the later 13th century, the area being free of vicarial tithe,[97] but attempts to improve the land further north near Yearsey had been frustrated earlier.[98] In 1497 St. Augustine's abbey, Bristol, owners of the rectory, had to make 35 perches of Severn wall.[99] The warths, those grasslands between the defences and the coast or river bank, were reclaimed and drained from the later 16th century.[1] The reclaimed land was highly valued and in the early 17th century entry fines for leases of pasture in the Hams were between £8 and £21 an acre.[2] Embanking, sometimes after deliberate breaches to prevent more serious damage, continued[3] and new closes south of the Hams comprised 150 a. added to the parish because the river had 'gradually shifted its bed and receded westwards'.[4] A warth in the northwest of the parish was regularly flooded in the mid 17th century,[5] but a wall was built to protect Great Yearsey Marsh and a second wall was added further south possibly in the late 18th century to enclose land gained as a result of the blocking of the channel east of Humble Island.[6] The new land, improved by the tenant, was known by 1832 as Great and Little Wharf.[7] Pawlett Wharf, further east, and land at Walpole had similarly been drained and protected by the earlier 19th century.[8]

A farming inventory of 1696 recorded 4 dairy cows, 6 plough beasts, 7 calves, 4 mares in foal,

73   *Accts. of St. Augustine's*, p. 190; below, church.
74   *H.M.C. Wells*, i. 444.
75   *Accts. of St. Augustine's*, pp. 188–9; *Cart. St. Mark's*, p. 35.
76   P.R.O., C 142/410, no. 104.
77   Above, intro.
78   S.R.O., DD/MLY 11.
79   Ibid. 7, 11.
80   Ibid. 12.
81   Ibid. 9; above.
82   S.R.O., D/D/Ca 274.
83   Ibid. DD/MLY 4, 11; Wimborne St. Giles, Shaftesbury MSS., map 1658.
84   S.R.O., DD/MLY 11.
85   Ibid. D/P/pawl 2/1/1; DD/MLY 8, 11.
86   Ibid. Q/REl 29/5; ibid. DD/MLY 1, 4, 5, 9; ibid. tithe award.
87   *S.R.S.* lxvii, p. 16; Wimborne St. Giles, Shaftesbury MSS., LE 1000.
88   S.R.O., DD/X/VIN 1; above.

89   S.R.O., tithe award.   90   *V.C.H. Som.* i. 497, 499.
91   *S.R.S.* xi, p. 151.
92   *Subsidy of 1334*, ed. R. E. Glasscock, 260.
93   S.R.O., DD/SAS NP 12.
94   *Accts. of St. Augustine's*, pp. 7, 35.
95   *Valor Eccl.* (Rec. Com.), i. 212.
96   *Cart. St. Mark's*, p. 10.
97   *H.M.C. Wells*, i. 389; S.R.O., tithe award.
98   *S.R.S.* xi, p. 166.
99   *Accts. of St. Augustine's*, p. 35.
1   M. Williams, *Draining of Som. Levels*, 94.
2   Wimborne St. Giles, Shaftesbury MSS., E/S 219.
3   S.R.O., DD/MLY 6–7; D/RA (C/2259); Wimborne St. Giles, Shaftesbury MSS., E/A 42, 127, 144; L 79; LE 1001; Williams, *Som. Levels*, 94.
4   S.R.O., tithe award.   5   Ibid. D/RA (C/2259).
6   Ibid. DD/CH 70/4; Williams, *Som. Levels*, 94. Also called the Island.
7   S.R.O., DD/CH 70/4; Clifford MSS., Som. estate, 1805.
8   S.R.O., DD/MLY 12; ibid. tithe award.

5 other horses, 53 sheep, at least 11 tons of hay, and 20 a. of wheat.[9] The Hams were usually let in blocks of between 40 a. and 100 a. but holdings elsewhere in the parish were scattered. One tenant with leases of 1697 and 1704 held a total of 58 a. most of it enclosed but about one sixth in the open arable fields; another tenant had 79 a. and a third 95 a. with smaller proportions of common arable.[10]

Each hamlet had its own open arable fields. Pawlett's north, south, and west fields were west of the village on the heavy clay of Pawlett Hill.[11] Smaller arable fields called Burhams and Bourdon fields lay south and north-east of the village.[12] Walpole had three fields, north, middle, and west,[13] the second divided and renamed by 1746 Churchpath and Little fields.[14] Grove field north of Stretcholt appears to have remained open arable in 1811.[15] The common arable fields were finally inclosed between the mid 18th century and 1838 beginning at Walpole and finishing in the fields south and west of Pawlett village.[16]

Pawlett common mead, east of Pawlett village, Walpole mead, and Stretcholt common mead provided each settlement with meadow, the first being shared with tenants from the two other manors.[17]

Dunball common in the south, partly in Puriton, was under salt water several times a year in the earlier 17th century, but changes in the course of the Parrett, improved drainage, and the construction of Dunball wall had increased the size of the common to at least 100 a. by 1707.[18] Grove Warth common, later Grove common, was a similar piece of common pasture west of Stretcholt.[19]

Clover was described as a new crop in 1711 and was mown twice, the second time to be kept for seed.[20] Wheat accounted for most of the arable crop on Pawlett Gaunts manor in 1810, followed by beans, vetches, clover and tares, and a small amount of barley. Several farmsteads then included dairies, and cider houses and a new apple orchard were recorded.[21] Withy beds were established at Stretcholt in the 18th century but of three beds recorded in 1838 one had been converted to orchard.[22] A new pound and sheep houses were ordered to be built on the Hams in 1777.[23] There were severe penalties for breaking pasture or meadow for tillage and in 1798 a man was charged with ploughing grassland for potatoes.[24]

By 1838 tithes were payable on 596 a. of arable,

1,734 a. of grass, and 62 a. of orchard, and a modus was paid on milk. Most holdings were less than 50 a. and many of those consisted of a single large field in the Hams. Ten holdings measured between 50 a. and 100 a. and 7 between 100 a. and 150 a.[25] Holdings were consolidated especially on Lord de Mauley's estates; by 1851 9 farmers worked more than 100 a. of whom 3 had more than 200 a. but none employed more than 4 labourers.[26] Lord de Mauley's agent later admitted that he had got rid of the smaller tenants and divided the farmhouses into cottages to house men employed to look after stock on the Hams.[27] From 1861 several farms were described as dairy farms and specialized labour included dairy men and maids. In 1871 3 farms of over 200 a. employed c. 29 labourers; by 1881 the number of labourers had fallen although one farm which had increased to 400 a. had 16 labourers.[28]

The Hams remained separate from the farms and were let annually from 1857. Fluctuations in livestock prices affected rents which fell by nearly half between 1871 and 1881. In 1879 1,700 a. in the Hams were let for £6,258.[29] By 1905 arable land had decreased to 357 a. and 2,794 a. were under permanent grass.[30] The de Mauleys owned most of the parish by 1920, with a rental of £14,235 a year of which £11,000 came from letting their 1,451 a. in the Hams. Most farms by that date specialized in grazing and dairying and Walpole Farm included two cheese rooms.[31] Grassland farming continued to be practised in the 1980s, and there were 7 farms over 50 ha. (124 a.). Returns made in 1982 for three quarters of the parish recorded 1,328 cattle, 1,271 sheep, 731 pigs, and 183 poultry. The main arable crops were wheat and barley, but potatoes were grown and some horticultural crops under glass.[32] In the 1920s and 1930s the West Somerset Nursery in Pound Lane had specialized in sweet peas.[33]

Alternative occupations included clothmaking in the 17th century[34] and fishing, mainly for salmon, in the 18th. The fisheries were associated with the Clifford estate at Yearsey[35] and Black Rock at West Stretcholt.[36] By the mid 19th century the de Mauleys claimed three sites in the river at Pawlett, Cannington, and Black Rock where four men had 1,000 putchers or butts, conical baskets for catching salmon. Between 1868 and 1873 the number of licensed butts fell from 1,360 to 450. The decline was blamed on the damming of Cannington brook which

9 S.R.O., DD/SP inventory, 1696.
10 Wimborne St. Giles, Shaftesbury MSS., E/S 16, 219; LE 1001–2.
11 S.R.O., T/PH/ea map 1780.
12 Wimborne St. Giles, Shaftesbury MSS., map 1658; S.R.O., T/PH/ea map 1780.
13 S.R.O., DD/S/WH 218.
14 Ibid. DD/ARN 12.
15 Wimborne St. Giles, Shaftesbury MSS., map 1658; S.R.O., DD/MLY 1.
16 S.R.O., DD/ARN 12; DD/MLY 6; DD/SAS (H/202) 4; ibid. tithe award.
17 Ibid. DD/MLY 3; DD/NW 63.
18 Ibid. D/RA (C/2259); DD/MLY 6; DD/S/WH 133.
19 Wimborne St. Giles, Shaftesbury MSS., map 1658; S.R.O., T/PH/ea map 1780.
20 Wimborne St. Giles, Shaftesbury MSS., E/T 61.

21 S.R.O., DD/MLY 6.
22 Ibid. 1; DD/X/BRC 10; ibid. tithe award.
23 Wimborne St. Giles, Shaftesbury MSS., E/C 32.
24 Ibid. M 209; S.R.O., DD/AH 20/5.
25 S.R.O., tithe award.   26 P.R.O., HO 107/1925.
27 Rep. Com. Employment in Agric. p. 483, H.C. (1868–9), xiii.
28 P.R.O., RG 9/1626, RG 10/2390, RG 11/2377.
29 Williams, Som. Levels, 214; Taunton Courier, 1 Feb. 1860; W. Som. Free Press, 29 Mar. 1879.
30 Statistics supplied by the then Bd. of Agric. 1905.
31 S.R.O., DD/KW 4.
32 Min. of Agric., Fisheries, and Food, agric. returns, 1982.
33 Kelly's Dir. Som. (1923–39); local inf.
34 S.R.O., Q/SR 21/77.
35 Clifford MSS., Som. estate, acct. 1770–1, 1795–6, c. 1808; S.R.O., DD/CH 70/3–4; D/RA 5/1.
36 S.R.O., DD/X/BRC 9; DD/MLY 11.

prevented salmon from reaching their spawning ground and on the shrimp putts which consisted of three baskets of diminishing size. Shrimp were valuable but the putts and hose nets used to catch them also took fry and other young fish.[37] Between 1841 and 1871 there were 6 to 8 fishermen in the parish[38] and 5 fishermen and 2 fish dealers in 1881.[39] Salmon putchers remained in the river in 1920 and were sold with the de Mauley estate.[40]

In the 16th and 17th centuries wine, coal, and timber were landed, probably at Pawlett reach or pill,[41] and a Pawlett merchant owned three ships and a share in a fourth between 1795 and 1819.[42] There were berthing facilities in 1861 and a boatbuilder was in business.[43]

Before the 19th century bricks may have been made in the wet land east of the village and in the Hams.[44] Thomas Parker began brickmaking on the river bank south of the church shortly before 1810[45] and by 1826 the site comprised brickyard, coalyard, counting house, and cottage.[46] In 1829 the yard was bought by Lady Barbara Ashley-Cooper's trustees.[47] In 1859 it was run by Browne and Co. and by 1894 belonged to the Somerset Trading Co.[48] By 1851 25 workers made brick and tile there[49] and by 1881 there were 33 brickyard workers in the parish including a foreman and an engine driver. Gaunt's Farm was converted into cottages for labourers and Browne's Buildings, a row of 15 houses, later called Mount View, were built by the company to house workers.[50] By 1886 the brickyard site comprised many buildings, ponds, cottages, and two landing stages.[51] The yard was last recorded in 1894[52] and the kilns and associated buildings had been demolished by 1904 although the landing stages remained.[53] In 1909 the claypits were said to be exhausted and the land was converted to a small farm.[54] By 1986 only one row of five cottages remained with the farmhouse and an outbuilding converted from part of the oldest brickyard building. The large water-filled pits were used by an angling club and the remains of a wharf and jetty could be seen.

A mill recorded on Pawlett Gaunts manor in 1377 was probably the windmill called Alderigge mill in 1528.[55] A windmill was mentioned until 1696.[56] It stood on a mound east of Mill Batch field on Pawlett Hill.[57] Mill Moot in South Field

in 1647[58] may represent an earlier site or another mill. A windmill was recorded on the Newports' manor of Pawlett in 1604.[59] A windmill was used to pump fresh water from Cannington under the Parrett into the rhynes in the late 19th century.[60]

In 1257 Henry de Gaunt, master of St. Mark's hospital, Bristol, was granted a three-day fair at the feast of the Decollation of St. John the Baptist (29 Aug.).[61] There is no further record of this fair but in the early 19th century a cattle fair was held on the last Monday in August.[62] An additional fair was held on the last Monday in October, said to be one of the most considerable cattle fairs in the west of England in 1860, when 300 graziers, farmers, and stock dealers petitioned for its retention.[63] It was last recorded in 1888.[64]

LOCAL GOVERNMENT. St. Mark's hospital was freed from suit to the hundred court c. 1243 in respect of Pawlett manor but suit was demanded again in 1277.[65] In 1274 Pawlett tithing was said to have withdrawn from the sheriff's tourn.[66] Stretcholt tithing alone attended the hundred court in the 14th and 15th centuries.[67] A third tithing, Walpole, had been formed out of Stretcholt by 1765.[68] Tenants of Yawesye, later Yearsey, owed suit and payments to the hundred.[69]

Court records survive for Pawlett Gaunts manor for 1377, 1474–7, 1661–74, 1737, and 1760–1808.[70] The court met twice a year in the 15th century, possibly in the chapel chamber at the manor house where the court was held in the 16th century, but in the 18th century every two or four years. There the tithingman was chosen, by the 17th century according to a rota. A hayward was appointed in the 17th century and in 1673 two men who were responsible for the rhynes.[71] Suit of court was owed to the Dodingtons' manor in the 18th century but their right to a court was later challenged.[72] Suit for a holding at Grove was owed twice a year in 1612 to Edward Tynte's unspecified court at Pawlett.[73] Walpole manor was administered with Bawdrip, and court rolls for both survive for 1479–82, 1537, and 1541–3.[74]

By the later 18th century four overseers were appointed in rotation, each serving for two years. Two constables each were appointed for Pawlett

37 Ibid. D/RA 5/1–2.
38 P.R.O., HO 107/953, HO 107/1925; ibid. RG 9/1626, RG 10/2390.   39 Ibid. RG 11/2377.
40 S.R.O., DD/KW 4.
41 Ibid. D/B/bw 1463, 1480, 1504, 1513, 1515.
42 Ibid. DD/FA 11/1–2.   43 P.R.O., RG 9/1626.
44 S.R.O., T/PH/ea map 1780; ibid. tithe award; Wimborne St. Giles, Shaftesbury MSS., E/C 32.
45 S.R.O., DD/MLY 8.
46 Ibid. D/P/pawl 13/1/1.
47 Ibid. DD/MLY 8.
48 P.O. Dir. Som. (1859); Kelly's Dir. Som. (1894).
49 P.R.O., HO 107/953, HO 107/1925.
50 Ibid. RG 11/2377.
51 O.S. Map 6", Som. XXXVIII. SE. (1886 edn.).
52 Kelly's Dir. Som. (1894).
53 O.S. Map 1/2,500, Som. XXXVIII. 15 (1904 edn.).
54 S.R.O., D/R/bw 15/3/21, 22/1/6.
55 Wimborne St. Giles, Shaftesbury MSS., M 205; LE 995.
56 Ibid. E/S 9, 12, 220.
57 S.R.O., tithe award; Wimborne St. Giles, Shaftesbury

MSS., map 1658.
58 Wimborne St. Giles, Shaftesbury MSS., LE 995, 1001.
59 P.R.O., CP 25(2)/345/2 Jas. I East.
60 S.R.O., DD/KW 11.
61 Cal. Chart. R. 1226–57, 472.
62 Som. Co. Gaz. Dir. (1840).
63 S.R.O., DD/MLY 12; P.O. Dir. Som. (1861).
64 Rep. Com. Market Rights and Tolls (1889).
65 S.R.O., DD/BR/bi 1; DD/S/HY 6/163.
66 Rot. Hund. (Rec. Com.), ii. 128.
67 S.R.O., DD/SAS NP 10, mm. 1–2; 15, m. 1.
68 Ibid. NP 10, mm. 2–3; DD/MLY 6.
69 Ibid. DD/SAS NP 10, mm. 5, 14, 15.
70 Wimborne St. Giles, Shaftesbury MSS., M 127, 130, 205–16.
71 S.R.S. xxviii. 18; Wimborne St. Giles, Shaftesbury MSS., LE 995; M 127, 205.
72 S.R.O., DD/AH 24/8; DD/MLY 1, 6; DD/SAS (H/202) 4; (H/212) 15.
73 Ibid. DD/S/WH 172.
74 P.R.O., SC 2/198/2; ibid. LR 3/123.

and Stretcholt. The vestry provided relief in cash and in kind, paid for an artificial leg in 1783 and an amputation in 1799, employed a surgeon by 1806 and a molecatcher from 1815.[75] A select vestry was appointed in 1824.[76] Paupers in the poorhouse were supplied with a wide range of food and goods including knitting needles and garden seeds.[77]

There was a poorhouse by 1778 and another house in Pound Lane was acquired on lease in 1792.[78] In 1807 and 1820 the vestry decided on extensions, probably to the original house, which in 1836 was let as two cottages. Standing on the lane to the brickyard it was sold in 1857.[79] The house in Pound Lane was divided by 1810[80] and in 1986 was a private house.

In the 19th century Pawlett had a jury of sewers to view rhynes and ditches[81] and by 1936 the parish had its own water board to supervise drainage and freshwater irrigation of the Hams. The board also appointed a herdsman and shepherd. It was absorbed into the Bridgwater and Pawlett drainage board in 1946.[82] Pawlett formed part of the Bridgwater poor-law union in 1836, Bridgwater rural district in 1894, and Sedgemoor district in 1974.[83]

CHURCH. The church was a dependent chapelry of North Petherton minster: payments to the mother church were made at Easter in the 13th century and a pension was paid to Buckland priory as appropriators of North Petherton until the Dissolution.[84] Pawlett evidently achieved virtual independence in the 12th century and Robert FitzHarding (d. 1171) gave the church to St. Augustine's abbey, Bristol, probably at its foundation c. 1140. Robert's son, also Robert, gave lands in the parish at the dedication of the abbey church in 1146.[85] The abbey did not formally appropriate the church until c. 1257, though a vicarage had been established by c. 1240.[86] The patronage remained with the abbey until its dissolution in 1539 and thereafter remained with the Crown. From 1974 the vicarage was held with Puriton, with which it was united in 1978, the Lord Chancellor exercising the Crown's patronage at every third vacancy.[87]

The vicarage was valued at nearly £11 net in 1535.[88] It was worth c. £50 in 1668,[89] and £264 net on average c. 1831.[90] About 1241 the vicar received oblations, small tithes, hay tithes, and all tithes of the abbey's demesne farm.[91] In 1535 the vicar's tithes amounted to £7 9s. 8d.[92] There was a dispute over modus payments c. 1711[93] and by 1838 tithes on gardens, orchards, meadows, milk, and pasture were paid by modus. The vicarial tithes were commuted for a rent charge of £200.[94]

The glebe c. 1241 comprised 1 a. of arable, on which the vicarage house stood, and 7½ a. of meadow, part of the former priest's holding.[95] In 1637 there were an orchard and garden, together with herbage, lopping, and topping in the churchyard.[96] The glebe amounted to 10 a. in 1838.[97] Some was exchanged in 1850 and sold c. 1926.[98] In 1637 the vicarage house had four lower and five upper rooms, a small barn, and a cowstall.[99] In 1806 a new house was built on the same site, south of the church.[1] Partly demolished c. 1954, it was sold in 1977.[2]

There was a stipendiary priest as well as a vicar c. 1535.[3] Thomas Sprint, vicar 1537–42, was attacked several times by one of his parishioners for declaring that laws made contrary to God's law were void and he was disciplined for demanding excessive tithe.[4] A fraternity had its own priest in 1544 and there was an endowed light in 1543.[5] The vicar was deprived for marriage in 1554.[6] A reader was paid for occasional services in 1575.[7] There were three services each Sunday in the 1630s.[8] Henry Ball, appointed vicar in 1648, remained in office until his death in 1667.[9] Most vicars were resident in the later 17th and the 18th century.[10] An Easter church ale survived until the mid 18th century, evidently providing income for the parish clerk.[11] There were 12 communicants c. 1776.[12] In 1815 the vicar also served Chedzoy but preached every Sunday at Pawlett; his successor in 1827 preached alternately morning and afternoon.[13] Two services with sermons were held each Sunday by 1840.[14] Psalms were sung by that same year, and in the late 1850s the band was replaced by an organ.[15] Communion was celebrated six times a year by 1870,[16] but more frequently in the early 20th century.[17]

The church house, part of Pawlett Gaunts manor, was let to a tenant in 1632, against the wishes of the churchwardens.[18]

The church of ST. JOHN THE BAPTIST evidently kept its patronal festival on the feast

75 S.R.O., D/P/pawl 9/1/1; 13/2/1–2.   76 Ibid. 9/1/2.
77 Ibid. 13/2/1.
78 Ibid.; ibid. DD/MLY 6.
79 Ibid. D/P/pawl 9/1/1, 13/2/6; DD/MLY 5.
80 Ibid. DD/MLY 6; ibid. tithe award.
81 Ibid. D/P/pawl 23/1.
82 Ibid. D/RA 4/4/4, 4/5/5.
83 Youngs, *Local Admin. Units*, i. 671, 673, 676.
84 *S.R.S.* ix, p. 239; xxv, p. 7; *V.C.H. Som.* ii. 148; *Valor Eccl.* (Rec. Com.), i. 211–12; *H.M.C. Wells*, i. 389.
85 *Accts. of St. Augustine's*, p. 190; J. C. Dickinson, 'Origins of St. Augustine's, Bristol', *Essays in Bristol & Glos. Hist.* ed. P. McGrath & J. Cannon (1976), 119–20.
86 *H.M.C. Wells*, i. 139, 389.
87 *Som. Incumbents*, ed. Weaver, 159; *Dioc. Dir.*
88 *Valor Eccl.* (Rec. Com.), i. 212.   89 S.R.O., D/D/Vc 24.
90 *Rep. Com. Eccl. Revenues*, pp. 148–9.
91 *H.M.C. Wells*, i. 389.
92 *Valor Eccl.* (Rec. Com.), i. 212.
93 Wimborne St. Giles, Shaftesbury MSS., E/T 61.
94 S.R.O., tithe award.   95 *H.M.C. Wells*, i. 389.

96 S.R.O., D/D/Rg 202.   97 Ibid. tithe award.
98 Ibid. D/P/pawl 3/3/1; inf. from Dioc. Office.
99 S.R.O., D/D/Rg 202.
1 Ibid. D/D/Bbm 17.
2 Ibid. DD/WBF 2; *Dioc. Dir.*
3 S.R.O., D/D/Vc 20.
4 *S.R.S.* lv, pp. 98, 165; Emden, *Biog. Reg. Univ. Oxf. 1500–40*; P.R.O., STAC 2/31/120.
5 P.R.O., STAC 2/31/120; *S.R.S.* ii, pp. 63, 246; xl. 78.
6 *V.C.H. Som.* ii. 66.
7 *S.D.N.Q.* xiv. 170.
8 S.R.O., D/D/Ca 297.
9 *L.J.* x. 380; S.R.O., D/P/pawl 2/1/1.
10 S.R.O., D/P/pawl 2/1/1.
11 Ibid. 4/1/1.   12 Ibid. D/D/Vc 88.
13 Ibid. D/D/Rb 1815, 1827.
14 Ibid. D/D/Va 1840.
15 Ibid. D/P/pawl 4/1/2.
16 Ibid. D/D/Va 1870.   17 Ibid. D/P/pawl 2/5/1.
18 Wimborne St. Giles, Shaftesbury MSS., E/S 219; S.R.O., D/D/Ca 314A.

of the Decollation of St. John (29 Aug.) by the mid 13th century.[19] The building comprises a chancel with north vestry, a nave with north and south transepts and south porch, and a west tower. The roof has decorative lead guttering, probably of the 19th century. The nave is of the 12th century and retains a south doorway of three orders with carved voussoirs, the outermost including beak-head ornament. The transepts were added in the later 13th century and probably at the same time the chancel was rebuilt. The north doorway of the nave and the window west of it were renewed and the south porch was added in the 14th century. The south windows of the nave were enlarged and the tower was added in the 15th or early 16th century. The chancel arch was also enlarged at that time and was provided with a richly carved rood screen. Some 17th-century mural painting survives beside the tower arch. The nave roof is said to have been ceiled in 1728 and the chancel roof was given a curved plaster ceiling with ornamental borders in 1779.[20] A singing gallery was built across the west end of the nave in 1781[21] and was said to have been removed in 1873.[22] The font was reconstituted from one of the 12th century and an octagonal font cover with lockable doors was provided in the 17th century. A new altar table was made in 1678 and the contemporary altar rails, which have turned balusters and enclose the altar on three sides, survive. Box pews in the chancel appear to have been made out of mid 17th-century panelling and the 17th-century pulpit was reset when the reader's desk was made out of panelling from box pews before 1915.[23]

The plate includes a chalice and paten of 1637 by 'R.W.' and a paten of 1707, possibly by Elston of Exeter and presented in 1827.[24] The five bells include one by either Roger or Richard Purdue of 1625 and three of the 18th century.[25] The registers date from 1667 and are complete.[26]

NONCONFORMITY. There was a Quaker in the parish in 1680[27] and the house of a man prosecuted for non-payment of tithes in 1710 was licensed for worship in 1706 and 1709.

Quaker meeting houses were licensed in 1731 and 1741.[28] There was a Baptist in the parish in 1791.[29]

Methodists registered a house for worship in 1803 and a chapel in 1810. John Carter's house at Stretcholt was licensed from 1819;[30] by 1845 a meeting house adjoined the dwelling.[31] In 1838 it was part of the Taunton Wesleyan circuit[32] and in 1841 a minister lodged in Carter's house.[33] Pawlett became part of the Bridgwater circuit in 1848.[34] The Carter memorial chapel was built on a new site north-west of Pawlett village in 1855.[35] A hall was added for a Sunday school in 1938. Average attendance at the chapel in 1960 was 35 in the morning and 15 in the evening.[36] It remained open in 1986.

EDUCATION. Anthony Ashley-Cooper, Lord Shaftesbury (d. 1811), paid £5 a year to a schoolmaster to teach poor children in the later 18th century.[37] The overseers paid a schoolmistress in the 1790s, possibly at the Sunday school which had 30 pupils in 1819.[38] Reopened in 1824, it had 50 children by 1835 and the teacher was paid out of the poor rate. Four day schools, begun in 1825, 1826, 1829, and 1830, had a total of 73 pupils in 1835, all educated at their parents' expense.[39] By 1846 three dame schools took 52 children, a day school 14 boys, and a Sunday school 43 children.[40] The dame schools were open in 1851 but two had closed by 1861 when a National school had been established near the church.[41] A girls' day school, possibly at Stretcholt and recorded in 1859, may have remained open in 1871,[42] and a Dissenting school had about 12 pupils in 1868.[43]

A school board for the parish was elected in 1887[44] and built a school on the National school site in 1888. In 1903 there were 58 children on the register and despite some fluctuations during the intervening years there were 53 children aged 5 to 11 on the books in 1975 and 75 in 1981.[45] A new County school opened west of the village in 1977 to replace the old building.[46]

CHARITIES FOR THE POOR. None known.

19 S.R.O., DD/S/WH 115; *S.R.S.* xl. 236; above, econ. hist. (fairs).
20 Plaque in ch.; S.R.O., D/D/Cf 1921/53; Wimborne St. Giles, Shaftesbury MSS., E/A 92.
21 S.R.O., D/P/pawl 4/1/1.
22 Ch. guide.
23 S.R.O., DD/X/COR 3.
24 *Proc. Som. Arch. Soc.* xlvii. 172–3; S.R.O., D/P/pawl 5/2/1.
25 S.R.O., DD/SAS CH 16/2.
26 Ibid. D/P/pawl 2/1/1–8.
27 *S.R.S.* lxxv. 137.
28 S.R.O., Q/RR meeting ho. lics.; *S.D.N.Q.* v. 294.
29 H. A. Hamblin & A. J. Whitby, *Baptists in Bridgwater*, 49.
30 S.R.O., D/D/Rm, box 2.
31 Ibid. DD/MLY 14, will of J. Carter.
32 Ibid. D/N/bmc 7/2.
33 P.R.O., HO 107/953.
34 S.R.O., D/N/bmc 7/2.
35 Inscr. on chapel.
36 S.R.O., D/N/bmc 3/2/2, 4/3/50; DD/X/HAG 1.
37 Wimborne St. Giles, Shaftesbury MSS., E/A 92, 127.
38 S.R.O., D/P/pawl 13/2/1; *Educ. of Poor Digest*, p. 793.
39 *Educ. Enq. Abstract*, p. 817; S.R.O., D/P/pawl 13/2/3–4.
40 Nat. Soc. *Inquiry, 1846–7*, Som. 14–15.
41 *P.O. Dir. Som.* (1861); P.R.O., HO 107/1925; RG 9/1626.
42 *P.O. Dir. Som.* (1859); P.R.O., RG 9/1626; RG 10/2390.
43 *Rep. Com. Employment in Agric.* p. 483, H.C. (1868–9), xiii.
44 *List of Sch. Boards, 1888*, [C. 5381], p. 67, H.C. (1888), lxxviii.
45 S.R.O., C/E 4/64, 4/390/316; O.S. Map 6", XXXVIII. SE. (1886 edn.).
46 Local inf.

NORTH PETHERTON

THE large parish of North Petherton[47] lies between the river Parrett, from which it takes its name,[48] and the lower slopes of the Quantocks. It measures 10 km. from east to west at its widest point, and 7 km. from north to south. It contains the large village of North Petherton, with North Newton village 1.5 km. to the south-east and Moorland or Northmoor Green 3 km. to the east. There are c. 14 other hamlets, of which Huntworth, 2 km. north-east, and Woolmersdon 0.5 km. north-west are the largest, and several farmsteads besides scattered houses and cottages. In 1886 land in the south and east was transferred to Lyng and Weston Zoyland leaving 10,484 a.[49] In 1933 St. Michaelchurch civil parish (46 a.) and 247 a. of Bridgwater Without civil parish were added, while 194 a. were transferred to Bridgwater Without.[50] In 1981, following minor changes in 1952, the civil parish measured 4,275 ha. (10,563 a.).[51]

The north-eastern boundary of the parish probably followed the Parrett's eastern branch, abandoned apparently in the 16th century for the western branch, leaving land beyond Moorland isolated across the river. Similar but smaller areas, such as Old River Ground,[52] were the result of deliberate straightening. The south-eastern boundary follows the probable earlier course of the river Tone, which was diverted in 1374–5.[53] The whole alluvial area is occupied by moor land known as Hay moor to the north, Little moor and Horlake moor around Moorland, and North moor in the south. The eastern third of the parish lies below the 15-m. contour on alluvium, with an 'island' of Burtle Beds occupied by the hamlet of Moorland, a small area of peat near Northmoor Corner, and beside the river some clay, used in brick and tile manufacture.[54]

Most of the remainder of the parish, rising from 15 m. to 46 m., is on Keuper marl and river deposits giving way further west to sandstone, with alluvium in the extreme north at Stock moor.[55] Quarrying took place at several sites,[56] and there is some evidence of lime burning near Shearston, south of Maunsel, and on the road from North Petherton to North Newton.[57] In the west, where the land rises steeply from 46 m. to 183 m. on the Quantocks, the parish occupies a ridge of Morte slates which falls steeply at King's Cliff to the stream which there forms the parish's northern boundary. Quarrying at King's Cliff had begun by the 14th century when a Langport slater worked there.[58] The quarry was regularly used in the 18th[59] and 19th centuries,[60] and gravel and sand were also extracted in the area in the 1960s.[61]

The principal route through the parish joined Bridgwater to Taunton. It entered the parish at Reed Bridge and crossed Stock moor by a causeway, created by 1603 and probably by 1502.[62] Until c. 1821 the road followed a tortuous route through North Petherton village.[63] From the village the main route to Taunton led via Farringdon and Shearston to Thurloxton,[64] but the present line was adopted by 1730 when it was turnpiked.[65] A second important route ran by the early 17th century along the Parrett bank linking Huntworth with Northmoor Green and Burrow Bridge.[66] The general direction of the Bridgwater–Taunton road was followed further south by the M5 motorway, opened in 1975.

A similar route, following the 15-m. contour, was taken by the Bridgwater and Taunton canal, opened in 1827.[67] From a basin beside the Parrett north of Huntworth it crossed the parish through four locks.[68] Cottages and stables were built around the basin, and several other cottages near Huntworth beside the canal. In 1841 the basin was abandoned and filled in when the canal was extended into Bridgwater. The Bristol–Exeter railway between Bridgwater and Taunton entered the parish where it crossed the Parrett by Somerset Bridge and followed the canal route. The stone bridge, designed by I. K. Brunel, was replaced before the line was opened in 1844 by a laminated timber structure on stone abutments which was in turn replaced in 1904 by a steel girder structure.[69] The bridge gave its name to a settlement which spread between canal and river around the brickyards and later included a school and a chapel.[70]

Evidence of mesolithic occupation has been found near North Newton and of Romano-British settlement at two sites near North Newton and one near West Newton.[71] North Petherton village, apparently established no earlier than the 10th century,[72] was probably the main focus of settlement in 1066 as the site of a minster church.[73] A second, pre-Conquest focus may have been St. Michaelchurch, by 1066 independent. In relation to St. Michaelchurch,

47 This article was written in 1984, with some later additions.
48 Ekwall, *Eng. Place-Names* (1960), 347.
49 *Census*, 1891.
50 S.R.O., GP/D, box 19.
51 Youngs, *Local Admin. Units*, i. 434; *Census*, 1981.
52 *S.R.S.* lxx, no. 1037; S.R.O., Q/REl 29/6D.
53 M. Williams, *Draining of Som. Levels*, 59.
54 Geol. Surv. Map 1/50,000, solid and drift, sheet 295 (1984 edn.); below, econ. hist. (trade and industry).
55 Geol. Surv. Map 1/50,000, solid and drift, sheet 295 (1984 edn.).
56 S.R.O., tithe award; O.S. Map 6", Som. LXI. NW., NE., SW. (1887 edn.).
57 S.R.O., tithe award; ibid. D/P/pet. n 13/1/9.
58 Ibid. DD/SAS NP 12, m. 9.

59 Ibid. DD/SL 3; D/P/pet. n 4/1/2.
60 Ibid. D/P/pet. n 9/1/1–3; ibid. tithe award.
61 O.S. Map 1/25,000, ST 23 (1959 edn.); *Som. C.C. Development Plan* (1964), 160.
62 *S.R.S.* xix. 27; xxiii. 26; S.R.O., Q/SR 115/76; Leland, *Itin.* ed. Toulmin Smith, i. 161.
63 S.R.O., T/PH/bb 3; ibid. Q/RUp 65.
64 J. Ogilby, *Britannia* (1675).
65 3 Geo. II, c. 34.   66 *S.R.S.* xxiii. 26.
67 S.R.O., Q/RUp 71; C. A. Buchanan, *Bridgwater and Taunton Canal*, 5.   68 S.R.O., tithe award.
69 B. J. Murless, *Bridgwater Docks and R. Parrett*, 21–3, 34.
70 Below, econ. hist. (trade and industry); nonconf.; educ.
71 Som. C.C., Sites and Mons. Rec.
72 *Proc. Som. Arch. Soc.* cxxi. 13–20.
73 *V.C.H. Som.* i. 435; below, churches.

North and West Newton were so named by the late 14th century, and Tuckerton was called Tokar Newton in the 13th century.[74] Other pre-Conquest holdings were at Melcombe, Shearston, and Shovel, which may have been single farmsteads in the Quantock foothills in the west; Hadworthy and Woolmersdon were farmsteads on the edge of moorland in the north; and Huntworth, perhaps in a woodland clearing, occupied a site just above the flood level of the Parrett in the north-east.[75] By the late 13th century more sites had been occupied around the margins of Stock moor in the north[76] and on the northern edges of North moor in the south and east, including settlements at Bankland and Primmore.[77] Farms had also been established by then on marginal land in the Quantocks.[78] Some of these sites, including the Domesday settlement at Hadworthy and the hamlets of Ballcombe and Ernesham, probably shrank in the 16th and 17th centuries.[79]

In contrast Moorland had spread by the early 17th century from the gravel 'island' beside the Parrett along the river bank north and south towards Huntworth and Burrow Bridge, and along the droves into the moor. Moorland House or Court, which retains at its south end the plan of a 17th-century three-roomed house, was extended northwards and westwards in the 18th century and it was largely refitted, extended further northwards, reroofed, refenestrated, and cased in red brick in the 19th century.

Huntworth became a nucleated hamlet containing several large 18th-century houses besides Huntworth House and Huntworth Park House. Huntworth House contains part of an older building at the south-west end which was remodelled and extended north-east and provided with a new staircase and drawing room c. 1830. Huntworth Park House was built in the mid 17th century but was greatly enlarged and altered in the 18th and 19th centuries.[80] Woolmersdon has houses dating from the 15th[81] to the 20th century, all of which lie away from the road except the 17th-century Orchard House and Woolmersdon House, built in the 1840s. Shearston is a scattered settlement mainly of 18th- and 19th- century houses. Chadmead, later Northmoor Corner, was an established squatter settlement by the late 18th century;[82] most of the houses appear to date from the 19th century but there are two older farmhouses towards North Newton called Coxhill and Turners, one of which is medieval, the other of the 17th century.[83] Bankland, further south and apparently more isolated, is on ground drained earlier, for of its two farmsteads one, Bankland Farm, is probably of the 16th century.

North Newton village appears to lie on a route from Clavelshay and the Quantocks to Petherton park. The church, there by the late 12th century,[84] occupies what may have been a green at the eastern end of the settlement. Routes to the north and south form a staggered crossroads at the centre of the village. Many of the surviving houses date from the 16th or the early 17th century. The Great House, rebuilt by Sir Thomas Wroth and his tenant c. 1671, has been altered but retains its 17th-century staircase and other features.[85]

North Petherton village seems to have developed around the church which stands on sloping ground above a stream. Land immediately west of the church which was settled before the mid 11th century had become a cemetery by 1302, but in the 15th century it reverted to domestic use.[86] The main street, north of the church, was probably known as High Street in the 17th century,[87] and later as Fore Street. It was lined by several inns and perhaps contained the shirehall (the use of which is unknown), court house, and guildhall in the 14th century.[88] The market place, possibly dating from the 14th century,[89] may have been on the north side of the church or further north-east between the present Clare and Queen Streets. South-west of the church is Hammet Street, perhaps in the 14th century Southbroke Street[90] and known as Hammer or Hammel Street in the 17th century.[91] Until the 19th century building was largely confined to those streets and a few adjoining them, Queen Street (formerly Back Street), Mill Street, the Newton road, High Street, Cliff Road, and Pilot's Elm or Helm. About 1821 the new Bridgwater road was built to provide a straighter route through the village; during the 19th century large suburban houses were built along it and houses were built on Tappers Lane west from Fore Street.[92]

In the 20th century houses were built north, south, and east of the village and by the 1970s the old orchards and gardens were largely obliterated. Most of the houses in the centre of the village appear to date from the 18th and the 19th century but a few have earlier features.

In the early 14th century there were two large open arable fields on the west side of the parish called Farringdon and Bulledones fields,[93] and there was an open field at North Newton called Brundon.[94] There were probably open fields which have not been recorded around other settlements. Landshares survived south of North Petherton village until the 18th century, small amounts of common arable at Woolmersdon in the late 18th century,[95] and strips north of North Newton in 1838. Common meadows

74   *V.C.H. Som.* i. 472; *S.R.S.* xiv, p. 180; xvii. 30–1; *Cal. Pat.* 1377–81, 145.
75   *V.C.H. Som.* i. 484–5, 511–12, 520–1.
76   *S.R.S.* xiv, p. 91; xxv, p. 2.
77   S.R.O., DD/SL 1; *S.R.S.* xiv, p. 180; xvii. 28; xxv, pp. 21–2.
78   *S.R.S.* iii. 244; xiv, p. 174; S.R.O., DD/BV 2, 4; below, manors.
79   S.R.O., DD/BV 2, 4, 16; DD/SL 1; below, manors.
80   S.R.O., DD/V/BWr 26.13.
81   Below, manors.
82   S.R.O., DD/SLM 2.
83   Ibid. DD/V/BWr 26.2.   84   Below, churches.

85   Devon R.O. 1148 M/add 6/17; S.R.O., DD/V/BWr 26.3, 7, 10, 14.
86   *Proc. Som. Arch. Soc.* cxxi. 13–20; S.R.O., DD/SAS NP 1, m. 8.
87   S.R.O., DD/BV 5.
88   *S.R.S.* xxv, p. 29; S.R.O., DD/SAS NP 1, m. 1; 5, m. 4.
89   Below, econ. hist. (markets and fairs).
90   P.R.O., E 326/8259.
91   S.R.O., DD/BV 5; DD/SAS (C/96) 17/2–3.
92   Ibid. tithe award; O.S. Map 1/2,500, Som. LXI. 6 (1905 edn.).
93   *S.R.S.* xii. 29.   94   *Cal. Pat.* 1338–40, 250.
95   S.R.O., DD/AH 6/10; DD/SLM (C/1795).

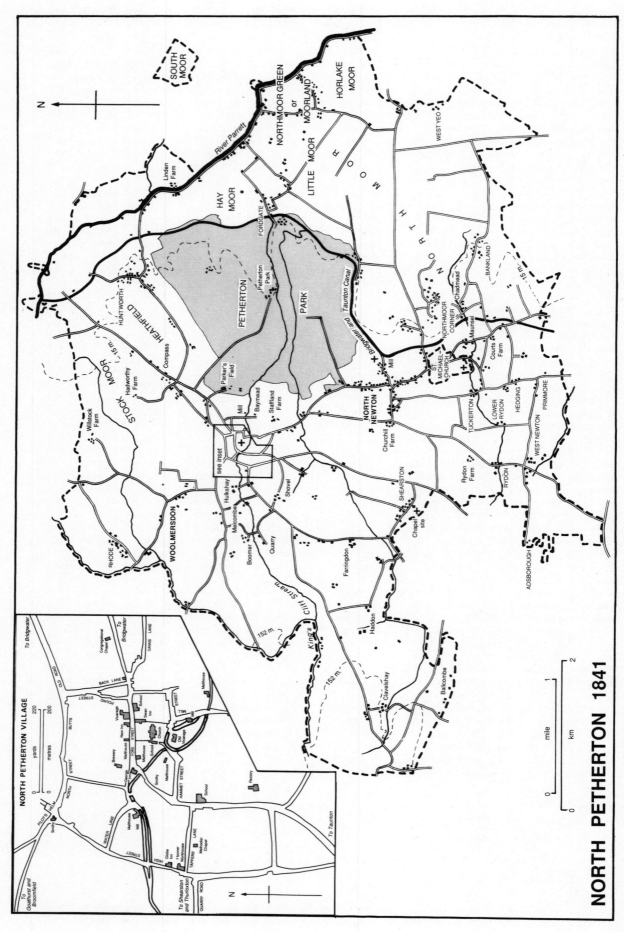

NORTH PETHERTON 1841

lay near the moors at Broadmead and Chadmead west of North moor, and at Pontage, Haygrove, and Horlake east of it.[96] Several small meadows at Woolmersdon were held in common until the later 18th century.[97]

There were four main areas of common pasture, North moor, Heathfield, King's Cliff, and Stock moor, and smaller areas at South moor in King's Sedgemoor, Lent moor in North Newton,[98] and Hurdown near Shearston. Stock moor was shared between Woolmersdon and Hadworthy manors and Hamp in Bridgwater by the mid 13th century,[99] and was probably inclosed before the end of the 17th.[1] Heathfield was gradually divided and inclosed in the 16th and 17th centuries,[2] and Hurdown by c. 1654.[3] The remaining common pasture, nearly 1,500 a. and mainly in North moor, was inclosed in 1798.[4]

Petherton park, probably a detached remnant of the Saxon royal forest of Quantock, was held from 1086 with that part of North Newton which came to be known as Newton Forester manor.[5] In Henry II's reign the forest jurisdiction was extended beyond the park to include much of North Petherton parish and manors and hamlets in Durston, Lyng, Creech St. Michael, North Curry, and Stoke St. Gregory. The earlier park or forest boundaries were re-established in 1298.[6] The boundaries of the park were marked in the late 13th century by watercourses and later by the Park brook on the east and south, by Baymead on the west, and by Heathfield on the north.[7] The park may have been walled in the early 14th century[8] and was 4 miles in circumference.[9] Entrances were Fordgate, probably the same as Highfordgate, Huntworth gate, English's gate, probably at North Newton, and Heathfield gate.[10] The area was disafforested and disparked in the 17th century.[11]

There was a park at Newton by 1339.[12] It was probably divided with the manor[13] but later belonged to Newton Wroth manor. It lay south of North Newton church and had been divided and let by 1671.[14] A park north-west of Huntworth village had been formed by the 1580s, a mile in circumference. A small part of it remained parkland in the late 19th century.[15] A park was created north of Maunsel House in the early 19th century.[16]

There was a warren in Petherton park, bounded on its southern side by Warren wall.[17] Warrens were also formed at Melcombe and Woolmersdon.[18]

In 1866–7 it was decided to establish a gas and coal company in the parish,[19] but no gas supply was provided and the street lighting recorded in 1896 appears to have been by gasolene lamps.[20] The North Petherton Gas and Carbide Co. produced acetylene gas between 1906 and 1931 for street and domestic lighting from October to March in premises in Mill Street. Street lighting was produced from dusk until 10 p.m. The spent carbide was used by farmers as fertilizer. Coal gas and electricity were supplied from Bridgwater from 1931.[21] A public library was opened in North Petherton in 1984 and a community centre west of the church c. 1988.

There were unlicensed alesellers in the parish in the 14th century, and 22 people were presented for breach of the assize of ale in 1349.[22] There was a tippler in 1594, a tippler and an innkeeper in 1619,[23] and an innholder in 1646.[24] Three alehouses, at Tuckerton, Primmore, and North moor, were suppressed in 1640[25] but a 'multitude' still remained in 1647.[26] Between the 1650s and the early 18th century the number of licensed premises fluctuated between three and ten;[27] in 1686 they could between them provide 11 beds and stabling for 21 horses.[28] Among them were the George, in Fore Street, first named in 1619.[29] It was built in the early 17th century and altered probably in the later 19th century when an assembly room was added to achieve hotel status.[30] Monthly petty sessions were held there in the 19th century.[31] It was still in business in 1984 but closed shortly afterwards. The White Horse was recorded in 1676[32] and the Anchor in 1699.[33] The Lion, mentioned in 1711,[34] may be the White Lion which was rebuilt before 1724 and was renamed the New Inn.[35] About 1897 the name was changed to the Clarence Hotel,[36] and c. 1978 to the Walnut Tree. The 18th-century inn, opposite the parish church in Fore Street, was extended in the 1930s[37] and again in the 1980s. The Nag's Head, possibly earlier the White Horse, was probably open in 1725.[38] It had closed by the later 18th century but the name survived until the 1830s. It stood in Fore Street west of the parish church.[39] The Swan, at the east side of the

96 S.R.O., tithe award.
97 Ibid. DD/AH 6/10, 8/3.
98 Cal. Pat. 1338–40, 250.
99 S.R.S. xi, p. 357; xiv, p. 149.
1 S.R.O., DD/AH 8/3; DD/DP 34/2; DD/S/WH 21/6.
2 Below, econ. hist. (agriculture).
3 S.R.O., DD/PT 2; DD/SAS (C/96) 7/8.
4 Ibid. DD/MK, inclosure map 1798.
5 V.C.H. Som. ii. 553–5; below, manors.
6 Collinson, Hist. Som. iii. 56–61.
7 S.R.O., tithe award; map opposite.
8 S.R.O., DD/SAS NP 1, m. 15.
9 S.R.S. xx. 137.
10 Devon R.O. 1148 M/add 2/71B, 9/23; P.R.O., HO 107/1926. Huntworth gate may have been the entrance to Huntworth park: S.R.O., tithe award.
11 Below, econ. hist. (agriculture).
12 Cal. Pat. 1338–40, 250.
13 S.R.O., DD/WM 1/113.
14 Devon R.O. 1148 M/add 6/17.
15 Greswell, Forests and Deerparks of Som. 258; S.R.O., tithe award; O.S. Map 6", Som. LXI. NE. (1887 edn.).
16 S.R.O., DD/SLM 14.

17 Devon R.O. 1148 M/add 6/17; S.R.O., tithe award.
18 Dors. R.O., D 10/M 245; S.R.O., tithe award.
19 Som. Co. Gaz. 15 Dec. 1866; inf. from Mr. D. Gledhill, Taunton.
20 S.R.O., D/PC/pet. n 1/2/1–2.
21 Proc. Som. Arch. Soc. cxxxi. 230; inf. from Mr. Gledhill.
22 S.R.O., DD/SAS NP 9, m. 1.
23 Ibid. D/D/Ca 98; ibid. Q/RLa 33.
24 Ibid. D/B/bw 1506–7.   25 S.R.S. lxxi, p. 2.
26 Ibid. xxviii. 22.   27 S.R.O., Q/RL.
28 P.R.O., WO 30/48.   29 S.D.N.Q. x. 300.
30 S.R.O., DD/SL 8, 9; DD/SLM 2; D/R/bw 16/11/1; P.R.O., RG 11/2369.
31 P.O. Dir. Som. (1861, 1875).
32 S.R.O., DD/SL 15.   33 Ibid. Q/SR 213/2, 9.
34 Ibid. D/P/pet. n 13/2/1.
35 Ibid.; DD/SLM, bk. of maps; DD/DHR, box 17, deed 1766.   36 Kelly's Dir. Som. (1897).
37 S.R.O., D/R/bw 22/1/39.
38 Ibid. Q/RL; ibid. DD/SL 8–9; DD/SLM 2.
39 Ibid. DD/SLM, bk. of maps; ibid. Q/REl 29/6; Post Med. Archaeology, xiii. 183, 185.

churchyard, was first recorded as an inn in 1727 although the building dates from the 17th century.[40] It had a fives court by 1838[41] and an assembly room by 1898.[42] It was still open in 1990. The Harp was open between 1765 and 1786[43] and may be the same as the Ring of Bells, Hammet Street, so named in 1840 and closed in 1924.[44] The Mitre, also in Hammet Street, had opened by 1798 and closed c. 1909.[45]

During the 19th century a number of public houses opened, including the Globe, still open in High Street in 1990, the Bird in Hand in Pound Street, the Royal Hotel in Back Lane, the William IV, the Lamb in Fore Street, open in 1990, and the Mason's Arms in Hammet Street.[46]

One or more inns at North Newton could provide three beds and stabling for three horses in 1686.[47] In 1688 there were three licensed victuallers there,[48] one of them probably at the Black Horse, recorded by name in 1711, and in business until the 1780s.[49] The Royal Oak, named in 1724,[50] was probably open between 1688 and 1779.[51] There were two unnamed beerhouses in 1851 and 1872,[52] but there is no later record of a public house in the village until the Harvest Moon was opened in 1962.[53]

There was a licensed victualler at Moorland in 1746, probably at the Fleur de Luce recorded from 1770 to 1786.[54] The Ferry Boat was open between 1838 and 1861 but probably closed shortly afterwards.[55] A second riverside house in 1851 may have been the later Thatcher's Arms, so named in 1871[56] and in business in 1990.

The Bell near Whitestock on the Taunton road and the Compass inn on the Bridgwater road were both open by 1851.[57] The Compass remained open in 1990. The Malt and Hops at Somerset Bridge was opened before 1851 by Samuel Fursland at his brick and tile works and it remained open until 1937.[58] The Boat and Anchor was in business by 1871 in a row of bargemen's cottages near the canal between Somerset Bridge and Huntworth. Extensions and a skittle alley replaced most of the cottages, and the inn remained open in 1990.[59] The Royal Oak at Northmoor Corner, recorded from 1871, was closed in 1924.[60] The Fordgate tavern, open between 1871 and 1939, lay beside the railway

north of a street of houses occupied mainly by railway workers.[61]

There was a friendly society in the 1790s which had a membership of 122 men in 1796.[62] Later known as the Old Blues, the club was still in existence in 1837.[63] In 1836 a new society was formed at the George inn by the vicar, James Toogood, and was known as the North Petherton friendly society.[64] In 1837 it was presented with a banner and had 74 members. Later in the century there were two clubs besides the Old Blues, known as the Tradesmen's and the Gentlemen's.[65] A penny club was founded in the 1830s to provide blankets for the poor.[66] A book club had been established by 1837[67] and a reading room was open between 1861 and 1894.[68] The North Petherton carnival, held since 1950, attracts many visitors.[69]

There were 811 communicants in North Petherton in 1547[70] and 236 households in the parish in 1563 including 13 at North Newton.[71] In 1667 nearly 320 people were recorded in North Newton tithing, which extended outside the parish.[72] The population of the parish was 2,346 in 1801 rising to 3,091 in 1821 and to 3,566 in 1831. Numbers reached a peak of 3,985 in 1871, falling gradually to 3,534 in 1901 and 3,179 in 1931. In 1933 the population of St. Michaelchurch and part of Bridgwater Without was added.[73] In 1981 there were 4,883 people in the civil parish.[74]

The poet Geoffrey Chaucer (d. 1400) was forester of Petherton park from 1391.[75] Tobias Venner, M.D. (1577–1660), who practised at North Petherton and, in the season, at Bath, was author of several medical works in the 1620s including an attack on tobacco and a book on the baths at Bath dedicated to Sir Francis Bacon.[76]

A skirmish between a royalist supply convoy and a parliamentary force took place in North Petherton in August 1644.[77]

BOROUGH. A burgage in North Petherton belonged to the serjeanty of Pignes in 1251–2.[78] North Petherton borough, which was separately represented neither at the eyres of 1225 and 1242–3[79] nor at the law hundreds of the 1430s,[80] yielded profits to the lord of North Petherton

40 S.R.O., D/P/pet. n 13/2/1.
41 Ibid. tithe award.
42 Ibid. D/R/bw 16/11/1, 18.
43 Ibid. Q/RL.
44 Ibid.; ibid. D/R/bw 15/1/2; ibid. Co. Lic. Cttee. min. bk. 2; Co. Gaz. Dir. Som. (1840).
45 S.R.O., Q/RL; QS/LIC 9.
46 Robson's Dir. (1839); Co. Gaz. Dir. Som. (1840); P. O. Dir. Som. (1859, 1861); P.R.O., RG 10/2381.
47 P.R.O., WO 30/48.
48 S.R.O. Q/RL.
49 Ibid.; ibid. D/P/pet. n. 13/2/1; Devon R.O. 1148 M/add 34/12.
50 Devon R.O. 1148 M/add 2/71B.
51 Ibid.; S.R.O., Q/RL.
52 P.R.O., HO 107/1924; Morris & Co. Dir. Som. (1872).
53 Inf. from clerk to magistrates.
54 S.R.O., Q/RL; ibid. DD/SLM, bk. of maps.
55 Ibid. tithe award; P.O. Dir. Som. (1861).
56 P.R.O., RG 10/3281.
57 Ibid. HO 107/1924.
58 Ibid.; S.R.O., tithe award; Bridgwater and District Dir. (1937–40).
59 P.R.O., RG 10/2381; Bridgwater Mercury, 2 Nov. 1983.

60 P.R.O., RG 10/2381; S.R.O., Q/RUp 562; ibid. Co. Lic. Cttee. min. bk. 2.
61 P.R.O., RG 10/2381; Kelly's Dir. Som. (1939).
62 S.R.O., D/P/pet. n 23/5; DD/SAS SE 8.
63 Ibid. DD/X/BUSH; Som. Co. Herald, 21 May 1921.
64 S.R.O., DD/X/BUSH; M. Fuller, W. Country Friendly Socs. 18, 40, 113; P.R.O., FS 1/618/464; FS 2/9.
65 Som. Co. Herald, 21 May 1921.
66 S.R.O., D/P/pet. n 9/1/2; DD/X/BUSH.
67 Ibid. DD/X/BUSH.
68 P.O. Dir. Som. (1861, 1866); Kelly's Dir. Som. (1883, 1894).
69 Bridgwater Mercury, 13 Nov. 1984.
70 S.R.S. ii. 59.
71 B.L. Harl. MS. 594, f. 55.
72 S.R.O., DD/WY 34.
73 Census; S.R.O., GP/D, box 19.
74 Census.   75 D.N.B.
76 Ibid.; S.R.O., DD/WO 59/4.
77 D. Underdown, Som. in Civil War, 77; S.R.O., D/P/pet. n 2/1/1.
78 Bk. of Fees, ii. 1266.
79 S.R.S. xi, pp. 40–1, 298–301.
80 S.R.O., DD/SAS NP 15.

hundred and manor, nearly £5 in 1297–8, nearly £6 in 1311–12, and £5 9s. 4d. in 1391–2. The profits came mostly from rents, but also from a borough court or portmote.[81] The lordship of the borough, linked with the tithing of Denizen in 1569[82] and yielding rents of £3 1s. in 1647,[83] descended with the hundred and manor until 1832 or later.[84]

MANORS AND OTHER ESTATES. In 1086 *NORTH PETHERTON* manor was part of the king's land and had never paid geld.[85] Its holders owed a fee farm to the Crown;[86] in 1761 the farm of 5 guineas was paid to Antony Duncombe, Baron Feversham (d. 1763),[87] presumably by grant. The fee farm was paid to the Crown in 1779[88] but by 1860 to William, Lord Radnor, son of Lord Feversham's daughter Anne.[89] It was later acquired by Anne (d. 1874), widow of Sir Henry Featherstonehaugh, Bt. In 1876 her successor Bullock Featherstonehaugh, probably her nephew, demanded payment, which was six years in arrears.[90] No further reference to the fee farm has been found.

The manor was said to have been given by Henry I to John of Erleigh.[91] John held it in 1157[92] and died c. 1162.[93] His successor was William of Erleigh, the king's chamberlain,[94] but John's widow, Adela or Alice, held part of the estate in 1166. William's lands were in the king's hands in 1166[95] and in 1169 Geoffrey de Mayenne accounted for North Petherton.[96] William, probably son of William of Erleigh, held the manor from 1170 until 1177 when his lands were confiscated. Henry II probably regranted the manor to him for a fee farm rent of 100s.[97] John of Erleigh had succeeded by 1189.[98] William of Erleigh was named as holding a fee in 1199, either in error for John or on behalf of John's son.[99] John of Erleigh held North-Petherton from 1202[1] until 1231 when he was succeeded by his brother Henry of Erleigh.[2] Henry (d. 1272)[3] was followed by his son Philip (d. c. 1275) and Philip by his son John, who came of age c. 1290[4] and died c. 1323. John of Erleigh, son of the last, died c. 1337, leaving a son (Sir) John, a minor.[5] Sir John sold the manor in 1371 to John Cole and his wife Margery.[6]

By 1388 Thomas Beaupyne was in possession, probably as tenant to the Coles from whom he bought the manor in 1391.[7] On the death of Thomas's widow Margaret in 1408 North Petherton passed to their daughter Agnes, wife first of John Bluet and then of John Bevyle.[8] Bevyle held the manor in 1412 but was dead by 1431.[9] Agnes was succeeded in 1442 by her son John Bluet.[10]

John Bluet (d. 1463)[11] was followed in turn by his son Walter (d. 1481) and his grandson Nicholas Bluet (d. 1522). Nicholas's heir was his grandson (Sir) Roger, son of Richard Bluet.[12] Roger came of age in 1524[13] and died c. 1566.[14] His son John (d. 1584) was followed by John's son Richard (d. 1615) and Richard's grandson John Bluet.[15] John died in 1634 leaving four daughters; his widow Elizabeth held the manor until her death c. 1637 when it passed to trustees.[16] The property was then divided like Chipstable manor[17] between the daughters, Anne, wife of Cadwallader Jones, Mary, wife successively of Sir James Stonehouse, Bt., and (Sir) John Lenthall, Dorothy, wife of Henry Wallop, and Susan, wife of John Basset. Anne sold her share to Dorothy, whose half of the manor formed part of the marriage settlement of Dorothy's younger son John Wallop and his wife Alice in 1683.[18] John (d. 1694) bought the Lenthall share in 1685, and settled it on his younger son John after Alice's death.[19] John's elder son Bluet inherited the half share but died without issue in 1707 leaving his brother John as heir.[20] John (cr. Baron Wallop and Vct. Lymington 1720, earl of Portsmouth 1743), held three quarters of the manor until 1742 when he acquired the remaining share from John Basset, great-grandson of Susan Bluet.[21] In 1754 the earl sold the entire North Petherton estate to Alexander Seymour Gapper who, unable to pay the purchase price, sold it back in 1755. The earl died in 1762 when his heir was his grandson John, who sold the manor to John Slade in 1768.[22] The manor descended from 1772 with the manor of Maunsel.[23]

No capital messuage for the manor has been

81 Ibid. 1, mm. 2, 17; 5, m. 4; below, local govt.
82 *S.R.S.* xx. 130–1.
83 S.R.O., DD/X/FRC (C/140).
84 P.R.O., CP 43/997, rot. 24; S.R.O., DD/SL 9; DD/SLM (C/1795).
85 *V.C.H. Som.* i. 435.
86 *Rot. Hund.* (Rec. Com.), ii. 140; *Cal. Pat.* 1391–6, 407.
87 S.R.O., DD/S/WH 26.
88 Ibid. DD/SL 3.
89 'Some payments by Thomas Mullins for Col. Tynte's Executrix', MS. in possession of Mr. J. S. Cox, Guernsey.
90 S.R.O., DD/SL 6, 40.
91 *Rot. Hund.* (Rec. Com.), ii. 140; *Cal. Inq. Misc.* i, p. 231.
92 *Pipe R.* 1156–8 (Rec. Com.), 98.
93 Ibid. 1162 (P.R.S. v), 22; ibid. 1163 (P.R.S. vi), 26.
94 *Red Bk. Exch.* (Rolls Ser.), i. 235.
95 *Pipe R.* 1166 (P.R.S. xi), 97.
96 Ibid. 1169 (P.R.S. xii), 4.
97 Ibid. 1170 (P.R.S. xv), 112; ibid. 1176 (P.R.S. xxv), 154; *S.D.N.Q.* xiv. 190; *Rot. Hund.* (Rec. Com.), ii. 140.
98 *Pipe R.* 1189 (Rec. Com.), 147.
99 *S.D.N.Q.* xiv. 70; *Red Bk. Exch.* (Rolls Ser.), i. 124.
1 *S.R.S.* xxv, p. 190; *S.D.N.Q.* xiv. 70.
2 *Cur. Reg. R.* 1230–2, p. 394; *Close R.* 1227–31, 518, 541.

3 *S.R.S.* xxv, p. xviii.
4 *Cal. Pat.* 1272–81, 100; *S.R.S.* xxv, p. 24; *Cal. Close,* 1288–96, 353.
5 S.R.O., DD/SAS NP 2, m. 2; *Cal. Inq. p.m.* vi, p. 297; viii, p. 58.
6 *Cal. Pat.* 1370–4, 136; *S.R.S.* xvii. 79.
7 *S.R.S.* xvii. 152; *Cal. Pat.* 1388–92, 503.
8 *S.R.S.* xxii. 11; P.R.O., C 137/71, no. 23.
9 *Feud. Aids*, iv. 433; vi. 513.
10 P.R.O., C 139/105, no. 10; *Cal. Fine R.* 1437–45, 228.
11 P.R.O., C 140/10, no. 25; *Cal. Close*, 1461–8, 174.
12 P.R.O., C 140/81, no. 56; C 142/39, no. 87; *Cal. Fine R.* 1471–85, 219–20.
13 *L. & P. Hen. VIII*, iv (1), p. 55.
14 S.R.O., DD/PM 3/4.
15 P.R.O., C 142/206, no. 87; C 142/351, nos. 104, 120; *S.R.S.* lxvii, p. 87.
16 P.R.O., C 142/475, no. 105; S.R.O., DD/PM 7; *Som. Wills*, ed. Brown, v. 20.
17 *V.C.H. Som.* v. 27.
18 S.R.O., DD/SL 5.   19 Ibid. 5, 17.
20 Ibid. 18; Burke, *Peerage* (1949), 1621.
21 S.R.O., DD/SL 5, 6, 18, 20; DD/BV 16.
22 Ibid. DD/SL 5; DD/SAS (C/96) 17/5.
23 Below, this section.

found but there was a court house in the 13th and 14th centuries.[24]

Lands, later known as *ACLAND'S* lands or North Petherton manor, were left by Baldwin Malet (d. 1533) to his wife Anne for life and then to their son John.[25] The estate descended to John's son Robert (fl. 1572) and to Robert's granddaughters Christina (d. 1590), wife of Robert Brett, and Eleanor, wife of Arthur Acland. In 1602 Eleanor, the sole survivor, sold her manor to Richard Bluet, lord of the principal manor of North Petherton.[26]

In 1225 Roger Baril, serjeant of Petherton hundred, had a house in the hundred and in the 1240s Roger Baril, possibly the same, held land in North Petherton, probably what was later called *VOWELL'S* lands.[27] In 1279 Roger's widow Alice released her dower to her heir John Baril who held land in 1270.[28] John is said to have received land near Petherton park and in Hay moor from Henry of Erleigh. He died without issue before 1296 and his land was held by the Erleighs in the early 14th century.[29] By 1466 Robert Baril held the land. Gillian Vowell, who held it by 1477[30] and in 1491 gave her estates in North Petherton and Huntworth to trustees to the uses of her will, was dead by 1492 when her estates, described as formerly Baril's, had passed to her son Richard Vowell.[31] Richard (d. 1498) was followed by his son William (d. 1552). William, probably William's son, with his wife Margaret and Thomas Vowell, sold the estate to Sir Roger Bluet in 1561.[32] It descended with the Bluets' manor of North Petherton.[33]

A house known as Baril's Place was recorded in the 18th century but had gone by 1770.[34]

Lands of St. Mary's chantry in the parish church were sold in 1550 to men probably acting for Sir Roger Bluet. He bequeathed the land to his son John in 1566,[35] and it descended with the Bluets' manor of North Petherton.[36] The chantry house, sold by the Crown in 1549, was also later acquired by the Bluets,[37] but it is not mentioned after 1677.[38]

The manor of North Petherton later known as *BUCKLAND FEE* belonged to Buckland priory before the Dissolution.[39] The Crown granted it in 1544 to William Portman and Alexander Popham.[40] It passed to Alexander's son Edward (d. 1586) and included lands in several parishes. It descended with the Pophams' manor of Huntworth until 1838 or later.[41] No later reference to the lordship has been found. The capital messuage was possibly that sold to Mr. Crosswell and may be the house north of the rectory, now demolished, in which Crosswell kept a school in the 19th century.[42]

A manor of *NORTH PETHERTON*, which can be traced to a holding of John Sydenham (d. 1468), included houses and lands which Margaret Mutton, probably wife of John's son Walter (d. 1469), held when she died in 1477.[43] Her son and heir John Sydenham of Brympton held land in Whitestock as a free tenant of Shearston manor in 1519.[44] In 1613 the Sydenhams' manor, held of the Bluets' manor of North Petherton, included lands in Moorland, Edington in Moorlinch, and Bridgwater, and probably less than half its land lay in North Petherton parish. John Sydenham (d. 1625) settled the manor on his son John for his marriage to Alice Hody,[45] and it descended with Combe Sydenham in Stogumber until 1674 or later.[46] No further reference to the lordship has been found and the land was probably dispersed.

William Brent (d. 1536) held a manor called *DUNWEAR* which may have been the *PETHERTON* manor held in 1552 by his son Richard (d. 1570).[47] Richard's heir was his daughter Anne, wife of Thomas Paulet.[48] Anne died before her husband, leaving a daughter Elizabeth, married to Giles Hoby.[49] The Hobys sold land in North Petherton to John Watts (d. 1622) who was succeeded by his son Nicholas (d. 1634). Nicholas left two infant daughters Jane and Walthean; the latter married John Newton.[50] The estate has not been traced further.

HULKSHAY manor was held of the Bluets' manor of North Petherton in 1485 and was so held until 1647 or later.[51] In 1397 John Brown held an estate in right of his wife Isabel with remainder to John Penny.[52] Penny conveyed it in 1428 to Martin Jacob, who with his wife Joan added land in 1446.[53] Joan Jacob died in 1485 and Hulkshay, sometimes called North Petherton manor, descended like Brompton Jacob in Brompton Ralph.[54] In 1701 Baldwin Malet appears to have sold the manor, and the lands were dispersed.[55] There is no further reference to the lordship.

The Jacob family had a house in the parish in 1428 and in 1443 they were granted a licence for

---

24 S.R.O., DD/SAS NP 1, mm. 1, 8–12, 14–15.
25 *S.R.S.* xxi, pp. 17–18; S.R.O., DD/MA 11.
26 P.R.O., C 142/230, no. 34; ibid. CP 25(2)/207/44 Eliz. I Trin.
27 *S.R.S.* vi. 143–4; xi, pp. 41, 299.
28 Ibid. xxv, pp. 27–8; *Cal. Chart. R.* 1257–1300, 157.
29 S.R.O., DD/SAS NP 1, mm. 8, 13; NP 8; Devon R.O., C.R. 1280.
30 Wells Cath. Libr., Vicars Choral MS. C/10; S.R.O., DD/CC 131912A/6.
31 S.R.O., DD/PM 3/1.
32 *Cal. Inq. p.m. Hen. VII*, ii, pp. 124–5; P.R.O., C 142/99, no. 82; ibid. CP 25(2)/204/3 & 4 Eliz. I Mich.
33 S.R.O., DD/SL 9; DD/S/WH 26; DD/X/FRC (C/140).
34 Ibid. DD/SL 9; DD/SLM, bk. of maps.
35 *S.R.S.* lxxvii, pp. 68–9; P.R.O., C 142/206, no. 1.
36 S.R.O., DD/X/FRC (C/140); DD/SL 8, 9.
37 *S.R.S.* lxxvii, p. 33; *Cal. Pat.* 1548–9, 430; S.R.O., DD/SL 16.
38 S.R.O., DD/SL 15.

39 P.R.O., C 142/211, no. 156.
40 *Proc. Som. Arch. Soc.* x. 76–8.
41 P.R.O., C 142/211, no. 156; S.R.O., tithe award; below, this section.
42 S.R.O., DD/PM 3/6; DD/PM 16; P.R.O., CRES 39/169; below, educ.
43 P.R.O., C 140/28, no. 22; C 140/32, no. 22; C 140/61, no. 36.   44 S.R.O., DD/PT, box 1.
45 Ibid. DD/SAS BK 87; P.R.O., C 142/525, no. 61.
46 *V.C.H. Som.* v. 181; S.R.O., DD/SL 16.
47 P.R.O., C 142/22, no. 43; C 142/41, no. 28; C 142/58, no. 6.   48 Ibid. C 142/156, no. 14.
49 Ibid. C 142/215, no. 245.
50 *S.R.S.* lxvii, p. 154; P.R.O., C 142/475, no. 78; ibid. CP 25(2)/592/1658 East.
51 *Cal. Inq. p.m. Hen. VII*, i, p. 58; S.R.O., DD/X/FRC (C/140).
52 S.R.O., DD/SAS NP 5, m. 2.
53 *S.R.S.* xii. 109, 143; xvii. 95, 171–2; xxii. 75; P.R.O., C 260/15, no. 26.   54 *V.C.H. Som.* v. 21–2.
55 S.R.O., DD/SAS (C/96) 17/6; DD/RN 8.

a private chapel there.[56] That house may be represented by Hulkshay Farm, built in the mid 18th century; part of the staircase, a fireplace with rococo plasterwork, and a stone porch survive. The house was refitted and partly refronted in the 19th century.

Ansger the cook, one of the king's serjeants, held *SHOVEL* in 1086. Two thegns had held it freely in 1066. Its 11th-century name, Siwoldestone, may record a former owner.[57] By the late 15th century Shovel was held by Adam Hamlyn of Bridgwater who died in 1493 leaving it to his younger daughter Margaret, wife of John Wyner.[58] In 1498 Margaret sold it to John Heyron (d. 1501) who in the following year was licensed to found a chantry at Langport endowed with lands at Shovel.[59] The Langport chantry estate was granted to Laurence Hyde of London in 1549.[60] Laurence died in 1590[61] and Edward Hyde of West Hatch in Tisbury (Wilts.), in possession in 1648,[62] sold it in 1659 to Walter Catford, who kept courts in 1684. In 1703 Walter's son, also Walter, sold Shovel to the tenant John Dobin. John or a son of the same name sold it to Joseph Gatcombe in 1763.[63] Joseph (d. 1777) was succeeded by his son William (d. 1816) and William by his son Joseph (d. 1820). Joseph's widow Anna died in 1847 and Shovel passed to Joseph's niece Matilda (d. 1889), wife of the Revd. William Chapman Kinglake (d. 1881).[64] They were succeeded by their second daughter Rosa, wife of Frederick Kinglake (d. 1900). Shovel was sold in 1910 to A. M. Wilson.[65] By 1925 it had been acquired by Herbert Nelson.[66]

Shovel House, also known as Gatcombe House and Shovel Hill, was built probably c. 1820.[67] It is a large double-pile brick villa with a five-bayed front and central porch, with a lower one-bayed wing, probably original, on the east and a symmetrical bay on the west added after 1841.[68] Further rooms were added later in the 19th century and the interior retains many original fittings and good contemporary plasterwork.

STAMFORDLANDS appears to have been severed from Melcombe Paulet manor in 1573 when it was bought by Richard Bidgood and William Tucker.[69] In 1578 Bidgood released his interest to Tucker who was succeeded by his son John (d. 1603).[70] In 1614 John's son William and

John Wroth sold the estate to John Musgrave (d. 1631)[71] who was succeeded by his son George (d. 1640). George's son Richard settled Stamfordlands in 1671 on his son George.[72] Richard died c. 1686 and George's estate was described as a manor in 1699.[73] The manor descended in the Musgrave family from George (d. 1721) to his son George (d. 1724) and then with Shearston to Juliana (d. 1810), wife of Sir James Langham, Bt.[74] By 1806 the estate had been dispersed and William Gatcombe held Stamfordlands farm,[75] which descended in the Gatcombe family with Shovel until 1893 when it was divided and sold.[76]

The house was described as new in 1573 and as newly erected in 1614.[77] It was replaced by Staffland Farm in the early 19th century.

An estate called *BAYMEAD*, including Nether Baymead, purchased by George Musgrave from the Ley or Farthing family in 1626,[78] was held with Stamfordlands, but in 1670 it was described as a separate manor.[79] It appears to have been sold in the 1760s[80] and had been divided by 1838.[81]

Saemer held an estate called *NEWTON*, later Estable Newton, in 1066 and John the usher held it in 1086; Stable held it under John.[82] Before 1199 Roger Stable granted it to William Wrotham.[83] In 1250 William's nephew Richard Wrotham held it of Roger Stable by service of a white wand.[84] It merged with the other estates of the Wrothams and had no further separate existence.

An estate at *NEWTON* which Osward held in 1066 was in 1086 held by Ansketil the parker apparently as a royal serjeanty.[85] It continued to be held by successive foresters of Petherton together with the bailiwick of Williton: Robert son of Bernard (d. c. 1184), Geoffrey FitzPeter in 1185, and Robert de Odburville until c. 1193.[86] William Wrotham received a grant of Newton in 1198.[87] Wrotham was forester from 1199 and from 1204 acquired land there called Deneysedon formerly of William Dacus.[88]

William Wrotham, who combined the forestership, the Stable and Odburville holdings, and the lands of William Dacus in an estate known as *NEWTON* or *NEWTON FORESTER*, was appointed archdeacon of Taunton c. 1204.[89] He was still alive in 1212, but by 1216 he had been succeeded by his nephew Richard,

56 *S.R.S.* xxii. 75; xlix, pp. 5–6.
57 *V.C.H. Som.* i. 521; *Dom. Bk.* ed. Thorn, 331. The usual spelling was Showel before the 18th century.
58 *S.R.S.* xvi. 310–11.
59 P.R.O., CP 25(1)/202/42/14 Hen. VII Trin.; *V.C.H. Som.* iii. 34; *S.R.S.* ii. 300; xix. 107; *Cal. Inq. p.m. Hen. VII*, iii, p. 446.
60 *S.R.S.* lxxvii. 29.
61 *Wilts. Visit. Peds. 1623* (Harl. Soc. cv–cvi), 98–9.
62 S.R.O., DD/SL 16.
63 Ibid. DD/DHR, box 17.
64 Ibid. DD/SL 34; D/P/pet. n 2/1/23.
65 Ibid. DD/DHR, boxes 15, 17, 18.
66 Ibid. D/R/bw 15/3/18; 16/11/8.
67 *S.R.S.* lxxvi, map 1822; *Proc. Som. Arch. Soc.* xliii. 52.
68 S.R.O., tithe award.   69 Ibid. DD/DP 33/2.
70 Ibid.; D/P/pet. n 2/1/1.
71 *S.R.S.* li, p. 198; *Som. Wills*, ed. Brown, i. 57.
72 S.R.O., DD/JL 83; DD/SAS (C/96) 17/2; *S.D.N.Q.* vi. 68.
73 S.R.O., DD/DP 33/7; DD/SAS (C/96) 17/18; *Som.*

Wills, ed. Brown, i. 57.
74 S.R.O., DD/JL 107; below, this section.
75 S.R.O., Q/REl 29/6.
76 Above, this section; S.R.O., DD/DHR, box 15.
77 S.R.O., DD/DP 33/2; *S.R.S.* li, p. 198.
78 S.R.O., DD/DP 33/2.
79 Ibid. DD/SAS (C/96) 17/3.
80 Ibid. DD/SAS (C/432) 33; ibid. Q/REl 29/6.
81 Ibid. tithe award.   82 *V.C.H. Som.* i. 520.
83 *Rot. Chart.* (Rec. Com.), 29; *Cur. Reg. R.* iii. 156.
84 *Cal. Inq. p.m.* i, p. 54.   85 *V.C.H. Som.* i. 521.
86 Ibid. v. 10–11; *Pipe R.* 1184 (P.R.S. xxxiii), 130; ibid. 1185 (P.R.S. xxxiv), 27; ibid 1194 (P.R.S. N.S. v), 19.
87 *Pipe R.* 1197 (P.R.S. N.S. viii), 139; *Rot. Chart.* (Rec. Com.), 29; *Proc. Som. Arch. Soc.* xci. 99–100.
88 *Proc. Som. Arch. Soc.* xci. 99–102; *Cal. Inq. p.m.* iii, p. 126; *Rot. Chart.* (Rec. Com.), 130–1; *V.C.H. Som.* iii. 231. In the late 13th century Hen. II was said to have given the stewardship of the park to William Wrotham: *Rot. Hund.* (Rec. Com.), ii. 140.
89 *S.R.S.* xi, p. 296; xliv. 218; *Pipe R.* 1204 (P.R.S. N.S. xviii), 218.

a minor.[90] Richard (d. *s.p.* 1250), known as Richard Forester, was succeeded by his nephew William de Plessis. Richard's estate at his death included, in addition to his inheritance from William Wrotham, land at Newton held of Stephen son of Michael[91] which may have been a half virgate in Estable Newton alienated in the time of Henry I.[92]

William de Plessis (d. *c.* 1274) was given custody of Petherton park in fee. His nephew and successor was Richard de Barbeflote or Plessis (d. 1289). Two thirds of his estate and the forestership passed to his sisters, Sabina, wife of Nicholas Pecche (d. 1295), Evelyn, wife of John Durant, and Emme, wife of John Heyron.[93] Richard's widow Margery (d. *c.* 1293) was to have her third for life, which was to revert to Evelyn and Emme; the forestership passed to Sabina.[94]

Sabina Pecche (d. *c.* 1307) left to her son Nicholas an estate later called a third of *NEWTON PLECY* or *NEWTON REGIS* manor. Nicholas Pecche (d. 1323) was succeeded by his son Richard (d. by 1330).[95] Richard's son Thomas (d. under age 1332) was followed by Richard's brother Matthew.[96] Matthew sold his estates in 1336 to Sir Richard Dammory, who granted a life interest to Matthew of Clevedon in 1342.[97] Matthew released his interest before 1351 when Dammory sold the manor and forestership to Roger Beauchamp. Roger sold them in turn to Roger Mortimer, earl of March, in 1359.[98] The estate passed with the earldom of March to the Crown and to Katharine and Anne, daughters of Edward IV. In 1511 it was recovered by the Crown and was granted, as the lordship and manor of North Petherton, in 1547 to Edward Seymour, duke of Somerset.[99] Following Somerset's attainder it was granted in 1553 to John Dudley, duke of Northumberland. The duke exchanged it for Syon House (Mdx.) in the same year with Sir Thomas Wroth (d. 1573).[1] Sir Thomas was involved in Suffolk's rebellion in 1554 and went into exile until Elizabeth's accession.[2]

Sir Thomas settled Newton Regis on his younger brother William in 1568 in trust for his own six younger sons. The sons shared the manor in 1586.[3] In 1623 the manor was settled on John, the only surviving son, and on Sir Thomas Wroth, son of John's brother Thomas (d. 1610). Sir Thomas, a member of the Long Parliament, was appointed to try Charles I but attended only one session of the trial.[4] John died in 1633 without issue[5] and Sir Thomas in 1672 when he was succeeded by his great-nephew, Sir John Wroth, Bt.[6] Sir John died *c.* 1677 leaving an infant son Sir Thomas (d. 1721). The estate passed to Sir Thomas's elder daughter Cecily, wife of Sir Hugh Acland, Bt., and on her death in 1761 to her son Sir Thomas Acland, Bt.[7] Sir Thomas died in 1785 and was followed in turn by his grandson Sir John Dyke Acland (d. 1785) and his own second son Sir Thomas Dyke Acland (d. 1794). The son of the last, Sir Thomas (d. 1871), sold most of the estate in 1834 to William Nation, but the lordship with some land was still retained by his son, also Sir Thomas (d. 1898), in 1872.[8]

A house called Newton Court was recorded in 1274 with a dovecot and gardens.[9] It probably stood in North Newton village. Park House was recorded in 1336, and the name was sometimes given to the park estate.[10] A house called the Lodge, probably in the park, was repaired in 1400.[11] William Wroth, resident keeper of the park under Henry VI, was said to have rebuilt the Court House, which may have stood on the edge of the park beside Parker's Field House, and was probably the moated lodge recorded by Leland.[12] The Lodge was said to have been pulled down in Elizabeth's reign but part was still standing in 1665.[13] Broad Lodge, built of materials from the earlier lodge, possibly *c.* 1582–6, was known as Petherton Park in the 17th century when it was the home of the Wroth family.[14] Sir Thomas Wroth (d. 1721) rebuilt the house *c.* 1700[15] as a double-piled structure. The stone west range has 11 bays with mullioned and transomed windows and a central doorway surmounted by a shell hood. The slightly shorter east range is of brick and has a recessed centre of five bays with similar windows and shell-hooded doorway. The interior retains many features of *c.* 1700 including a fine central staircase with arched landing, several rooms with bolection-moulded panelling and moulded plaster cornices, and in the upper part of the north-east corner a large room with three tall sash windows to the north. Some alterations appear to have been made inside in the 19th century at which time panelling dated 1601 was introduced into one of the principal ground-floor rooms. To the west is a small walled court with two gateways and, beyond, a stable building of *c.* 1700. In 1984 the house was divided and was known as Park Farm and Manor House Farm.

90 *Bk. of Fees*, i. 84; *Rot. Litt. Claus.* (Rec. Com.), 278, 352.
91 *S.R.S.* xi, p. 40; *Cal. Inq. p.m.* i, p. 54; *Cal. Pat.* 1247–58, 98.
92 *Testa de Nevill* (Rec. Com.), 172, where Newton is printed Abbetton.
93 *Cal. Inq. p.m.* ii, pp. 61, 442–3; *Cal. Fine R.* 1272–1307, 33.
94 *Cal. Inq. p.m.* iii, p. 58; *Cal. Close*, 1288–96, 13, 49–50, 301–2.
95 *Cal. Inq. p.m.* v, p. 2; vi, p. 277; *Cal. Fine R.*, 1327–41, 165.
96 *Cal. Inq. p.m.* vii, p. 314.
97 Collinson, *Hist. Som.* iii. 61; *Cal. Pat.* 1343–5, 46, 205.
98 *Cal. Pat.* 1350–4, 181; *S.R.S.* xvii. 180, 185.
99 *Cat. Anct. D.* iv, A 7551; *Cal. Pat.* 1547–8, 126.
1 *Cal. Pat.* 1553, 181; S.R.O., DD/SL 6.
2 *D.N.B.*

3 P.R.O., CP 25(2)/204/10 Eliz. I Hil.; S.R.O., DD/AH 21/2; Devon R.O. 1148 M/add 9/23.
4 S.R.O., DD/SAS (C/96) 17/2; *D.N.B.*
5 P.R.O., C 142/526, no. 12.
6 *Som. Wills*, ed. Brown, ii. 84; G.E.C. *Baronetage*, iii. 131.
7 *Som. Wills*, ed. Brown, ii. 85; S.R.O., DD/AH 1/3; DD/FD 7.
8 Burke, *Peerage* (1949), 14–15; Devon R.O. 1148 M/add 1/61; S.R.O., tithe award.
9 P.R.O., C 133/7, no. 4.
10 S.R.O., DD/AH 21/2; *S.R.S.* xvii. 180.
11 P.R.O., SC 6/973/23.
12 Leland, *Itin.* ed. Toulmin Smith, i. 161.
13 Collinson, *Hist. Som.* iii. 62, 67.
14 Devon R.O. 1148 M/add 9/23; *Cal. S.P. Dom.* 1635, 377.
15 S.R.O., DD/SAS SE 24.

To the east earthworks mark the layout of a former garden: James Veitch was planting and fencing at Petherton Park in 1815.[16]

Parker's Field House stands just outside the park boundary, possibly near the site of Court House. It dates from the late 16th century and has a main range of two rooms separated by a central passage, with a jointed cruck roof. Wings were added in the 17th century, probably before 1651 when the house was described as new.[17] A wing was added to the north-west in the late 18th century.

Evelyn Durant died in 1312 and her share of Newton Plecy, later called *NEWTON WROTH*, passed successively to her son Richard Durant (d. 1333)[18] and Richard's son Thomas (d. 1349).[19] Thomas's daughter Maud married first Sir John Wroth and second Baldwin of Raddington (d. 1401).[20] From her son and heir William Wroth (d. 1408) the estate passed in the direct male line to William (an infant in 1408, d. 1450),[21] John (d. 1480),[22] John (an infant in 1480, d. 1517), Robert (d. 1535),[23] and Sir Thomas Wroth (d. 1573), who had also acquired Newton Regis manor. Sir Thomas left Newton Wroth to his wife Mary for her life.[24] His eldest son Sir Robert died in 1606 and Sir Robert's grandson, also Sir Robert, in 1614, leaving an infant son James.[25] James died in 1616 when John Wroth, brother of Sir Robert (d. 1606), settled the manor on John, brother of Sir Robert (d. 1614). The younger John and his wife Maud held the manor in 1621.[26] In 1634 John sold the manor to Sir Thomas and Sir Peter Wroth (d. 1644), sons of Thomas (d. 1610), brother of Sir Robert (d. 1606).[27] Sir Thomas was succeeded in 1672 by his great-nephew Sir John Wroth, Bt., grandson of Sir Peter.[28] Sir John died c. 1677 leaving an infant son Thomas; the manor then descended with Newton Regis. No reference to the lordship has been found after 1872.[29]

There was a capital messuage in 1638,[30] known as Pyms in 1739.[31] It may have been the house called Newton Place in 1776[32] and now Church Farm House, east of North Newton church. It has cob walls and the roof at the east end is cruck framed, probably of the 16th century. Some refitting was carried out in the 18th and 19th centuries.[33]

John Heyron, husband of Emme, died in 1326 holding her share of Newton Plecy,[34] later called *NEWTON CHANTRY*. Their son John died without issue in 1335 and his heirs were his nephew John Garton and his sister Margaret Heyron.[35] The nephew died in 1362, by then probably holding Margaret's share; he was followed by his son John and that John in 1376 by his son John, a minor.[36] The last gave a life interest to Richard Mayne before 1401 and sold the reversion to Richard Bruton and William Gascoigne in 1417. Gascoigne died in 1423 in possession of the whole estate. His heir was his brother Thomas who died possibly c. 1424.[37] William Gascoigne, perhaps Thomas's son, was dead by 1462 when his daughter Christine and her husband John Keyrell were in possession.[38] In 1467 they gave the manor to the vicars choral of Wells cathedral. During the Interregnum it was purchased by Sir Thomas Wroth,[39] but it was returned to the vicars choral c. 1660 and was transferred to the Ecclesiastical (later Church) Commissioners before 1875. The Commissioners were lords of the manor in 1984.[40]

A capital messuage, probably belonging to the manor, was mentioned in 1326.[41] In 1362 the hall and chamber were repaired with stone tiles.[42] The house was mentioned in 1450.[43] In Elizabeth's reign the vicars choral were said to have used the materials from Newton chapel to build a court house.[44] It can perhaps be identified with Newton House, west of the church, a late 16th-century building with a main hall range and north wing. The present wing is probably of the 18th century, but contains reused 17th-century windows. The hall contains a canopied fireplace and a framed ceiling. The parlour has a ribbed plaster ceiling with moulded foliage decoration.[45]

The tithes of the former chantry in North Newton chapel were let by the Crown in reversion to Thomas Tallis and William Byrd in 1578[46] and by 1585 they had been let to William Lacey.[47] They were sold to William Wroth and others in reversion in 1592 when they were assessed at £3 17s. a year,[48] and were held by John Wroth (d. 1633). Usually known as *NEWTON CHANTRY*, the tithe estate descended with Newton Wroth manor.[49] In 1664 it was agreed that all great and small tithes, oblations, obventions, and mortuaries due within the chapelry should be paid to Sir Thomas Wroth.[50] The perpetual curate was said in 1838 to be

16 Devon R.O. 1148 M/add, Som. estate acct. 1815.
17 Ibid. 2/71B.
18 Cal. Inq. p.m. v, p. 192; vii, pp. 359–60; S.R.O., DD/SAS NP 1, m. 18.
19 Cal. Inq. p.m. ix, p. 311.
20 P.R.O., C 137/30, no. 17.
21 Ibid. C 137/71, no. 18; C 139/137, no. 6.
22 Ibid. C 140/74, no. 28.
23 Ibid. C 142/32, no. 83; C 142/57, no. 33.
24 Ibid. C 142/171, no. 97.
25 Ibid. C 142/294, no. 87; S.R.S. lxvii, p. 212.
26 D.N.B.; P.R.O., CP 43/136, rot. 70; CP 25(2)/387/19 Jas. I East.
27 P.R.O., CP 25(2)/480/10 Chas. I Mich.; S.R.O., DD/SAS H 47/3/9; Som. Wills, ed. Brown, ii. 86.
28 Som. Wills, ed. Brown, ii. 84; G.E.C. Baronetage, iii. 131.
29 Above, this section; Devon R.O. 1148 M/add 1/61.
30 S.R.O., DD/SAS H 47/3/9.
31 Devon R.O. 1148 M/add 2/71A.
32 S.R.O., DD/SF 3994.

33 The house features in J. B. Bickle, Village of Rosemary (1965).
34 Cal. Inq. p.m. vi, p. 467.
35 Ibid. vii, p. 462.
36 Ibid. xi, pp. 265–6; xiv, p. 264; Cal. Fine R. 1369–77, 364.
37 H.M.C. Wells, ii. 652, 664–6; S.R.S. xxii. 53; P.R.O., C 139/7, no. 56.
38 H.M.C. Wells, ii. 81, 90, 683.
39 S.R.O., DD/CC 131921A/6; DD/AH 19/15; H.M.C. Wells, ii. 685.
40 Inf. from Church Commissioners.
41 Cal. Inq. p.m. vi, p. 467.
42 S.R.O., DD/WM 1/138.
43 Wells Cath. Libr., Vicars Choral MS. B/29.
44 S.R.O., DD/AH 21/2.   45 Ibid. DD/V/BWr 26.11.
46 S.R.S. lxxvii, pp. 117–18; below, churches.
47 P.R.O., E 123/10, p. 371; E 123/12, p. 135.
48 S.R.S. lxxvii, pp. 117–18.
49 P.R.O., C 142/526, no. 12; CP 25(2)/347/21 Jas. I Trin.; Berks. R.O., DD/ED T 209; above, this section.
50 Devon R.O. 1148 M/add 6/17.

entitled to the tithe of the district, *c.* 260 a., except for the £3 paid to the vicar of North Petherton, but in 1841 the rent charge of £70 was awarded to Sir Thomas Dyke Acland as impropriator under a corrected award.[51]

The land of the former North Newton chantry, lying in North Newton and St. Michaelchurch, and worth £2 1s. a year in 1547,[52] was granted to John Hulson and William Pendred in 1549[53] and later regranted to Richard Bluet, who died in possession in 1566.[54] The land descended with the Bluets' manor of North Petherton and was usually known as the manor of *NEWTON PLACET*.[55]

The estate later known as *PLAYSTREET* was owned by the Heyron family who used it to endow their chantry at Langport.[56] In 1549 the estate was sold to Laurence Hyde[57] whose grandson Edward Hyde held it until 1656 or later.[58] By 1655 it had been acquired by the Catford family of Melcombe Paulet who sold it to Sir Thomas Wroth in 1696.[59] The estate descended as part of Newton Wroth manor and the name was lost.[60]

BALLCOMBE manor was probably held of the Bluets' manor of North Petherton.[61] It was held by Henry Blunt who died before 1515 leaving a son John Blunt or Swell. John's son Robert sold it in 1545 to William Fouracre of Hillfarrance and his wife Joan.[62] In 1605 Matthew Fouracre of Broadclyst (Devon), with his wife Mary and Hannah, probably his mother, sold Ballcombe to John Parsons. In 1618 John settled the estate on his son William for his marriage to Alice Gredge of Ballcombe.[63] William was succeeded by Henry Parsons before 1669 and by William Parsons (fl. 1692–1705). William was followed by Thomas Parsons, a London grocer, who with his wife Frances sold Ballcombe manor to William Hodgson in 1714. In 1721 Hodgson sold it to Charles Challis (d. *c.* 1745). In 1758 John Lock and his wife Mary, a daughter of Charles Challis, sold Ballcombe to Jeremiah Dewdney.[64] Dewdney (d. 1776) was succeeded by his great-nephew Jeremiah Dewdney Parsons (d. 1842), the owner in 1838.[65] In 1919 the surviving heirs of Jeremiah Dewdney Parsons sold Ballcombe to the Portman trustees.[66]

Athelney abbey by grants from John of Erleigh and members of the Clavil family between the early 13th century and *c.* 1400 acquired land in Clavelshay and Farringdon[67] which came to be known as *CLAVELSHAY* manor and remained with the abbey until the Dissolution.[68] The Crown sold the manor in 1544 to (Sir) William Portman and Alexander Popham.[69] Portman died in sole possession in 1557[70] and the manor descended in the direct male line to Sir Henry (d. 1591), John (cr. Bt., d. 1612), and Sir Henry (d. 1621).[71] Henry was followed in turn by his three brothers John (d. 1624), Hugh (d. 1629), and William (d. 1645).[72] Clavelshay manor descended after 1641 in the Portman family like Bere manor in Wayford to Henry Berkeley Portman, Viscount Portman (d. 1923). Claud Berkeley Portman, Viscount Portman (d. 1929), brother of the last, was followed by his son Edward Claud Berkeley Portman (d. 1942) whose brother Seymour Berkeley Portman, Viscount Portman, in 1944 sold Clavelshay to the Crown. All manorial incidents were then said to have been enfranchised.[73] In 1984 the estate comprised two farms, Higher and Lower Clavelshay, formerly Clavelshay and Clavelshay farm.

A capital messuage recorded in 1539[74] may have been the precursor of the 17th-century house called Classeys.[75] In 1735 the capital messuage comprised hall, parlour, kitchen, and service rooms, five chambers, 'cold bath', and servants' rooms.[76] The present house called Lower Clavelshay, formerly Clavelshay Farm, is a substantial 18th-century house which had ten bedrooms in 1946 before the demolition of a wing.[77] It has a symmetrical west front and nearly contemporary outshuts. In 1699 there were fishponds in the vicinity[78] and from the 19th century the house had a terraced garden on the west, falling to two small lakes.[79]

The Knights Hospitallers held land at Farringdon which they exchanged in 1310 and 1312 for land owned by Hugh de Reigny and his wife Gillian.[80]

In 1066 Sired held *SHEARSTON* and in 1086 Robert Herecom held it of Roger de Courcelles.[81] The overlordship descended with that of Kilve until 1363 or later. A mesne lordship held by Matthew de Furneaux in 1253 descended with Kilve also until 1363 or later.[82]

Simon son of Simon Brett was tenant in 1195, but Shearston passed to the Reigny family, probably by 1253.[83] John de Reigny held it in 1285, and before 1291 Joan de Reigny owned

51 S.R.O., tithe award.
52 *S.R.S.* ii. 238.
53 Ibid. lxxvii, p. 47.
54 P.R.O., C 142/144, no. 164.
55 S.R.O., DD/X/FRC (C/140).
56 *Cal. Inq. p.m. Hen. VII*, iii, pp. 446–7; *S.R.S.* ii. 301; P.R.O., C 145/25, no. 42.
57 *S.R.S.* lxxvii, p. 29; *Cal. Pat.* 1549, 290.
58 Devon R.O. 1148 M/add 6/17, 9/22; S.R.O., DD/SAS H 47/3/31.
59 Devon R.O. 1148 M/add 6/17.
60 Ibid. 2/71B; S.R.O., DD/SAS H 47/3/31.
61 S.R.O., DD/X/FRC (C/140).
62 P.R.O., C 1/287/35; S.R.O., DD/BV 2.
63 S.R.O., DD/BV 2–4.
64 Ibid. 2–4, 16.
65 Ibid. 2; DD/DHR, box 26; ibid. tithe award.
66 P.R.O., CRES 38/1891.
67 *S.R.S.* xiv, pp. 157, 163–5, 173–6; xvii. 73: date of fine erroneous; *Cal. Pat.* 1364–7, 213; *Cal. Inq. Misc.* vi, p. 33.

68 *Tax. Eccl.* (Rec. Com.), 204; *Valor Eccl.* (Rec. Com.), i. 206.
69 *L. & P. Hen. VIII*, xix (2), p. 313.
70 *S.R.S.* xxi. 188; P.R.O., C 142/108, no. 94.
71 P.R.O., C 142/229, no. 101; *S.R.S.* lxvii, pp. 47–50, 137–8.
72 P.R.O., C 142/406, no. 67; S.R.O., DD/PM 1/6; D/P/orch. p 2/1/1.
73 *V.C.H. Som.* iv. 71; Burke, *Peerage* (1949), 1618–19; P.R.O., CRES 35/1149.
74 P.R.O., SC 6/Hen. VIII/3144.
75 S.R.O., DD/V/BWr 26/15.   76 Ibid. DD/POt 167.
77 P.R.O., CRES 35/1149, 39/171.
78 S.R.O., Q/SR 212/17.
79 Ibid. tithe award; O.S. Map 6", Som. LXI. SW. (1887 edn.).
80 *S.R.S.* xii. 9, 29; *Cal. Pat.* 1307–13, 271.
81 *V.C.H. Som.* i. 485.
82 Ibid. v. 97–8; *Cal. Close*, 1360–4, 449; *S.R.S.* xxv, p. 99; xxxv. 66.
83 *S.R.S.* xi, p. 418; xxv, p. 90.

rents there.[84] Shearston was held with Rhode manor until 1616 when it was sold to George Blanchflower, probably in reversion.[85] By 1652 it had passed to George's son the Revd. Thomas Blanchflower (d. 1661)[86] whose land at Shearston was settled in 1663 on his eldest son George.[87] George (d. 1664) left the manor to his infant son George. The younger George died without issue c. 1686 and Charles Blanchflower (d. 1693), his uncle and heir, appears to have sold the manor to Valentine Gardiner.[88] Valentine held the estate c. 1691 but it was later sold to Thomas Musgrave.[89] Thomas (d. 1724) was followed by his great-nephew George Musgrave (also d. 1724) and George by his second son Thomas Frederick, an infant. Thomas Frederick, who settled the manor on his wife Mary in 1761, died c. 1780.[90] After Mary's death the estate was held by her niece Juliana (d. 1810), wife of Sir James Langham, Bt.[91] It passed to her son Sir William (d. Mar. 1812), to his son also Sir William (d. May 1812) and to the latter's uncle Sir James Langham (d. 1833).[92] Sir James's second son Herbert sold the estate in 1859 and 1860, without reference to the lordship.[93]

A capital messuage was recorded c. 1392.[94] A house recorded in 1663[95] was known as Shearston Farm in the 18th century and was described as the capital messuage in 1776.[96] By 1838 it was known as Chapel Hill or Chapel Hill Farm and in 1859 was described as a six-bedroomed farmhouse.[97] The house has a front range of cob probably dating from the 17th century. It was enlarged and extensively altered in the 19th century.

SHEARSTON CHANTRY manor originated in the land of Shearston chapel given to Buckland priory in 1189.[98] In 1548 the estate, including a mill and nine tenements, was granted to John Aylworth and William Lacey.[99] In 1584 the manor was held by John Bluet and descended with North Petherton manor.[1] In 1615 Shearston Chantry manor was said to be held both of Humphrey Sydenham's manor of Dulverton and of the king.[2] By the late 18th century the manor had lost its separate identity and most of the land, called Shearston farm or Woolcott's, was sold in 1772 to James Woolcott, whose family had been tenants since the 17th century.[3] By 1838 a small farm known as Shearston remained in North Petherton manor.[4] In 1777

Woolcott sold Shearston to Thomas Pyke. The Jolliffe family bought the estate in 1818 and sold it in 1858 to Edward Portman, Lord Portman.[5]

Saric held *MELCOMBE* in 1066 and Robert de Odburville in 1086.[6] The two Melcombe manors may have been divisions of that estate. The manor later called *MELCOMBE PAULET* appears to have been held of the Erleighs' manor of North Petherton in 1293 and later,[7] but in 1431 Melcombe Paulet was said to be held in socage,[8] and suit and quit rents for the manor were claimed by the Wroths and the Vicars Choral of Wells from the 15th to the early 17th century.[9]

The lands of John de Reigny of Melcombe were in John of Erleigh's hands in 1293.[10] Joan de Reigny of Melcombe, mentioned between 1291 and 1296, may have been succeeded by John de Reigny by 1312.[11] Melcombe is said to have passed from Elizabeth, John de Reigny's daughter and wife of John Paulet, to her son Sir John Paulet (d. 1391).[12] William Paulet of Melcombe, son of Sir John, held the manor by 1412.[13] William died c. 1436 and his son Sir John Paulet in 1437.[14] John Paulet, son of the last, died c. 1470; his son, also John, was alive in 1519 but had died probably by 1539 when his eldest son William was created Baron St. John of Basing. William, created marquis of Winchester in 1551, died in 1572, when his son John sold the manor with 430 a. to Richard Bidgood and William Tucker of North Petherton.[15]

Bidgood died in 1581 as sole owner of the manor, which he devised to his wife Joan for life and then to Catherine, wife of his son Richard. Joan died c. 1587 and in 1592 Richard and Catherine conveyed the manor to William Gough.[16] In 1622 Richard Gough, possibly William's son, sold it to Robert Catford.[17] Robert (d. 1623) was succeeded by his son Robert (d. s.p. 1625), whose heir was his brother Walter (d. 1653). Walter's son Robert (d. 1672) left the manor to his daughter Elizabeth (d. 1696). Elizabeth's heir was her cousin Walter Catford (d. 1706) whose widow Jane and son Charles sold the manor in 1723 to John Morley, husband of Charles's cousin Katharine Catford.[18] John died in 1727 and Katharine held the manor in 1763. Their son John died in 1765 and his son John was in possession in 1792 but the estate had been reduced and was known as Melcombe farm.[19] By

84 *Feud. Aids*, iv. 278; *Cal. Inq. Misc.* i, p. 436.
85 Below, this section; P.R.O., CP 25(2)/346/14 Jas. I Mich.
86 S.R.O., DD/SAS (C/96) 7/8; DD/SAS (C/432) 13; D/P/gst 2/1/2.   87 Ibid. DD/SAS H 47/3/16.
88 *Som. Wills*, ed. Brown, iii. 11; S.R.O., DD/DP 33/2; D/P/gst 2/1/3.
89 S.R.O., DD/DP 33/2; DD/JL 77, 109; *Som. Wills*, ed. Brown, iii. 40.
90 S.R.O., DD/JL 77, 79–80, 107, 109; DD/SF 3994.
91 Ibid. DD/SF 3325.
92 Burke, *Peerage* (1949), 1163.
93 S.R.O., DD/PM 4; DD/SF 3325.
94 Pole MS. 2560; incorrectly dated.
95 S.R.O., DD/SAS H 47/3/16; *Som. Wills*, ed. Brown, v. 108.
96 S.R.O., DD/JL 107; DD/SF 3994.
97 Ibid. tithe award; ibid. DD/SF 3325.
98 *S.R.S.* xxv, p. 8.
99 Ibid. ii. 238; P.R.O., E 315/68, p. 332.
1 P.R.O., C 142/206, no. 1.
2 *S.R.S.* lxvii, pp. 87–8; P.R.O., C 142/351, no. 104.
3 S.R.O., DD/SAS (C/96) 17/6; DD/SL 15.

4 Ibid. tithe award.
5 Ibid. DD/PM 4; DD/SAS (C/96) 17/6.
6 *V.C.H. Som.* i. 520.
7 S.R.O., DD/SAS NP 1, m. 2; P.R.O., C 142/447, no. 71.
8 *Feud. Aids*, iv. 435.
9 Devon R.O. 1148 M/add 6/17; Wells Cath. Libr., Vicars Choral MS. C/10, 66.
10 S.R.O., DD/SAS NP 1, m. 2.
11 Ibid. DD/SAS NP 1, mm. 1, 17; 8, m. 1; *Cal. Inq. Misc.* i, p. 436.
12 C. Winn, *Pouletts of Hinton St. George*, 15; *Cal. Fine R. 1391–9*, 47.   13 *S.R.S.* xxii. 11; *Feud. Aids*, vi. 508.
14 *S.R.S.* xvi. 139, 142–3.
15 Burke, *Peerage* (1949), 2153; *Cal. Pat.* 1569–72, p. 406; S.R.O., DD/PT, box 1; DD/S/VY 6/3.
16 S.R.O., DD/S/VY 6/3; DD/X/SR 5.
17 Ibid. DD/S/CMB.
18 Ibid. D/P/pet. n 2/1/3; DD/CH 73/2; P.R.O., CP 25(2)/1195/11 Geo. I Mich.
19 S.R.O., DD/CH 73/2; D/P/pet. n 2/1/3; DD/S/WH 26; DD/SLM (C/1795).

1806 the estate was held by Richard King, the owner in 1838.[20] No further reference to the lordship has been found but the estate was acquired by the Kinglake family of Shovel and sold by them in 1893 and 1901.[21]

A hall at Melcombe was repaired in 1293 and a court house was built there in the same year.[22] The capital messuage was referred to in 1581 and 1723 but had gone by 1838.[23]

Richard Bidgood and William Tucker sold an estate at *RHODE*, part of Melcombe Paulet manor, to Nicholas Chute in 1574. In 1594 Robert, Nicholas's son and heir, conveyed it to (Sir) Nicholas Halswell, who leased it to the Woodhouse family.[24] Halswell added an estate called Roadbrooks and before 1665 the Halswells added land there which had belonged to the Paulets and later further land formerly held with Woolmersdon manor.[25] By 1838 the estate, having descended with Halswell in Goathurst to the Tyntes, had shrunk in size and was known as Road farm.[26]

The house, now called the Chantry, is a substantial early 17th-century house with a main range of three rooms with short rear wings at each end, one containing a staircase. The northern wing was extended in brick in the 19th century to provide outbuildings. Many original windows remain, mostly in moulded oak, but those of the entrance front ground floor are of Ham stone. A first-floor room has a plaster heart bearing the date 1655 and initials 'I.W.'[27] There is a carved wooden cornice on the south-east front.

The manor of *RHODE* seems to have been held of North Petherton manor in 1311–12, and its lords were described as free tenants of John Slade's manor of North Petherton in 1770.[28] Thomas de Reigny was lord c. 1256, and may have been succeeded by John de Reigny (fl. 1285–93).[29] In 1308 John de Reigny the younger granted land in Shearston and Rhode to another John de Reigny and his son John for their lives in succession.[30] John de Reigny paid a relief for Rhode in 1311–12.[31] The manor appears to have descended with Melcombe Paulet manor to Sir John Paulet (d. 1391).[32] Sir John's widow Elizabeth held the manor in 1412[33] and Sir John's grandson William, son of Thomas Paulet, held it in 1428. Rhode descended with Hinton St. George manor until 1538 when Sir Amias

Poulett settled Rhode on his son Henry for life.[34] Henry died probably before 1559 when his brother Sir Hugh was in possession.[35] Rhode continued to descend with Hinton St. George until 1600 when Anthony Poulett was succeeded by his brother George Paulet.[36] George probably settled it on his son Edward, whose second wife Elizabeth was married to Thomas Yeates by 1647.[37] She still held the manor in 1676 although the inheritance had been divided between Edward's daughters.[38]

Elizabeth had been succeeded by Edward's grandson, Paulet Payne (d. 1707), by 1701 when he settled the manor on his son John (d. 1717). John's son Paulet (d. 1726) was succeeded by his sisters Mary and Elizabeth who married their step-brothers Edmund and John Jeane.[39] In 1783 Mary Jeane and Elizabeth's son Thomas Jeane (d. 1791) divided the estate for the benefit of their respective sons, both called John.[40] Mary's son John Jeane (d. 1790) of Binfords in Broomfield left his share to his daughter Elizabeth (d. 1859) who married the Revd. Thomas Coney.[41] Thomas's son John Jeane of West Monkton (d. s.p. 1798) was succeeded by his nephew Thomas Jeane Buncombe.[42] There was no reference to the lordship after the 1780s.

There was a house at Rhode by 1316.[43] Rhode Farm, on the Coneys' share of the estate in the 19th century, can perhaps be identified with a house of c. 1690 which had a hall, parlour, kitchen, brewhouse, and six chambers.[44] It was almost completely rebuilt in 1855.[45]

The three sons of Robert Whiting (d. 1500) may have shared the manor of *WEST MELCOMBE* or *BOOMER*. It was held of the Bluets' manor of North Petherton. Christopher Whiting died in 1501 in possession of a third, which passed to his brother John.[46] John Whiting settled the whole manor on his wife Anne in 1511. When he died in 1529 his heirs were his five daughters Mary, Agnes, Isabel, Joan or Jane, and Elizabeth.[47] Elizabeth died evidently soon after 1533, and her share was divided among her sisters, giving rise to the name Four Lords Land.[48] Mary Whiting married Humphrey Keynes and died in 1548 leaving a son John.[49] John Keynes sold his share to Robert Halswell in 1565.[50] Robert died in 1570 leaving a young son (Sir) Nicholas, who leased his share, then called a quarter, to Robert Catford in 1608

20 S.R.O., DD/SLM, bk. of maps; ibid. tithe award.
21 Ibid. DD/DHR, box 15; above, this section (Shovel).
22 S.R.O., DD/SAS NP 1, m. 2.
23 Ibid. DD/CH 73/2; DD/S/VY 6/3; ibid. tithe award.
24 Ibid. DD/S/WH 3, 27; DD/S/VY 6/3.
25 Ibid. DD/SAS (C/96) 17/2; DD/S/WH 27; *Som. Wills*, ed. Brown, iii. 54.
26 S.R.O., tithe award; above, Goathurst, manors.
27 In 1708 Jasper Woodhouse was tenant (S.R.O., DD/S/WH 218) and his father and grandfather had the same name.
28 S.R.O., DD/SAS NP 1, m. 17; DD/SLM, bk. of maps.
29 *S.R.S.* xiv, p. 159; *Feud. Aids*, iv. 278; S.R.O., DD/SAS NP 1, m. 2.
30 *S.R.S.* xii. 2.
31 S.R.O., DD/SAS NP 1, m. 17.
32 Above, this section.
33 *Feud. Aids*, vi. 514.
34 Ibid. iv. 345; *V.C.H. Som.* iv. 42; P.R.O., C 142/61, no. 14.

35 S.R.O., DD/PT, box 1.
36 P.R.O., C 142/260, no. 143.
37 S.R.O., DD/S/WH 116; DD/X/FRC (C/140).
38 P.R.O., CP 25(2)/592/1653 Trin.; CP 25(2)/593/1654 Mich.; S.R.O., DD/SAS H 47/3/33.
39 S.R.O., DD/RN 37; D/P/gst 2/1/2; DD/X/SR 5.
40 Ibid. DD/RN 8, 37; D/P/west m 2/1/2.
41 Ibid. DD/RN 36; DD/CCH 81; Burke, *Land. Gent.* (1914), 419–20.
42 S.R.O., DD/ALN 4/6; DD/RN 36–7; D/P/west m 2/1/2.
43 *S.R.S.* i. 108.
44 *Som. Wills*, ed. Brown, iii. 54; S.R.O., DD/SP inventory, 1690.
45 Plan in possession of Mr. and Mrs. Adams, Rhode.
46 *Cal. Inq. p.m. Hen. VII*, i. p. 457; ii, pp. 315–16; P.R.O., C 142/50, no. 154.
47 P.R.O., C 142/50, no. 154.
48 *S.R.S.* xxi. 20–2; S.R.O., DD/S/WH 290.
49 P.R.O., C 142/99, no. 29.
50 *S.R.S.* li, p. 68; S.R.O., DD/S/WH 27.

and sold it to him in 1620.[51] Agnes Whiting was succeeded in 1555 by her son Humphrey Walrond.[52] Humphrey's four sons seem to have entered the estate in 1584, two years before their father's death.[53] William Walrond, the eldest, leased his share of West Melcombe to Robert Catford in 1598. In 1627 William's son Henry sold a quarter of the manor to William Catford, Robert's son.[54] Isabel Whiting married Nicholas Ashford and was probably dead by 1573 when a quarter share of the manor was settled on Nicholas's son Roger and his wife Elizabeth.[55] In 1599 the estate was settled on Roger's son Henry Ashford who leased his share to Robert Catford in 1608 and sold it to him in 1618.[56] Joan or Jane Whiting had married Robert FitzJames by 1538.[57] Joan and Robert were dead by 1592 when her heir was her daughter Thomasin, wife of Thomas Stoton, who leased the estate. In 1599 the lease was assigned to Robert Catford and by 1605 Joan's share of West Melcombe was in the hands of Sir John Sydenham.[58] In 1620 it was settled on Sir John's younger son Sir Ralph Sydenham. Sir Ralph leased it to Robert Catford in 1621 and it was probably sold to the Catfords shortly after Robert's death in 1623.[59]

Robert Catford (d. 1623) was succeeded in turn by his sons Robert (d. 1625) and William (d. 1644).[60] William was succeeded in turn by his sons William (d. 1655) and Walter (d. 1662).[61] Walter's heir was his infant son William, and the manor may have been in the hands of trustees; John Gatcombe and his wife Elizabeth kept the manor courts in 1665.[62] William Catford died in 1698 leaving a son William, a minor. William (d. 1744) was succeeded by his son William Hardy Catford, who mortgaged the estate and put it up for sale in 1748. Some of the land was sold in 1751, but the manor was conveyed in 1761 to John Slade.[63] Slade retained the manor until 1779 when it was dismembered; the lordship with some land was sold to Sir Charles Kemeys-Tynte (d. 1785)[64] and after his widow's death passed to his niece Jane Hassell, wife of John Johnson who took the name Kemeys-Tynte. In 1799 Jane settled West Melcombe on her son Charles Kemeys Kemeys-Tynte.[65] There is no further reference to the lordship, but the estate descended with Halswell in Goathurst until 1953 when it was sold by Charles Kemeys-Tynte, Baron Wharton.[66]

The capital messuage of West Melcombe, usually called Boomer House, was recorded in 1592.[67] In 1644 the house comprised porch, hall,

parlour, study, kitchen, 4 service rooms, 2 cellars, 8 chambers, 2 servants' rooms, 2 lofts, and some 15 outbuildings and produce stores.[68] Boomer House has a five-bayed front with central, three-storeyed porch. It appears originally to have been L-shaped, with a main front range and a back kitchen wing on the north side. Some plasterwork of the early 17th century survives on the first floor above the kitchen and some internal fittings from the 1680s. Rainwater heads are dated 1681. An extensive remodelling c. 1740 gave the main south front a new entrance archway with rusticated architrave. Much of the interior was panelled and provided with new fireplaces and staircases. A new kitchen block was added in the angle between the older ranges.

In 1066 Alwig held *WOOLMERSDON*. In 1086 Alfred d'Epaignes held Woolmersdon, which formed part of the barony of Nether Stowey until 1605 or later.[69] In the late 13th century the honor of Dundon claimed overlordship, probably because of confusion with Woolstone in Stogursey.[70]

The terre tenant in 1086 was Walter d'Epaignes.[71] In 1166 Woolmersdon was held by Geoffrey de Vere, who was succeeded possibly by Baldwin de Vere (fl. 1234).[72] Geoffrey of Woolmersdon was in possession from 1239 until 1248 or later, and Gilbert of Woolmersdon was recorded in 1268.[73] John of Woolmersdon held the manor in 1285 but was dead by c. 1298, was survived by Rose, probably his widow (still alive 1338), and by Sibyl, wife of Roger Arundel, possibly his stepmother. Sibyl died c. 1298, and Roger held ½ knight's fee at Woolmersdon in 1303.[74]

The estate was divided by 1338 between Joan, daughter of John of Woolmersdon and wife of Vincent Trivet, Susan, possibly her sister, wife of Edmund Trivet, and Rose, probably John's widow. Edmund and Susan sold their share and their reversion of Rose's interest to Peter Trivet, Edmund's brother, in 1337. Peter was dead by 1377 when his son John held lands in Woolmersdon and Hadworthy.[75] John's son Peter died without issue before 1420 and his heirs were probably his sisters Joan, wife of Roger Pym, and Margaret, wife of Roger Tremayle.[76] In 1423 and 1429 Peter's half of the manor was settled on Margaret and her children.[77] The estate known in the 16th century as Woolmersdon and Hadworthy descended to Margaret's son John Tremayle (fl. 1440–52) and to John's son Sir Thomas Tremayle (d. 1508).[78] Sir Thomas's son

51 P.R.O., C 142/154, no. 86; S.R.O., DD/S/WH 27.
52 P.R.O., C 142/106, no. 74.
53 Ibid. C 142/209, no. 41; ibid. CP 25(2)/260/26 Eliz. I East.; *Som. Wills*, ed. Brown, i. 61.
54 S.R.O., DD/SL 16; DD/S/WH 27.
55 *S.R.S.* xxi. 20–2; S.R.O., DD/SF 3142.
56 S.R.O., DD/SF 681; DD/S/WH 27.
57 *S.R.S.* xxi. 20–2; P.R.O., CP 25(2)/52/373/30 Hen. VIII East.
58 S.R.O., DD/S/WH 27; DD/SL 16.
59 Ibid. DD/SL 3.
60 P.R.O., C 142/447, no. 71; S.R.O., D/P/pet. n 2/1/1; DD/X/FRC (C/140).
61 S.R.O., D/P/pet. n 2/1/1; DD/X/FRC (C/140); *Som. Wills*, ed. Brown, ii. 48–9.
62 S.R.O., DD/SAS H 47/3/22.
63 Ibid. DD/BV 4, 5; DD/SL 3, 17; D/P/pet. n 2/1/3.
64 Ibid. DD/BV 2; DD/SL 3.
65 Ibid. DD/S/WH 26; P.R.O., CP 25(2)/1401/39 Geo. III Trin.; Burke, *Land. Gent.* (1914), 1915.
66 Above, Goathurst, manors; S.R.O., DD/X/BID.
67 S.R.O., DD/S/WH 27.
68 Ibid. DD/SL 4.
69 *V.C.H. Som.* i. 511; *S.R.S.* lxvii, pp. 45–6.
70 *S.R.S.* xxxv, p. 66.   71 *V.C.H. Som.* i. 511.
72 *Red Bk. Exch.* (Rolls Ser.), i. 231; *Cal. Close, 1231–4*, 540.
73 *S.R.S.* vi. 108; xi, p. 357; xxxvi. 35.
74 *Feud. Aids*, iv. 278, 300; S.R.O., DD/AH 66/10.
75 *S.R.S.* xii. 187; xvii. 92–3; Devon R.O. 2530 M/T 6/2/1–2.
76 *S.R.S.* lvii, p. 39; *Visit. Som. 1531 and 1573*, ed. Weaver, 85.
77 *S.R.S.* xxii. 183; lvii, p. 41.
78 Devon R.O. 2530 M/L 6/6/1A; M/T 6/2/3–4; *Cal. Inq. p.m. Hen. VII*, iii, p. 312.

Philip died in 1520 leaving a daughter Florence, wife of William Ashleigh.[79] By 1544 the estate was divided between Alexander Popham and Nicholas Halswell.[80] Popham died in 1556 and his share passed to his son Edward and descended with Huntworth until 1641, although it was leased to John Popham in 1580.[81] It was retained by Thomas Popham (d. 1653) and his son Thomas, but George Musgrave acquired it in 1676. Musgrave died in 1692 leaving as his heir his nephew George Musgrave of Nettlecombe.[82] Musgrave's share of the manor descended with Stamfordlands and was sold to tenants c. 1800.[83] Nicholas Halswell's share of Woolmersdon and Hadworthy descended with Halswell manor in Goathurst. There was no reference to the lordship after 1799 and most of the lands were sold before 1838.[84]

Joan and Vincent Trivet settled their share of Woolmersdon in 1338 on Vincent's heirs.[85] Vincent was dead by 1343 when Joan released her right to land in Woolmersdon to Ralph Verney (d. 1350) and his brother Roger. Ralph had married Maud Trivet, said to be a daughter and coheir of Thomas Trivet of Durborough, possibly heir to Vincent.[86] The Verneys' third share of Joan's estate descended in the direct male line with Fairfield in Stogursey until 1482 when it was held by Alexander Verney, half-brother of William Verney of Fairfield. In 1488 Alexander gave all his lands in Woolmersdon to William and the manor, also called Petherton manor, continued to descend with Fairfield.[87] From 1488 to 1592 it was said to be held of the Paulets' manor of Rhode, possibly indicating that some of the Verney estate came from another fee.[88] The holding was enlarged in 1723 and in 1771 the manor was known as Woolmersdon and Bridgwater.[89] It was broken up in sales of 1799, 1815, and 1836–8.[90]

Another third share of Joan Trivet's estate was held in 1383[91] by John Pokeswell (d. 1400) and his wife Eleanor (d. by 1400).[92] Their son John (came of age 1408, d. 1413) left two sons who died young[93] and a widow Elizabeth (d. 1432), who married Thomas Tame.[94] John's nephew and heir John Pokeswell[95] was succeeded in 1505 by his son Thomas. Thomas's son Thomas (d. 1537) left as heirs his daughters Eleanor and Elizabeth.[96] By 1578 Eleanor and her husband

John Roynon held Woolmersdon,[97] which they sold in 1584 to George Smythe. George's son Sir Nicholas was succeeded in 1622 by his son Nicholas,[98] whose son George died an infant in 1631. George's uncle and heir George[99] conveyed the estate in 1634 to Benjamin Bull, who sold it in 1641 to Henry Harvey[1] (d. c. 1658). Henry's son Henry (d. 1671) left as heir his uncle John Harvey (d. 1673), whose heir was his brother Francis (d. 1682).[2] In 1715 the owner was John Harvey who had bought lands at Hadworthy in 1678 and was succeeded in turn by his sons Francis (d. by 1764) and John.[3] No further reference to the lordship has been found but the Hadworthy lands were sold to George Musgrave, owner of another part of Woolmersdon, in 1685.[4]

The capital messuage on the Pokeswells' estate was possibly Ball's Farm. The rendered and colourwashed house retains the roof and walls of a small late-medieval hall into which an upper floor and chimney stack were inserted probably in the 17th century. At about the same time a wing was added at the back of the south end.

The remaining third of Joan Trivet's estate was divided between the heirs of Cecily (d. 1361), wife successively of John Stapleton and of Stephen Laundy.[5] Those heirs were first the Dodingtons, who in 1544 sold part to the Newports;[6] secondly, the Orchards whose estate passed by marriage after 1420 to the Careys and was sold in 1564 to Nicholas Halswell;[7] and thirdly the Crewkernes, who appear to have sold their share before 1431.[8]

A capital messuage, also known as Barret's, was recorded in 1717 on the former Dodington estate.[9] It was later known as Bell's Farm and was demolished c. 1982. Built of rubble, it had a three-roomed plan with smoke-blackened trusses and evidence of two possible open hearths.[10]

In 1066 Algar held *HADWORTHY*, and in 1086 Roger de Courcelles held it with Robert as his tenant.[11] In 1287 John de Columbers held Hadworthy of the honor of Compton Dundon.[12] By 1239 Geoffrey of Woolmersdon held land at Hadworthy, which from 1429 apparently descended with part of Woolmersdon manor,[13] whose lords, the Halswells and their successors, retained the lordship of Hadworthy in 1736,

79 *L. & P. Hen. VIII*, xiii, p. 312.
80 P.R.O., CP 25(2)/36/239/31 Hen. VIII Mich.
81 *S.R.S.* xxi. 180; P.R.O., C 142/211, no. 156; below, this section (Huntworth).
82 S.R.O., DD/DP 33/2, 4, 7.
83 Ibid. 2; DD/SAS (C/432) 33; above, this section (Stamfordlands).
84 Above, Goathurst, manors; P.R.O., CP 25(2)/1401/39 Geo. III Trin.; S.R.O., tithe award.
85 *S.R.S.* xii. 195–6.
86 S.R.O., DD/AH 65/6.
87 Ibid. DD/AH 13/6, 65/6; above, Stogursey, manors; above, this section (Rhode).
88 S.R.O., DD/AH 65/6; P.R.O., WARD 7/24, no. 129.
89 S.R.O., DD/AH 1/3, 6/10, 8/3.
90 Ibid. 10/1; 14/3, 16; 24/1; 60/2; DD/SL 23.
91 *S.R.S.* xvii. 115–16.
92 P.R.O., C 137/55, no. 40; *Cal. Fine R.* 1399–1405, 82; *Cal. Pat.* 1401–5, 104; *Cat. Anct. D.* iii, D 681.
93 *Cal. Close*, 1405–9, 333; *Cal. Fine R.* 1413–22, 2; *Cal. Pat.* 1413–16, 99, 118; P.R.O., C 138/4, no. 48.
94 P.R.O., C 139/58, no. 28.
95 Ibid. C 139/45, no. 30.

96 *Cal. Inq. p.m. Hen. VII*, ii, p. 603; P.R.O., C 142/59, no. 53.
97 P.R.O., CP 25(2)/205/20 Eliz. I East.
98 Ibid. CP 25(2)/205/26 Eliz. I East.; C 142/399, no. 151; C 142/461, no. 87.
99 Ibid. C 142/486, no. 128.
1 Ibid. CP 25(2)/480/10 Chas. I East.; CP 25(2)/480/17 Chas. I Mich.
2 S.R.O., DD/SF 884–5; D/B/bw 2/1/2.
3 Ibid. DD/DP 33/7; 34/2, 7; DD/SF 3932; DD/SAS (C/96) 17/2; D/B/bw 2/1/2.
4 Ibid. DD/DP 33/2; above, this section.
5 *Cal. Inq. p.m.* viii, pp. 251–2; xi, pp. 279, 390.
6 *Feud. Aids*, iv. 364; vi. 513; P.R.O., C 142/141, no. 17.
7 *Feud. Aids*, vi. 507; P.R.O., C 140/42, no. 43; ibid. CP 25(2)/204/6 Eliz. I Hil.
8 *Feud. Aids*, iv. 364, 434; P.R.O., C 137/89, no. 13.
9 S.R.O., DD/SL 14.
10 Ibid. DD/V/BWr 26.16.
11 *V.C.H. Som.* i. 484.
12 *S.R.S.* xxxv. 30, 66.
13 Ibid. vi. 108; above, this section (Woolmersdon).

although they had only *c.* 8 a. of land there by 1708.[14]

William of Erleigh gave *WILLSTOCK* to Buckland priory in the 12th century.[15] Alexander Popham may have acquired it in 1544.[16] Alexander's son John gave it to his brother Edward[17] and it descended with Huntworth until 1615 when it was settled on Thomas, a younger son of Alexander Popham (d. 1602).[18] Sir William Portman probably bought Willstock in 1652, and sold it to George Musgrave in 1679.[19] George (d. 1692) left it to his wife Dorothy for life and then to his nephews Richard and William Musgrave, who conveyed their interest to their elder brother George (d. 1721).[20] Dorothy was followed by Mary, widow of George Musgrave's son George (d. 1724).[21] Willstock descended with Combe Sydenham in Stogumber[22] until 1795 when Juliana Langham sold it to Thomas Southwood, who retained a message and 110 a. and sold the rest.[23] In 1838 it belonged to the Coate family, who had been tenants in the 18th century.[24]

Alwig Banneson held *HUNTWORTH* in 1066 and Richard Demeri as tenant of Alfred d'Epaignes in 1086.[25] The manor was held of Alfred's honor of Stowey until 1586 or later.[26]

Huntworth was said to have passed from Jordan Rufus (fl. 1200) to his daughter Joan, wife of Walter of Kentisbere, and to her son Sir Walter of Kentisbere.[27] The son (fl. *c.* 1248–68) was probably succeeded by Stephen of Kentisbere (fl. 1275)[28] and Stephen by his sister or daughter Joan, wife of Sir Hugh Popham, who held Huntworth in 1285.[29] Sir Hugh (d. by 1326) was followed by his son John (d. *c.* 1345), John by his son Hugh (d. *c.* 1361),[30] and Hugh by John Popham (d. by 1428). Thomas Popham, probably John's son, held Huntworth in 1428 and 1438, and was succeeded by William Popham (d. 1479).[31] William's widow Agnes, who had a life interest, married Alexander Sydenham, survived until 1525, and was followed by her son John Popham.[32] John died in 1536 and was followed in turn by his son Alexander (d. 1556), his grandson Edward Popham (d. 1586), and Edward's son Alexander (d. 1602).[33] Alexander's son Edward, outlawed for debt between 1623 and 1625, had conveyed Huntworth and

other estates in 1621 to trustees.[34] Edward died without surviving issue in 1641 leaving Huntworth to Sir William Portman.[35] Portman died in 1645 and was succeeded by his son William. The manor descended in the Portman family with Clavelshay and Bere in Wayford to Claud Berkeley Portman, Viscount Portman (d. 1929), and was divided and sold in 1930, when no reference was made to the lordship.[36]

Huntworth House, built in the late 16th century, had a symmetrical front including a central hall range between a projecting three-storeyed porch and wing on one side and a projection, possibly for a stair, and a similar wing on the other.[37] By 1799 the house, known as Huntworth Farm, was let and it was demolished *c.* 1828. Some of the materials, including a royal coat of arms, were used to make a garden house in the grounds of the present Huntworth House.[38]

Dunwear hamlet was said to be held by John of Erleigh in 1298,[39] and *DUNWEAR* manor, held of North Petherton in 1630 and 1770,[40] can perhaps be traced back to the mid 13th century when Henry of Erleigh gave land there to Lawrence Wild (fl. 1260–7). Wild's son and heir John left a brother Richard,[41] who in 1307 settled 2 messuages and 95 a. in Standenhay and Dunwear on himself for life with remainder to John Popham, and other lands on members of the Paris family.[42] Richard was dead by 1349.[43] John Popham's grandson Thomas Popham of Postridge in Aisholt died *c.* 1410 leaving a son or grandson John Popham (d. *c.* 1473) who held lands at Dunwear. John's son John (d. *c.* 1510) was probably father of Margaret, wife of Cuthbert Clavelshay (d. 1523).[44] Margaret died *c.* 1546 leaving a son Richard Clavelshay (d. *c.* 1554) who held land at Dunwear.[45] Richard's heir was his son John whose daughter Mary married Robert Jennings. Mary's son Marmaduke Jennings bought an estate called Dunwear manor from Richard Clavelshay, probably John's male heir, and his wife in 1609.[46]

Marmaduke died in 1625 and his son Robert in 1630.[47] Robert left Dunwear to his second son Robert, but the eldest son Marmaduke (d. by 1662) took possession. After Marmaduke's death Robert entered the estate but in 1670 sold it to John Selleck, archdeacon of Bath.[48] Selleck (d.

14 S.R.O., DD/S/WH 168, 218.
15 *S.R.S.* xxv, p. 2.
16 *Proc. Som. Arch. Soc.* x. 76–8.
17 P.R.O., C 142/211, no. 156.
18 S.R.O., DD/PM 3/2; below, this section (Huntworth).
19 S.R.O., DD/PM 3/2; DD/DP 33/2.
20 Ibid. DD/JL 74; M.I. in W. Monkton ch.
21 S.R.O., DD/SAS (C/96) 17/5.
22 *V.C.H. Som.* v. 181.
23 S.R.O., DD/MT 53, 59.
24 Ibid. DD/SAS (C/96) 17/5; ibid. tithe award.
25 *V.C.H. Som.* i. 512.
26 P.R.O., C 142/211, no. 156.
27 *Cur. Reg. R.* i. 257; S.R.O., DD/AH 21/2.
28 *S.R.S.* vi. 197, 223; xiv, p. 149; xli, p. 29.
29 Ibid. xliv, p. 139; *Feud. Aids,* iv. 278.
30 *S.R.S.* xii. 110, 222; *Feud. Aids,* i. 344; P.R.O., E 326/6062; Pole MS. 3782.
31 *S.R.S.* xlviii, no. 226; *Feud. Aids,* iv. 364; S.R.O., DD/PM 3/4; P.R.O., C 140/66, no. 29.
32 P.R.O., C 142/44, no. 96.
33 Ibid. C 142/58, no. 81; C 142/211, no. 156; C 142/271, no. 149; *S.R.S.* xxi. 180–1; *Som. Wills,* ed. Brown, v. 107.
34 S.R.O., DD/DP 33/7; DD/PM 7; *Som. Wills,* ed.

Brown, v. 107.
35 S.R.O., DD/PM 3/2; *Som. Wills,* ed. Brown, v. 107; F. W. Popham, *West Country Fam.* 29.
36 Above, this section (Clavelshay); *V.C.H. Som.* iv. 71; S.R.O., DD/KW 20.
37 Taunton Castle, Braikenridge Colln., wash drawing by W. W. Wheatley, reproduced below, plate facing p. 296.
38 S.R.O., DD/PM 15; ibid. T/PH/bb 3; ibid. tithe award; Popham, *West Country Fam.* pl. III; above, intro.
39 Collinson, *Hist. Som.* ii. 60 n.
40 P.R.O., C 142/454, no. 56; S.R.O., DD/SLM 2. There was another manor of Dunwear in N. Petherton (above, this section) and one in Bridgwater.
41 *S.R.S.* xli. 17, 173; lxviii, pp. 8–9.
42 Ibid. vi. 351; xii. 20, 94; xli. 17, 214–15.
43 S.R.O., DD/SAS NP 9, m. 1.
44 Popham, *West Country Fam.* 18; *S.R.S.* xxii. 120; *Visit. Dors. 1623* (Harl. Soc. xx), 16.
45 S.R.O., DD/X/SR 5; P.R.O., C 142/104, no. 68.
46 P.R.O., C 3/292/29; ibid. CP 25(2)/385/5 Jas. I East.; *Visit. Som. 1623* (Harl. Soc. xi), 61.
47 P.R.O., C 142/417, no. 14; C 142/454, no. 56.
48 Ibid. CP 25(2)/715/16 Chas. II Mich.; CP 25(2)/716/22 Chas. II Mich.

1690) was succeeded in turn by his second son Nathaniel (d. *c.* 1699) and by Nathaniel's son John (d. 1732).[49] By 1766 John Stradling held at least part of the estate and in 1767 was said to hold the manor.[50] By 1770, however, it was in the possession of Benjamin Allen (d. 1791), and was said to have been held by his father Dr. John Allen (d. 1741). Dunwear manor descended to Benjamin's son Jeffreys Allen (d. 1844) who left it in trust for his son John,[51] but the manor lands in North Petherton parish had been sold to William Kinglake before 1838 and were later known as Hales farm.[52]

There was a house on Richard Wild's estate in 1316 when he had a licence for a private chapel.[53] No more is known of it.

In 1370 Matthew Clevedon held an estate in Moorland which Alexander Clevedon held in 1412 when it was called *NEW HITCHINGS*.[54] By 1458 it was held by Sir Edward Brooke, Lord Cobham (d. 1464), who was succeeded by his son John and daughter Elizabeth whose shares were bought by Sir Edward's nephew John Brooke in 1496 and 1502.[55] In 1650 Edward Court held the manors of *OLD HITCHINGS*, New Hitchings, and Moorland,[56] and in 1677 he and his wife sold New Hitchings and Moorland manors to Samuel Reynolds.[57] Samuel was dead by 1694 and his heir was his daughter Anne who with her husband Edward Leigh sold New Hitchings in 1711 to John Travers,[58] who in the same year sold it to Francis Newton.[59] James Byrt Newton had succeeded by 1742 and was dead by 1761 when his heirs were his cousins Elizabeth, wife of Thomas Putt, and Margaret, wife of Benjamin Incledon who sold New Hitchings and Moorland to Charles Chichester.[60] No further reference to the lordship has been found but most of the lands were acquired by John Chapman (d. *c.* 1776) and Richard Gatcombe (d. 1782).[61]

WELY manor at Moorland can be traced to a holding of William le Bole in the late 13th century. His unnamed heir, a minor in 1300, held Wely. In 1307 Nicholas Cralle was holding Wely from Hugh Popham but by 1323 John le Bole was in possession. John had died probably by 1332.[62] For most of the 14th century the Wely family held lands at Moorland.[63] Richard Wild (fl. 1329) also held land at Moorland. His heir Thomas Cave, a minor in 1349,[64] married Alice Wely. Cave and Richard Wely held courts jointly at Moorland in 1369.[65] In 1394 Richard Wely and Christine his wife held 'Kewelwere'[66] and *MOORLAND*.[67] John Cave of Wely, recorded in 1415, was probably son of Thomas and brother of Thomas Cave the younger (d. by 1438). Thomas's son Richard Cave married Joan, sister and heir of John Sydenham, whose family had held land at Moorland in the 14th and 15th centuries. Richard was succeeded by his son Philip who died in possession of Moorland in 1471.[68] He was succeeded by his son William, who was dead by 1527 when his son John settled the manors of Moorland and Wely on himself and his wife Elizabeth. John died *c.* 1529 and Elizabeth married James Hadley of Withycombe. In 1533 the manors were settled on Elizabeth and James for life; a statement in 1535 that Thomas Michell held Wely, Moorland, and 'Culawere' of the heirs of John Whiting, lord of West Melcombe, may be erroneous.[69] James Hadley was dead by 1539 but Elizabeth probably survived him.[70] The manor passed to John Cave's nephew George Perceval, who in 1566 sold Moorland to James Boyes of Bridgwater.[71] James left his lands to his elder son Simon[72] but his younger son John was holding Moorland by 1581 and sold it to Henry Andrews or Fry of Cannington. In 1599 Henry sold Moorland to John Cornish who in 1602 gave it to Nicholas Halswell in exchange for Stretcholt in Pawlett.[73] Moorland was settled on Nicholas and his male heirs in 1608 and descended with Halswell in Goathurst to the Tyntes.[74] In 1636 it was said to be held of Nether Stowey manor.[75] No reference to the lordship has been found after 1800. In 1838 the estate consisted of farms in Northmoor Green.[76]

In 1504 Alexander Sydenham acquired land at Moorland from Gilbert Collins. Alexander, who lived at Huntworth, gave all his estates in Moorland, Dunwear, and Chadmead to his son Sylvester and to Sylvester's wife Joan in 1511.[77] Alexander died in 1523, Sylvester in 1526, and Joan in 1547. Sylvester's nephew John held an estate called *MOORLAND* manor in 1578.[78] John was dead by 1603 when the manor was in the hands of Sir John Poyntz of Iron Acton (Glos.), husband of Elizabeth, daughter and heir of Alexander Sydenham, John's brother. In 1603 Sir John let and then sold the manor to Thomas Webber of Luxborough.[79] Thomas (d. *c.* 1609) was succeeded by his son John (d. 1627) and

49 S.R.O., DD/BR/lp 1, 4.
50 Ibid. Q/REl 29/6D; DD/SL 9.
51 *D.N.B.*; S.R.O., DD/SLM 2; DD/SPK, box 11; DD/S/ST 21.
52 S.R.O., tithe award; O.S. Map 1/25,000 ST 33 (1963 edn.).
53 S.R.O., D/D/B reg. 1, f. 97.
54 Ibid. DD/HI 4; *Feud. Aids*, vi. 514.
55 B.L. Add. Ch. 6144; *Cal. Close*, 1485–1500, 283; 1500–9, 30–1.
56 P.R.O., CP 25(2)/592/1650 East. Old Hitchings was not described as a manor thereafter.
57 P.R.O., CP 25(2)/717/28 & 29 Chas. II Hil.
58 S.R.O., DD/SAS (C/96) 17/13; P.R.O., CP 25(2)/962/10 Anne Mich.   59 S.R.O., DD/CH 96/1.
60 Ibid. DD/AY 16; DD/CH 96/1; DD/DP 23/8.
61 Ibid. Q/REl 29/6D; ibid. DD/ALN 6/1; DD/DHR, box 17; D/P/pet. n 2/1/3.
62 S.R.O., DD/SAS NP 1, mm. 5, 12; 2, mm. 1, 7.
63 Ibid. DD/AH 66/9; *S.R.S.* xlviii, no. 172; liii, p. 12.
64 S.R.O., DD/SAS NP 9, m. 1; DD/S/WH 64.
65 *Visit. Som. 1531 and 1573*, ed. Weaver, 99; S.R.O., DD/S/WH 64.
66 Possibly the 'Were' in Bridgwater: *S.R.S.* xlviii, p. 162; lviii, p. 45.   67 *S.R.S.* xvii. 159.
68 Ibid. lviii, nos. 575, 665, 685; P.R.O., C 140/38, no. 43.
69 S.R.O., DD/SG 4; P.R.O., C 142/57, no. 66.
70 P.R.O., C 142/61, no. 97; *S.R.S.* xxi. 13.
71 S.R.O., DD/SG 4; DD/S/WH 12.
72 *Som. Wills*, ed. Brown, iii. 50; P.R.O., C 142/191, no. 74.
73 S.R.O., DD/S/WH 12; above, Pawlett, manors.
74 P.R.O., C 142/475, no. 96; above, Goathurst, manors.
75 MS. in possession of Miss B. Harris, Taunton.
76 S.R.O., DD/S/WH 166; ibid. tithe award.
77 *Cat. Anct. D.* iv, A 8578; v, A 12554; G. F. Sydenham, *Hist. Sydenham Fam.* 208–9.
78 *S.R.S.* xix. 221; *Cat. Anct. D.* v, A 12415; P.R.O., C 142/44, no. 101.
79 S.R.O., DD/BR/pc 1; P.R.O., CP 25(2)/345/1 Jas. I Mich.

John by his son Thomas.[80] Thomas held the manor in 1640 but was dead by 1667 and probably by 1647. His son John (d. c. 1673) left his estate to his widow Gertrude (d. c. 1675).[81]

Alexander Kinglake had acquired the manor by 1693 probably from the heirs of John Webber. It may have passed to Alexander's son John (d. 1739) and to John's son Alexander in 1766.[82] Alexander mortgaged and subsequently sold parts of Moorland in 1771 and conveyed his remaining estate c. 1780 to his brother John (d. 1784).[83] John's son John (d. 1809) was succeeded by his widow Anna (d. 1847) and she by his brother William and his brother Robert's son John Alexander.[84] No reference has been found to the lordship after 1836. Some land was sold, but William Kinglake's son Alexander (d. 1891) bought the remainder of his cousin's share.[85] In 1897 Alexander's brother John Hamilton Kinglake gave it to his son Hamilton Alexander Kinglake as part of Saltmoor manor in Stoke St. Gregory.[86]

In 1370 Richard Coker held land at Moorland[87] which probably descended to James Coker. James's heir was his kinsman John Coker whose estates passed to his daughter Margaret, wife successively of Alexander Hody (d. 1461) and Sir Reynold Stourton.[88] Margaret died in 1489 in possession of the manor of *MOORLAND* by inheritance from her father. Her heir was John Seymour, grandson of her uncle Robert Coker.[89] The subsequent descent of this manor has not been traced.

Robert Broughton (d. 1631) settled land at Moorland on his daughter and coheir Jane, wife of James Clarke, in 1606.[90] In 1632 Jane, then a widow, sold *MOORLAND* manor to her daughter Bridget. In 1635 Bridget conveyed the manor to Alexander Bulpan.[91] Alexander and his sons Alexander and John were dead by 1666 when the manor was divided between their heirs, namely Joan, wife of John Phelps, and Mary, wife of Edward Batt. Mary sold her share to George Musgrave.[92] In 1672 Musgrave sold all or part of the estate to John Ballam. John had been succeeded by his son John by 1695, but the estate may have been forfeited under a mortgage, as land called Ballams formed part of the Tyntes' manor of Moorland in 1708.[93] John Phelps died in 1672; his son John mortgaged an estate at Moorland in 1685 to Sir Halswell Tynte.[94] No

further reference to the lordship has been found nor has later ownership of the land been traced.

In 1288 Walter le Lyf held land in North Petherton and la More.[95] Joan, wife of Walter Tilley, and Amice, wife of Baldwin Malet, co-heirs of Richard Lyf, held an estate, probably at *MOORLAND*, in 1401.[96] Walter and Joan appear to have acquired Amice's share c. 1416.[97] Walter probably died shortly afterwards and Joan married William Pym. She died c. 1426 when her heir was Thomas Blanchard, her son by her first husband.[98] Thomas's half-brother Leonard Tilley settled Moorland in 1463 on Joan, wife of John Speccote, for life and on his own children.[99] Thomas Tilley, probably Leonard's son or grandson, died in 1536 in possession of a manor of Moorland held of North Petherton.[1] Thomas was succeeded by his grandson James Tilley (d. 1557) and James by his son George (d. 1590).[2] George's heirs were his daughters Anne, wife of William Walton, and Elizabeth who later married Sir Edward Parham. In 1604 Walton obtained Elizabeth's share.[3] He died in 1617 survived by Anne and leaving a son Francis, a minor.[4] By 1647 the estate appears to have been acquired by the Court family, and descended with their manor of New Hitchings.[5]

John Bowyer owned land in *MOORLAND* in 1552. Before 1555 he acquired the reversion of more, and in 1586 held Moorland manor.[6] Bowyer died in 1599 when his heir was his son Edmund.[7] Edmund (d. 1625) was followed by his son Edmund (d. 1665) and by his grandson, also Edmund Bowyer (d. 1670).[8] Edmund, son of the last, assigned Moorland to William Browne in 1702.[9] The estate was dispersed in 1714 on behalf of William's son William, a minor;[10] subsequent ownership has not been traced.

St. John's hospital, Bridgwater, acquired estates in North Petherton in 1349 and 1357.[11] After the Dissolution the hospital's estate, in the east part of the parish, was divided and sold in 1544, 1553, and 1610.[12] Athelney abbey had lands at *WEST YEO* which were sold to John Leigh in 1543.[13]

An estate called Newton, held by Brictwold in 1066 and by Ralph under Roger Arundel in 1086, has been identified[14] as *MAUNSEL* manor, which was held of the Erleighs' manor

80 P.R.O., C 60/453, no. 61; C 142/439, no. 19.
81 S.R.O., DD/SAS (C/96) 17/13; DD/X/FRC (C/140).
82 Ibid. DD/SAS (C/96) 17/13; ibid. Q/REl 19/6D.
83 Ibid. Q/REl 29/6D; ibid. DD/SAS (C/114) 10; DD/DHR, box 27.
84 Ibid. DD/CH 96/4; DD/CC 111544.
85 Ibid. DD/CH 96/4; DD/AY 33B.
86 Ibid. DD/AY 34.
87 Ibid. DD/S/WH 64–5.
88 *S.R.S.* xxii. 127, 145–6; *Cal. Inq. p.m.* (Rec. Com.) iv, p. 311.
89 *Cal. Inq. p.m. Hen. VII*, i, p. 267.
90 P.R.O., C 145/534/29, no. 172; S.R.O., DD/DP 33/3.
91 S.R.O., DD/SAS (C/96) 17/13; DD/X/FRC (C/140).
92 Ibid. DD/SAS H 47/3/25; DD/SP 364.
93 Ibid. DD/SAS H 47/3/30; DD/DP 34/2; DD/S/WH 218.
94 Ibid. DD/HYD 30; DD/SAS H 47/3/30.
95 *S.R.S.* vi. 271.
96 Ibid. xxii. 158, 161; Collinson, *Hist. Som.* i. 239.
97 *S.R.S.* xxii. 178.

98 *Cal. Fine R.* 1422–30, 147.
99 *Cal. Close*, 1461–8, 253–4.
1 P.R.O., C 142/59, no. 79.
2 Ibid. C 142/57, no. 69; C 142/114, no. 53; C 142/228, no. 78.
3 Ibid. CP 25(2)/345/2 Jas. I Mich.
4 S.R.O., D/P/shap 2/1/1; *Som. Wills*, ed. Brown, v. 83.
5 S.R.O., DD/X/FRC (C/140); above, this section (New Hitchings).
6 S.R.O., DD/HI 4; DD/MVB 41; P.R.O., C 3/17/27.
7 *Som. Wills*, ed. Brown, i. 28; P.R.O., C 142/257, no. 57.
8 P.R.O., C 142/419, no. 42; S.R.O., DD/MVB 8; *Som. Wills*, ed. Brown, iv. 82.
9 S.R.O., DD/BR/py 21.
10 Bailey-Everard MSS., in possession of Messrs. Crosse & Wyatt, S. Molton, Devon.
11 *Cal. Pat.* 1348–50, 407; 1354–8, 525.
12 *L. & P. Hen. VIII*, xix (2), p. 313; *Cal. Pat.* 1553, 55, 159; Wilts. R.O. 753/1.
13 *L. & P. Hen. VIII*, xix (1), p. 39.
14 *Proc. Som. Arch. Soc.* xcix–c. 42.

of North Petherton in the 13th century.[15] By 1539, however, Maunsel was held of Buckland priory's manor of North Petherton, later known as Buckland Fee. That overlordship continued until 1566 or later.[16]

William of Erleigh is said to have given Maunsel to Philip Arblaster in the late 12th century in free marriage with William's daughter Mabel. Her mother Aziria confirmed the grant for Philip's son Philip, surnamed Maunsel.[17] Philip may have been succeeded by Roger Maunsel (fl. 1242–3) and Walter Maunsel (fl. 1276–80).[18] Geoffrey Maunsel was probably holding the manor in 1287 and died c. 1302 when his lands were in the custody of his widow Hawise during the minority of his heir.[19] Philip Maunsel, probably Geoffrey's heir, was dead by 1349. He was probably succeeded by William Maunsel (fl. 1366) who was dead by 1398 when his son Richard held the manor.[20] Richard was probably succeeded by his son John before 1423. John the elder, possibly the same, was at Maunsel in 1457. He was M.P. for Bridgwater in 1449 and 1454 and was still alive in 1469.[21] By 1500 he had been succeeded by Robert Maunsel. Marmaduke Maunsel (d. 1544) had inherited the manor by 1533 when he settled it on his son John for his marriage to Catherine Vowell.[22] In 1570 Catherine, then a widow, gave Maunsel to her son John Maunsel in return for an annuity. John died in 1586 leaving his son Richard a minor.[23] Richard, who came of age in 1587, was in possession of Maunsel in 1609. In 1631 his widow Elizabeth and heir John sold the manor to John Harvey of Taunton.[24]

Harvey sold Maunsel to William Bacon of Broomfield in 1648. William (d. 1663) was followed by his son William (d. 1690). In 1689 Maunsel was settled on William's son Thomas for his marriage. Thomas (d. 1722) left four daughters, Dorothy, Grace, Susan, and Elizabeth, who in 1726–7 released their shares to Henry Portman. Portman died in 1728 and was succeeded by his nephew Sir Edward Seymour, Bt., who in the same year conveyed the manor to his son Alexander. Alexander died c. 1733 leaving Maunsel to his sister Letitia for life and then to her son Alexander Seymour Gapper.[25]

Gapper mortgaged the estate heavily and in 1765 he left it to John Nichols (d. c. 1769). In 1771 John's sons John and William Nichols released Maunsel to the mortgagee Richard Scrafton, to enable John Slade to buy the manor in 1772.[26] John Slade (d. 1801) was succeeded by his son John (later Gen. Sir John Slade, Bt., d. 1859) who held command under Sir John Moore in 1808 and was defeated at Llera in 1812.

Sir John's third son Sir Frederick (d. 1863) was followed by his son Sir Alfred (d. 1890) and Alfred by his son Sir Cuthbert (d. 1908). Cuthbert's eldest son Sir Alfred died in 1960 and his second son Sir Michael in 1962. Michael's son Sir Benjamin Slade was the owner in 1983.[27]

Maunsel House or Grange was recorded as Maunsel Place in 1544.[28] An east–west range at the south end of the house comprises a medieval hall, screens passage, and cross wing. The hall became a kitchen when the main north–south range was added in the early 16th century. That range comprises a ground-floor hall and a first-floor great chamber which has an arch-braced roof of eight bays with cusped windbraces. The porch may be a later 16th-century addition. During the early 17th century the medieval hall was ceiled and a rear wing added at the north end of the main range. The rooms there have plastered intersecting beamed ceilings and two first-floor rooms contain contemporary panelling. Probably during the 18th century the great chamber was ceiled to provide an attic storey: John Bastard of Blandford (Dors.) worked on the house in 1727.[29] In the mid 18th century, probably when Sir John Slade bought the house, the staircase was rebuilt and several rooms were refitted. During the late 1820s extensive internal alterations were made by the architect Richard Carver including the removal of the great chimney stack from the hall. He built the dining room and extended the great hall northwards.[30] In the 19th century single-storeyed service rooms and a passage were added on the west and the porch was rebuilt. In the 1860s a library and billiard room were added west of the dining room and a canted bay was built above the main staircase.

By the early 18th century 4 a. around the house included a dovehouse, stables, barns, gardens, orchards, and a large fishpond with an island.[31] A canal was constructed in the early 18th century, possibly from earlier fishponds. Further south a lodge, called the dairy, on the site of the former mill, probably dates from the late 18th or early 19th century and incorporates a semi-circular thatched room. A northern lodge was rebuilt in the early 20th century. The park north of the house was established between 1823 and 1838, probably c. 1828 when the north drive was made, hedges removed, and a haha reconstructed.[32] In 1839 James Veitch of Exeter supplied many ornamental trees which were planted along the north drive, around the canal, and in a copse east of the house.[33] A partly walled kitchen garden lay west of the house.

ERNESHAM, recorded in the 13th century,[34] belonged to Richard Wely and his wife Christine

[15] Cal. Close, 1272–9, 410; S.R.S. xiv, p. 160.
[16] T. Hugo, Hist. Mynchin Buckland Priory & Preceptory (1861), 139–42; S.R.S. xxi. 180–1; P.R.O., C 142/71, no. 74.
[17] S.R.O., DD/AH 21/2.
[18] S.R.S. xi, p. 301; xiv, p. 160; xliv. 218; Cal. Close, 1272–9, 410.
[19] S.R.S. vi. 268; S.R.O., DD/SAS NP 8, mm. 7, 9, 13.
[20] S.R.O., DD/SAS NP 2, mm. 1, 3; 9, m. 1; 12, m. 7.
[21] Ibid. DD/SL 1; S.R.S. xiv, p. 197; xxii. 137; lx, pp. 54, 71; Cat. Anct. D. iv, A 9690.
[22] P.R.O., CP 25(1)/202/42/15 Hen. VII East.; ibid. C 142/71, no. 74.
[23] S.R.O., DD/SL 16; DD/X/SR 5.
[24] Ibid. DD/PH 28; DD/SL 10.

[25] Ibid. DD/SL 10; DD/NW 63, 64; Som. Wills, ed. Brown, iv. 11.
[26] S.R.O., DD/SL 10; DD/SLM 2; P.R.O., CP 25(2)/1398/12 Geo. III East.
[27] S.R.O., DD/SL 37, 40; DD/SLM 10; Burke, Peerage (1970), 2462–3; D.N.B.
[28] P.R.O., C 142/71, no. 74.
[29] Ibid. C 107/126.
[30] S.R.O., DD/SL 38/1–2; MS. in possession of Sir B. Slade, London.
[31] S.R.O., DD/SL 10.
[32] Ibid. DD/SL 38/1; DD/SLM, bk. of maps, map 1823; ibid. tithe award.   [33] Ibid. DD/SLM 14.
[34] Ibid. DD/SL 1.

North Petherton: Huntworth Manor, *c.* 1845

Chilton Trinity: Bere Manor, *c.* 1730

THE RIVER PARRETT BELOW BRIDGWATER, *c.* 1800

WEMBDON CHURCH AND CHURCH HOUSE, WITH VIEW OF BRIDGWATER SPIRE, *c.* 1800

in 1394.[35] In 1457 it was held by the Maunsel family[36] but by the early 17th century it was divided.[37] In 1613 Robert Catford sold an estate at Ernesham to Marmaduke Ling (d. 1641), who was succeeded by Marmaduke Ling (d. 1682).[38] Eleanor, widow of the last, died in 1683 and left as coheirs Eleanor, wife of Simon Court, and Joan, wife of James Porter, possibly her grand-daughters.[39] Simon Court (d. 1726) settled his share of Ernesham on his son Thomas (d. by 1733)[40] who was succeeded by his son Thomas (d. by ?1740) and his daughter Eleanor.[41] Eleanor was dead by 1759 when the estate, including the house later known as Court's Farm, had been bought by Jeremiah Dewdney who also acquired the Porters' share.[42] Dewdney's great-nephew Jeremiah Dewdney Parsons sold Court's farm to William Webber c. 1822.[43] Court's Farm prob-ably dates from the early 18th century and is built of brick with a pantile roof. The five-bayed front has a central door with wrought iron porch.

BUCKLAND SORORUM manor probably originated in estates held by Buckland priory in North Petherton. They were let to Edward Rogers before the Dissolution and in 1544 were granted to William Parr, earl of Essex, Edward Rogers, and others.[44] The manor descended with Chadmead in the Rogers family[45] and was some-times called the manor of Buckland Sororum cum Chadmead. From the 18th century it was also known as Buckland Tithe Free.[46] By 1838 much of the estate had been sold to Richard Meade King, Thomas Stacey, Sir Charles Kemeys-Tynte, and Sir John Slade, Bt.[47] There does not appear to have been a capital messuage.

CHADMEAD manor, also known as Brick-land, Bankland, or Bankland Chadmead,[48] was held of the Bluets' manor of North Petherton in 1485.[49] In 1298 Henry of Somerset held Chad-mead and Holbrook.[50] Ralph of Middleney (d. 1363) held an estate at Chadmead which passed at his death to his widow with reversion to his granddaughter Katharine, second wife of Tho-mas Berkeley. Katharine died in 1385 and was succeeded by Thomas Berkeley (d. 1417), her husband's grandson. Thomas's heir was his daughter Elizabeth (d. 1422), wife of Richard Beauchamp, earl of Warwick. Chadmead ap-pears to have descended to her eldest daughter Margaret (d. 1467), wife of John Talbot, earl of

Shrewsbury, and to their son John, Lord Lisle.[51] John's widow was in possession of deeds of Chadmead c. 1457, but the land was probably sold to the Newburghs. John Newburgh pos-sessed land at Chadmead in 1423.[52] Sir John Newburgh (d. by 1441), probably his son, was followed by his son John. That John's grandson John Newburgh (d. 1485)[53] was succeeded by his brother Roger who with his wife Elizabeth sold Chadmead to Alexander Sydenham in 1498.[54] Alexander settled the manor on his son Sylvester in 1511,[55] and in 1557 it was held by George Sydenham and his wife Eleanor,[56] who may have been the daughter of Sylvester. In 1586 the manor was in the possession of Joan or Jane Rogers, widow of Sir George Rogers of Cannington and granddaughter of Sylvester Sydenham.[57]

Joan Rogers died in 1602 and her son Edward in 1627.[58] Sir Francis Rogers (d. 1638), son of Edward, was succeeded by his son Hugh, a minor, and Hugh (d. 1653) by his uncle Henry Rogers. Henry died in 1672 leaving a life interest to Hugh's grandson Alexander Popham of Littlecote (Wilts.).[59] Alexander died without male issue in 1705 and by 1712 the manor had reverted to Sir Copplestone Warwick Bamp-fylde, heir to Warwick Bampfylde, nephew of Henry Rogers.[60] Sir Copplestone sold the manor to Sir Thomas Wroth in 1720.[61] The manor then descended with the Wroth estate in Lyng until the death of Elizabeth Acland in 1806, when her daughter Elizabeth Grove and her son Wroth Palmer Acland held it for the remainder of certain terms. In 1815 part was put up for sale and in 1829 that portion known as Little Bankland was sold to Sir John Slade.[62] The remainder of the estate, called Eames, was re-tained by John Acland's son Peregrine in 1838 as part of Buckland Sororum manor.[63]

There was a house on the estate in 1423[64] and the capital messuage, called Chadmead or Eames, probably after a former tenant, was let in 1720.[65] In 1754 Arthur Acland reserved the right to hold courts in the house but in 1767 the house was described as unfinished and the barn and offices were down. By 1771 the house had fallen into decay and had been demolished.[66]

BANKLAND was held by John Bluet in 1573[67] and descended as part of North Petherton

35 *S.R.S.* xvii. 159.
36 *Cat. Anct. D.* iv, A 9690.
37 *S.R.S.* lxvii, pp. 55–6; S.R.O., DD/BV 5; DD/S/BT 17.
38 S.R.O., DD/BV 5; D/P/pet. n 2/1/1; DD/X/FRC (C/140); DD/SP inventory, 1682.
39 Ibid. DD/X/SR 5.
40 Ibid.; ibid. DD/BV 5; DD/CCH 1.
41 Ibid. DD/BV 16; DD/CCH 1.
42 Ibid. DD/BV 2, 16; ibid. Q/REl 29/6A.
43 Ibid. DD/DHR, box 26; ibid. Q/REl 29/6A.
44 Hugo, *Hist. Mynchin Buckland*, 70; *L. & P. Hen. VIII*, xvii, p. 700; xix (1), p. 504.
45 Below, this section.
46 S.R.O., DD/AH 66/11; DD/DHR, box 26; ibid. tithe award.
47 Ibid. DD/AH 10/1, 24/1; ibid. tithe award.
48 Ibid. DD/AH 1/3, 66/11.
49 *Cal. Inq. p.m. Hen. VII*, i, p. 17.
50 Collinson, *Hist. Som.* iii. 60 n.
51 *Proc. Som. Arch. Soc.* lxi. 154–5; Burke, *Peerage* (1949), 1830; *Complete Peerage*, xii (2), 381–2.

52 P.R.O., E 326/10032; *S.R.S.* xxii. 183.
53 Dors. R.O., D 10/M 241–2; Hutchins, *Hist. Dors.* i. 135; *Cal. Inq. p.m. Hen. VII*, i, p. 17.
54 P.R.O., CP 25(1)/202/42/13 Hen. VII East.
55 *Cat. Anct. D.* v, A 12554; P.R.O., STAC 2/24/203.
56 P.R.O., CP 25(2)/83/712/3 & 4 Phil. & Mary East.
57 Ibid. CP 25(2)/261/28 Eliz. I Trin.; ibid. C 142/148, no. 28; *Som. Wills*, ed. Brown, ii. 91.
58 P.R.O., C 142/440, no. 91; *Proc. Som. Arch. Soc.* civ. 80.
59 P.R.O., C 142/486, no. 114; *S.R.S.* lxvii, p. 145; *Proc. Som. Arch. Soc.* civ. 80; *Som. Wills*, ed. Brown, ii. 92; S.R.O., DD/BR/bn 2; DD/AH 8/2, 5.
60 S.R.O., DD/AH 8/2; *Proc. Som. Arch. Soc.* civ. 83.
61 S.R.O., DD/AH 1/3, 66/11.
62 Above, Lyng, manors; S.R.O., DD/AH 14/3, 55/5; DD/SLM 13.
63 S.R.O., DD/AH 24/1; ibid. tithe award.
64 *S.R.S.* xxii. 183.
65 S.R.O., DD/AH 8/5, 65/15.
66 Ibid. 9/3, 66/11.
67 Ibid. DD/MI 5.

manor until 1855 or later.[68] A capital messuage recorded between 1573 and 1757[69] may have been Bankland Farm,[70] which dates from the 16th century with a three-roomed plan and cross passage. The rear wing was added in the 18th century when the house was reroofed and refitted.

It has been suggested that *TUCKERTON* formed part of Newton,[71] and during the early 13th century the name is recorded as Tokar Newton. It was held as of Nether Stowey manor in the 13th and 14th centuries.[72] Before 1216 the Hospitallers of Buckland received land at Tuckerton from Robert Bacon given to him by Robert son of Bernard and from Gerard of Brocton given to him by Robert Bacon. Stephen son of Michael de Perers also gave land there to the Hospitallers.[73] The Hospitallers held Tuckerton until 1428[74] and probably until the Dissolution.

After the Dissolution Tuckerton was probably granted with other lands of Buckland priory to William Portman and Alexander Popham in 1544.[75] Alexander Popham in 1551 gave Tuckerton manor to his son Edward (d. 1586) and Edward's wife Jane.[76] Jane (d. 1610) was succeeded by her grandson Edward Popham.[77] Edward was outlawed for debt in 1628 and the Crown granted the manor of Tuckerton and Clayhanger, probably after 1635, to William Dowthwayte of Bridgwater, who assigned it in 1638 to Emmanuel Sandys and William Dawe.[78] In 1671 Tuckerton belonged to Robert Hunt, in 1680 to John Hunt, and in 1703 to John Jeanes.[79] John Jeanes, apparently another, held it in 1766 and Miss Jeanes in 1770. By 1791 Sir John Durbin had acquired the estate, probably by marriage.[80] Joseph Jeanes Durbin, son of Sir John, sold the estate in 1839 to Sir John Slade.[81] There is no further reference to the lordship and the estate descended with Maunsel until 1870 or later.[82] Tuckerton farm was sold to the Portman family before 1897.[83]

Athelney abbey received rent for land at Primmore in the 13th century and held an estate at Tuckerton in 1338.[84] It was granted to John Leigh in 1543[85] but subsequent ownership has not been traced.

HEDGING belonged to Buckland priory by the late 13th century.[86] In 1706 Sir Philip Sydenham sold a house and c. 40 a. at Hedging to Giles Gardner (d. 1719) whose son Giles conveyed them to Henry Selleck in 1720. Henry's son John sold Hedging to George Coombe in 1742. George (d. c. 1762) was succeeded by his son George (d. c. 1823).[87] In 1838 George's nephew George Coombe was holding Hedging from Elizabeth Coles.[88] James Coles was the owner in 1858.[89]

Hedging Barton was a two-bayed open hall house with a one-bayed service block to the south. It was extended in the 17th century with the addition of a cross passage and a third room and a semi-attic upper storey.[90]

PRIMMORE belonged to the Hospitallers at Buckland[91] and was later held by Thomas Musgrave of West Monkton (d. 1627)[92] whose son Edward (d. 1684) was succeeded by his son or grandson Edward Musgrave (d. 1719). Thomas (d. 1760), son of the last,[93] settled the estate on his wife Martha (d. 1772) and his daughter, also Martha,[94] who died in 1800 and was followed by William Beadon, husband of her niece Martha Hammet and owner in 1838.[95]

In 1066 Lewin held *WEST NEWTON*, also known as *NEWTON COMITIS* and *NEWTON HAWYS*, and in 1086 Alfred of Marlborough held it of Eustace, count of Boulogne.[96] Eustace's fee passed to the Crown through the marriage of his daughter to Stephen of Blois, later King Stephen.[97] In 1524 West Newton was said to be held of the abbot of Athelney, and in 1600 and 1618 of Sir John Leigh's manor of Lyng, evidently in succession to the abbey.[98] No further reference to the overlordship has been found.

Alfred of Marlborough's lands were granted to Harold son of Ralph, earl of Hereford, during the reign of William Rufus. Harold was succeeded by his son Robert (d. after 1147) and by Robert's son Robert who died in 1198 leaving a daughter Sibyl, wife of Robert Tregoz. Sibyl died in 1236 leaving a son Robert Tregoz (d. 1265).[99] By 1241 West Newton had been subinfeudated; the mesne lordship passed from Robert's son John (d. 1300) to his daughter Sibyl, wife of William Grandison, and to John Warre, son of his daughter Clarice. John died in 1347.[1] No further reference to the mesne lordship has been found.

Reynold of Newton had been succeeded as terre tenant by his son Robert by 1241. Robert,

68   S.R.O., DD/SL 8, 22.
69   Ibid. DD/MI 5; Devon R.O. 48/51/8/24A–B.
70   S.R.O., DD/SL 22.
71   *Dom. Bk.*, ed. Thorn, 360.
72   *S.R.S.* xiv, p. 180; xxv, pp. 37–41.
73   Ibid. xxv, pp. 37–41.
74   *Feud. Aids*, iv. 279, 301, 345, 365.
75   *Proc. Som. Arch. Soc.* x. 76–8.
76   P.R.O., C 142/211, no. 156.
77   Ibid. C 142/271, no. 149.
78   Devon R.O. 1148 M/add 9/22; S.R.O., DD/DP 33/4, 7. The name Clayhanger was recorded in the early 14th century: S.R.O., DD/SAS NP 2, m. 3. It survived as a field name E. of Tuckerton in 1838: ibid. tithe award.
79   P.R.O., CP 25(2)/718/32 Chas. II Trin.; S.R.O., DD/MK 1.
80   S.R.O., Q/REl 29/6G; DD/SLM, bk. of maps; Collinson *Hist. Som.* iii. 72.
81   S.R.O., DD/SL 31; DD/SLM 13; MSS. in possession of Sir B. Slade, London; Burke, *Land. Gent* (1914), 163.
82   MSS. in possession of Sir B. Slade; above, this section.

83   S.R.O., D/R/bw 15/1/2.
84   *S.R.S.* xiv, p. 163.
85   *L. & P. Hen. VIII*, xix (1), p. 39.
86   *S.R.S.* xxv, p. 21; Collinson, *Hist. Som.* iii. 61.
87   S.R.O., DD/CCH 67/1, 73/1–2.
88   Ibid. tithe award.
89   Ibid. DD/DHR, box 12.
90   Ibid. DD/V/BWr 26.1.
91   *S.R.S.* xxv, pp. 21–2.
92   *S.D.N.Q.* vi. 68; S.R.O., DD/JL 69.
93   S.R.O., DD/JL 14, 17, 70, 75.
94   Ibid. 17, 26.
95   Ibid. 81; ibid. tithe award.
96   *V.C.H. Som.* i. 472; *S.R.S.* vi. 310; xii. 30–1; xxv, p. 8.
97   Sanders, *Eng. Baronies*, 151; *S.R.S.* iii. 10.
98   P.R.O., C 142/41, no. 47; C 142/260, no. 115; S.R.O., DD/MI 5.
99   Sanders, *Eng. Baronies*, 43.
1   *Feud. Aids*, iv. 278; *Cal. Inq. p.m.* iii, p. 454; Sanders, *Eng. Baronies*, 43.

alive in 1269, probably died shortly afterwards.[2] He had had a son called Richard but seems to have been succeeded by his brother Richard before 1280.[3] Richard held Newton in 1285 and 1303[4] but was dead by 1305 leaving a son Robert and a widow Sarah as tenant for life.[5] In 1346 Philip Luccombe and Agnes Trivet, possibly Robert's widow, were said to hold the fee.[6] By 1355 the manor was divided, part being held by Margaret, wife of John Payn.[7] Philip Luccombe's wife Agatha was possibly daughter of Robert Newton, and in 1385 Alice, daughter and heir of the Luccombes' son Geoffrey and wife of John Copplestone, held the entire manor.[8] John Copplestone's brother Richard bought the manor in 1385 and died leaving John Copplestone as his heir. John may have been still alive in 1423 but by 1428 Thomas Copplestone, possibly John's son, had succeeded.[9] Thomas Copplestone, possibly the same, and his wife Anne held the manor in 1477.[10] He died in 1480 leaving four daughters:[11] Catherine, wife of John Sydenham; Joan, wife successively of Simon Littlecote, Sir Morgan Kidwelly, and Sir Edmund Gorges; Margaret, wife successively of William Hymerford and Henry Thornton; and Elizabeth, wife of William Seymour. Catherine appears to have died by 1524 leaving her three sisters as her heirs.[12]

Joan died in 1524 holding one third. Her heir was William Thornborough, son of her daughter Alice.[13] William (d. 1535) left an infant son John, but he or his widow seems to have sold their share to William Hymerford whose son Andrew sold it to William Hawley (d. 1567). The estate descended in the Hawley family with Durston until 1618 when Sir Henry Hawley sold his share to Henry Cheeke (d. 1630),[14] who acquired most of the other shares.

In 1529 Margaret settled her share on William Hymerford her son and heir, on whose death it was divided between his two daughters Margaret, wife of William Vowell, and Joan, wife of John Hambridge.[15] John Willoughby bought Margaret's sixth share in 1555 and died in 1559. His son Richard sold it to Richard Galhampton and George Cheeke (d. c. 1589) in 1580.[16] The share passed to Cheeke's son Henry (d. 1594) and to Henry's son also Henry (d. 1630).[17] Joan Hambridge, holder of the other sixth share, was dead by 1542 and her share probably descended on the death of her husband in 1569 to her son

Richard, and from Richard passed by sale like other family land to George Harrison and then to John Bowyer of Beere in Chilton Trinity.[18] Bowyer died in 1599 and his son Edmund held a sixth share in 1602.[19] Edmund died in 1625 and his son Edmund sold his share to Sir Robert Phelips in 1626.[20] In 1668 that share was reunited with the rest of the manor.

Elizabeth died before her husband William Seymour (d. 1532). Her daughter Agnes, wife of Henry Fortescue,[21] was succeeded by her son John. John's son William[22] held a third of the manor in 1588 and died in 1599 leaving a son Francis under age.[23] In 1617 Francis sold his estate to Henry Cheeke.[24]

Henry Cheeke held five sixths of the manor at his death in 1630.[25] His son Henry (d. 1654) left a daughter Dorothy who in 1658 married John Bury (d. 1667) and in 1668 (Sir) Edward Phelips of Montacute (d. 1698), holder of the remaining share of the manor.[26] Dorothy Phelips died in 1678. Her only child, also Dorothy Phelips, may have predeceased her as the manor formed part of the marriage settlement of Sir Edward and his second wife Edith in 1683.[27] From Edith (d. 1728) the manor passed to her youngest daughter Edith (d. 1772), wife of Carew Mildmay, and to the younger Edith's nephew Edward Phelips (d. 1797) who in 1778 gave it to his elder son Edward (d. 1792). That Edward was succeeded by his brother the Revd. William Phelips.[28] The manor descended with Montacute manor until 1810 when John Phelips sold it to Thomas Warre. Thomas died in 1824 leaving as his heir his nephew John Ashley Warre.[29] No later reference to the lordship has been found, but John was succeeded in 1860 by his son, also John, who died in 1894 leaving West Newton to his niece Mary Elliott. Her father Arthur Warre seems to have occupied the estate. West Newton was bought by the tenant in 1904.[30] Showerings Ltd. bought the estate in 1958 and owned it in 1984.[31]

The manor house, formerly called Court House and in 1984 the Manor, may date from the 14th century.[32] It is of rubble, of two storeys, and formerly had a three-roomed frontage with cross-passage entrance; it is two rooms deep, and is probably a double-aisled hall house. The two-storeyed north porch has a moulded arch. Parts of smoke-blackened roof posts and some arch braces survive. The house was remodelled

2   *S.R.S.* vi. 108; xiv, p. 159; xxv, p. 37.
3   Ibid. xiv, p. 159; xxv, p. 30.
4   *Feud. Aids*, iv. 278, 300.
5   *S.R.S.* iii. 244; vi. 339; xxv, p. 36.
6   *Feud. Aids*, iv. 345.
7   *S.R.S.* xvii. 30–1.
8   Ibid. 125–6; P.R.O., CP 40/491, rot. 569.
9   C. E. H. Chadwyck Healey, *Hist. W. Som.* 450; *S.R.S.* xvii. 125–6; *Feud. Aids*, iv. 394.
10   *S.R.S.* xxii. 148.
11   P.R.O., C 140/74, no. 22.
12   Chadwyck Healey, *Hist. W. Som.* 105; P.R.O., C 142/41, no. 47.
13   P.R.O., C 142/41, no. 47; Chadwyck Healey, *Hist. W. Som.* 106.
14   Above, Durston, manors; P.R.O., C 142/145, no. 18; S.R.O., DD/PH 27.
15   Chadwyck Healey, *Hist. W. Som.* 105–6; P.R.O., C 142/67, no. 151.
16   S.R.O., DD/WO 11/4, 44/3, 53/1.

17   Ibid. DD/SAS (C/96) 17/9; D/P/pet. n 2/1/1.
18   Ibid. D/P/cok. e 2/1/1; P.R.O., C 142/152, no. 126; Chadwyck Healey, *Hist. W. Som.* 108, 112.
19   P.R.O., C 142/257, no. 57; S.R.O., DD/MVB 41.
20   P.R.O., C 142/419, no. 42; S.R.O., DD/PH 27.
21   P.R.O., C 142/54, no. 106.
22   S.R.O., DD/PH 27.
23   Ibid. DD/MI 5; P.R.O., C 142/260, no. 115.
24   S.R.O., DD/PH 27.
25   Ibid. D/P/pet. n 2/1/1.
26   Ibid.; ibid. DD/PH 27; DD/SAS (C/96) 17/9.
27   Ibid. DD/SAS (C/96) 17/9; DD/PH 27.
28   *Som. Wills*, ed. Brown, i. 78; S.R.O., DD/PH 27, 224/114, 300.
29   *V.C.H Som.* iii. 214; S.R.O., DD/PH 300; ibid. tithe award.
30   S.R.O., D/R/bw 15/1/2; Burke, *Land. Gent.* (1914), 1971.
31   *Proc. Som. Arch. Soc.* cxxiii. 63.
32   *S.R.S.* xvii. 125–6.

in the 17th century. The north porch bears the date 1622 and the initials of Henry Cheeke and his second wife Katharine. Also from the 17th century, possibly including some later work by the Phelipses, are ceiling beams in rooms at the west end, a staircase, and other fittings, and ovolo-moulded casements. There was probably some alteration in the later 18th century and a wing was added in the 20th century.[33]

Margery Lyte held *RYDON* in the early 16th century. In 1561 her son John Lyte sold it to Nicholas Halswell[34] who conveyed it to John Phelps in 1620.[35] He or another of that name died in 1678[36] and his son John sold Rydon to Andrew Moore in 1685.[37] Moore enlarged his estate at Rydon and was followed by his nephew Andrew Moore (d. 1743). Andrew's son William (d. 1768) left a widow Elizabeth,[38] who in 1792 with her then husband, the Revd. John Chaunter, settled Rydon on William Moore's nephew Hill Dawe.[39] In 1826 the Revd. Thomas Coney bought Rydon[40] which in 1984 was a county council smallholding.

In 1086 3 virgates of land were attached to the church of North Petherton. The church was in the king's hands but had formerly belonged to Peter, bishop of Chester (d. *c.* 1084).[41] The land may have been granted to John of Erleigh with the royal manor of North Petherton. The church and lands of Walter the priest were given to the canons of Buckland by William of Erleigh in the later 12th century. Walter may have held the land there as priest of the church or as heir to his father Robert and grandfather Leofric.[42] The gift was confirmed in 1186 for the support of the sisters at Buckland.[43] The priory continued in possession until the Dissolution and in 1539 the land and tithes, then known as the *RECTORY*, were let to John Worth.[44] Worth continued to hold it under the Crown[45] until his death in 1546,[46] when he was succeeded by a son of the same name. John Worth died in 1568[47] leaving his lease to his wife Margaret, who died while their son Thomas was under age.[48] William Lacey was probably lessee by 1557.[49] Alexander Popham, who was granted a reversionary lease in 1579,[50] died in 1602 and left part of the rectory estate to his wife Dulcibella.[51] His son Edward sold the rectory to William Rolfe in 1629, but subsequent litigation awarded part of the estate to Sir Peter Vanlore, Kt. and Bt. In 1639 Sir Peter assigned his share to his daughter Mary, wife of Henry Alexander, earl of Stirling. She seems to have acquired the whole by 1648, and was dead by 1659.[52] She was followed in turn by her son Henry, earl of Stirling (d. 1691), and Henry by his son Henry (d. 1739). The heirs of the last were two of his sisters, Mary, wife of

John Philips, and Judith, wife of Sir William Trumbell. Mary had three sons, Charles, Robert, and William, and Judith had one son, William. William Trumbell (d. 1760), of Easthampstead Park (Berks.), acquired the entire estate in 1743.[53] It passed to his daughter Mary (d. 1769), wife of Martin Sandys, whose daughter, also Mary, married in 1786 Arthur Hill, Viscount Fairford (d. 1801), who succeeded his father as marquess of Downshire in 1793. In 1811 Mary (cr. Baroness Sandys 1802), released the rectory to her son Arthur, marquess of Downshire (d. 1845),[54] and he in 1813 sold it to Richard King and others. King sold most of the tithes to individual landowners, retaining small plots of land in North Petherton and Moorland.[55]

In 1813 the rectory house stood in North Petherton and there was a barn and barton at Moorland.[56] The site of the house is not known. Between 1816 and 1838 Richard King or his successor, Richard Meade King, built a house, then called the Rectory[57] and in 1984 Wood Lea. It is a large, three-bayed house with a stucco front.

ECONOMIC HISTORY. AGRICULTURE. The

parish included 13 estates in 1066 of which by far the largest was the royal manor of North Petherton; that manor contained land outside the parish including what later became Chedzoy manor. On the 49 recorded ploughlands the villagers had 30½ teams and demesne holdings 13½ teams. The royal manor accounted for 30 ploughlands, but it had only 3 demesne teams compared with the 23 teams of its villagers. Newton, divided into 5 manors by 1066, totalled 9½ ploughlands in 1086, 3 of which were demesne. Of the estates whose value was given, besides the royal manor, 5 had increased in value, 4 considerably, between 1066 and 1086, but one of the Newton holdings had decreased. The royal manor accounted for 66 of the 172 inhabitants recorded. Also recorded were 151 a. of meadow, 69 a. and 2 leagues of pasture, and 30 a. of moor. Total stock comprised 325 sheep, nearly one third on the royal manor, 42 cattle of which 21 were on the Courcelles manor at North Newton, and 33 pigs, 20 on the same Newton estate, besides those on the royal manor where 20 pigmen were noted. There were 10 goats on another estate at Newton, 3 cows at Melcombe, and a cob at Hadworthy. No stock was mentioned at Shovel or on two of the manors at North Newton.[58]

By 1274 the estate of William de Plessis at North Newton, the only one to show decline in the later 11th century, had *c.* 168 a. of demesne,

33 S.R.O., DD/V/BWr 26.6.   34 Ibid. DD/S/WH 9.
35 Ibid. DD/HYD 30.
36 Ibid. D/P/pet. n 2/1/1.
37 Ibid. DD/HYD 30; DD/SAS FA 22.
38 Ibid. DD/HYD 30, 39, 49; DD/GC 24.
39 Ibid. DD/HYD 30; ibid. C/C, box 28.
40 Ibid. C/C, box 28; ibid. tithe award.
41 *V.C.H. Som.* i. 471; *V.C.H. Dors.* iii. 118.
42 *S.R.S.* xxv, pp. 1–2.   43 Ibid. p. 9.
44 P.R.O., SC 6/Hen. VIII/3137.
45 *L. & P. Hen. VIII*, xv, p. 557.
46 S.R.O., DD/BTL 29.
47 *Som. Wills*, ed. Brown, ii. 81.

48 P.R.O., C 3/52/33.
49 *Som. Incumbents*, ed. Weaver, 415.
50 S.R.O., DD/SL 25.
51 P.R.O., C 142/271, no. 149; *Som. Wills*, ed. Brown, v. 107.
52 Berks. R.O., D/ED T 208.
53 S.R.O., DD/PM 3/5; DD/SL 25.
54 Ibid. DD/SL 25; *Complete Peerage*, xi. 451; xii (i). 252–3.
55 P.R.O., CRES 38/1895; S.R.O., DD/AH 10/1; DD/SL 30; DD/S/VY 6/3; DD/BV, bundle 2.
56 P.R.O., CRES 38/1895.
57 S.R.O., T/PH/bb 3; ibid. tithe award.
58 *V.C.H. Som.* i. 435, 471–2, 484–5, 494, 511–12, 520–1.

mainly arable, worth £3 4s. 6d. and other income including aids from villein tenants worth 33s. 4d. Rents were worth £4 12s.[59] Wheat, rye, barley, oats, peas, and vetches were grown on the Woolmersdon demesne in 1298, cheese was produced, and stock sold comprised oxen, cows, and calves.[60] Oats were grown at Melcombe, wheat and oats on the royal manor; and apart from producing hay, the moors supported pigs and geese.[61] Wheat, barley, and oats were the chief crops in the earlier 14th century at Newton Plecy where seed was bought for the following year, and pasture, hay, and wood were sold.[62] By 1360 the 40-a. demesne was let and more than three quarters of the manorial income was from rents.[63] By the mid 15th century the same estate was entirely let for cash rents, and the level of rent remained almost the same until the 19th century.[64]

In the 15th century estates at Woolmersdon[65] and Chadmead[66] produced mainly rents and court profits; loss of rents at the first was usually offset by the sale of winter herbage from land which had fallen in hand. At Chadmead in the 1470s land in hand accounted for over half the estate, but sales offset the loss of rent. In 1474 a tenant there took all the land remaining in hand for a fine of 2 capons and reduced rent, pulled down old cottages, and replaced them with a single large house. Five tenants from three different families did fealty to a new lord in 1479. Shearston manor produced only rents and court profits by the early 16th century.[67]

By the 17th century most of the land outside North moor was in closes. Part of the Heathfield known as Wells Heathfield was inclosed by 1547[68] and was entirely let by 1605.[69] Other parts, known as Inner and Outer Newton Heathfields or Wroth's Heathfield,[70] were held in ½-a. and 1-a. plots until inclosure in the late 1670s.[71] Common pasture called Hurdown or Horedown belonging to Shearston manor was inclosed c. 1654.[72]

Towards the end of the 16th century sales of wood and pasture in Petherton park produced c. £150 a year, and by 1584 some of the park was enclosed and let. The average income from sales and rents between 1582 and 1585 was over £380 a year.[73] Sir Thomas Wroth agreed to compound for disafforestation in 1638.[74] By 1655 the park was divided between 11 holdings, and by 1676 between 15, all on short leases, with a total rental of £889. Four holdings were significantly larger

than the rest, and Thomas Gatcombe paid £230 a year.[75] By 1724 several of those holdings had been amalgamated, and there were four principal farms, Petherton Park, Parker's Field,[76] Impens, and Fordgate. Impens Farm is a building of the 16th or early 17th century with 17th-century plaster work and fittings including an overmantel dated 1649. A post and truss barn nearby was evidently built from oaks felled in the park during the Civil War.[77] Fordgate was recorded in 1675,[78] but the house was rebuilt c. 1812.[79]

Other houses of similar date such as the Chantry at Rhode, occupied and probably built by the Woodhouse family, and Great House in North Newton, built by Sir Thomas Wroth and his tenant, suggest by their quality the agricultural prosperity of the parish.[80] The Wroths and other owners of former Crown and monastic land such as the Bluets, Pophams, and Portmans were absentees in the early 17th century, but the Catfords of Melcombe and the Cheekes of West Newton were resident.[81] At the same time there emerged substantial tenants such as the Gatcombes, Webbers, and Woodhouses[82] who rented from the larger owners. Sir Thomas Wroth was said to hold 1,400 a. worth £1,400 a year in 1638 and during the Interregnum acquired lands worth a further £552 a year.[83] William Catford of West Melcombe (d. 1644) left goods worth over £2,600, including farm stock (£283), corn in the ground (£121), wool (£31), 543 lb. of mature cheese, c. 70 bu. of wheat and barley, and quantities of peas and malt.[84] Other 17th century inventories indicate the importance of dairying and cheesemaking; most farmers at the time kept a variety of stock and a few grew hops, leeks,[85] clover, carrots,[86] or grey, white, or blue peas.[87] The Huntworth demesne produced successive crops of wheat, barley, beans, peas, and oats between 1668 and 1672.[88]

Improvements on the Wroth estate from 1660 included the use of earth, probably clay or silt, and sand as dressing on wet land[89] and lime on sheep pasture in the park[90] and elsewhere. In 1673 two tenants were encouraged to test soap ashes instead of lime, and others were directed to plant withies by meadow ditches.[91] William Gatcombe, a tenant farmer at Huntworth, died in 1716 probably one of the wealthiest men in the parish. His goods, stock, and leasehold estate were valued for probate at over £5,200. He owned over 2,000 sheep on the moor and others elsewhere, and grew barley, wheat, beans, peas,

59 P.R.O., C 133/7, no. 4.
60 S.R.O., DD/AH 66/10.
61 Ibid. DD/SAS NP 1, mm. 1–2; Devon R.O., C.R. 1280.
62 S.R.O., DD/WM 1/103; Wells Cath. Libr., Vicars Choral MS. B/1.
63 S.R.O., DD/WM 1/113.
64 Ibid. DD/CC 121468, 131921/1.
65 Dors. R.O., D 10/M 348.
66 Ibid. M 241–3.
67 S.R.O., DD/PT, box 1.
68 Wells Cath. Libr., Vicars Choral MS. ct. bk. 1542–57.
69 Ibid. acct. bk. 1604–20.
70 Ibid. ct. bk. 1578–98.
71 Devon R.O. 1148 M/add 6/17, 7/35.
72 S.R.O., DD/PT, box 2; DD/SAS (C/96) 7/8.
73 Devon R.O. 1148 M/add 9/23.
74 Cal. S.P. Dom. 1638–9, 203.
75 Devon R.O. 1148 M/add 6/17.

76 Above, manors (Newton).
77 S.R.O., DD/V/BWr 26.8; Devon R.O. 1148 M/add 6/17.
78 S.R.O., DD/AH 8/5.
79 Devon R.O. 1148 M/add Som. estate acct. 1811–13.
80 Above, manors (Rhode, Newton Wroth).
81 Above, manors.
82 S.R.O., DD/SP inventories; DD/SAS SE 24; DD/S/WH 51, 166.
83 Devon R.O. 1148 M/add 6/17.
84 S.R.O., DD/SL 4.
85 Ibid. DD/SP inventory, 1646.
86 Ibid. 1667, 1669, 1672, 1675, 1680, 1684; DD/SAS H 47/3/34.
87 Ibid. Q/SR 112/99.
88 Ibid. DD/PM 7.
89 Devon R.O. 1148 M/add 6/17.
90 Ibid. 7/35.
91 Ibid. 6/17.

and clover. Most farms continued to be mixed in the 18th century, although some seem to have concentrated on pig-fattening, stock-breeding, and withy-growing.[92] Flax was grown around Rhode and Woolmersdon in the 1750s and 1760s,[93] and in the west part of the parish in the 1780s and 1790s.[94] Clover and turnips were produced on the large pastoral upland farm at Clavelshay,[95] and potatoes at North Newton.[96] John Kinglake (d. 1809), farming on a substantial scale from 1784, raised cattle, sheep, and horses, largely on the moors, and grew wheat, beans, barley, oats, and, after the inclosure of North moor, withies.[97]

Attempts had been made by the 13th century[98] to drain and enclose small areas of North moor, but most of the land remained subject to common rights for pasture and fuel.[99] Draught animals and other stock were grazed there in the Middle Ages,[1] and cattle and geese were grazed around Moorland in the 17th century.[2] In 1638 North moor measured 1,415 a.[3] By the mid 18th century there were between 60 and 70 cottages with gardens and orchards which were illegal encroachments.[4] The commoners were responsible for the upkeep of the main drains or brooks around the edge of North moor and in return had rights known as 'ox-shoots', for each of which they could pasture a horse, two oxen, three yearlings, or ten sheep. Commoners could also cut sedge on the moor. Improved drainage of North moor was suggested in 1770 and may have been carried out, but in 1798 the moor, the remaining common pastures at Heathfield and King's Cliff, and the greens at Rhode, Primmore, and Hedging were all inclosed and allotted.[5] In the late 18th century North moor, Stock moor, and Hay moor still remained subject to flooding, Stock moor being under water for four months each year.[6] North moor district drainage board was established in 1867 and an engine was installed at Moorland in 1868 to drain 2,500 a. of land.[7] The pump house was extended and new engines were installed in 1940–1.[8]

In 1821 two thirds of the 603 families in the parish were employed in agriculture.[9] By 1838 about half the land was arable, much of it concentrated around North Newton. Seven farms measured over 300 a., led by Clavelshay (497 a.), Park (417 a.), Boomer (312 a.), Hunt-

worth (309 a.), and Impens (302 a.). Two more, Fordgate and West Newton, were over 200 a., 10 between 100 a. and 200 a., and more than 60 others over 25 a. There were more than 135 holdings of less than 25 a., and hundreds of freeholds and leaseholds of one or two fields.[10] By 1851 Henry Paramore rented all four farms in the former park, together c. 1,300 a., and he employed at least 59 labourers, 2 master dairymen, and 2 dairymaids.[11] He was noted for his extensive manuring, and his use of fodder crops.[12] At the same date Clavelshay farm had increased to 650 a. with 40 labourers.[13] In 1881 the farm covered 800 a. and 30 men and boys were employed there. There were then dairies at Moorland and Bankland.[14]

In 1905 nearly 3,500 a. were under arable and 5,802 a. were under grass.[15] Land suitable for corn was put to grass, partly because of shortage of labour.[16] Flax was grown in the parish during the First World War,[17] and by the end of the Second World War the area was known for its peas and potatoes.[18] Wheat, oats, barley, and green crops were the chief crops in the 1930s.[19] By 1982, when arable had increased to c. 5,500 a. (2,313 ha.), wheat and barley were by far the commonest crops, with oats, maize, potatoes, rape, and fodder crops accounting for only a quarter of the area. Of the 96 holdings then making a return, 26 specialized in dairying or sheep and cattle rearing. Two holdings specialized in cereals, another 8 were mainly arable.[20]

Market gardens had been established at North Petherton, at West Newton, and near Shovel by 1851[21] and by 1881 there were many more mainly around North Newton but also at Huntworth and Rydon.[22] In 1906 there were 11 market gardeners in the North Newton area, including Tuckerton, and 8 elsewhere in North Petherton.[23] In 1982 horticultural crops, including orchards, covered at least 126 ha. (c. 302 a.) and two holdings specialized in vegetable production.[24]

Apples and cider were sold from Petherton manor in the 13th century,[25] and cider was made at Melcombe in the 1290s.[26] Gardens, fruit gardens, and orchards were distinguished from each other in the early 16th century,[27] and in the early 17th apples were tithed by a modus that varied depending on whether they were sold on

92 S.R.O., DD/SP inventories, 1713–14, 1716, 1721.
93 Ibid. D/P/pet. n 3/2/1.
94 Ibid. Q/RLh 24, 28, 35.
95 Ibid. DD/WY 197.
96 Ibid. D/P/pet. n 3/2/1.
97 Ibid. DD/X/VEA; Proc. Som. Arch. Soc. cxxix. 161–70.
98 S.R.S. xiv, p. 159; Cal. Inq. Misc. i, p. 478; Cal. Chart. R. 1327–41, 314; S.R.O., DD/SL 1.
99 S.R.S. xiv, pp. 153, 157–9; xxv, pp. 25–6; Cur. Reg. R. xv, p. 214; S.R.O., DD/SAS NP 8, mm. 2–3.
1 Cur. Reg. R. xv, p. 214; S.R.O., DD/SAS NP 1, mm. 1–5.
2 S.R.O., Q/SR 125/12; ibid. DD/SP inventories.
3 P.R.O., LR 2/202.
4 S.R.O., DD/SL 9.
5 Ibid. DD/SLM 2; DD/SLM, bk. of maps; DD/MK, inclosure map 1798; D/RA D7A.
6 Ibid. DD/AH 66/11.
7 Ibid. D/RA North moor DB 1; DD/MK 14; date on bldg.

8 S.R.O., D/RA (C/2785) North moor.
9 Census, 1821.   10 S.R.O., tithe award.
11 P.R.O., HO 107/1924.
12 Acland and Sturge, Farming of Som. (1851), 38–40.
13 P.R.O., HO 107/1924.
14 Ibid. RG 11/2369.
15 Statistics supplied by the then Bd. of Agric. (1905).
16 H. Rider Haggard, Rural Eng. (1902), i. 248–52.
17 Bridgwater Mercury, 10 July 1918.
18 S.R.O., DD/QK 143.
19 Kelly's Dir. Som. (1939).
20 Min. of Agric., Fisheries, and Food, agric. returns, 1982.
21 P.R.O., HO 107/1924.
22 Ibid. RG 11/2369.
23 Kelly's Dir. Som. (1906).
24 Min. of Agric., Fisheries, and Food, agric. returns, 1982. Returns also include St. Michaelchurch.
25 S.R.O., DD/SAS NP 1, m. 1.
26 Devon R.O., C.R. 1280.
27 S.R.S. ii. 241–2.

the tree, consumed at home, made into cider, or kept for sale later. Pears were tithed in a similar manner except wardens which were tithed in kind.[28] Tenements at Moorland in 1646 were either 'well-fruited' or had 'no great store of fruit',[29] and cider presses, apple chambers, apples, and cider were recorded in 1670 and 1675.[30] Cider was produced in quantity for sale by larger farmers,[31] of whom John Kinglake (d. 1809) also sold apple trees at Moorland and West Yeo to customers in Somerset and Devon.[32] Hopyards were recorded at Petherton Park in 1670[33] and at Woolmersdon in 1695,[34] and there was a small cherry orchard at Boomer in 1782.[35]

By 1838 there were extensive orchards at Moorland and around Huntworth, North Petherton village, and North Newton.[36] The acreage under orchard increased especially at Moorland and North Petherton village, which were almost entirely surrounded by orchards in 1887.[37] By the later 20th century new housing had reduced the acreage around North Petherton but there were large orchards at West Newton, belonging to Showerings Ltd., at Moorland, and at Petherton Park, where new orchards were laid out between Parker's Field and Park Farm.[38] In 1982 there were 68 ha. (163 a.) of commercial cider orchard.[39]

MILLS. Three mills were recorded in 1086.[40] By the 14th century there were said to be 14.[41] During the 16th century large numbers of millstones were imported through Bridgwater.[42]

The mill on the royal manor in 1086[43] was said to be worth 20s. a year in 1276.[44] It was probably the mill usually known as Baril's Mill in the early 14th century[45] and as New Mill in 1349.[46] Baril's Mill was held with Vowell's lands[47] until after 1770.[48] By 1838 it was owned by the miller.[49] Known as Petherton mills, it remained in use until c. 1920 powered by water and steam.[50] It lay on the north-east side of High Street. The pond has been filled in and the buildings have been demolished.

The mill at West Newton in 1086[51] was mentioned in the 15th century[52] and until the 1750s.[53] The mill house was recorded in 1794 but no mill,[54] and by 1810 even the house had gone.[55]

The mill was at Lower Rydon where a pond survived in 1838.[56]

The mill on the Melcombe estate in 1086[57] was probably on the later West Melcombe manor where two mills were called Kingsmills by 1349.[58] Melcombe mill was farmed in 1294[59] and was held by the lord of North Petherton manor in 1349, probably on the death of John de Reigny of Melcombe.[60] From the early 16th century until 1761 or later there were two mills called Kingsmills, probably under one roof.[61] In 1770 there was one mill, called Boomer mill,[62] which was leased to a baker in 1779[63] but had gone by 1838.[64]

The mill at Baymead was first recorded in 1549[65] and was attached to Huntworth manor. In 1747 there were two grist mills, probably under one roof;[66] from 1787 only one mill was recorded.[67] The mill was still in use as a water and steam mill in 1906 but had gone out of use by 1910.[68] It was south-east of North Petherton village and the house, called Baymead Mill, survived in 1984.

The mill attached to the manor of Buckland Fee was probably Higher Baymead Mill,[69] and may have been that belonging to North Petherton church in 1235.[70] By the 18th century there was a malt mill beside the grist mill.[71] The mill survived until 1899[72] south of the churchyard and gave its name to Mill Street. It survived as a private house called the Old Mill in 1984.

A mill near Clavelshay in the late 17th century, possibly at King's Cliff,[73] had gone by 1764.[74] It may have been Mrs. Popham's mill recorded c. 1630.[75] A mill, probably at Hulkshay, was held by the Musgraves, owners of Stamfordlands, probably in the 1630s.[76] In 1646 the waterwheel was said to stand in a cistern and was probably an overshot wheel.[77] No mill was listed at Stamfordlands in 1699[78] but the Musgraves held a mill called Poles Mill in the 1760s.[79] No later reference to it has been found.

Lower Mill near Maunsel House was recorded in 1631,[80] and its ownership descended with North Petherton manor. It was described in 1770 as lying by the canals in the grounds of Maunsel House,[81] and had gone out of use by 1838,[82] when it was used as a lodge called the

28 S.R.O., DD/SAS PR 233.   29 Ibid. DD/MVB 46.
30 Ibid. DD/SP inventories.
31 Ibid. 1714; ibid. DD/X/VEA.
32 Ibid. DD/X/VEA.
33 Devon R.O. 1148 M/add 6/17.
34 S.R.O., DD/AH 10/5.
35 Ibid. DD/S/WH 202.   36 Ibid. tithe award.
37 O.S. Map 6", Som. LXI. NE., SE. (1887 edn.).
38 Ibid. 1/50,000, ST 182 (1974 edn.).
39 Min. of Agric., Fisheries, and Food, agric. returns, 1982.
40 V.C.H. Som. i. 435, 472, 520.
41 S.R.S. xxv, pp. 13–14.
42 S.R.O., D/B/bw 1463–4, 1470–2.
43 V.C.H. Som. i. 435.   44 Cal. Close, 1272–9, 410.
45 S.R.O., DD/SAS NP 1, m. 13.
46 Ibid. 9, mm. 1–2.
47 Ibid. DD/SL 9; ibid. Q/REl 29/6; ibid. T/PH/dev 3; P.R.O., CP 25(2)/203/3 & 4 Eliz. I Mich.; above, manors.
48 S.R.O., DD/SLM, bk. of maps.
49 Ibid. tithe award.
50 P.O. Dir. Som. (1875); Kelly's Dir. Som. (1919, 1923).
51 V.C.H. Som. i. 472.
52 S.R.O., DD/SAS NP 15, m. 1.
53 Ibid. D/P/pet. n 3/2/1.   54 Ibid. DD/PH 27.
55 Ibid. DD/MY 35.   56 Ibid. tithe award.
57 V.C.H. Som. i. 520.
58 S.R.O., DD/SAS NP 9, m. 1.
59 Devon R.O., C.R. 1280.
60 S.R.O., DD/SAS NP 9, m. 1.
61 P.R.O., C 142/50, no. 154; S.R.O., DD/SL 3.
62 S.R.O., DD/SLM, bk. of maps.
63 Ibid. DD/S/WH 202.
64 Ibid. tithe award.
65 Ibid. DD/S/WH 116.
66 Ibid. DD/PM 19.   67 Ibid. 20.
68 Kelly's Dir. Som. (1906, 1910).
69 S.R.O., DD/PM 19.
70 S.R.S. xxv, pp. 25–6.
71 S.R.O., DD/PM 3/6.
72 Kelly's Dir. Som. (1899).
73 S.R.O., DD/DP 33/2, 7.
74 Ibid. DD/WY 197.
75 Ibid. T/PH/dev (add.).
76 Ibid. DD/DP 33/2.
77 Ibid. DD/SAS (C/96) 17/2.
78 Ibid. 17/18.
79 Ibid. (C/432) 33.
80 Ibid. DD/SL 10, 18; D/P/pet. n 4/1/1; ibid. T/PH/dev 3.
81 Ibid. DD/SLM, bk. of maps.
82 Ibid. tithe award.

dairy. In 1984 it was known as Dairy Mead Cottage.

Melcombe mills, attached to Melcombe Paulet manor, were recorded in 1402 when the two were let separately.[83] In 1575 one was sold as a fulling mill and was described as being near Hulkshay.[84] Later record has not been found unless it was the mill owned in the 1630s by the Musgraves.[85] The other mill was retained with the capital messuage[86] and by 1723 was described as two grist mills under one roof.[87] In 1901 there were two pairs of stones and an overshot wheel.[88] The mills were still in use in 1910 but had closed by 1914.[89] They lay south of the former capital messuage, west of North Petherton village. The mill house, known as Melcombe Farm, survived in 1984.

Moorland mill was probably in existence by 1656 when land known as Milshuts was recorded.[90] The mill was mentioned in 1670.[91] In 1684 Sir William Portman sold it to Sir Thomas Wroth[92] and in 1723 Cecily Acland owned it.[93] It was last recorded in 1808[94] and no trace survived by 1838.[95] It may have lain in the moor north-east of Fordgate.

Newton mill, attached to Newton Plecy manor, was shared by the lords of its three parts. Recorded in 1274,[96] it was rebuilt in 1356–7[97] and in 1360 repairs were made to the mill equipment.[98] The mill was let in the 15th century[99] but had fallen into disrepair by the 1480s.[1] By the late 16th century it appears to have been held with Newton Regis manor although the Wroths continued to owe suit for the mill to the Vicars Choral for their share[2] and reserved the right to have their grain ground free for two weeks every year.[3] A new mill brook was ordered to be made in 1799.[4] The mill remained in use until 1906 with the aid of steam power and was later converted to diesel power. It went out of use c. 1945.[5] The mill lay immediately south of Newton chapel, where Mill House and the mill brook survive.

There was a mill in Petherton park in the 1670s.[6] It had gone by 1838, but the field name Mill close survived south of Park Farm.[7] A mill at Shearston, perhaps existing in the 14th century,[8] in 1547 belonged to the chapel there.[9] It may have lain north of the hamlet where the name Haggots Pool survived in 1770.[10]

WOODLAND. Petherton park was well wooded and grants of timber, mostly oak but also alder, maple, hazel, and thorn,[11] were regularly made from the early 13th century for building works at Bridgwater[12] and Stogursey[13] castles, Somerton gaol,[14] Cleeve and Glastonbury abbeys,[15] Buckland priory,[16] the houses of the friars in Bridgwater and Ilchester,[17] and Somerton and Bridgwater churches.[18] Wood for fuel was supplied to Buckland priory from 1228 until the Dissolution, and sales of timber provided a steady income,[19] up to £200 a year in the 1580s,[20] but c. 140 of the best oaks were destroyed during the Civil War.[21]

Wood was sold from Woolmersdon in the 13th century,[22] and from North moor and Newton Plecy in the 14th.[23] In 1510 the abbot of Athelney and John Sydenham were said to have forged a lease of 100 a. of wood at Clavelshay in Clavelshay and Halsey woods,[24] but by 1544 the two woods together had shrunk to 15 a.,[25] the rest probably being converted to pasture.[26] Small oaks were being sold from Woolmersdon in 1635[27] and planting of oak, ash, and elm was encouraged at Hadworthy in 1668.[28] Elsewhere many of the old woods had been cleared for arable, meadow, and pasture land by the late 17th century[29] and field names at Melcombe, Rhode, Shovel, Clavelshay, and West Newton indicate their position.[30] By the late 18th century there were no woods or coppices on North Petherton manor and the timber on the moors was said to be of no value.[31] In 1791 hedgerow trees may have given North Petherton the appearance of being in 'a woody flat',[32] but there were only 73 a. of woodland in 1838, mainly at King's Cliff, with a few small coppices and plantations at Clavelshay, established after 1764, and near the larger houses of the parish.[33] By 1905 woodland had increased to over 166 a.[34] and during the 1920s there was considerable planting of both hardwoods and conifers on the Portman estate at Clavelshay and King's Cliff.[35]

83 *S.R.S.* xxii. 11.
84 S.R.O., DD/DP 33/2.
85 Above (this section).
86 S.R.O., DD/X/SR 5.
87 Ibid. DD/CH 73/2.
88 Ibid. DD/DHR, box 15.
89 *Kelly's Dir. Som.* (1910, 1914).
90 S.R.O., T/PH/dev 3.
91 Devon R.O. 1148 M/add 6/17.
92 S.R.O., DD/PM 19.
93 Ibid. DD/AH 1/3.
94 Devon R.O. 1148 M/add 1/61.
95 S.R.O., tithe award.
96 P.R.O., C 133/7, no. 4.
97 Wells Cath. Libr., Vicars Choral MS. B/2.
98 S.R.O., DD/WM 1/113.
99 Ibid. DD/CC 131912A/6; Wells Cath. Libr., Vicars Choral MS. VI/58.
1 Wells Cath. Libr., Vicars Choral MS. C/10.
2 S.R.O., DD/CC 110016, 116013; Devon R.O. 1148 M/add 2/71B.
3 Devon R.O. 1148 M/add 6/17; *S.D.N.Q.* vi. 68.
4 S.R.O., DD/SLM 2.
5 *Kelly's Dir. Som.* (1906); local inf.
6 Devon R.O. 1148 M/add 6/17.
7 S.R.O., tithe award.

8 *S.R.S.* iii. 243.   9 Ibid. ii. 238.
10 S.R.O., DD/SLM, bk. of maps.
11 *S.R.S.* xxv, pp. 32–3; P.R.O., C 260/154, no. 11.
12 *Rot. Litt. Claus.* (Rec. Com.), i. 274; ii. 506, 533.
13 *Cal. Close*, 1302–7, 121.   14 Ibid. 160.
15 *Close R.* 1231–4, 77; *V.C.H. Som.* ii. 554.
16 *Close R.* 1227–31, 402; 1234–7, 282.
17 Ibid. 1247–51, 312; 1256–9, 221; *V.C.H. Som.* ii. 554.
18 *S.R.S.* xlviii, p. 163; liii, p. 189; *V.C.H. Som.* ii. 554.
19 *Pat. R.* 1226–32, 199; P.R.O., SC 6/973/23.
20 Devon R.O. 1148 M/add 9/23.
21 Ibid. 6/17.
22 *S.R.S.* xi, p. 357.
23 S.R.O., DD/SAS NP 1, m. 7; DD/WM 1/113.
24 P.R.O., C 1/463/62.
25 *L. & P. Hen. VIII*, xix (2), p. 313.
26 S.R.O., DD/WY 197.
27 Devon R.O. 1148 M/add 9/22.
28 S.R.O., DD/AH 8/3.
29 e.g. Devon R.O. 1148 M/add 6/17.
30 S.R.O., tithe award.
31 Ibid. DD/SL 9.
32 Collinson, *Hist. Som.* iii. 54.
33 S.R.O., tithe award; ibid. DD/WY 197.
34 Statistics supplied by the then Bd. of Agric. (1905).
35 P.R.O., CRES 35/1150.

MARKETS AND FAIRS. In 1318 John of Erleigh was granted a weekly market on Saturdays and a three-day fair from 7 September.[36] The market, its day changed to Tuesday in 1536,[37] may have survived until the late 18th century, but had ceased by 1830 when it was said to have been large, mainly for corn.[38]

In 1556 Sir Roger Bluet was allowed, despite opposition from Bridgwater,[39] to change the fair date to 30 April, also for three days, and to receive stallage, picage, tolls, customs, and profits from the piepowder court.[40] By 1798 a second fair was being held on the Monday before 13 November.[41] In the late 18th and early 19th century the spring fair, held on 1 May, was attended by graziers looking for lean stock to fatten.[42] It survived until the late 19th century and was then noted for shoes.[43]

TRADE AND INDUSTRY. The position of the parish on both the road and the river between Bridgwater and Taunton was of significance in its economic development. Heavy carts were using the road in the later 13th century[44] and traders then and later had stalls in both Bridgwater[45] and Taunton.[46] By the 16th century local carriers such as the Ash and Nation families, Arthur Bidgood, and Mr. Glasse brought in a wide range of goods, including cargoes from London,[47] some of which were taken up river by traders from Moorland to Hook, probably near Burrow Bridge.[48] The river and the road carried a slightly narrower range of goods in the 17th century,[49] and by then several people had shares in river craft.[50] The canal, opened in 1827, brought an increase in business. By 1851 more than 40 boatmen lived at Moorland and along the canal between Fordgate and the old basin at Huntworth.[51] Barge traffic was dominated by a few families such as the Meades, who occupied cottages called Meades Buildings,[52] and the Goodland family of Moorland.[53] Business along the river and canal had ended by the late 19th century.[54]

Cloth was made in the parish in the 15th century[55] and many craftsmen were employed in the 17th and 18th centuries.[56] The main product was serge, but a clothier had 140 lb. of worsted wool put out to spinners in 1640.[57] A man described as a worsted comber in 1680 had at his death yarn, wool, three looms, and a shop full of mercery wares.[58] There were four weavers in North Newton in 1667[59] and elsewhere weavers, several with more than one loom, combined their craft with farming, brewing, or cidermaking.[60] Many had servants or apprentices.[61] Cloth finishing seems to have been less important: woad was imported in the 16th and 17th centuries,[62] but Dyer's Green on the North Newton road and Dye House meadow near Mill Street are the only direct evidence of dyeing and only two field names indicated cloth racking.[63]

Leather production had been established by the 1630s,[64] and there was a tanner in North Newton in 1667 and a tanhouse at Primmore in 1677.[65] Skins polluted the water supply in North Petherton village in 1707[66] and there was a tanhouse at Maunsel during the 18th century.[67] A fellmonger in 1731 left 700 pellskins, 65 dozen hides of white and tan leather, and 54 horse, dog, sheep, and calf skins.[68]

Malting was practised widely from the 17th century.[69] A malthouse stood in Hammet Street in 1816[70] and in 1838 there were others in Mill Street, at Petherton mill, and two in Fore Street.[71] Samuel Burston, in business in Hammet Street between 1830 and 1854, supplied malt to Bristol and Taunton.[72] A brewery developed from Thomas Starkey's Fore Street malting and by 1871 employed 20 men.[73] By 1898 Starkey and Co. owned the brewery and two malthouses in Fore Street and seven public houses in the parish.[74] Starkey, Knight, Ford, and Co. continued to brew in the parish until c. 1906 when they opened their brewery in Bridgwater.[75]

The planting of withies on the moors after inclosure[76] introduced commercial basketmaking. In 1830 there were 2 basketmakers in the parish,[77] 5 by 1840,[78] and at least 6 in 1851, 2 of whom employed 11 men between them.[79] Numbers declined in the 20th century, but there

36 Cal. Chart. R. 1300–26, 395.
37 Cal. Pat. 1555–7, p. 279.
38 Pigot, Nat. Com. Dir. (1830).
39 S.R.O., D/B/bw 1839.
40 Cal. Pat. 1555–7, p. 279.
41 S.R.O., DD/X/VEA; P.O. Dir. Som. (1859).
42 Billingsley, Agric. of Som. (1797), 245; S.R.O., DD/X/VEA.
43 Proc. Som. Arch. Soc. lxxxii. 139.
44 S.R.S. xli. 99.
45 Ibid. xlviii, no. 29; S.R.O., D/B/bw 1433.
46 S.R.O., DD/SP inventory, 1697.
47 Ibid. D/B/bw 1436–40, 1462–4, 1470–2, 1480–3, 1488–9.
48 Ibid. 1472, 1493; ibid. Q/SR 14/3.
49 Ibid. D/B/bw 1497–8, 1503–4, 1506–7.
50 Ibid. DD/SP inventories, 1683, 1691, 1693.
51 P.R.O., HO 107/1924; above, intro.
52 P.R.O., RG 10/2381; O.S. Map 6", Som. LXI. NE., SE. (1887 edn.). The cottages were on the site of the Boat and Anchor.
53 S.R.O., 'The Family of Goodland' (TS. n.d.).
54 The last commercial journey from Bridgwater (to Stoke St. Gregory) was made in 1895: E. Hembrow, Winter Harvest, 19.
55 S.R.S. xvi. 327.
56 S.R.O., DD/SP inventories; DD/SAS (C/96) 17/3; DD/SAS (C/432) 13; DD/PM 18–20; ibid. Q/SR 114/45, 120/9, 137/7.
57 Ibid. DD/SP inventory, 1640.
58 Ibid. 1680.   59 Ibid. DD/WY 34.
60 Ibid. DD/SP inventories, 1662, 1666, 1670, 1680, 1687; ibid. Q/SR 220/4.
61 Ibid. Q/SR 114/45, 234/3.
62 Ibid. D/B/bw 1460, 1503–4.
63 Ibid. tithe award; ibid. DD/PM 20; Devon R.O. 1148 M/add 2/71B.
64 Proc. Som. Arch. Soc. cxii. 66.
65 S.R.O., DD/WY 34; DD/DP 93/7.
66 B.L. Add. Ch. 71735.
67 S.R.O., DD/SL 10; DD/SLM 2.
68 Ibid. DD/SP inventory, 1731.
69 Ibid. 1666; DD/X/VEA; ibid. Q/SR 220/4.
70 Ibid. DD/CH 73/2.   71 Ibid. tithe award.
72 Ibid. DD/X/BRS; Pigot, Nat. Com. Dir. (1830); P.R.O., HO 107/1924.
73 Pigot, Nat. Com. Dir. (1830); P.O. Dir. Som. (1859, 1861); Morris & Co. Dir. Som. (1872); S.R.O., tithe award; P.R.O., RG 10/2381.
74 P.R.O., RG 11/2369; S.R.O., D/R/bw 16/11/1.
75 S.R.O., D/R/bw 15/3/18, 16/11/8; Kelly's Dir. Som. (1906).
76 e.g. S.R.O., DD/X/VEA.
77 Pigot, Nat. Com. Dir. (1830).
78 Co. Gaz. Dir. Som. (1840).
79 P.R.O., HO 107/1924.

was also a manufacturer of wicker furniture.[80] Withies were still processed in the parish in the early 1940s.[81]

Bricks were made in the southern part of Petherton park in 1670.[82] By 1838 two small brickyards had been established, one on either side of the Parrett near the canal basin, one of which was also a tileworks, and a third was in business by the river south of Moorland.[83] By 1851 William Symons had opened his yard and employed at least 17 men from the parish; there was also a drainage-pipe maker.[84] By 1859 Fursland and Co. and Colthurst, Symons, and Co. were the leading brickmakers.[85] In 1877 Thomas Colthurst took a new lease from Lord Portman of the brickyard, including kilns, manager's house, and cottages, and various fields at an increasing rent with a charge of £60 an acre for digging clay. He was required to fill the clay pits at the end of the term.[86] By 1881 large numbers were employed, 85 by one manufacturer.[87] The largest yard was the Crossway Brick and Tile Works of Colthurst, Symons, and Co. which won international medals.[88] By 1887 there were three yards, Crossway, Fursland's Somerset Yard, and New Yard.[89] New Yard was held by William Symons in 1898, when another yard across the Parrett was worked by the Somerset Trading Co. of Bridgwater.[90] In the early 20th century the industry declined and most yards closed.

There were several shops in the parish in the 17th century. In 1629 two men were licensed to sell wine and tobacco[91] and in 1669 Thomas Hooper kept a shop selling small wares.[92] Several craftsmen had retail shops including a shoemaker of North Newton who had two, one to sell his own products, the other a 'ware' shop stocked with fruit, sugar, tobacco, and brandy.[93] An apothecary kept a shop in the parish in 1681 and his inventory recorded books on physic.[94] Thomas Win or Wright (d. 1713), a blacksmith, left 2 anvils, 100 new horse shoes, 2,020 lb. of old and new iron, 17½ lb. of new steel, 2 dozen pig rings, and tools of every kind, some for his own use and others, including scythes, shears, hatchets, and shovels, for sale. Nearly £200 was owed him. He kept a flock of sheep, some cattle, and probably pigs as he had 340 lb. of bacon.[95] More modest craftsmen included a wheelwright at Shearston in 1672[96] and a mason working lias in 1675.[97] Craftsmen in the 18th-century included a soap-boiler and a roper.[98] Other crafts in the late 18th and early 19th century included coopering and mop making.[99] In 1840 there were milliners, a cabinet maker, a clockmaker, a hairdresser, and saddlers.[1] There were many shops in North Petherton village by the early 19th century and several wine and spirit merchants.[2] One man in 1839 was a saddler and harness manufacturer, grocer, tea dealer, linen draper, hosier, and haberdasher.[3] In 1840 there were 9 grocers, 5 bakers, 4 butchers, and a confectioner.[4] In 1851 North Petherton village had a clock and watchmaker, a tinman and brazier, straw bonnet makers, shirt and stay makers, glovers, saddlers, a glass and china man, a cheese and bacon factor, confectioners, bakers, butchers, fruiterers, grocers, and linen drapers. Most of the other settlements in the parish had their own shops, smithies, and craftsmen. Huntworth had a shopkeeper and an ironmonger; there were a shopkeeper, a baker, and three butchers at Moorland; a grocer, a shopkeeper, three bakers, and three butchers at North Newton, and a fruit dealer at Shearston. A portrait painter and a barm dealer lived at Compass and there was a veterinary surgeon at Hedging. A master machine maker was recorded at North Newton and a foundry at Hedging.[5] By 1859 there were a chemist and a stationer in North Petherton village[6] and by 1872 the portrait painter was also taking photographs.[7] By 1906 there was a coach and carriage business at North Newton.[8] Although shops disappeared from the smaller settlements a variety of shops and small businesses survived in North Petherton village in 1984 including a plastics engineering firm.

LOCAL GOVERNMENT. The parish was divided into a number of tithings. The borough was possibly the tithing of North Petherton recorded in 1242–3, and was later represented by Denizen or Town Denizen tithing.[9] Buckland fee tithing was also recorded in 1242–3 as the Hospitallers' jurisdiction.[10] Newton Plecy tithing, apparently the same as North Newton and in Freemanors hundred,[11] was recorded in 1396 along with Huntworth and West Newton tithings. Shearston, Tuckerton (sometimes Tuckerton and Hedging), and Woolmersdon tithings were recorded from the early 15th century.[12] The part of North Petherton village that was in Andersfield hundred in the 1670s[13] probably formed a separate tithing then as in 1841 when it was known as Petherton limit.[14] Tithings called Moorland and

80 S.R.O., D/R/bw 22/1/39; *Kelly's Dir. Som.* (1906, 1939).
81 S.R.O., D/RA (C/2785) North moor, min. bk.
82 Devon R.O. 1148 M/add 6/17.
83 S.R.O., tithe award.
84 P.R.O., HO 107/1924.
85 *P.O. Dir. Som.* (1859).
86 S.R.O., DD/CN 34/3.
87 P.R.O., RG 11/2369.
88 S.R.O., DD/CN 34/3.
89 O.S. Map 6", Som. L. SE. (1887 edn.).
90 S.R.O., D/R/bw 16/11/1.
91 *S.D.N.Q.* viii. 88.
92 S.R.O., Q/SR 112/57.
93 Ibid. DD/SP inventory, 1688.
94 Ibid. 1681.
95 Ibid. 1713.
96 Ibid. 1672.
97 Ibid. 1675.
98 Ibid. DD/PM 3/6; DD/FD 20.
99 Dwelly, *Par. Rec.* xii.
1 *Co. Gaz. Dir. Som.* (1840).
2 Pigot, *Nat. Com. Dir.* (1830).
3 S.R.O., D/P/pet. n 4/1/4.
4 *Co. Gaz. Dir. Som.* (1840).
5 P.R.O., HO 107/1924.
6 *P.O. Dir. Som.* (1859).
7 Morris & Co. *Dir. Som.* (1872).
8 *Kelly's Dir. Som.* (1906).
9 *S.R.S.* xi, p. 301; xx. 127–32; above, borough.
10 *S.R.S.* xi, p. 298; xxviii. 128.
11 *V.C.H. Som.* v. 10–11.
12 S.R.O., DD/AH 11/9; DD/SAS NP 15, mm. 6d. and 7.
13 Dwelly, *Hearth Tax*, ii. 44.
14 *S.R.S.* iii. 327.

Bankland had been formed by 1766,[15] following the growth of settlement in North moor.

North moor was administered by a moorward until the end of the 18th century.[16] Henry of Erleigh, lord of North Petherton, granted the hereditary office of moorward to Philip Maunsel in the mid 13th century.[17] The office, held with Maunsel manor, was usually exercised by deputy, who accounted for issues of the moor, collected grazing rents, and presumably supervised the regular chase or drive of the moor.[18]

A borough court, described as a portmote between 1308 and 1331,[19] and later simply as a court, was held monthly in the 1390s,[20] but no reference to it has been found after 1399. A portreeve was in office in 1293[21] and from 1299 until 1399 or later two borough reeves.[22] In the 1390s there was also a catchpole.[23]

Court rolls for the inner (*intrinsecus*) hundred or the manor of North Petherton survive for the years 1296, 1332–3, 1349–50, 1382, 1389–90, 1397–8, 1401, 1417, 1420, 1431–3, 1484,[24] and for 1653.[25] Seven sessions were held in 1293–4,[26] and between 10 and 14 each year in the period 1386–9.[27] Leets with view of frankpledge were held twice a year. The officers of the court were a bailiff and a clerk shared with the foreign hundred, and in 1397–8 an aletaster.[28] Business included civil pleas, tenures, and orders for roads, bridges, and rhynes, and the court maintained a pillory and held prisoners.[29] There was a court house in 1290. A new hall was built there in 1304–5, part of which was let in 1328–9.[30] Courts leet for the inner hundred were held each autumn between 1767 and 1779. The court appointed constables and tithingmen, and presentments included encroachments on manorial waste and the lord's failure to erect gateposts and to maintain stocks and pillory.[31]

Each part of Newton manor seems to have exercised leet jurisdiction. A record of one meeting for Newton Plecy survives for 1398.[32] A court was held in the 'largest and fittest lower room' at Parker's Field in the 17th century.[33] A court was also held for Newton Wroth manor, usually twice a year in the 1630s.[34] By the 18th century Newton Wroth and Newton Regis were administered together, and shared a court leet every other year, alternating with the court for Newton Chantry and sharing some profits and a pound.[35]

Court rolls for Newton Chantry manor survive

for various years between 1453 and 1610,[36] for 1613–38,[37] 1661–5,[38] and for most years 1689–1864.[39] There are presentments for every alternate year from 1794 to 1864.[40] In the mid 15th century the leet, view of frankpledge, and halimote were held twice a year, the halimote on the same day as the presentment of the homage but separately from it. In the 18th century only the leet and view were held, and by the end of the century presentments were made every other year.[41] A court baron for property transactions was held by the vicars choral at Wells twice a year in the 17th century.[42] The leet appointed tithingmen and reeves in the 15th century,[43] and surveyors were recorded in 1589 and 1619.[44] In the 18th century two constables assisted the reeve and tithingmen, then chosen in rotation by tenement.[45] A pound keeper was appointed in 1816 and a hayward from 1826. In the 15th century courts dealt with breaches of assizes and nuisances. In the 16th and 17th centuries the court made orders to control animals, prevent flooding, and repair buildings and hedges. In the 16th century the vicars choral of Wells, as lords of the manor, were said to have built an alehouse and stables for holding court, and they provided stocks, cucking stool, and pillory.[46] A reeve's dinner was held at Michaelmas 1661.[47] By the 18th century tenants of ten holdings in rotation provided accommodation for the court.[48]

Court rolls for Chadmead manor survive for various years between 1441 and 1485. The court normally met once a year, at Michaelmas or in early summer. Officers included a steward, bailiff, and rent collector.[49] There is a record of one court for Hulkshay in 1511.[50] The manors of Huntworth and Buckland Fee were administered together by the 18th century but court rolls survive only for 1728. The court appointed a tithingman for Buckland Fee and the leet jury were entitled to a dinner or 4d. in lieu. Buckland Fee had its own pound.[51] In 1611 a court for the Halswells' manors of West Melcombe and Moorland was held with that for Woolmersdon and Hadworthy.[52] Rhode and Shearston shared manorial officers but each had its own homage and records. Court rolls survive for 1519, 1530,[53] 1553–4,[54] 1559, and 1562–72,[55] and the court dealt with property transactions and nuisances.[56] For West Newton manor copies of court rolls survive from 1558, 1619, and 1631[57] and a court was held in 1798.[58] There was a pound at West

15 S.R.O., DD/SL 9 (1776).
16 Ibid. DD/SL 1; DD/SLM 2.
17 Ibid. DD/SL 1, 10; DD/SLM 2.
18 Ibid. DD/SAS NP 1, m. 12; 2, m. 4, 7.
19 Ibid. 1, m. 14; 2, m. 6.   20 Ibid. 6, m. 1.
21 P.R.O., E 326/7512.
22 S.R.O., DD/SAS NP 1, m. 5; 6, m. 4.
23 Ibid. 5, mm. 4, 6.   24 Ibid. 8–15.
25 Ibid. DD/PM 7.   26 Devon R.O., C.R. 1280.
27 S.R.O., DD/SAS NP 4, mm. 1, 8.
28 Ibid. 12, mm. 3–6.   29 Ibid. 1.
30 Ibid. 1, mm. 1, 8–12, 14–15.   31 Ibid. DD/SL 9.
32 P.R.O., SC 2/200/13, m. 4.
33 Devon R.O. 1148 M/add 7/35.   34 Ibid. 9/22.
35 S.R.O., DD/AH 21/2; DD/CC 116001; Bodl. MS. Rawl. D. 1481, ff. 88–90.
36 Wells Cath. Libr., Vicars Choral MS. C/6–7, 10–11, 17, 25, 28, 79–81; VI/58; ibid. ct. bks.; S.R.O., DD/CC 131909/22; 131912A/4, 6; 131913A/6; 131921/1.
37 Wells Cath. Libr., Vicars Choral MS. ct. bks.; C/85, 92–3.
38 Ibid. C/97.   39 S.R.O., DD/CC 110015–17.
40 Ibid. 116001.   41 Ibid. 110015, 116001.
42 Ibid. 110015–17.
43 Ibid. 131912A/6; Wells Cath. Libr., Vicars Choral MS. C/6.
44 Wells Cath. Libr., Vicars Choral MS. C/85; ct. bk. 1578–98.
45 S.R.O., DD/CC 110015 (1736, 1742).
46 Ibid. DD/AH 21/2.
47 Wells Cath. Libr., Vicars Choral MS. C/97.
48 Ibid. lease bks.
49 Dors. R.O., D 10/M 241–3.
50 S.R.O., DD/AH 11/9.
51 Ibid. DD/PM 19.
52 Ibid. DD/S/WH 211.
53 Ibid. DD/PT, box 1.
54 Ibid. DD/SS 1.
55 Ibid. DD/PT, box 1; DD/SS 1.
56 Ibid. DD/PT, box 1.   57 Ibid. DD/MI 5.
58 Ibid. DD/PH 153.

Newton in 1800.[59] At Woolmersdon the Pokeswells employed a steward in 1445–6.[60] The Halswells and their heirs held courts for their share of the manor of Woolmersdon and Hadworthy during the 17th and 18th centuries: in 1611 a court was held jointly with courts for Moorland and West Melcombe. Each manor had its own jury and a separate record.[61] Rolls for the court baron of the Verneys' manor of Woolmersdon survive for 1382, 1508, 1511, and 1516.[62] There were manorial courts from the 16th to the 18th century for Buckland Sororum, Chadmead,[63] and the Sydenhams' manor of North Petherton.[64] Suit of court was owed by tenants of Clavelshay,[65] Maunsel,[66] West Melcombe, where courts were held twice a year,[67] three of the Moorland estates,[68] and Shearston Chantry.[69] A court was held twice a year for Stamfordlands manor in the 17th century[70] and Bankland tenants attended a court at Lyng 1741–6.[71]

A forest court or swanimote was held for Petherton park twice a year and there are court rolls for 1396–8 and 1400.[72] The court had two verderers, four foresters, and a jury of regarders. The court was attended by the moorward of North moor and the tithingmen and their attendants from Huntworth, Newton Plecy, West Newton, Durston, and Lyng.[73]

Strong parochial administration emerged in the 17th century when the parish was divided between Town, South, and Moorland each with its own officers. There were three churchwardens until the 19th century, assisted by three sidesmen,[74] and normally three overseers.[75] The division of the parish into three was used by the waywardens in the 17th century, but between then and the early 19th century the waywardens reorganized their areas three times.[76] In 1843 the parish appointed 22 constables for 11 divisions.[77] An Easter vestry had been established by 1671,[78] and in 1718 a parish meeting held in the chancel of the parish church drew up a list of orders for parish government, church maintenance, and poor relief. Among particular concerns were unlicensed alehouses, strangers, unemployed dependents, and drunkenness on and around May Day.[79] By the early 19th century the vestry met about four times a year and additionally to bind out apprentices. In 1811 a clerk was appointed, in 1816 an inspector-general of accounts, and in 1819 an assistant overseer.[80] By 1823 a select vestry was formed.[81] In 1846 a collector of taxes

was employed and in 1850 the salaries of officers including the sexton and the clerk were burdensome and had to be reduced.[82] A burial board was appointed in 1855 after the virtual closure of the churchyard,[83] and Heathfield cemetery was opened in 1856.[84] A police station was established in 1860.[85] A parish council, created in 1894, met in private and appointed overseers and waywardens.[86] Parish meetings discussed general concerns such as street lighting and the council set up committees for lighting and fire-fighting. In 1912 fire inspectors were appointed and in 1917 a corps of firemen was established for Moorland and Somerset Bridge.[87] A town council, headed by a town mayor, replaced the parish council in 1974.

Poor relief in the 18th century divided regular recipients, described as in the calendar, from the rest.[88] The vestry in 1718 attempted to reduce costs by fixing maximum prices for supplies and funerals and by refusing to employ a surgeon except for fractures 'or such extraordinary occasion'.[89] Money was given in 1625 and 1698 towards building a workhouse,[90] and one was built in 1737–8, probably in High Street near Tappers Lane.[91] Until then the only lodging for paupers was probably the former church house,[92] known by 1709 as the poorhouse. It was evidently rebuilt, on the same site west of the church, in 1720, and was maintained by the wardens and overseers.[93] It was apparently abandoned after 1738. In the 18th century inmates of the workhouse were supplied with a wide variety of food, fuel, and clothing, and kept a pig.[94] In the early 19th century the governor farmed the poor for a small salary and 3s. 6d. per head a day.[95] In 1831 the workhouse was enlarged to house the assistant overseer,[96] and from 1836 to 1838, following the creation of the Bridgwater poor-law union, it was used as an annexe, where inmates were allegedly ill-treated, and for illegitimate children.[97] It may have been sold after 1838[98] and by 1851 it was divided into nine dwellings.[99] It may have been the almshouse recorded in 1871.[1]

The parish became part of the Bridgwater rural district in 1894 and of Sedgemoor district in 1974.[2]

CHURCHES. North Petherton church was probably a minster of royal foundation. Chedzoy, Pawlett, and probably St. Michaelchurch

59 Ibid. 169.   60 Dors. R.O., D 10/M 245, 348.
61 S.R.O., DD/S/WH 168, 211.
62 Ibid. DD/AH 11/9–10, 66/9.   63 Ibid. 22/13, 24/11.
64 Ibid. DD/SAS BK 87.   65 Ibid. DD/PM 3/2; 20.
66 Ibid. DD/MI 5; DD/SL 20.
67 Ibid. DD/S/WH 26–7.
68 Ibid. 166; DD/MVB 41; DD/SAS (C/96) 17/17.
69 Ibid. DD/SL 15.   70 Ibid. DD/SAS (C/96) 17/2.
71 Ibid. DD/AH 22/13, 24/11.
72 P.R.O., SC 2/200/13; SC 6/1113/14.
73 Ibid. SC 2/200/13.
74 S.R.O., D/P/pet. n 4/1/1–3; D/D/Rg 279.
75 Devon R.O. 1148 M/add 17/1/3; S.R.O., D/P/pet. n 13/2/1.
76 S.R.O., T/PH/dev 3; ibid. DD/SP 364; D/P/pet. n 9/1/3; 13/2/1, 3.
77 Ibid. D/P/pet. n 9/1/3.
78 Ibid. 4/1/1.   79 Ibid. 13/2/1.
80 Ibid. 9/1/1, 13/1/1.   81 Ibid. 9/1/2.

82 Ibid. 9/1/3.   83 Ibid. 3/5/3, 9/1/3.
84 Ibid. 3/5/4, 9/4/5; D/PC/pet. n 4/1/11.
85 Ibid. Q/AP 44; P.O. Dir. Som. (1861).
86 S.R.O., D/PC/pet. n 1/2/1.
87 Ibid. 1/2/1–2; 5/1/1.
88 Ibid. D/P/pet. n 13/2/1–18.   89 Ibid. 13/2/1.
90 Ibid. DD/BV 5; DD/X/SR 5.
91 Ibid. DD/SL 9; P.R.O., HO 107/1920.
92 Below, churches.
93 S.R.O., D/P/pet. n 4/1/2, 13/2/1.
94 Ibid. 13/2/7–8.
95 Ibid. 9/1/1, 13/1/1, 13/2/7–8, 13.
96 Ibid. 9/1/2, 13/2/18.
97 Ibid. DD/X/BUSH; L.J. lxx. 332, 403; Rep. Sel. Cttee. on Poor Law, H.L. (1837–8), xix (i–ii) passim.
98 S.R.O., D/P/pet. n 9/1/3, 13/2/18.
99 P.R.O., HO 107/1934.
1 Ibid. RG 10/2381.
2 Youngs, Local Admin. Units, i. 673, 676.

were in origin dependent upon it.[3] Peter, the king's clerk, afterwards bishop of Chester, held the church in 1066, and his nephew Ranulph succeeded to the income from the church on Peter's death c. 1084.[4] King Stephen gave a church that was either North or South Petherton to Wells cathedral,[5] but William of Erleigh included the church in his foundation grant to Buckland priory.[6] Vicars seem to have been appointed before 1186, and a vicarage was endowed probably by the end of the century.[7] The ecclesiastical parish, which in 1186 included five dependent chapelries,[8] was reduced in the 19th century by the formation of the parishes of North Newton and Moorland; the livings of North Petherton and Moorland were united in 1976.[9]

The advowson belonged to the Hospitallers by virtue of the grant to Buckland priory until the Dissolution and then to the Crown. Richard Ware presented in 1546. By 1557 the patron was William Lacey of Hartrow in Stogumber, possibly as a Crown lessee. Robert and John Musgrave and Alexander Popham presented in 1598 and the Crown in 1613.[10] In 1618 the advowson was held by Edward Popham, owner of the rectory.[11] The Laceys, however, apparently acquired it by 1624[12] and it descended with Hartrow manor until the late 18th century.[13] Peter Hoskins, possibly a trustee or lessee, presented in 1662 and the bishop by lapse in 1715. In 1780 the patron was Betty Wood who presented John Wood, possibly her husband.[14] After 1797 the vicar, Joseph Aldridge, acquired the advowson[15] which passed by purchase or descent to successive vicars or their relatives until the 1890s.[16] In 1906 the patronage was held by A. M. Hertzberg, rector of Ashton-on-Mersey (Ches.), in 1914 by Mrs. Boyd, and from 1919 by the Pascoe family.[17] From 1931 the patronage was vested in Miss Pascoe's trustees, and from 1984 in Dr. John Addy.[18]

In the late 12th century the vicar received £39 2s. a year, out of which he owed a pension of £3 6s. 8d. to Buckland priory and presumably had to find two chaplains at the mother church and at two dependent chapels.[19] The living was valued at £7 in 1291, £3 6s. 8d. in 1295,[20] more than £27 net in 1535, less than £22 in 1547,[21] c. £80 in 1668,[22] and £520 in 1804.[23] In the late 12th century the vicar received all offerings due

to the parish church and its chapels, all small tithes, and an allowance of hay from Buckland priory.[24] In 1804 the vicar took some tithes in kind.[25] In 1838 his tithes were commuted for £893 16s. 3d. and the lay impropriators of grain and hay tithes received £1,179 3s. 1d. between them. The total tithe rent charge on the parish was £2,146 6s. 10d.[26]

Early in the 13th century the vicar had an inn (hospicium) called Caldocum, a garden, and a vineyard.[27] The vicarage house was mentioned in 1606.[28] In 1613 it included a hall, parlour, kitchen, and buttery, with two outhouses and 1 a. of garden.[29] A few years later it was described as a mansion with 5 upper chambers and 2 studies, a brewhouse, and a stable.[30] In the late 18th century many alterations were made to the house and in 1797 a new parlour was completed 'at great expense'.[31] In 1804, however, the house was described as ruinous and the vicar's income was said to be insufficient to repair it. It was sold in the same year.[32] The Old Vicarage south of the church is a late 16th- or early 17th-century house reconstructed and enlarged in Gothick style in the 19th century. There are remains of a framed ceiling at the north end.[33] A large house in Fore Street that replaced the vicarage was described in 1804 as newly built on the site of three dwellings.[34] In 1834 it was enlarged and improved,[35] and was sold c. 1965. It lies on the north side of Fore Street opposite the Swan inn and is a four-bayed, late 18th-century house with a front to the road of the 1830s. The Dower House adjoining the Old Vicarage became the vicar's residence c. 1965.[36]

There were two anniversary chaplains in 1450, probably serving the chantries.[37] A chantry of St. Mary within the parish church had been established by 1356.[38] Sir William Paulet was patron in 1461, which suggests a link with Melcombe Paulet manor. Its altar may have been in the south or Melcombe aisle.[39] In 1535 the priest's stipend was £6[40] and when the chantry was dissolved in 1549 its land in the parish was let for c. £7 a year.[41]

A second chantry in the parish church may have been dedicated to All Souls and seems to have been established by Buckland priory in memory of Henry of Erleigh (d. 1272). In 1526 the sisters at Buckland allowed the chaplain £5 6s. 8d., a house, 4s. for bread and wax, a linen

3 S.R.S. xxv, pp. 7, 104–5; H.M.C. Wells, i. 389; above, Chedzoy, Pawlett; below, St. Michaelchurch.
4 V.C.H Som. i. 471; V.C.H. Dors. iii. 118.
5 Reg. Regum Anglo-Norm. iii, pp. 336–7.
6 S.R.S. xxv, pp. 1–2.
7 Ibid. pp. 8, 11–12.
8 Ibid. pp. 7–8.
9 Dioc. Dir.
10 Som. Incumbents, ed. Weaver, 415.
11 P.R.O., CP 25(2)/346/16 Jas. I Mich.; above, manors (Rectory).
12 S.R.O., DD/DR 32.
13 Ibid. D/D/B reg. 27; D/D/Vc 88; V.C.H. Som. v. 182.
14 Som. Incumbents, ed. Weaver, 415; S.R.O., D/D/Vc 88.
15 S.R.O., D/D/Vc 88; Collinson, Hist. Som. iii. 74.
16 S.R.O., DD/S/WH 283; DD/X/BUSH; Rep. Com. Eccl. Revenues, pp. 148–9; P.O. Dir. Som. (1861); Kelly's Dir. Som. (1883, 1894).
17 Kelly's Dir. Som. (1906–23).
18 Ibid. (1931); Dioc. Dir.; inf. from Dioc. Office.
19 S.R.S. xxv, pp. 10–12.

20 Tax. Eccl. (Rec. Com.), 204; S.R.S. xxv, pp. 12–13.
21 Valor. Eccl. (Rec. Com.), i. 214; S.R.S. ii. 59.
22 S.R.O., D/D/Vc 24.
23 Ibid. DD/WM 1/386.
24 S.R.S. xxv, pp. 10–12.
25 S.R.O., DD/WM 1/386A; D/P/pet. n 3/2/2.
26 Ibid. tithe award. Total includes N. Newton and tithes due to neighbouring parishes.
27 S.R.S. xxv, pp. 10–11.
28 S.R.O., D/D/Ca 151.
29 Ibid. 180; D/D/Rg 279.
30 Ibid. D/D/Rg 279.
31 Ibid. D/P/pet. n 2/1/3.
32 Ibid. D/D/Bg 9; DD/WM 1/386.
33 Ibid. DD/V/BWr 26.19.
34 Ibid. D/D/Bg 9.
35 Ibid. DD/WM 1/386C; DD/X/BUSH.
36 Dioc. Dir.   37 S.R.S. xlix, p. 139.
38 Ibid. xiv, pp. 160–1.
39 Ibid. lx, no. 823; S.R.O., D/B/bw 908.
40 Valor Eccl. (Rec. Com.), i. 214.
41 S.R.S. ii. 58–9, 240–1.

gown, 2 loads of fuel, and the lease of an orchard. In 1535 the income was £6 13s. 4d.[42] The chantry seems to have survived until c. 1542.[43]

There was a guildhall in 1392, possibly connected with the parish fraternity and perhaps a predecessor of the church house.[44] The church house in 1570 was north of a house in Hammet Street.[45] It may have been the house called 'the Church' probably held in trust for the poor in 1641.[46] It probably became the parish poorhouse although the name church house survived c. 1770.[47]

John Harrow, vicar 1476–1523, was fined for his involvement in the Cornish rebellion.[48] In the 1530s there was a fraternity known as Our Lady store.[49] There were two principal altars besides the high altar, and by 1541 a light before the high cross was endowed with a rent charge, perhaps that on lands at Rydon recorded from the 13th century.[50] Emery Tuckfield, vicar 1543–6, was chaplain to Henry VIII,[51] and John Rose (also known as Wyllie or Williams) was deprived in 1554 as a married priest.[52] Richard Edon, vicar 1554–6, was a former Cistercian monk from Hailes (Glos.), who joined the restored monastery at Westminster.[53] John Rose, restored in 1558, died in 1576 in possession of medical and theological books.[54] John Tanner, vicar 1598–1613, became bishop of Derry.[55] Under John Morley, appointed vicar in 1615 and deprived before 1646,[56] the altar was railed in 1635, but the rails were removed in 1642 and an organ installed by 1625 was removed c. 1645.[57] Morley was restored in 1660 and died two years later.[58] There were said to have been eight or nine ministers during the Interregnum.[59] In 1672 a new organ was bought and a salaried organist was employed,[60] and in 1716 seats were put in the gallery for singers.[61] Another new organ was built in 1752.[62]

William George, vicar 1801–35, was resident and held two services every Sunday in 1815; he also served St. Michaelchurch and North Newton.[63] James Toogood, vicar 1835–51, tried to revive the choir which had once been 'very celebrated', and in 1840 introduced daily services and monthly communions, abolishing an arrangement whereby rich and poor received communion on different Sundays.[64] In 1843, in addition to daily services, there were two or three sermons every Sunday.[65] By 1880 communion was celebrated weekly and morning prayers were held daily.[66] In 1896 cottage services were held at Somerset Bridge.[67]

The church of *ST. MARY*, so dedicated by 1086,[68] comprises a chancel with east sacristy and north and south chapels, an aisled and clerestoried nave with north and south porches, and a west tower. The north aisle was known in the 17th century as Mr. Popham's, later the Huntworth aisle, and the south as the Melcombe aisle.[69] A late 13th-century recess in the south wall of the nave, the 14th-century font, and a brass indent of Eleanor Paulet (d. 1413) in the south aisle are all that remain from before the rebuilding of nave, chancel, and aisles in rubble in the 15th century. The tower, of lias with Ham stone dressings, apart from the battlements added in 1704, belongs to the first decade of the 16th century,[70] and the sacristy is slightly later. New seating was added in the late 16th and earlier 17th century,[71] and some of the bench ends still survive in the nave and in the tower gallery. A gallery connecting with the upper floor of the south porch was built in 1623 and was used by the Wroth family under an agreement of 1627.[72] Sir Hugh Acland still owned the gallery and chamber in 1724.[73] There was an organ loft by 1631 and a gallery at the west end of the nave by 1632.[74] Work on the fabric in the 18th century included the ceiling of the nave in 1752.[75] Galleries at the west ends of the aisles, approached by corner turrets, were removed and the tower arch was reopened in 1838–9, and the church was repewed, using some old bench ends in a restoration by Richard Carver.[76] There were further extensive repairs in the 1880s, when a rood loft stairway door was uncovered, and again in the early 20th century.[77] The carved wooden pulpit is of the 15th century, there are brasses of a priest in the sacristy and of Katharine Morley (d. 1652) in the nave, glass by C. E. Kempe (1896) and Sir Henry Holiday (1911–18), and a screen of 1909 topped by a later rood. The brass chandelier is of 1984.

A western enlargement of the churchyard was apparently abandoned by the later 14th century.[78] An extension in the later 18th century probably took its boundary northwards to Fore Street.[79] The churchyard cross probably dates from the 15th century. All that remains is an octagonal socket on two steps. The alternate

42 *Valor Eccl.* (Rec. Com.), i. 210, 214; *S.R.S.* xxv, p. xxv.
43 S.R.O., DD/X/SR 5; *S.R.S.* ii. 59.
44 S.R.O., DD/SAS NP 5, m. 4.
45 Ibid. DD/SAS (C/96) 17/1.
46 *Som. Wills*, ed. Brown, ii. 48.
47 S.R.O., DD/SLM, bk. of maps.
48 *V.C.H. Som.* ii. 30.
49 *Wells Wills*, ed. Weaver, 123.
50 Ibid.; S.R.O., DD/X/SR 5; DD/SL 1; *S.R.S.* ii. 242.
51 *S.R.S.* lv, pp. 102, 114.
52 S.R.O., D/D/Ca 18, 22.
53 Knowles, *Religious Orders*, iii. 427; E. H. Pearce, *Monks of Westminster*, 216.
54 S.R.O., DD/X/SR 5; *S.D.N.Q.* xiii. 270.
55 *Cal. S.P. Dom.* 1612–18, 190.
56 *Walker Revised*, ed. A. G. Matthews, 316.
57 S.R.O., T/PH/dev (add.); ibid. D/P/pet. n 4/1/1.
58 *Walker Revised*, ed. A. G. Matthews, 316.
59 Ibid.; S.R.O., DD/BTL 29.
60 S.R.O., D/P/pet. n 4/1/1.

61 Ibid. 4/2/2.
62 Ibid. 4/1/3.
63 Ibid. D/D/Rb 1815.
64 Ibid. DD/X/BUSH.
65 Ibid. D/D/Va 1843.
66 *The Gospeller* (N. Petherton edn.), Jan. 1880.
67 *Rep. Som. Cong. Union* (1896).
68 *V.C.H. Som.* i. 471.
69 *Som. Wills*, ed. Brown, iv. 125; S.R.O., D/P/pet. n 4/1/1; DD/MK 1.
70 S.R.O., D/P/pet. n 4/1/2.
71 Ibid. D/D/Ca 180.
72 Date on gallery; S.R.O., T/PH/dev (add.).
73 S.R.O., D/P/pet. n 4/1/2.
74 Ibid. 4/1/1.
75 Ibid. 4/1/2–3.
76 Ibid. T/PH/bb 3; ibid. DD/X/BUSH; Taunton Castle, Pigott Colln., N. Petherton ch., drawing by J. Buckler, 1832, reproduced below, plate facing p. 312.
77 S.R.O., DD/BTL 29; *The Gospeller* (N. Petherton edn.), Oct. 1883; Taunton Castle, Som. print colln.
78 S.R.O., DD/SAS NP 1, m. 8; *Proc. Som. Arch. Soc.* cxxi. 15–16.
79 S.R.O., DD/PM 20.

panels of the socket are decorated with quatrefoils and there were St. Andrew's crosses on the lower east and west faces of the shaft which survived into the 19th century.[80]

There are six bells of 1895 by Mears and Stainbank.[81] The plate includes a cup and cover by 'I.P.' dated 1573, a paten of 1630,[82] and a silver flagon given in 1631.[83] The registers date from 1558 and are complete except for marriages 1631–45.[84] During the Interregnum a parish registrar was appointed who kept a duplicate book.[85]

In 1186 there were dependent chapels at Huntworth, North Newton, West Newton, Shearston, and Woolmersdon. One of them may have been the chapel of St. Catherine, served by the vicar of North Petherton two days a week in the late 12th century.[86] There is no further record of the chapels of Huntworth and Woolmersdon.

The chapel at North Newton was granted in 1186 with the mother church of North Petherton to Buckland priory by William of Erleigh.[87] Under the will of his uncle William de Plessis (d. c. 1274) Sir Richard de Plessis established a chantry in the chapel,[88] to which as a perpetual chantry or as a free chapel he and his successors appointed chaplains until the Dissolution.[89] In 1547 the chaplain was pensioned and the chapel property was seized,[90] but the parishioners repaired the building and paid a chaplain;[91] in 1555 all services and sacraments except christenings and burials were provided there.[92] In 1592 the advowson was excepted from the sale of the chantry lands to Sir Thomas Wroth[93] and the chapel had gone out of use.[94] In the 1630s Sir Thomas's private chaplain served the chapelry and from 1637 the Wroths and their successors regarded the chaplaincy as a donative.[95] When the chaplaincy was endowed by Queen Anne's Bounty in 1742 it became a perpetual curacy,[96] and in 1880 a vicarage was established when North Newton became a separate ecclesiastical parish.[97] Sir Thomas Dyke Acland sold the advowson, probably c. 1880, to the Gibbs family of Tyntesfield, Wraxall.[98] After the death of Anthony Gibbs in 1907[99] the advowson was held by trustees until c. 1960 when it was transferred to the bishop.[1] Boundary changes were made in 1961[2] and in the following year the parish was united with St. Michaelchurch. North Newton has been held with Thurloxton from 1975 and with Durston from 1978.[3]

Sir Richard de Plessis endowed the chantry with all tithes of his demesne at Newton and the tithes of the park, which the parochial chaplain had formerly received, 35½ a. of land, and pasture rights.[4] The endowment was worth £5 a year in 1418[5] and £5 3s. 2d. net in 1535.[6] During the 17th century the chaplain received an annual stipend of £20 or £30 from Sir Thomas Wroth who bound himself and his heirs to a minimum of £10, with £3 to the vicar of North Petherton to maintain the fabric.[7] In 1742 the chaplain received an endowment of £200 from Queen Anne's Bounty. A further £200 was given in 1760 to match a similar sum given by the assistant curate, Richard Abraham. In 1770 the endowment was used to buy land in Aisholt, later known as French's farm.[8] In 1827 the value of the living was said to be less than £40 a year of which £20 was paid to an assistant curate.[9] By then the Aclands were no longer paying the incumbent.[10] The average income of the benefice was assessed at £53 in 1835.[11] The endowment of the vicarage in 1880 amounted to £11 13s. 4d. and a yearly rent charge of £50 out of the vicarage of North Petherton.[12]

There was a chaplain's house at North Newton in the later 13th century.[13] It was still held by the priest in 1549.[14] No further reference to it has been found. In 1880 £1,000 was given to provide a vicarage house at North Newton[15] and a large house was built on the road to North Petherton.[16] The house, in 1984 known as Newton Grange, was sold c. 1976.[17]

In 1348 Robert Roser, chaplain of North Newton, was allowed to celebrate three days a week at St. Michaelchurch.[18] In 1418 the chaplain carried out parochial duties at Newton besides serving the chantry,[19] and in 1425 the living was said to be a cure with resident chaplain and parishioners.[20] Timothy Batt, appointed curate in 1637, had puritan views like his patron and became a Presbyterian after the Restoration.[21] In 1815 services were held once a fortnight by the

80 C. Pooley, *Old Crosses of Som.* (1877), 173; Taunton Castle, Braikenridge Colln., drawing by W. W. Wheatley, 1850.
81 S.R.O., D/P/pet. n 8/4/1, 9/1/1; DD/SAS CH 16/1.
82 Ibid. T/PH/dev (add.).
83 *Proc. Som. Arch. Soc.* xlvii, 160–1.
84 S.R.O., D/P/pet. n 2/1/1–25.
85 Ibid. 2/1/2.
86 *S.R.S.* xxv, pp. 7–8, 11–12.
87 Ibid. p. 8.
88 Ibid. xxx, pp. 331–2; P.R.O., E 210/1987.
89 *S.R.S.* xxx, pp. 329–32; lv, p. 18.
90 Ibid. ii, pp. xxi, 58.
91 S.R.O., DD/SH 21/2.
92 Ibid. D/D/Ca 22.
93 *S.R.S.* lxxvii, p. 118.
94 S.R.O., D/D/Cd 59.
95 Devon R.O., 1148 M/add 6/17; *Rep. Com. Eccl. Revenues*, pp. 146–7.
96 *Rep. Com. Eccl. Revenues*, pp. 146–7; below (this section).
97 S.R.O., D/P/new. n 2/9/1.
98 *P.O. Dir. Som.* (1875); *Kelly's Dir. Som.* (1883).
99 Burke, *Peerage* (1949), 34.
1 S.R.O., D/P/car 23/7; *Crockford* (1959–60); *Dioc. Dir.*

(1960–1).
2 S.R.O., D/P/new. n 22/3/1.
3 Ibid. 2/9/2.
4 *S.R.S.* xxx, pp. 331–2.
5 Ibid. p. 330.
6 *Valor Eccl.* (Rec. Com.), i. 214.
7 Devon R.O. 1148 M/add 6/17.
8 C. Hodgson, *Queen Anne's Bounty*, p. ccxliii; S.R.O., DD/X/JES 1; ibid. tithe award, Aisholt.
9 S.R.O., D/D/Rb 1827.
10 City of Westminster, R.I.C.S. Libr., sale partic., Petherton Park, 1833.
11 *Rep. Com. Eccl. Revenues*, pp. 146–7.
12 S.R.O., D/P/new. n 2/9/1.
13 *S.R.S.* xxx, pp. 331–2.
14 Ibid. lxxvii, p. 47.
15 S.R.O., D/P/new. n 2/9/1.
16 Ibid. 3/4/1.
17 Ibid. 2/9/2; DD/WBF 2, N. Newton.
18 *S.R.S.* x, p. 618.
19 Ibid. xxx, p. 330.
20 Ibid. xxxi, p. 7.
21 T. H. Peake, 'Clergy and Church Cts. in Dioc. of Bath and Wells 1625–42' (Bristol Univ. M. Litt. thesis, 1978), 283.

vicar of North Petherton.[22] Neither the perpetual curate nor his assistant curate was resident in 1827.[23] Even after North Newton became a parish with a vicarage house, the church was normally left in the care of curates until the 1920s.[24]

The church of *ST. PETER*, so dedicated by the late 13th century,[25] comprises a chancel, nave with north vestry and south aisle, and a west tower. The tower, said variously to be Saxon,[26] of the 12th,[27] and of the 13th century,[28] was rebuilt in 1360.[29] Its lower parts are probably medieval and are in sandstone with limestone dressings. It was heightened and given new openings of Ham stone apparently *c.* 1635 and was substantially rebuilt after 1850.[30] The body of the church, perhaps partly dismantled when the vicars choral of Wells used some material for an alehouse and stables *c.* 1600,[31] was still standing in 1615.[32] It was rebuilt in 1635 and consecrated in 1637.[33] The south aisle was added in 1840.[34] The nave roof, said to have been remade in 1635 with older timbers, had a decorated plaster vault with an angel frieze.[35] By 1879 the church was out of repair and too small, and all but the tower was demolished and rebuilt on a much larger scale in local sandstone with freestone dressings in 1884.[36]

Surviving from before 1884 are an early 17th-century wooden screen of five bays, carved with female figures, additional parts of which are incorporated in the 19th-century lectern, some 17th-century bench ends re-used as panelling in the sanctuary, re-used woodwork in the tower, a pulpit of the 1630s, and the vestry door, bearing carvings of the wise and foolish virgins, which was originally the west entrance door.[37]

In 1547 a gilt chalice was confiscated.[38] The plate includes a cup, paten, and two flagons of 1637, probably given by Sir Thomas Wroth.[39] In 1547 the single bell was sold.[40] In 1984 there were tubular bells. The registers date from 1778 and are complete except for marriages, which were registered at North Petherton.[41]

The chapel of West Newton was mentioned in 1186 and in the later 15th century.[42]

Shearston chapel was confirmed as a possession of Buckland priory by 1186.[43] By the 14th century it was sometimes called a perpetual chantry; the Reigny family, lords of Shearston manor, and their successors the Paulets

presented chaplains until its dissolution in 1548.[44] In 1535 its lands were worth £3 10s. 5d.,[45] and in 1546 its goods included a silver gilt chalice, two pairs of vestments, and a bell.[46]

The chapel site, south-west of Chapel Hill Farm on the boundary with Thurloxton, was retained by the lords of Shearston manor.[47] It was surrounded by a moat, and the remains of a bridge on the north side could be seen in 1963.[48]

A church built at Moorland or Northmoor Green at the instigation of the vicar, J. J. Toogood, to serve a community often cut off by flooding was consecrated in 1844[49] and assigned a district chapelry in 1845.[50] It was served from North Petherton until 1852 when a perpetual curacy (later a vicarage) was endowed by the Ecclesiastical Commissioners; Queen Anne's Bounty further endowed it in 1865. The living was in the gift of the vicar of North Petherton.[51] From 1969 to 1976 it was held with Burrowbridge, and thereafter was united with North Petherton.[52] The vicarage house, later called Glebe House, is dated 1892.

In 1866 disturbances in the church and parish over the introduction of ritual and vestments led to the departure of the vicar, James Hunt, and curates served in his place until his unexpected return *c.* 1898.[53] In 1870 communion was celebrated monthly and there were two services with sermons each Sunday.[54]

The church of *ST. PETER AND ST. JOHN*, designed by Benjamin Ferrey,[55] has an undivided chancel and nave under a steeply pitched roof, with a south porch and western bell turret. The furnishings include a chest dated 1687, a much restored medieval wooden lectern from North Petherton church, and tall candlesticks made from balusters formerly in the corporation pew at St. Mary's, Bridgwater.[56] A large wood carving of St. Peter the fisherman by 'V.M.W.' was given by a former vicar.

There is one bell, dated 1844, and the registers date from the same year.[57]

NONCONFORMITY. Members of the Maunsel family, their servants, and others were presented for recusancy from the 1590s to the 1620s.[58] A local recusant was convicted at the assizes in 1674.[59] There was a meeting, probably

22 S.R.O., D/D/Rb 1815. 23 Ibid. 1827.
24 Ibid. D/P/new. n 2/1/2.
25 *S.R.S.* xxx, pp. 332.
26 N. Pevsner, *S. & W. Som.* 259; the statement that the Alfred jewel was found at N. Newton church is incorrect: the exact findspot is uncertain but was probably near Parker's Field.
27 S.R.O., D/P/new. n 8/3/1.
28 Ibid. 8/4/1.
29 Ibid. DD/WM 1/113.
30 Taunton Castle, Braikenridge Colln., drawing by W. W. Wheatley, 1850.
31 S.R.O., DD/AH 21/2.
32 Wells Cath. Libr., Vicars Choral MS. survey bk. 1615.
33 Devon R.O., 1148 M/add 6/17.
34 L. H. King, *Short Acct. of Ch. and Par. of St. Peter's, N. Newton* (1899).
35 S.R.O., D/P/new. n 8/3/1; painting by W. Cartwright, 1865, in ch., reproduced above, plate facing p. 153.
36 S.R.O., D/P/new. n 6/1/1, 8/3/1, 8/4/1.
37 Ibid. 8/3/1, 8/4/1.   38 *S.R.S.* ii. 58.
39 S.R.O., D/P/new. n 5/2/1.   40 *S.R.S.* ii. 58.

41 S.R.O., D/P/new. n 2/1/1–4.
42 *S.R.S.* xxv, pp. 7–8; P.R.O., C 1/31/473.
43 *S.R.S.* xxv, p. 8.
44 Ibid. x, p. 454; liv, pp. 56, 132; P.R.O., C 142/61, no. 14; Pole MS. 2560.
45 *Valor Eccl.* (Rec. Com.), i. 216; above, manors (Shearston chantry).   46 P.R.O., E 117/8/23B, m. 34.
47 Above, manors (Shearston); S.R.O., tithe award.
48 *Som. Co. Herald*, 13 July 1963.
49 S.R.O., DD/X/BUSH.
50 *Lond. Gaz.* 11 Feb. 1845, 394.
51 Inf. from Ch. Comm.; *Kelly's Dir. Som.* (1906).
52 *Dioc. Dir.*
53 *Som. Co. Gaz.* 7 Apr. 1866; par. rec. in ch.
54 S.R.O., D/D/Va 1870.
55 Ibid. DD/X/BUSH.   56 Par. rec. in ch.
57 Ibid.; J. E. King, *Som. Parochial Docs.* 256.
58 *S.D.N.Q.* v. 114; *S.R.S.* xliii. 99; *Recusant Roll*, ii (Cath. Rec. Soc. lvii), 114; S.R.O., D/D/Ca 98, 160, 175, 180, 235.
59 *S.R.S.* xxxiv. 182.

BRIDGWATER CHURCH IN 1828

NORTH PETHERTON CHURCH IN 1832

ST. MICHAELCHURCH CHURCH, *c.* 1900

CHEDZOY CHURCH IN 1838

of Baptists, at Rydon in the 1650s.[60] There were two Quaker meeting places in the parish in 1669 and Friends were active in the 1670s. In 1672 licences for Presbyterian and Congregational worship were granted, and in all the parish had six nonconformist teachers with 90 hearers in 1669.[61] Licences for unspecified denominations were issued in 1696 and 1706 but by 1776 there were said to be only three dissenters in the parish.[62] Further licences were issued in 1807, 1822, 1823, 1824, and 1845, and for houses in North Newton in 1809 and 1851.[63]

An Independent minister was living in the parish in 1795, and in the early 19th century services and a Sunday school were held in a cottage. A Congregational meeting house was licensed in 1824 and a chapel was built in 1833 on the Bridgwater road with seats for 600 people.[64] It was given an Italianate facade by Edwin Down in 1869[65] and remained open as a United Reformed church in 1984. The school-room was rebuilt in 1922.[66]

In 1851 an Independent meeting house was licensed at North Newton,[67] and in 1865 a chapel, known as the Free Chapel, was built. In 1896 there was a Sunday school, services were 'well attended', and the chapel was the centre of an evangelist's district.[68] The chapel, south-west of North Newton church, had closed by 1972[69] and was later taken over for industrial use.

In 1863 Congregationalists began cottage services at Fordgate, and later in the same year a chapel was built there. In 1864 a Sunday school was started.[70] The chapel had closed by 1944 and in 1954 it was sold.[71] It has since been demolished. In the 1860s Bridgwater Congregationalists held cottage services at Somerset Bridge. In 1865 a chapel and schoolroom were built and in 1889 an evangelist was appointed to work at Huntworth, Northmoor Green, and Northmoor Corner. In 1896 a mission station was recorded at Northmoor Corner and the Somerset Bridge church had 51 members.[72] The chapel stood immediately south-west of the railway bridge. Recorded in 1914[73] but closed later, the chapel had become an ice-cream factory by 1966[74] and was so used until burnt down in 1984. The Union chapel at Hedging, built in 1863, was in the care of the Taunton village evangelist by 1896 and was shared with the Baptists.[75] A schoolroom was added in 1918.[76] The chapel probably closed c. 1964,[77] and was used as a storeroom by 1982.

A meeting house for Methodists was licensed in 1805.[78] In 1832 the Tappers Lane Wesleyan chapel was opened with 90 seats and in 1840 there were two Sunday services and one on a weekday. The schoolroom was said to have been built also in 1832 for 70 children.[79] There were three services each week in 1920 but by 1960 one evening service was held with an average attendance of six and in 1961 the chapel was closed.[80] In 1982 it was a private house. There may have been Methodist services at North Newton in 1889 and 1894.[81]

In 1839 Baptists from Burrowbridge formed a church at Northmoor Green.[82] A chapel was built in 1844 and restored in 1897.[83] It closed between 1939 and 1965[84] and in 1982 it was a private house. A Bible Christian chapel at Northmoor Green had two Sunday services in 1867. In 1868 the chapel was said to have been loaned to them and may have been the Baptist chapel.[85]

EDUCATION. There were two unlicensed schoolmasters in the parish in 1606,[86] and Gregory Ball was described as a schoolmaster at his burial there in 1625.[87] In 1635 Timothy Batt was licensed to teach and may have continued until 1643.[88] A charity school was established at Rydon c. 1687.[89] Another was started in North Petherton village under the will of Sir Thomas Wroth (d. 1721) who left £20 a year to clothe and educate 10 poor boys,[90] for which land was bought at Lyng in 1763 and which c. 1776 had 20 boys. After a further small endowment had been given by Sir Thomas Bacon, John Slade built a schoolroom in Pound Street, North Petherton, between 1787 and 1796. By that time pupils provided their own books but were given clothes of blue cloth, and the school was known as the Blue Coat school.[91] In 1840 the school was merged with the National school, some of whose pupils were elected to the Wroth foundation.[92] From the 1870s the charity income was distributed among all the board schools in the parish as prizes for attendance.[93] Under a Scheme of 1980 half the charity income was used to provide additional benefits for schools and half to promote the education of needy young people in the parish.[94]

In 1819 a Sunday school had 40 children and three boarding schools and several day schools

60 D. Jackman, *Baptists in the West Country*, 1; *Confessions of the Faith of several Churches of Christ in Som.* (1656).
61 *Cal. S.P. Dom.* 1672, 239, 677; *Orig. Rec. Early Nonconf.* ed. G. L. Turner, i. 9, 522, 562; *S.R.S.* lxxv. 98, 106; S.R.O., DD/SFR 8/1.
62 S.R.O., Q/RR meeting ho. lics.; ibid. D/D/Vc 88.
63 Ibid. D/D/Rm, box 2.
64 Ibid.; *Rep. Som. Cong. Union* (1896); *Co. Gaz. Dir. Som.* (1840).
65 Morris & Co. *Dir. Som.* (1872).
66 Inscr. on building.
67 S.R.O., D/D/Rm, box 2.
68 *North Street Cong. Ch. Taunton 1843–1943*, 24; *Rep. Som. Cong. Union* (1896).
69 S.R.O., D/N/np. c (S/2356).
70 *Rep. Som. Cong. Union* (1896).
71 S.R.O., D/N/np. c (S/2356).
72 *Rep. Som. Cong. Union* (1896).
73 Crippen, *Nonconf. in Som.* 50.
74 O.S. Map 1/1,250, ST 3135 NW. (1966 edn.).

75 *Rep. Som. Cong. Union* (1896).
76 Datestone; S.R.O., D/R/bw 22/1/9.
77 S.R.O., D/N/np. c (S/2356).
78 Ibid. D/D/Rm, box 2.
79 Ibid. D/N/bmc 4/3/50; 7/2.
80 Ibid. 3/2/2, 3/2/12, 4/3/50.
81 *Kelly's Dir. Som.* (1889, 1894).
82 Crippen, *Nonconf. in Som.* 50.
83 Inscr. on chapel.
84 *Kelly's Dir. Som.* (1939); G.R.O. Worship Reg. no. 10769.
85 S.R.O., D/N/bmc 3/2/5, 4/2/4.
86 Ibid. D/D/Ca 151.
87 Ibid. DD/X/SR 5; D/P/pet. n 2/1/1.
88 T. H. Peake, 'Clergy and Church Cts. in Dioc. of Bath and Wells 1625–42' (Bristol Univ. M. Litt. thesis, 1978), 283–4.
89 Below, this section.
90 *Som. Wills*, ed. Brown, ii. 85.
91 *15th Rep. Com. Char.* 433; S.R.O., D/D/Vc 88; DD/WRO 7.
92 S.R.O., DD/X/BUSH. 93 Ibid. DD/WRO 9.
94 Char. Com. reg.

had *c.* 250 children, in addition to Wroth's charity school and schools in North Newton.[95] In 1835 the whole parish had 11 day schools with 240 children taught either at parents' expense or by charities. There was also a church Sunday school with 150 pupils, held in a cottage; a Sunday school with 160 at the Congregational chapel; and a Wesleyan Sunday school with 70 pupils.[96]

A year later several dame schools were said to teach as many as 500 children. In that year the vicar, J. J. Toogood, established, as a continuation of the church Sunday school, a day school which was later affiliated to the National Society. It was for 70 children and was free to those whose parents could not afford to pay. Within a year it had 90 pupils, who were taught reading, needlework, and religious knowledge. The building, on two floors, stood immediately west of the church *c.* 1837.[97] By 1846 there were as many as 193 children attending.[98] In 1875 the school was transferred to a board for North Petherton and St. Michaelchurch.[99] A new school was built east of the church in 1877.[1] By 1903 there were 378 children in three classrooms and an evening continuation school was held.[2] Numbers fell to 254 in 1915, to 230 in 1945, and to 174 in 1955 but there were 232 children on the books in 1965. From 1967 the school took juniors only. A new infant school to the south was opened in 1967, and in 1983 there were 106 infants on the register and 135 juniors.[3]

The Congregational church maintained a British day school in 1861 and until *c.* 1878.[4] Three dame schools in North Petherton village had 71 pupils in 1846.[5] One was probably Elizabeth Mulford's infant school in Fore Street which existed from 1840 until 1872.[6] There was a second day school in Fore Street from 1861 to 1866.[7] Of several boarding schools in the village in the 19th century one kept by James Crosswell between 1816 and 1830 was run by Thomas Simons Crosswell until 1859;[8] in 1851 it had 13 boys aged between 10 and 15[9] in a large house south-west of the church. The Alexanders kept schools east of the church by 1830 and until 1866 or later when they moved to Bridgwater; in 1851 there were six boarders and an English teacher in addition to the family. There was a girls' boarding school with several proprietors between 1830 and 1859.[10]

At Rydon, Dorothy Cheeke by will dated 1687 endowed a school for six or more children. In 1701 the endowment was increased by Henry Stodgell for four more children. By 1786 the school had closed but the tenants of the school house and land contributed towards teaching poor children. After 1819 a private school was kept in the old schoolroom[11] and by 1835 the charity school had reopened.[12] After a second closure and accusations of mismanagement in the 1860s the school was reopened.[13] It continued into the early 1920s.[14] In 1933 the Cheeke and Stodgell educational foundation was established in its place to promote the education of poor children.[15] The schoolroom, standing opposite Rydon Farm, was rebuilt further north after 1838.[16]

At Northmoor Green in 1837 a school had 60 children paying 1*d.* a week.[17] It was probably the dame school which in 1846 had 26 pupils.[18] In 1857 a National school was built, which was enlarged or rebuilt *c.* 1865.[19] It closed in the late 1860s because of local religious controversy[20] and a school was established in its place by local farmers. The National school had reopened by 1875 and was then enlarged and administered by the school board.[21] In 1903 there were 76 children on the books and an evening continuation school was held.[22] Numbers fell to 28 in 1935 and 22 in 1955 but rose to 56 in 1975. In 1983 there were 27 children on the register.[23] The school is on the west side of the Bridgwater road 400 m. north of Northmoor Green church.

At North Newton in 1837 a school was supported by Sir Thomas Acland and the parents.[24] It may have continued until taken over by the school board in 1875.[25] A new building was erected in 1877 and part of the old one was sold for a vicarage house.[26] The school had 176 pupils in 1903 and held evening continuation classes.[27] Numbers fluctuated but fell from 112 in 1935 to 69 in 1955 and to 33 in 1975. In 1983 there were 37 children on the books.[28]

At Buncombe brook, south of North Petherton village, a school was established by Lady Slade and Richard Meade King *c.* 1836 when it taught up to 100 children and was supported by voluntary contributions and fees. The children were taught reading, writing, arithmetic, needlework, and grammar with one day devoted to religious instruction. The school closed *c.* 1837 after the

95 *Educ. of Poor Digest,* p. 793; below, this section.
96 *Educ. Enq. Abstract,* p. 818.
97 S.R.O., DD/X/BUSH.
98 Nat. Soc. *Inquiry, 1846–7,* Som. 14–15.
99 *Lond. Gaz.* 26 Mar. 1875, p. 1832.
1 S.R.O., C/E 4/183.
2 Ibid. 4/380/292.
3 Ibid. 4/64.
4 *P.O. Dir. Som.* (1861); *Rep. Som. Cong. Union* (1896); inf. from Mr. A. W. Turner, Edinburgh, grandson of a teacher there.
5 Nat. Soc. *Inquiry, 1846–7,* Som. 14–15.
6 *Co. Gaz. Dir. Som.* (1840); Morris & Co. *Dir. Som.* (1872).
7 *P.O. Dir. Som.* (1861, 1866).
8 MS. Jnl. of J. A. Giles, in possession of Miss M. M. Cheetham, Bondleigh, Devon; Pigot, *Nat. Com. Dir.* (1830); *P.O. Dir. Som.* (1859); S.R.O., DD/X/KLT (C/983); ibid. tithe award.
9 P.R.O., HO 107/1924.
10 Pigot, *Nat. Com. Dir.* (1830); *P.O. Dir. Som.* (1859,

1866); P.R.O., HO 107/1924.
11 *Char. Don.* pp. 1068–9; *15th Rep. Com. Char.* 457–8; *Educ. of Poor Digest,* p. 793.
12 S.R.O., DD/X/BUSH.
13 Ibid. D/P/pet. n 9/1/3; ibid. C/E 4/183.
14 Local inf.
15 Char. Com. reg.
16 S.R.O., tithe award.
17 Ibid. DD/X/BUSH; *Educ. Enq. Abstract,* p. 818.
18 Nat. Soc. *Inquiry, 1846–7,* Som. 14–15.
19 S.R.O., C/E 4/380/293; C/T 5.
20 Above, church.
21 S.R.O., C/E 4/183; Moorland par. rec. in ch.
22 S.R.O., C/E 4/380/293.
23 Ibid. 4/64.
24 Ibid. DD/X/BUSH; *Educ. Enq. Abstract,* p. 818.
25 S.R.O., C/E 4/183; Nat. Soc. *Inquiry, 1846–7,* Som. 14–15.
26 S.R.O., C/E 4/183.
27 Ibid. 4/380/294.
28 Ibid. 4/64.

opening of the National school in North Petherton village.[29] There was a school at Fordgate in 1838.[30]

A county school at Somerset Bridge, opened in 1903, had 168 pupils in 1910, 160 in 1915, and 192 in 1935. In 1983 there were 102 children on the register.[31] The school also serves part of Bridgwater.

CHARITIES FOR THE POOR. Margery Morley by will dated 1728 gave £20 for bread on St. Stephen's day (26 Dec.) and Mary Jeane by will dated 1785 gave £25 for an annual distribution of bread. In 1766 William Brown gave a £2 rent charge to the poor of North Newton for bread on St. Stephen's day. Richard King, by will dated 1828, provided for an annual distribution of bread on 30 November.[32] All these charities appear to have been lost.[33]

Mary Moggridge by will dated 1725 gave £20 for bread on St. Stephen's day.[34] Mary Escott by will dated 1809 gave £100 to the poor; under a scheme of 1871 the income was used in 1879 to provide cheap coal for the poor.[35] Sarah Ivyleafe by will dated 1816 provided for an annual distribution of coal on St. Stephen's day.[36] The income from those three charities was in the 1980s being allowed to accumulate.[37]

ST. MICHAELCHURCH

THE parish of St. Michaelchurch, usually called Michaelchurch, and measuring only 46 a., is an enclave in the southern part of North Petherton parish.[38] It may have originated as the area dependent on a church founded there by the 11th century.[39] Its only natural boundary is a stream on the south, but on parts of the north and east the parish boundary follows roads. The parish lies mainly on Upper Sandstone near the 15-m. contour, with a narrow band of alluvium beside the stream in the south.[40] It was united with North Petherton for civil purposes in 1933.[41]

The parish lies astride the road from North Newton to Lower Durston; a road to North moor forms part of its northern boundary.[42] A road from North moor to Chadmead which followed part of the eastern boundary was recorded in 1401[43] but fell out of use when the Bridgwater and Taunton canal was cut across it in the 1820s.[44] Field names like Woodcroft, the Wood, and Hamwood indicate that the parish was formerly wooded although no woodland was recorded in 1086.[45] By 1839 some land in the eastern half of the parish had been taken to form Maunsel park and two cottages were used as staff cottages, one as a lodge for the new park.[46] In 1663 there were said to be 14 or 15 'ancient inhabited tenements besides cottages' in the parish.[47] The site of those tenements is unknown and from the 18th century the scattered dwellings have declined in number: four were demolished in the 1820s and 1830s.[48] The population was 41 in 1801 rising to 50 in 1821 but falling to 32 in 1831. Thereafter the number remained stable at c. 30 until 1901. It had fallen to 24 by 1931[49] and was only c. 10 in 1984.[50]

MANOR AND OTHER ESTATES. The manor of *MICHAELCHURCH* was held of the honor of Trowbridge, later part of the Duchy of Lancaster, by 1324 and until 1604 or later.[51]

In 1066 Alwi held Michaelchurch and in 1086 it was held by Ansger the cook, holding by serjeanty.[52] It had come into the possession of the Erleigh family by the 13th century,[53] and continued to be held by them until 1373 or later with North Petherton.[54] In 1377–8 the manor was settled by trustees on William Cheddar of Bristol,[55] and in 1380 he gave it to Robert Cheddar, possibly his brother, and to Robert's wife Joan.[56] Joan and her second husband Sir Thomas Brooke held the manor in 1409.[57] After Sir Thomas's death in 1418 Joan continued to hold the manor,[58] probably until 1425 when their son Thomas conveyed it to John Seymour (d. 1438) and Elizabeth his wife.[59] Elizabeth survived her husband and died in 1457 in possession; the manor passed to her son Sir Thomas Seymour.[60] Michaelchurch descended like Durston until 1799 when Henry Seymour and his son, also Henry, conveyed it to John Slade of Maunsel in North Petherton. By then

[29] Ibid. DD/X/BUSH.
[30] Ibid. tithe award.
[31] Ibid. C/E 4/64.
[32] *Char. Don.* pp. 1068–9; Char. Com. reg.
[33] Inf. from Mr. T. M. Folkes, clerk, N. Petherton town cncl.
[34] *Char. Don.* pp. 1068–9.
[35] *15th Rep. Com. Char.* 351; Char. Com. reg.; *The Gospeller* (N. Petherton edn.), Oct. 1879.
[36] Char. Com. reg.
[37] Inf. from Mr. Folkes.
[38] O.S. Map 1/25,000, ST 32 (1958 edn.); ST 33 (1960 edn.); *Census*, 1891; S.R.O., tithe map. This article was completed in 1984.
[39] Below, church.
[40] Geol. Surv. Map 1", sheet 295, drift (1950 edn.).
[41] Youngs, *Local Admin. Units*, i. 436.
[42] O.S. Map 1/25,000, ST 33 (1960 edn.); S.R.O., DD/SLM, bk. of maps, St. Michaelchurch 1823.
[43] S.R.O., DD/SL 1.

[44] Ibid. Q/RUp 71; ibid. N. Petherton tithe map.
[45] Ibid. DD/SL 1; ibid. tithe award; *V.C.H. Som.* i. 521.
[46] S.R.O., tithe award.
[47] Ibid. DD/SAS PR 314.
[48] Ibid. DD/SL 19–21; S.R.O., DD/SLM, bk. of maps, St. Michaelchurch 1823, schedule 1831; ibid. tithe map.
[49] *Census*.
[50] Local inf.
[51] *Cal. Inq. p.m.* vi, p. 298, wrongly defined as Creech St. Michael in the index; *S.R.S.* lxvii, p. 61; *V.C.H. Wilts*, vii. 128–9; above, Durleigh, manors.
[52] *V.C.H. Som.* i. 521.
[53] S.R.O., DD/SL 1.
[54] B.L. Harl. Ch. 49 H 15; above, N. Petherton, manors.
[55] P.R.O., E 326/10803; *S.R.S.* xvii. 97–9.
[56] B.L. Harl. Ch. 48 A 24.
[57] *S.R.S.* xxii, pp. 34–5; *Proc. Som. Arch. Soc.* xliv. 14.
[58] *Cal. Close*, 1413–19, 478.
[59] P.R.O., C 139/92, no. 40.
[60] Ibid. C 139/167, no. 2.

the estate had shrunk to 26 a. in the parish from 125 a. or more in several parishes in the 14th and 15th centuries.[61] The manor descended with Maunsel;[62] no capital messuage has been traced.

A small estate called Ellerhaye belonged to Newton Plecy chantry from the later 13th century.[63] A cottage and land called Hamwood were added later and in 1549 the holding was granted with other chantry lands to John Hulson and William Pendred of London.[64] The estate descended with the Bluets' manor of North Petherton to the Slade family.[65]

By 1338 Buckland priory, Durston, had probably appropriated the 'little church'.[66] The rectory of Buckland alias Michaelchurch was granted to William Parr, earl of Essex, (Sir) Edward Rogers, and others in 1544.[67] In 1554 Rogers was in sole possession.[68] He died in 1567 and was followed in turn by his son Sir George (d. 1582), Sir George's son Edward (d. 1627), and Edward's son Sir Francis Rogers (d. 1638). Hugh Rogers, son of Sir Francis, was a minor in 1638.[69] No later reference to the rectory has been found, but by the mid 18th century the tithes belonged to the incumbent.[70]

Henry of Erleigh (d. 1272) gave a house and lands in St. Michaelchurch, later known as Rawlin's Cross,[71] and other land in the parish to Philip Maunsel and another small estate to John Wyter.[72] The Maunsels' estate lay probably north of Maunsel House on the eastern side of the parish and descended with the manor of Maunsel in North Petherton.[73] In 1417 Richard Maunsel acquired the land which had been John Wyter's.[74]

ECONOMIC HISTORY. In the 11th century 1 ploughland was recorded at St. Michaelchurch suggesting an estate much larger than the later parish.[75] During the Middle Ages the manor certainly included lands in neighbouring parishes and in 1377 four stalls in Taunton market.[76] By the 17th century farming in the parish was mainly arable, producing wheat, barley, and beans.[77] A farming inventory of 1639 included apples, cider, and cheese besides 4 rother cattle, poultry, and a horse.[78] Towards the end of the century a farmer's widow had 10 hogsheads of cider, but corn accounted for nearly half the value of her possessions.[79] The 14 or 15 holdings recorded in 1663[80] cannot have been very large, and in the 18th century houses were let with

between 2 a. and 13 a.[81] In 1823 there were seven holdings of between 2 a. and 13 a. and although two tenants had more than one holding there were nine dwellings in the parish.[82] By 1839 there were five smallholdings and the mill; 25½ a. were arable and 7 a. orchard. The only pasture land was Maunsel park and there was one meadow by the mill.[83] For the rest of the century there remained the mill house, the lodge occupied by the gardener of Maunsel, and three other houses. The tenant of the principal house, Michaelchurch Farm, farmed about 200 a. and employed up to 6 labourers, but only about 15 a. lay within the parish.[84] The farmhouse fell into disuse in the later 20th century and was demolished c. 1955.[85]

There is some evidence of serge-weaving in the 17th century,[86] and during the 18th century there was a family of tanners[87] and also a carpenter.[88] A tanning office was used as a school in the late 18th century.[89] Occupations recorded in the 19th century included carpenter,[90] butcher, mason,[91] dressmaker, and market gardener.[92]

MILL. A watermill at St. Michaelchurch was included in the gift of Henry of Erleigh (d. 1272) to Philip Maunsel.[93] The mill, usually known as Maunsel mill, descended in the Maunsel family with Maunsel in North Petherton. The house was rebuilt in the early 18th century and with the mill formed part of Maunsel manor.[94] By then the two Maunsel mills, one in St. Michaelchurch and one near Maunsel House in North Petherton, were usually held together.[95] The St. Michaelchurch mill appears to have ceased milling by the 1930s.[96] A reference to Brookwall in 1401 suggests that the watercourse was not a natural one,[97] and traces of walling diverting water along a higher level to the mill still survive. The mill also survived in 1984 with the remains of an overshot wheel and other machinery.

LOCAL GOVERNMENT. Michaelchurch was the name of a limit in Durston tithing in North Petherton hundred which also included a large part of North Petherton parish.[98] For the manor one court roll survives for 1632 when courts were held twice a year; courts were still held in the 1760s and 1770s.[99] During the late 16th and early 17th century there were two churchwardens[1] and in the 18th century there

61 *S.R.S.* xvii. 97–9; xxii. 34–5; S.R.O., DD/SL 30; above, Durston, manors.
62 Above, N. Petherton, manors.
63 *S.R.S.* xxx, p. 331; above, N. Petherton, churches.
64 *S.R.S.* lxxvii, p. 47; *Cal. Pat.* 1549–51, 131.
65 Above, N. Petherton, manors.
66 *Knights Hospitallers in Eng.* (Camd. Soc. [1st ser.], lxv), 17.
67 *L. & P. Hen. VIII*, xix (1), p. 504.
68 S.R.O., D/D/Ca 22.
69 P.R.O., C 142/148, no. 28; C 142/197, no. 52; C 142/440, no. 91; C 142/486, no. 114.
70 S.R.O., Q/REl 29/4.
71 Ibid. DD/SL 20.
72 Ibid. 1.
73 Above, N. Petherton, manors.
74 S.R.O., DD/SL 1.
75 *V.C.H. Som.* i. 521.
76 P.R.O., E 326/10803; *S.R.S.* xvii. 97–9.

77 S.R.O., DD/SP inventory, 1671.   78 Ibid. 1639.
79 Ibid. 1689.   80 Ibid. DD/SAS PR 314.
81 Ibid. DD/SL 19–21.
82 Ibid. DD/SLM bk. of maps, St. Michaelchurch 1823.
83 Ibid. tithe award.
84 P.R.O., HO 107/1924; RG 10/2382; RG 11/2372.
85 S.R.O., D/R/bw 13/2/1; local inf.
86 S.R.O., DD/SP inventory, 1666.
87 Ibid. DD/AH 9/3.
88 Ibid. DD/SL 18.   89 Ibid. DD/SLM, bk. of maps.
90 *P.O. Dir. Som.* (1875).
91 P.R.O., RG 10/2382.
92 Ibid. RG 11/2372.
93 S.R.O., DD/SL 1.   94 Ibid. 18.
95 Ibid.; above, N. Petherton, mills.
96 Local inf.   97 S.R.O., DD/SL 1.
98 Ibid. Q/REl 29/4.
99 B.L. Add. Ch. 28283; S.R.O., DD/SL 19–21.
1 S.R.O., D/D/Rr St. Michaelchurch; D/D/Ca 180.

were a churchwarden and a sidesman who may have been the retiring warden.[2] In 1654 it was proposed that St. Michaelchurch should be united with North Petherton under the same register.[3] There appears to have been a vestry in the 19th century.[4] The parish formed part of the Bridgwater poor-law union in 1836 and the Bridgwater rural district in 1894. As part of the civil parish of North Petherton it formed part of Sedgemoor district in 1974.[5]

CHURCH. The Domesday name Michelscerca[6] and parts of the present building[7] are evidence for an 11th-century church. It was probably part of the minster parish of North Petherton and linked with an independent, perhaps pre-Conquest, manor. By the 13th century it was described as a chapel when Henry of Erleigh (d. 1272) is said to have given it to Athelney abbey.[8] There is no further evidence for Athelney's possession, and by 1338 it was probably the 'little church' appropriated to Buckland priory.[9] Curates were paid by the priory until the Dissolution.[10] In 1541 the chapel acquired parochial status when a churchyard was made around it.[11] In 1628 it was known as a free chapel.[12] In the 18th and 19th centuries it was variously described as a vicarage, a rectory, a parish church, and a chapel with cure, and the incumbent was known as a perpetual curate.[13] The living was united with North Newton in 1962; it was held with Thurloxton from 1975, and a united benefice of North Newton with St. Michaelchurch, Thurloxton, and Durston was created in 1978.[14]

Successive owners of the chapel presumably appointed curates until the Dissolution and were probably followed by the owners of the rectory. Mrs. Anne Wyndham (d. 1748), heir to the estates of Sir Thomas Wroth, was patron in 1746, and was succeeded by her daughter Elizabeth, wife of Arthur Acland (d. 1771).[15] The patronage descended with Fairfield in Stogursey until 1883[16] but from 1897 until 1902 it was held by Antony Gibbs of Tyntesfield, Wraxall.[17] Since 1906 the advowson has been held by the Slade family of Maunsel, who in 1984 held one turn in four.[18]

In 1535 the tithes and offerings of St. Michaelchurch and Buckland together were worth only 12s. 5d.[19] The curate received a stipend of 106s. 8d., paid by the Crown after the Dissolution and charged to the grantees of the rectory in 1544.[20] In 1575 the curate was paid £6.[21] By the mid 18th century the curate had acquired the tithes, worth 8s. a year.[22] The living was augmented between 1740 and 1790 with £800 from Queen Anne's Bounty,[23] with which was bought 22 a. of land at Ham in Creech St. Michael.[24] In 1829–31 the average income was said to be £80 a year[25] and in 1839 the rent charge was £22.[26] There were nearly 21 a. of glebe in 1978.[27] No reference to a curate's house has been found.

During a vacancy in 1349 the chaplain of North Newton was allowed to celebrate at St. Michaelchurch on three days a week.[28] In 1603 a layman usually read the sermon[29] but in 1613 there was said to have been no sermon for three years.[30] The curate also served Lyng from 1689.[31] In 1815 an afternoon service was held on alternate Sundays but by 1827 there was a service every Sunday with communion on great festivals.[32] There was said to be only one resident parishioner in 1840 although a service was held every Sunday, alternately morning and afternoon, with communion three times a year but no catechizing.[33] During the early 19th century the parish was usually served by assistant curates from North Petherton and Bridgwater.[34] William Jeffreys Allen served the cure in the early 1850s when he lived at Maunsel House.[35] His successors usually lived at North Newton and served both churches.[36] By 1910 services were held weekly with monthly communion.[37]

The church of ST. MICHAEL comprises an undivided chancel and nave with north and south aisles, and a north tower above a porch. The proportions of the building and part of the north wall of the nave apparently survive from the 11th century. Some rebuilding took place in the 15th century at the west end. The east window is of the 15th or early 16th century and in 1840 the church retained square-headed windows of the same period.[38] The lay rectors were regularly presented in the 16th and 17th centuries for failing to maintain the church.[39] In 1663 it was said to be ruined and to have been so for some years, and the parishioners received

---

2   Ibid. D/D/Vc 3, 14.
3   S.R.S. xxviii. 230.
4   S.R.O., D/D/Rb 1840.
5   Youngs, Local Admin. Units, i. 436, 671, 673.
6   V.C.H. Som. i. 521.
7   Below, this section.
8   Collinson, Hist. Som. iii. 99, referring to part of an Athelney register which does not survive.
9   Knights Hospitallers in Eng. 17.
10   T. Hugo, Hist. Mynchin Buckland Priory and Preceptory (1861), 74–5.
11   L. & P. Hen. VIII, xvi, p. 502.
12   P.R.O., C 142/440, no. 91.
13   S.R.O., D/P/s. mi 2/2/1; D/D/Vc 87; D/D/Bs 42, 43; Rep. Com. Eccl. Revenues, pp. 144–5.
14   S.R.O., D/P/new. n 2/9/2.
15   Ibid. D/D/Vc 87; above, Lyng.
16   S.R.O., DD/AH 5/1; above, Stogursey, manors.
17   Kelly's Dir. Som. (1883, 1897, 1902).
18   Ibid. (1906); Dioc. Dir.
19   Valor Eccl. (Rec. Com.), i. 211.
20   Hist. Mynchin Buckland Priory, 74–5.

21   S.D.N.Q. xiii. 271.
22   S.R.O., Q/REl 29/4.
23   C. Hodgson, Queen Anne's Bounty (1864), p. ccxliii.
24   S.R.O., Q/REl 2/3; ibid. D/P/new. n 3/1/1, 3/4/1; D/P/s. mi 4/4/1, 5/2/1.
25   Rep. Com. Eccl. Revenues, pp. 144–5.
26   S.R.O., tithe award.
27   Inf. from Dioc. office.
28   S.R.S. x, pp. 618–19.
29   S.R.O., D/D/Ca 134.
30   Ibid. 180.
31   Ibid. D/D/Bs 42–3.
32   Ibid. D/D/Rb 1815, 1827.
33   Ibid. D/D/Va 1840.
34   Ibid. D/D/Rb 1815, 1827.
35   Ibid. DD/SLM 13; P.R.O., HO 107/1924.
36   e.g. Morris & Co. Dir. Som. (1872); S.R.O., D/P/car 23/7.
37   S.R.O., D/P/s. mi 2/5/1.
38   Taunton Castle, Pigott colln., wash drawing by J. Buckler, 1840.
39   S.R.O., D/D/Ca 22, 57, 235, 310.

support from the parishes of the diocese to pay for its rebuilding.[40] After 1823 a long south transept at the west end of the nave was removed.[41] Later in the century north and south aisles of three bays were built, the north known as the Maunsel aisle and the south built by Sir Alfred Slade in 1868,[42] possibly by the architect who was extending Maunsel House the same year. In 1840 the church had a west gallery with an outside staircase.[43] Communion rails dated 1635 were said to have been removed to the Priory, Chilton Polden.[44] There is a plain octagonal medieval font. The tower contains one bell dated 1670,[45] recast in 1938.[46] The church possesses a small Elizabethan cup and cover.[47] The registers date from 1695 and are complete.[48]

NONCONFORMITY. A woman was presented for not receiving communion in 1630.[49]

EDUCATION. A school run by Mrs. Slade at St. Michaelchurch was recorded c. 1770.[50] In 1874 the parish joined a united school board for North Petherton and St. Michaelchurch, and the children attended North Newton school.[51]

CHARITIES FOR THE POOR. John Slade of Maunsel House, by will proved 1801, gave an annuity of £2 a year to buy tools of husbandry for the use of the labouring poor of the parish.[52] No distributions have been made within living memory.[53]

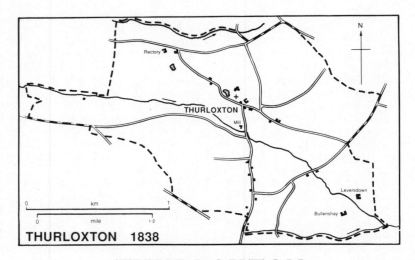

THURLOXTON 1838

THURLOXTON

THURLOXTON, probably taking its name from Reyner Thurlac, the 12th-century lord,[54] lies on the south-eastern slopes of the Quantocks, 6.5 km. north-east of Taunton. It is a small, compact parish 2.5 km. from east to west at its widest point and 1.5 km. from north to south. The parish occupies a shallow combe formed by a stream flowing east and south-east from Clavelshay in North Petherton, between the 137-m. and 46-m. contours. The village of Thurloxton lies in the centre and spreads south towards Adsborough in Creech St. Michael. Parts of the boundary with Creech on the south and with North Petherton on the east and north follow streams.[55] The ancient parish and the civil parish

are coterminous and measure 228 ha. (c. 540 a.).[56]

Most of the parish lies on Ilfracombe slate with an area of Upper Sandstone in the east. There were quarries in the centre of the village near the church and mill.[57]

The parish was probably once within the area of the minster church of North Petherton. It may represent the principal part of the estate recorded in 1086 as Tetesberge,[58] a name apparently surviving as Adsborough in Creech St. Michael, where the rest of the estate may have lain.[59] Thurloxton formerly had open fields, as indicated by furlong names.[60] There were 2 a. of woodland in 1086.[61] Although the parish was

40 S.R.O., DD/SAS PR 248, 314.
41 Ibid. DD/SLM, bk. of maps, St. Michaelchurch 1823.
42 Morris & Co. Dir. Som. (1872); for a photo., above, plate facing p. 313.
43 Taunton Castle, Pigott colln., wash drawing by J. Buckler, 1840.
44 W. Stradling, Priory of Chilton super Polden (1839), 5.
45 S.R.O., DD/SAS CH 16.
46 Ibid. D/P/s. mi 6/1/1.
47 Proc. Som. Arch. Soc. xlvii. 160; S.R.O., D/P/s. mi 5/2/1.
48 S.R.O., D/P/s. mi 2/1/1–4, 2/2/1.
49 Ibid. D/D/Ca 274.
50 Ibid. DD/SLM, bk. of maps.

51 Ibid. C/E 4/183/1; Lond. Gaz. 26 Mar. 1875, p. 1832.
52 Ibid. DD/SL 37; Char. Com. reg.
53 Inf. from the Revd. S. W. Davies, rector.
54 Below, manor.
55 O.S. Map 1/50,000, sheets 182, 193 (1976, 1979 edn.). This article was completed in 1985.
56 Census.
57 Geol. Surv. Map 1", drift, sheet 295 (1956 edn.); S.R.O., tithe award; O.S. Map 1/2,500, Som. LXI. 14 (1904 edn.).
58 V.C.H. Som. i. 501.
59 Above, Creech St. Michael.
60 B.L. Add. Ch. 16332.
61 V.C.H. Som. i. 501.

said to be well wooded in the late 18th century,[62] only 22 perches were recorded in 1838.[63]

Until the mid 19th century Thurloxton village lay scattered, principally along the road running south from the church to Adsborough; the northern part of the road was called Mill Lane, and the southern once formed part of the Bridgwater–Taunton turnpike route.[64] Several east–west lanes cross the parish. From Howell's Lane in the north, linking Clavelshay with Shearston in North Petherton, another lane runs south-east by the church to the turnpike road, forming from the mid 19th century a second line of settlement, including the Rectory at its western end, Manor House (which is not known to have been a manor house), and the school. The eastern part of the lane was known as Knotcroft Lane. Further south, Boez or Bowes Lane runs west from Mill Lane up the combe towards the Quantock ridge.[65] The Bridgwater–Taunton road was turnpiked in two stages, the part as far as the Green Dragon inn at the junction with Mill Lane by the Bridgwater trust in 1730,[66] and the remainder by the Taunton trust in 1751–2.[67] A tollgate was built between 1838 and 1851,[68] but both trusts ceased in the 1870s.[69] Improvements to the line of the road appear to have been suggested in 1822[70] but it was not until 1924–8 that, to provide relief work for the unemployed, a shorter route was made cutting across the angle on which the Green Dragon stands.[71]

Most of the houses in the village are of the later 19th century including Manor House and Thurloxton House, later called Hill View or Hill Cottage. The former mill house dates from the 16th century and the Cottage probably from the 17th. East of the village are the outlying habitations of Leversdown and Bullenshay Farm.

There was a tippler in the parish in 1619[72] and three licences were issued in 1674.[73] The Green Dragon was recorded by name in 1763[74] but was almost certainly licensed from 1660.[75] It closed before 1968 but reopened as a licensed restaurant in 1986.[76]

There were 25 houses in the parish in 1791[77] and 28 in 1801 when the population was 136. Numbers fluctuated during the 19th century: there were 156 inhabitants in 1811, 229 in 1831, 161 in 1881, and 210 in 1891. The total fell to 157 in 1901 and to 124 in 1981.[78]

Eight men from Thurloxton were fined for involvement in the Cornish rebellion in 1497,[79] and three men fought for the king in 1647.[80] The 18th-century diarist James Woodforde lived briefly at Thurloxton.[81]

MANOR AND OTHER ESTATES.

Until 1066 six thegns held in parage an estate called Tetesberge, which William de Mohun, lord of Dunster, held in 1086 with Hugh as his under tenant.[82] Before 1177, presumably following the death of his tenant, another William de Mohun had custody of Toteberga,[83] which probably soon after acquired the name THURLOXTON from Reyner Tornach or Thurlac, tenant of William for 1½ knight's fee in 1166.[84] Thurloxton was still held of the honor of Dunster in 1520.[85]

Reyner's daughter is said to have married Simon le Brett, who had evidently died by 1195 leaving a son Simon and a daughter Cecily. Cecily inherited Thurloxton[86] and married John of Bigbury, perhaps also called John of Thurloxton. Cecily gave land in Thurloxton perhaps including the manor to Taunton priory. Her son Henry of Bigbury confirmed her gift,[87] and in 1258 the priory held the manor.[88] By 1291 the income was assigned to the pittancer of the priory;[89] in the 15th century it was paid to the prior, pittancer, sacrist, steward, and cellarer.[90] The priory continued to hold the manor until the Dissolution.[91]

The Crown let the manor to Sir Thomas White in 1554[92] and in 1557 granted it in fee to William Babington and his wife Elizabeth.[93] Babington sold it to Henry Portman and others in 1564.[94] In 1566 Portman's fellow purchasers released their rights to him[95] and the manor descended in the Portman family like Clavelshay in North Petherton. All the land had been enfranchised by 1943.[96]

There is no record of a capital messuage. A dovecot was mentioned in the 15th and 16th centuries.[97] Thurloxton Farm, adjoining the churchyard, was said in 1763 to be 'good enough for any nobleman'[98] and in 1791 was 'a small house with neat gardens'.[99] It was substantially rebuilt in the mid 19th century, but incorporates the structure of an earlier house.

John Bole was a free tenant of Thurloxton manor in 1539,[1] and in 1548 John Hodges or

62   Collinson, *Hist. Som.* iii. 102.
63   S.R.O., tithe award.
64   *S.R.S.* lxxvi, Day and Masters map; S.R.O., tithe award.
65   O.S. Map 6", Som. LXI. SW. (1887 edn.).
66   3 Geo. II, c. 34.
67   25 Geo. II, c. 54.
68   S.R.O., tithe award; P.R.O., HO 107/1924.
69   J. B. Bentley and B. J. Murless, *Som. Roads* (1985), 21, 53.
70   S.R.O., Q/AB 35.
71   Ibid. DD/SIAS 29.
72   Ibid. Q/RLa 33.
73   Ibid. Q/RL.
74   *Ansford Diary of Jas. Woodforde*, ed. R. C. Winstanley (1980), i. 75.
75   S.R.O., Q/RL.
76   *Bridgwater Mercury*, 24 Sept. 1986.
77   Collinson, *Hist. Som.* iii. 102.
78   *Census.*
79   S.R.O., DD/BTL 25.

80   *Cal. Cttee. for Compounding*, iv. 3129.
81   Below, church.
82   *Dom. Bk.* ed. Thorn, 25.3 and p. 327.
83   *Pipe R.* 1177 (P.R.S. xxvi), 25; the identity of Thurloxton, held by the Bretts in the 12th cent., with Tetesberge, held by Hugh in 1086, is supported by the fact that Torweston was similarly held at those dates: *S.R.S.* extra ser. 143:
84   *S.R.S.* xxxiii, p. 4.   85   Ibid. p. 267.
86   Ibid. xxv, p. 90; lxi, p. 9; extra ser. 143–5.
87   Ibid. xiv, p. 177; *Cal. Chart. R.* 1327–41, 316.
88   *S.R.S.* xxxiii, p. 37.   89   *Tax. Eccl.* (Rec. Com.), 204.
90   B.L. Add. Ch. 16333, 25873.
91   *Valor Eccl.* (Rec. Com.), i. 168.
92   *Cal. Pat.* 1553–4, 318.   93   Ibid. 1555–7, 480.
94   Ibid. 1563–6, p. 3; S.R.O., DD/PM 3/1.
95   S.R.O., DD/PM 3/1.
96   Above, N. Petherton, manors; P.R.O., CRES 35/1149.
97   B.L. Add. Ch. 16333; S.R.O., DD/PM 3/1.
98   *Ansford Diary of Jas. Woodforde*, i. 76.
99   Collinson, *Hist. Som.* iii. 102.
1   P.R.O., SC 6/Hen. VIII/3137.

Balle held Bollyshay or *BULLENSHAY*,[2] which by the late 18th century belonged to the Harrisons, owners of Leversdown.[3]

LEVERSDOWN belonged to John Pratt (d. 1600). Pratt is said to have married Catherine Popham, possibly the daughter of Marmaduke (d. 1558), who held land in Thurloxton in 1555.[4] Leversdown passed from Pratt to successive sons, John (d. 1643), John (d. 1668), John (d. 1731), and John, who died in 1741 without issue and whose sister Mary married John Keyt, lord of Creech St. Michael manor.[5] Mary (d. 1757) settled Leversdown on Elizabeth Blake of Glastonbury in 1752 for her marriage to William Harrison of Thurloxton.[6] Harrison was succeeded in 1788 by his son William (d. 1811). Francis, a younger son of William, owned Leversdown in 1838;[7] he lived at Bullenshay Farm and was dead by 1861. He was probably succeeded by his nephew Dr. Richard Strong (d. 1867).[8] By 1894 the estate had been split up and Leversdown House was owned by Col. N. Lowis.[9] Mr. A. H. D. Gibson owned the house in 1985.

The old house at Leversdown, described as a large stone building in 1791, is said to have stood north of the present house.[10] It was probably demolished *c.* 1834,[11] and the new house erected by 1840.[12] Part of it had been taken down by 1887,[13] leaving a roughcast, two-storeyed, three-bayed house with a recessed central porch.

ECONOMIC HISTORY. The estate held by Hugh of William de Mohun in 1086 comprised 4 ploughlands. There was 1 ploughteam on the demesne farm of 3 virgates worked by 3 *servi*, and 1¼ hide was shared between 6 *villani* and 12 bordars with 3½ teams. There were 6 a. of meadow, 100 a. of pasture, and 10 a. of moor.[14] In 1319 the demesne farm was in hand,[15] but by 1437 it was let. Rents and entry fines, amercements, capon rents, and chevage of a neif then amounted to less that £20.[16] Freeholds were recorded in the 1460s, including one called Benetshay.[17] Demesnes and customary holdings were distinguished in 1535,[18] but by 1539 all the lands were accounted as customary, except three small freeholds,[19] probably including Bullenshay.[20]

In 1086 demesne stock comprised three beasts and a pig.[21] Pigs and geese were mentioned in 1539.[22] Sheep figured in 16th-century wills: one man distributed a flock of 40 among members of his family in 1558, another gave a lamb for church repairs.[23] In 1634 the rector received tithes and moduses on cider, apples, wool, colts, pigs, lambs, cows, and calves and on pasture let to non-parishioners.[24] Sheep continued to be important in the later 17th century and one farmer had a flock worth £34 in 1666.[25] Farming, however, was mixed: cheese and cider were made, and peas and vetches were grown.[26]

In 1784 flax was grown on 6 a. at Leversdown which produced a crop weighing over 200 stone.[27] At that period the parish was described as well cultivated, the land being very good and mainly in tillage.[28] In 1838 farms were small: 18 had between 5 a. and 25 a., 5 between 25 a. and 40 a., and the two largest holdings were the glebe (61 a.) and Thurloxton farm (63 a.).[29] During the later 19th century holdings were amalgamated but few men farmed more than 100 a. or employed more than two or three labourers. In 1861 Thurloxton farm had over 440 a. and 20 labourers but only half the land lay within the parish.[30] By 1943 the former Portman estate in the parish comprised three farms: Thurloxton (330 a.), Keirles (78 a.), and Glebe (76 a.), the last without a house.[31]

In 1838 *c.* 345 a. were arable, 150 a. meadow and pasture, and 56 a. orchards and gardens.[32] A lease of 1845 required the tenant to sow at least four of his 42 a. with artificial grass seed in the last year of his term, not to sow beans, and to feed sheep only. During the last two years he was limited to only 3 a. of potatoes.[33] By 1905 the parish was divided almost equally between arable and permanent grass.[34] In 1982 a return from four holdings covering almost the whole parish indicated the predominance of arable and horticultural crops, with only 60 ha. (*c.* 144 a.) under grass. The principal crops were wheat, barley, oilseed rape, potatoes, fruit, and green vegetables. Of the four farms, one produced general horticultural crops and another specialized in growing fruit for direct public sale. Livestock consisted of 323 sheep and a few cattle and poultry.[35]

A water mill kept in hand by the lords in 1437 and 1439, when a fulling mill was built or rebuilt,[36] was probably the mill sold to Henry Portman with the manor in 1566.[37] The mill, in

  2   P.R.O., C 142/99, no. 31.
  3   S.R.O., Q/REl 29/8.
  4   Ibid. DD/BTL 25; DD/X/SR 5; DD/SS 1; *Cal. Pat. 1554-5*, 175.
  5   S.R.O., D/P/thu 2/1/1-2.
  6   *Som. Wills*, ed. Brown, v. 63.
  7   S.R.O., D/P/thu 2/1/2-3; ibid. tithe award; ibid. Q/REl 29/8.
  8   P.R.O., HO 107/1924; S.R.O., D/P/thu 2/1/8; *P.O. Dir. Som.* (1861); M.I. in ch.
  9   S.R.O., D/R/bw 15/2/8; *Kelly's Dir. Som.* (1894).
 10   Collinson, *Hist. Som.* iii. 102; *S.D.N.Q.* xviii. 118-19.
 11   S.R.O., D/P/thu 4/1/1.
 12   *S.D.N.Q.* xviii. 118-19.
 13   O.S. Map 6", Som. LXI. SW. (1887 edn.).
 14   *V.C.H. Som.* i. 501.
 15   B.L. Add. Ch. 16332.
 16   Ibid. 16333, 25873.
 17   *S.R.S.* xxxiii, pp. 229-30.
 18   *Valor Eccl.* (Rec. Com.), i. 168.
 19   P.R.O., SC 6/Hen. VIII/3137.

 20   Above, manors.
 21   *V.C.H. Som.* i. 501.
 22   P.R.O., SC 6/Hen. VIII/3137.
 23   S.R.O., DD/X/SR 5.
 24   *S.D.N.Q.* xvi. 268-71.
 25   S.R.O., DD/SP inventory, 1666.
 26   Ibid. 1666, 1668, 1682, 1695.
 27   Ibid. Q/RLh 8.
 28   Collinson, *Hist. Som.* iii. 102.
 29   S.R.O., tithe award.
 30   P.R.O., HO 107/1924; ibid. RG 9/1622; S.R.O., D/R/bw 15/2/8.
 31   P.R.O., CRES 35/1149.
 32   S.R.O., tithe award.
 33   Ibid. DD/TBR 31.
 34   Statistics supplied by the then Bd. of Agric. (1905), relating to an acreage more than that of the parish.
 35   Min. of Agric., Fisheries, and Food, agric. returns, 1982; inf. from Thurloxton Fruit Growers.
 36   B.L. Add. Ch. 16333, 25873.
 37   S.R.O., DD/PM 3/1.

Mill Lane on the stream north of the road to Clavelshay,[38] had a malt mill by 1765 and was let to the Hopkins family,[39] the tenants in 1838.[40] It appears to have gone out of use by 1841.[41] The mill house, now Keirles Farm, dates from the 16th century, with 17th-century alterations and additions.[42] No trace of the mill remains.

In 1563 a man from Thurloxton imported wine and grindstones through Bridgwater,[43] and in 1617 another was a gunpowder maker.[44] In 1668 a man growing grain and peas for sale had a stock of oak and ash timber, 14 dozen and 9 pairs of stockings, some described as Irish, and a quantity of Irish cloth.[45] There was a maltster in 1695.[46] Other craftsmen in the 17th and 18th centuries included blacksmiths and a tallow chandler.[47] In 1821 8 out of 35 families were not engaged in agriculture.[48] By the later 19th century there were shoemakers, carpenters, dressmakers, butchers, and a wheelwright. One carpenter and builder employed five men in 1871 and kept a shop.[49]

LOCAL GOVERNMENT. The parish formed a single tithing in North Petherton hundred.[50] Court rolls for the manor survive for 1319–20;[51] courts were held three times a year in 1437–9 at Christmas, Hockday, and Michaelmas. In 1438 the cellarer of Taunton priory attended two courts with the steward.[52] Tenants owed suit to the Portmans' court for the manor in 1815.[53]

The stocks of the tithing were out of repair in 1650[54] and the churchwardens provided a lock and iron for them in 1777.[55] Two churchwardens and two sidesmen were appointed in the early 17th century[56] but by the later 18th century only one warden and one overseer.[57] The church house may have been used as a poorhouse in the 18th century.[58] About 1843 the vestry ordered the poorhouse to be sold. Roads were maintained by waywardens, and in 1838 the vestry agreed to employ a man for turnpike maintenance.[59] The parish formed part of Bridgwater poor-law union in 1836, Bridgwater rural district in 1894, and Sedgemoor district in 1974.[60]

CHURCH. The church of Thurloxton may have been one of the daughter churches and chapels of the minster church of North Petherton, in which residuary rights were granted to Buckland priory before 1176.[61] By 1195 and probably much earlier it had become an independent rectory, and by that year a temporary vicarage had been established.[62] The rectory remained a sole benefice until 1896; it was held 1896–1904 with Durston, with which it was united 1904–61.[63] From 1961 until 1975 it was again a sole living.[64] From 1975 Thurloxton was held with North Newton and St. Michaelchurch and in 1978 the united benefice of North Newton with St. Michaelchurch, Thurloxton, and Durston was created.[65]

The church evidently belonged to the lords of the manor in the 12th century, and the advowson passed to Taunton priory either with the manor by gift of Cecily la Brett or by her brother Simon le Brett's gift to William Wroth and the gift to the priory[66] of William's great-nephew Geoffrey of Scoland (d. c. 1288).[67] Until the Dissolution the priory held the advowson,[68] which presumably passed with the manor. By the early 17th century it belonged to the Portman family,[69] who held it until 1944 when patronage was transferred to the bishop.[70]

In 1535 the rectory was worth £7 4s. a year gross[71] and c. 1688 about £80.[72] Average annual income 1829–31 was put at £180.[73] In 1535 tithes and offerings amounted to £4 4s.[74] Tithes and moduses were let in the early 19th century[75] and were commuted for a rent charge of £102 17s. 2d. in 1838.[76] The glebe lands were valued at £3 a year in 1535[77] and in 1613 comprised 86 a., of which 26 a. were in North Petherton parish.[78] In 1877 c. 50 a. in Thurloxton and North Petherton were exchanged with Edward Portman, Viscount Portman.[79] In 1930 Glebe farm, then 76 a., was sold to the Portman trustees,[80] leaving c. 6½ a. which remained in 1978, mainly around the old rectory house.[81]

The medieval rectory house probably stood south of the church[82] on land known in 1838 as Parsonage plot.[83] By 1613 it had been replaced by a house north-west of the church, comprising a hall, kitchen, and buttery with chambers over and outbuildings.[84] From 1623 the house was regularly presented as being in need of repair,[85] notably in 1637 when the patron, Sir William Portman, took the rector to the ecclesiastical

38 Ibid. tithe award.   39 Ibid. DD/PM 19.
40 Ibid. tithe award.   41 Ibid. P.R.O., HO 107/953.
42 S.R.O., DD/V/BWr 33.1.
43 Ibid. D/B/bw 1463.
44 Ibid. D/D/Cd 50.
45 Ibid. DD/SP inventory, 1668.
46 Ibid. 1695.
47 Ibid. DD/X/SR 5.
48 Census, 1821.
49 P.R.O., HO 107/1924; ibid. RG 9/1622; RG 10/2383; RG 11/2372; Morris & Co. Dir. Som. (1872); P.O. Dir. Som. (1875).
50 S.R.S. xx. 129; S.R.O., Q/REl 29/3.
51 B.L. Add. Ch. 16332.
52 Ibid. 16333, 25873.
53 S.R.O., DD/PM 19.
54 S.R.S. xxviii. 123.
55 S.R.O., D/P/thu 4/1/1.
56 S.D.N.Q. xvi. 268–71.
57 S.R.O., D/P/thu 4/1/1.
58 Below, church.
59 S.R.O., D/P/thu 9/1/1.
60 Youngs, Local Admin. Units, i. 671, 673, 676.

61 B.L. Cott. Tib. E. 9, f. 23.   62 S.R.S. xxv, p. 90.
63 S.R.O., D/P/durn 2/1/2; D/P/thu 2/1/4, 2/9/1.
64 Ibid. D/P/lyn 22/3/1.
65 Ibid. D/P/new. n 2/9/2; Dioc. Dir.
66 S.R.S. xxv, p. 90; Cal. Chart. R. 1327–41, 316.
67 Cal. Inq. p.m. i, p. 54; Geoffrey was nephew of William's nephew Richard: above, N. Petherton, manors (Newton Forester).
68 Som. Incumbents, ed. Weaver, 456.
69 S.R.O., D/D/Cd 72; above, manor.
70 S.R.O., D/P/thu 2/9/2.
71 Valor Eccl. (Rec. Com.), i. 216.   72 S.R.O., D/D/Vc 24.
73 Rep. Com. Eccl. Revenues, pp. 156–7.
74 Valor Eccl. (Rec. Com.), i. 216.
75 S.R.O., DD/DP 108.
76 Ibid. tithe award.
77 Valor Eccl. (Rec. Com.), i. 216.
78 S.D.N.Q. xvi. 268–71.
79 Ibid. D/P/thu 3/1/2.
80 P.R.O., CRES 38/1891.
81 S.R.O., D/P/thu 3/1/2; inf. from Dioc. Office.
82 S.D.N.Q. xvi. 268–71.
83 S.R.O., tithe award.   84 S.D.N.Q. xvi. 268.
85 S.R.O., D/D/Ca 235, 266, 274, 310.

court.[86] A new house was built, possibly c. 1799,[87] on a slightly different site,[88] and was enlarged in 1868 by the addition of a new front containing two rooms and an entrance hall.[89] Built of stone and cob, it had six bedrooms, two reception rooms, study, kitchen, coach house, and stable when it was offered for sale in 1962. A new house was completed in 1964 nearer the church.[90]

There was a brotherhood in the parish in 1532.[91] The church lacked a chalice and service books in 1554[92] and in 1594 a bible and book of homilies.[93] From 1600 rectors were often non-resident: in 1603 the parish was served by an unlicensed curate and in 1606 by an illiterate parish clerk.[94] The parish shared a curate with St. Michaelchurch in 1606 and 1609.[95] A deacon was made rector in 1689.[96] James Woodforde was curate for three months in 1763.[97] His successor served as resident curate for 44 years.[98] About 1800 there were only 12 communicants.[99] In the early 19th century successive vicars of Creech St. Michael served the cure[1] and there was only one Sunday service at Thurloxton.[2] In 1843 communion was celebrated three times a year and the Sunday service alternated between morning and afternoon.[3] In 1904 Robert Bartlett resigned after being resident rector for 45 years.[4]

A church house mentioned in 1698 appears to have been a dwelling.[5] It was repaired by the churchwardens in 1766 and 1770 and was last recorded in 1777. It may have been used as a poorhouse.[6]

The church of *ST. GILES*, so dedicated by 1529,[7] comprises a chancel with north vestry, a nave with north aisle and south porch, and a west tower. The south wall of the nave and chancel, and possibly the tower, date from the 12th century. The chancel was enlarged in the 13th century, and was in need of repair in 1318.[8] The east window dates from the 14th century, and the tower was also then remodelled and given a new west window. The west door was probably inserted in 1500, the date on the external west wall. The south porch was added in the late 16th or early 17th century. A gallery was inserted before c. 1800.[9] After a storm in 1840 the pinnacles were removed from the tower.[10] The vestry was added shortly after 1856[11] and the north aisle was built in 1868 when the church was restored.[12] At a further restoration in 1881 new ceilings were installed and the gallery was taken down.[13]

The plain font, perhaps of c. 1100, has an octagonal, crocketted cover of the 14th century. The communion table is Elizabethan; the screen and pulpit both contain 17th-century woodwork, probably remodelled in the mid 18th century. The pulpit has figures similar to those at North Newton and an angel bearing a shield with the date 1634. The screen bears the date 1750 painted over the names of the churchwardens of 1634.[14] The pews at the west end were made in 1773[15] but others date from the 17th century.

The five bells include one of c. 1350 from Bristol, a late medieval bell from Exeter, and another of the late 16th-century by Roger Semson.[16] The plate includes a cup and cover by Ions of Exeter c. 1574 and a salver given by Mary Keyt in 1749.[17] The registers date from 1558 and are complete.[18]

NONCONFORMITY. Baptists are said to have met in the parish in the 1830s.[19]

EDUCATION. In 1819 there were two schools, one of which, supported by voluntary contributions, had 20 children and one paid teacher.[20] Both schools appear to have closed before 1825.[21] In 1861 a Sunday school was held in a cottage adjoining the rectory[22] and in 1862 a church day school was built south-east of the church. By 1903 there were 72 children on the books, with two teachers. A Sunday school and an evening continuation school were held on the premises.[23] Numbers fell from 66 in 1905 to 25 in 1935 and 14 in 1968 when the school was closed, the children going to West Monkton and North Petherton.[24] In 1985 the building was used as a village hall.

CHARITIES FOR THE POOR. None known.

86 S.R.O., D/D/Cd 72.
87 Ibid. DD/DP 108; D/D/Bbm 16.
88 *S.D.N.Q.* xvi. 271.
89 S.R.O., D/D/Bbm 159.
90 Ibid. D/P/thu 3/4/2–4.
91 *Wells Wills*, ed. Weaver, 171.
92 S.R.O., D/D/Ca 22.
93 Ibid. 98.
94 Ibid. 134, 151.
95 Ibid. 151, 160.
96 Ibid. D/D/Bs 43.
97 *Ansford Diary of Jas. Woodforde*, i. 75–88; ii. 46.
98 S.R.O., D/P/thu 2/1/2.
99 Ibid. D/D/Vc 88.
1 Ibid. D/D/Bo; D/D/Bp.
2 Ibid. D/D/Rb 1827.
3 Ibid. D/D/Va 1843.
4 Ibid. D/P/thu 2/1/4.
5 Ibid. Q/SR 207/8.
6 Ibid. D/P/thu 4/1/1.

7 *S.R.S.* lv, p. 29.
8 Ibid. i. 12.   9 S.R.O., D/P/thu 4/1/1.
10 *S.D.N.Q.* xvi. 305.
11 S.R.O., DD/BTL 29.
12 Ibid. D/P/thu 2/1/4.
13 Ibid. DD/BTL 29; D/P/thu 2/1/4; 8/2/1, 4.
14 F. B. Bond and B. Camm, *Roodscreens and Roodlofts* (1909), 195.
15 S.R.O., D/P/thu 4/1/1.
16 Ibid. DD/SAS CH 16/2.
17 *Proc. Som. Arch. Soc.* xlvii. 162.
18 S.R.O., D/P/thu 2/1/2–8.
19 Creech St. Michael, Zion Bapt. Ch. duplicated newsletter, Oct. 1974, 6.
20 *Educ. of Poor Digest*, p. 800.
21 *Ann. Rep. B. & W. Dioc. Assoc. S.P.C.K.* (1825–6); *Educ. Enq. Abstract*, p. 825.
22 *P.O. Dir. Som.* (1861).
23 S.R.O., C/E 4/380/395.
24 Ibid. 4/64, 306.

WEMBDON

THE main part of the ancient parish of Wembdon lay close to the town of Bridgwater on the north-west side.[25] A small part of it was within Bridgwater borough from 1835,[26] and the south-east corner has been increasingly occupied since the 1840s by the expanding suburbs of Bridgwater. North-east of the town a detached part of Wembdon parish, c. 170 a.,[27] including Sydenham which gave its name to a medieval estate, lay between the Parrett and Horsey rhyne, much of its boundary formed by a curving ditch which may mark a former course of the river.

From 1 km. beyond the town's west gate the southern boundary of the main part of the parish ran for 3 km. west, first along the road to Wembdon village and then along a hedge, part of which may have been the northern edge of Queen's wood in Bridgwater parish.[28] From that line the parish stretched northwards for more than 5 km. to the river Parrett. The western boundary with Cannington followed a stream, called in succession from south to north Perrymoor brook, Cannington brook, and Fenlyns rhyne. In the north the parish boundary followed the limit of high water in a wide curve of the Parrett and ditches and embankments around detached parts of Chilton Trinity parish. The irregular eastern boundary, from 1802 modified by the inclosure of Chilton common,[29] is marked in part by the Chilton road at Crowpill.

The boundaries were altered in 1886, when parts of Wembdon including the part in Bridgwater borough and the detached area of Sydenham, containing together 21 houses and 81 persons in 1891, were transferred to Bridgwater parish, and a part containing 1 house and 9 persons was transferred to Chilton Trinity, while uninhabited parts of Bridgwater and Chilton Trinity parishes were added to Wembdon. A further part of Wembdon, containing 270 houses and 1,141 persons in 1901, was transferred to Bridgwater borough and civil parish in 1896, reducing the area of Wembdon from 2,470 a. (1,000 ha.) to 2,351 a., and another 69 a., uninhabited in 1921 but with 6 persons in 1931, were transferred in 1933.[30] In 1938 Wembdon successfully resisted Bridgwater's attempt to absorb the rest of the parish.[31] The history of Sydenham, taken into the borough under Acts of 1928 and 1938,[32] is treated here with that of Wembdon.

Most of the northern part of the parish and the whole of the Sydenham area lies on alluvium below the 8-m. contour, with small areas of Burtle Beds in the centre;[33] sand was dug at Sandford in the early 15th century[34] and sandstone occurs north of Wembdon village near Perry Court.[35] The southern part, formed largely of Keuper marl, comprises two parallel east–west ridges, both reaching over 30 m. above sea level, the valley between them drained by the Kidsbury rhyne. The northern ridge, its centre known as Mount Radford from the mid 18th century, from a messuage named Mount Rodburd c. 1727,[36] contains a deposit of Upper Sandstone which was quarried from 1842 until after 1909.[37]

A watercourse known as Crowpill channel was dug before 1439,[38] Bradelake was mentioned c. 1540,[39] Fichet's rhyne in 1579,[40] Great or Wildmarsh rhyne in 1705,[41] and Pippins rhyne in 1802.[42]

Saxon burials have been discovered on the northern ridge where Wembdon Hill and Moore's and Hollow lanes may outline a triangular defensive site of the Bronze Age and later.[43] The hill gives the second element of the name of the parish. Traces of Romano-British settlement have been found further north near Perry Court and enclosures of uncertain date southwest of Perry Green.[44]

Wembdon village remained small until the 1840s, confined largely to the ridge between Mount Radford in the west and the church and parsonage house in the east. Houses were thereafter built along the road to Bridgwater, first detached houses south of the village in the 1840s on what came to be called Wembdon Rise and later terraces and semidetached houses stretching along Wembdon Road.[45] By 1851 a street of small terraced houses called Provident Place had been built,[46] and by the 1880s Newtown had been established as a suburb of Bridgwater for workers at the docks,[47] and higher-quality dwellings at Washington Terrace in Malt Shovel Lane (later Victoria Road) and Alexandra Villas, later Alexandra Road. By the same date there were larger houses on the ridge in Wembdon village, including Elm Grove (later Down House) and Mount Radford, Hoxton House, and Prospect Cottage, besides terraced cottages at 'Top of the Hill' and others called Sunny Banks, later Sandbanks.[48] In the 1920s building began off

25 Above, map on p. 192. This article was completed in 1988.
26 V.C.H. Som. ii. 347, 352.
27 S.R.O., tithe award.
28 O.S. Map 6", Som. XXXVIII. SW., L. NW., SW., NE., SE. (1886 edn.).
29 S.R.O., Q/RDe 29.
30 Census, 1891; Sydenham was entirely in Bridgwater parish by 1891: O.S. Map 6", Som. L. NE., SE. (1889, 1891 edn.); cf. above, map on p. 194. Between 1901 and 1911 the acreage given in Census increased to 2,365 a., either through recalculation or because of changes in the river's course.
31 Squibbs, Bridgwater, 130.
32 Bridgwater Corporation Act, 1928; Bridgwater (Extension) Act, 1938; S.R.O., GP/D 19, Som. Review Order.
33 Geol. Surv. Map 1", drift, sheet 295 (1956 edn.); Proc.

Som. Arch. Soc. lxxxiii. 178.   34 S.R.S. lviii, p. 52.
35 Geol. Surv. Map 1", drift, sheet 295 (1956 edn.).
36 S.R.O., DD/CH 45; D/P/wem 9/1/1; cf. P.N. Devon (E.P.N.S.), ii. 437.
37 Plaque in quarry; S.R.O., D/R/bw 15/3/26.
38 S.R.S. lviii, no. 690.   39 P.R.O., LR 3/123, f. 14A.
40 S.R.O., DD/WG 16/8.
41 Ibid. DD/WG, box 6.   42 Ibid. Q/RDe 29.
43 Suggested by Mr. H. Woods, archaeologist, Wembdon; inf. from Mr. R. A. Croft, County Archaeologist.
44 Som. C.C., Sites and Mons. Rec.
45 S.R.O., tithe award; below, econ. hist.
46 P.R.O., HO 107/1925; R. Jarman, Hist. Bridgwater (1889), 261.   47 P.R.O., RG 11/2376.
48 O.S. Map 6", Som. L. SW. (1886 edn.); S.R.O., D/R/bw 15/3/26.

Wembdon Road in Hillgrove and Orchard lanes, and in the 1930s smaller houses on Wembdon Hill.[49] More houses were built off Church Road in the 1950s,[50] and in the valley west of Wembdon Road (later Wembdon Rise) in the 1970s and 1980s.[51]

Perry and Sandford were the most populous areas of the parish in the earlier 14th century; Wembdon tithing, presumably including Wembdon village, had only 5 taxpayers in 1327 compared with 28 in Perry tithing.[52] West Perers or West Perry was a distinct settlement in the later 13th and the earlier 14th century,[53] and was perhaps an earlier name for Perry Green. There is some evidence of depopulation there, possibly in the 17th century.[54] Earthworks south of Sandford Manor may represent a change of site of the manor house rather than a lost village.[55]

Sydenham may have been only a single farmstead until the division of the estate in the 15th century.[56] By 1881 there were some cottages and a group of substantial farm buildings called Mile End barn along the Bristol road.[57] Much of the southern part of Sydenham was from 1935 covered by the factory of British Cellophane Ltd.[58]

Cheslade Farm, later known as Chislett, lay in the north end of the parish and was the centre of an estate by the mid 13th century, surviving as a single dwelling until the 1920s;[59] west of it by 1670 was a farm known as Hillocks.[60] After the inclosure of the commons in 1802[61] a farm was established beside Harp common, known in 1809 as Wallen and later as Waldings or Waldrons farm.[62] In the earlier 14th century there was a small settlement at Kidsbury,[63] 0.5 km. SSE. of Wembdon church. At least one house survived there in the mid 18th century,[64] but by 1841 only fields bore the name.[65] The spring below Wembdon Hill, whose curative properties were discovered in 1464,[66] was then known as St. John's well, and later as Holywell or Holowell.[67] The well head was rebuilt in 1855.[68] The name Medigdon given to land near Wembdon village in the later 13th century[69] may be the origin of Haddington Green, named in the 16th and the 17th century.[70]

The Saxon burial site on Mount Radford lies beside an east–west route which seems to have linked a possible crossing-point of the Parrett at Crowpill with Cannington, passing close to the site of Wembdon church. It may have given its name to a field called Hareway.[71] By the 14th century two other routes through the parish from Bridgwater seem to have been formed, one through Kidsbury,[72] the other further south to Bridgwater park.[73] The southern route later turned north-west as the main route to Cannington, leaving the parish church on a side road. It was turnpiked in 1730.[74] A toll house and gate were erected at the foot of Wembdon Hill;[75] by 1886 the house was used as a police station[76] and in 1987 was no. 119 Wembdon Road. There was also a toll gate at the crossroads on Wembdon Hill west of the village, where Moore's and Skimmerton lanes joined the Cannington road.[77] In 1922 a new route, called Quantock Road, was made further south to bypass Wembdon village and rejoin the former turnpike road just within Cannington parish.[78]

A medieval route further north snaked along a causeway at the edge of the marsh, linking Chilton Trinity village with Perry. One part of the route was described in 1340 as the highway to Cannington,[79] and it may be the route indicated by the field name Rudgeway.[80] Roads were created in Harp and Chilton commons after inclosure, and were extended in the mid 19th century.[81]

Open-field arable farming has been traced south-west of Wembdon village where there were fields called Waeforland, Godyvelond, Blackland, and Checkacre;[82] and also on Wembdon hill.[83] A *cultura* called Cokke at Sydenham was mentioned in 1414, a north field there in 1507, and Sydenham field in 1573 and 1604.[84] There was still a common arable field on Perry Furneaux manor in 1582.[85]

A common meadow called Monemede or Mowing mead, near Perry, was mentioned in 1397,[86] and by the later 16th century there was common grassland called Perry moor, Chilton moor, Harewey, and Langland, all north of Wembdon hill.[87] Bound stones in Perry moor were reported down in 1747 and stones and posts were replaced in 1785 by stones marked 'O' to

49 S.R.O., D/R/bw 16/19/1, 22/1/23.
50 C. Rayner-Smith, *Wembdon and its Church* (1959), 5.
51 Local inf.
52 *S.R.S.* iii. 242–3.
53 Pole MS. 2366, 2558, 2692, 2837.
54 Hants R.O. 7M54/20; S.R.O., DD/WG, box 6 (1705 survey).
55 Suggested by Mr. H. Woods.
56 Below, manors (Sydenham).
57 P.R.O., RG 11/2372.
58 C. H. Ward-Jackson, *The 'Cellophane' Story* (priv. print. 1977), 84, 89.
59 Below, manors; P.R.O., RG 11/2376; O.S. Map 6", Som. L. NW. (1886 edn.); inf. from Mr. A. H. Sparkes, Pury Court Farm, Wembdon.
60 S.R.O., DD/DP 73/2; *S.R.S.* iii. 243 (John Hillok); inf. from Mr. A. H. Sparkes.
61 Below, this section.
62 *S.R.S.* lxxvi, intro., p. 25.
63 Ibid. xlviii, no. 83.
64 S.R.O., D/P/wem 9/1/1.
65 Ibid. tithe award.
66 *S.R.S.* xlix, p. 414.
67 S.R.O., DD/S/WH 247; P.R.O., SC 6/Hen. VIII/3137; below, church.

68 Plaque on building.
69 S.R.O., DD/S/WH 68.
70 Ibid. DD/SP inventory, 1668/5; DD/PAM 8 (sale partic. Wembdon manor).
71 Dors. R.O., D.1. MW/M4.
72 *S.R.S.* xlviii, nos. 52, 83, 85, 95, 124.
73 Ibid. nos. 93, 212; liii, nos. 386, 449; lviii, nos. 503, 588, 623, 629, 635, 651–2.
74 S.R.O., DD/SAS (C/2402) 34; J. B. Bentley and B. J. Murless, *Som. Roads* (1985), i. 23.
75 S.R.O., tithe award.
76 O.S. Map 6", Som. L. SW. (1886 edn.).
77 *Cat. of MSS. offered for sale by A. J. Coombes* (1982).
78 Squibbs, *Bridgwater*, 122.
79 S.R.O., DD/SAS PD 31.
80 Dors. R.O., D.1. MW/M4.
81 S.R.O., D/P/wem 4/1/1, accts. of waywardens.
82 *S.R.S.* xlviii, nos. 2, 67, 86, 101, 110, 204; lviii, no. 565.
83 Ibid. lviii, no. 632; Dors. R.O., D.1. MW/M4; S.R.O., tithe award.
84 S.R.O., DD/L P36/6; DD/SG 20.
85 Ibid. T/PH/vch 65.
86 Pole MS. 4033.
87 S.R.O., T/PH/vch 65.

define the limits of the Oglanders' manor of Perry Furneaux.[88]

Extensive common grazing north of Wembdon village[89] included Chislett Warth, also called Sheepsleight or Sheepwalk, in the extreme north beside the Parrett in both Wembdon and Chilton Trinity parishes.[90] There was also common adjoining on Potter's Slyme,[91] and elsewhere. A second common called Sheepsleight, on the east bank of the Parrett, belonged to Sydenham.[92]

Wildmarsh and Harp common seem to have been names for common land shared between Wembdon, Durleigh, Chilton, and Bridgwater parishes north-west of Chilton Trinity village. In 1705 the common was variously known as Wildmarsh, Harp common, Chilton common, Wembdon common, Wembdon marsh, and Wembdon warth.[93] During the 18th century parts of the common were inclosed by agreement, and the remainder, about 260 a. of common meadow and pasture mostly in Durleigh and Bridgwater, was allotted in 1802 under an Act of 1798. Included were c. 23 a. in Wembdon.[94] There was a small piece of common near Wembdon church in the 18th century.[95]

There were 55 a. of woodland recorded in the parish in 1086, most of it evidently on the low-lying ground around Perry.[96] A coppice with oak and ash standards lay on Perry Furneaux manor in 1586 near a field called Rams Park.[97] A wood formerly called the king's wood adjoined Cokers farm in the south in 1664.[98] By 1841 there were 4 a. of wood in the parish.[99]

A field between Bridgwater and Kidsbury was called Euyn churchyard in 1540 and Jews Churchyard in the 19th century.[1] The origin of the name is not known.

In 1659 an unlicensed tippler was reported in the parish.[2] Victuallers had been licensed by 1674 and two were in business in 1690. A further licence was issued in 1741.[3] The Malt Shovel inn had been established at the junction of the Wembdon road and Kidsbury Lane by 1785,[4] and the present building replaced it in 1904.[5] The Rest and Be Thankful inn was open in 1856, the Cottage inn, combined with a grocer's shop, in 1861, and Templer's inn, probably later the Rock House inn, in 1875.[6] The Rock House continued as an inn until 1899 or later;[7] the Cottage inn was in business in 1987. In 1881 the George coffee tavern was open in Wembdon village and the British Flag public house in Chilton Street, Newtown.[8] In 1947 a private

house called Halesleigh or Halesleigh Tower, at the junction of Wembdon and Quantock roads, was converted into the Quantock Gateway Hotel.[9]

The Wembdon friendly society was established c. 1852 and was evidently re-formed in 1868. It was dissolved c. 1907.[10]

The population of the parish in 1801 was 244. It rose to 296 in 1811 and with minor fluctuations reached 370 in 1841. In the next decade it increased to 819, and by 1871 reached 1,107, much of the increase housed in those parts of the parish within Bridgwater borough. By 1881 the total was 1,299 and in 1901 1,842. The total continued to rise as houses were built in the part of Wembdon that had been added to Bridgwater. In 1921 the population within the ancient parish of Wembdon was 2,162 and in 1931 3,612. There was little increase in the next two decades and in 1951 the total of 4,011 comprised 3,116 in Bridgwater borough and 895 in Wembdon civil parish. In 1971 the total in the civil parish was 1,574 and in 1981 1,778.[11]

MANORS AND OTHER ESTATES. Merlesuain held *WEMBDON* in 1066; Walter of Douai held it in 1086.[12] The overlordship seems to have passed by the late 12th century to William Brewer (d. 1226),[13] and then through one of William's daughters, Alice, wife of Reynold Mohun (d. 1213), to Reynold's son Reynold (d. 1258). From William Mohun of Ottery Mohun (Devon), the younger Reynold's son by his second wife, it passed to William's daughter Eleanor, wife of John de Carru. In 1329 the overlord was John and Eleanor's son John, and the manor was held as of Ottery Mohun manor.[14] In 1487 and 1616 it was said to be held as of North Petherton manor.[15]

A mesne lordship was ascribed in 1284–5, 1303, and 1329 to Richard de Grenville (d. by 1327), possibly a descendant of William Brewer whose granddaughter Isabel Pagnell married Eustace de Grenville.[16] Theobald Grenville succeeded his father Henry as mesne lord in 1327,[17] but no later record of the lordship has been found.[18]

Walter of Douai's tenant in 1086 was Ludo.[19] Jordan of Wembdon, his son John the parson, and Jordan's granddaughter Sarah were successive owners of land in Wembdon which Sarah granted to William Brewer.[20] In 1268 William

88 Ibid. DD/X/DS 4.
89 Ibid. T/PH/vch 65.
90 Hants R.O. 7M54/199/21.
91 S.R.O., DD/DP 33/3.
92 Ibid. DD/SG 20; ibid. T/PH/no 3; P.R.O., E 178/6028.
93 S.R.O., DD/WG, box 6.
94 Ibid. Q/RDe 29.
95 Hants R.O. 7M54/200.
96 V.C.H. Som. i. 484–5, 499; below, manors (Perry Fichet).
97 Dors. R.O., D.1. MW/M4.
98 Hants R.O. 7M54/196/17.
99 S.R.O., tithe award.
1 Longleat House, Seymour Papers, XII, Seymour Rental, f. 16; S.R.O., DD/OS 76; ibid. tithe award.
2 S.R.S. xxviii. 371.
3 S.R.O., Q/RL vict. recog.
4 Ibid. D/P/bw. m 13/2/16.

5 Squibbs, *Bridgwater*, 12.
6 P.R.O., FS 2/9; *P.O. Dir. Som.* (1861, 1866, 1875).
7 *Kelly's Dir. Som.* (1883, 1899).
8 P.R.O., RG 11/2376.
9 Squibbs, *Bridgwater*, 134.
10 *Bridgwater Mercury*, 15 June 1870; M. Fuller, *W. Country Friendly Soc.* 100, 107, 144; P.R.O., FS 2/9.
11 *V.C.H. Som.* ii. 347, 352; *Census*, giving figures for the ecclesiastical parish, nearly equivalent to the ancient parish.
12 *V.C.H. Som.* i. 499.   13 P.R.O., DL 25/299.
14 *Cal. Inq. p.m.* vii, pp. 87–8; Sanders, *Eng. Baronies*, 114; Burke, *Ext., Dorm., & Abeyant Peerages* (1840), 352.
15 P.R.O., C 142/440, no. 89; *Cal. Inq. p.m. Hen. VII*, i, pp. 114–15.
16 *Feud. Aids*, iv. 278, 300, 332; *Bk. of Fees*, i. 248.
17 *Cal. Inq. p.m.* vii, pp. 87–8.
18 Cf. below, this section (Sydenham).
19 *V.C.H. Som.* i. 499.
20 P.R.O., DL 25/299; DL 42/11, f. 7v.

Testard had land in Wembdon, and in 1284–5 he held the manor as ⅔ knight's fee.[21] Robert Testard held ½ fee in 1303 and 1316 but was dead by 1346.[22] The manor passed, possibly with Clayhill in Cannington, to Thomas Michell before 1428,[23] and Walter Michell died in 1487 in possession of the manor.[24] Thereafter it descended with East Chilton manor in Durleigh,[25] and in the earlier 17th century was said to comprise land in Wembdon, Cannington, Durleigh, and Stogursey.[26] A settlement of 1753 divided the manor between eight beneficiaries,[27] one of whom, Richard Gould, paid land tax on the estate until 1790 or later.[28] The Revd. David Reynell, husband of another beneficiary, was described as lord of Wembdon manor in 1838,[29] but by 1841 he had only 7 a. in the parish.[30] No further reference to the manor has been found.

Thomas Michell (d. 1539), lord of the manor, owned a house called Perry Court,[31] which was the capital messuage in the earlier 17th century.[32] By 1753 it was occupied by a tenant. It was offered for sale with c. 98 a. in 1773 and Jonas Coles, then tenant, was owner in 1777; from him it passed c. 1806 to Richard Morley. In 1816 it was held of Morley by Thomas Gulliford and Benjamin Jennings Marshall,[33] and they occupied it in 1841.[34] It was occupied by Marshall's two sons in 1851 with 20 a. of land.[35]

In 1269 Robert Coker, described as chief lord of a fee in Wembdon,[36] perhaps held what was later called COKERS. He may have been succeeded by William Coker.[37] Matthew Coker was a substantial taxpayer in Wembdon tithing in 1327[38] and in 1343 Richard Coker established his claim to c. 120 a. in Wembdon, Chilton, and Bridgwater.[39] William Coker of Wembdon was referred to in 1348.[40] James, son and heir of William, had a burgage in Bridgwater in 1362,[41] and Matthew and probably another James Coker were owners of land in Wembdon in 1407.[42] Matthew was still alive in 1412.[43] By 1464 a large and scattered estate including land in Wembdon had come to Margaret, daughter and heir of John Coker and wife of Sir Reynold Stourton.[44] Margaret died in 1489 owning an estate called Wembdon manor, said to be held of Robert Testard; her heir was John Seymour, son of a daughter of John Coker's brother Robert.[45] The descent thereafter has not been traced until 1664

when the owner, Gregory Hockmore, also lord of the principal manor of Wembdon, leased to William Clarke of Sandford the capital messuage called Cokers and a farm of 120 a.[46] The farm continued to descend with Wembdon manor, and from the mid 18th century was let to Samuel Sealy. Richard Gould paid land tax on it in 1781 and 1794, but by the following year it had passed to John Cridland.[47] The farm was later sold and divided, and in 1841 comprised 67 a.[48] By 1866 it was known as Cokehurst farm,[49] and later as Cokerhurst farm.

Cokerhurst Farm dates from the 15th or earlier 16th century and incorporates an open hall with jointed crucks.

Of four estates called Perry in 1086 Roger de Courcelles held two. The largest, which four thegns held in parage in 1066 as 1 hide and 1 ferling,[50] descended as *PERRY FICHET* with Kilve in the Malet fee,[51] being held of Enmore manor in the late 14th century for a rent called Maletstorm[52] and in 1472.[53] In 1497 it was said to be held of Sir Giles Daubeney as of his manor of South Petherton.[54]

In 1086 Roger de Courcelles's tenant was Geoffrey de Vautort.[55] By the late 12th century Richard Fichet held the manor in succession to unnamed ancestors.[56] Hugh Fichet, Richard's successor at Spaxton, seems to have held Perry in 1251.[57] The manor descended with Spaxton in the Fichet, Hill, and Waldegrave families.[58] James Waldegrave, Earl Waldegrave (d. 1763), retained Perry when he sold Spaxton, but his heir, John, Earl Waldegrave, sold it in 1777 to Richard Cridland the elder of Milverton. Cridland was succeeded by his son John (d. 1798) and by his grandson, also John Cridland (d. 1826). In 1862 a third John, son of the last, sold most of the land but not the lordship, together with Sandford farm, to the executors of Mrs. Stuckey, late of Langport.[59] The estate passed to her son-in-law, the Revd. James Stratton Coles (d. 1872),[60] and in or before 1878 to William Brice of Bridgwater. The Revd. Edward Henry Brice sold it in 1906 to Miss E. M. Brice (d. 1961). The estate then comprised Grabham's farm, Walronds, and Perry Court. Miss Brice left her land to her two agents, L. H. and C. D. Palmer, and it was conveyed jointly to the daughters of each, Mrs. S. Barnes and Miss E.

21 *S.R.S.* vi. 224–5; *Feud. Aids*, iv. 278.
22 *Feud. Aids*, iv. 300, 332, 344.
23 Ibid. 364; above, Cannington, manors.
24 *Cal. Inq. p.m. Hen. VII*, i, pp. 114–15.
25 Above, Durleigh, manors.
26 P.R.O., E 178/5607.
27 S.R.O., DD/PAM 8.
28 Ibid. Q/REl 29/9C.
29 Burke, *Commoners* (1833–8), iv. 455.
30 S.R.O., tithe award.
31 *S.R.S.* xxvii. 222.
32 P.R.O., E 178/5607.
33 S.R.O., DD/PAM 8, sale partic. 1773; ibid. Q/REl 29/9C.
34 Ibid. tithe award.
35 P.R.O., HO 107/1925.
36 *S.R.S.* xxxvi. 78.
37 Pole MS. 2692.
38 *S.R.S.* iii. 243.
39 Ibid. lvii, pp. 31–2.
40 *Cal. Close*, 1346–9, 568.

41 *S.R.S.* xlviii, no. 200.
42 Pole MS. 4034.
43 *Feud. Aids*, vi. 513.
44 *S.R.S.* xxii. 127.
45 *Cal. Inq. p.m. Hen. VII*, i, pp. 266–7.
46 Hants R.O. 7M54/196/17; above, this section (Wembdon).
47 S.R.O., D/P/wem 9/1/1; ibid. Q/REl 29/9.
48 Ibid. DD/X/SQ; ibid. tithe award.
49 *P.O. Dir. Som.* (1866); *Kelly's Dir. Som.* (1906).
50 *V.C.H. Som.* i. 484–5.
51 Ibid. v. 97.
52 *Cal. Inq. p.m.* xvi, p. 402; *S.R.S.* lxviii, p. 24.
53 P.R.O., C 140/42, no. 51.
54 *Cal. Inq. p.m. Hen. VII*, ii, p. 51; *S.R.S.* lxviii, p. 24.
55 *V.C.H. Som.* i. 484.
56 *S.R.S.* lxviii, p. 25; *Cat. Anct. D.* ii, B 2966.
57 *S.R.S.* lxviii, pp. 24–5.
58 Above, Spaxton, manors.
59 S.R.O., DD/PAM 8, abs. of title.
60 *P.O. Dir. Som.* (1866); M. Churchman, *The Stuckeys of Som.* (TS. in Local Hist. Libr., Taunton), 21, 44.

M. Palmer. The estate was partitioned in 1982, Mrs. Barnes receiving most of the former Perry Fichet land.[61]

The capital messuage of the manor, held with a farm of c. 46 a. in 1705, was known as Wembdon House.[62] No reference to the house has been found after 1717.[63] Its site may have been north of the present Perry Wood Farm.

The second estate of Roger de Courcelles in 1086 had been added to one called 'Ulveronetone' which has not been identified or traced later. The suggestion that 'Ulveronetone' was Waldrons ignores the fact that Waldrons was created only after 1802, and the similarity of detail given for 'Ulveronetone' and the estate called Perry added to it may indicate that the two were in fact the same.[64] In 1066 'Ulveronetone' was held as 1 hide and 1 ferling by Alwig, Perry as 1 hide by Alweard.[65] The overlordship descended from Roger de Courcelles in the Malet fee, and was held with Kilve from 1251.[66]

Roger's tenant in 1086 was one William.[67] The manor may have been what was later called *PERRY FURNEAUX*, being held in 1251 with Kilve by Matthew Furneaux.[68] He or a namesake held it in 1284–5, and it descended with Kilve to Alice Blount (d. 1414), wife first of Sir Richard Stafford and secondly of Sir Richard Stury.[69] In 1419, as heirs to a quarter of Alice's estate, Ralph Bush and Eleanor his wife sold their interest in Perry Furneaux to John Rogers of Bryanston (Dors.),[70] but in 1421 a partition assigned Perry, with Stringston,[71] to Joan, descended from the Furneaux family, and her husband Robert Greyndour (d. 1443).[72] Joan married secondly Sir John Barre and died in 1485 leaving as her heir William Strode of Somerton.[73]

The manor descended from William Strode with Stringston to the Oglander family.[74] Sir Henry Oglander, Bt., died childless in 1874; on his widow Louisa's death in 1894 the manor passed to trustees.[75] No further trace of it has been found.

In 1352 Sir Thomas Fichet was pardoned for burning the house of Simon Furneaux at Perry.[76] The manor house and some land were let both by Alice Stury and, in 1443–4, by Joan Greyndour.[77] The house was again let in the 16th century.[78] In the 17th and 18th centuries the capital messuage was known variously as the Farm, Perryfurneaux Manor, and Wembdon

Farm.[79] Wembdon Manor Farmhouse is a large building of the 18th century considerably altered in the 19th.

A third manor of *PERRY*, held in 1066 by Ordgar as rather more than ½ hide and in 1086, apparently as a serjeanty, by John the usher whose tenant was one Robert, may have been the land later known as Cheslade or Chislett.[80] In 1251–2 Walter of Cheslade held 1½ virgate in Cheslade which was said to have been alienated from the serjeanty of Pignes, in Chilton Trinity, in the reign of Henry II.[81] That land may have been the estate of more than 1 virgate in which Robert had succeeded his father Warner by 1201.[82] Another Walter of Cheslade sold a larger estate in Cheslade to Simon Michell in 1307,[83] and Walter Michell died in 1487 holding *CHESLADE* manor of Nicholas Bluet as of North Petherton manor. Walter was succeeded by his son William,[84] but no further trace of the estate has been found.

Another estate at Cheslade was settled by Henry Brent on Robert and Clarice Brent in 1318.[85] John Brent, great-grandson of Robert, held land there in 1412 which in 1417 was called *CHESLADE* manor when it was settled on John's daughter Joan, wife of John Trethek.[86] Tenements there held of Nicholas Bluet descended to Robert Brent, grandson of John Brent, which on Robert's death in 1508 passed to his son, also John.[87] Richard Brent (d. 1570), grandson of the last John, settled Cheslade and other lands in 1552 on Thomas Broughton of Sandford, on the proposed marriage of Richard's daughter and heir, Anne, with Broughton's heir.[88] The marriage did not take place but Broughton seems to have retained Cheslade, which descended on his death in 1579 to his son Robert.[89] Described as Cheslade farm, the estate passed with Sandford manor[90] until 1682 when William Clarke sold it to John Trenchard. Two years later Trenchard sold it to Richard Musgrave (d. c. 1686) of Nettlecombe,[91] and the farm then descended with Stamfordlands in North Petherton to Richard's son George (d. 1721) and to his grandson, also George Musgrave (d. 1724).[92] Mary, widow of the last George, held it in 1737[93] and it passed from their son George (d. 1742) to his son Thomas (d. 1766). Thomas's sister and heir Juliana married Sir James Langham (d. 1795), on whose death it was sold[94] to Edward Gore. Edward (d. 1801) was followed

61   S.R.O., DD/PAM 9–11; inf. from Miss E. M. Palmer, Wembdon.
62   S.R.O. DD/WG, box 6.
63   Ibid. Q/RR.
64   *Dom. Bk.* ed. Thorn, 21.6; *S.R.S.* lxxvi (intro.), 25.
65   *V.C.H. Som.* i. 484–5.
66   Ibid. v. 97; *S.R.S.* lxviii, pp. 24–5; P.R.O., C 141/5, no. 10.
67   *V.C.H. Som.* i. 484–5.
68   *S.R.S.* lxviii, pp. 24–5; P.R.O., C 141/5, no. 10.
69   *V.C.H. Som.* v. 98; *Feud. Aids,* iv. 278; *Cal. Inq. p.m.* x, p. 395; Pole MS. 2345, 2511, 2528–9, 2532, 2545.
70   *S.R.S.* xxii. 180.
71   Above, Stringston.
72   *S.D.N.Q.* xvi. 282; *Cal. Close,* 1441–7, 177.
73   Pole MS. 2740, 2778; Dors. R.O., D.1. MW/M4, p. 47; *Cal. Pat.* 1485–94, 364.
74   Above, Stringston.
75   Burke, *Land. Gent.* (1914), 1421–2; *Kelly's Dir. Som.* (1889, 1894, 1897).

76   *Cal. Pat.* 1350–4, 377.
77   Pole MS. 2778.
78   S.R.O., T/PH/vch 65.
79   Dors. R.O., D.1. MW/M4, M5, M6; ibid. D279/E4.
80   *V.C.H. Som.* i. 520; O.S. Map 6", Som. L. NW. (1886 edn.).
81   *Bk. of Fees,* ii. 1266.
82   *S.R.S.* xi, pp. 11–12.   83   Ibid. vi. 360.
84   *Cal. Inq. p.m. Hen. VII,* i, pp. 114–15.
85   *S.R.S.* xli. 79.
86   *Feud. Aids,* vi. 510; *S.R.S.* xxii. 181; above, Bawdrip, manors.
87   *Cal. Inq. p.m. Hen. VII,* iii, pp. 309–10.
88   P.R.O., C 142/156, no. 14.
89   *Som. Wills,* ed. Brown, i. 47.
90   Below, this section.
91   S.R.O., DD/SAS (C/114) 21/2; DD/DP 33/3; Hants R.O. 7M54/196/32.
92   S.R.O., DD/DP 33/7; DD/SAS (C/114) 21/3–6.
93   Ibid. DD/SAS (C/114) 21/5.
94   Ibid. T/PH/no 3.

by his second son, the Revd. Charles Gore (d. 1841), and Charles by his eldest son Montagu (d. unmarried 1864).[95] Thereafter the estate seems to have been divided and absorbed into neighbouring farms.

A farmhouse was recorded at Cheslade in 1684.[96] Chislett House was occupied by a landless family in 1851[97] and was later demolished.

A fourth manor of Perry, held in 1066 as ½ hide by Wulfric and in 1086 by Roger Arundel with one Ralph as his tenant,[98] may have been what became *WEST PERRY* manor, so called by 1487 when it was held by Walter Michell.[99] The manor descended in the Michell family with East Chilton in Durleigh to Sir Bartholomew Michell (d. 1616). Presumably thereafter it became part of the Hockmores' estate,[1] and its lands became merged with those of Wembdon manor around Perry Green.

In what became Wembdon parish Roger Arundel also held Sandford and Sydenham in 1086. Aethelweard had held Sandford as a little more than 1 hide in 1066, and Roger's tenant in 1086 was Ralph, perhaps he who held Roger's estate at Perry.[2] The overlordship descended with the barony of Poorstock (Dors.)[3] and the manor of Rodway in Cannington to the Fitzpayn family, and thence to the earls of Northumberland, of whom it was held until 1631 or later.[4] In 1236 Geoffrey de la Rode held a fee at *SANDFORD*, in 1482 called *SAMPFORD BICKFOLD*.[5] In 1280 and 1284–5 Henry of Bickfold held 1 knight's fee in Sandford, part of which was subinfeudated to John of Bickfold.[6] In 1303 John of Bickfold and Roger of Bickfold held Sandford as ½ knight's fee of Robert Fitzpayn, the tenant in chief; Roger was one of the lords in 1316, and Maud of Bickfold was one of the main taxpayers in Sandford in 1327.[7] John of Bickfold had an interest in a manor called Bickfold which William Sambrook and his wife settled in reversion on their daughter Richard in 1371.[8] In 1428 and 1431 Thomas Sambrook of Bickfold and Edward Culliford of Sandford held ½ knight's fee formerly held by John and Roger of Bickfold.[9]

In 1435 Alexander Hody, possibly acting as a trustee, seems to have acquired the reversion of land in Sandford, Wembdon, and Bridgwater in which Edward Culliford, William Paulet of Melcombe, and William Broughton and his wife Elizabeth had interests,[10] but Edward Culliford alone was described as lord in 1442–3.[11] By 1472 John Broughton held Sandford manor. He was succeeded in 1492 by his son also John.[12] John (d. 1529) was followed by his son Thomas (d. 1579) and Thomas by his son Robert (d. 1631).[13]

Robert Broughton was succeeded by his elder daughter Jane, wife of James Clarke, on whom the manor, Cheslade farm, and other land had been settled in 1606.[14] Jane settled the estate in 1636 on her son Robert Clarke[15] (d. *c*. 1658) whose son William (d. 1688)[16] in 1687 sold Sandford to the mortgagee Edmund Bourne.[17]

Bourne died in 1695.[18] His widow Anne outlived her second husband, Humphrey Steare, and in 1733 sold Sandford, subject to her own life interest, to John Clarke of Salisbury, to whom she leased the manor in 1736.[19] Clarke (d. 1746)[20] was succeeded by his son John, and the son by his sister Elizabeth (d. 1781), wife of James Harris (d. 1780). Their son James (cr. Baron Malmesbury 1788, earl of Malmesbury 1800) sold the estate in 1794 to John Cridland of Milverton.[21] Sandford descended with Perry Fichet[22] until 1982 when on a partition of the estate Miss E. M. Palmer became sole owner of Sandford.[23]

Sandford Manor, formerly Sandford Farm, has a **T**-shaped plan with a long range forming the south front and a broad arm to the north. The entrance is by a porch-like pedimented doorway which is dated 1570 in the east face of the north range. The central position of that doorway and foundations of other buildings to the north suggest that the east front was symmetrical. If so then the service rooms were in the north wing adjacent to a yard which is still partly surrounded by outbuildings. The principal rooms are now in the south range which was built in the later 16th century and has a garderobe turret at its north-west corner. The north range accommodates minor rooms on the ground floor but within its roof fragments of two smoke-blackened timbers are evidence of its former importance as a medieval open hall with a base-cruck central truss. On the first floor there is much late 16th- and early 17th-century panelling, some of which is reset.

At *SYDENHAM*, which Cypping held as 1 virgate in 1066, Roger Arundel's tenant in 1086 was one William.[24] By 1280 a fee there was held of the honor of Dunster, and lands and tenements there were still considered part of that honor in 1520.[25] The manor was said in 1626 to be held of John Bluet, probably as of North Petherton manor.[26] A mesne lordship was held by Richard de Grenville, mesne lord of

95 S.R.O., DD/BR/lch 22; DD/GB 36; Burke, *Land. Gent.* (1851), i. 692; *D.N.B.*
96 S.R.O., DD/DP 33/3.
97 P.R.O., HO 107/1925.
98 *V.C.H. Som.* i. 494.
99 *Cal. Inq. p.m. Hen. VII*, i, pp. 114–15.
1 P.R.O., E 178/5607; above, Durleigh, manors.
2 *V.C.H. Som.* i. 494.
3 Sanders, *Eng. Baronies*, 72.
4 P.R.O., C 142/763, no. 172.
5 *Bk. of Fees*, i. 581; *Cal. Inq. p.m. Hen. VII*, iii, p. 348.
6 *S.R.S.* xliv. 282; *Feud. Aids* iv. 278.
7 *Feud. Aids* iv. 301, 332; *S.R.S.* iii. 243.
8 *S.R.S.* xvii. 79.
9 *Feud. Aids*, iv. 364, 434.
10 *S.R.S.* xxii. 87.
11 P.R.O., SC 6/1119/17.
12 Ibid. C 140/42, no. 51; *Cal. Inq. p.m. Hen. VII*, iii, p. 348.

13 P.R.O., C 142/51, no. 87; C 142/191, no. 96; C 142/763, no. 172; Hants R.O. 7M54/196; *Som. Wills*, ed. Brown, i. 47.
14 P.R.O., C 142/763, no. 172; Hants R.O. 7M54/196/5, 199/1; S.R.O., DD/DP 33/3.
15 S.R.O., DD/DP 33/3.
16 Hants R.O. 7M54/196/12; *Som. Wills*, ed. Brown, iii. 32.
17 Hants R.O. 7M54/199/21.
18 *Som. Wills*, ed. Brown, v. 80.
19 Hants R.O. 7M54/199; S.R.O., pedigree in catalogue of DD/GL.
20 Hants R.O. 7M54/202.
21 S.R.O., DD/PAM 1–2.
22 Above, this section.
23 S.R.O., DD/PAM 11; inf. from Miss Palmer.
24 *V.C.H. Som.* i. 495.
25 *S.R.S.* xxxiii. 50, 272.
26 P.R.O., C 145/525, no. 61.

Wembdon, in 1284–5 and 1303[27] and by John Grenville the younger in 1471.[28]

Robert Russell had ⅓ of ⅕ knight's fee in Sydenham in 1228[29] which in 1242–3 was awarded to his illegitimate son Walter Russell,[30] also perhaps known as Walter of Sydenham. William son of Walter of Sydenham held land in Wembdon parish in 1268,[31] and in 1279 Walter and John of Sydenham held 1 knight's fee in Sydenham.[32] Walter of Sydenham held it in 1284–5,[33] and he or another of the same name held ½ fee in 1303 and 1316.[34] Ralph, son and heir of Walter, was mentioned in 1328–9[35] and 1332.[36] In 1346 the heirs of William of Sydenham were said to have held ½ fee there.[37] Roger Sydenham was lord in 1341–2[38] and John Sydenham seems to have succeeded by 1386 and survived until 1402.[39] Richard Sydenham held 1 knight's fee in 1402–3 and was followed by John Sydenham, lord in 1406–7 and 1410.[40]

John Sydenham's heir was his sister Joan, wife first of Richard Cave and secondly of Robert Bozun.[41] Joan and Robert settled the manor in 1417 on Walter Tilley, probably father-in-law of Joan's heir Philip Cave.[42] In 1428 Robert Bozun, Philip Cave, John Gosse, and Agnes Sydenham shared ½ knight's fee.[43]

John Sydenham let some land at Sydenham in 1435[44] and John Sydenham of Combe Sydenham owed suit to Dunster in respect of his holding there in 1446.[45] Richard Sydenham of North Petherton had land there c. 1508,[46] and Sir John Sydenham (d. 1625) was succeeded by his son, also John,[47] who retained possession until 1665.[48] No further trace of the family holding there has been found.

The estate of Philip Cave (d. 1471) passed to his son William.[49] William's son (Sir) John (d. s.p. c. 1529) left a widow Elizabeth (d. in or after 1548), later wife of James Hadley. William Cave's great-grandson[50] George Perceval seems to have succeeded in 1553–4[51] and occupied the estate until his death c. 1600.[52] His son Richard, who deciphered the coded Spanish invasion plans found in 1586, mortgaged and in 1613 sold Sydenham to William Bull.[53]

Bull died in 1622 and was followed in turn by his son William (d. 1676), his grandson Henry Bull (d. 1692), and Henry's son Henry (d. 1695).[54] The last was succeeded by his sister Eleanor (d. c. 1714), wife of George Dodington. George (d. 1720) was succeeded by his nephew George Bubb, later Dodington (cr. Baron Melcombe 1761, d. 1762), and the latter by Richard Grenville, Earl Temple (d. 1779). Richard's nephew and heir, George Grenville (cr. marquess of Buckingham 1784, d. 1813), was succeeded by his son Richard (cr. duke of Buckingham and Chandos 1822).[55]

Between 1814 and 1823[56] part of the estate, known as Little Sydenham, was sold to the Pleydell family of Horsey in Bridgwater. The remainder was offered for sale in 1824,[57] 1827,[58] and 1833.[59] It was eventually sold in 1837 to the Revd. Thomas Frederick Dymock, who in turn sold it in 1847 to Gabriel and Joseph Poole. In 1848 the Pooles conveyed the manor house and c. 10 a. of land to Joseph Boon of Wembdon, while the rest of the estate was divided, part passing to the owners of Hawkers farm in Chilton Trinity. Joseph Boon died in 1894 and the house passed to William Bourchier. Bourchier sold it in 1916 to Col. S. H. Lynn, who sold it to Philip Sturdy in 1921. Sturdy also bought some land in 1927 but in 1935 sold both house and land to British Cellophane Ltd. The house, its grounds, and surrounding fields became part of the growing industrial site.[60]

The eastern side of Sydenham Manor, including the tower-like block at its north-east corner, is of the later 15th or earlier 16th century. It probably formed the cross wing to a medieval hall range which lay to the west, served by the pair of two-centred doorways in the main passageway. The hall was probably removed in the earlier 17th century when the house was remodelled, either by the Bull family or by Francis Galhampton, tenant from 1620.[61] The passageway was extended across a new north range to a two-storeyed porch, which incorporated an earlier doorway bearing the arms probably of Cave and Perceval.[62]

The south end of the medieval cross wing was also extended west and the ground-floor room was given a moulded plaster ceiling. The staircase in the angle between the north range and the cross wing has turned balusters of the mid 17th century. The house was restored in the 1960s and again in the 1980s, and in 1987 served as a conference and hospitality centre for British Cellophane Ltd.[63]

In the later 12th or earlier 13th century Robert of Pereton sold to William Brewer (d. 1226) a virgate of land in *KIDSBURY* held of Jordan

27 *Feud. Aids*, iv. 279, 300; *S.R.S.* xxxiii. 63, 65.
28 P.R.O., C 140/38, no. 43.
29 *S.R.S.* vi. 72, 106–7.
30 Ibid. xi, pp. 139–40.
31 Ibid. vi. 224.
32 *Cal. Inq. p.m.* ii, p. 179.
33 *S.R.S.* xxxiii. 63; *Feud. Aids*, iv. 279; *Cal. Inq. p.m.* ii, p. 353.
34 *Feud. Aids*, iv. 300, 332.
35 Pole MS. 731.
36 *S.R.S.* xii. 162.
37 *Feud. Aids*, iv. 344.
38 Collinson, *Hist. Som.* iii. 86.
39 *S.R.S.* xvii. 132; *Cal. Close*, 1399–1402, 497.
40 *S.R.S.* xxxiii. 116, 129; lviii, no. 553.
41 Collinson, *Hist. Som.* iii. 86–7.
42 *S.R.S.* xxii. 53.
43 *Feud. Aids*, iv. 364.
44 S.R.O., DD/L P36, lease 1435.
45 *S.R.S.* xxxiii. 221.

46 S.R.O., DD/L P36/6.
47 P.R.O., C 145/525, no. 61.
48 Ibid. CP 25(2)/715/17 Chas. II Trin.
49 Ibid. C 140/38, no. 43.
50 Ibid. C 142/56, no. 24; C 142/97, no. 79; S.R.O., DD/SG 4; DD/S/WH 116.
51 P.R.O., C 60/367, no 15.
52 S.R.O., DD/L P36/6; DD/WG 16/16.
53 Hist. MSS. Com. *Egmont*, i (1), 120; i (2), 487–8.
54 S.R.O., DD/SG 4, 9, 17–18; Collinson, *Hist. Som.* iii. 428.
55 S.R.O., DD/SG 9, 18; *V.C.H. Som.* v. 66.
56 S.R.O., T/PH/vch 56, rental 1814; ibid. DD/X/SQ.
57 Ibid. DD/HC, box 6N.   58 Ibid. DD/HWD 19.
59 Ibid. DD/AH 14/3, 20/5.
60 Sydenham Manor, British Cellophane Ltd., deeds; C. H. Ward-Jackson, The 'Cellophane' Story; local inf.; below, econ. hist.   61 S.R.O., DD/SG 20.
62 Cf. above, this section.
63 C. H. Ward-Jackson, *Sydenham Manor Ho.* (priv. print. 1962); local inf.

of Wembdon for suit of court and a pair of gilt spurs.[64] The estate was held of Richard de Grenville as of Wembdon in 1303[65] and the capital messuage was still held of Wembdon manor in 1627–8.[66]

In 1234 Roger of Sydenham held 1/50 knight's fee outside Bridgwater of William Brewer, perhaps the land at Kidsbury which Walter of Sydenham held in 1303 and which descended with Sydenham manor until the 15th century.[67] By 1428 it seems likely that Kidsbury had passed to John Gosse,[68] and Richard Gosse was living there in 1446.[69] In 1475–6 William Gosse held land there of Edward Grey, Lord Lisle,[70] which passed with Haygrove manor to the Seymour family and in 1547 to the Crown.[71] The Crown sold it to Henry Counsell and Robert Pistor in 1570.[72]

Hercules Holworthy (d. 1619–20) held the capital messuage called Kidsbury and lands in Chilton, Durleigh, and Wembdon.[73] His son William died in 1628[74] and the estate was divided between his three sisters, the eldest, Mary, later wife of John Were of Halberton (Devon), having the capital messuage and some land from 1639.[75] She sold them to George Crane of Bridgwater, her tenant, in 1665.[76] No further trace of the house has been found, but by c. 1640 lands at Kidsbury were owned by the Tynte family.[77] Lands called 'late Crane' and Kidsbury were held c. 1740 and in 1753 by the Revd. Samuel Lea and until 1803 by Mrs. Lea.[78]

The RECTORY estate was held by St. John's hospital, Bridgwater, from 1285 until the Dissolution.[79] In 1535 it was charged with the maintenance of five boys at school in the hospital.[80] The estate also included land and offerings at Holowell chapel.[81] The Crown leased it in 1553 to Nicholas Chute, formerly the hospital's tenant,[82] and sold it in 1560 to Ralph Bosseville.[83] Bosseville presumably sold it to Nicholas Halswell, who died in possession in 1564.[84] Robert Halswell, son of Nicholas, died in 1570 and was succeeded by his son Sir Nicholas (d. 1633). Henry Halswell, second son of Sir Nicholas,[85] sold the rectory, which included 40 a. of land, in 1634 to John Bourne (d. 1656) of Gothelney in Charlinch. His widow Elizabeth (d. 1660) was succeeded by her son Roger (d. 1672–3). Roger's daughter Florence died in 1673 and the eventual heir was Roger's brother Gilbert (d. 1686). Gilbert's son Edmund[86] (d. 1695) settled the rectory with Sandford manor on his wife Anne.

The rectory descended with Sandford;[87] it included 43 a. in 1754[88] and 36 a. in 1823.[89] John Cridland was in 1841 awarded a rent charge of £200 in lieu of the great tithes.[90]

In the mid 13th century the nuns of Barrow had a piece of meadow in Sydenham.[91] Athelney abbey had a close of land in Wembdon in 1535.[92]

ECONOMIC HISTORY. The seven estates that in 1086 made up the later parish of Wembdon[93] were assessed at nearly 6¾ hides and had land for 18 ploughteams. The recorded teams numbered 14, of which the demesnes accounted for 6½, with 4 of the hides; the agricultural tenants, 13 villani and 20 bordars, had 7½ teams with the remaining 2½ hides. Wembdon, the largest of the manors, had land for 8 teams, 2 teams in demesne with 1 servus, and 5 villani and 6 bordars with 4 teams; Sandford, having land for 3 teams, 1 team in demesne with 3 servi, and 2 villani and 4 bordars with 1 team, was next in value. No tenants were recorded on the Perry manor which Ralph held of Roger Arundel or on Sydenham manor. Meadow, totalling 78 a., was recorded on all the manors except Sydenham, the largest extent being 33 a. on Sandford; pasture, also totalling 78 a., was recorded on Wembdon, Sydenham, and two of the Perry manors; woodland, totalling 55 a. of which 37 a. was on Geoffrey de Vautort's Perry manor, was recorded also on the Perry manor which William held of Roger de Courcelles. The recorded livestock were 88 sheep, 48 swine, 30 beasts, 17 she-goats, and a riding horse, of which all the goats, the riding horse, and roughly half the other animals were on Wembdon manor. Three of the manors had increased in value; none was recorded as having declined.[94]

In the 14th and the 15th century scattered holdings in the parish were accumulated by such families as the Brents, who held land in Cheslade, Perry, Sandford, and Wembdon between 1318 and 1439.[95] Richard de St. Clare in 1444 held in Wembdon, Sandford, Sydenham, and elsewhere.[96] The Coker family, freeholders in the parish since the earlier 13th century,[97] and in addition tenants of the Michells in the mid 14th century,[98] had an estate which had grown to c. 1,000 a. at the death of James Coker in the mid 15th century.[99] The Michells were tenants of the Furneaux family in Perry in the later 13th century[1] and by the mid 14th century had

64 P.R.O., DL 42/11, f. 7v.
65 Feud. Aids, iv. 300.
66 P.R.O., C 142/436, no. 41.
67 Bk. of Fees, i. 400; Feud. Aids, iv. 300; above.
68 Feud. Aids, iv. 364.
69 Cal. Pat. 1446–52, 27.
70 P.R.O., SC 6/969/22.
71 Above, Bridgwater, manors; P.R.O., E 326/5686; Longleat House, Seymour Papers, XII, f. 16; Cal. Inq. p.m. Hen. VII, i, pp. 325–6; ii, p. 521.
72 Cal. Pat. 1569–72, p. 42.
73 P.R.O., C 142/436, no. 41; Som. Wills, ed. Brown, ii. 24.
74 P.R.O., C 142/760, no. 58.
75 S.R.O., DD/L 2/153/2, 2/154/2A.
76 Ibid. DD/L 2/153/2.
77 Ibid. DD/S/BW 5; DD/RN 53.
78 Ibid. D/P/wem 4/1/1, 9/1/1.
79 Below, church; V.C.H. Som. ii. 154–6.

80 Valor Eccl. (Rec. Com.), i. 208; V.C.H. Som. ii. 155.
81 P.R.O., SC 6/Hen. VIII/3137.
82 S.R.O., DD/SH 108, pt. 2; D/B/bw 2406.
83 Cal. Pat. 1558–60, 457.
84 P.R.O., C 142/141, no. 18; C 142/154, no. 86.
85 Ibid. C 142/475, no. 96.
86 Hants R.O. 7M54/196, 199/13; Som. Wills, ed. Brown, v. 79.   87 Above, this section.
88 Hants R.O. 7M54/200.   89 S.R.O., DD/X/SQ.
90 Ibid. tithe award.   91 Ibid. DD/S/WH 68.
92 Valor Eccl. (Rec. Com.), i. 207.
93 Excluding 'Ulveronetone', which is not to be identified with Waldron; if it was not the same as one of the estates called Perry is was not necessarily within the later parish: cf. above, manors.
94 V.C.H. Som. i. 484–5, 494–5, 499, 520.
95 S.R.S. xii. 79; Pole MS. 523, 527.
96 S.R.S. xxii. 107.   97 S.R.O., DD/S/WH 68.
98 Ibid. 218; S.R.S. lvii, pp. 31–2.
99 S.R.S. xxii. 145.   1 Pole MS. 2518.

extended their holding to Wembdon tithing and Bridgwater.[2] Walter Michell bought well over 100 a. in Wembdon, Cannington, and elsewhere in 1470[3] and at his death in 1487 held Wembdon, Cheslade, and West Perry manors in Wembdon parish and other lands in Bridgwater, Cannington, Durleigh, and Chilton, partly acquired from the Cokers.[4]

Some tenants of Perry Furneaux manor held leases for lives from the 1350s, including two who each held a furlong.[5] Tenants on Perry Fichet manor paid cash rents of over £310 by 1414, together with geese, cocks, and hens for churchscot.[6] By 1442 the manor also included burgages and other tenements in Bridgwater.[7] By 1473 the demesne of Perry Fichet, comprising three pasture closes, was let at farm; the tenants' land, evidently mostly arable, was divided between five holdings.[8]

In 1586 Perry Furneaux manor, containing c. 500 a., had 18 tenants of former demesne and 17 others, the largest with c. 32 a.[9] Rack renting was introduced in 1726,[10] but four copyholders still remained in 1779.[11] Sydenham manor comprised c. 270 a. in 1621 divided between two principal farms, the later Great (92 a.) and Little Sydenham (60 a.), and other small holdings, the whole let to 15 tenants;[12] c. 1590 the rent of its land at Dunwear had included a day's work at harvest time,[13] and in 1621 Little Sydenham was still held for two days' work at haymaking or a rent of 6d.[14] In 1705 Perry Fichet comprised c. 280 a. shared between 16 tenants, and the largest farm, called Wembdon House, measured c. 46 a.[15] In the later 18th century Thomas Grabham and his son of the same name occupied 93 a. in several separate tenancies, and John Holway had 51 a. on several leases including a house called Pury Place.[16]

By the earlier 17th century grassland in closes predominated in the northern and eastern parts of the parish. Arable on Perry Furneaux manor was mostly in severalty by 1582,[17] and common arable was inclosed by licence on Perry Fichet manor from 1603.[18] Langland common meadow had been inclosed by c. 1664,[19] and shortly afterwards c. 70 a. of Chislett Warth were inclosed to form part of Cheslade farm, which was increased in size when further riverside land was inclosed in the later 17th century.[20] Sydenham field had become pasture by the later 16th century and both meadow and pasture grounds there were said to be higher in value than the

former arable.[21] Owners or tenants at Sandford and the two manors at Perry had grazing rights for sheep and horses in the common pastures: in the earlier 18th century Chilton common was stinted at a mare and foal for each house or house site and two sheep for each acre.[22] Sandford manor and Cheslade farm had a share of the common at Chislett for 700 sheep in 1664,[23] but by 1705 tenants of Perry Fichet manor were complaining that large flocks established there by other tenants, notably Mr. Hawker, prevented the small tenant farmers from obtaining much benefit.[24] In the later 17th century the largest local flock belonging to a resident tenant numbered 30, and several farmers had no sheep at all, while two leases granted to outsiders in 1664 were each for 126 sheep.[25] Tenants of Wembdon manor and the rectory had no common rights.[26]

Field names current by the mid 17th century suggest that dairying was well established on Sandford manor. By 1686 water meadows had been created there.[27] Small farmers grew wheat, barley, beans, peas, clover, and leeks;[28] one cultivated reeds.[29] The lessee of the rectory had to plough in vetches, and a tenant of Perry Fichet manor in 1766 was allowed a rent reduction for drainage work.[30] Commoners on Wildmarsh and Harp were charged with maintenance of the Great or Wildmarsh rhyne.[31]

In 1773 Wembdon manor comprised 919 'computed' acres in the parish and other lands in Bridgwater, Cannington, and Stogursey parishes. Coker's farm (126 a.), Benham's Leaze (120 a.), and Perry Court (98 a.) were the largest farms and the most substantial tenant, Jonas Coles of Perry Court, farmed a total of 206 a.[32] In 1841 the largest individual holdings were Sandford farm (229 a.), William Horseman's Wembdon farm (198 a.), and Burnt House farm (154 a.).[33] Ten years later there were twelve substantial farms. Wembdon farm had been increased to 300 a. and employed 11 labourers; Sandford farm had 7 labourers; Burnt House farm had only 4 labourers.[34]

In 1841 there were 720 a. under arable cultivation and 1,730 a. under grass.[35] By 1905 the arable had been reduced to 418 a.[36] In 1982 a partial return of agricultural holdings included nearly 500 a. of grass and 205 a. of arable, mostly sown with wheat.[37] Dairying was of growing importance from the later 19th century: Walden or Waldrons was a specialist dairy farm by 1889,

2 S.R.S. xii. 218; xvii. 10.
3 Ibid. xxii. 139.
4 Cal. Inq. p.m. Hen. VII, i, pp. 114–15.
5 Pole MS. 2532, 2545, 2563.
6 P.R.O., SC 6/977/1–2.
7 Ibid. SC 6/1119/17.
8 Ibid. SC 6/977/13–14, 16, 18, 21, 23.
9 S.R.O., T/PH/vch 65.
10 Dors. R.O., D.1. MW/M5, M6, M7; ibid. D279/E4.
11 Hants R.O. 7M54/202.
12 S.R.O., DD/SG 4, 20.
13 Ward-Jackson, Sydenham Manor Ho.
14 S.R.O., DD/SG 20.
15 Ibid. DD/WG, box 6, survey.
16 Ibid. DD/WG 8/2A; 9/4, 5A; 12/2; 13/1.
17 Ibid. T/PH/vch 65.
18 Ibid. DD/WG 16/17.
19 Ibid. DD/X/CHK.
20 Ibid. DD/DP 33/3; DD/SAS (C/114) 21; ibid. T/PH/no

3; P.R.O., E 178/6028; Hants R.O. 7M54/196/32.
21 S.R.O., DD/SG 20.
22 Ibid. DD/WG, box 6; ibid. DD/SAS (C/114) 21.
23 Hants R.O. 7M54/202.
24 S.R.O., DD/WG, box 6.
25 Ibid. DD/SP inventories, 1667/11, 1669/63, 1670/27; ibid. DD/DP 76/7.
26 Hants R.O. 7M54/202.
27 Ibid. 7M54/196/17; 199/3, 21.
28 S.R.O., DD/SP inventories, 1667/11, 1670/27, 1671/31, 1681/14.
29 Ibid. 1669/88.
30 Ibid. DD/WG 8/2A.
31 Ibid. box 6.
32 Ibid. DD/PAM 1.   33 Ibid. tithe award.
34 P.R.O., HO 107/1925.
35 S.R.O., tithe award.
36 Statistics supplied by the then Bd. of Agric. 1905.
37 Min. of Agric., Fisheries, and Food, agric. returns, 1982.

Perry Court by 1894; by 1939 nine farmers described themselves as dairymen, and three milk retailers were in business in the village.[38]

The quarry in Wembdon village remained in use until 1909 or later.[39] In 1899 there were in business a grocer, a stationer, a builder, and a cab proprietor, and in 1902 two grocers and a florist. A motor engineer was established in 1919 and by 1939 both a garage and a motor car proprietor.[40] There was a brewer in the parish in 1851.[41] The Wembdon Brewery was built c. 1852 and continued production until 1914 or later.[42] The premises were taken over by the Ministry of Food as a fruit pulping station, but by 1923 were occupied by a private firm, the Somerset Fruit Products Co. Ltd., known by 1931 as the Quantock Preserving Co. Ltd.[43] The company was making a range of jams in 1988.[44] British Cellophane Ltd., part of the Courtauld Group, opened a factory at Sydenham in 1937 on a site of 59 a. which has since been extended.[45] In 1988 three separate factories on the site were producing cellulose and polythene film and bonded fibre fabric.[46] S. Leffman Ltd., makers of foundation garments, opened a factory in Provident Place in 1939 and were in business in 1988.[47]

There was a water mill on Robert Clarke's estate in the parish, presumably at Sandford, in 1636.[48] No further trace of it has been found.

In 1296 Matthew Furneaux had a grant of a fair at Perry to be held on the vigil, feast, and morrow of St. George's day (23 April).[49] In 1301 Matthew received £30 damages for the seizure at the fair of measures and tolls by the lord of the hundred.[50] The profits were let with the capital messuage of Perry Furneaux manor in 1571[51] and again in 1586,[52] but no later reference to the fair has been found.

LOCAL GOVERNMENT. In the later Middle Ages and the 16th century the parish was divided between the tithings of Sandford, Perry, and Wembdon; Sydenham was grouped with other parishes in 1569.[53] The constable of Wembdon hundred mentioned in 1648 was probably the petty constable of the parish or of Wembdon tithing.[54]

Rolls survive for Perry Fichet manor court for 1579, 1588, 1594, 1600, and 1602–5,[55] and extracts for 1382–3, 1402–3,[56] 1423–4, and 1427.[57] Courts were normally held twice a year in the 15th century.[58] In the 18th lessees were required to attend the court when summoned.[59] In 1402–3 a neif was appointed manorial bailiff for life.[60] Unrepaired houses and an unscoured watercourse were reported in 1427.[61] Scouring and repair of ditches were required in 1579.[62]

A book of extracts from rolls of Perry Furneaux manor court covers the period 1653 to 1806. In the later 18th century the court was held at Wembdon Farm and elsewhere in the parish, and a special court to take a surrender was held at the tenant's house in Salisbury.[63] From 1586 the tenant of the capital messuage collected rents and provided food and lodging twice a year for the steward.[64] Bartholomew Allen (d. 1657) held the capital messuage in return for serving as manorial bailiff. Most court business concerned the admission of tenants, but repairs were demanded in the 1650s, 1740s, and 1790s, a pound was ordered to be set up in 1658, and absent freeholders were amerced in 1709.[65]

A survey court for Sydenham manor was held in 1623.[66] No court records for Sandford or Wembdon manors have been found.

Before the mid 18th century the parish was administered by two churchwardens and two overseers, all chosen by virtue of their holdings, and by four or fewer other ratepayers who comprised the vestry. In 1761 one warden was chosen by the vicar, the other by the parish. Highway surveyors were appointed from 1757. A select vestry of vicar, wardens, overseers, and 11 or 12 others met from 1823. A medical officer was appointed from 1829 and a salaried waywarden from 1839. From 1751 the parish officers had a table in church from which to give out parish pay.[67]

A poorhouse had been established by 1777 west of the churchyard on a site belonging to the lords of Wembdon manor.[68] It was probably the former church house, a two-storeyed building with an outside stone stair, which the parish had rented in 1747 or earlier.[69] The vestry agreed in 1801 to buy the site and in 1803 decided to rebuild part of the house.[70] The building remained in use until 1884 when it was demolished and its site taken into the churchyard.[71]

The parish became part of the Bridgwater poor-law union in 1836 and part of Bridgwater rural district in 1894. The whole ancient parish, including the parts that had been taken into Bridgwater borough, became part of Sedgemoor district in 1974.[72]

38 Kelly's Dir. Som. (1889, 1894, 1939).
39 S.R.O., D/R/bw 15/3/26.
40 Kelly's Dir. Som. (1899, 1902, 1919, 1939).
41 P.R.O., HO 107/1925.
42 Bridgwater Times, 1 Apr. 1852, p. 2, advt. for builders' tenders; Kelly's Dir. Som. (1897, 1914); Bridgwater Mercury, 15 May 1984.
43 Kelly's Dir. Som. (1919, 1923, 1931).
44 Local inf.
45 Ward-Jackson, The 'Cellophane' Story, 84.
46 Local inf.
47 Bridgwater Mercury, 26 Apr. 1988.
48 P.R.O., CP 43/216, rot. 42.
49 Cal. Chart. R. 1257–1300, 465.
50 Abbrev. Plac. (Rec. Com.), 243; Pole MS. 2525.
51 S.R.O., T/PH/vch 65.
52 Dors. R.O., D.1. MW/M4, p. 43.
53 S.R.S. iii. 242–3; xx. 136, 243.

54 Cal. S.P. Dom. 1648–9, 33.
55 S.R.O., DD/WG, box 16.
56 S.R.S. lxviii, pp. 26–7.
57 P.R.O., SC 2/200/27–8.
58 Ibid. SC 6/977/1, 18.
59 S.R.O., DD/WG, box 6.
60 S.R.S. lxviii, p. 27.   61 P.R.O., SC 6/977/18.
62 S.R.O., DD/WG, box 16.
63 Ibid. DD/X/DS 4.
64 Dors. R.O., D.1. MW/M4, p. 43.
65 S.R.O., DD/X/DS 4.   66 Ibid. DD/SG 20.
67 Dwelly, Hearth Tax, ii. 134; S.R.O., D/P/wem 4/1/1, 9/1/1.
68 S.R.O., D/P/wem 4/1/1.
69 Ibid. 4/1/4 (1821–2), 4/1/4 (2).
70 Ibid. 9/1/1; above, plate facing p. 297.
71 S.R.O., D/P/wem 4/1/4 (2); ibid. tithe award.
72 Youngs, Local Admin. Units, i. 441, 673; S.R.O., GP/D 19.

CHURCH. There was a church at Wembdon by the late 12th century, when both a rector and a chaplain were mentioned.[73] In 1284 William Testard, lord of Wembdon manor, was licensed to alienate the advowson to St. John's hospital, Bridgwater.[74] The hospital appropriated the rectory in 1285 and a portion was set aside for the vicar.[75] A vicarage ordained between 1293 and 1302 was confirmed in 1304.[76] The living was a sole vicarage in 1987.[77]

The hospital appointed vicars until the Dissolution except in 1531 when the presentation was made by John Court.[78] In 1539 the advowson passed to the Crown, which presented in 1554.[79] In 1560 the Crown probably sold the advowson with the rectory,[80] and both descended to Henry Halswell. Henry, having sold the rectory, shortly before his death in 1636 settled the advowson on his brother Hugh.[81] The advowson descended with Goathurst manor to the Tynte family,[82] which held it until 1843 when Charles Kemeys Kemeys-Tynte sold it to the Revd. Edward Elton. Elton sold it in the following year to Charles W. H. Alston, who became vicar in 1845. Alston's daughters, Emma and Caroline Alston, presented Arthur Newman to the living in 1870 and sold him the advowson in 1871.[83] Newman presented his successor in 1885.[84] W. Brice was recorded as patron in 1889 and 1894,[85] and J. M. Evans presented himself in 1895 and his successor in 1908.[86] After 1910 Evans conveyed the patronage to P. S. Douglas-Hamilton, who in 1928 conveyed it to the Church Association Trust, later the Church Society Trust, patron in 1987.[87]

The vicarage was valued at £9 16s. 9d. in 1535.[88] The reputed value was £40 c. 1668,[89] and the average net income in 1829–31 was £612.[90]

Between 1293 and 1302 the vicar was assigned all offerings, casual fees, small tithes, and an allowance of grain from Bridgwater hospital.[91] By 1535 the grain allowance had been commuted to a pension of 34s. Tithes of wool and lambs (not usually paid to a vicar) were valued at 50s., other predial tithes at 60s. 8d., and personal offerings and tithes at 43s. 5d.[92] In 1841 the vicar was awarded a rent charge of £566 10s. in lieu of tithes.[93] Glebe in 1535 was valued at 8s. 8d.;[94] in 1620 it amounted to 6½ a., and in 1841 to just

over 6 a.[95] In 1916 there were over 10 a.,[96] but apparently none by 1978.[97]

In 1620 the vicarage comprised a parlour, hall, and kitchen, with three rooms above.[98] In 1815 the house was said to be too small for the curate, and in 1827 it was described as a cottage.[99] The building, west of the church, survived until 1871 when it was demolished to make way for a new church school.[1] The benefice had no house thereafter:[2] in 1881 the vicar was living at what was in 1987 nos. 41 and 41A Wembdon Rise.[3] In 1903 the vicar personally bought the house called Hill Grove in Wembdon Hill,[4] and his successors received an allowance to cover the mortgage charge.[5] The house, containing 21 rooms,[6] was sold c. 1943. From that time the vicars lived in a house on Wembdon Road until a new house was built in 1957 at no. 12, Greenacre.[7]

In 1554 it was reported that a canopy and pyx had not been set up for the restored liturgy and that no sermons had been preached for five years.[8] Hugh Halswell, vicar for just over a year from 1623, lived in Oxford, but the cure was said to have been well served.[9] John Musgrave, vicar from 1624, was deprived of his living c. 1652 but was restored in 1660 and remained until 1671.[10] There were generally fewer than 30 communicants in the later 18th century.[11] Henry Parsons, vicar 1791–1845 and prebendary of Wells, lived at his rectory house at Goathurst; his curate in 1815 lived at Bridgwater.[12] By 1827 two sermons were preached each Sunday and there was a resident curate,[13] but in 1840 the curate was an absentee and the vestry requested that he should live in the parish to provide weekly duty as well as services on Sunday afternoons.[14] Communion was held at least four times a year by 1843.[15] Charles Alston, vicar 1845–70, was also chaplain to the earl of Bessborough.[16] Three vicars before 1904 were also incumbents of Durleigh.[17]

In 1326 Matthew Coker had licence to alienate land in Wembdon and Chilton to provide a chaplain to celebrate in the church daily.[18] No further trace of the endowment has been found, but in 1333 St. John's hospital, Bridgwater, gave a messuage in the parish for a chantry for the Wigborough family. The chantry was to be in

73 S.R.S. lxviii, p. 25; Cat. Anct. D. ii, B 2966; P.R.O., DL 25/299; DL 42/11, f. 7v.
74 Above, manors; Cal. Pat. 1281–92, 132, 147.
75 Dugdale, Mon. vi. 662–3; Cal. Pat. 1313–17, 258.
76 S.R.S. i. 267–8.
77 Dioc. Dir.
78 S.R.S. lv, p. 62.
79 Cal. Pat. 1554–5, 253; S.R.S. lv, p. 137.
80 Cal. Pat. 1558–60, 457; above, manors (rectory).
81 P.R.O., C 142/492, no. 121; Som. Wills, ed. Brown, vi. 94–6.
82 Above, Goathurst, manors.
83 Inf. from Church Society Trust.
84 S.R.O., D/D/B reg 40, f. 207v.
85 Dioc. Kal.
86 S.R.O., D/D/B reg 41, f. 151v.; ibid. 42, p. 128.
87 Dioc. Dir. 1910, 1914; inf. from Church Society Trust.
88 Valor Eccl. (Rec. Com.), i. 214.
89 S.R.O., D/D/Vc 24.
90 Rep. Com. Eccl. Revenues, pp. 156–7.
91 S.R.S. i. 267–8.
92 Valor Eccl. (Rec. Com.), i. 214.
93 S.R.O., tithe award.
94 Valor Eccl. (Rec. Com.), i. 214.
95 S.R.O., D/D/Rg 687; ibid. tithe award.
96 Ibid. D/D/R, inventory 1916.
97 Inf. from Dioc. Office.
98 S.R.O., D/D/Rg 687.
99 Ibid. D/D/Rb 1815, 1827.
1 Ibid. tithe award; ibid. DD/EDS 6740; painting in vestry.   2 Dioc. Kal.
3 P.R.O., RG 11/2376.
4 S.R.O., D/D/Bbm 310.
5 Dioc. Dir.
6 S.R.O., D/D/R, inventory 1916.
7 Inf from the vicar, the Revd. Peter Bannister.
8 S.R.O., D/D/Ca 22.
9 Ibid. 235.
10 Walker Revised, ed. A. G. Matthews, 317.
11 S.R.O., D/D/Vc 88.
12 Ibid. D/D/Rb 1815; Le Neve, Fasti, 1541–1857, Bath and Wells, 63.
13 S.R.O., D/D/Rb 1827.
14 Ibid. D/D/Va 1840; ibid. D/P/wem 9/1/1.
15 Ibid. D/D/Va 1843.
16 Clergy List, 1857, 1869.
17 Above, Durleigh, church.
18 Cal. Pat. 1324–7, 246.

that family's patronage, and mass was to be said at the altar of the Virgin in Wembdon church.[19] No reference to the chantry has been found after 1349.[20]

A church house, owned by the lords of Wembdon manor, was probably the later poorhouse.[21]

Until it was substantially rebuilt after fire destroyed the nave roof in 1868, the church of *ST. GEORGE*, so called in 1285,[22] comprised a chancel with north vestry, a four-bayed nave with north and south aisles, and a west tower. The chancel was rebuilt and the north aisle added in the 13th century, the south aisle, porch, nave roof, and tower in the 14th century, probably after the building had been described as a ruin.[23] Windows were replaced at the same time in the earlier rear arches in the chancel. The font, a stair tower, rood loft, and screen were added in the later 15th century. In 1725 the chancel arch was filled to convert the chancel to a vestry and the nave was decorated with murals. A new vestry was made on the north side of the chancel in 1824, approached from the clerk's desk through the former doorway to the rood stair. The chancel arch was then reopened.[24]

After the fire the church was virtually rebuilt by J. M. Hay of Bath. The nave was extended one bay eastwards, the chancel arch was removed to the east end of the north aisle, and a vestry was added south of the chancel.[25] Most of the furnishings were replaced.

There are six bells, the oldest the tenor of 1710 by Thomas Wroth.[26] The plate includes a dish of 1712, and a cup, cover, and flagon of 1728 by James Wilkes.[27] The registers date from 1665.[28] In the churchyard are the base and shaft of a 15th-century cross and a set of stocks.

In 1539 there was a chapel called Holowell, near the well below Wembdon Hill.[29] No further trace of the chapel has been found.

NONCONFORMITY. John Temblett's house at Perry Green was licensed for nonconformist worship in 1845, and Thomas Granger's, elsewhere in the parish, in 1846.[30] No further evidence of nonconformist meetings has been found.

EDUCATION. From 1814 the parish clerk was paid by the churchwardens to teach children.[31] In 1819 he was paid £5 a year by the vicar to teach up to 30.[32] In 1825 a day and Sunday school for 24 children was supported by voluntary contributions and weekly payments by parents.[33] The number had fallen to 15 by 1835, when the vicar paid part of the cost.[34] In 1846 a Sunday school for 15 boys and 35 girls was held in church, its master being paid by subscriptions, and a dame school taught 7 children.[35] The Sunday school probably became the parochial school mentioned in 1861,[36] the buildings of which were used by the congregation after the church was damaged in 1868.[37] A new school on the site of the former vicarage house was opened in 1871 and housed 153 pupils.[38] In 1902 there were 192 children with 5 teachers.[39] From the 1920s there were fewer children but in 1955, when the school accepted Voluntary Controlled status and took pupils between 5 and 15 years, there were 201 on the books. From 1957 only infants and juniors were taught, but in 1971 there were 220 pupils. In that year St. George's Voluntary Controlled junior school was opened in Brentwood Road, leaving the older buildings to house a county infants school. In 1988 there were 126 children at the infants school and 142 at the junior school.[40]

Christchurch Unitarian church, Bridgwater, established a school for *c.* 130 infants in Provident Place in 1850; it remained there until 1862.[41] In 1861 there was a boarding school for boys at Oakfield House, and also a school for girls elsewhere in the parish.[42] Grove House school, a girls' boarding and day school, had been established by the 1930s and was still operating *c.* 1954.[43] Down Hall preparatory school was in existence *c.* 1939,[44] and in the later 1950s there was a private co-educational boarding and day school known as Wembdon High School.[45] Part of St. Margaret's school, Bridgwater, was housed in Wembdon Road by *c.* 1967, and survived until 1987.[46]

CHARITY FOR THE POOR. Sir Bartholomew Michell (d. 1616)[47] by will gave £40 to the poor. By 1714 the capital sum had increased to £50 and a further £10 was added to buy land at Chilton Marsh. In 1786 the annual income was £5 1s. In 1714 the charity distributed clothing.[48] In 1958 the income from investments was £13 16s. 4d. and was distributed to 29 recipients;[49] in 1988 the income was between £40 and £50, shared between 6 or 8 people.[50]

19 *S.R.S.* ix, p. 321.
20 Ibid. x, p. 608.
21 Above, local govt.
22 *Cal. Pat.* 1313–17, 258; for the church *c.* 1800, above, plate facing p. 297.
23 *S.R.S.* i. 257–8.
24 *Bridgwater Mercury*, 9 Nov. 1870; S.R.O., D/D/R, inventory 1916; ibid. D/P/wem 4/1/1–2; D/D/Cf 1869/1; Hawarden, St. Deiniol's Libr., Church Notes of Sir Stephen Glynne, vol. 49, ff. 12–13.
25 S.R.O., D/D/R, inventory 1916; D/D/Cf 1869/1; *County Herald*, 7 Nov. 1959.
26 S.R.O., DD/SAS CH 16/2.
27 *Proc. Som. Arch. Soc.* xlvii. 163.
28 S.R.O., D/P/wem 2/1/1–20.
29 P.R.O., SC 6/Hen. VIII/3137.
30 S.R.O., D/D/Rm, box 2.
31 Ibid. D/P/wem 4/1/4.
32 *Educ. of Poor Digest*, p. 802.
33 *Ann. Rep. B. & W. Assoc. S.P.C.K.* (1825–6).
34 *Educ. Enq. Abstract*, p. 827.

35 Nat. Soc. *Inquiry, 1846–7*, Som. 18–19.
36 *P.O. Dir. Som.* (1861).
37 S.R.O., D/P/wem 1/1/3, 4/1/2.
38 Ibid. DD/EDS 6740; D/D/WBf 9/3.
39 Ibid. C/E 4/380/431.
40 Ibid. 4/64.
41 S.R.O., D/N/bw. chch 4/2/1, 6/3/1.
42 *P.O. Dir. Som.* (1861).
43 S.R.O., C/E 4/362/4–9; *Bristol, Devon, Dors., & Som. Schs. Handbk.* (*c.* 1954).
44 *Som., Wilts., and Dors. Trades Dir.* (1939–40).
45 *Bristol, Devon, Dors., & Som. Schs. Handbk.* (*c.* 1954); Whitby, Light, and Lane, *Bridgwater Dir.* (1957).
46 *Indep. Schs. of Som. & Glos.* (*c.* 1967); *Thomson Local Dir., Taunton area* (1987–8); local inf.
47 Above, Durleigh, manors (E. Chilton).
48 *Char. Don.* pp. 1068–9; *15th Rep. Com. Char.* pp. 459–60.
49 C. Rayner-Smith, *Wembdon and its Ch.* (1959), 28.
50 Inf. from the vicar.

INDEX

NOTE. An italic page-number denotes an illustration on that page or facing it. The pages containing the substantive history of a parish or hundred are indicated by bold-face type.

Percy:
  Algernon, earl of Northumberland, 137
  Alice, m. Rob. de Glastonia, 7
  Eleanor, *see* Poynings
  Gerbert de, 7, 14, 259
  Hen., earl of Northumberland (d. 1461), 89, 136
  Hen., earl of Northumberland (d. 1489), 136
  Hen., earl of Northumberland (d. 1537), 136
  Hen., earl of Northumberland (d. 1585), 137, 156
  Hen., earl of Northumberland (d. 1632), 137, 210
  Hen. Algernon, earl of Northumberland, 136, 259
  Joceline, earl of Northumberland, 137
  Maud, *see* Arundel
  Sibyl, 259
  Thos., earl of Northumberland, 65, 137
  fam., 150, 259
Perers, Mic. de, and his s. Stephen, 298
Pereton, Rob. of, 329
Periam, fam., 270
Perrett (Perrot):
  Edw., 269
  fam., 166
Perry, in Chilton Trinity and Wembdon, 10, 114, 179–80, 252–3, 324, 328, 330
  commons, 324
  cts., 332
  fields, 324
  man., 325–8, 331–2
  nonconf., 334
  Perry Ct., 323, 326, 331–2
  Perry Green, 323–4, 328, 334
  tithing, 181, 324, 332
  West Perry (West Perers), 324, 328, 331
  woodland, 325
Perry Mill, *see* Stringston
Peryman:
  Agnes, m. Wal. Michell, 32, 81–2
  Dorothy, m. Phil. Courtenay, 82, 210
  Edith, w. of John, 82
  Joan, m. Bart. Coombe, 82, 115, 210
  John, 82, 210
Peter, bp. of Chester, 300, 309
Petherhams Marsh, *see* Cannington: Pedredham
Petherton, North, 179, **278–315**
  adv., 309
  agric. 300–3
  almsho., 308
  archit., 279, 285–93, 296–301, 310–11
  Ballcombe, 22, 279, 288
  Bankland, 61, 180–1, 279, 297, 302, 307–8
  Baymead, 303
  Boomer, *see* Melcombe, West
  boro., 180, 282–3, 306–7
  Brickland, 297
  Buckland Fee, 180–1, 296, 306–7
  Buckland Sororum, 297, 308
  Chadmead (Northmoor Corner), 79, 142, 278–9, 282, 294, 297, 301, 307–8
  chantries, 284, 309–10, 316
  chapels, 285, 289, 294, 309, 311
  chaplains, 309
  char., 313–15
  ch., 278–9, 284, 300, 303, 308–12, *312*
  ch. ho., 308, 310
  Civil War, 282
  Clavelshay, *q.v.*
  Clayhanger, 298
  commons, 279, 281, 302
  Compass, 306
  ct. ho., 279, 284, 290, 307

cts., 61, 227, 283, 285, 291, 297, 301, 305, 307–8
Denizen tithing, 180, 283, 306
Dunwear, *q.v.*
Ernesham, 296–7
fair, 305
fms., 301–2
Farringdon, 288
fields, 279, 301–2
Fordgate, 305, 313, 315
fraternity, 310
friendly soc., 282
greens, 302
guildhall, 279, 310
Hadworthy, *q.v.*
Hedging, 52, 54, 298, 302, 306, 313
Hitchings, 294–5
Holbrook, 297
Hulkshay, *q.v.*
hund., 1, 4, 58, 67, **179–81**, 227, 259, 264, 275, 282–4, 307, 316, 321–2
  cts., 180–1, 275
  officers, 181, 284
Huntworth, *q.v.*
incl., 192, 281, 301–2, 305
ind., 305
inns, 181, 279, 281–2, 305, 307–8, 312
King's Cliff, 278, 281, 302–4
limits, 180, 284
man., 1, 10, 22, 32, 141, 179–81, 210, 246, 259, 283–300, 307, 316, 325, 327–8
mkt., 305
Maunsel, *q.v.*
Melcombe, 279, 281, 285, 288–90
Melcombe, West, *q.v.*
mills, 289, 296, 303
Moorland, *q.v.*
moors, 278–9, 281, 300–2, 305
Newton, North, *q.v.*
Newton, West, *q.v.*
nonconf., 29, 278, 312–13
North moor, 53–5, 58–9, 61, 179, 301–2, 304, 307–8
Northmoor Corner, *see* Petherton, North: Chadmead
Northmoor Green, *see* Moorland
officers, 307–8
par. council, 308
park, *see* Petherton park
Playstreet, 288
poorho., 308, 310
pop., 282
prehist. rem., 278
Primmore, 279, 281, 298, 302, 305
public services, 281, 308
rectory, 300, 309; ho., 284, 300
Rhode, *q.v.*
rly., 278, 282
Rom. rem., 278
Rydon, 300, 302–3, 310, 313–14
schs., 278, 284, 313–15, 322
Shearston, *q.v.*
shirehall, 279
Shovel (Siwoldestone), 24, 279, 285, 290, 300, 302, 304
Somerset Bridge, 193, 278, 282, 308, 313, 315
Stamfordlands, 114, 139, 292, 303, 308, 327
Standenhay, 293
streets, 279
tithes, 287, 300, 302–3, 309
tithings, 180–1, 282–3, 306
trade, 306
Tuckerton, *q.v.*
vestry, 308
vicarage, 309, 311; ho., 309
vicars, 288, 309, 311–12; *and see* Toogood, Jas.
warrens, 281
Wely, 294
Whitestock, 282, 284
Willstock, 293
woodland, 279, 304

Woolmersdon, *q.v.*
workho., 308
Yeo, West, 295, 303
otherwise mentioned, 5, 22, 24, 34, 45, 52–3, 56–7, 186, 205, 213, 223, 247, 249, 253, 259, 261–2, 264, 276, 317–18, 329
Petherton, South, 262, 309, 326
  mills, 262
  Wigborough, 253
Petherton, park, 1, 5, 56, 61, 156, 179, 181, 197, 264, 279, 281–2, 284–7, 301–4, 306, 308, 311
  ct., 308
  officers, 308
Peyton, Chris., 254
Phelips:
  Dorothy, da. of Sir Edw., 299
  Dorothy, w. of Sir Edw., *see* Cheeke
  Edith, m. Carew Mildmay, 299
  Edith, w. of Sir Edw., 299
  Sir Edw. (d. 1698), 299
  Edw. (d. 1792), 299
  Edw. (d. 1797), 85, 145, 299
  John (fl. 1601), 58
  John (fl. 1810), 299
  Sir Rob., 299
  Wm., 145
  Revd. Wm., 299
  fam., 58, 300
  and see Philips
Phelps:
  Joan, w. of John, 295
  John (fl. 1620), 300
  John (d. 1678), 295, 300
  John (fl. 1685), 300
Philadelphia (U.S.A.), 216
Philips (Phillips):
  Chas., 300
  John (fl. *c.* 1560), 231
  John (fl. 1739), 300
  John (fl. 1804), 22
  Mary, *see* Alexander
  Rob., 300
  Wm., 300
  and see Phelips
Phillpotts, Hen., bp. of Exeter, 206
pigeon houses, *see* dovecots
piggery, 5, 59
Pightley, *see* Spaxton
Pignes, in Chilton Trinity, 179–80, 212, 215, 251–3, 255, 282, 327
  man., 256
  priest, 255–6
  tithing, 181, 251, 256
Pigott, John Smyth-, 124
Pillock:
  Wm., 83
  fam., 83
Pillock, *see* Cannington
pillory, 128, 202, 223–4, 307
Pincerna:
  Cecily, 107
  Helewise, *see* FitzBernard
  Hugh, 107
Pincombe, trustees of Mrs., 15, 43, 61
Pirou:
  Alex. de, 246
  Alf. de, 246
  Ric. de, 246
  Wm. de, 246
Pistor, Rob., 210, 330
Pitminster, *see* Poundisford
Pitt:
  Jane, *see* Hockmore
  Sam., 32
  Wm., 32, 210, 230
Plainsfield:
  Adam of, *see* Chandos, Adam of
  Wal. of, 162
Plainsfield, *see* Stowey, Over
Plainsfield, Lower, *see* Spaxton
Plantagenet:
  Alice, *see* Lacy
  Anne, 286
  Art., Vct. Lisle, 209